FINANCIAL ACCOUNTING

FIFTH CANADIAN EDITION

FINANCIAL ACCOUNTING

WALTER T. HARRISON, JR.
BAYLOR UNIVERSITY

CHARLES T. HORNGREN
STANFORD UNIVERSITY

C. WILLIAM (BILL) THOMAS
BAYLOR UNIVERSITY

GREG BERBERICH
UNIVERSITY OF WATERLOO

CATHERINE SEGUIN
UNIVERSITY OF TORONTO

TORONTO

To Jeanette, Simon, and Juliana
—Greg Berberich

To Dennis, Andrea, Allison, and Mark
—Catherine I. Seguin

Vice-President, Cross Media & Publishing Services: Gary Bennett
Managing Editor, Business Publishing: Claudine O'Donnell
Acquisitions Editor: Megan Farrell
Marketing Manager: Claire Varley
Developmental Editor: Rebecca Ryoji
Lead Project Manager: Avinash Chandra
Project Manager: Sarah Gallagher
Manufacturing Coordinator: Jane Schell/Karen Bradley
Production Editor: Carrie Fox, Electronic Publishing Services Inc., NYC
Copy Editor: Audra Gorgiev
Proofreader: Megan Smith-Creed
Compositor: Aptara, Inc.
Text Permissions: Electronic Publishing Services Inc., NYC
Photo Permissions: Q2A/Bill Smith
Art Director: Julia Hall
Interior Designer: Miguel Acevedo
Cover Designer: Anthony Leung
Cover Image: Getty Images

Credits and acknowledgments for material borrowed from other sources and reproduced, with permission, in this textbook appear on the appropriate page within the text.

10 9 8 7 6 5 4 3 2 1 [CKV]

Library and Archives Canada Cataloguing in Publication

Harrison, Walter T., author
Financial accounting / Walter T. Harrison Jr, Baylor University, Charles T. Horngren, Stanford University, C. William (Bill) Thomas, Baylor University, Greg Berberich, University of Waterloo, Catherine Seguin, University of Toronto. — Fifth Canadian edition.

Includes index.

Revision of: Financial accounting. 4th Canadian ed. 2011.

ISBN 978-0-13-297927-6 (bound)

1. Accounting—Textbooks.   I. Horngren, Charles T., 1926-, author
II. Thomas, C. William, author   III. Seguin, Catherine I., author
IV. Berberich, Greg, 1968-, author   V. Title.
HF5635.F43095 2014   657'.044   C2013-902937-0

ISBN: 978-0-13-297927-6

Contents

About the Authors

Walter T. Harrison, Jr., is Professor Emeritus of Accounting at the Hankamer School of Business, Baylor University. He received his BBA degree from Baylor University, his MS from Oklahoma State University, and his PhD from Michigan State University.

Harrison, recipient of numerous teaching awards from student groups as well as from university administrators, has also taught at Cleveland State Community College, Michigan State University, the University of Texas, and Stanford University.

A member of the American Accounting Association and the American Institute of Certified Public Accountants, Harrison has served as Chairman of the Financial Accounting Standards Committee of the American Accounting Association, on the Teaching/Curriculum Development Award Committee, on the Program Advisory Committee for Accounting Education and Teaching, and on the Notable Contributions to Accounting Literature Committee.

Harrison has lectured in several foreign countries and published articles in numerous journals, including *The Accounting Review, Journal of Accounting Research, Journal of Accountancy, Journal of Accounting and Public Policy, Economic Consequences of Financial Accounting Standards, Accounting Horizons, Issues in Accounting Education,* and *Journal of Law and Commerce.* He is coauthor of *Financial Accounting,* Seventh Edition, 2006 (with Charles T. Horngren) and *Accounting,* Eighth Edition (with Charles T. Horngren and Linda S. Bamber) published by Pearson Prentice Hall. Harrison has received scholarships, fellowships, research grants, or awards from Price Waterhouse & Co., Deloitte & Touche, the Ernst & Young Foundation, and the KPMG Peat Marwick Foundation.

Charles T. Horngren is the Edmund W. Littlefield Professor of Accounting, Emeritus, at Stanford University. A graduate of Marquette University, he received his MBA from Harvard University and his PhD from the University of Chicago. He is also the recipient of honourary doctorates from Marquette University and DePaul University.

A Certified Public Accountant, Horngren served on the U.S. Accounting Principles Board for six years, the Financial Accounting Standards Board Advisory Council for five years, and the Council of the American Institute of Certified Public Accountants for three years. For six years, he served as a trustee of the Financial Accounting Foundation, which oversees the Financial Accounting Standards Board and the Government Accounting Standards Board in the United States.

A member of the American Accounting Association, Horngren has been its President and its Director of Research. He received its first annual Outstanding Accounting Educator Award.

The California Certified Public Accountants Foundation gave Horngren its Faculty Excellence Award and its Distinguished Professor Award. He is the first person to have received both awards.

Horngren was named Accountant of the Year, Education, by the international professional accounting fraternity Beta Alpha Psi and is a member of the U.S. Accounting Hall of Fame.

Horngren is also a member of the Institute of Management Accountants, where he has received its Distinguished Service Award. He was a member of the Institute's Board of Regents, which administers the Certified Management Accountant examinations.

Horngren is the author of other accounting books published by Pearson Prentice Hall and Pearson Canada Inc.: *Cost Accounting: A Managerial Emphasis,* Fifth Canadian Edition, 2010 (with George Foster, Srikant Datar, and Maureen Gowing) and *Accounting,* Canadian Eighth Edition, 2010 (with Walter T. Harrison, Linda S. Bamber, W. Morley Lemon, Peter R. Norwood, and Jo-Ann Johnston).

Horngren is the Consulting Editor of the Charles T. Horngren Series in Accounting.

Charles William (Bill) Thomas is the J. E. Bush Professor of Accounting and a Master Teacher at Baylor University. A Baylor University alumnus, he received both his BBA and MBA there and went on to earn his PhD from The University of Texas at Austin.

With primary interests in the areas of financial accounting and auditing, Bill Thomas has served as the J.E. Bush Professor of Accounting since 1995. He has been a member of the faculty of the Accounting and Business Law Department of the Hankamer School of Business since 1971 and served as chair of the department from 1983 until 1995. He was recognized as an Outstanding Faculty Member of Baylor University in 1984 and Distinguished Professor for the Hankamer School of Business in 2002. Dr. Thomas has received several awards for outstanding teaching, including the Outstanding Professor in the Executive MBA Programs in 2001, 2002, and 2006. In 2004, he received the designation as Master Teacher.

Thomas is the author of textbooks in auditing and financial accounting, as well as many articles in auditing, financial accounting and reporting, taxation, ethics, and accounting education. His scholarly work focuses on the subject of fraud prevention and detection, as well as ethical issues among accountants in public practice. His most recent publication of national prominence is "The Rise and Fall of the Enron Empire," which appeared in the April 2002 Journal of Accountancy, and which was selected by Encyclopedia Britannica for inclusion in its Annals of American History. He presently serves as both technical and accounting and auditing editor of *Today's CPA*, the journal of the Texas Society of Certified Public Accountants, with a circulation of approximately 28,000.

Thomas is a certified public accountant in Texas. Prior to becoming a professor, Thomas was a practicing accountant with the firms of KPMG, LLP, and BDO Seidman, LLP. He is a member of the American Accounting Association, the American Institute of Certified Public Accountants, and the Texas Society of Certified Public Accountants.

Greg Berberich, CPA, CA, PhD, is the Director of the Masters of Accounting program in the School of Accounting and Finance at the University of Waterloo, where he has been a Lecturer since 2011. Before that, he was a faculty member at Wilfrid Laurier University for nine years. He obtained his BMath and PhD from the University of Waterloo and completed his CPA and CA in Ontario.

Berberich has taught financial accounting, auditing, and a variety of other courses at the undergraduate and graduate levels. He has presented papers at a variety of academic conferences in Canada and the United States and has served on the editorial board of the journal *Issues in Accounting Education*. Berberich was also the Treasurer of the Society for Teaching and Learning in Higher Education and the Associate Director of Teaching and Learning in Waterloo's School of Accounting and Finance. He has written a number of cases for use in university courses and professional training programs. This is Berberich's first time coauthoring a textbook.

Catherine I. Seguin, MBA, CGA, is a Senior Lecturer at the University of Toronto Mississauga. In addition to her books *Accounting for Not-for-Profit Organizations* for Carswell (Thomson-Reuters) and *Not-for-Profit Accounting*, published by CGA Canada, she revised the study guide that accompanied the third edition of this textbook. She also coauthored a practice book on management accounting and wrote a test bank for a financial accounting book for McGraw-Hill.

At the University of Toronto Mississauga, Catherine initiated, organized, and continues to run an internship course where fourth-year Bachelor of Commerce and Bachelor of Business Administration students are given an opportunity to gain practical business experience to complement their field of studies. She has organized, co-hosted, and chaired ongoing workshops that invite all University of Toronto Mississauga professors teaching first-year classes to discuss and learn what pedagogical and organizational issues they face. She serves as Dean's Designate for academic offences in the Social Sciences.

In the business community, she has participated in the consultation of the reform of the Canada Corporations Act for not-for-profit organizations. In the past, she has served on several boards of not-for-profit organizations and has been a professional development speaker for CGA Ontario on the topic of not-for-profit accounting. Currently, she serves as Treasurer on the board of a small not-for-profit organization.

Preface

Helping Students Build a Solid *Financial Accounting* Foundation

Financial Accounting introduces the financial statements and the conceptual framework that underlies them in Chapter 1 and builds on this foundation throughout the remaining 12 chapters. The concepts and procedures that form the accounting cycle are also described and illustrated early in the text (Chapters 2 and 3) and are then applied consistently in the chapters that follow. By introducing financial accounting's most critical concepts and procedures early in the book and then repeatedly applying them in the context of new material in later chapters, students will finish the textbook with a sound grasp of introductory financial accounting principles.

This book also features a new coauthor, Greg Berberich, from the University of Waterloo, who brings 25 years of experience practising and teaching accounting to the Fifth Canadian Edition textbook. Greg contributed to seven of the book's 13 chapters and also suggested some of its new or revised pedagogical features.

Visual Walkthrough

UPDATED! Learning Objectives on the first page of every chapter clearly specify what students should be able to do once they have finished reading the chapter and completing the accompanying exercises, problems, and cases. Each objective also serves as the heading of the chapter section in which the related concepts are presented, providing students with a clear link between the objectives and the material that will help them achieve those objectives.

UPDATED! Chapter-Opening Vignettes provide students with clear links between chapter topics and the business decisions made by many familiar real-world companies. Some of the companies students will encounter include Apple, Le Château, WestJet, and TELUS.

UPDATED! User-Oriented Approach focuses students' attention on the relevance and interpretation of information in the financial statements by adding coverage of several new ratios, which will enhance their ability to evaluate a company's liquidity, turnover, and profitability. New end-of-chapter problems give students additional practice using these new ratios.

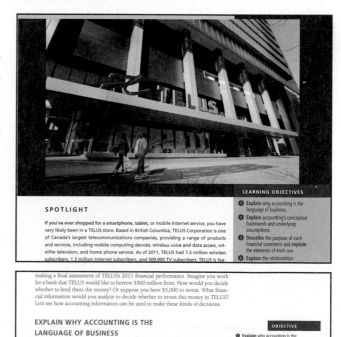

NEW! Focus on Analysis sections use the company TELUS Corporation, one of Canada's largest and most successful telecommunications companies, to illustrate key concepts throughout the book. Each chapter also features two problems that require students to analyze TELUS's financial statements, so they can clearly see how the concepts they are learning help them understand a real and well-known company's financial situation.

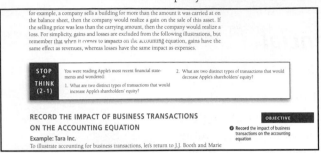

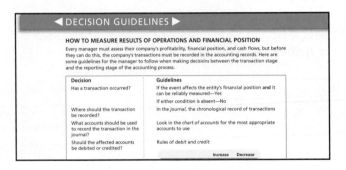

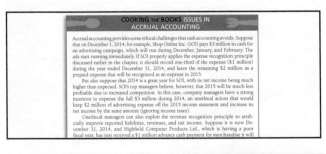

UPDATED! Stop + Think problems offer students the opportunity to pause in their reading and apply what they've just read to basic but realistic problems. The solutions to these problems have been moved to the end of each chapter, so students can't glance at them as they read the problems.

NEW! Decision Guidelines show students how managers, investors, and creditors would apply key financial accounting concepts to make critical business decisions.

NEW! Cooking the Books highlight real fraud cases in relevant sections throughout the text, giving students context to the material they are learning through real-life business situations.

NEW! IFRS-ASPE Differences are summarized at the end of several chapters to identify the differences that exist between these two sets of Canadian generally accepted accounting principles. Appendix B also contains a summary of all the IFRS-ASPE differences mentioned in the book.

UPDATED! End-of-Chapter Summaries clearly highlight the key concepts related to each learning objective so that students will finish each chapter with an overview of its most critical material.

UPDATED! Summary Problems and Solutions appear at the midpoint and end of the chapters, providing students with guidance on how to solve in-depth problems using concepts that have just been discussed in the text.

NEW! Microsoft Excel™ in MyAccountingLab

- Now students can get real-world Excel practice in their classes.
- Instructors have the option to assign students End-of-Chapter questions that can be completed in an Excel-simulated environment.
- Questions will be auto-graded, reported to, and visible in the grade book.
- Excel remediation will be available to students.

Changes to the Fifth Canadian Edition

Students and instructors will benefit from numerous changes incorporated into this latest edition of *Financial Accounting*. New student-friendly boxes called **Decision Guidelines** show students how managers, investors, and creditors would apply key financial accounting concepts to make critical business decisions. New topical **Cooking the Books** boxes highlight real fraud cases in relevant sections throughout the text, giving students context to the material they are learning through real-life business situations. New comprehensive **IFRS-ASPE Differences tables** summarized at the end of several chapters identify the differences that exist between these two sets of Canadian generally accepted accounting principles. Appendix B also contains a summary of all the IFRS-ASPE differences mentioned in the book. All material has been updated to reflect the IFRS and ASPE principles in effect at the time of writing (February 2013), or (in some cases) expected to be in effect by the time of the book's publication in 2014. The following is a summary of other significant changes made to this edition:

Chapter 1	• The first chapter has been rewritten to present key concepts with greater clarity and to eliminate redundancies with material covered in detail in later chapters.
	• The coverage of the main financial statements and their elements has been revised to incorporate formal IFRS terminology and definitions and to better highlight differences between IFRS and ASPE.
	• Most of the accounting vocabulary terms have been rewritten so they are consistent with IFRS/ASPE definitions.
Chapter 2	• The chapter title and learning objectives have been revised to better reflect the main purpose of the chapter and the outcomes to be achieved.
	• Much of the chapter has been rewritten to present key concepts and related examples more clearly.
	• This chapter now includes a Decision Guidelines section that summarizes the flow of accounting information from the transaction stage through to the financial statements.
Chapter 3	• The material on revenue and expense recognition has been rewritten to thoroughly reflect the IFRS/ASPE criteria that guide the recognition of these items. The accompanying examples have also been revised to clearly illustrate the application of each recognition principle to different scenarios.
	• The coverage of adjusting entries has been revised to eliminate redundancies and to describe each major type of adjusting entry using terminology that is consistent with the rewritten revenue and expense recognition principles described above.
	• Detailed coverage of the current ratio and debt ratio has been added, including illustrations of the impacts of transactions on the ratios, accompanied by a Decision Guidelines section that summarizes the use of these ratios.
Chapter 6	• More detailed explanations of how to apply the weighted-average and FIFO costing methods under both perpetual and periodic inventory systems are provided in this chapter.

- The end-of-chapter material includes several new problems on applying the weighted-average costing method under a perpetual inventory system.

Chapter 7
- This chapter now includes coverage of the return on assets, asset turnover, and net profit margin ratios, along with coverage of how to interpret these ratios using DuPont analysis.
- The end-of-chapter material has several new problems that require students to use these new ratios.

Chapter 8
- The coverage of long-term investments has been moved up several chapters to Chapter 8 to immediately follow the chapters that discuss the asset side of the balance sheet.
- Coverage of the time value of money has been moved from the appendix to this chapter, and end-of-chapter problems on this topic have been added.

Chapter 9
- This chapter now has coverage of the accounts payable turnover and leverage ratios, along with new end-of-chapter problems requiring the use of these ratios.
- Material on short-term borrowings, such as bank overdrafts and lines of credit, as well as term loans, has been added.

Chapter 10
- Much of this chapter has been rewritten to present key concepts with greater clarity and to eliminate redundancies with material covered in detail in other chapters.
- Coverage of the DuPont analysis has been added, which provides a more detailed and useful way of analyzing a company's return on equity.

Chapter 11
- Information on the statements of comprehensive income and changes in shareholders' equity has been updated to reflect proper terminology and presentation of these statements.
- Coverage of the auditor's report has also been updated to reflect new standards and wording for this report.
- Many of the accounting vocabulary terms have been rewritten so they are consistent with IFRS/ASPE definitions.

Chapter 12
- Most of this chapter has been rewritten to provide additional guidance and to improve clarity on difficult concepts, especially regarding the classification of operating, investing, and financing activities, and the treatment of changes in non-cash operating working capital accounts. Related terminology and definitions are now consistent with IFRS and ASPE.
- A mid-chapter summary problem with a focus on the operating activities section has been added, as well as a Stop + Think box with a focus on using information in the statement of cash flows.
- Most of the accounting vocabulary terms have been revised to be consistent with IFRS/ASPE definitions.

Chapter 13
- Coverage of accounts payable turnover, leverage, and the cash conversion cycle has been added to this chapter, along with end-of-chapter problems related to this new material.

Student Resources

MyAccountingLab is a powerful online learning tool that not only provides opportunities for limitless practice, but recreates the "I get it" moments from the classroom. MyAccountingLab provides a rich suite of learning tools, including:

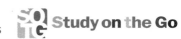

- Static and algorithmic versions of exercises and problems from the textbook
- An online, interactive Accounting Cycle Tutorial
- Mini-Cases
- Help Me Solve It question-specific interactive coaching
- A dynamic eText with links to media assets
- Accounting videos, animations, and DemoDocs

Study on the Go

Featured at the end of each chapter, you will find a unique barcode providing access to Study on the Go. Study on the Go brings material from your textbook to you and your smartphone. Now wherever you are—whatever you are doing—you can study by listening to the Audio Summaries, quizzing yourself, or using the awesome Glossary Flashcards. Go to one of the sites below to see how you can download an app to your smartphone for free. Once the app is installed, your phone will scan the code and link to a website containing Pearson's Study on the Go content that you can access anytime.

ScanLife
http://get.scanlife.com/

NeoReader
http://get.neoreader.com/

QuickMark
http://www.quickmark.com.tw/

Premium Online Courseware

Pearson's **MyAccountingCourse** is a premium online course solution that combines fully customizable course lessons and tutorials with the personalized homework and assessment features of MyAccountingLab. Designed to be used in fully online or blended learning environments, MyAccountingCourse can accommodate various term lengths and includes an integrated eText and comprehensive Instructor Resource Guide.

MyAccountingCourse

Features of MyAccountingCourse include:

- A flexible, customizable solution where an instructor may add to, delete, and reorganize content. Each topic-based MyAccountingCourse module is built to specific learning outcomes, and MyAccountingCourse includes a comprehensive Instructor Resource Guide complete with course outcomes, lesson objectives, and teaching tips.
- Interactive lesson presentations with a proven learning model, robust content, and relevant video, audio, eText, downloadable MP3 lectures, and other rich media assets.
- Rich MyAccountingLab-based assessment, pre-tests, quizzes, homework, and tests.

CourseSmart for Students

CourseSmart goes beyond traditional expectations—providing instant, online access to the textbooks and course materials you need at an average savings of 60%. With instant access from any computer and the ability to search your text, you'll find the content you need quickly, no matter where you are. And with online tools like highlighting and note-taking, you can save time and study efficiently. See all the benefits at www.coursesmart.com/students.

Pearson eText

Pearson eText gives you access to the text whenever and wherever you have access to the Internet. eText pages look exactly like the printed text, offering powerful new functionality for students and instructors. Users can create notes, highlight text in different colours, create bookmarks, zoom, click hyperlinked words and phrases to view definitions, and view in single-page or two-page view. Pearson eText allows for quick navigation to key parts of the eText using a table of contents and provides full-text search.

Technology Specialists

Pearson's Technology Specialists work with faculty and campus course designers to ensure that Pearson technology products, assessment tools, and online course materials are tailored to meet your specific needs. This highly qualified team is dedicated to helping schools take full advantage of a wide range of educational resources, by assisting in the integration of a variety of instructional materials and media formats. Your local Pearson Education sales representative can provide you with more details on this service program.

Instructor's Resources

🍎 Instructor's Teaching Tips Digital eText Resource

Instructors can easily locate useful teaching tips and resources throughout the eText located in MyAccountingLab. Easily identified by an apple icon throughout each chapter, intructors will find Chapter Overviews and Outlines, Assignment Grids, Ten-Minute Quizzes, and other valuable teaching resources including how to integrate MyAccountingLab into your course. Collated versions of this resource can also be downloaded from the Instructor Resources page at MyAccountingLab.

The following instructor resources are available to all adopters of this textbook:

- **Instructor's Solutions Manual:** This manual contains full solutions for all end-of-chapter material.
- **Instructor's Resource Manual:** This manual contains valuable resources, including chapter outlines, teaching tips, and assignment grids. The Instructor's Resource Manual is available in the eText via the MyAccountingLab.
- **Pearson TestGen:** Over 1,500 test questions, including multiple-choice, true-or-false, and essay questions, are provided in TestGen format. TestGen is a testing software that enables instructors to view and edit the existing questions, add questions, generate tests, and distribute the tests in a variety of formats.

Powerful search and sort functions make it easy to locate questions and arrange them in any order desired. TestGen also enables instructors to administer tests on a local area network, have the tests graded electronically, and have the results prepared in electronic or printed reports. TestGen is compatible with Microsoft and Apple operating systems and can be downloaded from the TestGen website located at www.pearsoned.com/testgen. Contact your local sales representative for details and access.

- **Microsoft PowerPoint Presentations:** PowerPoint presentations offer an outline of the key points for each chapter. A new template is utilized and new content is added for this edition of the PowerPoint program.
- **Image Library:** An Image Library provides access to many of the figures and tables in the textbook.

All of these instructor supplements, except for the Instructor's Resource Manual, are also available for download from a password-protected section of Pearson Canada's online catalogue (vig.pearsoned.ca). Navigate to your book's catalogue page to view a list of those supplements that are available. See your local sales representative for details and access.

Pearson Advantage: For qualified adopters, Pearson Education is proud to introduce the **Pearson Advantage**. The Pearson Advantage is the first integrated Canadian service program committed to meeting the customization, training, and support needs for your course. Our commitments are made in writing and in consultation with faculty. Your local Pearson Education sales representative can provide you with more details on this service program.

Innovative Solutions Team: Pearson's Innovative Solutions Team works with faculty and campus course designers to ensure that Pearson technology products, assessment tools, and online course materials are tailored to meet your specific needs. This highly qualified team is dedicated to helping schools take full advantage of a wide range of educational technology by assisting in the integration of a variety of instructional materials and media formats.

Pearson Custom Publishing

We know that not every instructor follows the exact order of a course text. Some may not even cover all the material in a given volume. Pearson Custom Publishing provides the flexibility to select the chapters you need, presented in the order you want, to tailor fit your text to your course and your students' needs. Contact your Pearson Education Canada Sales and Editorial Representative to learn more. We hope you enjoy *Financial Accounting*.

Acknowledgments

Thanks are extended to TELUS for permission to include portions of their annual report in Appendix A and MyAccountingLab. Appreciation is also expressed to the following individuals and organizations:

The annual reports of a number of Canadian companies
Professors Tom Harrison, Charles Horngren, and Bill Thomas

Particular thanks are also due to the following instructors for reviewing the manuscript for the Fifth Canadian Edition and offering many useful suggestions:

Howard Leaman, *University of Guelph/Humber*
Amy Kwan, *Certified Management Accountants of Ontario*
Peggy Wallace, *Trent University*
Gordon Holyer, *Vancouver Island University*
Scott M. Sinclair, *University of British Columbia*
Sherif Elbarrad, *Grant MacEwan University*
Ken MacAulay, *St. Francis Xavier University*
Rob Anderson, *Thompson Rivers University*
Ian Dunn, *Western University*
Anna Schiavi, *Vanier College*
Anita Braaksma, *Kwantlen Polytechnic University*
Ron Baker, *University of Guelph*
Mingzhi Liu, *University of Manitoba*
Andrea Chance, *University of Guelph* and *George Brown College*
Larry Webster, *NAIT*
Elisabetta Ipino, *Concordia University*

The authors acknowledge with gratitude the professional support received from Pearson Canada. In particular we thank Megan Farrell, Aquisition Editor; Rebecca Ryoji, Developmental Editor; Imee Salumbides, Media Content Editor; Sarah Gallagher, Project Manager; Carrie Fox, Production Editor; Audra Gorgiev, Copy Editor; and Claire Varley, Marketing Manager.

Greg Berberich also acknowledges the patience and support of Jeanette, Simon, and Juliana, who endured many stressful moments while he was working on this book. He is also grateful for the IFRS and ASPE advice provided by Al Foerster, as well as the good cheer and perspective supplied by Melanie Davis throughout the writing process. All of them have made invaluable contributions to this book.

Prologue

Accounting Careers: Much More Than Counting Things

What kind of career can you have in accounting? Almost any kind you want. A career in accounting lets you use your analytical skills in a variety of ways, and it brings both monetary and personal rewards. Professional accountants work as executives for public companies, partners at professional services firms, and analysts at investment banks, among many other exciting positions.

Accounting as an art is widely believed to have been invented by Fra Luca Bartolomeo de Pacioli, an Italian mathematician and Franciscan friar in the sixteenth century. Pacioli was a close friend of Leonardo da Vinci and collaborated with him on many projects.

Accounting as the profession we know today has its roots in the Industrial Revolution during the eighteenth and nineteenth centuries, mostly in England. However, accounting did not attain the stature of other professions such as law, medicine, or engineering until early in the twentieth century. Professions are distinguished from trades by the following characteristics: (1) a unifying body of technical literature, (2) standards of competence, (3) codes of professional conduct, and (4) dedication to service to the public.

An aspiring accountant must obtain a university degree, pass several professional examinations, and gain two or three years of on-the-job training before they can receive a professional accounting designation. Historically, the most common accounting designations in Canada were the CA (Chartered Accountant), CMA (Certified Management Accountant), and CGA (Certified General Accountant) designations. Recently, however, the Canadian accounting profession has become more unified, so now the most prevalent designation is the CPA, which stands for Chartered Professional Accountant, although the three legacy designations are still used in some jurisdictions.

When you hold one of these designations, employers know what to expect about your education, knowledge, abilities, and personal attributes. They value your analytical skills and extensive training. Your professional designation gives you a distinct advantage in the job market, and instant credibility and respect in the workplace. It's a plus when dealing with other professionals, such as bankers, lawyers, auditors, and federal regulators. In addition, your colleagues in private industry tend to defer to you when dealing with complex business matters, particularly those involving financial management.

Where Accountants Work

Where can you work as an accountant? There are four main types of employers.

Professional Accounting Firms

You can work for a professional accounting firm, which could range in size from a small local firm to a large international firm such as KPMG or Ernst & Young. These firms provide assurance, tax, and consulting services to a variety of clients, allowing you to gain a broad range of experience if you so choose. Many accountants begin their careers at a professional accounting firm and then move into more senior positions in one of the job categories described below. Others may stay on, or join one of these firms after working elsewhere, to take advantage of the many rewarding careers these firms offer.

Public or Private Companies

Rather than work for an accounting firm and provide your expertise to a variety of clients, you can work for a single company that requires your professional knowledge. Your role may be to analyze financial information and communicate that information to managers who use it to plot strategy and make decisions. Or you may be called upon to help allocate corporate resources or improve financial performance. For example, you might do a cost-benefit analysis to help decide whether to acquire a company or build a factory. Or you might describe the financial implications of choosing one business strategy over another. You might work in areas such as internal auditing, financial management, financial reporting, treasury management, and tax planning. The most senior financial position in these companies is the chief financial officer (CFO) role; some CFOs rise further to become chief executive officers (CEOs) of their companies.

Government and Not-for-Profit Entities

Federal, provincial, and local governmental bodies also require accounting expertise. You could be helping to evaluate how government agencies are being managed, or advise politicians on how to allocate resources to promote efficiency. The RCMP hires accountants to investigate the financial aspects of white-collar crime. You might find yourself working for the Canadian Revenue Agency, one of the provincial securities commissions, or a federal or provincial Auditor General.

As an accountant, you might also decide to work in the not-for-profit sector. Colleges, universities, public and private primary and secondary schools, hospitals, and charitable organizations such as churches and the United Way all have accounting functions. Accountants in the not-for-profit sector provide many of the same services as those in the for-profit sector, but their focus is less on turning a profit than on making sure the organizations spend their money wisely and operate efficiently and effectively.

Education

Finally, you can work at a college or university, advancing the thought and theory of accounting and teaching future generations of new accountants. On the research side of education, you might study how companies use accounting information. You might develop new ways of categorizing financial data, or study accounting practices in different countries. You then publish your ideas in journals and books and present them to colleagues at meetings around the world. On the education side, you can help others learn about accounting and give them the tools they need to be their best.

Regardless of which type of organization you work for, as an accountant, your knowledge will be highly valued by your clients, colleagues, and other important stakeholders. As the economy becomes increasingly global in scope, accounting standards, tax laws, and business strategies will grow more complex, so it's safe to say that the expertise provided by professional accountants will continue to be in high demand. This book could serve as the first step on your path to a challenging and rewarding career as a professional accountant!

FINANCIAL ACCOUNTING

The Financial Statements

LEARNING OBJECTIVES

1. **Explain** why accounting is the language of business
2. **Explain** accounting's conceptual framework and underlying assumptions
3. **Describe** the purpose of each financial statement and **explain** the elements of each one
4. **Explain** the relationships among the financial statements
5. **Make** ethical business decisions

SPOTLIGHT

If you've ever shopped for a smartphone, tablet, or mobile Internet service, you have very likely been in a TELUS store. Based in British Columbia, TELUS Corporation is one of Canada's largest telecommunications companies, providing a range of products and services, including mobile computing devices, wireless voice and data access, satellite television, and home phone service. As of 2011, TELUS had 7.3 million wireless subscribers, 1.3 million Internet subscribers, and 509,000 TV subscribers. TELUS is featured throughout this textbook as a way of connecting new financial accounting concepts to the actual business activities and financial statements of a familiar Canadian corporation.

As you can see from its Consolidated Statements of Income on the next page, TELUS sells a lot of mobile devices and services—about $10.3 billion worth for the year ended December 31, 2011 (line 3). After deducting a variety of expenses incurred during 2011 (lines 6–9, 12, and 14), TELUS earned net income of over $1.2 billion for the year (line 15).

These terms—revenues, expenses, and net income—may be unfamiliar to you now, but after you read this chapter, you'll be able to explain these and many other accounting terms. Welcome to the world of accounting!

TELUS Corporation
Consolidated Statements of Income (Adapted)
For the Years Ended December 31, 2011 and 2010

(in millions of dollars)	2011	2010
Operating Revenues		
1. Service	$ 9,606	$9,131
2. Equipment	719	611
3.	10,325	9,742
4. Other operating income	72	50
5.	10,397	9,792
Operating Expenses		
6. Goods and services purchased	4,726	4,236
7. Employee benefits expense	1,893	1,906
8. Depreciation	1,331	1,339
9. Amortization of intangible assets	479	402
10.	8,429	7,883
11. **Operating Income**	1,968	1,909
12. Financing costs	377	522
13. **Income Before Income Taxes**	1,591	1,387
14. Income taxes	376	335
15. **Net Income**	$ 1,215	$1,052

Each chapter of this book begins with an actual financial statement—in this chapter, it's the Consolidated Statements of Income of TELUS Corporation for the years ended December 31, 2011 and 2010. The core of financial accounting revolves around the basic financial statements:

- Income statement (sometimes known as the statement of profit or loss)
- Statement of retained earnings (sometimes included in the statement of changes in owners' equity)
- Balance sheet (also known as the statement of financial position)
- Cash flow statement (also known as the statement of cash flows)
- Statement of other comprehensive income

Financial statements are the reports that companies use to convey the financial results of their business activities to various user groups, which can include managers, investors, creditors, and regulatory agencies. In turn, these parties use the reported information to make a variety of decisions, such as whether to invest in or loan money to the company. To learn accounting, you must learn to focus on decisions. In this chapter, we explain generally accepted accounting principles, their underlying assumptions and concepts, and the bodies responsible for issuing accounting standards. We discuss the judgment process that is necessary to make good accounting decisions. We also discuss the contents of the four basic financial statements that report the results of those decisions. In later chapters, we will explain in more detail how to construct the financial statements, as well as how user groups typically use the information contained in them to make business decisions.

Using Accounting Information

TELUS Corporation's managers make a lot of decisions. Which tablet is selling the best? Which smartphone is earning the most profit? Should TELUS expand its offerings

MyAccountingLab

MyAccountingLab provides students with a variety of resources including a personalized study plan, assignable Excel simulated questions, videos and animations, and an interactive Accounting Cycle Tutorial (ACT). Margin logos that appear throughout Chapters 2 and 3 direct you to the appropriate ACT section and material. There are three buttons on the opening page of each chapter module: **Tutorial** helps you review major concepts, **Application** gives you practice exercises, and **Glossary** allows you to review key terms.

in Eastern Canada to match those in B.C. and Alberta? Accounting information helps company managers make these decisions.

Take a look at TELUS Corporation's Consolidated Statements of Income on page 2. Focus on net income (line 15). Net income is the excess of revenues over expenses. You can see that TELUS earned $1,215 million in net income for the year ended December 31, 2011. That's good news because it means that TELUS's revenues exceeded its expenses by over $1.2 billion in 2011.

TELUS's Consolidated Statements of Income convey more great news. Operating revenues grew from $9,742 million in 2010 to $10,325 million in 2011 (line 3), an increase of about 6%. Also, TELUS's 2011 net income of $1,215 million was 15.5% higher than its 2010 net income of $1,052 million (line 15). Based on these key numbers, TELUS's 2011 operating performance improved significantly from 2010.

There would, however, be much more accounting information to analyze before making a final assessment of TELUS's 2011 financial performance. Imagine you work for a bank that TELUS would like to borrow $500 million from. How would you decide whether to lend them the money? Or suppose you have $5,000 to invest. What financial information would you analyze to decide whether to invest this money in TELUS? Let's see how accounting information can be used to make these kinds of decisions.

EXPLAIN WHY ACCOUNTING IS THE LANGUAGE OF BUSINESS

OBJECTIVE

❶ **Explain** why accounting is the language of business

Accounting is an information system that measures and records business activities, processes data into reports, and reports results to decision makers. Accounting is "the language of business." The better you understand the language, the better you can make decisions using accounting information.

Accounting produces the financial statements that report information about a business entity. The financial statements report a business's financial position, operating performance, and cash flows, among other things. In this chapter, we focus on TELUS's 2011 financial statements. By the end of the chapter, you will have a basic understanding of these statements.

Don't confuse bookkeeping and accounting. Bookkeeping is a mechanical part of accounting, just as arithmetic is a mechanical part of mathematics. Accounting, however, requires an understanding of the principles used to accurately report financial information, as well as the professional judgment needed to apply them and then interpret the results. Exhibit 1-1 illustrates the flow of accounting information and helps illustrate accounting's role in business. The accounting process starts and ends with people making decisions.

Who Uses Accounting Information?

Almost everyone uses accounting information! Students use it to decide how much of their income to save for next year's tuition. Managers use it to decide if they should expand their business. Let's take a closer look at how these and other groups use accounting information.

MANAGERS. Managers have to make many business decisions. Should they introduce a new product line? Should the company set up a regional sales office in Australia or South Africa? Should they consider acquiring a competitor? Should the company extend credit to a potential major customer? Accounting information helps managers make these decisions.

EXHIBIT 1-1
The Flow of Accounting Information

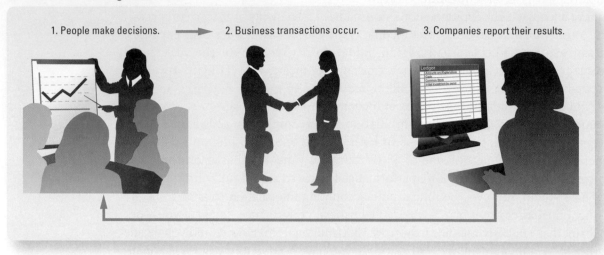

1. People make decisions.　　2. Business transactions occur.　　3. Companies report their results.

INVESTORS AND CREDITORS. Investors and creditors provide the money to finance a business's activities. Investors want to know how much income they can expect to earn on their investment. Creditors want to know if and how a business is going to pay them back. Accounting information allows investors and creditors to make these decisions.

GOVERNMENT AND REGULATORY BODIES. Many government and regulatory bodies use accounting information. For example, the federal government requires businesses, individuals, and other organizations to pay income and sales taxes. The Canada Revenue Agency uses accounting information to ensure these organizations pay the correct amount of taxes. The Ontario Securities Commission requires companies whose stock is traded publicly to provide the Commission with many kinds of periodic financial reports. All of these reports contain accounting information.

INDIVIDUALS. People like you manage bank accounts and decide whether to rent an apartment or buy a house. They also determine their monthly income and then decide how much to spend and save each month. Accounting provides the information needed to make these decisions.

NOT-FOR-PROFIT ORGANIZATIONS. Not-for-profit organizations—churches, hospitals, and charities, such as Habitat for Humanity and the Canadian Red Cross—base their decisions on accounting information. In addition, accounting information is the basis of a not-for-profit's reporting on the organization's stewardship of funds received and its compliance with the reporting requirements of the Canada Revenue Agency.

Two Kinds of Accounting: Financial Accounting and Management Accounting

Accounting information falls into two categories: financial accounting and management accounting. The distinction is based primarily on who uses the information in each category. Both *internal and external users* rely on financial accounting information, whereas management accounting information is used by *internal users only*.

Financial accounting provides information for managers inside the business and for decision makers outside the organization, such as investors, creditors, government agencies, and the public. This information must be relevant for the needs of decision makers and must provide a faithful representation of the entity's economic activities. This textbook focuses on financial accounting.

Management accounting generates inside information for the managers of the organization. Examples of management accounting information include budgets, forecasts, and projections that are used to make strategic business decisions. Internal information must be accurate and relevant for the decision needs of managers. Management accounting is covered in a separate course.

Organizing a Business

Accounting is used in every type of business. A business generally takes one of the following forms:

- Proprietorship
- Partnership
- Corporation

Exhibit 1-2 compares ways to organize a business.

PROPRIETORSHIPS. A **proprietorship** is an unincorporated business with a single owner, called the proprietor. Dell Computer started out in the college dorm room of Michael Dell, the owner. Proprietorships tend to be small businesses or individual professional organizations, such as physicians, lawyers, and accountants. From a legal perspective, the business *is* the proprietor, and the proprietor is personally liable for all business debts. But for accounting, a proprietorship is an entity separate from its proprietor. Thus, the business records do not include the proprietor's personal finances.

PARTNERSHIPS. A **partnership** is an unincorporated business with two or more parties as co-owners, and each owner is a partner. Individuals, corporations, partnerships, or other types of entities can be partners. The income (or loss) of the partnership "flows through" to the partners and they recognize it based on their agreed-upon percentage interest in the business. The partnership is not a taxpaying entity. Instead, each partner takes a proportionate share of the entity's taxable income and pays tax according to that partner's individual or corporate rate. Many retail establishments and

EXHIBIT 1-2
The Various Forms of Business Organization

	Proprietorship	Partnership	Corporation
Owner(s)	Proprietor—one owner	Partners—two or more owners	Shareholders—generally many owners
Life of entity	Limited by owner's choice or death	Limited by owners' choices or death	Indefinite
Personal liability of owner(s) for business debts	Proprietor is personally liable	Partners are usually personally liable	Shareholders are not personally liable
Accounting status	Accounting entity is separate from proprietor	Accounting entity is separate from partners	Accounting entity is separate from shareholders

some professional organizations of physicians, lawyers, and accountants are partnerships. Most partnerships are small or medium-sized, but some are very large, with several hundred partners. Accounting treats the partnership as a separate organization, distinct from the personal affairs of each partner. But the law views a partnership as the partners: Normally, each partner is personally liable for all the partnership's debts. For this reason, partnerships can be quite risky. Recently, professional partnerships such as public accounting firms and law firms have become limited liability partnerships (LLPs), which limits claims against the partners to their partnership assets.

CORPORATIONS. A **corporation** is an incorporated business owned by its **shareholders**, who own **shares** representing partial ownership of the corporation. One of the major advantages of a corporation is the ability to raise large sums of capital by issuing shares to the public. Individuals, partnerships, other corporations, or other types of entities may be shareholders in a corporation. Most well-known companies, such as TD Bank, Rogers, and Apple, are corporations. As with TELUS Corporation, their legal names include *Corporation* or *Incorporated* (abbreviated *Corp.* and *Inc.*) to indicate they are corporations. Some, like the Ford Motor Company, bear the name *Company* to denote this fact.

A corporation is formed under federal or provincial law. From a legal perspective, unlike proprietorships and partnerships, a corporation is distinct from its owners. The corporation is like an artificial person and possesses many of the rights that a person has. Unlike proprietors and partners, the shareholders who own a corporation have no personal obligation for its debts; so we say shareholders have limited liability, as do partners in an LLP. Also, unlike the other forms of organization, a corporation pays income taxes. In the other two cases, income tax is paid personally by the proprietor or partners.

A corporation's ownership is divided into shares of stock. One becomes a shareholder by purchasing the corporation's shares. TELUS, for example, has issued more than 300 million shares of stock. Any investor can become a co-owner of TELUS by buying shares of its stock through the Toronto Stock Exchange (TSX).

The shares of a public corporation like TELUS are widely held, which means they are owned by thousands of different shareholders who buy and sell the shares on a stock exchange. Shares of a private corporation are typically owned by a small number of shareholders, often including the founder and other family members.

The ultimate control of a corporation rests with the shareholders. They normally get one vote for each voting share they own. Shareholders also elect the members of the **board of directors**, which sets policy for the corporation and appoints officers. The board elects a chairperson, who is the most powerful person in the corporation and may also carry the title chief executive officer (CEO), the top management position. Most corporations also have vice-presidents in charge of sales, manufacturing, accounting and finance, and other key areas.

OBJECTIVE

❷ **Explain** accounting's conceptual framework and underlying assumptions

EXPLAIN ACCOUNTING'S CONCEPTUAL FRAMEWORK AND UNDERLYING ASSUMPTIONS
Generally Accepted Accounting Principles

Accountants prepare financial accounting information according to professional guidelines called **generally accepted accounting principles (GAAP)**. GAAP specify the standards for how accountants must record, measure, and report financial information.

In Canada, GAAP are established by the Canadian Institute of Chartered Accountants (CICA), one of the country's three professional accounting bodies.

Canada actually has multiple sets of GAAP, with each set being applicable to a specific type of entity or organization. **Publicly accountable enterprises (PAEs)**, which are corporations and other organizations that have issued or plan to issue shares or debt in public markets such as the Toronto Stock Exchange, *must* apply **International Financial Reporting Standards (IFRS)**. IFRS are set by the International Accounting Standards Board and have been adopted by over 100 countries in an effort to enhance the comparability of the financial information reported by public enterprises around the world.

Private enterprises, which have not issued and do not plan to issue shares or debt on public markets, *have the option* of applying IFRS. Because IFRS are relatively complex and costly to apply, however, very few Canadian private enterprises have adopted them. Instead, they apply another set of GAAP known as **Accounting Standards for Private Enterprises (ASPE)**, which have been set by the CICA. At the introductory financial accounting level, there are very few major differences between IFRS and ASPE, but we will discuss them where they do exist and also summarize them at the end of each chapter. In addition, all the IFRS-ASPE differences we discuss in the book have been compiled in Appendix B.

There are other sets of GAAP applicable to not-for-profit organizations, pension plans, and government entities, but they are too specialized to cover at the introductory level. If you choose to pursue accounting as a career, you will learn about them in the future.

Now let's examine the conceptual framework and assumptions underlying IFRS and ASPE.

Accounting's Conceptual Framework

Exhibit 1-3 gives an overview of the joint conceptual framework of accounting developed by the IASB and the Financial Accounting Standards Board (FASB) in the United States. This conceptual framework, along with several underlying assumptions, provides the foundation for the specific accounting principles included in IFRS and ASPE, though there are some small differences between the frameworks for the two sets of standards. The overall *objective* of accounting is to provide financial information about the reporting entity that is useful to current and future investors and creditors when making investing and lending decisions.

Fundamental Qualitative Characteristics

To be useful, information must have two *fundamental qualitative characteristics*:

- **relevance** and
- **faithful representation**.

To be **relevant**, information must have *predictive value, confirmatory value*, or both. Information has predictive value if it can be employed by users to predict an entity's future business or financial outcomes. It has confirmatory value if it confirms or changes prior evaluations of an entity. In addition, the information must be **material**, which means that it is significant enough in nature or magnitude that omitting or misstating it could affect the decisions of an informed user. All material information must be recorded or disclosed (listed or discussed) in the financial statements.

EXHIBIT 1-3
Accounting's Conceptual Framework

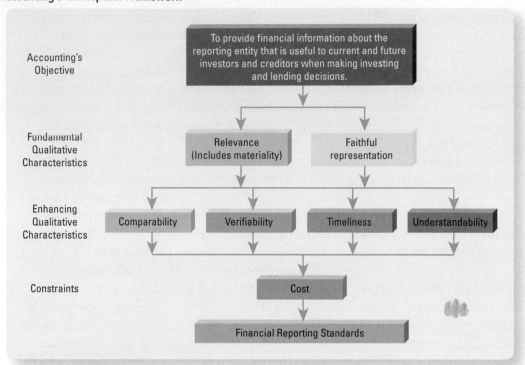

For accounting information to provide a faithful representation to users, it must reflect the *economic substance* of a transaction or event, which may not be the same as its legal form. The information must also be complete, neutral (free of bias), and accurate (free of material error). When accounting information possesses these facets of faithful representation, it is *reliable* to users.

Enhancing Qualitative Characteristics

To be useful, accounting information must also possess four *enhancing qualitative characteristics*:

- **comparability**,
- **verifiability**,
- **timeliness**, and
- **understandability**.

For accounting information to be *comparable*, it must be reported in a way that makes it possible to compare it to similar information being reported by other companies. It must also be reported in a way that is consistent with how it was reported in previous accounting periods.

Accounting information is *verifiable* when it can be checked for accuracy, completeness, and reliability. Verifiability enhances the chance that accounting information reflects a faithful representation of the economic substance of a transaction or event.

Timeliness means reporting accounting information to users in time for it to influence their decisions. Accounting information tends to become less relevant as it gets older, so it should be reported to users as soon after the end of the accounting period as possible, without sacrificing the other qualitative characteristics in the process.

Accounting information is *understandable* when it is clearly and concisely classified and presented to reasonably knowledgeable and diligent users of the information. At times, however, even informed and careful users will require assistance in understanding certain complex transactions and events.

The Cost Constraint

Accounting information is costly to produce. A primary constraint in the decision to disclose accounting information is that the cost of disclosure should not exceed the expected benefits to users. Management of an entity is primarily responsible for preparing accounting information. Managers must exercise judgment in determining whether the information is necessary for complete understanding of underlying economic facts and not excessively costly to provide.

This book introduces you to the basic financial reporting standards that have been devised using this conceptual framework. Before we begin exposing you to these standards, let's examine the assumptions that underlie this conceptual framework.

Assumptions Underlying the Conceptual Framework

The conceptual framework has only one explicit underlying assumption: the **going-concern assumption**. There are, however, three other assumptions that are implicit in the framework, so we present them here as well. They are the **separate-entity**, **historical-cost**, and **stable-monetary-unit assumptions**.

GOING-CONCERN ASSUMPTION. We typically prepare financial information under the assumption that the reporting entity is a going concern, which means that we expect it to continue operating normally for the foreseeable future. A company that is not a going concern is at risk of going bankrupt or closing down, so it may need to significantly scale down its operations or sell some of its assets at heavily discounted rates. When this risk is present, the financial statements are typically prepared on a basis that differs from the usual standards in IFRS or ASPE. If a different basis is used in such circumstances, it must be clearly disclosed to the users of the financial statements.

SEPARATE-ENTITY ASSUMPTION. We also prepare financial statements under the assumption that the business activities of the reporting entity are separate from the activities of its owners, so we do not mix the assets, liabilities, income, or expenses of the entity with those of its owners when reporting the entity's operating performance and financial position. Consider Gerald Schwartz, the chairman, president, chief executive officer, and major shareholder of ONEX Corporation, a large Canadian public company. Mr. Schwartz personally owns a house, automobiles, and investments in various companies. His personal assets, however, would not be included among the land, buildings, vehicles, and investments reported on ONEX's financial statements because his assets are separate from those of the entity he owns and operates. The separate-entity assumption draws a clear boundary around the business activities of the reporting entity, and only the activities within this boundary are reported in the entity's financial statements.

HISTORICAL-COST ASSUMPTION. The historical-cost assumption states that assets should be recorded at their *actual cost*, measured on the date of purchase as the amount of cash paid plus the dollar value of all non-cash consideration (other assets, privileges, or rights) also given in exchange. For example, suppose TELUS purchases a building for a new store. The building's current owner is asking for $600,000 for the building. The management of TELUS believes the building is worth $585,000, and offers the present owner that amount. Two real estate professionals appraise the building at $610,000. The two parties compromise and agree on a price of $590,000 for the building. The historical-cost assumption requires TELUS to initially record the building at its actual cost of $590,000—not at $585,000, $600,000, or $610,000—even though those amounts were what some people believed the building was worth. At the point of purchase, $590,000 is both the *relevant* amount for the building's worth and the amount that *faithfully represents* a reliable figure for the price the company paid for it.

The historical-cost and the going-concern assumptions also maintain that TELUS's accounting records should continue to use historical cost to value the asset for as long as the business holds it. Why? Because cost is a *verifiable* measure that is relatively *free from bias*. Suppose that TELUS owns the building for six years and that real estate prices increase during this period. As a result, at the end of the period, the building can be sold for $650,000. Should TELUS increase the value of the building on the company's books to $650,000? No. According to the historical-cost assumption, the building remains on TELUS's books at its historical cost of $590,000. According to the going-concern assumption, TELUS intends to stay in business and keep the building, not to sell it, so its historical cost is the most relevant and the most faithful representation of its value. It is also the most easily verifiable amount. Should the company decide to sell the building later at a price above or below its recorded value, it will record the cash received, remove the value of the building from the books, and record a gain or a loss for the difference at that time.

The historical-cost assumption is not used as extensively as it once was. Accounting is moving in the direction of reporting more assets and liabilities at their fair values. **Fair value** is the amount that the business could sell the asset for, or the amount that the business could pay to settle the liability. IFRS permit certain types of assets and liabilities to be periodically adjusted to reflect their fair values rather than leaving them on the books at their historical costs. With rare exceptions, ASPE still require assets and liabilities to be kept on the books at their historical costs. Fair-value accounting is generally beyond the scope of this textbook, but in later chapters we will highlight where this option exists.

STABLE-MONETARY-UNIT ASSUMPTION. The vast majority of Canadian entities report their financial information in Canadian dollars (or monetary units), although some choose to report in U.S. dollars instead. Regardless of the reporting currency used, financial information is always reported under the assumption that the value of the currency is stable, despite the fact that its value does change due to economic factors such as inflation. By assuming that the purchasing power of the reporting currency is stable, we can add and subtract dollar values from different reporting periods without having to make adjustments for changes in the underlying value of the currency.

Now that you have an understanding of the conceptual framework and assumptions underlying the financial statements, let's take an introductory look at each of the statements that you will learn more about as you progress through this book.

STOP + THINK (1-1)

It is September 24, 2014, and your company is considering the purchase of land for future expansion. The seller is asking $50,000 for the land, which cost them $35,000 four years ago. An independent appraiser assigns the land a value of $47,000. You offer the seller $44,000 for the land and they come back with a counter-offer of $48,000. You and the seller end up settling on a purchase price of $46,000 for the land.

1. When you record the purchase of this land in your accounting records, at what value will you record it?

2. Assume that four years later someone approaches your company and offers to purchase this land, which you have yet to develop, for $60,000. You know this to be a fair price given a recent appraisal you had done on the land. You decline the offer because you have plans to begin developing the land next year. What adjustment would you make to the value of the land in your accounting records?

DESCRIBE THE PURPOSE OF EACH FINANCIAL STATEMENT AND EXPLAIN THE ELEMENTS OF EACH ONE

OBJECTIVE

❸ **Describe** the purpose of each financial statement and **explain** the elements of each one

The financial statements present a company's financial results to users who wish to answer questions about the company's financial performance. What would users want to know about a company's performance? The answer to this question will vary by user, but Exhibit 1-4 presents four main questions most users would ask, as well as the financial statement that would be used to answer each question.

Each of the four financial statements reports transactions and events by grouping them into broad classes according to their economic characteristics. These broad classes are termed the *elements of financial statements*. Exhibit 1-4 presents the main elements of each financial statement. Let's examine each statement and its elements, beginning with the income statement.

The Income Statement Measures Operating Performance

The **income statement** (or **statement of profit or loss**) measures a company's operating performance for a *specified period of time*. The period of time covered by an income statement is typically a month, a quarter (three months), or a year, and will always be

EXHIBIT 1-4
The Financial Statements and Their Elements

Question	Financial Statement	Elements
1. How well did the company perform during the year?	Income statement	Total income (revenues + gains) − Total expenses (expenses + losses) Net income (or Net loss)
2. Why did the company's retained earnings change during the year?	Statement of retained earnings	Beginning retained earnings + Net income + Other comprehensive income (IFRS only) − Dividends Ending retained earnings
3. What is the company's financial position at the end of the year?	Balance sheet	Assets = Liabilities + Owners' equity
4. How much cash did the company generate and spend during the year?	Statement of cash flows	Operating cash flows ± Investing cash flows ± Financing cash flows Increase (or decrease) in cash

EXHIBIT 1-5
Consolidated Statements
of Income and Other
Comprehensive Income
(Adapted)

TELUS Corporation
Consolidated Statements of Income and Other Comprehensive Income (Adapted)
For the Years Ended December 31, 2011 and 2010

(in millions of dollars)	2011	2010
Operating Revenues		
1. Service	$ 9,606	$9,131
2. Equipment	719	611
3.	10,325	9,742
4. Other operating income	72	50
5.	10,397	9,792
Operating Expenses		
6. Goods and services purchased	4,726	4,236
7. Employee benefits expense	1,893	1,906
8. Depreciation	1,331	1,339
9. Amortization of intangible assets	479	402
10.	8,429	7,883
11. **Operating Income**	1,968	1,909
12. Financing costs	377	522
13. **Income Before Income Taxes**	1,591	1,387
14. Income taxes	376	335
15. **Net Income**	$ 1,215	$1,052
Other Comprehensive Income		
16. Items that may be reclassified to income	10	54
17. Items that will not be reclassified to income	(846)	(218)
18. **Comprehensive Income**	$ 379	$ 888

specified in the heading of the income statement. In the heading of TELUS's income statement in Exhibit 1-5, we can see that it covers the years ended December 31, 2011 and 2010. Financial statements for the current year are easier to analyze and interpret when they can be compared to the prior year's statements, so you will always see the prior year's results presented beside those of the current year (unless it is an entity's first year of operations). TELUS's *fiscal year* ends on December 31, so like most companies it has a *calendar year-end*, but a company can choose whatever fiscal year-end date it desires. Most of Canada's big banks, for example, have a fiscal year-end of October 31. The income statement has two main elements, income and expenses, which are discussed in more detail below.

INCOME. A company's **income** includes both **revenue** and **gains**. Revenue consists of amounts earned by a company in the course of its ordinary, day-to-day business activities. The vast majority of a company's revenue is earned through the sale of its primary goods and services. Loblaws, for example, earns most of its revenue by selling groceries and other household goods. An accounting firm such as KPMG earns revenue by providing accounting, tax, and other professional services to its clients. TELUS's ordinary business activities include the sale of services such as wireless phone and Internet access, as well as goods like the smartphones and tablets that access these services. On lines 1 and 2 of TELUS's 2011 income statement, we see that it earned "Service revenues" of $9,606 million and "Equipment revenues" of $719 million in 2011. Revenue is referred to by a variety of different names, including sales, fees, interest, dividends, royalties, and rent. You will learn more about revenue and how to account for it in Chapter 3.

Gains represent other items that result in an *increase* in economic benefits to a company and may, but usually do not, occur in the course of the company's ordinary business activities. If, for example, TELUS sold one of the buildings it owned for an amount that exceeded what it was last recorded at in the financial statements, the excess would be recognized as a gain on the income statement. When gains are recognized in the income statement, they are usually listed separately, either directly in the statement or in the notes to the financial statements (discussed on page 22), because knowledge of these gains is useful for making decisions. TELUS does not explicitly report any gains on its 2011 income statement, but the notes to the financial statements disclose that there are $20 million in gains included in TELUS's "Other operating income" of $72 million on line 4 of the income statement. The *other income* line on an income statement generally includes categories of revenues and gains that are not sufficiently material to report on separate lines of the statement. You will learn more about some common types of gains in Chapters 7 and 8.

EXPENSES. A company's expenses consist of **losses** as well as those expenses that are incurred in the course of its ordinary business activities. Expenses consist mainly of the costs incurred to purchase the goods and services a company needs to run its business on a day-to-day basis. For TELUS, these expenses would include the cost of the smartphones, tablets, and other goods it sells to customers, which is an expense commonly known as the *cost of goods sold* or *cost of sales*, an item you will learn more about in Chapter 6. This cost, as well as the wages it pays its employees, the rent it pays on its stores, and many more expenses, would be included in the $4,726 million of "Goods and services purchased" on line 6 of TELUS's income statement. On line 7, we see that TELUS incurred "Employee benefits expense" of $1,893 million, which would include expenses related to medical and dental plans, pensions, and other benefits paid to employees during 2011. The "Depreciation" of $1,331 million on line 8 relates to the use of TELUS's buildings and equipment during 2011. You will learn more about this type of expense, as well as the "Amortization" on line 9, in Chapter 7. On line 12, we see that TELUS incurred "Financing costs" of $377 million, which consist mostly of the interest expense it paid on the money it has borrowed from banks and other lenders, a topic that will be covered in Chapter 9. The last expense on TELUS's income statement is "Income taxes" of $376 million (line 14). You likely know a little bit about this kind of expense already, but it will be discussed more in Chapter 11. There are many more expenses that companies incur on a day-to-day basis but are not typically disclosed separately on the income statements of public companies, either because they are not sufficiently material or because they are too sensitive to disclose to competing companies. You will encounter many of these expenses as you progress through the book.

Losses are the opposite of gains, and represent items that result in a *decrease* in economic benefits to a company. Like gains, they may, but usually do not, occur in the course of the company's ordinary business activities. If, for example, TELUS sold some equipment it owned for an amount that was less than what it was last recorded at in the financial statements, the difference would be recognized as a loss on the income statement. Losses are usually listed separately in the statement or disclosed in the notes to the financial statements. TELUS does not report any losses on its 2011 income statement or in the notes to the financial statements. You will learn more about some common types of losses in Chapters 7 and 8.

The income statement also reports the company's **net income**, which is calculated as follows:

Net Income = Total Revenues and Gains − Total Expenses and Losses

In accounting, the word *net* refers to the amount of something that is left after something else has been deducted from an initial total. In this case, *net income* is the amount of *income* that is left after *total expenses* (expenses + losses) have been deducted from *total income* (revenues + gains) for the period. When total expenses exceed total income, the result is called a **net loss**. Net income is sometimes known as **net earnings** or **net profit**, and is *usually considered the most important amount in a company's financial statements*. It is a key component of many financial ratios, including return on equity and earnings per share, which you will learn about in later chapters of this book.

A company whose net income is consistently increasing is usually regarded by investors and creditors as a healthy and high-quality company. In the long run, the company's value should increase. On line 15 of TELUS's income statement, we see that its net income increased from $1,052 in 2010 to $1,215 million in 2011, so TELUS's managers, investors, and creditors should have been pleased with its 2011 operating performance. You will see TELUS's net income of $1,215 carried forward to its statement of retained earnings, which is discussed in the next section.

Appended to the bottom of TELUS's income statement in Exhibit 1-5 is another financial statement called the *statement of other comprehensive income*, which under IFRS reports other types of income and expenses that are not included in a company's net income. It includes items that are generally complex to determine, such as gains and losses from foreign currency translations, financial derivatives, and employee pension plans. As you can see on line 18, TELUS's $379 million in comprehensive income for 2011 is far less than its net income of $1,215, which is due to the large loss of $846 million reported on line 17. This additional financial statement, which is not reported under ASPE, is discussed briefly in Chapter 11 and covered in more depth in intermediate accounting courses.

The Statement of Retained Earnings Reports Changes in Retained Earnings

A company's **retained earnings** represent the accumulated net income (or net earnings) of the company since the day it started business, less any net losses and dividends declared during this time. When the accumulated amount is negative, the term **deficit** is used to describe it. The **statement of retained earnings** reports the changes in a company's retained earnings during the same period covered by the income statement. Under ASPE, this statement is often added to the bottom of the income statement, although it may also be presented as a completely separate statement. Under IFRS, information on the changes in retained earnings is included in the *statement of changes in owners' equity*, which you will learn more about in Chapter 11. At the beginning of 2011, TELUS had retained earnings of $2,126 million (line 1 of Exhibit 1-6). Let's look at the major changes to TELUS's retained earnings during 2011.

- Because retained earnings represent a company's accumulated net income, the first addition to the opening balance is TELUS's 2011 net income of $1,215 million (line 2), which comes directly from line 15 of the income statement in Exhibit 1-5.

- TELUS reports an "other comprehensive income" of $846 million on line 3, which comes directly from line 17 of the statement of comprehensive income at the bottom of Exhibit 1-5. Under IFRS, this amount represents a special type of loss that TELUS incurred during 2011, a loss that it will never include in its regular net income. It is therefore deducted from retained earnings here to reflect the decrease in earnings available for future distribution to shareholders.

EXHIBIT 1-6
Consolidated Statements of
Retained Earnings (Adapted)

TELUS Corporation
Consolidated Statements of Retained Earnings (Adapted)
For the Years Ended December 31, 2011 and 2010

(in millions of dollars)	2011	2010
1. Balance, beginning of year	$2,126	$1,934
2. Net income	1,215	1,052
3. Other comprehensive income	(846)	(218)
4. Dividends	(715)	(642)
5. Balance, end of year	$1,780	$2,126

- On line 4, we see that TELUS declared dividends of $715 million during 2011. Dividends represent the distribution of past earnings to current shareholders of the company. You will learn more about dividends in Chapter 10.

After accounting for all the changes during 2011, TELUS reports a closing retained earnings balance of $1,780 million on line 5. This balance will be carried forward to the owners' equity section of the balance sheet, which is the next financial statement we will introduce to you.

The Balance Sheet Measures Financial Position

A company's financial position consists of three elements: the assets it controls, the liabilities it is obligated to pay, and the equity its owners have accumulated in the business. These elements are reported in the **balance sheet**, which under IFRS is also known as the **statement of financial position**. (For simplicity, this financial statement will be referred to as the balance sheet throughout the textbook.) The balance sheet reports a company's financial position *as at a specific date*, which always falls on the last day of a monthly, quarterly, or annual reporting period. Because it is presented as at a specific date, you can think of the balance as a snapshot of the company's financial position at a particular point in time. The TELUS balance sheet in Exhibit 1-7 reports its financial position as at the year-end dates of December 31, 2011 and 2010.

The balance sheet takes its name from the fact that the assets it reports must *always* equal—or be in balance with—the sum of the liabilities and equity it reports. This relationship is known as the **accounting equation**, and it provides the foundation for the double-entry method of accounting you will begin to learn in Chapter 2. Exhibit 1-8 illustrates the equation using the figures from TELUS's 2011 balance sheet in Exhibit 1-7.

IFRS and ASPE define assets, liabilities, and equity using different terms, but the definitions are essentially equivalent. The IFRS definitions are used below, primarily because they are more concise than the ASPE definitions.

ASSETS. An **asset** is a resource controlled by the company as a result of past events and from which the company expects to receive future economic benefits. Let's use two of TELUS's assets to illustrate this formal definition. One of TELUS's assets is its "accounts receivable" (line 2), which arose from past sales to customers who purchased TELUS's products and services on account (or on credit), with the promise to pay off the accounts at a later date. In the future, when customers do pay off their accounts, TELUS will receive the economic benefit of "cash" (line 1), another asset, which it can

EXHIBIT 1-7
Consolidated Balance
Sheets (Adapted)

TELUS Corporation
Consolidated Balance Sheets (Adapted)
As at December 31, 2011 and 2010

(in millions of dollars)	2011	2010
Current assets		
1. Cash and temporary investments, net	$ 46	$ 17
2. Accounts receivable	1,428	1,318
3. Inventories	353	283
4. Prepaid expenses	144	113
5. Other current assets	80	66
6.	2,051	1,797
Non-current assets		
7. Property, plant and equipment, net	7,964	7,831
8. Goodwill and intangible assets, net	9,814	9,724
9. Investments	21	37
10. Other long-term assets	81	235
11.	17,880	17,827
12. **Total assets**	$19,931	$19,624
Current liabilities		
13. Short-term borrowings	$ 404	$ 400
14. Accounts payable and accrued liabilities	1,419	1,477
15. Income and other taxes payable	25	6
16. Dividends payable	188	169
17. Advance billings and customer deposits	655	658
18. Provisions	88	122
19. Current maturities of long-term debt	1,066	847
20. Other current liabilities	-	419
21.	3,845	4,098
Non-current liabilities		
22. Long-term debt	5,508	5,209
23. Other long-term liabilities	1,465	853
24. Deferred income taxes	1,600	1,683
25.	8,573	7,745
26. **Total liabilities**	12,418	11,843
Shareholders' equity		
27. Share capital	5,556	5,456
28. Contributed surplus	166	176
29. Retained earnings	1,780	2,126
30. Accumulated other comprehensive income	11	1
31. Non-controlling interests	-	22
32.	7,513	7,781
33. **Total liabilities and shareholders' equity**	$19,931	$19,624

use to fund future business activities. We classify assets into two categories on the balance sheet: **current assets** and **non-current assets**. We classify an asset as current when we expect to convert it to cash, sell it, or consume it *within one year* of the balance sheet date, or within the business's normal operating cycle if it is longer than one year. Current assets are listed in order of their **liquidity**, which is a measure of how quickly they can be converted to cash, the most liquid asset. At the end of 2011, TELUS had $2,051 million in current assets (line 6). Let's examine TELUS's major current assets, all of which will be covered in more detail in later chapters.

- TELUS had "cash and temporary investments" of $46 million at the end of 2011 (line 1). You know what cash is, so no explanation is necessary. Temporary

EXHIBIT 1-8
The Accounting Equation
(in millions of dollars)

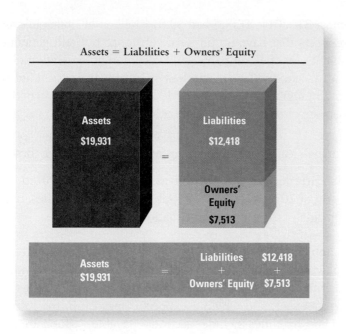

investments include stocks, bonds, and other investments the company intends to sell within the next year. They are also known as *short-term investments*, and you will learn more about them in Chapter 5.

- On line 2, we see that TELUS had $1,428 million in "accounts receivable" on December 31, 2011. This balance represents the amount of money TELUS expects to collect within the next year from customers who bought smart-phones, wireless access, and other goods and services on account (or on credit) prior to year-end. You will read more about this asset in Chapter 5 as well.

- At the end of 2011, TELUS held $353 million of "inventories" (line 3), which include the phones, tablets, and other products the company expects to sell to customers in 2012. Inventories are covered in detail in Chapter 6.

- The last major current asset on TELUS's 2011 balance sheet is "prepaid expenses" of $144 million (line 4), which, as the name suggests, represent expenses that TELUS has paid for but not yet consumed as at the end of the year. If, for example, on December 15, 2011, TELUS paid $500,000 for TV advertising time during the Super Bowl at the end of January 2012, this amount would be included in prepaid expenses on December 31, 2011, because TELUS will not realize the benefit of this expense until after year-end. Prepaid expenses are discussed in Chapter 3.

All assets that do not qualify as current are classified as non-current assets, which are also known as **long-term assets**. TELUS had $17,880 million of non-current assets on December 31, 2011. We will take a brief look at the major components of this total now and revisit them in more depth later in the book.

- TELUS had "property, plant, and equipment" of $7,964 million at the end of 2011 (line 7). This balance consists of the land (property), buildings (plant), and equipment that TELUS uses to carry out its business activities. Plant and equipment assets are usually reported at their **carrying amount**, which is their original cost *net* of accumulated depreciation (or amortization). The accumulated depreciation represents the amount of the original cost of the asset that has been *used up* to generate economic benefits for the company. You will learn more about these non-current assets in Chapter 7.

- On December 31, 2011, TELUS had $9,814 million of "intangible assets" (line 8), which are assets that have no physical substance but still generate future economic benefits for the company. TELUS's intangible assets include customer lists, software, goodwill, and wireless spectrum licences. Like property and equipment, intangible assets are recorded net of any accumulated amortization. These assets are also covered in detail in Chapter 7.

- On line 9, TELUS reports "investments" in the shares of other companies of $21 million. You will learn more about long-term investments like these in Chapter 8.

Between its current and non-current assets, TELUS reported total assets of $19,931 at the end of 2011. Next we will look at TELUS's liabilities, the first component on the right side of the accounting equation.

LIABILITIES. A **liability** is a present obligation of the entity arising from past events, the settlement of which is expected to result in an outflow from the entity of resources embodying economic benefits. In simpler terms, a liability is a debt the entity owes as a result of a past event, and which it expects to pay off in the future using some of its assets. TELUS's liabilities include "accounts payable," which are debts they owe to companies that have supplied them with goods and services in the past. TELUS's largest liability is its "long-term debt," which represents money they have borrowed in the past from banks and other financial institutions to help them fund asset purchases and other business activities. In the future, TELUS will use some of its cash to pay off both of these liabilities. Like assets, we classify liabilities as **current liabilities** or **non-current liabilities** (or **long-term liabilities**), with the distinction based on how soon after year-end the company expects to pay off the debt. Current liabilities are debts the company expects to pay off *within one year* of the balance sheet date, or within the company's normal operating cycle if it is longer than one year. TELUS reported current liabilities of $3,845 million at the end of 2011. Let's look at the individual liabilities that make up this total.

- TELUS had "short-term borrowings" of $404 million at the end of 2011 (line 13). This amount represents money TELUS has borrowed on a short-term basis to cover temporary shortfalls in cash it needs to run its business.

- At December 31, 2011, TELUS owed $1,419 million in "accounts payable and accrued liabilities" (line 14), which comprise debts related to goods and services the company has purchased on credit from its suppliers. Essentially, this liability is the opposite of the accounts receivable current asset discussed above. You will learn more about these liabilities in Chapters 3 and 9.

- TELUS had $25 million of "income and other taxes payable" as at December 31, 2011 (line 15). This balance comprises the income and other taxes, such as the Harmonized Sales Tax (HST), Goods and Services Tax (GST), and various provincial sales taxes, that TELUS owes to various government entities at the end of the year. Sales taxes are discussed in Chapter 9 and income taxes are covered in Chapter 11.

- At the end of 2011, TELUS had "dividends payable" of $188 million (line 16). This balance represents the dividends that TELUS's board of directors declared prior to year-end, but that will not be paid until after December 31, 2011.

- On line 17 is a liability of $655 million related to "advance billings and customer deposits." This liability represents money TELUS has received from customers *in advance* of providing them with the goods and services they have paid for. Most liabilities are paid off using cash, but this type of liability—known more commonly as *deferred revenue* or *unearned revenue*—is actually paid off by providing the customers with the goods and services they are owed. It will be discussed in more detail in Chapters 3 and 9.

- TELUS had a liability for "provisions" of $88 million at the end of 2011 (line 18). Provisions represent *estimated* liabilities for things such as product warranties that the company expects to have to pay at some point in the future, but for which the exact amount cannot be determined. Chapter 9 presents more information on this type of liability.

- TELUS reports "current maturities of long-term debt" totalling $1,066 million (line 19). This balance represents the portion of long-term debt that TELUS must pay off within one year of the balance sheet date. The long-term portion is discussed below, and these liabilities are discussed more in Chapter 9.

In total, TELUS reported $3,845 million in liabilities that it expected to pay off before the end of its next fiscal year on December 31, 2012 (line 21). It also reported total non-current (or long-term) liabilities of $8,573 million (line 25), which are debts the company expects to pay off beyond one year from the balance sheet date of December 31, 2011. Here are a few details on the major liabilities TELUS expects to pay off after December 31, 2012:

- On line 22, TELUS reports $5,508 million of "long-term debt," which is composed of notes, debentures, and bonds payable at the end of 2011. These types of long-term debts will be covered in depth in Chapter 9.

- TELUS's other major long-term liability at December 31, 2011 is "deferred income taxes" of $1,600 million (line 24). This liability arises because there are differences between how income taxes payable are calculated for accounting purposes and how they are calculated according to the Canadian *Income Tax Act*. This is an advanced topic that is covered in intermediate financial accounting courses.

In total, TELUS reported liabilities of $12,418 million at the end of 2011 (line 26). Let's now examine the last major element of the balance sheet, owners' equity.

OWNERS' EQUITY. Owners' equity is the owners' remaining interest in the assets of the company after deducting all its liabilities. In effect, it represents the owners' claim on the company's assets *net* of the company's liabilities, so it is sometimes referred to as the **net assets** of the company. For incorporated companies like TELUS, it is often called **shareholders' equity**. We can rearrange the accounting equation to clearly express the nature of this balance sheet element:

$$\textbf{Owners' Equity} = \textbf{Assets} - \textbf{Liabilities}$$

Owners' equity has four common components. Let's look at each one using TELUS's 2011 balance sheet as an example.

- TELUS had "share capital" of $5,556 million on December 31, 2011 (line 27). This balance represents amounts contributed by shareholders in exchange for shares in TELUS. You will learn more about share capital in Chapter 10.

- On line 28, TELUS reports $166 million of "contributed surplus," which consists of amounts contributed by shareholders *in excess* of amounts allocated to share capital.

- TELUS's ending "retained earnings" of $1,780 million is carried over from the statement of retained earnings to line 29 on the balance sheet.
- The last component of TELUS's owners' equity is "accumulated other comprehensive income" of $11 million (line 30). IFRS require companies to report this amount, which is an accumulation of past earnings not included in retained earnings. This equity item is discussed in detail in Chapter 11. ASPE do not require companies to account for this item.

At December 31, 2011, TELUS had total owners' equity of $7,513 (line 32). Now let's take another look at how the three main elements of TELUS's balance sheet fit into the accounting equation:

$$\begin{array}{ccccc} \text{Assets} & = & \text{Liabilities} & + & \text{Owners' Equity} \\ \$19,931 & = & \$12,418 & + & \$7,513 \end{array}$$

STOP + THINK (1-2)

1. If the assets of a business are $240,000 and the liabilities are $80,000, how much is the owners' equity?
2. If the owners' equity in a business is $160,000 and the liabilities are $130,000, how much are the assets?
3. A company reported total monthly income of $129,000 and total expenses of $85,000. What is the result of operations for the month?
4. If the beginning balance of retained earnings is $100,000, total income is $75,000, expenses total $50,000, and the company pays a $10,000 dividend, what is the ending balance of retained earnings?

The Statement of Cash Flows Measures Cash Receipts and Payments

The **statement of cash flows** (or cash flow statement under ASPE) reports a company's cash receipts and cash payments for the same fiscal period covered by the income statement. This statement shows users the specific business activities that generated cash receipts or resulted in cash payments during the period. These activities are classified into three categories:

1. **Operating activities**
2. **Investing activities**
3. **Financing activities**

Exhibit 1-9 presents TELUS's statements of cash flows for 2011 and 2010. Let's use it to learn more about each of these business activities.

OPERATING ACTIVITIES. These activities comprise the main revenue-producing activities of a company, and generally result from the transactions and other events that determine net income. Common operating activities include cash receipts from a company's sales of its primary goods and services as well as cash payments to suppliers and employees for the goods and services they provide to generate these sales. When TELUS pays Apple for the iPhones it sells to its customers, for example, the payment is an operating activity that results in a cash outflow. Similarly, when a customer pays TELUS for one of these iPhones, it results in a cash inflow from operating activities.

On line 1 of TELUS's statement of cash flows, we see that the determination of cash flows from operating activities begins with the $1,215 million in net income it

EXHIBIT 1-9
Consolidated Statements of
Cash Flows (Adapted)

TELUS Corporation
Consolidated Statements of Cash Flows (Adapted)
For the Years Ended December 31, 2011 and 2010

(in millions of dollars)	2011	2010
Operating activities		
1. Net income	$ 1,215	$ 1,052
Adjustments to reconcile net income to cash		
provided by operating activities:		
2. Depreciation and amortization	1,810	1,741
3. Deferred income taxes	205	217
4. Share-based compensation	(12)	(30)
5. Net employee defined benefit plans expense	(32)	(9)
6. Employer contributions to employee defined benefit plans	(298)	(140)
7. Other	(83)	(42)
8. Net change in non-cash operating working capital	(255)	(119)
9. **Cash provided by operating activities**	2,550	2,670
Investing activities		
10. Capital expenditures	(1,847)	(1,721)
11. Acquisitions and other	(110)	-
12. Proceeds from the sale of property and other assets	4	10
13. Other	-	4
14. Net change in non-cash investing working capital	(15)	(24)
15. **Cash used by investing activities**	(1,968)	(1,731)
Financing activities		
16. Non-voting shares issued	24	15
17. Dividends paid	(642)	(473)
18. Issuance and repayment of short-term borrowing	4	(100)
19. Long-term debt issued	4,068	3,725
20. Redemptions and repayment of long-term debt	(3,946)	(4,119)
21. Other	(61)	(11)
22. **Cash used by financing activities**	(553)	(963)
Cash position		
23. Increase (decrease) in cash and temporary investments, net	29	(24)
24. Cash and temporary investments, net, beginning of period	17	41
25. **Cash and temporary investments, net, end of period**	$ 46	$ 17

reported on line 15 of its income statement in Exhibit 1-6. In total, the company generated over $2.5 billion in cash inflows from operating activities in 2011 (line 9). This is a sign of excellent financial health. A company that does not regularly generate sufficient cash flows from operating activities will eventually suffer cash flow problems and may go bankrupt.

INVESTING ACTIVITIES. These activities include the purchase and sale of long-term assets and other investments that result in cash inflows or outflows related to resources used for generating future income and cash flows. Cash payments to acquire property, plant, and equipment, and the cash received upon the sale of these assets, are common investing activities. Investing activities also include cash flows from the purchase and sale of investments in other companies, and those related to loans made to other entities.

In 2011, TELUS spent $1,847 million in cash on "capital expenditures" (line 10), which included purchases of property, plant, equipment, and a variety of intangible assets. They also spent $110 million on "acquisitions" of other companies (line 11). TELUS received $4 million in "proceeds from the sale of property and other assets" (line 12). Like its operating activities, TELUS's 2011 investing activities indicate excellent future prospects for the company because they show that the company invested almost $2 billion in new long-term assets (line 15) that will help it earn additional revenues in coming years.

FINANCING ACTIVITIES. These activities result in changes in the size and composition of a company's contributed equity and borrowings. Common financing activities include the issuance and acquisition of shares, the payment of cash dividends, the cash proceeds from borrowings, and the repayment of amounts borrowed.

In this section of TELUS's statement of cash flows, we see that it received $24 million in cash from "non-voting shares issued" during the year (line 16). There was also a cash outflow of $642 million for "dividends paid" to shareholders (line 17). Lines 18, 19, and 20 report the cash inflows and outflows related to TELUS's short-term and long-term borrowings during the year. In total, TELUS reported total cash outflows from financing activities of $553 million for 2011.

Overall, TELUS's business activities resulted in a net increase in cash of $29 million for 2011 (line 23; TELUS includes temporary investments in its cash balance). When this is added to its $17-million cash balance at the beginning of the year (line 24), TELUS ended 2011 with $46 million in cash (line 25). You can trace this cash balance to line 1 of TELUS's balance sheet in Exhibit 1-7 for an illustration of the link between the statement of cash flows and the balance sheet.

The Notes to the Financial Statements Provide Additional Information

The notes to the financial statements are an integral part of the financial statements and should be read carefully as part of a review of the financial statements. The notes provide information that cannot be reported conveniently on the face of the financial statements. For example, the notes tell the readers information such as what accounting policies were used in preparing the financial statements, and what methods were used to account for inventories and depreciation. An example of these notes can be found in Appendix A: Annual Report for TELUS Corporation. Notice that at the bottom of each of TELUS's financial statements is this reminder to users: *The accompanying notes are an integral part of these financial statements.*

Let's now summarize the relationships among the financial statements.

OBJECTIVE

❹ **Explain** the relationships among the financial statements

EXPLAIN THE RELATIONSHIPS AMONG THE FINANCIAL STATEMENTS

Exhibit 1-10 presents summarized financial statements for the fictional Huron Ltd. This exhibit highlights the relationships among each of the four financial statements you just studied. These relationships apply to the financial statements of every organization, so examine them carefully to ensure you understand the nature of each relationship.

EXHIBIT 1-10
Relationships Among the
Financial Statements

Huron Ltd.
Income Statement
For the Year Ended December 31, 2014

Income	$ 700,000
Expenses	670,000
Net income	$ 30,000

Huron Ltd.
Statement of Retained Earnings
For the Year Ended December 31, 2014

Beginning retained earnings	$ 120,000
Net income	30,000
Cash dividends	(10,000)
Ending retained earnings	$ 140,000

Huron Ltd.
Balance Sheet
As at December 31, 2014

Assets	
Cash	$ 25,000
All other assets	275,000
Total assets	$ 300,000
Liabilities	
Total liabilities	$ 120,000
Shareholders' Equity	
Common shares	40,000
Retained earnings	140,000
Total liabilities and shareholders' equity	$ 300,000

Huron Ltd.
Statement of Cash Flows
For the Year Ended December 31, 2014

Net cash provided by operating activities	$ 90,000
Net cash used for investing activities	(110,000)
Net cash provided by financing activities	40,000
Net increase in cash	20,000
Beginning cash balance	5,000
Ending cash balance	$ 25,000

Specifically, note the following:

1. The income statement measures Huron's operating performance for the year ended December 31, 2014, by:
    a. Reporting all income and expenses for the year.
    b. Reporting net income if total income exceeds total expenses, or a net loss if expenses exceed income.

2. The statement of retained earnings reports changes in Huron's retained earnings balance for the year ended December 31, 2014, by:

   a. First adding the net income (or subtracting the net loss) from the income statement (link 1 in Exhibit 1-10) to the retained earnings balance at the beginning of the year.

   b. Then deducting dividends declared during the year to arrive at the retained earnings balance at the end of the year.

3. The balance sheet reports Huron's financial position at December 31, 2014, by:

   a. Reporting all assets, liabilities, and shareholders' equity as at the end of the year.

   b. Within the shareholders' equity section of the statement, reporting the retained earnings balance at the end of the year, which comes from the statement of retained earnings (link 2).

◄ DECISION GUIDELINES ►

WHAT DO DECISION MAKERS LOOK FOR WHEN EVALUATING A COMPANY?

These Decision Guidelines illustrate how people use financial statements. Decision Guidelines appear throughout the book to show how accounting information aids decision making.

   Suppose you are considering an investment in TELUS Corporation stock. How do you proceed? Where do you get the information you need? What do you look for?

Decision	Guidelines
1. Can the company sell its products and services?	**1.** Sales revenue on the income statement: Are sales growing or falling?

2. Is the company making money?	**2. a.** Gross profit (Sales – Cost of goods sold)
	   b. Operating income (Gross profit – Operating expenses)
	   c. Net income (bottom line of the income statement)
	All three income measures should be increasing over time.

3. What percentage of sales revenue ends up as profit?	**3.** Divide net income by sales revenue. Examine the trend of the net income percentage from year to year.
4. Can the company collect its accounts receivable?	**4.** From the balance sheet, compare the percentage increase in accounts receivable to the percentage increase in sales. If receivables are growing much faster than sales, collections may be too slow, and a cash shortage may result.

5. Can the company pay its:
   a. current liabilities?
   b. total liabilities?
	5. From the balance sheet, compare:
	   a. current assets to current liabilities. Current assets should be somewhat greater than current liabilities.
	   b. total assets to total liabilities. Total assets must be somewhat greater than total liabilities.

6. Where is the company's cash coming from? How is cash being used?	**6.** On the statement of cash flows, operating activities should provide the bulk of the company's cash during most years. Otherwise, the business will fail. Examine investing cash flows to see if the company is purchasing long-term assets—property, plant, and equipment and intangibles (this signals growth).

4. The statement of cash flows reports Huron's cash receipts and cash payments for the year ended December 31, 2014, by:
   a. Reporting cash provided by (or used in) the company's operating, investing, and financing activities during the year.
   b. Reporting the net change in the company's cash balance during the year and adding it to the beginning cash balance to arrive at the cash balance as at the end of the year, which is also reported on the balance sheet (link 3).

MAKE ETHICAL BUSINESS DECISIONS

OBJECTIVE

❺ **Make** ethical business decisions

Running a business requires sound decision making, which in turn requires the exercise of good judgment, both at the individual and corporate levels. For example, you may work for or eventually run a company like Tim Hortons that devotes a percentage of its net income to a variety of charitable organizations and activities. Will this be profitable in the long run, or would it be more sensible to devote those resources to other, less-charitable activities? Making a business decision like this requires careful ethical judgment. Can that be profitable in the long run?

As an accountant, you may have to decide whether to record a $50,000 expenditure as an asset on the balance sheet or an expense on the income statement. Or, you may have to decide whether $25 million of goods delivered to customers in late 2014 should be recorded as revenue in 2014 or in 2015. As mentioned earlier, the application of IFRS and ASPE frequently requires the use of professional judgment because accounting standards contain few clear-cut rules on how to account for transactions and events. Depending on the type of business, the facts and circumstances surrounding accounting decisions may not always make them clear cut, and yet the decision may determine whether the company shows a profit or a loss in a particular period! What are the factors that influence business and accounting decisions, and how should these factors be weighed? Generally, three factors influence business and accounting decisions: *economic, legal, and ethical factors*.

The *economic* factor states that the decision being made should *maximize the economic benefits* to the decision maker. Based on economic theory, every rational person faced with a decision will choose the course of action that maximizes his or her own welfare, without regard to how that decision impacts others. In summary, the combined outcome of each person acting in his or her own self-interest will maximize the benefits to society as a whole.

The *legal* factor is based on the proposition that free societies are governed by laws. Laws are written to provide clarity and to prevent abuse of the rights of individuals or society. Democratically enacted laws both contain and express society's collective moral standards. Legal analysis involves applying the relevant laws to each decision and then choosing the action that complies with those laws. A complicating factor for a global business may be that what is legal in one country might not be legal in another. In that case, it is usually best to abide by the laws of the most restrictive country.

The *ethical* factor recognizes that while certain actions might be both economically profitable and legal, they may still not be right. Therefore, most companies, and many individuals, have established ethical standards for themselves to enforce a higher level of conduct than that imposed by law. These standards govern how we treat others and the way we restrain our selfish desires. This behaviour and its underlying beliefs are the essence of ethics. **Ethical standards** are shaped by our cultural, socioeconomic, and religious backgrounds. An *ethical analysis* is often needed to guide judgment when making business decisions.

When performing an ethical analysis, our challenge is to identify our specific ethical responsibilities and the stakeholders to whom we owe these responsibilities. As with legal issues, a complicating factor in making global ethical decisions may be that what is considered ethical in one country is not considered ethical in another.

Among the questions you may ask in making an ethical analysis are the following:

- *Which options are most honest, open, and truthful?*
- *Which options are most kind and compassionate, and build a sense of community?*
- *Which options create the greatest good for the greatest number of stakeholders?*
- *Which options result in treating others as I would want to be treated?*

Ethical training starts at home and continues throughout our lives. It is reinforced by the teaching that we receive in our church, synagogue, mosque, or other house of worship; the schools we attend; and by the persons and companies we associate with.

In addition, each of Canada's professional accounting bodies—the Canadian Institute of Chartered Accountants, the Certified General Accountants Association of Canada, and the Society of Management Accountants of Canada—have codes of professional conduct that help their members make ethical judgments and decisions. Members who violate these codes are subject to a variety of disciplinary actions, including expulsion from their profession for serious violations.

Occasionally, a company will report falsified accounting information. It may, for example, overstate profits or understate the company's debts. In recent years, Livent Inc., the theatrical production company, was convicted of keeping two sets of accounting records and falsifying its financial statements. Several well-known U.S. companies were charged with reporting misleading information. Enron Corporation (at the time, one of the largest companies in the United States) admitted understating its liabilities and overstating its profits. Xerox and WorldCom were accused of overstating their profits. Investors and creditors of companies that falsify their financial statements usually lose significant amounts of money and are forced to file lawsuits to recover their losses. Company executives caught falsifying accounting information often pay significant fines, and in some cases go to prison. Applying relevant accounting standards in a way that reports a faithful representation of the company's financial position and operating performance is always the most ethical course of action.

A thorough understanding of ethics requires more study than we can accomplish in this book. However, remember that when you are making accounting decisions, you should not check your ethics at the door!

In a business setting, sound ethical judgment begins "at the top." When employees see the top executives of their company promoting a strong ethical culture and regularly acting in a socially responsible manner, they are more likely to emulate this behaviour when making their own decisions. *Corporate Knights* magazine annually publishes a list of the most socially responsible corporations in Canada. Its 2012 list includes companies such as Desjardins Group, Hydro One, Royal Bank of Canada, Loblaws, and Mountain Equipment Co-op. It is easier to act ethically when you work for companies that recognize the importance of ethical business practices. These companies have learned from experience that, in the long run, ethical conduct pays big rewards, not only socially, morally, and spiritually, but economically as well!

◄ DECISION GUIDELINES ►

DECISION FRAMEWORK FOR MAKING ETHICAL JUDGMENTS

Making tough ethical judgments in business and accounting requires a decision framework. Answering the following four questions will help you to make ethical business decisions:

Decision	Guidelines
1. What is the issue?	**1.** The issue will usually deal with making a judgment about an accounting measurement or disclosure that results in economic consequences, often to numerous parties.
2. Who are the stakeholders, and what are the consequences of the decision to each of them?	**2.** Stakeholders include anyone who might be affected by the decision—you, your company, and potential users of the information (investors, creditors, regulatory agencies). Consequences can be economic, legal, or ethical in nature.
3. What are the decision alternatives, and how do they affect each stakeholder?	**3.** Analyze the impact of the decision on all stakeholders, using economic, legal, and ethical criteria. Ask, "Who will be helped or hurt, whose rights will be exercised or denied, and in what way?"
4. What decision alternative will you choose?	**4.** Choose the alternative that best balances your economic, legal, and ethical responsibilities to your stakeholders. Also, assess how your decision makes you feel. If it makes you feel uneasy, determine why and consider choosing another alternative.

To simplify, we might ask three questions:

1. Is the action legal? If not, steer clear, unless you want to go to jail or pay monetary damages to injured parties. If the action is legal, go on to questions (2) and (3).

2. Who will be affected by the decision and how? Be as thorough about this analysis as possible, and analyze it from all three standpoints (economic, legal, and ethical).

3. How will this decision make me feel afterward? How would it make me feel if my family reads about it in the newspaper?

In later chapters we will apply this model to different accounting decisions.

Summary of IFRS-ASPE Differences

Concepts	IFRS	ASPE
Application of IFRS and ASPE (p. 7)	Publicly accountable enterprises or those enterprises planning to become one must apply IFRS.	Private enterprises have the option of applying IFRS, but almost all apply ASPE, which is simpler and less costly for these smaller enterprises.
Historical-cost assumption (p. 10)	Certain assets and liabilities are permitted to be recorded at their fair values rather than being kept on the books at their historical costs.	With rare exceptions, assets and liabilities are carried at their historical costs for as long as the company owns or owes them.
Changes in retained earnings during an accounting period (p. 14)	These changes are reported in the statement of changes in owners' equity.	These changes are reported in the statement of retained earnings.
The balance sheet (p. 15)	This financial statement is called the statement of financial position.	This financial statement is called the balance sheet.
The income statement (p. 11)	This financial statement is called the statement of profit or loss.	This financial statement is called the income statement.
The cash flow statement (p. 20)	This financial statement is called the statement of cash flows.	This financial statement is called the cash flow statement.
The statement of other comprehensive income (p. 14)	This statement is required.	This statement is not required.

SUMMARY OF CHAPTER 1

LEARNING OBJECTIVE	SUMMARY
1. **Explain** why accounting is the language of business	Accounting is an information system that measures and records business activities, processes data into reports, and reports results to decision makers. The better you understand the language used to prepare and report accounting information, the better you can make decisions using this information.
2. **Explain** accounting's conceptual framework and underlying assumptions	In Canada there are two main sets of GAAP. Publicly accountable enterprises (or those planning to become one) must use International Financial Reporting Standards (IFRS), whereas private enterprises have the option of applying IFRS or Accounting Standards for Private Enterprises (ASPE). Most private enterprises choose the ASPE because it is simpler and less costly to apply.
	Both IFRS and ASPE rest on a conceptual framework, which helps ensure that accounting information is useful for decision-making purposes. This framework includes the fundamental qualitative characteristics of relevance and faithful representation, as well as four enhancing qualitative characteristics: comparability, verifiability, timeliness, and understandability. The cost of obtaining certain types of accounting information is sometimes a constraint on what is reported to the users of financial statements.
	Underlying the conceptual framework are four assumptions: the going-concern, separate-entity, historical-cost, and stable-monetary-unit assumptions.

3. **Describe** the purpose of each financial statement and **explain** the elements of each one

The income statement (or statement of operations) measures a company's operating performance for a specified period of time. The income statement has two main elements, income and expenses, and also reports a company's net income for the period (Total Income − Total Expenses).

The statement of retained earnings reports the changes in a company's retained earnings during the same period covered by the income statement. Under ASPE, this statement is often added to the bottom of the income statement, whereas under IFRS, information on the changes in retained earnings is included in the statement of changes in owners' equity. In its basic form, this statement adds net income to and deducts dividends from the opening retained earnings balance for the period to arrive at the ending retained earnings balance.

The balance sheet (or statement of financial position) reports a company's financial position as at a specific date, which almost always falls on the last day of a monthly, quarterly, or annual reporting period. A company's financial position consists of three elements: the assets it controls, the liabilities it is obligated to pay, and the equity its owners have accumulated in the business. The balance sheet takes its name from the fact that the assets it reports must always equal—or be in balance with—the sum of the liabilities and equity it reports. This relationship is known as the accounting equation, and it provides the foundation for the double-entry method of accounting you will begin to learn in Chapter 2.

The statement of cash flows reports the specific business activities that generated cash receipts or resulted in cash payments during the same period covered by the income statement. These business activities are classified into three categories: operating, investing, and financing activities.

4. **Explain** the relationships among the financial statements

Certain key financial statement items serve as links among the financial statements:
1. Net income from the income statement is included in the calculation of retained earnings on the statement of retained earnings (which is included as part of the statement of changes in owners' equity under IFRS).
2. The closing retained earnings balance from the statement of retained earnings is included in the calculation of owners' equity on the balance sheet.
3. The closing cash balance from the statement of cash flows appears as an asset on the balance sheet.

5. **Make** ethical business decisions

Accountants must often use professional judgment when applying IFRS and ASPE because many accounting standards do not have clear-cut rules that specify how transactions or events should be accounted for. When using professional judgment, the accountant's goal is to make a decision that fulfills their ethical responsibilities to every party with a stake in the decision. Professional accountants are governed by rules of professional conduct, which provide guidance meant to ensure that ethical standards are upheld when applying professional judgment.

J. J. Booth and Marie Savard incorporated Tara Inc., a consulting engineering company, and began operations on April 1, 2014. During April, the business provided engineering services for clients. It is now April 30, and J. J. and Marie wonder how well Tara Inc. performed during its first month. They also want to know the business's financial position as at April 30 and cash flows during the month.

The following data are listed in alphabetical order:

Accounts payable	$ 1,800	Land	$ 18,000
Accounts receivable	2,000	Office supplies	3,700
Adjustments to reconcile net income to net cash provided by operating activities	(3,900)	Payments of cash:	
		Acquisition of land	40,000
		Dividends	2,100
Cash balance at beginning of April	0	Rent expense	1,100
Cash balance at end of April	33,300	Retained earnings at beginning of April	0
Cash receipts:			
Issuance (sale) of shares	50,000	Retained earnings at end of April	?
Sale of land	22,000	Salary expense	1,200
Common shares	50,000	Service revenue	10,000
		Utilities expense	400

Requirements

1. Prepare the income statement, the statement of retained earnings, and the statement of cash flows for the month ended April 30, 2014, and the balance sheet as at April 30, 2014. Draw arrows linking the pertinent items in the statements.
2. Answer the investors' underlying questions.
   a. How well did Tara Inc. perform during its first month of operations?
   b. Where does Tara Inc. stand financially at the end of the first month?

ANSWERS

Requirement 1

Financial Statements of Tara Inc.

The title must include the name of the company, "Income Statement," and the specific period of time covered. It is critical that the time period be defined.

Gather all the income and expense accounts from the account listing. List the income accounts first. List the expense accounts next.

Tara Inc.
Income Statement
For the Month Ended April 30, 2014

Income:		
Service revenue		$10,000
Expenses:		
Salary expense	$1,200	
Rent expense	1,100	
Utilities expense	400	
Total expenses		2,700
Net income		$ 7,300

Tara Inc.
Statement of Retained Earnings
For the Month Ended April 30, 2014

Retained earnings, April 1, 2014...................................	$ 0
Add: Net income for the month	7,300
	7,300
Less: Dividends..	(2,100)
Retained earnings, April 30, 2014.................................	$5,200

① The title must include the name of the company, "Statement of Retained Earnings," and the specific period of time covered. It is critical that the time period be defined.

The net income amount (or net loss amount) is transferred from the income statement. Retained earnings at the end of the period is the result of a calculation, and is an accumulation of the corporation's performance since it began.

Tara Inc.
Balance Sheet
As at April 30, 2014

② The title must include the name of the company, "Balance Sheet," and the date of the balance sheet. It shows the financial position at the end of the day.

Assets		Liabilities	
Cash.....................................	$33,300	Accounts payable	$ 1,800
Accounts receivable.............	2,000	**Shareholders' Equity**	
Office supplies	3,700	Common shares	50,000
Land	18,000	Retained earnings................	5,200
		Total shareholders' equity...	55,200
		Total liabilities and	
Total assets	$57,000	shareholders' equity	$57,000

Gather all the asset, liability, and equity accounts from the account listing. List assets first, then liabilities, then equity accounts. The retained earnings amount is transferred from the statement of retained earnings.

It is imperative that total assets = total liabilities + shareholders' equity.

Tara Inc.
Statement of Cash Flows
For the Month Ended April 30, 2014

The title must include the name of the company, "Statement of Cash Flows," and the specific period of time covered. It is critical that the time period be defined.

③

Cash flows from operating activities:		
Net income...		$ 7,300
Adjustments to reconcile net income to net cash		
provided by operating activities		(3,900)
Net cash provided by operating activities.................		3,400
Cash flows from investing activities:		
Acquisition of land	$(40,000)	
Sale of land..	22,000	
Net cash used for investing activities		(18,000)
Cash flows from financing activities:		
Issuance (sale) of shares..	$ 50,000	
Payment of dividends..	(2,100)	
Net cash provided by financing activities..................		47,900
Net increase in cash..		$33,300
Cash balance, April 1, 2014		0
Cash balance, April 30, 2014		$33,300

Net income comes from the income statement. The adjustments amount was provided. In later chapters, you will learn how to calculate this amount.

Include all transactions that involve investing the company's cash, which involve any changes in the property, plant, and equipment.

Include all cash transactions relating to shares and long-term debt obligations.

Requirement 2

2. a. The company performed rather well in April. Net income was $7,300—very good in relation to service revenue of $10,000. Tara was able to pay cash dividends of $2,100.

b. The business ended April with cash of $33,300. Total assets of $57,000 far exceed total liabilities of $1,800. Shareholders' equity of $55,200 provides a good cushion for borrowing. The business's financial position at April 30, 2014, is strong.

The company has plenty of cash, and assets far exceed liabilities. Operating activities generated positive cash flow in the first month of operations. Lenders like to see these features before making a loan.

Consider the net income from the income statement.

Consider net worth, which is total assets minus total liabilities.

STOP + THINK (1-1)

ANSWERS

1. According to the historical-cost assumption, the land would be recorded at a value of $46,000, its initial actual cost.

2. According to the historical-cost and going-concern assumptions, no adjustment would be made to the value of the land despite its increase in value to $60,000. IFRS do permit companies to adjust assets such as land to their fair values, but it is rare for companies to actually make these adjustments. Even under IFRS, assets are almost always left on the books at their historical costs.

STOP + THINK (1-2)

ANSWERS

1. $160,000 ($240,000 − $80,000)

2. $290,000 ($160,000 + $130,000)

3. Net income of $44,000 ($129,000 − $85,000); income minus expenses.

4. $115,000 [$100,000 beginning balance + net income of $25,000 ($75,000 − $50,000) − dividends of $10,000]

Review the Financial Statements

QUICK CHECK (ANSWERS ARE GIVEN ON PAGE 53.)

1. All of the following statements are true except one. Which statement is false?
   a. Bookkeeping is only a part of accounting.
   b. A proprietorship is a business with several owners.
   c. Professional accountants are held to a high standard of ethical conduct.
   d. The organization that formulates generally accepted accounting principles is the Canadian Institute of Chartered Accountants (CICA).

2. The recorded cost of assets at time of purchase is based on
   a. the amount paid for the asset.
   b. what it would cost to replace the asset.
   c. current fair value as established by independent appraisers.
   d. selling price.

3. The accounting equation can be expressed as
   a. Assets + Liabilities = Shareholders' Equity
   b. Shareholders' Equity − Assets = Liabilities
   c. Assets = Liabilities − Shareholders' Equity
   d. Assets − Liabilities = Shareholders' Equity

4. The nature of an asset is best described as
   a. something with physical form that's valued at cost of purchase in the accounting records.
   b. an economic resource representing cash or the right to receive cash in the near future.
   c. a resource controlled by the company as a result of past events and from which the company expects to receive future economic benefits.
   d. something owned by a business that has a ready market value.

5. Which financial statement covers a period of time?
   a. Balance sheet
   b. Income statement
   c. Statement of cash flows
   d. Both b and c

6. How would net income be most likely to affect the accounting equation?
   a. Increase assets and increase shareholders' equity.
   b. Increase liabilities and decrease shareholders' equity.
   c. Increase assets and increase liabilities.
   d. Decrease assets and decrease liabilities.

7. During the year, ChemDry Ltd. has $100,000 in revenues, $40,000 in expenses, and $3,000 in dividend payments. Shareholders' equity changed by
   a. +$27,000
   (b.) +$57,000
   c. +$12,000
   d. −$8,000

8. ChemDry Ltd. in Question 7 had
   a. net income of $100,000.
   b. net income of $57,000.
   c. net income of $60,000.
   d. net loss of $40,000.

9. Leah Corporation holds cash of $5,000 and owes $25,000 on accounts payable. Leah has accounts receivable of $30,000, inventory of $20,000, and land cost of $50,000. How much are Leah's total assets and shareholders' equity?

	Total assets	Shareholders' equity
a.	$100,000	$25,000
b.	$105,000	$80,000
c.	$105,000	$25,000
d.	$25,000	$105,000

10. Which item(s) is (are) reported on the balance sheet?
    a. Retained earnings
    b. Accounts payable
    c. Inventory
    d. All of the above

11. During the year, Mason Inc.'s shareholders' equity increased from $30,000 to $40,000. Mason earned net income of $15,000. How much in dividends did Mason declare in the year?
    a. $6,000
    b. $0
    c. $8,000
    d. $5,000

12. Stuebs Corporation had total assets of $300,000 and total shareholders' equity of $100,000 at the beginning of the year. During the year, assets increased by $50,000, and liabilities increased by $40,000. Shareholders' equity at the end of the year is
    a. $90,000
    b. $110,000
    c. $140,000
    d. $150,000

Accounting Vocabulary

accounting An information system that measures and records business activities, processes data into reports, and reports results to decision makers.   (p. 3)

accounting equation Assets = Liabilities + Owners' Equity. Provides the foundation for the double-entry method of accounting.   (p. 15)

Accounting Standards for Private Enterprises (ASPE) Canadian accounting standards that specify the *generally accepted accounting principles* applicable to *private enterprises* that are required to follow *GAAP* and choose not to apply *IFRS*.   (p. 7)

asset A resource owned or controlled by a company as a result of past events and from which the company expects to receive future economic benefits.   (p. 15)

balance sheet Reports a company's financial position as at a specific date. In particular, it reports a company's assets, liabilities, and owners' equity. Also called the *statement of financial position*.   (p. 15)

board of directors Group elected by the shareholders to set policy for a corporation and to appoint its officers.   (p. 6)

carrying amount The historical cost of an asset net of its accumulated depreciation.   (p. 17)

comparability Investors like to compare a company's financial statements from one year to the next. Therefore, a company must consistently use the same accounting method each year.   (p. 8)

corporation An incorporated business owned by one or more *shareholders*, which according to the law is a legal "person" separate from its owners.   (p. 6)

current asset An asset that is expected to be converted to cash, sold, or consumed during the next 12 months, or within the business's normal operating cycle if longer than a year.   (p. 16)

current liability A debt due to be paid within one year or within the entity's operating cycle if the cycle is longer than a year.   (p. 18)

deficit The term used when *retained earnings* is a negative balance.   (p. 14)

ethical standards Standards that govern the way we treat others and the way we restrain our selfish desires. They are shaped by our cultural, socioeconomic, and religious backgrounds.   (p. 25)

expense A cost incurred to purchase the goods and services a company needs to run its business on a day-to-day basis. The opposite of revenue.   (p. 12)

fair value The amount that a business could sell an asset for, or the amount that a business could pay to settle a liability.   (p. 10)

faithful representation A fundamental qualitative characteristic of accounting information. Information is a faithful representation if it is complete, neutral, accurate, and reflects the economic substance of the underlying transaction or event.   (p. 7)

financial accounting The branch of accounting that provides information for managers inside a business and for decision makers outside the business.   (p. 5)

financial statements The reports that companies use to convey the financial results of their business activities to various user groups, which can include managers, investors, creditors, and regulatory agencies.   (p. 2)

financing activities Activities that result in changes in the size and composition of a company's contributed equity and borrowings.   (p. 20)

gain A type of income other than revenue that results in an increase in economic benefits to a company, and usually occurs outside the course of the company's ordinary business activities.   (p. 12)

generally accepted accounting principles (GAAP) The guidelines of financial accounting, which specify the standards for how accountants must record, measure, and report financial information.   (p. 6)

going-concern assumption The assumption that an entity will continue operating normally for the foreseeable future.   (p. 9)

historical-cost assumption Holds that assets should be recorded at their actual cost, measured on the date of purchase as the amount of cash paid plus the dollar value of all non-cash consideration (other assets, privileges, or rights) also given in exchange.   (p. 10)

income Consists of a company's *revenues* and *gains*.   (p. 12)

income statement The financial statement that measures a company's operating performance for a specified period of time. In particular, it reports income, expenses, and net income. Also called the *statement of profit or loss*.   (p. 11)

International Financial Reporting Standards (IFRS) International accounting standards that specify the *generally accepted accounting principles* which must be applied by *publicly accountable enterprises* in Canada and over 100 other countries.   (p. 7)

investing activities Activities that include the purchase and sale of long-term assets and other investments that result in cash inflows or outflows related to resources used for generating future income and cash flows.   (p. 20)

liability An obligation (or debt) owed by a company, which it expects to pay off in the future using some of its assets.   (p. 18)

liquidity A measure of how quickly an asset can be converted to cash. The higher an asset's liquidity, the more quickly it can be converted to cash.   (p. 16)

long-term asset Another term for *non-current asset*.   (p. 17)

long-term liability Another term for *non-current liability*.   (p. 19)

loss A type of expense that results in a decrease in economic benefits to a company, and usually occurs outside the course of the company's ordinary business activities. The opposite of a gain.   (p. 13)

management accounting The branch of accounting that generates information for the internal decision makers of a business, such as top executives.   (p. 5)

material Accounting information is material if it is significant enough in nature or magnitude that omitting or misstating it could affect the decisions of an informed user.   (p. 7)

net assets Another name for *owners' equity*.   (p. 19)

net earnings Another name for *net income*.   (p. 14)

net income The excess of a company's total income over its total expenses.   (p. 14)

net loss Occurs when a company's total expenses exceed its total income.   (p. 14)

net profit Another term for *net income*.   (p. 13)

non-current asset Any asset that is not classified as a current asset.   (p. 16)

non-current liability A liability a company expects to pay off beyond one year from the balance sheet date.   (p. 18)

operating activities Activities that comprise the main revenue-producing activities of a company, and generally result from the transactions and other events that determine net income.   (p. 20)

owners' equity The company owners' remaining interest in the assets of the company after deducting all its liabilities.   (p. 19)

partnership An unincorporated business with two or more parties as co-owners, with each owner being a partner in the business.   (p. 5)

private enterprise An entity that has not issued and does not plan to issue shares or debt on public markets.   (p. 7)

proprietorship An unincorporated business with a single owner, called the proprietor.   (p. 5)

publicly accountable enterprises (PAEs) Corporations that have issued or plan to issue shares or debt in a public market.   (p. 7)

relevance A fundamental qualitative characteristic of accounting information. Information is relevant if it has predictive value, confirmatory value, or both, and is *material*.   (p. 7)

retained earnings Represent the accumulated net income of a company since the day it started business, less any net losses and dividends declared during this time.   (p. 14)

revenue Consists of amounts earned by a company in the course of its ordinary, day-to-day business activities. The vast majority of a company's revenue is earned through the sale of its primary goods and services.   (p. 12)

separate-entity assumption Holds that the business activities of the reporting entity are separate from the activities of its owners.   (p. 9)

shareholder A party who owns shares of a corporation.   (p. 6)

shareholders' equity Another term for *owners' equity*.   (p. 19)

shares Legal units of ownership in a corporation.   (p. 6)

stable-monetary-unit assumption Holds that regardless of the reporting currency used, financial information is always reported under the assumption that the value of the currency is stable, despite the fact that its value does change due to economic factors such as inflation.   (p. 10)

statement of cash flows Reports cash receipts and cash payments classified according to the entity's major activities: operating, investing, and financing.   (p. 20)

statement of financial position Another name for the *balance sheet*.   (p. 15)

statement of profit or loss Another name for the *income statement*.   (p. 11)

statement of retained earnings Summary of the changes in the retained earnings of a corporation during a specific period.   (p. 14)

verifiability The ability to check financial information for accuracy, completeness, and reliability.   (p. 8)

Assess Your Progress

MyAccountingLab   Make the grade with MyAccountingLab: The Exercises, Quizzes, and Problems (A set) marked in red can be found on MyAccountingLab. You can practise them as often as you want, and most feature step-by-step guided instructions to help you find the right answer.

SHORT EXERCISES

S1-1 Accounting definitions are precise, and you must understand the vocabulary to properly use accounting. Sharpen your understanding of key terms by answering the following questions:

1. How do the *assets* and *shareholders' equity* of TELUS differ from each other? Which one (assets or shareholders' equity) must be at least as large as the other? Which one can be smaller than the other?
2. How are TELUS's *liabilities* and *shareholders' equity* similar? How are they different?

LEARNING OBJECTIVE ❸

Distinguish between assets, liabilities, and equity

S1-2 Use the accounting equation to show how to determine the amount of the missing term in each of the following situations.

LEARNING OBJECTIVE ❸

Apply the accounting equation

Total Assets	=	Total Liabilities	+	Shareholders' Equity
a. $?		$150,000		$150,000
b. 290,000		90,000		?
c. 220,000		?		120,000

S1-3 Review the accounting equation on page 19.

1. Use the accounting equation to show how to determine the amount of a company's owners' equity. How would your answer change if you were analyzing your own household or a single Dairy Queen restaurant?
2. If you know assets and owners' equity, how can you measure liabilities? Give the equation.

LEARNING OBJECTIVE ❸

Use the accounting equation

S1-4 Consider Walmart, the world's largest retailer. Classify the following items as an asset (A), a liability (L), or an owners' equity (E) item for Walmart:

LEARNING OBJECTIVE ❸

Classify assets, liabilities, and owners' equity

_____ a. Accounts payable		_____ g. Accounts receivable
_____ b. Common shares		_____ h. Long-term debt
_____ c. Cash		_____ i. Merchandise inventories
_____ d. Retained earnings		_____ j. Notes payable
_____ e. Land		_____ k. Accrued expenses payable
_____ f. Prepaid expenses		_____ l. Equipment

S1-5

1. Identify the two basic categories of items on an income statement.
2. What do we call the bottom line of the income statement?

LEARNING OBJECTIVE ❸

Use the income statement

S1-6 Split Second Wireless Inc. began 2014 with total assets of $110 million and ended 2014 with assets of $160 million. During 2014, Split Second earned revenues of $90 million and had expenses of $20 million. Split Second paid dividends of $10 million in 2014. Prepare the company's income statement for the year ended December 31, 2014, complete with the appropriate heading.

LEARNING OBJECTIVE ❸

Prepare an income statement

S1-7 Mondala Ltd. began 2014 with retained earnings of $200 million. Revenues during the year were $400 million and expenses totalled $300 million. Mondala declared dividends of $40 million. What was the company's ending balance of retained earnings? To answer this question, prepare Mondala's statement of retained earnings for the year ended December 31, 2014, complete with its appropriate heading.

LEARNING OBJECTIVE ❸

Prepare a statement of retained earnings

S1-8 At December 31, 2014, Skate Sharp Limited has cash of $13,000, receivables of $2,000, and inventory of $40,000. The company's equipment totals $75,000, and other assets amount to $10,000. Skate Sharp owes accounts payable of $10,000 and short-term notes payable of $5,000, and also has long-term debt of $70,000. Contributed capital is $15,000. Prepare Skate Sharp Limited's balance sheet at December 31, 2014, complete with its appropriate heading.

LEARNING OBJECTIVE ❸

Prepare a balance sheet

LEARNING OBJECTIVE ③

Prepare a statement of cash flows

S1-9 Brazos Medical, Inc., ended 2013 with cash of $24,000. During 2014, Brazos earned net income of $120,000 and had adjustments to reconcile net income to net cash provided by operations totalling $20,000 (this is a negative amount).

Brazos paid $300,000 for equipment during 2014 and had to borrow half of this amount on a long-term note. During the year, the company paid dividends of $15,000 and sold old equipment, receiving cash of $60,000.

Prepare Brazos' statement of cash flows with its appropriate heading for the year ended December 31, 2014. Follow the format in the summary problem on page 31.

LEARNING OBJECTIVE ②

Apply accounting assumptions

S1-10 John Grant is chairman of the board of The Grant Group Ltd. Suppose Grant has just founded this company, and assume that he treats his home and other personal assets as part of The Grant Group. Answer these questions about the evaluation of The Grant Group.

1. Which accounting assumption governs this situation?
2. How can the proper application of this accounting assumption give John Grant a realistic view of The Grant Group? Explain in detail.

LEARNING OBJECTIVE ⑤

Make ethical judgments

S1-11 Accountants follow ethical guidelines in the conduct of their work. What are these standards of professional conduct designed to produce? Why is this goal important?

LEARNING OBJECTIVE ③

Classify items on the financial statements

S1-12 Suppose you are analyzing the financial statements of a Canadian company. Identify each item with its appropriate financial statement, using the following abbreviations: income statement (IS), statement of retained earnings (SRE), balance sheet (BS), and statement of cash flows (SCF).

Three items appear on two financial statements, and one item shows up on three statements.

a. Dividends _____
b. Salary expense _____
c. Inventory _____
d. Sales revenue _____
e. Retained earnings _____
f. Net cash provided by operating activities _____
g. Net income _____

h. Cash _____
i. Net cash provided by financing activities _____
j. Accounts payable _____
k. Common shares _____
l. Interest revenue _____
m. Long-term debt _____
n. Net increase or decrease in cash _____

EXERCISES

LEARNING OBJECTIVE ①

Organize a business

E1-13 Quality Environmental Inc. needs funds, and Mary Wu, the president, has asked you to consider investing in the business. Answer the following questions about the different ways in which Wu might organize the business. Explain each answer.

a. What form of organization will enable the owners of Quality Environmental to limit their risk of loss to the amount they have invested in the business?
b. What form of business organization will give Wu the most freedom to manage the business as she wishes?
c. What form of organization will give creditors the maximum protection in the event that Quality Environmental fails and cannot pay its liabilities?

If you were Wu and could organize the business as you wish, what form of organization would you choose for Quality Environmental? Explain your reasoning.

LEARNING OBJECTIVE ③

Describe the purpose of the financial statements

E1-14 Ed Eisler wants to open a café in Digby, Nova Scotia. In need of cash, he asks the Bank of Montreal for a loan. The bank requires financial statements to show likely results of operations for the year and the expected financial position at year-end. With little knowledge of accounting, Eisler doesn't understand the request. Explain to him the information provided by the income statement and the balance sheet. Indicate why a lender would require this information.

[handwritten: Assumptions & Principles]

E1-15 Identify the accounting assumption that best applies to each of the following situations.

a. Wendy's, the restaurant chain, sold a store location to Burger King. How can Wendy's determine the sale price of the store: by a professional appraisal, Wendy's cost, or the amount actually received from the sale?

b. If Trammel Crow Realtors had to liquidate its assets, their value would be less than carrying amounts of the assets. *[handwritten: going concern principle]*

c. Toyota Canada wants to determine which division of the company—Toyota or Lexus—is more profitable. *[handwritten: entity]*

d. You get an especially good buy on a laptop, paying only $399 for a computer that normally costs $799. What is your accounting value for this computer? *[handwritten: historical cost]*

LEARNING OBJECTIVE **2**

Apply accounting assumptions

E1-16 Compute the missing amount in the accounting equation for each company (amounts in millions):

LEARNING OBJECTIVE **3**

Use the accounting equation

	Assets =	Liabilities +	Shareholders' Equity
TELUS	$ *[handwritten: 16,987]* ?	$10,061	$ 6,926
Scotiabank	411,510	*[handwritten: 392,706]* ?	18,804
Shoppers Drug Mart	5,644	2,434	*[handwritten: 3,210]* ?

E1-17 Assume Maple Leaf Foods Inc. has current assets of $633.6 million, capital assets of $1,126.7 million, and other assets totalling $1,237.5 million. Current liabilities are $591.2 million and long-term liabilities total $1,245.2 million.

LEARNING OBJECTIVE **3**

Use the accounting equation; evaluating a business

Requirements

1. Use these data to write Maple Leaf Foods' accounting equation.
2. How much in resources does Maple Leaf Foods have to work with?
3. How much does Maple Leaf Foods owe creditors?
4. How much of the company's assets do the Maple Leaf Foods shareholders actually own?

E1-18 We Store For You Ltd.'s comparative balance sheets at December 31, 2014, and December 31, 2013, report the following (in millions):

LEARNING OBJECTIVE **3**

Apply the accounting equation

	2014	2013
Total assets	$40	$30
Total liabilities	10	8

Requirements

Below are three situations about We Store For You's issuance of shares and payment of dividends during the year ended December 31, 2014. For each situation, use the accounting equation and statement of retained earnings to compute the amount of We Store For You's net income or loss during the year ended December 31, 2014.

1. We Store For You issued shares for $2 million and paid no dividends.
2. We Store For You issued no shares and paid dividends of $3 million.
3. We Store For You issued shares for $11 million and paid dividends of $2 million.

E1-19 Answer these questions about two companies:

LEARNING OBJECTIVE **3**

Apply the accounting equation

1. Mortimer Limited began the year with total liabilities of $400,000 and total shareholders' equity of $300,000. During the year, total assets increased by 20%. How much are total assets at the end of the year?

2. Aztec Associates began a year with total assets of $500,000 and total liabilities of $200,000. Net income for the year was $100,000 and no dividends were paid. How much is shareholders' equity at the end of the year?

E1-20 Assume MySpace Inc. is expanding into the United States. The company must decide where to locate, and how to finance the expansion. Identify the financial statement in which decision makers can find the following information about MySpace Inc. In some cases, more than one statement will report the needed data.

a. Common shares
b. Income tax payable
c. Dividends
d. Income tax expense
e. Ending balance of retained earnings
f. Total assets
g. Long-term debt
h. Revenue
i. Cash spent to acquire equipment

j. Selling, general, and administrative expenses
k. Adjustments to reconcile net income to net cash provided by operations
l. Ending cash balance
m. Current liabilities
n. Net income
o. Cost of goods sold

E1-21 Amounts of the assets and liabilities of Torrance Associates Inc., as of December 31, 2014, are given as follows. Also included are revenue and expense figures for the year ended on that date (amounts in millions):

Property and equipment, net	$ 4	Total revenue	$ 35
Investment	72	Receivables	253
Long-term liabilities	73	Current liabilities	290
Other expenses	14	Common shares	12
Cash	28	Interest expense	3
Retained earnings, beginning	19	Salary and other employee expense	9
Retained earnings, ending	?	Other assets	43

Requirement

Prepare the balance sheet of Torrance Associates Inc. at December 31, 2014. Use the accounting equation to compute ending retained earnings.

E1-22 This exercise should be worked only in connection with exercise E1-21. Refer to the data of Torrance Associates Inc. in E1-21.

Requirements

1. Prepare the income statement of Torrance Associates Inc. for the year ended December 31, 2014.
2. What amount of dividends did Torrance declare during the year ended December 31, 2014? Hint: Prepare a statement of retained earnings.

E1-23 Groovy Limited began 2014 with $95,000 in cash. During 2014, Groovy earned net income of $300,000, and adjustments to reconcile net income to net cash provided by operations totalled $60,000, a positive amount. Investing activities used cash of $400,000, and financing activities provided cash of $70,000. Groovy ended 2014 with total assets of $250,000 and total liabilities of $110,000.

Requirement

Prepare Groovy Limited's statement of cash flows for the year ended December 31, 2014. Identify the data items that do not appear on the statement of cash flows and indicate which financial statement reports these items.

E1-24 Assume a FedEx Kinko's at the University of Saskatchewan ended the month of July 2014 with these data:

Payments of cash:		Cash receipts:	
Acquisition of equipment	$36,000	Issuance (sale) of shares to	
Dividends	2,000	owners	$35,000
Retained earnings at July 1, 2014	0	Rent expense	700
Retained earnings at July 31, 2014	?	Common shares	35,000
Utilities expense	200	Equipment	36,000
Adjustments to reconcile net income		Office supplies expense	1,200
to cash provided by operations	3,200	Accounts payable	3,200
Salary expense	4,000	Service revenue	14,000
Cash balance July 1, 2014	0		
Cash balance July 31, 2014	8,100		

Requirement

Prepare the income statement and the statement of retained earnings of this FedEx Kinko's for the month ended July 31, 2014.

E1-25 Refer to the data in the preceding exercise. Prepare the balance sheet of the FedEx Kinko's at July 31, 2014.

E1-26 Refer to the data in exercise E1-24. Prepare the statement of cash flows of the FedEx Kinko's at the University of Saskatchewan for the month ended July 31, 2014. Draw arrows linking the pertinent items in the statements you prepared for exercises E1-24 through E1-26.

E1-27 This exercise should be used in conjunction with exercises E1-24 through E1-26. The owner of the FedEx Kinko's now seeks your advice as to whether the University of Saskatchewan store should cease operations or continue operating. Write a report giving the owner your opinion of operating results, dividends, financial position, and cash flows during the company's first month of operations. Cite specifics from the financial statements to support your opinion. Conclude your report with advice on whether to stay in business or cease operations.

E1-28 Apply your understanding of the relationships among the financial statements to answer these questions:
a. How can a business earn large profits but have a small balance of retained earnings?
b. Give two reasons why a business can have a steady stream of net income over a five-year period and still experience a cash shortage.
c. If you could pick a single source of cash for your business, what would it be? Why?
d. How can a business suffer net losses for several years in a row and still have plenty of cash?

QUIZ

Test your understanding of the financial statements by answering the following questions. Select the best choice from among the possible answers given.

Q1-29 The *primary* objective of financial reporting is to provide information
a. useful for making investment and credit decisions.
b. about the profitability of the enterprise.
c. on the cash flows of the company.
d. to the federal government.

Q1-30 For a business of a certain size, which type of business organization provides the least amount of protection for bankers and other creditors of the company?

a. Proprietorship   c. Both a and b

b. Partnership   d. Corporation

Q1-31 International Financial Reporting Standards (IFRS) were developed because

a. Canadian GAAP were outdated.

b. corporations wanted to change their reporting.

c. different GAAP in countries of the world made global comparisons difficult.

d. new assumptions were defined.

Q1-32 During January, assets increased by $20,000, and liabilities increased by $4,000. Shareholders' equity must have

a. increased by $16,000.   c. decreased by $16,000.

b. increased by $24,000.   d. decreased by $24,000.

Q1-33 The amount a company expects to collect from customers appears on the

a. income statement in the expenses section.

b. balance sheet in the current assets section.

c. balance sheet in the shareholders' equity section.

d. statement of cash flows.

Q1-34 All of the following are current assets except

a. cash.   c. inventory.

b. accounts receivable.   d. sales revenue.

Q1-35 Revenues are

a. increases in share capital resulting from the owners investing in the business.

b. increases in income resulting from selling products or performing services.

c. decreases in liabilities resulting from paying off loans.

d. All of the above.

Q1-36 The financial statement that reports revenues and expenses is called the

a. statement of retained earnings.   c. statement of cash flows.

b. income statement.   d. balance sheet.

Q1-37 Another name for the balance sheet is the

a. statement of operations.

b. statement of earnings.

c. statement of profit and loss.

d. statement of financial position.

Q1-38 Baldwin Corporation began the year with cash of $35,000 and a computer that cost $20,000. During the year, Baldwin earned sales revenue of $140,000 and had the following expenses: salaries, $59,000; rent, $8,000; and utilities, $3,000. At year-end, Baldwin's cash balance was down to $16,000. How much net income (or net loss) did Baldwin experience for the year?

a. ($19,000)   c. $107,000

b. $70,000   d. $140,000

Q1-39 Quartz Instruments had retained earnings of $145,000 at December 31, 2013. Net income for 2014 totalled $90,000, and dividends for 2014 were $30,000. How much retained earnings should Quartz report at December 31, 2014?

a. $205,000   c. $140,000

b. $235,000   d. $175,000

Q1-40 Net income appears on which financial statement(s)?

a. Income statement   c. Both a and b

b. Statement of retained earnings   d. Balance sheet

Q1-41 Cash paid to purchase a building appears on the statement of cash flows among the
a. operating activities.
b. financing activities.
c. investing activities.
d. shareholders' equity.

Q1-42 The shareholders' equity of Chernasky Company at the beginning and end of 2014 totalled $15,000 and $18,000, respectively. Assets at the beginning of 2014 were $25,000. If the liabilities of Chernasky Company increased by $8,000 in 2014, how much were total assets at the end of 2014? Use the accounting equation.
a. $36,000
b. $16,000
c. $2,000
d. Some other amount (fill in the blank)

Q1-43 Drexler Company had the following on the dates indicated:

	12/31/14	12/31/13
Total assets	$750,000	$520,000
Total liabilities	300,000	200,000

Drexler had no share transactions in 2014, and thus, the change in shareholders' equity for 2014 was due to net income and dividends. If dividends were $50,000, how much was Drexler's net income for 2014? Use the accounting equation and the statements of retained earnings.
a. $100,000
b. $130,000
c. $180,000
d. Some other amount (fill in the blank)

PROBLEMS

(Group A)

P1-44A Assume that the Special Contract Division of FedEx Kinko's experienced the following transactions during the year ended December 31, 2014:

a. Suppose the division provided copy services to TELUS for the discounted price of $250,000. Under normal conditions, Kinko's would have provided these services for $280,000. Other revenues totalled $50,000.
b. Salaries cost the division $20,000 to provide these services. The division had to pay employees overtime. Ordinarily, the salary cost for these services would have been $18,000.
c. Other expenses totalled $240,000. Income tax expense was 30% of income before tax.
d. FedEx Kinko's has two operating divisions. Each division is accounted for separately to indicate how well each is performing. At year-end, FedEx Kinko's combines the statements of divisions to show results for FedEx Kinko's as a whole.
e. Inflation affects the amounts that FedEx Kinko's must pay for copy machines. To show the effects of inflation, net income would drop by $3,000.
f. If FedEx Kinko's were to go out of business, the sale of its assets would bring in $150,000 in cash.

LEARNING OBJECTIVE ❷

Use financial statements and apply assumptions and characteristics to the income statement

Requirements

1. Prepare the Special Contracts Division income statement for the year ended December 31, 2014.
2. As CEO, identify the accounting assumption or characteristics used in accounting for the items described in a through f. State how you have applied the assumption or characteristic in preparing the division income statement.

P1-45A Compute the missing amounts (shown by a ?) for each company (in millions).

	Link Ltd.	Chain Inc.	Fence Corp.
Beginning			
Assets	$ 78	$ 30	?
Liabilities	47	19	$ 2
Common shares	6	1	2
Retained earnings	?	10	3
Ending			
Assets	?	$ 48	$ 9
Liabilities	$ 48	30	?
Common shares	6	1	2
Retained earnings	27	?	4
Dividends	$ 3	$ 2	$ 0
Income statement			
Revenues	$216	?	$20
Expenses	211	$144	19
Net income	?	9	1

At the end of the year, which company has the
- highest net income?
- highest percentage of net income to revenues?

Hint: Prepare a statement of retained earnings to help with your calculations.

P1-46A Dan Shoe, the manager of STRIDES Inc., prepared the company's balance sheet while the accountant was ill. The balance sheet contains numerous errors. In particular, Shoe knew that the balance sheet should balance, so he plugged in the shareholders' equity amount needed to achieve this balance. The shareholders' equity amount is *not* correct. All other amounts are accurate.

STRIDES Inc.
Balance Sheet
For the Month Ended July 31, 2014

Assets		Liabilities	
Cash	$ 25,000	Accounts receivable	$ 20,000
Store fixtures	10,000	Sales revenue	80,000
Accounts payable	16,000	Interest expense	800
Rent expense	4,000	Note payable	9,000
Salaries expense	15,000	Total	109,800
Land	44,000		
Advertising expense	3,000	Shareholders' Equity	
		Shareholders' equity	7,200
Total assets	$117,000	Total liabilities and	
		shareholders' equity	$117,000

Requirements
1. Prepare the correct balance sheet and date it properly. Compute total assets, total liabilities, and shareholders' equity.
2. Is STRIDES Inc. actually in better or worse financial position than the erroneous balance sheet reports? Give the reason for your answer.

3. Identify the accounts listed on the incorrect balance sheet that are not reported on the balance sheet. State why you excluded them from the correct balance sheet you prepared for Requirement 1. On which financial statement should these accounts appear?

LEARNING OBJECTIVE ②③
Understand the balance sheet, entity assumption

P1-47A Alexa Markowitz is a realtor. She buys and sells properties on her own, and she also earns commission as an agent for buyers and sellers. She organized her business as a corporation on March 16, 2014. The business received $60,000 cash from Markowitz and issued common shares in return. Consider the following facts as of March 31, 2014:

a. Markowitz has $5,000 in her personal bank account and $14,000 in the business bank account.
b. Office supplies on hand at the real estate office total $1,000.
c. Markowitz's business spent $25,000 for a ReMax franchise, which entitles her to represent herself as an agent. ReMax is a national affiliation of independent real estate agents. This franchise is a business asset.
d. The business owes $60,000 on a note payable for some undeveloped land acquired for a total price of $110,000.
e. Markowitz owes $100,000 on a personal mortgage on her personal residence, which she acquired in 2005 for a total price of $350,000.
f. Markowitz owes $1,800 on a personal charge account with Holt Renfrew.
g. Markowitz acquired business furniture for $10,000 on March 25. Of this amount, the business owes $6,000 on accounts payable at March 31.

Requirements

1. Prepare the balance sheet of the real estate business of Alexa Markowitz Realtor Inc. at March 31, 2014.
2. Does it appear that the realty business can pay its debts? How can you tell?
3. Explain why some of the items given in the preceding facts were not reported on the balance sheet of the business.

LEARNING OBJECTIVE ④
Prepare and use the income statement, statement of retained earnings, and balance sheet

P1-48A The assets and liabilities of Web Services Inc. as of December 31, 2014 and revenues and expenses for the year ended on that date are listed here.

Land	$ 8,000	Equipment	$ 11,000
Note payable	32,000	Interest expense	4,000
Property tax expense	2,000	Interest payable	2,000
Rent expense	15,000	Accounts payable	15,000
Accounts receivable	25,000	Salary expense	40,000
Service revenue	150,000	Building	126,000
Supplies	2,000	Cash	8,000
Utilities expense	3,000	Common shares	15,000

Beginning retained earnings were $60,000, and dividends totalled $30,000 for the year.

Requirements

1. Prepare the income statement of Web Services Inc. for the year ended December 31, 2014.
2. Prepare the company's statement of retained earnings for the year.
3. Prepare the company's balance sheet at December 31, 2014.
4. As CEO of Web Services Inc., answer the following questions and then decide if you would be pleased with Web Services' overall performance in 2014?
   a. Was Web Services profitable during 2014? By how much?
   b. Did retained earnings increase or decrease? By how much?
   c. Which is greater: total liabilities or total equity? Who owns more of Web Services' assets: creditors or Web Services' shareholders?

LEARNING OBJECTIVE ❸

Prepare a statement of cash flows

P1-49A The following data are from financial statements of Stuart Inc. for the fiscal year ended March 1, 2014 (in millions):

Purchases of capital assets and other assets	$ 144	Accounts receivable	$168
Issuance of long-term debt	164	Repurchase of common shares	177
Net loss	(251)	Payment of dividends	31
Adjustments to reconcile net income (loss) to cash provided by operations	397	Common shares	715
		Issuance of common shares	1
		Sales of capital assets and other assets	1
Revenues	1,676	Retained earnings	752
Cash, beginning of year	41	Repayment of long-term debt	1
Cash, end of year	0		
Cost of goods sold	1,370		

Requirements

1. Prepare a statement of cash flows for the fiscal year ended March 1, 2014. Follow the format of the summary problem on page 31. Not all items given are reported in the statement of cash flows.
2. What was the largest source of cash? Is this a sign of financial strength or weakness?

LEARNING OBJECTIVE ❸❹

Analyze a company's financial statements; explain relationships among the financial statements

P1-50A Summarized versions of the Gonzales Corporation's financial statements are given below for two years.

	(in thousands)	
	2014	2013
Statement of Income		
Revenues	$ k	$ 16,000
Cost of goods sold	11,500	a
Other expenses	1,300	1,200
Earnings before income taxes	4,000	3,700
Income taxes (35% tax rate)	1	1,300
Net earnings	$ m	$ b
Statement of Retained Earnings		
Beginning balance	$ n	$ 3,500
Net earnings	o	c
Dividends	(300)	(200)
Ending balance	$ p	$ d
Balance Sheet		
Assets:		
Cash	$ q	$ e
Capital assets	3,000	1,800
Other assets	r	11,200
Total assets	$ s	$ 15,000
Liabilities:		
Current liabilities	$ t	$ 5,600
Notes payable and long-term debt	4,500	3,200
Other liabilities	80	200
Total liabilities	$ 9,100	$ f

Shareholders' Equity:				
Common shares..	$	300	$	300
Retained earnings		u		g
Total shareholders' equity		v		6,000
Total liabilities and shareholders' equity....................	$	w	$	h

Statement of Cash Flows				
Net cash provided by operating activities............................	$	x	$	1,900
Net cash used for investing activities		(1,000)		(900)
Net cash used for financing activities.................................		(700)		(1.010)
Increase (decrease) in cash...		400		i
Cash at beginning of year..		y		2,010
Cash at end of year	$	z	$	j

Requirements

1. Determine the missing amounts denoted by the letters.
2. As Gonzales Corporation's CEO, use the financial statements to answer these questions about the company. Explain each of your answers, and identify the financial statement where you found the information.
   a. Did operations improve or deteriorate during 2014?
   b. What is the company doing with most of its income—retaining it for use in the business or using it for dividends?
   c. How much in total resources does the company have to work with as it moves into the year 2015?
   d. At the end of 2013, how much did the company owe outsiders? At the end of 2014, how much did the company owe? Is this trend good or bad in comparison to the trend in assets?
   e. What is the company's major source of cash? Is cash increasing or decreasing? What is your opinion of the company's ability to generate cash?

(Group B)

P1-51B Snap Fasteners Inc. experienced the following transactions during the year ended December 31, 2014:

LEARNING OBJECTIVE ❷❸❹

Apply assumptions and characteristics to the income statement

a. All other expenses, excluding income taxes, totalled $14.9 million for the year. Income tax expense was 35% of income before tax.
b. Snap has several operating divisions. Each division is accounted for separately to show how well each division is performing. However, Snap's financial statements combine the statements of all the divisions to report on the company as a whole.
c. Inflation affects Snap's cost to manufacture goods. If Snap's financial statements were to show the effects of inflation, assume the company's reported net income would drop by $0.250 million.
d. If Snap were to go out of business, the sale of its assets might bring in over $5 million in cash.
e. Snap sold products for $56.2 million. Company management believes that the value of these products is approximately $60.5 million.
f. It cost Snap $40.0 million to manufacture the products it sold. If Snap had purchased the products instead of manufacturing them, Snap's cost would have been $43.0 million.

Requirements

1. Prepare Snap's income statement for the year ended December 31, 2014.
2. For items a through f, identify the accounting assumption or characteristic that determined how you accounted for the item described. State how you have applied the assumption or characteristic in preparing Snap's income statement.

LEARNING OBJECTIVE ❸❹

Apply the accounting equation;
understand the financial statements

P1-52B Compute the missing amounts (?) for each company (in millions).

	Gas Limited	Groceries Inc.	Bottlers Corp.
Beginning			
Assets	$11,200	$ 3,256	$ 909
Liabilities	4,075	1,756	564
Ending			
Assets	$12,400	$?	$1,025
Liabilities	4,400	1,699	563
Owners' Equity			
Issuance (Repurchase) of shares	$ (36)	$ (0)	$?
Dividends	341	30	0
Income Statement			
Revenues	$11,288	$11,099	$1,663
Expenses	?	10,879	1,568

Which company has the
- highest net income?
- highest percentage of net income to revenues?

Hint: Prepare a statement of owners' equity, which begins with opening shareholders' equity and adds and subtracts changes to conclude with closing shareholders' equity.

LEARNING OBJECTIVE ❸

Understand the balance sheet

P1-53B Ned Robinson, the manager of Lunenberg Times Inc., prepared the balance sheet of the company while the accountant was ill. The balance sheet contains numerous errors. In particular, the manager knew that the balance sheet should balance, so he plugged in the shareholders' equity amount needed to achieve this balance. The shareholders' equity amount, however, is *not* correct. All other amounts are accurate.

Lunenberg Times Inc.
Balance Sheet
For the Month Ended October 31, 2014

Assets		Liabilities	
Cash	$ 25,000	Accounts receivable	$ 10,000
Office furniture	15,000	Sales revenue	70,000
Note payable	16,000	Salary expense	20,000
Rent expense	4,000	Accounts payable	8,000
Inventory	30,000		
Land	34,000	**Shareholders' Equity**	
Advertising expense	2,500	Shareholders' equity	18,500
Total assets	$126,500	Total liabilities	$126,500

Requirements

1. Prepare the correct balance sheet, and date it properly. Compute total assets, total liabilities, and shareholders' equity.
2. Is Lunenberg Times Inc. actually in better or worse financial position than the erroneous balance sheet reports? Give the reason for your answer.
3. Identify the accounts listed in the incorrect balance sheet that are *not* reported on the corrected balance sheet. State why you excluded them from the correct balance sheet you prepared for Requirement 1. Which financial statement should these accounts appear on?

P1-54B Luis Fantano is a realtor. He buys and sells properties on his own and also earns commission as an agent for buyers and sellers. Fantano organized his business as a corporation on July 10, 2014. The business received $75,000 from Fantano and issued common shares in return. Consider these facts as of July 31, 2014:

a. Fantano owes $5,000 on a personal charge account with Visa.

b. Fantano's business owes $80,000 on a note payable for some undeveloped land acquired for a total price of $135,000.

c. Fantano has $5,000 in his personal bank account and $10,000 in the business bank account.

d. Office supplies on hand at the real estate office total $1,000.

e. Fantano's business spent $35,000 for a Century 21 real estate franchise, which entitles him to represent himself as a Century 21 agent. Century 21 is a national affiliation of independent real estate agents. This franchise is a business asset.

f. Fantano owes $125,000 on a personal mortgage on his personal residence, which he acquired in 2004 for a total price of $300,000.

g. Fantano acquired business furniture for $18,000 on July 15. Of this amount, his business owes $10,000 on open account at July 31.

Requirements

1. Prepare the balance sheet of the realty business of Luis Fantano Realtor Inc. at July 31, 2014.
2. Does it appear that Fantano's realty business can pay its debts? How can you tell?
3. Identify the personal items given in the preceding facts that would not be reported on the balance sheet of the business.

P1-55B The assets and liabilities of Auto Mechanics Ltd. as of December 31, 2014, and revenues and expenses for the year ended on that date follow.

Interest expense	$ 4,000	Accounts receivable	$ 25,000
Land	95,000	Advertising expense	10,000
Note payable	95,000	Building	140,000
Accounts payable	21,000	Salary expense	85,000
Rent expense	6,000	Salary payable	12,000
Cash	10,000	Service revenue	210,000
Common shares	75,000	Supplies	3,000
Furniture	20,000	Property tax expense	5,000

Beginning retained earnings were $40,000, and dividends totalled $50,000 for the year.

Requirements

1. Prepare the income statement of Auto Mechanics Ltd. for the year ended December 31, 2014.
2. Prepare the Auto Mechanics Ltd. statement of retained earnings for the year.
3. Prepare Auto Mechanics' balance sheet at December 31, 2014.
4. Use the information prepared in Requirements 1 through 3 to answer the following:
   a. Was Auto Mechanics Ltd. profitable during 2014? By how much?
   b. Did retained earnings increase or decrease? By how much?
   c. Which is greater: total liabilities or total equity? Who has a claim against more of Auto Mechanics Ltd.'s assets: the creditors or the shareholders?

P1-56B The data below are adapted from the financial statements of Long Boat Ltd. at the end of a recent year (in thousands).

LEARNING OBJECTIVE ❷❸

Understand the balance sheet, entity assumption

LEARNING OBJECTIVE ❸❹

Understand the income statement, statement of retained earnings, balance sheet; explain relationships among the financial statements

LEARNING OBJECTIVE ❸

Prepare a statement of cash flows

Adjustments to reconcile net income to cash provided by operations....	$ 65	Sales of capital assets........................	$ 2
		Payment of long-term debt..............	26
Revenues	3,870	Cost of goods sold...........................	3,182
Bank overdraft, beginning of year	(11)	Common shares...............................	212
Cash, end of year.............................	23	Accounts receivable.........................	271
Purchases of capital assets...............	123	Issuance of common shares.............	4
Long-term debt................................	234	Change in bank loan.......................	(44)
Net income......................................	180	Payment of dividends.....................	24
Retained earnings	1,000		

Requirements

1. Prepare Long Boat's statement of cash flows for the year. Follow the solution to the summary problem starting on page 30. Not all the items given appear on the statement of cash flows.
2. Which activities provided the bulk of Long Boat's cash? Is this a sign of financial strength or weakness?

LEARNING OBJECTIVE ❸❹

Analyze a company's financial statements; explain relationships among the financial statements

P1-57B Condensed versions of Your Phone Ltd.'s financial statements, with certain amounts omitted, are given for two years.

	(thousands)	
	2014	2013
Statement of Income		
Revenues	$94,500	$ a
Cost of goods sold..	k	65,400
Other expenses..	15,660	13,550
Income before income taxes	5,645	9,300
Income taxes	1,975	3,450
Net income..	$ l	$ b
Statement of Retained Earnings		
Beginning balance..	$ m	$10,000
Net income...	n	c
Dividends..	(480)	(450)
Ending balance...	$ o	$ d
Balance Sheet		
Assets:		
Cash...	$ p	$ 400
Capital assets	23,790	e
Other assets...	q	17,900
Total assets...	$ r	$38,500
Liabilities:		
Current liabilities...	$11,100	$10,000
Long-term debt and other liabilities.........................	s	12,500
Total liabilities...	24,500	f
Shareholders' Equity:		
Common shares..	$ 400	$ 600
Retained earnings	t	g
Total shareholders' equity	u	16,000
Total liabilities and shareholders' equity................	$ v	$ h
Statement of Cash Flows		
Net cash provided by operating activities.................	$ w	$ 3,600
Net cash used for investing activities	(2,700)	(4,150)
Net cash provided by financing activities.................	250	900
Increase (decrease) in cash.....................................	50	i
Cash at beginning of year	x	50
Cash at end of year..	$ y	$ j

Requirements

1. Determine the missing amounts denoted by the letters.
2. Use Your Phone's financial statements to answer these questions about the company. Explain each of your answers.
   a. Did operations improve or deteriorate during 2014?
   b. What is the company doing with most of its income—retaining it for use in the business or using it for dividends?
   c. How much in total resources does the company have to work with as it moves into 2015? How much in total resources did the company have at the end of 2013?
   d. At the end of 2013, how much did the company owe outsiders? At the end of 2014, how much did the company owe?
   e. What is the company's major source of cash? What is your opinion of the company's ability to generate cash? How is the company using most of its cash? Is the company growing or shrinking?

Apply Your Knowledge

Decision Cases

Case 1. Two businesses, Web Services and PC Providers, have sought business loans from you. To decide whether to make the loans, you have requested their balance sheets.

LEARNING OBJECTIVE ❸

Evaluate business operations; use financial statements

Web Services
Balance Sheet
As at October 31, 2014

Assets		Liabilities	
Cash	$ 11,000	Accounts payable	$ 13,000
Accounts receivable	4,000	Notes payable	377,000
Furniture	36,000	Total liabilities	390,000
Software	79,000	**Shareholders' Equity**	
Computers	300,000	Shareholders' equity	40,000
		Total liabilities and	
Total assets	$430,000	shareholders' equity	$430,000

PC Providers Inc.
Balance Sheet
As at October 31, 2014

Assets		Liabilities	
Cash	$ 9,000	Accounts payable	$ 12,000
Accounts receivable	24,000	Note payable	28,000
Merchandise inventory	85,000	Total liabilities	40,000
Furniture and fixtures	9,000		
Building	82,000	**Shareholders' Equity**	
Land	14,000	Shareholders' equity	183,000
		Total liabilities and	
Total assets	$223,000	shareholders' equity	$223,000

Requirements

1. Using only these balance sheets, to which entity would you be more comfortable lending money? Explain fully, citing specific items and amounts from the respective balance sheets.
2. Is there other financial information you would consider before making your decision? Be specific.

LEARNING OBJECTIVE 3

Analyze a company's financial statements

Case 2. After you have been out of college for a year, you have $5,000 to invest. A friend has started My Dream Inc., and she asks you to invest in her company. You obtain My Dream Inc.'s financial statements, which are summarized at the end of the first year as follows:

My Dream Inc.
Income Statement
For the Year Ended December 31, 2014

Revenues	$80,000
Expenses	60,000
Net income	$20,000

My Dream Inc.
Balance Sheet
As at December 31, 2014

Cash	$13,000	Liabilities	$35,000
Other assets	67,000	Equity	45,000
Total assets	$80,000	Total liabilities and equity	$80,000

Visits with your friend turn up the following facts:

a. The company owes an additional $10,000 for TV ads that was incurred in December but not recorded in the books.

b. Software costs of $20,000 were recorded as assets. These costs should have been expensed. My Dream paid cash for these expenses and recorded the cash payment correctly.

c. Revenues and receivables of $10,000 were overlooked and omitted.

Requirements

1. Prepare corrected financial statements.
2. Use your corrected statements to evaluate My Dream's results of operations and financial position.
3. Will you invest in My Dream? Give your reason.

Ethical Issue

LEARNING OBJECTIVE 5

Make ethical business decisions

You are studying frantically for an accounting exam tomorrow. You are having difficulty in this course, and the grade you make on this exam can make the difference between receiving a final grade of B or C. If you receive a C, it will lower your grade point average to the point that you could lose your academic scholarship. An hour ago, a friend, also enrolled in the course but in a different section under the same professor, called you with some unexpected news. In her sorority test files, she has just found a copy of an old exam from the previous year. In looking at the exam, it appears to contain questions that come right from the class notes you have taken, even the very same numbers. She offers to make a copy for you and bring it over.

You glance at your course syllabus and find the following: "You are expected to do your own work in this class. Although you may study with others, giving, receiving, or obtaining information pertaining to an examination is considered an act of academic dishonesty, unless such action is authorized by the instructor giving the examination. Also, divulging the contents of an essay or objective examination designated by the instructor as an examination is considered an act of academic dishonesty. Academic dishonesty is considered a violation of the student honour code and will subject the student to disciplinary procedures, which can include suspension from the university." Although you have heard a rumour that fraternities and sororities have cleared their exam files with professors, you are not sure.

Requirements

1. What is the ethical issue in this situation?
2. Who are the stakeholders? What are the possible consequences to each?
3. Analyze the alternatives from the following standpoints: (a) economic, (b) legal, and (c) ethical.
4. What would you do? How would you justify your decision? How would your decision make you feel afterward?
5. How is this similar to a business situation?

Focus on Financials

TELUS Corporation

This case is based on the financial statements of TELUS, which you can find in Appendix A at the back of the book. As you work with TELUS's financial statements throughout this course, you will develop the ability to use actual financial statements.

LEARNING OBJECTIVE ❸
Evaluate business operations

Requirements

1. Suppose you own shares in TELUS. If you could pick one item on the company's income statement to increase year after year, what would it be? Why is this item so important? Did this item increase or decrease during the year ended December 31, 2011? Is this good news or bad news for the company?
2. What was TELUS's largest expense each year? In your own words, explain the meaning of this item. Give specific examples of items that make up this expense. Why is this expense less than sales revenue?
3. Use the balance sheet as at December 31, 2011, to answer these questions. At December 31, 2011, how much in total resources did TELUS have to work with? How much did the company owe? How much of its assets did the company's shareholders actually own? Use these amounts to write TELUS's accounting equation at December 31, 2011 (express all items in thousands of dollars).
4. How much cash, including temporary investments, did TELUS have at December 31, 2010? How much cash did it have at December 31, 2011? Where does TELUS get most of its cash? How does the company spend its cash?

Focus on Analysis

TELUS Corporation

This case is based on the financial statements of TELUS, which can be found in Appendix A at the back of the book. As you work with TELUS throughout this course, you will develop the ability to analyze financial statements of actual companies.

LEARNING OBJECTIVE ❸
Evaluate a company by using financial statements

Requirements

1. Does TELUS's financial condition look strong or weak? How can you tell?
2. What was the result of TELUS's operations during 2011? Identify both the name and the dollar value of the result of operations for 2011. Does an increase (decrease) signal good news or bad news for the company and its shareholders?
3. Examine shareholders' equity on the balance sheet and the statement of changes in owners' equity. What were the changes in shareholders' equity during 2011? What caused these changes?
4. Which statement reports cash as part of TELUS's financial position? Which statement tells why cash increased (or decreased) during the year? What items caused TELUS's cash to change the most in 2011?

Group Project

Project 1. As instructed by your professor, obtain an annual report of a Canadian company.

Requirements

1. Take the role of a loan committee of the Royal Bank of Canada. Assume the company has requested a loan from your bank. Analyze the company's financial statements and any other information you need to reach a decision regarding the largest amount of money you would be willing to lend. Go as deeply into the analysis and the related decision as you can. Specify the following:
   a. Any restrictions you would impose on the borrower.
   b. The length of the loan period (that is, over what period you will allow the company to pay you back).

Note: The long-term debt note to the financial statements gives details of the company's liabilities.

2. Write your group decision in a report addressed to the bank's board of directors. Limit your report to two double-spaced word-processed pages.
3. If your professor directs you to, present your decision and analysis to the class. Limit your presentation to 10–15 minutes.

Project 2. You are the owner of a company that is about to "go public" (that is, issue its shares to outside investors). You wish to make your company look as attractive as possible to raise $1 million in cash to expand the business. At the same time, you want to give potential investors a reliable and relevant picture of your company.

Requirements

1. Design a presentation to portray your company in a way that will enable outsiders to reach an informed decision as to whether to invest in your company. The presentation should include the following:
   a. Name and location of your company.
   b. Nature of the company's business (be specific and detailed to provide a clear picture of the nature, history, and future goals of the business).
   c. How you plan to spend the money you raise.
   d. The company's comparative income statement, statement of retained earnings, balance sheet, and statement of cash flows for two years: the current year and the preceding year. Make the data as realistic as possible with the intent of receiving $1 million.
2. Prepare a word-processed presentation that does not exceed five pages.
3. If directed by your professor, distribute copies of your presentation to the class with the intent of enticing your classmates to invest in your company. Make a 10- to 15-minute investment pitch to the class. Measure your success by the amount of investment commitment you receive.

Quick Check Answers

1. *b*
2. *a*
3. *d*
4. *c*
5. *d*
6. *a*
7. *b* ($100,000 − $40,000 − $3,000 = $57,000)
8. *c* ($100,000 − $40,000 = $60,000)
9. *b* [*Total assets = $105,000 ($5,000 + $30,000 + $20,000 + $50,000)*
   Shareholders' equity: $80,000 ($105,000 − $25,000)]
10. *d*
11. *d* [*$30,000 + Net income ($15,000) − Dividends = $40,000; Dividends = $5,000*]
12. *b*

	Assets	=	Liabilities	+	Equity
Beginning	$300,000	=	$200,000	+	$100,000
Increase	50,000	=	40,000	+	10,000*
Ending	350,000	=	240,000	+	110,000*

*Must solve for these amounts.

Study on the Go

Featured at the end of each chapter, you will find a unique barcode providing access to Study on the Go. Study on the Go brings material from your textbook to you and your smartphone. Now wherever you are—whatever you are doing—you can study by listening to the Audio Summaries, quizzing yourself, or using the awesome Glossary Flashcards. Go to one of the sites below to see how you can download an app to your smartphone for free. Once the app is installed, your phone will scan the code and link to a website containing Pearson's Study on the Go content that you can access anytime.

ScanLife
http://get.scanlife.com/

NeoReader
http://get.neoreader.com/

QuickMark
http://www.quickmark.com.tw/

2

Recording Business Transactions

© FocusDigital/Alamy

SPOTLIGHT

How do you manage information in your busy life? You may use many of thousands of apps on Apple's iPhone for texting, listening to music, or checking the weather or sports scores. You may use an iPad for reading your favourite books or playing your favourite game. The iPhone, iPod, and iPad, in addition to the company's popular MacBook computers, have generated billions of dollars in profits for the company.

Apple Inc. is a U.S.-based multinational corporation that designs and manufactures consumer electronics. The company operates more than 300 retail stores worldwide and an online store where hardware and software products are sold. How does Apple determine its revenues, expenses, and net income? Like all other companies, Apple has a comprehensive accounting system. Apple's income statement is displayed on the next page. The income statement shows that during fiscal year 2011, Apple made over $100 billion of sales and earned net income of almost $26 billion. Where did those figures come from? In this chapter, we'll show you.

Apple Inc. Income Statement (Adapted) Fiscal Year Ended September 24, 2011	
(in billions)	2011
Net sales	$108.2
Cost of goods sold	64.4
Gross profit	43.8
Operating expenses:	
Research and development expense	2.4
Selling, general, and adminstrative expense	7.6
Total operating expense	10.0
Operating income	33.8
Other income	0.4
Income before income taxes	34.2
Income tax expense	8.3
Net income	$ 25.9

Businesses engage in many different activities, and most of these activities result in transactions that are recorded in the accounting records. A **transaction** is any event that has a financial impact on a business and that can be reliably measured. For example, Apple pays programmers to create iTunes software. Apple also sells computers, buys other companies, and repays debts—three different kinds of transactions.

But not all events qualify as transactions. The iPhone may be featured in TV ads, for example, motivating people to *consider* buying one, but no transaction occurs until someone *actually buys* an Apple product, creating a financial impact on the company. A transaction must occur before Apple records anything.

Every transaction has two sides, and we always record both sides in the accounting records. Before we can record it, however, we must be able to reliably assign a dollar value to the transaction, so that we have a measure of its financial impact on the business.

DESCRIBE COMMON TYPES OF ACCOUNTS

OBJECTIVE

❶ **Describe** common types of accounts

Recall the accounting equation introduced in Chapter 1:

$$\text{Assets} = \text{Liabilities} + \text{Shareholders' Equity}$$

Each asset, liability, and element of shareholders' equity has its own **account**, which is used to record all the transactions affecting the related asset, liability, or element of shareholders' equity during an accounting period. Before we start learning how to record transactions in accounts, let's review some common types of accounts that companies such as Apple have in their accounting records.

Asset Accounts

Most companies have the following asset accounts in their accounting records:

CASH. Cash consists of bank account balances, paper currency and coins, and undeposited cheques.

ACCOUNTS RECEIVABLE. Accounts Receivable represent the amounts owing from customers who have purchased goods or services on credit.

INVENTORY. Inventory includes the goods a company sells to its customers. Companies that make the products they sell also have inventory consisting of the raw materials used to produce the finished products and any partially finished products.

PREPAID EXPENSES. Prepaid Expenses consist of expenses a company has paid in advance of actually using the product or service it has purchased. If, for example, a company pays up front for a one-year insurance contract, the payment would be recorded as a Prepaid Insurance Expense.

LAND. This account includes any land a company uses in its operations.

BUILDINGS. Any office buildings, factories, and other buildings owned by a company are included in the Buildings account.

EQUIPMENT, FURNITURE, AND FIXTURES. These accounts include a variety of office, computer, and manufacturing equipment, as well as any furniture and fixtures owned by a company.

Liability Accounts

You will see the following liability accounts in the accounting records of many companies:

ACCOUNTS PAYABLE. Accounts Payable represent the amounts a company owes to suppliers who have sold the company goods or services on credit. They are the opposite of Accounts Receivable.

ACCRUED LIABILITIES. An accrued liability is a liability for an expense that has not been billed for or paid. Examples include interest payable on bank loans, salaries payable to employees, and income taxes payable to governments.

LOANS PAYABLE. Loans Payable include money a company has borrowed from banks and other creditors to fund its business activities.

Shareholders' Equity Accounts

The Shareholders' Equity accounts found in a corporation's accounting records include the following:

SHARE CAPITAL. The Share Capital account includes the capital a company has received from its owners in exchange for shares of the company. This account is sometimes called Common Shares, which is the most basic element of equity.

RETAINED EARNINGS. The Retained Earnings account shows the cumulative net income earned by the company over its lifetime, minus its cumulative net losses and dividends.

DIVIDENDS. The Dividends account includes dividends that have been declared during the current fiscal period. Dividends are payments to shareholders that represent the distribution of a portion of the company's past earnings.

REVENUES. Revenues are a form of income that increase shareholders' equity. Companies typically earn revenue through the sale of their primary goods and services. For example, a lawyer provides legal services for clients and uses a Service Revenue account to record the revenue. Scotiabank loans money to an outsider and uses an Interest Revenue account. If the business rents a building to a tenant, it needs a Rent Revenue account.

EXPENSES. Expenses decrease shareholders' equity and consist mainly of the costs incurred to purchase the goods and services a company needs to run its business. Common types of expenses include Salary Expense, Rent Expense, Advertising Expense, and Utilities Expense. Companies strive to minimize expenses and thereby maximize net income.

GAINS AND LOSSES. Gains and losses also affect shareholder's equity via their impact on net income and retained earnings. Gains, which usually occur outside the course of a company's ordinary business activities, are another form of income, so they *increase* shareholders' equity. Losses, which also typically occur outside of ordinary business activities, are a type of expense, so they *reduce* shareholders' equity. If, for example, a company sells a building for more than the amount it was carried at on the balance sheet, then the company would realize a gain on the sale of this asset. If the selling price was less than the carrying amount, then the company would realize a loss. For simplicity, gains and losses are excluded from the following illustrations, but remember that when it comes to impacts on the accounting equation, gains have the same effect as revenues, whereas losses have the same impact as expenses.

STOP + THINK (2-1)

You were reading Apple's most recent financial statements and wondered:

1. What are two distinct types of transactions that would increase Apple's shareholders' equity?

2. What are two distinct types of transactions that would decrease Apple's shareholders' equity?

RECORD THE IMPACT OF BUSINESS TRANSACTIONS ON THE ACCOUNTING EQUATION

OBJECTIVE

❷ **Record** the impact of business transactions on the accounting equation

To illustrate accounting for business transactions, let's return to J.J. Booth and Marie Savard. You met them in Chapter 1, when they opened a consulting engineering company on April 1, 2014, and incorporated it as Tara Inc. (Tara for short).

We consider 11 transactions and analyze the effects of each one on Tara's accounting equation. In the latter part of the chapter, we will record these same 11 transactions using the formal accounting records of Tara.

TRANSACTION 1. Booth, Savard, and several fellow engineers invest $50,000 to begin Tara, and the business issues common shares to the shareholders. The effects of this transaction on the accounting equation are as follows:

	ASSETS Cash	=	LIABILITIES	+	SHAREHOLDERS' EQUITY Share Capital	TYPE OF SHAREHOLDERS' EQUITY TRANSACTION
(1)	+ 50,000				+ 50,000	Issued shares

For every transaction, the net amount on the left side of the equation must equal the net amount on the right side so that the equation stays in balance. The first transaction causes Cash on the left side to increase by $50,000, with a corresponding increase in Share Capital on the right side. To the right of the transaction we write "Issued shares" to record the reason for the $50,000 increase in shareholders' equity.

Tara Inc.
Balance Sheet
As at April 1, 2014

Assets		Liabilities	
Cash..	$50,000	None	
		Shareholders' Equity	
		Share Capital..............................	$50,000
		Total shareholders' equity........	50,000
		Total liabilities and	
Total assets	$50,000	shareholders' equity	$50,000

Every transaction affects the financial statements, and we can prepare the statements after one, two, or any number of transactions. Tara, for example, could prepare the above balance sheet after its first transaction. This balance sheet reports that Tara has $50,000 in cash, no liabilities, and share capital of $50,000 as at April 1, 2014, its first day of operations.

As a practical matter, entities report their financial statements at the end of an accounting period—not after each transaction. But an accounting system can produce statements whenever managers need to know where the business stands.

TRANSACTION 2. Tara purchases land for an office location and pays cash of $40,000. The effect of this transaction on the accounting equation is:

	ASSETS				LIABILITIES	+	SHAREHOLDERS' EQUITY
	Cash	+	Land				Share Capital
Balance	50,000						50,000
(2)	−40,000		+ 40,000	=			
Bal.	10,000		40,000				50,000
		50,000					50,000

The purchase increases one asset (Land) and decreases another asset (Cash) by the same amount. After the transaction, Tara has cash of $10,000, land of $40,000, and no liabilities. Shareholders' equity is unchanged at $50,000. Note that total assets must always equal total liabilities plus equity.

TRANSACTION 3. Tara buys stationery and other office supplies on account, agreeing to pay $3,700 within 30 days. This transaction increases both the assets and the liabilities of the business. Its effect on the accounting equation is:

		ASSETS				LIABILITIES	+	SHAREHOLDERS' EQUITY
	Cash	+	Office Supplies	+	Land	Accounts Payable	+	Share Capital
Bal.	10,000				40,000			50,000
(3)			+3,700			+3,700		
Bal.	10,000		3,700		40,000	3,700		50,000
		53,700					53,700	

The new asset is Office Supplies (which is a prepaid expense), and the liability is Accounts Payable.

TRANSACTION 4. Tara earns service revenue by providing engineering services. Assume the business earns $7,000 and collects this amount in cash. The effect on the accounting equation is an increase in the asset Cash and an increase in Retained Earnings, a shareholders' equity account:

| | ASSETS | | | | LIABILITIES | + | SHAREHOLDERS' EQUITY | | | TYPE OF SHAREHOLDERS' EQUITY TRANSACTION |
	Cash	+	Office Supplies	+ Land	Accounts Payable	+	Share Capital	+	Retained Earnings	
Bal.	10,000		3,700	40,000	3,700		50,000			
(4)	+7,000								7,000	Service revenue
Bal.	17,000		3,700	40,000	3,700		50,000		7,000	
		60,700					60,700			

To the right we record "Service revenue" to show where the $7,000 increase in Retained Earnings came from.

TRANSACTION 5. Tara performs services on account, which means that Tara lets customers pay later. Tara earns revenue but doesn't receive the cash immediately. In this transaction, Tara provides $3,000 in engineering services for King Contracting Ltd., and King promises to pay Tara within one month. This promise represents an asset for Tara in the form of an account receivable. The impact of this transaction on the accounting equation is as follows:

| | ASSETS | | | | LIABILITIES + | | SHAREHOLDERS' EQUITY | | | TYPE OF SHAREHOLDERS' EQUITY TRANSACTION |
	Cash +	Accounts Receivable	+ Office Supplies	+ Land	Accounts Payable	+	Share Capital	+	Retained Earnings	
Bal.	17,000		3,700	40,000	3,700		50,000		7,000	
(5)		+3,000							+3,000	Service revenue
Bal.	17,000	3,000	3,700	40,000	3,700		50,000		10,000	
		63,700					63,700			

Tara records (or recognizes) revenue when it performs the service, regardless of whether it receives the cash now or later. You will learn more about revenue recognition in the next chapter.

TRANSACTION 6. During the month, Tara pays for the following expenses: office rent, $1,100; employee salary, $1,200; and utilities, $400. The effect on the accounting equation is:

	ASSETS					LIABILITIES	+	SHAREHOLDERS' EQUITY			TYPE OF SHAREHOLDERS' EQUITY TRANSACTION
	Cash +	Accounts Receivable +	Office Supplies +	Land		Accounts Payable	+	Share Capital +	Retained Earnings		
Bal.	17,000	3,000	3,700	40,000	=	3,700		50,000	10,000		
(6)	–1,100								–1,100		Rent expense
	–1,200								–1,200		Salary expense
	– 400								– 400		Utilities expense
Bal.	14,300	3,000	3,700	40,000		3,700		50,000	7,300		
		61,000						61,000			

The expenses decrease Tara's Cash and Retained Earnings. We list each expense separately to keep track of its amount.

TRANSACTION 7. Tara pays $1,900 of the balance owing to the store from which it purchased Office Supplies in Transaction 3. The transaction decreases Cash and also decreases Accounts Payable as follows:

	ASSETS					LIABILITIES	+	SHAREHOLDERS' EQUITY		
	Cash +	Accounts Receivable +	Office Supplies +	Land		Accounts Payable	+	Share Capital +	Retained Earnings	
Bal.	14,300	3,000	3,700	40,000	=	3,700		50,000	7,300	
(7)	–1,900					– 1,900				
Bal.	12,400	3,000	3,700	40,000		1,800		50,000	7,300	
		59,100						59,100		

TRANSACTION 8. J.J. Booth paid $30,000 to remodel his home. This event is a personal transaction of J.J. Booth, so according to the separate-entity assumption from Chapter 1, we do not record it in the accounting records of Tara. Business transactions must be kept separate from the transactions of the business's owners.

TRANSACTION 9. In Transaction 5, Tara Inc. performed services for King Contracting on account. The business now collects $1,000 from King Contracting, which means Tara will record an increase in Cash and a decrease in Accounts Receivable. This is not service revenue now because Tara already recorded the revenue in Transaction 5. The effect of this transaction is:

	ASSETS					LIABILITIES	+	SHAREHOLDERS' EQUITY		
	Cash +	Accounts Receivable +	Office Supplies +	Land		Accounts Payable	+	Share Capital +	Retained Earnings	
Bal.	12,400	3,000	3,700	40,000	=	1,800		50,000	7,300	
(9)	+1,000	–1,000								
Bal.	13,400	2,000	3,700	40,000		1,800		50,000	7,300	
		59,100						59,100		

TRANSACTION 10. Tara sells part of the land purchased in Transaction 2 for $22,000, which is the same amount Tara paid for that part of the land. Tara receives $22,000 cash, and the effect on the accounting equation is:

	ASSETS					LIABILITIES	+	SHAREHOLDERS' EQUITY		
	Cash +	Accounts Receivable +	Office Supplies +	Land		Accounts Payable	+	Share Capital	+	Retained Earnings
Bal.	13,400	2,000	3,700	40,000	=	1,800		50,000		7,300
(10)	+22,000			−22,000						
Bal.	35,400	2,000	3,700	18,000		1,800		50,000		7,300
		59,100						59,100		

TRANSACTION 11. Tara pays the shareholders a $2,100 cash dividend. The effect on the accounting equation is:

	ASSETS					LIABILITIES +		SHAREHOLDERS' EQUITY			TYPE OF SHARHOLDERS' EQUITY TRANSACTION
	Cash +	Accounts Receivable +	Office Supplies +	Land		Accounts Payable	+	Share Capital	+	Retained Earnings	
Bal.	35,400	2,000	3,700	18,000	=	1,800		50,000		7,300	
(11)	−2,100									−2,100	Dividends
Bal.	33,300	2,000	3,700	18,000		1,800		50,000		5,200	
		57,000						57,000			

The dividend decreases both the asset Cash and the Retained Earnings of the business. *But dividends are not an expense*—they cause a direct reduction in Retained Earnings.

Transactions and Financial Statements

Exhibit 2-1 summarizes the 11 preceding transactions. Panel A gives the details of the transactions, and Panel B shows the transaction analysis for each one that affects the business. As you study the exhibit, note that every transaction in Panel B keeps the accounting equation in balance.

Panel B in Exhibit 2-1 provides the data needed to prepare Tara's financial statements:

- *Income statement* data appear as revenues and expenses under Retained Earnings. The revenues increase Retained Earnings; the expenses decrease Retained Earnings.
- The *balance sheet* data are composed of the ending balances of the assets, liabilities, and shareholders' equity shown at the bottom of the exhibit. The accounting equation shows that total assets ($57,000) equal total liabilities plus shareholders' equity ($57,000).
- The *statement of retained earnings* reports net income (or net loss) from the income statement. Dividends are subtracted. Ending retained earnings is the final result.
- Data for the *statement of cash flows* are aligned under the Cash account. Cash receipts increase cash, and cash payments decrease cash.

EXHIBIT 2-1
Transaction Analysis: Tara Inc.

Panel A—Transaction Details

(1) Received $50,000 cash and issued shares to the owners
(2) Paid $40,000 cash for land
(3) Bought $3,700 of office supplies on account
(4) Received $7,000 cash from customers for service revenue earned
(5) Performed services for customers on account, $3,000
(6) Paid cash for expenses: rent, $1,100; employee salary, $1,200; utilities, $400

(7) Paid $1,900 on the account payable created in Transaction 3
(8) Shareholder uses personal funds to remodel home, which is *not* a transaction of the business
(9) Received $1,000 of the accounts receivable created in Transaction 5
(10) Sold land for cash at its cost of $22,000
(11) Declared and paid a dividend of $2,100 to the shareholders

Panel B—Transaction Analysis

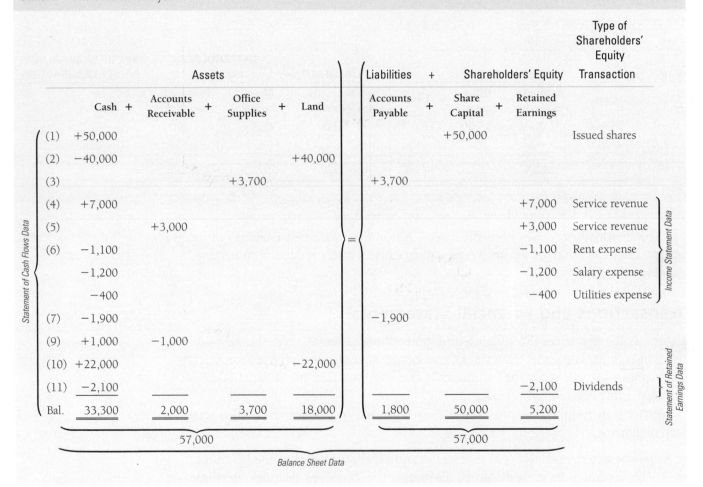

	Cash +	Accounts Receivable +	Office Supplies +	Land	=	Accounts Payable +	Share Capital +	Retained Earnings	Type of Shareholders' Equity Transaction
(1)	+50,000						+50,000		Issued shares
(2)	−40,000			+40,000					
(3)			+3,700			+3,700			
(4)	+7,000							+7,000	Service revenue
(5)		+3,000						+3,000	Service revenue
(6)	−1,100							−1,100	Rent expense
	−1,200							−1,200	Salary expense
	−400							−400	Utilities expense
(7)	−1,900					−1,900			
(9)	+1,000	−1,000							
(10)	+22,000			−22,000					
(11)	−2,100							−2,100	Dividends
Bal.	33,300	2,000	3,700	18,000		1,800	50,000	5,200	

Assets: 57,000   Liabilities + Shareholders' Equity: 57,000

Statement of Cash Flows Data (left bracket)
Income Statement Data (right bracket for transactions 4–6)
Statement of Retained Earnings Data (bracket for transaction 11)
Balance Sheet Data (bottom bracket)

Exhibit 2-2 shows the Tara Inc. financial statements for April, the company's first month of operations. Follow the flow of data to observe the following:

1. The income statement reports revenues, expenses, and either a net income or a net loss for the period. During April, Tara earned net income of $7,300. The income statement includes only two types of accounts: revenues and expenses.

2. The statement of retained earnings starts with the beginning balance of Retained Earnings (zero for a new business). Add net income for the period (arrow ①), subtract dividends, and obtain the ending balance of Retained Earnings ($5,200).

3. The balance sheet lists the assets, liabilities, and shareholders' equity of the business at the end of the period. Included in shareholders' equity is Retained Earnings, which comes from the statement of retained earnings (arrow ②).

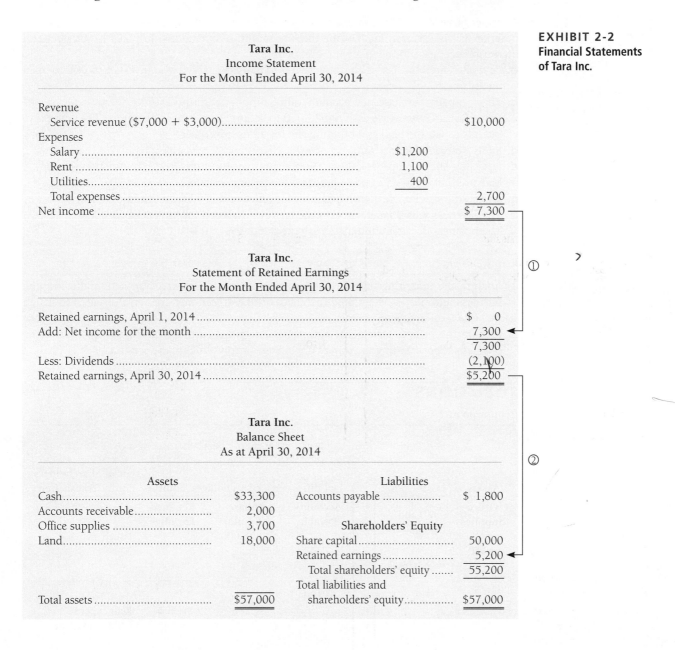

EXHIBIT 2-2
Financial Statements of Tara Inc.

Tara Inc.
Income Statement
For the Month Ended April 30, 2014

Revenue		
Service revenue ($7,000 + $3,000)...		$10,000
Expenses		
Salary	$1,200	
Rent	1,100	
Utilities..	400	
Total expenses		2,700
Net income		$ 7,300

Tara Inc.
Statement of Retained Earnings
For the Month Ended April 30, 2014

Retained earnings, April 1, 2014..	$ 0
Add: Net income for the month	7,300
	7,300
Less: Dividends	(2,100)
Retained earnings, April 30, 2014..	$5,200

Tara Inc.
Balance Sheet
As at April 30, 2014

Assets		Liabilities	
Cash.................................	$33,300	Accounts payable	$ 1,800
Accounts receivable.........................	2,000		
Office supplies	3,700	**Shareholders' Equity**	
Land..	18,000	Share capital...............................	50,000
		Retained earnings.......................	5,200
		Total shareholders' equity	55,200
		Total liabilities and	
Total assets	$57,000	shareholders' equity................	$57,000

①

②

MID-CHAPTER SUMMARY PROBLEM

Margaret Jarvis opens a research services business near a college campus. She names the corporation Jarvis Research Inc. During the first month of operations, July 2014, Margaret and the business engage in the following transactions:

a. Jarvis Research Inc. issues common shares to Margaret Jarvis, who invests $25,000 to open the business.

b. The company purchases, on account, office supplies costing $350.

c. Jarvis Research Inc. pays cash of $20,000 to acquire a lot near the campus. The company intends to use the land as a building site for a business office.

d. Jarvis Research Inc. performs services for clients and receives cash of $1,900.

e. Jarvis Research Inc. pays $100 on the account payable it created in Transaction (b).

f. Margaret Jarvis pays $2,000 in personal funds for a vacation.

g. Jarvis Research Inc. pays cash expenses for office rent ($400) and utilities ($100).

h. The business sells a small parcel of the land it purchased for its cost of $5,000.

i. The business declares and pays a cash dividend of $1,200.

Name: Jarvis Research Inc.
Industry: Research services
Fiscal Period: Month of July 2014
Key Facts: New business

Requirements

1. Analyze the preceding transactions. First determine if each is a transaction affecting the business and, if it is, determine the effect on the accounting equation of Jarvis Research Inc. Use Exhibit 2-1 as a guide.

2. Prepare the income statement, statement of retained earnings, and balance sheet of the business after recording the transactions. Draw arrows linking the statements.

SOLUTIONS

Requirement 1

	Assets				Liabilities +	Shareholders' Equity		Type of Shareholders' Equity Transaction
	Cash	+	Office Supplies	+ Land	Accounts Payable +	Share Capital +	Retained Earnings	
a.	+25,000					+25,000		Issued shares
b.			+350		+350			
c.	−20,000			+20,000				
d.	+ 1,900						+1,900	Service revenue
e.	−100				−100			
g.	−400						−400	Rent expense
	−100						−100	Utilities expense
h.	+ 5,000			−5,000				
i.	−1,200						−1,200	Dividends
Balance	10,100		350	15,000	250	25,000	200	
	25,450					25,450		

Add all the asset balances and add all the liabilities and shareholders' equity balances. Make sure that Total assets = Total liabilities + Shareholders' equity.

Requirement 2

Jarvis Research Inc.
Income Statement
For the Month Ended July 31, 2014

Revenue		
Service revenue		$1,900
Expenses		
Rent	$400	
Utilities	100	
Total		500
Net income		$1,400

The title must include the name of the company, "Income Statement," and the specific period of time covered. It is critical that the time period be defined.

Use the revenue and expense amounts from the Retained Earnings column and names from the Type of Shareholders' Equity Transaction column.

Jarvis Research Inc.
Statement of Retained Earnings
For the Month Ended July 31, 2014

Retained earnings, July 1, 2014	$ 0
Add: Net income for the month	1,400
	1,400
Less: Dividends	(1,200)
Retained earnings, July 31, 2014	$ 200

① The title must include the name of the company, "Statement of Retained Earnings," and the specific period of time covered. It is critical that the time period be defined.

Beginning retained earnings is $0 because this is the first year of operations. The net income amount is transferred from the income statement. The dividends amount is from the Retained Earnings column.

Jarvis Research Inc.
Balance Sheet
As at July 31, 2014

Assets		Liabilities	
Cash	$10,100	Accounts payable	$ 250
Office supplies	350		
Land	15,000	**Shareholders' Equity**	
		Share capital	25,000
		Retained earnings	200
		Total shareholders' equity	25,200
		Total liabilities and	
Total assets	$25,450	shareholders' equity	$25,450

② The title must include the name of the company, "Balance Sheet," and the date of the balance sheet. It shows the financial position at the end of business on a specific date.

Gather the asset, liability, and shareholders' equity accounts. Insert the final balances for each account from the Balance row. The retained earnings amount is transferred from the statement of retained earnings. It is imperative that Total assets = Total liabilities + Shareholders' equity.

RECORD BUSINESS TRANSACTIONS IN T-ACCOUNTS

We could use the accounting equation to record all of a business's transactions, but it would be very cumbersome, even for a small business with a low volume of transactions. In this section, we introduce the **double-entry system** of accounting, which is the method that all but the smallest of businesses use to record transactions.

It is called the double-entry system because every transaction has two sides and affects two (or more) accounts. When Tara Inc. issued common shares for $50,000 in cash, for example, one side of the transaction was a $50,000 increase in the Cash account and the other side was a $50,000 increase in the Share Capital account. We must record both sides of every transaction to keep the accounting equation in balance. If we record only a single entry for the $50,000 increase in Cash, the accounting equation would be out of balance, so we must make a second entry in Share Capital to account for the $50,000 increase in equity.

Chart of Accounts

An organization uses a **chart of accounts** to keep track of all its accounts. The chart of accounts lists the name of every account and its unique account number, but it does not provide the account balances. If an accountant is unsure about what account to use when recording a transaction, they can consult the chart of accounts to help them choose the most appropriate one. If the chart of accounts does not contain an appropriate account, the accountant can add a new account to the chart and use it to record the transaction.

Exhibit 2-3 presents Tara Inc.'s chart of accounts. The gaps between account numbers leave room to insert new accounts. In the illustrations that follow, we leave out the account numbers to avoid cluttering the presentation.

EXHIBIT 2-3
Chart of Accounts—Tara Inc.

Balance Sheet Accounts		
Assets	**Liabilities**	**Shareholders' Equity**
101 Cash	201 Accounts Payable	301 Share Capital
111 Accounts Receivable	231 Notes Payable	311 Dividends
141 Office Supplies		312 Retained Earnings
151 Office Furniture		
191 Land		

	Income Statement Accounts (Part of Shareholders' Equity)	
	Revenues	**Expenses**
	401 Service Revenue	501 Rent Expense
		502 Salary Expense
		503 Utilities Expense

The T-Account

We can represent an account using the letter T, which we call a *T-account*. The vertical line divides the account into left (debit) and right (credit) sides, while the account title rests on the horizontal line. The Cash T-account, for example, looks like this:

Cash	
(Left side)	**(Right side)**
Debit	*Credit*

The left side of the account is called the **debit** side, and the right side is called the **credit** side. Students are often confused by the words *debit* and *credit*, so it may help to remember that for every account:

Debit = Left side	Credit = Right side

Using these terms, we can refine our description of a transaction as having two sides: a debit side and a credit side. The double-entry system records both sides and requires that *the debit side equals the credit side* so that the accounting equation stays in balance.

Increases and Decreases in the Accounts: The Rules of Debit and Credit

The way we record increases and decreases to an account under the double-entry system varies by account type. *The rules of debit and credit* are as follows (see Exhibit 2-4 for an illustration):

- *Increases* in assets are recorded on the *left* (*debit*) side of the T-account, whereas *decreases* are recorded on the *right* (*credit*) side. When a business receives cash, the Cash account *increases*, so we *debit* the *left side* of the Cash account to record the increase in this asset. When a business makes a cash payment, we *credit* the *right* side of the Cash account to record the *decrease* in this account.

- Conversely, *increases* in liabilities and shareholders' equity are recorded on the *right* (*credit*) side of the T-account, whereas *decreases* are recorded on the *left* (*debit*) side. When a business receives a loan, the Loan Payable account *increases*, so we *credit* the *right side* of the Loan Payable account to record the increase in this liability. When a business makes a loan payment, we *debit* the *left* side of the Loan Payable account to record the *decrease* in this account.

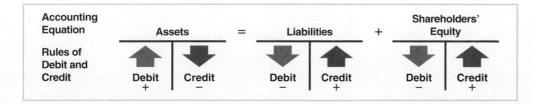

EXHIBIT 2-4
Accounting Equation and the Rules of Debit and Credit

Let's use Tara Inc.'s first two transactions to apply the rules of debit and credit illustrated in Exhibit 2-4. In Transaction (1), Tara received $50,000 in cash and issued common shares in return. As a result, we debit the left side of the Cash account to record the increase in this asset and credit the right side of the Share Capital account to record the increase in shareholders' equity. These two entries are illustrated in the T-accounts in Exhibit 2-5. After recording both sides of this transaction, the debits equal the credits ($50,000 each), so the accounting equation is in balance.

In Transaction (2), Tara purchased land for $40,000 in cash. To record the two sides of this transaction, we debit the left side of the Land account to record the increase in this asset and credit the right side of the Cash account to record the decrease in this asset. Again, the debits equal the credits ($40,000 each) after recording both sides of this transaction.

EXHIBIT 2-5
T-accounts After Tara Inc.'s First Two Transactions

Cash				Share Capital	
(1) Debit for increase	50,000	(2) Credit for decrease	40,000		(1) Credit for increase 50,000
Balance	10,000				Balance 50,000

Land		
(2) Debit for increase	40,000	
Balance	40,000	

MyAccountingLab

Accounting Cycle Tutorial:
Balance Sheet Accounts and
Transactions - Tutorial

After both transactions, the Cash account has a $10,000 debit balance, the Land account a $40,000 debit balance, and the Share Capital account a $50,000 credit balance. The total of the debit balances ($50,000) equals the only credit balance, so the accounting equation is in balance after these transactions, as illustrated in Exhibit 2-6.

EXHIBIT 2-6
The Accounting Equation After Tara Inc.'s First Two Transactions

Assets	=	Liabilities	+	Shareholders' Equity
Cash $10,000 Land $40,000 $50,000				Share Capital $50,000

The Expanded Accounting Equation

MyAccountingLab

Accounting Cycle Tutorial:
Balance Sheet Accounts and
Transactions - Application Exercise 2

Because several accounts from three separate financial statements affect shareholders' equity, we can expand the accounting equation to explicitly reflect the impact of changes in these accounts on shareholders' equity, as shown in Exhibit 2-7. Revenues and expenses are shown in parentheses to indicate their inclusion in the calculation of net income.

EXHIBIT 2-7
The Expanded Accounting Equation

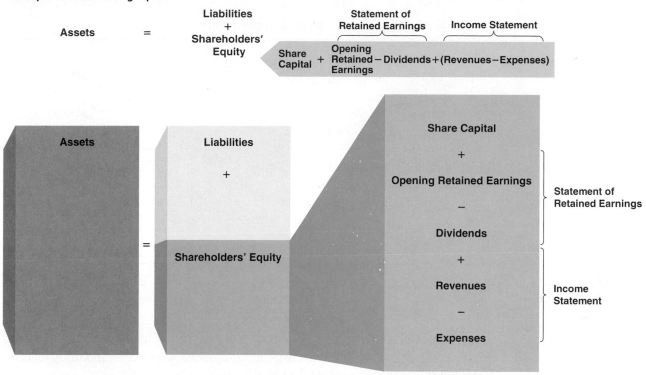

Based on this expanded equation, we can express the rules of debit and credit in more detail, as shown in Exhibit 2-8. *You should not proceed until you have learned these rules*, and you must remember the following:

- To record an increase in assets, use a debit.
- To record a decrease in assets, use a credit.

For liabilities and shareholders' equity, these rules are reversed:

- To record an increase in liabilities or shareholders' equity, use a credit.
- To record a decrease in liabilities or shareholders' equity, use a debit.

Recall that *increases* in Dividends and Expenses result in *decreases* to shareholders' equity, so applying the last rule above means that increases to Dividends and Expenses are recorded using debits, which is the opposite of the "increase = credit" rule for all other shareholders' equity accounts.

Exhibit 2-8 also highlights which side of each account the *normal balance* (debit or credit) falls on, which is the side where increases to the account are recorded (denoted by a "+" sign).

Analyzing Transactions Using Only T-Accounts

We can quickly assess the financial impact of a proposed business transaction by analyzing it informally using T-accounts. Assume, for example, that a manager is considering (a) taking out a $100,000 loan to (b) purchase $100,000 worth of equipment. The manager could record these proposed transactions in T-accounts as follows:

Cash		Equipment		Loan Payable	
(a) 100,000	(b) 100,000	(b) 100,000			(a) 100,000

MyAccountingLab

Accounting Cycle Tutorial:
Income Statement Accounts and
Transactions - Tutorial

MyAccountingLab

Accounting Cycle Tutorial:
The Journal and the Ledger
Application Exercises 1 and 2

EXHIBIT 2-8
The Expanded Rules of Debit and Credit

ASSETS	=	LIABILITIES	+	SHAREHOLDERS' EQUITY		

Assets		Liabilities		Share Capital		Retained Earnings		Dividends	
Debit	Credit	**Debit**	**Credit**	**Debit**	**Credit**	**Debit**	**Credit**	**Debit**	Credit
+	−	−	+	−	+	−	+	+	−
Normal balance			Normal balance		Normal balance		Normal balance	Normal balance	

						Revenues		Expenses	
						Debit	**Credit**	**Debit**	**Credit**
						−	+	+	−
							Normal balance	Normal Balance	

This informal analysis shows the manager that the net impact of these proposed transactions will be a $100,000 increase in Equipment, with a corresponding increase in the Loan Payable account. Managers who can analyze proposed transactions this way can make business decisions with a clear idea of their impact on the company's financial statements.

RECORD BUSINESS TRANSACTIONS IN THE JOURNAL AND POST THEM TO THE LEDGER

When recording transactions, accountants use a chronological record called a **journal**. The recording process follows these three steps:

1. Specify each account affected by the transaction.
2. Determine whether each account is increased or decreased by the transaction; use the rules of debit and credit to increase or decrease each account.
3. Record the transaction in the journal, including a brief explanation for the entry and the date of the transaction. The debit side is entered on the left margin, and the credit side is indented to the right.

Step 3 is also called "recording the journal entry" or "journalizing the transaction." Let's apply the steps to journalize the first transaction of Tara Inc.

Step 1   The business receives cash and issues shares. Cash and Share Capital are affected.

Step 2   Both Cash and Share Capital increase. Debit Cash to record an increase in this asset. Credit Share Capital to record an increase in this equity account.

Step 3   Record the journal entry for the transaction, as illustrated in Panel A of Exhibit 2-9.

EXHIBIT 2-9
Recording a Journal Entry and
Posting it to the Ledger

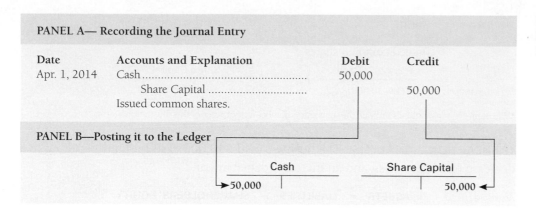

PANEL A— Recording the Journal Entry

Date	Accounts and Explanation	Debit	Credit
Apr. 1, 2014	Cash	50,000	
	Share Capital		50,000
	Issued common shares.		

PANEL B—Posting it to the Ledger

Cash	Share Capital
50,000	50,000

Posting From the Journal to the Ledger

The journal is a chronological record containing all of a company's transactions. The journal does not, however, indicate the balances in any of the company's accounts. To obtain these balances, we must transfer information from the journal to the **ledger**, which is an accounting process we call **posting**.

The ledger contains all of a company's accounts, along with their balances as of the most recent posting date. Posting is a simple process of directly transferring information from the journal to the ledger: debits in the journal are posted as debits in the ledger accounts, and likewise for credits. Exhibit 2-9 shows the posting of Tara Inc.'s first transaction from the journal to the ledger.

The Flow of Accounting Data

Exhibit 2-10 summarizes the flow of accounting data from the business transaction to the ledger. Let's practise using this process by revisiting Tara Inc.'s transactions for the month of April 2014. We will analyze each transaction, record it in Tara's journal (if necessary), then post it to the ledger.

MyAccountingLab

Accounting Cycle Tutorial:
The Journal and the Ledger - Tutorial

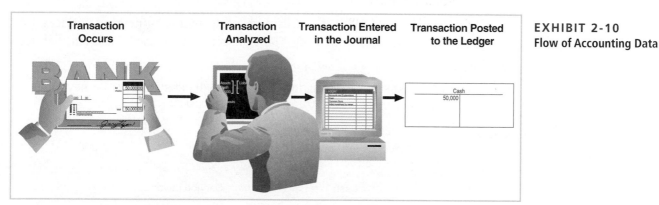

Transaction Occurs	Transaction Analyzed	Transaction Entered in the Journal	Transaction Posted to the Ledger

EXHIBIT 2-10
Flow of Accounting Data

TRANSACTION 1 ANALYSIS. Tara received $50,000 cash from shareholders and in turn issued Share Capital to them. The accounting equation, journal entry, and posting details for this transaction are as follows:

Accounting equation

ASSETS	=	LIABILITIES	+	SHAREHOLDERS' EQUITY
+50,000	=	0	+	50,000

Journal entry   Cash...   50,000
                      Share Capital...   50,000
                   Issued common shares.

	Cash		Share Capital	
The ledger accounts	(1)* 50,000			(1)* 50,000

*The numbers in parentheses indicate the transaction number for purposes of this illustration.

TRANSACTION 2 ANALYSIS. The business paid $40,000 cash for land, resulting in a decrease (credit) to Cash and an increase (debit) in Land.

Accounting equation

ASSETS	**=**	**LIABILITIES**	**+**	**SHAREHOLDERS' EQUITY**
+40,000	=	0	+	0
−40,000				

Journal entry   Land..   40,000
                      Cash   40,000
                   Paid cash for land.

	Cash		Land	
The ledger accounts	(1) 50,000	(2) 40,000	(2) 40,000	

TRANSACTION 3 ANALYSIS. The business purchased $3,700 in office supplies on account. The purchase increased Office Supplies, an asset, and Accounts Payable, a liability.

Accounting equation

ASSETS	**=**	**LIABILITIES**	**+**	**SHAREHOLDERS' EQUITY**
+3,700	=	+3,700	+	0

Journal entry   Office Supplies   3,700
                      Accounts Payable...............................   3,700
                   Purchased office supplies on account.

	Office Supplies		Accounts Payable	
The ledger accounts	(3) 3,700			(3) 3,700

TRANSACTION 4 ANALYSIS. The business performed engineering services for clients and received cash of $7,000. The transaction increased Cash and Service Revenue.

Accounting equation

ASSETS	**=**	**LIABILITIES**	**+**	**SHAREHOLDERS' EQUITY**	**+**	**REVENUES**
+7,000	=	0	+	0	+	7,000

Journal entry   Cash..   7,000
                      Service Revenue...................................   7,000
                   Performed services for cash.

	Cash		Service Revenue	
The ledger accounts	(1) 50,000	(2) 40,000		(4) 7,000
	(4) 7,000			

TRANSACTION 5 ANALYSIS. Tara performed $3,000 in services for King Contracting on account. The transaction increased Accounts Receivable and Service Revenue.

Accounting equation

ASSETS	**=**	**LIABILITIES**	**+**	**SHAREHOLDERS' EQUITY**	**+**	**REVENUES**
+3,000	=	0			+	3,000

Journal entry	Accounts Receivable............................... 3,000	
	Service Revenue.................................	3,000
	Performed services on account.	

Accounts Receivable	Service Revenue
The ledger accounts (5) 3,000	(4) 7,000
	(5) 3,000

TRANSACTION 6 ANALYSIS. Tara paid cash for the following expenses: office rent, $1,100; employee salary, $1,200; and utilities, $400. Debit each expense account for the amount of the expense and credit Cash for the sum of these expenses.

Accounting equation

ASSETS	=	LIABILITIES	+	SHAREHOLDERS' EQUITY	−	EXPENSES
−2,700	=	0			−	2,700

Journal entry

Rent Expense... 1,100
Salary Expense 1,200
Utilities Expense.................................... 400
    Cash... 2,700
Paid expenses.

Cash		Rent Expense
The ledger accounts (1) 50,000	(2) 40,000	(6) 1,100
(4) 7,000	(6) 2,700	

Salary Expense	Utilities Expense
(6) 1,200	(6) 400

TRANSACTION 7 ANALYSIS. The business paid $1,900 on the account payable created in Transaction 3. Credit Cash for the payment. The payment decreased a liability, so debit Accounts Payable.

Accounting equation

ASSETS	=	LIABILITIES	+	SHAREHOLDERS' EQUITY
−1,900	=	−1,900	+	0

Journal entry

Accounts Payable..................................... 1,900
    Cash.. 1,900
Paid cash on account.

Cash		Accounts Payable	
The ledger accounts (1) 50,000	(2) 40,000	(7) 1,900	(3) 3,700
(4) 7,000	(6) 2,700		
	(7) 1,900		

TRANSACTION 8 ANALYSIS. J.J. Booth, a shareholder of Tara Inc., remodelled his personal residence. This is not a transaction of the engineering consultancy, so Tara does not record it.

TRANSACTION 9 ANALYSIS. The business collected $1,000 cash on account from the client in Transaction 5. Debit Cash for the increase in this asset, and credit Accounts Receivable for the decrease in this asset.

Accounting equation

ASSETS	=	LIABILITIES	+	SHAREHOLDERS' EQUITY
+1,000	=	0	+	0
−1,000				

Journal entry

Cash... 1,000
    Accounts Receivable 1,000
Collected cash on account.

	Cash			Accounts Receivable	
The ledger accounts	(1) 50,000	(2) 40,000		(5) 3,000	(9) 1,000
	(4) 7,000	(6) 2,700			
	(9) 1,000	(7) 1,900			

TRANSACTION 10 ANALYSIS. Tara sold a portion of its land at cost for $22,000, receiving cash in return. This transaction resulted in an increase to Cash and a decrease in Land.

Accounting equation	**ASSETS**	**=**	**LIABILITIES**	**+**	**SHAREHOLDERS' EQUITY**
	+22,000	=	0	+	0
	−22,000				

Journal entry
Cash.. 22,000
    Land..   22,000
Sold land.

	Cash			Land	
The ledger accounts	(1) 50,000	(2) 40,000		(2) 40,000	(10) 22,000
	(4) 7,000	(6) 2,700			
	(9) 1,000	(7) 1,900			
	(10) 22,000				

TRANSACTION 11 ANALYSIS. Tara paid its shareholders cash dividends of $2,100. We credit Cash for the decrease in this asset, and debit Dividends to account for the decrease in shareholders' equity.

Accounting equation	**ASSETS**	**=**	**LIABILITIES**	**+**	**SHAREHOLDERS' EQUITY**	**−**	**DIVIDENDS**
	−2,100	=	0			−	2,100

Journal entry
Dividends.. 2,100
    Cash   2,100
Declared and paid dividends.

	Cash			Dividends	
The ledger accounts	(1) 50,000	(2) 40,000		(11) 2,100	
	(4) 7,000	(6) 2,700			
	(9) 1,000	(7) 1,900			
	(10) 22,000	(11) 2,100			

MyAccountingLab

Accounting Cycle Tutorial:
The Journal and the Ledger –
Application Exercise 1

Accounts After Posting to the Ledger

Exhibit 2-11 presents Tara Inc.'s ledger accounts after all transactions have been posted to them. For each account, a horizontal line separates the transaction amounts from the account balance (Bal.) at the end of the month. If the sum of an account's debits exceeds the sum of its credits, then the account will have a debit balance at the end of the period, as illustrated by the Cash debit balance of $33,300. If total credits exceed total debits, a credit balance results, as reflected in the Accounts Payable credit balance of $1,800.

MyAccountingLab

Accounting Cycle Tutorial:
The Journal and the Ledger –
Application Exercise 2

Analyzing Accounts

You can increase your understanding of how transactions affect accounts by analyzing the accounts to compute missing information. While you will likely never encounter

EXHIBIT 2-11
Tara Inc.'s Ledger Accounts After Posting

Assets		=	Liabilities		+		Shareholders' Equity	

Cash			Accounts Payable			Share Capital		Dividends	
(1) 50,000	(2) 40,000		(7) 1,900	(3) 3,700			(1) 50,000	(11) 2,100	
(4) 7,000	(6) 2,700			Bal. 1,800			Bal. 50,000	Bal. 2,100	
(9) 1,000	(7) 1,900								
(10) 22,000	(11) 2,100					REVENUE		EXPENSES	
Bal. 33,300						Service Revenue		Rent Expense	
							(4) 7,000	(6) 1,100	
Accounts Receivable							(5) 3,000	Bal. 1,100	
(5) 3,000	(9) 1,000						Bal. 10,000		
Bal. 2,000								Salary Expense	
								(6) 1,200	
Office Supplies								Bal. 1,200	
(3) 3,700									
Bal. 3,700								Utilities Expense	
								(6) 400	
Land								Bal. 400	
(2) 40,000	(10) 22,000								
Bal. 18,000									

situations like this in practice, this kind of analysis will help you determine how different transactions are recorded in the accounts.

Suppose, for example, that Tara Inc. began May with a Cash balance of $1,000, received cash of $8,000 during the month, and ended May with $3,000 in the account. We can enter the known information in the Cash ledger account and then compute Tara's cash payments for May (x) as follows:

Cash			
Beginning balance	1,000		
Cash receipts	8,000	Cash payments	$x = 6,000$
Ending balance	3,000		

Similarly, if we know Tara's beginning and ending Accounts Receivable balances and its total credit sales for a period, we can compute the amount of cash it collected on account during the period (x):

Accounts Receivable			
Beginning balance	6,000		
Sales on account	10,000	Collections on account	$x = 11,000$
Ending balance	5,000		

We can also determine Tara's payments on account for a month (x) if we are given its beginning and ending Accounts Payable balances and the purchases it made on account:

Accounts Payable			
Payments on account	$x = 4{,}000$	Beginning balance	9,000
		Purchases on account	6,000
		Ending balance	11,000

Similar kinds of analysis can be performed on any account for any business if you are given any three of the four key figures in an account for a particular accounting period.

PREPARE A TRIAL BALANCE

OBJECTIVE

❺ **Prepare** a trial balance

A **trial balance** lists all of a business's ledger accounts and their balances. Asset accounts are listed first, followed by the liability accounts, and then all the accounts that affect shareholders' equity. We add all the debit balances and all the credit balances and place the totals at the bottom of the trial balance. If the total debits equal the total credits, we can go on to prepare the financial statements using the account balances from the trial balance. Exhibit 2-12 presents Tara Inc.'s trial balance at the end of April 2014.

EXHIBIT 2-12
Tara Inc.'s Trial Balance

Tara Inc.
Trial Balance
April 30, 2014

Account Title	Balance Debit	Balance Credit
Cash	33,300	
Accounts receivable	2,000	
Office supplies	3,700	
Land	18,000	
Accounts payable		1,800
Share capital		50,000
Dividends	2,100	
Service revenue		10,000
Rent expense	1,100	
Salary expense	1,200	
Utilities expense	400	
Total	61,800	61,800

MyAccountingLab
Accounting Cycle Tutorial:
The Journal and the Ledger –
Glossary Terminology

MyAccountingLab
Accounting Cycle Tutorial:
The Journal and the Ledger –
Glossary Quiz

◄ DECISION GUIDELINES ►

HOW TO MEASURE RESULTS OF OPERATIONS AND FINANCIAL POSITION

Every manager must assess their company's profitability, financial position, and cash flows, but before they can do this, the company's transactions must be recorded in the accounting records. Here are some guidelines for the manager to follow when making decisions between the transaction stage and the reporting stage of the accounting process.

Decision	Guidelines
Has a transaction occurred?	If the event affects the entity's financial position **and** it can be reliably measured—Yes
	If either condition is absent—No
Where should the transaction be recorded?	In the *journal*, the chronological record of transactions
What accounts should be used to record the transaction in the journal?	Look in the *chart of accounts* for the most appropriate accounts to use
Should the affected accounts be debited or credited?	Rules of *debit* and *credit*:

	Increase	Decrease
Assets	Debit	Credit
Liabilities	Credit	Debit
Share capital	Credit	Debit
Retained earnings	Credit	Debit
Dividends	Debit	Credit
Revenues	Credit	Debit
Expenses	Debit	Credit

Decision	Guidelines
Where are all the transactions for each account summarized?	In the *ledger*, the book of accounts
Where are all the accounts and their balances listed?	In the *trial balance*
Where are the results of operations reported?	In the *income statement* (Revenues – Expenses = Net income or net loss)
Where is the financial position reported?	In the *balance sheet* (Assets = Liabilities + Shareholders' equity)
Where are the cash flows reported?	In the *statement of cash flows*

SUMMARY OF CHAPTER 2

LEARNING OBJECTIVE	SUMMARY
1. **Describe** common types of accounts	A business transaction is any event that has a financial impact on a business and that can be reliably measured. Business transactions are recorded in the accounts affected by the transactions. An account is the record of all transactions affecting a particular asset, liability, or element of shareholders' equity. Here are the common accounts of each type: **Assets:** Cash, Accounts Receivable, Inventory, Prepaid Expenses, Land, Buildings, Equipment **Liabilities:** Accounts Payable, Accrued Liabilities, Loans Payable **Shareholders' equity:** Share Capital, Retained Earnings, Dividends, Revenues, Expenses
2. **Record** the impact of business transactions on the accounting equation	Recall the accounting equation introduced in Chapter 1: $$\text{Assets} = \text{Liabilities} + \text{Shareholders' Equity}$$ Every business transaction affects at least one element of the accounting equation. When a company issues shares in exchange for $50,000 in cash, for example, the Cash asset increases by $50,000 and so does the Share Capital component of shareholders' equity. After each transaction is recorded in the accounting equation, the equation must remain in balance, as it is in our example, with $50,000 on each side of the equation. If the equation is out of balance, the transaction has been recorded incorrectly and must be revised.
3. **Record** business transactions in T-accounts	We can represent an account using the letter T, which we call a T-account. The vertical line divides the account into left (debit) and right (credit) sides, while the account title rests on the horizontal line. The left side of the account is called the debit side, and the right side is called the credit side. We can use these T-accounts to record transactions instead of using the cumbersome accounting equation approach. When using T-accounts to record transactions, we apply the following rules of debit and credit, which help us translate the impacts of transactions on the accounting equation into impacts on specific accounts: • To record an increase in assets, use a debit. • To record a decrease in assets, use a credit. For liabilities and shareholders' equity, these rules are reversed: • To record an increase in liabilities or shareholders' equity, use a credit. • To record a decrease in liabilities or shareholders' equity, use a debit. Recall that increases in Dividends and Expenses result in decreases to shareholders' equity, so applying the last rule above means that increases to Dividends and Expenses are recorded using debits, which is the opposite of the "increase = credit" rule for all other shareholders' equity accounts. Every transaction involves at least one debit and one credit, and after recording a transaction, the total debits must equal the total credits. This ensures that the accounting equation remains in balance after each transaction. The normal balance of each account falls on the same side as where the increases to the account are recorded. The normal balance of an asset account, for example, falls on the left (debit) side, whereas the normal balance of a liability falls on the right (credit) side of the account.

4. **Record** business transactions in the journal and **post** them to the ledger	When formally recording transactions in the accounting records, accountants use a journal, a chronological record of all a business's transactions. When making a journal entry to record a transaction, we follow these three steps:
	1. Specify each account affected by the transaction.
	2. Determine whether the transaction increases or decreases each account affected by the transaction, and apply the rules of debit and credit to determine whether each account should be debited or credited.
	3. Record the transaction in the journal, including a brief explanation of the transaction and its date.
	Before we can obtain the balance of an account at the end of an accounting period, we must post all of the transactions from the journal to the ledger. The ledger contains all of a business's accounts, and posting is a simple process of directly transferring information from the journal to the ledger. Debits in the journal are posted as debits to the ledger accounts, and likewise for credits.
5. **Prepare** a trial balance **There are no differences between IFRS and ASPE in this chapter.**	A trial balance lists all of a business's ledger accounts and their balances. Asset accounts are listed first, followed by the liability accounts, and then all the accounts that affect shareholders' equity. We add all the debit balances and all the credit balances and place the totals at the bottom of the trial balance. If the total debits equal the total credits, we can go on to prepare the financial statements using the account balances from the trial balance.

END-OF-CHAPTER SUMMARY PROBLEM

The trial balance of Bos Personnel Services Inc. on March 1, 2014, lists the entity's assets, liabilities, and shareholders' equity on that date.

	Balance	
Account Title	Debit	Credit
Cash	$26,000	
Accounts receivable	4,500	
Accounts payable		$ 2,000
Share capital		10,000
Retained earnings		18,500
Total	$30,500	$30,500

During March, the business completed the following transactions:

a. Borrowed $70,000 from the bank, with C. Bos signing a note payable in the name of the business.

b. Paid cash of $60,000 to a real estate company to acquire land.

c. Performed service for a customer and received cash of $5,000.

d. Purchased supplies on credit, $300.

e. Performed customer service and earned revenue on account, $4,000.

Name: Bos Personnel Services Inc.
Industry: Human Resources
Fiscal Period: Month of March 2014
Key Fact: An existing, ongoing business

f. Paid $1,200 on account.
g. Paid the following cash expenses: salary, $3,000; rent, $1,500; and interest, $400.
h. Received $3,100 on account.
i. Received a $200 utility bill that will be paid next month.
j. Declared and paid a dividend of $300.

Requirements

Prepare a T-account for each account name. Place the opening balance in the T-account, remembering that the normal balance in an asset account is a debit, in a liability or equity account is a credit, in a revenue account is a credit, and in an expense account is a debit.

For each transaction, ensure that Debits = Credits.

1. Open the following accounts, with the balances indicated, in the ledger of Bos Personnel Services Inc. Use the T account format.
   - Assets—Cash, $26,000; Accounts Receivable, $4,500; Supplies, no balance; Land, no balance
   - Liabilities—Accounts Payable, $2,000; Note Payable, no balance
   - Shareholders' Equity—Share Capital, $10,000; Retained Earnings, $18,500; Dividends, no balance
   - Revenues—Service Revenue, no balance
   - Expenses—Salary Expense, Rent Expense, Interest Expense, Utilities Expense (none have balances)

Refer to the rules of debit and credit shown in Exhibit 2-8 on page 70.

2. Journalize the transactions listed above. Key the journal entries by transaction letter.
3. Post all transactions to the ledger and show the balance in each account after all the transactions have been posted.
4. Prepare the trial balance of Bos Personnel Services Inc. at March 31, 2014.
5. To determine the net income or net loss of the entity during the month of March, prepare the income statement for the month ended March 31, 2014. List expenses in order from the largest to the smallest.

ANSWERS

Requirement 1

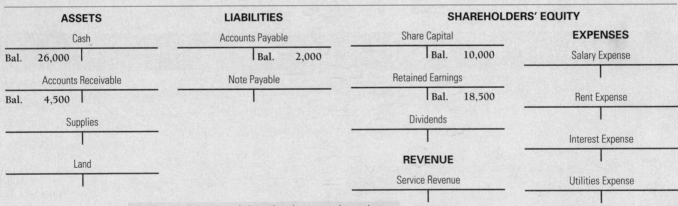

ASSETS	LIABILITIES	SHAREHOLDERS' EQUITY	
Cash	**Accounts Payable**	**Share Capital**	**EXPENSES**
Bal. 26,000	Bal. 2,000	Bal. 10,000	Salary Expense
Accounts Receivable	**Note Payable**	**Retained Earnings**	
Bal. 4,500		Bal. 18,500	Rent Expense
Supplies		**Dividends**	
			Interest Expense
Land		**REVENUE**	
		Service Revenue	Utilities Expense

To make sure all the account balances have been entered correctly, trace each T-account's balance back to the March 1, 2014, trial balance given on the previous page.

Requirement 2

Accounts and Explanation	Debit	Credit	Accounts and Explanation	Debit	Credit
a. Cash	70,000		g. Salary Expense	3,000	
Note Payable		70,000	Rent Expense	1,500	
Borrowed cash on note payable.			Interest Expense	400	
b. Land	60,000		Cash		4,900
Cash		60,000	Paid cash expenses.		
Purchased land for cash.			h. Cash	3,100	
c. Cash	5,000		Accounts Receivable		3,100
Service Revenue		5,000	Received on account.		
Performed service and received cash.			i. Utilities Expense	200	
d. Supplies	300		Accounts Payable		200
Accounts Payable		300	Received utility bill.		
Purchased supplies on account.			j. Dividends	300	
e. Accounts Receivable	4,000		Cash		300
Service Revenue		4,000	Declared and paid dividends.		
Performed service on account.					
f. Accounts Payable	1,200				
Cash		1,200			
Paid on account.					

Selected transactions explained more fully:

d. Increase Supplies (asset) and increase Accounts Payable (liability) because supplies were purchased on credit. Cash will be paid for the supplies in the future.

e. Increase Accounts Receivable (asset) and increase Service Revenue (revenue) because the service was performed on account. Cash will be received for the service in the future.

g. This transaction could also have been recorded with three journal entries, with a debit to the expense and a credit to Cash for each of the expenses.

I. Increase Utilities Expense (expense) and increase Accounts Payable (liability) because cash will be paid for the utility bill in the future.

Requirement 3

ASSETS

Cash

Bal.	26,000	(b)	60,000
(a)	70,000	(f)	1,200
(c)	5,000	(g)	4,900
(h)	3,100	(j)	300
Bal.	37,700		

Accounts Receivable

Bal.	4,500	(h)	3,100
(e)	4,000		
Bal.	5,400		

Supplies

(d)	300		
Bal.	300		

Land

(b)	60,000		
Bal.	60,000		

LIABILITIES

Accounts Payable

(f)	1,200	Bal.	2,000
		(d)	300
		(i)	200
		Bal.	1,300

Note Payable

		(a)	70,000
		Bal.	70,000

SHAREHOLDERS' EQUITY

Share Capital

		Bal.	10,000

Retained Earnings

		Bal.	18,500

Dividends

(j)	300		
Bal.	300		

REVENUE

Service Revenue

		(c)	5,000
		(e)	4,000
		Bal.	9,000

EXPENSES

Salary Expense

(g)	3,000		
Bal.	3,000		

Rent Expense

(g)	1,500		
Bal.	1,500		

Interest Expense

(g)	400		
Bal.	400		

Utilities Expense

(i)	200		
Bal.	200		

Make sure each transaction is posted to the proper T-account, and make sure no transactions were missed. Make sure that Assets = Liabilities + Shareholders' Equity for each transaction before going to the next transaction.

Requirement 4

The title must include the name of the company, "Trial Balance," and the date of the trial balance. It shows the account balances on one specific date.

List all the accounts that have a balance in their T-accounts. Write the "Bal." amount for each account from Requirement 3 into the debit or credit column of the trial balance. Make sure that the total of the Debit column equals the total of the Credit column. Double-underline the totals to show that the columns have been added and the totals are final.

Bos Personnel Services Inc.
Trial Balance
March 31, 2014

Account Title	Balance Debit	Credit
Cash	$ 37,700	
Accounts receivable	5,400	
Supplies	300	
Land	60,000	
Accounts payable		$ 1,300
Note payable		70,000
Share capital		10,000
Retained earnings		18,500
Dividends	300	
Service revenue		9,000
Salary expense	3,000	
Rent expense	1,500	
Interest expense	400	
Utilities expense	200	
Total	$108,800	$108,800

Requirement 5

The title must include the name of the company, "Income Statement," and the specific period of time covered. It is critical that the time period be defined. Prepare the income statement by listing the revenue and expense account names from the trial balance. Then transfer the amounts from the trial balance to the income statement.

Bos Personnel Services Inc
Income Statement
For the Month Ended March 31, 2014.

Revenue		
Service revenue		$9,000
Expenses		
Salary expense	$3,000	
Rent expense	1,500	
Interest expense	400	
Utilities expense	200	
Total expenses		5,100
Net income		$3,900

STOP + THINK (2-1)

ANSWERS

1. The issuance of shares and the sale of electronics products

2. The declaration and payment of dividends and the payment of expenses

Review the Recording of Business Transactions

QUICK CHECK (ANSWERS ARE GIVEN ON PAGE 104.)

1. A debit entry to an account
  a. increases liabilities.
  b. increases shareholders' equity.
  c. increases assets.
  d. both a and c.

2. Which of the following account types normally have a credit balance?
  a. Liabilities
  b. Revenues
  c. Expenses
  d. Both a and b.

3. An attorney performs services of $800 for a client and receives $200 cash with the rest on account. The journal entry for this transaction would be which of the following?
  a. Debit Cash, debit Accounts Receivable, credit Service Revenue
  b. Debit Cash, credit Accounts Receivable, credit Service Revenue
  c. Debit Cash, credit Service Revenue
  d. Debit Cash, debit Service Revenue, credit Accounts Receivable

4. Accounts Payable had a normal beginning balance of $1,000. During the period, there were debit postings of $400 and credit postings of $600. What was the ending balance?
  a. $800 debit
  b. $800 credit
  c. $1,200 debit
  d. $1,200 credit

5. The list of all accounts with their balances is the
  a. trial balance.
  b. chart of accounts.
  c. journal.
  d. balance sheet.

6. The record of all transactions affecting a specific asset, liability, or element of shareholders' equity is the
  a. ledger.
  b. account.
  c. journal.
  d. trial balance.

7. The beginning Cash balance was $5,000. At the end of the period, the balance was $6,000. If total cash paid out during the period was $24,000, the amount of cash receipts was
  a. $23,000.
  b. $13,000.
  c. $25,000.
  d. $35,000.

8. In a double-entry accounting system
  a. a debit entry is recorded on the left side of a T-account.
  b. half of all the accounts have a normal credit balance.
  c. liabilities, owners' equity, and revenue accounts all have normal debit balances.
  d. Both a and c are correct.

9. Which accounts appear on which financial statement?

	Balance sheet	Income statement
a.	cash, revenues, land	expenses, payables
b.	receivables, land, payables	revenues, supplies
c.	expenses, payables, cash	revenues, receivables, land
d.	cash, receivables, payables	revenues, expenses

10. A doctor purchases medical supplies of $670 and pays $200 cash with the rest on account. The journal entry for this transaction would be
  a. Supplies
         Accounts Payable
           Cash
  b. Supplies
         Cash
           Accounts Payable
  c. Supplies
         Accounts Receivable
           Cash
  d. Supplies
         Accounts Payable
           Cash

11. Which is the correct sequence of accounting procedures?
  a. Journal, ledger, trial balance, financial statements
  b. Ledger, trial balance, journal, financial statements
  c. Financial statements, trial balance, ledger, journal
  d. Ledger, journal, trial balance, financial statements

Accounting Vocabulary

account The record of the changes that have occurred in a particular asset, liability, or element of shareholders' equity during a period.   (p. 55)

chart of accounts List of a company's accounts and their account numbers.   (p. 66)

credit The right side of an account.   (p. 67)

debit The left side of an account.   (p. 67)

double-entry system An accounting system that uses debits and credits to record the dual effects of each business transaction.   (p. 66)

journal The chronological accounting record of an entity's transactions.   (p. 70)

ledger The book of accounts and their balances.   (p. 71)

posting Transferring amounts from the journal to the ledger.   (p. 71)

transaction An event that has a financial impact on a business and that can be reliably measured.   (p. 55)

trial balance A list of all the ledger accounts with their balances.   (p. 76)

Assess Your Progress

MyAccountingLab

Make the grade with MyAccountingLab: The Exercises, Quizzes, and Problems (A set) marked in red can be found on MyAccountingLab. You can practise them as often as you want, and most feature step-by-step guided instructions to help you find the right answer.

SHORT EXERCISES

LEARNING OBJECTIVE ❷

Analyze a transaction

S2-1 Sue Deliveau opened a software consulting firm that immediately paid $2,000 for a computer. Was this event a transaction for the business?

LEARNING OBJECTIVE ❷

Analyze the effects of transactions

S2-2 Hourglass Software began with cash of $10,000. Hourglass then bought supplies for $2,000 on account. Separately, Hourglass paid $5,000 for a computer. Answer these questions:

1. How much in total assets does Hourglass have?

2. How much in liabilities does Hourglass owe?

LEARNING OBJECTIVE ❸

Analyze transactions using T-accounts

S2-3 Marsha Solomon, a physiotherapist, opened a practice. The business completed the following transactions:

May	1	Solomon invested $25,000 cash to start her practice. The business issued shares to Solomon.
	1	Purchased medical supplies on account totalling $9,000.
	2	Paid monthly office rent of $4,000.
	3	Recorded $8,000 revenue for service rendered to patients, received cash of $2,000, and sent bills to patients for the remainder.

After these transactions, how much cash does the business have to work with? Use T-accounts to show your answer.

LEARNING OBJECTIVE ❸

Analyze transactions using T-accounts

S2-4 Refer to exercise S2-3. Which of the transactions of Marsha Solomon, P.T., increased the total assets of the business? For each transaction, identify the asset or liability that was increased or decreased.

S2-5 After operating for several months, artist Paul Marciano completed the following transactions during the latter part of June:

LEARNING OBJECTIVE ❹
Journalize transactions

June	15	Borrowed $25,000 from the bank, signing a note payable.
	22	Painted a portrait for a client on account totalling $9,000.
	28	Received $5,000 cash on account from clients.
	29	Received a utility bill of $600, which will be paid during July.
	30	Paid monthly salary of $2,500 to gallery assistant.

Journalize the transactions of Paul Marciano, Artist. Include an explanation with each journal entry.

S2-6 Architect Sonia Biaggi purchased supplies on account for $5,000. Later, Biaggi paid $3,000 on account.

LEARNING OBJECTIVE ❹
Journalize transactions; post

1. Journalize the two transactions on the books of Sonia Biaggi, Architect. Include an explanation for each transaction.
2. Open a T-account for Accounts Payable and post to Accounts Payable. Compute the balance and denote it as Bal.
3. How much does Biaggi's business owe after both transactions? In which account does this amount appear?

S2-7 Family Services Centre (The Centre) performed service for a client who could not pay immediately. The Centre expected to collect the $500 the following month. A month later, The Centre received $100 cash from the client.

LEARNING OBJECTIVE ❹
Journalize transactions; post

1. Record the two transactions on the books of Family Services Centre. Include an explanation for each transaction.
2. Open these T-accounts: Cash, Accounts Receivable, and Service Revenue. Post to all three accounts. Compute each account balance and denote as Bal.
3. Answer these questions based on your analysis:
  a. How much did The Centre earn? Which account shows this amount?
  b. How much in total assets did The Centre acquire as a result of the two transactions? Show the amount of each asset.

S2-8 Assume that Lululemon Athletica Inc. reported the following summarized data at December 31, 2014. Accounts appear in no particular order; dollar amounts are in millions.

LEARNING OBJECTIVE ❺
Prepare and use a trial balance

Revenues	$275
Other liabilities	38
Other assets	101
Cash and other current assets	53
Accounts payable	5
Expenses	244
Shareholders' equity	80

Prepare the trial balance of lululemon at December 31, 2014. List the accounts in their proper order, as on page 76. How much was lululemon's net income or net loss?

LEARNING OBJECTIVE ⑤

Use a trial balance

S2-9 Blackburn Inc.'s trial balance follows:

Blackburn Inc.
Trial Balance
June 30, 2014

	Debit	Credit
Cash	$ 6,000	
Accounts receivable	13,000	
Supplies	4,000	
Equipment	22,000	
Land	50,000	
Accounts payable		$ 19,000
Note payable		20,000
Share capital		10,000
Retained earnings		8,000
Service revenue		70,000
Salary expense	21,000	
Rent expense	10,000	
Interest expense	1,000	
Total	$127,000	$127,000

Compute these amounts for Blackburn:

1. Total assets
2. Total liabilities
3. Total shareholders' equity
4. Net income or loss during June

LEARNING OBJECTIVE ⑤

Prepare a trial balance

S2-10 The accounts of Custom Pool Service, Inc., follow with their normal balances at June 30, 2014. The accounts are listed in no particular order.

Account	Balance	Account	Balance
Share capital	$ 8,300	Dividends	$ 5,800
Accounts payable	4,100	Utilities expense	1,700
Service revenue	22,300	Accounts receivable	15,200
Land	29,600	Delivery expense	900
Loan payable	11,500	Retained earnings	24,700
Cash	9,200	Salary expense	8,500

Prepare the company's trial balance at June 30, 2014, listing accounts in proper sequence, as illustrated in the chapter. For example, Accounts Receivable comes before Land. List the expense with the largest balance first, the expense with the next largest balance second, and so on.

LEARNING OBJECTIVE ①②③④

Use key accounting terms

S2-11 Accounting has its own vocabulary and basic relationships. Match the accounting terms at left with the corresponding definition or meaning at right.

___ **1.** Debit
___ **2.** Expense
___ **3.** Net income
___ **4.** Ledger
___ **5.** Posting
___ **6.** Normal balance
___ **7.** Payable
___ **8.** Journal
___ **9.** Receivable
___**10.** Owners' equity

A. The cost of operating a business; a decrease in shareholders' equity
B. Always a liability
C. Revenues – Expenses
D. Grouping of accounts
E. Assets – Liabilities
F. Record of transactions
G. Always an asset
H. Left side of an account
I. Side of an account where increases are recorded
J. Copying data from the journal to the ledger

S2-12 Canadian Prairies Investments began by issuing common shares for cash of $100,000. The company immediately purchased computer equipment on account for $60,000.

1. Set up the following T-accounts for the company: Cash, Computer Equipment, Accounts Payable, Share Capital.
2. Record the transactions directly in the T-accounts without using a journal.
3. Show that total debits equal total credits.

LEARNING OBJECTIVE ❸

Record transactions using T-accounts

EXERCISES

E2-13 Assume The Gap has opened a store in Ottawa. Starting with cash and shareholders' equity (common shares) of $100,000, Susan Harper, the store manager, signed a note payable to purchase land for $40,000 and a building for $130,000. She also paid $50,000 for store fixtures and $40,000 for inventory to use in the business. All these were paid for in cash.

Suppose the head office of Gap requires a weekly report from store managers. Write Harper's memo to the head office to report on her borrowing and purchases. Include the store's balance sheet as the final part of your memo. Prepare a T-account to compute the balance for cash.

LEARNING OBJECTIVE ❸

Analyze transactions using T-accounts

E2-14 During April, Spokes Ltd. completed a series of transactions. For each of the following items, give an example of a business transaction that has the described effect on the accounting equation of Spokes Ltd.
a. Increase one asset, and decrease another asset.
b. Decrease an asset, and decrease shareholders' equity.
c. Decrease an asset, and decrease a liability.
d. Increase an asset, and increase shareholders' equity.
e. Increase an asset, and increase a liability.

LEARNING OBJECTIVE ❷

Understand transactions and the accounting equation

E2-15 The following selected events were experienced by either Problem Solvers Inc., a corporation, or Pierce Laflame, the major shareholder. State whether each event (1) increased, (2) decreased, or (3) had no effect on the total assets of the business. Identify any specific asset affected.
a. Received $9,000 cash from customers on account. – nothing
b. Laflame used personal funds to purchase a swimming pool for his home. – nothing (personal) corporation
c. Sold land and received cash of $60,000 (the land was carried on the company's books at – nothing
   $60,000).
d. Borrowed $50,000 from the bank. – Go up asset
e. Made cash purchase of land for a building site, $85,000. – nothing
f. Received $20,000 cash and issued shares to a shareholder. up assets
g. Paid $60,000 cash on accounts payable. down assets
h. Purchased equipment and signed a $100,000 promissory note in payment. up assets
i. Purchased supplies on account for $15,000. up assets
j. The business paid Laflame a cash dividend of $4,000. down assets

LEARNING OBJECTIVE ❷

Analyze transactions using the accounting equation

E2-16 Joseph Ohara opens a dental practice. During the first month of operation (March), the practice, titled Joseph Ohara Dental Clinic Ltd., experienced the following events:

LEARNING OBJECTIVE ❷

Analyze transactions using the accounting equation

March	6	Ohara invested $50,000 in the business, which in turn issued its common shares to him.
	9	The business paid cash for land costing $30,000. Ohara plans to build a professional services building on the land.
	12	The business purchased dental supplies for $3,000 on account.
	15	Joseph Ohara Dental Clinic Ltd. officially opened for business.
	15–31	During the rest of the month, Ohara treated patients and earned service revenue of $10,000, receiving cash for half the revenue earned.
	15–31	The practice paid cash expenses: employee salaries, $1,400; office rent, $1,000; utilities, $300.
	31	The practice used dental supplies with a cost of $250.
	31	The practice borrowed $10,000, signing a note payable to the bank.
	31	The practice paid $2,000 on account.

Requirements

1. Analyze the effects of these events on the accounting equation of the practice of Joseph Ohara Dental Clinic Ltd. Use a format similar to that of Exhibit 2-1, Panel B, with headings for Cash, Accounts Receivable, Dental Supplies, Land, Accounts Payable, Note Payable, Share Capital, and Retained Earnings.

2. After completing the analysis, answer these questions about the business:
  a. How much are total assets?
  b. How much does the business expect to collect from patients?
  c. How much does the business owe in total?
  d. How much of the business's assets does Ohara really own?
  e. How much net income or net loss did the business experience during its first month of operations?

LEARNING OBJECTIVE ❹

Journalize transactions

E2-17 Refer to exercise E2-16. Record the transactions in the journal of Joseph Ohara Dental Clinic Ltd. List the transactions by date, and give an explanation for each transaction.

LEARNING OBJECTIVE ❹

Journalize transactions

E2-18 Perfect Printers Inc. completed the following transactions during October 2014, its first month of operations:

Oct.	1	Received $25,000, and issued common shares.
	2	Purchased $800 of office supplies on account.
	4	Paid $20,000 cash for land to use as a building site.
	6	Performed service for customers, and received cash of $5,000.
	9	Paid $100 on accounts payable.
	17	Performed service for Waterloo School Board on account totalling $1,500.
	23	Collected $1,000 from Waterloo School Board on account.
	31	Paid the following expenses: salary, $1,000; rent, $500.

Requirement

1. Record the transactions in the journal of Perfect Printers Inc. Key transactions by date, and include an explanation for each entry, as illustrated in the chapter.

LEARNING OBJECTIVE ❹❺

Post to the ledger and prepare and using a trial balance

E2-19 Refer to exercise E2-18.

Requirements

1. After journalizing the transactions of exercise E2-18, post the entries to the ledger using T-accounts. Key transactions by date. Date the ending balance of each account October 31, 2014.

2. Prepare the trial balance of Perfect Printers Inc., at October 31, 2014.

3. How much are total assets, total liabilities, and total shareholders' equity on October 31, 2014?

LEARNING OBJECTIVE ❹

Journalize transactions

E2-20 The first seven transactions of Splash Water Park Ltd. have been posted to the company's accounts as follows:

Cash		Supplies		Equipment		Land	
(1) 20,000	(3) 8,000	(4) 1,000	(5) 100	(6) 8,000		(3) 31,000	
(2) 7,000	(6) 8,000						
(5) 100	(7) 400						

Accounts Payable		Note Payable		Share Capital	
(7) 400	(4) 1,000		(2) 7,000		(1) 20,000
			(3) 23,000		

Requirement

Prepare the journal entries that served as the sources for the seven transactions. Include an explanation for each entry. As Splash Water Park moves into the next period, how much cash does the business have? How much does Splash Water Park owe?

E2-21 The accounts of Victoria Garden Care Ltd. follow with their normal balances at September 30, 2014. The accounts are listed in no particular order.

LEARNING OBJECTIVE **5**

Prepare and use a trial balance

Account	Balance	Account	Balance
Dividends..............................	6,000	Share capital..............................	8,500
Utilities expense	1,400	Accounts payable.......................	4,300
Accounts receivable....................	17,500	Service revenue	24,000
Delivery expense	300	Equipment	29,000
Retained earnings......................	21,400	Note payable	13,000
Salary expense...........................	8,000	Cash..	9,000

Requirements

1. Prepare the company's trial balance at September 30, 2014, listing accounts in proper sequence, as illustrated in the chapter. For example, Accounts Receivable comes before Equipment. List the expense with the largest balance first, the expense with the next largest balance second, and so on.
2. Prepare the financial statement for the month ended September 30, 2014, that will tell the company's top managers the results of operations for the month.

E2-22 The trial balance of Sam's Deli Inc. at October 31, 2014, does not balance:

LEARNING OBJECTIVE **5**

Correct errors in a trial balance

Cash	$ 4,200	
Accounts receivable	13,000	
Inventory...	17,000	
Supplies...	600	
Land..	55,000	
Accounts payable...		$12,000
Share capital..		47,900
Sales revenue		32,100
Salary expense...	1,700	
Rent expense	800	
Utilities expense	700	
Total..	$93,000	$92,000

The accounting records contain the following errors:

a. Recorded a $1,000 cash revenue transaction by debiting Accounts Receivable. The credit entry was correct.
b. Posted a $1,000 credit to Accounts Payable as $100.
c. Did not record utilities expense or the related account payable in the amount of $200.
d. Understated Share Capital by $1,100.
e. Omitted insurance expense of $1,000 from the trial balance.

Requirement

Prepare the correct trial balance at October 31, 2014, complete with a heading. Journal entries are not required.

E2-23 Set up the following T-accounts: Cash, Accounts Receivable, Office Supplies, Office Furniture, Accounts Payable, Share Capital, Dividends, Service Revenue, Salary Expense, and Rent Expense.

LEARNING OBJECTIVE **3**

Record transactions in T-accounts

Record the following transactions directly in the T-accounts without using a journal. Use the letters to identify the transactions. Calculate the account balances and denote as Bal.

a. In the month of May 2014, Sonia Rothesay opened an accounting firm by investing $10,000 cash and office furniture valued at $5,000. Organized as a professional corporation, the business issued common shares to Rothesay.

b. Paid monthly rent of $1,600.

c. Purchased office supplies on account, $600.

d. Paid employees' salaries of $2,000.

e. Paid $200 of the account payable created in transaction (c).

f. Performed accounting service on account, $12,100.

g. Declared and paid dividends of $2,000.

LEARNING OBJECTIVE ❺

Prepare and use a trial balance

E2-24 Refer to exercise E2-23.

Requirements

1. After recording the transactions in exercise E2-23, prepare the trial balance of Sonia Rothesay, Accountant, at May 31, 2014.

2. How well did the business perform during its first month? Give the basis for your answer.

SERIAL EXERCISE

Exercise E2-25 begins an accounting cycle that is completed in Chapter 3.

LEARNING OBJECTIVE ❸❹❺

Journalize and post business transactions and prepare a trial balance

E2-25 Web Marketing Services Inc. completed these transactions during the first part of January 2014:

Jan.	2	Received $5,000 cash from investors, and issued common shares.
	2	Paid monthly office rent, $500.
	3	Paid cash for a Dell computer, $3,000, with the computer expected to remain in service for five years.
	4	Purchased office furniture on account, $6,000, with the furniture projected to last for five years.
	5	Purchased supplies on account, $900.
	9	Performed marketing service for a client, and received cash for the full amount of $800.
	12	Paid utility expenses, $200.
	18	Performed marketing service for a client on account, $1,700.

Requirements

1. Set up T-accounts for Cash, Accounts Receivable, Supplies, Equipment, Furniture, Accounts Payable, Share Capital, Dividends, Service Revenue, Rent Expense, Utilities Expense, and Salary Expense.

2. Journalize the transactions. Explanations are not required.

3. Post to the T-accounts. Key all items by date and denote an account balance on January 18 as Bal.

4. Prepare a trial balance at January 18. In the Serial Exercise of Chapter 3, we add transactions for the remainder of January and will require a trial balance at January 31, 2014.

CHALLENGE EXERCISES

LEARNING OBJECTIVE ❸

Analyze transactions using T-accounts

E2-26 The manager of Canadiana Gallery Ltd. needs to compute the following information:

a. Total cash paid during March. Analyze Cash.

b. Cash collections from customers during March. Analyze Accounts Receivable.

c. Cash paid on a note payable during March. Analyze Notes Payable.

Here are additional data you need to analyze:

Account	Balance Feb. 28	Balance Mar. 31	Additional Information for the Month of March
1. Cash...	10,000	5,000	Cash receipts, $80,000
2. Accounts Receivable.................	26,000	24,000	Sales on account, $50,000
3. Note Payable............................	13,000	21,000	New borrowing, $25,000

Prepare a T-account to compute the amounts for (a) through (c).

E2-27 The trial balance of You Build Inc. at December 31, 2014, does not balance.

LEARNING OBJECTIVE ❸❺

Analyze transactions using T-accounts; use a trial balance

Cash..	$ 3,900	Share capital.........................	$20,000
Accounts receivable...........................	7,200	Retained earnings................	7,300
Land..	34,000	Service revenue	9,100
Accounts payable	5,800	Salary expense......................	3,400
Note payable	5,000	Advertising expense	900

Requirements
1. How much out of balance is the trial balance? Determine the out-of-balance amount. The error lies in the Accounts Receivable account. Add the out-of-balance amount to, or subtract it from, Accounts Receivable to determine the correct balance of Accounts Receivable.
2. You Build Inc. also failed to record the following transactions during December:
  a. Purchased additional land for $60,000 by signing a note payable.
  b. Earned service revenue on account, $10,000.
  c. Paid salary expense of $1,400.
  d. Purchased a TV advertisement for $1,000 on account. This account will be paid during January.
    Add these amounts to, or subtract them from, the appropriate accounts to properly include the effects of these transactions. Then prepare the corrected trial balance of You Build Inc.
3. After correcting the accounts, advise the top management of You Build Inc. on the company's:
  a. Total assets
  b. Total liabilities
  c. Net income or loss

E2-28 This question concerns the items and the amounts that two entities, City of Regina and Public Health Organization, Inc. (PHO), should report in their financial statements.

LEARNING OBJECTIVE ❷

Analyze transactions

During August, PHO provided City of Regina with medical checks for new school pupils and sent a bill for $30,000. On September 7, Regina sent a cheque to PHO for $25,000. Regina began August with a cash balance of $50,000; PHO began with cash of $0.

Requirement
For this situation, show everything that both Regina and PHO will report on their August and September income statements and on their balance sheets at August 31 and September 30. Use the following format for your answer:

Regina:		
Income statement	August	September
Balance sheet	August 31	September 30
PHO:		
Income statement	August	September
Balance sheet	August 31	September 30

After showing what each company should report, briefly explain how the City of Regina and PHO data relate to each other. Be specific.

QUIZ

Test your understanding of business transactions by answering the following questions. Select the best choice from among the possible answers.

Q2-29 An investment of cash into the business will
a. decrease total assets.
b. decrease total liabilities.
c. increase shareholders' equity.
d. have no effect on total assets.

Q2-30 Purchasing a computer on account will
a. increase total assets.
b. increase total liabilities.
c. have no effect on shareholders' equity.
d. All of the above.

Q2-31 Performing a service on account will
a. increase total assets.
b. increase shareholders' equity.
c. Both a and b.
d. increase total liabilities.

Q2-32 Receiving cash from a customer on account will
a. have no effect on total assets.
b. increase total assets.
c. decrease liabilities.
d. increase shareholders' equity.

Q2-33 Purchasing computer equipment for cash will
a. increase both total assets and total liabilities.
b. decrease both total assets and shareholders' equity.
c. decrease both total liabilities and shareholders' equity.
d. have no effect on total assets, total liabilities, or shareholders' equity.

Q2-34 Purchasing a building for $100,000 by paying cash of $20,000 and signing a note payable for $80,000 will
a. increase both total assets and total liabilities by $100,000.
b. increase both total assets and total liabilities by $80,000.
c. decrease total assets, and increase total liabilities by $20,000.
d. decrease both total assets and total liabilities by $20,000.

Q2-35 What is the effect on total assets and shareholders' equity of paying the electric bill as soon as it is received each month?

	Total assets	Shareholders' equity
a.	Decrease	No effect
b.	No effect	No effect
c.	Decrease	Decrease
d.	No effect	Decrease

Q2-36 Which of the following transactions will increase an asset and increase a liability?
a. buying equipment on account
b. purchasing office equipment for cash
c. issuing shares
d. making a payment on account

Q2-37 Which of the following transactions will increase an asset and increase shareholders' equity?
a. collecting cash from a customer on an account receivable
b. performing a service on account for a customer
c. borrowing money from a bank
d. purchasing supplies on account

Q2-38 Where do we first record a transaction?
a. ledger
b. trial balance
c. account
d. journal

Q2-39 Which of the following is not an asset account?
a. Share Capital
b. Salary Expense
c. Service Revenue
d. None of the above accounts is an asset.

Q2-40 Which of the following statements is false?
a. Revenues are increased by credits.
b. Assets are increased by debits.
c. Dividends are increased by credits.
d. Liabilities are decreased by debits.

Q2-41 The journal entry to record the receipt of land and a building and issuance of common shares
a. debits Land and Building, and credits Share Capital.
b. debits Land, and credits Share Capital.
c. debits Share Capital, and credits Land and Building.
d. credits Land and Building, and debits Share Capital.

Q2-42 The journal entry to record the purchase of supplies on account
a. credits Supplies, and debits Cash.
b. debits Supplies, and credits Accounts Payable.
c. debits Supplies Expense, and credits Supplies.
d. credits Supplies, and debits Accounts Payable.

Q2-43 If the credit to record the purchase of supplies on account is not posted,
a. liabilities will be understated.
b. expenses will be overstated.
c. assets will be understated.
d. shareholders' equity will be understated.

Q2-44 The journal entry to record a payment on account will
a. debit Accounts Payable, and credit Retained Earnings.
b. debit Cash, and credit Expenses.
c. debit Expenses, and credit Cash.
d. debit Accounts Payable, and credit Cash.

Q2-45 If the credit to record the payment of an account payable is not posted,
a. liabilities will be understated.
b. expenses will be understated.
c. cash will be overstated.
d. cash will be understated.

Q2-46 Which statement is false?
a. A trial balance lists all the accounts with their current balances.
b. A trial balance is the same as a balance sheet.
c. A trial balance can verify the equality of debits and credits.
d. A trial balance can be taken at any time.

Q2-47 A business's purchase of a $100,000 building with an $85,000 mortgage payable and issuance of $15,000 of common shares will
a. increase shareholders' equity by $15,000.
b. increase assets by $15,000.
c. increase assets by $85,000.
d. increase shareholders' equity by $100,000.

Q2-48 A new company completed these transactions:
1. Shareholders invested $50,000 cash and inventory worth $25,000.
2. Sales on account, $12,000.
What will total assets equal?
a. $75,000
b. $87,000
c. $63,000
d. $62,000

PROBLEMS

(Group A)

LEARNING OBJECTIVE ❺
Analyze a trial balance

P2-49A The trial balance of Amusement Specialties Inc. follows:

Amusement Specialties Inc.
Trial Balance
December 31, 2014

Cash	$ 14,000	
Accounts receivable	11,000	
Prepaid expenses	4,000	
Equipment	171,000	
Building	100,000	
Accounts payable		$ 30,000
Note payable		120,000
Share capital		102,000
Retained earnings		40,000
Dividends	22,000	
Service revenue		86,000
Rent expense	14,000	
Advertising expense	3,000	
Wage expense	32,000	
Supplies expense	7,000	
Total	$378,000	$378,000

Sue Sibalius, your best friend, is considering investing in Amusement Specialties Inc. She seeks your advice in interpreting this information. Specifically, she asks how to use this trial balance to compute the company's total assets, total liabilities, and net income or net loss for the year.

Requirement
Write a short note to answer Sue's questions. In your note, state the amounts of Amusement Specialties' total assets, total liabilities, and net income or net loss for the year. Also, show how you computed each amount.

LEARNING OBJECTIVE ❷
Analyze transactions with the accounting equation and prepare the financial statements

P2-50A The following amounts summarize the financial position of Blythe Spirit Consulting, Inc. on May 31, 2014:

ASSETS				=	LIABILITIES	+	SHAREHOLDERS' EQUITY		
Cash +	Accounts Receivable	+ Supplies +	Land	=	Accounts Payable	+	Common Shares	+	Retained Earnings
1,300	1,000		12,000		8,000		4,000		2,300

During June 2014, the business completed these transactions:

a. Received cash of $5,000, and issued common shares.
b. Performed services for a client, and received cash of $7,600.
c. Paid $4,000 on accounts payable.
d. Purchased supplies on account, $1,500.
e. Collected cash from a customer on account, $1,000.
f. Consulted on the design of a business report, and billed the client for services rendered, $2,500.
g. Recorded the following business expenses for the month: paid office rent, $900; paid advertising, $300.
h. Declared and paid a cash dividend of $2,000.

Requirements

1. Analyze the effects of the preceding transactions on the accounting equation of Blythe Spirit Consulting, Inc. Adapt the format of Exhibit 2-1, Panel B.
2. Prepare the income statement of Blythe Spirit Consulting, Inc. for the month ended June 30, 2014. List expenses in decreasing order by amount.
3. Prepare the entity's statement of retained earnings for the month ended June 30, 2014.
4. Prepare the balance sheet of Blythe Spirit Consulting, Inc. at June 30, 2014.

P2-51A Use this problem in conjunction with problem P2-50A.

LEARNING OBJECTIVE ❹

Journalize transactions; post

Requirements

1. Journalize the transactions of Blythe Spirit Consulting, Inc. Explanations are not required.
2. Set up the following T-accounts: Cash, Accounts Receivable, Supplies, Land, Accounts Payable, Share Capital, Retained Earnings, Dividends, Service Revenue, Rent Expense, and Advertising Expense. Insert in each account its balance as given (example: Cash $1,300). Post the transactions to the accounts.
3. Compute the balance in each account. For each asset account, each liability account, and for Share Capital, compare its balance to the ending balance you obtained in problem P2-50A. Are the amounts the same or different? (In Chapter 3, we complete the accounting process. There you will learn how the Retained Earnings, Dividends, Revenue, and Expense accounts work together in the processing of accounting information.)

P2-52A Mountain View Estates Ltd. experienced the following events during the organizing phase and its first month of operations. Some of the events were personal and did not affect the business. Others were business transactions.

LEARNING OBJECTIVE ❷❹

Analyze transactions with the accounting equation; journalize transactions

Sept.	4	Gayland Jet, the major shareholder of the company, received $50,000 cash from an inheritance.
	5	Jet deposited $50,000 cash in a new business bank account titled Mountain View Estates Ltd. The business issued common shares to Jet.
	6	The business paid $300 cash for letterhead stationery for the new office.
	7	The business purchased office furniture. The company paid cash of $20,000 and agreed to pay the account payable for the remainder, $5,000, within three months.
	10	Jet sold Telus shares, which he had owned for several years, receiving $30,000 cash from his stockbroker.
	11	Jet deposited the $30,000 cash from the sale of the Telus shares in his personal bank account.
	12	A representative of a large company telephoned Jet and told him of the company's intention to put a down payment of $10,000 on a lot.
	18	Jet finished a real estate deal on behalf of a client and submitted his bill for services, $10,000. Jet expects to collect from this client within two weeks.
	21	The business paid half its account payable for the furniture purchased on September 7.
	25	The business paid office rent of $4,000.
	30	The business declared and paid a cash dividend of $2,000.

Requirements

1. Classify each of the preceding events as one of the following:
   a. A business-related event but not a transaction to be recorded by Mountain View Estates Ltd.
   b. A personal transaction for a shareholder, not to be recorded by Mountain View Estates Ltd.
   c. A business transaction to be recorded by the business of Mountain View Estates Ltd.

2. Analyze the effects of the preceding events on the accounting equation of Mountain View Estates Ltd. Use a format similar to that in Exhibit 2-1, Panel B.
3. At the end of the first month of operations, Jet has a number of questions about the financial standing of the business. Explain the following to him:
   a. How the business can have more cash than retained earnings.
   b. How much in total resources the business has, how much it owes, and what Jet's ownership interest is in the assets of the business.
4. Record the transactions of the business in its journal. Include an explanation for each entry.

LEARNING OBJECTIVE 4

Journalize and post transactions

P2-53A During October, All Pets Veterinary Clinic Ltd. completed the following transactions:

Oct.	1	Dr. Squires deposited $8,000 cash in the business bank account. The business issued common shares to her.
	5	Paid monthly rent, $1,000.
	9	Paid $5,000 cash, and signed a $25,000 note payable to purchase land for an office site.
	10	Purchased supplies on account, $1,200.
	19	Paid $600 on account.
	22	Borrowed $10,000 from the bank for business use. Dr. Squires signed a note payable to the bank in the name of the business.
	31	Revenues earned during the month included $7,000 cash and $5,000 on account.
	31	Paid employees' salaries ($2,000), advertising expense ($1,500), and utilities ($1,100).
	31	Declared and paid a cash dividend of $3,000.

The clinic uses the following accounts: Cash, Accounts Receivable, Supplies, Land, Accounts Payable, Notes Payable, Share Capital, Dividends, Service Revenue, Salary Expense, Rent Expense, Utilities Expense, and Advertising Expense.

Requirements
1. Journalize each transaction of All Pets Veterinary Clinic Ltd. Explanations are not required.
2. Prepare T-accounts for Cash, Accounts Payable, and Notes Payable. Post to these three accounts.
3. After these transactions, how much cash does the business have? How much in total does it owe?

LEARNING OBJECTIVE 4 5

Journalize and post transactions; prepare and use a trial balance

P2-54A During the first month of operations, May 2014, New Pane Windows Inc. completed the following transactions:

May	2	New Pane received $30,000 cash and issued common shares to shareholders.
	3	Purchased supplies, $1,000, and equipment, $2,600, on account.
	4	Performed services, and received cash, $1,500.
	7	Paid cash to acquire land for an office site, $22,000.
	11	Repaired a window, and billed the customer $500.
	16	Paid for the equipment purchased May 3 on account.
	17	Paid the telephone bill, $95.
	18	Received partial payment from client on account, $250.
	22	Paid the water and electricity bills, $400.
	29	Received $2,000 cash for installing a new window.
	31	Paid employee salary, $1,300.
	31	Declared and paid dividends of $1,500.

Requirements

Set up the following T-accounts: Cash, Accounts Receivable, Supplies, Equipment, Land, Accounts Payable, Share Capital, Dividends, Service Revenue, Salary Expense, and Utilities Expense.

1. Record each transaction in the journal, using the account titles given. Key each transaction by date. Explanations are not required.
2. Post the transactions to the T-accounts, using transaction dates as posting references. Label the ending balance of each account Bal., as shown in the chapter.
3. Prepare the trial balance of New Pane Windows, at May 31, 2014.
4. The manager asks you how much in total resources the business has to work with, how much it owes, and whether May 2014 was profitable (and by how much). Calculate the amounts needed to answer her questions.

P2-55A During the first month of operations (January 2014), Music Services Ltd. completed the following selected transactions:

a. The business has cash of $10,000 and a building valued at $50,000. The corporation issued common shares to the shareholders.
b. Borrowed $50,000 from the bank, and signed a note payable.
c. Paid $60,000 for music equipment.
d. Purchased supplies on account, $1,000.
e. Paid employees' salaries, $1,500.
f. Received $800 for service performed for customers.
g. Performed service to customers on account, $4,500.
h. Paid $100 of the account payable created in transaction (d).
i. Received a $600 utility bill that will be paid in the near future.
j. Received cash on account, $3,100.
k. Paid the following cash expenses: rent, $1,000; advertising, $800.

LEARNING OBJECTIVE ❸❺

Record transactions in T-accounts; prepare and use a trial balance

Requirements

1. Set up the following T-accounts: Cash, Accounts Receivable, Office Supplies, Music Equipment, Building, Accounts Payable, Note Payable, Share Capital, Service Revenue, Salary Expense, Rent Expense, Advertising Expense, and Utilities Expense.
2. Record the foregoing transactions directly in the T-accounts without using a journal. Use the letters to identify the transactions.
3. Prepare the trial balance of Music Services Ltd. at January 31, 2014.
4. The bank manager is afraid that the total liabilities of the business exceed the total assets. He also fears that the business suffered a net loss during January. Compute the amounts needed to answer his questions.

(Group B)

P2-56B The owners of Opera Tours Inc. are selling the business. They offer the trial balance that appears at the top of the next page to prospective buyers.

Your best friend is considering buying Opera Tours. She seeks your advice in interpreting this information. Specifically, she asks whether this trial balance provides the data to prepare a balance sheet and an income statement.

LEARNING OBJECTIVE ❺

Analyze a trial balance

Requirement

Write a memo to answer your friend's questions. Indicate which accounts go on the balance sheet and which accounts go on the income statement. State the amount of net income that Opera Tours earned in 2014, and explain your computation.

Opera Tours Inc.
Trial Balance
December 31, 2014

Cash	$ 12,000	
Accounts receivable	45,000	
Prepaid expenses	4,000	
Equipment	231,000	
Accounts payable		$105,000
Note payable		92,000
Share capital		30,000
Retained earnings		32,000
Service revenue		139,000
Salary expense	69,000	
Tour expenses	26,000	
Rent expense	7,000	
Advertising expense	4,000	
Total	$398,000	$398,000

LEARNING OBJECTIVE ❷

Analyze transactions with the accounting equation and prepare the financial statements

P2-57B Doug Hanna operates and is the major shareholder of an interior design studio called DH Designers, Inc. The following amounts summarize the financial position of the business on April 30, 2014:

	ASSETS				=	LIABILITIES	+	SHAREHOLDERS' EQUITY		
Cash	+	Accounts Receivable	+ Supplies +	Land	=	Accounts Payable	+	Common Shares	+	Retained Earnings
Bal. 1,700		2,200		24,100		5,400		10,000		12,600

During May 2014, the business completed these transactions:

a. Hanna received $30,000 as a gift and deposited the cash in the business bank account. The business issued common shares to Hanna.

b. Paid $1,000 on accounts payable.

c. Performed services for a client and received cash of $5,100.

d. Collected cash from a customer on account, $700.

e. Purchased supplies on account, $800.

f. Consulted on the interior design of a major office building and billed the client for services rendered, $15,000.

g. Received cash of $1,700 and issued common shares to a shareholder.

h. Recorded the following expenses for the month: paid office rent, $2,100; paid advertising, $1,600.

i. Declared and paid a cash dividend of $2,000.

Requirements

In order to guide Doug Hanna:

1. Analyze the effects of the preceding transactions on the accounting equation of DH Designers, Inc. Adapt the format of Exhibit 2-1, Panel B.

2. Prepare the income statement of DH Designers, Inc. for the month ended May 31, 2014. List expenses in decreasing order by amount.

3. Prepare the statement of retained earnings of DH Designers, Inc. for the month ended May 31, 2014.

4. Prepare the balance sheet of DH Designers, Inc. at May 31, 2014.

P2-58B Use this problem in conjunction with problem P2-57B.

LEARNING OBJECTIVE ❹

Journalize and post transactions

Requirements
1. Journalize the transactions of DH Designers, Inc. Explanations are not required.
2. Set up the following T-accounts: Cash, Accounts Receivable, Supplies, Land, Accounts Payable, Share Capital, Retained Earnings, Dividends, Service Revenue, Rent Expense, and Advertising Expense. Insert in each account its balance as given (example: Cash $1,700). Post to the accounts.
3. Compute the balance in each account. For each asset account, each liability account, and for Share Capital, compare its balance to the ending balance you obtained in problem P2-57B. Are the amounts the same or different? (In Chapter 3, we complete the accounting process. There you will learn how the Retained Earnings, Dividends, Revenue, and Expense accounts work together in the processing of accounting information.)

P2-59B Lane Kohler opened a consulting practice that he operates as a corporation. The name of the new entity is Lane Kohler, Consultant, Inc. Kohler experienced the following events during the organizing phase of his new business and its first month of operations. Some of the events were personal transactions of the shareholder and did not affect the consulting practice. Others were transactions that should be accounted for by the business.

LEARNING OBJECTIVE ❷❹

Record transactions using the accounting equation and journal entries

March	1	Kohler sold 1,000 shares of RIM stock and received $100,000 cash from his stockbroker.
	2	Kohler deposited in his personal bank account the $100,000 cash from sale of the RIM shares.
	3	Kohler received $150,000 cash through an inheritance from his grandfather.
	5	Kohler deposited $50,000 cash in a new business bank account titled Lane Kohler, Consultant, Inc. The business issued common shares to Kohler.
	6	A representative of a large company telephoned Kohler and told him of the company's intention to give $15,000 of consulting business to Kohler.
	7	The business paid $450 cash for letterhead stationery for the consulting office.
	9	The business purchased office furniture. Kohler paid cash of $5,000 and agreed to pay the account payable for the remainder, $10,500, within three months.
	23	Kohler finished an analysis for a client and submitted his bill for services, $4,000. He expected to collect from this client within one month.
	29	The business paid $5,000 of its account payable on the furniture purchased on March 9.
	30	The business paid office rent of $2,100.
	31	The business declared and paid a cash dividend of $1,000.

Requirements
1. Classify each of the preceding events as one of the following:
   a. A personal transaction of a shareholder not to be recorded by the business of Lane Kohler, Consultant, Inc.
   b. A business transaction to be recorded by the business of Lane Kohler, Consultant, Inc.
   c. A business-related event but not a transaction to be recorded by the business of Lane Kohler, Consultant, Inc.
2. Analyze the effects of the preceding events on the accounting equation of the business of Lane Kohler, Consultant, Inc. Use a format similar to Exhibit 2-1, Panel B.
3. At the end of the first month of operations, Kohler has a number of questions about the financial standing of the business. Answer the following questions for him:
   a. How can the business have more cash than retained earnings?
   b. How much in total resources does the business have? How much does it owe? What is Kohler's ownership interest in the assets of the business?
4. Record the transactions of the business in its journal. Include an explanation for each entry.

LEARNING OBJECTIVE ❹

Journalize and post transactions

P2-60B Wimberley Glass, Inc. has shops in the shopping malls of a major metropolitan area. The business completed the following transactions:

June	1	Received cash of $25,000, and issued common shares to a shareholder.
	2	Paid $10,000 cash, and signed a $30,000 note payable to purchase land for a new glassworks site.
	7	Received $20,000 cash from sales, and deposited that amount in the bank.
	10	Purchased supplies on account, $1,000.
	15	Paid employees' salaries, $2,800, and rent on a shop, $1,800.
	15	Paid advertising expense, $1,100.
	16	Paid $1,000 on account.
	17	Declared and paid a cash dividend of $2,000.

Wimberley Glass, Inc. uses the following accounts: Cash, Supplies, Land, Accounts Payable, Note Payable, Share Capital, Dividends, Sales Revenue, Salary Expense, Rent Expense, and Advertising Expense.

Requirements
1. Journalize each transaction. Explanations are not required.
2. Prepare T-accounts for Cash, Accounts Payable, and Notes Payable. Post to these three accounts.
3. After these transactions, how much cash does the business have? How much does it owe in total?

LEARNING OBJECTIVE ❹❺

Journalize and post transactions; prepare and use a trial balance

P2-61B During the first month of operations, October 2014, Barron Environmental Services Inc. completed the following transactions:

Oct.	3	Received $20,000 cash, and issued common shares.
	4	Performed services for a client, and received $5,000 cash.
	6	Purchased supplies, $300, and furniture, $2,500, on account.
	7	Paid $15,000 cash to acquire land for an office site.
	7	Worked for a client, and billed the client $1,500.
	16	Received partial payment from a client on account, $500.
	24	Paid the telephone bill, $110.
	24	Paid the water and electricity bills, $400.
	28	Received $2,500 cash for helping a client meet environmental standards.
	31	Paid secretary's salary, $1,200.
	31	Paid $2,500 of the account payable created on October 6.
	31	Declared and paid dividends of $2,400.

Requirements
Set up the following T-accounts: Cash, Accounts Receivable, Supplies, Furniture, Land, Accounts Payable, Share Capital, Dividends, Service Revenue, Salary Expense, and Utilities Expense.

1. Record each transaction in the journal, using the account titles given. Key each transaction by date. Explanations are not required.
2. Post the transactions to the T-accounts, using transaction dates as posting references. Label the ending balance of each account Bal., as shown in the chapter.
3. Prepare the trial balance of Barron Environmental Services Inc. at October 31, 2014.
4. Report to the shareholder how much in total resources the business has to work with, how much it owes, and whether October was profitable (and by how much).

LEARNING OBJECTIVE ❸❺

Record transactions directly in T-accounts; prepare and use a trial balance

P2-62B During the first month of operations (June 2014), Schulich Graphics Service Inc. completed the following selected transactions:

a. Began the business with an investment of $20,000 cash and a building valued at $60,000. The corporation issued common shares to the shareholders.
b. Borrowed $90,000 from the bank, and signed a note payable.

c. Paid $35,000 for computer equipment.

d. Purchased office supplies on account for $1,300.

e. Performed computer graphic service on account for a client, $2,500.

f. Received $1,200 cash on account.

g. Paid $800 of the account payable created in transaction (d).

h. Received a $500 bill for advertising expense that will be paid in the near future.

i. Performed service for clients, and received $1,100 in cash.

j. Paid employees' salaries totalling $2,200.

k. Paid the following cash expenses: rent, $700; utilities, $400.

Requirements

1. Set up the following T-accounts: Cash, Accounts Receivable, Office Supplies, Computer Equipment, Building, Accounts Payable, Note Payable, Share Capital, Service Revenue, Salary Expense, Advertising Expense, Rent Expense, and Utilities Expense.

2. Record each transaction directly in the T-accounts without using a journal. Use the letters to identify the transactions.

3. Prepare the trial balance of Schulich Graphics Service Inc. at June 30, 2014.

Apply Your Knowledge

Decision Cases

Case 1. A friend named Tom Tipple has asked what effect certain transactions will have on his company. Time is short, so you cannot apply the detailed procedures of journalizing and posting. Instead, you must analyze the transactions without the use of a journal. Tipple will continue the business only if he can expect to earn monthly net income of $10,000. The following transactions occurred this month:

LEARNING OBJECTIVE ❸❺

Record transactions directly in T-accounts, prepare a trial balance, and measure net income or loss

a. Tipple deposited $10,000 cash in a business bank account, and the corporation issued common shares to him.

b. Paid $300 cash for supplies.

c. Purchased office furniture on account, $4,400.

d. Earned revenue on account, $7,000.

e. Borrowed $5,000 cash from the bank, and signed a note payable due within one year.

f. Paid the following cash expenses for one month: employee's salary, $1,700; office rent, $600.

g. Collected cash from customers on account, $1,200.

h. Paid on account, $1,000.

i. Earned revenue, and received $2,500 cash.

j. Purchased advertising in the local newspaper for cash, $800.

Requirements

1. Set up the following T-accounts: Cash, Accounts Receivable, Supplies, Furniture, Accounts Payable, Notes Payable, Share Capital, Service Revenue, Salary Expense, Advertising Expense, and Rent Expense.

2. Record the transactions directly in the accounts without using a journal. Key each transaction by letter.

3. Prepare a trial balance at the current date. List expenses with the largest amount first, the next largest amount second, and so on. The business name will be Tipple Networks, Inc.

4. Compute the amount of net income or net loss for this first month of operations. Why would you recommend that Tipple continue or not continue in business?

Case 2. Barbara Boland opened a flower shop. Business has been good, and Boland is considering expanding with a second shop. A cousin has produced the following financial statements at December 31, 2014, the end of the first three months of operations:

Barbara Boland Blossoms Inc. Income Statement Quarter Ended December 31, 2014	
Sales revenue	$36,000
Share capital	10,000
Total revenue	46,000
Accounts payable	8,000
Advertising expense	5,000
Rent expense	6,000
Total expenses	19,000
Net income	$27,000

Barbara Boland Blossoms Inc. Balance Sheet As at December 31, 2014	
Assets	
Cash	$ 6,000
Cost of goods sold (expense)	22,000
Flower inventory	5,000
Store fixtures	10,000
Total assets	$43,000
Liabilities	
None	
Owners' Equity	$43,000

In these financial statements, all amounts are correct except for Owners' Equity. Boland's cousin heard that total assets should equal total liabilities plus owners' equity, so he plugged in the amount of owners' equity at $43,000 to make the balance sheet come out evenly.

Requirements

Barbara Boland has asked whether she should expand the business. Her banker says Boland may be wise to expand if (a) net income for the first quarter reaches $5,000 and (b) total assets are at least $25,000. It appears that the business has reached these milestones, but Boland doubts her cousin's understanding of accounting. Boland needs your help in making this decision. Prepare a corrected income statement and balance sheet. (Remember that Retained Earnings, which was omitted from the balance sheet, should equal net income for the period; there were no dividends.) After preparing the statements, give Boland your recommendation as to whether she should expand the flower shop.

Ethical Issues

Issue 1. Scruffy Murphy is the president and principal shareholder of Scruffy's Bar and Grill Limited. To expand, the business is applying for a $250,000 bank loan. The bank requires the company to have shareholders' equity of at least as much as the loan. Currently, shareholders' equity is $150,000. To get the loan, Murphy is considering two options for beefing up the shareholders' equity of the business:

Option 1. Issue $100,000 of common shares for cash. A friend has been wanting to invest in the company. This may be the right time to extend the offer.
Option 2. Transfer $100,000 of Murphy's personal land to the business, and issue common shares to Murphy. Then, after obtaining the loan, Murphy can transfer the land back to himself and cancel the common shares.

Requirement 1

Journalize the transactions required by each option.

Requirement 2

Use the Framework for Making Ethical Judgments in Chapter 1 (p. 27) to determine which plan would be ethical.

Issue 2. Community Charities has a standing agreement with Royal Bank of Canada (RBC). The agreement allows Community Charities to overdraw its cash balance at the bank when donations are running low. In the past, Community Charities managed funds wisely and rarely used this privilege. Recently, however, Beatrice Grand has been named president of Community Charities. To expand operations, she is acquiring office equipment and spending a lot for fundraising. During Grand's presidency, Community Charities has maintained a negative bank balance of about $3,000.

Requirements

What is the ethical issue in this situation? Do you approve or disapprove of Grand's management of Community Charities' and RBC's funds? Why? Use the Framework for Making Ethical Judgments in Chapter 1 (p. 27) in answering this question.

Focus on Financials

TELUS Corporation

Refer to the TELUS financial statements in Appendix A at the back of the book. Assume that TELUS completed the following selected transactions during the year ended December 31, 2011 (all amounts in millions).

LEARNING OBJECTIVE ❹
Journalize and post transactions

a. Sold services on account, $3,101.
b. Sold services for cash, $6,505.
c. Collected accounts receivable, $2,991.
d. Paid cash for inventory, $741.
e. Sold inventory that cost $671. Debit "Goods and services purchased."
f. Purchased goods and services on account, $4,055.
g. Paid accounts payable, $4,113.
h. Repaid long-term debt, $1,413.
i. Purchased property, plant, and equipment for cash, $3,200.

Requirements

1. For the following items, set up T-accounts with the given opening balances (note that the debits do not equal the credits because this is only a subset of TELUS's accounts):
   a. Cash and Temporary Investments, debit balance of $17
   b. Accounts Receivable, debit balance of $1,318
   c. Inventories, Debit balance of $283
   d. Property, Plant, and Equipment, debit balance of $7,831
   e. Accounts Payable and Accrued Liabilities, credit balance of $1,477
   f. Long-Term Debt, credit balance of $5,209
   g. Service Revenue, balance of $0
   h. Goods and Services Purchased, balance of $0
2. Record TELUS's transactions (a) through (i) in the journal. Explanations are not required.
3. Post the transactions in part (2) to the T-accounts (key them by letter) and compute the balance in each account.
4. For each of the following accounts, compare your balance to the actual balance in TELUS's financial statements in Appendix A. Your balances should agree with the actual balances.
   a. Cash and Temporary Investments
   b. Accounts Receivable
   c. Inventories
   d. Accounts Payable and Accrued Liabilities
   e. Service Revenue
   f. Goods and Services Purchased

Focus on Analysis

TELUS Corporation

Refer to the TELUS Corporation financial statements in Appendix A at the end of the book. Suppose you are an investor considering buying TELUS's shares. The following questions are important:

1. Explain which of TELUS's sales or collections from customers was the largest amount during the year ended December 31, 2011. Analyze net receivables to answer this question.

2. A major concern of lenders, such as banks, is the amount of long-term debt a company owes. How much long-term debt does TELUS owe at December 31, 2011? What must have happened to TELUS's long-term debt during the 2011 fiscal year?

3. Investors are vitally interested in a company's revenues and profits, and its trends of revenues and profits over time. Consider TELUS's operating revenues and net income during the year ended December 31, 2011. Compute the percentage change in operating revenue and also in net income or loss during this period. Which item changed more during this period, operating revenue or net income? (For convenience, show dollar amounts in millions.) Which provides a better indicator of business success? Give the reason for your answer.

Group Projects

You are promoting a concert in your area. Your purpose is to earn a profit, so you need to establish the formal structure of a business entity. Assume you organize as a corporation.

Requirements

1. Make a detailed list of 10 factors you must consider as you establish the business.
2. Describe 10 of the items your business must arrange to promote and stage the concert.
3. Identify the transactions that your business can undertake to organize, promote, and stage the concert. Journalize the transactions, and post to the relevant T-accounts. Set up the accounts you need for your business ledger.
4. Prepare the income statement, statement of retained earnings, and balance sheet immediately after the concert; that is, before you have had time to pay all the business bills and collect all receivables.
5. Assume that you will continue to promote concerts if the venture is successful. If it is unsuccessful, you will terminate the business within three months after the concert. Discuss how to evaluate the success of your venture and how to decide whether to continue in business.

Quick Check Answers

1. *c*	4. *d*	7. *c*	10. *d*
2. *d*	5. *a*	8. *a*	11. *a*
3. *a*	6. *b*	9. *d*	

Accrual Accounting and the Financial Statements

3

egory Holmgren/Alamy

SPOTLIGHT

Le Château has been selling fashion apparel, footwear, and accessories in Canada for over 50 years. What started as a single, family-owned store in Montreal in 1959 is now a global fashion brand, with its merchandise sold in 235 stores in Canada and 10 more in the Middle East. As the company's promotional materials state, Le Château's "fashion-forward image continues to inspire and engage its stylish clientele at home and abroad."

As you can see from Le Château's statement of loss on the next page, the company sold over $300 million in merchandise in its fiscal 2012 year. Unfortunately, its expenses for the year were slightly higher, so it ended up reporting a net loss of about $2.4 million. How does Le Château determine when to recognize the revenues and expenses it reports on this statement? Read on and you will find out!

Le Château Inc.
Consolidated Statement of Loss (Adapted)
For the Year Ended January 28, 2012

	(in thousands of dollars)
Income	
Sales	$302,707
Finance income	217
Total income	302,924
Expenses	
Cost of sales	96,145
Selling	168,035
General and administrative	39,752
Finance costs	1,974
Total expenses	305,906
Loss before income taxes	(2,982)
Income tax recovery	(596)
Net loss	$ (2,386)

Chapter 2 focused on measuring and recording transactions up to the trial balance. This chapter completes our coverage of the accounting cycle by discussing the adjustment process, the preparation of financial statements, and the closing of the books at the end of the period. It also includes a discussion of accounting principles that govern the recognition of revenue and expenses. At the end of the chapter, you will learn how to evaluate a company's debt-paying ability.

OBJECTIVE

❶ **Explain** how accrual accounting differs from cash-basis accounting

EXPLAIN HOW ACCRUAL ACCOUNTING DIFFERS FROM CASH-BASIS ACCOUNTING

Managers want to earn a profit. Investors search for companies whose share prices will increase. Banks seek borrowers who will pay their debts. Accounting provides the information these people use for decision making. Accounting information can be prepared using either the cash basis or the accrual basis of accounting.

When using **cash-basis accounting**, we record only business transactions involving the receipt or payment of cash. All other business transactions are ignored. If a business makes a $1,000 sale on account, for example, with the customer taking delivery of the goods but not paying for them until a later date, we would not record the sale transaction until we receive the cash payment from the customer. Similarly, the business would not record the purchase of $2,000 of inventory on account until it actually pays cash for the goods at some future date, despite having already received the inventory items from its supplier.

In contrast, when using **accrual accounting**, *the receipt or payment of cash is irrelevant* to deciding whether a business transaction should be recorded. What matters is whether the business has acquired an asset, earned revenue, taken on a liability, or incurred an expense. If it has, the transaction is recorded in the accounting records.

After the above sale on account, for example, the business has both gained an asset and earned revenue despite receiving no cash. Recall from Chapter 1 that an asset is a resource controlled by a company as a result of a past event and from which it expects to receive future economic benefits. The sale on account creates a $1,000 account receivable, which is an asset because it entitles the company to receive the economic benefit of cash at a future date when the customer pays off its account. The business has also earned $1,000 in revenue by delivering goods to the customer, which is a key activity in its day-to-day business operations. Because this transaction results in both an asset and revenue, we record it under the accrual basis of accounting.

Similarly, after the preceding purchase of inventory on account, the business has acquired $2,000 in assets in the form of goods it can sell to its customers in return for cash at some future date. It also has an obligation—in the form of a $2,000 account payable—that it must settle by paying cash to its supplier at some future date, so the business has also taken on a liability. Since this transaction results in an asset and a liability, we must record it under the accrual basis of accounting.

If the business were using the cash basis of accounting, neither of these initial transactions would have been recorded, leading to the following understatements in the business's financial statements: $3,000 in assets, $2,000 in liabilities, and $1,000 in revenue and net income. As a result, users relying on these cash-basis financial statements would have incomplete information about the company's financial position and results of operations, which would likely lead them to make poor business decisions.

Because the cash basis of accounting is inconsistent with the conceptual framework of accounting introduced in Chapter 1, it is not permitted by IFRS or ASPE, both of which provide extensive guidance on how to apply the accrual basis of accounting to prepare financial statements that present a relevant and faithful representation of a company's business activities.

Let's look at a simple example that illustrates the differences between the two methods of accounting. Suppose Pointz Corporation has the following transactions during July 2014:

1. Provides services to a customer for $500 in cash.
2. Provides services to a customer for $800 on account.
3. Pays employees' salaries of $450 in cash.
4. Receives a $50 hydro bill for electricity used during July.

The income statements for Pointz Corporation under the accrual basis and the cash basis of accounting appear as follows:

Pointz Corporation
Income Statement Using Accrual Accounting
For the Month Ended July 31, 2014

Revenue	$1,300
Expenses:	
Salaries	450
Hydro	50
Net income	$ 800

Pointz Corporation
Income Statement Using Cash-Basis Accounting
For the Month Ended July 31, 2014

Revenue	$500
Expenses:	
Salaries	450
Hydro	0
Net income	$ 50

The accrual-accounting statement reports an additional $800 in revenue because we have recorded the sale on account that is ignored in the cash-basis statement. The accrual statement also includes the $50 cost of hydro consumed during the month, which we have excluded from the cash statement because it remained unpaid at the end of the month. As a result of these differences, we report an additional $750 in net income for the month ($800 in revenue less $50 in expenses) on the accrual basis compared to the cash basis.

Next we discuss the formal principles used to determine when revenues and expenses should be recognized under accrual accounting.

OBJECTIVE

❷ **Apply** the revenue and expense recognition principles

APPLY THE REVENUE AND EXPENSE RECOGNITION PRINCIPLES

The Revenue Recognition Principle

In Chapter 1 we provided you with a basic definition of revenue, which stated that it consists of amounts earned by a company in the course of its ordinary, day-to-day business activities, primarily through the sale of goods and services. Now that you are more familiar with many fundamental accounting terms and concepts, we will provide the formal IFRS definition of revenue. IFRS define revenue as "the gross inflow of economic benefits during the period arising in the course of the ordinary activities of an entity when those inflows result in increases in equity, other than increases relating to contributions from equity participants" (ASPE has a fundamentally equivalent definition of revenue). Restating this in terms of the accounting equation, revenue is earned when ordinary business activities result in increases to both assets and shareholders' equity, other than when shareholders contribute capital to the business. When a business delivers goods to a customer who pays cash for them, the Cash asset increases and so does Shareholders' Equity (via Retained Earnings), so the business has earned revenue. But when a shareholder purchases additional shares in the business, which also increases Cash and Shareholders' Equity (via Share Capital), no revenue has been earned because the shareholder has simply injected more capital into the business.

IFRS and ASPE have revenue recognition principles which specify the conditions that must be met before a business can recognize revenue from a transaction. The principles are generally consistent across the two sets of standards, and while they both contain several criteria that must be met before recognizing revenue, we will focus on the three most fundamental criteria at this early stage in your accounting learning. A transaction must satisfy *all three* of these conditions before the business can recognize revenue:

1. The control and benefits of the goods have been transferred to the customer, or the services have been provided to the customer.
2. The amount of revenue can be reliably measured.
3. It is probable that the business will receive the economic benefits associated with the transaction, which usually come in the form of cash receipts.

To illustrate the application of these criteria, suppose you go shopping at Le Château and purchase a pair of pants for $75, which you pay cash for and take home with you. After this transaction, Le Château can recognize revenue because all three conditions have been met: (1) you possess the pants, along with the benefit of wearing them; (2) the pants have a price of $75; (3) Le Château received $75 in cash from you. Suppose, instead, that you find a pair of $75 pants you like but the store does not have your size in stock, so the sales clerk orders a pair in your size from another store, and tells you to come back to pick up and pay for them in three days. At this point, you do not have the pants, so you cannot benefit from wearing them, which leaves the first recognition condition unmet. In addition, after leaving the store, you may change your mind about the pants and never return to purchase them, which creates doubt about the third recognition condition. Le Château therefore cannot recognize revenue in this situation. Only if you return to the store to pick up and pay for the pants will Le Château be able to recognize any revenue.

As an example of service revenue recognition, assume a plumber comes to fix a leaky pipe under your bathroom sink, taking one hour and charging you $75, which you pay for by credit card. The plumbing company can recognize $75 in revenue here because all three recognition conditions have been met. In contrast, assume you simply call the plumbing company to arrange for a plumber to come to your home in two days to fix the leaky pipe, which the company estimates will take one hour and cost $75. In this case, none of the three conditions has been met, so the plumbing company cannot yet recognize any revenue.

The Expense Recognition Principle

In Chapter 1 we defined expenses as costs incurred to purchase the goods and services a company needs to run its business on a day-to-day basis. As with revenue recognition, IFRS and ASPE contain formal principles which set out the criteria that must be satisfied before an expense can be recognized:

1. There has been a decrease in future economic benefits caused by a decrease in an asset *or* an increase in a liability.

2. The expense can be reliably measured.

So, for example, once you have left the store with your new pants, Le Château's pants inventory (an asset) decreases by one pair, so the first expense recognition condition has been met. Le Château can check its inventory records to determine the cost of the pants it sold you, so the expense can be reliably measured. Both conditions have now been satisfied, so Le Château can recognize an expense in the form of Cost of Goods Sold. As for the situation where you are waiting for pants to be shipped from another store, Le Château cannot recognize an expense because its pants inventory will not decrease until you have actually purchased the pants.

In the case of the plumber who has fixed your leaky pipe, the plumbing company that employs him is now obligated to pay him for the one hour of work he did for you, which increases the company's Wages Payable liability. The plumber's hourly wage rate can be used to reliably measure the expense, so with both conditions satisfied, the company can recognize the wage expense associated with the plumber's work on your pipe. As for the situation where you have to wait two days for the plumber to come and fix your pipe, the plumbing company is not yet obligated to pay the plumber

MyAccountingLab

Accounting Cycle Tutorial: Income Statement Accounts and Transactions - Tutorial

because he has not done the work for you. Without an increase in the Wages Payable liability, the first condition has not been met, so no expense can be recognized.

STOP + THINK (3-1)

1. A client pays Windsor Group Ltd. $900 on March 15 for consulting service to be performed April 1 to June 30. Assuming the company uses accrual accounting, has Windsor Group Ltd. earned revenue on March 15? When will Windsor Group Ltd. earn the revenue?

2. Windsor Group Ltd. pays $4,500 on July 31 for office rent for the next three months. Has the company incurred an expense on July 31?

OBJECTIVE

❸ **Record** adjusting journal entries

RECORD ADJUSTING JOURNAL ENTRIES

At the end of a period, the business prepares its financial statements. This process begins with the trial balance introduced in Chapter 2. We refer to this trial balance as *unadjusted* because the accounts are not yet ready for the financial statements. In most cases, the simple label "Trial Balance" means "Unadjusted Trial Balance."

Because IFRS and ASPE require accrual accounting, we must record adjusting journal entries to ensure that all assets and liabilities have been recorded at period end, and that all revenues earned and expenses incurred during the period have been included in the accounts. These entries are recorded at the end of the accounting period, just before the financial statements are prepared.

Types of Adjusting Entries

There are three main types of adjusting entries: deferrals, depreciation, and accruals. We will use a variety of transactions and related adjusting entries for the fictional Moreau Ltd. to illustrate each main type of adjustment. Other miscellaneous adjusting entries are usually required at the end of an accounting period. We will address some of these as they arise in later chapters of the book. The table below provides an overview of the main types of adjusting entries.

Main Types of Adjusting Entries

Type	Description
Deferrals	An adjusting entry must be recorded when a company receives (pays) cash in advance of providing (receiving) the related good or service that has been paid for. This type of adjusting entry results in the *deferral* of the recognition of the related revenue (expense) until the future period in which the economic benefit is actually provided.
Depreciation	An adjusting entry must be recorded to reflect that the future economic benefits of a tangible asset decline with age. This type of adjusting entry, which can be considered a special form of deferral, results in the *depreciation* (amortization under ASPE) of the value of the asset over its useful life by expensing the portion of the asset's economic benefits that has been used up during an accounting period.
Accruals	An adjusting entry must be recorded when a company delivers (or receives) a good or service in advance of it being billed and paid for. This type of adjusting entry results in the *accrual* of the related revenue (expense) in the period in which the good or service is actually provided, regardless of the fact that it will not be billed or paid for until a future period.

Deferrals—Prepaid Expenses   Assets.

A prepaid expense is an expense a company has paid for in advance of actually using the benefit. Because it will provide a future economic benefit to the company, it is recorded as an asset when the cash payment is made. Recording the initial transaction this way results in the **deferral** of the expense to the future period in which the related benefit is realized. Let's look at the initial and adjusting entries for prepaid rent and supplies.

PREPAID RENT. Rent is usually paid in advance of the rented item being used, creating an asset for the renter, who gains the benefit of using the rented item during the future rental period. Suppose Moreau Ltd. prepays three months' office rent ($3,000) on April 1. The journal entry for the prepayment of three months' rent is as follows:

Apr. 1	Prepaid Rent ($1000 × 3)	3,000	
	Cash..		3,000
	Paid three months' rent in advance.		

The accounting equation shows that one asset increases and another decreases. Total assets are unchanged.

ASSETS	=	LIABILITIES	+	SHAREHOLDERS' EQUITY
3,000	=	0	+	0
−3,000				

After posting, the Prepaid Rent account appears as follows:

Prepaid Rent	
Apr. 1 3,000	

At the end of April, Moreau has only two months of future rental benefits remaining (2/3 of $3,000), so we must adjust the Prepaid Rent account to reflect this and to expense the $1,000 in Prepaid Rent used up during April (1/3 of $3,000).[*]

Apr. 30	Rent Expense.......................................	1,000	
Adjusting entry a	Prepaid Rent		1,000
	To record rent expense.		

Both assets and shareholders' equity decrease.

ASSETS	=	LIABILITIES	+	SHAREHOLDERS' EQUITY	
−1,000	=	0	−	1,000	Rent Expense

After posting, Prepaid Rent and Rent Expense appear as follows:

Prepaid Rent			Rent Expense	
Apr. 1 3,000	Apr. 30 1,000	→	Apr. 30 1,000	
Bal. 2,000			Bal. 1,000	

SUPPLIES. Businesses often have a stock of unused supplies on hand at the end of an accounting period, which represents an asset that will be used up in future periods. These unused supplies are another type of prepaid expense. On April 2, Moreau paid cash for $700 of office supplies, requiring the following journal entry:

Apr. 2	Supplies..	700	
	Cash..		700
	Paid cash for supplies.		

---

[*]See Exhibit 3-6, page 122, for a summary of adjustments a through g.

ASSETS	=	LIABILITIES	+	SHAREHOLDERS' EQUITY
700	=	0	+	0
−700				

Moreau used some of these supplies during April, so to expense their use and adjust the Supplies asset to reflect the future benefit remaining at April 30, we need an adjusting entry. By counting and valuing the supplies on hand at April 30, we can determine the amount of the adjustment needed. If Moreau's count shows that $400 in supplies remain at April 30, then we know that $300 worth of supplies have been used during April ($700 − $400), and we can record this adjusting entry:

Apr. 30	Supplies Expense ($700 – $400).	300	
Adjusting entry b	Supplies		300
	To record supplies expense.		

ASSETS	=	LIABILITIES	+	SHAREHOLDERS' EQUITY	
−300	=	0	−	300	Supplies Expense

After posting, the Supplies and Supplies Expense accounts appear as follows:

	Supplies						Supplies Expense	
Apr. 2	700	Apr. 30	300	→	Apr. 30	300	
Bal.	400				Bal.	300	

STOP + THINK (3-2)

At the beginning of the month, supplies were $5,000. During the month, $7,000 of supplies were purchased. At month's end, $3,000 of supplies were still on hand.

What adjusting entry is needed to account for the supplies, and what is the ending balance in the Supplies account?

Deferrals—Unearned Revenues *liability*

Businesses sometimes receive cash from customers before providing them with the goods or services they have paid for. Because the goods or services have not been delivered, the revenue recognition principle deems this to be **unearned revenue**. In fact, the business now has an obligation to provide the goods or services at some future date, which requires it to record a liability instead of revenue. Recording such transactions in this way results in a deferral of revenue recognition until the liability has been settled by providing the goods or services to the customer.

Suppose a customer engages Moreau Ltd. to provide consulting services over the next year, agreeing to pay Moreau $450 per month for nine hours of services ($50/hour), effective immediately. If Moreau receives the first $450 payment on April 20, it records this entry to reflect the unearned revenue:

Apr. 20	Cash	450	
	Unearned Service Revenue		450
	Received cash in advance of providing services.		

ASSETS	=	LIABILITIES	+	SHAREHOLDERS' EQUITY
450	=	450	+	0

After posting, the liability account appears as follows:

Unearned Service Revenue	
	Apr. 20 450

Unearned Service Revenue is a liability because Moreau Ltd. is obligated to perform nine hours of services for the client. During the last 10 days of April, Moreau performed three hours of services for the client, so by April 30, Moreau has settled one-third of the liability and earned one-third of the revenue ($450 × 1/3 = $150). The following adjusting entry is needed to reflect these events:

Apr. 30	Unearned Service Revenue..................	150	
Adjusting entry c	Service Revenue.............................		150
	To adjust unearned service revenue that has been earned ($450 × 1/3).		

ASSETS	=	LIABILITIES	+	SHAREHOLDERS' EQUITY	
0	=	−150	+	150	Service Revenue

This adjusting entry shifts $150 of the total amount received ($450) from liability to revenue. After posting, Unearned Service Revenue is reduced to $300, and Service Revenue is increased by $150, as follows:

Unearned Service Revenue				Service Revenue		
Apr. 30	150	Apr. 20	450			7,000
		Bal.	300		Apr. 30	150
					Bal.	7,150

Any time a business receives cash from a customer in advance of providing the related goods or services, similar initial and adjusting entries are required to properly reflect the obligation and defer the recognition of revenue until the goods or services have been provided.

Also note that one company's unearned revenue is another company's prepaid expense. As at April 30, for example, the $300 in Unearned Service Revenue on Moreau's books would be reflected as $300 in Prepaid Consulting Services on its customer's books. Under accrual accounting, the deferral of revenue by one company will result in the deferral of an expense by another company.

Depreciation of Property, Plant, and Equipment

Property, plant, and equipment, such as buildings, furniture, and machinery, are long-term tangible assets that provide several years of economic benefits to a company. Because the future benefits of a tangible asset decline with age, however, we must reduce its carrying value each year to reflect this decline. To accomplish this, we record adjusting entries for **depreciation** (amortization under ASPE), which gradually reduce the value of the asset over its useful life by expensing the portion of the asset's economic benefits that has been used up during each accounting period. An exception is made for land, which we do not depreciate because it has an unlimited useful life, so its future economic benefits generally do not decline with age.

To illustrate depreciation, suppose that on April 3, Moreau Ltd. purchased $16,500 of office furniture, including desks, chairs, and storage cabinets, on account. The entry to record this purchase is as follows:

Apr. 3   Furniture 16,500
                Accounts Payable   16,500
            Purchased office furniture on account.

ASSETS	=	LIABILITIES	+	SHAREHOLDERS' EQUITY
16,500	=	16,500	+	0

After posting, the Furniture account appears as follows:

Furniture	
Apr. 3 16,500	

Moreau Ltd.'s furniture is expected to remain useful for five years and then be worthless. One way to *estimate* the amount of depreciation for each year is to divide the cost of the asset ($16,500 in our example) by its expected useful life (five years). This procedure—called the straight-line depreciation method—yields annual depreciation of $3,300, or monthly depreciation of $275 ($3,300/12). (Chapter 7 covers depreciation and property, plant, and equipment in more detail.)

The adjusting entry to record depreciation for April is therefore:

Apr. 30   Depreciation Expense—Furniture............................ 275
Adjusting entry d   Accumulated Depreciation—Furniture   275
                  To record depreciation.

ASSETS	=	LIABILITIES	+	SHAREHOLDERS' EQUITY	
−275	=	0	−	275	Depreciation

Note that the adjusting entry does not decrease Assets by directly crediting the Furniture asset account. Instead, we decrease Assets by crediting an account called Accumulated Depreciation—Furniture, which is known as a contra asset account. A **contra account** has two distinguishing features:

1. It always has a companion account.
2. Its normal balance is opposite that of the companion account.

In this case, the Furniture account is the companion to the Accumulated Depreciation contra account. Since the Furniture account's normal balance is a debit, the normal balance of the Accumulated Depreciation account is a credit.

As its name suggests, the **Accumulated Depreciation** account accumulates all the depreciation recorded on the asset(s) included in the related companion account, so its balance increases over the life of the related assets being depreciated. A business's chart of accounts normally contains a separate Accumulated Depreciation account for each major category of depreciable asset.

After posting, the furniture-related accounts of Moreau Ltd. are as follows:

Furniture		Accumulated Depreciation—Furniture		Depreciation Expense—Furniture	
Apr. 3 16,500		Apr. 30 275		Apr. 30 275	
Bal. 16,500		Bal. 275		Bal. 275	

As at April 30, the **carrying amount** of Moreau's furniture is $16,225, which is obtained by deducting the asset's accumulated depreciation ($275) from its original cost ($16,500). All long-term tangible assets are reported at their carrying amounts on the balance sheet, with the details of their original costs and accumulated depreciation normally disclosed in a note to the financial statements.

STOP + THINK (3-3)	What will the carrying amount of Moreau Ltd.'s furniture be at the end of May 2014?

Accruals—Accrued Expenses

Businesses often incur expenses they have not yet been billed for, let alone paid. Utility bills, for example, usually arrive after the business has consumed the electricity or gas being billed. For some types of expenses, such as salaries or loan interest, no bills will ever be received. At the end of each accounting period, businesses must record adjusting entries called **accruals** to get these unbilled, unpaid expenses, which we call **accrued expenses**, into the books. By recording these accruals, we ensure the related expenses and liabilities are properly reflected in the financial statements for the period.

Let's use Salary Expense to illustrate this concept. Suppose Moreau Ltd. has one employee that receives a monthly salary of $1,900, which is paid in equal $950 amounts on the 15th and last day of each month. If a payday falls on a weekend, the salary is paid on the following Monday. The following calendar illustrates Moreau's pay days for April:

		April				
Sun.	Mon.	Tue.	Wed.	Thur.	Fri.	Sat.
					1	2
3	4	5	6	7	8	9
10	11	12	13	14	⑮	16
17	18	19	20	21	22	23
24	25	26	27	28	29	㉚

On April 15, a Friday, Moreau records this entry to account for the first half-month's salary:

```
Apr. 15   Salary Expense.............................................   950
              Cash.......................................................           950
          To pay salary.
```

ASSETS	=	LIABILITIES	+	SHAREHOLDERS' EQUITY	
−950	=	0	−	950	Salary Expense

After posting, the Salary Expense account is:

Salary Expense	
Apr. 15 950	

Because April 30 falls on a Saturday, the employee will not receive the second half of the salary for April until Monday, May 2, two days after the end of the April accounting period. In this case, the business has incurred a half-month of Salary Expense that it owes the employee as at April 30. To reflect these facts, we record this accrual adjusting entry:

Apr. 30	Salary Expense....................................	950	
Adjusting entry e	Salary Payable		950
	To accrue salary expense.		

The accounting equation shows that an accrued expense increases liabilities and decreases shareholders' equity:

ASSETS	=	LIABILITIES	+	SHAREHOLDERS' EQUITY	
0	=	950	−	950	Salary Expense

After posting, the Salary Payable and Salary Expense accounts appear as follows:

Salary Payable			Salary Expense	
	Apr. 30 950		Apr. 15 950	
	Bal. 950		Apr. 30 950	
			Bal. 1,900	

After the accrual, Moreau's accounts contain accurate salary information for April: it incurred $1,900 in Salary Expense during the month and owed $950 of this amount as at April 30. All accrued-expense adjustments are typically recorded this way—by debiting an expense account and crediting a liability account.

Accruals—Accrued Revenues

At the end of each accounting period, we must also consider the need to record accruals to account for **accrued revenues**, which are the opposite of accrued expenses. Businesses sometimes earn revenues they have not yet billed their customers for, let alone collected cash for. Service businesses such as accounting firms, for example, often provide services to their clients prior to invoicing for the work. Some types of revenues, such as loan interest, will never be invoiced. By recording accruals for these unbilled, uncollected revenues, we ensure that the related assets and revenues are properly reflected in the financial statements for the period.

To illustrate this type of accrual, assume that during the last half of April, Moreau performed $250 worth of services for a client that were not invoiced until early May. The adjusting entry to record this accrual is as follows:

Apr. 30	Accrued Service Revenue	250	
Adjusting entry f	Service Revenue		250
	To accrue service revenue.		

ASSETS	=	LIABILITIES	+	SHAREHOLDERS' EQUITY	
250	=	0	+	250	Service Revenues

This entry increases Assets, in the form of Accrued Service Revenue, because Moreau will receive the economic benefit of cash after it bills and collects the $250 from its client. Note that we have used Accrued Service Revenue instead of Accounts Receivable because the customer has not yet been billed, so no formal account receivable exists. This entry also increases Service Revenue by the same amount to reflect the revenue it has earned by providing the services in April. After posting, these accounts appear as follows:

Accrued Service Revenue			Service Revenue	
	2,250			7,000
Apr. 30	250		Apr. 30	150
			Apr. 30	250
Bal.	2,500		Bal.	7,400

In May, when Moreau invoices the client for the work in April, it will record an entry that debits Accounts Receivable and credits Accrued Service Revenue for $250, since there is now a formal account receivable from this client.

We record similar accrual entries for other kinds of accrued revenues—an accrued revenue account is debited and a revenue account is credited.

| STOP + THINK (3-4) | Suppose Moreau Ltd. holds a loan receivable from a client. At the end of April, $125 of interest revenue | has been earned but not received. Prepare the adjusting entry at April 30. |

Summary of the Adjusting Process

At the end of every accounting period, we must record adjusting journal entries to ensure that we properly measure income for the period and that we accurately reflect the business's financial position as at the end of the period. Exhibit 3-1 summarizes the main types of adjusting entries, along with the types of accounts they affect.

Exhibit 3-2 details the specific deferral and accrual adjusting entries needed at the end of each accounting period, as well as the journal entries to record the transactions that precede the deferrals and succeed the accruals.

MyAccountingLab
Accounting Cycle Tutorial:
Adjustments - Tutorial

EXHIBIT 3-1
Summary of Adjusting Entries

	Type of Account	
Type of Adjusting Entry	Debit	Credit
Deferral—Prepaid Expense	Expense	Asset
Deferral—Unearned Revenue	Liability	Revenue
Depreciation	Expense	Contra asset
Accrual—Accrued Expense	Expense	Liability
Accrual—Accrued Revenue	Asset	Revenue

Adapted from material provided by Beverly Terry.

EXHIBIT 3-2
Deferral and Accrual Adjusting Entries

DEFERRALS—Cash First

	First				Later		
Prepaid expenses	Pay cash and record an asset:			→	Record an expense and decrease the asset:		
	Prepaid Expense	XXX			Expense	XXX	
	Cash		XXX		Prepaid Expense		XXX
Unearned revenues	Receive cash and record unearned revenue:			→	Record a revenue and decrease unearned revenue:		
	Cash	XXX			Unearned Revenue	XXX	
	Unearned Revenue		XXX		Revenue		XXX

ACCRUALS—Cash Later

	First				Later		
Accrued expenses	Accrue expense and a payable:			→	Pay cash and decrease the payable:		
	Expense	XXX			Payable	XXX	
	Payable		XXX		Cash		XXX
Accrued revenues	Accrue revenue:			→	Invoice customer and record a receivable:		
	Accrued Revenue	XXX			Receivable	XXX	
	Revenue		XXX		Accrued Revenue		XXX

COOKING THE BOOKS ISSUES IN ACCRUAL ACCOUNTING

Accrual accounting provides some ethical challenges that cash accounting avoids. Suppose that on December 1, 2014, for example, Shop Online Inc. (SOI) pays $3 million in cash for an advertising campaign, which will run during December, January, and February. The ads start running immediately. If SOI properly applies the expense recognition principle discussed earlier in the chapter, it should record one-third of the expense ($1 million) during the year ended December 31, 2014, and leave the remaining $2 million as a prepaid expense that will be recognized as an expense in 2015.

But also suppose that 2014 is a great year for SOI, with its net income being much higher than expected. SOI's top managers believe, however, that 2015 will be much less profitable due to increased competition. In this case, company managers have a strong incentive to expense the full $3 million during 2014, an unethical action that would keep $2 million of advertising expense off the 2015 income statement and increase its net income by the same amount (ignoring income taxes).

Unethical managers can also exploit the revenue recognition principle to artificially improve reported liabilities, revenues, and net income. Suppose it is now December 31, 2014, and Highfield Computer Products Ltd., which is having a poor fiscal year, has just received a $1 million advance cash payment for merchandise it will deliver early in January. If top managers are unethical, the company can "manufacture" revenue and net income by recording the $1 million cash payment as revenue in 2014 instead of as unearned revenue (a liability) at the end of the year.

MyAccountingLab

Accounting Cycle Tutorial:
Adjustments - Application Exercise 1

Exhibit 3-3 summarizes the adjusting process we followed for Moreau Ltd. as at April 30, 2014. Panel A contains the information used to record each adjusting entry in Panel B, while Panel C presents all of Moreau's ledger accounts, with each adjusting entry keyed with the corresponding letter from Panel A.

Exhibit 3-3 includes an additional accrual adjustment (*entry g*) to accrue the income tax expense Moreau owes for April. This is typically the last adjusting entry a business makes at the end of an accounting period because it is based on the net income for the period, which can only be determined after all other adjusting entries have been posted to the accounts. If we assume Moreau owes $540 of income tax for April, the adjusting entry is as follows:

Apr. 30	Income Tax Expense............................	540	
Adjusting entry g	Income Tax Payable		540
	To accrue income tax expense.		

The Adjusted Trial Balance

MyAccountingLab

Accounting Cycle Tutorial:
Adjustments - Application Exercise 3

Before we prepare the financial statements, it is helpful to compile an **adjusted trial balance** listing all of the ledger accounts and their adjusted balances, which are what we need to report on the financial statements. Exhibit 3-4 contains the adjusted trial balance for Moreau Ltd. Note how clearly the adjusted trial balance presents the adjustments made to the account balances contained in the initial unadjusted trial balance. This presentation format makes it easy for us to see the impacts of all our adjusting entries on the accounts in the ledger. We see, for example, that we adjusted Supplies downward by $300 to arrive at the account's $400 balance as at April 30, 2014.

EXHIBIT 3-3
The Adjusting Process of Moreau Ltd.

Panel A—Information for Adjustments at April 30, 2014

(a) Prepaid rent expired, $1,000
(b) Supplies on hand, $400.
(c) Amount of unearned service revenue that has been earned, $150.
(d) Depreciation on furniture, $275.

(e) Accrued salary expense, $950. This entry assumes the pay period ended April 30 and the employee was paid May 2.
(f) Accrued service revenue, $250
(g) Accrued income tax expense, $540.

Panel B—Adjusting Entries

(a) Rent Expense...	1,000	
Prepaid Rent...		1,000
To record rent expense.		
(b) Supplies Expense..	300	
Supplies...		300
To record supplies used.		
(c) Unearned Service Revenue	150	
Service Revenue..		150
To record unearned revenue that has been earned.		
(d) Depreciation Expense—Furniture	275	
Accumulated Depreciation—Furniture....................................		275
To record depreciation.		
(e) Salary Expense	950	
Salary Payable...		950
To accrue salary expense.		
(f) Accrued Service Revenue..	250	
Service Revenue..		250
To accrue service revenue.		
(g) Income Tax Expense...	540	
Income Tax Payable...		540
To accrue income tax expense.		

Panel C—Ledger Accounts

Assets

Cash
Bal. 24,800	

Accrued Service Revenue
2,250	
(f) 250	
Bal. 2,500	

Supplies
700	(b) 300
Bal. 400	

Prepaid Rent
3,000	(a) 1,000
Bal. 2,000	

Furniture
Bal. 16,500	

Accumulated Depreciation—Furniture
	(d) 275
	Bal. 275

Liabilities

Accounts Payable
	Bal. 13,100

Salary Payable
	(e) 950
	Bal. 950

Unearned Service Revenue
(c) 150	450
	Bal. 300

Income Tax Payable
	(g) 540
	Bal. 540

Shareholders' Equity

Share Capital
	Bal. 20,000

Retained Earnings
	Bal. 11,250

Dividends
Bal. 3,200	

Revenue

Service Revenue
	7,000
	(c) 150
	(f) 250
	Bal. 7,400

Expenses

Rent Expense
(a) 1,000	
Bal. 1,000	

Salary Expense
950	
(e) 950	
Bal. 1,900	

Supplies Expense
(b) 300	
Bal. 300	

Depreciation Expense—Furniture
(d) 275	
Bal. 275	

Utilities Expense
Bal. 400	

Income Tax Expense
(g) 540	
Bal. 540	

EXHIBIT 3-4
**Worksheet for the Preparation
of Adjusted Trial Balance**

Moreau Ltd.
Preparation of Adjusted Trial Balance
April 30, 2014

Account Title	Unadjusted Trial Balance Debit	Credit	Adjustments Debit	Credit	Adjusted Trial Balance Debit	Credit	
Cash	24,800				24,800		
Accrued service revenue	2,250		(f) 250		2,500		
Supplies	700			(b) 300	400		
Prepaid rent	3,000			(a) 1,000	2,000		
Furniture	16,500				16,500		
Accumulated depreciation—furniture				(d) 275		275	**Balance Sheet** *(Exhibit 3-7)*
Accounts payable		13,100				13,100	
Salary payable				(e) 950		950	
Unearned service revenue		450	(c) 150			300	
Income tax payable				(g) 540		540	
Share capital		20,000				20,000	
Retained earnings		11,250				11,250	**Statement of Retained Earnings** *(Exhibit 3-6)*
Dividends	3,200				3,200		
Service revenue		7,000		(f) 250 (c) 150		7,400	
Rent expense			(a) 1,000		1,000		
Salary expense	950		(e) 950		1,900		**Income Statement** *(Exhibit 3-5)*
Supplies expense			(b) 300		300		
Depreciation expense—furniture			(d) 275		275		
Utilities expense	400				400		
Income tax expense			(g) 540		540		
	51,800	51,800	3,465	3,465	53,815	53,815	

PREPARE THE FINANCIAL STATEMENTS

The April 2014 financial statements of Moreau Ltd. can be prepared from the adjusted trial balance in Exhibit 3-4. The right side of the exhibit highlights which financial statement(s) the accounts are reported on.

- The income statement (Exhibit 3-5) reports the revenue and expense accounts.
- The statement of retained earnings (Exhibit 3-6) reports the changes in retained earnings.
- The balance sheet (Exhibit 3-7) reports assets, liabilities, and shareholders' equity.
- The arrows in Exhibits 3-5, 3-6, and 3-7 show the flow of data from one statement to the next.

EXHIBIT 3-5
Income Statement

MyAccountingLab

Accounting Cycle Tutorial:
Financial Statements - Application
Exercise 2

Moreau Ltd.
Income Statement
For the Month Ended April 30, 2014

Revenue:		
Service revenue		$7,400
Expenses:		
Salary	$1,900	
Rent	1,000	
Utilities	400	
Supplies	300	
Depreciation	275	3,875
Income before tax		3,525
Income tax expense		540
Net income		$2,985

①

EXHIBIT 3-6
Statement of
Retained Earnings

Moreau Ltd.
Statement of Retained Earnings
For the Month Ended April 30, 2014

Retained earnings, April 1, 2014	$11,250
Add: Net income	2,985
	14,235
Less: Dividends	(3,200)
Retained earnings, April 30, 2014	$11,035

EXHIBIT 3-7
Balance Sheet

②

Moreau Ltd.
Balance Sheet
As at April 30, 2014

Assets			Liabilities		
Cash		$24,800	Accounts payable		$13,100
Accrued service revenue		2,500	Salary payable		950
Supplies		400	Unearned service revenue		300
Prepaid rent		2,000	Income tax payable		540
Furniture	16,500		Total liabilities		14,890
Less accumulated					
depreciation	(275)	16,225	**Shareholders' Equity**		
			Share capital		20,000
			Retained earnings		11,035
			Total shareholders' equity		31,035
			Total liabilities and		
Total assets		$45,925	shareholders' equity		$45,925

Why is the income statement prepared first and the balance sheet last?

1. The income statement is prepared first because it reports net income (revenues minus expenses), which is needed to prepare the statement of retained earnings. This link is illustrated by arrow 1 between Exhibits 3-5 and 3-6.

2. The balance sheet is prepared last because it relies on the ending balance from the statement of retained earnings to complete the shareholders' equity section of the statement. This link is illustrated by arrow 2 between Exhibits 3-6 and 3-7.

You will note that the statement of cash flows is not included in the list of statements that are prepared from the adjusted trial balance. The reason it is not included, as you will discover in Chapter 12, is that the statement of cash flows is not prepared from the adjusted trial balance, but rather from the comparative balance sheets, the income statement, and other sources.

Formats for the Financial Statements

Companies can format their balance sheets and income statements in various ways. Here we will highlight some of the most common balance sheet and income statement formats.

BALANCE SHEET FORMATS. In Chapter 1 we introduced you to the difference between current and non-current (or long-term) assets. Recall that a current asset is an asset we expect to convert to cash, sell, or consume *within one year* of the balance sheet date, or within the business's normal operating cycle if it is longer than one year. A non-current asset is any asset that does not qualify as a current asset. We make a similar distinction between current and non-current liabilities, with a current liability being one we expect to repay within one year of the balance sheet date, or within the business's normal operating cycle if it is longer than one year; while a non-current liability will be repaid beyond one year or the normal operating cycle. A **classified balance sheet** separates current assets from non-current assets and current liabilities from non-current liabilities, and it also subtotals the current assets and current liabilities. Exhibit 3-8 contains the classified balance sheet of Le Château as at January 28, 2012. An unclassified balance sheet does not separate current and non-current assets or liabilities. Regardless of which of these two formats is used, current assets are always listed in order of decreasing **liquidity**, which is a measure of how quickly they can be converted to cash, the most liquid asset. IFRS and ASPE require the use of classified balance sheets.

A balance sheet prepared in **report format** lists assets at the top, followed by liabilities, and then shareholders' equity. Le Château's balance sheet in Exhibit 3-8 is in report format.

A balance sheet prepared in **account format** uses a T-account as a framework, with assets (debits) listed on the left side and liabilities and shareholders' equity (credits) on the right. The Moreau Ltd. balance sheet in Exhibit 3-7 is in account format. Companies are free to choose the report format or the account format when preparing their balance sheets.

INCOME STATEMENT FORMATS. A **single-step income statement** lists all the revenues together under a heading such as Revenues or Income. The expenses are also

EXHIBIT 3-8
Classified Balance Sheet
of Le Château Inc.

Le Château Inc.
Consolidated Balance Sheet (Adapted)
As at January 28, 2012

	(in thousands of dollars)
ASSETS	
Current assets	
Cash and cash equivalents	$ 7,193
Accounts receivable	2,358
Income taxes refundable	2,137
Derivative financial instruments	129
Inventories	119,325
Prepaid expenses	1,564
Total current assets	132,706
Property and equipment	95,744
Intangibles	5,344
Total assets	$ 233,794
LIABILITIES AND SHAREHOLDERS' EQUITY	
Current liabilities	
Trade and other payables	$ 21,820
Deferred revenue	3,918
Current portion of provisions	300
Current portion of long-term debt	16,323
Total current liabilities	42,361
Long-term debt	29,145
Provisions	120
Deferred income taxes	2,954
Deferred lease credits	16,109
Total liabilities	90,689
Shareholders' equity	
Share capital	37,729
Contributed surplus	2,328
Retained earnings	102,956
Accumulated other comprehensive income	92
Total shareholders' equity	143,105
Total liabilities and shareholders' equity	$ 233,794

listed together in a single category titled Expenses, or Expenses and Losses. This format contains only a single step: the subtracting of Total Expenses from Total Revenues to arrive at Net Income. Le Château's statement of loss at the opening of the chapter is in single-step format.

A **multi-step income statement** contains a number of subtotals to highlight important relationships among revenues and expenses. Le Château's multi-step statement of loss in Exhibit 3-9 highlights gross profit, results from operating activities, and loss before income taxes prior to arriving at the net loss reported at the bottom of the statement. We will discuss the components of the income statement in more detail in Chapter 11.

Companies are free to use either format for their income statements, or they can use a format of their own design if it better suits their reporting needs.

EXHIBIT 3-9
Multi-Step Statement of Loss
for Le Château Inc.

Le Château Inc.
Consolidated Statement of Loss (Adapted)
For the Year Ended January 28, 2012

	(in thousands of dollars)
Sales	$302,707
Cost of sales	96,145
Gross profit	206,562
Operating expenses	
Selling	168,035
General and administrative	39,752
Total operating expenses	207,787
Results from operating activities	(1,225)
Finance costs	1,974
Finance income	(217)
Loss before income taxes	(2,982)
Income tax recovery	(596)
Net loss	$ (2,386)

MID-CHAPTER SUMMARY PROBLEM

The trial balance of Goldsmith Inc. shown below pertains to December 31, 2014, which is the end of its fiscal year. Data needed for the adjusting entries include the following (all amounts in thousands):

√a. Supplies on hand at year-end, $2.
√b. Depreciation on furniture and fixtures, $20.
√c. Depreciation on building, $10.
√d. Salary owed but not yet paid, $5.
√e. Accrued service revenue, $12.
√f. Of the $45 balance of unearned service revenue, $32 was earned during the year.
g. Accrued income tax expense, $35.

Requirements

1. Open the ledger accounts with their unadjusted balances. Show dollar amounts in thousands, as shown for Accounts Receivable:

Accounts Receivable
370 I

2. Journalize the Goldsmith Inc. adjusting entries at December 31, 2014. Key entries by letter, as in Exhibit 3-3, page 119. Make entries in thousands of dollars.
3. Post the adjusting entries.
4. Copy the trial balance to a worksheet, enter the adjusting entries, and prepare an adjusted trial balance, as shown in Exhibit 3-4.
5. Prepare the income statement, the statement of retained earnings, and the balance sheet. (At this stage, it is not necessary to classify assets or liabilities as current or long term.) Draw arrows linking these three financial statements.

Name: Goldsmith Inc.
Industry: Service corporation
Fiscal Period: Year ended December 31, 2014

Goldsmith Inc.
Trial Balance
December 31, 2014

	(in thousands)	
Cash	$ 198	
Accrued service revenue	370	
Supplies	6	
Furniture and fixtures	100	
Accumulated depreciation—furniture and fixtures		$ 40
Building	250	
Accumulated depreciation—building		130
Accounts payable		380
Salary payable		
Unearned service revenue		45
Income tax payable		
Share capital		100
Retained earnings		193
Dividends	65	
Service revenue		286
Salary expense	172	
Supplies expense		
Depreciation expense—furniture and fixtures		
Depreciation expense—building		
Income tax expense		
Miscellaneous expense	13	
Total	$1,174	$1,174

ANSWERS

Requirements 1 and 3 (amounts in thousands)

Assets

Cash

| Bal. | 198 | | |

Accrued Service Revenue

	370		
(e)	12		
Bal.	382		

Supplies

| | 6 | (a) | 4 |
| Bal. | 2 | | |

Furniture and Fixtures

| Bal. | 100 | | |

Accumulated Depreciation— Furniture and Fixtures

			40
		(b)	20
		Bal.	60

Liabilities

Accounts Payable

| | | Bal. | 380 |

Salary Payable

| | | (d) | 5 |
| | | Bal. | 5 |

Unearned Service Revenue

| (f) | 32 | | 45 |
| | | Bal. | 13 |

Shareholders' Equity

Share capital

| | | Bal. | 100 |

Retained Earnings

| | | Bal. | 193 |

Dividends

| Bal. | 65 | | |

Expenses

Salary Expense

	172		
(d)	5		
Bal.	177		

Supplies Expense

| (a) | 4 | | |
| Bal. | 4 | | |

Depreciation Expense— Furniture and Fixtures

| (b) | 20 | | |
| Bal. | 20 | | |

Depreciation Expense— Building

| (c) | 10 | | |
| Bal. | 10 | | |

	Building	
Bal.	250	

Income Tax Payable		
	(g)	35
	Bal.	35

Income Tax Expense		
(g)	35	
Bal.	35	

Accumulated Depreciation—Building		
		130
	(c)	10
	Bal.	140

Miscellaneous Expense		
Bal.	13	

For Requirement 1, create a T-account for each account name listed in the December 31, 2014, trial balance. Insert the opening balances into the T-accounts from the trial balance, ensuring debit and credit balances in the trial balance are debit and credit balances in the T-accounts. To make sure all the account balances have been entered correctly, trace each T-account's balance back to the December 31, 2014, trial balance.

For Requirement 3, make sure each transaction is posted to the proper T-account, and make sure no transactions were missed.

Revenue

Service Revenue

		286
	(e)	12
	(f)	32
	Bal.	330

Requirement 2

2014			(amounts in thousands)	
(a) Dec. 31	Supplies Expense		4	
	Supplies			4
	To record supplies used ($6 − $2).			
(b) Dec. 31	Depreciation Expense—Furniture and Fixtures		20	
	Accumulated Depreciation—Furniture and Fixtures			20
	To record depreciation expense on furniture and fixtures.			
(c) Dec. 31	Depreciation Expense—Building		10	
	Accumulated Depreciation—Building			10
	To record depreciation expense on building.			
(d) Dec. 31	Salary Expense		5	
	Salary Payable			5
	To accrue salary expense.			
(e) Dec. 31	Accrued Service Revenue		12	
	Service Revenue			12
	To accrue service revenue.			
(f) Dec. 31	Unearned Service Revenue		32	
	Service Revenue			32
	To record unearned service revenue that has been earned.			
(g) Dec. 31	Income Tax Expense		35	
	Income Tax Payable			35
	To accrue income tax expense.			

Refer to the rules of debit and credit shown in Chapter 2, Exhibit 2-8, on page 70.

Make sure that Assets = Liabilities + Shareholders' Equity for each transaction before going to the next transaction.

Requirement 4

Goldsmith Inc.
Preparation of Adjusted Trial Balance
December 31, 2014

(amounts in thousands)

	Unadjusted Trial Balance		Adjustments				Adjusted Trial Balance	
	Debit	Credit	Debit		Credit		Debit	Credit
Cash	198						198	
Accrued service revenue	370		(e)	12			382	
Supplies	6				(a)	4	2	
Furniture and fixtures	100						100	
Accumulated depreciation— furniture and fixtures		40			(b)	20		60
Building	250						250	
Accumulated depreciation—building		130			(c)	10		140
Accounts payable		380						380
Salary payable					(d)	5		5
Unearned service revenue		45	(f)	32				13
Income tax payable					(g)	35		35
Share capital		100						100
Retained earnings		193						193
Dividends	65						65	
Service revenue		286			(e)	12		330
					(f)	32		
Salary expense	172		(d)	5			177	
Supplies expense			(a)	4			4	
Depreciation expense— furniture and fixtures			(b)	20			20	
Depreciation expense—building			(c)	10			10	
Income tax expense			(g)	35			35	
Miscellaneous expense	13						13	
	1,174	1,174	118		118		1,256	1,256

Create a worksheet with columns for the unadjusted trial balance, adjustments, and the adjusted trial balance. List all the account names that have a balance in their T-accounts. Write the account balances from the December 31, 2014, trial balance in the first two columns. Write the adjustment amounts in the next two columns. Write the "Bal." amounts from the T-accounts in the Adjusted Trial Balance columns. Ensure total debits equal total credits for each pair of columns. Double-check the Adjusted Trial Balance amounts by adding the Adjustments to the Unadjusted Trial Balance amounts. Double-underline the totals to show that the columns have been added and the totals are final.

Requirement 5

The title must include the name of the company, "Income Statement," and the specific period of time covered. It is critical that the time period is defined.

Gather all the revenue and expense account names and amounts from the Debit and Credit Adjusted Trial Balance columns of the worksheet.

Notice that income tax expense is always reported separately from the other expenses, and it appears as the last item before net income (or net loss).

Goldsmith Ltd.
Income Statement
For the Year Ended December 31, 2014

		(amounts in thousands)
Revenue:		
Service revenue		$330
Expenses:		
Salary	$177	
Depreciation—furniture and fixtures	20	
Depreciation—building	10	
Supplies	4	
Miscellaneous	13	224
Income before tax		106
Income tax expense		35
Net income		$ 71

The title must include the name of the company, "Statement of Retained Earnings," and the specific period of time covered. It is critical that the time period is defined.

Beginning retained earnings and dividends are from the Adjusted Trial Balance columns of the worksheet.

The net income amount is transferred from the income statement.

Goldsmith Inc.
Statement of Retained Earnings
For the Year Ended December 31, 2014

	(amounts in thousands)
Retained earnings, January 1, 2014	$193
Add: Net income	71
	264
Less: Dividends	(65)
Retained earnings, December 31, 2014	$199

The title must include the name of the company, "Balance Sheet," and the date of the balance sheet. It shows the financial position on one specific date.

Gather all the asset, liability, and equity accounts and amounts from the Adjusted Trial Balance columns of the worksheet. The retained earnings amount is transferred from the statement of retained earnings.

It is imperative that Total assets = Total liabilities + Shareholders' equity.

Goldsmith Inc.
Balance Sheet
As at December 31, 2014

(amounts in thousands)

Assets			Liabilities	
Cash		$198	Accounts payable	$380
Accounts receivable		382	Salary payable	5
Supplies		2	Unearned service revenue	13
Furniture and fixtures	$100		Income tax payable	35
Less accumulated			Total liabilities	433
depreciation	(60)	40		
			Shareholders' Equity	
Building	$250		Share capital	100
Less accumulated			Retained earnings	199
depreciation	(140)	110	Total shareholders' equity	299
			Total liabilities and	
Total assets		$732	shareholders' equity	$732

RECORD CLOSING JOURNAL ENTRIES

⑤ Record closing journal entries

Recall that a business's Retained Earnings represent the accumulated net income of the business since its inception, less any net losses and dividends declared during this time. To keep track of this balance, at the end of each fiscal year we must record **closing entries**, which are journal entries that transfer the balances in all revenue, expense, and dividend accounts into the Retained Earnings account. After these entries, all the income statement and dividend accounts have zero balances, leaving them ready to begin tracking revenues, expenses, and dividends for the next fiscal year.

Because the revenue, expense, and dividend accounts are closed at the end of each year, we call them **temporary accounts**. In effect, they temporarily contain a business's revenues, expenses, and dividends for a year, and then are returned to zero balances before starting the next fiscal year. In contrast, all the asset, liability, and shareholders' equity accounts we report on the balance sheet are **permanent accounts** because their balances carry forward from year to year. The balances in these accounts at the end of one fiscal year become the beginning balances of the next fiscal year.

To record and post the closing journal entries at the end of a fiscal year, follow this process:

① Debit each revenue account for the amount of its credit balance. Credit Retained Earnings for the sum of the revenues. Now the sum of the revenues has been added to Retained Earnings.

② Credit each expense account for the amount of its debit balance. Debit Retained Earnings for the sum of the expenses. The sum of the expenses has now been deducted from Retained Earnings.

③ Credit the Dividends account for the amount of its debit balance. Debit Retained Earnings for the same amount. The dividends have now been deducted from Retained Earnings.

④ Post all of the closing journal entries to the ledger to close the accounts for the year.

Exhibit 3-10 illustrates the process of journalizing and posting the closing entries for Moreau Ltd. at the end of April. Panel A contains the closing journal entries, which have been prepared using the revenue, expense, and dividend account balances contained in Moreau's adjusted trial balance in Exhibit 3-4. Panel B shows these entries being posted to the ledger accounts. Note that after the closing entries have been posted, the ending credit balance of $11,035 in the Retained Earnings account matches the Retained Earnings balance in the statement of retained earnings in Exhibit 3-6 and the balance sheet in Exhibit 3-7. If the ending balance in the Retained Earnings account does not match the balance reported in these financial statements, then you know you have made an error in the closing process.

MyAccountingLab
Accounting Cycle Tutorial: Adjusting and Closing Entries - Tutorial

MyAccountingLab
Accounting Cycle Tutorial: Adjusting and Closing Entries - Application Exercise 2

EXHIBIT 3-10
Journalizing and Posting
Closing Entries

PANEL A—Journalizing the Closing Entries

Closing Entries

①	Apr.	30	Service Revenue...	7,400	
			Retained Earnings...................................		7,400
②		30	Retained Earnings.......................................	4,415	
			Rent Expense..		1,000
			Salary Expense......................................		1,900
			Supplies Expense....................................		300
			Depreciation Expense—Furniture		275
			Utilities Expense....................................		400
			Income Tax Expense.................................		540
③		30	Retained Earnings.......................................	3,200	
			Dividends...		3,200

PANEL B—Posting to the Accounts

Rent Expense			
Adj.	1,000		
Bal.	1,000	Clo	1,000

Salary Expense			
	950		
Adj.	950		
Bal.	1,900	Clo.	1,900

Supplies Expense			
Adj.	300		
Bal.	300	Clo.	300

Depreciation Expense			
Adj.	275		
Bal.	275	Clo.	275

Utilities Expense			
	400		
Bal.	400	Clo.	400

Income Tax Expense			
Adj.	540		
Bal.	540	Clo.	540

Service Revenue			
			7,000
		Adj.	250
		Adj.	150
Clo.	7,400	Bal.	7,400

Retained Earnings			
Clo.	4,415		11,250
Clo.	3,200	Clo.	7,400
		Bal.	11,035

Dividends			
Bal.	3,200	Clo.	3,200

Adj. = Amount posted from an adjusting entry
Clo. = Amount posted from a closing entry
Bal. = Balance
As arrow ② in Panel B shows, it is not necessary to make a separate closing entry for each expense. In one closing entry, we record one debit to Retained Earnings and a separate credit to each expense account.

ANALYZE AND EVALUATE A COMPANY'S DEBT-PAYING ABILITY

OBJECTIVE

❻ Analyze and evaluate a company's debt-paying ability

As we have noted, managers, investors, and creditors use accounting information to make business decisions. A bank considering lending money must predict whether the borrower can repay the loan. If the borrower already has a lot of debt compared to its assets, the probability of repayment may be low. If the borrower owes relatively little, however, the odds of repayment are higher. To evaluate a company's debt-paying ability, decision makers examine data and ratios calculated using information in the financial statements. Let's see how this process works.

Net Working Capital

Net working capital (or simply working capital) is a figure that indicates a company's liquidity. In this context, liquidity refers to the ease with which a company will be able to use its current assets to pay off its current liabilities. The higher a company's liquidity, the easier it will be able to pay off its current liabilities. The calculation for net working capital is:

$$\text{Net working capital} = \text{Total current assets} - \text{Total current liabilities}$$

Generally, a company is considered to be liquid when its current assets sufficiently exceed its current liabilities. The sufficiency of the excess is usually evaluated using the current ratio, which we discuss below, and typically varies by industry.

Using the balance sheet data in Exhibit 3-8, we can calculate Le Château's net working capital at the end of 2012 (all dollar amounts in thousands from here on):

$$\text{Net working capital} = \$132,706 - \$42,361 = \$90,345$$

Le Château's current assets exceed its current liabilities by $90,345, meaning that after the company pays all of its current liabilities, it will still have almost $100,000 in current assets to fund other business activities. For a company of its size, Le Château would be considered highly liquid.

Current Ratio

Another means of evaluating a company's liquidity using its current assets and current liabilities is via the **current ratio**, which is calculated as follows:

$$\text{Current ratio} = \frac{\text{Total current assets}}{\text{Total current liabilities}}$$

The higher the current ratio, the better we consider the company's liquidity. As a rule of thumb, a company's current ratio should be at least 1.50, which indicates the company has $1.50 in current assets for every $1.00 in current liabilities. The threshold does, however, vary by industry, and in some cases can be as low as 1.00 or as high as 2.00. A current ratio of less than 1.00 is considered low by any standard, as it indicates that current liabilities exceed current assets, or that the net working capital is negative.

Le Château's current ratio at January 28, 2012 was:

$$\text{Current ratio} = \frac{\text{Total current assets}}{\text{Total current liabilities}} = \frac{\$132,706}{\$42,361} = 3.13$$

By any measure, Le Château's current ratio of 3.13 is outstanding and indicates to current and potential lenders that the company will have no trouble paying its current liabilities. With a current ratio that high, the company could even take on significant additional current debt and pay it off with no difficulty.

Debt Ratio

We can also evaluate a company's debt-paying ability using the **debt ratio**, which is calculated as follows:

$$\text{Debt ratio} = \frac{\text{Total liabilities}}{\text{Total assets}}$$

This ratio indicates the proportion of a company's assets that is financed with debt, which helps evaluate the company's ability to pay both current and long-term debts (total liabilities). In contrast to the current ratio, a low debt ratio is better than a high debt ratio because it indicates a company has not used an excessive amount of debt to finance its assets, which means it should be easier for the company to use its assets to generate the cash needed to pay off its liabilities. Companies with low debt ratios are less likely to encounter financial difficulty.

Le Château's debt ratio at January 28, 2012 was:

$$\text{Debt ratio} = \frac{\text{Total liabilities}}{\text{Total assets}} = \frac{\$90,689}{\$233,794} = 0.39$$

As with the current ratio, the threshold for an acceptable debt ratio varies by industry, but most companies have a ratio between 0.60 and 0.70 (60% and 70%). Le Château's debt ratio of 0.39 (39%) is therefore well below the norm, and indicates the company will have little difficulty paying down its debts. When considered along with its very high current ratio, we can say with great confidence that Le Château has a very high debt-paying ability at the end of 2012.

How Do Transactions Affect the Ratios?

Companies such as Le Château are keenly aware of how transactions affect their ratios. Lending agreements often require that a company's current ratio not fall below a certain level, or that its debt ratio not rise above a specified threshold. When a company fails to meet one of these conditions, it is said to default on its lending agreements. The penalty for default can be severe, and in the extreme can require immediate repayment of the loan. As noted, Le Château's debt-paying ability is very high, so it is not in danger of default. Companies that do face this danger can pursue a variety of strategies to avoid default, including:

- Increase sales to enhance both net income and current assets.
- Decrease expenses to improve net income and reduce liabilities.
- Sell additional shares to increase cash and shareholders' equity.

Let's use Le Château Inc. to examine the effects of some transactions on the company's current ratio and debt ratio. As shown in the preceding section, Le Château's ratios are as follows:

$$\text{Current ratio} = \frac{\$132,706}{\$42,361} = 3.13 \qquad \text{Debt ratio} = \frac{\$90,689}{\$233,794} = 0.39$$

The managers of any company would be concerned about how inventory purchases, collections on account, expense accruals, and depreciation would affect its ratios. Let's see how Le Château would be affected by some typical transactions. For each transaction, the journal entry helps identify the effects on the ratios. Note that the impact of each transaction is being analyzed in isolation.

a. Issued shares and received cash of $5 million (all journal entry amounts in thousands of dollars).

Journal entry: Cash 5,000
                                   Share capital   5,000

The increase in Cash, a current asset, affects both ratios as follows:

$$\text{Current ratio} = \frac{\$132,706 + \$5,000}{\$42,361} = 3.25 \qquad \text{Debt ratio} = \frac{\$90,689}{\$233,794 + \$5,000} = 0.38$$

The issuance of shares slightly improves both ratios, as current assets increase while liabilities remain unchanged.

b. Paid cash to purchase buildings for $2 million.

Journal entry: Buildings...................................... 2,000
                                   Cash   2,000

Cash, a current asset, decreases, but total assets stay the same; liabilities are unchanged.

$$\text{Current ratio} = \frac{\$132,706 - \$2,000}{\$42,361} = 3.09 \qquad \text{Debt ratio} = \frac{\$90,689}{\$233,794 - \$2,000 + \$2,000} = 0.39$$

The cash purchase of a building hurts the current ratio but doesn't affect the debt ratio.

c. Sold inventory that had been purchased at a cost of $20 million.

Journal entry: Cost of Sales................................ 20,000
                                   Inventory...................................   20,000

This transaction causes a decrease in current and total assets but leaves liabilities unchanged:

$$\text{Current ratio} = \frac{\$132,706 - \$20,000}{\$42,361} = 2.661 \qquad \text{Debt ratio} = \frac{\$90,689}{\$233,794 - \$20,000} = 0.424$$

As a result, both ratios are worse after this entry is recorded.

d. Collected accounts receivable of $1 million.

Journal entry: Cash 1,000
                                   Accounts Receivable   1,000

$$\text{Current ratio} = \frac{\$132,706 + \$1,000 - \$1,000}{\$42,361} = 3.13 \qquad \text{Debt ratio} = \frac{\$90,689}{\$233,794 + \$1,000 - \$1,000} = 0.39$$

This transaction has no effect on total current assets, total assets, or total liabilities, so the ratios do not change.

e. Accrued expenses of $3 million.

Journal entry: Operating Expenses 3,000
                                   Accrued Expenses Payable   3,000

$$\text{Current ratio} = \frac{\$132,706}{\$42,361 + \$3,000} = 2.93 \qquad \text{Debt ratio} = \frac{\$90,689 + \$3,000}{\$233,794} = 0.40$$

After this entry, current and total liabilities increase while assets remain unchanged, so both ratios are slightly hurt by this accrual.

f. Recorded depreciation of $15 million.

Journal entry: Depreciation Expense................... 15,000
                                   Accumulated Depreciation......... 15,000

No liabilities or current assets are affected, but the credit to Accumulated Depreciation reduces total assets, so the debt ratio increases.

$$\text{Current ratio} = \frac{\$132,706}{\$42,361} = 3.13 \qquad \text{Debt ratio} = \frac{\$90,689}{\$233,794 - \$15,000} = 0.41$$

g. Made cash sales of $30 million.

Journal entry: Cash 30,000
                                   Sales Revenue 30,000

These cash sales improve both the current ratio and the debt ratio as follows:

$$\text{Current ratio} = \frac{\$132,706 + \$30,000}{\$42,361} = 3.841 \qquad \text{Debt ratio} = \frac{\$90,689}{\$233,794 + \$30,000} = 0.344$$

The following Decision Guidelines summarize the key factors to consider when evaluating a company's debt-paying ability.

◀ DECISION GUIDELINES ▶

EVALUATE DEBT-PAYING ABILITY USING NET WORKING CAPITAL, THE CURRENT RATIO, AND THE DEBT RATIO

In general, a *larger* amount of net working capital is preferable to a smaller amount. Similarly, a *high* current ratio is preferable to a low current ratio. *Increases* in net working capital and *increases* in the current ratio improve debt-paying ability. By contrast, a *low* debt ratio is preferable to a high debt ratio. Improvement in debt-paying ability is indicated by a decrease in the debt ratio.

   No single ratio gives the whole picture about a company. Therefore, lenders and investors use many ratios to evaluate a company. Let's apply what we have learned. Suppose you are a loan officer at the Bank of Montreal, and Le Château has asked you for a $20 million loan to remodel its stores. How will you make this loan decision? The Decision Guidelines show how bankers and investors use two key ratios.

USING NET WORKING CAPITAL AND THE CURRENT RATIO

Decision	Guidelines
How can you measure a company's ability to pay current liabilities with current assets?	Net working capital = Total current assets − Total current liabilities $$\text{Current ratio} = \frac{\text{Total current assets}}{\text{Total current liabilities}}$$
Who uses net working capital and the current ratio for decision making?	*Lenders and other creditors*, who must predict whether a borrower can pay its current liabilities. *Investors*, who know that a company that cannot pay its debts is not a good investment because it may go bankrupt. *Managers*, who must have enough cash to pay the company's current liabilities.
What are good net working capital and current ratio values?	There is no correct answer for this. It depends on the industry as well as the individual entity's ability to quickly generate cash from operations. An entity with strong operating cash flow can operate successfully with a low amount of net working capital as long as cash comes in through operations at least as fast as accounts payable become due. A current ratio of, say, 1.10–1.20 is sometimes sufficient. An entity with relatively low cash flow from operations needs a higher current ratio of, say, 1.30–1.50. Traditionally, a current ratio of 2.00 was considered ideal. Recently, acceptable values have decreased as companies have been able to operate more efficiently. Today, a current ratio of 1.50 is considered strong. Although not ideal, cash-rich companies can operate with a current ratio below 1.0.

USING THE DEBT RATIO

Decision	Guidelines
How can you measure a company's ability to pay total liabilities?	$$\text{Debt ratio} = \frac{\text{Total liabilities}}{\text{Total assets}}$$
Who uses the debt ratio for decision making?	*Lenders and other creditors,* who must predict whether a borrower can pay its debts. *Investors*, who know that a company that cannot pay its debts is not a good investment because it may go bankrupt. *Managers*, who must have enough assets to pay the company's debts.
What is a good debt ratio value?	Depends on the industry: A company with strong cash flow can operate successfully with a high debt ratio of, say, 0.70–0.80. A company with weak cash flow needs a lower debt ratio of, say, 0.50–0.60. Traditionally, a debt ratio of 0.50 was considered ideal. Recently, values have increased as companies have been able to operate more efficiently. Today, a normal value of the debt ratio is around 0.60–0.70.

SUMMARY OF CHAPTER 3

LEARNING OBJECTIVE	SUMMARY
1. **Explain** how accrual accounting differs from cash-basis accounting	When using the cash basis of accounting, we record only business transactions involving the receipt or payment of cash. All other business transactions are ignored. In contrast, when using accrual accounting, *the receipt or payment of cash is irrelevant* to deciding whether a business transaction should be recorded. What matters is whether the business has acquired an asset, earned revenue, taken on a liability, or incurred an expense. If it has, the transaction is recorded in the accounting records.
2. **Apply** the revenue and expense recognition principles	According to the revenue recognition principle, a transaction must satisfy *all three* of these conditions before the business can recognize revenue: 1. The control and benefits of the goods have been transferred to the customer, or the services have been provided to the customer. 2. The amount of revenue can be reliably measured. 3. It is probable that the business will receive the economic benefits associated with the transaction, which usually come in the form of cash receipts. The expense recognition principle sets out the two criteria that must be satisfied before an expense can be recognized: 1. There has been a decrease in future economic benefits caused by a decrease in an asset *or* an increase in a liability. 2. The expense can be reliably measured.
3. **Record** adjusting journal entries	Under accrual accounting, we must record adjusting journal entries at the end of each accounting period to ensure that all assets and liabilities have been recorded at period end and that all revenues earned and expenses incurred during the period have been included in the accounts. There are three main types of adjusting entries: deferrals, depreciation (amortization under ASPE), and accruals. Deferrals include adjustments related to transactions for which a business has received or paid cash in advance of delivering or receiving goods and services. Depreciation adjustments are made to expense the benefits of capital assets that have been used up during the period. Accruals include adjustments related to revenues earned or expenses incurred prior to any cash or invoices changing hands.
4. **Prepare** the financial statements	The financial statements can be prepared using the account balances from the adjusted trial balance. The income statement is prepared first, followed by the statement of retained earnings, and then the balance sheet. A classified balance sheet reports current assets and liabilities separately from their non-current counterparts. A balance sheet prepared using a report format lists assets first, followed by liabilities, and then shareholders' equity. A balance sheet in account format lists assets on the left and liabilities and shareholders' equity on the right. A single-step income statement reports all revenue items together, followed by all expense items, whereas a multi-step income statement splits revenues and expenses into two or more categories to highlight important subtotals (e.g., gross profit, income from operations) useful to decision makers.

5. **Record** closing journal entries

At the end of each fiscal year we must record closing entries, which are journal entries that transfer the balances in all revenue, expense, and dividend accounts into the Retained Earnings account. After these entries, all the income statement and dividend accounts have zero balances, leaving them ready to begin tracking revenues, expenses, and dividends for the next fiscal year.

6. **Analyze** and **evaluate** a company's debt-paying ability

There are no differences between IFRS and ASPE in this chapter.

We can evaluate a company's debt-paying ability using net working capital, the current ratio, and the debt ratio. A business's net working capital equals its total current assets minus its total current liabilities, and this figure should be sufficiently in excess of zero for a company to avoid debt-paying troubles. The current ratio equals total current assets divided by total current liabilities, so a higher current ratio is correlated with a stronger debt-paying ability. The debt ratio is calculated by dividing total liabilities by total assets, so for this ratio, a lower ratio indicates a higher debt-paying ability.

END-OF-CHAPTER SUMMARY PROBLEM

This problem follows on the mid-chapter summary problem that begins on page 124.

Requirements

1. Make Goldsmith Inc.'s closing entries at December 31, 2014. Explain what the closing entries accomplish and why they are necessary.
2. Post the closing entries to Retained Earnings and compare Retained Earnings' ending balance with the amount reported on the balance sheet on page 128. The two amounts should be the same.
3. Prepare Goldsmith Inc.'s classified balance sheet to identify the company's current assets and current liabilities. (Goldsmith Inc. has no long-term liabilities.) Then compute the company's current ratio and debt ratio at December 31, 2014.
4. The top management of Goldsmith Inc. has asked you for a $500,000 loan to expand the business. They propose to pay off the loan over a 10-year period. Recompute Goldsmith Inc.'s debt ratio assuming you make the loan.

Name: Goldsmith Inc.
Industry: Service corporation
Fiscal Period: Year ended December 31, 2014
Key Fact: Existing, ongoing business

ANSWERS

Requirement 1

2014			(in thousands)	
Dec. 31	Service Revenue		330	
	Retained Earnings			330
31	Retained Earnings		259	
	Salary Expense			177
	Depreciation Expense—Furniture and Fixtures			20
	Depreciation Expense—Building			10
	Supplies Expense			4
	Income Tax Expense			35
	Miscellaneous Expense			13
31	Retained Earnings		65	
	Dividends			65

To close revenue accounts, debit each revenue account for the amounts reported on the income statement, and credit Retained Earnings for the total of the debits.

To close expense accounts, credit each expense account for the amounts reported on the income statement, and debit Retained Earnings for the total of the credits.

To close the dividend accounts, credit each dividend account for the amounts reported on the statement of retained earnings, and debit Retained Earnings for the total of the credits.

Explanation of Closing Entries

The closing entries set the balance of each revenue, expense, and Dividends account back to zero for the start of the next accounting period. They also add the year's net income to and deduct any dividends declared from Retained Earnings, so this account accurately reflects the earnings that have been retained by the company.

Requirement 2

The balance in the Retained Earnings T-account should equal the Retained Earnings balance reported on the balance sheet.

Retained Earnings

Clo.	259		193
Clo.	65	Clo.	330
		Bal.	199

The balance in the Retained Earnings account agrees with the amount reported on the balance sheet, as it should.

Requirement 3

The title must include the name of the company, "Balance Sheet," and the date of the balance sheet. It shows the financial position on one specific date.

The classified balance sheet uses the same accounts and balances as those on page 128. However, segregate current assets (assets expected to be converted to cash within one year) from capital assets, and segregate current liabilities (liabilities expected to be paid or settled within one year) from other liabilities.

Goldsmith Inc.
Balance Sheet
As at December 31, 2014

(amounts in thousands)

Assets			Liabilities	
Current assets			Current liabilities	
Cash		$198	Accounts payable	$380
Accounts receivable		382	Salary payable	5
Supplies........................		2	Unearned service revenue	13
Total current assets		582	Income tax payable	35
Capital assets			Total current liabilities	433
Furniture and fixtures	$100			
Less Accumulated			**Shareholders' Equity**	
depreciation..............	(60)	40	Share capital	100
Building........................	$250		Retained earnings.................	199
Less Accumulated			Total shareholders' equity.....	299
depreciation..............	(140)	110	Total liabilities and	
Total assets		$732	shareholders' equity	$732

$$\text{Current ratio} = \frac{\text{Current assets}}{\text{Current liabilities}}$$

$$\text{Debt ratio} = \frac{\text{Total liabilities}}{\text{Total assets}}$$

$$\text{Current ratio} = \frac{\$582}{\$433} = 1.34 \qquad \text{Debt ratio} = \frac{\$433}{\$732} = 0.59$$

Requirement 4

You must add $500,000 to the current liabilities and total assets to account for the additional $500,000 loan.

$$\text{Debt ratio assuming the loan is made} = \frac{\$433 + \$500}{\$732 + \$500} = \frac{\$933}{\$1,232} = 0.76$$

STOP + THINK (3-1)	**ANSWERS**
	1. No, Windsor Group has yet to perform any services, so it cannot recognize revenue. It can begin to recognize revenue as it performs the services the customer has paid for.	2. No, Windsor group has not experienced a decrease in future economic benefits, so it has not incurred an expense. This transaction results in prepaid rent, an asset that will benefit the company over the next three months.

STOP + THINK (3-2)	**ANSWERS**

Supplies Expense ($5,000 + $7,000 − $3,000) 9,000

    Supplies...   9,000

To adjust supplies at period end.

The ending balance in the Supplies account is $3,000, the value of supplies on hand at the end of the month.

STOP + THINK (3-3)	**ANSWERS**

$16,500 − $275 − $275 = $15,950.

STOP + THINK (3-4)	**ANSWERS**

Interest Receivable 125

    Interest Revenue   125

To accrue interest revenue.

Review Accrual Accounting and Income

QUICK CHECK   (ANSWERS ARE GIVEN ON PAGE 169.)

1. On September 1, Lost Forest Apartments Ltd. received $3,600 from a tenant for three months' rent. The receipt was credited to Unearned Rent Revenue. What adjusting entry is needed on September 30?

    a. Unearned Rent Revenue 2,400

        Rent Revenue.......................   2,400

    b. Rent Revenue 1,200

        Unearned Rent Revenue   1,200

    c. Unearned Rent Revenue 1,200

        Rent Revenue.......................   1,200

    d. Cash... 1,200

        Rent Revenue.......................   1,200

2. The following normal balances appear on the _adjusted_ trial balance of Ojibway Industries:

Equipment	$90,000
Accumulated depreciation, equipment	15,000
Depreciation expense, equipment......................................	5,000

The carrying amount of the equipment is
   a. $85,000.
   b. $70,000.
   c. $75,000.
   d. $60,000.

3. Jones Company Ltd. purchased supplies for $1,000 during 2014. At year-end Jones had $300 of supplies left. The company had no supplies at the beginning of the year. The adjusting entry should
   a. debit Supplies, $700.
   b. debit Supplies Expense, $700.
   c. credit Supplies, $300.
   d. debit Supplies, $300.

4. The accountant for Moreau Ltd. failed to make the adjusting entry to record depreciation for the current year. The effect of this error is
   a. assets are overstated; shareholders' equity and net income are understated.
   b. assets and expenses are understated, and net income is understated.
   c. net income is overstated, and liabilities are understated.
   d. assets, net income, and shareholders' equity are all overstated.

5. Interest due on a loan payable at December 31 equals $125. What adjusting entry is required to accrue this expense?
   a. Dr. Interest Payable for $125, Cr. Interest Expense for $125
   b. Dr. Interest Expense for $125, Cr. Cash for $125
   c. Dr. Interest Receivable for $125, Cr. Interest Revenue for $125
   d. Dr. Interest Expense for $125, Cr. Interest Payable for $125

6. If a real estate company fails to accrue commission revenue,
   a. liabilities are overstated, and owners' equity is understated.
   b. assets are understated, and net income is understated.
   c. net income is understated, and shareholders' equity is overstated.
   d. revenues are understated, and net income is overstated.

7. All of the following statements are true except one. Which statement is false?
   a. Adjusting entries are required for a business that uses the cash basis.
   b. Accrual accounting produces better information than cash-basis accounting.
   c. Expenses are identified and recorded as they are incurred and deducted from revenue earned during the same period.
   d. A fiscal year does not have to end on December 31.

8. The account Unearned Revenue is a(n)
   a. revenue.
   b. expense.
   c. asset.
   d. liability.

9. Adjusting entries
   a. are recorded at the end of an accounting period.
   b. are needed to measure the period's net income or net loss.
   c. update the accounts.
   d. All of the above

10. An adjusting entry that debits an expense and credits a related liability is which type?
    a. Accrued expense
    b. Cash expense
    c. Prepaid expense
    d. Depreciation expense

Use the following data for Questions 11 and 12.

Here are key figures from the balance sheet of Davis Ltd. at the end of 2014 (in thousands):

	December 31, 2014
Total assets (of which 40% are current)	$4,000
Current liabilities	800
Loan payable (long-term)	1,200
Share capital	1,500
Retained earnings	500
Total liabilities and shareholders' equity	$4,000

11. Davis's current ratio at the end of 2014 is
    a. 6.25.
    b. 2.0.
    c. 3.75.
    d. 2.24.

12. Davis's debt ratio at the end of 2014 is
    a. 42% (rounded).
    b. 17% (rounded).
    c. 60%.
    d. 50%.

13. On a trial balance, which of the following would indicate that an error has been made?
    a. Service Revenue has a debit balance.
    b. Salary Expense has a debit balance.
    c. Accumulated Depreciation has a credit balance.
    d. All of the above indicate errors.

14. The entry to close Management Fees Revenue would be
    a. Management Fees Revenue does not need to be closed out.
    b. Dr. Retained Earnings   Cr. Management Fees Revenue
    c. Dr. Management Fees Revenue   Cr. Retained Earnings
    d. Dr. Management Fees Revenue   Cr. Service Revenue

15. Which of the following accounts is not closed out at the end of each year?
    a. Accumulated Depreciation
    b. Depreciation Expense
    c. Dividends
    d. Interest Revenue

16. Suppose Starbucks Corporation borrows $50 million on a 10-year loan payable. How does this transaction affect the company's current and debt ratios?
    a. Improves both ratios.
    b. Improves the current ratio and hurts the debt ratio.
    c. Hurts both ratios.
    d. Hurts the current ratio and improves the debt ratio.

Accounting Vocabulary

account format A balance sheet format that lists assets on the left side and liabilities above shareholders' equity on the right side. (p. 122)

accrual An adjustment related to revenues earned or expenses incurred prior to any cash or invoice changing hands. (p. 115)

accrual accounting A basis of accounting that records transactions based on whether a business has acquired an asset, earned rev-enue, taken on a liability, or incurred an expense, regardless of whether cash is involved. (p. 106)

accrued expense An expense that has been incurred but not yet paid or invoiced. (p. 115)

accrued revenue A revenue that has been earned but not yet collected or invoiced. (p. 116)

accumulated depreciation The account showing the sum of all depreciation expense from the date of acquiring a capital asset.   (p. 114)

adjusted trial balance A list of all the ledger accounts with their adjusted balances.   (p. 118)

carrying amount (of a capital asset) The asset's cost minus accumulated depreciation.   (p. 114)

cash-basis accounting Accounting that records only transactions in which cash is received or paid.   (p. 106)

classified balance sheet A balance sheet that shows current assets separate from long-term assets, and current liabilities separate from long-term liabilities.   (p. 122)

closing entries Entries that transfer the revenue, expense, and dividend balances from these respective accounts to the Retained Earnings account.   (p. 129)

contra account An account that always has a companion account and whose normal balance is opposite that of the companion account.   (p. 114)

current ratio Current assets divided by current liabilities. Measures a company's ability to pay current liabilities with current assets.   (p. 131)

debt ratio Ratio of total liabilities to total assets. States the proportion of a company's assets that is financed with debt.   (p. 132)

deferral An adjustment related to a transaction for which a business has received or paid cash in advance of delivering or receiving goods or services.   (p. 111)

depreciation An expense to recognize the portion of a capital asset's economic benefits that has been used up during an accounting period.   (p. 113)

liquidity Measure of how quickly an item can be converted to cash.   (p. 122)

multi-step income statement An income statement that contains subtotals to highlight important relationships between revenues and expenses.   (p. 123)

net working capital Current assets − current liabilities. Measures the ease with which a company will be able to use its current assets to pay off its current liabilities.   (p. 131)

permanent accounts Assets, liabilities, and shareholders' equity accounts, which all have balances that carry forward to the next fiscal year.   (p. 129)

report format A balance sheet format that lists assets at the top, followed by liabilities and then shareholders' equity.   (p. 122)

single-step income statement Lists all revenues together and all expenses together; there is only one step in arriving at net income.   (p. 122)

temporary accounts Revenue, expense, and dividend accounts, which do not have balances that carry forward to the next fiscal year.   (p. 129)

unearned revenue A liability that arises when a business receives cash from a customer prior to providing the related goods or services.   (p. 112)

Assess Your Progress

MyAccountingLab   Make the grade with MyAccountingLab: The Exercises, Quizzes, and Problems (A set) marked in red can be found on MyAccountingLab. You can practise them as often as you want, and most feature step-by-step guided instructions to help you find the right answer.

SHORT EXERCISES

LEARNING OBJECTIVE ❶
Apply accrual accounting

S3-1 Marquis Inc. made sales of $700 million during 2014. Of this amount, Marquis Inc. collected cash for all but $30 million. The company's cost of goods sold was $300 million, and all other expenses for the year totalled $350 million. Also during 2014, Marquis Inc. paid $400 million for its inventory and $280 million for everything else. Beginning cash was $100 million. Marquis Inc.'s top management is interviewing you for a job and you are asked two questions:

a. How much was Marquis Inc.'s net income for 2014?
b. How much was Marquis Inc.'s cash balance at the end of 2014?

LEARNING OBJECTIVE ❶
Apply accrual accounting

S3-2 Great Sporting Goods Inc. began 2014 owing notes payable of $4.0 million. During 2014, the company borrowed $2.6 million on notes payable and paid off $2.5 million of notes payable from prior years. Interest expense for the year was $1.0 million, including $0.2 million of interest payable accrued at December 31, 2014. Show what Great Sporting Goods Inc. should report for these facts on the following financial statements:

- Income Statement
    Interest expense

- Balance Sheet
    Notes payable
    Interest payable

S3-3 Ford Canada sells large fleets of vehicles to auto rental companies, such as Budget and Avis. Suppose Budget is negotiating with Ford to purchase 1,000 Explorers. Write a short paragraph to explain to Ford when the company should, and should not, record this sales revenue and the related cost of goods sold.

LEARNING OBJECTIVE ❷

Apply the revenue and expense recognition principles

S3-4 Answer the following questions about prepaid expenses:

a. On November 1, World Travel Ltd. prepaid $6,000 for three months' rent. Give the adjusting entry to record rent expense at December 31. Include the date of the entry and an explanation. Then post all amounts to the two accounts involved, and show their balances at December 31. World Travel adjusts the accounts only at December 31.

b. On December 1, World Travel paid $800 for supplies. At December 31, World Travel has $500 of supplies on hand. Make the required journal entry at December 31. Post all accounts to the accounts and show their balances at December 31.

LEARNING OBJECTIVE ❸

Record adjusting journal entries

S3-5 Suppose that on January 1, Roots Ltd. paid cash of $30,000 for computers that are expected to remain useful for three years. At the end of three years, the computers' values are expected to be zero.

1. Make journal entries to record (a) the purchase of the computers on January 1, and (b) the annual depreciation on December 31. Include dates and explanations, and use the following accounts: Computer Equipment; Accumulated Depreciation—Computer Equipment; and Depreciation Expense—Computer Equipment.
2. Post to the accounts and show their balances at December 31.
3. What is the computers' carrying amount at December 31?
4. Which account(s) will Roots report on the income statement for the year? Which accounts will appear on the balance sheet of December 31? Show the amount to report for each item on both financial statements.

LEARNING OBJECTIVE ❸❹

Record depreciation and prepare financial statements

S3-6 During 2014, Many Miles Trucking paid salary expense of $40 million. At December 31, Many Miles accrued salary expense of $2 million. Many Miles paid $1.9 million to its employees on January 3, 2015, the company's next payday after the end of the 2014 year. For this sequence of transactions, show what Many Miles would include on its 2014 income statement and its balance sheet at the end of 2014.

LEARNING OBJECTIVE ❷

Apply the revenue and expense recognition principles

S3-7 Schwartz & Associates Inc. borrowed $100,000 on October 1 by signing a note payable to Scotiabank. The interest expense for each month is $500. The loan agreement requires Schwartz & Associates Inc. to pay interest on December 31.

1. Make Schwartz & Associates Inc.'s adjusting entry to accrue interest expense and interest payable at October 31, at November 30, and at December 31. Date each entry and include its explanation.
2. Post all three entries to the Interest Payable account. You need not take the balance of the account at the end of each month.
3. Record the payment of three months' interest at December 31.

LEARNING OBJECTIVE ❸

Record adjusting journal entries

S3-8 Return to the situation in S3-7. Here you are accounting for the same transactions on the books of Scotiabank, which lent the money to Schwartz & Associates Inc. Perform all three steps in S3-7 for Scotiabank using the bank's own accounts.

LEARNING OBJECTIVE ❸

Record adjusting journal entries

S3-9 Write a paragraph explaining why unearned revenues are liabilities instead of revenues. In your explanation, use the following actual example: *Maclean's* magazine collects cash from subscribers in advance and later delivers magazines to subscribers over a one-year period. Explain what happens to the unearned subscription revenue over the course of a year as *Maclean's* delivers magazines to subscribers. Into what account does the unearned subscription revenue go as *Maclean's* delivers magazines?

Give the journal entries that *Maclean's* would make to:

a. Collect $40,000 of subscription revenue in advance.
b. Record earning $10,000 of subscription revenue.

LEARNING OBJECTIVE ❷❸

Apply the revenue recognition principle and record adjusting journal entries

LEARNING OBJECTIVE ❸
Report prepaid expenses

S3-10 Birdie Golf Ltd. prepaid three months' rent ($6,000) on January 1. At March 31, Birdie prepared a trial balance and made the necessary adjusting entry at the end of the quarter. Birdie adjusts its accounts every quarter of the fiscal year, which ends December 31.

What amount appears for Prepaid Rent on

a. Birdie's unadjusted trial balance at March 31?
b. Birdie's adjusted trial balance at March 31?

What amount appears for Rent Expense on

a. Birdie's unadjusted trial balance at March 31?
b. Birdie's adjusted trial balance at March 31?

LEARNING OBJECTIVE ❸
Record adjusting journal entries

S3-11 Josie Inc. collects cash from customers two ways:

1. Accrued Revenue. Some customers pay Josie after Josie has performed service for the customer. During 2014, Josie made sales of $50,000 on account and later received cash of $40,000 on account from these customers.
2. Unearned Revenue. A few customers pay Josie in advance, and Josie later performs service for the customer. During 2014, Josie collected $7,000 cash in advance and later earned $6,000 of this amount.

Journalize the following for Josie:

a. Earning service revenue of $50,000 on account and then collecting $40,000 on account
b. Receiving $7,000 in advance and then earning $6,000 as service revenue

LEARNING OBJECTIVE ❹
Prepare the financial statements

S3-12 Entertainment Centre Ltd. reported the following data at March 31, 2014, with amounts adapted and in thousands:

Retained earnings, March 31, 2014.....	$ 1,300	Cost of goods sold....................	$126,000
Accounts receivable.........................	27,700	Cash...	900
Net revenues	174,500	Property and equipment, net....	7,200
Total current liabilities.....................	53,600	Share capital.............................	26,000
All other expenses	45,000	Inventories	33,000
Other current assets	4,800	Long-term liabilities	13,500
Other assets.....................................	24,300	Dividends.................................	0

You are the CFO responsible for reporting Entertainment Centre Ltd. (ECL) results. Use these data to prepare ECL's income statement for the year ended March 31, 2014, the statement of retained earnings for the year ended March 31, 2014, and the classified balance sheet at March 31, 2014. Use the report format for the balance sheet. Draw arrows linking the three statements to explain the information flows between the statements.

LEARNING OBJECTIVE ❺
Prepare closing entries

S3-13 Use the Entertainment Centre Ltd. data in S3-12 to make the company's closing entries at March 31, 2014. Then set up a T-account for Retained Earnings and post to that account. Compare Retained Earnings' ending balance to the amount reported on ECL's statement of retained earnings and balance sheet. What do you find? Why is this important?

LEARNING OBJECTIVE ❻
Evaluate a company's debt-paying ability

S3-14 Use the Entertainment Centre Ltd. data in S3-12 to compute ECL's

a. Current ratio
b. Debt ratio

Round to two decimal places. Report to the CEO whether these values look strong, weak, or middle-of-the-road.

LEARNING OBJECTIVE ❻
Use the financial statements

S3-15 Use the Entertainment Centre Ltd. data in S3-12 to answer the following questions.

1. Was the net revenue high enough to cover all of ECL's costs?
2. What could you do to improve this situation?

EXERCISES

E3-16 During 2014, Organic Foods Inc. made sales of $4,000 (assume all on account) and collected cash of $4,100 from customers. Operating expenses totalled $800, all paid in cash. At December 31, 2014, Organic Foods' customers owed the company $400. Organic Foods owed creditors $700 on account. All amounts are in millions.

1. For these facts, show what Organic Foods Inc. would report on the following 2014 financial statements:
   • Income statement
   • Balance sheet
2. Suppose Organic Foods had used cash-basis accounting. What would Organic Foods Ltd. have reported for these facts?

LEARNING OBJECTIVE ❶
Apply accrual and cash-basis accounting

E3-17 During 2014, Valley Sales Inc. earned revenues of $500,000 on account. Valley Sales collected $410,000 from customers during the year. Expenses totalled $420,000, and the related cash payments were $400,000. Show what Valley Sales would report on its 2014 income statement under the

a. Cash basis
b. Accrual basis

Compute net income under both bases of accounting. Which basis measures net income more appropriately? Explain your answer.

LEARNING OBJECTIVE ❶
Apply accrual and cash-basis accounting

E3-18 During 2014, Dish Networks Inc. earned revenues of $700 million. Expenses totalled $540 million. Dish collected all but $20 million of the revenues and paid $530 million on its expenses. Dish's top managers are evaluating the year, and they ask you the following questions:

a. Under accrual accounting, what amount of revenue should the company report for 2014? Is the $700 million revenue earned, or is it the amount of cash actually collected?
b. Under accrual accounting, what amount of total expense should Dish report for the year—$540 million or $530 million?
c. Which financial statement reports revenues and expenses? Which statement reports cash receipts and cash payments?

LEARNING OBJECTIVE ❷
Recognize revenue and record expenses under accrual basis of accounting

E3-19 Write a short paragraph to explain in your own words the concept of depreciation as used in accounting.

LEARNING OBJECTIVE ❷
Apply expense recognition principles

E3-20 Answer each of the following questions.

a. Employees earned wages of $20,000 during the current month, but were not paid until the following month. Should the employer record any expenses at the end of the current month?
b. The current year has been a poor one, so the business is planning to delay the recording of some expenses until they are paid early the following year. Is this acceptable?
c. A dentist performs a surgical operation and bills the patient's insurance company. It may take three months to collect from the insurance company. Should the dentist record revenue now or wait until cash is collected?
d. A construction company is building a highway system, and construction will take three years. How do you think it should record the revenue it earns—over the year or over three years?
e. A utility bill is received on December 30 and will be paid next year. When should the company record utility expense?

LEARNING OBJECTIVE ❷
Apply revenue and expense recognition principles

E3-21 An accountant made the following adjustments at December 31, the end of the accounting period:

a. Prepaid insurance, beginning, $700. Payments for insurance during the period, $2,100. Prepaid insurance, ending, $800.
b. Interest revenue accrued, $900.

LEARNING OBJECTIVE ❸
Record adjusting journal entries and analyze their effects on net income

c. Unearned service revenue, beginning, $800. Unearned service revenue, ending, $300.
d. Depreciation, $6,200.
e. Employees' salaries owed for three days of a five-day work week; weekly payroll, $9,000.
f. Income before income tax expense, $20,000. Income tax rate is 25%.

Requirements

1. Journalize the adjusting entries.
2. Suppose the adjustments were not made. Compute the overall overstatement or understatement of net income as a result of the omission of these adjustments.

LEARNING OBJECTIVE **1**

Apply accrual accounting

E3-22 Green Leaf Fertilizer Ltd. experienced four situations for its supplies. Compute the amounts indicated by question marks for each situation. For situations 1 and 2, journalize the needed transaction. Consider each situation separately.

	Situation			
	1	2	3	4
Beginning supplies	$ 500	$1,000	$ 300	$ 900
Payments for supplies during the year	?	3,100	?	1,100
Total amount to account for	$1,300	?	?	2,000
Ending supplies	400	500	700	?
Supplies expense	$ 900	$?	$ 700	$1,400

LEARNING OBJECTIVE **3**

Record adjusting entries

earned in prior year: post last Dec.

get rid of unearned Revenue.

½ earned.

E3-23 Clark Motors Ltd. faced the following situations. Journalize the adjusting entry needed at year-end (December 31, 2014) for each situation. Consider each fact separately.

a. The business has interest expense of $9,000 early in January 2015.
b. Interest revenue of $3,000 has been earned but not yet received.
c. When the business collected $12,000 in advance three months ago, the accountant debited Cash and credited Unearned Revenue. The client was paying for two cars, one delivered in December, the other to be delivered in February 2015.
d. Salary expense is $1,000 per day—Monday through Friday—and the business pays employees each Friday. For example purposes, assume that this year, December 31 falls on a Tuesday.
e. The unadjusted balance of the Supplies account is $3,100. The total cost of supplies on hand is $800.
f. Equipment was purchased at the beginning of this year at a cost of $60,000. The equipment's useful life is five years. Record the depreciation for this year and then determine the equipment's carrying amount.

LEARNING OBJECTIVE **3**

Record adjusting entries directly in T-accounts

E3-24 The accounting records of Lalonde Ltée include the following unadjusted balances at May 31: Accounts Receivable, $1,300; Supplies, $900; Salary Payable, $0; Unearned Service Revenue, $800; Service Revenue, $14,400; Salary Expense, $4,200; Supplies Expense, $0. As Lalonde's accountant you have developed the following data for the May 31 adjusting entries:

a. Supplies on hand, $300
b. Salary owed to employees, $2,000
c. Service revenue accrued, $600
d. Unearned service revenue that has been earned, $700

Open the foregoing T-accounts with their beginning balances. Then record the adjustments directly in the accounts, keying each adjustment amount by letter. Show each account's adjusted balance. Journal entries are not required.

E3-25 The adjusted trial balance of Honeybee Hams Inc. follows.

LEARNING OBJECTIVE ❹

Prepare the financial statements

Honeybee Hams Inc.
Adjusted Trial Balance
December 31, 2014

	Adjusted Trial Balance	
(in thousands)	Debit	Credit
Cash	$ 3,300	
Accounts receivable	1,800	
Inventories	1,100	
Prepaid expenses	1,900	
Capital assets	6,600	
Accumulated depreciation		$ 2,400
Other assets	9,900	
Accounts payable		7,700
Income tax payable		600
Other liabilities		2,200
Share capital		4,900
Retained earnings (December 31, 2013)		4,500
Dividends	1,700	
Sales revenue		41,000
Cost of goods sold	25,000	
Selling, administrative, and general expense	10,000	
Income tax expense	2,000	
	$63,300	$63,300

Requirement

Prepare Honeybee Hams' income statement and statement of retained earnings for the year ended December 31, 2014, and its balance sheet on that date. Draw arrows linking the three statements.

E3-26 The adjusted trial balances of Tower Development Inc. for March 31, 2013, and March 31, 2014, include these amounts (in millions):

LEARNING OBJECTIVE ❹

Determine financial statement amounts

	2014	2013
Receivables	$300	$200
Prepaid insurance	180	110
Accrued liabilities (for other operating expenses)	700	600

Tower Development completed these transactions during the year ended March 31, 2014.

Collections from customers	$20,800
Payment of prepaid insurance	400
Cash payments for other operating expenses	4,100

Compute the amount of sales revenue, insurance expense, and other operating expense to report on the income statement for the year ended March 31, 2014.

LEARNING OBJECTIVE ❹

Report on the financial statements

E3-27 This question deals with the items and the amounts that two entities, Mountain Services Inc. (Mountain) and City of Squamish (Squamish), should report in their financial statements.

1. On March 31, 2014, Mountain collected $12,000 in advance from Squamish, a client. Under the contract, Mountain is obligated to provide consulting services for Squamish evenly during the year ended March 31, 2014. Assume you are Mountain.

   Mountain's income statement for the year ended December 31, 2014, will report _____ of $_____.
   Mountain's balance sheet at December 31, 2014, will report _____ of $_____.

2. Assume that you are Squamish. Squamish's income statement for the year ended December 31, will report _____ of $_____.

   Squamish's balance sheet at December 31, 2014, will report _____ of $_____.

LEARNING OBJECTIVE ❶

Apply accrual accounting

E3-28 This exercise builds from a simple situation to a slightly more complex situation. Rogers, a wireless phone service provider, collects cash in advance from customers. All amounts are in millions.

   Assume Rogers collected $400 in advance during 2014 and at year-end still owed customers phone service worth $90.

Requirements

1. Show what Rogers will report for 2014 on its

   • Income statement
   • Balance sheet

2. Use the same facts for Rogers as in Requirement 1. Further, assume Rogers reported unearned service revenue of $80 at the end of 2013.

   Show what Rogers will report for 2014 on the same financial statements. Explain why your answer differs from your answer to Requirement 1.

LEARNING OBJECTIVE ❺

Record closing entries

E3-29 Prepare the required closing entries for the following selected accounts from the records of SouthWest Transport Inc. at December 31, 2014 (amounts in thousands):

Cost of services sold	$11,600	Service revenue	$23,600
Accumulated depreciation	17,800	Depreciatiation expense	4,100
Selling, general, and		Other revenue	600
administrative expense	6,900	Income tax expense	400
Retained earnings,		Dividends	400
December 31, 2013	1,900	Income tax payable	300

How much net income did SouthWest Transport Inc. earn during the year ended December 31, 2014? Prepare a T-account for Retained Earnings to show the December 31, 2014, balance of Retained Earnings.

E3-30 The unadjusted trial balance and the income statement amounts from the December 31, 2014, adjusted trial balance of Yosaf Portraits Ltd. are given below.

LEARNING OBJECTIVE ❸❺

Identify and record adjusting and closing entries

Yosaf Portraits Ltd.
Trial Balance
December 31, 2014

Account Title	Unadjusted Trial Balance		From the Adjusted Trial Balance	
Cash	10,200			
Prepaid rent	1,100			
Equipment	32,100			
Accumulated depreciation		3,800		
Accounts payable		4,600		
Salary payable				
Unearned service revenue		8,400		
Income tax payable				
Note payable, long term		10,000		
Share capital		8,700		
Retained earnings		1,300		
Dividends	1,000			
Service revenue		12,800		19,500
Salary expense	4,000		4,900	
Rent expense	1,200		1,400	
Depreciation expense			300	
Income tax expense			1,600	
	49,600	49,600	8,200	19,500
Net income			11,300	
			19,500	19,500

Requirement

Journalize the adjusting and closing entries of Yosaf Portraits Ltd. at December 31, 2014. There was only one adjustment to Service Revenue.

E3-31 Refer to exercise E3-30.

LEARNING OBJECTIVE ❹❻

Prepare a classified balance sheet and evaluate a company's debt-paying ability

Requirements

1. After solving E3-30, use the data in that exercise to prepare Yosaf Portraits Ltd.'s classified balance sheet at December 31, 2014. Use the report format. First you must compute the adjusted balance for several balance sheet accounts.
2. Compute Yosaf Portraits Ltd.'s current ratio and debt ratio at December 31, 2014. A year ago, the current ratio was 1.55 and the debt ratio was 0.45. Indicate whether the company's ability to pay its debts—both current and total—improved or deteriorated during the current year.

E3-32 Le Gasse Inc. reported this information at December 31:

LEARNING OBJECTIVE ❻

Evaluate debt-paying ability

	2014	2013	2012
Current assets	$ 20	$ 15	$ 8
Total assets	50	57	35
Current liabilities	10	8	6
Total liabilities	20	20	10
Sales revenue	204	190	175
Net income	28	20	25

Requirements

1. Using this information, calculate the current ratio and the debt ratio for 2014, 2013, and 2012.
2. Explain whether each ratio improved or deteriorated over the three years. In each case, what does your answer indicate?

SERIAL EXERCISE

Exercise E3-33 continues the Web Marketing Services Inc. situation begun in exercise E2-25 of Chapter 2 (p. 90).

LEARNING OBJECTIVE ❸❹❺❻

Adjust the accounts, prepare the financial statements, close the accounts, and use financial statements to evaluate the business

E3-33

Refer to exercise E2-25 of Chapter 2. Start from the trial balance and the posted T-accounts prepared at January 18, 2014. Later in January, the business completed these transactions:

2014		
Jan.	21	Received $900 in advance for marketing work to be performed evenly over the next 30 days
	21	Hired a secretary to be paid on the 15th day of each month
	26	Paid $900 on account
	28	Collected $600 on account
	31	Declared and paid dividends of $1,000

Requirements

1. Open these T-accounts: Accumulated Depreciation—Equipment, Accumulated Depreciation—Furniture, Salary Payable, Unearned Service Revenue, Retained Earnings, Depreciation Expense—Equipment, Depreciation Expense—Furniture, and Supplies Expense. Also, use the T-accounts opened for exercise E2-25.
2. Journalize the transactions of January 21 through 31.
3. Post the January 21 to January 31 transactions to the T-accounts, keying all items by date. Denote account balances as Bal.
4. Prepare a trial balance at January 31. Also, set up columns for the adjustments and for the adjusted trial balance, as illustrated in Exhibit 3-4, on page 120.
5. At January 31, the following information is gathered for the adjusting entries:
   a. Accrued service revenue, $1,000
   b. Earned $300 of the service revenue collected in advance on January 21
   c. Supplies on hand, $300
   d. Depreciation expense—equipment, $100; furniture, $200
   e. Accrued expense for secretary's salary, $1,000

   Make these adjustments directly in the adjustments columns and complete the adjusted trial balance at January 31, 2014.
6. Journalize and post the adjusting entries. Denote each adjusting amount as Adj. and an account balance as Bal.
7. Prepare the income statement and statement of retained earnings of Web Marketing Services Inc. for the month ended January 31, 2014, and the classified balance sheet at that date. Draw arrows to link the financial statements.
8. Journalize and post the closing entries at January 31, 2014. Denote each closing amount as Clo. and an account balance as Bal.
9. Using the information you have prepared, compute the current ratio and the debt ratio of Web Marketing Services Inc. (to two decimals) and evaluate these ratio values as indicative of a strong or weak financial position.

CHALLENGE EXERCISES

E3-34 Valley Bleu Ltée reported the following current accounts at December 31, 2013 (amounts in thousands):

LEARNING OBJECTIVE ❸❹❻

Compute financial statement amounts, analyze debt-paying ability

a. Cash	$1,700
b. Receivables	5,600
c. Inventory	1,800
d. Prepaid expenses	800
e. Accounts payable	2,400
f. Unearned revenue	1,200
g. Accrued expenses payable	1,700

During 2014, Valley Bleu completes these transactions:

- Used inventory of $3,800
- Sold services on account, $6,500
- Depreciation expense, $400
- Paid for accrued expenses, $500
- Collected from customers on account, $7,500
- Accrued expenses, $1,300
- Purchased inventory of $3,500 on account
- Paid on account, $5,000
- Used up prepaid expenses, $600

Compute Valley Bleu's current ratio at December 31, 2013, and again at December 31, 2014. Did the current ratio improve or deteriorate during 2014? Comment on the company's current ratio.

E3-35 The accounts of Maritime Specialists Ltd. prior to the year-end adjustments are given below.

LEARNING OBJECTIVE ❸❹

Compute financial statement amounts

Cash	$ 4,000	Share capital	$ 10,000
Accounts receivable	7,000	Retained earnings	43,000
Supplies	4,000	Dividends	16,000
Prepaid insurance	3,000	Service revenue	155,000
Building	107,000	Salary expense	32,000
Accumulated depreciation—building	14,000	Depreciation expense—building	0
Land	51,000	Supplies expense	0
Accounts payable	6,000	Insurance expense	0
Salary payable	0	Advertising expense	7,000
Unearned service revenue	5,000	Utilities expense	2,000

Adjusting data at the end of the year include:

a. Unearned service revenue that has been earned, $1,000
b. Accrued service revenue, $2,000
c. Supplies used in operations, $3,000
d. Accrued salary expense, $3,000
e. Prepaid insurance expired, $1,000
f. Depreciation expense, building, $2,000

Jon Whale, the principal shareholder, has received an offer to sell Maritime Specialists. He needs to know the following information within one hour:

a. Net income for the year covered by these data
b. Total assets
c. Total liabilities

d. Total shareholders' equity
e. Proof that Total assets = Total liabilities + Total shareholders' equity, after all items are updated

Requirement

Without opening any accounts, making any journal entries, or using a worksheet, provide Whale with the requested information. The business is not subject to income tax. Show all computations.

QUIZ

Test your understanding of accrual accounting by answering the following questions. Select the best choice from among the possible answers given.

Questions 36 through 38 are based on the following facts:

Freddie Handel began a music business in July 2014. Handel prepares monthly financial statements and uses the accrual basis of accounting. The following transactions are Handel Company's only activities during July through October:

July	14	Bought music on account for $10, with payment to the supplier due in 90 days
Aug.	3	Performed a job on account for Joey Bach for $25, collectible from Bach in 30 days. Used up all the music purchased on July 14
Sept.	16	Collected the $25 receivable from Bach
Oct.	22	Paid the $10 owed to the supplier from the July 14 transaction

Q3-36 In which month should Handel record the cost of the music as an expense?
a. July
b. August
c. September
d. October

Q3-37 In which month should Handel report the $25 revenue on its income statement?
a. July
b. August
c. September
d. October

Q3-38 If Handel Company uses the *cash* basis of accounting instead of the accrual basis, in what month will Handel report revenue and in what month will it report expense?

	Revenue	Expense
a.	September	October
b.	September	July
c.	August	October
d.	September	August

Q3-39 In which month should revenue be recorded?
a. In the month that goods are ordered by the customer
b. In the month that goods are shipped to the customer
c. In the month that the invoice is mailed to the customer
d. In the month that cash is collected from the customer

Q3-40 On January 1 of the current year, Aladdin Company paid $600 rent to cover six months (January through June). Aladdin recorded this transaction as follows:

Prepaid Rent	600	
Cash		600

Aladdin adjusts the accounts at the end of each month. Based on these facts, the adjusting entry at the end of January should include

a. a credit to Prepaid Rent for $500.
b. a debit to Prepaid Rent for $500.
c. a debit to Prepaid Rent for $100.
d. a credit to Prepaid Rent for $100.

Q3-41 Assume the same facts as in the previous problem. Aladdin's adjusting entry at the end of February should include a debit to Rent Expense in the amount of

a. $0.
b. $500.
c. $200.
d. $100.

Q3-42 What effect does the adjusting entry in Question 3-41 have on Aladdin's net income for February?

a. increase by $100
b. increase by $200
c. decrease by $100
d. decrease by $200

Q3-43 An adjusting entry recorded March salary expense that will be paid in April. Which statement best describes the effect of this adjusting entry on the company's accounting equation at the end of March?

a. Assets are not affected, liabilities are decreased, and shareholders' equity is decreased.
b. Assets are decreased, liabilities are increased, and shareholders' equity is decreased.
c. Assets are not affected, liabilities are increased, and shareholders' equity is decreased.
d. Assets are decreased, liabilities are not affected, and shareholders' equity is decreased.

Q3-44 On April 1, 2014, Metro Insurance Company sold a one-year insurance policy covering the year ended April 1, 2015. Metro collected the full $1,200 on April 1, 2014. Metro made the following journal entry to record the receipt of cash in advance:

Cash	1,200	
Unearned Revenue		1,200

Nine months have passed, and Metro has made no adjusting entries. Based on these facts, the adjusting entry needed by Metro at December 31, 2014, is

a.	Unearned Revenue	300	
	Insurance Revenue		300
b.	Insurance Revenue	300	
	Unearned Revenue		300
c.	Unearned Revenue	900	
	Insurance Revenue		900
d.	Insurance Revenue	900	
	Unearned Revenue		900

Q3-45 The Unearned Revenue account of Dean Incorporated began 2014 with a normal balance of $5,000 and ended 2014 with a normal balance of $12,000. During 2014, the Unearned Revenue account was credited for $19,000 that Dean will earn later. Based on these facts, how much revenue did Dean earn in 2014?

a. $5,000
b. $19,000
c. $24,000
d. $12,000

Q3-46 What is the effect on the financial statements of recording depreciation on equipment?

a. Assets are decreased, but net income and shareholders' equity are not affected.
b. Net income, assets, and shareholders' equity are all decreased.
c. Net income and assets are decreased, but shareholders' equity is not affected.
d. Net income is not affected, but assets and shareholders' equity are decreased.

Q3-47 For 2014, Monterrey Company had revenues in excess of expenses. Which statement describes Monterrey's closing entries at the end of 2014?

a. Revenues will be debited, expenses will be credited, and retained earnings will be debited.

b. Revenues will be credited, expenses will be debited, and retained earnings will be debited.

c. Revenues will be debited, expenses will be credited, and retained earnings will be credited.

d. Revenues will be credited, expenses will be debited, and retained earnings will be credited.

Q3-48 Which of the following accounts would not be included in the closing entries?

a. Accumulated Depreciation

b. Service Revenue

c. Depreciation Expense

d. Retained Earnings

Q3-49 A major purpose of preparing closing entries is to

a. zero out the liability accounts.

b. close out the Supplies account.

c. adjust the asset accounts to their correct current balances.

d. update the Retained Earnings account.

Q3-50 Selected data for Austin Company follow:

Current assets	$50,000	Current liabilities	$40,000
Capital assets	70,000	Long-term liabilities	35,000
Total revenues	30,000	Total expenses	20,000

Based on these facts, what are Austin's ratios?

	Current ratio	Debt ratio
a.	2 to 1	0.5 to 1
b.	0.83 to 1	0.5 to 1
c.	1.25 to 1	0.625 to 1
d.	2 to 1	0.633 to 1

PROBLEMS

(Group A)

LEARNING OBJECTIVE ❶❹

Apply accrual accounting and prepare financial statements

P3-51A Lewitas Ltd. earned revenues of $35 million during 2014 and ended the year with income of $8 million. During 2014, Lewitas Ltd. collected $33 million from customers and paid cash for all of its expenses plus an additional $1 million for accounts payable. Answer these questions about Lewitas's operating results, financial position, and cash flows during 2014:

Requirements

1. How much were the company's total expenses? Show your work.

2. Identify all the items that Lewitas will report on its 2014 income statement. Show each amount.

3. Lewitas began 2014 with receivables of $4 million. All sales were on account. What was the company's receivables balance at the end of 2014? Identify the appropriate financial statement, and show how Lewitas will report ending receivables in the 2014 annual report.

4. Lewitas began 2014 owing accounts payable totalling $9 million. How much in accounts payable did the company owe at the end of the year? Identify the appropriate financial statement, and show how Lewitas will report these accounts payable in its 2014 annual report.

2. Evaluate Marciano's debt position as strong or weak, giving your reason. Assess whether Marciano's ability to pay both current and total debts improved or deteriorated during 2014. In order to complete your evaluation, compute Marciano's current and debt ratios at March 31, 2014, rounding to two decimal places. At March 31, 2013, the current ratio was 1.30 and the debt ratio was 0.30.

P3-60A The balance sheet at December 31, 2012, 2013, and 2014 and income statement for the years ended December 31, 2012, 2013, and 2014 for Ojibway Inc. include the following data:

LEARNING OBJECTIVE ⑥

Evaluate debt-paying ability

Ojibway Inc.
Balance Sheet
As at December 31
(in thousands)

	2014	2013	2012
Assets			
Current assets			
Cash	$ 3.0	$ 1.0	$ 0.5
Accounts receivable	8.0	5.0	3.5
Total current assets	11.0	6.0	4.0
Furniture and equipment, net	16.0	9.5	3.0
Total assets	$ 27.0	15.5	$ 7.0
Liabilities			
Current liabilities			
Accounts payable	$ 5.0	$ 4.5	$ 3.0
Salaries payable	1.5	1.0	0.5
Total current liabilities	6.5	5.5	3.5
Notes payable	9.0	5.0	3.5
Total liabilities	15.5	10.5	7.0
Shareholders' equity			
Shareholders' equity	11.5	5.0	0.0
Total liabilities and shareholders' equity	$ 27.0	$ 15.5	$ 7.0

Ojibway Inc.
Income Statement
For the year ended December 31
(in thousands)

	2014	2013	2012
Revenue			
Service revenue	$100.0	$ 90.0	$ 64.0
Expenses			
Salary	60.0	57.5	46.0
Rent	18.0	16.0	12.0
Supplies	4.0	3.0	2.0
Utilities	4.5	4.0	2.0
Depreciation	5.0	3.0	2.0
Total expenses	91.5	83.5	64.0
Income before taxes	8.5	6.5	0.0
Income tax expense	2.0	1.5	
Net income	$ 6.5	$ 5.0	$ 0.0

Requirements

Use the years of data to answer the following:

1. Calculate the current ratio for 2012, 2013, and 2014.
2. Calculate the debt ratio for 2012, 2013, and 2014.

3. Evaluate each ratio and determine if the ratio has improved or deteriorated over the three years. Explain what the changes mean.

(Group B)

LEARNING OBJECTIVE ❸❹
Apply accrual accounting and prepare financial statements

P3-61B During 2014, Schubert Inc. earned revenues of $19 million from the sale of its products. Schubert ended the year with net income of $4 million. Schubert collected cash of $20 million from customers.

Answer these questions about Schubert's operating results, financial position, and cash flows during 2014:

1. How much were Schubert's total expenses? Show your work.
2. Identify all the items that Schubert will report on its income statement for 2014. Show each amount.
3. Schubert began 2014 with receivables of $6 million. All sales are on account. What was Schubert's receivables balance at the end of 2014? Identify the appropriate financial statement and show how Schubert will report its ending receivables balance in the company's 2014 annual report.
4. Schubert began 2014 owing accounts payable of $9 million. Schubert incurs all expenses on account. During 2014, Schubert paid $18 million on account. How much in accounts payable did Schubert owe at the end of 2014? Identify the appropriate financial statement and show how Schubert will report these accounts payable in its 2014 annual report.

LEARNING OBJECTIVE ❶
Apply accrual and cash-basis accounting

P3-62B Fred's Catering Ltd. had the following selected transactions during May 2014:

May	1	Received $800 in advance for a banquet to be served later
	5	Paid electricity expenses, $700
	9	Received cash for the day's sales, $2,000
	14	Purchased two food warmers, $1,800
	23	Served a banquet, receiving a note receivable, $700
	31	Accrued salary expense, $900
	31	Prepaid $3,000 building rent for June and July

Requirements

1. Show how each transaction would be handled using the cash basis and the accrual basis. Under each column, give the amount of revenue or expense for May. Journal entries are not required. Use the following format for your answer, and show your computations. Ignore depreciation expense.

Fred's Catering Ltd.
Amount of Revenue (Expense) for May 2014

Date	Cash Basis	Accrual Basis

2. Compute income (loss) before tax for May under the two accounting methods.
3. Which method better measures income and assets? Use the last transaction to explain.

LEARNING OBJECTIVE ❶❷
Explain accrual accounting and expense recognition

P3-63B As the controller of Stuart Enterprises Inc. you have hired a new employee, whom you must train. She objects to making an adjusting entry for accrued utilities at the end of the period. She reasons, "We will pay the utilities soon. Why not wait until payment to record the expense? In the end, the result will be the same." Write a reply to explain to the employee why the adjusting entry is needed for accrued utility expense.

P3-64B Journalize the adjusting entry needed on December 31, 2014, the end of the current accounting period, for each of the following independent cases affecting Lee Computer Systems Inc. (LCSI). Include explanations for each entry.

LEARNING OBJECTIVE ❸
Record adjusting journal entries

a. Each Friday, LCSI pays employees for the current week's work. The amount of the payroll is $5,000 for a five-day work week. The current accounting period ends on Tuesday.

b. LCSI has received notes receivable from some clients for services. During the current year, LCSI has earned accrued interest revenue of $1,100, which will be received next year.

c. The beginning balance of Supplies was $1,800. During the year, LCSI purchased supplies costing $12,500, and at December 31 the inventory of supplies on hand is $2,900.

d. LCSI is developing software for a client and the client paid LCSI $20,000 at the start of the project. LCSI recorded this amount as Unearned Service Revenue. The software development will take several months to complete. LCSI executives estimate that the company has earned three-quarters of the total fee during the current year.

e. Depreciation for the current year includes Computer Equipment, $6,300, and Building, $3,700. Make a compound entry.

f. Details of Prepaid Insurance are shown in the Prepaid Insurance account. LCSI pays the annual insurance premium (the payment for insurance coverage is called a premium) on September 30 each year. At December 31, nine months of insurance is still prepaid.

Prepaid Insurance

Jan. 1	Bal.	1,800
Sept. 30		3,600

P3-65B Consider the unadjusted trial balance of Creative Advertising Ltd. at October 31, 2014, and the related month-end adjustment data.

LEARNING OBJECTIVE ❸❹❻
Record adjusting entries, prepare financial statements, and evaluate debt-paying ability

Creative Advertising Ltd.
Trial Balance
October 31, 2014

Cash	$16,300	
Accounts receivable	7,000	
Prepaid rent	4,000	
Supplies	600	
Computers	36,000	
Accumulated depreciation		$ 3,000
Accounts payable		8,800
Salary payable		
Share capital		15,000
Retained earnings (September 30, 2013)		21,000
Dividends	4,600	
Advertising revenue		25,400
Salary expense	4,400	
Rent expense		
Utilities expense	300	
Depreciation expense		
Supplies expense		
Total	$73,200	$73,200

Adjustment data:

a. Accrued advertising revenue at October 31, $2,900

b. Prepaid rent expired during the month: The unadjusted prepaid balance of $4,000 relates to the period October 2014 through January 2015.

c. Supplies used during October, $200

d. Depreciation on computers for the month: The computers' expected useful life is three years.

e. Accrued salary expense at October 31 for Monday through Thursday; the five-day weekly payroll is $2,000.

Requirements

1. Using Exhibit 3-4, page 120, as an example, prepare the adjusted trial balance of Creative Advertising Ltd. at October 31, 2014. Key each adjusting entry by letter.

2. Prepare the income statement, the statement of retained earnings, and the classified balance sheet. Draw arrows linking the three financial statements.

3. **a.** Compare the business's net income for October to the amount of dividends paid to the owners. Suppose this trend continues into November. What will be the effect on the business's financial position, as shown by its accounting equation?

   b. Will the trend make it easier or more difficult for Creative Advertising Ltd. to borrow money if the business gets in a bind and needs cash? Why?

   c. Does either the current ratio or the cash position suggest the need for immediate borrowing? Explain.

LEARNING OBJECTIVE ❸❹

Record adjusting entries and prepare a balance sheet

P3-66B Your Talent Agency Ltd.'s unadjusted and adjusted trial balances at December 31, 2014, are shown below.

Your Talent Agency Ltd.
Adjusted Trial Balance
December 31, 2014

Account Title	Trial Balance Debit	Trial Balance Credit	Adjusted Trial Balance Debit	Adjusted Trial Balance Credit
Cash	$ 4,100		$ 4,100	
Accounts receivable	11,200		12,400	
Supplies	1,000		700	
Prepaid insurance	2,600		900	
Office furniture	21,600		21,600	
Accumulated depreciation		$ 8,200		$ 9,300
Accounts payable		6,300		6,300
Salary payable				900
Interest payable				400
Note payable		6,000		6,000
Unearned commission revenue		1,500		1,100
Share capital		5,000		5,000
Retained earnings		3,500		3,500
Dividends	18,300		18,300	
Commission revenue		72,800		74,400
Depreciation expense			1,100	
Supplies expense			300	
Utilities expense	4,900		4,900	
Salary expense	26,600		27,500	
Rent expense	12,200		12,200	
Interest expense	800		1,200	
Insurance expense			1,700	
	$103,300	$103,300	$106,900	$106,900

Requirements

1. Make the adjusting entries that account for the difference between the two trial balances.
2. Compute Your Talent Agency Ltd.'s total assets, total liabilities, total equity, and net income.
3. Prove your answer with the accounting equation.

P3-67B The adjusted trial balance of Reid and Campbell Ltd. at December 31, 2014, appears below.

LEARNING OBJECTIVE ❹❻

Prepare financial statements and evaluate debt-paying ability

Reid and Campbell Ltd.
Adjusted Trial Balance
December 31, 2014

Cash	$ 11,600	
Accounts receivable	41,400	
Prepaid rent	1,300	
Store furnishings	67,600	
Accumulated depreciation		$ 12,900
Accounts payable		3,600
Deposits		4,500
Interest payable		2,100
Salary payable		900
Income tax payable		8,800
Note payable		26,200
Share capital		12,000
Retained earnings, Dec. 31, 2013		20,300
Dividends	48,000	
Sales		165,900
Depreciation expense	11,300	
Salary expense	44,000	
Rent expense	12,000	
Interest expense	1,200	
Income tax expense	18,800	
Total	$257,200	$257,200

Requirements

1. Prepare Reid and Campbell Ltd.'s 2014 income statement, statement of retained earnings, and balance sheet. List expenses in decreasing order on the income statement and show total liabilities on the balance sheet. Draw arrows linking the three financial statements.
2. Compute Reid and Campbell Ltd.'s debt ratio at December 31, 2014, rounding to two decimal places. Evaluate the company's debt ratio as strong or weak.

P3-68B The accounts of For You eTravel Inc. at December 31, 2014, are listed in alphabetical order.

LEARNING OBJECTIVE ❺

Record closing journal entries

Accounts payable	$ 5,100	Other assets	3,600
Accounts receivable	6,600	Retained earnings,	
Accumulated depreciation—furniture	11,600	December 31, 2013	5,300
Advertising expense	2,200	Salary expense	24,600
Cash	7,300	Salary payable	3,900
Depreciation expense	1,300	Service revenue	93,500
Dividends	47,400	Share capital	15,000
Furniture	41,400	Supplies	7,700
Interest expense	800	Supplies expense	5,700
Note payable, long term	$10,600	Unearned service revenue	3,600

Requirements

1. All adjustments have been journalized and posted, but the closing entries have not been made. Journalize For You eTravel Inc.'s closing entries at December 31, 2014.
2. Set up a T-account for Retained Earnings and post to that account. Compute For You's net income for the year ended December 31, 2014. What is the ending balance of Retained Earnings?
3. Did Retained Earnings increase or decrease during the year? What caused the increase or the decrease?

LEARNING OBJECTIVE ❹❻

Prepare a balance sheet and evaluate debt-paying ability

P3-69B Refer to Problem 3-68B.

1. Use the For You eTravel Inc. data in problem P3-68B to prepare the company's classified balance sheet at December 31, 2014. Show captions for total assets, total liabilities, and total liabilities and shareholders' equity.
2. Evaluate For You's debt position as strong or weak, giving your reason. Assess whether For You's ability to pay both current and total debts improved or deteriorated during 2014. In order to complete your evaluation, compute For You's current and debt ratios at December 31, 2014, rounding to two decimal places. At December 31, 2013, the current ratio was 1.50 and the debt ratio was 0.45.

LEARNING OBJECTIVE ❻

Evaluate debt-paying ability

P3-70B A company's balance sheet at December 31, 2012, 2013, and 2014 and income statement for the years ended December 31, 2012, 2013, and 2014 include the data on pages 164–165.

Requirements

Use the years of data to answer the following:
1. Calculate the current ratio for 2012, 2013 and 2014.
2. Calculate the debt ratio for 2012, 2013, and 2014.
3. Evaluate each ratio and determine if the ratio has improved or deteriorated over the three years. Explain what the changes mean.

Balance Sheet
As at December 31
(in thousands)

	2014	2013	2012
Assets			
Current assets			
Cash	$ 6.0	$ 4.0	$ 3.5
Accounts receivable	11.0	8.0	6.5
Total current assets	17.0	12.0	10.0
Furniture and equipment, net	19.0	12.5	6.0
Total assets	$36.0	$24.5	$16.0
Liabilities			
Current liabilities			
Accounts payable	$ 8.0	$ 7.0	$ 6.0
Salaries payable	4.5	4.0	3.5
Total current liabilities	12.5	11.0	9.5
Notes payable	12.0	6.0	5.5
Total liabilities	24.5	17.0	15.0
Shareholders' equity			
Shareholders' equity	11.5	7.5	1.0
Total liabilities and shareholders' equity	$36.0	$24.5	$16.0

Income Statement
For the year ended December 31
(in thousands)

	2014	2013	2012
Revenue			
Service revenue	$110.0	$99.0	$75.0
Expenses			
Salary	65.0	59.0	48.0
Rent	20.0	18.0	17.0
Supplies	7.5	6.0	3.0
Utilities	6.0	4.5	3.5
Depreciation	6.0	3.0	2.0
Total expenses	104.5	90.5	73.5
Income before taxes	5.5	8.5	1.5
Income tax expense	1.5	2.0	.5
Net income	$ 4.0	$ 6.5	$ 1.0

Apply Your Knowledge

Decision Cases

Case 1. Below is a list of accounts of Patel Consulting Ltd. at January 31, 2014. The unadjusted trial balance of Patel Consulting Ltd. at January 31, 2014, does not balance. In addition, the trial balance needs to be updated before the financial statements at January 31, 2014, can be prepared. The manager needs to know the current ratio of Patel Consulting Ltd.

LEARNING OBJECTIVE ❸ ❻

Adjust and correct the accounts; evaluating debt-paying ability

Patel Consulting Ltd.
List of Accounts
January 31, 2014

Cash	$ 6,000	
Accounts receivable	2,200	
Supplies	800	
Prepaid rent	12,000	
Land	41,000	
Accounts payable		10,000
Salary payable		0
Unearned service revenue		1,500
Note payable, due in three years		25,400
Share capital		15,000
Retained earnings		7,300
Service revenue		9,100
Salary expense	3,400	
Rent expense	0	
Advertising expense	900	
Supplies expense	0	
	?	?

Requirements

1. How much *out of balance* is the trial balance? The error is in the Land account.
2. Patel Consulting Ltd. needs to make the following adjustments at January 31:
    a. Supplies of $600 were used during January.

b. The balance of Prepaid Rent was paid on January 1 and covers the rest of 2014. No adjustment was made January 31.

c. At January 31, Patel Consulting owes employees $400.

d. Unearned service revenue of $800 was earned during January.

Prepare a corrected, adjusted trial balance. Give Land its correct balance.

3. After the error is corrected and after these adjustments are made, compute the current ratio of Patel Consulting Ltd. If your business had this current ratio, could you sleep at night?

LEARNING OBJECTIVE ❹

Prepare financial statements and make an expansion decision

Case 2. On October 1, Sue Skate opened a restaurant named Silver Skates Ltd. After the first month of operations, Skate is at a crossroads. The October financial statements paint a glowing picture of the business, and Skate has asked you whether she should expand Silver Skates.

To expand the business, Sue Skate wants to be earning net income of $10,000 per month and have total assets of $35,000. Based on the financial information available to her, Skate believes she is meeting both goals.

To start the business, she invested $20,000, not the $10,000 amount reported as "Share capital" on the balance sheet. The bookkeeper plugged the $10,000 "Share capital" amount into the balance sheet to make it come out even. The bookkeeper made other mistakes too. Skate shows you the following financial statements that the bookkeeper prepared.

Silver Skates Ltd.
Income Statement
For the Month Ended October 31, 2014

Revenues:		
Investments by owner	$20,000	
Unearned banquet sales revenue	3,000	
		$23,000
Expenses:		
Wages expense	$ 5,000	
Rent expense	4,000	
Dividends	3,000	
Depreciation expense—fixtures	1,000	
		13,000
Net income (Net loss)		$10,000

Silver Skates Ltd.
Balance Sheet
October 31, 2014

Assets:		Liabilities:	
Cash	$ 6,000	Accounts payable	$ 5,000
Prepaid insurance	1,000	Sales revenue	32,000
Insurance expense	1,000	Accumulated depreciation—	
Food inventory	3,000	fixtures	1,000
Cost of goods sold (expense)	14,000		38,000
Fixtures (tables, chairs, etc.)	19,000	Owners' equity:	
Dishes and silverware	4,000	Share capital	10,000
	$48,000		$48,000

Requirements

Prepare a corrected income statement, statement of retained earnings, and balance sheet for Silver Skates Ltd. Then, based on your corrected statements, recommend to Sue Skate whether she should expand her business.

LEARNING OBJECTIVE ❹

Prepare financial statements and compute a purchase price

Case 3. Walter Liu has owned and operated LW Media Inc. since its beginning 10 years ago. Recently, Liu mentioned that he would consider selling the company for the right price.

Assume that you are interested in buying this business. You obtain its most recent monthly trial balance, which follows. Revenues and expenses vary little from month to month, and June is a typical month. Your investigation reveals that the trial balance does not include the effects of monthly revenues of $5,000 and expenses totalling $1,100. If you were to buy LW Media Inc., you would hire a manager so you could devote your time to other duties. Assume that your manager would require a monthly salary of $6,000.

Requirements

1. Assume that the most you would pay for the business is 20 times the monthly net income *you could expect to earn* from it. Compute this possible price.
2. Walter Liu states that the least he will take for the business is 1.5 times shareholders' equity on June 30, 2014. Compute this amount.
3. Under these conditions, how much should you offer Liu? Give your reason.

LW Media Inc.
Trial Balance
June 30, 2014

Cash	$ 10,000	
Accounts receivable	4,900	
Prepaid expenses	3,200	
Equipment	115,000	
Accumulated depreciation		$ 76,500
Land	158,000	
Accounts payable		13,800
Salary payable		
Unearned revenue		56,700
Share capital		50,000
Retained earnings		88,000
Dividends	9,000	
Revenue		20,000
Rent expense		
Salary expense	4,000	
Utilities expense	900	
Depreciation expense		
Supplies expense		
Total	$305,000	$305,000

Ethical Issues

Issue 1. ARAS Inc. is in its third year of operations and the company has grown. To expand the business, ARAS borrowed $1 million from Royal Bank of Canada. As a condition for making this loan, the bank required that ARAS maintain a current ratio of at least 1.50 and a debt ratio of no more than 0.50.

Business recently has been worse than expected. Expenses have brought the current ratio down to 1.47 and the debt ratio up to 0.51 at December 15. Shane Rollins, the general manager, is considering the implication of reporting this current ratio to the bank. Rollins is considering recording this year some revenue on account that ARAS will earn next year. The contract for this job has been signed, and ARAS will perform the service during January.

Requirements

1. Journalize the revenue transaction, omitting amounts, and indicate how recording this revenue in December would affect the current ratio and the debt ratio.
2. State whether it is ethical to record the revenue transaction in December. Identify the accounting principle relevant to this situation.
3. Propose to ARAS a course of action that is ethical.

Issue 2. The net income of Accent Photography Company Ltd. decreased sharply during 2014. Mark Smith, owner of the company, anticipates the need for a bank loan in 2015. Late in 2014, he instructed the accountant to record a $20,000 sale of portraits to the Smith family, even though the photos will not be shot until January 2015. Smith also told the accountant *not* to make the following December 31, 2014, adjusting entries:

Salaries owed to employees..	$5,000
Prepaid insurance that has expired...	1,000

Requirements

1. Compute the overall effect of these transactions on the company's reported income for 2014. Is income overstated or understated?
2. Why did Smith take these actions? Are they ethical? Give your reason, identifying the parties helped and the parties harmed by Smith's action.
3. As a personal friend, what advice would you give the accountant?

Focus on Financials

LEARNING OBJECTIVE ❸❻

Record journal entries and evaluate debt-paying ability

Like all other businesses, TELUS adjusts accounts prior to year-end to measure assets, liabilities, revenues, and expenses for the financial statements. Examine TELUS's balance sheet in Appendix A, and pay particular attention to (a) Prepaid Expenses and (b) Accounts Payable and Accrued Liabilities.

Requirements

1. Why aren't Prepaid Expenses "true" expenses?
2. Open T-accounts for the Prepaid Expenses account and the Accounts Payable and Accrued Liabilities account. Insert TELUS's balances (in millions) at December 31, 2010.
3. Journalize the following for the year ended December 31, 2011. Key entries by letter, and show accounts in millions. Explanations are not required.
   a. Paid the beginning balance of Accounts Payable and Accrued Liabilities.
   b. Allocated Prepaid Expenses of $113 to Goods and Services Purchased.
   c. Recorded Accounts Payable and Accrued Liabilities in the amount of $1,419. Assume this relates to Goods and Services Purchased.
   d. Recorded a prepayment of $144 in services to Prepaid Expenses.
4. Post these entries and show that the balances in Prepaid Expenses and in Accounts Payable and Accrued Liabilities agree with the corresponding amounts reported in the December 31, 2011, balance sheet.
5. Compute the current ratios and debt ratios for TELUS at December 31, 2011, and at December 31, 2010. Did the ratio values improve, deteriorate, or hold steady during the year ended December 31, 2011? Do the ratio values indicate financial strength or weakness?

Focus on Analysis

LEARNING OBJECTIVE ❷

Explain revenue and expense recognition principles

TELUS Corporation

During the fiscal year ended 2011, TELUS had numerous accruals and deferrals. As a new member of TELUS's accounting and financial staff, it is your job to explain the effects of accruals and deferrals on TELUS's net income for 2011. The accrual and deferral data follow, along with questions that TELUS's shareholders have raised (all amounts in millions):

1. Beginning total receivables for 2011 were $1,318. Ending receivables for 2011 are $1,428. Which of these amounts did TELUS earn in 2010? Which amount did TELUS earn in 2011? Which amount is included in TELUS's revenue for 2011?

2. Accumulated depreciation on property, plant, and equipment stood at $19,629 at December 31, 2010, and at $20,347 as at December 31, 2011. Accumulated depreciation was reduced by

$253 for assets sold during the year. Calculate the depreciation expense for the year, and compare to the depreciation expense reported on the 2011 statement of income in Appendix A.

3. Certain income-statement accounts are directly linked to specific balance-sheet accounts other than cash. Examine TELUS's income statement in Appendix A. For each revenue and expense account that you can do so, identify the related balance sheet account(s) (other than cash).

Group Project

Matt Davis formed a lawn service company as a summer job. To start the business on May 1, he deposited $1,000 in a new bank account in the name of the corporation. The $1,000 consisted of an $800 loan from his father and $200 of his own money. The corporation issued 200 common shares to Davis.

Davis rented lawn equipment, purchased supplies, and hired high-school students to mow and trim his customers' lawns. At the end of each month, Davis mailed bills to his customers. On August 31, Davis was ready to dissolve the business and return to Simon Fraser University for the fall semester. Because he had been so busy, he had kept few records other than his chequebook and a list of amounts owed by customers.

At August 31, Davis's chequebook shows a balance of $1,390, and his customers still owe him $560. During the summer, he collected $5,150 from customers. His chequebook lists payments for supplies totalling $400, and he still has gasoline, weed whacker cord, and other supplies that cost a total of $50. He paid his employees wages of $1,900, and he still owes them $200 for the final week of the summer.

Davis rented some equipment from Ludwig Tool Company. On May 1, he signed a six-month lease on mowers and paid $600 for the full lease period. Ludwig will refund the unused portion of the prepayment if the equipment is in good shape. To get the refund, Davis has kept the mowers in excellent condition. In fact, he had to pay $300 to repair a mower that ran over a hidden tree stump.

To transport equipment to jobs, Davis used a trailer that he bought for $300. He figures that the summer's work used up one-third of the trailer's service potential. The business chequebook lists an expenditure of $460 for dividends paid to Davis during the summer. Also, Davis paid his father back during the summer.

Requirements

1. Prepare the income statement of Davis Lawn Service Inc. for the four months May through August. The business is not subject to income tax.
2. Prepare the classified balance sheet of Davis Lawn Service Inc. at August 31.

Quick Check Answers

1. *c*	5. *d*	9. *d*	13. *a*
2. *c*	6. *b*	10. *a*	14. *c*
3. *b*	7. *a*	11. *b*	15. *a*
4. *d*	8. *d*	12. *d*	16. *b*

4

Internal Control and Cash

© Hero Images Inc./Alamy

LEARNING OBJECTIVES

1 **Describe** fraud and its impact

2 **Explain** the objectives and components of internal control

3 **Prepare** and **use** a bank reconciliation

4 **Apply** internal controls to cash receipts and cash payments

5 **Construct** and **use** a budget to manage cash

SPOTLIGHT

COOKING THE BOOKS: GREBRU PRODUCTS INC. TAKES A HIT

The following is adapted from a true story:

"I've never been so shocked in my life!" exclaimed Lee Riffe, manager of the GreBru Products Inc. office in Vancouver, B.C. "I never thought this could happen to us. We are such a close-knit organization where everyone trusts everyone else. Why, people at GreBru feel like family! I feel betrayed, violated."

Riffe had just returned from the trial of Alec Jones, who had been convicted of embezzling over $600,000 from GreBru over a six-year period. Jones had been one of GreBru's most trusted employees for 10 years. A single father with two teenage daughters, Jones had pulled himself up by his own bootstraps, putting himself through community college where he had obtained an associate's degree in accounting. Riffe had hired him as a part-time bookkeeper at GreBru while Jones was in college to help him out. He had done such a good job that, when he completed his degree, Riffe asked him to stay on and assigned him the additional role of cashier, in charge of accumulating the daily cash receipts from customers and taking them to the night depository at the bank each day after work. Through the years, he also awarded him what he considered good raises, compensating him at a rate that was generally higher than other employees with his education and experience levels.

Jones rapidly became the company's "go-to" financial employee. He was eager to learn, dependable, responsible. In 10 years he never took a day of vacation, choosing instead to take advantage of the company's policy that allowed employees to draw additional compensation for vacation accrued but not taken at the end of each year. Riffe grew to depend on Jones more and more each month, as the business grew to serve over 1,000 customers. Jones's increased involvement on the financial side of the business freed Riffe to spend his time working on new business, spending less and less time on financial matters. Riffe had noticed that, in the past few years, Jones had begun to wear better clothes and drive a shiny late-model convertible around town. Both of his teenagers also drove late-model automobiles, and the family had recently moved into a new home in an upscale subdivision of the city. Riffe had been pleased that he had contributed to Jones's success. But in recent months, Riffe was becoming worried because, in spite of increasing revenues, the cash balances and cash flows from operations at GreBru had been steadily deteriorating, sometimes causing the company difficulty in paying its bills on time.

Jones, on the other hand, had felt underappreciated and underpaid for all of his hard work. Having learned the system well, and observing that no one was monitoring him, Jones fell into a simple but deadly trap. As cashier, he was in charge of receiving customer payments that came in by mail. Unknown to Riffe, Jones had been **lapping** accounts receivable, an embezzlement scheme nicknamed "robbing Peter to pay Paul." Jones began by misappropriating (stealing) some of the customers' cheques, endorsing them, and depositing them to his own bank account. To cover up the shortage in a particular customer's account, Jones would apply the collections received later from another customer's account. He would do this just before the monthly statements were mailed to the first customer, so that the customer wouldn't notice when she or he received the statement that someone else's payment was being applied to the amount owed GreBru. Of course, this left the second customer's account short, so Jones had to misapply the collection from a third customer to straighten out the discrepancy in the second customer's account. He did this for many customers, over a period of many months, boldly stealing more and more each month. With unlimited access to both cash and customer accounts, and with careful planning and constant diligence, Jones became very proficient at juggling entries in the books to keep anyone from discovering his scheme. This embezzlement went on for six years, allowing Jones to misappropriate $622,000 from the company. The customer accounts that were misstated due to the fraud eventually had to be written off.

What tipped off Riffe to the embezzlement? Jones was involved in a skiing accident and couldn't work for two weeks. The employee covering for Jones was swamped with telephone calls from customers wanting to discuss unexplained differences in their billing statements for amounts they could prove had been paid. The ensuing investigation pointed straight to Jones, and Riffe turned the case over to the authorities.

The excerpt from the GreBru Products Inc. balance sheet on the following page reports the company's assets. Focus on the top line, Cash and cash equivalents. At December 31, 2014, GreBru reported cash of $8,000. Due to Jones's scheme, the company had been cheated of $622,000 over several years that it could have used to buy new equipment, expand operations, or pay off debts.

GreBru Products Inc.
Balance Sheet (Partial, Adapted)
As at December 31, 2014

Assets

Cash and cash equivalents	$ 8,000
Accounts receivable	128,000
Inventories	247,000
Prepaid expenses	1,400
Property, plant, and equipment (net of accumulated depreciation of $97,000)	213,600
Other assets	15,000
Total assets	$613,000

GreBru Products has now revamped its internal controls. The company has hired a separate person, with no access to cash, to keep customer accounts receivable records. The company now uses a **lockbox system** for all cheques received by mail. They are sent to GreBru's bank lock box, where they are gathered by a bank employee and immediately deposited. The remittance advices accompanying the cheques are electronically scanned and forwarded to GreBru's accounts receivable bookkeeper where they are used as the source documents for posting amounts collected from customers. A summary of cash received goes to Riffe, who reviews it for reasonableness and compares it with the daily bank deposit total. Another employee, who has neither cash handling nor customer bookkeeping responsibilities, reconciles GreBru's monthly bank statement, and reconciles the total cash deposited per the daily listings with the total credits to customer accounts receivable. Now Riffe requires every employee to take time off for earned vacation, and rotates other employees through those positions while those employees are away.

Lapping is a type of fraud known as misappropriation of assets. Although it does not take a genius to accomplish, lapping requires some motivation, and is usually rationalized by distorted and unethical thinking. The opportunity to commit this type and other types of frauds arises through a weak internal control system. In this case, the fact that Jones had access to cash and the customer accounts receivable, along with the fact that Riffe failed to monitor Jones's activities, proved to be the deadly combination that provided the opportunity for this fraud.

This chapter begins with a discussion of fraud, its types, and common characteristics. We then discuss internal controls, which are the primary means by which fraud as well as unintentional financial statement errors are prevented. We also discuss how to account for cash. These three topics—fraud, internal control, and cash—go together. Internal controls help prevent fraud. Cash is probably the asset that is most often misappropriated through fraud.

The discussion of fraud in this chapter reinforces the notion that it is important for managers to understand accounting and internal control if they are to be effective in their job. Well-designed and properly implemented internal controls can protect a company from fraud and error, but managers must have enough of an understanding of internal controls to determine if their internal controls are properly designed and implemented to be effective.

DESCRIBE FRAUD AND ITS IMPACT

Fraud is an intentional misrepresentation of facts, made for the purpose of persuading another party to act in a way that causes injury or damage to that party. For example, in the chapter opening story, Alec Jones intentionally misappropriated money from GreBru and covered it up by making customer accounts look different than they actually were. In the end, his actions caused $622,000 in damages to GreBru.

A recent survey on occupational fraud conducted by the Association for Certified Fraud Examiners (ACFE) that examined occupational fraud revealed that:

- Approximately 5% of an organization's revenue is lost to fraud each year.
- A majority of the cases were committed by people working in the accounting, operations, sales, executive/upper manager, customer service, or purchasing departments.
- Private companies were more affected than public companies.

Fraud has exploded with the expansion of e-commerce via the Internet. In addition, studies have shown that the percentage of losses related to fraud from transactions originating in "third world" or developing countries via the Internet is even higher than in economically developed countries.

What are the most common types of fraud? What causes fraud? What can be done to prevent it?

There are many types of fraud. Some examples are insurance fraud, cheque forgery, credit card fraud, and identity theft. The two most common types of fraud that impact financial statements are:

- **Misappropriation of assets.** This type of fraud is committed by employees of an entity who steal assets from the company and cover it up through erroneous entries in the books. The GreBru case is an example of the misappropriation of cash assets. Other examples of asset misappropriation include theft of inventory, falsifying invoices, forging or altering cheques, or overstatement of expense reimbursement requests.
- **Fraudulent financial reporting.** This type of fraud is committed by company managers who make false and misleading entries in the books, making financial results of the company appear to be better than they actually are. The purpose of this type of fraud is to deceive investors and creditors into making decisions they might otherwise not have made if given accurate financial information.

Research has indicated that managers engage in such fraud for a variety of reasons. Several such reasons and the related frauds are:

- To meet profit targets set by market analysts so that the company's share price will increase. An example would be where the company's earnings are actually $1.12 a share but analysts predicted $1.18 a share. The fraud: management reverses bad debt write-downs, reducing expenses to increase earnings to $1.18.
- To meet loan covenants so the lender won't demand payment of a loan. An example would be where the company has a loan covenant requiring it to maintain a current ratio of 2:1 and the actual ratio at year-end is 1.8:1. The fraud: management reverses an inventory write-down to increase the value of inventory so that the new ratio is 2.1:1.

- To meet an earnings target that will result in a management bonus. The fraud: management overstates revenue by recording subsequent-year sales in the current year, resulting in a misstated net income number so that the desired bonus is achieved.

- To convert a loss to a profit. The company suffers a net loss. The fraud: management overstates revenue to turn the loss into a profit.

Both misappropriation of assets and fraudulent financial reporting involve making false or misleading entries in the books of the company. We call this *cooking the books*. Of these two types, asset misappropriation is the most common, but fraudulent financial reporting is by far the most expensive. Perhaps two of the most notorious cases involving fraudulent financial reporting occurred in the United States and involved Enron Corporation in 2001 and WorldCom Corporation in 2002. These two scandals alone rocked the U.S. economy and impacted financial markets across the world. Enron committed fraudulent financial reporting by overstating profits through bogus sales of nonexistent assets with inflated values. When Enron's banks found out, they stopped loaning the company money to operate, causing it to go out of business almost overnight. WorldCom reported expenses as property, plant, and equipment and overstated both profits and assets. The company's internal auditor blew the whistle on WorldCom, resulting in the company's eventual collapse. Sadly, the same international accounting firm, Arthur Andersen LLP, had audited both companies' financial statements. Because of these and other failed audits, the once mighty firm of Arthur Andersen was forced to close its doors in 2002.

Each of these frauds, and many others revealed at about the same time, involved losses in the billions of dollars and thousands of jobs when the companies went out of business. Widespread media coverage sparked adverse market reaction, loss of confidence in the financial reporting system, and losses through declines in stock values that ran in the trillions of dollars!

Livent Inc. was a Canadian public company listed on the Toronto Stock Exchange. The company produced several successful musicals, such as *The Phantom of the Opera, Joseph and the Amazing Technicolor Dreamcoat, Show Boat,* and *Ragtime.* In the late 1990s, Livent declared bankruptcy in the United States. There were criminal investigations in Canada and the United States. Company co-founders Garth Drabinsky and Myron Gottlieb were indicted for fraud and misappropriation in the United States. In Canada, the co-founders and several other executives were charged with fraud. Drabinsky and Gottlieb were found guilty of fraud and forgery in an Ontario court for misstating the company's financial statements. In 2009, they were sentenced to time in prison.

We will discuss some of these cases throughout the remaining chapters of the text as examples of how accounting principles were deliberately misapplied to cook the books in environments characterized by *weak internal controls*.

Exhibit 4-1 explains in graphic form the elements that make up virtually every fraud. We call it the **fraud triangle**.

The first element in the fraud triangle is *motive*. This usually results from either critical need or greed on the part of the person who commits the fraud (the perpetrator). Sometimes, it is a matter of just never having enough (because some persons who commit fraud are already rich by most people's standards). Other times, the perpetrator of the fraud might have a legitimate financial need, such as a medical emergency, but he or she uses illegitimate means to meet that need. In any case, the

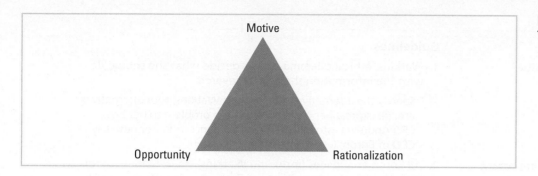

EXHIBIT 4-1
The Fraud Triangle

prevailing attitude on the part of the perpetrator is, "I want it, and someone else has it, so I'm going to do whatever I have to do to get it."

The second element in the fraud triangle is *opportunity*. As in the case of GreBru, the opportunity to commit fraud usually arises through weak internal controls. It might be a breakdown in a key element of controls, such as improper *segregation of duties* and/or improper *access to assets*. Or it might result from a weak control environment, such as a domineering CEO, a weak or conflicted board of directors, or lax ethical practices, allowing top management to override whatever controls the company has placed in operation for other transactions.

The third element in the triangle is *rationalization*. The perpetrator engages in distorted thinking, such as: "I deserve this"; "Nobody treats me fairly"; "No one will ever know"; "Just this once; I won't let it happen again"; or "Everyone else is doing it."

Fraud and Ethics

As we pointed out in our decision framework for making ethical accounting and business judgments introduced in Chapter 1, the decision to engage in fraud is an act with economic, legal, and ethical implications. The perpetrators of fraud usually do so for their own short-term *economic gain*, while others incur *economic losses* that may far outstrip the gains of the fraudsters. Moreover, fraud is *illegal*. Those who are caught and found guilty of fraud ultimately face penalties that include imprisonment, fines, and monetary damages. Finally, from an *ethical* standpoint, fraud violates the rights of many for the temporary betterment of a few, and for the ultimate betterment of no one. At the end of the day, everyone loses!

◀ DECISION GUIDELINES ▶

MAKE AN ETHICAL BUSINESS JUDGMENT

A Real-World Example

Sherron Watkins was a vice-president of Enron Corporation, one of the largest energy companies in the world in 2000. In the process of her work, she discovered that Enron's CFO, Andy Fastow, was involved in a significant fraud that resulted in Enron's financial statements being materially misstated. Watkins faced a tough decision that had an ethical dimension. The following discussion uses the framework for making ethical decisions developed in Chapter 1 to examine how Watkins worked through the ethical dilemma.

Decision	Guidelines
1. What is the issue?	**1.** Watkins' ethical dilemma was to decide what she should do with the information she had uncovered.
	Specify the alternatives. For Sherron Watkins, four alternatives are: (a) express her concern about the problem to her boss, CFO Andrew Fastow; (b) express her concern to Kenneth Lay, CEO of Enron; (c) do nothing; or (d) resign.
2. Who are the important stakeholders?	**2.** *All* Enron employees (including Watkins), shareholders, creditors, and the U.S. Securities and Exchange Commission (SEC) are stakeholders.
3. What are the alternatives and consequences?	**3. a.** If Watkins approached Fastow, he might have penalized her, or he might have rewarded her for careful work. This would have preserved her integrity and led Fastow to correct the situation and preserve Enron's public trust, but Fastow might have fired Watkins for insubordination.
	b. If Watkins took her concerns to the CEO, who was Fastow's boss—going over Fastow's head—her integrity would have been preserved. Her relationship with Fastow would surely have been strained and it might have been difficult for them to work together in the future. Watkins might have been rewarded for careful work, but if Fastow's boss had colluded with Fastow in setting up the partnerships, Watkins could have been penalized. If the situation was corrected and outsiders were notified, Enron could have been reprimanded by the SEC if the company's financial statement data proved inaccurate.
	c. and d. If Watkins had done nothing, or resigned, she would have avoided a confrontation with Fastow or Lay. But, the public might have suffered if investors and creditors relied on faulty data, and Watkins' conscience would likely have troubled her.
4. What should be done?	**4.** Identifying the best choice is difficult. Watkins had to balance the likely effects on the various people against the dictates of her own conscience. This framework identifies the relevant factors. As it turned out, Watkins took her concerns to CEO Kenneth Lay, and he launched an investigation into the situation. Unfortunately, however, enough damage had already been done and Enron filed for Chapter 11 bankruptcy protection from its creditors. Enron fired Andrew Fastow, who has since pleaded guilty to a number of charges and is now in jail.

EXPLAIN THE OBJECTIVES AND COMPONENTS OF INTERNAL CONTROL

OBJECTIVE

❷ **Explain** the objectives and components of internal control

The primary way that fraud and unintentional errors are prevented, detected, or corrected in an organization is through a proper system of internal control. How critical are internal controls? They're so important that the Ontario Legislature passed a law[*] to require public companies—those that sell their shares to the public—to maintain a system of internal controls. Exhibit 4-2 provides an excerpt from Loblaw Companies

---

[*]Bill 198 (Chapter 22, Statutes of Ontario, 2002) *An Act to Implement Budget Measures and Other Initiatives of the Government.*

Loblaws 2011 Annual Report
Management is also responsible to provide reasonable assurance that assets are safeguarded and that relevant and reliable financial information is produced. Management is required to design a system of internal controls and certify as to the design and operating effectiveness of internal controls over financial reporting. A dedicated control compliance team reviews and evaluates internal controls, the results of which are shared with management on a quarterly basis.

EXHIBIT 4-2
Loblaw Companies Limited's Management's Statement of Responsibility for Financial Reporting (Partial) From the 2011 Annual Report

Limited's Management's Statement of Responsibility for Financial Reporting, taken from the 2011 annual report.

Internal control is a plan of organization and system of procedures designed, implemented, and maintained by company management and the board of directors to deal with risks to the business that have been identified and that relate to

- the reliability of the company's financial records and financial reporting,
- the company's ability to operate effectively and efficiently, and
- the company's compliance with legal requirements.

THE RELIABILITY OF THE COMPANY'S FINANCIAL RECORDS AND FINANCIAL REPORTING. The system of internal control should be designed to ensure that the accounting records are accurate, reliable, and timely. Without reliable records, the business cannot know if it is profitable and investors and creditors cannot know if the financial statements are a faithful representation of the company's operations.

THE COMPANY'S ABILITY TO OPERATE EFFECTIVELY AND EFFICIENTLY. The system of internal control should be designed to ensure that assets and records are safeguarded. No company can afford to waste physical or reputational resources. It is important that employees follow company policy; everyone in the company must work towards the same goal. Company policies should be designed so that employees and customers are treated fairly.

THE COMPANY'S COMPLIANCE WITH LEGAL REQUIREMENTS. The system of internal control should be designed to ensure that the board of directors can be confident that employees of the company from management on down are complying with all laws and regulations that affect the company.

These three goals can be achieved by satisfying five objectives:

- Safeguard assets, including records against waste, inefficiency, and fraud.
- Encourage all employees, managers, and staff to follow company policy.
- Promote operational efficiency to minimize waste.
- Ensure accurate, reliable accounting records.
- Comply with legal and regulatory requirements.

The *Sarbanes-Oxley Act* (SOX)

As the Enron and WorldCom scandals unfolded, many people asked, "How can these things happen? If such large companies that we have trusted commit such acts, how can we trust any company to be telling the truth in its financial statements? Where were the auditors?" To address public concern, U.S. Congress passed the *Sarbanes-Oxley Act of 2002*, abbreviated as SOX. SOX revamped corporate governance in the United States and also had sweeping effects on the accounting profession. Securities regulators in Canada and around the world revised their own regulations in light of the SOX requirements.

Canadian-listed public companies, whose shares or debt are sold to the public, are regulated by one of the 13 (10 provinces and 3 territories) securities commissions in Canada. The 13 securities commissions have formed an umbrella organization called the Canadian Securities Administrators (CSA), which issues Staff Notices and National Instruments on behalf of the 13 securities commissions.

The CSA began work on developing a Canadian strategy incorporating some or all of the rules in SOX for Canadian public companies. As a result, National Instrument (NI) 52-109 was issued. It requires public companies to provide certain disclosures in the Management Discussion and Analysis (MD&A) of their annual report. The MD&A provides users of financial statements with management's explanation of the company's past performance, financial condition, and future prospects. The MD&A is not part of the financial statements, but it is included in the annual report. Some of the requirements of NI 52-109 include the following:

- "The [chief executive officer] CEO and [chief financial officer] CFO [certifying officers] must certify that they have evaluated the effectiveness of the issuer's internal controls over financial reporting (ICFR) and disclosed in the annual MD&A their conclusions about the effectiveness of ICFR at the financial year-end. The evaluation must be completed using a control framework."*

- MD&A disclosure is required for each material weakness related to ICFR. Issuers are not required to remediate a material weakness; however, they must disclose plans or actions already taken to do so.

- The CEO and CFO to certify each quarter, among other things, that they have designed disclosure controls and procedures (DC&P) and ICFR and disclosed changes in ICFR that have materially affected or are reasonably likely to materially affect the issuer's ICFR.

Exhibit 4-3 diagrams the shield that internal controls provide for an organization. Protected by this shield from fraud, waste, and inefficiency, companies can do business in a trustworthy manner that ensures public confidence, an extremely important element in maintaining the stability of financial markets around the world. The next section identifies the components of internal control.

EXHIBIT 4-3
The Shield of Internal Control

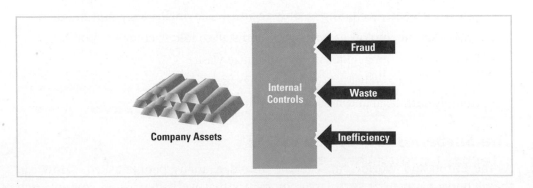

---

*Source: "Certification of Internal Controls: Final Certification Rules" KPMG LLP, September 2008.

The Components of Internal Control

As noted earlier, management is responsible for establishing and maintaining adequate internal control over financial reporting. In order to achieve this, internal control procedures are designed for all employees within the organization to follow. Before we discuss these procedures, it is important to take a look at the five components of an effective internal control system.

CRISCM

CONTROL ENVIRONMENT. The control environment is the "tone at the top" of the business. It starts with the CEO and the top managers. They must behave honourably to set a good example for company employees. They must demonstrate the importance of internal controls if they expect employees to take the controls seriously. A key ingredient in the control environment of many companies is a corporate code of conduct that communicates the company's policies on integrity and ethical values.

RISK ASSESSMENT. A company must be able to identify its business risks, then establish procedures for dealing with those risks to minimize their impact on the company. For example, CN Rail faces the business risk of derailment. Air Canada faces the risk of high fuel costs. Kraft Foods faces the risk that its food products may harm people. All companies face the risk of bankruptcy. The management of companies, supported by their boards, have to identify these business risks and do what they can to prevent those risks from causing financial or other harm to the company, its employees, its owners, and its creditors.

INFORMATION SYSTEMS. Management of a business needs accurate information to keep track of assets and measure profits and losses. Every system within the business that processes accounting data should have the ability to capture transactions as they occur, record those transactions in an accurate and timely manner, post those transactions to the ledger, and report those transactions in the form of account balances or footnotes in the financial statements.

CONTROL PROCEDURES. Control procedures are designed to ensure that the company's goals are achieved. Examples include the proper separation of duties, comparisons and other checks, adequate records, proper approvals, and physical safeguards to protect assets from theft. The next section discusses internal control procedures.

MONITORING OF CONTROLS. Monitoring provides "eyes and ears," so that no one person or group of persons can process a transaction completely without being seen and checked by another person or group. With modern computerized systems, much of the monitoring of day-to-day activity is done through controls programmed into a company's information systems. In addition, companies hire auditors to monitor their controls. Internal auditors monitor company controls from the inside to safeguard the company's assets, and external auditors test the controls from the outside to ensure that the accounting records are accurate and reliable.

Internal Control Procedures

Whether the business is Telus, Gildan Activewear, GreBru Products, or a Petro-Canada gas station, every major class of transactions needs to have the following internal control procedures.

SMART HIRING PRACTICES. In a business with good internal controls, no important duty is overlooked. Each person in the information chain is important. The chain should start with hiring. Background checks should be conducted on job applicants. Proper training and supervision, as well as paying competitive salaries, helps ensure that all employees are sufficiently competent for their jobs. Employee responsibilities should be clearly laid out in position descriptions. For example, the treasurer's department should be in charge of cash handling, as well as signing and approving cheques. Warehouse personnel should be in charge of storing and keeping track of inventory. With clearly assigned responsibilities, all important jobs get done.

SEPARATION OF DUTIES. In processing transactions, smart management separates three key duties: *asset handling, record keeping, and transaction approval.* For example, in the case of GreBru Products, separation of the duties of cash handling from record keeping for customer accounts receivable would have removed Alec Jones's opportunity to engage in fraud, because it would have made it impossible for him to have lapped accounts receivable if another employee had been keeping the books. Ideally, someone else should also review customer accounts for collectability and be in charge of writing them off if they become completely uncollectible.

The accounting department should be completely separate from the operating departments, such as production and sales. What would happen if sales personnel, who were compensated based on a percentage of the amount of sales they made, were also responsible for recording sales transactions in the accounting records? Sales figures could be inflated and might not reflect the actual amount sold to customers.

No employee should have responsibility for both handling cash and recording cash transactions in the accounting records. If one employee has both cash-handling and accounting duties, that person can steal cash and conceal the theft. This is what happened at GreBru Products.

For companies that are too small to hire separate persons to do all of these functions, the key to good internal control is getting the owner involved, usually by having the owner approve all large transactions, make bank deposits, or reconcile the monthly bank account.

PROPER MONITORING. All internal controls must be regularly monitored to ensure they are operating effectively and efficiently. When flaws are discovered, they should be promptly corrected.

One of the most effective tools for monitoring compliance with management's policies is the use of **operating budgets** and **cash budgets**. A **budget** is a quantitative financial plan that helps control day-to-day management activities. Management may prepare these budgets on a yearly, quarterly, monthly, or more frequent basis. Operating budgets are budgets of future periods' net income. Cash budgets, discussed in depth later in this chapter, are budgets of future periods' cash receipts and cash disbursements. Often these budgets are "rolling," being constantly updated by adding a time period a year away while dropping the time period that has just passed. Computer systems are programmed to prepare exception reports for data that are out of line with expectations. This data can include variances for each account from budgeted amounts. Department managers are required to explain the variances and to take corrective actions in their operating plans to keep the budgets in line with expectations. This is an example of the use of **exception reporting**.

To validate the accounting records and monitor compliance with company policies, many companies have an audit. An **audit** is an examination of the company's financial statements and its accounting system, including its controls.

Audits can be internal or external. *Internal auditors* are employees of the business. They ensure that employees are following company policies and operations are running efficiently. Internal auditors also determine whether the company is following legal requirements.

External auditors are completely independent of the business. They are hired to determine whether or not the company's financial statements agree with generally accepted accounting principles. Auditors examine the client's financial statements and the underlying transactions in order to form a professional opinion on the accuracy and reliability of the company's financial statements.

ADEQUATE RECORDS. Adequate records provide the details of business transactions. The general rule is that all major groups of transactions should be supported by either hard-copy documents or electronic records. Examples of documents include sales invoices, shipping records, customer remittance advices, purchase orders, vendor invoices, receiving reports, and cancelled (paid) cheques. Documents should be prenumbered to assure completeness of processing and proper transaction cut-off, and to prevent theft and inefficiency. A gap in the numbered document sequence draws attention to the possibility that transactions might have been omitted from processing.

LIMITED ACCESS. To complement separation of duties, company policy should limit access to assets to only those persons that have custodial responsibilities for those assets. Cash receipts, for example, might be processed through a lockbox system. Access to inventory should be limited to persons in the company warehouse where inventories are stored, or to persons in the shipping and receiving functions. Likewise, the company should limit access to records to those persons who have record-keeping responsibilities. All manual records of the business should be protected by lock and key, and electronic records should be protected by **passwords**. Only authorized persons should have access to certain records. Individual computers in the business should be protected by user identification and password. Electronic data files should be encrypted to prevent their recognition if accessed by a hacker or other unauthorized person.

PROPER APPROVALS. No transaction should be processed without management's general or specific approval. The bigger the transaction, the more specific approval it requires. For individual small transactions, management might delegate approval to a specific department. For example:

- Sales to customers on account should all be approved by a separate credit department that reviews all customers for creditworthiness before sales are made on credit. This helps assure that the company doesn't make sales to customers who cannot afford to pay their bills.

- Purchases of all items on credit should be approved by a separate purchasing department that specializes in that function. Among other things, a purchasing department should only buy from approved vendors, on the basis of competitive bids, to assure that the company gets the highest quality products for the most competitive prices.

- All personnel decisions, including hiring, firing, and pay adjustments, should be handled by a separate human resources (HR) department that specializes in personnel-related matters.

Very large transactions should generally be approved by top management, and may even go to the board of directors for approval.

INFORMATION TECHNOLOGY. Accounting systems are relying less on manual procedures and more on information technology (IT) than ever before for record keeping, asset handling, approval, and monitoring, as well as physically safeguarding the assets. For example, retailers such as The Hudson Bay Company control inventory by attaching an electronic sensor to merchandise. The cashier must remove or demagnetize the sensor before the customer can walk out of the store. If a customer tries to leave the store with the sensor attached, an alarm sounds. According to Checkpoint Systems, these devices reduce theft by as much as 50%. Bar codes speed up the checkout process at retail stores, performing multiple operations in a single step. When the sales associate scans the merchandise at the register, the computer records the sale, removes the item from inventory, and computes the amount of cash to be tendered.

When a company employs sophisticated IT, the basic attributes of internal control do not change, but the procedures by which these attributes are implemented change substantially. For example, separation of duties is often accomplished by separating the IT department from user departments (e.g., **controller**, sales, purchasing, receiving, credit, HR, treasurer) and restricting access to the IT department only to authorized personnel. Within the IT department, programmers should be separated from computer operators and data librarians. Access to sensitive data files is protected by **password** and data encryption. Electronic records must be saved routinely, or they might be written over or erased. Comparisons of data (such as cash receipts with total credits to customer accounts) that might otherwise be done by hand are performed by the computer. Computers can monitor inventory levels by item, generating a purchase order for inventory when it reaches a certain level.

The use of computers has the advantage of speed and accuracy (when programmed correctly). However, a computer that is *not* programmed correctly can corrupt *all* the data, making it unusable. It is therefore important to hire experienced and competent people to run the IT department, to restrict access to sensitive data and the IT department only to authorized personnel, to check data entered into and retrieved from the computer for accuracy and completeness, and to test and retest programs on a regular basis to assure data integrity and accuracy.

SAFEGUARD CONTROLS. Businesses keep important documents in fireproof vaults. Burglar alarms safeguard buildings, and security cameras safeguard other property. Loss-prevention specialists train employees to spot suspicious activity.

Employees who handle cash are in a tempting position. Many businesses purchase fidelity bonds on cashiers. The bond is an insurance policy that reimburses the company for any losses due to employee theft. Before issuing a fidelity bond, the insurance company investigates the employee's background.

Mandatory vacations and job rotation improve internal control. Companies move employees from job to job; this improves morale by giving employees a broad view of the business. Also, knowing someone else will do your job next month keeps you honest. GreBru Products didn't rotate employees to different jobs, and it cost the company $622,000.

STOP + THINK (4-1)	An employee stole $2.2 million from her employer by diverting cheques received in the mail and used them to conceal thefts of cash from the daily bank deposits. Removing and destroying invoices for which the cheques	were payment against concealed the theft. Because she had access to incoming receipts and the related invoices, it gave her the opportunity to steal and alter the records to cover the theft. How could this have been avoided?

Internal Controls for E-Commerce

E-commerce creates its own risks. Hackers may gain access to confidential information such as account numbers and passwords. The pitfalls of including e-commerce as part of a business's operations include:

- Stolen credit-card numbers
- Computer viruses and Trojan horses
- Phishing expeditions

STOLEN CREDIT-CARD NUMBERS. Suppose you buy music from iTunes. To make the purchase, your credit-card number must travel through cyberspace. Wireless networks (Wi-Fi) are creating new security hazards.

Amateur hacker Carlos Salgado, Jr., used his home computer to steal 100,000 credit-card numbers with a combined limit exceeding $1 billion. Salgado was caught when he tried to sell the numbers to an undercover police officer.

COMPUTER VIRUSES AND TROJAN HORSES. A **computer virus** is a malicious program that (a) enters program code without consent and (b) performs destructive actions in the victim's computer files or programs. A **Trojan horse** is a malicious computer program that hides inside a legitimate program and works like a virus. Viruses can destroy or alter data, make bogus calculations, and infect files. Most firms have had a problem with viruses.

PHISHING EXPEDITIONS. **Phishing** can involve creating neat-sounding but bogus Web sites that attract lots of visitors. The thieves then set about obtaining account numbers and passwords from unsuspecting people. Another way thieves obtain personal information from people is by sending e-mails from what appears to be legitimate banks or businesses, requesting bank account information or usernames and passwords. Of course, the thieves then use this information for illicit purposes.

Security Measures

To address the risks posed by e-commerce, companies have devised a number of security measures, including:

- Encryption
- Firewalls

ENCRYPTION. The company's computer server holding confidential information may not be secure. One technique for protecting customer data is encryption. **Encryption** rearranges messages by using a mathematical process. The encrypted message can't be read by those who don't know the code. An accounting example uses check-sum digits for account numbers. Each account number has its last digit equal to the sum of the previous digits. For example, consider Customer Number 2237, where 2 + 2 + 3 = 7. Any account number that fails this test triggers an error message.

FIREWALLS. A **firewall** limits access into a local network. Members can access the network but nonmembers can't. Usually, several firewalls are built into the system. Think of a fortress with multiple walls protecting the company's computerized records in the centre. At the point of entry, passwords, PINs (personal identification numbers), and signatures are used. More sophisticated firewalls are used deeper in the network. The following illustration demonstrates this layered security, starting with Firewall 1.

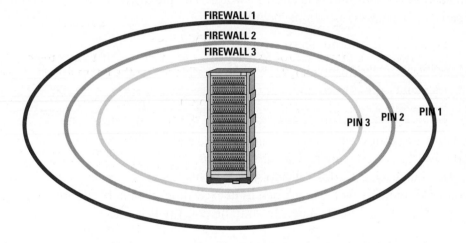

STOP + THINK (4-2)	A student received an e-mail from her bank instructing her to upgrade her bank account, with a convenient	link for her to click on. She felt something was not quite right. What she should do?

Limitations of Internal Control—Costs and Benefits

Unfortunately, most internal control measures can be overcome. Systems designed to thwart one person's fraud can be beaten by two or more employees working together—*colluding*—to defraud the firm. Consider the Galaxy Theatre. Ralph, who sells tickets, and Lana, who takes the tickets, can design a scheme in which Ralph sells tickets and pockets the cash from 10 customers. Lana admits 10 customers without tickets. Ralph and Lana split the cash. To prevent this situation, Colleen, the manager, must take additional steps, such as matching the number of people in the theatre against the number of ticket stubs retained, but that takes time away from her other duties.

The stricter the internal control system, the more it costs. A too-complex system of internal control can strangle the business with red tape. How tight should the controls be? Internal controls must be judged in light of their costs and benefits. An example of a good cost/benefit relationship: A security guard at a Walmart store costs about $28,000 a year. On average, each guard prevents about $50,000 of theft. The net savings to Walmart is $22,000.

◀ DECISION GUIDELINES ▶

INTERNAL CONTROL SYSTEM

An effective internal control system provides reasonable assurance regarding the reliability of financial reporting. Managers are responsible for establishing and maintaining a system of internal control and procedures.

Decision	Guidelines
How is an internal control system used in decision making?	*Managers,* who have to sign the certification, need to be confident that the internal controls over financial reporting are effective, because there are penalties when the certifying officers knew or should have known that they were not effective.
	Investors and creditors will then have more confidence that the financial statements fairly present the financial position of the company and the results of its operations.

PREPARE AND USE A BANK RECONCILIATION

OBJECTIVE

❸ **Prepare** and **use** a bank reconciliation

Cash is the most liquid asset because it is the medium of exchange, but it is easy to conceal and relatively easy to steal. As a result, most businesses have specific controls for cash.

Keeping cash in a bank account helps control cash. This is an important option because banks have established procedures for safeguarding customers' money. Following are the documents used to control bank accounts.

Signature Card

Banks require each person authorized to sign on an account to provide a *signature card*. This protects against forgery.

Deposit Slip

Banks supply standard account forms such as *deposit slips*. The customer fills in the amount of each deposit. As proof of the transaction, the customer keeps a deposit receipt.

EXHIBIT 4-4
Cheque With Remittance
Advice

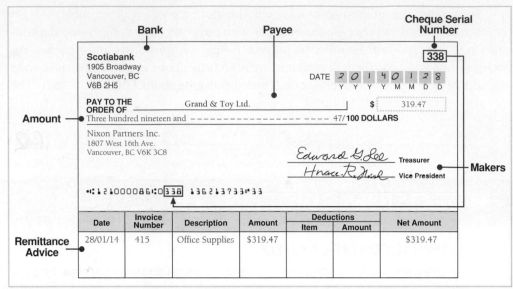

Cheque

To pay cash, the depositor can write a **cheque**, which tells the bank to pay the designated party a specified amount. There are three parties to a cheque:

- the maker, who signs the cheque,
- the payee, to whom the cheque is paid, and
- the bank on which the cheque is drawn.

Exhibit 4-4 shows a cheque drawn by Nixon Partners Inc., the maker. The cheque has two parts, the cheque itself and the **remittance advice** below it. This optional attachment, which may often be scanned electronically, tells the payee the reason for the payment and is used as a source document for posting the proper accounts.

Bank Statement

Banks may send monthly statements to customers in paper form or the statements may be available on the bank's website. A **bank statement** reports the activity in a bank account. The statement shows the account's beginning and ending balances, cash receipts, and payments. Exhibit 4-5 is the January 2014 bank statement of Nixon Partners Inc.

Electronic funds transfer (EFT) moves cash by electronic communication. It is cheaper for a company to pay employees by EFT (direct deposit) than by issuing payroll cheques. Many people pay their regular bills, such as mortgage, rent, and utilities, by EFT.

Bank Reconciliation

There are two records of a business's cash:

1. The Cash account in the company's general ledger. Exhibit 4-6 shows that Nixon Partners Inc.'s ending cash balance is $3,294.21.

EXHIBIT 4-5
Bank Statement

ACCOUNT STATEMENT

Scotiabank
1905 Broadway Vancouver, BC V6B 2H5

Nixon Partners Inc.
1807 West 16th Avenue
Vancouver, BC V6K 3C8

BUSINESS CHEQUING ACCOUNT 136–213733

CHEQUING ACCOUNT SUMMARY AS OF 01/01/14

BEGINNING BALANCE	TOTAL DEPOSITS	TOTAL WITHDRAWALS	SERVICE CHARGES	ENDING BALANCE
6,556.12	4,352.64	4,963.00	14.25	5,931.51

━━━━━━━━ BUSINESS CHEQUING ACCOUNT TRANSACTIONS ━━━━━━━━

DEPOSITS	DATE	AMOUNT
Deposit	Jan04	1,000.00
Deposit	Jan04	112.00
Deposit	Jan06	194.60
EFT—Collection of rent	Jan10	904.03
Bank Collection	Jan16	2,114.00
Interest	Jan20	28.01

CHARGES	DATE	AMOUNT
Service Charge	Jan31	14.25
Cheques:		

CHEQUES			BALANCES			
Number	Date	Amount	Date	Balance	Date	Balance
332	Jan06	3,000.00	Dec31	6,556.12	Jan16	7,378.75
656	Jan06	100.00	Jan04	7,616.12	Jan20	7,045.76
333	Jan10	150.00	Jan06	4,710.72	Jan25	5,945.76
334	Jan12	100.00	Jan10	5,464.75	Jan31	5,931.51
335	Jan12	100.00	Jan12	5,264.75		
336	Jan25	1,100.00				

OTHER CHARGES	DATE	AMOUNT
NSF	Jan04	52.00
EFT—Insurance	Jan20	361.00

MONTHLY SUMMARY

Withdrawals: 8	Minimum Balance: 4,710.72	Average Balance: 6,215.00

EXHIBIT 4-6
Cash Records of Nixon Partners Inc.

ACCOUNT Cash

Date		Item	Debit	Credit	Balance
2014					
Jan.	1	Balance			6,556.12
	2	Cash receipt	1,112.00		7,668.12
	5	Cash receipt	194.60		7,862.72
	31	Cash payments		6,160.14	1,702.58
	31	Cash receipt	1,591.63		3,294.21

Cash Payments

Cheque No.	Amount	Cheque No.	Amount
332	$3,000.00	338	$ 319.47
333	510.00	339	83.00
334	100.00	340	203.14
335	100.00	341	458.53
336	1,100.00		
337	286.00	Total	$6,160.14

2. The bank statement, which shows the cash receipts and payments transacted through the bank. In Exhibit 4-5, the bank shows an ending balance of $5,931.51 for Nixon Partners.

The books and the bank statement usually show different cash balances. Differences arise because of a time lag in recording transactions. Here are two examples:

- When you write a cheque, you immediately record it in your chequebook as a deduction. But the bank does not subtract the cheque from your account until the payee cashes it at a later date. Likewise, you immediately record the cash receipts for all your deposits as additions. But it may take a day or two for the bank to add deposits to your balance.
- Your EFT payments and cash receipts are recorded by the bank before you learn of them.

To ensure accurate cash records, you need to update your cash record—either online or after you receive your bank statement. The result of this updating process allows you to prepare a **bank reconciliation**. The bank reconciliation explains all differences between your cash records and your bank statement balance.

The person who prepares a company's bank reconciliation should have no other cash duties and be independent of cash activities. Otherwise, he or she can steal cash and manipulate the reconciliation to conceal the theft.

Preparing the Bank Reconciliation

Here are the items that appear on a bank reconciliation. They all cause differences between the bank balance and the book balance to occur. We call your cash record (also known as a "chequebook") the "books."

BANK SIDE OF THE RECONCILIATION.

1. Items to show on the *Bank* side of the bank reconciliation include the following:
   a. *Deposits in transit* (outstanding deposits). You have recorded these deposits, but the bank has not. Add **deposits in transit** on the bank reconciliation.
   b. *Outstanding cheques.* You have recorded these cheques, but the payees have not yet cashed them. Subtract **outstanding cheques.**
   c. *Bank errors.* Correct all bank errors on the Bank side of the reconciliation. For example, the bank may erroneously subtract from your account a cheque written by someone else.

BOOK SIDE OF THE RECONCILIATION.

1. Items to show on the *Book* side of the bank reconciliation include the following:
   a. *Bank collections.* **Bank collections** are cash receipts that the bank has recorded for your account. But you haven't recorded the cash receipt yet. Many businesses have their customers pay directly to their bank. This is called a *lockbox system* and reduces theft. An example is a bank collecting an account receivable for you. Add bank collections on the bank reconciliation.
   b. *Electronic funds transfers.* The bank may receive or pay cash on your behalf. An electronic funds transfer (EFT) may be a cash receipt or a cash payment.

EFTs are set up with a bank using a code and bank account number for the company. It allows electronic cheques to be sent (or received) digitally to (or from) the bank who then disburses the money from (or deposits the money to) the company account. Add EFT receipts and subtract EFT payments.

c. *Service charge.* This cash payment is the bank's fee for processing your transactions. Subtract service charges.

d. *Interest income.* On certain types of bank accounts, you earn interest if you keep enough cash in your account. The bank statement tells you of this cash receipt. Add interest income.

e. *Nonsufficient funds (NSF) cheques.* **Nonsufficient funds (NSF) cheques** are cash receipts from customers who do not have sufficient funds in their bank account to cover the amount. NSF cheques (sometimes called bad cheques) are treated as cash payments on your bank reconciliation. Subtract NSF cheques.

f. *The cost of printed cheques.* This cash payment is handled like a service charge. Subtract this cost.

g. *Book errors.* Correct all book errors on the Book side of the reconciliation. For example, you may have recorded a $120 cheque that you wrote as $210.

In a business, the bank reconciliation can be a part of internal control if it is done on a regular basis and if someone independent of the person preparing the bank reconciliation (for example, someone from another department) reviews the reconciliation.

BANK RECONCILIATION ILLUSTRATED. The bank statement in Exhibit 4-5 indicates that the January 31 bank balance of Nixon Partners Inc. is $5,931.51. However, Exhibit 4-6 shows that the company's Cash account on the books has a balance of $3,294.21. This situation calls for a bank reconciliation. Exhibit 4-7, Panel A, lists the reconciling items for easy reference, and Panel B shows the completed reconciliation.

After the reconciliation in Exhibit 4-7, the adjusted bank balance equals the adjusted book balance. This equality checks the accuracy of both the bank and the books.

RECORDING TRANSACTIONS FROM THE BANK RECONCILIATION. The bank reconciliation is an accountant's tool separate from the journals and ledgers. It does *not* account for transactions in the journal. To get the transactions into the accounts, we must record journal entries and post them to the ledger. All items on the *Book* side of the bank reconciliation require journal entries.

The bank reconciliation in Exhibit 4-7 requires Nixon Partners to make journal entries to bring the Cash account up to date. These journal entries are detailed below. Numbers in parentheses correspond to the reconciling items listed in Exhibit 4-7, Panel A.

(4) Jan.	31	Cash	904.03		
		Interest revenue		904.03	
		Receipt of interest revenue.			
(5) Jan.	31	Cash	2,114.00		
		Note receivable		1,900.00	
		Interest revenue		214.00	
		Note receivable collected by bank.			
(6) Jan.	31	Cash	28.01		
		Interest revenue		28.01	
		Interest earned on bank balance.			
(7) Jan.	31	Cash	360.00		
		Accounts payable—Brown Co. Ltd.		360.00	
		Correction of cheque no. 333.			

(8) Jan.	31	Bank service charge expense	14.25		
		Cash		14.25	
		Bank service charge.			
(9) Jan.	31	Accounts receivable—L. Ross	52.00		
		Cash		52.00	
		NSF customer cheque returned by bank.			
(10) Jan.	31	Insurance expense	361.00		
		Cash		361.00	
		Payment of monthly insurance.			

EXHIBIT 4-7
Bank Reconciliation

PANEL A—Reconciling Items

Bank side:

1. Deposit in transit, $1,591.63
2. Bank error: The bank deducted $100.00 on January 6 for a cheque written by another company. Add $100.00 to the bank balance.
3. Outstanding cheques—total of $1,350.14

Cheque No.	Amount
337	$286.00
338	319.47
339	83.00
340	203.14
341	458.53

Book side:

4. EFT receipt of your interest revenue earned on an investment, $904.03.
5. Bank collection of your note receivable, including interest of $214.00, $2,114.00.
6. Interest revenue earned on your bank balance, $28.01.
7. Book error: You recorded cheque no. 333 for $510.00. The amount you actually paid on account was $150.00. Add $360.00 to your book balance.
8. Bank service charge, $14.25.
9. NSF cheque from a customer, $52.00. Subtract $52.00 from your book balance.
10. EFT payment of insurance expense, $361.00.

PANEL B—Bank Reconciliation

Nixon Partners Inc.
Bank Reconciliation
January 31, 2014

Bank			Books		
Balance, January 31		$5,931.51	Balance, January 31		$3,294.21
Add:			Add:		
1. Deposit in transit		1,591.63	4. EFT receipt of interest revenue		904.03
2. Correction of bank error		100.00	5. Bank collection of note		
		7,623.14	receivable		2,114.00
			6. Interest revenue earned on		
			bank balance		28.01
			7. Correction of book error—		
Less:			overstated our cheque no. 333		360.00
3. Outstanding cheques					6,700.25
No. 337	$286.00				
No. 338	319.47		Less:		
No. 339	83.00		8. Service charge	$ 14.25	
No. 340	203.14		9. NSF cheque	52.00	
No. 341	458.53	(1,350.14)	10. EFT payment of insurance expense	361.00	(427.25)
Adjusted bank balance		$6,273.00	Adjusted bank balance		$6,273.00

These amounts should agree.

Summary of the Various Reconciling Items:

Bank Balance—Always:
- *Add* deposits in transit.
- *Subtract* outstanding cheques.
- *Add* or *subtract* corrections of bank errors.

Book Balance—Always:
- *Add* bank collections, interest revenue, and EFT receipts.
- *Subtract* service charges, NSF cheques, and EFT payments.
- *Add* or *subtract* corrections of book errors.

The entry for the NSF cheque (entry 9) needs explanation. Upon learning that a customer's $52.00 cheque to us was not good, we must credit Cash to update the Cash account. Unfortunately, we still have a receivable from the customer, so we must debit Accounts Receivable to reinstate our receivable.

Online Banking

Online banking allows you to pay bills and view your account electronically—you don't have to wait until the end of the month to get a bank statement. With online banking you can reconcile transactions at any time and keep your account current whenever you wish.

STOP + THINK (4-3)

You have been asked to prepare a bank reconciliation and are given the following information. The bank statement balance is $4,500 and shows a service charge of $15, interest earned of $5, and an NSF cheque for $300. Deposits in transit total $1,200; outstanding cheques are $575. You recorded as $152 a cheque of $125 in payment of an account payable.

1. What is the adjusted bank balance?

2. What was the book balance of cash before the reconciliation?

Using the Bank Reconciliation to Control Cash

The bank reconciliation is a powerful control device. Julie Brox is an accountant in Regina, Saskatchewan. She owns several apartment complexes that are managed by her uncle, Herman Klassen. Her uncle signs up tenants, collects the monthly rents, arranges custodial and maintenance work, hires and fires employees, writes the cheques, and performs the bank reconciliation. In short, he does it all. This concentration of duties in one person is evidence of weak internal control. Brox's uncle could be stealing from her or making mistakes, and as a a accountant she is aware of this possibility.

Brox trusts her uncle because he is a member of the family. Nevertheless, she exercises some controls over his management of her apartments. Brox periodically drops by her properties to see whether the maintenance staff is keeping the property in good condition. To control cash, Brox regularly examines the bank reconciliation that her uncle has performed. Brox would know immediately if her uncle were writing cheques to himself. By examining each cheque, Brox establishes control over cash payments.

Brox has a simple method for controlling cash receipts. She knows the occupancy level of her apartments. She also knows the monthly rent she charges. She multiplies the number of apartments—20—by the monthly rent (which averages $800 per unit) to arrive at an expected monthly rent revenue of $16,000. By tracing the $16,000 revenue to the bank statement, Brox can tell if all her rent money went into her bank account. To keep her uncle on his toes, Brox lets him know that she periodically audits his work.

Control activities such as these are critical. If there are only a few employees, separation of duties may not be feasible. The owner must control operations, or the assets may slip away. These controls are called *executive controls*.

MID-CHAPTER SUMMARY PROBLEM

The Cash account of Chima Inc. at February 28, 2014, is as follows:

Cash					
Feb. 1	Balance	3,995	Feb. 5		400
6		800	12		3,100
15		1,800	19		1,100
22		1,100	26		500
28		2,400	27		900
Feb. 28	Balance	4,095			

Aneil Chima deposits all cash receipts in the bank and makes all cash payments by cheque. Chima Inc. receives this bank statement on February 28, 2014 (as always, negative amounts are in parentheses):

Name: Chima Inc.
Accounting Period: Month of February 2014

Bank Statement for February 2014		
Beginning balance		$ 3,995
Deposits:		
Feb. 7	$ 800	
15	1,800	
23	1,100	3,700
Cheques (total per day):		
Feb. 8	$ 400	
16	3,100	
23	1,100	(4,600)
Other items:		
Service charge		(10)
NSF cheque from M. E. Crown		(700)
Bank collection of note receivable		1,000*
EFT—monthly rent expense		(330)
Interest on account balance		15
Ending balance		$ 3,070

*Includes interest of $119

Requirements

1. Prepare the bank reconciliation of Chima Inc. at February 28, 2014.
2. Record the journal entries based on the bank reconciliation.

ANSWERS

Requirement 1

<table>
<tr><td colspan="3" align="center">Chima Inc.
Bank Reconciliation
February 28, 2014</td></tr>
<tr><td colspan="3">Bank:</td></tr>
<tr><td>Balance, February 28, 2014...</td><td></td><td>$ 3,070</td></tr>
<tr><td>Add: Deposit of February 28 in transit...............................</td><td></td><td>2,400</td></tr>
<tr><td></td><td></td><td>5,470</td></tr>
<tr><td>Less: Outstanding cheques issued on
        Feb. 26 ($500) and Feb. 27 ($900)............................</td><td></td><td>(1,400)</td></tr>
<tr><td>Adjusted bank balance, February 28, 2014 ....</td><td></td><td>$ 4,070</td></tr>
<tr><td colspan="3">Books:</td></tr>
<tr><td>Balance, February 28, 2014...</td><td></td><td>$ 4,095</td></tr>
<tr><td>Add: Bank collection of note receivable, including interest of $119 ....</td><td></td><td>1,000</td></tr>
<tr><td>   Interest earned on bank balance.................................</td><td></td><td>15</td></tr>
<tr><td></td><td></td><td>5,110</td></tr>
<tr><td>Less: Service charge ....</td><td>$ 10</td><td></td></tr>
<tr><td>   NSF cheque...</td><td>700</td><td></td></tr>
<tr><td>   EFT—Rent expense...</td><td>330</td><td>(1,040)</td></tr>
<tr><td>Adjusted book balance, February 28, 2014.........................</td><td></td><td>$ 4,070</td></tr>
</table>

Before creating the bank reconciliation, compare the Cash account and the bank statement. Cross out all items that appear in both places. The items that remain are the reconciling items.

Begin with the ending balance on the bank statement.
- Add deposits (debits) from the Cash account not on the bank statement.
- Deduct cheques (credits) from the Cash account not on the bank statement.

Begin with the ending balance in the Cash general ledger account.
- Add money received by the bank on behalf of the company (increases to the bank statement balance).
- Deduct bank charges, NSF cheques, or pre-authorized payments (decreases to the bank statement balance).

Requirement 2

Feb. 28	Cash..	1,000		Feb. 28	Accounts receivable—M. E. Crown	700	
	Note receivable ($1,000 − $119)		881		Cash..		700
	Interest revenue................................		119		NSF cheque returned by bank.		
	Note receivable collected by bank.			28	Rent expense	330	
28	Cash..	15			Cash..		330
	Interest revenue................................		15		Monthly rent expense.		
	Interest earned on bank balance.						
28	Bank service charge expense...............	10					
	Cash..		10				
	Bank service charge.						

Prepare journal entries for all reconciling items from the "Books" section of the bank reconciliation.

APPLY INTERNAL CONTROLS TO CASH RECEIPTS AND CASH PAYMENTS

Cash requires some specific internal controls because cash is relatively easy to steal and it's easy to convert to other forms of wealth. Moreover, all transactions ultimately affect cash. That is why cash is called "the eye of the needle." Let's see how to control cash receipts.

All cash receipts should be deposited for safekeeping in the bank—quickly. Companies receive cash over the counter and through the mail. Each source of cash requires its own security measures.

Cash Receipts Over the Counter

Exhibit 4-8 illustrates a cash receipt over the counter in a grocery store. The point-of-sale terminal provides control over the cash receipts. Consider a Sobeys store. For each transaction, a Sobeys sales associate issues a receipt to the customer as proof of purchase. The cash drawer opens when all the purchases have been entered, and the machine electronically transmits a record of the sale to the store's main computer. At the end of each shift, the sales associate delivers his or her cash drawer to the office, where it is combined with cash from all other terminals and delivered by armoured car to the bank for deposit. Later, a separate employee in

EXHIBIT 4-8
Cash Receipts Over the Counter

Monkey Business

the accounting department reconciles the electronic record of the sales per terminal to the record of the cash turned in. These measures, coupled with oversight by a manager, discourage theft.

Point-of-sale terminals also provide effective control over inventory. For example, in a restaurant, these devices track sales by menu item and total sales by cash, type of credit card, gift card redeemed, etc. They create the daily sales journal for that store, which, in turn, interfaces with the general ledger. Managers can use records produced by point-of-sale terminals to check inventory levels and compare them against sales records for accuracy. For example, in a restaurant, an effective way to monitor sales of expensive wine is for a manager to perform a quick count of the bottles on hand at the end of the day and compare it with the count at the end of the previous day, plus the record of any purchased. The count at the end of the previous day, plus the record of bottles purchased, minus the count at the end of the current day should equal the amount sold as recorded by the point-of-sale terminals in the restaurant.

An effective control for many chain retail businesses, such as restaurants, grocery stores, or clothing stores, to prevent unauthorized access to cash as well as to allow for more efficient management of cash, is the use of "depository bank accounts." Cash receipts for an individual store are deposited into a local bank account (preferably delivered by armoured car for security reasons) on a daily basis. The corporate headquarters arranges for its centralized bank to draft the local depository accounts on a frequent (perhaps daily) basis to get the money concentrated into the company's centralized account, where it can be used to pay the corporation's bills. Depository accounts are "one-way" accounts where the local management may only make deposits. They have no authority to write cheques on the account or take money out of the store's account.

Cash Receipts by Mail

Most companies receive cheques by mail. Exhibit 4-9 shows how some companies control cash received by mail. All incoming mail is opened by a mailroom employee. The person opening the mail should also make a list of the receipts as an independent control from the treasurer/accounting department. The mailroom then sends all customer cheques to the treasurer, who has the cashier deposit the money in the bank. The remittance advices go to the accounting department for journal entries to

EXHIBIT 4-9
Receipts of Cheques by Mail

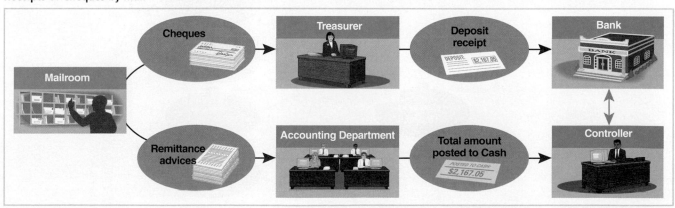

Cash and to the appropriate customers' accounts receivable. As a final step, the controller compares the following records for the day:

- Bank deposit amount from the treasurer
- Debit to Cash from the accounting department

The debit to Cash should equal the amount deposited in the bank. All cash receipts are safe in the bank, and the company books are up to date.

Many companies use a lockbox system. Customers send their cheques directly to the company's bank account. Internal control is tight because company personnel never touch incoming cash. The lockbox system puts your cash to work immediately.

Controls Over Payment by Cheque

Companies make most payments by cheque. Let's see how to control cash payments by cheque.

As we have seen, you need a good separation of duties between (a) operations and (b) writing cheques for cash payments. Payment by cheque is an important internal control, as follows:

- The cheque provides a record of the payment.
- The cheque must be signed by an authorized official.
- Before signing the cheque, the official should study the evidence supporting the payment.

CONTROLS OVER PURCHASE AND PAYMENT. To illustrate the internal control over cash payments by cheque, suppose GreBru Products buys some of its inventory from Gildan Activewear Inc. The purchasing and payment process follows the steps shown in Exhibit 4-10. Start with the box for GreBru Products on the left side.

1. GreBru e-mails a *purchase order* to Gildan. GreBru says, "Please send us 100 T-shirts."
2. Gildan ships the goods and e-mails an *invoice* back to GreBru.

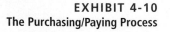

EXHIBIT 4-10
The Purchasing/Paying Process

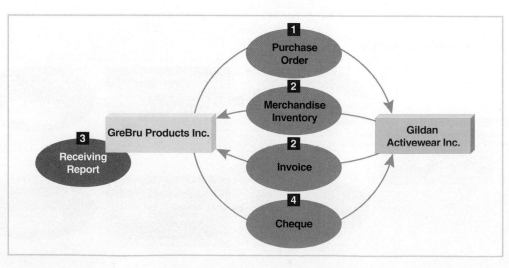

3. GreBru receives the *inventory* and prepares a *receiving report* to list the goods received.

4. After approving all documents, GreBru says, "Okay, we'll pay you" and sends a cheque to Gildan.

For good internal control, the purchasing agent should neither receive the goods nor approve the payment. If these duties aren't separated, a purchasing agent can buy goods and have them shipped to his or her home. Or a purchasing agent can spend too much on purchases, approve the payment, and split the excess with the supplier. To avoid these problems, companies distribute the following duties among different employees:

- Purchasing goods
- Receiving goods
- Approving the invoice for goods
- Signing the cheque or approving the EFT

Exhibit 4-11 shows GreBru's payment packet of documents.

Before approving the payment, the treasurer's department should examine the packet to ensure that all the documents agree. Only then does the company know:

1. It received the goods ordered.
2. It pays only for the goods received.

After payment, the person in the treasurer's department who has authorized the disbursement stamps the payment packet "paid" or punches a hole through it to prevent it from being submitted a second time. Dishonest people have tried to run a bill through twice for payment. The stamp or hole shows that the bill has been paid. If cheques are used, they should then be mailed directly to the payee without being allowed to return to the department that prepared them. To do so would violate separation of the duties of cash handling and record keeping, as well as unauthorized access to cash.

PETTY CASH. It would be wasteful to write separate cheques for an executive's taxi fare, name tags needed right away, or delivery of a package across town. To pay such minor amounts, companies keep a small **petty cash** fund on hand in the care of a single employee.

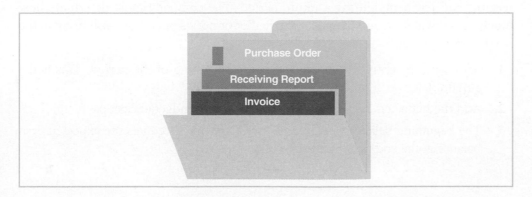

EXHIBIT 4-11
Payment Packet

The petty cash fund is opened with a particular amount of cash. A cheque for that amount is issued to Petty Cash. Assume that on February 28, CHC Helicopter Corp. establishes a petty cash fund of $500 in a sales department. The custodian of the petty cash fund cashes the cheque and places $500 in the fund, which may be a cash box or other device.

For each petty cash payment, the custodian prepares a petty cash slip to list the item purchased. The sum of the cash in the petty cash fund plus the total of the slip amounts should equal the opening balance at all times—in this case, $500. The Petty Cash account keeps its prescribed $500 balance at all times. Maintaining the Petty Cash account at this balance, supported by the fund (cash plus slips), is how an **imprest system** works. The control feature of an imprest system is that it clearly identifies the amount for which the custodian is responsible.

STOP + THINK (4-4)	While its accountant was on vacation, a company discovered that it was the victim of a phony invoice scheme, having paid more than $2.3 million to two non-existent companies. It was the accountant's job to review and approve invoices and sign the cheques to ensure they were paid. What should the company do to prevent this from happening again?

CONSTRUCT AND USE A BUDGET TO MANAGE CASH

Managers control their organizations with an operating budget. As mentioned earlier in the chapter, a *budget* is a financial plan that helps managers coordinate business activities. Cash is the item that is budgeted most often.

How, for example, does TELUS Corp. decide when to invest millions in new wireless technology? How will TELUS Corp. decide how much to spend? Will borrowing be needed, or can TELUS Corp. finance the purchase with internally generated cash? What do ending cash balances need to be in order to provide a "safety margin" so the company won't unexpectedly run out of cash? A cash budget for a business works on roughly the same concept as a personal budget. Similarly, by what process do you decide how much to spend on your education? On an automobile? On a house? All of these decisions depend to some degree on the information that a cash budget provides.

A **cash budget** helps a company or an individual manage cash by planning receipts and payments during a future period. The company must determine how much cash it will need and then decide whether or not its operations will bring in the needed cash. Managers proceed as follows:

1. Start with the entity's cash balance at the beginning of the period. This is the amount left over from the preceding period.

2. Add the budgeted cash receipts and subtract the budgeted cash payments.

3. The beginning balance plus receipts minus payments equals the expected cash balance at the end of the period.

4. Compare the expected ending cash balance to the budgeted cash balance at the end of the period. Managers know the minimum amount of cash they need (the budgeted balance). If the budget shows excess cash, managers can invest the excess. But if the expected cash balance falls below the budgeted balance, the company will need additional financing. The budget is a valuable tool for helping the company plan for the future.

The budget period can span any length of time—a day, a week, a month, or a year. Exhibit 4-12 shows a cash budget for The Country Store Ltd. for the year ended January 31, 2014. Study it carefully, because at some point you will use a cash budget.

The Country Store Ltd.'s cash budget in Exhibit 4-12 begins with $12.0 million of cash (line 1). Then the budgeted cash receipts are added and budgeted payments subtracted. In this case, The Country Store expects to have $4.6 million of cash available at the year end (line 11). The Country Store managers need to maintain a cash balance of at least $13.5 million (line 12). Line 13 shows that The Country Store must arrange the financing of $8.9 million in order to achieve its goals for 2014.

Reporting Cash on the Balance Sheet

Most companies have numerous bank accounts, but they usually combine all cash amounts into a single total called "Cash and cash equivalents." **Cash equivalents** include liquid assets such as treasury bills, commercial paper, and money market funds, which are interest-bearing accounts that can often be withdrawn with no penalty. Slightly less liquid than cash, cash equivalents are sufficiently similar to be reported along with cash.

EXHIBIT 4-12
Cash Budget

The Country Store Ltd.
Cash Budget (Hypothetical)
For the Year Ended January 31, 2014

		(in millions)	
(1)	Cash balance, February 1, 2013		$ 12.0
	Estimated cash receipts:		
(2)	Collections from customers	$360.0	
(3)	Interest and dividends on investments	6.2	
(4)	Sale of store fixtures	4.9	371.1
			383.1
	Estimated cash payments:		
(5)	Purchases of inventory	245.0	
(6)	Operating expenses	82.5	
(7)	Expansion of existing stores	14.6	
(8)	Opening of new stores	12.4	
(9)	Payment of long-term debt	16.0	
(10)	Payment of dividends	8.0	(378.5)
(11)	Cash available (needed) before new financing		4.6
(12)	Budgeted cash balance, January 31, 2014		13.5
(13)	Cash available for additional investments (New financing needed)		$ (8.9)

SUMMARY OF CHAPTER 4

LEARNING OBJECTIVE	SUMMARY
1. **Describe** fraud and its impact	Fraud is the intentional misrepresentation of facts, made for the purpose of persuading another party to act in a way that causes injury or damage to that party. Fraud is a huge problem that may cause significant losses to companies.
2. **Explain** the objectives and components of internal control	Internal control is a plan of organization and system of procedures designed, implemented, and maintained by company management and the board of directors to deal with risks to the business that have been identified and that relate to the reliability of the company's financial records. The components of internal control are the control environment, risk assessment, information system, control procedures, and monitoring of controls.
3. **Prepare** and **use** a bank reconciliation.	To ensure accurate cash records, a bank reconciliation is prepared. It explains all differences between cash records and the bank statement.
4. **Apply** internal controls to cash receipts and cash payments	Cash receipts and payments need internal controls because cash is easy to steal. Duties of handling cash and recording cash should be separated.
5. **Construct** and **use** a budget to manage cash	Budgets are a means by which managers control the finances of their organizations. The budget is a future-oriented financial plan that helps companies coordinate their business activities.

There are no differences between IFRS and ASPE in this chapter.

END-OF-CHAPTER SUMMARY PROBLEM

Assume the following situation and transactions for TransAlta Corporation. At December 31, 2013, TransAlta had total assets of $9,762 million, which included cash and cash equivalents of $82 million. At December 31, 2013, TransAlta had long-term obligations of $4,724 million, of which it expected to pay $63 million during 2014. Suppose at the end of 2013, Brian Burden, CFO of TransAlta, is preparing the budget for the next year.

Suppose Burden makes the following assumption. During 2014, Burden expects TransAlta to collect $2,103 million from customers. TransAlta expects to pay $1,000 million for fuel and purchased power, and $950 million for operations and other cash expenses. To remain competitive, TransAlta plans to spend $500 million to upgrade facilities and purchase new property, plant, and equipment. Sale of property, plant, and equipment will provide cash of $120 million. TransAlta will pay dividends of $275 million.

Because of the increased level of activity planned for 2015, Burden budgets the need for a minimum cash balance of $160 million at December 31, 2014.

Requirements

Name: TransAlta Corporation
Industry: Energy corporation
Document: Cash budget
Fiscal Period: Year ended December 31, 2014

1. How much must TransAlta borrow during 2014 to keep its cash balance from falling below $160 million? Prepare the 2014 cash budget to answer this important question.
2. Consider the company's need to borrow $643 million. TransAlta can avoid the need to borrow money in 2014 by delaying one particular cash payment until 2015 or later. Identify the item, and state why it might be unwise to delay its payment.

ANSWERS

Requirement 1

TransAlta Corporation
Cash Budget (Hypothetical)
For the Year Ended December 31, 2014

	(in millions)
Cash and cash equivalents, December 31, 2013	$ 82
Estimated cash receipts:	
Collections from customers	2,103
Sale of assets..	120
	$ 2,305
Estimated cash payments:	
Payment of fuel and purchased power.. $1,000	
Purchases of operating expenses... 950	
Upgrading of facilities and purchase of property, plant, and equipment 500	
Payment of dividends... 275	
Payment of long-term debt.. 63	(2,788)
Cash available (needed) before new financing	(483)
Budgeted cash balance, December 31, 2014..	160
Cash available for additional investments (New financing needed)..........	$ (643)

A cash budget helps a company estimate its cash inflows and cash outflows for a future period. The period of time covered must be specified in the heading of the cash budget.

Use only the cash amounts from the data that are given.

Cash receipts from:
- Ordinary sales
- Extraordinary sales

Cash payments for:
- Purchases from suppliers
- Cash dividends
- Debt repayments

Requirement 2

TransAlta can eliminate the need for borrowing most of the $643 million by delaying the $500 million payment to *upgrade the company's facilities and purchase property, plant, and equipment*. Investors and creditors could consider the delay to be unwise because TransAlta needs the upgrading and new property, plant, and equipment to remain competitive.

Consider delaying cash payments to upgrade facilities since the upgrades are not necessary to generate the current level of income.

STOP + THINK (4-1)

ANSWERS

- Separate the duties of cash handling from record keeping.

- Require employees to take vacations. That way, other employees must review the work of the one on vacation.

- Routinely check on the work of employees. Discrepancies can then be detected.

- Mail questionnaires to customers with accounts and ask them to confirm their account balances to a responsible official of the company. Investigate all discrepancies.

STOP + THINK (4-2)

ANSWERS

The student should not respond to the e-mail—it is "phishing" for the student's bank account and password. This request should be ignored and the message deleted. More importantly, she should also refrain from clicking on any links included in the message. A bank (or most any business, for that matter) would never ask for personal information through an e-mail. She should notify her bank immediately to inform them the bank's name is being used for phishing purposes.

STOP + THINK (4-3)	**ANSWERS**

1. $5,125 ($4,500 + $1,200 − $575).

2. $5,408 ($5,125 + $15 − $5 + $300 − $27).

The adjusted book and bank balances are the same. The answer can be determined by working backward from the adjusted balance.

STOP + THINK (4-4)	**ANSWERS**

Simple measures, such as dividing up duties between approving the invoices and signing the cheques for payment, and having regular external audits and external evaluations of an organization's internal controls, can help provide protection against the potential for employee fraud.

Review Internal Control and Cash

QUICK CHECK (ANSWERS ARE GIVEN ON PAGE 221.)

1. Internal control has its own terminology. On the left are some key internal control concepts. On the right are some key terms. Match each internal control concept with its term by writing the appropriate letter in the space provided. Not all letters are used.

_____ This procedure limits access to sensitive data.
_____ This type of insurance policy covers losses due to employee theft.
_____ Trusting your employees can lead you to overlook this procedure.
___C___ The most basic purposes of internal control.
_____ Internal control cannot always safeguard against this problem.
_____ Often mentioned as the cornerstone of a good system of internal control.
___a___ Pay employees enough to require them to do a good job.

a. Competent personnel
b. Encryption
c. Separation of duties
d. Safeguarding assets
e. Fidelity bond
f. Collusion
g. Firewalls
h. Supervision
i. External audits

2. Each of the following is an example of a control procedure, *except*
   a. sound personnel procedures.
   b. a sound marketing plan.
   c. separation of duties.
   d. limited access to assets.

3. Which of the following is an example of poor internal control?
   a. The accounting department compares goods received with the related purchase order.
   b. Employees must take vacations.
   c. Rotate employees through various jobs.
   d. The mailroom clerk records daily cash receipts in the journal.

4. A private organization has internal controls because
   a. it has a responsibility to safeguard assets.
   b. it makes operations easier for employees.
   c. it wants to be businesslike.
   d. None of the above.

Use the following information for Questions 5–8.

Lawrence Corporation has asked you to prepare its bank reconciliation at the end of the current month. Answer Questions 5–8 using the following code letters to indicate how the item described would be reported on the bank reconciliation.

- **a.** Deduct from the book balance
- **b.** Does not belong on the bank reconciliation
- **c.** Add to the bank balance
- **d.** Deduct from the bank balance
- **e.** Add to the book balance

5. A cheque for $835 written by Lawrence during the current month was erroneously recorded as a $358 payment.

6. A $400 deposit made on the last day of the current month did not appear on this month's bank statement.

7. The bank statement showed interest earned of $65.

8. The bank statement included a cheque from a customer that was marked NSF.

9. Which of the following reconciling items does not require a journal entry?
   - **a.** Bank service charge
   - **b.** Bank collection of a note receivable
   - **c.** NSF cheque
   - **d.** Deposit in transit

10. A cheque was written for $542 to purchase supplies. The cheque was recorded in the journal as $425. The entry to correct the error would
    - **a.** increase Supplies, $117.
    - **b.** decrease Cash, $117.
    - **c.** decrease Supplies, $117.
    - **d.** Both a and b.

11. A cash budget helps control cash by
    - **a.** helping to determine whether additional cash is available for investments or new financing is needed.
    - **b.** developing a plan for increasing sales.
    - **c.** ensuring accurate cash records.
    - **d.** All of the above.

Accounting Vocabulary

audit A periodic examination of a company's financial statements and the accounting systems, controls, and records that produce them.   (p. 181)

bank collections Collections of money by the bank on behalf of a depositor.   (p. 188)

bank reconciliation A document explaining the reasons for the difference between a depositor's records and the bank's records about the depositor's cash.   (p. 188)

bank statement Document showing the beginning and ending balances of a particular bank account and listing the month's transactions that affected the account.   (p. 186)

budget A quantitative expression of a plan that helps managers coordinate the entity's activities.   (p. 180)

cash budget A budget that helps a company or an individual manage cash by planning receipts and payments during a future period.   (p. 198)

cash equivalents Investments such as term deposits, guaranteed investment certificates, or high-grade government securities that are considered so similar to cash that they are combined with cash for financial disclosure purposes on the balance sheet.   (p. 199)

cheque Document instructing a bank to pay the designated person or business the specified amount of money.   (p. 186)

computer virus A malicious program that enters a company's computer system by e-mail or other means and destroys program and data files.   (p. 182)

controller The chief accounting officer of a business who accounts for cash.   (p. 180)

deposits in transit A deposit recorded by the company but not yet recorded by its bank.   (p. 188)

electronic funds transfer (EFT) System that transfers cash by electronic communication rather than by paper documents.   (p. 186)

encryption Mathematical rearranging of data within an electronic file to prevent unauthorized access to information.   (p. 184)

exception reporting Identifying data that is not within "normal limits" so that managers can follow up and take corrective action. Exception reporting is used in operating and cash budgets to keep company profits and cash flow in line with management's plans.   (p. 181)

firewall An electronic barrier, usually protected by passwords, around computerized data files to protect local area networks of computers from unauthorized access.   (p. 184)

fraud An intentional misrepresentation of facts, made for the purpose of persuading another party to act in a way that causes injury or damage to that party.   (p. 173)

fraud triangle The three elements that are present in almost all cases of fraud. These elements are motive, opportunity, and rationalization on the part of the perpetrator.   (p. 174)

fraudulent financial reporting Fraud perpetrated by management by preparing misleading financial statements.   (p. 173)

imprest system A way to account for petty cash by maintaining a constant balance in the petty cash account, supported by the fund (cash plus payment slips) totalling the same amount.   (p. 198)

internal control Organizational plan and related measures adopted by an entity to safeguard assets, encourage adherence to company policies, promote operational efficiency, ensure accurate and reliable accounting records, and comply with legal requirements.   (p. 177)

lapping A fraudulent scheme to steal cash through misappropriating certain customer payments and posting payments from other customers to the affected accounts to cover it up. Lapping is caused by weak internal controls (i.e., not segregating the duties of cash handling and accounts receivable bookkeeping, allowing the bookkeeper improper access to cash, and not appropriately monitoring the activities of those who handle cash).   (p. 171)

lockbox system A system of handling cash receipts by mail whereby customers remit payment directly to the bank, rather than through the entity's mail system.   (p. 172)

misappropriation of assets Fraud committed by employees by stealing assets from the company.   (p. 173)

nonsufficient funds (NSF) cheque A cheque for which the payer's bank account has insufficient money to pay the cheque. NSF cheques are cash receipts that turn out to be worthless.   (p. 189)

operating budget A budget of future net income. The operating budget projects a company's future revenue and expenses. It is usually prepared by line item of the company's income statement.   (p. 180)

outstanding cheques Cheques issued by the company and recorded on its books but not yet paid by its bank.   (p. 188)

password A special set of characters that must be provided by the user of computerized program or data files to prevent unauthorized access to those files.   (p. 182)

petty cash Fund containing a small amount of cash that is used to pay minor amounts.   (p. 197)

phishing Creating bogus Web sites or sending phony e-mails for the purpose of stealing unauthorized data, such as names, addresses, social security numbers, bank account, and credit card numbers.   (p. 183)

remittance advice An optional attachment to a cheque (sometimes a perforated tear-off document and sometimes capable of being electronically scanned) that indicates the payer, date, and purpose of the cash payment. The remittance advice is often used as the source document for posting cash receipts or payments.   (p. 186)

Trojan horse A malicious program that hides within legitimate programs and acts like a computer virus.   (p. 183)

Assess Your Progress

SHORT EXERCISES

LEARNING OBJECTIVE ❶

Learn about fraud

S4-1 Define "fraud." List and briefly discuss the three major components of the "fraud triangle."

LEARNING OBJECTIVE ❷

Understand the components of internal control

S4-2 List the components of internal control. In your own words briefly describe each component.

LEARNING OBJECTIVE ❷

Understand the characteristics of an effective system of internal control

S4-3 Explain in your own words why separation of duties is such an important procedure for safeguarding assets. Describe what can happen if the same person has custody of an asset and also accounts for it.

LEARNING OBJECTIVE ❷

Understand the components of internal control

S4-4 Identify the other control procedures usually found in a company's system of internal control besides separation of duties, and tell why each is important.

LEARNING OBJECTIVE ❸

Prepare a bank reconciliation

S4-5 The Cash account of SWITZER Ltd. reported a balance of $2,500 at August 31, 2014. Included were outstanding cheques totalling $900 and an August 31 deposit of $500 that did not appear on the bank statement. The bank statement, which came from HSBC Bank, listed an August 31, 2014, balance of $3,405. Included in the bank balance was an August 30 collection of $550 on account from a customer who pays the bank directly. The bank statement also shows a $20 service charge, $10 of interest revenue that SWITZER earned on its bank balance, and an NSF cheque for $35.

Prepare a bank reconciliation to determine how much cash SWITZER actually has at August 31, 2014.

S4-6 After preparing the SWITZER Ltd. bank reconciliation in exercise S4-5, make the company's journal entries for transactions that arise from the bank reconciliation. Include an explanation with each entry.

LEARNING OBJECTIVE ❸

Record transactions from a bank reconciliation

S4-7 Jordan Quinn manages the local homeless shelter. He fears that a trusted employee has been stealing from the shelter. This employee receives cash from supporters and also prepares the monthly bank reconciliation. To check on the employee, Quinn prepares his own bank reconciliation as in Exhibit 4-7 on page 190.

LEARNING OBJECTIVE ❸

Use a bank reconciliation as a control device

Homeless Shelter
Bank Reconciliation
August 31, 2014

Bank		Books	
Balance, August 31	$ 3,300	Balance, August 31	$2,820
Add		Add	
Deposits in transit	400	Bank collections	800
		Interest revenue	10
Less		Less	
Outstanding cheques	(1,100)	Service charge	(30)
Adjusted bank balance	$ 2,600	Adjusted book balance	$3,600

Does it appear that the employee stole from the shelter? If so, how much? Explain your answer. Which side of the bank reconciliation shows the shelter's true cash balance?

S4-8 Gina Rolande sells memberships to the symphony in Winnipeg. The symphony's procedure requires Rolande to write a patron receipt for all memberships sold. The receipt forms are pre-numbered. Rolande is having personal financial problems, and she stole $500 received from a member. To hide her theft, Rolande destroys the symphony copy of the receipt she gave the member. What will alert manager Tom Jelnick that something is wrong?

LEARNING OBJECTIVE ❹

Apply internal control over cash receipts

S4-9 Answer the following questions about internal control over cash payments:

1. Payment by cheque carries three basic controls over cash. What are they?

2. Suppose a receptionist opens the mail, records payments received, and makes the bank deposit. How could a dishonest receptionist cheat the company? How do companies avoid this internal control weakness?

LEARNING OBJECTIVE ❹

Apply internal control over cash payments

S4-10 Briefly explain how a cash budget works and what it accomplishes with its last few lines of data.

LEARNING OBJECTIVE ❺

Use a cash budget

S4-11 Dairy Farmers of Ontario (DFO) is the marketing group for Ontario's dairy farms. Suppose the organization begins 2014 with cash of $28 million. DFO estimates cash receipts during the year will total $15 million. Planned payments for the year will total $14 million. To meet member commitment, DFO must maintain a cash balance of at least $25 million. Prepare the organization's cash budget for 2014.

LEARNING OBJECTIVE ❺

Prepare a cash budget

S4-12 Jane Hill, an accountant for Stainton Hardware Inc., discovers that her supervisor, Drew Armour, made several errors last year. Overall, the errors overstated Stainton Hardware's net income by 20%. It is not clear whether the errors were deliberate or accidental. What should Jane Hill do?

LEARNING OBJECTIVE ❶

Learn about fraud and make an ethical judgment

EXERCISES

LEARNING OBJECTIVE ❷

Understand e-commerce pitfalls

LEARNING OBJECTIVE ❷

Explain the role of internal control

LEARNING OBJECTIVE ❶❷

Learn about fraud; identify internal control weaknesses

E4-13 How do computer viruses, Trojan horses, and phishing expeditions work? How can these e-commerce pitfalls hurt you? Be specific.

E4-14 Answer the following questions on internal control:
a. Separation of duties is an important internal control procedure. Why is this so?
b. Cash may be a small item on the financial statements. Nevertheless, internal control over cash is very important. Why is this true?
c. Crane Company requires that all documents supporting a cheque be cancelled by punching a hole through the packet. Why is this practice required? What might happen if it were not?

E4-15 Identify the internal control weakness in the following situations. State how the person can hurt the company.
a. Jerry Miller works as a security guard at U Park parking in Calgary. Miller has a master key to the cash box where commuters pay for parking. Each night Miller prepares the cash report that shows (a) the number of cars that parked on the lot and (b) the day's cash receipts. Sandra Covington, the U Park treasurer, checks Miller's figures by multiplying the number of cars by the parking fee per car. Covington then deposits the cash in the bank.
b. Sharon Fisher is the purchasing agent for Manatee Golf Equipment. Fisher prepares purchase orders based on requests from division managers of the company. Fisher faxes the purchase orders to suppliers who then ship the goods to Manatee. Fisher receives each incoming shipment and checks it for agreement with the purchase order and the related invoice. She then routes the goods to the respective division managers and sends the receiving report and the invoice to the accounting department for payment.
c. The external auditor for Mattson Financial Services takes a global view of the audit. To form his professional opinion of Mattson's financial statements, the auditor runs no tests of Mattson's financial statements or of the underlying transactions. Instead, the auditor computes a few ratios and compares the current-year ratio values to the ratio values a year ago. If the ratio values appear reasonable, the auditor concludes that Mattson's financial statements are okay.

LEARNING OBJECTIVE ❷

Identify internal control strengths and weaknesses

E4-16 The following situations describe two cash payment situations and two cash receipt situations. In each pair, one set of internal controls is better than the other. Evaluate the internal controls in each situation as being either strong or weak, and give the reason for your answer.

Cash payments:
a. Jim McCord Construction's policy calls for construction supervisors to request the equipment needed for their jobs. The home office then purchases the equipment and has it shipped to the construction site.
b. Granite & Marble Inc.'s policy calls for project supervisors to purchase the equipment needed for jobs. The supervisors then submit the paid receipts to the home office for reimbursement. This policy enables supervisors to get the equipment quickly and keep construction jobs moving.

Cash receipts:
a. At McClaren Chevrolet, cash received by mail goes straight to the accountant, who debits Cash and credits Accounts Receivable to record the collections from customers. The McClaren accountant then deposits the cash in the bank.
b. Cash received by mail at Fleur de Lys Orthopedic Clinic goes to the mailroom, where a mail clerk opens envelopes and totals the cash receipts for the day. The mail clerk forwards customer cheques to the cashier for deposit in the bank and forwards the remittance slips to the accounting department for posting credits to customer accounts.

E4-17 A former chief information officer of the Council of Ontario Universities (COU) was accused of embezzling $600,000 from the organization. She is alleged to have arranged the payment of funds for invoices for services never produced and which instead were allegedly siphoned off by her. In addition, her chief academic credentials—a Canadian university degree and a Ph.D. from the United States—were found to be bogus. The fraud was not discovered until after her departure from COU when an audit was launched due to irregularities noticed by her successor at COU.

How could she have embezzled the funds from COU? Give your opinion on how COU might have prevented the fraud, and the actions taken when irregularities were discovered.

LEARNING OBJECTIVE ❶❷

Learn about fraud; correct an internal control weakness

E4-18 The following items appear on a bank reconciliation:

_____ **1.** Outstanding cheques

_____ **2.** Bank error: The bank credited our account for a deposit made by another bank customer.

_____ **3.** Service charge

_____ **4.** Deposits in transit

_____ **5.** NSF cheque

_____ **6.** Bank collection of a note receivable on our behalf

_____ **7.** Book error: We debited Cash for $100. The correct debit was $1,000.

Classify each item as (a) an addition to the bank balance, (b) a subtraction from the bank balance, (c) an addition to the book balance, or (d) a subtraction from the book balance.

LEARNING OBJECTIVE ❸

Classify bank reconciliation items

E4-19 LeAnn Bryant's chequebook lists the following:

LEARNING OBJECTIVE ❸

Prepare a bank reconciliation

Date	Cheque No.	Item	Cheque	Deposit	Balance
Nov. 1					$ 705
4	622	Direct Energy	$ 19		686
9		Dividends		$116	802
13	623	Canadian Tire	43		759
14	624	Petro-Canada	58		701
18	625	Cash	50		651
26	626	St. Mark's Church	25		626
28	627	Bent Tree Apartments	275		351
30		Paycheque		846	1,197

The November bank statement shows:

Balance...			$ 705
Add deposits			116
Deduct cheques	No.	Amount	
	622	$19	
	623	43	
	624	85*	
	625	50	(197)
Other charges:			
NSF cheque...		$ 8	
Service charge		12	(20)
Balance..			$ 604

*This is the correct amount for cheque number 624.

Requirement

Prepare Bryant's bank reconciliation at November 30.

LEARNING OBJECTIVE ❸

Prepare a bank reconciliation

E4-20 Tim Wong operates a FedEx Kinko's store. He has just received the monthly bank statement at May 31, 2014, from Royal Bank of Canada, and the statement shows an ending balance of $595. Listed on the statement are an EFT customer collection of $300, a service charge of $12, two NSF cheques totalling $120, and a $9 charge for printed cheques. In reviewing his cash records, Wong identifies outstanding cheques totalling $603 and a May 31 deposit in transit of $1,788. During May, he recorded a $290 cheque for the salary of a part-time employee as $29. Wong's Cash account shows a May 31 cash balance of $1,882. How much cash does Wong actually have at May 31?

LEARNING OBJECTIVE ❸

Journalize transactions from bank
reconciliations

E4-21 Use the data from exercise E4-20 to make the journal entries that Wong should record on May 31 to update his Cash account. Include an explanation for each entry.

LEARNING OBJECTIVE ❹

Evaluate internal control over cash
receipts

E4-22 A chain of shoe stores uses point-of-sale terminals as cash registers. The register shows the amount of each sale, the cash received from the customer, and any change returned to the customer. The machine also produces a customer receipt but keeps no record of transactions. At the end of the day, the clerk counts the cash in the register and gives it to the cashier for deposit in the company bank account. Write a memo to convince the store manager that there is an internal control weakness over cash receipts. Identify the weakness that gives an employee the best opportunity to steal cash and state how to prevent such a theft.

LEARNING OBJECTIVE ❹

Evaluate internal control over cash
payments

E4-23 Tee Golf Company manufactures a popular line of golf clubs. Tee Golf employs 140 workers and keeps their employment records on time sheets that show how many hours the employees work each week. On Friday, the shop foreman collects the time sheets, checks them for accuracy, and delivers them to the payroll department for preparation of paycheques. The treasurer signs the paycheques and returns the cheques to the payroll department for distribution to the employees.

Identify the main internal control weakness in this situation, state how the weakness can hurt Tee Golf, and propose a way to correct the weakness.

LEARNING OBJECTIVE ❺

Prepare a cash budget

E4-24 Wireless Communications Inc. is preparing its cash budget for 2014. Wireless ended 2013 with cash of $81 million, and managers need to keep a cash balance of at least $75 million for operations.

Collections from customers are expected to total $11,284 million during 2014, and payments for the cost of services and products should reach $6,166 million. Operating expense payments are budgeted at $2,543 million.

During 2014, Wireless expects to invest $1,825 million in new equipment and sell older assets for $115 million. Debt payments scheduled for 2014 will total $597 million. The company forecasts net income of $890 million for 2014 and plans to pay dividends of $338 million.

Prepare Wireless Communications' cash budget for 2014. Will the budgeted level of cash receipts leave Wireless with the desired ending cash balance of $75 million, or will the company need additional financing? If it does, how much will it need?

LEARNING OBJECTIVE ❶

Resolve an ethical challenge

E4-25 Sunbelt Bank recently appointed the accounting firm of Baker, Jackson, and Trent as the bank's auditor. Sunbelt quickly became one of Baker, Jackson, and Trent's largest clients. Subject to banking regulations, Sunbelt must provide for any expected losses on notes receivable that Sunbelt may not collect in full.

During the course of the audit, Baker, Jackson, and Trent determined that three large notes receivable of Sunbelt seem questionable. Baker, Jackson, and Trent discussed these loans with Stephanie Carson, controller of Sunbelt. Carson assured the auditors that these notes were good and that the makers of the notes will be able to pay their notes after the economy improves.

Baker, Jackson, and Trent stated that Sunbelt must record a loss for a portion of these notes receivable to account for the likelihood that Sunbelt may never collect their full amount.

Carson objected and threatened to dismiss Baker, Jackson, and Trent if the auditor demands that the bank record the loss. Baker, Jackson, and Trent want to keep Sunbelt as a client. In fact, Baker, Jackson, and Trent were counting on the revenue from the Sunbelt audit to finance an expansion of the firm.

Apply the framework for making ethical decisions outlined in the Decision Guidelines in Make an Ethical Business Judgment on page 176 to decide how the accounting firm of Baker, Jackson, and Trent should proceed.

CHALLENGE EXERCISES

E4-26 Morris Cody, the owner of Parkwood Apartments, has delegated management of the apartment building to Mario daSilva, a friend. Cody drops by to meet tenants and check up on rent receipts, but daSilva manages building maintenance and handles cash payments. Rentals have been very good lately, and cash receipts have kept pace with the apparent level of rent. However, for a year or so, the amount of cash on hand has been too low. When asked about this, daSilva explains that building maintenance has been required and suppliers are charging more for goods than in the past. During the past year, daSilva has taken two expensive vacations, and Cody wonders how daSilva can afford these trips on his $60,000 annual salary.

List at least three ways daSilva could be defrauding Cody of cash. In each instance, also identify how Cody can determine whether daSilva's actions are ethical. Limit your answers to the building's cash payments. The business pays all suppliers by cheque (no EFTs).

LEARNING OBJECTIVE ❶❷❸
Learn about fraud; evaluate internal controls over cash payments

E4-27 Dan Davis, the chief financial officer, is responsible for The Furniture Mart's cash budget for 2014. The budget will help Davis determine the amount of long-term borrowing needed to end the year with a cash balance of $150 thousand. Davis's assistants have assembled budget data for 2014, which the computer printed in alphabetical order. Not all the data items reproduced below are used in preparing the cash budget.

LEARNING OBJECTIVE ❺
Prepare and use a cash budget

(Assumed Data)	(in thousands)
Actual cash balance December 31, 2013	$ 140
Budgeted total assets	22,977
Budgeted total current assets	7,776
Budgeted total current liabilities	4,860
Budgeted total liabilities	11,488
Budgeted total shareholders' equity	7,797
Collections from customers	18,527
Dividend payments	237
Issuance of shares	627
Net income	1,153
Payment of long-term and short-term debt	950
Payment of operating expenses	2,349
Purchases of inventory items	14,045
Purchase of property and equipment	1,518

Requirements
1. Prepare the cash budget of The Furniture Mart for 2014.
2. Compute The Furniture Mart's budgeted current ratio and debt ratio at December 31, 2014. Based on these ratio values, and on the cash budget, would you lend $100,000 to The Furniture Mart? Give the reason for your decision.

QUIZ

Test your understanding of internal control and cash by answering the following questions. Select the best choice from among the possible answers given.

Q4-28 All of the following are objectives of internal control *except*
a. to comply with legal requirements.
b. to safeguard assets.
c. to maximize net income.
d. to ensure accurate and reliable accounting records.

Q4-29 All of the following are internal control procedures *except*
a. electronic devices.
b. *Sarbanes-Oxley* reforms.
c. assignment of responsibilities.
d. internal and external audits.

Q4-30 Requiring that an employee with no access to cash do the accounting is an example of which characteristic of internal control?
a. Separation of duties
b. Competent and reliable personnel
c. Mandatory vacations
d. Monitoring of controls

Q4-31 Which of the following is *not* a control for cash received over the counter?
a. The customer should be able to see the amounts entered into the cash register.
b. A printed receipt must be given to the customer.
c. The cash drawer should open only when the sales clerk enters an amount on the keys.
d. The sales clerk must have access to the cash register tape.

Q4-32 In a bank reconciliation, an outstanding cheque is
a. added to the book balance.
b. deducted from the book balance.
c. added to the bank balance.
d. deducted from the bank balance.

Q4-33 In a bank reconciliation, a bank collection of a note receivable is
a. added to the book balance.
b. deducted from the book balance.
c. added to the bank balance.
d. deducted from the bank balance.

Q4-34 In a bank reconciliation, an EFT cash payment is
a. added to the book balance.
b. deducted from the book balance.
c. added to the bank balance.
d. deducted from the bank balance.

Q4-35 If a bookkeeper mistakenly recorded a $58 deposit as $85, the error would be shown on the bank reconciliation as a(n)
a. $27 addition to the book balance.
b. $85 deduction from the book balance.
c. $27 deduction from the book balance.
d. $85 addition to the book balance.

Q4-36 If a bank reconciliation included a deposit in transit of $670, the entry to record this reconciling item would include which of the following?
a. Credit to prepaid insurance for $670
b. Credit to cash for $670
c. Debit to cash for $670
d. No journal entry is required.

Q4-37 In a bank reconciliation, interest revenue earned on your bank balance is
a. added to the book balance.
b. deducted from the book balance.
c. added to the bank balance.
d. deducted from the bank balance.

Q4-38 Before paying an invoice for goods received on account, the controller or treasurer should ensure that
a. the company is paying for the goods it ordered.
b. the company is paying for the goods it actually received.
c. the company has not already paid this invoice.
d. All of the above.

Q4-39 La Petite France Bakery is budgeting cash for 2014. The cash balance at December 31, 2013, was $10,000. La Petite budgets 2014 cash receipts at $85,000. Estimated cash payments include $40,000 for inventory, $30,000 for operating expenses, and $20,000 to expand the store. La Petite needs a minimum cash balance of $10,000 at all times. La Petite expects to earn net income of $40,000 during 2014. What is the final result of the company's cash budget for 2014?

a. $10,000 is available for additional investments.

b. $5,000 is available for additional investments.

c. La Petite must arrange new financing for $5,000.

d. La Petite must pay off $10,000 of debt.

PROBLEMS

(Group A)

P4-40A Avant Garde Imports is an importer of silver, brass, and furniture items from Mexico. Kay Jones is the general manager of Avant Garde Imports. Jones employs two other people in the business. Marco Gonzalez serves as the buyer for Avant Garde. He travels throughout Mexico to find interesting new products. When Gonzalez finds a new product, he arranges for Avant Garde to purchase and pay for the item. He helps the Mexican artisans prepare their invoices and then faxes the invoices to Jones in the company office.

LEARNING OBJECTIVE **❶❷**

Learn about fraud; identify internal control weaknesses

Jones operates out of an office in Montreal, Quebec. The office is managed by Rita Bowden, who handles the mail, keeps the accounting records, makes bank deposits, and prepares the monthly bank reconciliation. Virtually all of Avant Garde's cash receipts arrive by mail—from sales made to Pier 1 Imports and Walmart.

Bowden also prepares cheques for payment based on invoices that come in from the suppliers who have been contacted by Gonzalez. To maintain control over cash payments, Jones examines the paperwork and signs all cheques.

Requirement

Identify all the major internal control weaknesses in Avant Garde's system and how the resulting action could hurt Avant Garde. Also, state how to correct each weakness.

P4-41A Each of the following situations reveals an internal control weakness.

a. Accounting firms use paraprofessional employees to perform routine tasks. For example, an accounting paraprofessional might prepare routine tax returns for clients. In the firm of Dunham & Lee, Rodney Lee, one of the partners, turns over a significant portion of his high-level accounting work to his paraprofessional staff.

b. In evaluating the internal control over cash payments of Butler Manufacturing, an auditor learns that the purchasing agent is responsible for purchasing diamonds for use in the company's manufacturing process, approving the invoices for payment, and signing the cheques. No supervisor reviews the purchasing agent's work.

c. Charlotte James owns an architecture firm. James's staff consists of 12 professional architects, and James manages the office. Often, James's work requires her to travel to meet with clients. During the past six months, James has observed that when she returns from a business trip, the architecture jobs in the office have not progressed satisfactorily. James learns that when she is away, two of her senior architects take over office management and neglect their normal duties. One employee could manage the office.

d. B.J. Tanner has been an employee of Crystal City for many years. Because the company is small, Tanner performs all accounting duties, plus opening the mail, preparing the bank deposit, and preparing the bank reconciliation.

e. Part of an internal auditor's job is to evaluate how efficiently the company is running. For example, is the company purchasing inventory from the least expensive supplier? After a particularly bad year, Long Photographic Products eliminates its internal audit department to reduce expenses.

LEARNING OBJECTIVE **❶❹**

Learn about fraud; identify internal control weaknesses

Requirements

1. Identify the missing internal control characteristic in each situation.

2. Identify each firm's possible problem.

3. Propose a solution to the problem.

LEARNING OBJECTIVE ❸

Prepare the bank reconciliation and use it as a control device

P4-42A The cash data of Alta Vista Toyota for June 2014 follow:

Cash

Date	Item	Jrnl. Ref.	Debit	Credit	Balance
June 1	Balance				5,011
30		CR6	10,578		15,589
30		CP11		10,924	4,665

Cash Receipts (CR)		Cash Payments (CP)	
Date	Cash Debit	Cheque No.	Cash Credit
June 2	$ 4,174	3113	$ 891
8	407	3114	147
10	559	3115	1,930
16	2,187	3116	664
22	1,854	3117	1,472
29	1,060	3118	1,000
30	337	3119	632
Total	$10,578	3120	1,675
		3121	100
		3122	2,413
		Total	$10,924

Alta Vista received the following bank statement on June 30, 2014:

Bank Statement for June 2014

Beginning balance...		$ 5,011
Deposits and other additions		
June 1..	$ 326 EFT	
4..	4,174	
9..	407	
12..	559	
17..	2,187	
22..	1,701 BC	
23..	1,854	11,208
Cheques and other deductions		
June 7..	$ 891	
13..	1,390	
14..	903 US	
15..	147	
18..	664	
21..	219 EFT	
26..	1,472	
30..	1,000	
30..	20 SC	(6,706)
Ending balance..		$ 9,513

Explanation: EFT—electronic funds transfer, BC—bank collection, US—unauthorized signature, SC—service charge

Additional data for the bank reconciliation include the following:

a. The EFT deposit was a receipt of a monthly car lease. The EFT debit was a monthly insurance payment.

b. The bank collection was of a note receivable.
c. The unauthorized signature cheque was received from a customer.
d. The correct amount of cheque number 3115, a payment on account, is $1,390. (Alta Vista's accountant mistakenly recorded the cheque for $1,930.)

Requirements

1. Prepare the Alta Vista Toyota bank reconciliation at June 30, 2014.
2. Describe how a bank account and the bank reconciliation help the general manager control Alta Vista's cash.

P4-43A The May 31 bank statement of Family Services Association (FSA) has just arrived from Scotiabank. To prepare the FSA bank reconciliation, you gather the following data:

a. FSA's Cash account shows a balance of $2,256.14 on May 31.
b. The May 31 bank balance is $4,023.05.
c. The bank statement shows that FSA earned $38.19 of interest on its bank balance during May. This amount was added to FSA's bank balance.
d. FSA pays utilities ($250) and insurance ($100) by EFT.
e. The following FSA cheques did not clear the bank by May 31:

LEARNING OBJECTIVE ❸

Prepare a bank reconciliation and the related journal entries

Cheque No.	Amount
237	$ 46.10
288	141.00
291	578.05
293	11.87
294	609.51
295	8.88
296	101.63

f. The bank statement includes a donation of $850, electronically deposited to the bank for FSA.
g. The bank statement lists a $10.50 bank service charge.
h. On May 31, the FSA treasurer deposited $16.15, which will appear on the June bank statement.
i. The bank statement includes a $300 deposit that FSA did not make. The bank added $300 to FSA's account for another company's deposit.
j. The bank statement includes two charges for returned cheques from donors. One is a $395 cheque received from a donor with the imprint "Unauthorized Signature." The other is a nonsufficient funds cheque in the amount of $146.67 received from a client.

Requirements

1. Prepare the bank reconciliation for FSA.
2. Journalize the May 31 transactions needed to update FSA's Cash account. Include an explanation for each entry.

P4-44A Sun Skin Care makes all sales on credit. Cash receipts arrive by mail, usually within 30 days of the sale. Nancy Brown opens envelopes and separates the cheques from the accompanying remittance advices. Brown forwards the cheques to another employee, who makes the daily bank deposit but has no access to the accounting records. Brown sends the remittance advices, which show the amount of cash received, to the accounting department for entry in the accounts receivable. Brown's only other duty is to grant allowances to customers. (An *allowance* decreases the amount that the customer must pay.) When Brown receives a customer cheque for less than the full amount of the invoice, she records the allowance in the accounting records and forwards the document to the accounting department.

LEARNING OBJECTIVE ❹

Identify internal control weakness in sales and cash receipts

Requirement

You are a new employee of Sun Skin Care. Write a memo to the company president identifying the internal control weakness in this situation. State how to correct the weakness.

LEARNING OBJECTIVE ❺

Prepare a cash budget and use cash flow information

P4-45A Kenneth Austin, chief financial officer of Morin Equipment Ltd., is responsible for the company's budgeting process. Austin's staff is preparing the Morin cash budget for 2014. A key input to the budgeting process is last year's statement of cash flows, which follows (amounts in thousands):

Morin Equipment Ltd.
Statement of Cash Flows
2013

	(in thousands)
Cash Flows From Operating Activities	
Collections from customers	$ 60,000
Interest received	100
Purchases of inventory	(44,000)
Operating expenses	(13,900)
Net cash provided by operations	2,200
Cash Flows From Investing Activities	
Purchases of equipment	(4,300)
Purchases of investments	(200)
Sales of investments	400
Net cash used for investing activities	(4,100)
Cash Flows From Financing Activities	
Payment of long-term debt	(300)
Issuance of shares	1,200
Payment of cash dividends	(500)
Net cash provided by financing activities	400
Cash	
Increase (decrease) in cash	(1,500)
Cash, beginning of year	2,700
Cash, end of year	$ 1,200

Requirements

1. Prepare the Morin Equipment Ltd. cash budget for 2014. Date the budget simply "2014" and denote the beginning and ending cash balances as "beginning" and "ending." Assume the company expects 2014 to be the same as 2013, but with the following changes:
   a. In 2014, the company expects a 15% increase in collections from customers and a 20% increase in purchases of inventory.
   b. There will be no sales of investments in 2014.
   c. Morin plans to issue no shares in 2014.
   d. Morin plans to end the year with a cash balance of $2,000 thousand.
2. Does the company's cash budget for 2014 suggest that Morin is growing, holding steady, or decreasing in size?

LEARNING OBJECTIVE ❶

Make an ethical judgment

P4-46A Larry Raborn is a branch manager of HSBC. Active in community affairs, Raborn serves on the board of directors of The Salvation Army. The Salvation Army is expanding rapidly and is considering relocating. At a recent meeting, The Salvation Army decided to buy 200 hectares of land on the edge of town. The owner of the property is Freda Rader, a major depositor in his branch. Rader is completing a bitter divorce, and Raborn knows that Rader is eager to sell her property. In view of Rader's difficult situation, Raborn believes Rader would accept a low offer for the land. Realtors have appraised the property at $2.2 million.

Requirement

Apply the framework for making the ethical decisions outlined in Chapter 1 to help Raborn decide what role he should play in The Salvation Army's attempt to buy the land from Rader.

(Group B)

P4-47B Trey Osborne, administrator of Valley View Clinic, seeks your advice. Valley View Clinic employs two people in the office, Jim Bates and Rhonda Clark. Osborne asks you how to assign the various office functions to the three people (including Osborne) to achieve good internal control. Here are the duties to be performed by the two office workers and Osborne:

a. Record cash payments

b. Record cash receipts

c. Receive incoming cash from patients

d. Reconcile the bank account

e. Deposit cash receipts

f. Sign cheques for payment

LEARNING OBJECTIVE ❷❹

Evaluate and apply internal control procedures

Requirements

1. Propose a plan that divides duties (a) through (f) to Bates, Clark, and Osborne. Your goal is to divide the duties so as to achieve good internal control for the clinic.
2. Identify several combinations of duties that should not be performed by the same person.

P4-48B Each of the following situations has an internal control weakness:

a. Retail stores such as Sobeys and Home Depot receive a significant portion of their sales revenue in cash. At the end of each day, sales clerks compare the cash in their own register with the record of sales kept within the register. They then forward the cash to a Brinks security officer for deposit in the bank.

b. The office supply company from which Martin Audiology Service purchases cash receipt forms recently notified Martin that the last-shipped sales receipts were not pre-numbered. Derek Martin, the owner, replied that he did not use the receipt numbers, so the omission is unimportant to him.

c. Azbell Electronics specializes in programs with musical applications. The company's most popular product prepares musical programs for large gatherings. In the company's early days, the owner and eight employees wrote the programs, lined up production of the programs, sold the products, and performed the general management of the company. As Azbell has grown, the number of employees has increased dramatically. Recently, the development of a new musical series stopped while the programmers redesigned Azbell's sound system. Azbell could have hired outsiders to do this task.

d. Paul Allen, who has no known sources of outside income, has been a trusted employee of Chapparall Cosmetics for 20 years. Allen performs all cash-handling and accounting duties, including opening the mail, preparing the bank deposit, accounting for cash and accounts receivable, and preparing the bank reconciliation. Allen has just purchased a new Lexus. Linda Altman, owner of the company, wonders how Allen can afford the new car on his salary.

e. Monica Wade employs three professional interior designers in her design studio. The studio is located in an area with a lot of new construction, and her business is booming. Ordinarily, Wade does all the purchasing of materials needed to complete jobs. During the summer, Wade takes a long vacation, and in her absence she allows each designer to purchase materials. On her return, Wade reviews operations and observes that expenses are higher and net income is lower than in the past.

LEARNING OBJECTIVE ❶❹

Learn about fraud; identify internal control weaknesses

Requirements

1. Identify the missing internal control characteristics in each situation.
2. Identify each firm's possible problem.
3. Propose a solution to the problem.

LEARNING OBJECTIVE ③

Use the bank reconciliation as a
control device

P4-49B The cash data of Navajo Products for September 2014 follow:

			Cash		
Date	**Item**	**Jrnl. Ref.**	**Debit**	**Credit**	**Balance**
Sept. 1	Balance				7,078
30		CR 10	9,106		16,184
30		CP 16		11,353	4,831

Cash Receipts (CR)		Cash Payments (CP)	
Date	Cash Debit	Cheque No.	Cash Credit
Sept. 1	$ 2,716	1413	$ 1,465
9	544	1414	1,004
11	1,655	1415	450
14	896	1416	8
17	367	1417	775
25	890	1418	88
30	2,038	1419	4,126
Total	$ 9,106	1420	970
		1421	200
		1422	2,267
		Total	$11,353

On September 30, 2014, Navajo received this bank statement:

Bank Statement for September 2014

Beginning balance			$ 7,078
Deposits and other additions			
Sept. 1		$ 625 EFT	
5		2,716	
10		544	
12		1,655	
15		896	
18		367	
25		890	
30		1,400 BC	9,093
Cheques and other deductions			
Sept. 8		$ 441 NSF	
9		1,465	
13		1,004	
14		450	
15		8	
19		340 EFT	
22		775	
29		88	
30		4,216	
30		25 SC	(8,812)
Ending balance			$ 7,359

Explanation: BC—bank collection, EFT—electronic funds transfer, NSF—nonsufficient funds cheque,
SC—service charge

Additional data for the bank reconciliation:

a. The EFT deposit was for monthly rent revenue. The EFT deduction was for monthly insurance expense.

b. The bank collection was of a note receivable.

c. The NSF cheque was received from a customer.

d. The correct amount of cheque number 1419, a payment on account, is $4,216. (The Navajo accountant mistakenly recorded the cheque for $4,126.)

Requirements

1. Prepare the bank reconciliation of Navajo Products at September 30, 2014.
2. Describe how a bank account and the bank reconciliation help managers control a firm's cash.

P4-50B The January 31 bank statement of Bed & Bath Accessories has just arrived from Royal Bank of Canada. To prepare the Bed & Bath bank reconciliation, you gather the following data:

a. The January 31 bank balance is $8,400.82.

b. Bed & Bath's Cash account shows a balance of $7,391.55 on January 31.

c. The following Bed & Bath cheques are outstanding at January 31:

Cheque No.	Amount
616	$403.00
802	74.02
806	36.60
809	161.38
810	229.05
811	48.91

LEARNING OBJECTIVE ❸
Prepare a bank reconciliation and the related journal entries

d. The bank statement includes two special deposits: $899.14, which is the amount of dividend revenue the bank collected from IBM on behalf of Bed & Bath; and $16.86, the interest revenue Bed & Bath earned on its bank balance during January.

e. The bank statement lists a $6.25 bank service charge.

f. On January 31 the Bed & Bath treasurer deposited $381.14, which will appear on the February bank statement.

g. The bank statement includes a $410.00 deduction for a cheque drawn by Bonjovi Music Company.

h. The bank statement includes two charges for returned cheques from customers. One is a nonsufficient funds cheque in the amount of $67.50 received from a customer. The other is a $195.03 cheque received from another customer. It was returned by the customer's bank with the imprint "Unauthorized Signature."

i. A few customers pay monthly bills by EFT. The January bank statement lists an EFT deposit for sales revenue of $200.23.

Requirements

1. Prepare the bank reconciliation for Bed & Bath Accessories at January 31.
2. Journalize the transactions needed to update the Cash account. Include an explanation for each entry.

P4-51B Nordhaus Energy Co. makes all sales on credit. Cash receipts arrive by mail, usually within 30 days of the sale. Dan Webster opens envelopes and separates the cheques from the accompanying remittance advices. Webster forwards the cheques to another employee, who makes the daily bank deposit but has no access to the accounting records. Webster sends the remittance advices, which show the amount of cash received, to the accounting department for entry in the accounts receivable. Webster's only other duty is to grant allowances to customers. (An *allowance* decreases the amount that the customer must pay.) When Webster receives a customer cheque for less than the full amount of the invoice, he records the allowance in the accounting records and forwards the document to the accounting department.

LEARNING OBJECTIVE ❹
Identify an internal control weakness in sales and cash receipts

Requirement

You are a new employee of Nordhaus Energy Co. Write a memo to the company president identifying the internal control weakness in this situation. Explain how to correct the weakness.

LEARNING OBJECTIVE ❺

Prepare a cash budget and use cash flow information

P4-52B Melissa Becker is chief financial officer of Valero Machines. She is responsible for the company's budgeting process. Becker's staff is preparing the Valero cash budget for 2014. The starting point is the statement of cash flows of the current year, 2013, which follows:

Valero Machines
Statement of Cash Flows
2013

	(in thousands)
Cash Flows From Operating Activities	
Collections from customers	$ 35,600
Interest received	100
Purchases of inventory	(11,000)
Operating expenses	(16,600)
Net cash provided by operating activities	8,100
Cash Flows From Investing Activities	
Purchases of property and equipment	(5,000)
Purchases of investments	(7,500)
Sales of investments	8,100
Net cash used by investing activities	(4,400)
Cash Flows From Financing Activities	
Payment of dividends	(2,700)
Payment of short-term debt	(1,000)
Long-term borrowings by issuing notes payable	1,200
Issuance of common shares	300
Net cash used by financing activities	(2,200)
Increase (decrease) in Cash	1,500
Cash, beginning of year	2,600
Cash, end of year	$ 4,100

Requirements

1. Prepare the Valero Machines cash budget for 2014. Date the budget simply "2014" and denote the beginning and ending cash balances as "beginning" and "ending." Assume the company expects 2014 to be the same as 2013, but with the following changes:
   a. In 2014, the company expects a 10% increase in collections from customers, a 5% increase in purchases of inventory, and a doubling of additions to property and equipment.
   b. Operating expenses will drop by $2,000.
   c. There will be no sales of investments in 2014.
   d. Becker plans to end the year with a cash balance of $3,000.
2. Does the company's cash budget for 2014 suggest that Valero is growing, holding steady, or decreasing in size?

LEARNING OBJECTIVE ❶

Make an ethical judgment

P4-53B A community bank has a loan receivable from IMS Chocolates. IMS is six months late in making payments to the bank, and Jan French, a bank vice-president, is assisting IMS to restructure its debt.

French learns that IMS is depending on landing a contract with Snicker Foods, another bank client. French also serves as Snicker Foods' loan officer at the bank. In this capacity, French is aware that Snicker is considering bankruptcy. No one else outside Snicker Foods knows this. French has been a great help to IMS, and IMS's owner is counting on French's expertise in loan workouts to advise the company through this difficult process. To help the bank collect on this large loan, French has a strong motivation to alert IMS of Snicker's financial difficulties.

Requirement

Apply the framework for making an ethical decision outlined in Chapter 1 to help French plan her next action.

Apply Your Knowledge

Decision Cases

Case 1. Green Construction Inc. has poor internal control. Recently, Jean Ouimet, the owner, has suspected the cashier of stealing. Here are some details of the business's cash position at June 30, 2014:

LEARNING OBJECTIVE ❶❸
Learn about fraud, use the bank reconciliation to detect a theft

a. The Cash account shows a balance of $10,402. This amount includes a June 30 deposit of $3,794 that does not appear on the June 30 bank statement.

b. The June 30 bank statement shows a balance of $8,224. The bank statement lists a $200 bank collection, an $8 service charge, and a $36 NSF cheque. The accountant has not recorded any of these items.

c. At June 30, the following cheques are outstanding:

Cheque No.	Amount
154	$116
256	150
278	853
291	990
292	206
293	145

d. The bookkeeper records all incoming cash and makes bank deposits. He also reconciles the monthly bank statement. Here is his June 30 reconciliation:

Balance per books, June 30		$10,402
Add: Outstanding cheques		1,460
Bank collection		200
Subtotal		12,062
Less: Deposits in transit	$3,794	
Service charge	8	
NSF cheque	36	(3,838)
Balance per bank, June 30		$ 8,224

Requirement

Ouimet has requested that you determine whether the cashier has stolen cash from the business and, if so, how much. He also asks you to explain how the cashier has attempted to conceal the theft. To make this determination, you perform your own bank reconciliation. There are no bank or book errors. Ouimet also asks you to evaluate the internal controls and to recommend any changes needed to improve them.

Case 2. Gilead Construction Inc., which is headquartered in Calgary, Alberta, built a small apartment building in Red Deer. The construction foreman, whose name was Jon Machenko, moved to Red Deer in May to hire the 20 workers needed to complete the project. Machenko hired the construction workers, had them fill out the necessary tax forms, and sent the employment documents to the home office, which opened a payroll file for each employee.

LEARNING OBJECTIVE ❶❷
Learning about fraud, correcting an internal control weakness

Work on the building began on June 1. Each Friday evening, Jon Machenko filled out a time card that listed the hours worked for each employee during the five-day work week ended at 5:00 p.m. on Friday. Machenko faxed the time sheets to the home office, which prepared the payroll cheques on Monday morning. Machenko drove to the home office after lunch on Monday, picked up the payroll cheques, and returned to the construction site. At 5:00 p.m. on Monday, Machenko distributed the payroll cheques to the workers.

a. Describe in detail the internal control weakness in this situation. Specify what negative result could occur because of the internal control weakness.
b. Describe what you would do to correct the internal control weakness.

Ethical Issue

Eric Thorman owns shoe stores in Halifax and Lunenburg. Each store has a manager who is responsible for sales and store expenses, and runs advertisements in the local newspaper. The managers transfer cash to Thorman monthly and prepare their own bank reconciliations. The manager in Lunenburg has been stealing large sums of money. To cover the theft, he understates the amount of the outstanding cheques on the monthly bank reconciliation. As a result, each monthly bank reconciliation appears to balance. However, the balance sheet reports more cash than Thorman actually has in the bank. While negotiating the sale of the shoe stores, Thorman shows the balance sheet to prospective investors.

Requirements

1. Identify two parties other than Thorman who can be harmed by this theft. In what ways can they be harmed?
2. Discuss the role accounting plays in this situation.

Focus on Financials

LEARNING OBJECTIVE ❷❹

Understand cash and internal control

TELUS Corporation

Refer to the TELUS financial statements in Appendix A at the end of the book. Suppose TELUS's year-end bank statement has just arrived at company headquarters. Further assume the bank statement shows TELUS's cash balance at $36,025 and that TELUS's Cash and Temporary Investments, Net account has a balance of $35,346 on the books.

1. You must determine how much to report for cash and temporary investments, net, on the December 31, 2011, balance sheet. Suppose you uncover these reconciling items (all amounts are assumed and in thousands):
   a. Interest earned on bank balance, $5
   b. Outstanding cheques, $7,525
   c. Bank collections of various items, $12,000
   d. Deposits in transit, $17,500
   e. Transposition error—TELUS overstated cash by $1,350
   f. Bank charges of $1

   Prepare a bank reconciliation to show how TELUS arrived at the correct amount of cash and temporary investments, net, to report on its December 31, 2011, balance sheet. Prove that your answer is the actual amount TELUS reported. Journal entries are not required.

2. NI 52-109 requires the CEO and CFO to certify compliance with the disclosures required under the standard. Locate the statement of compliance in TELUS's MD&A in MyAccountingLab and compare it to the requirements under NI 52-109 reported in Chapter 4.
   a. Does TELUS meet the requirements with respect to certification by the certifying officers? Who are identified as TELUS's certifying officers?
   b. Does the MD&A identify the control framework used? If so, what framework was used?

Focus on Analysis

TELUS Corporation

Refer to the TELUS financial statements in Appendix A at the end of the book.

LEARNING OBJECTIVE ❷❹

Analyze internal control and cash flows

1. Focus on cash and temporary investments, net. Why did cash change during the year ended December 31, 2011? The statement of cash flows holds the answer to this question. Analyze the four largest *individual* items on the cash flow statement (exclude net income) over $1,000 million. For each of the four individual items, state how TELUS's action affected cash. Show amounts in millions.
2. TELUS's shares are listed on the Toronto Stock Exchange (TSX) and the New York Stock Exchange (NYSE). The U.S. listing requires TELUS to comply with *Sarbanes-Oxley*, which requires TELUS's auditor, Deloitte, LLP, to provide an opinion on the effectiveness of TELUS's internal control over financial reporting. Locate the auditor's report in TELUS's annual report in Appendix A and compare it to the certification in TELUS's MD&A. What is the major difference between the two?

Group Project

You are promoting a rock concert in your area. Assume you organize as a corporation, with each member of your group purchasing $10,000 of the corporation's shares. Therefore, each of you is risking some hard-earned money on this venture. Assume it is April 1 and that the concert will be performed on June 30. Your promotional activities begin immediately, and ticket sales start on May 1. You expect to sell all the firm's assets, pay all the liabilities, and distribute all remaining cash to the group members by July 31.

Requirements

Write an internal control manual that will help safeguard the assets of the business. The manual should address the following aspects of internal control:

1. Assign responsibilities among the group members.
2. Authorize individuals, including group members and any outsiders that you need to hire, to perform specific jobs.
3. Separate duties among the group and any employees.
4. Describe all documents needed to account for and safeguard the business's assets.

Quick Check Answers

1. *g, e, h, d, f, c, a Unused: b, i*   5. *a*   9. *d*
2. *b*   6. *c*   10. *d*
3. *d*   7. *e*   11. *a*
4. *a*   8. *a*

5 Short-Term Investments and Receivables

Mario Beauregard/Canadian Press Images

LEARNING OBJECTIVES

1. **Account** for short-term investments
2. **Account for** and **control** accounts receivables
3. **Estimate** and **account for** uncollectible accounts receivable
4. **Account** for notes receivable
5. **Explain** how to improve cash flows from sales and receivables
6. **Evaluate** a company's liquidity

SPOTLIGHT

Did you know that CGI Group Inc. is the largest independent information technology and business process services firms in the world? They provide IT services to clients in Canada, the United States, Europe, and the Asia Pacific region.

Take a look at CGI's comparative balance sheets (excerpt) for 2010 and 2011 on the following page. Notice how accounts receivable is the largest component of CGI's current assets. This balance represents the amount of money customers owe CGI at the end of the year.

Another category of current assets is short-term investments. As you can see on CGI's balance sheet, CGI had about $10 million of short-term investments at the end of 2011. You'll notice that short-term investments are listed on the balance sheet immediately after cash and before receivables. Let's see why.

CGI Group Inc.
Consolidated Balance Sheets (Excerpt, Adapted)
As at September 30, 2010 and 2011 (in thousands, Canadian dollars)

	2011	2010
Assets		
Current Assets		
Cash and cash equivalents	$ 157,761	$ 127,824
Short-term investments	10,166	13,196
Accounts receivable	494,755	423,926
Work in progress	400,203	358,984
Prepaid expenses and other	104,170	76,844
Income taxes	4,252	7,169
Future income taxes	3,522	16,509
Other current assets	247,622	248,695
Total current assets	$1,422,451	$1,273,147

This chapter shows how to account for short-term investments and receivables. We also examine short-term investments to compare their liquidity relative to receivables. Short-term investments are the next most-liquid current assets after cash. (Recall that liquid means close to being cash.) We begin our discussion with short-term investments.

ACCOUNT FOR SHORT-TERM INVESTMENTS

OBJECTIVE

❶ **Account** for short-term investments

Short-term investments, also called **marketable securities** or *temporary investments*, are investments that a company plans to hold for one year or less. These investments allow the company to invest excess cash for a short period of time and earn a return until the cash is needed.

Because short-term investments are the next most-liquid asset after cash, we report short-term investments immediately after cash and before receivables on the balance sheet. Investments in marketable securities fall into one of three categories:

Short-term investments	Long-term investments in shares (including available-for-sale) **	Long-term investment in bonds
Covered in this section of the chapter	Covered in Chapter 8	Covered in Chapter 8

**Available-for-sale investments are usually classified as long-term unless they mature in the current period.

An investor, such as CGI Group Inc., expects to hold its short-term investments for a few months at most. Therefore, all such investments are current assets. Other categories of investments are either short term or long term, depending on how long management intends to hold them. One common type of short-term investment is a held-for-trading investment. Let's look at the characteristics of this investment.

Held-for-Trading Investments

The purpose of owning a **held-for-trading investment** is to hold it for a short time and then sell it for more than its cost. Held-for-trading investments can be shares or bonds in another company. Suppose CGI purchases shares in TransCanada Corporation, intending to sell the shares in a few months. If the fair value (or market price) of the TransCanada shares increases, CGI will have a gain; if TransCanada's share price decreases, CGI will have a loss. Along the way, CGI may receive dividend revenue from TransCanada.

Suppose CGI buys the TransCanada shares on September 18, 2012, paying $100,000 cash. CGI records the purchase of the investment at cost:

2012			
Sept. 18	Short-Term Investments............................	100,000	
	Cash..		100,000
	Purchased investment.		

Short-Term Investments	
100,000	

ASSETS	=	LIABILITIES	+	SHAREHOLDERS' EQUITY
+100,000				
−100,000	=	0	+	0

Assume on September 27 CGI receives a cash dividend of $800 from TransCanada. CGI records the receipt of the dividend as follows:

2012			
Sept. 27	Cash	800	
	Dividend Revenue....................................		800
	Received cash dividend.		

ASSETS	=	LIABILITIES	+	SHAREHOLDERS' EQUITY
+800	=	0	+	800 Revenue

UNREALIZED GAINS AND LOSSES. Held-for-trading investments are reported on the balance sheet at their fair value. An investment's **fair value** is the amount a willing buyer would pay to a willing seller to acquire the investment. CGI's fiscal year ends on September 30, 2012. Assume the TransCanada shares have risen in value by $2,000, and on September 30, 2012, CGI's investment has a fair value (current market price) of $102,000. CGI has an *unrealized gain* on the investment.

- It is *unrealized* because CGI has not yet sold the investment.
- It is a *gain* because the fair value ($102,000) is greater than CGI's investment cost. A gain has the same effect on owners' equity as a revenue.

On September 30, 2012, CGI would record the following adjusting entry to account for the unrealized gain:

2012			
Sept. 30	Short-Term Investments............................	2,000	
	Unrealized Gain on Investments		2,000
	Adjusted investment to fair value.		

Short-Term Investments		Unrealized Gain on Investments	
100,000			2,000
2,000			
102,000			

After the adjustment, CGI's investment account appears as shown above. The Short-Term Investments account is ready to be reported on the balance sheet at fair value of $102,000. The unrealized gain of $2,000 will be reported on the income statement.

If CGI's investment in TransCanada shares had decreased in value, say, to $95,000, then CGI would have reported an *unrealized loss*. A loss has the same effect on owners' equity as an expense. In this case, CGI would make a different entry at September 30, 2012, for an unrealized loss of $5,000.

2012			
Sept. 30	Unrealized Loss on Investments.................	5,000	
	Short-Term Investments.........................		5,000
	Adjusted investment to fair value.		

Short-Term Investments		Unrealized Loss on Investments	
100,000	5,000	5,000	
95,000			

REALIZED GAINS AND LOSSES. A *realized* gain or loss occurs only when the investor sells an investment. The result may be a:

- Realized gain → Sale price *greater than* investment carrying amount
- Realized loss → Sale price *less than* investment carrying amount

Suppose CGI sells its TransCanada shares on October 19, 2012. The sale price is $98,000, and CGI makes the following journal entry:

2012			
Oct. 19	Cash	98,000	
	Loss on Sale of Investments	4,000	
	Short-Term Investments.........................		102,000
	Sold short-term investments at a loss.		

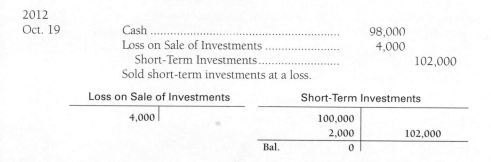

Loss on Sale of Investments		Short-Term Investments	
4,000		100,000	
		2,000	102,000
	Bal.	0	

Accountants rarely use the word "Realized" in the account title. A gain (or a loss) is understood to be a realized gain (or loss) arising from a sale transaction. Unrealized gains and losses are clearly labelled as *unrealized*.

NOTES TO THE FINANCIAL STATEMENTS. The notes to the financial statements should disclose the details of the specific types of short-term investments owned at the end of the year. Below are the details of CGI's actual short-term investments as at September 30, 2012:

Note 1. Summary of Significant Accounting Policies (Adapted)
SHORT-TERM INVESTMENTS
Short-term investments, comprised of term deposits, have remaining maturities over three months, but not more than one year, at the date of purchase.

Under IFRS, companies can elect to report all gains and losses from short-term investments not held for trading as part of other comprehensive income instead of net income. Under ASPE, the private enterprise records these unrealized and realized gains and losses through net income.

Reporting in the Financial Statements

THE BALANCE SHEET. Short-term investments are current assets. They appear on the balance sheet immediately after cash because short-term investments are almost as liquid as cash. Short-term investments are reported at their *fair value*.

INCOME STATEMENT. Investments earn interest revenue and dividend revenue. Investments also create gains and losses. For short-term investments, these items are reported on the income statement in a section below operating revenues and expenses, as shown in Exhibit 5-1.

EXHIBIT 5-1
Reporting Short-Term Investments and the Related Revenues, Gains, and Losses

Balance sheet			Income statement		
Current assets:			Revenues		$ XXX
Cash	$	XXX	Expenses		XXX
Short-term investments, at			Other revenue, gains, and (losses)		
fair value		102,000	Interest revenue		XXX
Accounts receivable		XXX	Dividend revenue		800
			Unrealized gain on investments		2,000
			Net income		$ XXX

MID-CHAPTER SUMMARY PROBLEM

Rogers Corporation is a leading Canadian communications company. Suppose one of the current assets on Rogers's balance sheet is Short-Term Investments. Their cost is $41.8 million; their fair value is $42.4 million.

What will Rogers report on the balance sheet at December 31, 2013? What will Rogers report on its 2013 income statement? Show the Short-Term Investments T-account.

Name: Rogers Corporation
Industry: Communications corporation
Accounting Period: Year ended December 31, 2013

ANSWER

Short-Term Investments are reported on the balance sheet as follows (amounts in millions):

	(in millions)
Current assets	
Short-term investments at fair value	$42.4

Short-term investments are included in current assets (amounts assumed).

An unrealized gain is the excess of the market value over the cost (amounts assumed).

Rogers's income statement will report:

	(in millions)
Other revenue, gains, and (losses):	
Unrealized gain on investment ($42.4 − $41.8 million)..........................	$ 0.6

Suppose Rogers sells the investments on February 7, 2014, for $41.4 million. Journalize the sale and then show the Short-Term Investments account as it would appear after the sale.

ANSWER

2014
Feb. 7   Cash 41,400,000
           Loss on Sale of Short-Term Investments........................ 1,000,000
               Short-Term Investments..   42,400,000
           Sold short-term investments at a loss.

Short-Term Investments		
41,800,000		
600,000	42,400,000	
Bal. 0		

OBJECTIVE

❷ Account for and control
receivables

ACCOUNT FOR AND CONTROL RECEIVABLES

Receivables are the third most-liquid asset after cash and short-term investments. Most of the remainder of this chapter shows how to account for receivables.

Types of Receivables

Receivables are monetary claims against others. They are acquired mainly by selling goods and services on account (accounts receivable) and by lending money (notes receivable). Journal entries to record receivables can be shown as follows:

Performing a Service on Account	Lending Money on a Note Receivable
Accounts Receivable XXX	Note Receivable XXX
Service Revenue........................ XXX	Cash XXX
Performed a service on account.	Loaned money to another company.

The two major types of receivables are accounts receivable and notes receivable. A business's *accounts receivable* are the amounts collectible from customers from the sale of goods and services. Accounts receivable, which are *current assets*, are sometimes called *trade receivables* or merely *receivables*.

The Accounts Receivable account in the general ledger serves as a *control account* that summarizes the total amount receivable from all customers. Companies also keep a *subsidiary ledger* of accounts receivable with a separate account for each customer, illustrated as follows:

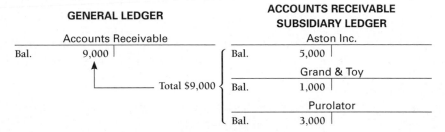

Notes receivable are more formal contracts than accounts receivable. The borrower signs a written promise to pay the creditor a definite sum at the *maturity* date. This is why notes receivable are also called promissory notes. The note may require the borrower to pledge *security* for the loan. This means that the borrower gives the lender permission to claim certain assets, called *collateral*, if the borrower fails to pay the amount due. We cover the details of notes receivable starting on page 237.

Other Receivables is a miscellaneous category that includes loans to employees and subsidiary companies. Some companies report other receivables under the heading Other Assets on the balance sheet.

Internal Controls Over Cash Collections on Account

Businesses that sell on credit receive most of their cash receipts from the collection of accounts receivable. Internal control over collections on account is important. Chapter 4 discussed control procedures for cash receipts, but another element of internal control deserves emphasis here—the separation of cash-handling and cash-accounting duties. Consider the following case:

> Franklin Supply Co. Ltd. is a small, family owned business that takes pride in the loyalty of its workers. Most employees have been with Franklin for at least five years. The company makes 90% of its sales on account.

The office staff consists of a bookkeeper and a supervisor. The bookkeeper maintains the general ledger and a subsidiary record of individual accounts receivable. He also makes the daily bank deposit. The supervisor prepares monthly financial statements and any special reports Franklin requires. She also takes sales orders from customers and serves as office manager.

Can you identify the internal control weakness here? The problem is that the bookkeeper makes the deposit. With this cash-handling duty, the bookkeeper could steal an incoming customer cheque and write off the customer's account as uncollectible. The customer doesn't complain because the bookkeeper has written the account off the books and Franklin, therefore, stops pursuing collection.

How can this weakness be corrected? The supervisor—not the bookkeeper—could open incoming mail and make the daily bank deposit. The bookkeeper should *not* be allowed to handle cash. Only the remittance advices would be forwarded to the bookkeeper to credit customer accounts receivable. Removing cash handling from the bookkeeper and keeping the accounts away from the supervisor separates duties and strengthens internal control.

How Do We Manage the Risk of Not Collecting?

Most companies sell on credit and thus hold accounts receivable. By selling on credit, all companies run the risk of not collecting some receivables, and unfortunately, customers sometimes don't pay their debts. The prospect that we may fail to collect from a customer provides the biggest challenge in accounting for receivables. How do we minimize this risk? The Decision Guidelines below provide some advice.

◀ DECISION GUIDELINES ▶

MANAGING AND ACCOUNTING FOR ACCOUNTS RECEIVABLE

Here are the management and accounting issues a company faces when it extends credit to customers. Let's look at a business situation: Suppose you and a friend open a health club near your school. Assume you will let customers use the club and charge bills to their accounts. What challenges will you encounter by extending credit to customers?

The main issues in *managing* receivables, along with a plan of action, are the following:

Decision	Guidelines
1. What are the benefits and the costs of extending credit to customers?	1. Benefit—increase in sales. Cost—risk of not collecting.
2. Extend credit only to creditworthy customers.	2. Run a credit check on prospective customers.
3. Separate cash-handling and accounting duties to keep employees from stealing the cash collected from customers.	3. Design the internal control system to separate duties.
4. Pursue collection from customers to maximize cash flow.	4. Keep a close eye on customer paying habits. Send second, and third, statements to slow-paying customers, if necessary. Do not extend credit to overdue accounts.

The main issues in accounting for receivables and the related plans of action are as follows (amounts are assumed):

Decision	Guidelines
How should receivables be reported?	Report receivables at net realizable value: **Balance sheet** Receivables $1,000 Less: Allowance for uncollectibles (80) Receivables, net $ 920 *Managers* This is the amount the company expects to collect and the appropriate amount to report for receivables. *Investors and Creditors* They are interested in seeing the net receivables because this is the amount the company actually expects to collect. They understand that legally the company is owed $1,000, but in reality, $920 is the amount expected to be collected.
How should the bad debt expense be reported?	This expense of not collecting from customers is called *bad debt expense* and is reported on the income statement. **Income statement** Sales (or service) revenue $8,000 Expenses: Bad debt expense 190 *Managers* The company measures and reports the expense associated with the failure to collect receivables. *Investors and Creditors* Because investors and creditors are interested in the profitability of the company, the bad debt expense on the income statement reflects the cost associated with selling goods on credit.

These guidelines lead to our next topic, accounting for uncollectible receivables.

3 Estimate and account for uncollectible accounts receivable

ESTIMATE AND ACCOUNT FOR UNCOLLECTIBLE ACCOUNTS RECEIVABLE

A company gets an account receivable only when it sells its product or service on credit. You'll recall that the entry to record the earning of revenue on account is (amount assumed):

Accounts Receivable 1,000
    Sales Revenue (or Service Revenue)   1,000
    Earned revenue on account.

Companies rarely collect all of their accounts receivable, so they must account for what they do not collect.

As stated above, selling on credit creates both a benefit and a cost:

- *Benefit*: Customers who cannot pay cash immediately can buy on credit, so company profits rise as sales increase.

- *Cost*: When a customer doesn't pay, the debt has gone bad, so this cost is commonly called an **uncollectible account expense**, a **doubtful account expense**, or a **bad debt expense**.

Accounts receivable are reported in the financial statements at cost minus an appropriate allowance for uncollectible accounts (that is, net realizable value). This is the amount a company expects to collect.

A company may present the allowance for uncollectible accounts in the notes to the financial statements, or disclose the information on the balance sheet as follows:

Accounts Receivable (net of allowance for
    uncollectible accounts of $120,000) $2,005,234

From this information we can determine several things about the company's receivables. From the amount of its allowance for uncollectible accounts, we can see that *it does not expect to collect* $120,000 of its accounts receivable at year-end. The *net realizable value* of its receivables is $2,005,234, which is the amount it *expects to collect* from its customers. If we add the uncollectible account to the net realizable value, we get the company's *total accounts receivable* at year-end; $2,125,234.

Bad debt expense is an expense associated with the failure to collect receivables. It is usually reported as an operating expense on the income statement. To measure bad debt expense, accountants use the *allowance method* or, in certain limited cases, the *direct write-off method* (which we discuss starting on page 235).

STOP + THINK (5-1)

You are considering an investment in Black Corporation and are looking at Black's June 30, 2013, financial statements, which are stated in thousands of dollars. In particular, you are focusing on Black's accounts receivable. The balance sheet includes the following:

	June 30	
	2013	2012
Accounts receivable trade, net of Allowance for uncollectible accounts of $3,974 as of June 30, 2013, and $2,089 as of June 30, 2012...	$134,396	$128,781

At June 30, 2013, how much did customers owe Black Corporation? How much did Black expect *not* to collect? How much of the receivables did Black expect to collect? What was the net realizable value of Black Corporation's receivables?

Allowance Method

The best way to measure bad debts is by the **allowance method**. This method records collection losses on the basis of estimates. Management does not wait to see which customers will not pay. Managers estimate bad debt expense on the basis of the company's collection experience. The company records the estimated amount as Bad Debt Expense and sets up an **Allowance for Uncollectible Accounts**. Other titles for this account are **Allowance for Doubtful Accounts** and **Allowance for Bad Debts**. This is a contra account to Accounts Receivable. The allowance shows the amount of the receivables that the business *does not expect* to collect.

When estimating their uncollectible accounts, companies typically rely on their history of collections from customers. There are two basic ways to estimate uncollectibles:

- Percentage-of-sales method
- Aging-of-receivables method

PERCENTAGE-OF-SALES METHOD. The **percentage-of-sales method** computes uncollectible-account expense as a percentage of revenue. This method takes an *income-statement approach* because it focuses on the amount of expense to be reported on the income statement. Assume it is June 30, 2013, and Black Corporation's accounts have these balances *before the year-end adjustments* (the following discussion expresses all amounts in thousands):

Accounts Receivable	Allowance for Uncollectible Accounts
138,370	346

Customers owe Black Corporation $138,370, and the Allowance amount is $346. Suppose the economy slows down, and Black's top managers know that the company will fail to collect more than $346. Based on the company's collection history, Black's credit department estimates that bad debt expense is 1/2 of 1% (0.005) of total revenues, which were $725,532 for 2013. The entry to record bad debt expense for the year also updates the allowance as follows:

```
2013
June 30    Bad Debt Expense ($725,532 × 0.005)..............    3,628
               Allowance for Uncollectible Accounts.............            3,628
           Recorded expense for the year.
```

The expense decreases assets, as shown by the accounting equation:

ASSETS	=	LIABILITIES	+	SHAREHOLDERS' EQUITY
−3,628	=	0		−3,628 Expense

Now the accounts are ready for reporting in the financial statements:

Accounts Receivable	Allowance for Uncollectible Accounts
138,370	346
	3,628
	3,974

Net accounts receivable, $134,396

Compare these amounts to the Stop + Think answer on page 249. They are the same.

Customers still owe Black Corporation $138,370, but now the Allowance for Uncollectible Accounts balance is realistic. Black's balance sheet actually reported accounts receivable at their net realizable value of $134,396 ($138,370 − $3,974).

Black's income statement included bad debt expense among the operating expenses for the period.

AGING-OF-RECEIVABLES METHOD. The other popular method for estimating uncollectibles is called the **aging-of-receivables method**. This method is a *balance-sheet approach* because it focuses on Accounts Receivable. In the aging method, individual receivables from specific customers are analyzed based on how long they have been outstanding.*

Accounting software packages are designed to age the company's accounts receivable. Exhibit 5-2 shows an assumed aging of receivables for Black at June 30, 2013. Black's receivables total $138,370 (in thousands of dollars). Of this amount, the aging schedule shows that the company will *not* collect $6,156, but the allowance for uncollectible accounts is not yet up to date. Suppose Black's accounts are as follows *before the year-end adjustment* (in thousands):

Accounts Receivable	Allowance for Uncollectible Accounts
138,370	346

Using the aging method, the accounts are listed in categories based on the number of days they have been outstanding. For example, in Exhibit 5-2, the total accounts receivable is $138,370. This amount is further divided into days outstanding: 0–30 days, 31–60 days, 61–90 days, and over 90 days.

If you look under the 0–30 days category, you will see that credit sales of $67,570 were made within the last 30 days and the company is still waiting to collect cash from the customers. Management estimated that 2% or $1,351 ($67,570 × 2%) would not be collected. The estimated percentages are based on management's past experience with collections. Under the 31–60 days category, $58,000 was sold on account more than 30 days ago but less than 60 days. Management estimates that 5% of the $58,000 will not be collected. Each of the other categories has its estimated percentage of uncollectible accounts indicated as well. Adding up the total estimated uncollectible accounts for each column ($1,351 + $2,900 + $1,030 + $875), it totals $6,156. This means that Black expects *not* to collect $6,156, but the allowance for bad debts is not yet up to date. The aging method will bring the balance of the allowance account

EXHIBIT 5-2
Aging the Accounts Receivable of Black Corporation

Customer	Total	Dollar Amounts (in thousands) Number of Days Outstanding			
		0–30	31–60	61–90	over 90
City of Regina	$ 500	$ 500			
IBM Canada	1,000	1,000			
Keady Pipe Corp.	2,100		$ 1,000	$ 1,100	
TorBar Inc.	200			200	
Others	134,570	66,070	57,000	9,000	$2,500
	$138,370	$67,570	$58,000	$10,300	$2,500
Estimated % Uncollectible		2%	5%	10%	35%
Total Estimated Uncollectible Accounts	$ 6,156	$ 1,351	$ 2,900	$ 1,030	$ 875

*Rather than preparing an aging schedule, the company could determine what the credit balance of the allowance for uncollectible accounts needs to be by calculating it as a percent of the total Accounts Receivable balance.

($346) to the needed amount ($6,156) as determined by the aging schedule in Exhibit 5-2. To update the allowance, Black Corporation would make this entry:

2013
June 30   Bad Debt Expense ($6,156 − $346)   5,810
                    Allowance for Uncollectible Accounts   5,810
                Recorded expense for the year.

Both assets and shareholders' equity decrease, as shown by the accounting equation.

ASSETS	=	LIABILITIES	+	SHAREHOLDERS' EQUITY
−5,810	=	0		−5,810 Expense

Now the balance sheet can report the amount that Black Corporation actually expects to collect from customers: $132,214 ($138,370 − $6,156). This is the net realizable value of Black's trade receivables. Black's accounts are now ready for the balance sheet, as follows:

Accounts Receivable		Allowance for Uncollectible Accounts	
138,370			346
		Adj.	5,810
		End. Bal.	6,156

Net accounts receivable, $132,214

Exhibit 5-3 compares the two methods of accounting for uncollectible accounts.

WRITING OFF UNCOLLECTIBLE ACCOUNTS. Suppose that early in July 2013, Black's credit department determines that Black cannot collect from customers Keady Pipe Corporation and TorBar Inc. (see Exhibit 5-2). Black Corporation then writes off the receivables from these two delinquent customers with the following entry (in thousands of dollars):

2013
July 12   Allowance for Uncollectible Accounts   2,300
                    Accounts Receivable—Keady Pipe Corporation..........   2,100
                    Accounts Receivable—TorBar Inc.   200
                Wrote off uncollectible receivables.

EXHIBIT 5-3
Comparing the Percentage-of-Sales and Aging-of-Receivables Methods for Estimating Uncollectible Accounts

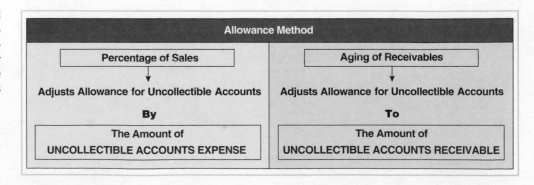

After the write-off, Black's accounts show these amounts:

Accounts Receivable—Keady Pipe Corp.		Accounts Receivable—TorBar Inc.		Allowance for Uncollectible Accounts	
2,100	2,100	200	200	2,300	6,156
					3,856

Accounts Receivable Others		Accounts Receivable—City of Regina	
134,570		500	

Accounts Receivable—IBM Canada	
1,000	

Total Accounts Receivable = $136,070   Allowance = $3,856

Accounts Receivable, Net = $132,214

The accounting equation shows that the write-off of uncollectibles has no effect on total assets; the net realizable value of accounts receivable is still $132,214. There is no effect on net income either, because no income statement account is affected.

ASSETS	=	LIABILITIES	+	SHAREHOLDERS' EQUITY
+2,300				
−2,300	=	0	+	0

STOP + THINK (5-2)   In the preceding accounting equation (for the write-off of uncollectible receivables), why is there no effect on total assets? Why is there no effect on net income?

Recovery of an Uncollectible Account

Even though an account has been written off as uncollectible, the customer still owes the money and will sometimes pay off the account, at least in part.

Some companies turn delinquent receivables over to a collection agency to help recover some of their cash. This is called the *recovery of an uncollectible account*. Recall that on July 12, 2013, Black Corporation wrote off the $200 account receivable from TorBar. Suppose it is now September 1, 2013, and the company unexpectedly receives the $200 from TorBar. To account for this recovery, the company makes two journal entries to (1) reverse the earlier write-off and (2) record the cash collection, as follows:

2013			
Sept. 1	Accounts Receivable—TorBar Inc.	200	
	Allowance for Uncollectible Accounts		200
	Reinstated TorBar's account receivable.		
	Cash..	200	
	Accounts Receivable—TorBar Inc.		200
	Collected on account.		

Direct Write-Off Method

There is another, less preferable, way to account for uncollectible receivables. Under the **direct write-off method**, the company waits until it decides that a specific customer's receivable is uncollectible. Then the accountant records bad debt expense and writes off the customer's account receivable as follows (using assumed data):

2014			
Jan. 30	Bad Debt Expense	2,000	
	Accounts Receivable—Jones Inc.		2,000
	Wrote off an uncollectible account by direct write-off method.		

This method is not appropriate for two reasons:

1. The direct write off method does not set up an allowance for uncollectible accounts. As a result, receivables are always reported at their full amount, which is more than the business expects to collect. *Assets on the balance sheet are overstated.*

2. In this example, the company made the sale to Jones Inc. in 2013 and should have recorded the expense during 2013. By recording the expense in 2014, the company *overstates net income in 2013.* Then, by recording the expense when it writes off the receivable in 2014, the company *understates net income in 2014.*

Because of these flaws, the direct write-off method should be used only when the total uncollectible accounts are immaterial for the reporting period.

Computing Cash Collections From Customers

A company earns revenue and then collects the cash from customers. For Black Corporation (and most other companies), there is a time lag between earning the revenue and collecting the cash. Collections from customers are the single most important source of cash for any business. You can compute a company's collections from customers by analyzing its Accounts Receivable account. Receivables typically hold only five different items, as follows (amounts assumed):

Accounts Receivable

Beg. balance (left from last period)	200	Write-offs of uncollectible accounts	100**
		Collections from customers	$X = 1,500^{\dagger}$
Sales (or service) revenue	1,800*		
End. balance (carries over to next period)	400		

*The journal entry that places revenue into the receivable account is:

Accounts Receivable	1,800	
Sales (or Service) Revenue..................		1,800

**The journal entry for write-offs is:

Allowance for Uncollectible Accounts....	100	
Accounts Receivable...........................		100

†The journal entry that places collections into the receivable account is:

Cash	1,500	
Accounts Receivable...........................		1,500

Suppose you know all these amounts except collections from customers. You can compute collections by solving for *X* in the T-account.*

Often write-offs are not known and must be omitted. Then the computation of collections becomes an approximation.

---

*An equation may help you solve for *X*. The equation is $\$200 + \$1,800 - X - \$100 = \$400$. $X = \$1,500$.

COOKING THE BOOKS SHIFTING SALES INTO THE CURRENT PERIOD

Suppose it is December 26. Late in the year a company's business dried up: Its profits are running below what everyone predicted. The company needs a loan and its banker requires financial statements to support the loan request. Unless the company acts quickly, it won't get the loan.

Fortunately, next year looks better. The company has standing orders for sales of $50,000. As soon as the company gets the merchandise, it can ship it to customers and record the sales. An old accounting trick can solve the problem. Book the $50,000 of sales in December. After all, the company will be shipping the goods on January 2 of next year. What difference does two days make?

It makes all the difference in the world. Shifting the sales into the current year will make the company look better immediately. Reported profits will rise, the current ratio will improve, and the company can then get the loan needed. But what are the consequences? If caught, the company will be prosecuted for fraud, and its reputation will be ruined. Remember that the company shifted next year's sales into the current year. Next year's sales will be lower than the true amount, and profits will suffer. If next year turns out to be like this year, the company will be facing the same shortage again. Also, something may come up to keep the company from shipping the goods on January 2.

ACCOUNT FOR NOTES RECEIVABLE

OBJECTIVE

❹ **Account** for notes receivable

As stated earlier, notes receivable are more formal than accounts receivable. Notes receivable due within one year or less are current assets. Notes due beyond one year are *long-term receivables* and are reported as non-current. Some notes receivable are collected in instalments. The portion due within one year is a current asset and the remainder is a long-term asset. Assume, for example, that a company issues a $20,000 note receivable to a customer, with quarterly instalments of $2,500 due over the next two years. If six instalments are still owing at year-end, then $10,000 of the note would be a current asset (four quarterly payments of $2,500), and the remaining $5,000 would be reported as a long-term asset.

Before launching into the accounting for notes receivable, let's define some key terms:

Creditor	The party to whom money is owed. The creditor is also called the *lender*. The debt is a *note receivable* from the *borrower*.
Debtor	The party that borrowed and owes money on the note. The debtor is also called the *maker* of the note or the *borrower*. The debt is a *note payable* to the *lender*.
Interest	Interest is the cost of borrowing money. The interest is stated as an annual percentage rate.
Maturity date	The date on which the debtor must pay the note.
Principal	The amount of money borrowed by the debtor.
Term	The length of time the debtor has to repay the note.

The debtor signs the note and thereby creates a contract with the creditor. Exhibit 5-4 shows a typical promissory note.

EXHIBIT 5-4
A Promissory Note

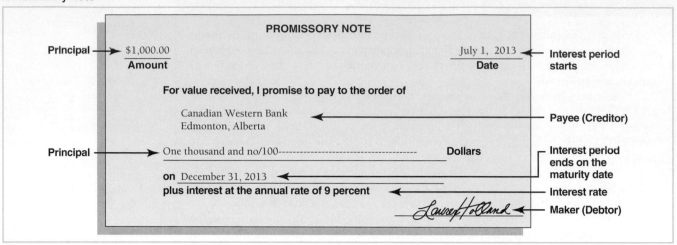

The *principal* amount of the note ($1,000) is the amount borrowed by the debtor and lent by the creditor. This six-month note runs from July 1, 2013, to December 31, 2013, when Lauren Holland (the maker) promises to pay Canadian Western Bank (the creditor) the principal of $1,000 plus 9% interest per year. *Interest* is revenue to the creditor and an expense to the debtor.

Accounting for Notes Receivable

Consider the promissory note shown in Exhibit 5-4. After Lauren Holland (the maker) signs the note, Canadian Western Bank gives her $1,000 cash. The bank would record the following journal entry:

2013			
July 1	Note Receivable—L. Holland...............................	1,000	
	Cash...		1,000
	Made a loan.		

Note Receivable—L. Holland	
1,000	

The bank gave one asset, cash, in return for another asset, a note receivable, so the total assets did not change:

ASSETS	=	LIABILITIES	+	SHAREHOLDERS' EQUITY
+1,000				
−1,000	=	0	+	0

Assume Canadian Western Bank has an October 31 year-end. The bank earns interest revenue during July, August, September, and October. At October 31, 2013, the bank accrues interest revenue for four months as follows:

2013			
Oct. 31	Interest Receivable ($1,000 × 0.09 × 4/12)..................	30	
	Interest Revenue..		30
	Accrued interest revenue.		

The bank's assets and its revenue increase.

The bank reports these amounts in its financial statements at October 31, 2013:

Balance sheet
Current assets:
Note receivable $1,000
Interest receivable 30
Income statement
Interest revenue .... $ 30

The bank collects the note on December 31, 2013, and records:

2013
Dec. 31   Cash 1,045
         Note Receivable—L. Holland 1,000
         Interest Receivable 30
         Interest Revenue ($1,000 × 0.09 × 2/12) 15
         Collected note at maturity.

This entry eliminates the Note Receivable and Interest Receivable and also records the interest revenue earned from November 1 to December 31, 2013.

Note Receivable—L. Holland	
1,000	1,000

In its 2014 financial statements, the only item that Canadian Western Bank will report is the interest revenue of $15 that was earned in November and December 2013, part of its 2014 fiscal period. There's no note receivable or interest receivable on the balance sheet because those items were zeroed out when the bank collected the note at maturity.

Three aspects of these entries deserve mention:

1. Interest rates are always for an annual period unless stated otherwise. In this example, the annual interest rate is 9%. At October 31, 2013, Canadian Western Bank accrues interest revenue for the four months the bank has held the note. The interest computation is:

$$\text{Principal} \times \text{Interest rate} \times \text{Time} = \text{Amount of Interest}$$
$$\$1,000 \times \quad 0.09 \quad \times 4/12 = \quad \$30$$

2. The time element (4/12) is the fraction of the year that the note has been in force during the year ended October 31, 2013.

3. Interest is often completed for a number of days. For example, suppose you loaned out $10,000 on April 10. The note receivable runs for 90 days and specifies interest at 8%.

   a. Interest starts accruing on April 10, the day the money is borrowed, and continues to accrue until the note comes due 90 days later (July 8):

Month	Number of Days That Interest Accrues
April	21
May	31
June	30
July	8
Total	90

   b. The interest computation is: $10,000 × 0.08 × 90/365 = $197

Some companies sell goods and services on notes receivable (versus selling on accounts receivable). This often occurs when the payment term extends beyond the customary accounts receivable period of 30 to 60 days.

Suppose that on March 20, 2013, West Fraser Timber Co. Ltd. sells lumber for $15,000 to Darmal Const. Inc. West Fraser receives Darmal's 90-day promissory note at 10% annual interest. The entries to record the sale and collection from Darmal follow the pattern illustrated previously for Canadian Western Bank and Lauren Holland, with one exception. At the outset, West Fraser would credit Sales Revenue (instead of Cash) because West Fraser is making a sale (and not lending money to Darmal). Short-term notes receivable are valued the same way as regular accounts receivable, so we must set up an appropriate allowance for any uncollectible short-term notes. Any notes with a maturity date beyond 365 days of year-end, however, must be valued at their amortized cost by discounting them to reflect the time value of money. This topic will be addressed in more detail in Chapter 8.

A company may also accept a note receivable from a trade customer whose account receivable is past due. The customer signs a note, and the company then credits the account receivable and debits a note receivable. We would say the company "received a note receivable from a customer on account."

For example, assume that on February 1, 2013, Power Ltd. purchased $5,000 of building supplies from Piercy's Building Supplies with 60-day credit terms. Piercy's records the sale as follows:

2013			
Feb. 1	Accounts Receivable—Power Ltd..................................	5,000	
	Sales..		5,000
	To record sale to Power Ltd.		

If on April 1, 2013, Power Ltd. agrees to sign a 30-day note receivable to replace the account receivable due on that date, then Piercy's would record the following journal entry:

2013			
Apr. 1	Notes Receivable...	5,000	
	Accounts Receivable—Power Ltd.		5,000
	To record conversion of account receivable		
	to note receivable.		

Now let's examine some strategies to speed up cash flow.

OBJECTIVE

❺ **Explain** how to improve cash flows from sales and receivables

EXPLAIN HOW TO IMPROVE CASH FLOWS FROM SALES AND RECEIVABLES

Most companies strive to convert their sales to cash receipts as quickly as possible so they can use the cash to pay liabilities and invest in new products, new technology, research, and development. Thus, companies find ways to collect cash immediately. There are several ways companies can hasten their cash receipts from sales.

CREDIT CARD SALES. The merchant sells merchandise and lets the customer pay with a credit card, such as VISA, MasterCard, or a company credit card such as HBC (Hudson's Bay Company). This strategy may dramatically increase sales, but the added revenue comes at a cost. Let's see how credit cards work from the seller's perspective.

Suppose you purchase an iPhone from TELUS in Fredericton, New Brunswick, for $500 and you pay with a MasterCard. TELUS would record the sale as follows:

Cash...	485	
Credit Card Fee...	15	
Sales Revenue...		500
Record credit card sale.		

ASSETS	=	LIABILITIES	+	SHAREHOLDERS' EQUITY
+485	=	0	+	+500 Revenue
				−15 Expense

TELUS enters the transaction in the credit-card machine. The machine, linked to a MasterCard server, automatically credits TELUS's account for a discounted portion—say, $485—of the $500 sales amount. MasterCard gets 3%, or $15 ($500 × 0.03 = $15). To the merchant, the credit card fee is an operating expense similar to interest expense.

DEBIT CARD SALES. The merchant sells merchandise, and the customer pays by swiping a bank card such as a Scotiabank ScotiaCard or a TD Canada Trust Green Card using the Interac System. In this case, the bank card is being used as a debit card. To a merchant or service provider, a debit card is just like cash; when the card is swiped and the personal identification number (PIN) is entered, the merchant receives payment immediately as the Interac System takes money directly from the cardholder's bank account and transfers the money to the merchant's bank account less a processing fee. As with credit cards, the merchant is charged a fee. To record a sale of groceries for $65.48, Sobeys would record this entry:

Cash...	64.48	
Interac Fee (assumed rate)	1.00	
Sales Revenue...		65.48
Record sale paid using Interac.		

ASSETS	=	LIABILITIES	+	SHAREHOLDERS' EQUITY
+64.48	=	0	+	+65.48 Revenue
				−1.00 Expense

One advantage for the merchant is that the payment is just like cash without the task of having to deposit the money. One advantage to the customer is that there is no need to carry cash. A second advantage to the cardholder is the cash-back feature (some merchants offer this service to their customers); the cardholder can ask for cash back, and the merchant will record an entry that includes the purchase plus the requested cash. Using the above date and assuming the carholder requested $40.00 cash back, the entry would be:

Cash...	104.48	
Interac Fee (assumed rate)	1.00	
Sales Revenue...		65.48
Cash (to cardholder)		40.00
Record sale paid using Interac and cash back of $40.00.		

SELLING (FACTORING) RECEIVABLES. Suppose Black Corporation makes normal sales on account, debiting Accounts Receivable and crediting Sales Revenue. Black can then sell its accounts receivable to another business, called a *factor*. The factor earns revenue by paying a discounted price for the receivables and then collecting the full amount from the customers. The benefit to the company is the immediate receipt of cash.

To illustrate, suppose Black wishes to speed up cash flow and therefore sells $100,000 of accounts receivable, receiving cash of $95,000. Black would record the sale of the receivables as follows:

Cash	95,000	
Financing Expense	5,000	
Accounts Receivable		100,000
Sold accounts receivable.		

The Financing Expense is typically reported as an operating expense, although some companies report it as a non-operating loss. Factoring a note receivable is similar to selling an account receivable; however, the credit is to Notes Receivable (instead of Accounts Receivable).

SALES DISCOUNTS. Sometimes businesses offer customers **sales discounts** for early payment in order to speed up cash flow. A typical sales discount incentive might be stated as follows:

2/10, n/30

This expression means that the seller is willing to discount the order by 2% if the buyer pays the invoice within 10 days. After that time, the seller withdraws the discount offer, and the buyer is supposed to pay in full within 30 days. Assume Black Corporation sells goods to a customer and invoices them for $1,500, 2/10, n/30. If the customer pays the invoice within 10 days, it is entitled to a $30 discount, making the full amount due to settle Black Corporation's invoice $1,470 rather than $1,500. The entry to record the collection of this sale would be as follows:

Cash	1,470	
Sales Discount	30	
Accounts Receivable		1,500

Companies with plenty of cash often take advantage of early payment discounts on their purchases, thus adding to their reported profits and cash flows.

SALES RETURNS AND ALLOWANCES. Retailers and consumers have a right to return unsatisfactory or damaged merchandise for a refund or exchange. This is called **sales returns and allowances**. Retailers keep track of sales returns over time to make sure they are not excessive. Returned merchandise means lost profits. For example, suppose that of the goods Black Corporation sold to a customer, $9 worth of goods are returned (or Black grants them an allowance) because they are damaged in shipment. Black Corporation would record the following entry:[*]

Sales Returns and Allowances	9	
Accounts Receivable		9

---

[*]In this example, we ignore the cost of the product to Black Corporation, which is accounted for at both the point of sale and the point of return. We will discuss this further when we cover inventories and cost of goods sold in Chapter 6.

Retailers, wholesalers, and manufacturers typically disclose sales revenue at the *net* amount, which means after the sales discounts and sales returns and allowances have been subtracted. Using hypothetical data for discounts and returns, Black Corporation's net sales (revenue) for 2014, compared with the last two years, is as follows:

Black Corporation
(2014, Adapted)

Gross revenue			$ 59,000
−Sales discounts			(900)
−Sales returns and allowances			(262)
=Net revenue			$ 57,838

	2014	2013	2012
Net revenue (in millions)	$57,838	$43,232	$43,251

Reporting on the Statement of Cash Flows

Receivables and short-term investments appear on the balance sheet as current assets. We saw these in CGI Group Inc.'s balance sheet at the beginning of the chapter. We've also seen how to report the related revenues, gains, and losses on the income statement. Because receivables and investment transactions affect cash, their effects must also be reported on the statement of cash flows.

Receivables bring in cash when the business collects from customers. These transactions are reported as *operating activities* on the statement of cash flows because they result from sales. Held-for-trading investment transactions are also reported as *operating activities* on the statement of cash flows. Chapter 12 shows how companies report their cash flows on the statement of cash flows. In that chapter, we will see exactly how to report cash flows related to receivables and investment transactions.

EVALUATE A COMPANY'S LIQUIDITY

Managers, investors, and creditors use ratios to evaluate the financial health of a company. They care about the liquidity of assets. Liquidity is a measure of how quickly an item can be converted to cash. Remember, a balance sheet lists current assets in order of relative liquidity:

OBJECTIVE

❻ **Evaluate** a company's liquidity

- *Cash and cash equivalents* come first because they are the most liquid assets.
- *Short-term investments* come next because they are almost as liquid as cash. They can be sold for cash whenever the owner wishes.
- *Current receivables* are less liquid than short-term investments because the company must collect the receivables.
- *Merchandise inventory* is less liquid than receivables because the goods must be sold first.
- *Prepaid expenses* are listed after inventories because they are expenses where cash has already been paid in advance.

We introduced the current ratio in Chapter 3. Recall that the current ratio is computed as follows:

$$\text{Current ratio} = \frac{\text{Total current assets}}{\text{Total current liabilities}}$$

The current ratio measures the company's ability to pay current liabilities with current assets.

Lending agreements often require the borrower to maintain a current ratio at some specified level, say 1.50 or greater. What happens when the borrower's current ratio falls below 1.50? The consequences can be severe:

- The lender can call the loan for immediate payment.
- If the borrower cannot pay, then the lender may pursue legal action to enforce collections.

Suppose it's December 10 and it looks like Black Corporation's current ratio will end the year at a value of 1.48. That would put Black in default on the lending agreement of maintaining a 1.50 or greater current ratio and create a bad situation. With three weeks remaining in the year, how can Black improve its current ratio?

There are several strategies for increasing the current ratio, such as the following:

1. Launch a major sales effort. The increase in cash and receivables will more than offset the decrease in inventory, total current assets will increase, and the current ratio will improve.

2. Pay off some current liabilities before year-end. Both current assets in the numerator and current liabilities in the denominator will decrease by the same amount. The proportionate impact on current liabilities in the denominator will be greater than the impact on current assets in the numerator, and the current ratio will increase. This strategy increases the current ratio when the current ratio is already above 1.0.

3. A third strategy, although questionable, reveals one of the accounting games that unethical companies sometimes play. Suppose Black has some long-term investments (investments that Black plans to hold for longer than a year—these are long-term assets). Before year-end, Black might choose to reclassify these long-term investments as current assets. The reclassification of these investments increases Black's current assets, and that increases the current ratio. This strategy would be acceptable if Black does in fact plan to sell the investments within the next year. But the strategy would be unethical and dishonest if Black in fact plans to keep the investments for longer than a year.

From this example you can see that accounting is not cut-and-dried or all black-and-white. It takes good judgment—which includes ethics—to become a successful accountant.

Other ratios, including the *acid-test* (or *quick ratio*) and the number of *days' sales in receivables*, also help investors measure liquidity.

Acid-Test (or Quick) Ratio

The **acid-test ratio** (or **quick ratio**) is a more stringent measure of a company's ability to pay current liabilities. The acid-test ratio is similar to the current ratio but it excludes inventory and prepaid expenses.

Inventory takes time to sell before the company is able to collect its cash. A company with lots of inventory may have an acceptable current ratio but find it hard to pay its bills. Prepaid expenses are also excluded from the acid-test ratio because the cash has already been paid for these assets that will be expensed as they are used up. The formula is:

$$\text{Acid-test ratio} = \frac{\text{Cash} + \text{Short-term investments} + \text{Net receivables}}{\text{Total current liabilities}}$$

Using CGI Group Inc.'s balance sheet in the chapter-opening story, the acid-test ratio is:

$$2011 \text{ CGI} = \frac{\$158 + \$10 + 495}{\$1,219^*} = 0.54$$

The higher the acid-test ratio, the easier it is to pay current liabilities. CGI's acid-test ratio of 0.54 means that CGI has $0.54 of quick assets to pay each $1.00 of current liabilities. Does this mean that CGI is in trouble? No, although CGI's quick ratio is relatively low, when analyzing ratios you might find it useful to consider other information found in the annual report. In CGI's case, over the past several years they have been busy expanding their business.

What is an acceptable acid-test ratio? The answer depends on the industry. Auto dealers can operate smoothly with an acid-test ratio of 0.20. How can auto dealers survive with so low an acid-test ratio? GM, Toyota, and the other auto manufacturers help finance their dealers' inventory. Most dealers, therefore, have a financial safety net. In general, a quick ratio of 1.0 is considered healthy for this industry.

Days' Sales in Receivables

After a business makes a credit sale, the next step is collecting the receivable. **Days' sales in receivables**, also called the *collection period*, tells how long it takes to collect the average level of receivables. Shorter is better because cash is coming in quickly. The longer the collection period, the less cash is available to pay bills and expand.

Days' sales in receivables can be computed in two logical steps, as follows. First, compute one day's sales ideally, only credit sales should be used. Then divide one day's sales into average receivables for the period. We show days' sales in receivables for CGI Group Inc. as follows:

For CGI Group Inc. (in thousands)*

1. One day's sales $= \dfrac{\text{Net sales}}{365 \text{ days}}$ $\qquad \dfrac{\$4,323^*}{365} = \$11.84 \text{ per day}$

2. $\dfrac{\text{Days' sales in}}{\text{receivables}} = \dfrac{\text{Average net accounts receivable}}{\text{One day's sales}} = \dfrac{\left(\begin{array}{c}\text{Beginning net} \quad \text{Ending net} \\ \text{receivables} + \text{receivables}\end{array}\right) \div 2}{\text{One day's sales}}$

$= \dfrac{(\$495 + 424)/2}{\$11.84} = 38.8 \text{ or } 39 \text{ days}$

*Taken from CGI Group Inc.'s 2011 income statement.

Net sales come from the income statement and the receivables amounts are taken from the balance sheet. Average receivables is the simple average of the beginning and ending balances.

*Amount taken from 2011 balance sheet in annual report.

The length of the collection period depends on the credit terms of the company's sales. For example, sales on "net 30" terms should be collected within approximately 30 days. CGI's days' sales in receivables was 39 days in the 2011 financial statements, compared to an industry average of 42 days. While CGI's collections were longer than 30 days, this was shorter than other companies operating in the same industry.

Companies watch their collection periods closely. Whenever the collections get slow, the business must find other sources of financing, such as borrowing cash or factoring receivables. During recessions, customers pay more slowly, and a longer collection period may be unavoidable.[*]

---

[*]Another ratio, **accounts receivable turnover**, captures the same information as days' sales in receivables. Receivable turnover is computed as follows: Net sales/Average net accounts receivable. The authors prefer days' sales in receivables because it is easier to interpret. Days' sales in receivables can be compared directly to the company's credit sale terms.

◀ DECISION GUIDELINES ▶

USING LIQUIDITY RATIOS IN DECISION MAKING

A company needs cash to pay their bills, buy more inventory, and finance new products and services. Two new ratios that measure liquidity were introduced in the chapter. Let's see how they are used in decision making.

Decision	Guidelines
How do you measure a company's ability to pay all current liabilities if they come due immediately?	$\text{Quick ratio} = \dfrac{\text{Cash} + \text{short-term investments} + \text{Net receivables}}{\text{Current liabilities}}$
How do you determine if a company is collecting cash from their customers in a timely manner?	$\text{Days' sales in receivables} = \dfrac{\text{Average net receivables}}{\text{Net sales}/365}$
Who uses the quick ratio and days' sales in receivables for decision making and why?	*Managers* need to ensure that cash is available to pay current liabilities if they come due immediately. They know that some of this cash is tied up in accounts receivables waiting for customers to pay them. This is why companies set up policies and procedures to ensure they can receive their cash from customers quickly so it is available to pay their current debt.
	Investors know that it is important for a company to have enough cash on hand to pay back liabilities, particularly if they are due immediately. Using these ratios helps them to determine how quickly the company is able to collect what is owed them and if this cash is enough to meet current obligations.
	Creditors are expecting to be repaid and look to see how much cash the company has on hand as well as any cash the company expects to receive in the near future. They look to see if the company is able to collect from their customers quickly and if this cash is enough to pay back current liabilities if they are due immediately.

Summary of IFRS-ASPE Differences

Concepts	IFRS	ASPE
Short-term investments (p. 223)	These investments are reported at fair value, with unrealized and realized gains and losses reported in net income, unless the company elects to report them in other comprehensive income.	These investments are reported at fair value, with unrealized and realized gains and losses reported in net income.

SUMMARY OF CHAPTER 5

LEARNING OBJECTIVE	SUMMARY
1. **Account** for short-term investments	Short-term (trading) investments are classified as current assets. When these investments are bought, they are recorded at cost, but at year-end they are reported on the balance sheet at fair value. Any unrealized gain or loss resulting from the change in value is recorded and reported on the income statement. When the investment is sold, any realized gain or loss is also reported on the income statement.
2. **Account for** and **control** receivables	Accounts receivable result from a company selling its products or services on credit. They are classified as a current asset because the company expects to collect cash from the customer within a short period of time. A note receivable is a written agreement in which the borrower agrees to pay a definite sum at a maturity date plus interest over the life of the note. Other receivables include loans to employees and subsidiary companies. Internal control for receivables relates to cash collections on account, where the cash handling and cash accounting duties are separated to prevent theft or fraud.
3. **Estimate** and **account for** uncollectible accounts receivable	Managers use the allowance method (percentage of sales method or aging of receivables method) to estimate the uncollectible accounts. An accounts receivable is written off when a company is not able to collect from a customer. Sometimes, though, an account receivable may be recovered after it has been written off. Rather than estimating uncollectibles, a direct write-off method can be used where the customer's receivable is written off once it is decided that it is uncollectible.
4. **Account** for notes receivable	Notes receivable are formal arrangements in which the debtor signs a promissory note, agreeing to pay back both the principal borrowed plus a stated percentage of interest on a certain date. The creditor has a note receivable and the debtor has a note payable.
5. **Explain** how to improve cash flows from sales and receivables	Rather than wait to collect cash from customers, a company can allow the customer to pay with a credit card or debit card, or the company can sell their receivables to another business. Collections from customers are reported as operating activities on the statement of cash flows.
6. **Evaluate** a company's liquidity	Key ratios used in decision making include the acid-test (quick ratio) and the days' sales in receivables. These ratios help managers, investors, and creditors measure the liquidity of the company. Liquidity relates to how quickly a company can obtain and pay cash.

END-OF-CHAPTER SUMMARY PROBLEM

CHC Helicopter Corporation is Vancouver-based and is the world's largest provider of helicopter services to the global offshore oil and gas industry. Assume the company's balance sheet at April 30, 2013, adapted, reported the following:

	(in millions)
Trade accounts receivable	$240.6
Allowance for uncollectible accounts	(8.4)

Requirements

1. How much of the April 30, 2013, balance of accounts receivable did CHC Helicopter Corporation expect to collect? Stated differently, what was the expected realizable value of these receivables?
2. Journalize, without explanations, 2014 entries for CHC Helicopter, assuming the following:
   a. The estimated Bad Debt Expense is $1.3 million, based on the percentage-of-sales method, all during the year.
   b. The write-offs of uncollectible accounts receivable total $8.0 million. Prepare a T-account for Allowance for Uncollectible Accounts as well, and post to this account. Show its unadjusted balance at April 30, 2014.
   c. The April 30, 2014, aging of receivables indicates that $3.1 million of the total receivables of $303.4 million is uncollectible at year-end. Post to Allowance for Uncollectible Accounts as well, and show its adjusted balance at April 30, 2014.
3. Show how CHC Helicopter's receivables and related allowance will appear on the April 30, 2014, balance sheet.
4. Show what CHC Helicopter's income statement will report for the foregoing transactions.

ANSWERS
Requirement 1

	(in millions)
Expected realizable value of receivables ($240.6 − $8.4)	$232.2

Requirement 2

a. Bad Debt Expense	1.3	
Allowance for Uncollectible Accounts		1.3
b. Allowance for Uncollectible Accounts	8.0	
Accounts Receivable		8.0

Allowance for Uncollectible Accounts

2014 Write-offs	8.0	April 30, 2013	8.4
		2014 Expense	1.3
		2014 Balance	1.7

c. Bad Debt Expense ($3.1−$1.7) ....　1.4
　　　Allowance for Uncollectible Accounts ....　　　　　1.4

Allowance for Uncollectible Accounts

	1.7
	1.4
	3.1

The final balance in the Allowance for Uncollectible Accounts must be $3.1 (estimated in 2c). The balance in the T-account is already $1.7 (calculated above). Therefore, Bad Debt Expense and Allowance for Uncollectible Accounts must be increased by the difference of $1.4.

Requirement 3

	(in millions)
Accounts receivable (net of allowance for uncollectibe accounts of $3.1)	$300.3

Accounts receivable are always shown at net realizable value, the amount actually expected to be collected.

Requirement 4

	(in millions)
Expenses: Bad Debt expense for 2014 ($1.3 + $1.4)	$2.7

Add all the Bad Debt Expense amounts from Requirement 2a, b, and c. The $2.7 includes estimates based on percentage of sales and aging of the receivables.

STOP + THINK (5-1)

ANSWER

	(in thousands)
Customers owed Black Corporation..	$138,370
Black expected not to collect..	3,974
Net realizable value (or the amount	
Black expected to collect)	$134,396

STOP + THINK (5-2)

ANSWER

There is no effect on total assets because the write-off of an uncollectible receivable decreases both Accounts Receivable and the Allowance for Uncollectible Accounts, a contra account. Both accounts are part of net receivables, so one effect offsets the other. The result is no effect on the net realizable value of the receivables and no effect on total assets. There is no effect on net income because the write-off of uncollectible accounts affects no expense account. (The expense account was affected when the Allowance for Uncollectible Accounts was created in an earlier period.)

Review Short-Term Investments and Receivables

QUICK CHECK (ANSWERS ARE GIVEN ON PAGE 269.)

1. Harvey Penick Golf Academy held trading investments valued at $55,000 at December 31, 2013. These investments cost Penick $50,000. What is the appropriate amount for Penick to report for these investments on the December 31, 2013, balance sheet?
   - a. $50,000
   - b. $55,000
   - c. $5,000 gain
   - d. Cannot be determined from the data given

2. Return to Harvey Penick Golf Academy in Question 1. What should appear on the Penick income statement for the year ended December 31, 2013, for the trading investments?
   - a. $50,000
   - b. $55,000
   - c. $5,000 unrealized gain
   - d. Cannot be determined from the data given

Use the following information to answer Questions 3 through 7.

Neal Company had the following information relating to credit sales in 2013:

Accounts receivable December 31, 2013	$ 9,500
Allowance for uncollectible accounts December 31, 2013 (before adjustment)	900
Credit sales during 2013	46,000
Cash sales during 2013	15,000
Collections from customers on account during 2013	49,500

3. Uncollectible accounts are determined by the percentage-of-sales method to be 2% of credit sales. How much is the bad debt expense for 2013?
   - a. $920 $46 1000 x .02
   - b. $2,000
   - c. $750
   - d. $20

4. Using the percentage-of-sales method, what is the adjusted balance in the Allowance account at year-end 2013?
   - a. $900
   - b. $920
   - c. $1,500
   - d. $1,820 $900 + 920

5. If uncollectible accounts are determined by the aging-of-receivables method to be $1,350, the bad debt expense for 2013 would be
   - a. $450.   1350 - 900
   - b. $900.
   - c. $920.
   - d. $1,350.

6. Using the aging-of-receivables method, the balance of the Allowance account after the adjusting entry would be
   - a. $450.
   - b. $900.
   - c. $920.
   - d. $1,350.

7. Assuming the aging-of-receivables method is used, the net realizable value of accounts receivable on the December 31, 2013, balance sheet would be
   - a. $8,580.
   - b. $8,150.   9500 - 1350
   - c. $8,600.
   - d. $9,500.

8. Accounts Receivable has a debit balance of $3,200, and the Allowance for Uncollectible Accounts has a credit balance of $300. A $100 account receivable is written off. What is the amount of net receivables (net realizable value) after the write-off?
   - a. $2,800
   - b. $2,900 (3200 - 100) - (300 - 100)
   - c. $3,000
   - d. $3,100

9. Ridgewood Corporation began 2014 with accounts receivable of $800,000. Sales for the year totalled $2,500,000. Ridgewood ended the year with accounts receivable of $900,000. Ridgewood's bad debt losses are minimal. How much cash did Ridgewood collect from customers in 2014?
   - a. $3,400,000
   - b. $2,940,000
   - c. $2,500,000
   - d. $2,400,000   800 + 2m - 900 K

10. Saturn Company received a four-month, 5%, $4,800 note receivable on December 1. The adjusting entry on December 31 will
   a. debit Interest Receivable $20.   **c.** Both a and b. $4800 \times .05 \times 1/12$
   b. credit Interest Revenue $20.   **d.** credit Interest Revenue $240.

11. What is the maturity value of a $25,000, 5%, six-month note?
   a. $20,000   **c.** $25,625 $25K + (25K \times .05 \times 6/12)$
   b. $25,000   **d.** $26,250

12. If the adjusting entry to accrue interest on a note receivable is omitted, then
   a. liabilities are understated, net income is overstated, and shareholders' equity is overstated.
   b. assets are overstated, net income is understated, and shareholders' equity is understated.
   c. assets, net income, and shareholders' equity are overstated.
   d. assets, net income, and shareholders' equity are understated.

13. Net sales total $730,000. Beginning and ending accounts receivable are $62,000 and $58,000, respectively. Calculate days' sales in receivables.
   a. 32 days   **c.** 43 days
   b. 23 days   **d.** 30 days

14. From the following list of accounts, calculate the quick ratio.

Cash	$3,000	Accounts payable	$ 8,000
Accounts receivable	6,000	Salary payable	3,000
Inventory	8,000	Notes payable (due in two years)	10,000
Prepaid insurance	2,000	Short-term investments	2,000

   a. 2.1   **c.** 1.0
   b. 1.3   **d.** 1.4

Accounting Vocabulary

accounts receivable turnover Net sales divided by average net accounts receivable.   (p. 246)

acid-test ratio Ratio of the sum of cash plus short-term investments plus net receivables to total current liabilities. It is an indicator of an entity's ability to pay its current liabilities if they become due immediately. Also called the *quick ratio*.   (p. 244)

aging-of-receivables method A way to estimate bad debts by analyzing accounts receivable according to the length of time they have been receivable from the customer. Also called the *balance-sheet approach* because it focuses on accounts receivable.   (p. 233)

allowance for bad debts Another name for *allowance for uncollectible accounts*.   (p. 232)

allowance for doubtful accounts Another name for *allowance for uncollectible accounts*.   (p. 232)

allowance for uncollectible accounts A contra account, related to accounts receivable, that holds the estimated amount of collection losses.   (p. 232)

allowance method A method of recording collection losses based on estimates of how much money the business will not collect from its customers.   (p. 231)

bad debt expense A cost to the seller of extending credit to customers. Arises from a failure to collect an account receivable in full.   (p. 231)

creditor The party to whom money is owed.   (p. 237)

days' sales in receivables Tells the company how long it takes to collect the average level of receivables.   (p. 245)

debtor The party who owes money.   (p. 237)

direct write-off method A method of accounting for bad debts in which the company waits until a customer's account receivable proves uncollectible and then debits Uncollectible-Account Expense and credits the customer's Account Receivable.   (p. 235)

doubtful account expense Another name for *bad debt expense*.   (p. 231)

fair value The amount a willing buyer would pay a willing seller to acquire an asset.   (p. 224)

held-for-trading investment A share or bond investment that is to be sold in the near future with the intent of generating profits on the sale.   (p. 224)

interest The borrower's cost of renting money from a lender. Interest is revenue for the lender and expense for the borrower.   (p. 237)

marketable securities Another name for *short-term investments*.   (p. 223)

maturity date The date on which a debt instrument must be paid.   (p. 237)

percentage-of-sales method Computes bad debt expense as a percentage of net sales. Also called the *income-statement approach* because it focuses on the amount of expense to be reported on the income statement.   (p. 232)

principal The amount borrowed by a debtor and lent by a creditor.   (p. 237)

quick ratio Another name for *acid-test ratio*.   (p. 244)

receivables Monetary claims against a business or an individual, acquired mainly by selling goods or services and by lending money.   (p. 228)

sales discount Percentage reduction of sale price by the seller as an incentive for early payment before the due date. A typical way to express a sales discount is "2/10, n/30." This means the seller will grant a 2% discount if the invoice is paid within 10 days, or the full amount is due within 30 days.   (p. 242)

sales returns and allowances Merchandise returned for credit or refunds for services provided.   (p. 242)

short-term investments Investments that a company plans to hold for one year or less. Also called *marketable securities*.   (p. 223)

term The length of time from inception to maturity.   (p. 237)

uncollectible account expense Another name for bad debt expense.   (p. 231)

Assess Your Progress

MyAccountingLab

Make the grade with MyAccountingLab: The Exercises, Quizzes, and Problems (A set) marked in red can be found on MyAccountingLab. You can practise them as often as you want, and most feature step-by-step guided instructions to help you find the right answer.

SHORT EXERCISES

LEARNING OBJECTIVE ❶

Account for short-term investments

S5-1 Answer these questions about investments.

1. Why is a held-for-trading investment always a current asset?

2. What is the amount to report on the balance sheet for a held-for-trading investment?

LEARNING OBJECTIVE ❶

Account for a short-term investment

S5-2 Bannister Corp. holds short-term trading investments. On November 16, Bannister paid $80,000 for a short-term trading investment in Black Corporation shares. At December 31, the fair value of the Black Corporation shares is $84,000. For this situation, show everything that Bannister would report on its December 31 balance sheet and on its income statement for the year ended December 31.

LEARNING OBJECTIVE ❶

Account for a short-term investment

S5-3 Beckham Investments paid $104,000 for a short-term investment in Black Corporation shares.

1. Suppose the Black Corporation shares decreased in value to $98,000 at December 31. Make the Beckham journal entry to adjust the Short-Term Investment account to fair value.

2. Show how Beckham would report the short-term investment on its balance sheet and the unrealized gain or loss on its income statement.

LEARNING OBJECTIVE ❷

Explain internal control over the collection of receivables

S5-4 Don Roose keeps the accounts receivable records of Zachary & Polk, a partnership. What duty will a good internal control system withhold from Roose? Why?

Short Exercises 5-5 through 5-7 should be used together.

LEARNING OBJECTIVE ❸

Apply the allowance method (percentage-of-sales) to account for uncollectibles

S5-5 During its first year of operations, Environmental Products Inc. had sales of $875,000, all on account. Industry experience suggests that Environmental Products' uncollectibles will amount to 2% of credit sales. At December 31, 2013, Environmental Products' accounts receivable total $80,000. The company uses the allowance method to account for uncollectibles.

1. Make Environmental Products' journal entry for bad debt expense using the percentage-of-sales method.

2. Show how Environmental Products could report accounts receivable on its balance sheet at December 31, 2013, by disclosing the allowance for uncollectible accounts.

LEARNING OBJECTIVE ❸

Apply the allowance method (percentage-of-sales) to account for uncollectibles

S5-6 This exercise continues the situation of exercise S5-5, in which Environmental Products ended the year 2013 with accounts receivable of $80,000 and an allowance for uncollectible accounts of $17,500. During 2014, Environmental Products completed the following transactions:

1. Credit sales, $1,000,000

2. Collections on account, $880,000

3. Write-offs of uncollectibles, $16,000

4. Bad debt expense, 1.5% of credit sales

Journalize the 2014 transactions for Environmental Products. Explanations are not required.

S5-7 Use the solution to exercise S5-6 to answer these questions about Environmental Products Inc. for 2014.

1. Start with Accounts Receivable's beginning balance ($80,000) and then post to the Accounts Receivable T-account. How much do Environmental Products' customers owe the company at December 31, 2014?

2. Start with the Allowance account's beginning credit balance ($17,500) and then post to the Allowance for Uncollectible Accounts T-account. How much of the receivables at December 31, 2014, does the company expect *not* to collect?

3. At December 31, 2014, what is the net realizable value of the company's accounts receivable?

LEARNING OBJECTIVE

Apply the allowance method (percentage-of-sales) to account for uncollectibles

S5-8 Gulig and Durham, a law firm, started 2014 with accounts receivable of $60,000 and an allowance for uncollectible accounts of $5,000. The 2014 service revenue on account was $400,000, and cash collections on account totalled $410,000. During 2014, Gulig and Durham wrote off uncollectible accounts receivable of $7,000. At December 31, 2014, the aging-of-receivables method indicated that Gulig and Durham will *not* collect $10,000 of its accounts receivable.

Journalize Gulig and Durham's (a) service revenue, (b) cash collections on account, (c) write-offs of uncollectible receivables, and (d) bad debt expense for the year. Explanations are not required. Prepare a T-account for Allowance for Uncollectible Accounts to show your computation of bad debt expense for the year.

LEARNING OBJECTIVE

Apply the allowance method (aging-of-receivables method) to account for uncollectibles

S5-9 Perform the following accounting for the receivables of Benoit, Brown & Hill, an accounting firm, at December 31, 2014.

1. Start with the beginning balances for these T-accounts:
   • Accounts Receivable, $80,000
   • Allowance for Uncollectible Accounts, $9,000
   Post the following 2014 transactions to the T-accounts:
   a. Service revenue of $850,000, all on account
   b. Collections on account, $790,000
   c. Write-offs of uncollectible accounts, $7,000
   d. Bad debt expense (allowance method), $8,000

2. What are the ending balances of Accounts Receivable and Allowance for Uncollectible Accounts?

3. Show two ways Benoit, Brown & Hill could report accounts receivable on its balance sheet at December 31, 2014.

LEARNING OBJECTIVE

Apply the allowance method (aging-of-receivables method) to account for uncollectibles

S5-10 Metro Credit Union in Charlottetown, Prince Edward Island, loaned $90,000 to David Mann on a six-month, 8% note. Record the following for Metro Credit Union:
a. Lending the money on March 6.
b. Collecting the principal and interest at maturity. Specify the date. Explanations are not required.

LEARNING OBJECTIVE

Account for a note receivable

S5-11

1. Compute the amount of interest during 2012, 2013, and 2014 for the following note receivable: On June 30, 2012, Scotiabank loaned $100,000 to Heather Hutchison on a two-year, 8% note.

LEARNING OBJECTIVE

Account for a note receivable

2. Which party has a (an)
- **a.** note receivable?
- **b.** note payable?
- **c.** interest revenue?
- **d.** interest expense?

3. How much in total would Scotiabank collect if Hutchison paid off the note early—say, on October 30, 2012?

LEARNING OBJECTIVE ❹

Account for a note receivable and interest thereon

S5-12 On May 31, 2013, Nancy Thomas borrowed $6,000 from Assiniboine Credit Union. Thomas signed a note payable, promising to pay the credit union principal plus interest on May 31, 2014. The interest rate on the note is 8%. The accounting year of Assiniboine Credit Union ends on December 31, 2013. Journalize Assiniboine Credit Union's (a) lending money on the note receivable at May 31, 2013, (b) accruing interest at December 31, 2013, and (c) collecting the principal and interest at May 31, 2014, the maturity date of the note.

LEARNING OBJECTIVE ❹

Report notes receivable

S5-13 Using your answers to exercise S5-12, show how the Assiniboine Credit Union will report the following:
- **a.** Whatever needs to be reported on the bank's classified balance sheet at December 31, 2013. (Ignore Cash).
- **b.** Whatever needs to be reported on the bank's income statement for the year ended December 31, 2013.
- **c.** Whatever needs to be reported on the bank's classified balance sheet at December 31, 2014. (Ignore Cash).
- **d.** Whatever needs to be reported on the bank's income statement for the year ended December 31, 2014.

LEARNING OBJECTIVE ❻

Evaluate the acid-test ratio and days' sales in receivables

S5-14 Botany Clothiers reported the following amounts in its 2014 financial statements. The 2013 figures are given for comparison.

		2014		2013
Current assets:				
Cash		$ 9,000		$ 7,000
Short-term investments		12,000		10,000
Accounts receivable	$60,000		$54,000	
Less allowance for uncollectibles	(5,000)	55,000	(5,000)	49,000
Inventory		170,000		172,000
Prepaid insurance		1,000		1,000
Total current assets		$247,000		$239,000
Total current liabilities		$ 80,000		$ 70,000
Net sales		$803,000		$750,000

Requirements

1. Compute Botany's acid-test ratio at the end of 2014. Round to two decimal places. How does the acid-test ratio compare with the industry average of 0.95?
2. Compare Botany's days' sales in receivables measure for 2014 with the company's credit terms of net 30 days.

LEARNING OBJECTIVE ❷❻

Report receivables and other accounts in the financial statements and evaluate liquidity

S5-15 Victoria Medical Service reported the following selected items (amounts in thousands):

Unearned revenues (current)	$ 207	Service revenue	$8,613
Allowance for		Other assets	767
doubtful accounts	109	Property, plant, and equipment	3,316
Other expenses	2,569	Operating expense	1,620
Accounts receivable	817	Cash	239
Accounts payable	385	Notes payable (long-term)	719

1. Classify each item as (a) income statement or balance sheet and as (b) debit balance or credit balance.

2. How much net income (or net loss) did Victoria report for the year?

3. Compute Victoria's current ratio. Round to two decimal places. Evaluate the company's liquidity position.

EXERCISES

E5-16 Research Capital, an investment banking company, has extra cash to invest. Suppose Research Capital buys 1,000 shares of Potash Corporation of Saskatchewan at $185 per share. Assume Research Capital expects to hold the Potash shares for one month and then sell them. The purchase occurs on December 15, 2014. At December 31, the market price of Potash is $195 per share.

LEARNING OBJECTIVE ❶
Account for a short-term investment

[handwritten annotations: temp. investment. — held for trading Inv. Dec.15 - Short term Inv - 185,000 Cash 185,000 Dec.30 - ST Invested - 10,000 Unrealized Gain - int: 10,000]

[handwritten annotations near problem: 3. Balance Sheet! current Ass et Cash xxxx Short term investment 195,000 Income Statement Revenue t/rom other Revenue Unrealized gain on inv. 10,000]

Requirements

1. What type of investment is this to Research Capital? Give the reason for your answer.
2. Record Research Capital's purchase of the Potash shares on December 15 and the adjustment to fair value on December 31.
3. Show how Research Capital would report this investment on its balance sheet at December 31 and any gain or loss on its income statement for the year ended December 31, 2014.

E5-17 On November 16, Edward Jones Co. paid $50,000 for a trading investment in shares of Royal Bank of Canada (RBC). On November 27, Edward Jones received a $500 cash dividend from RBC. It is now December 31, and the fair value of the RBC shares is $49,500. For this investment, show what Edward Jones should report in its income statement and balance sheet.

LEARNING OBJECTIVE ❶
Account for a short-term investment

E5-18 TELUS reports short-term investments on its balance sheet. Suppose a division of TELUS completed the following short-term investment transactions during 2013 and 2014:

LEARNING OBJECTIVE ❶
Account for a short-term investment

2013		
Nov.	6	Purchased 1,000 shares of Canadian Pacific Railway Limited (CPR) for $60,000. TELUS plans to sell the shares at a profit in the near future.
	27	Received a cash dividend of $0.25 per share on the CPR shares.
Dec.	31	Adjusted the investment in CPR shares. Current fair value is $65,000. TELUS plans to sell the shares in early 2014.
2014		
Jan.	11	Sold the CPR shares for $66,000.

Requirement

Prepare T-accounts for Cash, Short-Term Investment, Dividend Revenue, Unrealized Loss or Gain on Investment, and Loss or Gain on Sale of Investment. Show the effects of TELUS's investment transactions. Start with a cash balance of $75,000. All of the other accounts start at zero.

E5-19 As a recent university graduate, you land your first job in the customer collections department of Backroads Publishing. Shawn Dugan, the manager, asks you to propose a system to ensure that cash received from customers by mail is handled properly. Draft a short memorandum to explain the essential element in your proposed plan. State why this element is important. Refer to Chapter 4 if necessary.

LEARNING OBJECTIVE ❷
Apply internal control to receivables

E5-20 At December 31, 2014, Credit Valley Nissan has an Accounts Receivable balance of $101,000. Allowance for Uncollectible Accounts has a credit balance of $2,000 before the year-end adjustment. Service revenue for 2014 was $800,000. Credit Valley estimates that bad debt expense for the year is 1% of sales. Make the December 31 entry to record bad debt

LEARNING OBJECTIVE ❸
Report uncollectible accounts by the allowance method

expense. Show how the accounts receivable and the allowance for uncollectible accounts are reported on the balance sheet. Use the reporting format "Accounts receivable, net of allowance for uncollectible accounts $—" in 2014. Insert the value you've calculated for the allowance.

LEARNING OBJECTIVE ❸

Use the allowance method for uncollectible accounts

E5-21 On June 30, 2014, Perfect Party Planners (PPP) had a $40,000 balance in Accounts Receivable and a $3,000 credit balance in Allowance for Uncollectible Accounts. During July, PPP made credit sales of $75,000. July collections on account were $60,000, write-offs of uncollectible receivables totalled $2,200, and an account of $1,000 was recovered. Bad debt expense is estimated as 2% of revenue.

Requirements

1. Journalize sales, collections, write-offs of uncollectibles, recovery of accounts receivable, and bad debt expense by the allowance method during July. Explanations are not required.
2. Show the ending balances in Accounts Receivable, Allowance for Uncollectible Accounts, and *Net* Accounts Receivable at July 31. How much does PPP expect to collect?
3. Show how PPP will report Accounts Receivable on its July 31 balance sheet. Use the format "Accounts Receivable, net of allowance for uncollectible accounts of $—" at July 31, 2014. Insert the value you've calculated for the allowance.

LEARNING OBJECTIVE ❸

Use the direct write-off method for uncollectible account

E5-22 Refer to exercise E5-21.

Requirements

1. Record bad debt expense for July by the direct write-off method.
2. What amount of accounts receivable would Perfect Party Planners (PPP) report on its July 31 balance sheet under the direct write-off method? Does PPP expect to collect the full amount?

LEARNING OBJECTIVE ❸

Use the aging method to estimate uncollectible accounts

E5-23 At December 31, 2014, before any year-end adjustments, the Accounts Receivable balance of Sunset Hills Clinic is $235,000. Allowance for Uncollectible Accounts has a $6,500 credit balance. Sunset Hills prepares the following aging schedule for accounts receivable:

Total Balance	Age of Accounts			
	0–30 Days	31–60 Days	61–90 Days	Over 90 Days
$235,000	$110,000	$60,000	$50,000	$15,000
Estimated uncollectible	0.5%	1.0%	6.0%	40%

Requirements

1. Based on the aging-of-receivables method, is the unadjusted balance of the allowance account adequate? Is it too high or too low?
2. Make the entry required by the aging schedule. Prepare a T-account for the allowance.
3. Show how Sunset Hills Clinic will report Accounts Receivable on its December 31 balance sheet. Include the two accounts that come before receivables on the balance sheet, using assumed amounts.

LEARNING OBJECTIVE ❸

Measure and account for uncollectibles

E5-24 University Travel experienced the following revenue and accounts receivable write-offs:

Month	Service Revenue	Accounts Receivable Write-Offs			
		January	February	March	Total
January	$ 6,800	$53	$ 86		$139
February	7,000		105	$ 33	138
March	7,500			115	115
	$21,300	$53	$191	$148	$392

University Travel estimates that 2% of revenues will become uncollectible.

Journalize service revenue (all on account), bad debt expense, and write-offs during March. Include explanations. Is an estimate of 2% of revenues being uncollectible reasonable?

E5-25 Record the following note receivable transactions in the journal of Town & Country Realty. How much interest revenue did Town & Country earn this year? Use a 365-day year for interest computations, and round interest amounts to the nearest dollar.

LEARNING OBJECTIVE ❹

Record notes receivable and accrue interest revenue

Oct.	1	Loaned $50,000 cash to Springfield Co. on a one-year, 9% note.
Nov.	3	Performed service for Joplin Corporation, receiving a 90-day, 12% note for $10,000.
Dec.	16	Received a $2,000, six-month, 12% note on account from Afton, Inc.
	31	Accrued interest revenue for the year.

E5-26 Mattson Loan Company completed these transactions:

LEARNING OBJECTIVE ❹

Report the effects of note receivable transactions on the balance sheet and income statement

2013		
Apr.	1	Loaned $20,000 to Charlene Baker on a one-year, 5% note.
Dec.	31	Accrued interest revenue on the Baker note.
2014		
Apr.	1	Collected the maturity value of the note from Baker (principal plus interest).

Show what Mattson would report for these transactions on its 2013 and 2014 balance sheets and income statements. Mattson's accounting year ends on December 31.

E5-27 Answer these questions about receivables and uncollectibles. For the true-false questions, explain any answers that are false.

LEARNING OBJECTIVE ❸❹

Understand receivables

1. True or false? Credit sales increase receivables. Collections and write-offs decrease receivables.
2. Which receivables figure, the *total* amount that customers *owe* the company or the *net* amount the company expects to collect, is more interesting to investors as they consider buying the company's shares? Give your reason.
3. Show how to determine net accounts receivable.
4. True or false? The direct write-off method of accounting for uncollectibles understates assets.
5. Caisse Desjardins lent $100,000 to Chicoutimi Ltée on a six-month, 6% note. Which party has interest receivable? Which party has interest payable? Which party has interest expense, and which has interest revenue? How much interest will these organizations record one month after Chicoutimi Ltée signs the note?
6. When Caisse Desjardins accrues interest on the Chicoutimi Ltée note, show the directional effects on the bank's assets, liabilities, and equity (increase, decrease, or no effect).

E5-28 Assume Black Corporation reported the following items at year-ends 2014 and 2013.

LEARNING OBJECTIVE ❺❻

Use the acid-test ratio and days' sales in receivables to evaluate a company

Black Corporation
Consolidated Balance Sheets (Summarized)
(amounts in millions)

	March 1, 2014	March 3, 2013		March 1, 2014	March 3, 2013
Current assets:			Current liabilities:		
Cash......................................	$1,184.4	$ 677.1	Accounts payable.............	$ 271.1	$ 130.3
Short-term investments ...	420.7	310.1	Other current liabilities....	1,203.3	416.3
Accounts receivable, net ..	1,174.7	572.6	Long-term liabilities.............	103.2	58.8
Inventories.........................	396.3	255.9			
Other current assets.........	301.3	103.6	Shareholders' equity.............	3,933.6	2,483.5
Capital assets	2,033.8	1,169.6			
Total assets...........................	$5,511.2	$3,088.9	Total liabilities and equity....	$5,511.2	$3,088.9

Income Statement (partial): 2014

Revenue	$6,009.4

Requirements

1. Compute Black's (a) acid-test ratio and (b) days' sales in average receivables for 2014. Evaluate each ratio value as strong or weak. Assume Black sells on terms of net 30 days.
2. Recommend two ways the company can speed up its cash flow.

LEARNING OBJECTIVE ⑥

Analyze a company's financial statements

E5-29 Assume Loblaw Companies Limited reported these figures in millions of dollars:

	2014	2013
Net sales	$29,384	$28,640
Receivables at end of year	885	728

Requirements

1. Compute Loblaw's average collection period during 2014.
2. Was Loblaw's collection period long or short? Potash Corporation of Saskatchewan takes 36 days to collect its average level of receivables. FedEx, the overnight shipper, takes 40 days. What causes Loblaw's collection period to be so different?

CHALLENGE EXERCISES

LEARNING OBJECTIVE ⑤

Determine whether to accept credit cards

E5-30 Ripley Shirt Company sells on credit and manages its own receivables. Average experience for the past three years has been as follows:

	Cash	Credit	Total
Sales	$300,000	$300,000	$600,000
Cost of goods sold	165,000	165,000	330,000
Bad debt expense	—	10,000	10,000
Other expenses	84,000	84,000	168,000

John Ripley, the owner, is considering whether to accept credit cards (VISA, MasterCard). Ripley expects total sales to increase by 10% but cash sales to remain unchanged. If Ripley switches to credit cards, the business can save $8,000 on other expenses, but VISA and MasterCard charge 2% on credit card sales. Ripley figures that the increase in sales will be due to the increased volume of credit card sales.

Requirement

Should Ripley Shirt Company start accepting credit cards? Show the computations of net income under the present plan and under the credit card plan.

LEARNING OBJECTIVE ②③

Reconstruct receivables and uncollectible-account amounts

E5-31 Nixtel Inc. reported net receivables of $2,583 million and $2,785 million at December 31, 2014, and 2013, after subtracting allowances of $62 million and $88 million at these respective dates. Nixtel earned total revenue of $10,948 million (all on account) and recorded bad debt expense of $2 million for the year ended December 31, 2014.

Requirements

Use this information to measure the following amounts for the year ended December 31, 2014:

a. Write-offs of uncollectible receivables
b. Collections from customers

QUIZ

Test your understanding of short-term investments and receivables by answering the following questions.

Q5-32 HSBC Bank Canada owns lots of investments. Assume that HSBC paid $600,000 for held-for-trading investments on December 3, 2014. Two weeks later, HSBC received a $45,000 cash dividend. At December 31, 2014, these held-for-trading investments were quoted at a market price of $603,000. HSBC's December income statement should report
a. dividend revenue of $45,000.
b. unrealized gain of $3,000.
c. Both a and b.
d. None of the above.

Q5-33 Refer to the HSBC data in question Q5-32. At December 31, the HSBC balance sheet should report
a. dividend revenue of $45,000.
b. unrealized gain of $3,000.
c. short-term investment of $603,000.
d. short-term investment of $600,000.

Q5-34 Under the allowance method for uncollectible receivables, the entry to record bad debt expense has what effect on the financial statements?
a. Increases expenses and increases owners' equity
b. Decreases assets and has no effect on net income
c. Decreases owners' equity and increases liabilities
d. Decreases net income and decreases assets

Q5-35 Snead Company uses the aging method to adjust the allowance for uncollectible accounts at the end of the period. At December 31, 2014, the balance of accounts receivable is $210,000 and the allowance for uncollectible accounts has a credit balance of $3,000 (before adjustment). An analysis of accounts receivable produced the following age groups:

Current	$150,000
60 days past due	50,000
Over 60 days past due	10,000
	$210,000

Based on past experience, Snead estimates that the percentages of accounts that will prove to be uncollectible within the three groups are 2%, 8%, and 20%, respectively. Based on these facts, the adjusting entry for bad debt expense should be made in the amount of
a. $3,000.
b. $6,000.
c. $9,000.
d. $13,000.

Q5-36 Refer to question Q5-35. The net receivables on the balance sheet are _____.

Q5-37 Harper Company uses the percentage-of-sales method to estimate uncollectibles. Net credit sales for the current year amount to $100,000 and management estimates 2% will be uncollectible. Allowance for Uncollectible Accounts prior to adjustment has a credit balance of $2,000. The amount of expense to report on the income statement will be
a. $30,000.
b. $32,000.
c. $28,000.
d. $2,000.

Q5-38 Refer to question Q5-37. The balance of Allowance for Uncollectible Accounts, after adjustment, will be
a. $2,000.
b. $4,000.
c. $6,000.
d. $12,000.
e. impossible to determine from the information given.

Q5-39 Draw a T-account to illustrate the information in questions Q5-37 and Q5-38. Early the following year, Harper wrote off $3,000 of old receivables as uncollectible. The balance in the Allowance account is now _____.

The next four questions use the following data:

On August 1, 2013, Maritimes Ltd. sold equipment and accepted a six-month, 9%, $10,000 note receivable. Maritimes' year-end is December 31.

Q5-40 How much interest revenue should Maritimes Ltd. accrue on December 31, 2013?
a. $225
c. $375
b. $450
d. Some other amount: _____

Q5-41 If Maritimes Ltd. fails to make an adjusting entry for the accrued interest, which of the following will happen?
a. Net income will be understated, and liabilities will be overstated.
b. Net income will be understated, and assets will be understated.
c. Net income will be overstated, and liabilities will be understated.
d. Net income will be overstated, and assets will be overstated.

Q5-42 How much interest does Maritimes Ltd. expect to collect on the maturity date (February 1, 2014)?
a. $450
c. $75
b. $280
d. Some other amount _____

Q5-43 Which of the following accounts will Maritimes Ltd. credit in the journal entry at maturity on February 1, 2014, assuming collection in full?
a. Interest Receivable
c. Interest Payable
b. Note Payable
d. Cash

Q5-44 Write the journal entry for question Q5-43.

Q5-45 Which of the following is included in the calculation of the acid-test ratio?
a. Cash and accounts receivable
c. Inventory and short-term investment
b. Prepaid expenses and cash
d. Inventory and prepaid expenses

Q5-46 A company with net sales of $1,217,000, beginning net receivables of $90,000, and ending net receivables of $110,000, has a days' sales in accounts receivable value of
a. 50 days.
c. 30 days.
b. 55 days.
d. 33 days.

Q5-47 The company in question Q5-46 sells on credit terms of "net 30 days." Its days' sales in receivables figure is
a. too high.
c. about right.
b. too low.
d. impossible to evaluate from the data given.

PROBLEMS

(Group A)

LEARNING OBJECTIVE ❶

Account for a short-term investment

P5-48A During the fourth quarter of 2013, Cablevision Inc. generated excess cash, which the company invested in securities, as follows:

Nov.	12	Purchased 1,000 common shares as a held-for-trading investment, paying $9 per share.
Dec.	14	Received cash dividend of $0.26 per share on the held-for-trading investment.
	31	Adjusted the held-for-trading investment to its fair value of $7.50 per share.

Requirements
1. Prepare T-accounts for Cash, beginning balance of $20,000; Short-Term Investment; Dividend Revenue; and Unrealized Gain on Investment or Unrealized Loss on Investment.
2. Journalize the foregoing transactions, and post to the T-accounts.

3. Show how to report the short-term investment on the Cablevision balance sheet at December 31.
4. Show how to report whatever should appear on Cablevision's income statement.
5. Cablevision sold the held-for-trading investment for $8,000 on January 10, 2014. Journalize the sale.

P5-49A Computer Giant Inc. makes all sales on account. Susan Phillips, accountant for the company, receives and opens incoming mail. Company procedure requires Phillips to separate customer cheques from the remittance slips, which list the amounts that Phillips posts as credits to customer accounts receivable. Phillips deposits the cheques in the bank. At the end of each day she computes the day's total amount posted to customer accounts and matches this total to the bank deposit slip. This procedure ensures that all receipts are deposited in the bank.

LEARNING OBJECTIVE ❷

Determine internal control of cash receipts from customers

Requirements

As a consultant hired by Computer Giant Inc., write a memo to management evaluating the company's internal controls over cash receipts from customers. If the system is effective, identify its strong features. If the system has flaws, propose a way to strengthen the controls.

P5-50A This problem takes you through the accounting for sales, receivables, and uncollectibles for FedEx Corporation, the overnight shipper. By selling on credit, FedEx cannot expect to collect 100% of its accounts receivable. Assume that at May 31, 2014 and 2013, respectively, FedEx reported the following on its balance sheet (adapted and in millions of U.S. dollars):

LEARNING OBJECTIVE ❷❸

Account for receivables, collections, and uncollectibles by the percentage-of-sales method

	May 31	
	2014	2013
Accounts receivable	$4,517	$4,078
Less: Allowance for uncollectibles	(318)	(136)
Accounts receivable, net	$4,199	$3,942

During the year ended May 31, 2014, FedEx earned service revenue and collected cash from customers. Assume bad debt expense for the year was 1% of service revenue and that FedEx wrote off uncollectible receivables.

Requirements

1. Prepare T-accounts for Accounts Receivable and Allowance for Uncollectibles, and insert the May 31, 2014, balances as given.
2. Journalize the following assumed transactions of FedEx for the year ended May 31, 2014. Explanations are not required.
   a. Service revenue on account, $37,953 million
   b. Collections on account, $37,314 million
   c. Bad debt expense, 1% of service revenue
   d. Write-offs of uncollectible accounts receivable, $200 million
   e. Recovered an account receivable, $2 million
3. Post your entries to the Accounts Receivable and the Allowance for Uncollectibles T-accounts.
4. Compute the ending balances for the two T-accounts, and compare your balances to the actual May 31, 2014 amounts. They should be the same.
5. Show what FedEx would report on its income statement for the year ended May 31, 2014.

P5-51A The September 30, 2014, records of First Data Communications include these accounts:

LEARNING OBJECTIVE ❸

Use the aging approach for uncollectibles

Accounts Receivable	$230,000
Allowance for Uncollectible Accounts	(8,500)

At year-end, the company ages its receivables and adjusts the balance in Allowance for Uncollectible Accounts to correspond to the aging schedule. During the last quarter of 2014, the company completed the following selected transactions:

2014		
Nov.	30	Wrote off as uncollectible the $1,100 account receivable from Rainbow Carpets and the $600 account receivable from Show-N-Tell Antiques.
Dec.	31	Adjusted the Allowance for Uncollectible Accounts, and recorded Bad Debt Expense at year-end, based on the aging of receivables, which follows.

		Age of Accounts		
Total Balance	0–30 Days	31–60 Days	61–90 Days	Over 90 Days
$230,000	$150,000	$40,000	$14,000	$26,000
Estimated uncollectible	0.2%	0.5%	5.0%	30.0%

Requirements

1. Record the transactions in the journal. Explanations are not required.
2. Prepare a T-account for Allowance for Uncollectible Accounts, and post to that account.
3. Show two ways First Data could report its accounts receivable on a comparative balance sheet for 2013 and 2014. At December 31, 2013, the company's Accounts Receivable balance was $212,000 and the Allowance for Uncollectible Accounts stood at $4,200.

LEARNING OBJECTIVE ❶❸❻

Account for short-term investments and uncollectibles, and use ratios to evaluate a business

P5-52A Assume Deloitte & Touche, the accounting firm, advises Pappadeaux Seafood that Pappadeaux's financial statements must be changed to conform to GAAP. At December 31, 2014, Pappadeaux's accounts include the following:

Cash	$ 51,000
Short-term trading investments, at cost	19,000
Accounts receivable	37,000
Inventory	61,000
Prepaid expenses	14,000
Total current assets	$182,000
Accounts payable	$ 62,000
Other current liabilities	41,000
Total current liabilities	$103,000

Deloitte & Touche advised Pappadeaux that:

- Cash includes $20,000 that is deposited in a compensating balance account that is tied up until 2016.
- The fair value of the short-term trading investments is $17,000. Pappadeaux purchased the investments a couple of weeks ago.
- Pappadeaux has been using the direct write-off method to account for uncollectible receivables. During 2014, Pappadeaux wrote off bad receivables of $7,000. Deloitte & Touche determines that bad debt expense for the year should be 2.5% of sales revenue, which totalled $600,000 in 2014.
- Pappadeaux reported net income of $92,000 in 2014.

Requirements

1. Restate Pappadeaux's current accounts to conform to GAAP.
2. Compute Pappadeaux's current ratio and acid-test ratio both before and after your corrections.
3. Determine Pappadeaux's correct net income for 2014.

P5-53A Assume that General Mills Canada, famous for Cheerios, Chex snacks, and Yoplait yogurt, completed the following selected transactions:

LEARNING OBJECTIVE ❹

Account for notes receivable and accrued interest revenue

2013		
Nov.	30	Sold goods to Sobeys Inc., receiving a $50,000, three-month, 5% note.
Dec.	31	Made an adjusting entry to accrue interest on the Sobeys note.
2014		
Feb.	28	Collected the Sobeys note.
Mar.	1	Received a 90-day, 5%, $6,000 note from Louis Joli Goût on account.
	1	Sold the Louis note to Caisse Populaire, receiving cash of $5,900.
Dec.	16	Loaned $25,000 cash to Betty Crocker Brands, receiving a 90-day, 8% note.
	31	Accrued the interest on the Betty Crocker Brands note.

Requirements

1. Record the transactions in General Mills' journal. Round interest amounts to the nearest dollar. Explanations are not required.
2. Show what General Mills will report on its comparative classified balance sheet at December 31, 2013, and December 31, 2014.

P5-54A The comparative financial statements of Sunset Pools Inc. for 2014, 2013, and 2012 included the following selected data:

LEARNING OBJECTIVE ❻

Use ratio data to evaluate a company's financial position

	(in millions)		
	2014	2013	2012
Balance sheet:			
Current assets:			
Cash	$ 86	$ 60	$ 70
Short-term investments	130	174	112
Receivables, net of allowance for uncollectible accounts			
of $27, $21, and $15, respectively	243	245	278
Inventories	330	375	362
Prepaid expenses	10	25	26
Total current assets	$ 799	$ 879	$ 848
Total current liabilities	$ 403	$ 498	$ 413
Income statement:			
Net sales	$2,898	$2,727	$2,206

Requirements

1. Compute these ratios for 2014 and 2013:
   a. Current ratio
   b. Acid-test ratio
   c. Days' sales in receivables
2. Write a memo explaining to top management which ratio values improved from 2013 to 2014 and which ratio values deteriorated. State whether the overall trend is favourable or unfavourable, and give the reason for your evaluation.
3. Recommend two ways for Sunset Pools to improve cash flow from receivables.

(Group B)

LEARNING OBJECTIVE ❶

Account for a short-term investment

P5-55B During the fourth quarter of 2013, the operations of Baris Carpet Centre generated excess cash, which the company invested in securities, as follows:

Dec.	10	Purchased 2,500 common shares as a held-for-trading investment, paying $15 per share.
	17	Received cash dividend of $0.50 per share on the held-for-trading investment.
	31	Adjusted the held-for-trading investment to its fair value of $40,000.

Requirements

1. Prepare T-accounts for Cash, balance of $85,000; Short-Term Investment; Dividend Revenue; and Unrealized Gain on Investment or Unrealized Loss on Investment.
2. Journalize the foregoing transactions, and post to the T-accounts.
3. Show how to report the short-term investment on Baris's balance sheet at December 31.
4. Show how to report whatever should appear on Baris's income statement.
5. On January 6, 2014, Baris sold the held-for-trading investment for $36,000. Journalize the sale.

LEARNING OBJECTIVE ❷

Determine internal control of cash receipts from customers

P5-56B Mountainview Software Sales makes all sales on credit, so virtually all cash receipts arrive in the mail. Shatel Patel, the company president, has just returned from a trade association meeting with new ideas for the business. Among other things, Patel plans to institute stronger internal controls over cash receipts from customers.

Requirements

Take the role of Shatel Patel, the company president. Write a memo to employees outlining procedures to ensure that all cash receipts are deposited in the bank and that the total amounts of each day's cash receipts are posted to customer accounts receivable.

LEARNING OBJECTIVE ❷❸

Account for receivables, collections, and uncollectibles by the percentage-of-sales method

P5-57B Brubacher Service Company sells for cash and on account. By selling on credit, Brubacher cannot expect to collect 100% of its accounts receivable. At December 31, 2014, and 2013, respectively, Brubacher reported the following on its balance sheet (in thousands of dollars):

	December 31	
	2014	2013
Accounts receivable	$500	$400
Less: Allowance for uncollectibles	(100)	(60)
Accounts receivable, net	$400	$340

During the year ended December 31, 2014, Brubacher earned service revenue and collected cash from customers. Bad debt expense for the year was 5% of service revenue and Brubacher wrote off uncollectible accounts receivable.

Requirements

1. Prepare T-accounts for Accounts Receivable and Allowance for Uncollectibles, and insert the December 31, 2013, balances as given.
2. Journalize the following transactions of Brubacher for the year ended December 31, 2014. Explanations are not required.
   a. Service revenue on account, $6,700 thousand
   b. Collections from customers on account, $6,300 thousand
   c. Bad debt expense, 5% of service revenue
   d. Write-offs of uncollectible accounts receivable, $300 thousand
   e. Recovered an account receivable, $5 thousand

3. Post to the Accounts Receivable and Allowance for Uncollectibles T-accounts.
4. Compute the ending balances for the two T-accounts, and compare to the Brubacher Service amounts at December 31, 2014. They should be the same.
5. Show what Brubacher should report on its income statement for the year ended December 31, 2014.

P5-58B The September 30, 2014, records of Synetics Computers show:

LEARNING OBJECTIVE ❹
Use the aging approach for uncollectibles

Accounts Receivable	$114,000
Allowance for Uncollectible Accounts	(4,100)

At year-end, Synetics ages its receivables and adjusts the balance in Allowance for Uncollectible Accounts to correspond to the aging schedule. During the last quarter of 2014, Synetics completed the following selected transactions:

2014		
Oct.	31	Wrote off the following accounts receivable as uncollectible: Cisco Foods, $300; Tindall Storage, $400; and Tiffany Energy, $1,100.
Dec.	31	Adjusted the Allowance for Uncollectible Accounts and recorded bad debt expense at year-end, based on the aging of receivables, which follows.

	Age of Accounts			
Total Balance	0–30 Days	31–60 Days	61–90 Days	Over 90 Days
$114,000	$80,000	$20,000	$4,000	$10,000
Estimated uncollectible	0.5%	1.0%	5.0%	40.0%

Requirements

1. Record the transactions in the journal. Explanations are not required.
2. Prepare a T-account for Allowance for Uncollectible Accounts, and post to that account.
3. Show two ways Synetics Computers could report its accounts receivable in a comparative balance sheet for 2013 and 2014. At December 31, 2013, the company's Accounts Receivable balance was $111,000 and the Allowance for Uncollectible Accounts stood at $3,700.

P5-59B The top managers of Whelan Gift Stores seek the counsel of Ernst & Young, the accounting firm, and learn that Whelan must make some changes to bring its financial statements into conformity with GAAP. At December 31, 2014, Whelan Gift Stores accounts include the following:

LEARNING OBJECTIVE ❶❸❻
Account for short-term investments, and uncollectibles by the percentage-of-sales method

Cash	$ 23,000
Short-term trading investments, at cost	24,000
Accounts receivable	54,000
Inventory	45,000
Prepaid expenses	17,000
Total current assets	$163,000
Accounts payable	46,000
Other current liabilities	69,000
Total current liabilities	$115,000

As the accountant from Ernst & Young, you draw the following conclusions:

- Cash includes $6,000 that is deposited in a compensating balance account that will be tied up until 2016.
- The fair value of the short-term trading investments is $32,000. Whelan Gift Stores purchased the investments in early December.

- Whelan Gift Stores has been using the direct write-off method to account for uncollectibles. During 2014, the company wrote off bad receivables of $4,000. Ernst & Young determines that bad debt expense should be 2% of sales, which for 2014 totalled $450,000.
- Whelan Gift Stores reported net income of $81,000 for 2014.

Requirements

1. Restate all current accounts to conform to GAAP.
2. Compute Whelan Gift Stores' current ratio and acid-test ratio both before and after your corrections.
3. Determine Whelan Gift Stores' correct net income for 2014.

LEARNING OBJECTIVE ❹

Account for notes receivable and
accrued interest revenue

P5-60B Lilley & Taylor, partners in an accounting practice, completed the following selected transactions:

2013		
Oct.	31	Performed service for Berger Manufacturing Inc., receiving a $30,000, three-month, 5% note.
Dec.	31	Made an adjusting entry to accrue interest on the Berger note.
2014		
Jan.	31	Collected the Berger note.
Feb.	18	Received a 90-day, 8%, $10,000 note from Emerson Ltd., on account.
	19	Sold the Emerson note to a financial institution, receiving cash of $9,700.
Nov.	11	Loaned $20,000 cash to Diaz Insurance Agency, receiving a 90-day, 9% note.
Dec.	31	Accrued the interest on the Diaz note.

Requirements

1. Record the transactions in Lilley & Taylor's journal. Round all amounts to the nearest dollar. Explanations are not required.
2. Show what Lilley & Taylor will report on its comparative classified balance sheet at December 31, 2014, and December 31, 2013.

LEARNING OBJECTIVE ❻

Use ratio data to evaluate a
company's financial position

P5-61B The comparative financial statements of New World Piano Company for 2014, 2013, and 2012 included the following selected data:

	(in millions)		
	2014	2013	2012
Balance sheet:			
Current assets:			
Cash	$ 67	$ 66	$ 62
Short-term investments	73	81	70
Receivables, net of allowance for uncollectible accounts of			
$7, $6, and $4, respectively	226	174	195
Inventories	398	375	349
Prepaid expenses	22	19	16
Total current assets	$ 786	$ 715	$ 692
Total current liabilities	$ 420	$ 405	$ 388
Income statement:			
Net sales	$2,071	$2,005	$1,965

Requirements

1. As a financial advisor to an investor in New World Piano Company, compute these ratios for 2014 and 2013:
   a. Current ratio
   b. Acid-test ratio
   c. Days' sales in receivables

2. Write a memo explaining to your client which ratio values showed improvement from 2013 to 2014 and which ratio values deteriorated. State whether the overall trend is favourable or unfavourable for the company, give the reason for your evaluation, and advise your client regarding its investment.

3. Recommend two ways to improve cash flow from receivables.

Apply Your Knowledge

Decision Cases

Case 1. A fire during 2014 destroyed most of the accounting records of Morris Financial Services Inc. The only accounting data for 2014 that Morris can come up with are the following balances at December 31, 2014. The general manager also knows that bad debt expense should be 5% of service revenue.

LEARNING OBJECTIVE ❷❸

Account for receivables, collections, and uncollectible accounts on receivables

Accounts receivable	$180,000
Less: Allowance for uncollectibles	(22,000)
Total expenses, excluding bad debt expense	670,000
Collections from customers	840,000
Write-offs of bad receivables	30,000
Accounts receivable, December 31, 2013	110,000

As the insurance claims officer, prepare a summary income statement for Morris Financial Services Inc. for the year ended December 31, 2014. The insurance claim will be affected by whether the company was profitable in 2014. Use a T-account for Accounts Receivable to compute service revenue.

Case 2. Suppose you work in the loan department of CIBC. Dean Young, owner of Dean Young Sports Equipment, has come to you seeking a loan for $500,000 to expand operations. Young proposes to use accounts receivable as collateral for the loan and has provided you with the following information from the company's most recent financial statements:

LEARNING OBJECTIVE ❸❻

Estimate the collectibility of accounts receivable and evaluate liquidity

	(in thousands)		
	2014	2013	2012
Sales	$1,475	$1,001	$902
Cost of goods sold	876	647	605
Gross profit	599	354	297
Other expenses	518	287	253
Net profit or (loss) before taxes	$ 81	$ 67	$ 44
Accounts receivable	$ 128	$ 107	$ 94
Allowance for uncollectible accounts	13	11	9

Requirement

Analyze the trends of sales, days' sales in receivables, and cash collections from customers for 2014 and 2013. Would you make the loan to Young? Support your decision with facts and figures.

Ethical Issue

Sunnyvale Loan Company is in the consumer loan business. Sunnyvale borrows from banks and loans out the money at higher interest rates. Sunnyvale's bank requires Sunnyvale to submit quarterly financial statements to keep its line of credit. Sunnyvale's main asset is

Notes Receivable. Therefore, Bad Debt Expense and Allowance for Uncollectible Accounts are important accounts for the company. Kimberly Burnham, the company's owner, prefers for net income to reflect a steady increase in a smooth pattern, rather than increase in some periods and decrease in other periods. To report smoothly increasing net income, Burnham underestimates Bad Debt Expense in some periods. In other periods, Burnham overestimates the expense. She reasons that the income overstatements roughly offset the income under-statements over time.

Requirement

Is Sunnyvale Loan's practice of smoothing income ethical? Why or why not?

Focus on Financials

LEARNING OBJECTIVE

Account for short-term investments and accounts receivable

TELUS Corporation

Refer to TELUS's financial statements in Appendix A at the end of the book.

1. In the notes to the financial statements are the following:

> Note 1(c)
>
> Short-term marketable securities investments are accounted for as held-for-trading and thus are measured at fair value through net income.

Assume that cash and cash equivalents, which included short-term money market instruments, were $100 at December 31, 2011, and $200 at December 31, 2010. Further assume that there were no fair value adjustments in 2010 and that the statement of cash flows reports that TELUS sold money market instruments for $150. How much gain or loss would TELUS have on the sale of the money market instruments?

2. How much were TELUS's receivables at December 31, 2011, and December 31, 2010? What can you assume from this information?

3. Assume that TELUS wrote off 1% of 2011 sales as uncollectible. How much did TELUS collect from customers during 2011?

Focus on Analysis

LEARNING OBJECTIVE

Analyze accounts receivable and liquidity

TELUS Corporation

Refer to TELUS's financial statements in Appendix A.

Requirements

1. Does TELUS disclose the Allowance for Uncollectible Accounts in its financial statements? How can you determine what TELUS expects to collect from its reported Accounts Receivable?*

2. Evaluate TELUS's liquidity as of December 31, 2011, and compare it with 2010. What other information might be helpful in your evaluation?

*Note: TELUS uses the term allowance for doubtful accounts in their financial statements; this is another term for allowance for uncollectible accounts.

Group Project

Jillian Michaels and Dee Childress worked for several years as sales representatives for Xerox Corporation. During this time, they became close friends as they acquired expertise with the company's full range of copier equipment. Now they see an opportunity to put their expertise to work and fulfill lifelong desires to establish their own business. Northern Lights College has a campus in their community, Fort St. John, British Columbia, and there is no copy centre within eight kilometres of the campus. Business in the area is booming, office buildings and apartments are springing up, and the population of the city of Fort St. John is growing.

Michaels and Childress want to open a copy centre, similar to FedEx Kinko's, near the campus. A small shopping centre across the street from the college has a vacancy that would fit their needs. Michaels and Childress each have $35,000 to invest in the business, but they forecast the need for $200,000 to renovate the store and purchase some of the equipment they will need. Xerox Corporation will lease two large copiers to them at a total monthly rental of $6,000. With enough cash to see them through the first six months of operation, they are confident they can make the business succeed. The two women work very well together, and both have excellent credit ratings. Michaels and Childress must borrow $130,000 to start the business, advertise its opening, and keep it running for its first six months.

Requirements

Assume two roles: (1) Michaels and Childress, the partners who will own Fort St. John Copy Centre; and (2) loan officers at North Peace Savings and Credit Union (NPSCU).

1. As a group, visit a copy centre to familiarize yourselves with its operations. Then write a loan request that Michaels and Childress will submit to NPSCU with the intent of borrowing $130,000 to be paid back over three years. The request should specify all the details of Michaels's and Childress's plan that will motivate the bank to grant the loan. Include a budget for each of the first six months of operation of the proposed copy centre.
2. As a loan officer in a bank, write NPSCU's reply to the loan request. Specify all the details that the bank should require as conditions for making the loan.
3. If necessary, modify the loan request or the bank's reply in order to reach agreement between the two parties.

Quick Check Answers

1. b
2. c
3. a ($46,000 × 0.02)
4. d ($900 + $920)
5. a ($1,350 − $900)
6. d
7. b ($9,500 − $1,350)
8. b ($3,200 − $100) − ($300 − $100)
9. d ($800,000 + $2,500,000 − $900,000)
10. c ($4,800 × 0.05 × 1/12)
11. c $25,000 + ($25,000 × 0.05 × 6/12)
12. d
13. d [($62,000 + $58,000)/2 ÷ ($730,000/365)]
14. c [($3,000 + $6,000 + $2,000) ÷ ($8,000 + $3,000)]

6

Inventory and Cost of Goods Sold

The Canadian Press Images/J.P. Moczulski

SPOTLIGHT

You have just graduated from university, taken a job, and are moving into an apartment. The place is unfurnished, so you will need a bed, dresser, sofa, table, and chairs to go with your TV and sound system. Where will you find these things? Leon's Furniture is a good source.

Leon's Furniture is known for its contemporary-styled, well-priced furnishings—just about right for a new graduate. The company operates 75 retail stores across Canada.

Leon's Furniture Limited's balance sheet (partial) is summarized on the next page. You can see that merchandise inventory (labelled simply as Inventory) is one of Leon's Furniture's biggest assets. That's not surprising since Leon's, like other retailers, attracts customers with goods they can purchase and take home immediately.

Leon's Furniture Limited
Consolidated Balance Sheets (partial, adapted)
As at December 31

	(millions)	
	2011	2010
Assets		
Current		
Cash and cash equivalents	$ 72.5	$ 71.6
Short-term investments	149.3	140.2
Trade receivables	28.9	28.6
Income taxes receivable	5.2	–
Inventories	87.8	85.4
Total current assets	343.7	325.8
Other assets	37.4	39.4
Property, plant, and equipment	214.2	201.5
Total Assets	$595.3	$566.7

We also present Leon's Furniture Limited's income statement. Even though sales were down in 2011, gross profit, as a percentage of sales, increased from 41.9% in 2010 to 42.3% in 2011.

Leon's Furniture Limited
Consolidated Income Statements (adapted)
Years ending December 31

	(millions)	
	2011	2010
Sales	$682.8	$710.4
Cost of sales	394.1	412.4
Gross profit	288.7	298.0
General and administrative expenses	96.0	98.7
Sales and marketing expenses	78.4	78.2
Other operating expenses	39.0	35.3
Operating profit	75.3	85.8
Other income	3.5	4.3
Profit before income tax	78.8	90.1
Income tax expense	22.1	26.9
Net income for the year	$ 56.7	$ 63.2

You can see that the *cost of sales* (another name for **cost of goods sold**) is by far Leon's Furniture's largest expense. The account titled Cost of Sales perfectly describes that expense. In short,

- Leon's buys inventory, an asset carried on the books at cost.
- the goods that Leon's sells are no longer Leon's Furniture's assets. The cost of inventory that's sold gets shifted into the expense account, Cost of Sales.

Merchandise inventory is the heart of a merchandising business, and cost of goods sold is the most important expense for a company that sells goods rather than services. This chapter covers the accounting for inventory and cost of goods sold. It also shows you how to analyze financial statements. Here, we focus on inventory, cost of goods sold, and gross profit.

❶ **Account** for inventory using the perpetual and periodic inventory systems

ACCOUNT FOR INVENTORY USING THE PERPETUAL AND PERIODIC INVENTORY SYSTEMS

We begin by showing how the financial statements of a merchandiser such as Leon's Furniture Limited differ from those of service entities such as Royal LePage Real Estate. Merchandisers have two accounts that service entities don't need: Inventory on the balance sheet and Cost of Goods Sold on the income statement. The financial statements in Exhibit 6-1 highlight these differences.

EXHIBIT 6-1
Contrasting a Service Company With a Merchandiser

Service Company
Royal LePage Real Estate
Income Statement
For the Year Ended December 31, 2011

Service revenue	$XXX
Expenses	
Operating and administrative	X
Depreciation	X
Income tax	X
Net income	$ X

Merchandising Company
Leon's Furniture Ltd.
Income Statement
For the Year Ended December 31, 2011

Amounts in millions

Sales revenue	$682.8
Cost of goods sold	394.1
Gross profit	$288.7
Operating *expenses*	
Operating and administrative	X
Depreciation	X
Income tax	X
Net income	$ 56.7

Royal LePage Real Estate
Balance Sheet
As at December 31, 2011

Assets

Current assets	
Cash	$X
Temporary investments	X
Accounts receivable, net	X
Prepaid expenses	X

Leon's Furniture Ltd.
Balance Sheet
As at December 31, 2011

Assets

Amounts in thousands

Current assets	
Cash	$ X
Temporary investments	X
Accounts receivable, net	X
Inventory	87.8
Prepaid expenses	X

Accounting for Inventory

The value of inventory affects two financial statement accounts: inventory, reported as a current asset on the balance sheet; and cost of goods sold, shown as an expense on the income statement. This basic concept of accounting for merchandise inventory can be illustrated with an example. Suppose Leon's Furniture has in stock three chairs that cost $300 each. Leon's Furniture marks the chairs up by $200 and sells two of the chairs for $500 each.

EXHIBIT 6-2
Inventory and Costs of Goods Sold When Inventory Cost Is Constant

Balance Sheet (Partial)		Income Statement (Partial)	
Current assets		Sales revenue	
Cash	$XXX	(2 chairs @ sales price of $500)	$1,000
Short-term investments	XXX	Cost of goods sold	
Accounts receivable	XXX	(2 chairs @ cost of $300)	600
Inventory (1 chair @ cost of $300)	300	Gross profit	$ 400
Prepaid expenses	XXX		

- Leon's Furniture's balance sheet reports the one chair that the company still holds in inventory.

- The income statement reports the cost of the two chairs sold, as shown in Exhibit 6-2.

Here is the basic concept of how we identify inventory, the asset, from cost of goods sold, the expense.

Inventory's cost shifts from asset to expense when the seller delivers the goods to the buyer.

Sales Price Versus Cost of Inventory

Note the difference between the sale price of inventory and the cost of inventory. In our Leon's Furniture example:

- Sales revenue is based on the *sale price* of the inventory sold ($500 per chair).

- Cost of goods sold is based on the *cost* of the inventory sold ($300 per chair).

- Inventory on the balance sheet is based on the *cost* of the inventory still on hand ($300 per chair).

Exhibit 6-2 shows these items.

Gross profit, also called **gross margin**, is the excess of sales revenue over cost of goods sold. It is called *gross profit* because operating expenses have not yet been subtracted. The actual inventory and cost of goods sold data (cost of sales) from the financial statements of Leon's Furniture Limited are:

Leon's inventory of $87.8 million represents:

$$\frac{\text{Inventory}}{\text{(balance sheet)}} = \frac{\text{Number of units of}}{\text{inventory } on \ hand} \times \frac{\text{Cost per unit}}{\text{of inventory}}$$

Leon's cost of goods sold ($394.1 million) represents:

$$\frac{\text{Cost of goods sold}}{\text{(income statement)}} = \frac{\text{Number of units of}}{\text{inventory } sold} \times \frac{\text{Cost per unit}}{\text{of inventory}}$$

Let's see what "units of inventory" and "cost per unit" mean.

NUMBER OF UNITS OF INVENTORY. This figure simply represents the number of units of inventory a business has on hand at a certain point in time. At each year-end, the business normally conducts a physical count of its inventory so it has an accurate record of the number of units on hand at that time. Leon's, for example, would conduct a physical inventory count on December 31 each year to determine the number of chairs, beds, tables, and other types of furniture it has on hand at year-end. Leon's needs an accurate count of inventory so it can properly determine the total cost of inventory to report on its year-end balance sheet.

The manager must also take into account inventory that has been shipped. Who owns it? Determining the ownership of inventory at the time of shipment depends on who has legal title. If inventory is shipped FOB (free on board) shipping point, it should be included on the books of the buyer, who has legal title, as soon as it leaves the shipper's dock. If the goods are shipped FOB destination, the inventory in transit still belongs on the books of the seller until it is delivered to the buyer.

COST PER UNIT OF INVENTORY. Determining the cost per unit of inventory poses a challenge because companies purchase goods at different prices throughout the year. Which unit costs go into the ending inventory for the balance sheet? Which unit costs go to cost of goods sold?

What Goes Into Inventory Cost?

The cost of merchandise in Leon's Furniture Limited's balance sheet represents all the costs that Leon's Furniture incurred to bring the inventory to the point of sale. Both IFRS and ASPE state the following:

> *The cost of inventories shall comprise all costs of purchase, costs of conversion and other costs incurred in bringing the inventories to their present location and condition.*

Inventory's cost includes its basic purchase price, plus freight-in, insurance while in transit, and any costs paid to get the inventory ready to sell, less returns, allowances, and discounts.

Once a product is sitting in a Leon's Furniture showroom, other costs incurred, such as advertising and delivery costs, are not included as the cost of inventory. Advertising, sales commissions, and delivery costs are expenses.

The next section shows how the different accounting methods determine the cost of ending inventory on the balance sheet and cost of goods sold for the income statement. First, however, you need to understand how inventory accounting systems work.

Accounting for Inventory in the Perpetual System

There are two main types of inventory accounting systems: the periodic system and the perpetual system. The **periodic inventory system** is mainly used by businesses that sell inexpensive goods. A dollar store or a convenience store, for example, may not keep a running record of every one of the hundreds of items they sell. Instead, these stores count their inventory periodically—at least once a year—to determine the quantities on hand. Businesses such as some restaurants and hometown nurseries also use the periodic inventory system because the accounting cost is low.

A **perpetual inventory system** uses computer software to keep a running record of inventory on hand. This system achieves control over goods such as parts at a Ford dealer, lumber at RONA, furniture at Leon's, and all the various groceries and other items that a Loblaws store sells. Today, most businesses use the perpetual inventory system.

Even with a perpetual system, the business still counts the inventory on hand annually. The physical count serves as a check on the accuracy of the perpetual records and confirms the accuracy of the inventory records for preparing the financial statements. The chart below compares the perpetual and periodic systems.

Perpetual Inventory System	*Periodic Inventory System*
• Used for all types of goods	• Used for inexpensive goods
• Keeps a running record of all goods bought, sold, and on hand	• Does not keep a running record of all goods bought, sold, and on hand
• Inventory counted at least once a year	• Inventory counted at least once a year

HOW THE PERPETUAL SYSTEM WORKS. Let's use an everyday situation to show how a perpetual inventory system works. Suppose you are buying a pair of Nike cross-trainer shoes from Sport Chek. The clerk scans the bar code on the product label of your purchase. Exhibit 6-3 illustrates a typical bar code. The bar code on the product or product label holds lots of information. The optical scanner reads the bar code, and the computer records the sale and updates the inventory records.

EXHIBIT 6-3
Bar Code for Electronic Scanner

0 72512 06581 5

RECORDING TRANSACTIONS IN THE PERPETUAL SYSTEM. Each purchase of inventory is recorded as a debit to Inventory and a credit to Cash or Accounts Payable.

When Leon's Furniture makes a sale, two entries are needed in the perpetual system:

- The company records the sale:
  Dr   Cash or Accounts Receivable
     Cr   Sales Revenue
- Leon's Furniture also records the cost of inventory sold:
  Dr   Inventory
     Cr   Cost of Goods Sold

RECORDING TRANSACTIONS IN THE PERIODIC SYSTEM. In the periodic inventory system, the business keeps no running record of the merchandise. Instead, at the end of the period, the business counts inventory on hand and applies the unit costs to determine the cost of ending inventory. This inventory figure appears on the balance sheet and is used to compute cost of goods sold.

In the periodic system, throughout the period the Inventory account carries the beginning balance left over from the preceding period. The business records purchases of inventory in the Purchases account (an expense). Then, at the end of the period, the Inventory account must be updated for the financial statements. A journal entry removes the beginning balance by crediting Inventory and debiting Cost of

Goods Sold. A second journal entry sets up the ending Inventory balance, based on the physical count. The final entry in this sequence transfers the amount of Purchases to Cost of Goods Sold. These end-of-period entries can be made during the closing process. When Leon's Furniture records a sale, the only journal entry needed in the periodic system is:

Dr   Cash or Accounts Receivable
   Cr   Sales Revenue

Exhibit 6-4 shows the accounting for inventory in a perpetual system and a periodic system. Panel A gives the journal entries and Panel B presents the income statement and the balance sheet. All amounts are assumed.

The cost of the inventory, $560,000,[*] is the net amount of the purchases, determined as follows (using assumed amounts):

Purchase price of the inventory from the seller	$600,000
+ **Freight-in** (transportation cost to move the goods from the seller to the buyer)	4,000
− **Purchase returns** for unsuitable goods returned to the seller	(25,000)
− **Purchase allowances** granted by the seller	(5,000)
− **Purchase discounts** for early payment	(14,000)
= Net purchases of inventory	$560,000

EXHIBIT 6-4
Recording and Reporting Inventory—Perpetual System (Amounts Assumed)

Perpetual System	Periodic System
PANEL A—Recording Transactions	**PANEL A—Recording Transactions (all amounts are assumed)**

	Perpetual System			Periodic System		
Jan. 2	Inventory	600,000		Jan. 2 Purchases	600,000	
	Accounts payable		600,000	Accounts payable		600,000
	Purchased 1,000 units on account.			Purchased 1,000 units on account.		
3	Inventory	4,000		3 Freight-in	4,000	
	Accounts payable		4,000	Accounts Payable		4,000
	Record freight fee on purchases.			Record freight fee on purchases.		
9	Accounts payable	25,000		9 Accounts payable	25,000	
	Inventory		25,000	Purchase returns and allowance		25,000
	Returned goods to supplier for credit.			Returned goods to supplier for credit.		
11	Accounts payable	5,000		11 Accounts payable	5,000	
	Inventory		5,000	Purchase allowance		5,000
	Record purchase allowance.			Record purchase allowance.		

[*]The price shown does *not* include Canada's goods and services tax (GST)/harmonized sales tax (HST).

16	Accounts payable	14,000			16	Accounts payable	14,000	
	Inventory		14,000			Purchase discount		14,000
	Record purchase discount.					Record purchase discount.		
16	Accounts payable	560,000			16	Accounts payable	560,000	
	Cash		560,000			Cash		560,000
	Record payment.					Record payment.		
31	Accounts receivable	900,000			31	Accounts receivable	900,000	
	Sales revenue		900,000			Sales revenue		900,000
	Record sales on account.					Record sales on account.		
31	Cost of goods sold	540,000			31	No entry.		
	Inventory		540,000					
	Update inventory and COGS.							
31	No adjustments required.				31	Cost of goods sold	540,000	
						Inventory,* ending balance	120,000	
						Purchase allowance	5,000	
						Purchase returns and allow.	25,000	
						Purchase discount	14,000	
						Purchases		600,000
						Freight-in		4,000
						Inventory, beginning		100,000
						Close out temporary accounts to COGS and record ending inventory.		

*Determined by physical count.

PANEL B—Reporting in the Financial Statements

Income Statement (Partial)

Sales revenue	$900,000
Cost of goods sold	**540,000**
Gross profit	$360,000

Ending Balance Sheet (Partial)

Current assets:

Cash	$	XXX
Temporary investments		XXX
Accounts receivable		XXX
Inventory		**120,000**
Prepaid expenses		XXX

PANEL B—Reporting in the Financial Statements

Income Statement (Partial)

Sales revenue		$900,000
Cost of goods sold:		
Beginning inventory	$100,000	
Purchases	560,000	
Goods available for sale	660,000	
Ending inventory	(120,000)	
Cost of goods sold		540,000
Gross profit		$360,000

Ending Balance Sheet (Partial)

Current Assets:

Cash	$	XXX
Temporary investments		XXX
Accounts receivable		XXX
Inventory		**120,000**
Prepaid expenses		XXX

Freight-in is the transportation cost paid by the buyer to move goods from the seller to the buyer. Freight-in is accounted for as part of the cost of inventory. A **purchase return** is a decrease in the cost of inventory because the buyer returned the goods to the seller. A **purchase allowance** also decreases the cost of inventory because the buyer got an allowance (a deduction) from the amount owed—often because of a merchandise defect. Throughout this book, we often refer to net purchases simply as purchases.

A **purchase discount** is a decrease in the cost of inventory that is earned by paying quickly. A common arrangement states payment terms of 2/10 n/30. This means the buyer can take a 2% discount for payment within 10 days, or pay the full amount within 30 days. Another common credit term is "net 30," which directs the customer to pay the full amount within 30 days.

In summary,

NET PURCHASES =	PURCHASES
	−PURCHASE RETURNS AND ALLOWANCES
	−PURCHASE DISCOUNTS
	+FREIGHT-IN

Net sales are computed as follows:

NET SALES =	SALES REVENUE
	−SALES RETURNS AND ALLOWANCES
	−SALES DISCOUNTS

Freight-out paid by the *seller* is not part of the cost of inventory. Instead, freight-out is a delivery expense. It is the seller's expense of delivering merchandise to customers. Now study Exhibit 6-4 above.

Since the various transactions that make up the $560,000 may occur on different dates, it is instructive to now view each entry separately for both the perpetual and the period inventory system with assumed dates in Exhibit 6-4.

OBJECTIVE

❷ **Explain** and **apply** three inventory costing methods.

EXPLAIN AND APPLY THREE INVENTORY COSTING METHODS

A manager must choose one of three costing methods to apply when valuing inventory for reporting purposes. The costing method selected affects the profits to be reported, the amount of income taxes to be paid, and the values of the ratios derived from the balance sheet.

Inventory Costing Methods

Determining the cost of inventory is easy when the unit cost remains constant, as in Exhibit 6-2, but unit cost usually changes. For example, prices often rise. Salomon snowboards that cost The Source Board Shop $150 in October may cost $160 in November and $180 in December. The Source Board Shop sells 50 snowboards in November. How many of the Salomon snowboards sold cost $150, how many cost $160, and how many cost $180?

To compute cost of goods sold and the cost of ending inventory still on hand, we must assign a unit cost to the items. Three generally accepted inventory methods are the following:

1. Specific identification cost
2. Weighted-average cost
3. First-in, first-out (FIFO) cost

As we shall see, these methods can have very different effects on reported inventory balances, cost of goods sold, income taxes, and cash flows. Therefore, companies select their inventory method with great care.

SPECIFIC IDENTIFICATION COST METHOD. Some businesses deal in unique inventory items, such as antique furniture, jewels, and real estate. These businesses cost their inventories at the specific cost of the particular unit. For instance, a Toyota dealer may have two vehicles in the showroom—a "stripped-down" model that cost

$22,000 and a "loaded" model that cost $29,000. If the dealer sells the loaded model, cost of goods sold is $29,000. The stripped-down auto will be the only unit left in inventory, so ending inventory is $22,000.

The **specific identification cost method** is too expensive to use for inventory items that have common characteristics, such as metres of lumber, litres of paint, or number of automobile tires.

The other acceptable inventory accounting methods—weighted-average and FIFO—do not use the specific cost of a particular unit. Instead, they assume different flows of inventory costs.

ILLUSTRATION OF WEIGHTED-AVERAGE AND FIFO COSTING METHODS. To illustrate weighted-average and FIFO costing, we will use a common set of data, given in Exhibit 6-5.

In Exhibit 6-5, Leon's began the period with 10 lamps that cost $11 each; the beginning inventory was therefore $110. During the period, Leon's bought 50 more lamps, sold 40 lamps, and ended the period with 20 lamps, summarized in the T-account in Exhibit 6-5 and as follows:

	Number of Units	Total Cost
Goods available for sale	= 10 + 20 + 15 + 15 = 60 units	$110 + $280 + $240 + $270 = $900
Cost of goods sold	= 40 units	?
Ending inventory	= 20 units	?

EXHIBIT 6-5
Inventory Data Used to Illustrate Inventory Costing Methods

Inventory					
Begin. bal.	(10 units @ $11)	110			
Purchases:			Cost of goods sold		
No. 1	(20 units @ $14)	280	(40 units @ $?)		?
No. 2	(15 units @ $16)	240			
No. 3	(15 units @ $18)	270			
Ending bal.	(20 units @ $?)	?			

The big accounting questions are:

1. What is the cost of goods sold for the income statement?
2. What is the cost of the ending inventory for the balance sheet?

The answers to these questions depend on which inventory method Leon's uses. Leon's actually uses FIFO, but we look at weighted-average costing first.

WEIGHTED-AVERAGE COST–PERPETUAL. The **weighted-average-cost method**, sometimes called the average cost method, is based on the average cost of inventory during the period. Since the inventory records are updated each time merchandise is bought and sold, a new average cost per unit is computed every time a purchase is made. To illustrate, we will use the data in Exhibit 6-5:

Inventory (at weighted-average cost–perpetual)

Begin. bal.	(10 units @$11)	110		
Purchases:				
No. 1	(20 units @$14)	280		
No. 2	(15 units @$16)	240	Cost of goods sold (40 units @ weighted-average cost of $14* per unit)	560
No. 3	(15 units @$18)	270		
Ending bal.	(20 units @ new weighted-average cost of $17** per unit)	340		

Since the 40 units were sold after Purchase No. 2, the weighted-average cost per unit is based on beginning inventory, Purchase No. 1 and the units in Purchase No. 2. The computations are:

$$*\text{Weighted-Average cost} = \frac{\overset{(\text{Beg. Inv. + Purch. 1 + Purch. 2})}{\$110 + \$280 + \$240}}{10 + 20 + 15} = \frac{\$630}{45} = \$14$$

$$\text{Cost of goods sold} = \frac{\overset{(\text{Number of units sold} \times \text{weighted-average cost per unit})}{40 \text{ units sold}} \times \$14 \text{ per unit}}{} = \$560$$

The cost of ending inventory is determined by taking the 5 units left over from Purchase No. 2 plus the 15 units bought from Purchase No. 3. The new weighted-average cost per unit is now:

$$\begin{aligned}\text{Ending inventory} &= 5 \text{ units left after sale of goods} @\$14 = \$\ 70 \\ &+ 15 \text{ units from Purchase No. 3} = \underline{\ \ 270} \\ & \hspace{9cm} \$340\end{aligned}$$

**New weighted-average cost = $340/20 units = $17 per unit

WEIGHTED-AVERAGE COST–PERIODIC. Under the periodic inventory system, the cost of inventory is based on the average cost of inventory for the entire period. The weighted-average cost per unit is determined as follows (data from Exhibit 6-5):

$$\text{Weighted-average cost per unit} = \frac{\text{Cost of goods available*}}{\text{Number of units available}} = \frac{\$110 + \$280 + \$240 + \$270}{10 + 20 + 15 + 15} = \frac{\$900}{60} = \$15$$

*Goods available = Beginning inventory + Purchases

$$\begin{aligned}\text{Cost of goods sold} &= \text{Number of units sold} \times \text{Weighted-average cost per unit} \\ &= \hspace{1cm} 40 \text{ units} \hspace{1.5cm} \times \hspace{1.5cm} \$15 \hspace{2cm} = \$600\end{aligned}$$

$$\begin{aligned}\text{Ending inventory} &= \text{Number of units on hand} \times \text{Weighted-average cost per unit} \\ &= \hspace{1cm} 20 \text{ units} \hspace{1.5cm} \times \hspace{1.5cm} \$15 \hspace{2cm} = \$300\end{aligned}$$

The following T-account shows the effects of weighted-average costing:

Inventory (at weighted-average cost–periodic)

Begin. bal.	(10 units @ $11)	110		
Purchases:				
No. 1	(20 units @ $14)	280		
No. 2	(15 units @ $16)	240	Cost of goods sold (40 units @ average cost of $15 per unit)	600
No. 3	(15 units @ $18)	270		
Ending bal.	(20 units @ average cost of $15 per unit)	300		

FIFO COST–PERPETUAL. Under the **first-in, first-out (FIFO) cost method**, the first costs into inventory are the first costs assigned to cost of goods sold—hence, the name *first-in, first-out.* The following T-account shows how to compute FIFO cost of goods sold and ending inventory for Leon's lamps (data from Exhibit 6-5):

Inventory (at FIFO cost–perpetual)

Begin. bal.	(10 units @$11)	110			
Purchases:					
No. 1	(20 units @$14)	280			
No. 2	(15 units @$16)	240	Cost of goods sold (40 units):		
			(10 units @$11)	110	
			(20 units @$14)	280	550
			(10 units @$16)	160	
No. 3	(15 units @$18)	270			
Ending bal.	(5 units @$16) = 80				
	(15 units @$18) = 270	350			

Under the periodic inventory system, all of the information for the entire period is taken into account. This means that FIFO assumes the oldest units are sold first. Looking at the Cost of goods sold, FIFO assumes that all of the 10 units in beginning inventory were sold along with the 20 units from Purchase No. 1 but only 10 of the 15 units from Purchase No. 2 were sold. The ending inventory contains the 5 units left from Purchase No. 2 and all of the 15 units from Purchases No. 3.

FIFO COST-PERIODIC. Just like the perpetual inventory system, the first costs into inventory are assigned to the first units sold. Using the data from Exhibit 6-5:

Inventory (at FIFO cost–periodic)

Begin. bal.	(10 units @ $11)	110			
Purchases:			Cost of goods sold (40 units):		
No. 1	(20 units @ $14)	280	(10 units @ $11)	110	
No. 2	(15 units @ $16)	240	(20 units @ $14)	280	550
No. 3	(15 units @ $18)	270	(10 units @ $16)	160	
Ending bal.	(5 units @ $16) = 80				
	(15 units @ $18) = 270	350			

Under the periodic inventory system, all of the information for the entire period is taken into account. This means that FIFO assumes that all of the 10 units in beginning inventory were sold, along with the 20 units from the No.1 purchase and 10 of the 15 units of the No. 2 purchase. The cost of ending inventory is based on the units remaining: 5 units from the No. 2 purchase and all of the 15 units from the No. 3 purchase. Notice how the amounts for cost of goods sold and ending inventory are the same under both the perpetual and periodic inventory method.

The Effects of FIFO and Weighted-Average Cost on Cost of Goods Sold, Gross Profit, and Ending Inventory

In our Leon's example, the cost of inventory rose from $11 to $14 and up to $18. When inventory unit costs change this way, the various inventory methods produce different cost-of-goods-sold figures. Exhibit 6-6 summarizes the income effects of the two inventory methods (remember that prices are rising). Study the exhibit carefully, focusing on cost of goods sold and gross profit assuming the periodic system.

EXHIBIT 6-6
Effects of the FIFO and Weighted-Average Inventory Methods

	FIFO	Weighted-Average
Sales revenue (assumed)	$1,000	$1,000
Cost of goods sold	550 (lowest)	600 (highest)
Gross profit	$ 450 (highest)	$ 400 (lowest)

Let's use the gross profit data from Exhibit 6-6 to illustrate the potential tax effects of the two methods in a period of rising prices:

	FIFO	Weighted-Average
Gross profit	$450	$400
Operating expenses (assumed)	260	260
Income before income tax	$190	$140
Income tax expense (35%)	$ 67 (rounded)	$ 49

Income tax expense is lower under weighted-average ($49) and higher under FIFO ($67).

Exhibit 6-7 demonstrates the effect of increasing and decreasing costs of inventory on cost of goods sold and ending inventory. Study this exhibit carefully; it will help you really understand the FIFO and weighted-average inventory methods.

In a period of rising prices, FIFO will generally lead to higher profits and higher taxes than weighted-average, while the opposite is true in a period of falling prices.

EXHIBIT 6-7
Cost of Goods Sold and Ending Inventory—FIFO and Weighted-Average; Increasing Costs and Decreasing Costs

When inventory costs are decreasing:

	Income Statement Effects Cost of Goods Sold (COGS)	Balance Sheet Effects Ending Inventory (EI)	Cash Flow Effects Income Taxes
FIFO	FIFO COGS is highest because it's based on the oldest costs, which are high. Gross profit is, therefore, the lowest.	FIFO EI is lowest because it's based on the most recent costs, which are low.	Less cash is paid for taxes, so FIFO could be used by firms seeking to minimize taxes.
Weighted-Average	Weighted-average COGS is lowest because it's based on an average of the costs for the period, which is lower than the oldest costs. Gross profit is, therefore, the highest.	Weighted-average EI is highest because the average cost for the period is higher than the most recent costs.	More cash is paid for taxes, but weighted-average may still be popular with firms seeking to maximize reported income.

When inventory costs are increasing:

	Income Statement Effects Cost of Goods Sold (COGS)	Balance Sheet Effects Ending Inventory (EI)	Cash Flow Effects Income Taxes
FIFO	FIFO COGS is lowest because it's based on oldest costs, which are low. Gross profit is, therefore, the highest.	FIFO EI is highest because it's based on the most recent costs, which are high.	More cash is paid for taxes, but FIFO may still be popular with firms seeking to maximize reported income.
Weighted-Average	Weighted-average COGS is highest because it's based on an average of the costs for the period, which is higher than the oldest costs. Gross profit is, therefore, the lowest.	Weighted-average EI is lowest because the average cost for the period is lower than the most recent costs.	Less cash is paid for taxes, so weighted-average could be used by firms seeking to minimize taxes.

The difference between the two methods on profit and income taxes may be small, and each of the two methods is appropriate for certain types of inventory.

Comparison of the Inventory Methods

Let's compare the weighted-average and FIFO inventory methods.

1. How well does each method measure income by allocating inventory expense—cost of goods sold—against revenue? Weighted-average results in the most realistic net income figure, it is an average that combines all costs (old costs and recent costs). In contrast, FIFO uses old inventory costs against revenue. FIFO income is therefore less realistic than weighted-average income.

2. Which method reports the most up-to-date inventory cost on the balance sheet? FIFO reports the most current inventory cost on the balance sheet. Weighted-average can value inventory at very old costs because weighted-average leaves the oldest prices in ending inventory.

3. What effects do the methods have on income taxes? As we have seen in Exhibit 6-7, in a period of rising costs, FIFO uses old inventory costs against revenue, resulting in higher income taxes. Weighted-average is an average that combines all costs (old costs and recent costs), which leads to lower profits and lower income taxes.

◄ DECISION GUIDELINES ►

MANAGING INVENTORY

Suppose Leon's Furniture stocks two basic categories of merchandise:

*   Furniture pieces, such as tables and chairs
*   Small items of low value, near the checkout stations, such as flower vases and other small accent pieces

Jacob Stiles, the store manager, is considering how accounting will affect the business. Let's examine several decisions that Stiles must make to achieve his goals for his company.

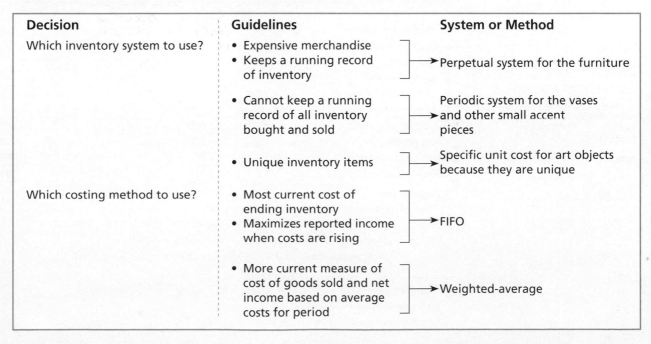

Decision	Guidelines	System or Method
Which inventory system to use?	• Expensive merchandise • Keeps a running record of inventory	Perpetual system for the furniture
	• Cannot keep a running record of all inventory bought and sold	Periodic system for the vases and other small accent pieces
	• Unique inventory items	Specific unit cost for art objects because they are unique
Which costing method to use?	• Most current cost of ending inventory • Maximizes reported income when costs are rising	FIFO
	• More current measure of cost of goods sold and net income based on average costs for period	Weighted-average

MID-CHAPTER SUMMARY PROBLEM

Suppose a division of DIY Building Products Inc. has these inventory records for January 2014:

Date		Item	Quantity	Unit Cost
Jan.	1	Beginning inventory	100 units	$ 8
	6	Purchase	60 units	9
	21	Purchase	150 units	9
	24	Sales	300 units	
	27	Purchase	90 units	10

Operating expense for January was $1,900, and the 300 units sold on January 24 generated sales revenue of $6,770.

Name: DIY Building Products Inc.
Industry: Building products
Fiscal Period: Month of January 2014
Key Fact: Perpetual inventory system and periodic inventory system

Requirements

1. Prepare the January income statement, showing amounts for FIFO and weighted-average cost assuming that ~~(a) a periodic inventory system~~ is used, and (b) a perpetual inventory system is used. Label the bottom line "Operating income." (Round figures to whole-dollar amounts.) Show your computations, and compute cost of goods sold.
2. Explain which inventory method would result in:
   a. Reporting the highest operating income
   b. Reporting inventory on the balance sheet at the most current cost
   c. Attaining the best measure of net income for the income statement

ANSWERS

Requirement 1(a) Periodic Inventory System

DIY Building Products Inc.
Income Statement for Division
For the Month Ended January 31, 2014

	FIFO	Weighted-Average
Sales revenue	$6,770	$6,770
Cost of goods sold:		
Beginning inventory	$ 800	$ 800
Purchases	2,790	2,790
Cost of goods available for sale	3,590	3,590
Ending inventory....................	(990)	(898)
Cost of goods sold	2,600	2,692
Gross profit	4,170	4,078
Operating expenses	1,900	1,900
Operating income......................	$2,270	2,178

Sales revenue is given.

Beginning inventory is given.

See the Computations section.

Beginning inventory + Purchases

See the Computations section.

Cost of goods available for sale − Ending inventory

Sales revenue − Cost of goods sold

Operating expenses are given.

Gross profit − Operating expenses

Computations:

Beginning inventory: 100 × $8 = $800
Purchases: (60 × $9) + (150 × $9) + (90 × $10) = $2,790
*Ending inventory—FIFO: (10 × $9) + (90 × $10) = $990
Weighted-average: 100 × $8.975** = $898 (rounded from $897.50)

*Number of units in ending inventory = 100 + 60 + 150 + 90 − 300 = 100

**$3,590/400 units† = $8.975 per unit
†Number of units available = 100 + 60 + 150 + 90 = 400

Requirement 1(b) Perpetual Inventory System

DIY Building Products Inc.
Income Statement for Division
For the Month Ended January 31, 2014

	FIFO	Weighted-Average
Sales Revenue	$6,770	$6,770
Cost of goods sold	2,600	2,603
Gross profit	4,170	4,167
Operating expenses	1,900	1,900
Operating income	$2,270	$2,267

Computations:

FIFO:

Cost of goods sold = $(100 \times \$8) + (60 \times \$9) + (140 \times \$9) = \$2,600$

Ending inventory = $(10 \times \$9) + (90 \times \$10) = \$990$

Weighted-average:

Cost of goods sold = $(100 \times \$8) + (60 \times \$9) + (150 \times \$9) = \$2,690$

$2,690/310$ units = 8.677 per unit

300 units sold $\times \$8.677$/unit = $2,603$ (rounded)

Ending inventory = 10 units left after sale (310 available − 300 units sold) $\times \$8.677 =$ 87 (rounded)

90 units bought $\times \$10 =$ 900

Ending inventory   = $987 ($87 + $900)

Requirement 2

a. Use FIFO to report the highest operating income. Income under FIFO is highest when inventory unit costs are increasing, as in this situation.

b. Use FIFO to report inventory on the balance sheet at the most current cost. The oldest inventory costs are expensed as cost of goods sold, leaving the most recent (most current) costs of the period in ending inventory.

c. Use weighted-average to attain the best measure of net income. Weighted-average inventory costs, which are expensed as part of goods sold, are closer to the most recent (most current) inventory costs than FIFO costs are.

> Use the quantities and unit costs given in the question to calculate beginning inventory and purchases. Recall that FIFO ending inventory calculations use the most current purchase prices. Weighted-average ending inventory calculations use the average purchase prices.

> Because beginning inventory, purchases, and operating expense are the same for both inventory methods, use the ending inventory and operating income amounts you calculated in Requirement 1 to help you answer these questions.

EXPLAIN HOW ACCOUNTING STANDARDS APPLY TO INVENTORY

OBJECTIVE

❸ **Explain** how accounting standards apply to inventory

It is important at this point that you consider two characteristics of accounting that have special relevance to inventories:

- Comparability
- Disclosure

Comparability

Investors like to compare a company's financial statements from one period to the next so they can use this information to make a decision. In order to do this, the company must use the same accounting method for inventory consistently from one accounting period to another.

Suppose you are analyzing Leon's Furniture's net income pattern over a two-year period. Now, suppose Leon's switched from one inventory method to another during that time and its net income increased dramatically, but only because of the change in inventory method. If you did not know about the change, you might believe that Leon's Furniture's income increased due to improved operations, which is not the case.

Recall from Chapter 1 that one of the enhancing qualitative characteristics of accounting information is **comparability**. For accounting information to be comparable, it must be reported in a way that makes it possible to compare it to similar information being reported by other companies and by comparing it with its own financial statements from one period to the next. It must also be reported in a way that is consistent with how it was reported in previous periods (**consistency principle**). This does not mean that a company is not permitted to change its accounting methods. Both IFRS and ASPE allow such a change, indicating that it is acceptable if it "results in the financial statements providing reliable and more relevant information." The change should normally be applied retrospectively, which means that prior years' financial statements should be restated to reflect the change. In addition, the effect of the change on the current financial statements should be disclosed, and would be found in the notes to the financial statements according to the disclosure principal.

Disclosure Principle

The **disclosure principle** holds that a company's financial statements should report enough information for outsiders to make informed decisions about the company. Companies are required to provide notes at the end of their financial statements to *disclose* the accounting policies used along with other *relevant* information about a company. That means disclosing inventory accounting methods. Without knowledge of the accounting method being used, a user such as a banker could make an unwise lending decision.

Suppose the banker is comparing two companies—one uses one inventory method and the other uses another method that leads to higher income. The latter reports higher net income, but only because of the inventory method being used. Without knowing the reason for the higher income, the banker could loan money to the less financially sound business.

Lower of Cost and Net Realizable Value

The **lower-of-cost-and-net-realizable-value (LCNRV) rule** is based on the premise that inventory can become obsolete or damaged or its selling price can decline. Both IFRS and ASPE require that inventory be reported in the financial statements at whichever is lower—the inventory's cost or its **net realizable value**, that is, the amount the business could get if it sold the inventory, less any costs incurred to sell it. If the net realizable value of inventory falls below its historical cost, the business must write down the value of its goods to net realizable value. On the balance sheet, the business reports ending inventory at its LCNRV. How is the write-down accomplished?

Suppose Klassen Furniture Inc. paid $3,000 for inventory on September 26. By December 31, Klassen determines that it will be able to sell this inventory for only

$2,000, net of selling costs. Because the inventory's net realizable value is less than its original cost, Klassen's December 31 balance sheet must report the inventory at $2,000. Exhibit 6-8 presents the effects of LCNRV on the balance sheet and the income statement. Before any LCNRV effect, cost of goods sold is $9,000.

An LCNRV write-down decreases Inventory and increases Cost of Goods Sold, as follows:

Dec. 31	Cost of Goods Sold	1,000	
	Inventory		1,000
	Write inventory down to net realizable value.		

Inventory	
Sept. 26 $3,000	
	$1,000 Dec. 31
Balance $2,000	

Inventory that has been written down to net realizable value should be reassessed each period. If the net realizable value has increased, the previous write-down should be reversed up to the new net realizable value. Of course, the inventory cannot be written up to a value that exceeds its original cost.

Assume that Klassen's inventory described above was still on hand at the end of the next period and that the net realizable value had increased to $2,400. The journal entry to reverse a previous write-down would be as follows:

Inventory	400	
Cost of Goods Sold		400
Write inventory up to the net realizable value.		

Companies disclose how they apply LCNRV in a note to their financial statements as shown in the following excerpt from Leon's 2011 audited annual report.

Summary of Significant Accounting Policies
Inventories

Inventories are valued at the lower of cost determined on a first-in, first-out basis, and net realizable value. . . .

EXHIBIT 6-8
Lower-of-Cost-and-Net-Realizable-Value (LCNRV) Effects on Inventory and Cost of Goods Sold

Balance Sheet

Current assets:	$	XXX
Cash		XXX
Short-term investments		XXX
Accounts receivable		XXX
Inventories, at net realizable value		
(which is lower than $3,000 cost)		2,000
Prepaid expenses		XXX
Total current assets		$X,XXX

Income Statement

Sales revenue	$21,000
Cost of goods sold ($9,000 + $1,000)	10,000
Gross profit	$11,000

OBJECTIVE

❹ **Analyze** and **evaluate** gross profit and inventory turnover

ANALYZE AND EVALUATE GROSS PROFIT AND INVENTORY TURNOVER

Managers, investors, and creditors use ratios to evaluate a business. Two ratios relate directly to inventory: the gross profit percentage and the rate of inventory turnover.

Gross Profit Percentage

Gross profit—sales minus cost of goods sold—is a key indicator of a company's ability to sell inventory at a profit. Merchandisers strive to increase **gross profit percentage**, also called the *gross margin percentage*. Gross profit percentage is stated as a percentage of sales. Gross profit percentage is computed as follows for Leon's Furniture. Data (in millions) for 2011 are taken from the financial statements, page 271.

$$\text{Gross profit percentage} = \frac{\text{Gross profit}}{\text{Net sales revenue}} = \frac{\$288.7}{\$682.8} = 0.423 = 42.3\%$$

Managers and investors watch the gross profit percentage carefully. A 42.3% gross margin means that each dollar of sales generates 42.3 cents of gross profit. On average, cost of goods sold consumes 57.7 cents of each sales dollar for Leon's. For most firms, the gross profit percentage changes little from year to year, so a small downturn may signal trouble.

Leon's gross profit was 40.3%, 42%, and 42.3% for the years 2009 through 2011, respectively. These figures indicate that there was a slight increase in gross profit from 2009 to 2010, but gross profit stayed relatively the same from 2010 to 2011. For Leon's, 2011 was a challenging year—consumers were spending less on furniture given the weak economy. However, this did not stop Leon's from opening up more stores in Canada and announcing their acquisition of The Brick in 2012. Leon's gross profit of 42.3% in 2011 was higher than Walmart (25%), but almost the same as Pier 1 (42.4%). Both Pier 1 and Leon's handle higher-priced merchandise than Walmart, which may explain their higher gross profit. Exhibit 6-9 graphs the gross profit for these three companies.

Inventory Turnover

Leon's strives to sell its inventory as quickly as possible because furniture and fixtures generate no profit until they are sold. The faster the sales, the higher the company's

EXHIBIT 6-9
Gross Profit Percentages of Three Leading Retailers

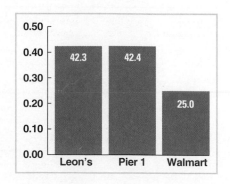

income; the slower the sales, the lower the company's income. **Inventory turnover**, the ratio of cost of goods sold to average inventory, indicates how rapidly inventory is sold. The 2011 computation for Leon's follows (data in millions from the financial statements, page 271):

$$\frac{\text{Inventory}}{\text{turnover}} = \frac{\text{Cost of goods sold}}{\text{Average inventory}} = \frac{\text{Cost of goods sold}}{\left(\frac{\text{Beginning}}{\text{inventory}} + \frac{\text{Ending}}{\text{inventory}}\right) \div 2}$$

$$= \frac{\$394.1}{(\$87.8 + \$85.4)/2} = \frac{4.55 \text{ or } 4.6 \text{ times per year}}{(\text{every } 79 \text{ days})}$$

The inventory turnover statistic shows how many times the company sold (or turned over) its average level of inventory during the year. Inventory turnover varies from industry to industry. To calculate how long it takes to sell inventory, take 365 days and divide by the inventory turnover. For Leon's, it would be 365/4.6 = 79 days.

Leon's and other specialty retailers turn their inventory over slowly. Retailers must keep lots of inventory on hand because visual appeal is critical in retailing. Department stores such as The Bay and discounters such as Walmart and Target also keep a lot of inventory on hand. Exhibit 6-10 shows the inventory turnover rates for three leading retailers.

STOP + THINK 6-1

You have received a gift of cash from your grandparents and are considering investing in the stock market. You have carefully researched the market and have decided that you will invest in one of three companies: Leon's Furniture, Pier 1, or Walmart. Assume your analysis has resulted in Exhibits 6-9 and 6-10. What do the ratio values in the two exhibits say about the merchandising (pricing) strategies of Leon's, Pier 1, and Walmart?

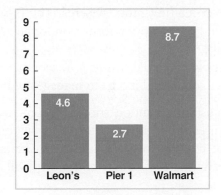

EXHIBIT 6-10
Inventory Turnover Rates of Three Leading Retailers

◄ DECISION GUIDELINES ►

Companies buy and sell inventory to generate revenue. Two ratios that relate directly to inventory are the inventory turnover and the gross profit percentage. Let's see how they are used in decision making.

Decision	Guidelines
Who uses the inventory turnover and the gross profit percentage ratios for decision making and why?	*Managers* keep their eye on inventory to make sure it is selling quickly. Slow-moving inventory could be a sign that it is outdated or no longer in demand. Also, determining the selling price for inventory affects gross profit and, ultimately, net income. If the gross profit is too low, it may indicate that the inventory is costing too much or the selling price is not high enough.
	Investors want to know if inventory is selling quickly because it affects revenue and, ultimately, net income. They examine gross profit to see if it is high enough to cover all the other expenses and still provide for a reasonable profit.
	Creditors are interested in how inventory is selling because the faster inventory is sold, the sooner the cash flows in and the company can pay its debts.

OBJECTIVE

❺ **Use** the cost-of-goods-sold (COGS) model to make management decisions

USE THE COST-OF-GOODS-SOLD (COGS) MODEL TO MAKE MANAGEMENT DECISIONS

Exhibit 6-11 presents the **cost-of-goods-sold model**. Some accountants view this model as related to the periodic inventory system. But it's used by all companies, including those with perpetual inventory systems. The model is extremely powerful because it captures all the inventory information for an entire accounting period. Study this model carefully.

Leon's Furniture uses a perpetual inventory accounting system. Let's see how Leon's can use the cost-of-goods-sold model to manage the business effectively.

1. What's the single most important question for Leon's to address?
   - What merchandise should Leon's offer to its customers? This is a *marketing* question that requires market research. If Leon's continually stocks the wrong merchandise, sales will suffer and profits will drop.

EXHIBIT 6-11
The Cost-of-Goods-Sold Model

Cost of goods sold:	
Beginning inventory	$ 92.9
+ Purchases	410.9
= Goods available for sale	503.8
− Ending inventory	(84.0)
= Cost of goods sold	$419.8

2. What's the second most important question for Leon's?

- How much inventory should Leon's buy? This is an *accounting* question that requires careful consideration. If Leon's buys too much merchandise, it will have to lower prices, the gross profit percentage will suffer, and it may lose money. If Leon's buys too little inventory, customers will go elsewhere. Buying the right quantity of inventory is critical for success. This question can be answered with the cost-of-goods-sold model. Let's see how it works.

By rearranging the cost-of-goods-sold formula, we can help a Leon's store manager know how much inventory to buy, as follows (using amounts from Exhibit 6-11):

		(millions)
1	Cost of goods sold (based on the budget for the next period).................	$419.8
2	+ Ending inventory (based on the budget for the next period)..................	84.0
3	= Goods available for sale as budgeted......................................	503.8
4	− Beginning inventory (actual amount left over from the prior period).......	92.9
5	= Purchases (how much inventory the manager needs to buy)	$410.9

In this case, the manager should buy $410.9 million of merchandise to work his plan for the upcoming period.

Estimating Inventory by the Gross Profit Method

Often a business must *estimate* the value of its goods. For example, suppose a company uses the periodic inventory system and needs to know the value of ending inventory to prepare their monthly financial statements. In this case, the business must estimate the cost of ending inventory because the periodic inventory system does not keep a record of inventory bought or sold and therefore it does not know how much inventory is on hand.

The **gross profit method**, also known as the *gross margin method*, is widely used to estimate ending inventory. This method uses the familiar cost-of-goods-sold model (amounts are assumed):

Beginning inventory...	$ 4,000
+ Purchases..	16,000
= Goods available for sale...	20,000
− Ending inventory	(5,000)
= Cost of goods sold...	$15,000

We rearrange *ending inventory* and *cost of goods sold* as follows:

Beginning inventory...	$ 4,000
+ Purchases..	16,000
= Goods available for sale...	20,000
− Cost of goods sold...	(15,000)
= Ending inventory	$ 5,000

To estimate ending inventory, Leon's would take beginning inventory, net purchases, and net sales, which can be taken directly from the accounting records. Using

EXHIBIT 6-12
The Gross Profit Method of
Estimating Inventory
(amounts assumed)

Beginning inventory		$18,000
Purchases		72,000
Goods available for sale		90,000
Cost of goods sold:		
Net sales revenue	$100,000	
Less estimated gross profit of 42.3%	(42,300)	
Estimated cost of goods sold		$57,700
Estimated cost of *ending inventory*		$32,300

Leon's *actual gross profit rate* of 42.3% (that is, gross profit divided by net sales), you can estimate the cost of goods sold. Then to estimate ending inventory, subtract cost of goods sold from goods available for sale. Exhibit 6-12 shows the calculations for the gross profit method with new amounts assumed for this illustration.

You can use the gross profit method to test the overall reasonableness of an ending inventory amount. This method also helps to detect large errors.

STOP + THINK (6-2)

Assume your business had a bad fire and you wish to calculate your inventory loss. Beginning inventory is $70,000, net purchases total $365,000, and net sales are $500,000. With a normal gross profit rate of 30% of sales, how much is ending inventory?

OBJECTIVE

❻ **Analyze** how inventory errors affect the financial statements

ANALYZE HOW INVENTORY ERRORS AFFECT THE FINANCIAL STATEMENTS

Inventory errors sometimes occur. In Exhibit 6-13, start with period 1, in which ending inventory is *overstated* by $5,000 and cost of goods sold is therefore *understated* by $5,000. Then compare period 1 with period 3, which is correct. *Period 1 should look exactly like period 3.*

EXHIBIT 6-13
Inventory Errors: An Example

	Period 1 Ending Inventory Overstated by $5,000		Period 2 Beginning Inventory Overstated by $5,000		Period 3 Correct	
Sales revenue		$100,000		$100,000		$100,000
Cost of goods sold:						
Beginning inventory	$10,000		$ 15,000		$10,000	
Purchases	50,000		50,000		50,000	
Cost of goods available for sale	60,000		65,000		60,000	
Ending inventory	(15,000)		(10,000)		(10,000)	
Cost of goods sold		45,000		55,000		50,000
Gross profit		$ 55,000		$ 45,000		$ 50,000

$ 100,000

Source: The authors thank Professor Carl High for this example.

Inventory errors counterbalance in two consecutive periods. Why? Recall that period 1's ending inventory becomes period 2's beginning inventory amount. Thus, the error in period 1 carries over into period 2. Trace the ending inventory of $15,000 from period 1 to period 2. Then compare periods 2 and 3. *All periods should look exactly like period 3.* The amounts **in bold type** in Exhibit 6-13 are incorrect.

Beginning inventory and ending inventory have opposite effects on cost of goods sold (beginning inventory is added; ending inventory is subtracted); therefore, after two periods, an inventory accounting error "washes out" (counterbalances) as illustrated in Exhibit 6-13. Notice that total gross profit for periods 1 and 2 combined is correct ($100,000), even though each period's gross profit is wrong by $5,000. The correct gross profit is $50,000 for each period as shown in period 3.

Note that there is a direct relationship between ending inventory (EI) and gross profit (GP), but an inverse relationship between beginning inventory (BI) and gross profit. That is, an understatement of ending inventory results in an understatement of gross profit, but an understatement of beginning inventory results in an overstatement of gross profit. (COGS = cost of goods sold)

EI ↓ results in COGS ↑ results in GP ↓ (**Direct relationship between EI and GP**)

BI ↓ results in COGS ↓ results in GP ↑ (**Inverse relationship between BI and GP**)

Inventory Errors

Inventory errors cannot be ignored simply because they counterbalance. Suppose you are analyzing trends in the operations of the company presented above.

Exhibit 6-13 shows a drop in gross profit from period 1 to period 2, followed by an increase in period 3. Did the company really get worse and then better again? No, that picture of operations is inaccurate because of the accounting error. The correct gross profit is $50,000 for each period. We must have accurate information for all periods. Exhibit 6-14 summarizes the effects of inventory accounting errors.

EXHIBIT 6-14
Effects of Inventory Errors

	Period 1		Period 2	
	Cost of	Gross Profit	Cost of	Gross Profit
Inventory Error	Goods Sold	and Net Income	Goods Sold	and Net Income
Period 1				
Ending inventory	Understated	Overstated	Overstated	Understated
overstated				
Period 1				
Ending inventory	Overstated	Understated	Understated	Overstated
understated				

Reporting on the Statement of Cash Flows

Inventories appear on the balance sheet as current assets. Since inventory transactions affect cash, their effects are reported on the statement of cash flows.

Inventory transactions are *operating activities* because the purchase and sale of merchandise drives a company's operations. The purchase of inventory requires a cash payment and the sale of inventory requires a cash receipt. We will see in Chapter 12 how to report inventory transactions on the statement of cash flows.

COOKING THE BOOKS WITH INVENTORY

No area of accounting has a deeper ethical dimension than inventory. Managers of companies whose profits do not meet shareholder expectations are sometimes tempted to "cook the books" to increase reported income. The increase in reported income may lead investors and creditors into thinking the business is more successful than it really is.

What do managers hope to gain from fraudulent accounting? In some cases, they are trying to keep their jobs. In other cases, their bonuses are tied to reported income: the higher the company's net income, the higher the managers' bonuses.

The easiest is simply to overstate ending inventory. The two most common ways to "cook the books" with inventory are (1) inserting fictitious inventory, thus overstating quantities; and (2) deliberately overstating unit prices used in the computation of ending inventory amounts. The upward-pointing arrows in the accounting equation indicate an overstatement: reporting more assets and equity than are actually present.

ASSETS	=	LIABILITIES	+	SHAREHOLDERS' EQUITY
↑	=	0	+	↑

SUMMARY OF CHAPTER 6

LEARNING OBJECTIVE	SUMMARY
1. **Account** for inventory using the perpetual and periodic inventory systems	When inventory is bought, it is a current asset on the balance sheet, and when it is sold, it is an expense on the income statement. A company can use either the perpetual inventory system or the periodic inventory system to account for its inventory. A perpetual inventory system keeps a continuous record of inventory bought and sold. A periodic inventory system does not keep a continuous record of inventory; a physical count is performed to determine ending inventory. Cost of goods sold is a computation.
2. **Explain** and **apply** three inventory costing methods	The three inventory methods are the specific identification; first-in, first-out (FIFO); and the weighted-average-cost method. Specific identification is used for unique inventory items where the company identifies the specific cost of the inventory item. Under the FIFO method, the first costs into inventory are the first costs assigned to cost of goods sold. The weighted-average-cost method assigns an average cost to inventory based on the cost of the inventory for the period.
3. **Explain** how accounting standards apply to inventory	Comparability (including consistency) says that businesses should use the same accounting methods and procedures from period to period so users can compare information. Disclosure says that a company's financial statements should report enough information for outsiders to be able to make knowledgeable decisions about the business. The lower-of-cost-and-net-realizable-value (LCNRV) rule requires that inventory be reported in the financial statements at the lower of its cost and net realizable value. Net realizable value is the amount the business could get if it sold the inventory less any costs of selling it.

4. **Analyze** and **evaluate** gross profit and inventory turnover	There are two ratios used to evaluate inventory:
	Gross profit percentage = Gross profit/Net sales revenue (the gross profit percentage indicates the company's ability to sell inventory at a profit)
	Inventory turnover = Cost of goods sold/Average inventory (inventory turnover shows how rapidly inventory is sold)
5. **Use** the cost-of-goods-sold (COGS) model to make management decisions	The cost-of-goods-sold model can be used to determine how much inventory to buy. It can also be used to estimate ending inventory when records are lost or destroyed or to test the overall reasonableness of ending inventory.
6. **Analyze** how inventory errors affect the financial statements **There are no differences between IFRS and ASPE in this chapter.**	Inventory errors, if not corrected, can affect the values of inventory on the balance sheet, and cost of goods sold, gross profit, and net income on the income statement.

END-OF-CHAPTER SUMMARY PROBLEM

During February 2014, its first month of operations, Blanc Company reported the following transactions:

Feb. 1	Purchased 20,000 units on account for $2.50 each
Feb. 15	Purchased 25,000 units on account for $2.75 each
Feb. 20	Sold on account 35,000 units for $3.25 each
Feb. 23	Purchased 10,000 units on account for $2.70 each
Feb. 25	Paid for the purchases made on Feb. 1
Feb. 27	Collected $75,000 from customers on account
Feb. 28	Incurred on account $11,000 in operating expenses

The company uses the perpetual inventory method and pays 35% income tax.

Requirements

1. Prepare journal entries to record the transactions for the month of February assuming the company uses the FIFO inventory method. Explanations are not required.
2. Determine the ending inventory assuming the company uses the FIFO inventory method. (Hint: You might find it helpful to use a T-account.)
3. Prepare the company's multi-step income statement for the month of February.
4. Compute the company's gross profit percentage and the inventory turnover for the month. How does this company compare with the industry average of 17% for the gross profit and an inventory turnover of three times? Round to one decimal place.
5. Assume instead that the company uses the weighted-average method to value inventory; calculate the cost of goods sold and the ending inventory value.

ANSWERS

Requirement 1

Feb. 1	Inventory (20,000 units × $2.50)	50,000	
	Accounts payable		50,000
Feb. 15	Inventory (25,000 units × $2.75)	68,750	
	Accounts payable		68,750
Feb. 20	Accounts receivable (35,000 × $3.25)	113,750	
	Sales Revenue		113,750
	Cost of goods sold (20,000 × $2.50 + 15,000 × $2.75)	91,250	
	Inventory		91,250
Feb. 23	Inventory (10,000 units × $2.70)	27,000	
	Accounts payable		27,000

Name: Blanc Company
Industry: Retail corporation
Fiscal Period: Year ended December 31, 2014
Key Fact: Perpetual inventory system

Because the company uses the perpetual inventory system, record inventory purchases and sales as they occur.

All merchandise is purchased on account.

All sales are made on account.

Use FIFO (oldest costs) to calculate cost of the 35,000 units sold:
Opening inventory: $0 (company just started)
From Feb. 1 purchase: $50,000 (20,000 units)
From Feb. 15 purchase: $68,750 (25,000 units)

Feb. 25	Accounts payable		50,000	
	Cash			50,000
Feb. 27	Cash		75,000	
	Accounts receivable			75,000
Feb. 28	Operating expenses		11,000	
	Accounts payable			11,000
Feb. 28	Income tax expense (from Requirement 3)		4,025	
	Tax payable			4,025

Operating expenses were incurred ($11,000).

Income tax expense is 35% of net income before taxes (Sales revenue − Cost of goods sold − Operating expenses).

Requirement 2

FIFO − Ending inventory = $50,000 + $68,750 − $91,250 + $27,000 = $54,500

FIFO ending inventory:
Beginning inventory + Purchases − Cost of goods sold

Inventory				
Feb. 1	50,000			
Feb. 15	68,750	91,250	Feb. 20	
Feb. 23	27,000			
Balance				
Feb. 28	54,500			

Requirement 3

Beginning inventory must be the same amount as the inventory on the previous year's balance sheet.
Blanc Company just started, so there is no previous year's balance.
Ending inventory must be the same amount as the inventory on this year's balance sheet.

Sales revenue − Cost of goods sold

Gross profit − Operating expenses

IFRS require that income tax expense be presented separately from all other expenses.

Blanc Company
Income Statement
For the Month Ended February 28, 2014

Sales revenue	$113,750
Cost of goods sold	91,250
Gross profit	$ 22,500
Operating expenses	11,000
Income before tax	$ 11,500
Income tax expense (35%)	4,025
Net income	$ 7,475

Requirement 4

Gross profit ÷ Sales revenue

Cost of goods sold ÷ Average inventory, where Average inventory = (Beginning inventory + Ending inventory) ÷ 2

Net income ÷ Sales revenue

Gross profit percentage = $22,500/$113,750 = 19.8%
Inventory turnover = $91,250/$54,500* = 1.7 times

Compared to the industry averages, Blanc Company's gross profit percentage is higher, which suggests that the company is able to sell its inventory at a profit. However, the inventory turnover is low, which means that the company has too much inventory on hand.

Requirement 5

Weighted average−calculate the unit cost = $\dfrac{\text{Cost of goods available for sale}}{\text{Number of units available for sale}}$

A new unit cost must be calculated after a purchase is made.

Feb. 15—New unit cost = $\dfrac{\$50,000 \text{ (Feb. 1)} + \$68,750 \text{ (Feb. 15)}}{20,000 + 25,000}$ = $2.64 each

Feb. 20—Cost of goods sold = 35,000 units sold × $2.64 = $92,400
Feb. 23—New unit cost is calculated as follows:
Units left after the sale on Feb. 20 (45,000 available − 35,000 sold) = 10,000 × $2.64 = $26,400
Units bought on Feb. 23 = 10,000 × $2.70 = $27,000
Total cost = $53,400 ($26,400 + $27,000) divided by 20,000 (number of units on hand) = $2.67
Therefore, ending inventory = $2.67 × 20,000 units = $53,400

*Since the company just started, there is no beginning inventory and, therefore, an average is not used.

STOP + THINK (6-1)	**ANSWER**
	It's obvious that both Leon's and Pier 1 sell higher-end merchandise. Leon's and Pier 1's gross profits are almost the same, and both have a much higher gross profit than Walmart. At the same time, Leon's turnover rate is higher than Pier 1 but lower than Walmart. Generally, the lower the price, the faster the turnover, and the higher the price, the slower the turnover.

STOP + THINK (6-2)	**ANSWER**
	$70,000 + $365,000 − (0.70 × $500,000) = $85,000

Review Inventory and Cost of Goods Sold

QUICK CHECK (ANSWERS ARE GIVEN ON PAGE 320.)

1. Which statement is true?
   a. The Sales account is used to record only sales on account.
   b. When inventory costs are increasing, FIFO COGS is highest.
   c. Gross profit is the excess of sales revenue over cost of goods sold.
   d. A service company purchases products from suppliers and then sells them.

2. Sales discounts should appear in the financial statements
   a. as an addition to inventory.
   b. as an addition to sales.
   c. as an operating expense.
   d. among the current liabilities.
   e. as a deduction from sales.

3. How is inventory classified in the financial statements?
   a. As an asset
   b. As a liability
   c. As an expense
   d. As a revenue
   e. As a contra account to Cost of Goods Sold

Questions 4 through 6 use the following data of King Ltd.

	Units	Unit Cost	Total Cost	Units Sold
Beginning inventory	25	$5	$125	
Purchase on May 23	30	6	180	
Purchase on Nov. 5	10	7	70	
Sales	50	?	?	

4. King uses a FIFO inventory system. Cost of goods sold for the period is
   a. $275. c. $255.
   b. $347. d. $375.

5. King's FIFO cost of ending inventory would be
   a. $161.   c. $208.
   b. $100. 10×7 + 5×6 = 100   d. $225.
6. King's weighted-average cost of ending inventory (rounded) is
   a. $87.   c. $100.
   b. $104. 15 × (125 +180 +70) ÷65 = 86.54 d. $330.
7. When applying the lower-of-cost-and-net-realizable-value rule, "net realizable value" generally means
   a. sales value.   c. selling price less costs of selling.
   b. original cost.   d. original cost less physical deterioration.
8. During a period of rising prices, the inventory method that will yield the highest net income and asset value is
   a. specific identification.
   b. weighted-average cost.
   c. FIFO.
9. Which statement is true?
   a. When inventory costs are increasing, the gross profit using FIFO is lowest.
   b. Application of the lower-of-cost-and-net-realizable-value rule often results in a lower inventory value.
   c. An error overstating ending inventory in 2014 will understate 2014 net income.
   d. When prices are rising, the inventory method that results in the lowest ending inventory value is FIFO.
10. The ending inventory of LaVal Co. is $64,000. If beginning inventory was $70,000 and goods available for sale totalled $124,000, the cost of goods sold is
   a. $112,000.   d. $50,000.
   b. $198,000.   e. None of the above ($_____)
   c. $60,000. (24,000 - 64,000 = 60K
11. Martin Company had cost of goods sold of $130,000. The beginning and ending inventories were $10,000 and $20,000, respectively. Purchases for the period must have been
   a. $82,000.   d. $140,000. 10,000 + x - 20K = 130. X = 140
   b. $94,000.   e. $138,000.
   c. $132,000.

Use the following information for Questions 12 through 14.

Tee Company had a $20,000 beginning inventory and a $24,000 ending inventory. Net sales were $180,000; purchases, $80,000; purchase returns and allowances, $4,000; and freight-in, $5,000.

12. Cost of goods sold for the period is
   a. $69,000.   d. $77,000. 20 + 80 - 4 + 5 + 24 = 77)?
   b. $49,000.   e. None of the above
   c. $85,000.
13. What is Tee's gross profit percentage (rounded to the nearest percentage)?
   a. 57% (180 - 77K / 180   c. 47%
   b. 88%   d. None of the above
14. What is Tee's rate of inventory turnover?
   a. 3.4 times   c. 6.4 times
   b. 3.5 times   d. 6.2 times
15. Beginning inventory is $60,000, purchases are $180,000, and sales total $300,000. The normal gross profit is 30%. Using the gross profit method, how much is ending inventory?
   a. $120,000   d. $30,000
   b. $106,400   e. None of the above ($_____)
   c. $244,000
16. An overstatement of ending inventory in one period results in
   a. no effect on net income of the next period.
   b. an understatement of net income of the next period.
   c. an overstatement of net income of the next period.
   d. an understatement of the beginning inventory of the next period.

Accounting Vocabulary

comparability Comparability is an enhancing qualitative characteristic. It allows the user to distinguish between similarities and differences by comparing a company's financial statement from one period to the next. (p. 286)

consistency principle A business must use the same accounting methods and procedures from period to period. (p. 286)

cost of goods sold Cost of the inventory the business has sold to customers. Also called *cost of sales*. (p. 271)

cost-of-goods-sold model Formula that brings together all the inventory data for the entire accounting period: Beginning inventory + Purchases = Goods available for sale. Then, Goods available for sale − Ending inventory = Cost of goods sold. (p. 290)

disclosure principle A business's financial statements must report enough information for outsiders to make knowledgeable decisions about the business. The company should report relevant, reliable, and comparable information about its economic affairs. (p. 286)

first-in, first-out (FIFO) cost method Inventory costing method by which the first costs into inventory are the first costs out to cost of goods sold. Ending inventory is based on the costs of the most recent purchases. (p. 281)

gross margin Another name for *gross profit*. (p. 273)

gross profit Sales revenue minus cost of goods sold. Also called *gross margin*. (p. 273)

gross profit method A way to estimate inventory based on a rearrangement of the cost-of-goods-sold model: Beginning inventory + Net purchases = Goods available for sale − Cost of goods sold = Ending inventory. Also called the *gross margin method*. (p. 291)

gross profit percentage Gross profit divided by net sales revenue. Also called the *gross margin percentage*. (p. 288)

inventory turnover Ratio of cost of goods sold to average inventory. Indicates how rapidly inventory is sold. (p. 289)

lower-of-cost-and-net-realizable-value (LCNRV) rule Requires that an asset be reported in the financial statements at whichever is lower—its historical cost or its net realizable value. (p. 286)

net realizable value The amount a business could get if it sold the inventory less the costs of selling it. (p. 286)

periodic inventory system An inventory system in which the business does not keep a continuous record of the inventory on hand. Instead, at the end of the period, the business makes a physical count of the inventory on hand and applies the appropriate unit costs to determine the cost of the ending inventory. (p. 274)

perpetual inventory system An inventory system in which the business keeps a continuous record for each inventory item to show the inventory on hand at all times. (p. 275)

purchase allowance A decrease in the cost of purchases because the seller has granted the buyer a discount (an allowance) from the amount owed. (p. 277)

purchase discount A decrease in the cost of purchases earned by making an early payment to the vendor. (p. 277)

purchase return A decrease in the cost of purchases because the buyer returned the goods to the seller. (p. 277)

specific identification cost method Inventory costing method based on the specific cost of particular units of inventory. (p. 279)

weighted-average-cost method Inventory costing method based on the average cost of inventory for the period. Weighted-average cost is determined by dividing the cost of goods available by the number of units available. Also called the *average cost method*. (p. 279)

Assess Your Progress

MyAccountingLab

Make the grade with MyAccountingLab: The Exercises, Quizzes, and Problems (A set) marked in red can be found on MyAccountingLab. You can practise them as often as you want, and most feature step-by-step guided instructions to help you find the right answer.

SHORT EXERCISES

LEARNING OBJECTIVE 1

Account for inventory transactions

S6-1 Journalize the following assumed transactions for Shoppers Drug Mart Corporation. Show amounts in millions.

- Cash purchases of inventory, $3,900 million
- Sales on account (including credit cards), $19,400 million
- Cost of goods sold (perpetual inventory system), $4,200 million
- Collections on account, $18,900 million

LEARNING OBJECTIVE 1

Account for inventory transactions

S6-2 Riley Kilgo Inc. purchased inventory costing $100,000 and sold 80% of the goods for $240,000. All purchases and sales were on account. Kilgo later collected 20% of the accounts receivable.

1. Journalize these transactions for Kilgo, which uses the perpetual inventory system.
2. For these transactions, show what Kilgo will report for inventory, revenues, and expenses on its financial statements. Report gross profit on the appropriate statement.

LEARNING OBJECTIVE ❷

Apply the weighted-average-cost and FIFO methods

S6-3 Allstate Sporting Goods started April with an inventory of 10 sets of golf clubs that cost a total of $1,500. During April, Allstate purchased 20 sets of clubs for $3,200. At the end of the month, Allstate had six sets of golf clubs on hand. The store manager must select an inventory costing method, and he asks you to tell him both cost of goods sold and ending inventory under these two accounting methods, assuming the periodic system is used.

a. Weighted-average cost
b. FIFO

LEARNING OBJECTIVE ❷

Apply the weighted-average-cost and FIFO methods

S6-4 University Copy Centre Ltd. uses laser printers. The company started the year with 100 containers of ink (weighted-average cost of $9.20 each, FIFO cost of $9 each). During the year, University Copy Centre purchased 700 containers of ink at $10 each and sold 600 units for $20 each. The company paid operating expenses throughout the year, to a total of $3,000. University Copy Centre is not subject to income tax. Prepare University Copy Centre Ltd.'s income statement for the year ended December 31, 2014, under the weighted-average and FIFO inventory costing methods assuming periodic system is used. Include a complete statement heading.

LEARNING OBJECTIVE ❷

Understand income tax effects of the inventory costing methods

S6-5 This exercise should be used in conjunction with exercise S6-4. Now assume that University Copy Centre in exercise S6-4 is a corporation subject to an 18% income tax. Compute University Copy Centre's income tax expense under the weighted-average cost and FIFO inventory costing methods. Which method would you select to (a) maximize income before tax and (b) minimize income tax expense?

LEARNING OBJECTIVE ❸

Understand accounting standards related to inventory

S6-6 You are opening a new bookstore catering to the students at Queen's University. Once you have established this operation, you plan to approach investors to support an expansion to locations in other Canadian university communities. Explain to your accountant what characteristics you expect him to maintain in accounting for inventory and the reasons for your expectations.

LEARNING OBJECTIVE ❸

Apply the lower-of-cost-and-net-realizable-value rule to inventory

S6-7 It is December 31, 2014, end of year, and the controller of Garcia Corporation is applying the lower-of-cost-and-net-realizable-value (LCNRV) rule to inventories. Before any year-end adjustments Garcia has these data:

Cost of goods sold..	$410,000
Historical cost of ending inventory,	
as determined by a physical count...	60,000

Garcia determines that the net realizable value of ending inventory is $49,000. Show what Garcia should report for ending inventory and for cost of goods sold. Identify the financial statement where each item appears.

LEARNING OBJECTIVE ❹

Use ratio data to evaluate operations

S6-8 Assume Gildan Activewear Inc. made sales of $964.4 million during 2012. Cost of goods sold for the year totalled $655.3 million. At the end of 2011, Gildan's inventory stood at $200.7 million, and Gildan ended 2012 with inventory of $240 million. Compute Gildan's gross profit percentage and rate of inventory turnover for 2012.

LEARNING OBJECTIVE ❺

Estimate ending inventory by the gross profit method

S6-9 Provincial Technology Inc. began the year with inventory of $300,000 and purchased $1,600,000 of goods during the year. Sales for the year are $3,000,000, and Provincial's gross profit percentage is 40% of sales. Compute Provincial's estimated cost of ending inventory by using the gross profit method.

LEARNING OBJECTIVE ❻

Assess the effect of an inventory error—one year only

S6-10 CWD Inc. reported these figures for its fiscal year (amounts in millions):

Net sales..	$1,700
Cost of goods sold...	1,180
Ending inventory..	360

Suppose CWD later learns that ending inventory was overstated by $10 million. What are CWD's correct amounts for (a) net sales, (b) ending inventory, (c) cost of goods sold, and (d) gross profit?

S6-11 Suppose Staples Inc.'s $1.9 million cost of inventory at its fiscal year-end on February 3, 2013, was understated by $0.5 million.

1. Would 2013's reported gross profit of $5.2 million be overstated, understated, or correct? What would be the correct amount of gross profit for 2013?
2. Will 2014's gross profit of $5.6 million be overstated, understated, or correct? What would be the correct amount of gross profit for 2014?

LEARNING OBJECTIVE ❻

Assess the effect of an inventory error on two years

S6-12 Determine whether each of the following actions in buying, selling, and accounting for inventories is ethical or unethical. Give your reason for each answer.

1. In applying the lower-of-cost-and-net-realizable-value rule to inventories, Terre Haute Industries recorded an excessively low net realizable value for ending inventory. This allowed the company to pay less income tax for the year.
2. Laminated Photo Film purchased lots of inventory shortly before year-end to increase the weighted-average cost of goods sold and decrease reported income for the year.
3. Madison Inc. delayed the purchase of inventory until after December 31, 2014, to keep 2014's cost of goods sold from growing too large. The delay in purchasing inventory helped net income in 2014 to reach the level of profit demanded by the company's investors.
4. Dover Sales Company deliberately overstated ending inventory in order to report higher profits (net income).
5. Roberto Corporation deliberately overstated purchases to produce a high figure for cost of goods sold (low amount of net income). The real reason was to decrease the company's income tax payments to the government.

LEARNING OBJECTIVE ❶❸

Understand ethical implications of inventory actions

S6-13 Capital Technologies Inc. began 2014 with inventory of $20,000. During the year, Capital purchased inventory costing $100,000 and sold goods for $140,000, with all transactions on account. Capital ended the year with inventory of $30,000. Journalize all the necessary transactions under the periodic inventory system.

LEARNING OBJECTIVE ❶

Record inventory transactions in the periodic system

S6-14 Use the data in exercise S6-13 to do the following for Capital Technologies Inc.:

1. Post to the Inventory and Cost of Goods Sold accounts.
2. Compute cost of goods sold by the cost-of-goods-sold model.
3. Prepare the December 2014 income statement of Capital Technologies Inc. through gross profit.

LEARNING OBJECTIVE ❶❺

Compute cost of goods sold and prepare the income statement—periodic system

EXERCISES

E6-15 Accounting records for Red Deer Tire Ltd. yield the following data for the year ended December 31, 2014 (amounts in thousands):

LEARNING OBJECTIVE ❶❷

Account for inventory transactions—perpetual system

Inventory, December 31, 2013	$ 550
Purchases of inventory (on account)..	1,200
Sales of inventory—80% on account; 20% for cash (cost $900)	2,000
Inventory at FIFO cost, December 31, 2014...	850

Requirements

1. Journalize Red Deer Tire's inventory transactions for the year under the perpetual system. Show all amounts in thousands. Use Exhibit 6-4 as a model, on page 276.
2. Report ending inventory, sales, cost of goods sold, and gross profit on the appropriate financial statement (amounts in thousands).

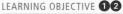

LEARNING OBJECTIVE ❶❷

Analyze inventory transactions—
perpetual system

E6-16 Langley Inc. inventory records for a particular development program show the following at October 31, 2014:

Oct. 1	Beginning inventory..................................	5 units @	$150 =	$ 750
15	Purchase	11 units @	160 =	1,760
26	Purchase	5 units @	170 =	850

At October 31, 10 of these programs are on hand. Langley uses the perpetual inventory system.

Requirements

1. Journalize for Langley:
   a. Total October purchases in one summary entry. All purchases were on credit.
   b. Total October sales and cost of goods sold in two summary entries. The selling price was $500 per unit, and all sales were on credit. Langley uses the FIFO inventory method.
2. Under FIFO, how much gross profit would Langley earn on these transactions? What is the FIFO cost of Langley's ending inventory?

LEARNING OBJECTIVE ❷

Determine ending inventory
and cost of goods sold by three
methods—perpetual system

E6-17 Use the data for Langley Inc. in exercise E6-16 to answer the following.

Requirements

1. Compute cost of goods sold and ending inventory, using each of the following methods:
   a. Specific unit cost, with two $150 units, three $160 units, and five $170 units still on hand at the end
   b. Weighted-average cost
   c. First-in, first-out cost
2. Which method produces the highest cost of goods sold? Which method produces the lowest cost of goods sold? What causes the difference in cost of goods sold?

LEARNING OBJECTIVE ❷

Compute the tax advantage of
weighted-average cost over FIFO

E6-18 Use the data in exercise E6-16 to illustrate Langley's income tax advantage from using weighted-average cost over FIFO cost. Sales revenue is $6,000, operating expenses are $1,100, and the income tax rate is 25%. How much in taxes would Langley save by using the weighted-average-cost method versus FIFO?

LEARNING OBJECTIVE ❶❷

Determine ending inventory and
cost of goods sold—FIFO versus
weighted-average cost–perpetual
system

E6-19 MusicBiz.net Ltd. specializes in sound equipment. Because each inventory item is expensive, MusicBiz uses a perpetual inventory system. Company records indicate the following data for a line of speakers:

Date		Item	Quantity	Unit Cost	Sale Price
June	1	Balance	6	$ 95	
	8	Sale	3		$155
	10	Purchase	11	100	
	30	Sale	5		160

Requirements

1. Determine the amounts that MusicBiz should report for cost of goods sold and ending inventory in the following two ways:
   a. FIFO
   b. Weighted-average cost
2. MusicBiz uses the FIFO method. Prepare MusicBiz's income statement for the month ended June 30, 2014, reporting gross profit. Operating expenses totalled $319, and the income tax rate was 25%.

E6-20 Suppose a Johnson store in Ottawa, Ontario, ended November 2014 with 800,000 units of merchandise that cost an average of $8 each. Suppose the store then sold 600,000 units for $5.0 million during December. Further, assume the store made two large purchases during December as follows:

LEARNING OBJECTIVE ❶❷

Measure gross profit—FIFO versus weighted-average cost, falling prices–periodic system

December	6	100,000 units	@ $7	=	$ 700,000
	26	400,000 units	@ 6	=	2,400,000

1. At December 31, the store manager needs to know the store's gross profit under both FIFO and weighted-average cost. Supply this information. Johnson uses the periodic inventory system.
2. What caused the FIFO and weighted-average cost gross profit figures to differ?

E6-21 Deitrick Guitar Company is nearing the end of its worst year ever. With three weeks until year-end, it appears that net income for the year will have decreased by 20% from the previous year. Jim Deitrick, the president and principal shareholder, is distressed with the year's results.

LEARNING OBJECTIVE ❷

Manage income taxes under the weighted-average-cost method

Deitrick asks you, the financial vice-president, to come up with a way to increase the business's net income. Inventory quantities are a little higher than normal because sales have been slow during the last few months. Deitrick uses the weighted-average-cost inventory method, and inventory costs have risen dramatically during the latter part of the year.

Requirement

Write a memorandum to Jim Deitrick to explain how the company can increase its net income for the year. Explain your reasoning in detail. Deitrick is a man of integrity, so your plan must be completely ethical.

E6-22 This exercise tests your understanding of accounting for inventory. Provide a word or phrase that best fits the description. Assume that the cost of inventory is rising.

LEARNING OBJECTIVE ❶❷❸

Identify effects of the inventory methods and evaluate operations

____ 1. Generally associated with saving income taxes.
____ 2. Results in a cost of ending inventory that is close to the current cost of replacing the inventory.
____ 3. Used to account for automobiles, jewellery, and art objects.
____ 4. Maximizes reported income.
____ 5. Inventory system that keeps a running record of all goods bought, sold, and on hand.
____ 6. Characteristic that enables investors to compare a company's financial statements from one period to the next.
____ 7. Writes inventory down when net realizable value drops below historical cost.
____ 8. Key indicator of a company's ability to sell inventory at a profit.
____ 9. A decrease in the buyer's cost of inventory earned by paying quickly.

E6-23 Tavistock Inc. uses a perpetual inventory system. Tavistock has these account balances at December 31, 2014, prior to making the year-end adjustments:

LEARNING OBJECTIVE ❸

Apply the lower-of-cost-and-net-realizable-value rule to inventories

Inventory		Cost of Goods Sold		Sales Revenue	
Beg. bal. 12,400					
End bal. 14,000		Bal. 78,000		Bal. 125,000	

A year ago, the net realizable value of Tavistock's ending inventory was $13,000, which exceeded cost of $12,400. Tavistock has determined that the net realizable value of the December 31, 2014, ending inventory is $12,000.

Requirement

Prepare Tavistock Inc.'s 2014 income statement through gross profit to show how the company would apply the lower-of-cost-and-net-realizable-value rule to its inventories.

LEARNING OBJECTIVE ⑤

Determine amounts for the income statement; use the cost-of-goods-sold model

E6-24 Supply the missing income statement amounts for each of the following companies (amounts in millions, at January 31, 2014):

Company	Net Sales	Beginning Inventory	Purchases	Ending Inventory	Cost of Goods Sold	Gross Profit
Myers Confectionary	$543	$29	$470	$24	(a)	(b)
Canada Computers	74	7	(c)	8	(d)	19
Best Taste Beverages	(e)	(f)	16	2	16	19
Value for $	31	2	24	(g)	23	(h)

Prepare the income statement for Myers Confectionary Ltd., in millions of dollars, for the year ended January 31, 2014. Use the cost-of-goods-sold model to compute cost of goods sold. Myers's operating and other expenses for the year were $204. Ignore income tax.

Note: Exercise E6-25 builds on exercise E6-24 with a profitability analysis of these actual companies.

LEARNING OBJECTIVE ④

Measure profitability

E6-25 Refer to the data in Exercise E6-24. Compute all ratio values to answer the following questions:
- Which company has the highest gross profit percentage? Which company has the lowest?
- Which company has the highest rate of inventory turnover? Which company has the lowest?

Based on your figures, which company appears to be the most profitable?

LEARNING OBJECTIVE ④⑤

Measure gross profit and report cash flows

E6-26 Suppose a company you are considering as an investment made sales of $54.8 billion in the year ended December 31, 2014. Collections from customers totalled $55 billion. The company began the year with $6.6 billion in inventories and ended with $7.9 billion. During the year, purchases of inventory added up to $39.8 billion. Of the purchases, the company paid $37.9 billion to suppliers.

As an investor searching for a good investment, you would identify several critical pieces of information about the company's operations during the year.

Compute the company's gross profit, gross profit percentage, and rate of inventory turnover during 2014. Use the cost-of-goods-sold model as needed. Would the information help you make your investment decision?

LEARNING OBJECTIVE ⑤

Budget inventory purchase

E6-27 Your company, Home Products Ltd., is preparing budgets for the fiscal year ended December 31, 2014, to help manage the company. During the preceding fiscal year, 2013, sales totalled $1,777 million and cost of goods sold was $1,175 million. At December 31, 2013, inventory stood at $366 million.

During the upcoming 2014 year, suppose you expect cost of goods sold to increase by 8%. The company budgets next year's ending inventory at $369 million.

Requirement

One of the most important decisions you make is how much inventory to buy. How much inventory will you purchase during the upcoming year to reach your budgeted figures?

LEARNING OBJECTIVE ⑤

Estimate inventory by the gross profit method

E6-28 Vacation Properties began March with concession inventory of $36,000. The business made net purchases of $79,500 for concessions and had net sales of $150,000 before a break-in when its concession inventory was stolen. For the past several years, Vacation Properties' gross profit percentage has been 45%. Estimate the cost of the concession inventory stolen. Would a manager use the gross profit method to estimate ending inventory under normal circumstances?

E6-29 Dijon Mustard Ltée. reported the following comparative income statement for the years ended September 30, 2013, and 2014:

LEARNING OBJECTIVE ❻

Correct an inventory error

Dijon Mustard Ltée.
Income Statement
For the Years Ended September 30

	2014		2013	
Sales revenue		$194,000		$158,000
Cost of goods sold				
Beginning inventory	$ 23,000		$ 16,000	
Purchases	97,000		86,000	
Goods available for sale	120,000		102,000	
Ending inventory	(21,000)		(23,000)	
Cost of goods sold		99,000		79,000
Gross profit		95,000		79,000
Operating expenses		20,000		20,000
Net income		$ 75,000		$ 59,000

Dijon's shareholders are thrilled by the company's boost in sales and net income during 2014. Then they discover that the 2013 ending inventory was understated by $10,000. How well did Dijon really perform in 2014, as compared with 2013?

E6-30 Suppose a technology company's inventory records for a particular computer chip indicate the following at October 31:

LEARNING OBJECTIVE ❶❷

Compute amounts for the inventory methods—periodic system

Oct. 1	Beginning inventory	5 units @ $160 = $ 800
8	Purchase	4 units @ 160 = 640
15	Purchase	11 units @ 170 = 1,870
26	Purchase	5 units @ 180 = 900

$4210 GAFS

The physical count of inventory at October 31 indicates that 8 units of inventory are on hand.

25
17

Requirements

Compute ending inventory and cost of goods sold using each of the following methods. Round all amounts to the nearest dollar.

1. Specific unit cost, assuming four $160 units and four $170 units are on hand
2. Weighted-average cost
3. First-in, first-out cost

E6-31 Use the data in exercise E6-30 to journalize the following for the periodic system:

LEARNING OBJECTIVE ❶❷

Journalize inventory transactions in the periodic system; compute cost of goods sold

1. Total October purchases in one summary entry. All purchases were on credit.
2. Total October sales in a summary entry. Assume that the selling price was $300 per unit and that all sales were on credit.
3. October 31 entries for inventory. The company uses weighted-average cost. Post to the Cost of Goods Sold T-account to show how this amount is determined. Label each item in the account.
4. Show the computation of cost of goods sold by the cost-of-goods-sold model.

E6-32 Assume a Roots outlet store began August 2014 with 40 units of inventory that cost $30 each. The sale price of these units was $60. During August, the store completed the following inventory transactions.

LEARNING OBJECTIVE ❶❷

Compute cost of goods sold and gross profit on sales—periodic system

			Units	Unit Cost	Unit Sale Price
Aug.	3	Sale	16	$30	$60
	8	Purchase........................	70	31	62
	11	Sale	24	30	60
	19	Sale	8	31	62
	24	Sale	30	31	62
	30	Purchase........................	28	32	73
	31	Sale	15	31	62

Requirements

1. Determine the store's cost of goods sold for August under the periodic inventory system. Assume the FIFO method.
2. Compute gross profit for August.

E6-33 Accounting records for Cookies for You Ltd. yield the following data for the year ended December 31, 2014 (amounts in thousands):

Inventory, December 31, 2013...	$ 410
Purchases of inventory (on account)	3,200
Sales of inventory—80% on account; 20% for cash	4,830
Inventory at the lower of FIFO cost and net realizable value, December 31, 2014...	600

Requirements

1. Journalize Cookies for You's inventory transactions for the year under the periodic system. Show all amounts in thousands.
2. Report ending inventory, sales, cost of goods sold, and gross profit on the appropriate financial statement (amounts in thousands). Show the computation of cost of goods sold.

CHALLENGE EXERCISES

E6-34 For each of the following situations, identify the inventory method that you would use or, given the use of a particular method, state the strategy that you would follow to accomplish your goal:

a. Inventory costs are increasing. Your company uses weighted-average cost and is having an unexpectedly good year. It is near year-end, and you need to keep net income from increasing too much in order to save on income tax.
b. Suppliers of your inventory are threatening a labour strike, and it may be difficult for your company to obtain inventory. This situation could increase your income taxes.
c. Inventory costs are decreasing, and your company's board of directors wants to minimize income taxes.
d. Inventory costs are increasing, and the company prefers to report high income.
e. Inventory costs have been stable for several years, and you expect costs to remain stable for the indefinite future. (Give the reason for your choice of method.)

E6-35 Suppose Holt Renfrew, the specialty retailer, had these records for ladies' evening gowns during 2014.

Beginning inventory (30 @ $1,000)...	$ 30,000
Purchase in February (25 @ $1,100)...	27,500
Purchase in June (60 @ $1,200)...	72,000
Purchase in December (25 @ $1,300)..	32,500
Goods available...	$162,000

Assume sales of evening gowns totalled 130 units during 2014 and that Holt's uses the weighted-average-cost method under the periodic inventory system to account for inventory. The income tax rate is 30%.

Requirements

1. Compute Holt's cost of goods sold for evening gowns in 2014.
2. Compute what cost of goods sold would have been if Holt had purchased enough inventory in December—at $1,300 per evening gown—to keep year-end inventory at the same level it was at the beginning of the year, 30 units.

E6-36 Cheri's Beauty Products Ltd. reported the figures below at December 31, 2014, 2013, and 2012. The business has declared bankruptcy. You have been asked to review the business and explain why it failed.

LEARNING OBJECTIVE ❹

Evaluate a company's profitability

Cheri's Beauty Products Ltd.
Statement of Income
For the Years Ended December 31, 2014, 2013, and 2012

Thousands	2014	2013	2012
Sales	$41.0	$39.5	$37.1
Cost of sales	32.7	30.9	28.9
Selling expenses	8.0	7.2	6.8
Other expenses	0.4	1.0	0.8
Net income (net loss)	$ (0.1)	$ 0.4	$ 0.6
Additional data:			
Ending inventory	9.2	8.6	7.7

Requirement

Evaluate the trend of Cheri's Beauty Products' results of operations during 2012 through 2014. Consider the trends of sales, gross profit, and net income. Track the gross profit percentage (to three decimal places) and the rate of inventory turnover (to one decimal place) in each year—2012, 2013, and 2014. Also, discuss the role that selling expenses must have played in Cheri's Beauty Products' difficulties.

QUIZ

Test your understanding of accounting for inventory by answering the following questions. Select the best choice from among the possible answers given.

Q6-37 Riverside Software began January with $3,500 of merchandise inventory. During January, Riverside made the following entries for its inventory transactions:

Inventory	6,000	
Accounts Payable		6,000
Accounts Receivable	7,200	
Sales Revenue		7,200
Cost of Goods Sold	5,500	
Inventory		5,500

What was the value of Riverside's inventory at the end of January?
a. $0
b. $4,000
c. $4,500
d. $5,500

Q6-38 Use the data in question Q6-37. What is Riverside's gross profit for January?

a. $0

b. $1,700

c. $5,500

d. $7,200

Q6-39 When does the cost of inventory become an expense?

a. When cash is collected from the customer

b. When inventory is purchased from the supplier

c. When payment is made to the supplier

d. When inventory is delivered to a customer

Questions Q6-40 and Q6-41 use the following facts. Leading Edge Frame Shop wants to know the effect of different inventory costing methods on its financial statements. The company uses the periodic inventory system. Inventory and purchases data for April follow.

			Units	Unit Cost	Total Cost
April	1	Beginning inventory	2,000	$10.00	$20,000
	4	Purchase	1,000	10.60	10,600
	9	Sale	(1,500)		

Q6-40 If Leading Edge uses the FIFO method, the cost of the ending inventory will be

a. $10,600.

b. $15,000.

c. $15,300.

d. $15,600.

Q6-41 If Leading Edge uses the weighted-average-cost method, cost of goods sold will be

a. $10,600.

b. $15,000.

c. $15,300.

d. $15,600.

Q6-42 In a period of rising prices,

a. gross profit under FIFO will be higher than under weighted-average cost.

b. weighted-average-cost inventory will be greater than FIFO inventory.

c. cost of goods sold under weighted-average cost will be less than under FIFO.

d. net income under weighted-average cost will be higher than under FIFO.

Q6-43 The income statement for Heritage Health Foods shows gross profit of $144,000, operating expenses of $130,000, and cost of goods sold of $216,000. What is the amount of net sales revenue?

a. $274,000

b. $246,000

c. $360,000

d. $490,000

Q6-44 The phrase "net realizable value" as used in "the lower of cost and net realizable value" generally means

a. original cost.

b. market value.

c. retail market price.

d. liquidation price.

Q6-45 The sum of ending inventory and cost of goods sold is

a. goods available for sale.

b. net purchases.

c. gross profit.

d. beginning inventory.

Q6-46 The following data come from the inventory records of Dodge Company:

Net sales revenue	$620,000
Beginning inventory...	60,000
Ending inventory	40,000
Net purchases	400,000

Based on these facts, the gross profit for Dodge Company is
a. $150,000.
c. $190,000.
b. $220,000.
d. some other amount ($ _200,000_).

Q6-47 Elizabeth Baker Cosmetics ended May with inventory of $20,000. Elizabeth Baker expects to end June with inventory of $15,000 after cost of goods sold of $90,000. How much inventory must Elizabeth Baker purchase during June to accomplish these results?

20000 + x -15000 = 90,000

a. $85,000
c. $105,000
b. $95,000
d. Cannot be determined from the data given.

Q6-48 Two financial ratios that clearly distinguish a discount chain such as Walmart from a high-end retailer such as Tiffany & Co. are the gross profit percentage and the rate of inventory turnover. Which set of relationships is most likely for Tiffany?

	Gross Profit Percentage	**Inventory Turnover**
a.	High	High
b.	Low	Low
c.	Low	High
d.	High	Low

Q6-49 Sales are $500,000, and cost of goods sold is $300,000. Beginning and ending inventories are $25,000 and $35,000, respectively. How many times did the company turn its inventory over during this period?

Inventory turnover.

a. 16.7 times $\frac{300,000}{30,000}$ c. 8 times
b. 6.7 times   d. 10 times

Q6-50 Tulsa Inc. reported the following data:

205,000 + 20,000 - 4,000 - 6000 = 215,000
490,000 - 10,000 = 480,000

Freight-in..........................	$ 20,000	Sales returns............................	$ 10,000
Purchases......................................	205,000	Purchase returns	6,000
Beginning inventory......................	50,000	Sales revenue............................	490,000
Purchase discounts........................	4,000	Ending inventory	40,000

215,000 = 265,000

COGS: 50000 + 215,000 - 40,000 = 225,000

Tulsa's gross profit percentage is
a. 47.9%.
c. 53.1%.
b. 52.1%.
d. 54.0%.

Q6-51 Sherman Tank Company had the following for the first quarter of 2013:

Beginning inventory, $50,000   Net purchases, $75,000   *125,000*
Net sales revenue, $90,000   Gross profit rate, 30%   *27,000 = GP*
63.

By the gross profit method, the ending inventory should be
a. $62,000.
c. $64,000.
b. $63,000.
d. $65,000.

Q6-52 An error understated Rice Corporation's December 31, 2013, ending inventory by $40,000. What effect will this error have on total assets and net income for 2013?

	Assets	**Net Income**
a.	No effect	No effect
b.	No effect	Overstate
c.	Understate	Understate
d.	Understate	No effect

Q6-53 What is the effect of Rice Corporation's 2013 inventory error on net income for 2014?
a. No effect
b. Understate
c. Overstate

PROBLEMS

(Group A)

LEARNING OBJECTIVE

Account for inventory in a perpetual system

P6-54A Best Buy purchases merchandise inventory by the crate; each crate of inventory is a unit. The fiscal year of Best Buy ends each February 28.

Assume you are dealing with a single Best Buy store in Toronto, Ontario, and that the store experienced the following: The store began fiscal year 2014 with an inventory of 20,000 units that cost a total of $1,000,000. During the year, the store purchased merchandise on account as follows:

April (30,000 units @ cost of $60)...	$1,800,000
August (50,000 units @ cost of $64)..	3,200,000
November (60,000 units @ cost of $70)	4,200,000
Total purchases	$9,200,000

Cash payments on account totalled $8,800,000.

During fiscal year 2014, the store sold 150,000 units of merchandise for $14,400,000. Cash accounted for $5,000,000 of this, and the balance was on account. Best Buy uses the FIFO method for inventories.

Operating expenses for the year were $4,000,000. The store paid 80% in cash and accrued the rest as accrued liabilities. The store accrued income tax at the rate of 33%.

Requirements

1. Make summary journal entries to record the store's transactions for the year ended February 28, 2014. Best Buy uses a perpetual inventory system.
2. Prepare a T-account to show the activity in the Inventory account.
3. Prepare the store's income statement for the year ended February 28, 2014. Show totals for gross profit, income before tax, and net income.

LEARNING OBJECTIVE ❶❷

Measure cost of goods sold and ending inventory—perpetual system

P6-55A Assume an outlet of The Runner's Store began August 2014 with 40 pairs of running shoes that cost the store $40 each. The sale price of these shoes was $70. During August, the store completed these inventory transactions:

			Units	Unit Cost	Unit Sale Price
Aug.	3	Sale	16		$70
	8	Purchase.....................	80	41	
	11	Sale	24		70
	19	Sale	9		72
	24	Sale	30		72
	30	Purchase.....................	18	42	

Requirement

Determine the store's cost of goods sold, gross profit, and ending inventory using (a) FIFO and (b) weighted-average assuming the perpetual system is used.

LEARNING OBJECTIVE ❶❷

Compute inventory by two methods—perpetual system

P6-56A Army-Navy Surplus Ltd. began March 2014 with 70 tents that cost $20 each. During the month, Army-Navy Surplus made the following purchases at cost:

March	4	100 tents	@ $22	=	$2,200
	19	160 tents	@ 24	=	3,840
	25	40 tents	@ 25	=	1,000

Army-Navy Surplus sold 320 tents (150 tents on March 22 and 170 tents on March 30), and at March 31 the ending inventory consists of 50 tents. The sale price of each tent was $45.

Requirements

1. Determine the cost of goods sold and ending inventory amounts for March under (a) weighted-average cost and (b) FIFO cost assuming the perpetual system is used. Round weighted-average cost per unit to four decimal places, and round all other amounts to the nearest dollar.
2. Explain why cost of goods sold is highest under weighted-average cost. Be specific.
3. Prepare Army-Navy Surplus's income statement for March 2014. Report gross profit. Operating expenses totalled $4,000. Army-Navy Surplus uses weighted-average costing for inventory. The income tax rate is 21%.

P6-57A The records of Armstrong Aviation Supply Inc. include the following accounts for inventory of aviation fuel at December 31, 2014:

LEARNING OBJECTIVE ❶❷

Apply the different inventory costing methods—periodic system

Inventory				
Jan.	1	Balance	700 units @ $7.00	4,900
Mar.	6	Purchase	300 units @ 7.05	2,115
June	22	Purchase	8,400 units @ 7.50	63,000
Oct.	4	Purchase	500 units @ 8.50	4,250

Sales Revenue		
Dec. 31	9,000 units	127,800

Requirements

1. Prepare a partial income statement through gross profit under the weighted-average-cost and FIFO methods assuming the periodic system is used. Round weighted-average cost per unit to four decimal places and all other amounts to the nearest dollar.
2. Which inventory method would you use to minimize income tax? Explain why this method causes income tax to be the lowest.

P6-58A AMC Trade Mart has recently had lacklustre sales. The rate of inventory turnover has dropped, and the merchandise is gathering dust. At the same time, competition has forced AMC's suppliers to lower the prices that AMC will pay when it replaces its inventory. It is now December 31, 2014, and the current net realizable value of AMC's ending inventory is $80,000 below what AMC actually paid for the goods, which was $190,000. Before any adjustments at the end of the period, the Cost of Goods Sold account has a balance of $780,000.

LEARNING OBJECTIVE ❸

Apply the lower-cost-and-net-realizable-value rule to inventories—perpetual system

What accounting action should AMC take in this situation? Give any journal entry required. At what amount should AMC report Inventory on the balance sheet? At what amount should the company report Cost of Goods Sold on the income statement? Discuss the accounting characteristic that is most relevant to this situation.

Are there circumstances that would allow AMC to increase the value of its inventory? Are there limits to which the value of the inventory may be increased?

P6-59A Chocolate Treats Ltd. and Coffee Bars Inc. are both specialty food chains. The two companies reported these figures, in thousands:

LEARNING OBJECTIVE ❹

Use gross profit percentage and inventory turnover to evaluate two companies

Chocolate Treats Ltd.		
Statement of Operations		
	Fiscal Year	
Thousands	**2014**	**2013**
Revenues:		
Net sales...	$543	$708
Costs and Expenses:		
Cost of goods sold.................................	475	598
General and administrative expenses......	68	55

Chocolate Treats Ltd.
Balance Sheet

| | January 31, | |
Thousands	2014	2013
Assets		
Current assets:		
Cash and cash equivalents......................	$17	$28
Receivables..	27	30
Inventories..	24	29

Coffee Bars Inc.
Statement of Earnings

| | Fiscal Year | |
Thousands	2014	2013
Net sales	$7,787	$6,369
Cost of goods sold......................................	3,179	2,605
Selling, general, and administrative expenses	2,948	2,363

Coffee Bars Inc.
Balance Sheet

| | Year End | |
Thousands	2014	2013
Assets		
Current assets:		
Cash and temporary investments	$313	$174
Receivables, net.......................................	224	191
Inventories...	636	546

Requirements

1. Compute the gross profit percentage and the rate of inventory turnover for Chocolate Treats and for Coffee Bars for 2014.
2. Based on these statistics, which company looks more profitable? Why? What other expense category should we consider in evaluating these two companies?

LEARNING OBJECTIVE ❺

Estimate inventory by the gross profit method; prepare the income statement

P6-60A Suppose an Indigo bookstore lost inventory in a fire. To file an insurance claim, Indigo must estimate its inventory by the gross profit method. For the past two years, Indigo's gross profit has averaged 40% of net sales. Indigo's inventory records reveal the following data:

Inventory, July 1, 2014	$ 360,000
Transactions during July	
Purchases..	628,000
Purchase discounts..	4,500
Purchase returns	9,000
Sales revenue	1,000,000
Sales returns..	170,000

Requirements

1. Estimate the cost of the lost inventory using the gross profit method.

2. Prepare the July 2014 income statement through gross profit. Show the detailed computation of cost of goods sold in a separate schedule.

P6-61A Here are condensed versions of Pontiac Convenience Store's most recent income statement and balance sheet. Income taxes are ignored.

LEARNING OBJECTIVE ❺

Determine the amount of inventory to purchase

Pontiac Convenience Store Income Statement For the Year Ended December 31, 2013	
Sales	$900,000
Cost of sales	700,000
Gross profit	200,000
Operating expenses	80,000
Net income	$120,000

Pontiac Convenience Store Balance Sheet As at December 31, 2013			
Assets		Liabilities and Capital	
Cash	$ 70,000	Accounts payable	$ 35,000
Inventories	35,000	Note payable	280,000
Land and		Total liabilities	315,000
buildings, net	360,000	Owner, capital	150,000
Total assets	$465,000	Total liabilities and capital	$465,000

The owner is budgeting for 2014. She expects sales and cost of goods sold to increase by 8%. To meet customer demand for the increase in sales, ending inventory will need to be $50,000 at December 31, 2014. The owner hopes to earn a net income of $160,000 next year.

Requirements

1. One of the most important decisions a manager makes is the amount of inventory to purchase. Compute the amount of inventory to purchase in 2014.

2. Prepare the store's budgeted income statement for 2014 to reach the target net income of $160,000.

P6-62A Columbia Video Sales Ltd. reported the following data. The shareholders are very happy with Columbia's steady increase in net income.

Auditors discovered that the ending inventory for 2012 was understated by $1 million and that the ending inventory for 2013 was also understated by $1 million. The ending inventory for 2014 was correct.

LEARNING OBJECTIVE ❻

Correct inventory errors over a three-year period

Columbia Video Sales Ltd. Income Statements for the Years Ended			
(Amounts in millions)	2014	2013	2012
Net sales revenue	$36	$33	$30
Cost of goods sold:			
Beginning inventory	$ 6	$ 5	$ 4
Purchases	26	24	22
Goods available for sale	32	29	26
Less: Ending inventory	(7)	(6)	(5)
Cost of goods sold	25	23	21
Gross profit	11	10	9
Total operating expenses	8	8	8
Net income	$ 3	$ 2	$ 1

Requirements

1. Show corrected income statements for each of the three years.

2. How much did these assumed corrections add to or take away from Columbia's total net income over the three-year period? How did the corrections affect the trend of net income?

3. Will Columbia's shareholders still be happy with the company's trend of net income? Give the reason for your answer.

(Group B)

LEARNING OBJECTIVE ❶❷

Account for inventory in a perpetual system

P6-63B Italian Leather Goods Inc. began 2014 with an inventory of 50,000 units that cost $1,500,000. During the year, the store purchased merchandise on account as follows:

March (40,000 units @ cost of $32)...	$1,280,000
August (40,000 units @ cost of $34)..	1,360,000
October (180,000 units @ cost of $35)..	6,300,000
Total purchases	$8,940,000

Cash payments on account totalled $8,610,000.

During 2014, the company sold 260,000 units of merchandise for $12,900,000. Cash accounted for $4,700,000 of this, and the balance was on account. Italian Leather Goods uses the FIFO method for inventories.

Operating expenses for the year were $2,080,000. Italian Leather Goods paid 60% in cash and accrued the rest as accrued liabilities. The company accrued income tax at the rate of 32%.

Requirements

1. Make summary journal entries to record the Italian Leather Goods transactions for the year ended December 31, 2014. The company uses a perpetual inventory system.
2. Prepare a T-account to show the activity in the Inventory account.
3. Prepare the Italian Leather Goods Inc. income statement for the year ended December 31, 2014. Show totals for gross profit, income before tax, and net income.

LEARNING OBJECTIVE ❶❷

Measure cost of goods sold and ending inventory—perpetual system

P6-64B Whitewater Sports Ltd. began July 2014 with 50 backpacks that cost $19 each. The sale price of each backpack was $36. During July, Whitewater completed these inventory transactions:

			Units	Unit Cost	Unit Sale Price
July	2	Purchase......................	12	$20	
	8	Sale	37		$36
	13	Sale	13		36
		Sale	4		37
	17	Purchase......................	24	20	
	22	Sale	15		37

Requirement

Determine the store's cost of goods sold, gross profit, and ending inventory using (a) FIFO and (b) weighted-average assuming the perpetual system is used.

LEARNING OBJECTIVE ❶❷

Compute inventory by two methods—perpetual system

P6-65B Spice Inc. began October 2014 with 100 shirts that cost $76 each. During October, the store made the following purchases at cost:

Oct.	3		200 @	$81	=	$16,200
	12		90 @	82	=	7,380
	24		240 @	85	=	20,400

Spice sold 500 shirts (320 shirts on October 18 and 180 shirts on October 28) and ended October with 130 shirts. The sale price of each shirt was $130.

Requirements

1. Determine the cost of goods sold and ending inventory amounts by the weighted-average-cost and FIFO cost methods assuming the perpetual system is used. Round weighted-average cost per unit to three decimal places, and round all other amounts to the nearest dollar.
2. Explain why cost of goods sold is highest under weighted-average cost. Be specific.
3. Prepare Spice's income statement for October 2014. Report gross profit. Operating expenses totalled $10,000. Spice uses the weighted-average-cost method for inventory. The income tax rate is 23%.

P6-66B The records of Sonic Sound Systems Inc. include the following for cases of CDs at December 31, 2014:

LEARNING OBJECTIVE ❶❷

Apply the different inventory costing methods—periodic system

Inventory					
Jan.	1	Balance	300 cases @ $300	121,500	
			100 cases @ 315		
May	19	Purchase	600 cases @ 335	201,000	
Aug.	12	Purchase	400 cases @ 350	140,000	
Oct.	4	Purchase	700 cases @ 370	259,000	

Sales Revenue			
Dec.	31	1,800 cases	910,000

Requirements

1. Prepare a partial income statement through gross profit under the weighted-average-cost and FIFO cost methods assuming the periodic system is used. Round weighted-average cost per unit to four decimal places and all other amounts to the nearest dollar.
2. Which inventory method would you use to report the highest net income? Explain why this method produces the highest reported income.

P6-67B Westside Copiers Ltd. has recently been plagued with lacklustre sales. The rate of inventory turnover has dropped, and some of the company's merchandise is gathering dust. At the same time, competition has forced some of Westside's suppliers to lower the prices that Westside will pay when it replaces its inventory. It is now December 31, 2014. The current net realizable value of Westside's ending inventory is $6,800,000, which is far less than the amount Westside paid for the goods, $8,900,000. Before any adjustments at the end of the period, Westside's Cost of Goods Sold account has a balance of $36,400,000.

LEARNING OBJECTIVE ❸

Apply the lower-of-cost-and-net-realizable-value rule to inventories—perpetual system

What accounting action should Westside Copiers take in this situation? Give any journal entry required. At what amount should Westside report Inventory on the balance sheet? At what amount should Westside report Cost of Goods Sold on the income statement? Discuss the accounting characteristic that is most relevant to this situation.

Are there circumstances that would allow Westside Copiers to increase the value of its inventory? Are there limits to which the value of inventory may be increased?

P6-68B Trans Canada Motors Ltd. and X Country Trucks Inc. are competitors. The companies reported the following amounts, in millions. In January 2014, you wish to make an investment in one of these companies. Results for 2013 are not yet available.

LEARNING OBJECTIVE ❹

Use gross profit percentage and inventory turnover to evaluate two leading companies

Trans Canada Motors Ltd.
Statement of Earnings

	Fiscal Years		
Amounts in millions	2012	2011	2010
Net sales	$84.2	$73.6	$68.9
Cost of sales	63.4	55.2	52.6
Selling, general, and administrative expenses	12.2	11.3	11.2

Trans Canada Motors Ltd.
Balance Sheet

Amounts in millions	Year-End 2012	Year-End 2011	Year-End 2010
Assets			
Cash and cash equivalents...	$11.3	$16.4	$13.9
Accounts receivable..	13.4	10.9	9.9
Inventories...	8.0	7.8	6.9

X Country Trucks Inc.
Statement of Operations

Amounts in millions	Fiscal Years 2012	Fiscal Years 2011	Fiscal Years 2010
Net sales	$24.0	$19.3	$13.9
Cost of sales...	15.9	13.7	9.9
Selling, general, and administrative expenses.............	3.0	2.4	1.9

X Country Trucks Inc.
Balance Sheet

Amounts in millions	Year-End 2012	Year-End 2011	Year-End 2010
Assets			
Cash and cash equivalents...	$9.4	$6.4	$3.5
Accounts receivable..	6.0	1.3	0.9
Inventories...	0.4	0.3	0.2

Requirements

1. Compute both companies' gross profit percentage and their rates of inventory turnover during 2012 and 2011.
2. Can you tell from these statistics which company should be more profitable in percentage terms? Why? What other important category of expenses do the gross profit percentage and the inventory turnover ratio fail to consider?

LEARNING OBJECTIVE ❺

Estimate inventory by the gross profit method; prepare the income statement

P6-69B Assume McMillan Tire Ltd. lost some inventory in a fire. To file an insurance claim, McMillan must estimate its ending inventory by the gross profit method. Assume that, for the past two years, McMillan's gross profit has averaged 40% of net sales. Suppose the company's inventory records reveal the following data at June 15, 2014, the date of the fire:

Inventory, January 1...	$1,200,000
Transactions during the year:	
Purchases..	6,500,000
Purchase discounts..	100,000
Purchase returns	10,000
Sales revenue	8,600,000
Sales returns	20,000

Requirements

1. Estimate the cost of the ending inventory lost in the fire using the gross profit method.
2. Prepare McMillan Tire Ltd.'s income statement through gross profit for the period up to the date of the fire. Date the statement "For the Period Up to the Fire." Show the detailed computations of cost of goods sold in a separate schedule.

P6-70B Margison Shoe Stores Ltd.'s income statement and balance sheet reported the following data. The owners are budgeting for 2014, and expect sales and cost of goods sold to increase by 10%. To meet customer demand, ending inventory will need to be $80,000 at December 31, 2014. The owners can lower operating expenses by $6,000 by doing some of the work themselves. They hope to earn a net income of $160,000 next year.

LEARNING OBJECTIVE 5

Determine the amount of inventory to purchase

Margison Shoe Stores Ltd.
Income Statement
For the Year Ended December 31, 2013

Sales	$960,000
Cost of goods sold	720,000
Gross profit	240,000
Operating expenses	110,000
Net income	$130,000

Margison Shoe Stores Ltd.
Balance Sheet
As at December 31, 2013

Assets		Liabilities and Equity	
Cash	$ 40,000	Accounts payable	$ 30,000
Inventories	70,000	Note payable	190,000
Land and		Total liabilities	220,000
buildings, net	270,000	Shareholders' equity	160,000
Total assets	$380,000	Total liabilities and equity	$380,000

Requirements

1. One of the most important decisions a business owner makes is the amount of inventory to purchase. Compute the amount of inventory to purchase in 2014.
2. Prepare the store's budgeted income statement for 2014 to reach the target net income of $160,000.

P6-71B The accounting records of Oriental Rugs show these data (in thousands).

As the auditor, you discovered that the ending inventory for 2012 was overstated by $100,000 and that the ending inventory for 2013 was understated by $50,000. The ending inventory at December 31, 2014, was correct.

LEARNING OBJECTIVE 6

Correct inventory errors over a three-year period

Oriental Rugs
Income Statements for the Years Ended

(Amounts in thousands)	2014	2013	2012
Net sales revenue	$1,400	$1,200	$1,100
Cost of goods sold:			
Beginning inventory	$ 400	$ 300	$200
Purchases	800	700	600
Goods available for sale	1,200	1,000	800
Less ending inventory	(500)	(400)	(300)
Cost of goods sold	700	600	500
Gross profit	700	600	600
Total operating expenses	500	430	450
Net income	$ 200	$ 170	$ 150

Requirements

1. Show correct income statements for each of the three years.
2. How much did these corrections add to, or take away from, Oriental Rugs' total net income over the three-year period? How did the corrections affect the trend of net income?

Apply Your Knowledge

Decision Cases

LEARNING OBJECTIVE ❶❷

Assess the impact of a year-end purchase of inventory—periodic system

Case 1. Duracraft Corporation is nearing the end of its first year of operations. Duracraft made inventory purchases of $926,000 during the year, as follows:

January	1,500 units	@	$120.00	=	$180,000
July	3,000		142.00		426,000
November	2,000		160.00		320,000
Totals	6,500				$926,000

Sales for the year are 6,000 units for $1,800,000 of revenue. Expenses other than cost of goods sold and income taxes total $425,000. The president of the company is undecided about whether to adopt the FIFO method or the weighted-average-cost method for inventories. The company uses the periodic inventory system. The income tax rate is 30%.

Requirements

1. To aid company decision making, prepare income statements under FIFO and under weighted-average cost.
2. Compare the net income under FIFO with net income under weighted-average cost. Which method produces the higher net income? What causes this difference? Be specific.

LEARNING OBJECTIVE ❷❸

Assess the impact of the inventory costing method on the financial statements

Case 2. The inventory costing method a company chooses can affect the financial statements and, thus, the decisions of the people who use those statements.

Requirements

1. Company A uses the weighted-average-cost inventory method and discloses this in notes to the financial statements. Company B uses the FIFO method to account for its inventory, but does not disclose which inventory method it uses. Company B reports a higher net income than Company A. In which company would you prefer to invest? Give your reason. Assume rising inventory costs.
2. The lower-of-cost-and-net-realizable-value rule is an accepted accounting concept. Would you want management to follow this rule in accounting for inventory if you were a shareholder or a creditor of a company? Give your reason.
3. Super Sports Company follows the lower-of-cost-and-net-realizable-value rule (LCNRV) and writes the value of its inventory of tents down to net realizable value, which has declined below cost. The following year, an unexpected camping craze results in a demand for tents that far exceeds supply, and the net realizable value increases above the previous cost. What effect will the LCNRV rule have on the income of Super Sports over the two years?

Ethical Issue

During 2013, Vanguard Inc. changed to the weighted-average-cost method of accounting for inventory. Suppose that during 2014, Vanguard changes back to the FIFO method, and the following year Vanguard switches back to weighted-average cost again.

Requirements

1. What would you think of a company's ethics if it changed accounting methods every year?
2. What accounting characteristic would changing methods every year violate?
3. Who can be harmed when a company changes its accounting methods too often? How?

Focus on Financials

TELUS CORPORATION

The notes are part of the financial statements. They give details that would clutter the statements. This case will help you learn to use a company's inventory notes. Refer to TELUS's statements and related notes in Appendix A at the end of the book and answer the following questions:

1. How much was TELUS's inventory at December 31, 2011? What about at December 31, 2010?
2. How does TELUS value its inventories? Which cost method does the company use?
3. Using the cost-of-goods-sold model, compute TELUS's purchase of inventory during the year ended December 31, 2011.
4. Did TELUS's gross profit percentage and rate of inventory turnover improve or deteriorate in 2011 (versus 2010)? Considering the overall effect of these two ratios, did TELUS improve during 2011? How did these factors affect the net income for 2011? (Hint: TELUS refers to COGS as "Goods and Services Purchased.")

LEARNING OBJECTIVE ❶❸❹

Analyze inventories

Focus on Analysis

TELUS CORPORATION

Refer to TELUS's financial statements in Appendix A at the end of the book to answer the following questions. Show amounts in millions.

1. Three important pieces of inventory information are (a) the cost of inventory on hand, (b) the cost of goods sold, and (c) the cost of inventory purchases. Identify or compute each of these items for TELUS at December 31, 2011. (Hint: TELUS refers to COGS as "Goods and Services Purchased.")
2. Which item in Requirement 1 is most directly related to cash flow? Why?
3. Assume that all inventory purchases were made on account, and that only inventory purchases increased Accounts Payable. Compute TELUS's cash payment for inventory during 2011.

Group Project

Obtain the annual reports of 10 companies, two from each of five different industries. Most companies' financial statements can be downloaded from their websites

1. Compute each company's gross profit percentage and rate of inventory turnover for the most recent two years. If annual reports are unavailable or do not provide enough data for multiple-year computations, you can gather financial statement data from the System for Electronic Document Analysis and Retrieval (SEDAR).
2. For the industries of the companies you are analyzing, obtain the industry averages for gross profit percentage and inventory turnover.
3. How well does each of your companies compare to the other company in its industry? How well do your companies compare to the average for their industry? What insight about your companies can you glean from these ratios?
4. Write a memo to summarize your findings, stating whether your group would invest in each of the companies it has analyzed.

LEARNING OBJECTIVE ❹

Compare companies' inventory turnover ratios

Quick Check Answers

1. *c*
2. *e*
3. *a*
4. *a* [(25 × $5) + (25 × $6) = $275]
5. *b* (10 × $7 + 5 × $6 = $100)
6. *a* [15 × ([$125 + $180 + $70] ÷ 65) = $86.54]
7. *c*
8. *c*
9. *b*
10. *c* ($124,000 − $64,000 = $60,000)
11. *d* ($10,000 + X − $20,000 = $130,000; X = $140,000)
12. *d* ($20,000 + $80,000 − $4,000 + $5,000 − $24,000 = $77,000)
13. *a* [($180,000 − $77,000)/$180,000 = 0.572]
14. *b* [$77,000 ÷ ($20,000 + $24,000)/2 = 3.5]
15. *d* [$60,000 + $180,000 − ($300,000 × [1 − 0.30]) = $30,000]
16. *b*

Property, Plant, and Equipment, and Intangible Assets

7

Andre Jenny Stock Connection Worldwide/Newscom

SPOTLIGHT

Have you ever gone to Canadian Tire to fill your car with gas? Ninety years ago, this company began operations by selling tires; today, Canadian Tire offers many products and services, including clothing, gas bars, and financial services. This Canadian company has grown substantially and has total assets worth over $12 billion.

Included in Canadian Tire's total assets are goodwill and intangible assets as well as property and equipment. A partial balance sheet along with the accompanying notes are presented on the following page. Let's begin by examining the various types of long-lived assets.

LEARNING OBJECTIVES

1 **Describe** the types of tangible and intangible assets a business may own

2 **Measure** and **account** for the cost of property, plant, and equipment

3 **Calculate** and **record** depreciation on property, plant, and equipment

4 **Explain** additional topics in accounting for long-lived tangible assets

5 **Account** for intangible assets

6 **Analyze** and **evaluate** a company's return on assets

7 **Interpret** tangible and intangible asset activities on the statement of cash flows

Canadian Tire
Partial Balance Sheet (adapted)
Long-Lived Assets

($ in millions)	As at Dec. 31, 2011	As at Jan. 1, 2011
Non-Current Assets		
Long-term receivables and other assets..	$ 705.7	$ 761.5
Long-term investments...	128.2	75.8
Goodwill and intangible assets (note 16)......................................	1,110.0	361.4
Investment property...	72.4	68.6
Property and equipment (note 18)	3,365.9	3,232.0

Note 16—Intangible assets:		Note 18—Property, Plant, and Equipment:	
Indefinite-life intangible assets:		Land	$ 748.8
Goodwill	$ 377.6	Buildings	1,574.8
Banners, label brands, trademarks, franchise agreements, etc.	380.9	Fixtures and equipment	280.4
		Leasehold improvements	496.0
Finite-life intangible assets:		Assets under finance lease	128.9
Customer relationships, private label brands, etc.	20.9	Construction in progress	137.0
Software	330.6	Total property, plant, and equipment	$3,365.9
Total goodwill and intangible assets	$1,110.0		

OBJECTIVE

❶ **Describe** the types of tangible and intangible assets a business may own

DESCRIBE THE TYPES OF TANGIBLE AND INTANGIBLE ASSETS A BUSINESS MAY OWN

Businesses use several types of assets that are classified as long-lived, such as property, plant, and equipment, and intangible assets. These assets are used in the business and are not held for sale.

Tangible long-lived assets are also called property, plant, and equipment. For example, buildings, airplanes, and equipment are tangible long-lived assets that do not last forever. Therefore, the cost of these assets must be expensed over their useful lives, and the expense associated with this is called depreciation. Of these assets, land is unique. Land is not expensed over time because its usefulness does not decrease. Many companies report tangible long-lived assets as property, plant, and equipment on the balance sheet. Canadian Tire calls them property and equipment. Looking at the partial balance sheet above, Canadian Tire owns $3,365.9 (million) in property and equipment. To find out what is included under this category, you need to read the notes that accompany the financial statements. These notes are used to explain the numbers reported. Reading Canadian Tire's Note 18 above reveals that these assets include land, buildings, fixtures, equipment, and leasehold improvements.

Intangible assets are useful because of the special rights they carry. They have no physical form. Patents, copyrights, and trademarks are intangible assets, as is goodwill. Accounting for intangibles, except goodwill, is similar to accounting for tangible long-lived assets. Canadian Tire has several intangible assets on its balance sheet, including goodwill. Reading Note 16 above indicates that Canadian Tire's intangible assets include items such as their store banners, trademarks, and franchise agreements.

Not all companies have both types of assets. For example, U-Haul, a subsidiary of Amerco, is a moving and storage company that owns land, buildings, equipment, rental trucks, and trailers, but does not own any intangible assets.

Asset Account (Balance Sheet)	Related Expense Account (Income Statement)
Tangible Long-Lived Assets	
Land	None
Buildings, machinery, and equipment	Depreciation
Furniture and fixtures	Depreciation
Computers	Depreciation
Intangible Assets	
Copyrights	Amortization
Patents	Amortization
Goodwill	Impairment losses

EXHIBIT 7-1
Long-Lived Asset and Related Expense Accounts

Accounting for long-lived tangible assets and intangibles has its own terminology. Different names apply to the individual assets and their corresponding expense accounts, as shown in Exhibit 7-1.

MEASURE AND ACCOUNT FOR THE COST OF PROPERTY, PLANT, AND EQUIPMENT

OBJECTIVE

❷ **Measure** and **account** for the cost of property, plant, and equipment

Here is a basic working rule for determining the cost of an asset:

The cost of any asset is the sum of all the costs incurred to bring the asset to its location and intended use. The cost of property, plant, and equipment includes its purchase price plus any taxes, commissions, and other amounts paid to make the asset ready for use. Because the specific costs differ for the various categories of property, plant, and equipment, we discuss the major groups individually.

Land

The cost of land includes its purchase price, real estate commission, survey fees, legal fees, and any back property taxes that the purchaser pays. Land cost also includes expenditures for grading and clearing the land and demolishing or removing unwanted buildings.

The cost of land does *not* include the cost of fencing, paving, sprinkler systems, and lighting. These are recorded in a separate account—called *land improvements*—and they are subject to depreciation.

Suppose Canadian Tire signs a $300,000 note payable to purchase 20 hectares of land for a new retail store. Canadian Tire also pays $10,000 for real estate commission, $8,000 of back taxes, $5,000 for removal of an old building, a $1,000 survey fee, and $260,000 to pave the parking lot—all in cash. What is Canadian Tire's cost of this land?

Purchase price of land		$300,000
Add related costs:		
Real estate commission	$10,000	
Back property tax	8,000	
Removal of building	5,000	
Survey fee	1,000	
Total related costs		24,000
Total cost of land		$324,000

Note that the cost to pave the parking lot, $260,000, is *not* included in the land's cost, because the pavement is a land improvement. Canadian Tire would record the purchase of this land as follows:

Land..	324,000	
Note Payable		300,000
Cash..		24,000
To record the purchase of land.		

ASSETS	=	LIABILITIES	+	SHAREHOLDERS' EQUITY
+324,000 −24,000	=	+300,000	+	0

The purchase increases both assets and liabilities. There is no effect on equity.

Buildings, Machinery, and Equipment

The cost of constructing a building includes architectural fees, building permits, contractors' charges, and payments for material, labour, and overhead. The company may also include as cost the interest on money borrowed to construct a building or buy machinery and equipment for the building until the point in time when the building, machinery, and equipment are ready for their intended use.

When an existing building (new or old) is purchased, its cost includes the purchase price, brokerage commission, sales and other taxes paid, and all expenditures to repair and renovate the building for its intended purpose.

The cost of machinery and equipment includes its purchase price plus transportation, insurance while in transit, non-refundable sales and other taxes, purchase commission, installation costs, and any expenditures to test the asset before it is placed in service. The equipment cost will also include the cost of any special platforms used to support the equipment. After the asset is up and running, insurance, taxes, and maintenance costs are recorded as expenses, not as part of the asset's cost.

Land Improvements and Leasehold Improvements

For the Canadian Tire building, the cost to pave a parking lot ($260,000) would be recorded in a separate account titled Land Improvements. This account includes costs for other items such as driveways, signs, fences, and sprinkler systems. Although these assets are located on the land, they are subject to decay, and their cost should therefore be depreciated.

An airline such as WestJet leases some of its airplanes and other assets. The company customizes these assets to meet its special needs. For example, WestJet paints its logo on airplanes. These improvements are assets of WestJet Airlines Ltd., even though the company does not own the airplane. The cost of improvements to leased assets may appear under Property, Plant, and Equipment, or Other Long-Term Assets. The cost of leasehold improvements should be depreciated over the term of the lease or the life of the asset, whichever is shorter.

Lump-Sum (or Basket) Purchases of Assets

Businesses often purchase several assets as a group, or in a "basket," for a single lump-sum amount. For example, Great-West Lifeco Inc. may pay one price for land and a building. The company must identify the cost of each asset. The total cost is divided among the assets according to their relative fair values.

Suppose Great-West purchases land and a building in St. John's, Newfoundland, for a sales office. The building sits on two hectares of land, and the combined purchase price of land and building is $2,800,000. An appraisal indicates that the land's fair value is $300,000 and that the building's fair value is $2,700,000.

Great-West first calculates the ratio of each asset's fair value to the total fair value. Total appraised value is $2,700,000 + $300,000 = $3,000,000. Thus, the land, valued at $300,000, is 10% of the total fair value. The building's appraised value is 90% of the total. These percentages are then used to determine the cost of each asset, as follows:

Asset	Fair Value		Total Fair Value		Percentage of Total Fair Value		Total Cost		Cost of Each Asset
Land	$ 300,000	÷	$3,000,000	=	10%	×	$2,800,000	=	$ 280,000
Building	2,700,000	÷	3,000,000	=	90	×	2,800,000	=	2,520,000
Total	$3,000,000				100%				$2,800,000

If Great-West pays cash, the entry to record the purchase of the land and building is:

Land..	280,000	
Building	2,520,000	
Cash..		2,800,000

ASSETS	=	LIABILITIES	+	SHAREHOLDERS' EQUITY
+ 280,000				
+2,520,000 =		0	+	0
−2,800,000				

Total assets don't change—merely the makeup of Great-West's assets.

> **STOP + THINK (7-1)**
>
> Why are land improvements and leasehold improvements depreciated?

Capital Expenditure Versus an Immediate Expense

When a company spends money on property, plant, and equipment, it must decide whether to record an asset or an expense. Examples of these expenditures range from WestJet Airlines' purchase of a flight simulator from CAE Electronics to replacing a tire on a plane.

Expenditures that increase the asset's productivity or extend its useful life are called **capital expenditures** (also called *betterments*). For example, the cost of a major overhaul that extends the useful life of a Canadian Tire truck is a capital expenditure. Capital expenditures are said to be *capitalized*, which means the cost is added to an asset account and not expensed immediately. A major decision in accounting for property, plant, and equipment is whether to capitalize or expense a certain cost.

Costs that do not extend the asset's productivity or its useful life, but merely maintain the asset or restore it to working order, are considered repairs and are recorded as expenses. The costs of repainting a Canadian Tire truck, repairing a dented fender, and replacing tires are also expensed immediately. Exhibit 7-2

Record an Asset for Capital Expenditures/Betterments	Record Repair and Maintenance Expense for an Expense
Extraordinary repairs:	*Ordinary repairs:*
Major engine overhaul	Repair of transmission or other mechanism
Modification of body for new use of van	Oil change, lubrication, and so on
Addition to storage capacity of van	Replacement tires, windshield, or a paint job

illustrates the distinction between capital expenditures and immediate expenses for van expenditures.

The distinction between a capital expenditure and an expense requires judgment: Does the expenditure extend the asset's productivity or its useful life? If so, capitalize it. If the cost merely repairs or maintains the asset or returns it to its prior condition, then record an expense.

Most companies expense all small costs, say, below $1,000. For higher costs, they follow the rule we gave above: they capitalize costs that extend the asset's usefulness or its useful life, and they expense all other costs. A conservative policy is one that avoids overstating assets and profits. A company that overstates its assets may get into trouble and have to defend itself in court. Whenever investors lose money because a company overstated its profits or its assets, the investors might file a lawsuit. The courts tend to be sympathetic to investor losses caused by shoddy accounting. The Cooking the Books scenario on the next page provides an example.

Accounting misstatements sometimes occur for asset costs. For example, a company may:

- Expense a cost that should have been capitalized. This error overstates expenses and understates net income in the year of the error.

- Capitalize a cost that should have been expensed. This error understates expenses and overstates net income in the year of the error.

CALCULATE AND RECORD DEPRECIATION ON PROPERTY, PLANT, AND EQUIPMENT

As we've seen in previous chapters, property, plant, and equipment are reported on the balance sheet at carrying amount, which is:

$$\text{Carrying amount of property, plant, and equipment} = \text{Cost} - \text{Accumulated depreciation}$$

Property, plant, and equipment wears out, grows obsolete, and loses value over time. To account for this process, we allocate an asset's cost to expense over its life—a process called **depreciation**. The depreciation process begins when an asset is available for use and continues until the asset is removed. In the private enterprise sector, it is referred to as amortization. Recall that depreciation expense (not accumulated depreciation) is reported on the income statement.

Only land has an unlimited life and is not depreciated for accounting purposes. Most property, plant, and equipment have limited lives because of:

- **Physical wear and tear.** For example, physical deterioration takes its toll on the usefulness of WestJet's airplanes, vehicles, and buildings.

- **Obsolescence**. Computers and other electronic equipment may be *obsolete* before they deteriorate. An asset is obsolete when another asset can do the job more efficiently. An asset's useful life may be shorter than its physical life. WestJet and other companies depreciate their computers over a short period of time—perhaps four years—even though the computers will remain in working condition much longer.

COOKING THE BOOKS
BY IMPROPER CAPITALIZATION

WORLDCOM

It is one thing to accidentally capitalize a plant asset, but quite another to do it intentionally, thus deliberately overstating assets, understating expenses, and overstating net income. One well-known company committed one of the biggest financial statement frauds in U.S. history in this way.

In 2002, WorldCom, Inc., was one of the largest telecommunications service providers in the world. The company had grown rapidly from a small, regional telephone company in 1983 to a giant corporation in 2002 by acquiring an ever-increasing number of other such companies. But 2002 was a bad year for WorldCom, as well as for many others in the telecom industry. The United States was reeling from the effects of a deep economic recession spawned by the "bursting dot-com bubble" in 2000 and intensified by the terrorist attacks on U.S. soil in 2001. Wall Street was looking high and low for positive signs, pressuring public companies to keep profits trending upward in order to support share prices (without much success, at least for the honest companies).

Bernard J. ("Bernie") Ebbers, WorldCom's chief executive officer, was worried. He began to press his chief financial officer, Scott Sullivan, to find a way to make the company's income statement look healthier. After all legitimate attempts to improve earnings failed, Sullivan concocted a scheme to cook the books.

Like all telecommunications companies, WorldCom had signed contracts with other telephone companies, paying them fees so that WorldCom customers could use their lines for telephone calls and Internet usage. GAAP require such fees to be expensed as incurred, rather than capitalized. Overestimating the growth of its business, WorldCom had incurred billions of dollars in such costs, about 15% more than its customers would ever use.

In direct violation of GAAP, Sullivan rationalized that the excessive amounts WorldCom had spent on line costs would eventually lead to the company's recognizing revenue in future years (thus extending their usefulness and justifying, in his mind, their classification as assets). Sullivan directed the accountants working under him to reclassify line costs as property, plant, and equipment assets, rather than as expenses, and to amortize (spread) the costs over several years rather than to expense them in the periods in which they were incurred. Over several quarters, Mr. Sullivan and his assistants transferred a total of $3.1 billion in such charges from operating expense accounts to property, plant, and equipment, resulting in the transformation of what would have been a net loss for all of 2001 and the first quarter of 2002 into a sizable profit. It was the largest single fraud in U.S. history to that point.

Sullivan's fraudulent scheme was discovered by the company's internal audit staff during a routine spot-check of the company's records for capital expenditures. The staff members reported Sullivan's (and his staff's) fraudulent activities to the head of the company's audit committee and its external auditor, setting in motion a chain of events that resulted in Ebbers' and Sullivan's firing, and the company's eventual bankruptcy. Ebbers, Sullivan, and several of their assistants went to prison for their participation in this fraudulent scheme.

Shareholders of WorldCom lost billions of dollars in share value when the company went down, and more than 500,000 people lost their jobs. The WorldCom scandal also rocked the financial world, causing global stock markets to plummet from lack of confidence.

Suppose WestJet buys a computer for use in scheduling flight crews. WestJet believes it will get four years of service from the computer, which will then be worthless. Under straight-line depreciation, WestJet expenses one-quarter of the asset's cost in each of its four years of use.

You've just seen what depreciation accounting is. Let's see what it is *not*.

1. **Depreciation is not a process of valuation.** Businesses do not record depreciation based on changes in the fair value of their property, plant, and equipment. Instead, businesses allocate the asset's cost to the periods of its useful life based on a specific depreciation method.

2. **Depreciation does not mean setting aside cash to replace assets as they wear out.** Any cash fund is entirely separate from depreciation.

How to Measure Depreciation

To measure depreciation for property, plant, and equipment, we must know its:

1. Cost

2. Estimated useful life

3. Estimated residual value

We have already discussed cost, which is a known amount. The other two factors must be estimated.

Estimated useful life is the length of service expected from using the asset. Useful life may be expressed in years, units of output, kilometres, or some other measure. For example, the useful life of a building is stated in years. The useful life of a WestJet airplane or van may be expressed as the total number of kilometres the aircraft or vehicle is expected to travel. Companies base such estimates on past experience and information from industry and government publications.

Estimated residual value—also called *scrap value* or *salvage value*—is the expected cash value of an asset at the end of its useful life. For example, WestJet may believe that a baggage-handling machine will be useful for seven years. After that time, WestJet may expect to sell the machine as scrap metal. The amount WestJet believes it can get for the machine is the estimated residual value. In computing depreciation, the asset's estimated residual value is *not* depreciated because WestJet expects to receive this amount from selling the asset. If there's no expected residual value, the full cost of the asset is depreciated. An asset's **depreciable cost** is measured as follows:

$$\text{Depreciable cost} = \text{Asset's cost} - \text{Estimated residual value}$$

Depreciation Methods

There are three main depreciation methods that will be discussed in this text:

- Straight-line

- Units-of-production

- Diminishing-balance—an accelerated depreciation method

These methods allocate different amounts of depreciation to each period. However, they all result in the same total amount of depreciation, which is the asset's depreciable cost. Exhibit 7-3 presents assumed data, which we will use to illustrate depreciation computations for a Canadian Tire van.

Data Item	Amount
Cost of van, January 1, 2014...	$41,000
Less estimated residual value..	(1,000)
Depreciable cost..	$40,000
Estimated useful life:	
Years..	5 years
Units of production..	100,000 units [kilometres]

EXHIBIT 7-3
Data for Depreciation Computations— A Canadian Tire Van

STRAIGHT-LINE METHOD. In the **straight-line (SL) method**, an equal amount of depreciation is assigned to each year (or period) of asset use. Depreciable cost is divided by useful life in years to determine the annual depreciation expense. Applied to the Canadian Tire van data from Exhibit 7-3, straight-line depreciation is:

$$\text{Straight-line depreciation per year} = \frac{\text{Cost} - \text{Residual value}}{\text{Useful life, in years}}$$

$$= \frac{\$41,000 - \$1,000}{5}$$

$$= \$8,000$$

The entry to record depreciation is:

Depreciation Expense......................................	8,000	
Accumulated Depreciation		8,000

ASSETS	=	LIABILITIES	+	SHAREHOLDERS' EQUITY
−8,000	=	0		−8,000 Expenses

Observe that depreciation decreases the asset (through Accumulated Depreciation) and also decreases equity (through Depreciation Expense). Let's assume that Canadian Tire purchased this van on January 1, 2014; Canadian Tire's fiscal year ends on December 31. Exhibit 7-4 gives a *straight-line depreciation schedule* for the van. The final column of the exhibit shows the *asset's carrying amount*, which is its cost less accumulated depreciation.

As an asset is used in operations, accumulated depreciation increases, and the carrying amount of the asset decreases. An asset's final carrying amount is its *residual value* ($1,000 in Exhibit 7-4). At the end of its useful life, the asset is said to be *fully depreciated*.

EXHIBIT 7-4
Straight-Line Depreciation Schedule for a Canadian Tire Van

Date	Asset Cost	Depreciation for the Year			Accumulated Depreciation	Asset Carrying Amount
		Depreciation Rate	Depreciation Cost	Depreciation Expense		
01-01-2014	$41,000					$41,000
31-12-2014		0.20* ×	$40,000 =	$8,000	$ 8,000	33,000
31-12-2015		0.20 ×	40,000 =	8,000	16,000	25,000
31-12-2016		0.20 ×	40,000 =	8,000	24,000	17,000
31-12-2017		0.20 ×	40,000 =	8,000	32,000	9,000
31-12-2018		0.20 ×	40,000 =	8,000	40,000	1,000

$*\dfrac{1}{5 \text{ Years}} = 0.20 \text{ per year}$

STOP + THINK (7-2)

Imagine a company purchased a machine for $13,000 that had a useful life of five years and residual value of $3,000. If the asset's carrying amount was $7,000, how many more years of use would the machine have?

UNITS-OF-PRODUCTION METHOD. In the **units-of-production (UOP) method**, a fixed amount of depreciation is assigned to each *unit of output*, or service, produced by the asset. Depreciable cost is divided by useful life—in units of production—to determine this amount. This per-unit depreciation expense is then multiplied by the number of units produced each period to compute depreciation. The units-of-production depreciation for the Canadian Tire van data in Exhibit 7-3 is:

$$\frac{\text{Units-of-production}}{\text{depreciation per unit of output}} = \frac{\text{Cost} - \text{Residual value}}{\text{Useful life, in units of production}}$$

$$= \frac{\$41,000 - \$1,000}{100,000 \text{ km}} = \$0.40/\text{km}$$

Assume that the van is driven 20,000 km during the first year, 30,000 during the second, 25,000 during the third, 15,000 during the fourth, and 10,000 during the fifth. Exhibit 7-5 shows the UOP depreciation schedule.

The amount of UOP depreciation varies with the number of units the asset produces. In our example, the total number of units produced is 100,000. UOP depreciation does not depend directly on time, as do the other methods.

DIMINISHING-BALANCE METHOD. An **accelerated depreciation method** writes off a larger amount of the asset's cost near the start of its useful life than the straight-line method does. Double-diminishing-balance is the main accelerated depreciation

EXHIBIT 7-5
Units-of-Production Depreciation Schedule for a Canadian Tire Van

| Date | Asset Cost | Depreciation for the Year | | | | Accumulated Depreciation | Asset Carrying Amount |
		Depreciation Rate	Number of Units		Depreciation Expense		
01-01-2014	$41,000						$41,000
31-12-2014		$0.40*	×	20,000	=	$ 8,000	$ 8,000	33,000
31-12-2015		0.40	×	30,000	=	12,000	20,000	21,000
31-12-2016		0.40	×	25,000	=	10,000	30,000	11,000
31-12-2017		0.40	×	15,000	=	6,000	36,000	5,000
31-12-2018		0.40	×	10,000	=	4,000	40,000	1,000

*($41,000 − $1,000)/100,000 km = $0.40/km.

method. The **double-diminishing-balance (DDB) method** computes annual depreciation by multiplying the asset's declining carrying amount by a constant percentage, which is two times the straight-line depreciation rate. Double-diminishing-balance amounts are computed as follows:

- *First*, compute the straight-line depreciation rate per year. A 5-year asset has a straight-line depreciation rate of 1/5, or 20% each year. A 10-year asset has a straight-line rate of 1/10, or 10%, and so on.

- *Second*, multiply the straight-line rate by 2 to compute the DDB rate. For a 5-year asset, the DDB rate is 40% (20% × 2). A 10-year asset has a DDB rate of 20% (10% × 2).

- *Third*, multiply the DDB rate by the period's beginning asset carrying amount (cost less accumulated depreciation). Under the DDB method, ignore the residual value of the asset in computing depreciation, except during the last year. The DDB rate for the Canadian Tire van in Exhibit 7-3 (page 329) is:

$$\text{DDB depreciation rate per year} = \frac{1}{\text{Useful life, in years}} \times 2$$

$$= \frac{1}{5 \text{ years}} \times 2$$

$$= 20\% \times 2$$

$$= 40\%$$

- *Fourth,* determine the final year's depreciation amount—that is, the amount needed to reduce the asset carrying amount to its residual value. In Exhibit 7-6, the fifth and final year's DDB depreciation is $4,314: the carrying amount of $5,314 less the $1,000 residual value. *The residual value should not be depreciated* but should remain on the books until the asset is disposed of.

The DDB method differs from the other methods in two ways:

1. Residual value is ignored initially; in the first year, depreciation is computed on the asset's full cost.

2. Depreciation expense in the final year is whatever amount is needed to reduce the asset's carrying amount to its residual value.

EXHIBIT 7-6
Double-Diminishing-Balance Depreciation Schedule for a Canadian Tire Van

Date	Asset Cost	DDB Rate		Asset Carrying Amount		Depreciation Expense	Accumulated Depreciation	Asset Carrying Amount
				Depreciation for the Year				
01-01-2014	$41,000							$41,000
31-12-2014		0.40	×	$41,000	=	$16,400	$16,400	24,600
31-12-2015		0.40	×	24,600	=	9,840	26,240	14,760
31-12-2016		0.40	×	14,760	=	5,904	32,144	8,856
31-12-2017		0.40	×	8,856	=	3,542	35,686	5,314
31-12-2018						4,314*	40,000	1,000

*Last-year depreciation is the amount needed to reduce the asset's carrying amount to the residual value ($5,314 − $1,000 = $4,314).

STOP + THINK (7-3) Using the company data described in the Stop + Think 7-2 on page 329, what would you expect DDB depreciation to be for each year?

Comparing Depreciation Methods

Let's compare the three methods in terms of the yearly amount of depreciation. The yearly amount of depreciation varies by method, but the total $40,000 depreciable cost is the same under all methods.

	Amount of Depreciation Per Year		
Year	Straight-Line	Units-of-Production	Accelerated Method Double-Diminishing-Balance
1	$ 8,000	$ 8,000	$16,400
2	8,000	12,000	9,840
3	8,000	10,000	5,904
4	8,000	6,000	3,542
5	8,000	4,000	4,314
Total	$40,000	$40,000	$40,000

IFRS directs a business to choose a depreciation method that reflects the pattern in which the asset will be used. For an asset that generates revenue evenly over time, the straight-line method best meets this criterion. The units-of-production method best fits those assets that wear out because of physical use rather than obsolescence. The accelerated method (DDB) applies best to assets that generate greater amounts of revenue earlier in their useful lives and less in later years.

Exhibit 7-7 graphs annual depreciation amounts for the straight-line, units-of-production, and accelerated (DDB) methods. The graph of straight-line depreciation is flat through time because annual depreciation is the same in all periods. Units-of-production depreciation follows no particular pattern because annual depreciation depends on the use of the asset. Accelerated depreciation is greatest in the first year and less in the later years.

Recent surveys of companies in Canada and the United States indicate that straight-line depreciation is used by more than 80% of them. Around 10% of companies use some form of accelerated depreciation, and the rest use units of production and other methods. Many companies use more than one method.

EXHIBIT 7-7
Depreciation Patterns Through Time

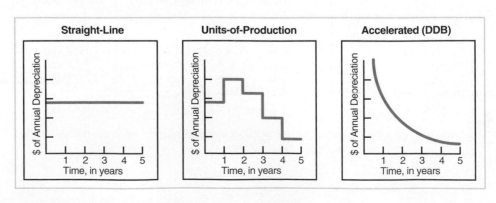

MID-CHAPTER SUMMARY PROBLEM

Suppose you are a manager at Canadian Tire. The company purchased equipment on January 1, 2014, for $44,000. The expected useful life of the equipment is 10 years or 100,000 units of production, and its residual value is $4,000. Under three depreciation methods, the annual depreciation expense and the balance of accumulated depreciation at the end of 2014 and 2015 are as follows:

| | Method A | | Method B | | Method C | |
| | Annual Depreciation Expense | Accumulated Depreciation | Annual Depreciation Expense | Accumulated Depreciation | Annual Depreciation Expense | Accumulated Depreciation |
Year						
2014	$4,000	$4,000	$8,800	$ 8,800	$1,200	$1,200
2015	4,000	8,000	7,040	15,840	5,600	6,800

Requirements

1. Your assistant has provided you with the above information. Identify the depreciation method used in each instance, and show the equation and computation for each. (Round to the nearest dollar.)
2. Assume continued use of the same method through the year 2016. Determine the annual depreciation expense, accumulated depreciation, and carrying amount of the equipment for 2014 through 2016 under each method, assuming 12,000 units of production in 2016.
3. How does a manager decide which method to use to depreciate their property, plant, and equipment?

Name: Canadian Tire
Industry: Retailer
Accounting Period: The years 2014, 2015, 2016

ANSWERS

Requirement 1

The straight-line method assigns the same depreciation expense to each year.

Method A: Straight-Line

$$\text{Depreciable cost} = \$40,000 \ (\$44,000 - \$4,000)$$
$$\text{Each year: } \$40,000/10 \text{ years} = \$4,000$$

Method B: Double-Diminishing-Balance

$$\text{Rate} = \frac{1}{10 \text{ years}} \times 2 = 10\% \times 2 = 20\%$$

2014: 0.20 × $44,000 = $8,800
2015: 0.20 × ($44,000 − $8,800) = $7,040

The double-diminishing-balance method assigns an expense amount that gets smaller every year. Do not include the residual value when using this method.

Method C: Units-of-Production

$$\text{Depreciation per unit} = \frac{\$44,000 - \$4,000}{100,000 \text{ units}} = \$0.40/\text{unit}$$

2014: $1,200 ÷ $0.40 = 3,000 units
2015: $5,600 ÷ $0.40 = 14,000 units

With the units-of-production method, there is a direct correlation to the number of units produced.

Subtract the residual value from the original cost. Calculate the depreciation per unit. Then divide the annual depreciation expense by the unit cost to determine the number of units produced each year.

Requirement 2

Use the same $4,000 annual depreciation expense used for the prior years.

Method A: Straight-Line

Year	Annual Depreciation Expense	Accumulated Depreciation	Carrying Amount
Start			$44,000
2014	$4,000	$ 4,000	40,000
2015	4,000	8,000	36,000
2016	4,000	12,000	32,000

The depreciation expense is calculated as 20% of the prior year's carrying amount.

Method B: Double-Diminishing-Balance

Year	Annual Depreciation Expense	Accumulated Depreciation	Carrying Amount
Start			$44,000
2014	$8,800	$ 8,800	35,200
2015	7,040	15,840	28,160
2016	5,632	21,472	22,528

Use the same $0.40 per unit amount used for the prior years. Multiply by the number of units produced during 2016.

Method C: Units-of-Production

Year	Annual Depreciation Expense	Accumulated Depreciation	Carrying Amount
Start			$44,000
2014	$1,200	$ 1,200	42,800
2015	5,600	6,800	37,200
2016	4,800	11,600	32,400

Computations for 2016

Straight-line	$40,000/10 years = $4,000
Double-diminishing-balance	0.20 × $28,160 = $5,632
Units-of-production	$0.40 × 12,000 units = $4,800

Requirement 3

Managers choose the method that best reflects the way in which the asset is used up. For example, buildings normally wear out over time, so the straight-line depreciation method might be used. Equipment that produces units would wear out after continued use, so the units of production might be the best method. Diminishing balance might be used for computer equipment because of new technology advancements.

EXPLAIN ADDITIONAL TOPICS IN ACCOUNTING FOR LONG-LIVED TANGIBLE ASSETS

OBJECTIVE

❹ **Explain** additional topics in accounting for long-lived tangible assets

Depreciation for Partial Years

Companies purchase property, plant, and equipment whenever they need them. They do not wait until the beginning of a year or a month. Therefore, companies must compute *depreciation for partial years*. Suppose the County Line Bar-B-Q restaurant in Edmonton purchases a building on April 1 for $500,000. The building's estimated life is 20 years, and its estimated residual value is $80,000. The restaurant's fiscal year ends on December 31. Let's consider how the company computes depreciation for April through December:

- First compute depreciation for a full year.
- Then multiply the full year's depreciation by the fraction of the year that the company held the asset.

Assuming the straight-line method, the year's depreciation for County Line's building is $15,750, as follows:

$$\text{Full-year depreciation} = \frac{\$500,000 - \$80,000}{20} = \$21,000$$

Partial-year depreciation: $21,000 \times 9/12 = \$15,750$

What if County Line bought the asset on April 18? Many businesses record no monthly depreciation on assets purchased after the 15th of the month, and they record a full month's depreciation on an asset bought on or before the 15th.

Most companies use computerized systems to account for property, plant, and equipment. Each asset has a unique identification number that links to the asset's cost, estimated life, residual value, and depreciation method. The system will automatically calculate the depreciation expense for each period. Accumulated Depreciation is automatically updated.

Changing the Useful Life of a Depreciable Asset

Managers must decide on an asset's useful life to compute its depreciation. After an asset is put into use, managers may refine their estimate on the basis of experience and new information. Such a change in accounting estimate is very rare in Canada.

An example from the United States is illustrative. The Walt Disney Company made such a change, called a *change in accounting estimate*. Disney recalculated depreciation on the basis of revised useful lives of several of its theme park assets. The following note in Walt Disney's financial statements reports this change in accounting estimate:

> *Note 5*
>
> . . . [T]he Company extended the estimated useful lives of certain theme park ride and attraction assets based upon historical data and engineering studies. The effect of this change was to decrease [depreciation] by approximately $8 million (an increase in net income of approximately $4.2 million . . .).

Assume that a Disney hot-dog stand cost $40,000 and that the company originally believed the asset had an eight-year useful life with no residual value. Using the straight-line method, the company would record $5,000 depreciation each year

($40,000/8 years = $5,000). Suppose Disney used the asset for two years. Accumulated depreciation reached $10,000, leaving a remaining depreciable carrying amount (cost *less* accumulated depreciation *less* residual value) of $30,000 ($40,000 − $10,000). From its experience, management believes the asset will remain useful for an additional 10 years. The company would spread the remaining depreciable carrying amount over the asset's remaining life as follows:

$$\begin{array}{ccccc} \text{Asset's remaining} & & \text{(New) Estimated} & & \text{(New) Annual} \\ \text{depreciable carrying amount} & \div & \text{useful life remaining} & = & \text{depreciation} \\ \$30,000 & \div & 10 \text{ years} & = & \$3,000 \end{array}$$

The yearly depreciation entry based on the new estimated useful life is:

Depreciation Expense—Hot-Dog Stand.........................	3,000	
Accumulated Depreciation—Hot-Dog Stand		3,000

ASSETS	=	LIABILITIES	+	SHAREHOLDERS' EQUITY
−3,000	=	0		−3,000 Expenses

STOP + THINK (7-4)

1. Suppose a company was having a bad year—net income was well below expectations and lower than last year's income. For depreciation purposes, the company extended the estimated useful lives of its depreciable assets. How would this accounting change affect the company's (a) depreciation expense, (b) net income, and (c) owners' equity?

2. Suppose that the company's accounting change turned a loss year into a profitable year. Without

the accounting change, the company would have reported a net loss for the year. The accounting change enabled the company to report net income. Under IFRS, the company's annual report must disclose the accounting change and its effect on net income. Would investors evaluate the company as better or worse for having made this accounting change?

Fully Depreciated Assets

A *fully depreciated asset* is an asset that has reached the end of its estimated useful life. Suppose Canadian Tire has fully depreciated equipment with zero residual value (cost was $40,000). Canadian Tire's accounts will appear as follows:

Equipment		Accumulated Depreciation	
40,000			40,000

The equipment's carrying amount is zero, but that doesn't mean the equipment is worthless. Canadian Tire may continue using the equipment for a few more years but will not take any more depreciation.

When Canadian Tire disposes of the equipment, it will remove both the asset's cost ($40,000) and its accumulated depreciation ($40,000) from the books. The next section shows how to account for disposals of property, plant, and equipment.

Derecognition of Property, Plant, and Equipment

Derecognition is a term IFRS uses to refer to property, plant, and equipment that is either no longer useful or has been sold. When this occurs, the related accounts are removed from the company's books and a gain or loss is recorded.

Eventually, property, plant, and equipment cease to serve a company's needs. The asset may wear out, become obsolete, or for some other reason cease to be useful. Before accounting for the disposal of the asset, the business should bring depreciation up to date to:

- Record the expense up to the date of sale
- Measure the asset's final carrying amount

To account for disposal, the asset and its related accumulated depreciation are removed from the books. Suppose the final year's depreciation expense has just been recorded to fully depreciate a machine that cost $50,000 and is estimated to have zero residual value. The machine's accumulated depreciation thus totals $50,000. Assuming that this asset is disposed of, not sold, the entry to record its disposal is:

Accumulated Depreciation—Machinery	50,000	
Machinery		50,000
To dispose of a fully depreciated machine.		

ASSETS	=	LIABILITIES	+	SHAREHOLDERS' EQUITY
+50,000 −50,000	=	0	+	0

There is no gain or loss on this disposal, so there is no effect on equity.

If assets are "junked" before being fully depreciated, the company incurs a loss on the disposal. Suppose M&M Meat Shops disposes of store fixtures that cost $4,000. Accumulated depreciation is $3,000, and the carrying amount is, therefore, $1,000. Junking these store fixtures results in a loss as follows:

Accumulated Depreciation—Store Fixtures	3,000	
Loss on Disposal of Store Fixtures	1,000	
Store Fixtures		4,000
To dispose of store fixtures.		

ASSETS	=	LIABILITIES	+	SHAREHOLDERS' EQUITY
+3,000 −4,000	=	0	+	−1,000 Loss

M&M Meat Shops got rid of an asset with a $1,000 carrying amount and received nothing. The result is a $1,000 loss, which decreases both total assets and equity.

The Loss on Disposal of Store Fixtures is reported as Other Income (Expense) on the income statement. Losses decrease net income exactly as expenses do. Gains increase net income in the same manner as revenues.

SELLING PROPERTY, PLANT, AND EQUIPMENT. Suppose M&M Meat Shops sells fixtures on September 30, 2014, that cost $10,000 when purchased on January 1, 2011, and have been depreciated on a straight-line basis. M&M Meat Shops originally estimated a 10-year useful life and no residual value. Prior to recording the sale, the M&M Meat Shops accountants must update the asset's depreciation. Suppose the business uses the calendar year as its accounting period. Partial-year depreciation must be recorded for the asset's expense from January 1, 2014, to the sale date. The straight-line depreciation entry at September 30, 2014, is:

Sept. 30	Depreciation Expense ($10,000/10 years × 9/12)	750	
	Accumulated Depreciation—Fixtures..................................		750
	To update depreciation.		

The Fixtures account and the Accumulated Depreciation—Fixtures account appear as follows. Observe that the fixtures' carrying amount is $6,250 ($10,000 − $3,750).

Fixtures		Accumulated Depreciation—Fixtures	
Jan. 1, 2011 10,000		Dec. 31, 2011	1,000
		Dec. 31, 2012	1,000
		Dec. 31, 2013	1,000
		Sep. 30, 2014	750
		Balance	3,750

Suppose M&M Meat Shops sells the fixtures for $7,000 cash. The gain on the sale is $750, determined as follows:

Cash received from sale of the asset..		$7,000
Carrying amount of asset sold:		
Cost...	$10,000	
Less accumulated depreciation	(3,750)	6,250
Gain on sale of the asset		$ 750

The entry to record the sale of the fixtures for $7,000 cash is:

Sept. 30	Cash	7,000	
	Accumulated Depreciation—Fixtures	3,750	
	Gain on Sale of Fixtures..		750
	Fixtures..		10,000
	To sell fixtures.		

ASSETS	=	LIABILITIES	+	SHAREHOLDERS' EQUITY
+ 7,000				
+ 3,750	=	0		+750 Gain
−10,000				

Gains are recorded as credits, in the same manner as revenues; losses are recorded as debits, in the same manner as expenses. Gains and losses on asset disposals appear on the income statement as other income (expense).

STOP + THINK (7-5)

Suppose you are reviewing WestJet Airlines's comparative income statement for 2014 and 2013 and notice these items (amounts assumed):

	(in millions)	
	2014	2013
Net revenues..	$1,600	$1,300
Income from operations..	150	165
Other income (expense)		
Gain on sale of maintenance building	20	
Income before income taxes...	$ 170	$ 165

Which would you decide was a better year for WestJet, 2014 or 2013?

Using T-Accounts to Analyze Property, Plant, and Equipment Transactions

You can perform quite a bit of analysis if you know how transactions affect the property, plant, and equipment accounts. The following are some of these accounts with descriptions of the activity in each.

Building (or Equipment)	
Beginning balance	
Cost of assets purchased	Cost of assets disposed of
Ending balance	

Accumulated Depreciation	
Accum. depreciation of assets	Beginning balance
	Depreciation expense for the current period
	Ending balance

Depreciation Expense	
Depreciation expense for the current period	

Gain on Sale of Building (or Equipment)	
	Gain on sale

Loss on Sale of Building (or Equipment)	
Loss on sale	

Example: Suppose you started the year with buildings that cost $100,000. During the year you bought another building for $150,000 and ended the year with buildings that cost $180,000. What was the cost of the building you sold?

Building			
Beginning balance	100,000		
Cost of assets purchased	150,000	Cost of assets sold	? = $70,000
Ending balance	180,000		

You can perform similar analyses to answer other interesting questions about what the business did during the period.

Special Issues in Accounting for Property, Plant, and Equipment

Long-lived assets such as property, plant, and equipment are complex because:

- Depreciation affects income taxes
- Significant components of property, plant, and equipment should be depreciated separately
- Assets should be tested regularly for impairment
- The revaluation method could be used to measure property, plant, and equipment assets

Depreciation for Tax Purposes

Many businesses use the straight-line method for reporting property, plant, and equipment on the balance sheet and depreciation expense on the income statement. However, for income tax purposes, they also keep a separate set of depreciation records. The *Income Tax Act* requires taxpayers to use accelerated and sometimes straight-line depreciation (up to specified capital cost allowance [CCA] maximums) for tax purposes. In other words, a taxpayer may use one method of depreciation for accounting purposes and another method for tax purposes.

Depreciating Significant Components

IFRS require that significant components of an item of property, plant, and equipment be depreciated separately. What does this mean? Take, for example, Air Canada or WestJet, which buy aircraft for use in their operations. Air Canada depreciates their aircraft and engines over 20-25 years, while the cabin and interior equipment are depreciated over the lesser of 5 years or the remaining useful life of the aircraft. Under ASPE, depreciating separate components is done only when practicable.

Impairment

At each reporting date, a company should review its property, plant, and equipment to see if an asset is impaired. Impairment occurs when the carrying amount exceeds its recoverable amount. Recoverable amount is determined to be the higher of an asset's fair value (less costs to sell) and its value in use. Value in use is the present value of estimated future cash flows expected to be earned from the continuing use of an asset and from its disposal at the end of its useful life.

Impairment may be caused by many factors, including obsolescence, physical damage, and loss in market value. The journal entry to record impairment is:

Loss on Impairment	XXX	
Accumulated Deprecation..		XXX

If the situation changes, IFRS do permit a company to reverse the impairment loss by writing the asset up to its carrying amount. The accounting standards for private enterprises require a company to review its property, plant, and equipment only when impairment is suspected. No reversal of the write-off is allowed.

In a note to its financial statements, Air Canada states that for its property, plant, and equipment,

> Assets that are subject to depreciation are reviewed for impairment whenever events or changes in circumstances indicate that the carrying amount may not be recoverable. An impairment test is performed by comparing the carrying amount of the asset or group of assets to their recoverable amount.

Revaluation Model

Throughout this chapter, we have shown you what IFRS refers to as the cost model. This means that a company measures property, plant, and equipment at cost less any accumulated depreciation less any accumulated impairment losses.

Another method a company could choose to measure property, plant, and equipment is called the revaluation model. Under this method, an asset would be recorded at cost when purchased but subsequently measured at its fair value less any accumulated depreciation less any accumulated impairment losses. Fair value is the price at which the asset could be sold, and a professional valuator would do this revaluation regularly. It may be revalued at year-end or when the company believes a change in the asset value has taken place. With every new change in the asset account, depreciation has to be revised accordingly based on the new carrying amount. To keep the example simple, depreciation is ignored, as this topic is discussed in greater detail in an intermediate accounting course.

Example: A company chooses to use the revaluation method for a building that was bought for $1.8 million and is being depreciated over 25 years, with no residual value. Subsequently, if the appraised value is $2 million, the increase of $200,000 will be recognized through equity by the following journal entry:

| Building | 200,000 | |
| Revaluation surplus | | 200,000 |

Revaluation Surplus is an equity account that is reported as other comprehensive income. Only the cost model is used under ASPE.

◄ DECISION GUIDELINES ►

USING PROPERTY, PLANT, AND EQUIPMENT AND RELATED EXPENSES IN DECISION MAKING

Companies must make decisions about how to account for property, plant, and equipment. Let's look at some ways property, plant, and equipment are used in decision making.

Decision	Guidelines
Capitalize or expense a cost?	*Managers*
(a) New asset	Capitalize all costs that bring the asset to its intended use, including asset purchase price, transportation charges, and taxes paid to acquire the asset.
(b) Existing asset	Capitalize only those costs that add to the asset's productivity or to its useful life.
	Expense all other costs as maintenance or repairs.
Which depreciation method to use?	*Managers*
	Use the method that best allocates the cost of an asset through depreciation expense against the revenues produced by the asset. As discussed earlier, each method will produce varying amounts of depreciation expense each year, but overall, they will result in the same total amount of depreciation. If the asset generates revenue evenly over time, the straight-line method is best; if it wears out through physical use, the units-of-production method should be used; if greater revenue is generated earlier in the asset's useful life, then diminishing-balance is the method to use.
	Investors and Creditors
	Both investors and creditors read the notes to the financial statements to see which depreciation methods management used. Why do they do this? As we have already seen, the depreciation method chosen affects both the income statement and the balance sheet. Remember, if management chooses to use the straight-line method, then depreciation expense will be the same amount each year. However, if the double-diminishing balance is used, then depreciation expense is highest in the early years of the asset's life, causing net income to be lower. This information is useful when comparing companies using different depreciation methods.

OBJECTIVE

❺ **Account** for intangible assets

ACCOUNT FOR INTANGIBLE ASSETS

As we saw earlier, *intangible assets* are long-lived assets with no physical form. Intangibles are valuable because they carry special rights from patents, copyrights, trademarks, franchises, and goodwill. Like buildings and equipment, an intangible asset is recorded at its acquisition cost. Intangibles are often the most valuable assets of high-tech companies and other companies that depend on research and development. The residual value of most intangibles is zero.

Intangible assets fall into two categories:

- Intangibles with *finite lives* that can be measured. We record **amortization** for these intangibles. Amortization is usually computed on a straight-line basis, but one of the other methods could be used.

- Intangibles with *indefinite lives*. No amortization for these intangibles is recorded. Instead, check them annually for any loss in value (impairment), and record a loss when it occurs. Goodwill is the most prominent example of an intangible asset with an indefinite life.

In the following discussions, we illustrate the accounting for both categories of intangibles.

Accounting for Specific Intangibles

Each type of intangible asset is unique, and the accounting can vary from one intangible to another.

PATENTS. **Patents** are federal government grants giving the holder the exclusive right for 20 years to produce and sell an invention. The invention may be a product or a process—for example, BlackBerry's new cellphone and IMAX's projection process. Like any other asset, a patent may be purchased. Suppose Bombardier pays $170,000 to acquire a patent on January 1, and the business believes the expected useful life of the patent is five years. Amortization expense is $34,000 per year ($170,000/5 years). Bombardier records the acquisition and amortization for this patent as follows:

Jan. 1	Patents	170,000	
	Cash		170,000
	To acquire a patent.		
Dec. 31	Amortization Expense—Patents ($170,000/5)................	34,000	
	Accumulated Amortization..		34,000
	To amortize the cost of a patent.		

ASSETS	=	LIABILITIES	+	SHAREHOLDERS' EQUITY
−34,000	=	0		−34,000 Expense

Amortization for an intangible decreases both assets and equity exactly as it does for equipment.

COPYRIGHTS. **Copyrights** are exclusive rights to reproduce and sell a book, musical composition, film, or other work of art. Copyrights also protect computer software programs, such as Corel's WordPerfect. Issued by the federal government, copyrights extend 50 years beyond the author's (composer's, artist's, or programmer's) death. The cost of obtaining a copyright from the government is low, but a company may pay a large sum to purchase an existing copyright from the owner. For example, a publisher may pay the author of a popular novel $1 million or more for the book copyright. A copyright is usually amortized over its useful life.

TRADEMARKS AND TRADE NAMES. **Trademarks** and **trade names** (or **brand names**) are distinctive identifications of products or services. You are probably familiar with McDonald's golden arches or Apple Inc.'s famous apple. Tim Hortons and Roots are names we all recognize. Advertising slogans, such as "Red Bull gives you wings," are also protected.

The cost of a trademark or trade name may be amortized over its useful life, but if the trademark is expected to generate cash flow for the indefinite future, the business should not amortize the trademark's cost.

FRANCHISES AND LICENCES. **Franchises and licences** are privileges granted by a private business or a government to sell a product or service in accordance with specified conditions. The Edmonton Oilers hockey organization is a franchise granted to its owner by the National Hockey League. Swiss Chalet restaurants and Canadian Tire are popular franchises. Companies purchase licences for the right to use computer software. Coca-Cola sells licences to companies around the world, which allow the companies to produce and distribute Coca-Cola beverages in specified markets. The useful lives of many franchises and licences are indefinite and, therefore, are not amortized.

GOODWILL. In accounting, **goodwill** has a very specific meaning. It is defined as the excess of the cost of purchasing another company over the sum of the market values of its net assets (assets minus liabilities). A purchaser is willing to pay for goodwill when it buys another company with abnormal earning power.

Canadian Tire expanded into another line of business when it acquired The Forzani Group in August 2011. The purchase price was $800.6 million. The fair value of the assets was $1,149.9 million, and the fair value of the liabilities was $657.7 million, so Canadian Tire paid $308.4 million for goodwill, computed as follows:

Purchase paid for The Forzani Group (FGL)	$ 800.6 million
Sum of the fair values of FGL's assets	$1,149.9 million
Less: Fair value of FLG's liabilities	657.7 million
Value of FLG's net assets	492.2 million
Excess is called *goodwill*	$ 308.4 million

Canadian Tire would consolidate The Forzani Group's financial statements, but if Canadian Tire were to combine FLG's records with its own, the entry, including goodwill, would be:

Assets (Cash, Receivables, Inventories, Property, Plant, and Equipment, Other Assets, all at fair value)	1,149,900,000	
Goodwill	308,400,000	
Liabilities		657,700,000
Cash		800,600,000

ASSETS	=	LIABILITIES	+ SHAREHOLDERS' EQUITY
+1,149,900,000			
+308,400,000	=	+657,700,000	+ 0
−800,600,000			

Note that Canadian Tire has acquired both The Forzani Group's assets and its liabilities.

Goodwill has special features, as follows:

1. Goodwill is recorded *only* when it is purchased in the acquisition of another company. A purchase transaction provides objective evidence of the value of goodwill. Companies never record goodwill that they have created for their own business.

2. Goodwill is not amortized because it has an indefinite life. As you will see below, if the value of goodwill is impaired, it must be written down.

Accounting for the Impairment of an Intangible Asset

Some intangibles—such as goodwill, licences, and some trademarks—have indefinite lives and, therefore, are not subject to amortization. But all intangibles are subject to a write-down when their recoverable amount is less than the carrying amount. The 2011 annual report of Hewlett-Packard (HP) reported that,

> In the fourth quarter of fiscal 2011, HP determined that it would wind down the manufacture and sale of webOS devices resulting from the Palm acquisition, including webOS smartphones and the HP TouchPad. The decision triggered an impairment review of the related goodwill and purchased intangible assets recorded in connection with the Palm acquisition.

As a result of the impairment test, HP recognized a goodwill impairment loss of $813 million. This impairment loss is recorded as an expense on the income statement. HP would record the write-down of goodwill as follows:

```
2011
Oct. 31       Goodwill Impairment ....................................................   $813
                  Goodwill ..................................................................          $813
```

ASSETS	=	LIABILITIES	+	SHAREHOLDERS' EQUITY
−813	=	0		− 813 Expense

Under IFRS, a company must check its intangible assets for impairment at each reporting date, whereas under ASPE, impairment of intangible assets with an indefinite life is tested only when there is an indication of impairment.

Accounting for Research and Development Costs

Accounting for research and development (R&D) costs is one of the most difficult issues the accounting profession has faced. R&D is the lifeblood of companies such as BlackBerry, Open Text, TELUS, and Bombardier because it is vital to the development of new products and processes. The cost of R&D activities is one of these companies' most valuable (intangible) assets.

Both IFRS and ASPE require *development costs* meeting certain criteria to be capitalized and then expensed over the life of the product, while *research costs* are to be expensed as incurred.

ANALYZE AND EVALUATE A COMPANY'S RETURN ON ASSETS

Evaluating company performance is a key goal of financial statement analysis. Shareholders entrust managers with the responsibility of developing a business strategy that utilizes company assets in a manner that both effectively and efficiently generates a profit. In this chapter, we begin to develop a framework by which company performance can be evaluated. The most basic framework for this purpose is **return on assets (ROA)**.

ROA, also known as *rate* of return on assets, measures how profitably management has used the assets that shareholders and creditors have provided the company. The basic formula for the ROA ratio is as follows:

$$\text{ROA} = \frac{\text{Net income*}}{\text{Average total assets}}$$

where Average total assets = (Beginning total assets + Ending total assets)/2

ROA measures how much the entity earned for each dollar of assets invested by both shareholders and creditors. Companies with high ROA have both selected assets and managed them more successfully than companies with low ROA. ROA is often computed on a divisional or product-line basis to help identify less profitable segments and improve their performance.

DuPont Analysis: A More Detailed View of ROA

To better understand why ROA increased or decreased over time, companies often perform a **DuPont analysis**,[**] which breaks ROA down into two component ratios that drive it:

$$\text{Net profit margin} = \frac{\text{Net income}}{\text{Net sales}}$$

$$\text{Total asset turnover} = \frac{\text{Net sales}}{\text{Average total assets}}$$

Net profit margin measures how much every sales dollar generates in profit. Recall that net profit can be increased in one of three ways: (1) increasing sales volume, or the amount of goods or services sold or performed; (2) increasing sales prices; or (3) decreasing cost of goods sold and operating expenses.

Total asset turnover measures how many sales dollars are generated for each dollar of assets invested. This is a measure of how effectively and efficiently the company manages its assets. Asset turnover can be increased by (1) increasing sales in the ways just described, (2) keeping less inventory on hand, or (3) closing unproductive facilities, selling idle assets, and consolidating operations to fewer places to reduce the amount of plant assets needed.

ROA is the product of net profit margin and total asset turnover:

$$\text{ROA} = \text{Net profit margin} \times \text{Total asset turnover}$$

$$\text{ROA} = \frac{\text{Net income}}{\text{Net sales}} \times \frac{\text{Net sales}}{\text{Average total assets}} = \frac{\text{Net income}}{\text{Average total assets}}$$

---

[*]For companies with significant debt, some analysts may add interest expense to net income. While it is theoretically correct to do so, in order to illustrate DuPont analysis, we do not. Adding back interest makes a material difference to ROA only when interest expense is relatively high compared to net income.

[**]The full DuPont analysis model actually contains three components: profit margin, asset turnover, and leverage.

By influencing the drivers of net profit margin and total asset turnover, management devises strategies to improve each one, thus increasing ROA. Successful manufacturing firms often choose between a mixture of two different strategies: *product differentiation* or *low-cost*. A company that follows a product differentiation strategy usually spends a great deal on research and development and advertising to convince customers that the company's products (usually higher priced) are worth the investment. Apple Inc. follows a product differentiation strategy, introducing innovative and attractive technology in the marketplace before any other competitor, and always at a higher price. Alternatively, a low-cost strategy usually relies on efficient management of inventory and productive assets to produce a high asset turnover. Dell Inc., a competitor of Apple's, follows a low-cost strategy. Of course, all companies would like to have the best of both worlds by maximizing both profit margin and asset turnover, but some companies have to settle for one or the other.

To illustrate, let's consider Masimo Corporation, a company that produces electronic instruments used in the health-care industry. The following table contains approximate financial data adapted from Masimo's income statements and balance sheets for 2013 and 2014:

Masimo Corporation
Selected (Adapted) Financial Data

	(Amounts in thousands)	
	2013	2014
Net sales..	$493,000	$439,000
Net income	65,000	64,000
Average total assets..	371,000	338,000

Masimo Corporation
DuPont Analysis

	Net profit margin × (Net income/Net sales) ×	Total asset turnover = (Net sales/Average total assets) =	ROA (Net income/Average total assets)
2013	$\dfrac{65,000}{493,000}$ ×	$\dfrac{493,000}{371,000}$ =	18%
2014	$\dfrac{64,000}{439,000}$ ×	$\dfrac{439,000}{338,000}$ =	19%

In 2013, the company's profit margin was 13.2% (65,000/493,000). Its asset turnover was 1.33 (493,000/371,000), meaning that it earned $1.33 of sales revenue for every $1 of assets invested. In 2014, the company improved its profit margin to 14.6% (64,000/439,000) even though overall sales decreased. In addition, Massimo sold unproductive plant assets, reducing total average assets from $371,000 to $338,000. With this decrease in sales, the asset turnover only declined slightly from 1.33 to 1.30. Overall, despite the decrease in net sales, the company was still able to increase its return on assets from 18% to 19%.

◄ DECISION GUIDELINES ►

USING THE RETURN ON ASSETS IN DECISION MAKING

The fundamental goal of a company is to earn a profit. The return on asset (ROA) measures how profitably a company uses its assets. Let's see how the ROA is used in making decisions.

Decision	Guidelines
How profitable was the company?	*Managers*
	Managers try to increase the profitability of the company, whether it is through increasing sales, reducing expenses, or a combination of both. They know that investors and creditors expect them to use the assets of the company to generate a profit.
	Investors and Creditors
	Since investors and creditors provide the financing for the assets that a company owns, they are looking to see if managers were able to use these assets to generate a profit. For the investor, share prices generally react favourably when the company is profitable—and the company will be able to pay them dividends. For the creditor, profitability means the company will be able to pay back their debt.

INTERPRET TANGIBLE AND INTANGIBLE ASSET ACTIVITIES ON THE STATEMENT OF CASH FLOWS

OBJECTIVE

❼ **Interpret** tangible and intangible asset activities on the statement of cash flows

Three main types of long-lived asset transactions appear on the statement of cash flows:

- Acquisitions
- Sales
- Depreciation and amortization

Acquisitions and sales of long-lived assets are *investing* activities. For example, a company invests in property, plant, and equipment by paying cash or incurring a liability. The purchase of buildings and equipment are investing activities that appear on the statement of cash flows. The sale of property, plant, and equipment results in a cash receipt, as illustrated in Exhibit 7-8, which excerpts data from the statement of cash flows of Canadian Tire. The acquisitions, sales, and depreciation of property, plant, and equipment and intangible assets are denoted in lines 2, 3, 6, 7, and 8.

Let's examine the investing activities first. During the year-end December 31, 2011, Canadian Tire paid $230.5 million for property and equipment and $128.9 million for intangible assets. Canadian Tire received $16.9 million from the disposal of these assets during the year. A gain or loss on the sale of these assets is not reported as an investing activity on the statement of cash flows.

EXHIBIT 7-8
Reporting Long-lived Asset
Transactions on Statement
of Cash Flows

Canadian Tire
Consolidated Statement of Cash Flows (partial, adapted)
For the Year Ended December 31, 2011

(amounts in millions)

Operating Activities:	
1. Net earnings	$ 467.0
Adjustments to reconcile net income	
to cash provided by operating activities:	
2. **Depreciation**...	229.8
3. **Amortization of intangible assets**	66.3
4. Other items (summarized)...	642.4
5. Cash provided by operating activities	1,405.5
Investing Activities:	
6. **Purchases of property and equipment**	(230.5)
7. **Additions to intangible assets**...	(128.9)
8. **Proceeds from disposals of assets**..	16.9
9. Other items (summarized)...	(818.9)
Cash used for investing activities...	(1,161.4)
Financing Activities:	
10. Cash used for financing activities..	(493.7)
11. Cash used in the year	(249.6)
12. Cash and cash equivalents at beginning of year	450.9
13. Effect of exchange rate on cash..	(0.3)
14. Cash and cash equivalents at end of year...................................	$ 201.0

Canadian Tire's statement of cash flows reports Depreciation (Amortization) in the operating activities section (line 2). You may be wondering why depreciation appears on the statement of cash flows—after all, depreciation does not affect cash. Depreciation (Amortization) decreases net income in the same way that all other expenses do, but it does not affect cash. Depreciation (Amortization) is therefore added back to net income to measure cash flows from operations under the indirect method.

Canadian Tire's cash flows are strong—cash provided by operating activities exceed net income by almost $1 billion. With this excess, the company has bought property and equipment as well as other intangible assets needed to expand and run its business.

STOP + THINK (7-6)

Test your ability to understand the statement of cash flows.

1. How much cash did Canadian Tire spend on purchases of property, plant, and equipment and intangibles during the year?

2. Suppose the carrying amount of the property, plant and equipment that Canadian Tire sold for $230.5

million was $231.5 million (a cost of $500 million minus accumulated depreciation of $268.5 millions). Write a sentence to explain why the sale transaction resulted in a loss for Canadian Tire.

3. Where would Canadian Tire report any gain or loss on the sale of the capital assets—on which financial statement, under which heading?

Summary of IFRS-ASPE Differences

Concepts	IFRS	ASPE
Depreciation (p. 326)	This concept is called depreciation.	This concept is called amortization.
Significant components of an item of property, plant, or equipment (p. 340)	Significant components shall be depreciated separately.	Significant components are amortized separately only when it is practical to do so.
Impairment (p. 340)	A company shall assess at the end of each reporting period whether there are any signs that an asset may be impaired. Irrespective of any signs of impairment, a company must annually review goodwill and intangible assets with indefinite useful lives for impairment. If an impaired asset subsequently increases in value, a company may reverse all or part of any previous write-down but not on goodwill.	A company shall test an asset for impairment whenever events or circumstances indicate its carrying amount may not be recoverable. A company may not reverse any write-downs, even if an impaired asset subsequently increases in value.
Revaluation (p. 340)	A company may choose to use the revaluation model to measure its property, plant, and equipment.	A company must use the cost method; no revaluation is permitted.

SUMMARY OF CHAPTER 7

LEARNING OBJECTIVE	SUMMARY
1. **Describe** the types of tangible and intangible assets a business may own	A company may own tangible long-lived assets such as land, buildings, and equipment, as well as intangible assets, including patents, copyrights, and trademarks. These assets are used in the business to help generate revenue.
2. **Measure** and **account** for the cost of property, plant, and equipment	The cost of property, plant, and equipment is the sum of all the costs incurred to bring the asset to its location and intended use. Costs incurred after the asset has been placed in use are either capitalized (if it increases the asset's productivity or extends its useful life) or expensed (if it maintains the asset and keeps it in good working order).
3. **Calculate** and **record** depreciation on property, plant, and equipment	Because assets decline in value either from wearing out, becoming obsolete, or losing value, depreciation is used to allocate their cost to the periods of their useful life. Three depreciation methods discussed include the straight-line method, the units-of-production method, and the diminishing or double diminishing-balance method. If an asset is bought during the year, depreciation is computed for the partial year. Managers may revise their estimate of an asset's useful life and recalculate depreciation. If a fully depreciated asset is still being used, it is left on the company's records.
4. **Explain** additional topics in accounting for long-lived tangible assets	Depreciation affects income taxes because the depreciation method used for accounting purposes may be different than the depreciation method required for tax purposes. Subsequent to the acquisition of property, plant, and equipment, a company can choose to measure these assets using either the cost method or the revaluation method. The cost method uses cost as its measurement, while the revaluation method uses fair value. Significant components of property, plant, and equipment shall be depreciated separately. Property, plant, and equipment are checked annually for any impairment.

5. **Account** for intangible assets

Intangible assets are long-lived assets with no physical form and include patents, copyrights, trademarks, franchises, and licences, and goodwill. Two categories of intangibles are those with finite lives (record amortization) and those with indefinite lives (no amortization is recorded). All intangible assets are checked each year for impairment, and a loss is recorded when it occurs.

6. **Analyze** and **evaluate** a company's return on assets

The return on assets ratio measures how profitably management has used the assets that shareholders and creditors have provided the company.

7. **Interpret** tangible and intangible asset activities on the statement of cash flows

On the statement of cash flows, acquisitions and sales of property, plant, and equipment and intangibles are recorded under investing activities, while the depreciation expense is added to net income under operating activities.

END-OF-CHAPTER SUMMARY PROBLEM

The figures that follow appear in the *Answers to the Mid-Chapter Summary Problem*, Requirement 2, on page 334, for Canadian Tire.

	Method A: Straight-Line			Method B: Double-Diminishing-Balance		
Year	Annual Depreciation Expense	Accumulated Depreciation	Carrying amount	Annual Depreciation Expense	Accumulated Depreciation	Carrying Amount
Start			$44,000			$44,000
2014	$4,000	$ 4,000	40,000	$ 8,800	$ 8,800	35,200
2015	4,000	8,000	36,000	7,040	15,840	28,160
2016	4,000	12,000	32,000	5,632	21,472	22,528

Name: Canadian Tire
Industry: Retailer
Accounting Period: The years 2014, 2015, 2016

Problem

Suppose Canadian Tire purchased the equipment described in the table on January 1, 2014. Management has depreciated the equipment by using the double-diminishing-balance method. On July 1, 2016, Canadian Tire sold the equipment for $27,000 cash.

Requirement

Record depreciation for 2016 and the sale of the equipment on July 1, 2016.

ANSWERS

Problem

To record depreciation to date of sale, and then the sale of the equipment:

Depreciation expense must first be recorded for the portion of the year that the asset was used before it was sold.

The gain on the sale is the excess of the cash received over the carrying amount of the asset.

2016				
July 1	Depreciation Expense—Equipment ($5,632 × 1/2 year)		2,816	
	Accumulated Depreciation—Equipment			2,816
	To update depreciation.			
July 1	Cash		27,000	
	Accumulated Depreciation—Equipment ($15,840 + $2,816)		18,656	
	Equipment			44,000
	Gain on Sale of Equipment			1,656
	To record sale of equipment.			

STOP + THINK (7-1)

ANSWER

These improvements wear out over time, and in the case of leasehold improvements, they expire once the terms of the lease are up.

STOP + THINK (7-2)

ANSWER

The yearly depreciation would be $2,000 [($13,000 − $3,000)/5]. Therefore, the years of use left would be 2 [($7,000 − $3,000)/($2,000)].

STOP + THINK (7-3)

ANSWERS

Yr. 1: $5,200 ($13,000 × 40%)
Yr. 2: $3,120 ($7,800 × 40%)
Yr. 3: $1,680 ($13,000 − $5,200 − $3,120 − $3,000)*

Yr. 4: $0
Yr. 5: $0

*The asset is not depreciated below residual value.

STOP + THINK (7-4)

ANSWERS

1. An accounting change that lengthens the estimated useful lives of depreciable assets
   (a) decreases depreciation expense, and
   (b, c) increases net income and owners' equity.

2. Investor reactions are not always predictable. There is research to indicate that companies cannot fool investors. In this case, investment advisors would *probably* subtract from the company's reported net income the amount added by the accounting change. Investors could then use the remaining net *loss* figure to evaluate the company's lack of progress during the year. Investors would probably view the company as worse for having made this accounting change. It is probably for this reason that such changes in accounting estimates are so rare in Canada.

STOP + THINK (7-5)

ANSWER

From a *revenue* standpoint, 2014 was better because revenues were higher. But from an *income* standpoint, 2013 was better.

In 2013, the company's core business generated $165 million of income from operations. In 2014, operations produced only $150 million of operating income.

Of the company's income in 2014, $20 million came from selling a maintenance building (gain of $20 million). A business cannot hope to continue on this path very long. This example shows why investors and creditors care about the sources of a company's profits, not just the final amount of net income.

STOP + THINK (7-6)

ANSWERS

1. Canadian Tire spent $230.5 million on property, plant, and equipment, and $128.9 million on intangible assets.

2. The company sold assets for $230.5 million that had a carrying amount of $231.5 million. The result of the sale was a loss of $1 million ($230.5 million received and $231.5 million carrying amount).

3. Report the loss on the *income statement* under the heading *Non-operating income (expense)*.

Review Property, Plant, and Equipment, and Intangible Assets

QUICK CHECK (ANSWERS ARE GIVEN ON PAGE 373.)

1. Argyle Corp. purchased a tract of land, a small office building, and some equipment for $1,500,000. The appraised value of the land was $850,000; the building, $675,000; and the equipment, $475,000. What is the cost of the land?
   a. $850,000
   b. $637,500
   c. $482,776
   d. None of the above

2. Which of the following statements about depreciation is false?
   a. Recording depreciation creates a fund to replace the asset at the end of its useful life.
   b. The cost of a building minus accumulated depreciation equals the building's carrying amount.
   c. Depreciation is a process of allocating the cost of property, plant, and equipment over its useful life.
   d. Depreciation is caused by physical wear and tear or obsolence.

Use the following data for Questions 3 through 6.

On August 1, 2013, Major Link Inc. purchased a new piece of equipment that cost $25,000. The estimated useful life is five years, and estimated residual value is $2,500.

3. Assume Major Link purchased the equipment on August 1, 2013. If Major Link uses the straight-line method for depreciation, what is the depreciation expense for the year ended December 31, 2013?
   a. $1,875
   b. $1,500
   c. $2,083
   d. $4,500

4. Assume Major Link purchased the equipment on January 1, 2013. If Major Link uses the straight-line method for depreciation, what is the asset's carrying amount at the end of 2014?
   a. $13,500
   b. $15,000
   c. $18,625
   d. $16,000

5. Assume Major Link purchased the equipment on January 1, 2013. If Major Link uses the double-diminishing-balance method of depreciation, what is the depreciation expense for the year ended December 31, 2014?
   a. $5,400
   b. $6,000
   c. $8,333
   d. $15,000

6. Return to Major Link's original purchase date of August 1, 2013. Assume that Major Link uses the straight-line method of depreciation and sells the equipment for $11,500 on August 1, 2017. Based on the result of the sale of the equipment, what gain (or loss) will Major Link realize?
   a. $4,500
   b. $13,500
   c. $(9,000)
   d. $0

7. A company bought a new machine for $17,000 on January 1. The machine is expected to last four years and to have a residual value of $2,000. If the company uses the double-diminishing-balance method, what is the accumulated depreciation at the end of year 2?
   a. $10,880
   b. $11,250
   c. $12,750
   d. $15,000

8. Which of the following is *not* a capital expenditure?
   a. The addition of a building wing
   b. A complete overhaul of an air-conditioning system
   c. A tune-up of a company vehicle
   d. Replacement of an old motor with a new one in a piece of equipment
   e. The cost of installing a piece of equipment

9. Which of the following assets is *not* subject to a decreasing carrying amount through amortization?
   a. Goodwill
   b. Intangibles
   c. Land improvements
   d. Land

10. Why would a business select an accelerated method of depreciation for reporting purposes?
    a. Accelerated depreciation results in a constant amount of depreciation.
    b. Accelerated depreciation generates a greater amount of depreciation over the life of the asset than does straight-line depreciation.
    c. Accelerated depreciation is easier to calculate because residual value is ignored.
    d. Accelerated depreciation generates higher depreciation expense immediately, and therefore lower net income in the early years of the asset's life.

11. A company sells an asset that originally cost $300,000 for $100,000 on December 31, 2014. The accumulated depreciation account had a balance of $120,000 after the current year's depreciation of $30,000 had been recorded. The company should recognize a(n)
    a. $200,000 loss on disposal.
    b. $80,000 loss on disposal.
    c. $80,000 gain on disposal.
    d. $50,000 loss on disposal.

12. Which item among the following is *not* an intangible asset?
    a. A trademark
    b. A copyright
    c. A patent
    d. Goodwill
    e. All of the above are intangible assets

13. An important measure of profitability is
    a. inventory turnover.
    b. quick (acid test) ratio.
    c. return on assets (ROA).
    d. net sales.

14. In 2014, total asset turnover for JBC Company has increased. This means that the
    a. company has become more effective.
    b. company has become more efficient.
    c. company has become more effective and more efficient.
    d. company has neither become more effective nor more efficient.

Accounting Vocabulary

accelerated depreciation method A depreciation method that writes off a relatively larger amount of the asset's cost nearer the start of its useful life than the straight-line method does. (p. 330)

amortization Allocation of the cost of an intangible asset with a finite life over its useful life (p. 342)

brand name A distinctive identification of a product or service. Also called a *trademark* or *trade name*. (p. 343)

capital expenditure Expenditure that increases an asset's capacity or efficiency, or extends its useful life. Capital expenditures are debited to an asset account. Also called *betterments*. (p. 325)

copyright Exclusive right to reproduce and sell a book, musical composition, film, other work of art, or computer program. Issued by the federal government, copyrights extend 50 years beyond the author's life. (p. 342)

depreciable cost The cost of a tangible asset minus its estimated residual value. (p. 328)

depreciation Allocation of the cost of property, plant, and equipment for its useful life. (p. 326)

double-diminishing-balance (DDB) method An accelerated depreciation method that computes annual depreciation by multiplying the asset's decreasing carrying amount by a constant percentage, which is two times the straight-line rate. (p. 331)

DuPont analysis A detailed approach to measuring return on assets (ROA). It breaks ROA into two components ratios: Net profit margin (Net income/Net sales) and Total asset turnover (Net sales/Average total assets). (p. 345)

estimated residual value Expected cash value of an asset at the end of its useful life. Also called *scrap value* or *salvage value*. (p. 328)

estimated useful life Length of service that a business expects to get from an asset. May be expressed in years, units of output, kilometres, or other measures. (p. 328)

franchises and licences Privileges granted by a private business or a government to sell a product or service in accordance with specified conditions. (p. 343)

goodwill Excess of the cost of an acquired company over the sum of the market values of its net assets (assets minus liabilities). (p. 343)

intangible assets Long-lived assets with no physical form that convey a special right to current and expected future benefits. (p. 322)

net profit margin Computed by the formula Net income/Net sales. This ratio measures the portion of each sales dollar generated in net profit. (p. 345)

obsolescence Occurs when an asset becomes outdated or no longer produces revenue for the company. (p. 327)

patent A federal government grant giving the holder the exclusive right for 20 years to produce and sell an invention. (p. 342)

physical wear and tear Occurs when the usefulness of the asset deteriorates. (p. 326)

return on assets (ROA) Measures how profitably management has used the assets that shareholders and creditors have provided the company. (p. 345)

straight-line (SL) method Depreciation method in which an equal amount of depreciation expense is assigned to each year of asset use. (p. 329)

tangible long-lived assets Also called property, plant, and equipment. (p. 322)

total asset turnover Measures a company's success in using assets to earn a profit. The formula is Net sales/Average total assets. Also known as asset turnover. (p. 345)

trademark, trade name A distinctive identification of a product or service. Also called a *brand name*. (p. 343)

units-of-production (UOP) method Depreciation method by which a fixed amount of depreciation is assigned to each unit of output produced by the plant asset. (p. 330)

Assess Your Progress

MyAccountingLab

Make the grade with MyAccountingLab: The Exercises, Quizzes, and Problems (A set) marked in red can be found on MyAccountingLab. You can practise them as often as you want, and most feature step-by-step guided instructions to help you find the right answer.

SHORT EXERCISES

LEARNING OBJECTIVE ❶❷

Measure the cost and carrying amount of a company's property, plant, and equipment

S7-1 Examine Riverside's assets as follows:

Riverside Corporation
Consolidated Balance Sheets (Partial, Adapted)

		May 31,	
(in millions)		2014	2013
1.	Assets		
2.	Current assets		
3.	Cash and cash equivalents	$ 2,088	$ 257
4.	Receivables, less allowances of $144 and $125	2,770	2,623
5.	Spare parts, supplies, and fuel	4,653	4,509
6.	Prepaid expenses and other	467	423
7.	Total current assets	9,978	7,812
8.	Property and equipment, at cost		
9.	Aircraft	2,392	2,392
10.	Package handling and ground support equipment	12,229	12,132
11.	Computer and electronic equipment	28,159	26,102
12.	Vehicles	581	452
13.	Facilities and other	1,432	1,589
14.	Total cost	44,793	42,667
15.	Less: Accumulated depreciation	(14,900)	(12,944)
16.	Net property and equipment	29,893	29,723
17.	Other long-term assets		
18.	Goodwill	722	722
19.	Prepaid pension cost	1,340	1,271
20.	Intangible and other assets	329	333
21.	Total other long-term assets	2,391	2,326
22.	Total assets	$ 42,262	$ 39,861

1. What is Riverside's largest category of assets? List all 2014 assets in the largest category and their amounts as reported by Riverside.

2. What was Riverside's cost of property and equipment at May 31, 2014? What was the carrying amount of property and equipment on this date? Why is book value less than cost?

LEARNING OBJECTIVE ❶❷

Measure the cost of property

S7-2 Page 323 of this chapter lists the costs included for the acquisition of land. First is the purchase price of the land, which is obviously included in the cost of the land. The reasons for including the related costs are not so obvious. For example, property tax is ordinarily an expense, not part of the cost of an asset. State why the related costs listed on page 323 are included as part of the cost of the land. After the land is ready for use, will these related costs be capitalized or expensed?

S7-3 Suppose you have purchased land, a building, and some equipment. At the time of the acquisition, the land has a current fair value of $75,000, the building's fair value is $60,000, and the equipment's fair value is $15,000. Journalize the lump-sum purchase of the three assets for a total cost of $140,000. Assume you sign a note payable for this amount.

LEARNING OBJECTIVE ❶❷

Measure and record the lump-sum purchase of assets

S7-4 Assume WestJet repaired one of its Boeing 737 aircraft at a cost of $0.8 million, which WestJet paid in cash. Further, assume that the WestJet accountant erroneously capitalized this cost as part of the cost of the plane.

Show the effects of the accounting error on WestJet's income statement and balance sheet. To answer this question, determine whether revenues, total expenses, net income, total assets, and shareholders' equity would be overstated or understated by the accounting error.

LEARNING OBJECTIVE ❶❷

Measure and account for equipment

S7-5 Assume that at the beginning of 2014, Porter Airlines purchased a Bombardier Q400 aircraft at a cost of $25,000,000. Porter expects the plane to remain useful for five years (5,000,000 km) and to have a residual value of $5,000,000. Porter expects the plane to be flown 750,000 km the first year and 1,250,000 km each year during years 2 through 4, and 500,000 km the last year.

1. Compute Porter's first-year depreciation on the plane using the following methods:
   a. Straight-line
   b. Units-of-production
   c. Double-diminishing-balance
2. Show the airplane's carrying amount at the end of the first year under each depreciation method.

LEARNING OBJECTIVE ❸

Compute depreciation by three methods—first year only

S7-6 Use the assumed Porter Airlines data in exercise S7-5 to compute Porter's fifth-year depreciation on the plane using the following methods:
a. Straight-line
b. Units-of-production
c. Double-diminishing-balance

LEARNING OBJECTIVE ❸

Compute depreciation by three methods—final year only

S7-7 Assume that on September 30, 2014, Swiss, the national airline of Switzerland, purchased an Airbus aircraft at a cost of €40,000,000 (€ is the symbol for the euro). Swiss expects the plane to remain useful for seven years (5,000,000 km) and to have a residual value of €5,000,000. Swiss expects the plane to be flown 500,000 km during the remainder of the first year ended December 31, 2014. Compute Swiss's depreciation on the plane for the year ended December 31, 2014, using the following methods:
a. Straight-line
b. Units-of-production
c. Double-diminishing-balance

Which method would produce the highest net income for 2014? Which method produces the lowest net income?

LEARNING OBJECTIVE ❹

Compute partial-year depreciation

S7-8 Canada's Wonderland paid $60,000 for a concession stand. Depreciation was recorded by the straight-line method over 10 years with zero residual value. Suppose that after using the concession stand for four years, Canada's Wonderland determines that the asset will remain useful for only three more years. How will this affect depreciation on the concession stand for year 5 by the straight-line method?

LEARNING OBJECTIVE ❹

Compute and record depreciation after a change in useful life of the asset

S7-9 On January 1, 2011, Big Rock Brewery purchased a van for $45,000. Big Rock expects the van to have a useful life of five years and a residual value of $5,000. The depreciation method used was straight-line. On December 31, 2014, the van was sold for $15,000 cash.

1. What was the carrying amount of the van on the date of sale?
2. Record the sale of the van on December 31, 2014.

LEARNING OBJECTIVE ❹

Record a gain or loss on derecognition under two depreciation methods

LEARNING OBJECTIVE ❺

Account for the amortization of a company's intangible assets

LEARNING OBJECTIVE ❺

Analyze a company's goodwill

S7-10 Define patents and goodwill, which are both intangible assets. Explain how the accounting differs between a patent and goodwill.

S7-11 Consider the purchase of a supplier by Canadian Tire.

1. Suppose the fair value of the net assets at the date of purchase (February 1, 2014) had been $180.3 million. What would the goodwill cost have been if Canadian Tire had paid $200 million?

2. Explain how Canadian Tire will have been accounting for this goodwill up to February 1, 2016.

LEARNING OBJECTIVE ❺

Account for patents and research cost

S7-12 This exercise summarizes the accounting for patents, which, like copyrights, trademarks, and franchises, provide the owner with a special right or privilege. It also covers research costs.

Suppose Jaguar Automobiles Ltd. paid $500,000 to research a new global positioning system. Jaguar also paid $1,200,000 to acquire a patent on a new motor. After readying the motor for production, Jaguar's sales revenue for the first year totalled $6,500,000. Cost of goods sold was $3,200,000, and selling expenses were $300,000. All these transactions occurred during fiscal 2014. Jaguar expects the patent to have a useful life of three years.

Prepare Jaguar's income statement for the fiscal year ended December 31, 2014, complete with a heading.

LEARNING OBJECTIVE ❼

Report investing activities on the statement of cash flows

S7-13 You are reviewing the financial statements of Rising Yeast Co. During 2014, Rising Yeast purchased two other companies for $17 million. Also during fiscal 2014, Rising Yeast made capital expenditures of $2 million to expand its market share. During the year, the company sold operations, receiving cash of $25 million, and experienced a gain of $6 million on the disposal. Overall, Rising Yeast reported net income of $1 million during 2014. What would you expect the section for cash flows from investing activities on its statement of cash flows for 2014 to report? What total amount for net cash provided by (used in) investing activities do you anticipate?

LEARNING OBJECTIVE ❻

Calculate return on assets

LEARNING OBJECTIVE ❻

Calculate return on assets

S7-14 In 2012, Artesia, Inc., reported $300 million in sales, $18 million in net income, and average total assets of $120 million. What is Artesia's return on assets in 2013?

S7-15 Ochoa Optical, Inc., provides a full line of designer eyewear to optical dispensaries. Ochoa reported the following information for 2013 and 2014:

	2014	2013
Sales revenue	$500,000	$450,000
Net income	$ 45,000	$ 42,500
Average total assets	$250,000	$240,000

Compute return on assets for 2013 and 2014.

EXERCISES

LEARNING OBJECTIVE ❶❷

Determine the cost of property

E7-16 Moody Inc. purchased land, paying $150,000 cash as a down payment and signing a $100,000 note payable for the balance. Moody also had to pay delinquent property tax of $5,000, title insurance costing $3,000, and $25,000 to level the land and to remove an unwanted building. The company paid $70,000 to remove earth for the foundation and then constructed an office building at a cost of $3,750,000. It also paid $100,000 for a fence around the property, $10,500 for the company sign near the property entrance, and $18,000 for lighting of the grounds. Determine the cost of the company's land, land improvements, and building.

E7-17 Assume Trois Cuisines Manufacturing bought three machines in a $100,000 lump-sum purchase. An independent appraiser valued the machines as follows:

Machine No.	Appraised Value
1	$27,000
2	45,000
3	36,000

Trois Cuisines paid one-third in cash and signed a note payable for the remainder. What is each machine's individual cost? Immediately after making this purchase, Trois Cuisines sold machine 2 for its appraised value. What is the result of the sale? Round to three decimal places.

E7-18 Assume Hershey Chocolate Ltd. purchased a piece of manufacturing machinery. Classify each of the following expenditures as an asset expenditure or an immediate expense related to machinery: (a) sales tax paid on the purchase price, (b) transportation and insurance while machinery is in transit from seller to buyer, (c) purchase price, (d) installation, (e) training of personnel for initial operation of the machinery, (f) special reinforcement to the machinery platform, (g) income tax paid on income earned from the sale of products manufactured by the machinery, (h) major overhaul to extend useful life by three years, (i) ordinary repairs to keep the machinery in good working order, (j) lubrication of the machinery before it is placed in service, and (k) periodic lubrication after the machinery is placed in service. What criteria differentiated an asset expenditure from an immediate expense?

E7-19 During 2014, Roberts Inc. paid $200,000 for land and built a restaurant in Collingwood, Ontario. Prior to construction, the City of Collingwood charged Roberts Inc. $2,250 for a building permit, which Roberts Inc. paid. Roberts Inc. also paid $20,000 for architect's fees. The construction cost of $700,000 was financed by a long-term note payable issued on January 1, 2014, with interest cost of $29,000 paid at December 31, 2014. The building was completed September 30, 2014. Roberts Inc. will depreciate the building by the straight-line method over 25 years, with an estimated residual value of $60,000.

1. Journalize transactions for the following (explanations are not required):
   a. Purchase of the land
   b. All the costs chargeable to the building, in a single entry
   c. Depreciation on the building

2. Report this transaction in the Property, Plant, and Equipment on the company's balance sheet at December 31, 2014.

3. What will Roberts Inc.'s income statement for the year ended December 31, 2014, report for the building?

E7-20 Assume you have a flower shop and you bought a delivery van for $30,000. You expect the van to remain in service for three years (150,000 km). At the end of its useful life, you estimate that the van's residual value will be $3,000. You estimate the van will travel 40,000 km the first year, 60,000 km the second year, and 50,000 km the third year. Prepare an estimate of the *depreciation expense* per year for the van under the three depreciation methods. Show your computations.

Which method do you think tracks the useful life cost on the van most closely?

E7-21 In January 2014, suppose a Starbucks franchise in Regina purchased a building, paying $50,000 cash and signing a $100,000 note payable. The franchise paid another $50,000 to remodel the facility. Equipment and store fixtures cost $50,000; dishes and supplies—a current asset—were obtained for $10,000.

The franchise is depreciating the building over 25 years by the straight-line method, with estimated residual value of $50,000. The equipment and store fixtures will be replaced at the end of five years; these assets are being depreciated by the double-diminishing-balance method, with zero residual value. At the end of the first year, the franchise has dishes and supplies worth $2,000.

Show what the franchise will report for supplies, property, plant, and equipment and cash flows at the end of the first year on its:
- Income statement
- Balance sheet
- Statement of cash flows (investing only)

Show all computations. (*Note:* The purchase of dishes and supplies is an operating cash flow because supplies are a current asset.)

LEARNING OBJECTIVE ⑥

Calculate return on assets

E7-22 Loblaws, one of the nation's largest grocery retailers, reported the following information (adapted) for its fiscal year ended January 31, 2014

	January 31, 2014	January 31, 2013
Net sales...	$48,815	$47,220
Net earnings..	$ 2,010	$ 1,783
Average total assets	$33,699	$33,005

Requirements
1. Compute profit margin for the year ended January 31, 2014.
2. Compute asset turnover for the year ended January 31, 2014.
3. Compute return on assets for the year ended January 31, 2014.

LEARNING OBJECTIVE ④

Change a building's useful life

E7-23 Assume The Salvation Army purchased a building for $900,000 and depreciated it on a straight-line basis over 30 years. The estimated residual value was $100,000. After using the building for 10 years, the Salvation Army realized that the building will remain useful for only 10 more years. Starting with the 11th year, the Salvation Army began depreciating the building over the newly revised total life of 20 years and decreased the estimated residual value to $75,000. What is the effect on depreciation expense on the building for years 11 and 12?

LEARNING OBJECTIVE ④

Record depreciation and the sale of equipment

E7-24 Assume that on January 2, 2013, a Pizza Hut franchise purchased fixtures for $15,000 cash, expecting the fixtures to remain in service five years. The restaurant has depreciated the fixtures on a double-diminishing-balance basis, with $1,000 estimated residual value. On June 30, 2014, Pizza Hut sold the fixtures for $5,000 cash. Record both the depreciation expense on the fixtures for 2014 and then the sale of the fixtures. Apart from your journal entries, also show how to compute the gain or loss on Pizza Hut's disposal of these fixtures.

LEARNING OBJECTIVE ①②③④

Measure equipment's cost, use UOP depreciation, and derecognize a used asset

E7-25 Bison Transport is a large trucking company that operates from Ontario to British Columbia in Canada and in the United States. Bison uses the units-of-production (UOP) method to depreciate its trucks because its managers believe UOP depreciation best measures wear and tear.

Bison Transport trades in its trucks often to keep driver morale high and maximize fuel efficiency. Assume that in 2011, the company acquired a tractor-trailer rig costing $280,000 and expected it to remain in service for five years or 1,000,000 km. Estimated residual value would be $40,000. During 2011, the truck was driven 130,000 km; during 2012, 180,000 km; and during 2013, 180,000 km. After 90,000 km in 2014, the company wishes to trade in the tractor-trailer rig for a new rig. Determine the carrying value of the rig and prepare the journal entry to derecognize the rig.

LEARNING OBJECTIVE ⑤

Analyze intangible assets

E7-26 Following is an excerpt from the balance sheet of On the Edge Technologies Inc.:

	(in thousands)	
	2014	2013
Goodwill (Note 4)	$60.7	$51.8
Intangible assets (Note 4)	48.4	42.4

A potential investor in On the Edge has asked you for advice. What information would you look for in the accompanying notes to the financial statements on which to base your advice about the investment decision?

E7-27 Holze Music Company purchased for $600,000 a patent for a new sound system. Although it gives legal protection for 20 years, the patent is expected to provide the company with a competitive advantage for only six years. Make journal entries to record (a) the purchase of the patent and (b) amortization for year 1.

LEARNING OBJECTIVE ❹❺

Record intangibles, amortization, and a change in the asset's useful life

After using the patent for two years, Holze Music Company's research director learns at a professional meeting that BOSE is designing a more powerful system. On the basis of this new information, Holze Music Company determines that the patent's total useful life is only four years. Record amortization for year 3.

E7-28 BlackBerry, the manufacturer of BlackBerry smartphones, recently reported in the statement of cash flows and notes to the financial statements in its annual report that it had made acquisitions of USD $6.2 million. Assume the balance sheet reported an increase in goodwill for the year in the amount of USD $4.5 million.

LEARNING OBJECTIVE ❺❼

Understand business acquisitions and statement of cash flows

Requirements

1. What is the definition of goodwill?
2. Explain the meaning of (a) the $6.2 million that BlackBerry reported on the statement of cash flows and (b) the $4.5 million increase in goodwill on the balance sheet.
3. BlackBerry's income statement and statement of cash flows do not show any charges for amortization of goodwill during the year. Explain the reason for the lack of charges.

E7-29 Assume that Google paid $18 million to purchase MySpace.com. Assume further that MySpace had the following summarized data at the time of the Google acquisition (amounts in millions of U.S. dollars).

LEARNING OBJECTIVE ❺

Measure and record goodwill

Assets		Liabilities and Equity	
Current assets	$10	Total liabilities	$24
Long-term assets	20	Shareholders' equity	6
	$30		$30

MySpace's long-term assets had a current value of only $15 million.

Requirements

1. Compute the cost of the goodwill purchased by Google.
2. Record the purchase of MySpace.
3. Explain how Google will account for goodwill in the future.

E7-30 The following items are excerpted from an annual report of a large retailer.

LEARNING OBJECTIVE ❼

Interpret a statement of cash flows

Consolidated Statement of Cash Flows (Partial, Adapted)
For the Year Ended December 30, 2014

	(amounts in millions)
Cash flow from operating activities:	
Net income	$ 185.1
Noncash items:	
Depreciation	90.9
Cash flow from investing activities:	
Property, plant, and equipment	$(233.6)
Other investments	(0.6)
Disposal of assets	17.0

Requirements

1. Why is depreciation listed on the statement of cash flows?
2. Explain in detail each investing activity.

LEARNING OBJECTIVE ➐

Report cash flows for property and equipment

E7-31 Assume Flowers to Go Ltd., a chain of flower shops, completed the following transactions. For each transaction, show what the company would report for investing activities on its statement of cash flows. Show negative amounts in parentheses.

a. Sold a building for $600,000. The building had cost $1,000,000, and at the time of the sale its accumulated depreciation totalled $400,000.
b. Lost a store building in a fire. The warehouse cost $300,000 and had accumulated depreciation of $180,000. The insurance proceeds received were $120,000.
c. Renovated a store at a cost of $400,000, paying cash.
d. Purchased store fixtures for $60,000. The fixtures are expected to remain in service for five years and then be sold for $10,000. Flowers to Go uses the straight-line depreciation method.

LEARNING OBJECTIVE ➏

Calculate return on assets

E7-32 Lowe's Companies, Inc. reported the following information (adapted) for its fiscal year ended January 31, 2014:

	January 31, 2014	January 31, 2013
Net sales	$82,189	$76,733
Net earnings	$ 1,116	$ 70
Average total assets	$23,505	$23,126

Requirements

1. Compute the profit margin for the year ended January 31, 2014.
2. Compute the asset turnover for the year ended January 31, 2014.
3. Compute the return on assets for the year ended January 31, 2014.

CHALLENGE EXERCISES

LEARNING OBJECTIVE ➌

Understand units-of-production depreciation

E7-33 Good Life Clubs purchased exercise equipment at a cost of $100,000 each. In addition, Good Life paid $2,000 for a special platform on which to stabilize the equipment for use. Freight costs of $2,500 to ship the equipment were paid by the equipment supplier. Good Life will depreciate the equipment by the units-of-production method, based on an expected useful life of 50,000 hours of exercise. The estimated residual value of the equipment is $10,000. How many hours of usage can Good Life expect from the equipment if budgeted depreciation expense is $10,304 for the year?

LEARNING OBJECTIVE ➍

Determine the gain or loss on sale of property and equipment

E7-34 Collicutt Energy Services Ltd. of Calgary, Alberta, reported the following for land, buildings, and equipment (in millions):

	December 31	
	2014	2013
Land, buildings, and equipment	$ 544.1	$ 575.1
Accumulated depreciation	(195.1)	(209.4)

During 2014, Collicutt Energy paid $74.2 million for new property and equipment. Depreciation for the year totalled $38.1 million. During 2014, Collicutt sold property and equipment for $20.2 million. How much was Collicutt's gain or loss on the sale of the property and equipment?

E7-35 Rindy Inc. has a popular line of beaded jewellery. Rindy reported net earnings of $21,000 for 2014. Rindy depreciates furniture, fixtures, equipment and automotive assets on a straight-line basis over five years and assumes no residual value. Depreciation expense for the year totaled $1,000 and the assets are four years old.

What would net income be for 2014 if Rindy used the double-diminishing balance (DDB) instead? The company's income tax rate is 25%.

LEARNING OBJECTIVE ❸❹

Determine net income after a change in depreciation method

E7-36 Air New Zealand (ANZ) is a Star Alliance member airline. Assume that early in 2014, ANZ purchased equipment at a cost of $200,000 (NZ). Management expects the equipment to remain in service for four years and the estimated residual value to be negligible. ANZ uses the straight-line depreciation method. Through an accounting error, ANZ expensed the entire cost of the equipment at the time of purchase.

LEARNING OBJECTIVE ❶❷

Determine equipment capitalizing versus expensing; measure the effect of an error

Requirement

Prepare a schedule to show the overstatement or understatement in the following items at the end of each year over the four-year life of the equipment. Ignore income taxes.

1. Total current assets   **2.** Equipment, net   **3.** Net income   **4.** Owners' equity

QUIZ

Test your understanding of accounting for property, plant, and equipment, and intangibles by answering the following questions. Select the best choice from among the possible answers given.

Q7-37 A capital expenditure
a. is expensed immediately.
b. records additional capital.
c. adds to an asset.
d. is a credit like capital (owners' equity).

Q7-38 Which of the following items should be accounted for as a capital expenditure?
a. Taxes paid in conjunction with the purchase of office equipment
b. The monthly rental cost of an office building
c. Costs incurred to repair leaks in the building's roof
d. Maintenance fees paid with funds provided by the company's capital

Q7-39 Suppose you buy land for $3,000,000 and spend $1,000,000 to develop the property. You then divide the land into lots as follows:

Category	Sale price per lot
10 Hilltop lots	$500,000
10 Valley lots	300,000

How much did each hilltop lot cost you?
a. $171,429
b. $228,571
c. $250,000
d. $400,000

Q7-40 Which statement about depreciation is false?
a. Depreciation is a process of allocating the cost of an asset to expense over its useful life.
b. Depreciation should not be recorded in years that the fair value of the asset has increased.
c. Residual value is the expected cash value of an asset at the end of its useful life.
d. Obsolescence as well as physical wear and tear should be considered when determining the period over which an asset should be depreciated.

Q7-41 TextDat, Inc., reported sales revenue of $600,000, net income of $45,000, and average total assets of $500,000. TextDat's return on assets is

a. 7.5%.

b. 9.0%.

c. 1.1%.

d. 83.3%.

$\frac{45,000}{500,000}$

Q7-42 The Blossom Shoppe's business activity fluctuates over its fiscal year, with December being its busiest month. Which method of depreciation would be most appropriate for its delivery van?

a. Straight-line

b. Diminishing-balance

c. Units-of-production

d. Some other method

Q7-43 Kramer Company failed to record depreciation of equipment. How does this omission affect Kramer's financial statements?

a. Net income is overstated, and assets are understated.

b. Net income is understated, and assets are understated.

c. Net income is understated, and assets are overstated.

d. Net income is overstated, and assets are overstated.

Q7-44 Jack's Stereo Inc. uses the double-diminishing-balance method for depreciation on its computers. Which item is not needed to compute depreciation for the first year?

a. Original cost

b. Estimated residual value

c. Expected useful life in years

d. All the above are needed.

Q7-45 Which of the following costs is reported on a company's income statement?

a. Accumulated depreciation

b. Land

c. Accounts payable

d. Depreciation expense

Q7-46 Which of the following items is reported on the balance sheet?

a. Net sales revenue

b. Accumulated depreciation

c. Gain on disposal of equipment

d. Cost of goods sold

Q7-47 Which of the following transactions does not appear on a statement of cash flows?

a. Purchase of plant, property, and equipment

b. Accumulated depreciation

c. Cash receipts from sale of property, plant, and equipment

d. Depreciation expense

Q7-48 Intangible assets are different from other assets for which of the following reasons?

a. They have special rights to current and expected future benefits.

b. They do not become obsolete.

c. They have no physical form.

d. They are not amortized.

Q7-49 Your self-storage company has purchased a moving company for $400,000. The fair value of the moving company's net assets is $325,000. How do you record the $75,000 difference?

a. As an expense on the income statement

b. As a property, plant, and equipment cost

c. As a long-term asset named goodwill

d. None of the above

Q7-50 A company has purchased the rights to a patent valued at $850,000. The company expects the useful life of the patent to be five years. The correct amortization for this asset would be which of the following?

a. Straight-line over five years

b. Units-of-production method based on a long-lived asset of $850,000

c. Diminishing-balance method based on a long-lived asset of $850,000

d. Units-of-production method based on a long-lived asset determined by the company

Q7-51 Suppose the *Globe and Mail* paid $1 million for a rural newspaper in Ontario three years ago. The newspaper's assets were valued at $1,000,000 and its liabilities at $150,000.

The company recorded $150,000 as goodwill at the time of the purchase. What *amortization* expense will be recorded for the current year?

a. $30,000 based on straight-line amortization over five years

b. No amortization, as review of the goodwill indicates there has been reduction in its value

c. No amortization, as the goodwill was fully expensed in the year of purchase

d. None of the above

PROBLEMS

(Group A)

P7-52A Assume Milne's Moving & Storage Ltd. (MMS) of Regina, Saskatchewan, incurred the following costs in acquiring land, making land improvements, and constructing and furnishing its own storage warehouse:

LEARNING OBJECTIVE ❶❷❸

Identify the elements of property and plant's cost

a. Purchase price of 4 acres of land, including an old building that will be used for an office (land fair value is $320,000, building fair value is $80,000)	$350,000
b. Landscaping (additional dirt and earth moving)	8,100
c. Fence around the land	31,600
d. Lawyer fee for title search on the land	1,000
e. Delinquent real estate taxes on the land to be paid by MMS	7,500
f. Company signs at front of the company property	3,400
g. Building permit for the warehouse	1,500
h. Architect fee for the design of the warehouse	24,500
i. Masonry, carpentry, roofing, and other labour to construct the warehouse	920,000
j. Renovation of the office building	50,200
k. Interest cost on construction loan for warehouse	9,700
l. Landscaping (trees and shrubs)	8,200
m. Parking lot, concrete walks, and lights on the property	57,600
n. Concrete, wood, and other materials used in the construction of the warehouse	234,300
o. Supervisory salary of construction supervisor (85% to warehouse, 5% to land improvements, 10% to office building)	60,000
p. Office furniture	115,700
q. Transportation and installation of furniture	2,300

Assume MMS depreciates buildings over 40 years, land improvements over 20 years, and furniture over 8 years, all on a straight-line basis with zero residual value.

Requirements

1. Set up columns for Land, Land Improvements, Warehouse, Office Building, and Furniture. Show how to account for each of MMS's costs by listing the cost under the correct account. Determine the total cost of each asset.

2. Assuming that all construction was complete and the assets were placed in service on September 1, 2014, record depreciation for the year ended December 31, 2014. Round to the nearest dollar.

3. Identify the management issues included in this problem and what effect they have on business operations.

P7-53A Lifestyle Lighting Ltd. reported the following on its balance sheet at December 31, 2013:

LEARNING OBJECTIVE ❶❷❸

Record property, plant, and equipment transactions; report on the balance sheet

Capital assets, at cost:	
Land	$ 150,000
Buildings	400,000
Less Accumulated depreciation	(87,500)
Equipment	600,000
Less Accumulated depreciation	(260,000)

In early July 2014, Lifestyle Lighting Ltd. expanded operations and purchased additional equipment at a cost of $100,000. The company depreciates buildings by the straight-line method over 20 years with residual value of $50,000. Due to obsolescence, the equipment has a useful life of only 10 years and is being depreciated by the double-diminishing-balance method with zero residual value.

Requirements

1. Journalize Lifestyle Lighting Ltd.'s capital equipment purchase and depreciation transactions for 2014.
2. Report capital assets on the December 31, 2014, balance sheet.

LEARNING OBJECTIVE ❶❷❸❹

Record property, plant, and equipment transactions, derecognition, and changes in useful life

P7-54A Assume that Inter-Provincial Transport Ltd.'s balance sheet includes the following assets under Property, Plant, and Equipment: Land, Buildings, and Motor-Carrier Equipment. Inter-Provincial has a separate accumulated depreciation account for each of these assets except land. Further, assume that Inter-Provincial completed the following transactions:

2014		
Jan.	2	Sold motor-carrier equipment with accumulated depreciation of $67,000 (cost of $130,000) for $70,000 cash. Purchased similar new equipment with a cash price of $176,000.
July	3	Sold a building that had cost $650,000 and had accumulated depreciation of $145,000 through December 31 of the preceding year. Depreciation is computed on a straight-line basis. The building had a 40-year useful life and a residual value of $250,000. Inter-Provincial received $100,000 cash and a $400,000 note receivable.
Oct.	29	Purchased land and a building for a single price of $420,000. An independent appraisal valued the land at $150,000 and the building at $300,000.
Dec.	31	Recorded depreciation as follows:
		New motor-carrier equipment has an expected useful life of six years and an estimated residual value of 5% of cost. Depreciation is computed on the double-diminishing-balance method.
		Depreciation on buildings is computed by the straight-line method. The new building carries a 40-year useful life and a residual value equal to 10% of its cost.

Requirement

Record the transactions in Inter-Provincial Transport Ltd.'s journal.

LEARNING OBJECTIVE ❸

Explain the concept of depreciation

P7-55A The board of directors of Special Services is reviewing its 2014 annual report. A new board member—a nurse with little business experience—questions the accountant about the depreciation amounts. The nurse wonders why depreciation expense has decreased from $200,000 in 2012 to $184,000 in 2013 to $172,000 in 2014. She states that she could understand the decreasing annual amounts if the company had been disposing of buildings each year, but that has not occurred. Further, she notes that growth in the city is increasing the values of company buildings. Why is the company recording depreciation when the property values are increasing?

Requirement

Write a paragraph or two to explain the concept of depreciation to the nurse and to answer her questions.

LEARNING OBJECTIVE ❸

Compute depreciation by three methods

P7-56A On January 3, 2013, B.W. Soffer Inc. paid $224,000 for a computer system. In addition to the basic purchase price, the company paid a setup fee of $6,200, $6,700 sales tax, and $3,100 for special installation. Management estimates that the computer will remain in service for five years and have a residual value of $20,000. The computer will process 50,000 documents the first year, decreasing annually by 5,000 during each of the next four years (that is, 45,000 documents in 2014, 40,000 documents in 2015, and so on). In trying to decide which depreciation method to use, the company president has requested a depreciation schedule for each of three depreciation methods (straight-line, units-of-production, and double-diminishing-balance).

Requirements

1. Prepare a depreciation schedule for each of the three depreciation methods listed, showing asset cost, depreciation expense, accumulated depreciation, and asset carrying amount.
2. B.W. Soffer Inc. reports to shareholders and creditors in the financial statements using the depreciation method that maximizes reported income in the early years of asset use. Consider the first year B.W. Soffer Inc. uses the computer system. Identify the depreciation method that meets the company's objectives. Discuss the advantages of each depreciation method.

P7-57A The excerpts that follow are adapted from financial statements of a Canadian not-for-profit organization.

LEARNING OBJECTIVE ❷❸❹❼

Analyze property, plant, and equipment transactions from a company's financial statements

| (amounts in thousands) | March 31 | |
Balance Sheet	2014	2013
Assets		
Total current assets	$277,631	$261,015
Property, plant, and equipment	68,406	61,225
Less accumulated depreciation	(26,909)	(22,725)
Long-term investments	108,302	147,165

| | For the Year Ended March 31 | |
Consolidated Statement of Cash Flows	2014	2013
Operating excess of revenues over expense	$13,068	$15,321
Noncash items affecting net income:		
Depreciation	4,184	3,748
Cash flows from investing activities:		
Additions to property, plant, and equipment	(7,781)	(8,623)
Reduction of (addition to) long-term investments	38,863	(96,316)

Requirements

1. How much was the entity's cost of property, plant, and equipment at March 31, 2014? How much was the carrying amount of capital assets? Show computations.
2. The financial statements give four pieces of evidence that the entity purchased property, plant, and equipment and sold long-term investments during 2014. What is the evidence?
3. Prepare T-accounts for Property, Plant and Equipment, Accumulated Depreciation, and Long-Term Investments. Then show all the activity in these accounts during 2014. Label each increase or decrease and give its dollar amount.
4. Why is depreciation added to net income on the statement of cash flows?

P7-58A Part 1. Sobeys Inc.'s balance sheet reports the asset Cost in Excess of Net Assets of Purchased Businesses. Assume that Sobeys acquired another company, which carried these figures:

LEARNING OBJECTIVE ❺

Account for intangibles and the related expenses

Carrying amount of net assets	$3.8 million
Fair value of assets	4.1 million

Requirements

1. What is the term used in Canadian financial reporting for the asset Cost in Excess of Net Assets of Purchased Businesses?
2. Record Sobeys Inc.'s purchase of the other company for $5.3 million cash.
3. Assume that Sobeys determined that the asset Cost in Excess of Net Assets of Purchased Businesses increased in value by $800,000. How would this transaction be recorded?

Then, suppose Cost in Excess of Net Assets of Purchased Businesses decreased in value by $800,000. How would this transaction be recorded? Discuss the basis for your decision in each case.

Part 2. Suppose Ford paid $2.6 million for a patent related to an integrated system, including hands-free cell phone, GPS, and iPod connectivity. The company expects to install this system in its automobiles for four years. Ford will sell this as an "extra" for $1,500. In the first year, 10,000 units were sold. All costs per unit totalled $835.

Requirements

1. As the CFO, how would you record transactions relating to the patent in the first year?
2. Prepare the income statement for the integrated system's operations for the first year. Evaluate the profitability of the integrated system's operations. Use an income tax rate of 38%.
3. Explain what items were recorded as assets and why.

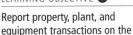
LEARNING OBJECTIVE ⑦

Report property, plant, and equipment transactions on the statement of cash flows

P7-59A At the end of 2013, Geothermal Heating Ltd. had total assets of $17.4 million and total liabilities of $9.2 million. Included among the assets were property, plant, and equipment with a cost of $4.8 million and accumulated depreciation of $3.4 million.

Assume that Geothermal Heating completed the following selected transactions during 2014. The company earned total revenues of $26.5 million and incurred total expenses of $21.3 million, which included depreciation of $1.7 million. During the year, Geothermal Heating paid $1.4 million for new equipment and sold old equipment for $0.3 million. The cost of the assets sold was $0.8 million, and their accumulated depreciation was $0.4 million.

Requirements

1. Explain how to determine whether Geothermal Heating had a gain or loss on the sale of old equipment during the year. What was the amount of the gain or loss, if any?
2. How will Geothermal Heating report property, plant, and equipment on the balance sheet at December 31, 2014, after all the year's activity? What will the carrying amount of property, plant, and equipment be?
3. How will Geothermal Heating report operating activities and investing activities on its statement of cash flows for 2014? The company's statement of cash flows starts with net income.

LEARNING OBJECTIVE ⑥

Calculate return on assets

P7-60A Target Corporation operates general merchandise and food discount stores in the United States. The company reported the following information for the three years ending January 31, 2014:

Target Corporation Income Statement (Adapted) For the years ended			
(in millions)	Jan 31, 2014	Jan 31, 2013	Jan 31, 2012
Total net revenue	$67,390	$65,357	$64,948
Cost of revenue	45,725	44,062	44,157
Selling, general, and administrative	16,413	16,622	16,389
Operating income or loss	5,252	4,673	4,402
Other revenue (expense)	(757)	(801)	(866)
Income before tax	4,495	3,872	3,536
Income tax expense	(1,575)	(1,384)	(1,322)
Net income	$ 2,920	$ 2,488	$ 2,214

Target Corporation
Partial Balance Sheet (Condensed)

(in millions)	Jan 31, 2014	Jan 31, 2013	Jan 31, 2012
Total current assets	$17,213	$18,424	$17,488
Property, plant, and equipment	25,493	25,280	25,756
Other assets	999	829	862
Total assets	$43,705	$44,533	$44,106

Requirements

1. Compute the profit margin for Target for the years ended January 31, 2014, and January 31, 2013.
2. Compute the asset turnover for Target for the years ended January 31, 2014, and January 31, 2013.
3. Compute return on assets for Target for the years ended January 31, 2014, and January 31, 2013.
4. What factors contributed to the change in return on assets during the year?

(Group B)

P7-61B McMillan Tire Inc. operates in several provinces. The head office incurred the following costs in acquiring land and a building, making land improvements, and constructing and furnishing a garage showroom:

LEARNING OBJECTIVE ❶❷❸

Identify the elements of property, plant, and equipment cost

a. Purchase price of land, including a building that will be enlarged to be a warehouse (land fair value is $150,000; building fair value is $50,000)	$180,000
b. Fence around the land	26,000
c. Company signs near front and rear approaches to the company property	25,000
d. Title insurance on the land acquisition	1,200
e. Renovation of the warehouse	21,300
f. Landscaping (additional dirt and earth moving)	3,550
g. Architect fee for the design of the garage/showroom	45,000
h. Building permit for the building	200
i. Delinquent real estate taxes on the land to be paid by McMillan	3,700
j. Concrete, wood, and other materials used in the construction of the garage/showroom	322,000
k. Supervisory salary of construction supervisor (90% to garage/showroom, 6% to land improvements, and 4% to building renovation)	55,000
l. Landscaping (trees and shrubs)	5,350
m. Masonry, carpentry, roofing, and other labour to construct the garage/showroom	234,000
n. Lights for the parking lot, walkways, and company signs	8,900
o. Parking lots and concrete walks on the property	17,450
p. Interest cost on construction loan for garage/showroom	3,300
q. Installation of equipment	8,000
r. Equipment for the garage/showroom	80,000

McMillan Tire depreciates buildings over 40 years, land improvements over 10 years, and equipment over 8 years, all on a straight-line basis with zero residual value.

Requirements

1. Determine the total cost of each asset. Set up columns for Land, Land Improvements, Garage/Showroom, Warehouse, and Equipment. Decide how to account for each of McMillan's costs by listing the cost under the correct account.

2. All construction was complete and the assets were placed in service on March 29. Record depreciation for the year ended December 31. Round figures to the nearest dollar.
3. Identify the issues of this problem, and discuss how your decisions would affect the results of McMillan Tire Inc.

LEARNING OBJECTIVE ① ②

Record property, plant, and equipment transactions; report on the balance sheet

P7-62B Moreau Lock & Key Ltd. has a hefty investment in security equipment, as reported in the company's balance sheet at December 31, 2013:

Property, plant, and equipment, at cost:	
Land	$ 200,000
Buildings	310,000
Less Accumulated depreciation	(40,000)
Security equipment	620,000
Less Accumulated depreciation	(370,000)

In early October 2014, Moreau Lock & Key purchased additional security equipment at a cost of $80,000. The company depreciates buildings by the straight-line method over 20 years with a residual value of $70,000. Due to obsolescence, security equipment has a useful life of only eight years and is being depreciated by the double-diminishing-balance method with zero residual value.

Requirements

1. How will Moreau Lock & Key's equipment purchase be recorded? What will the 2014 depreciation expense be?
2. Report property, plant, and equipment on the company's December 31, 2014, balance sheet.

LEARNING OBJECTIVE ① ② ③ ④

Record property, plant, and equipment transactions

P7-63B Schmaltz Cable Company's balance sheet reports the following assets under Property, Plant, and Equipment: Land, Buildings, Office Furniture, Communication Equipment, and Televideo Equipment. The company has a separate accumulated depreciation account for each of these assets except land. Assume that Schmaltz Cable completed the following transactions:

2014	
Jan. 4	Sold communication equipment with accumulated depreciation of $85,000 (cost of $96,000) for $18,000. Purchased new equipment for $118,000.
June 30	Sold a building that had cost $495,000 and had accumulated depreciation of $255,000 through December 31 of the preceding year. Depreciation is computed on a straight-line basis. The building has a 40-year useful life and a residual value of $95,000. The company received $50,000 cash and a $250,000 note receivable.
Nov. 4	Purchased used communication and televideo equipment from Rogers Cable Company. Total cost was $80,000 paid in cash. An independent appraisal valued the communication equipment at $75,000 and the televideo equipment at $25,000.
Dec. 31	Depreciation is recorded as follows: Equipment is depreciated by the double-diminishing-balance method over a five-year life with zero residual value. Depreciation is recorded separately on the equipment purchased on January 4 and on November 4.

Requirement

If Schmaltz Cable has recorded these transactions correctly, what should your review of the company's records show?

LEARNING OBJECTIVE ③

Explain the concept of depreciation

P7-64B The board of directors of the Canadian Red Cross is having its regular quarterly meeting. Accounting policies are on the agenda, and depreciation is being discussed. A new board member, a social worker, has some strong opinions about two aspects of depreciation policy.

The new board member argues that depreciation must be coupled with a fund to replace company assets. Otherwise, there is no substance to depreciation, he argues. He also challenges the three-year estimated life over which the Canadian Red Cross is depreciating association computers. He notes that the computers will last much longer and should be depreciated over at least 10 years.

Requirement

Write a paragraph or two to explain the concept of depreciation to the new board member and to answer his arguments.

P7-65B On January 2, 2014, Yuki Sporting Goods Ltd. purchased branding equipment at a cost of $63,000. Before placing the equipment in service, the company spent $2,200 for delivery, $4,000 to customize the equipment, and $800 for installation. Management estimates that the equipment will remain in service for six years and have a residual value of $16,000. The equipment can be expected to brand 18,000 pieces in each of the first four years and 14,000 pieces in each of the next two years. In trying to decide which depreciation method to use, George Yuki requests a depreciation schedule for each method (straight-line, units-of-production, and double-diminishing-balance).

LEARNING OBJECTIVE **3**

Compute depreciation by three methods

Requirements

1. Prepare a depreciation schedule for each of the depreciation methods listed, showing asset cost, depreciation expense, accumulated depreciation, and asset carrying value.
2. Yuki Sporting Goods reports to its banker in the financial statements using the depreciation method that maximizes reported income in the early years of asset use. Consider the first year that Yuki Sporting Goods uses the equipment. Identify the depreciation method that meets the company's objectives. Explain your choice.

P7-66B CrossCanada Transport Inc. (CC) provides warehouse and distribution services. The excerpts that follow are adapted from CC's financial statements for fiscal year 2014.

LEARNING OBJECTIVE **2 3 4 5 7**

Analyze property, plant, and equipment transactions from a company's financial statements

(amounts in thousands)	October 31	
Balance Sheet	2014	2013
Assets		
Total current assets	$237,936	$208,530
Premises and equipment	5,941	5,246
Less Accumulated depreciation	(3,810)	(3,428)
Goodwill	4,752	4,304

	For the Year Ended October 31	
Statement of Cash Flows (in millions)	2014	2013
Cash provided from operating activities:		
Net income from continuing operations	$5,492	$4,757
Noncash items affecting net income:		
Depreciation	434	405
Cash used in investing activities:		
Acquisition of premises and equipment	(706)	(511)
Cash used in acquisitions (including $41 of premises and equipment)	(373)	(256)

Requirements

1. How much was CC's cost of property and equipment at October 31, 2014? How much was the carrying amount of premises and equipment? Show computations.
2. The financial statements give four pieces of evidence that CC purchased premises and equipment during 2014. What are they?

3. Prepare T-accounts for Premises and Equipment and Accumulated Depreciation. Then show all the activity in these accounts during 2014. Did CC dispose of any assets and, if so, what was the carrying amount?
4. Why has goodwill not been amortized?

LEARNING OBJECTIVE 5

Account for intangibles and the related expenses

P7-67B Part 1. The Coca-Cola Company's (CCC) balance sheet reports the asset Goodwill. Assume that CCC purchased an asset to be included in Goodwill as part of the acquisition of another company, which carried these figures (thousands of dollars):

Carrying amount of long-term assets	$34,550
Fair value of assets	49,000
Liabilities	4,500

Requirements

1. Explain the terms *carrying amount of assets*, *fair value of assets*, and *goodwill*. On what would you base the purchase price of the acquisition?
2. Make the journal entry to record CCC's purchase of the other company for $50,000 cash.

Part 2. Joshua Thomas has written a new dance song which Luv Sound Inc. would like to record. Joshua is negotiating the rights to the new song. It is estimated that Luv Sound will sell about 500,000 recordings either on CD, to radio station airings, or to iPod sales. Joshua would like to receive $2,000,000 for the copyright to this song.

Requirements

1. As the CFO of Luv Sound, decide whether $2,000,000 is an appropriate amount to pay for the copyright for Joshua Thomas's song.
2. If you chose to purchase the copyright, show how you would record the transaction.
3. What would be the accumulated amortization after 300,000 copies of the song had been sold by Luv Sound Inc.?

LEARNING OBJECTIVE 7

Report property, plant, and equipment transactions on the statement of cash flows

P7-68B At the end of 2013, a telecommunications company had total assets of $15.3 billion and total liabilities of $10.7 billion. Included among the assets were property, plant, and equipment with a cost of $16.4 billion and accumulated depreciation of $9.1 billion.

Suppose that the company completed the following selected transactions during 2014. The company earned total revenues of $11.6 billion and incurred total expenses of $9.89 billion, which included depreciation of $1.84 billion. During the year, the company paid $1.8 billion for new property, plant, and equipment, and sold old property, plant, and equipment for $0.2 billion. The cost of the assets sold was $0.29 billion and their accumulated depreciation was $0.29 billion.

Requirements

1. Explain how to determine whether the company had a gain or a loss on the sale of the old property, plant, and equipment. What was the amount of the gain or loss, if any?
2. Show how the company would report property, plant, and equipment on the balance sheet at December 31, 2014.
3. Show how the company would report operating activities and investing activities on its statement of cash flows for 2014. The company's statement of cash flows starts with net income.

LEARNING OBJECTIVE 6

Calculate return on assets

P7-69B Kohl's Corporation operates family oriented department stores that sell moderately priced apparel and housewares. The company reported the following information (adapted) for the three years ending January 31, 2014:

Kohl's Corporation
Income Statement (Adapted)

	Jan 31, 2014	Jan 31, 2013	Jan 31, 2012
Net sales	$18,391	$17,178	$16,389
Cost of merchandise sold	11,359	10,680	10,334
Selling, general, and administrative	5,118	4,786	4,519
Operating income	1,914	1,712	1,536
Other revenue (expense)	(132)	(124)	(111)
Income before tax	1,782	1,588	1,425
Provision for income tax	(668)	(597)	(540)
Net income	$ 1,114	$ 991	$ 885

Kohl's Corporation
Partial Balance Sheet

	Jan 31, 2014	Jan 31, 2013	Jan 31, 2012
Total current assets	$ 5,645	$ 5,485	$ 3,728
Long-term investments	386	336	333
Property, plant, and equipment	7,256	7,018	6,984
Other assets	277	321	318
Total assets	$13,564	$13,160	$11,363

Requirements

1. Compute the profit margin for Kohl's for the years ended January 31, 2014, and January 31, 2013.
2. Compute the asset turnover for Kohl's for the years ended January 31, 2014, and January 31, 2013.
3. Compute the return on assets for Kohl's for the years ended January 31, 2014, and January 31, 2013.
4. What factors contributed to the change in return on assets during the year?

Apply Your Knowledge

Decision Cases

Case 1. Suppose you are considering investing in two businesses, La Petite France Bakery and Burgers Ahoy Inc. The two companies are virtually identical, and both began operations at the beginning of the current year.

In early January, both companies purchased equipment costing $175,000 that had a 10-year estimated useful life and a $10,000 residual value. La Petite France uses the depreciation method that maximizes income for reporting purposes. In contrast, Burgers Ahoy uses the double-diminishing-balance method for depreciation purposes. Assume that both companies' trial balances at December 31 included the following:

Sales revenue	$350,000
Cost of goods sold	94,000
Operating expenses before depreciation	50,000

The income tax rate is 25%.

LEARNING OBJECTIVE ❸❹

Measure profitability based on different depreciation methods

Requirements

1. Prepare both companies' income statements.
2. Write an investment newsletter to address the following questions for your clients. Which company appears to be more profitable? If prices continue rising over the long term, in which company would you prefer to invest? Why?

LEARNING OBJECTIVE ❷❺

Understand property, plant, and equipment and intangible assets

Case 2. The following questions are unrelated except that they all apply to property, plant, and equipment and intangible assets:

1. The manager of Fashion Forward Ltd. regularly buys property, plant, and equipment and debits the cost to Repairs and Maintenance Expense. Why would she do that, since she knows this action violates IFRS?

2. The manager of Greytown Express Inc. regularly debits the cost of repairs and maintenance of property, plant, and equipment to Plant and Equipment. Why would he do that, since he knows he is violating IFRS?

3. It has been suggested that because many intangible assets have no value except to the company that owns them, they should be valued at $1.00 or zero on the balance sheet. Many accountants disagree with this view. Which view do you support? Why?

Ethical Issue

Vitner's Ltd. purchased land and a building for the lump sum of $6.0 million. To report a higher net income, Mary Drink allocated 60% of the purchase price to the building and only 40% to the land. A more realistic allocation would have been 80% to the building and 20% to the land.

Requirements

1. Explain the advantage of allocating too little to the building and too much to the land.
2. Was Vitner's allocation ethical? If so, state why. If not, why not? Identify who was harmed.

Focus on Financials

LEARNING OBJECTIVE ❸❹❼

Explain property, plant, and equipment activity

TELUS Corporation

Refer to TELUS's financial statements in Appendix A at the end of this book, and answer the following questions.

1. Which depreciation method does TELUS use for reporting to shareholders and creditors in the financial statements?

2. During 2011, TELUS sold property, plant, and equipment (assets). What were the proceeds? What was the cost of the property, plant, and equipment disposed of?

3. How much did TELUS pay for property and equipment during 2011? What about in 2010? Evaluate the trend in these expenditures as to whether it conveys good news for TELUS.

4. During 2011, TELUS added new property, plant, and equipment. Therefore, it is possible that the company's property and equipment at the end of 2011 were proportionately newer than the assets the company held at the end of 2010. Were property and equipment proportionately newer or older at the end of 2011 (versus 2010)?

Focus on Analysis

LEARNING OBJECTIVE ❸❹❺❼

Analyze property, plant, and equipment and intangible assets

TELUS Corporation

Refer to TELUS'S financial statements in Appendix A at the end of the book, and answer the following questions:

1. How much was TELUS's depreciation and amortization expense during fiscal year 2011? How much was TELUS's accumulated depreciation and amortization at the end of year

2010? Explain why accumulated depreciation and amortization exceeds depreciation and amortization expense for the year 2011.

2. Explain why TELUS adds depreciation and amortization expenses back to net income in the computation of net cash from operating activities.

3. Does TELUS have any goodwill? In 2011, was amortization on goodwill charged? TELUS describes intangible assets. What are they? How much amortization of intangible assets did TELUS record in 2011?

Group Project

Obtain the annual report of two public Canadian companies from the same industry. Most annual reports can be downloaded from their websites. Examine the notes and other information that may be useful to analyze property, plant, and equipment, as well as intangible assets, including goodwill.

Requirements

1. What additions and disposals did the company make during the year? If there were any new additions, did they have to borrow money to help finance the cost of these assets? How can you tell?

2. Was there any impairment of long-lived assets? If so, what contributed to this impairment? How did it impact the financial statements?

3. Compute the return on assets for both companies for the two most recent years. Which company is using their assets more efficiently?

4. Write a memo to summarize your findings, stating which company you would invest in.

Quick Check Answers

1. *b* [($850,000/[$850,000 + $675,000 + $475,000]) × $1,500,000 = $637,500]
2. *a*
3. *a* [($25,000 − $2,500)/5 × 5/12 = $1,875]
4. *d* [($25,000 − $2,500)/5 × 2 = $9,000; $25,000 − $9,000 = $16,000]
5. *b* [$25,000 × 2/5 = $10,000; ($25,000 − $10,000) × 2/5 = $6,000]
6. *a* [($25,000 − $2,500)/5 × 4 = $18,000; $25,000 − $18,000 = $7,000; $11,500 − $7,000 = gain of $4,500, therefore, a gain will be realized]
7. *c* [$17,000 × 2/4 = $8,500; ($17,000 − $8,500) × 2/4 = $4,250; $8,500 + $4,250 = $12,750]
8. *c*   9. *a*   10. *d*   11. *b*
12. *e*   13. *c*   14. *c*

8

Long-Term Investments and the Time Value of Money

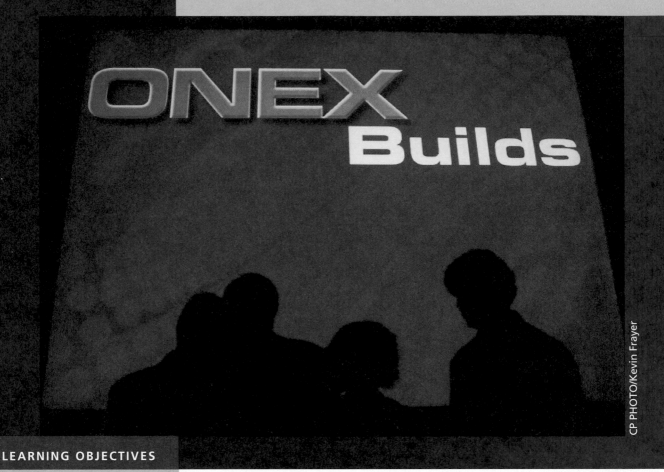

CP PHOTO/Kevin Frayer

LEARNING OBJECTIVES

❶ **Analyze** and **report** non-strategic investments

❷ **Analyze** and **report** investments in affiliated companies using the equity method

❸ **Analyze** and **report** controlling interests in other corporations using consolidated financial statements

❹ **Analyze** and **report** long-term investments in bonds

❺ **Report** investing activities on the statement of cash flows

❻ **Explain** the impact of the time value of money on certain types of investments

SPOTLIGHT

ONEX Corporation holds several different types of investments. Have you ever wondered what you will do with all the money you will be earning once you graduate? Maybe you will start investing through a retirement or savings plan at work, and you may make some investments on your own. The reasons people invest are for current income (interest and dividends) and for appreciation of the investment's value (stocks and real estate, for example). Some very wealthy individuals invest in a wide variety of traditional and non-traditional investments in order to obtain significant influence over, or even to control, corporate entities and to maximize their wealth.

Businesses like ONEX, Canadian Tire Corporation, and TELUS invest their money for the same reasons. If you look at ONEX's balance sheet on the next page, you will see that of the $29,446 million of total assets they own, they have $5,415 million in long-term investments. In this chapter you'll learn how to account for investments of all types. You will also learn how companies like these do business across international borders and the impact that cross-border business has on their financial statements.

ONEX Corporation
Consolidated Balance Sheet (Partial, Adapted)
As at December 31, 2011

	(in millions of U.S. dollars)
Assets	
Current assets	
Cash and cash equivalents	$ 2,448
Short-term investments	749
Accounts receivable	3,272
Inventories	4,428
Other current assets	1,186
Total Current Assets	12,083
Property, plant, and equipment	5,102
Long-term investments	5,415
Other non-current assets	1,813
Intangible assets	2,599
Goodwill	2,434
Total Assets	$ 29,446

Founded in 1983, ONEX is an investment firm that buys significant interests in companies with the intention of controlling their operations. Once a company is acquired, they work with the company's management to help them become a leader in their industry. The many companies ONEX has acquired significant control of include Celestica and Cineplex. These investments are reflected in various asset accounts, such as inventory; property, plant, and equipment; and goodwill. In addition, ONEX has short-term investments.

Throughout this course, you have become increasingly familiar with the financial statements of companies such as TELUS Corporation, Leon's Furniture, and CGI Group. You have seen most of the items that appear in a set of financial statements. One of your learning goals should be to develop the ability to interpret whatever you encounter in real-company statements. This chapter will help you advance toward that goal.

The first part of the chapter shows how to account for long-term investments, including a brief overview of consolidated financial statements. The second half of the chapter covers accounting for international operations and the time value of money.

Share Investments: A Review

Investments come in all sizes and shapes—ranging from a few shares to the acquisition of an entire company, to interests in other types of investments, such as corporate bonds. In this chapter, we will introduce you to the accounting for various types of long-term investments from the perspective of the purchaser, or investor.

To consider investments, we need to define two key terms. The entity that owns shares in a corporation is the *investor*. The corporation that issued the shares is the *investee*. If you own ONEX common shares, you are an investor and ONEX is the investee.

Share Prices

Investors buy more shares in transactions among themselves than directly from large companies, such as ONEX. Each share is issued only once, but it may be traded

EXHIBIT 8-1
**Share Price Information
for ONEX Corporation**

	52-Week		Stock			Net
Hi		Lo	Symbol	Div	Close	Change
$40.26		$28.01	OCX	$0.11	$38.76	−$0.34

among investors many times thereafter. You may log onto the Internet or consult a newspaper to learn ONEX's current share price.

Exhibit 8-1 presents information on ONEX common shares from the *Globe and Mail Investor* for August 31, 2012. During the previous 52 weeks, ONEX shares reached a high price of $40.26 and a low price of $28.01 per share. The annual cash dividend is $0.11 per share. At the end of the day, the price of the shares closed at $38.76, down $0.34 from the closing price of the shares on August 30, 2012.

Reporting Investments on the Balance Sheet

An investment is an asset to the investor. The investment may be short term or long term. *Short-term investments* are current assets and are sometimes called *temporary investments* or *marketable securities*. To be listed as short term on the balance sheet,

- the investment must be *liquid* (readily convertible to cash).
- the investor must intend either to convert the investment to cash within one year or to use it to pay a current liability. We saw how to account for short-term investments in Chapter 5.

Investments that are not short term are classified as **long-term investments**, a category of non-current assets. Long-term investments include shares and bonds that the investor expects to hold for longer than one year. Exhibit 8-2 shows the positions of short-term and long-term investments on the balance sheet.

Accounting for Long-Term Investments in Shares

IFRS describe three categories of long-term share investments. The category an investment falls into depends on the percentage of ownership held by the investor.

1. *Non-strategic investments.* **Non-strategic investments** are investments where the investor owns less than 20% of the voting shares of the investee and thus is presumed to exercise no influence over the affairs of the investee. The investor records the investment at the price paid and adjusts the investment account

EXHIBIT 8-2
**Reporting Investments on
the Balance Sheet**

Current Assets:	
Cash	$X
Short-term investments	X
Accounts receivable	X
Inventories	X
Prepaid expenses	X
Total current assets	$X
Long-term investments [or simply Investments]	X
Property, plant, and equipment (net)	X
Intangible assets (net)	X
Other assets	X

for changes in fair value either through net income or through other comprehensive income. If the fair value is not available, then the investment is recorded at cost and no adjustments are made to its value (the cost method). Until January 1, 2015, the investor accounts for the investment using the cost method by which the investor's share of dividends paid by the investee is treated as income by the investor. After this date, under IFRS 9, the investor will record the initial investment at cost and, at each reporting date, record any changes in fair value through either other comprehensive income (currently referred to as "Available-for-Sale Investments"[*]) or through profit or loss (net income). This chapter will illustrate IFRS 9 because Canadian companies can choose to adopt this approach early. Under ASPE, a company can use either the cost method or fair value, with any changes in fair value reported through net income.

2. *Investments subject to significant influence.* An investee is generally described as being subject to significant influence when the investor owns between 20% and 50% of the voting shares of the investee. Significant influence allows the investor to direct the affairs of the investee. The investor accounts for the investment using the *equity method* by which the investor's proportionate share of the investee's profits and losses are treated as income or loss by the investor. The investor's share of dividends paid by the investee are treated as a return of investment and are credited to the investment account. Under ASPE, a company can choose to use either the equity method or the cost method. If the share investments are quoted in an active market, fair value replaces the cost method with any changes in fair value reported through net income.

3. *Investments in subsidiaries.* A subsidiary is a company controlled by another company (the parent), which is entitled to the rewards and bears the risks of the subsidiary. Generally a parent will own more than 50% of the voting shares of the subsidiary. The financial statements of the investee are consolidated with those of the investor. Under ASPE, a company can choose to either consolidate its financial statements or account for its investment using either the equity method or the cost method. If the share investments are quoted in an active market, fair value replaces the cost method with any changes in fair value reported through net income.

ANALYZE AND REPORT NON-STRATEGIC INVESTMENTS

An investor may make a non-strategic (or passive) investment where the purpose is similar to that of short-term investing; the investor will hold the investment to earn dividend revenue and/or capital appreciation but has no interest in directing the affairs of investee. The investor usually holds less than 20% of the voting shares and would normally play no important role in the investee's operations.

Non-strategic investments are accounted for at fair value because the company expects to sell the investment at its current market price. *Cost* is used as the initial amount for recording the investments. These investments are reported on the balance sheet at *fair value* unless the shares are not traded in an active market. If that is the case, then cost becomes the reported value of the investment.

---

[*]The "Available for Sale" category will disappear as of January 1, 2015.

Suppose ONEX purchases 1,000 Agrium Inc. common shares at the market price of $50.00 on July 10, 2014. Assume ONEX has no significant influence over Agrium and intends to hold this investment for longer than a year. This type of investment is classified as a non-strategic investment. ONEX's entry to record the investment is:

2014
July 10   Long-Term Investment (1,000 × $50.00)............   50,000
                     Cash   50,000
                 Purchased investment.

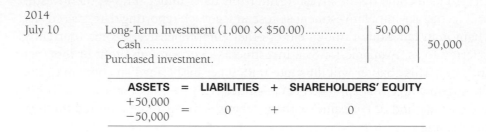

ASSETS	=	LIABILITIES	+	SHAREHOLDERS' EQUITY
+50,000 −50,000	=	0	+	0

Assume on October 5, 2014 that ONEX receives a $0.14 per share cash dividend on the Agrium Inc. shares. ONEX's entry to record receipt of the dividend is:

2014
Oct. 5   Cash (1,000 × $0.14)   140
                     Dividend Revenue...   140
                 Received cash dividend.

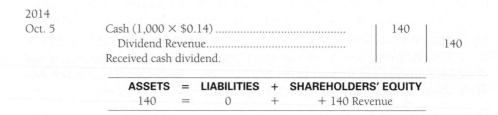

ASSETS	=	LIABILITIES	+	SHAREHOLDERS' EQUITY
140	=	0	+	+ 140 Revenue

What Value of an Investment Is Most Relevant?

Fair value is the amount for which you can buy or sell an investment. Because of the relevance of fair values for decision making, non-strategic investments in shares are reported on the balance sheet at their fair value. On the balance sheet date we therefore adjust non-strategic investments from their last carrying amount to current fair value. Assume that the fair value of the Agrium common shares is $53,000 on December 31, 2014. As previously discussed, at initial recognition the investor can choose to report the changes in fair value in long-term non-strategic investments either through net income or through other comprehensive income (currently referred to as "Available-for-Sale Investment"). Shown below are the journal entries to report changes in fair value under both approaches.

Company chooses to report changes in fair value through net income:	Company chooses to report changes in fair value through other comprehensive income:

Long-term Investment   3,000
   Unrealized gain   3,000
Adjusted investment to fair value.
	Long-Term Investment 3,000
	   Other Comprehensive Income 3,000
	Adjusted investment to fair value.

Unrealized gains are reported under "Other Income" on the Income statement.	Other Comprehensive Income is reported below net income on the statement of comprehensive income.

The increase in the investment's fair value creates additional equity for the investor.

ASSETS	=	LIABILITIES	+	SHAREHOLDERS' EQUITY
+3,000	=	0	+	+3,000 Unrealized gain

The Long-Term Investment account and the Other Comprehensive Income or Unrealized Gain account would appear as follows:

Long-Term Investment	Other Comprehensive Income or Unrealized Gain
50,000	
3,000	3,000

If the investment's fair value declines, the Long-Term Investment account is credited. The corresponding debit is to Other Comprehensive Income or Unrealized Loss. *Unrealized* gains and losses result from changes in fair value, not from sales of investments.

Unrealized gains and unrealized losses on non-strategic investments that occur in a fiscal year are reported in two places in the financial statements:

- *Other Comprehensive Income* is reported in a separate section below net income on the *statement of comprehensive income*. For example, assume the Consolidated Statement of Comprehensive Income section of Leon's Furniture Limited's 2011 annual report states:

  Other Comprehensive Income, Net of Tax
    Unrealized Gain on Financial Assets Arising
      During the Year (Net of Tax of $45) $223

- *Accumulated Other Comprehensive Income*, which is a separate section of shareholders' equity below retained earnings on the *balance sheet*. The Shareholders' Equity section of the Leon's Furniture Limited's 2011 balance sheet reports:

  Accumulated Other Comprehensive Income .... $(142)

At December 31, 2014, ONEX would close the Other Comprehensive Income account to the shareholders' equity account Accumulated Other Comprehensive Income as follows:

2014			
Dec. 31	Other Comprehensive Income..............................	3,000	
	Accumulated Other Comprehensive Income.....		3,000
	To Close Out the Unrealized Gain on the Investment to		
	Accumulated Other Comprehensive Income.		

Under ASPE, all unrealized gains and losses flow through net income.

If the company chooses to recognize the changes in fair value in the investment through income (called profit or loss), unrealized gains or unrealized losses would be used instead of other comprehensive income. These unrealized gains and losses are reported under Other Income on the income statement.

Selling a Non-strategic Investment

The sale of a non-strategic investment can result in a *realized* gain or loss. Realized gains and losses measure the difference between the amount received from the sale of the investment and the carrying amount of the investment.

Suppose ONEX sells its investment in Agrium Inc. shares for $57,000 during 2015. ONEX would record the sale as follows:

Company chooses to report changes in fair value through net income:			Company chooses to report changes in fair value through other comprehensive income:		
Cash	57,000		Cash	57,000	
Long-Term Investment		53,000	Long-Term Investment		53,000
Gain on Sale of Investment		4,000	Other Comprehensive Income		4,000
Realized gains and losses are reported under "Other Income" on the income statement.			Realized gains are reported under Other Comprehensive Income on the statement of comprehensive income.		

ONEX would report the Gain on Sale of Investments as an "Other" item on the income statement.

STOP + THINK (8-1)

Suppose Ardnas Holdings Ltd. holds the following securities as long-term investments at March 31, 2014:

Shares	Cost	Current Market Value
Canadian Tire Corp..	$70,000	$47,500
Quebecor	26,000	16,000
	$96,000	$63,500

Show how Ardnas Holdings will report long-term investments on its March 31, 2014, balance sheet.

OBJECTIVE

❷ Analyze and report investments in affiliated companies using the equity method

ANALYZE AND REPORT INVESTMENTS IN AFFILIATED COMPANIES USING THE EQUITY METHOD

An investor who holds less than 20% of the investee's voting shares usually plays no important role in the investee's operations. But an investor with a larger share holding—between 20% and 50% of the investee's voting shares—may significantly influence how the investee operates the business. Such an investor can probably affect the investee's decisions on dividend policy, product lines, and other important matters. The investor will also likely hold one or more seats on the board of directors of the investee company. We use the **equity method** to account for these types of investments.

Accounting for Investments Using the Equity Method

Investments accounted for by the equity method are recorded initially at cost. Suppose NPC Corporation paid $611 million for 32% of the common shares of Bruce Power. NPC's entry to record the purchase of this investment is (in millions):

2014
Jan. 2   Long-Term Investment..   611
                 Cash   611
            To purchase equity investment.

ASSETS	=	LIABILITIES	+	SHAREHOLDERS' EQUITY
+611	=	0	+	0
−611				

THE INVESTOR'S PERCENTAGE OF INVESTEE INCOME. Under the equity method, NPC, as the investor, applies its percentage of ownership (32% in our example) in recording its share of the investee's net income. Suppose Bruce reports net income of $100 million for 2014; NPC would record 32% of this amount as follows (in millions):

2014
Dec. 31   Long-Term Investment ($100 × 0.32)..................   32
                 Investment Revenue...   32
            To record investment revenue.

ASSETS	=	LIABILITIES	+	SHAREHOLDERS' EQUITY
32	=	0	+	+ 32 Revenue

Because of the close relationship between NPC and Bruce, the investor increases the Investment account and records Investment Revenue when the investee reports income. As Bruce's equity increases, so does the Investment account on NPC's books.

RECEIVING DIVIDENDS UNDER THE EQUITY METHOD. NPC Corporation records its proportionate part of cash dividends received from Bruce. Assume Bruce declares and pays a cash dividend of $9,375,000. NPC receives 32% of this dividend and records this entry (in millions):

Dec. 31   Cash ($9,375,000 × 0.32)   3
                 Long-Term Investment.......................................   3
            To receive cash dividend on equity investment.

ASSETS	=	LIABILITIES	+	SHAREHOLDERS' EQUITY
3	=	0	+	0
−3				

The Investment account is *decreased* for the receipt of a dividend on an equity method investment. Why? Because the dividend decreases the investee's equity and thus the investor's investment.

After the preceding entries are posted, NPC's Long-Term Investment account would include its equity in the net assets of Bruce as follows (in millions):

		Long-Term Investment				
2014	Jan. 2	Purchase	611	Dec. 31	Dividends	3
	Dec. 31	Net income	32			
	Dec. 31	Balance	640			

NPC reports long-term investments on the balance sheet and the investment revenue on the income statement as follows:

	(in millions)
Balance sheet (partial):	
Assets	
Total current assets	$XXX
Long-term investments..	640
Property, plant, and equipment, net..	XXX
Income statement (partial):	
Income from operations	$XXX
Other revenue:	
Revenue from equity investments	32
Net income	$XXX

The gain or loss on the sale of an equity-method investment is measured as the difference between the sale proceeds and the carrying amount of the investment. For example, NPC Corporation's financial statements show that the investment in Bruce Power at December 31, 2014, was $640 million. Suppose NPC sold 10% of its interest in Bruce Power on January 10, 2015, for $62 million. The entry to record the sale would be:

2015			
Jan. 10	Cash	62	
	Loss on Sale of Investment..	2	
	Long-Term Investment ($640 million × 0.10).........		64
	Sold 10% of investment.		

ASSETS	=	LIABILITIES	+	SHAREHOLDERS' EQUITY
62	=	0	+	−2 Loss
−64				

When there has been a loss in value in an equity investment other than a temporary decline, the investment is written down to reflect the loss. This is different than adjusting the value to fair value, which is done whether the decline is temporary or not.

SUMMARY OF THE EQUITY METHOD. The following T-account illustrates the accounting for equity-method investments.

Equity-Method Investment	
Original cost	Share of losses
Share of income	Share of dividends
Balance	

ANALYZE AND REPORT CONTROLLING INTERESTS IN OTHER CORPORATIONS USING CONSOLIDATED FINANCIAL STATEMENTS

OBJECTIVE

❸ **Analyze** and **report** controlling interests in other corporations using consolidated financial statements

Companies buy a significant stake in another company to *influence* the other company's operations. In this section, we cover the situation in which a corporation buys enough of another company to actually *control* that company.

Why Buy Another Company?

Most large corporations own controlling interests in other companies. A **controlling** (or **majority**) **interest** is the ownership of more than 50% of the investee's voting shares. Such an investment enables the investor to elect a majority of the members of the investee's board of directors and thus control the investee. The investor is called the **parent company**, and the investee company is called the **subsidiary company**. For example, ONEX Partners is a subsidiary of ONEX, the parent. Therefore, the shareholders of ONEX control ONEX Partners, as shown in Exhibit 8-3.

EXHIBIT 8-3
Ownership Structure of ONEX Partners and ONEX

Consolidation Accounting

Consolidation accounting is a method of combining the financial statements of all the companies controlled by the same parent company. This method reports a single set of financial statements for the consolidated entity, which carries the name of the parent company. Exhibit 8-4 summarizes the accounting methods used for long-term share investments.

Consolidated statements combine the balance sheets, income statements, and other financial statements of the parent company with those of its subsidiaries. The result is as if the parent and its subsidiaries were one company. Users can gain a better perspective on total operations than they could by examining the reports of the parent and each individual subsidiary separately.

In consolidated financial statements, the assets, liabilities, revenues, and expenses of each subsidiary are added to the parent's accounts. For example, the balance in the Cash account of ONEX Partners is added to the balance in the ONEX Cash account, and the sum of the two amounts is presented as a single amount in the ONEX consolidated balance sheet at the beginning of the chapter. Each account balance of a subsidiary loses its identity in the consolidated statements, which bear the name of the parent company, ONEX.

Percentage of Ownership	Accounting Method
Less than 20%	Fair Value
20% to 50%	Equity
Greater than 50%	Consolidation

EXHIBIT 8-4
Accounting Methods for Long-Term Investments

Goodwill and Non-controlling Interests

Goodwill and Non-Controlling Interests are two accounts that only a consolidated entity can have. *Goodwill*, which we studied in Chapter 7 (see p. 343), arises when a parent company pays more to acquire a subsidiary company than the fair value of the subsidiary's net assets. As we saw in Chapter 7, goodwill is the intangible asset that represents the parent company's excess payment to acquire the subsidiary. ONEX reports goodwill of $2,434 million on its December 31, 2011, balance sheet.

Non-controlling interest arises when a parent company purchases less than 100% of the shares of a subsidiary company. For example, ONEX owns less than 100% of some of the companies it controls. The remainder of the subsidiaries' shares is a non-controlling interest to ONEX. Non-controlling interest is included within shareholders' equity on the balance sheet of the parent company. ONEX reports non-controlling interest on its balance sheet in the amount of $3,862 (millions).

Income of a Consolidated Entity

The income of the parent company is combined with the income of each subsidiary beginning with sales revenue. All intercompany sales and expenses are eliminated, but that is a subject for an advanced accounting text. The following example is a very simplified version of a complex topic. Suppose Parent Company owns all the shares of Subsidiary S-1 and 60% of the shares of Subsidiary S-2. During the year just ended, Parent earned net income of $330,000, S-1 earned $150,000, and S-2 had a net loss of $100,000. Parent Company would report net income of $420,000, computed as follows:

	Net Income (Loss) of Each Company		Parent's Ownership of Each Company		Parent's Consolidated Net Income
Parent Company	$ 330,000	×	100%	=	$330,000
Subsidiary S-1	150,000	×	100%	=	150,000
Subsidiary S-2	(100,000)	×	60%	=	(60,000)
Consolidated net income........					$420,000

Consolidation of Foreign Subsidiaries

Many Canadian companies do large parts of their business abroad. Bank of Nova Scotia, Magna International Inc., and BlackBerry Limited, among many others, are very active in other countries. Exhibit 8-5 shows the percentages of international sales for these companies.

The complexities of foreign currency translation are normally covered in an advanced accounting course. Accordingly, the following discussion is intended to provide you with a basic understanding of foreign currency translation in the context of international trade and the context of international investment by Canadian companies.

EXHIBIT 8-5
Extent of International Business

Company	Percentage of International Revenue
Bank of Nova Scotia	43%
Magna International Inc.	71%
BlackBerry Limited	93%

FOREIGN CURRENCIES AND EXCHANGE RATES Most countries use their own national currencies. An exception is a group of European nations; the European Union (EU)—France, Germany, Italy, Belgium, and others—use a common currency, the *euro*, whose symbol is €. If Bombardier Inc., a Canadian company, sells aircraft to Air France, will Bombardier receive Canadian dollars or euros? If the transaction takes place in dollars, Air France must buy dollars to pay Bombardier in Canadian currency. If the transaction is in euros, Bombardier will collect euros and sell the euros for dollars.

The price of one nation's currency may be stated in terms of another country's monetary unit. This measure of one currency against another is called the **foreign-currency exchange rate**. In Exhibit 8-6, the dollar value of a euro is $1.2405. This means that one euro can be bought for about $1.2405. Other currencies are also listed in Exhibit 8-6.

EXHIBIT 8-6
Foreign-Currency Exchange Rates

Country	Monetary Unit	Canadian Dollar Value	Country	Monetary Unit	Canadian Dollar Value
Hong Kong	Dollar	$0.128	Japan	Yen (¥)	0.01264
France	Euro (€)	1.2405	Mexico	Peso (P)	0.07413
Germany	Euro (€)	1.2405	United Kingdom	Pound (£)	1.5676
Italy	Euro (€)	1.2405	United States	Dollar ($)	0.9926

Source: The Bank of Canada, August 30, 2012

We can convert the cost of an item in one currency to its cost in a second currency. We call this conversion a *translation*. Suppose an item costs 200 euros. To compute its cost in dollars, we multiply the amount in euros by the conversion rate: 200 euros × $1.2405 = $248.10.

FOREIGN-CURRENCY TRANSLATION ADJUSTMENT. The process of translating a foreign subsidiary's financial statements into dollars usually creates a *foreign-currency translation adjustment*. This item appears in the financial statements of most multinational companies and is reported as other comprehensive income in a separate section below net income on the statement of comprehensive income. Under ASPE, the foreign-currency translation adjustment is reported as a separate component of shareholders' equity unless the subsidiary is in a highly inflationary environment. In that type of situation, the translation adjustment would be reported on the income statement.

A translation adjustment arises due to changes in the foreign exchange rate over time. In general,

- *assets* and *liabilities* are translated into dollars at the current exchange rate on the date of the statements;
- income and expenses are translated into dollars at the current exchange rates on the dates of the transactions;
- *shareholders' equity* is translated into dollars at older, historical exchange rates. Paid-in capital accounts are translated at the historical exchange rate when the subsidiary was acquired. Retained earnings are translated at the average exchange rates applicable over the period in which interest in the subsidiary has been held.

This difference in exchange rates creates an out-of-balance condition on the balance sheet. The translation adjustment brings the balance sheet back into balance. Let's see how the translation adjustment works.

EXHIBIT 8-7
Translation of a Foreign
Currency Balance Sheet
Into Dollars

Italian Imports, Inc., Accounts	Euros	Exchange Rate	Dollars
Assets	800,000	$1.20	$960,000
Liabilities	500,000	1.20	$600,000
Shareholders' equity			
Share capital	100,000	1.35	135,000
Retained earnings	200,000	1.30	260,000
Accumulated other comprehensive income:			
Foreign-currency translation adjustment			(35,000)
	800,000		$960,000

Suppose Intel has an Italian subsidiary whose financial statements are expressed in euros (the European Union currency). Intel must consolidate the Italian subsidiary's financials into its own statements. When Intel acquired the Italian company in 2009, a euro was worth $1.35 (assumed). When the Italian firm earned its retained income during 2009–2012, the average exchange rate was $1.30 (assumed). On the balance sheet date in 2012, a euro is worth only $1.20 (assumed). Exhibit 8-7 shows how to translate the Italian company's balance sheet into dollars.

The foreign-currency translation adjustment is the balancing amount that brings the dollar amount of liabilities and equity of a foreign subsidiary into agreement with the dollar amount of total assets (in Exhibit 8-7, total assets equal $960,000). Only after the translation adjustment of $35,000 do total liabilities and equity equal total assets stated in dollars.

What caused the negative translation adjustment? The euro weakened after the acquisition of the Italian company.

- When Intel acquired the foreign subsidiary in 2009, a euro was worth $1.35.
- When the Italian company earned its income during 2009 through 2012, the average exchange rate was $1.30.
- On the balance sheet date in 2012, a euro is worth only $1.20.
- Thus, the Italian company's equity (assets minus liabilities) is translated into only $360,000 ($960,000 – $600,000).
- To bring shareholders' equity to $360,000 requires a $35,000 negative adjustment.

A negative translation adjustment is like a loss, reported as a negative item in the statement of other comprehensive income. Losses and gains from translation adjustments are eventually transferred to accumulated other comprehensive income in the shareholders' equity section of the balance sheet, as shown in Exhibit 8-7. The Italian firm's dollar figures in Exhibit 8-7 reflect what Intel would include in its consolidated balance sheet.

ANALYZE AND REPORT LONG-TERM INVESTMENTS IN BONDS

The major investors in bonds are financial institutions, pension plans, mutual funds, and insurance companies, such as Manulife Financial Corporation. The relationship between the issuing corporation and the investor (bondholder) may be diagrammed as follows:

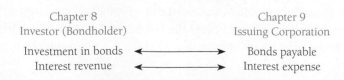

Chapter 8		Chapter 9
Investor (Bondholder)		Issuing Corporation
Investment in bonds	⟷	Bonds payable
Interest revenue	⟷	Interest expense

An investment in bonds is classified either as short term (a current asset) or as long term. Short-term investments in bonds are rare. Here, we focus on long-term investments in bonds.

Bonds of public companies are traded on the open market, just as shares are. Bonds are usually issued in $1,000 face (par) denominations, but they typically do not sell at par value. Market prices of bonds fluctuate with market interest rates. If market rates on competing instruments are higher than the interest the company is paying on a particular bond, the bond sells at a discount (below 100% of par, or face value). For example, a quoted bond price of 96.5 means that the $1,000 bond is selling for 96.5% of par, or $965. If market rates are lower, the bond sells at a premium (above 100% of par)—a quoted bond price of 102.5 means that the bond is selling for 102.5% of par, or $1,025 (a premium over par). Bondholders receive interest, usually semi-annually.

IFRS require bond investments that are held to maturity to be valued at amortized cost, which determines the carrying amount. **Bond investments** are initially recorded at cost (market price as a percentage × par value of bonds issued). At each semi-annual interest payment date, the investor records interest revenue. In addition, whenever there is a premium or discount on the bond, it is amortized by adjusting the carrying amount of the bond upward or downward toward its par or face value. The amortization of the discount or premium is calculated using the effective interest method (see Chapter 9). Under ASPE, amortization is calculated using either the straight-line method or the effective interest method.

Suppose an investor purchases $100,000 of 5% Government of Canada bonds at a price of $95,735 on June 1, 2014. The bonds pay interest on June 1 and December 1. The investor intends to hold the bonds until their maturity on June 2, 2019. The bonds will be outstanding for five years (10 interest periods). The investor paid a discounted price for the bonds of $95,735 (an effective interest rate of 6%). The investor must amortize the bonds' carrying amount from cost of $95,735 up to $100,000 over their term to maturity. The following are the entries for this long-term investment:

2014			
June 1	Long-Term Investment in Bonds ($100,000 × 95.735)............................	95,735	
	Cash..		95,735
	To purchase bond investment.		
Dec. 1	Cash ($100,000 × 0.05 × 1/2)...	2,500	
	Interest Revenue..		2,500
	To receive semi-annual interest.		
	Long-Term Investment in Bonds ([$95,735 × 0.06 × 1/2] − $2,500)......	373[*]	
	Interest Revenue..		372[*]
	To amortize bond investment.		

*Rounded

At December 31, the year-end adjustments are:

Dec. 31	Interest Receivable ($100,000 × 0.05 × 1/12)	417[*]	
	Interest Revenue..		417[*]
	To accrue interest revenue.		
Dec. 31	Long-Term Investment in Bonds ([$96,108 × 0.06 × 1/12] − $417).......	64[*]	
	Interest Revenue..		64[*]
	To amortize bond investment.		

*Rounded

This amortization entry has two effects:

1. It increases the Long-Term Investment account on its march toward maturity value.

2. It increases the interest by the amount of the increase in the carrying amount of the investment.

The financial statements at December 31, 2014, report the following for this investment in bonds:

Balance sheet at December 31, 2014:
    Current assets:
        Interest receivable... $ 417
        Long-term investments in bonds ($95,735 + $373 + $64)............................... 96,172
        Property, plant, and equipment .... X,XXX
Income statement for the year ended December 31, 2014:
    Other revenues:
        Interest revenue ($2,500 + $373 + $417 + $64).. $ 3,354

◄ DECISION GUIDELINES ►

ACCOUNTING METHODS FOR LONG-TERM INVESTMENTS

These guidelines show which accounting method to use for each type of long-term investment. A company can have all types of investments—stock, bonds, 25% interests, and controlling interests. How should a company account for its various investments?

Type of Long-Term Investment	Accounting Method
Non-strategic investments	Fair value
Significantly influenced investments	Equity method
Controlled investments	Consolidation
Investment in bonds	Amortized cost

As we have seen in this chapter, investments may be bought in order to earn either dividend revenue and/or capital appreciation (called *non-strategic*), or they are bought with the intent to significantly influence or control the company's operations (referred to as *strategic*). Let's see how long-term investments are used in decision making.

Decision	Guidelines
Who uses long-term investments in decision making, and why?	*Managers* buy investments with one or more of these intentions in mind. If the company has excess cash on hand, they may decide to invest this cash in a non-strategic investment rather than have it sit in a bank account where it earns little interest. On the other hand, the company may decide to buy another company's shares with a plan to be involved in the company's operations.
	Investors might consider the type of investment. If the investment was non-strategic, they would look at the statements and notes to see whether or not the investment increased or decreased in value and the amount of dividend revenue the company received. If it was a strategic investment, the investor would look to see whether or not this investment generated a reasonable profit for the company.
	Creditors are always looking to see if a company would be a good candidate for a loan and whether there was sufficient profit from operations or investment income to cover current and potentially increased interest costs.

COOKING the BOOKS
WITH INVESTMENTS AND DEBT

ENRON CORPORATION

In 2000, Enron Corporation in Houston, Texas, employed approximately 22,000 people and was one of the world's leading electricity, natural gas, pulp and paper, and communications companies, with reported revenues of nearly $101 billion. *Fortune* had named Enron "America's Most Innovative Company" for six consecutive years. To many outside observers, Enron was the model corporation.

Enron's financial statements showed that the company was making a lot of money, but in reality, most of its profits were merely on paper. Rather than from operations, the great majority of the cash Enron needed to operate on a day-to-day basis came from bank loans. It was very important, therefore, that Enron keep its debt ratio (discussed in Chapter 3) as well as its return on assets (ROA, discussed in Chapter 7) at acceptable levels, so the banks would continue to view the company as creditworthy. Enron's balance sheets contained large misstatements in the liabilities and shareholders' equity sections over a period of years. Many of the off-setting misstatements were in long-term assets. Specifically, Enron owned numerous long-term investments, including power plants; water rights; broadband cable; and sophisticated, complex, and somewhat dubious derivative financial instruments in such unusual things as the weather! Many of these investments actually had questionable value, but Enron had abused fair market value accounting to estimate them at grossly inflated values.

To create paper profits, Andrew Fastow, Enron's chief financial officer, created a veritable maze of "special purpose entities" (SPEs), financed with bank debt. He valued these investments using "mark-to-market" (fair-value accounting), using un-realistic assumptions that created inflated asset values on the financial statements. He then "sold" the dubious investments to the SPEs to get them off Enron's books. Enron recorded millions of dollars in "profits" from these transactions. Fastow then used Enron stock to collateralize the bank debt of the SPEs, making the transactions entirely circular. Unknown to Enron's board of directors, Fastow or members of his own family owned most of these entities, making them related parties to Enron. Enron was, in fact, the owner of the assets, and was, in fact, obligated for the debts of the SPEs because those debts were collateralized with Enron stock. When Enron's fraud was discovered in late 2001, the company was forced to consolidate the assets of the SPEs, as well as all of their bank debt, into its own financial statements. The inflated assets had to be written down to impaired market values. The end result of the restatement impacted Enron's debt ratio and ROA so much that the banks refused to loan the company any more money to operate. Enron's energy trading business vir-tually dried up overnight, and it was bankrupt within 60 days. An estimated $60 billion in shareholder value, and 22,000 jobs, were lost. Enron's CEO, Jeffrey Skilling, its CFO, Andrew Fastow, and Board Chairman Kenneth Lay were all convicted of fraud. Skilling and Fastow both went to prison. Lay died suddenly of a heart attack before being sentenced.

Enron's audit firm, Arthur Andersen LLP, was accused of trying to cover up its knowledge of Enron's practices by shredding documents. The firm was indicted by the U.S. Justice Department in March 2002. Because of the indictment, Andersen lost all of its public clients and was forced out of business. As a result, over 58,000 persons lost their jobs worldwide. A U.S. Supreme Court decision in 2005 eventu-ally led to withdrawal of the indictment, but it came much too late for the once "gold-plated" CPA firm. Allegations about the quality of its work on Enron, as well as another well-publicized case WorldCom (p. 327), who was also a client, doomed Arthur Andersen.

MID-CHAPTER SUMMARY PROBLEM

1. Identify the appropriate accounting method for each of the following long-term investment situations:
   a. Investment in 25% of investee's shares
   b. 10% investment in shares
   c. Investment in more than 50% of investee's shares
2. At what amount should the following long-term investment portfolio be reported on the June 30, 2014, balance sheet? All the investments are less than 5% of the investee's shares and are classified as non-strategic. The investor chooses to record any changes in fair value through other comprehensive income.

Shares	Investment Cost	Fair Value
Bank of Montreal	$75,000	$52,000
Canadian Tire Corp.	24,000	31,000
Jean Coutu Group	32,000	36,000

Journalize any adjusting entry required by these data.
3. Investor Corporation paid $67,900 to acquire a 40% equity-method investment in the common shares of Investee Corporation. At the end of the first year, Investee's net income was $80,000, and Investee declared and paid cash dividends of $55,000. What is Investor's ending balance in its Equity-Method Investment account? Use a T-account to answer.

ANSWERS

For investments:
Less than 20%→Fair value;
20% to 50%→Equity;
Greater than 50%→Consolidation

1. a. Equity
   b. Fair value
   c. Consolidation

Determine the fair value for each investment in the portfolio. Then create the journal entry for any change from investment cost to current fair value.

2. Report the investments at fair value ($119,000) as follows:

Shares	Investment Cost	Fair Value
Bank of Montreal	$ 75,000	$ 52,000
Canadian Tire	24,000	31,000
Jean Coutu Group	32,000	36,000
Totals	$131,000	$119,000

Adjusting entry:

Other Comprehensive Income ($131,000 − $119,000)............................	12,000	
Long-Term Investments...		12,000
To adjust investments to current fair value.		

3. Equity-Method Investment

The Equity-Method Investment
T-account includes:
100% of the cost of the investment
+40% of the investee's net income
−40% of the investee's cash dividends

Equity-Method Investment

Cost	67,900	Dividends	22,000**
Income	32,000*		
Balance	77,900		

*$80,000 × 0.40 = $32,000
**$55,000 × 0.40 = $22,000

REPORT INVESTING ACTIVITIES ON THE STATEMENT OF CASH FLOWS

OBJECTIVE

❺ **Report** investing activities on the statement of cash flows

Investing activities include many types of transactions. In Chapter 7, we covered investing transactions in which companies purchase and sell long-lived assets, such as property, plant, and equipment. In this chapter, we examined long-term investments in shares and bonds. These are also investing activities reported on the statement of cash flows.

Investing activities are usually reported on the statement of cash flows as the second category, after operating activities and before financing activities. Exhibit 8-8 provides excerpts from ONEX's statement of cash flows. During 2011, ONEX spent $646 million on new property, plant, and equipment and $1,155 million to acquire other companies. They also received $45 million in interest and dividends from their investments. Alternatively, ONEX could also have reported the interest and dividends as an operating activity. Overall, ONEX invested $12 million.

EXHIBIT 8-8
ONEX Corporation
Consolidated Statement of Cash Flows

ONEX Corporation
Consolidated Statement of Cash Flows (Partial, Adapted)
For the Year Ended December 31, 2011

	(in millions of U.S. dollars)
Investing Activities	
Acquisition of operating companies	$(1,155)
Purchase of property, plant, and equipment	(646)
Cash interest and dividends received	45
Decrease due to other investing activities	(286)
Cash flows from investing activities of discontinued operations	2,030
	$ (12)

EXPLAIN THE IMPACT OF THE TIME VALUE OF MONEY ON CERTAIN TYPES OF INVESTMENTS

Future Value

OBJECTIVE

❻ **Explain** the impact of the time value of money on certain types of investments

Which would you rather receive: $1,000 today, or $1,000 a year from today? A logical person would answer: "I'd rather have the cash now, because if I get it now, I can invest it so that a year from now I'll have more." The term **future value** means the amount of money that a given current investment will be worth at a specified time in the future, assuming a certain interest rate. The term *time value of money* refers to the fact that money earns interest over time. *Interest* is the cost of using money. To borrowers, interest is the fee paid to the lender for the period of the loan. To lenders, interest is the revenue earned from allowing someone else to use our money for a period of time.

Whether making investments or borrowing money, we must always recognize the interest we receive or pay. Otherwise, we overlook an important part of the transaction. Suppose you invest $4,545 in corporate bonds that pay 10% interest each year. After one year, the value of your investment has grown to $5,000, as shown in the following diagram:

End of Year	Interest	Future Value
0	—	$4,545
1	$4,545 × 0.10 = $455	5,000
2	5,000 × 0.10 = 500	5,500
3	5,500 × 0.10 = 550	6,050
4	6,050 × 0.10 = 605	6,655
5	6,655 × 0.10 = 666	7,321

The difference between your original investment (present value of $4,545) and the future value of the investment ($5,000) is the amount of interest revenue you will earn during the year ($455). Interest becomes more important as the time period lengthens because the amount of interest depends on the span of time the money is invested. The time value of money plays a key role in measuring the value of certain long-term investments, as well as long-term debt.

If the money were invested for five years, you would have to perform five calculations like the one described above. You would also have to consider the compound interest that your investment is earning. *Compound interest* is not only the interest you earn on your principal amount, but also the interest you receive on the interest you have already earned. Most business applications include compound interest.

To calculate the future value of an investment, we need three inputs: (1) the *amount of initial payment (or receipt)*, (2) the length of *time* between investment and future receipt (or *payment*), and (3) the *interest rate*. The table above shows the interest revenue earned on the original $4,545 investment each year for five years at 10%. At the end of five years, your initial $4,545 investment will be worth $7,321.

Present Value

Often a person knows or is able to estimate a future amount and needs to determine the related present value (PV). The term **present value** means the value on a given date of a future payment or series of future payments, discounted to reflect the time value of money. In Exhibit 8-9, present value and future value are on opposite ends of the same timeline. Suppose an investment promises to pay you $5,000 at the *end* of one year. How much would you pay *now* to acquire this investment? You would be willing to pay the present value of the $5,000 future amount, which, at 10% interest, is $4,545.

Like future value, present value depends on three factors: (1) the *amount of payment (or receipt)*, (2) the length of *time* between investment and future receipt (or

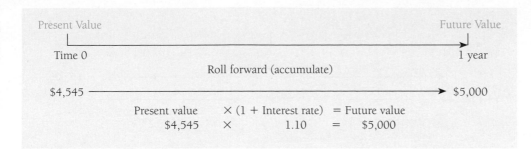

EXHIBIT 8-9
Future Value of an Investment

payment), and (3) the *interest rate*. The process of computing a present value is called *discounting* because the present value is *less* than the future value.

In our investment example, the future receipt is $5,000. The investment period is one year. Assume that you demand an annual interest rate of 10% on your investment. With all three factors specified, you can compute the present value of $5,000 at 10% for one year:

$$\text{Present value} = \frac{\text{Future value}}{1 + \text{Interest rate}} = \frac{\$5,000}{1.10} = \$4,545$$

By turning the data around into a future-value problem, we can verify the present-value computation:

Amount invested (present value)...	$4,545
Expected earnings ($4,545 × 0.10)	455
Amount to be received one year from now (future value)..............	$5,000

This example illustrates that present value and future value are based on variations of the same equation:

$$\text{Future value} = \text{Present value} \times (1 + \text{Interest rate})^n$$
$$\text{Present value} = \frac{\text{Future value}}{(1 + \text{Interest rate})^n}$$
$$\text{where } n = \text{number of periods}$$

If the $5,000 is to be received two years from now, you will pay only $4,132 for the investment, as shown in Exhibit 8-10. By turning the data around, we verify that $4,132 accumulates to $5,000 at 10% for two years:

Amount invested (present value)...	$4,132
Expected earnings for first year ($4,132 × 0.10)	413
Value of investment after one year...	4,545
Expected earnings for second year ($4,545 × 0.10)......................	455
Amount to be received two years from now (future value)	$5,000

$$\text{Formula: Present value} = \frac{\text{Future value}}{(1 + \text{Interest rate})^n}$$
$$4,132 = \frac{5,000}{(1 + 0.10)^2}$$
$$\text{Future value} = \text{Present value} \times (1 + \text{Interest rate})^n$$
$$5,000 = \$4,132 \times (1 + 0.10)^2$$

EXHIBIT 8-10
Present Value: An Example

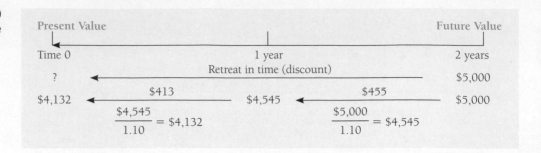

You would pay $4,132—the present value of $5,000— to receive the $5,000 future amount at the end of two years at 10% per year. The $868 difference between the amount invested ($4,132) and the amount to be received ($5,000) is the return on the investment, the sum of the two interest receipts: $413 + $455 = $868.

Present-Value Tables

We have shown the simple formula for computing present value. However, figuring present value "by hand" for investments spanning many years is time-consuming and presents too many opportunities for arithmetic errors. Present-value tables simplify our work. Let's re-examine our examples of present value by using Exhibit 8-11, Present Value of $1.

For the 10% investment for one year, we find the junction of the 10% column and row 1 in Exhibit 8-11. The figure 0.909 is computed as follows: 1/1.10 = 0.909. This work has been done for us, and only the present values are given in the table. To figure the present value for $5,000, we multiply 0.909 by $5,000. The result is $4,545, which matches the result we obtained by hand.

For the two-year investment, we read down the 10% column and across row 2. We multiply 0.826 (computed as 0.909/1.10 = 0.826) by $5,000 and get $4,130, which confirms our earlier computation of $4,132 (the difference is due to rounding in the present-value table). Using the table, we can compute the present value of any single future amount.

EXHIBIT 8-11
Present Value of $1

Period	4%	5%	6%	7%	8%	10%	12%	14%	16%
1	0.962	0.952	0.943	0.935	0.926	0.909	0.893	0.877	0.862
2	0.925	0.907	0.890	0.873	0.857	0.826	0.797	0.769	0.743
3	0.889	0.864	0.840	0.816	0.794	0.751	0.712	0.675	0.641
4	0.855	0.823	0.792	0.763	0.735	0.683	0.636	0.592	0.552
5	0.822	0.784	0.747	0.713	0.681	0.621	0.567	0.519	0.476
6	0.790	0.746	0.705	0.666	0.630	0.564	0.507	0.456	0.410
7	0.760	0.711	0.665	0.623	0.583	0.513	0.452	0.400	0.354
8	0.731	0.677	0.627	0.582	0.540	0.467	0.404	0.351	0.305
9	0.703	0.645	0.592	0.544	0.500	0.424	0.361	0.308	0.263
10	0.676	0.614	0.558	0.508	0.463	0.386	0.322	0.270	0.227
11	0.650	0.585	0.527	0.475	0.429	0.350	0.287	0.237	0.195
12	0.625	0.557	0.497	0.444	0.397	0.319	0.257	0.208	0.168
13	0.601	0.530	0.469	0.415	0.368	0.290	0.229	0.182	0.145
14	0.577	0.505	0.442	0.388	0.340	0.263	0.205	0.160	0.125
15	0.555	0.481	0.417	0.362	0.315	0.239	0.183	0.140	0.108
16	0.534	0.458	0.394	0.339	0.292	0.218	0.163	0.123	0.093
17	0.513	0.436	0.371	0.317	0.270	0.198	0.146	0.108	0.080
18	0.494	0.416	0.350	0.296	0.250	0.180	0.130	0.095	0.069
19	0.475	0.396	0.331	0.277	0.232	0.164	0.116	0.083	0.060
20	0.456	0.377	0.312	0.258	0.215	0.149	0.104	0.073	0.051

Present Value of an Annuity

Return to the investment example at the top of page 394. That investment provided the investor with only a single future receipt ($5,000 at the end of two years). *Annuity investments* provide multiple receipts of an equal amount at fixed intervals over the investment's duration.

Consider an investment that promises *annual* cash receipts of $10,000 to be received at the end of each of three years. Assume that you demand a 12% return on your investment. What is the investment's present value? That is, what would you pay today to acquire the investment? The investment spans three periods, and you would pay the sum of three present values. The computation follows.

Year	Annual Cash Receipt	Present Value of $1 at 12% (Exhibit 8-11)	Present Value of Annual Cash Receipt
1	$10,000	0.893	$ 8,930
2	10,000	0.797	7,970
3	10,000	0.712	7,120
Total present value of investment...............			$24,020

The present value of this annuity is $24,020. By paying this amount today, you will receive $10,000 at the end of each of the three years while earning 12% on your investment.

This example illustrates repetitive computations of the three future amounts, a time-consuming process. One way to ease the computational burden is to add the three present values of $1 (0.893 + 0.797 + 0.712) and multiply their sum (2.402) by the annual cash receipt ($10,000) to obtain the present value of the annuity ($10,000 × 2.402 = $24,020).

An easier approach is to use a present-value-of-an-annuity table. Exhibit 8-12 shows the present value of $1 to be received periodically for a given number of periods. The present value of a three-period annuity at 12% is 2.402 (the junction of row 3 and the 12% column). Thus, $10,000 received annually at the end of each of three years, discounted at 12%, is $24,020 ($10,000 × 2.402), which is the present value.

Using Present Value to Compute the Fair Value of Investments

Recall that, at the end of each year, investors are required to adjust the portfolio of non-strategic investments to fair values. Some types of investments (publicly traded stocks and bonds) have quoted prices in active markets. Determining fair value for these investments is easy: merely obtain the quoted price from the financial media (usually the Internet or the *Globe and Mail* on the year-end). Other types of non-traditional investments (e.g., notes, non–publicly traded bonds or stocks, contracts, annuities) may not have daily quoted market prices in active markets. Therefore, the company may use financial models that predict expected cash flows from these investments over a period of time and discount those cash flows back to the balance sheet date.

EXHIBIT 8-12
Present Value of Annuity of $1

						Present Value of Annuity of $1				
Period	4%	5%	6%	7%	8%	10%	12%	14%	16%
1	0.962	0.952	0.943	0.935	0.926	0.909	0.893	0.877	0.862
2	1.886	1.859	1.833	1.808	1.783	1.736	1.690	1.647	1.605
3	2.775	2.723	2.673	2.624	2.577	2.487	2.402	2.322	2.246
4	3.630	3.546	3.465	3.387	3.312	3.170	3.037	2.914	2.798
5	4.452	4.329	4.212	4.100	3.993	3.791	3.605	3.433	3.274
6	5.242	5.076	4.917	4.767	4.623	4.355	4.111	3.889	3.685
7	6.002	5.786	5.582	5.389	5.206	4.868	4.564	4.288	4.039
8	6.733	6.463	6.210	5.971	5.747	5.335	4.968	4.639	4.344
9	7.435	7.108	6.802	6.515	6.247	5.759	5.328	4.946	4.608
10	8.111	7.722	7.360	7.024	6.710	6.145	5.650	5.216	4.833
11	8.760	8.306	7.887	7.499	7.139	6.495	5.938	5.453	5.029
12	9.385	8.863	8.384	7.943	7.536	6.814	6.194	5.660	5.197
13	9.986	9.394	8.853	8.358	7.904	7.103	6.424	5.842	5.342
14	10.563	9.899	9.295	8.745	8.244	7.367	6.628	6.002	5.468
15	11.118	10.380	9.712	9.108	8.559	7.606	6.811	6.142	5.575
16	11.652	10.838	10.106	9.447	8.851	7.824	6.974	6.265	5.669
17	12.166	11.274	10.477	9.763	9.122	8.022	7.120	6.373	5.749
18	12.659	11.690	10.828	10.059	9.372	8.201	7.250	6.467	5.818
19	13.134	12.085	11.158	10.336	9.604	8.365	7.366	6.550	5.877
20	13.590	12.462	11.470	10.594	9.818	8.514	7.469	6.623	5.929

Present Value of an Investment in Bonds

The present value of a bond—its market price—is the present value of the future principal amount at maturity plus the present value of the future stated interest payments. The principal is a *single amount* to be received by the investor and paid by the debtor at maturity. The interest is an *annuity* because it occurs periodically.

Let's compute the present value of 9% five-year bonds of Air Canada from the standpoint of an investor. The face value of the bonds is $100,000, and the face interest rate is 9% annually. Because bonds typically pay interest twice per year, these bonds pay 4 1/2% semi-annually. At issuance, the market interest rate is assumed to be 10% annually, but it is computed at 5% semi-annually (again, because the bonds pay interest twice a year). Therefore, the effective (market) interest rate for each of the 10 semi-annual periods is 5%. We thus use 5% in computing the present value of the maturity and of the interest. The market price of these bonds is $96,149, as follows:

	Annual Market Interest Rate ÷ 2	**Number of Semi-annual Interest Payments**	
PV of principal:			
$100,000 × PV of single amount at 5%		for 10 periods	
$100,000 × 0.614 (Exhibit 8-11)			$61,400
PV of stated (cash) interest:			
$100,000 × 0.045 × PV of annuity at 5%		for 10 periods	
$4,500 × 7.722 (Exhibit 8-12)			34,749
PV (market price) of bonds			$96,149

The fair value of the Air Canada bonds on the investor's balance sheet would be $96,149.[*]

We discuss accounting for these bonds from the debtor's point of view in Chapter 9.

---

[*]The process of estimating fair value using discounted cash flow models is similar for all types of investments.

Summary of IFRS-ASPE Differences

Concepts	IFRS	ASPE
Non-strategic investments (p. 376)	These investments are reported at fair value, with unrealized and realized gains and losses reported in net income, unless the company elects to report them in other comprehensive income.	These investments are reported at fair value, with unrealized and realized gains and losses reported in net income.
Investments subject to significant influence (p. 377)	A company shall apply the equity method to account for these investments.	A company may choose to apply either the equity method or the cost method. If the share investments are quoted in an active market, then the fair value method replaces the cost method as an option, with any changes in fair value reported through net income.
Investments in controlled subsidiaries (p. 383)	A company shall consolidate its financial statements with those of its subsidiaries.	A company may choose to account for its subsidiaries using the cost method, the equity method, or the consolidation method. If share investments are quoted in an active market, then the fair value method replaces the cost method, with any changes in fair value reported through net income.
Amortization of the discount or premium relating to long-term investments in bonds (p. 386)	The effective-interest method must be used to amortize discounts and premiums.	The straight-line method or the effective-interest method may be used to amortize discounts and premiums.
Foreign-currency translation resulting from consolidation (p. 384)	Translation adjustments are included in other comprehensive income.	Translation adjustments are included in a separate category in shareholders' equity, unless they relate to a self-sustaining subsidiary in a highly inflationary environment, in which case they are included in the determination of net income.

SUMMARY OF CHAPTER 8

LEARNING OBJECTIVE	SUMMARY
1. **Analyze** and **report** non-strategic investments	Non-strategic investments are initially recorded at cost and subsequently reported on the balance sheet at fair value. Any changes in value are recorded through net income (profit or loss) or under "other comprehensive income". The cost method is used for investments where the market price is not available.
2. **Analyze** and **report** investments in affiliated companies using the equity method	If the company (investor) owns between 20% and 50% of the voting shares of the investee and exercises significant influence over the investee, the equity method is used to account for the investment. This means that the investor recognizes their share of the investee's net income as their own. The investor's share of dividends is treated as a return of investment.
3. **Analyze** and **report** controlling interests in other corporations using consolidated financial statements	If the company (investor) owns more than 50% of the investee's shares and exercises control over the investee, the financial statements of the investee are consolidated (combined) with those of the investor. The result is as if the parent and subsidiary are one company. Goodwill and Non-controlling interest are two accounts that only a consolidated entity would have. Goodwill results when a company pays more for the subsidiary company than the fair value of the subsidiary's net assets. Non-controlling interest occurs when a company buys less than 100% of the company they control.
4. **Analyze** and **report** long-term investment in bonds	When a company buys a long-term investment in bonds, they are recorded at the price paid. When there is a premium or discount, the bonds are amortized to account for interest revenue and the bond's carrying amount. These bonds are reported on the balance sheet at its amortized cost.
5. **Report** investing activities on the statement of cash flows	Buying and selling long-term investments in shares and bonds are reported under investing activities. Any increase (decrease) in cash due to changes in foreign exchange rates are reported in a separate category underneath the operating, investing, and financing activities.
6. **Explain** the impact of the time value of money on certain types of investments	Time value of money refers to the fact that money earns interest over time, and it plays a key role in measuring the value of certain long-term investments a well as long-term debt. Interest is the cost of using money. The difference between your original (present) investment and the future value of the investment is the amount of interest revenue you will earn.

END-OF-CHAPTER SUMMARY PROBLEM

Translate the balance sheet of the Brazilian subsidiary of The Jean Shop Corporation, a Canadian company, into dollars. When The Jean Shop acquired this subsidiary, the exchange rate of the Brazilian currency, the real, was $0.45. The average exchange rate applicable to retained earnings is $0.52. The real's current exchange rate is $0.53.

Before performing the translation, predict whether the translation adjustment will be positive or negative. Does this situation generate a foreign-currency translation gain or loss? Give your reasons.

	Reals
Assets	900,000
Liabilities	600,000
Shareholders' equity:	
Common shares	30,000
Retained earnings	270,000
	900,000

ANSWERS

Translation of foreign-currency balance sheet:

This situation will generate a *positive* translation adjustment, which is like a gain. The gain occurs because the real's current exchange rate, which is used to translate net assets (assets minus liabilities), exceeds the historical exchange rates used for shareholders' equity.

The calculation follows.

> The current exchange rate is higher than the rate in effect at the time of the investment purchase. This results in an increase in the value of the investment and, accordingly, a gain.

	Reals	Exchange Rate	Dollars
Assets	900,000	$0.53	$477,000
Liabilities	600,000	0.53	$318,000
Shareholders' equity:			
Common shares	30,000	0.45	13,500
Retained earnings	270,000	0.52	140,400
Foreign-currency translation adjustment	—		5,100
	900,000		$477,000

> The foreign-currency translation adjustment is the "plug" figure that makes total assets equal total liabilities plus shareholders' equity after translation. A positive figure is like a foreign-currency translation gain. A negative figure is like a foreign-currency translation loss.

STOP + THINK (8-1)	ANSWER	
	Assets	
	Long-term investments	$63,500

Review Long-Term Investments and the Time Value of Money

QUICK CHECK (ANSWERS ARE GIVEN ON PAGE 415.)

1. A company's investment in less than 1% of GE's shares, which it expects to hold for two years and then sell, is which type of investment?
   - a. Held-for-trading
   - b. Equity
   - c. Non-strategic
   - d. Consolidation
2. DuBois Corporation purchased a non-strategic investment in 1,000 shares of Scotiabank (BNS) for $31 per share. On the next balance sheet date, BNS is quoted at $35 per share. DuBois' *balance sheet* should report
   - a. unrealized loss of $4,000.
   - b. unrealized gain of $31,000.
   - c. investments of $31,000.
   - d. investments of $35,000.

3. Use the DuBois Corporation data in question 2. The company reports changes in fair value through net income DuBois' *income statement* should report
   a. unrealized gain of $4,000.
   b. unrealized loss of $4,000.
   c. investments of $31,000.
   d. nothing because DuBois hasn't sold the investment.

4. Use the DuBois Corporation data in question 2. DuBois sold the Scotiabank shares for $40,000 two years later. DuBois' *income statement* should report
   a. unrealized gain of $4,000.
   b. gain on sale of $9,000.
   c. gain on sale of $5,000.
   d. investments of $40,000.

5. Alexander Moving & Storage Inc. paid $100,000 for 20% of the common shares of Sellers Ltd. Sellers earned net income of $50,000 and paid dividends of $25,000. Alexander accounts for the investment using the equity method. The carrying value of Alexander's investment in Sellers is
   a. $100,000.
   b. $105,000.
   c. $125,000.
   d. $150,000.

6. Tarrant Inc. owns 80% of Rockwall Corporation, and Rockwall owns 80% of Kaufman Company. During 2014, these companies' net incomes are as follows before any consolidations:
   - Tarrant, $100,000
   - Rockwall, $68,000
   - Kaufman, $40,000

   How much net income should Tarrant report for 2014?
   a. $100,000
   b. $164,000
   c. $180,000
   d. $204,000

7. TRULINE Inc. holds an investment in Manulife bonds that pay interest each June 30. TRULINE's *balance sheet* at December 31 should report
   a. interest receivable.
   b. interest payable.
   c. interest revenue.
   d. interest expense.

8. You are going on a vacation to France, and you buy euros for $1.60. On your return, you cash in your unused euros for $1.50. During your vacation,
   a. the dollar lost value.
   b. the euro rose against the dollar.
   c. the euro gained value.
   d. the dollar rose against the euro.

9. Grey County, Ontario, purchased earth-moving equipment from a U.S. company. The cost was $1,000,000 in U.S. dollars, and the U.S. dollar was quoted at $1.25. A month later, Grey County paid its debt, and the Canadian dollar was quoted at $1.27. What was Grey County's cost of the equipment?
   a. $20,000
   b. $1,250,000
   c. $950,000
   d. $1,020,000

10. ATCO owns numerous foreign subsidiary companies. When ATCO consolidates its Australian subsidiary, ATCO should translate the subsidiary's assets into Canadian dollars at the
    a. historical exchange rate when ATCO purchased the Australian company.
    b. average exchange rate during the period ATCO owned the Australian subsidiary.
    c. current exchange rate.
    d. None of the above. There's no need to translate the subsidiary's assets into Canadian dollars.

Accounting Vocabulary

bond investments Bonds and notes are debt instruments that an investor intends to hold until maturity. (p. 387)

consolidated statements Financial statements of the parent company plus those of majority-owned subsidiaries as if the combination were a single legal entity. (p. 383)

controlling (majority) interest Ownership of more than 50% of an investee company's voting shares and can exercise control over the investee. (p. 383)

equity method The method used to account for investments in which the investor has 20–50% of the investee's voting shares and can significantly influence the decisions of the investee. (p. 381)

foreign-currency exchange rate The measure of one country's currency against another country's currency. (p. 385)

future value Measures the future sum of money that a given current investment is "worth" at a specified time in the future, assuming a certain interest rate.   (p. 391)

long-term investments Any investment that does not meet the criteria of a short-term investment; any investment that the investor expects to hold for longer than a year.   (p. 376)

majority interest Ownership of more than 50% of an investee company's voting shares.   (p. 383)

non-controlling interest A subsidiary company's equity that is held by shareholders other than the parent company. (p. 384)

non-strategic investments Investments in which the investor owns less than 20% of the voting shares of the investee and is presumed to exercise no influence.   (p. 376)

parent company An investor company that owns more than 50% of the voting shares of a subsidiary company.   (p. 383)

present value The value on a given date of a future payment or series of future payments, discounted to reflect the time value of money   (p. 392)

subsidiary company An investee company in which a parent company owns more than 50% of the voting shares and can exercise control over the subsidiary.   (p. 383)

Assess Your Progress

MyAccountingLab

Make the grade with MyAccountingLab: The Exercises, Quizzes, and Problems (A set) marked in red can be found on MyAccountingLab. You can practise them as often as you want, and most feature step-by-step guided instructions to help you find the right answer.

SHORT EXERCISES

LEARNING OBJECTIVE **1**

Analyze and report a non-strategic investment

S8-1 Assume Knowlton Holdings Ltd. completed these long-term non-strategic investment transactions during 2014:

2014	
Feb. 10	Purchased 300 shares of BCE, paying $25 per share.
	Knowlton intends to hold the investment for the indefinite future.
Dec. 1	Received a cash dividend of $0.36 per share on the BCE shares.
Dec. 31	Adjusted the BCE investment to its current fair value of $7,000.

1. Journalize Knowlton's investment transactions assuming the company reports any changes in fair value through other comprehensive income. Explanations are not required.

2. Show how to report the investment and any unrealized gain or loss on Knowlton's balance sheet at December 31, 2014. Ignore income tax.

LEARNING OBJECTIVE **1**

Account for the sale of a non-strategic investment

S8-2 Use the data given in exercise S8-1. On May 19, 2015, Knowlton sold its investment in BCE shares for $26 per share.

1. Journalize the sale. No explanation is required.

2. How does the gain or loss that you recorded here differ from the gain or loss that was recorded at December 31, 2014?

LEARNING OBJECTIVE **2**

Analyze and report a 40% investment in another company

S8-3 Suppose on February 1, 2014, General Motors paid $41 million for a 40% investment in ABC Ltd., an auto parts manufacturer. Assume ABC earned net income of $6 million and paid cash dividends of $2 million during 2014.

1. What method should General Motors use to account for the investment in ABC? Give your reason.

2. Journalize these three transactions on the books of General Motors. Show all amounts in millions of dollars, and include an explanation for each entry.

3. Post to the Long-Term Investment T-account. What is its balance after all the transactions are posted?

LEARNING OBJECTIVE **2**

Account for the sale of an equity-method investment

S8-4 Use the data given in exercise S8-3. Assume that in November 2015, General Motors sold half its investment in ABC to Toyota. The sale price was $14 million. Compute General Motors' gain or loss on the sale.

S8-5 Answer these questions about consolidation accounting:

1. Define *parent company*. Define *subsidiary company*.
2. How do consolidated financial statements differ from the financial statements of a single company?
3. Which company's name appears on the consolidated financial statements? How much of the subsidiary's shares must the parent own before reporting consolidated statements?

S8-6 Two accounts that arise from consolidation accounting are Goodwill and Non-Controlling Interest.

1. What is *goodwill*, and how does it arise? Which company reports goodwill, the parent or the subsidiary? Where is goodwill reported?
2. What is non-controlling interest and which company reports it, the parent or the subsidiary? Where is non-controlling interest reported?

S8-7 Suppose Prudential Bache (PB) buys $1,000,000 of CitiCorp bonds at a price of 101. The CitiCorp bonds pay cash interest at the annual rate of 7% and mature at the end of five years.

1. How much did PB pay to purchase the bond investment? How much will PB collect when the bond investment matures?
2. How much cash interest will PB receive each year from CitiCorp?
3. Will PB's annual interest revenue on the bond investment be more or less than the amount of cash interest received each year? Give your reason.
4. Compute PB's first-year interest revenue on this bond investment. Use the effective interest of 6.75% to amortize the investment.

S8-8 Return to exercise S8-7, the Prudential Bache (PB) investment in CitiCorp bonds. Journalize the following on PB's books:
a. Purchase of the bond investment on January 2, 2014. PB expects to hold the investment to maturity.
b. Receipt of annual cash interest on December 31, 2014
c. Amortization of the bonds on December 31, 2014
d. Collection of the investment's face value at the maturity date on January 2, 2019. (Assume the receipt of 2018 interest and the amortization of bonds for 2018 have already been recorded, so ignore these entries.)

S8-9 Calculate the present value of the following amounts:

1. $10,000 at the end of five years at 8%
2. $10,000 a year at the end of the next five years at 8%

S8-10 Arnold Financing leases airplanes to airline companies. Arnold has just signed a 10-year lease agreement that requires annual lease payments of $1,000,000. What is the present value of the lease using a 10% interest rate?

S8-11 Companies divide their cash flows into three categories for reporting on the statement of cash flows.

1. List the three categories of cash flows in the order they appear on the statement of cash flows. Which category of cash flows is most closely related to this chapter?
2. Identify two types of transactions that companies report as cash flows from investing activities.

EXERCISES

E8-12 Journalize the following long-term non-strategic investment transactions of Solomon Brothers Department Stores assuming the company reports changes in fair value through net income:

a. Purchased 400 shares of Royal Bank of Canada at $40 per share, with the intent of holding the shares for the indefinite future

b. Received cash dividend of $0.50 per share on the Royal Bank of Canada investment

c. At year-end, adjusted the investment account to current fair value of $35 per share

d. Sold the shares for the market price of $30 per share

E8-13 Dow-Smith Ltd. bought 3,000 common shares of Shoppers Drug Mart at $50.00 common shares of Bank of Montreal (BMO) at $42.50, and 1,400 common shares of EnCana at $93.36, all as non-strategic investments. At December 31, TSX Online reports Shoppers' shares at $48.05, BMO's shares at $31.25, and EnCana's shares at $56.96. The company reports changes in fair value through other comprehensive income

LEARNING OBJECTIVE ❶

Analyze and report non-strategic investments

Requirements

1. Determine the cost and the fair value of the long-term investment portfolio at December 31.
2. Record Dow-Smith's adjusting entry at December 31.
3. What would Dow-Smith report on its income statement and balance sheet for the information given? Make the necessary disclosures. Ignore income tax.

E8-14 BlackBerry owns equity-method investments in several companies. Suppose BlackBerry paid $1,000,000 to acquire a 25% investment in Thai Software Company. Thai Software reported net income of $640,000 for the first year and declared and paid cash dividends of $420,000.

LEARNING OBJECTIVE ❷

Account for transactions under the equity method

1. Record the following in BlackBerry's journal: (a) purchase of the investment, (b) BlackBerry's proportion of Thai Software's net income, and (c) receipt of the cash dividends.
2. What is the ending balance in BlackBerry's investment account?

E8-15 Without making journal entries, record the transactions of exercise E8-14 directly in the BlackBerry account, Long-Term Investment in Thai Software. Assume that after all the noted transactions took place, BlackBerry sold its entire investment in Thai Software for cash of $2,700,000. How much is BlackBerry's gain or loss on the sale of the investment?

LEARNING OBJECTIVE ❷

Analyze gains or losses on equity-method investments

E8-16 Oaktree Financial Inc. paid $500,000 for a 25% investment in the common shares of eTrav Inc. For the first year, eTrav reported net income of $200,000 and at year-end declared and paid cash dividends of $100,000. On the balance sheet date, the fair value of Oaktree's investment in eTrav shares was $384,000.

LEARNING OBJECTIVE ❷

Apply the appropriate accounting method for a 25% investment

Requirements

1. Which method is appropriate for Oaktree Financial to use in accounting for its investment in eTrav? Why?
2. Show everything that Oaktree would report for the investment and any investment revenue in its year-end financial statements.

E8-17 Assume that on September 30, 2014, Manulife Financial paid 91 for 7% bonds of Hydro-Québec as a long-term bond investment. The effective interest rate was 8%. The maturity value of the bonds will be $20,000 on September 30, 2019. The bonds pay interest on March 31 and September 30.

LEARNING OBJECTIVE ❹

Analyze and report bond investment transactions

Requirements

1. What method should Manulife use to account for its investment in the Hydro-Québec bonds?
2. Using the effective interest method of amortizing the bonds, journalize all of Manulife's transactions on the bonds for 2014.
3. Show how Manulife would report everything related to the bond investment on its balance sheet at December 31, 2014.

E8-18 Brinkman Corp. purchased ten $1,000, 5% bonds of General Electric Corporation when the market rate of interest was 4%. Interest is paid annually on the bonds, and the bonds will mature in six years. Compute the price Brinkman paid (the present value) on the bond investment.

LEARNING OBJECTIVE ❻

Calculate the present value of a bond investment

LEARNING OBJECTIVE ❸

Translate a foreign-currency balance sheet into dollars

E8-19 Translate into dollars the balance sheet of Assiniboine Leather Goods Inc.'s Spanish subsidiary. When Assiniboine Leather Goods acquired the foreign subsidiary, a euro was worth $1.60. The current exchange rate is $1.70. During the period when retained earnings were earned, the average exchange rate was $1.58 per euro.

	Euros
Assets	500,000
Liabilities	300,000
Shareholders' equity:	
Common shares	50,000
Retained earnings	150,000
	500,000

During the period covered by this situation, which currency was stronger, the dollar or the euro?

LEARNING OBJECTIVE ❺

Prepare and use a statement of cash flows

E8-20 During fiscal year 2014, Donuts 'R' Us Inc. reported net loss of $135.8 million. Donuts received $1.0 million from the sale of other businesses. Donuts made capital expenditures of $10.4 million and sold property, plant, and equipment for $7.3 million. The company purchased long-term investments at a cost of $12.2 million and sold other long-term investments for $2.5 million.

Requirement

Prepare the investing activities section of the Donuts 'R' Us statement of cash flows. Based solely on Donuts' investing activities, does it appear that the company is growing or shrinking? How can you tell?

LEARNING OBJECTIVE ❺

Use statement of cash flows

E8-21 At the end of the year, Blue Chip Properties Ltd.'s statement of cash flows reported the following for investment activities:

Blue Chip Properties Ltd.
Consolidated Statement of Cash Flows (Partial)

Cash Flows from Investing Activities	
Notes receivable collected	$ 3,110,000
Purchases of short-term investments	(3,457,000)
Proceeds from sales of equipment	1,409,000*
Proceeds from sales of investments (cost of $450,000)	461,000
Expenditures for property, plant, and equipment	(1,761,000)
Net cash used by investing activities	$ (238,000)

*Cost $5,100,000; Accumulated depreciation, $3,691,000

Requirement

For each item listed, make the journal entry that placed the item on Blue Chip's statement of cash flows.

CHALLENGE EXERCISES

LEARNING OBJECTIVE ❻

Calculate the present value of competing investments

E8-22 Which option is better: receive $100,000 now or $20,000, $25,000, $30,000, $25,000, and $20,000, respectively, over the next five years?

Requirements

1. Assuming a 5% interest rate, which investment opportunity would you choose?
2. If you could earn 10%, would your choice change?
3. What would the cash flow in year 5 have to be in order for you to be indifferent to the options mentioned above?

E8-23 Big-Box Retail Corporation reported shareholders' equity on its balance sheet at December 31, 2014, as follows:

LEARNING OBJECTIVE ❶

Explain and analyze accumulated other comprehensive income

Big-Box Retail Corporation
Balance Sheet (Partial)
December 31, 2014

	millions
Shareholders' Equity:	
Common shares, $0.10	
800 million shares authorized, 300 million shares issued	$1,113
Retained earnings	6,250
Accumulated other comprehensive income (loss)	(?)

Requirements

1. Identify two components that were discussed in this chapter that are included in accumulated other comprehensive income.
2. For each component of accumulated other comprehensive income, describe the event that can cause a *positive* balance. Also describe the events that can cause a negative balance for each component.
3. At December 31, 2013, Big-Box's accumulated other comprehensive loss was $53 million. Then, during 2014, Big-Box had a positive foreign-currency translation adjustment of $29 million and an unrealized loss of $16 million on non-strategic investments. Assume Big-Box chooses to record any changes in fair value through other comprehensive income. What was Big-Box's balance of accumulated other comprehensive income (loss) at December 31, 2014?

QUIZ

Test your understanding of long-term investments and international operations by answering the following questions. Select the best choice from among the possible answers given.

Questions 8-24 through 8-26 use the following data:

Assume that Maritimes Holdings Inc. owns the following long-term non-strategic investments and reports any changes in fair value through other comprehensive income:

December 31, 2014

Company	Number of Shares	Cost per Share	Current Fair Value per Share	Dividend per Share
Airbus Corp.	1,000	$60	$71	$2
Whole Grains Inc.	200	9	11	1.50
MySpace Ltd.	500	20	24	1

Q8-24 Maritime's balance sheet at December 31, 2014, should report
a. investments of $85,200.
b. investments of $81,200.
c. dividend revenue of $2,800.
d. unrealized loss of $13,400.

Q8-25 Maritime's 2014 income statement should report

a. investments of $71,800.

c. unrealized gain of $13,400.

b. gain on sale of investment of $13,400.

d. dividend revenue of $2,800.

Q8-26 Suppose Maritime sells the Airbus shares for $68 per share on February 2, 2015. Journalize the sale.

Q8-27 Dividends received on an equity-method investment

a. increase the investment account.

b. decrease the investment account.

c. increase dividend revenue.

d. increase owners' equity.

Q8-28 The starting point in accounting for all investments is

a. fair value on the balance sheet date.

c. cost.

b. equity value.

d. cost minus dividends.

Q8-29 Consolidation accounting

a. combines the accounts of the parent company and those of the subsidiary companies.

b. eliminates all liabilities.

c. reports the receivables and payables of the parent company only.

d. All of the above

Q8-30 On January 1, 2014, Vallée Bleue Ltée purchased $100,000 face value of the 7% bonds of Mail Frontier Inc. at 105. Interest is paid on January 1. The bonds mature on January 1, 2015. For the year ended December 31, 2014, Vallée Bleu received cash interest of

a. $5,000.

c. $6,400.

b. $6,000.

d. $7,000.

Q8-31 Return to Vallée Bleue's bond investment in question Q8-30. Assume an effective interest rate of 6%. For the year ended December 31, 2014, Vallée Bleu earned interest revenue of

a. $5,000.

c. $7,000.

b. $6,300.

d. $7,700.

Q8-32 Yukon Systems purchased inventory on account from Panasonic. The price was ¥100,000, and a yen was quoted at $0.0129. Yukon paid the debt in yen a month later, when the price of a yen was $0.0134. Yukon

a. debited Inventory for $1,290.

b. debited Inventory for $1,340.

c. recorded a Foreign-Currency Transaction Gain of $50.

d. None of the above

Q8-33 One way to avoid a foreign-currency transaction loss is to

a. pay in the foreign currency.

b. collect in your own currency.

c. offset foreign-currency inventory and plant assets.

d. pay debts as late as possible.

Q8-34 Foreign-currency transaction gains and losses are reported on the

a. balance sheet.

c. statement of cash flows.

b. consolidation worksheet.

d. income statement.

Q8-35 Consolidation of a foreign subsidiary usually results in a

a. gain on consolidation.

b. loss on consolidation.

c. foreign-currency translation adjustment.

d. foreign-currency transaction gain or loss.

PROBLEMS

(Group A)

P8-36A Winnipeg Exchanges Ltd. completed the following long-term investment transactions during 2014:

LEARNING OBJECTIVE ❶❷

Analyze and report various long-term investment transactions on the balance sheet and income statement

2014

May 12	Purchased 20,000 shares, which make up 35% of the common shares of Fellingham Corporation at a total cost of $370,000	
July 9	Received annual cash dividend of $1.26 per share on the Fellingham investment	
Sept. 16	Purchased 800 common shares of Tomassini Inc. as a non-strategic investment, paying $41.50 per share	
Oct. 30	Received cash dividend of $0.30 per share on the Tomassini investment	
Dec. 31	Received annual report from Fellingham Corporation. Net income for the year was $510,000.	

At year-end the current fair value of the Tomassini shares is $30,600. The fair value of the Fellingham shares is $652,000. The company reports changes in fair value through other comprehensive income.

Requirements

1. For which investment is current fair value used in the accounting? Why is fair value used for one investment and not the other?
2. Show what Winnipeg Exchanges Ltd. would report on its year-end balance sheet and income statement for these investment transactions. It is helpful to use a T-account for the Long-Term Investment in Fellingham Shares account. Ignore income tax.

P8-37A The beginning balance sheet of New Technology Corporation included the following:

LEARNING OBJECTIVE ❶❷

Analyze and report non-strategic and equity-method investments

Long-Term Investment in MSC Software (equity-method investment)........................	$619,000

New Technology completed the following investment transactions during the year 2014:

Mar. 16	Purchased 2,000 shares of ATI Inc. as a long-term non-strategic investment, paying $12.25 per share
May 21	Received cash dividend of $0.75 per share on the ATI investment
Aug. 17	Received cash dividend of $81,000 from MSC Software
Dec. 31	Received annual report from MSC Software. Net income for the year was $550,000. Of this amount, New Technology's proportion is 22%.

At year-end, the fair values of New Technology's investments are ATI, $25,700, and MSC, $700,000. The company reports any changes in fair value through net income.

Requirements

1. Record the transactions in the journal of New Technology Corporation.
2. Post entries to the T-account for Long-Term Investment in MSC and determine its balance at December 31, 2014.
3. Show how to report the Long-Term Non-strategic Investment and the Long-Term Investment in MSC accounts on New Technology's balance sheet at December 31, 2014.

P8-38A This problem demonstrates the dramatic effect that consolidation accounting can have on a company's ratios. ABC Company owns 100% of ABC Credit Corporation, its financing subsidiary. ABC's main operations consist of manufacturing automotive products. ABC Credit

LEARNING OBJECTIVE ❸

Analyze consolidated financial statements

Corporation mainly helps people finance the purchase of automobiles from ABC and its dealers. The two companies' individual balance sheets are adapted and summarized as follows (amounts in billions):

	ABC (Parent)	ABC Credit (Subsidiary)
Total assets	$94.8	$179.0
Total liabilities	$68.4	$164.7
Total shareholders' equity	26.4	14.3
Total liabilities and equity	$94.8	$179.0

Requirements

1. Compute the debt ratio of ABC Company considered alone.
2. Determine the consolidated total assets, total liabilities, and shareholders' equity of ABC Company after consolidating the financial statements of ABC Credit into the totals of ABC, the parent company.
3. Recompute the debt ratio of the consolidated entity. Why do companies prefer not to consolidate their financing subsidiaries into their own financial statements?

LEARNING OBJECTIVE ❹

Analyze and report a bond investment

P8-39A Insurance companies and pension plans hold large quantities of bond investments. Prairie Insurance Corp. purchased $600,000 of 5% bonds of Eaton Inc. for 104.5 on March 1, 2014, when the effective interest rate was 4%. These bonds pay interest on March 1 and September 1 each year. They mature on March 1, 2019. At February 28, 2015, the market price of the bonds is 103.5.

Requirements

1. Journalize Prairie's purchase of the bonds as a long-term investment on March 1, 2014 (to be held to maturity), receipt of cash interest and amortization of the bond investment on September 1, 2014, and accrual of interest revenue and amortization at February 28, 2015. Use the effective-interest method for amortizing the bond investment.
2. Show all financial statement effects of this long-term bond investment on Prairie Insurance Corp.'s balance sheet and income statement at February 28, 2015.

LEARNING OBJECTIVE ❻

Explain the impact of the time value of money on valuation of investments

P8-40A Annual cash flows from two competing investment opportunities are given. Each investment opportunity will require the same initial investment at the end of each year.

	Investment	
Year	A	B
1	$10,000	$ 8,000
2	8,000	8,000
3	6,000	8,000
	$24,000	$24,000

Requirement

Assuming a 12% interest rate, which investment opportunity would you choose?

LEARNING OBJECTIVE ❸

Measure and explain the foreign-currency translation adjustment

P8-41A Assume that Blackberry has a subsidiary company based in Japan.

Requirements

1. Translate into dollars the foreign-currency balance sheet of the Japanese subsidiary of BlackBerry.

	Yen
Assets	300,000,000
Liabilities	80,000,000
Shareholders' equity:	
Common shares	20,000,000
Retained earnings	200,000,000
	300,000,000

When Blackberry acquired this subsidiary, the Japanese yen was worth $0.0134. The current exchange rate is $0.0137. During the period when the subsidiary earned its income, the average exchange rate was $0.0135 per yen.

Before you perform the foreign-currency translation calculations, indicate whether Blackberry has experienced a positive or a negative translation adjustment. State whether the adjustment is a gain or a loss, and show where it is reported in the financial statements.

2. To which company does the foreign-currency translation adjustment "belong"? In which company's financial statements will the translation adjustment be reported?

P8-42A Excerpts from Smart Pro Inc.'s statement of cash flows appear as follows:

LEARNING OBJECTIVE ❺

Use the statement of cash flows

Smart Pro Inc.
Consolidated Statement of Cash Flows (Partial, Adapted)
For the Years Ended December 31

(in millions)	2014	2013
Cash and cash equivalents, beginning of year	$ 2,976	$ 3,695
Net cash provided by operating activities	8,654	12,827
Cash flows provided by (used for) investing activities:		
Additions to property, plant, and equipment	(7,309)	(6,674)
Acquisitions of other companies	(883)	(2,317)
Purchases of investments	(7,141)	(17,188)
Sales of investments	15,138	16,144
Net cash (used for) investing activities	(195)	(10,035)
Cash flows provided by (used for) financing activities:		
Borrowing	329	215
Repayment of long-term debt	(10)	(46)
Proceeds from issuance of shares	762	797
Repurchase of common shares	(4,008)	(4,007)
Payment of dividends to shareholders	(538)	(470)
Net cash (used for) financing activities	(3,465)	(3,511)
Net increase (decrease) in cash and cash equivalents	4,994	(719)
Cash and cash equivalents, end of year	$ 7,970	$ 2,976

Requirement

As the chief executive officer of Smart Pro Inc., your duty is to write the management letter to your shareholders to explain Smart Pro's investing activities during 2014. Compare the company's level of investment with the preceding year, and indicate the major way the company financed its investments during 2014. Net income for 2014 was $1,291 million.

(Group B)

LEARNING OBJECTIVE ❶❷

Analyze and report various long-term investment transactions on the balance sheet and income statement

P8-43B Homestead Financial Corporation owns numerous investments in the shares of other companies. Homestead Financial completed the following long-term investment transactions:

2014		
May	1	Purchased 8,000 shares, which make up 25% of the common shares of Mars Company at total cost of $450,000
Sept.	15	Received a cash dividend of $1.40 per share on the Mars investment
Oct.	12	Purchased 1,000 common shares of Mercury Corporation as a non-strategic investment, paying $22.50 per share
Dec.	14	Received a cash dividend of $0.75 per share on the Mercury investment
	31	Received annual report from Mars Company. Net income for the year was $350,000.

At year-end the current fair value of the Mercury shares is $19,200. The fair value of the Mars shares is $740,000. The company reports changes in fair value through net income.

Requirements
1. For which investment is current fair value used in the accounting? Why is fair value used for one investment and not the other?
2. Show what Homestead Financial will report on its year-end balance sheet and income statement for these investments. (It is helpful to use a T-account for the Long-Term Investment in Mars Shares account.) Ignore income tax.

LEARNING OBJECTIVE ❶❷

Analyze and report non-strategic and equity-method investments

P8-44B The beginning balance sheet of Dealmaker Securities Limited included the following:

Long-Term Investments in Affiliates (equity-method investments).............................	$409,000

Dealmaker completed the following investment transactions during the year:

Feb.	16	Purchased 10,000 shares of BCM Software common shares as a long-term non-strategic investment, paying $9.25 per share
May	14	Received cash dividend of $0.82 per share on the BCM investment
Oct.	15	Received cash dividend of $29,000 from an affiliated company
Dec.	31	Received annual reports from affiliated companies. Their total net income for the year was $620,000. Of this amount, Dealmaker's proportion is 25%.

The fair values of Dealmaker's investments are BCM, $89,000, and affiliated companies, $947,000. The company reports changes in fair value through other comprehensive income.

Requirements
1. Record the transactions in the journal of Dealmaker Securities.
2. Post entries to the Long-Term Investments in Affiliates T-account, and determine its balance at December 31.
3. Show how to report Long-Term Non-strategic Investments and Long-Term Investments in Affiliates on Dealmaker's balance sheet at December 31.

LEARNING OBJECTIVE ❹

Analyze and report a bond investment

P8-45B Financial institutions hold large quantities of bond investments. Suppose Sun Life Financial purchases $500,000 of 6% bonds of General Components Corporation for 88 on January 1, 2014, when the effective interest rate is 8%. These bonds pay interest on January 1 and July 1 each year. They mature on January 1, 2022. At December 31, 2014, the market price of the bonds is 90.

Requirements

1. Journalize Sun Life's purchase of the bonds as a long-term investment on January 1, 2014 (to be held to maturity), receipt of cash interest and amortization of the bond investment on July 1, 2014, and accrual of interest revenue and amortization at December 31, 2014. Use the effective-interest method for amortizing the bond investment.
2. Show all financial statement effects of this long-term bond investment on Sun Life's balance sheet and income statement at December 31, 2014.

P8-46B Annual cash flows from two competing investment opportunities are given. Each investment opportunity will require the same initial investment.

LEARNING OBJECTIVE 6

Explain the impact of the time value of money on the valuation of investments

Year	Investment	
	X	Y
1	$15,000	$10,000
2	10,000	10,000
3	5,000	10,000
	$30,000	$30,000

Requirement

Assuming a 10% interest rate, which investment opportunity would you choose?

P8-47B Arte Fabrics Ltd. owns a subsidiary based in France.

LEARNING OBJECTIVE 3

Measure and explain the foreign-currency translation adjustment

Requirements

1. Translate the foreign-currency balance sheet of the French subsidiary of Arte Fabrics Ltd. into dollars. When Arte Fabrics acquired this subsidiary, the euro was worth $1.60. The current exchange rate is $1.80 per euro. During the period when the subsidiary earned its income, the average exchange rate was $1.70 per euro.

	Euros
Assets	3,000,000
Liabilities	1,000,000
Shareholders' equity:	
Common shares	300,000
Retained earnings	1,700,000
	3,000,000

Before you perform the foreign-currency translation calculation, indicate whether Arte Fabrics has experienced a positive or a negative foreign-currency translation adjustment. State whether the adjustment is a gain or a loss, and show where it is reported in the financial statements.

2. To which company does the translation adjustment "belong"? In which company's financial statements will the translation adjustment be reported?

LEARNING OBJECTIVE ❺

Use the statement of cash flows

P8-48B Marine Transport Ltd.'s statement of cash flows, as adapted, appears as follows:

Marine Transport Ltd.
Consolidated Statement of Cash Flows
For the Years Ended December 31 (Stated in thousands of Canadian dollars)

	2014	2013
Cash flows from (used in):		
Operating activities:		
Net earnings	$192,833	$114,676
Items not involving cash:		
Depreciation and amortization	127,223	111,442
Amortization of other liabilities	(897)	(868)
Amortization of hedge settlements	1,400	1,427
Net realized loss on cash flow hedge	18	—
Loss on derecognition of property and equipment and ship parts	32,773	394
Stock-based compensation expense	20,058	21,205
Future income tax expense	41,775	46,635
Unrealized foreign exchange loss (gain)	13,813	(346)
Decrease in non-cash working capital	112,069	43,707
	541,065	338,272
Financing activities:		
Increase in long-term debt	141,178	418,581
Repayment of long-term debt	(156,516)	(132,559)
Decrease in obligations under capital lease	(356)	(480)
Share issuance costs	—	(10)
Shares repurchased	(21,250)	—
Issuance of common shares	1,551	—
Increase in other assets	(20,897)	(27,830)
Increase in non-cash working capital	(3,000)	(1,071)
	(59,290)	256,631
Investing activities:		
Ship additions	(191,437)	(438,906)
Ship disposals	1,975	3,822
Other property and equipment additions	(24,639)	(43,590)
Other property and equipment disposals	13,819	1,611
	(200,282)	(477,063)
Cash flow from operating, financing, and investing activities	281,493	117,840
Effect of exchange rate on cash	(5,452)	37
Net change in cash	276,041	117,877
Cash, beginning of year	377,517	259,640
Cash, end of year	$653,558	$377,517

Cash is defined as cash and cash equivalents.

Requirement

As a member of an investment club, you have been asked to review Marine Transport's major investing activities during 2014. Compare the company's level of investment with the previous year, and indicate how the company financed its investments during 2014.

Apply Your Knowledge

Decision Cases

Case 1. Infografix Corporation's consolidated sales for 2014 were $26.6 million and expenses totalled $24.8 million. Infografix operates worldwide and conducts 37% of its business outside Canada. During 2014, Infografix reported the following items in its financial statements (amounts in millions):

LEARNING OBJECTIVE ❶❸
Make an investment decision

Foreign-currency translation adjustments...	$(202)
Unrealized holding on non-strategic investments	(328)

As you consider an investment in Infografix shares, some concerns arise. Answer the following questions:

1. What do the parentheses around the two dollar amounts signify?
2. Are these items reported as assets, liabilities, shareholders' equity, revenues, or expenses? Are they normal-balance accounts, or are they contra accounts?
3. Are these items reason for rejoicing or sorrow at Infografix? Are Infografix's emotions about these items deep or only moderate? Why?
4. Did Infografix include these items in net income? Did it include these items in retained earnings? In the final analysis, how much net income did Infografix report for 2014?
5. Should these items scare you away from investing in Infografix shares? Why or why not?

Case 2. Cathy Talbert is the general manager of Barham Ltd., which provides data-management services for physicians in the Regina, Saskatchewan, area. Barham is having a rough year. Net income trails projections for the year by almost $75,000. This shortfall is especially important—Barham plans to issue shares early next year and needs to show investors that the company can meet its earnings targets.

LEARNING OBJECTIVE ❶❷❹
Make an investment sale decision

Barham holds several investments purchased a few years ago. Even though investing in shares is outside Barham's core business of data-management services, Talbert thinks these investments may hold the key to helping the company meet its net income goal for the year. She is considering what to do with the following investments:

1. Barham owns 50% of the common shares of Prairie Office Systems, which provides the business forms that Barham uses. Prairie Office Systems has lost money for the past two years but still has a retained earnings balance of $550,000. Talbert thinks she can get Prairie's treasurer to declare a $160,000 cash dividend, half of which would go to Barham.
2. Barham owns a bond investment with a 4% coupon rate and an annual interest payment. The bond was purchased eight years ago for $293,000. The purchase price represents a discount from the bonds' maturity value of $400,000 based on an effective rate of 8%. These bonds mature two years from now, and their current market value is $380,000. Ms. Talbert has checked with a Scotiabank investment representative and Talbert is considering selling the bonds. A charge of 1% commission would be made on the sale transaction.
3. Barham owns 5,000 Royal Bank of Canada (RBC) shares valued at $53 per share. One year ago, RBC was worth only $28 per share. Barham purchased the RBC shares for $37 per share. Talbert wonders whether Barham should sell the RBC shares.

Requirement

Evaluate all three actions as a way for Barham Ltd. to generate the needed amount of income. Recommend the best way for Barham to achieve its net income goal.

Ethical Issue

Media One owns 15% of the voting shares of Online Inc. The remainder of the Online shares are held by numerous investors with small holdings. Austin Cohen, president of Media One and a member of Online's board of directors, heavily influences Online's policies.

Under the fair-value method of accounting for investments, Media One's net income increases as it receives dividend revenue from Online. Media One pays President Cohen a bonus, computed as a percentage of Media One's net income. Therefore, Cohen can control his personal bonus to a certain extent by influencing Online's dividends.

A recession occurs in 2014, and Media One's income is low. Cohen uses his power to have Online pay a large cash dividend. The action requires Online to borrow in order to pay the dividend.

Requirements

1. In getting Online to pay the large cash dividend, is Cohen acting within his authority as a member of the Online board of directors? Are Cohen's actions ethical? Whom can his actions harm?
2. Discuss how using the equity method of accounting for investment would decrease Cohen's potential for manipulating his bonus.

Focus on Financials

LEARNING OBJECTIVE ❸❺

Analyze investments, consolidated statements, and international operations

TELUS Corporation

TELUS's financial statements are given in Appendix A at the end of this book.

1. Does TELUS have any subsidiaries? How can you tell?
2. Is TELUS expanding or contracting its operations? How can you tell?
3. Does TELUS engage in foreign-currency transactions? If so, what is the nature of these transactions?

Focus on Analysis

LEARNING OBJECTIVE ❸

Analyze goodwill, consolidated subsidiaries, and investments

TELUS Corporation

TELUS's financial statements are given in Appendix A at the end of this book.

1. TELUS has subsidiaries. What is TELUS's percentage of ownership? How can you tell?
2. TELUS reports long-term investments on its consolidated balance sheet. Did they buy or sell any of these investments during the year? How can you tell?
3. Did TELUS's goodwill suffer any impairment during the year? How can you tell?

Group Project

Pick a stock from the *Globe and Mail* or other database or publication. Assume that your group purchases 1,000 shares as a long-term investment and that your 1,000 shares are less than 20% of the company's outstanding shares. Research the shares to determine whether the company pays cash dividends and, if so, how much and at what intervals.

Requirements

1. Track the shares for a period assigned by your professor. Over the specified period, keep a daily record of the share price to see how well your investment has performed. Keep a record of any dividends you would have received. End the period of your analysis with a month-end, such as September 30 or December 31.

2. Journalize all transactions that you have experienced, including the share purchase, dividends received (both cash dividends and stock dividends), and any year-end adjustment required by the accounting method that is appropriate for your situation. Assume you will prepare financial statements on the ending date of your study.

3. Show what you will report on your company's balance sheet, income statement, and statement of cash flows as a result of your investment transactions.

Quick Check Answers

1. *c*
2. *d (1,000 shares × $35 = $35,000)*
3. *a ($35,000 − $31,000 = $4,000)*
4. *c [$40,000 − (1,000 shares × $35) = $5,000]*
5. *b [$100,000 + 0.20 ($50,000 − $25,000) = $105,000]*
6. *c ($100,000 + 0.80 [$68,000 + 0.80($40,000)] = $180,000)*
7. *a*
8. *d*
9. *b ($1,000,000 in U.S. dollars × $1.25 = $1,250,000)*
10. *c*

9

Liabilities

© GerryRousseau/Alamy

SPOTLIGHT

WESTJET AIRLINES: A SUCCESS STORY

WestJet began operations in 1996 by serving five cities in Western Canada and now flies across Canada and to many destinations in the United States, Mexico, and the Caribbean. The airline decided at its start to operate with a single type of plane, the Boeing 737, in order to reduce operating costs. WestJet also decided to encourage share ownership by employees, so the front-desk staff, pilots, and flight attendants also own part of the company. This has led to a high level of service, which encourages passengers to "fly WestJet."

Airlines have some interesting liabilities. WestJet collects fares in advance and recognizes the revenue when the passenger actually takes the trip. Thus, WestJet had a liability called "advance ticket sales" of about $450 million on its balance sheet at March 31, 2012. When passengers change or cancel flights, they receive credits that they can apply toward future WestJet flights. This "nonrefundable guest credits" liability was $44 million at March 31, 2012. In this chapter, you will learn more about these and other types of liabilities commonly found on financial statements.

WestJet
Consolidated Balance Sheet (Adapted)
As at March 31, 2012 (in millions)

Assets		Liabilities and Shareholders' Equity	
Current Assets		Current Liabilities	
Cash and cash equivalents..............	$1,401	Accounts payable and	
Other current assets	165	accrued liabilities........................	$ 401
Total current assets........................	1,566	Advance ticket sales.......................	452
		Nonrefundable guest credits..........	44
		Current portion of obligations	
		under finance leases...................	1
		Current portion of long-term debt ...	162
		Total current liabilities...................	1,060
Property and equipment...................	1,921	Obligations under finance leases	3
Other long-lived assets.....................	141	Long-term debt	662
		Other long-term liabilities	490
			2,215
		Shareholders' Equity	
		Shareholders' equity.........................	1,413
		Total liabilities and	
Total assets	$3,628	shareholders' equity.......................	$3,628

This chapter shows how to account for liabilities—both current and long-term. We begin with current liabilities.

EXPLAIN AND ACCOUNT FOR CURRENT LIABILITIES

OBJECTIVE

❶ **Explain** and **account** for current liabilities

Current liabilities are obligations due within one year, or within the company's normal operating cycle if it is longer than one year. Obligations due beyond that are classified as *long-term liabilities*.

Current liabilities are of two kinds:

* Known amounts
* Estimated amounts

We look first at current liabilities of a known amount.

Current Liabilities of Known Amount

SHORT-TERM BORROWINGS. Companies sometimes need to borrow money on a short-term basis to cover temporary shortfalls in cash needed to run their businesses. For example, a ski resort that earns most of its revenues during the winter months may need to temporarily borrow money to supplement the minimal cash flows it generates from operations during the summer. A **line of credit** allows a company to access credit on an as-needed basis up to a maximum amount set by the lender. The ski resort, for example, could arrange with its bank to borrow up to $250,000 to help run its business over the slow summer months.

ACCOUNTS PAYABLE. Amounts owed for products or services purchased on credit are **accounts payable**. For example, WestJet purchases on account the food and beverages it serves its passengers. We have seen many other examples of accounts payable in previous chapters. One of a merchandiser's most common transactions is the credit purchase of inventory. The Hudson's Bay Company and Sobeys buy their inventory on account.

ACCRUED LIABILITIES (ACCRUED EXPENSES). An accrued liability results from an expense the business has incurred but has not yet been billed for or paid. Therefore, an accrued expense creates a liability, which explains why it is also called an *accrued expense*.

For example, WestJet's salaries and wages payable accrue as employees work for the company. Interest expense accrues with the passage of time. Common types of accrued liabilities are:

- Salaries and Wages Payable
- Interest Payable
- Income Taxes Payable

Salaries and Wages Payable is the liability for salaries, wages, and related payroll expenses not yet paid at the end of the period (see the Payroll Liabilities section below for more details on this accrual). This category also includes payroll deductions withheld from employee paycheques. *Interest Payable* is the company's interest payable on notes, loans, and bonds payable. *Income Taxes Payable* is the amount of income tax the company still owes at year-end.

SHORT-TERM NOTES PAYABLE. In Chapter 5 we introduced you to promissory notes from a lender's perspective, so we called them notes *receivable*. When we record these same notes in the borrower's books, they are notes *payable*. **Short-term notes payable** are notes payable due within one year. Robertson Construction Inc. may issue short-term notes payable to borrow cash or to purchase assets. For its notes payable, Robertson must accrue interest expense at the end of each reporting period. The following sequence of entries covers the purchase of inventory, accrual of interest expense, and payment of a short-term note payable:

2014			
Oct. 1	Inventory...	8,000	
	Note Payable, Short-Term		8,000
	Purchase of inventory by issuing a six-month 10% note payable.		

This transaction increases both an asset and a liability:

				SHAREHOLDERS'
ASSETS	**=**	**LIABILITIES**	**+**	**EQUITY**
+8,000	=	+8,000		

Assume Robertson Construction's year-end is December 31. At year-end, Robertson must accrue interest expense at 10% per year for October through December. (For ease of exposition, accrued interest has been calculated based on months rather than days. In practice, days are typically used.)

2014
Dec. 31   Interest Expense ($8,000 × 0.10 × 3/12)   200
             Interest Payable...   200
       Adjusting entry to accrue interest expense at year-end.

Liabilities increase, and equity decreases because of the expense:

ASSETS	=	LIABILITIES	+	SHAREHOLDERS' EQUITY
0	=	+200		−200 Interest Expense

The balance sheet at year-end will report the note payable of $8,000 and the related interest payable of $200 as current liabilities. The income statement will report interest expense of $200.

The following entry records the note's payment at March 31, 2015:

2015
Mar. 31   Note Payable, Short-Term   8,000
         Interest Payable   200
         Interest Expense ($8,000 × 0.10 × 3/12)   200
             Cash [$8,000 + ($8,000 × 0.10 × 6/12)]   8,400
         Payment of a note payable and interest at maturity.

ASSETS	=	LIABILITIES	+	SHAREHOLDERS' EQUITY
−8,400	=	−8,000		−200 Interest Expense
		− 200		

The debits eliminate the two payables and also record Robertson's interest expense for January, February, and March.

SALES TAX PAYABLE. The federal government and most provinces levy taxes on the sale of goods and services. Sellers collect these taxes from customers, creating **sales tax payable** to the government levying the tax. Canada has three types of sales taxes:

- Goods and services tax (GST) is a value-added tax levied by the federal government. At the time of writing, the tax is 5%. It applies to most goods and services.

- Provincial or regional sales tax (PST) is a retail tax applied to goods and services purchased by individuals or businesses *for their own use,* not for resale, with the rates varying by province or region. At the time of writing, Alberta, the Northwest Territories, Nunavut, and Yukon do not levy a provincial or regional sales tax.

- Harmonized sales tax (HST), which combines PST and GST, is also a value-added tax. Prince Edward Island, New Brunswick, Newfoundland and Labrador, Nova Scotia, and Ontario, together with the federal government, levy an HST.

The final consumer of a GST- or HST-taxable product or service bears the tax, while entities farther down the supply chain from the end consumer do pay GST or HST, but receive an input tax credit (ITC) equal to the tax they have paid. These ITCs are deducted from any GST or HST collected to arrive at the net GST or HST payable to the government. For example, if a company collected $10,000 in HST on its sales and paid $8,000 in HST on goods and services it purchased, then it would end the period with HST payable of $2,000 ($10,000 in HST collected less $8,000 in ITCs).

GST or HST payable is always a current liability, as it is payable annually, quarterly, or monthly, depending on the collector's volume of business. GST and HST are remitted to the Canada Revenue Agency (CRA), which in turn remits the provincial portion of the HST to the respective provinces, with all GST and the federal portion of the HST being remitted to the federal government.

GST and HST are accounted for in the same way, so the following illustration using GST is applicable for HST as well, except for the difference in tax rates. Assume Kitchen Hardware Ltd., of Brandon, Manitoba, purchases lawn rakes for $3,000 plus 5% GST for a total of $3,150. Subsequently, Kitchen sells the rakes for $6,000 plus GST of $300 (provincial sales tax is ignored for this example but is covered below). The entries to record the purchase of the rakes, the sale of the rakes, and the remittance of the GST payable by Kitchen are as follows:

Inventory	3,000	
GST Recoverable	150	
Accounts Payable		3,150
To record purchase of inventory.		
Accounts Receivable	6,300	
Cost of Goods Sold	3,000	
Sales		6,000
Inventory		3,000
GST Payable		300
To record sale of inventory.		
GST Payable	300	
GST ITC		150
Cash		150
To record payment of GST collected less GST paid.		

PST is levied at the point of sale to the final consumer, unlike GST and HST. It would apply to Kitchen Hardware when it purchases a cash register and to Mary Fortin, a customer of Kitchen, when she purchases light bulbs. Because only the final consumer pays PST, there are no ITCs for provincial taxes (except for Quebec's QST). PST payable is always a current liability as it is payable quarterly or monthly, depending on the payer's volume of business.

With respect to Kitchen Hardware's sale of rakes for $6,000, the GST would be $300 and the PST would be $420, as Manitoba's tax rate is 7%. So the total price to the consumer would be $6,720. The entries to record the sale of the rakes (including GST and PST payable) and the remittance of the PST payable by Kitchen are as follows:

Accounts Receivable	6,720	
Cost of Goods Sold	3,000	
Sales		6,000
Inventory		3,000
GST Payable		300
PST Payable		420
To record sale of inventory.		
PST Payable	420	
Cash		420
To record payment of PST collected.		

PAYROLL LIABILITIES. **Payroll**, also called *employee compensation*, is a major expense for most companies. For service organizations—such as law firms, real estate brokers, and accounting firms—compensation is *the* major expense, just as cost of goods sold is the major expense for a merchandising company.

Employee compensation takes different forms. A *salary* is employee pay stated at a yearly or monthly rate. A *wage* is employee pay stated at an hourly rate. Sales employees often earn a *commission*, which is a percentage of the sales the employee has made. A *bonus* is an amount over and above regular compensation. Accounting for all forms of compensation follows the same pattern, as illustrated in Exhibit 9-1 (using assumed figures).

Salary expense represents *gross pay* (that is, pay before subtractions for taxes and other deductions). Salary expense creates several payroll entries, expenses, and liabilities:

- *Salaries and Wages Payable* is the employees' net (take-home) pay.
- *Employee Withholdings Income Tax Payable* is the employees' income tax that has been withheld from paycheques.
- *Canada Pension Plan Payable* and *Employment Insurance Payable* are the employees' contributions to those two government programs that have been withheld from their paycheques, along with the employer's contributions to these programs. In Quebec, the Quebec Pension Plan replaces the CPP and employees and employers must also contribute to the Quebec Parental Insurance Plan.
- *Canada Pension Plan and Employment Insurance Expense* is the cost of the employer's contribution to these two government programs. The two credits to liabilities totalling $751 represent the liability for the employer's contribution.

EXHIBIT 9-1
Accounting for Payroll Expenses and Liabilities

Salary Expense	10,000	
Employee Withholdings Income Tax Payable		1,350
Canada Pension Plan Payable		495
Employment Insurance Payable		183
Salary and Wages Payable [take-home pay]		7,972
To record salary expense and employee withholdings.		
Canada Pension Plan and Employment Insurance Expense	751	
Canada Pension Plan Payable		495
Employment Insurance Payable		256
To record employer's share of Canada Pension Plan and Employment Insurance.		

ASSETS	=	LIABILITIES	+	SHAREHOLDERS' EQUITY
		+1,350		
		+ 495		
0	=	+ 183		−10,000 Salary Expense
		+7,972		
0	=	+ 495		−751 CPP and EI Expense
		+ 256		

UNEARNED REVENUES. A business sometimes collects cash from its customers before it provides the goods or services the customer has paid for. This creates a liability called **unearned revenues** because the business owes goods or services to the customer.

WestJet, for example, sells tickets and collects cash in advance of passengers actually taking their flights. WestJet therefore reports Advance Ticket Sales for airline tickets sold in advance. At March 31, 2012, WestJet owed customers $452 million of air travel (see page 417). Let's see how WestJet accounts for unearned ticket revenue.

Assume that on September 1 WestJet collects $800 for a round-trip ticket from Vancouver to Montreal, departing September 26 and returning October 10. WestJet's entries would be as follows:

Sept. 1	Cash	800	
	Advance Ticket Sales...		800
	To record cash received for future return airfare from Vancouver to Montreal.		

Advance Ticket Sales
800

WestJet's assets and liabilities increase equally. There is no revenue yet.

ASSETS	=	LIABILITIES	+	SHAREHOLDERS' EQUITY
+800	=	+800	+	0

When the passenger flies from Vancouver to Montreal on September 26, WestJet can record $400 of revenue because it has provided half of the air travel it owes the customer:

Sept. 26	Advance Ticket Sales	400	
	Ticket Revenue ($800/2)..................................		400
	To record revenue earned that was collected in advance.		

The liability decreases and revenue increases:

Advance Ticket Sales		Ticket Revenue
400 800		400

At September 30, WestJet reports:

- $400 of advance ticket sales (a liability) on the balance sheet for the return flight it still owes the customer
- $400 of ticket revenue on the income statement

When the customer returns to Vancouver on October 10, WestJet has earned the remaining $400 of revenue:

Oct. 10	Advance Ticket Sales	400	
	Ticket Revenue ($800/2)..................................		400
	Earned revenue that was collected in advance.		

Now the liability balance is zero because WestJet has provided both of the flights it owed the customer.

CURRENT PORTION OF LONG-TERM DEBT. The **current portion of long-term debt** is the amount of long-term debt that is payable within the next year. At the end of each year, a company reclassifies (from long-term debt to a current liability) the amount of its long-term debt that must be paid during the upcoming year. We will cover the accounting for long-term debt in the second half of this chapter.

Current Liabilities That Must Be Estimated

A business may know that it has a present obligation and that it is *probable* it will have to settle this obligation in the future, but it may be uncertain of the timing or amount of the liability. Despite this uncertainty, IFRS require the business to estimate and record a **provision** for this obligation in its financial statements. A provision is a specific type of contingent liability (see page 424 for further information on contingent liabilities).

Estimated liabilities vary among companies and include such things as warranties, employee pension obligations, and corporate restructuring costs. Warranty liabilities are quite common, so we will use them to illustrate the accounting for estimated liabilities.

ESTIMATED WARRANTY PAYABLE. Many companies guarantee their products under *warranty* agreements that cover some period of time after their customers purchase them. Automobile companies accrue liabilities for vehicle warranties, which usually extend for several years. The sale of a product with a warranty attached is a past event that creates a present obligation, which will require company resources (repair or replacement) to settle at some future date. At the time of the sale, however, the company does not know which products will be defective or how much it will cost to fix or replace them. The exact amount of warranty expense cannot be known with certainty, so the business must estimate warranty expense and the related warranty liability.

Assume that Black & Decker Canada Inc., which manufactures power tools, sold 4,000 tools subject to one-year warranties. If, in past years, between 2% and 4% of products proved defective and it cost an average of $50 to replace each tool, Black & Decker could estimate that 3% of the products it sells this year will require repair or replacement. In that case, Black & Decker would estimate warranty expense of $6,000 (4,000 × 0.03 × $50) for the period and make the following entry:

Warranty Expense	6,000	
Estimated Warranty Payable		6,000
To accrue warranty expense.		

Estimated Warranty Payable	
	6,000

If Black & Decker actually ends up replacing 100 defective tools with new tools costing $4,800, it would record the following:

Estimated Warranty Payable	4,800	
Inventory		4,800
To replace defective products sold under warranty.		

Estimated Warranty Payable

4,800		6,000
	Bal.	1,200

At the end of the year, Black & Decker will report Estimated Warranty Payable of $1,200 as a current liability. The income statement reports Warranty Expense of $6,000 for the year. Then, next year Black & Decker will repeat this process. The Estimated Warranty Payable account probably won't ever zero out.

Vacation pay is another expense that must be estimated. Income taxes must also be estimated because the final amount isn't determined until early the next year.

Contingent Liabilities

Contingent liabilities are possible obligations that will become actual obligations only if some uncertain future event occurs. They also include present obligations for which there is doubt about the need for the eventual outflow of resources to settle the obligation, or for which the amount of the obligation cannot be reliably estimated. Lawsuits in progress, debt guarantees, and audits by the Canada Revenue Agency are examples of contingent liabilities.

Under ASPE, contingent liabilities that are *likely* to occur and can be *reasonably estimated* are accrued as liabilities, similar to the above treatment for provisions under IFRS. Other less-certain contingent liabilities, under both IFRS and ASPE, are simply disclosed in the notes. Even note disclosure is not required if there is only a remote chance the contingent liability will occur. Determining the proper accounting treatment of contingent liabilities is beyond the scope of this text.

Are All Liabilities Reported on the Balance Sheet or Disclosed in the Notes?

The big danger with liabilities is that a company may fail to report a debt on its balance sheet. What is the consequence of not reporting a liability? The company would definitely understate its liabilities and would probably overstate its net income. In short, its financial statements would make the company look stronger than it really is. Any such misstatement, if significant, hurts a company's credibility.

Contingent liabilities are very easy to overlook because they aren't actual debts. How would you feel if you owned shares in a company that failed to report a contingency that put the company out of business? In this case, you would hire a lawyer to file suit against the company for negligent financial reporting. If you had known of the contingency, you could have sold the shares and avoided the loss.

Summary of Current Liabilities

Let's summarize what we've covered thus far. A company can report its current liabilities on the balance sheet as follows:

Hudson Ltd.
Balance Sheet
December 31, 2014

Assets		Liabilities	
Current assets		**Current liabilities**	
Cash		Accounts payable	
Short-term investments		Salary payable*	
Etc.		Interest payable*	
		HST/GST payable**	
		PST payable*	
		CPP payable*	
		EI payable*	
		Income tax payable	
Property, plant, and equipment:		Unearned revenue	
Land		Estimated warranty payable	
Etc.		Notes payable, short-term	
		Current portion of long-term debt	
		Total current liabilities	
Other assets:		**Long-term liabilities**	
		Shareholders' Equity	
		Share capital	
		Retained earnings	
Total assets	$XXX	Total liabilities and shareholders' equity	$XXX

*These items are often combined and reported in a single total as "Accrued Liabilities" or "Accrued Expenses Payable."
**ASPE requires separate disclosure of the amount payable with respect to government remittances (other than income taxes), either on the face of the balance sheet or in the notes.

COOKING THE BOOKS WITH LIABILITIES

CRAZY EDDIE, INC.

Accidentally understating liabilities is one thing, but doing it intentionally is quite another. When unethical management decides to cook the books in the area of liabilities, its strategy is to *deliberately understate recorded liabilities*. This can be done by intentionally under-recording the amount of existing liabilities or by omitting certain liabilities altogether.

Crazy Eddie, Inc., was a large electronics retailer that used multiple tactics to overstate its financial position over a period of four consecutive years from 1984 to 1987. In addition to overstating inventory (thus understating cost of goods sold and overstating income), the management of the company deliberately understated accounts payable by issuing fictitious debit memos from suppliers. A debit memo is issued for goods returned to a supplier, such as Sony. When a debit memo is issued, accounts payable are debited (reduced), thus reducing current liabilities and increasing the current ratio. Eventually, expenses are also decreased, and profits are correspondingly increased through reduction of expenses. Crazy Eddie, Inc., issued $3 million of fictitious debit memos in one year, making the company's current ratio and working capital look better than they actually were, as well as overstating profits.

MID-CHAPTER SUMMARY PROBLEM

Assume that Korvar Plastics Inc., a manufacturer of plastic pipe for the construction industry and located in Red Deer, Alberta, faced the following liability situations at June 30, 2014, the end of the company's fiscal year:

a. Long-term debt totals $10 million and is payable in annual instalments of $1 million each. The interest rate on the debt is 7%, and interest is paid each December 31.

b. Salary expense for the last payroll period of the year was $90,000. Of this amount, employees' income tax of $12,000 was withheld, and other withholdings and employee benefits were $6,000. These payroll amounts will be paid early in July.

c. Since the last reporting period, GST of $200,000 had been collected and ITCs of $76,000 had been earned.

d. On fiscal year 2014 sales of $40 million, management estimates warranty expense of 2%. One year ago, at June 30, 2013, Estimated Warranty Liability stood at $100,000. Warranty payments were $300,000 during the year ended June 30, 2014.

Show how Korvar Plastics Inc. would report these liabilities on its balance sheet at June 30, 2014.

ANSWER

a. Current liabilities:

Current portion of long-term debt	$1,000,000
Interest payable ($10,000,000 × 0.07 × 6/12)	350,000
Long-term debt ($10,000,000 − $1,000,000)	9,000,000

b. Current liabilities:

Salary payable ($90,000 − $12,000 − $6,000)	$ 72,000
Employee withheld income tax payable	12,000
Other employee withholdings and benefits payable	6,000

c. Current liabilities:

GST payable ($200,000 − $76,000)	$ 124,000

d. Current liabilities:

Estimated warranty payable	$ 600,000
[$100,000 + ($40,000,000 × 0.02) − $300,000]	

EXPLAIN THE TYPES, FEATURES, AND PRICING OF BONDS PAYABLE

Large companies, such as Bombardier, Canadian Tire, and TransCanada, cannot borrow billions of dollars from a single lender. So how do large corporations borrow huge amounts? They issue (sell) bonds to the public. **Bonds payable** are groups of notes issued to multiple lenders, called *bondholders*. Bombardier can borrow large amounts by issuing bonds to thousands of investors, who each lend a modest amount to Bombardier. Here, we treat bonds and long-term notes payable together because their accounting is similar.

Bonds: An Introduction

Each bond that is issued is, in effect, a long-term note payable. Bonds payable are debts of the issuing company.

Each bond has a *principal* amount which is typically stated in units of $1,000; principal is also called the bond's **face value** or *maturity value*. The bond obligates the issuing company to pay the debt at a specific future time called the *maturity date*.

Interest is the rental fee on money borrowed. The bond states the interest rate that the issuer will pay the holder and the dates that the interest payments are due (generally twice a year).

Issuing bonds usually requires the services of a securities firm (for example, RBC Dominion Securities) to act as the underwriter of the bond issue. The **underwriter** purchases the bonds from the issuing company and resells them to its clients, or it may hold some of the bonds for its own account and sell them at a later time.

TYPES OF BONDS. All the bonds in a particular issue may mature at a specified time (**term bonds**) or in instalments over a period of time (**serial bonds**). Serial bonds are like instalment notes payable. Some of TransCanada Corporation's long-term debts are serial in nature because they come due in instalments.

Secured, or *mortgage*, *bonds* give the bondholder the right to take specified assets of the issuer if the company *defaults*, that is, fails to pay interest or principal. *Unsecured bonds*, called **debentures**, are backed only by the good faith of the borrower. Debentures carry a higher rate of interest than secured bonds because debentures are riskier investments.

BOND PRICES. Investors buy and sell bonds through bond markets. Bond prices are quoted at a percentage of their maturity value. For example:

- A $1,000 bond quoted at 100 is bought or sold for $1,000, which is 100% of its face value.

- The same bond quoted at 101.5 has a market price of $1,015 (101.5% of face value = $1,000 × 1.015). Any excess of the bond's price over its face value is called a **bond premium**.

- A $1,000 bond quoted at 88.375 is priced at $883.75 ($1,000 × 0.88375). When the price of a bond is below its face value, the difference is called a **bond discount**.

As with stocks, bond prices are reported in a wide variety of online sources. For example, on May 25, 2012, the *Globe and Mail* website reported price information for Province of Manitoba bonds. On that day, Province of Manitoba $1,000 face value bonds with an interest rate of 4.30% and maturity date of March 1, 2016, were quoted at a price of 109.59, so it would have cost you $1,095.90 to purchase one of these bonds ($1,000 face value + bond premium of $95.90). Bond prices change regularly due to changes in market demand and supply.

BOND INTEREST RATES DETERMINE BOND PRICES. Bonds are always sold at their **market price**, which is the amount investors are willing to pay. A bond's market price is determined by its present value, which equals the present value of the future principal payment plus the present value of the future interest payments. Interest is usually paid semi-annually. Some issuers pay annually or quarterly.

Two interest rates determine the price of a bond:

- The **stated interest rate** (or *coupon rate*) is the actual interest rate of the bond. The stated interest rate determines the amount of interest the borrower pays—and the investor receives—each year. For example, the Province of Manitoba's 4.3% bonds have a stated interest rate of 4.3%. Thus, Manitoba pays $43 of interest annually on each $1,000 bond. Each semi-annual interest payment is $215 ($1,000 × 0.043 × 6/12).

- The **market interest rate**, or *effective interest rate*, is the rate that investors demand for loaning their money. The market rate varies by the minute.

An entity may issue bonds with a stated interest rate that differs from the prevailing market interest rate. In fact, the two interest rates often differ because the issuer often has to finalize details of the bond weeks or months before the bonds are actually issued.

Exhibit 9-2 shows how the stated interest rate and the market interest rate interact to determine the price of a bond payable for three separate cases. If the stated interest rate does happen to equal the market rate, the bond will be issued at face value (Case A).

Manitoba may, however, issue 6% bonds when the market rate has risen to 7%. Will the Manitoba bonds attract investors in this market? No, because investors can earn 7% on other bonds of similar risk. Therefore, investors will purchase Manitoba bonds only at a *discount* (Case B). Conversely, if the market interest rate is 5%, Manitoba's 6% bonds will be so attractive that investors will pay a *premium* for them (Case C). It is useful to remember that there is an inverse relationship between the market rate and bond prices—a market rate higher than the stated rate results in a discounted bond price, whereas a market rate lower than the stated rate results in a premium price.

EXHIBIT 9-2
How the Stated Interest Rate and the Market Interest Rate Interact to Determine the Price of a Bond

				Issuance Price of Bonds Payable
Case A:				
Stated interest rate on a bond payable	equals	Market interest rate	implies	Face price
Example: 6%	=	6%	→	*Face: $1,000 bond issued for $1,000*
Case B:				
Stated interest rate on a bond payable	less than	Market interest rate	implies	Discount price (price *below* face value)
Example: 6%	<	7%	→	*Discount: $1,000 bond issued for a price below $1,000*
Case C:				
Stated interest rate on a bond payable	greater than	Market interest rate	implies	Premium price (price *above* face value)
Example: 6%	>	5%	→	*Premium: $1,000 bond issued for a price above $1,000*

ACCOUNT FOR BONDS PAYABLE

Issuing Bonds at Face Value

Suppose Great-West Lifeco Inc. plans to issue $50,000 in 6% bonds that mature in five years. Assume that Great-West issues these bonds at face value on January 1, 2014. The issuance entry is as follows:

2014			
Jan. 1	Cash	50,000	
	Bonds Payable...		50,000
	To issue 6%, five-year bonds at face value.		

Bonds Payable	
	50,000

ASSETS	=	LIABILITIES	+	SHAREHOLDERS' EQUITY
+50,000	=	+50,000		

Great-West, the borrower, makes a one-time entry to record the receipt of cash and the issuance of bonds. Afterwards, investors buy and sell the bonds through the bond markets. These buy-and-sell transactions between outside investors do *not* involve Great-West at all.

Interest payments occur each January 1 and July 1. Great-West's entry to record the first semi-annual interest payment is as follows:

2014			
July 1	Interest Expense	1,500	
	Cash		1,500
	To pay semi-annual interest. ($50,000 × 0.06 × 6/12)		

ASSETS	=	LIABILITIES	+	SHAREHOLDERS' EQUITY
−1,500	=			−1,500 Interest Expense

At year-end, Great-West must accrue interest expense and interest payable for six months (July through December), as follows:

2014			
Dec. 31	Interest Expense ($50,000 × 0.06 × 6/12)	1,500	
	Interest Payable...		1,500
	To accrue interest.		

ASSETS	=	LIABILITIES	+	SHAREHOLDERS' EQUITY
0	=	+1,500		−1,500 Interest Expense

At maturity, Great-West will pay off the bonds as follows (any interest owing will be paid separately):

2019			
Jan. 1	Bonds Payable	50,000	
	Cash		50,000
	To pay bonds payable at maturity.		

Bonds Payable	
50,000	50,000
	Bal. 0

				SHAREHOLDERS'
ASSETS	=	LIABILITIES	+	EQUITY
−50,000	=	−50,000		

Issuing Bonds at a Discount

Market conditions may force a company to issue bonds at a discount. Suppose TELUS issues $100,000 of its 9% five-year bonds when the market interest rate is 10%. The market price of the bonds drops, and TELUS receives $96,149[*] at issuance. The transaction is recorded as follows:

2014				
Jan. 1	Cash..	96,149		
	Discount on Bonds Payable.................................	3,851		
	Bonds Payable...		100,000	
	To issue 9%, five-year bonds at a discount.			

				SHAREHOLDERS'
ASSETS	=	LIABILITIES	+	EQUITY
+96,149	=	−3,851		
		+100,000		

Now the bond accounts have a net balance of $96,149 as follows:

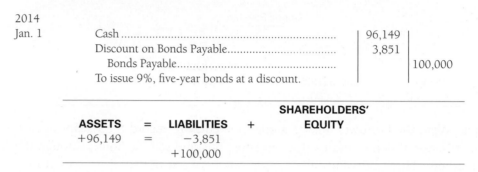

Bonds Payable		Discount on Bonds Payable	= Net carrying amount of bonds payable
100,000	+	3,851	= $96,149

TELUS's balance sheet immediately after issuance of the bonds would report the following:

Total current liabilities...		$ XXX
Long-term liabilities		
Bonds payable, 9%, due 2019	$100,000	
Less: Discount on bonds payable...................................	(3,851)	96,149

Discount on Bonds Payable is a contra account to Bonds Payable, which decreases the company's liabilities. Subtracting the discount from Bonds Payable yields the *carrying amount* of the bonds. Thus, TELUS's liability is $96,149, which is the amount the company borrowed.

OBJECTIVE

❹ Calculate and account for interest expense on bonds payable

CALCULATE AND ACCOUNT FOR INTEREST EXPENSE ON BONDS PAYABLE

TELUS pays interest on its bonds semi-annually, which is common practice. Each semi-annual interest *payment* remains the same over the life of the bonds:

$$\text{Semi-annual interest payment} = \$100,000 \times 0.09 \times 6/12$$
$$= \$4,500$$

[*]Appendix B at the end of this book shows how to determine the price of this bond.

EXHIBIT 9-3
Debt Amortization for a Bond Discount

PANEL A—Bond Data

Issue date—January 1, 2014

Maturity (face) value—$100,000

Stated interest rate—9%

Interest paid—4½% semi-annually, $4,500 = $100,000 × 0.09 × 6/12

Market interest rate at time of issue—10% annually, 5% semi-annually

Issue price—$96,149

Maturity date—January 1, 2019

PANEL B—Amortization Table

	A	B	C	D	E
Semi-Annual Interest Date	Interest Payment (4½% of Maturity Value)	Interest Expense (5% of Preceding Bond Carrying Amount)	Bond Discount Amortization (B − A)	Bond Discount Account Balance (Preceding D − C)	Bond Carrying Amount ($100,000 − D)
Jan. 1, 2014				$3,851	$ 96,149
July 1	$4,500	$4,807	$307	3,544	96,456
Jan. 1, 2015	4,500	4,823	323	3,221	96,779
July 1	4,500	4,839	339	2,882	97,118
Jan. 1, 2016	4,500	4,856	356	2,526	97,474
July 1	4,500	4,874	374	2,152	97,848
Jan. 1, 2017	4,500	4,892	392	1,760	98,240
July 1	4,500	4,912	412	1,348	98,652
Jan. 1, 2018	4,500	4,933	433	915	99,085
July 1	4,500	4,954	454	461	99,539
Jan. 1, 2019	4,500	4,961*	461	0	100,000

*Adjusted for the effect of rounding.

Notes

*Column A   The semi-annual interest payments are constant—(fixed by the bond contract).

*Column B   The interest expense each period = Preceding bond carrying amount × Market interest rate.
　　　　　　　Interest expense increases as the bond carrying amount (E) increases.

*Column C   The excess of interest expense (B) over interest payment (A) is the discount amortization (C) for the period.

*Column D   The discount balance (D) decreases when amortized.

*Column E   The bond carrying amount (E) increases from $96,149 at issuance to $100,000 at maturity.

This payment amount is fixed by the bond contract. But TELUS's interest *expense* increases from period to period as the bonds march toward maturity. Remember, these bonds were issued at a discount.

Panel A of Exhibit 9-3 summarizes the TELUS bond data used above. Panel B provides an amortization table that:

- determines the periodic interest expense (column B)

- shows the bond carrying amount at each semi-annual interest date (column E)

Study the exhibit carefully because the amounts we will be using come directly from the amortization table. This exhibit shows the *effective-interest method of amortization*, which is the required way of amortizing bond premiums and discounts under IFRS. ASPE permit this method, as well as the *straight-line method*, which is discussed briefly later in this section.

Interest Expense on Bonds Issued at a Discount

In Exhibit 9-3, TELUS borrowed $96,149 cash but must pay $100,000 when the bonds mature. What happens to the $3,851 balance of the discount account over the life of the bond issue?

EXHIBIT 9-4
Interest Expense on Bonds
Payable Issued at a Discount

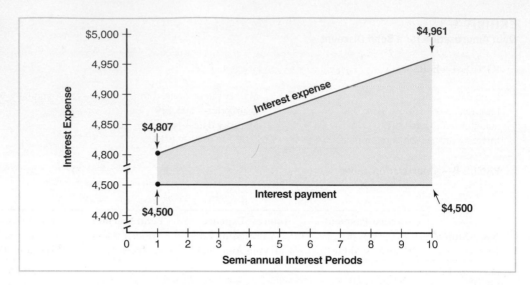

The $3,851 is additional interest expense to TELUS over and above the stated interest that TELUS pays each six months. Exhibit 9-4 graphs the interest expense and the interest payment on the TELUS bonds over their lifetime. Observe that the semi-annual interest payment is fixed—by contract—at $4,500 (column A in Exhibit 9-3), but the amount of interest expense (column B) increases each period as the bond carrying amount moves upward toward maturity.

The discount is allocated to interest expense through amortization each period over the term of the bonds. Exhibit 9-5 illustrates the amortization of the bonds' carrying value from $96,149 at the start to $100,000 at maturity using the effective interest method. These amounts come from Exhibit 9-3, column E.

Now let's see how to account for the TELUS bonds issued at a discount. In our example, TELUS issued its bonds on January 1, 2014. On July 1, TELUS made the first $4,500 semi-annual interest payment. But TELUS's interest expense is greater than $4,500. TELUS's journal entry to record interest expense and the interest payment for the first six months follows (with all amounts taken from Exhibit 9-3):

2014			
July 1	Interest Expense	4,807	
	Discount on Bonds Payable...............................		307
	Cash		4,500
	To pay semi-annual interest and amortize bond discount.		

EXHIBIT 9-5
Amortizing Bonds Payable
Issued at a Discount

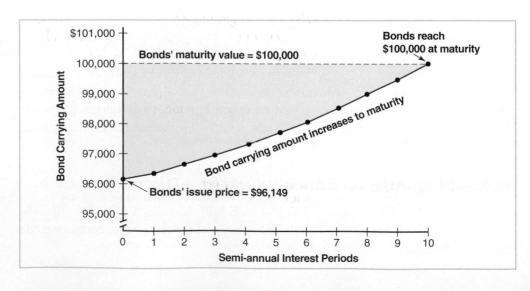

The credit to Discount on Bonds Payable serves two purposes:

- It adjusts the bonds' carrying amount as the bonds approach maturity value.
- It amortizes the discount to interest expense.

ASSETS	=	LIABILITIES	+	SHAREHOLDERS' EQUITY
−4,500	=	+307		−4,807 Interest Expense

At December 31, 2014, TELUS accrues interest and amortizes the bond discount for July through December with this entry (amounts from Exhibit 9-3):

2014
Dec. 31   Interest Expense   4,823
             Discount on Bonds Payable.............................   323
             Interest Payable..   4,500
             To accrue semi-annual interest and amortize bond discount.

ASSETS	=	LIABILITIES	+	SHAREHOLDERS' EQUITY
0	=	+323		−4,823 Interest Expense
		+4,500		

At December 31, 2014, TELUS's bond accounts appear as follows:

Bonds Payable		Discount on Bonds Payable	
	100,000	3,851	307
			323
		Bal. 3,221	

Bond carrying amount, $96,779 = $100,000 − $3,221 from Exhibit 9-3

STOP + THINK (9-2)

What would you expect TELUS Communications Inc.'s 2014 income statement and year-end balance sheet to report for these bonds?

Partial-Period Interest Amounts

Companies don't always issue bonds at the beginning or the end of their accounting year. They issue bonds when market conditions are most favourable, and that may be on May 16, August 1, or any other date. To illustrate partial-period interest, assume Goldcorp Inc. issues $100,000 of 8% bonds payable at 96 on August 31, 2014. The market rate of interest was 9%, and these bonds pay semi-annual interest on February 28 and August 31 each year. The first few lines of Goldcorp's amortization table are as follows:

Semi-Annual Interest Date	4% Interest Payment	4½% Interest Expense	Discount Amortization	Discount Account Balance	Bond Carrying Amount
Aug. 31, 2014				$4,000	$96,000
Feb. 28, 2015	$4,000	$4,320	$320	3,680	96,320
Aug. 31, 2015	4,000	4,334	334	3,346	96,654

Goldcorp's accounting year ends on December 31, so at year-end Goldcorp must accrue interest and amortize the bond discount for four months (September through December). At December 31, 2014, Goldcorp will make this entry:

2014
Dec. 31   Interest Expense ($4,320 × 4/6)   2,880
                Discount on Bonds Payable ($320 × 4/6)............   213
                Interest Payable ($4,000 × 4/6)..........................   2,667
           To accrue interest and amortize discount at year-end.

The year-end entry at December 31, 2014, uses 4/6 of the upcoming semi-annual amounts at February 28, 2015 because the September–December period covers four of the six months of interest to be paid on that date. This example clearly illustrates the benefit of an amortization schedule.

Issuing Bonds at a Premium

Let's modify the TELUS bond example to illustrate issuance of the bonds at a premium. Assume that on January 1, 2014, TELUS Communications Inc. issues $100,000 of five-year, 9% bonds that pay interest semi-annually. If the bonds are issued when the market interest rate is 8%, their issue price is $104,100.[*] The premium on these bonds is $4,100, and Exhibit 9-6 shows how to amortize the bonds by the effective-interest method.

TELUS's entries to record issuance of the bonds on January 1, 2014, and to make the first interest payment and amortize the bonds on July 1, are as follows:

2014
Jan. 1   Cash   104,100
                Bonds Payable...   100,000
                Premium on Bonds Payable   4,100
           To issue 9%, five-year bonds at a premium.

At the beginning, TELUS's liability is $104,100—not $100,000. The accounting equation makes this clear.

ASSETS	=	LIABILITIES	+	SHAREHOLDERS' EQUITY
+104,100	=	+100,000		
		+4,100		

2014
July 1   Interest Expense   4,164
           Premium on Bonds Payable   336
                Cash   4,500
           To pay semi-annual interest and amortize bond premium.

ASSETS	=	LIABILITIES	+	SHAREHOLDERS' EQUITY
−4,500	=	−336		−4,164 Interest Expense

---

[*]Again, Appendix B at the end of the book shows how to determine the price of this bond.

Immediately after issuing the bonds at a premium on January 1, 2014, TELUS would report the bonds payable on the balance sheet as follows:

Total current liabilities..	$	XXX
Long-term liabilities:		
Bonds payable	$100,000	
Add: Premium on bonds payable...	4,100	104,100

The premium is *added* to the balance of bonds payable to determine the carrying amount.

In Exhibit 9-6, TELUS borrowed $104,100 cash but must pay only $100,000 at maturity. The $4,100 premium on the bonds results in a reduction in TELUS's interest expense over the term of the bonds. Exhibit 9-7 graphs TELUS's interest payments (column A from Exhibit 9-6) and interest expense (column B).

EXHIBIT 9-6
Debt Amortization for a Bond Premium

PANEL A—Bond Data

Issue date—January 1, 2014
Maturity (face) value—$100,000
Contract interest rate—9%
Interest paid—4½% semi-annually, $4,500 = $100,000 × 0.09 × 6/12

Market interest rate at time of issue—8% annually, 4% semi-annually
Issue price—$104,100
Maturity date—January 1, 2019

PANEL B—Amortization Table

	A	B	C	D	E
Semi-Annual Interest Date	Interest Payment (4½% of Maturity Value)	Interest Expense (4% of Preceding Bond Carrying Amount)	Bond Premium Amortization (A − B)	Bond Premium Account Balance (Preceding D − C)	Bond Carrying Amount ($100,000 + D)
Jan. 1, 2014				$4,100	$104,100
July 1	$4,500	$4,164	$336	3,764	103,764
Jan. 1, 2015	4,500	4,151	349	3,415	103,415
July 1	4,500	4,137	363	3,052	103,052
Jan. 1, 2016	4,500	4,122	378	2,674	102,674
July 1	4,500	4,107	393	2,281	102,281
Jan. 1, 2017	4,500	4,091	409	1,872	101,872
July 1	4,500	4,075	425	1,447	101,447
Jan. 1, 2018	4,500	4,058	442	1,005	101,005
July 1	4,500	4,040	460	545	100,545
Jan. 1, 2019	4,500	3,955*	545	0	100,000

*Adjusted for the effect of rounding.

Notes
- Column A The semi-annual interest payments are constant—(fixed by the bond contract).
- Column B The interest expense each period = Preceding bond carrying amount × Market interest rate.
  Interest expense decreases as the bond carrying amount (E) decreases.
- Column C The excess of each interest payment (A) over interest expense (B) is the premium amortization (C) for the period.
- Column D The premium balance (D) decreases when amortized.
- Column E The bond carrying amount (E) decreases from $104,100 at issuance to $100,000 at maturity.

EXHIBIT 9-7
Interest Expense on Bonds
Payable Issued at a Premium

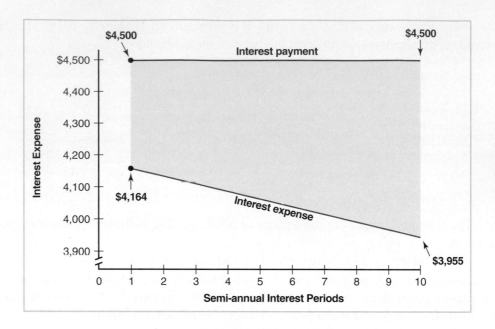

EXHIBIT 9-7
Interest Expense on Bonds
Payable Issued at a Premium

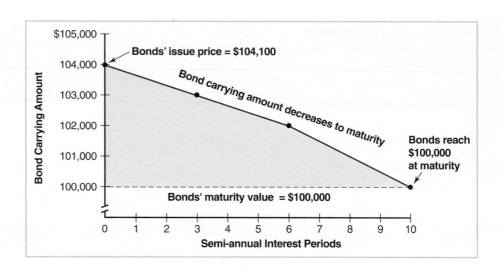

EXHIBIT 9-8
Amortizing Bonds Payable
Issued at a Premium

Through amortization, the premium decreases interest expense each period over the term of the bonds. Exhibit 9-8 diagrams the amortization of the bond carrying amount from the issue price of $104,100 to the maturity value of $100,000. All amounts are taken from Exhibit 9-6.

The Straight-Line Amortization Method

ASPE permit a simpler method of amortizing discounts and premiums. The *straight-line amortization method* divides a bond discount (or premium) into equal periodic amounts over the bond's term. The amount of interest expense is the same for each interest period.

Let's apply the straight-line method to the TELUS bonds issued at a discount and illustrated in Exhibit 9-3. The amortization for each semi-annual period is calculated by dividing the total bond discount of $3,851 by 10, which is the number of semi-annual interest periods over the life of the bond. This method results in the following semi-annual interest expense:

Semi-annual cash interest payment ($100,000 × 0.09 × 6/12)	$4,500
+Semi-annual amortization of discount ($3,851 ÷ 10).......................................	385
=Semi-annual interest expense	$4,885

The straight-line amortization method uses these same amounts every period over the term of the bonds.

TELUS's entry to record interest and amortization of the bond discount under the straight-line amortization method would be the same for every semi-annual interest period:

Interest Expense	4,885	
Discount on Bonds Payable..		385
Cash		4,500
To pay semi-annual interest and amortize bond discount.		

EXPLAIN THE ADVANTAGES AND DISADVANTAGES OF FINANCING WITH DEBT VERSUS EQUITY

OBJECTIVE

❺ **Explain** the advantages and disadvantages of financing with debt versus equity

Managers must decide where to get the money needed to fund acquisitions, expansion, and other operational activities. There are three main ways to finance business activities:

- By using excess cash not needed for operating activities
- By raising capital from issuing shares
- By borrowing money using loans, bonds, or notes

1. To use *excess cash*, a company must have saved enough cash and short-term investments from past profitable operations so that it can self-finance its desired business activities. This is a low-risk and low-cost option because it does not require taking on more debt or issuing more shares.

2. *Raising capital by issuing new shares* creates no new liabilities and requires no interest payments, so it does not increase a company's credit risk. Dividend payments on shares are usually optional, so they can be avoided if cash flows are poor or the company has other needs for its cash. Issuing shares, however, can cost a lot in legal and other financing fees, and can also dilute the control and earnings per share of existing shareholders.

3. *Borrowing money* does not dilute control of the company because no shares are being issued, but it can still be somewhat costly in terms of financing fees paid to arrange the debt. Taking on more debt can also increase a company's credit risk, and it requires the company to make regular principal and interest payments, which cannot be postponed when cash flows are poor. The leverage gained by borrowing money can often increase the company's earnings per share, which is beneficial to shareholders.

Earnings per share (EPS) represents the amount of net income (or loss) earned by each of a company's outstanding common shares. It is useful for evaluating the earnings performance of a company and also assessing the impact of various financing options on earnings.

Suppose Athens Corporation needs $500,000 for expansion. Assume Athens has net income of $300,000 and 100,000 common shares outstanding. Management is considering two financing plans. Plan 1 is to issue $500,000 of 6% bonds, and plan 2 is to issue 50,000 common shares for $500,000. Management believes the new cash can be invested in operations to earn income of $200,000 before interest and taxes.

Exhibit 9-9 shows the earnings-per-share advantage of borrowing. As you can see, Athens Corporation's EPS amount is higher if the company borrows by issuing bonds (compare lines 9 and 10). Athens earns more on the investment ($102,000) than the interest it pays on the bonds ($30,000).

In this case, borrowing results in higher earnings per share than issuing shares. Borrowing has its disadvantages, however. Interest expense may be high enough to eliminate net income and lead to losses. Also, borrowing creates liabilities that must be paid during bad years as well as good years. In contrast, a company that issues shares can omit its dividends during a bad year.

◄ DECISION GUIDELINES ►

FINANCING WITH DEBT OR WITH STOCK

Suppose you are the owner of El Taco, a regional chain of tex-mex restaurants in western Canada. You are planning to expand into central Canada, so you must make some key decisions about how to finance the expansion.

Decision	Guidelines
How will you finance El Taco's expansion?	Your financing plan depends on El Taco's ability to generate cash flow, your willingness to give up some control of the business, the amount of financing risk you are willing to take, and El Taco's credit rating.
Do El Taco's operations generate enough cash to meet all its financing needs?	If yes, the business needs little outside financing. There is no need to borrow.
	If no, the business will need to issue additional stock or borrow the money.
Are you willing to give up some of your control of the business?	If yes, then issue stock to other shareholders, who can vote their shares to elect the company's directors.
	If no, then borrow from bondholders, who have no vote in the management of the company.
How much leverage (financing risk) are you willing or able to take?	If much, then borrow as much as you can, and you may increase El Taco's earnings per share. But this will increase the business's debt ratio and the risk of being unable to pay its debts.
	If little, then borrow sparingly. This will hold the debt ratio down and reduce the risk of default on borrowing agreements, but El Taco's earnings per share may be lower than if you were to borrow.
How good is the business's credit rating?	The better the credit rating, the easier it is to borrow on favourable terms. A good credit rating also makes it easier to issue stock. Neither shareholders nor creditors will entrust their money to a company with a bad credit rating.

EXHIBIT 9-9
Earnings-per-Share Advantage of Borrowing

	Plan 1		Plan 2	
	Borrow $500,000 at 6%		Issue 50,000 Common Shares for $500,000	
1. Net income before expansion..		$300,000		$300,000
2. Expected project income before interest and income tax.......................	$200,000		$200,000	
3. Less interest expense ($500,000 × 0.06)..	(30,000)		0	
4. Expected project income before income tax......................................	170,000		200,000	
5. Less income tax expense (40%)	(68,000)		(80,000)	
6. Expected project net income...		102,000		120,000
7. Total company net income...		$402,000		$420,000
8. Earnings per share after expansion:				
9. Plan 1 Borrow ($402,000/100,000 shares)......................................		$ 4.02		
10. Plan 2 ($420,000/150,000 shares)..				$ 2.80

ANALYZE AND EVALUATE A COMPANY'S DEBT-PAYING ABILITY

OBJECTIVE

❻ Analyze and evaluate a company's debt-paying ability

ACCOUNTS PAYABLE TURNOVER. In Chapter 3 we used working capital and the current ratio to analyze a company's liquidity. Another important measure of liquidity for a business is **accounts payable turnover (T/O)**, which measures the number of times a year a company is able to pay its accounts payable. The ratio is computed as follows:

> Accounts payable turnover (T/O) = Cost of goods sold ÷ Average accounts payable
> Turnover expressed in days = 365 ÷ T/O (computed above)

The average accounts payable amount is calculated using the year's opening and closing balances. Once the turnover is computed, it is usually expressed in number of days, or **days payable outstanding (DPO)**, by dividing the turnover into 365. Here are recent comparative ratios for accounts payable turnover for Best Buy and RadioShack, two large consumer electronics retailers:

(In millions)	Best Buy	RadioShack
Cost of goods sold..	$37,611	$2,462
Average accounts payable	5,085	268
Accounts payable turnover (T/O)	7.40	9.19
Turnover in days (365 ÷ T/O), or days payable outstanding (DPO)......	49 days	40 days

Because different industries have different business models and standard business practices, it is important to compare companies with competitors in the same industry. Since Best Buy and RadioShack are both in the consumer electronics industry, purchasing many of their products from the same vendors, it is reasonable to compare them on the basis of accounts payable turnover. RadioShack pays its accounts payable in about 40 days, whereas Best Buy takes 49 days to pay its accounts payable. If you were a supplier of these two giant companies, which would you rather do business with, on the basis of this ratio? If cash collections are important to you in order to pay your own bills, the obvious answer is RadioShack, based strictly on this ratio.

What makes an accounts payable turnover ratio strong or weak in the eyes of creditors and investors? Generally, a high turnover ratio (short period in days) is better than a low turnover ratio. Companies with shorter payment periods are generally better credit risks than those with longer payment periods. However, some companies with strong credit ratings strategically follow shrewd cash management policies, withholding payment to suppliers as long as possible, while speeding up collections, in order to conserve cash. For example, Walmart's accounts payable turnover is about 37 days, which is longer than a typical 30-day credit period. The company strategically stretches its payment period, which is tough on suppliers, but because of Walmart's size, market share, and buying power, few suppliers can afford not to do business with the company.

To be sure, credit and sales decisions are based on far more information than accounts payable turnover, so it's wise not to oversimplify. However, combined with inventory turnover (discussed in Chapter 6) and accounts receivable turnover (discussed in Chapter 5), all expressed in days, accounts payable turnover is an important ingredient in computing the *cash conversion cycle*, which is an overall measure of liquidity. Combined with the current ratio (discussed in Chapter 3) and the quick ratio (discussed in Chapter 5), studying the cash conversion cycle helps users of financial statements determine the overall liquidity of a company. We will discuss the cash conversion cycle in more depth in Chapter 13.

The Leverage Ratio

As discussed and illustrated above, financing with debt can be advantageous, but management of a company must be careful not to incur too much debt. Chapter 3 discussed the debt ratio, which measures the proportion of total liabilities to total assets, two elements of the fundamental accounting equation:

$$\text{Debt ratio} = \frac{\text{Total debt (liabilities)}}{\text{Total assets}}$$

We can rearrange this relationship between total assets, total liabilities, and shareholders' equity in a different manner to illustrate the impact that leverage can have on profitability. The **leverage ratio** is commonly calculated as follows, although other methods are sometimes used:

$$\text{Leverage ratio} = \frac{\text{Total assets}}{\text{Total shareholders' equity}}$$

This ratio shows a company's total assets per dollar of shareholders' equity. A leverage ratio of exactly 1.0 would mean a company has no debt, because total assets would exactly equal total shareholders' equity. This condition is almost nonexistent, because virtually all companies have liabilities, and, therefore, have leverage ratios in excess of 1.0. In fact, as we have shown previously, having a healthy amount of debt can actually enhance a company's profitability, in terms of the shareholders' investment. The leverage ratio is the third element of the *DuPont analysis* model, introduced in part with the discussion of return on assets in Chapter 7.[*] The higher the leverage ratio, the more it magnifies return on shareholders' equity (Net Income/Average Shareholders' Equity, or ROE). If net income is positive, return on assets (ROA) is positive. The leverage ratio magnifies this positive return to make return on equity (ROE) even more positive. This is because the company is using borrowed money to earn a profit (a concept known as *trading on the equity*). However, if earnings are negative (losses), ROA is negative, and the leverage ratio makes ROE even more negative. We will discuss DuPont analysis and ROE in more detail as we discuss Shareholders' Equity in Chapter 10. For now, let's just focus on understanding the meaning of the leverage ratio by looking at two U.S. airlines, Southwest and United Continental. Here are the leverage ratios and debt ratios for the two companies:

(In millions)	Southwest	United Continental
1. Total assets	$15,463	$40,552
2. Shareholders' equity	$ 6,237	$ 1,912
3. Leverage ratio (1 ÷ 2)	2.48	21.2
4. Total debt (1 − 2)	$ 9,226	$38,640
5. Debt ratio (4 ÷ 1)	59.7%	95.3%

These figures show that Southwest has $2.48 of total assets for each dollar of shareholders' equity. This translates to a debt ratio of 59.7%, which we learned in Chapter 3 is about normal for many companies. However, United Continental has a leverage ratio of 21.2, meaning there are $21.20 of assets for each dollar of shareholders' equity. Rearranging the elements to show debt to total assets, United Continental has an astonishing ratio of 95.3%. This company is drowning in debt!

The Times-Interest-Earned Ratio

The debt ratio measures the effect of debt on the company's *financial position* but says nothing about the ability to pay interest expense. Analysts use a second ratio—the **times-interest-earned ratio**—to relate income to interest expense. To compute this ratio, we divide *income from operations* (also called *operating income* or *earnings before interest and taxes*) by interest expense. This ratio measures the number of times that operating income can *cover* interest expense. The ratio is also called the **interest-coverage ratio**. A high times-interest-earned ratio indicates ease in paying interest expense; a low value suggests difficulty. Let's see how Sobeys Inc. and Loblaw Companies Limited, two leading grocery chains, compare on the times-interest-earned ratio.

			Sobeys Inc.	Loblaw Companies Limited
Times-interest-earned ratio	=	$\dfrac{\text{Operating income}}{\text{Interest expense}}$ =	$\dfrac{\$406 \text{ million}}{\$60 \text{ million}}$	$\dfrac{\$1,205 \text{ million}}{\$269 \text{ million}}$
			= 6.8 times	= 4.5 times

[*]The DuPont model provides a detailed analysis of return on equity (ROE). It is the product of three elements: Net income/Net sales; Net sales/Total assets; and Total assets/Total shareholders' equity. Notice that elements cross-cancel so that the model reduces to Net income/Shareholders' equity. See Chapter 10 for a more complete discussion of ROE. A modified version of the model considers only the first two elements to calculate return on assets, as discussed in Chapter 7.

Sobeys' income from operations covers its interest expense 6.8 times. Loblaw's interest-coverage ratio is 4.5 times. Both companies have healthy ratios, but Sobeys' higher ratio indicates less risk relative to Loblaw's ratio.

STOP + THINK (9-3)	Suppose you are a loan officer at a bank and you must decide which of the two companies below would present a lower risk to the bank if you were to loan it money. Which company would you prefer to loan money to?		
		Company A	**Company B**
	Total assets...	$4,858	$14,991
	Total liabilities..	$4,178	$ 8,718
	Total Shareholders' equity	680	6,273
	Total liabilities and Shareholders' equity....................	$4,858	$14,991
	Operating income	$ 241	$ 1,068
	Interest expense	$ 101	$ 211

OBJECTIVE

❼ **Describe** other types of long-term liabilities

DESCRIBE OTHER TYPES OF LONG-TERM LIABILITIES

Term Loans

Companies can often satisfy their long-term financing needs without resorting to the issuance of bonds in a public market. **Term loans** are a common form of long-term financing, which, like bonds, allow a company to borrow a fixed amount of money up front and repay it over a specified number of years at a stated interest rate. Unlike bonds, however, a term loan is typically arranged with a single lender, such as a bank or other financial institution. A term loan is usually secured by certain assets of the borrower, often the assets acquired using the proceeds of the loan. WestJet, for example, had over $800 million in term loans payable at March 31, 2012. Each of the 53 loans comprising this balance was secured by the airplane WestJet had purchased with the original loan proceeds. Term loans secured by real property, such as land and buildings, are called **mortgages**. As with other forms of long-term debt, term loans are split between their current and long-term portions on the balance sheet, and the terms of the loans, including principal repayments over the next five years, are disclosed in the notes.

Leases

A **lease** is a rental agreement in which the renter (**lessee**) agrees to make rent payments to the property owner (**lessor**) in exchange for the use of the asset for an agreed period of time. Leasing allows the lessee to acquire the use of a needed asset without having to make the large upfront payment that purchase agreements require. WestJet, for example, may lease some of its planes instead of buying them outright. Accountants distinguish between two types of leases: finance leases and operating leases. ASPE uses the term capital leases instead of finance leases. For simplicity, this section uses the term finance leases.

IFRS and ASPE are consistent in their definitions of **finance leases**: they are leases that transfer to the lessee substantially all the risks and rewards incidental to the ownership of an asset, even though formal legal title of the asset may remain with the lessor. For an **operating lease**, substantially all the risks and rewards of ownership remain with the lessor. Both sets of standards indicate that the substance of a leasing transaction determines whether it should be accounted for as a finance lease or an operating lease. Making this determination is beyond the scope of this text, so the decision criteria are not presented here. Also note that at the date of publication, a new draft IFRS lease accounting standard proposed that all leases be treated as finance leases, possibly removing the distinction between operating and finance leases under IFRS in the future.

Because a finance lease transfers to the lessee substantially all the risks and rewards incidental to the ownership of an asset, the lessee records the leased property as an asset on its financial statements, following all of the relevant accounting standards presented for property, plant, and equipment in Chapter 7. The finance lease contract also creates a formal legal obligation for the lessee, so the lessee must record a liability that reflects the future payments to be made according to the terms of the lease. Finance lease obligations are split into their current and long-term portions for balance sheet presentation purposes, just as with other forms of long-term debt. In its March 31, 2012, balance sheet at the beginning of the chapter, WestJet showed total finance lease obligations of $4 million, with $1 million of this being current. The detailed accounting for finance leases is beyond the scope of this text.

Under an operating lease, the risks and rewards of ownership do not transfer to the lessee, so they record neither an asset nor a liability. IFRS and ASPE simply require the lessee to expense the operating lease payments as they come due, and also to disclose at least the next five years of operating-lease commitments in the notes to the financial statements. In the notes to its March 31, 2012, financial statements, WestJet disclosed $1.1 billion in operating lease commitments.

Post-Employment Benefits

Employee benefits are forms of consideration given by a company in exchange for services rendered by employees. **Post-employment benefits** are a special type of employee benefits that do not become payable until after a person has completed employment with the company. They include such things as pension benefits, medical and dental insurance, and prescription drug benefits. A company's obligations for these future benefits must be recorded as liabilities on its balance sheet, split into current and long-term portions where applicable. The formal accounting for these benefits is complex and beyond the scope of this text.

REPORT LIABILITIES ON THE BALANCE SHEET

Exhibit 9-10 again presents the liabilities of WestJet as at March 31, 2012.

Investors and creditors need the information illustrated in Exhibit 9-10 and discussed below in order to evaluate WestJet's balance sheet and the company.

Exhibit 9-10 includes Note 9 (adapted) from WestJet's financial statements, which gives additional information about the Company's long-term debt. This note shows that WestJet's long-term debt consists of three tranches of term loans that have been used to finance the purchase of aircraft and a hangar in Calgary. The current portion of this debt, about $162 million, can be traced to the balance sheet presented above the note.

Note 15 in Exhibit 9-10 presents the details of WestJet's operating leases. We can see that they leased a variety of items, including aircraft, computer hardware, and

OBJECTIVE

❽ **Report** liabilities on the balance sheet

EXHIBIT 9-10
Reporting Liabilities
of WestJet

WestJet
Consolidated Balance Sheet (Partial, Adapted)
As at March 31, 2012

	(amounts in thousands)
Current Liabilities:	
Accounts payable and accrued liabilities....................................	$ 401,435
Advance ticket sales..	451,995
Nonrefundable guest credits..	44,065
Current portion of obligations under capital leases....................	76
Current portion of long-term debt......................................	161,919
Total current liabilities	1,059,490
Obligations under finance leases	3,155
Long-term debt (Note 9)..	662,466
Other long-term liabilities..	490,286
	$2,215,397

9. LONG-TERM DEBT (Partial, Adapted)

Term loans—purchased aircraft.......................................	$ 788,619
Term loan—purchased aircraft	35,303
Term loan—Calgary hangar facility	463
	824,385
Current portion..	161,919
	$ 662,466

15. COMMITMENTS (Partial, Adapted)
(b) Operating leases and commitments

   The Corporation has entered into operating leases and commitments for aircraft, land, buildings, equipment, computer hardware, software licences and satellite programming. As at March 31, 2012, the future payments in under operating leases and commitments, are as follows:

Within 1 year	$ 216,794
1–5 years	654,553
Over 5 years	231,374
	$1,102,721

satellite programming. Their total commitments under operating leases was about $1.1 billion at March 31, 2012.

   Working back and forth between the financial statements and the notes to the financial statements is an important part of financial analysis. You now have the tools to understand the liabilities on an actual balance sheet.

Reporting Financing Activities on the Statement of Cash Flows

The WestJet Airlines consolidated balance sheet (p. 417) shows that the company finances about 60% of its operations with debt. WestJet's debt ratio is about 60%. Let's examine WestJet's financing activities as reported on its statement of cash flows. Exhibit 9-11 is an excerpt from WestJet's consolidated statement of cash flows.

EXHIBIT 9-11
Consolidated Statement of Cash Flows (Partial, Adapted) for WestJet Airlines Ltd.

WestJet Airlines Ltd.
Consolidated Statement of Cash Flows (Adapted)
Quarter Ended March 31, 2012

in thousands	
Cash flow from operating activities:	
Net cash provided by operating activities	$ 258,166
Cash flow from investing activities:	
Net cash used for investing activities	$ (56,244)
Cash flow from financing activities:	
Proceeds of long-term debt	35,303
Payments of long-term debt and finance lease obligations	(39,650)
Other financing payments (net)	(39,783)
Net cash used for financing activities	(44,130)
Cash flow from operating, investing, and financing activities	$ 157,792

You can learn a lot about WestJet's financing activities by examining this statement. During the quarter ended March 31, 2012, WestJet took on new long-term debt of $35.3 million, but also paid off long-term debt and finance lease obligations of $39.7 million. The other financing payments of $39.8 million during the quarter include cash interest payments of $11.2 million. It is critical to analyze the details in this section of the statement of cash flows to ensure you gain a complete understanding of a company's financing activities during the period.

Summary of IFRS-ASPE Differences

Concepts	IFRS	ASPE
Provisions and contingent liabilities (p. 424)	A contingent liability is recorded as a provision when it is probable that an outflow of economic benefits will be required to settle the liability. *Probable* is generally considered to mean that an outflow is *more likely than not* to occur.	A contingent liability is recorded as a liability when it is likely that an outflow of economic benefits will be required to settle the liability. *Likely* is generally considered to be a higher threshold to meet than *probable*, so fewer contingent liabilities will be recorded under ASPE than under IFRS.
Government remittances (p. 425)	No separate disclosure of these liabilities is required.	Government remittances (other than income taxes) such as sales taxes, Employment Insurance, and Canada Pension Plan payable must be disclosed separately, either on the balance sheet or in the notes.
Amortization of discounts and premiums (p. 431)	The effective-interest method must be used to amortize discounts and premiums.	The straight-line method is available as an amortization option.
Finance leases (p. 442)	Leases that transfer substantially all the risks and rewards incidental to the ownership of assets to the lessee are called finance leases.	The equivalent term is capital leases. There are no differences in accounting for these leases.

SUMMARY OF CHAPTER 9

LEARNING OBJECTIVE	SUMMARY
1. **Explain** and **account** for current liabilities	Current liabilities are obligations due within one year of the balance sheet date, or within the company's operating cycle if it is longer than one year. Obligations due beyond that time period are long-term liabilities. Current liabilities are of two kinds: (1) known amounts, such as short-term borrowings, accounts payable, short-term notes payable, sales taxes, accrued liabilities, payroll liabilities, unearned revenues, and the current portion of long-term debts; and (2) estimated amounts, such as warranties payable and contingent liabilities.
2. **Explain** the types, features, and pricing of bonds payable	Bonds payable are groups of notes issued to multiple lenders. Bonds may be term bonds, which have a fixed maturity date, or serial bonds, which mature in instalments over a certain period of time. Some bonds are secured by specific assets of the issuing company, whereas others are debentures, which are unsecured bonds. Bonds are bought and sold through bond markets. The price of a bond is dependent on the relationship between the stated interest rate on the bond and the current market interest rate. When the stated rate exceeds the market rate, the bond is issued at a premium above face value; when the opposite is true, the bond is issued at a discount below face value.
3. **Account** for bonds payable	Bonds payable are initially recorded as long-term liabilities at their face value less (plus) any bond discount (premium). Bond discounts and premiums are amortized to interest expense over the life of the bonds, so that by the time the bonds mature, any related discounts or premiums have been eliminated. Any bonds maturing within one year of the balance sheet date are classified as current liabilities.
4. **Calculate** and **account** for interest expense on bonds payable	Bonds pay interest semi-annually at their stated interest rate times the face value of the bonds. The interest expense is equal to the interest payment plus (minus) the amortization of any discount (premium). IFRS require interest expense to be calculated using the effective-interest method, whereas ASPE also permit use of the simpler straight-line method.
5. **Explain** the advantages and disadvantages of financing with debt versus equity	A company that wishes to fund expansion, acquisitions, or other operational activities has three main options: using excess cash, issuing new shares, or borrowing money. Each of these methods has advantages and disadvantages related to the dilution of control, the flexibility of cash payments, and impact on earnings per share.

6. **Analyze** and **evaluate** a company's debt-paying ability	Accounts payable turnover (Cost of goods sold/Average accounts payable) measures the number of times during the year a company is able to fully pay off its accounts payable. It is an important indicator of a company's liquidity, or its ability to pay off its short-term debts.
	The leverage ratio (Total assets/Total shareholders' equity) shows how many dollars of assets a company has per dollar of shareholders' equity. A leverage ratio above 1.0 can enhance returns to shareholders because it means the company is using debt to invest in additional assets, which will presumably generate additional net income to be shared among the owners. An excessive leverage ratio can be dangerous, however, as it often leads to a company's inability to meet its debt payments.
	The times-interest-earned ratio (Operating income/Interest expense) measures the number of times a company's operating income can cover its interest payments. The higher the ratio, the easier it is for a company to make its payments.
7. **Describe** other types of long-term liabilities	A term loan is a long-term loan at a stated interest rate, typically from a single lender such as a bank, which must be repaid over a specified number of years. It is usually secured by specific assets of the borrower, often the ones acquired using the loan proceeds. A mortgage is a term loan secured by real property such as land and buildings.
	A lease is a rental agreement in which the lessee agrees to make rent payments to the lessor (property owner) in exchange for the use of property. There are two types of leases: a finance (or capital) lease that transfers to the lessee substantially all the risks and rewards incidental to the ownership of the property; and an operating lease, in which the lessor retains the risks and rewards of ownership. Finance leases are recorded as liabilities and accounted for in the same way as other long-term debts, whereas operating lease payments are expensed as they come due.
	Post-employment benefits are a special type of employee benefits that do not become payable until after a person has completed employment with the company. They include such things as pension benefits, medical and dental insurance, and prescription drug benefits.
8. **Report** liabilities on the balance sheet	Financial statement users should review all of the current and long-term liabilities reported on a company's balance sheet. In order to properly interpret this information, users should also consult related information in the statement of cash flows and the notes to the financial statements.

END-OF-CHAPTER SUMMARY PROBLEM

TransCanada Corporation has a number of bond issues outstanding in various amounts with various interest rates and maturities. Assume TransCanada has outstanding an issue of 8% bonds that mature in 2024. Suppose the bonds are dated October 1, 2014, and pay interest each April 1 and October 1.

Requirements

1. Complete the following effective-interest amortization table through October 1, 2016:
   Bond Data
   Maturity value—$100,000
   Contract interest rate—8%
   Interest paid—4% semi-annually, $4,000 ($100,000 × 0.08 × 6/12)

Market interest rate at the time of issue—9% annually, 4½% semi-annually
Issue price—93.80

Amortization Table

Semi-Annual Interest Date	A Interest Payment (4% of Maturity Amount)	B Interest Expense (4½% of Preceding Bond Carrying Amount)	C Bond Discount Amortization (B − A)	D Bond Discount Account Balance (Preceding D − C)	E Bond Carrying Amount ($100,000 − D)
01-10-14					
01-04-15					
01-10-15					
01-04-16					
01-10-16					

Name: TransCanada Corporation
Industry: Pipeline provider
Accounting Period: The years 2014, 2015, 2016

2. Using the amortization table, record the following transactions:
   a. Issuance of the bonds on October 1, 2014.
   b. Accrual of interest and amortization of the bonds on December 31, 2014.
   c. Payment of interest and amortization of the bonds on April 1, 2015.

ANSWERS
Requirement 1

The semi-annual interest payment is constant ($4,000). The interest expense is calculated as 4.5% of the previous period's carrying value. The discount account balance reflects that the issue price of $93.80 is less than $100.00.

Semi-Annual Interest Date	A Interest Payment (4% of Maturity Amount)	B Interest Expense (4½% of Preceding Bond Carrying Amount)	C Bond Discount Amortization (B − A)	D Bond Discount Account Balance (Preceding D − C)	E Bond Carrying Amount ($100,000 − D)
01-10-14				$6,200	$93,800
01-04-15	$4,000	$4,221	$221	5,979	94,021
01-10-15	4,000	4,231	231	5,748	94,252
01-04-16	4,000	4,241	241	5,507	94,493
01-10-16	4,000	4,252	252	5,255	94,745

Requirement 2

The bonds were issued for less than $100,000, reflecting a discount. Use the amounts from columns D and E for 01-10-14 from the amortization table.

a. 2014

Oct. 1   Cash 93,800
         Discount on Bonds Payable 6,200
            Bonds Payable 100,000
         To issue 8%, ten-year bonds at a discount.

The accrued interest is calculated, and the bond discount is amortized. Use 3/6 of the amounts from columns A, B, and C for 01-04-15 from the amortization table.

b. Dec. 31   Interest Expense ($4,221 × 3/6) 2,111
           Discount on Bonds Payable ($121 × 3/6)............. 111
           Interest Payable ($4,000 × 3/6)............................ 2,000
         To accrue interest and amortize the bonds.

The semi-annual interest payment is made ($4,000 from column A). Only the January-to-March 2015 interest expense is recorded, because the October-to-December interest expense was already recorded in Requirement 2(b). The same is true for the discount on bonds payable. Reverse Interest Payable from Requirement 2(b), because cash is paid now.

c. 2015

Apr. 1   Interest Expense 2,110
        Interest Payable 2,000
           Discount on Bonds Payable ($121 × 3/6)............. 110[*]
           Cash 4,000
         To pay semi-annual interest, part of which was
         accrued, and amortize the bonds.

[*]The total amortization was $221, of which $111 was recognized at December 31, 2014.

STOP + THINK (9-1)	**ANSWERS**
	1. $824 million ($162 current portion + $662 long-term portion)
	2. Pay by March 31, 2013: $162 million; pay thereafter: $662 million

STOP + THINK (9-2)

ANSWERS

Income Statement for 2014

Interest expense ($4,807 + $4,823)	$9,630

Balance Sheet at December 31, 2014

Current liabilities:		
Interest payable..		$4,500
Long-term liabilities:		
Bonds payable..	$100,000	
Less: Discount on bonds payable	(3,221)	96,779

STOP + THINK (9-3)

ANSWERS

	Company A	Company B
Debt ratio	86.0%	58.2%
Leverage ratio	7.14	2.39
Times-interest-earned ratio	2.39	5.06

Based on the ratios above, Company B shows a higher debt-paying ability, so it would present a lower risk to the bank than Company A. B's debt ratio is within the comfort range of 60%–70%, whereas A's is well above this range at 86%. A is also more highly leveraged than B (7.14 vs. 2.39) and has a much lower interest-coverage ratio, at only 2.39 compared to B's much more comfortable ratio of 5.06. I would therefore prefer to loan money to the less-risky Company B.

Review Liabilities

QUICK CHECK (ANSWERS ARE GIVEN ON PAGE 473.)

1. Which of the following is *not* an estimated liability?
   a. Allowance for bad debts
   b. Product warranties
   c. Income taxes
   d. Vacation pay
2. Recording estimated warranty expense in the current year *best* follows which accounting principle?
   a. Comparability
   b. Materiality
   c. Full disclosure
   d. Historical cost
   e. Relevance
3. Lotta Sound grants a 90-day warranty on all stereos. Historically, approximately 2½% of all sales prove to be defective. Sales in June are $200,000. In July, $2,900 of defective units are returned for replacement. What entry must Lotta Sound make at the end of June to record the warranty expense?
   a. Debit Warranty Expense, and credit Estimated Warranty Payable, $2,900.
   b. Debit Warranty Expense, and credit Cash, $4,865.
   c. Debit Warranty Expense, and credit Estimated Warranty Payable, $5,000.
   d. No entry is needed at June 30.

4. Outback Camera Co. was organized to sell a single product that carries a 60-day warranty against defects. Engineering estimates indicate that 5% of the units sold will prove defective and require an average repair cost of $40 per unit. During Outback's first month of operations, total sales were 400 units; by the end of the month, six defective units had been repaired. The liability for product warranties at month-end should be which of the following?

   a. $270
   b. $530
   c. $560

   d. $810
   e. None of these

5. Dart Corporation's leverage ratio increased from 2.5 in 2013 to 3.0 in 2014. Without looking at the financial statements, which statement best describes what may have occurred?

   a. The company incurred new debt financing in 2014, making it more profitable.
   b. The company incurred new equity financing in 2014, making it less profitable.
   c. The company incurred new debt financing in 2014, but it may or may not have been more profitable.
   d. The company incurred new equity financing in 2014, but it may or may not have been more profitable.

6. An unsecured bond is a

   a. registered bond.
   b. mortgage bond.
   c. term bond.

   d. serial bond.
   e. debenture bond.

7. The Discount on Bonds Payable account

   a. is a contra account to Bonds Payable.
   b. is a miscellaneous revenue account.
   c. is an expense account.
   d. is expensed at the bond's maturity.
   e. has a normal credit balance.

8. The discount on a bond payable becomes

   a. additional interest expense the year the bonds are sold.
   b. additional interest expense over the life of the bonds.
   c. a reduction in interest expense the year the bonds mature.
   d. a reduction in interest expense over the life of the bonds.
   e. a liability in the year the bonds are sold.

9. A bond that matures in instalments is called a

   a. secured bond.
   b. zero coupon.
   c. serial bond.

   d. term bond.
   e. callable bond.

10. The carrying value of Bonds Payable equals

   a. Bonds Payable – Premium on Bonds Payable.
   b. Bonds Payable – Discount on Bonds Payable.
   c. Bonds Payable + Discount on Bonds Payable.
   d. Bonds Payable + Accrued Interest.

11. A corporation issues bonds that pay interest each March 1 and September 1. The corporation's December 31 adjusting entry may include a

   a. debit to Cash.
   b. credit to Cash.
   c. credit to Interest Expense.

   d. debit to Interest Payable.
   e. credit to Discount on Bonds Payable.

Use this information to answer Questions 12 through 16.

McLennan Corporation issued $200,000 of 9½% five-year bonds. The bonds are dated and sold on January 1, 2014. Interest payment dates are January 1 and July 1. The bonds are issued for $196,140 to yield the market interest rate of 10%. Use the effective-interest method for Questions 12 through 15.

12. What is the amount of interest expense that McLennan Corporation will record on July 1, 2014, the first semi-annual interest payment date?

   a. $9,807   196,140 × .10 × 6/12 –
   b. $9,926

   c. $10,000
   d. $19,000

13. What is the amount of discount amortization that McLennan Corporation will record on July 1, 2014, the first semi-annual interest payment date?
    a. $0　　　　　　　　　　　　　　　　c. $193
    b. $74　　　　　　　　　　　　　　　(d.) $307

14. What is the total cash payment for interest for each 12-month period?
    a. $10,000　　　　　　　　　　　　　c. $19,614
    (b.) $19,000　　　　　　　　　　　　d. $20,000

15. What is the carrying amount of the bonds on the December 31, 2014, balance sheet?
    a. $196,140　　　　　　　　　　　　(c.) $196,769
    b. $196,526　　　　　　　　　　　　d. $196,912

16. Using straight-line amortization, the carrying amount of McLennan Corporation's bonds at December 31, 2014, is which of the following?
    a. $196,140　　　　　　　　　　　　c. $196,769
    b. $196,526　　　　　　　　　　　(d.) $196,912

Accounting Vocabulary

account payable A liability for goods or services purchased on credit and backed by the general reputation and credit standing of the debtor.　(p. 417)

accounts payable turnover (T/O) A liquidity ratio that measures the number of times per year a company was able to repay its accounts payable in full. Calculated by dividing the cost of goods sold by the average accounts payable balance for the year.　(p. 439)

bond discount Excess of a bond's face (par) value over its issue price.　(p. 427)

bond market price The price investors are willing to pay for the bond. It is equal to the present value of the principal payment plus the present value of the interest payments.　(p. 427)

bonds payable Groups of notes payable issued to multiple lenders called *bondholders*.　(p. 426)

bond premium Excess of a bond's issue price over its face value.　(p. 427)

contingent liability A possible obligation that arises from past events and whose existence will be confirmed only by the occurrence or non-occurrence of one or more uncertain future events not wholly within the control of the company.　(p. 424)

current portion of long-term debt The amount of the principal that is payable within one year. Also called *current instalment of long-term debt*.　(p. 422)

days payable outstanding (DPO) Another way of expressing the accounts payable turnover ratio, this measure indicates how many days it will take to pay off the accounts payable balance in full. Calculated by dividing the *accounts payable turnover* into 365.　(p. 439)

debentures Unsecured bonds—bonds backed only by the good faith of the borrower.　(p. 427)

earnings per share (EPS) Amount of a company's net income per outstanding common share.　(p. 437)

face value of bond The principal amount payable by the issuer. Also called *maturity value*.　(p. 427)

finance lease Under IFRS, a lease that transfers substantially all the risks and rewards incidental to ownership of assets to the lessee.　(p. 442)

interest-coverage ratio Another name for the *times-interest-earned ratio*.　(p. 441)

lease Rental agreement in which the tenant (lessee) agrees to make rent payments to the property owner (lessor) in exchange for the use of the asset.　(p. 442)

lessee Tenant in a lease agreement.　(p. 442)

lessor Property owner in a lease agreement.　(p. 442)

leverage ratio Shows the ratio of a company's total assets to total shareholders' equity. It is an alternative way of expressing how much debt a company has used to fund its assets, or in other words, how much leverage it has used.　(p. 440)

line of credit A method of short-term borrowing that provides a company with as-needed access to credit up to a maximum amount specified by its lender.　(p. 417)

market interest rate Interest rate that investors demand for loaning their money. Also called *effective interest rate*.　(p. 428)

mortgage A *term loan* secured by real property, such as land and buildings.　(p. 442)

operating lease A lease in which the risks and rewards of asset ownership are not transferred to the lessee.　(p. 442)

payroll Employee compensation, a major expense of many businesses.　(p. 421)

post-employment benefits A special type of employee benefits that do not become payable until after a person has completed employment with the company. They include such things as pension benefits, medical and dental insurance, and prescription drug benefits.　(p. 443)

provision Under IFRS, a present obligation of uncertain timing or amount that is recorded as a liability because it is probable that economic resources will be required to settle it.　(p. 423)

sales tax payable The amount of HST, GST, and provincial sales tax owing to government bodies.　(p. 419)

serial bonds Bonds that mature in instalments over a period of time.　(p. 427)

short-term notes payable Notes payable due within one year.　(p. 418)

stated interest rate Interest rate printed on the bond certificate that determines the amount of cash interest the borrower pays and the investor receives each year. Also called the *coupon rate* or *contract interest rate*.　(p. 428)

term bonds Bonds that all mature at the same time for a particular issue.　(p. 427)

term loan A long-term loan at a stated interest rate, typically from a single lender such as a bank, which must be repaid over a specified number of years. Usually secured by specific assets of the borrower, often the ones acquired using the loan proceeds. (p. 442)

times-interest-earned ratio Ratio of income from operations to interest expense. Measures the number of times that operating income can cover interest expense. Also called the *interest-coverage ratio*. (p. 441)

underwriter Organization that purchases the bonds from an issuing company and resells them to its clients or sells the bonds for a commission, agreeing to buy all unsold bonds. (p. 427)

unearned revenue A liability for goods or services customers have paid for but not yet received. (p. 421)

Assess Your Progress

MyAccountingLab

Make the grade with MyAccountingLab: The Exercises, Quizzes, and Problems (A set) marked in red can be found on MyAccountingLab. You can practise them as often as you want, and most feature step-by-step guided instructions to help you find the right answer.

SHORT EXERCISES

LEARNING OBJECTIVE ❶

Account for a note payable

S9-1 Jasper Sports Limited purchased inventory costing $10,000 by signing a 10% short-term note payable. The purchase occurred on March 31, 2014. Jasper pays annual interest each year on March 31. Journalize Jasper's (a) purchase of inventory, (b) accrual of interest expense on December 31, 2014, and (c) payment of the note plus interest on March 31, 2015.

LEARNING OBJECTIVE ❽

Report a short-term note payable and the related interest in the financial statements

S9-2 This short exercise works with exercise S9-1.

1. Refer to the data in S9-1. Show what the company would report on its balance sheet at December 31, 2014, and on its income statement for the year ended on that date.

2. What one item will the financial statements for the year ended December 31, 2015, report? Identify the financial statement, the item, and its amount.

LEARNING OBJECTIVE ❶

Account for warranty expense and estimated warranty payable

S9-3 General Motors of Canada Limited guarantees automobiles against defects for five years or 160,000 km, whichever comes first. Suppose GM Canada can expect warranty costs during the five-year period to add up to 3% of sales.

Assume that Forbes Motors in Waterloo, Ontario, made sales of $2,000,000 on their Buick line during 2014. Forbes received cash for 10% of the sales and took notes receivable for the remainder. Payments to satisfy customer warranty claims totalled $50,000 during 2014.

1. Record the sales, warranty expense, and warranty payments for Forbes. Ignore any reimbursement that Forbes may receive from GM Canada.

2. Post to the Estimated Warranty Payable T-account. The beginning balance was $40,000. At the end of 2014, how much in estimated warranty payable does Forbes owe its customers?

LEARNING OBJECTIVE ❶❽

Report warranties in the financial statements

S9-4 Refer to the data given in exercise S9-3. What amount of warranty expense will Forbes report during 2014? Does the warranty expense for the year equal the year's cash payments for warranties? Explain the relevant accounting principle as it applies to measuring warranty expense.

LEARNING OBJECTIVE ❻

Analyze accounts payable turnover

S9-5 Wardlow Sales, Inc.'s comparative income statements and balance sheets show the following selected information for 2013 and 2014:

	2014	2013
Cost of goods sold	$2,700,000	$2,500,000
Average accounts payable	$ 300,000	$ 250,000

Requirements

1. Calculate the company's accounts payable turnover and days payable outstanding (DPO) for 2013 and 2014.
2. On the basis of this computation alone, has the company's liquidity position improved or deteriorated during 2014?

S9-6 Compute the price of the following bonds:
a. $1,000,000 quoted at 89.75
b. $500,000 quoted at 110.375
c. $100,000 quoted at 97.50
d. $400,000 quoted at 102.625

LEARNING OBJECTIVE ❷❸

Price bonds

S9-7 Determine whether the following bonds will be issued at face value, a premium, or a discount:
a. The market interest rate is 9%. Star Inc. issues bonds with a stated rate of 8½%.
b. Charger Corporation issued 7½% bonds when the market rate was 7½%.
c. Explorer Corporation issued 8% bonds when the market interest rate was 6⅞%.
d. Tundra Company issued bonds that pay cash interest at the stated interest rate of 7%. At the date of issuance, the market interest rate was 8¼%.

LEARNING OBJECTIVE ❷❸

Determine bond prices at face value, a discount, or a premium

S9-8 Suppose Scotiabank issued a six-year $10,000 bond with stated interest rate of 6.25% when the market interest rate was 6¼%. Assume that the accounting year of Scotiabank ends on October 31. Journalize the following transactions, including an explanation for each entry.
a. Issuance of the bond, payable on May 1, 2014
b. Accrual of interest expense on October 31, 2014 (rounded to the nearest dollar)
c. Payment of cash interest on November 1, 2014
d. Payment of the bonds at maturity (give the date)

LEARNING OBJECTIVE ❷❸

Journalize basic bond payable transactions

S9-9 Standard Autoparts Inc. issued $100,000 of 7%, 10-year bonds at a price of 87 on January 31, 2014. The market interest rate at the date of issuance was 9%, and the standard bonds pay interest semi-annually.

1. Prepare an effective-interest amortization table for the bonds through the first three interest payments. Use Exhibit 9-3, page 431, as a guide, and round amounts to the nearest dollar.
2. Record Standard's issuance of the bonds on January 31, 2014, and payment of the first semi-annual interest amount and amortization of the bonds on July 31, 2014. Explanations are not required.

LEARNING OBJECTIVE ❷❸

Record bond transactions and calculate interest using the effective-interest method

S9-10 Use the amortization table that you prepared for Standard Autoparts in exercise S9-9 to answer these questions about the company's long-term debt:

1. How much cash did Standard Autoparts borrow on January 31, 2014? How much cash will Standard Autoparts pay back at maturity on January 31, 2015?
2. How much cash interest will Standard Autoparts pay each six months?
3. How much interest expense will Standard Autoparts report on July 31, 2014, and on January 31, 2015? Why does the amount of interest expense increase each period? Explain in detail.

LEARNING OBJECTIVE ❹

Analyze interest on long-term debt

S9-11 Max Industries Ltd. borrowed money by issuing a $10,000 6.5%, 10-year bond. Assume the issue price was 94 on July 1, 2014.

1. How much cash did Max Industries receive when it issued the bond?
2. How much must Max Industries pay back at maturity? When is the maturity date?
3. How much cash interest will Max Industries pay each six months? Carry the interest amount to the nearest cent.
4. How much interest expense will Max Industries report each six months? Assume the straight-line amortization method, and carry the interest amount to the nearest cent.

LEARNING OBJECTIVE ❷❸❹

Determine bonds payable amounts; amortize bonds by the straight-line method

LEARNING OBJECTIVE ❸❹

Record bond transactions and calculate interest using the straight-line method

S9-12 Return to the Max Industries bond in exercise S9-11. Assume that Max Industries issued the bond on July 1, 2014, at a price of 90. Also assume that Max Industries' accounting year ends on December 31. Journalize the following transactions for Max Industries, including an explanation for each entry:

a. Issuance of the bonds on July 1, 2014.

b. Accrual of interest expense and amortization of bonds on December 31, 2014. (Use the straight-line amortization method, and round amounts to the nearest dollar.)

c. Payment of the first semi-annual interest amount on January 1, 2015.

LEARNING OBJECTIVE ❻

Calculate the leverage ratio, debt ratio, and times-interest-earned, and evaluate debt-paying ability

S9-13 Examine the following selected financial information for Best Buy Co., Inc., and Walmart Stores, Inc.:

(in millions)	Best Buy Co., Inc.	Walmart Stores, Inc.
1. Total assets	$17,849	$180,663
2. Shareholders' equity	$ 7,292	$ 71,247
3. Operating income	$ 2,114	$ 25,542
4. Interest expense	$ 87	$ 1,928
5. Leverage ratio		
6. Total debt		
7. Debt ratio		
8. Times interest earned		

1. Complete the table, calculating all the requested information for the two companies.

2. Evaluate each company's long-term debt-paying ability (strong, medium, weak).

LEARNING OBJECTIVE ❻

Compute and evaluate three ratios

S9-14 Evensen Plumbing Products Ltd. reported the following data in 2014 (in millions):

	2014
Net operating revenues	$ 29.1
Operating expenses	25.0
Operating income	4.1
Nonoperating items:	
Interest expense	(1.1)
Other	(0.2)
Net income	$ 2.8
Total assets	$100.0
Total shareholders' equity	40.0

Compute Evensen's leverage ratio, debt ratio, and times-interest-earned ratio, and write a sentence to explain what those ratio values mean. Would you be willing to lend Evensen $1 million? State your reason.

LEARNING OBJECTIVE ❽

Report liabilities, including capital lease obligations

S9-15 Trinidad Industries Inc. has the following selected accounts at December 31, 2014:

GST Payable (net of ITC)	$ 17,000
Bonds payable	300,000
Equipment	120,000
Current portion of bonds payable	40,000
Notes payable, long-term	100,000
Interest payable (due March 1, 2015)	10,000
Accounts payable	44,000
Discount on bonds payable (all long-term)	10,000
Accounts receivable	34,000

Prepare the liabilities section of Trinidad's balance sheet at December 31, 2014, to show how Trinidad would report these items. Report total current liabilities and total liabilities.

EXERCISES

E9-16 The accounting records of Audio-Video Inc. included the following balances before the year-end adjustments:

LEARNING OBJECTIVE ❶❽

Account for and report warranty expense and the related liability

Estimated Warranty Payable	Sales Revenue	Warranty Expense
Beg. bal. 8,000	150,000	

In the past, Audio-Video's warranty expense has been 6% of sales. During the current period, the business paid $9,400 to satisfy the warranty claims of customers.

Requirements

1. Record Audio-Video's warranty expense for the period and the company's cash payments to satisfy warranty claims. Explanations are not required.
2. Show everything Audio-Video will report on its income statement and balance sheet for this situation.
3. Which data item from Requirement 2 will affect Audio-Video's current ratio? Will Audio-Video's current ratio increase or decrease as a result of this item?

E9-17 *Ontario Traveller Magazine* completed the following transactions during 2014:

LEARNING OBJECTIVE ❶❽

Record and report current liabilities

Aug. 31	Sold one-year subscriptions, collecting cash of $1,500, plus HST of 13%.
Dec. 31	Remitted (paid) HST to Canada Revenue Agency (CRA).
31	Made the necessary adjustment at year-end.

Journalize these transactions (explanations are not required). Then report any liability on the company's balance sheet at December 31.

E9-18 Penske Talent Search has an annual payroll of $150,000. At December 31, Penske owes salaries of $7,600 on which employee withholdings payable are $1,200 and employee benefits payable by the company are $1,000. The company has calculated its share of Canada Pension Plan, Employment Insurance, and other employee benefits to be 6% of payroll expense. The company will pay these amounts early next year. Show what Penske will report for the foregoing on its income statement and year-end balance sheet.

LEARNING OBJECTIVE ❽

Report payroll expense and liabilities

E9-19 Joy's Bar and Grill completed the following note-payable transactions:

LEARNING OBJECTIVE ❶

Record note-payable transactions

2014	
Aug. 1	Purchased kitchen equipment costing $60,000 by issuing a one-year, 5% note.
Dec. 31	Accrued interest on the note payable.
2015	
Aug. 1	Paid the note payable at maturity.

Answer these questions for Joy's Bar and Grill:

1. How much interest expense must be accrued at December 31, 2014?
2. Determine the amount of Joy's final payment on July 31, 2015.
3. How much interest expense will Joy's report for 2014 and for 2015?

LEARNING OBJECTIVE ❶❻❽

Analyze current and long-term liabilities; evaluate debt-paying ability

E9-20 Geodesic Domes, Inc., builds environmentally sensitive structures. The company's 2014 revenues totalled $2,800 million. At December 31, 2014, and 2013, the company had $661 million and $600 million in current assets, respectively. The December 31, 2014, and 2013, balance sheets and income statements reported the following amounts:

At Year-End (in millions)	2014	2013
Liabilities and shareholders' equity		
Current liabilities		
Accounts payable..	$ 110	$ 182
Accrued expenses..	97	177
Employee compensation and benefits..........................	45	15
Current portion of long-term debt..............................	7	20
Total current liabilities..	259	394
Long-term debt	1,394	1,315
Post-retirement benefits payable..................................	102	154
Other liabilities...	8	20
Shareholders' equity..	1,951	1,492
Total liabilities and shareholders' equity	$3,714	$3,375
Year-end (in millions)		
Cost of goods sold...	$1,656	$1,790

Requirements

1. Describe each of Geodesic Domes, Inc.'s liabilities and state how the liability arose.
2. What were the company's total assets at December 31, 2014? Evaluate the company's leverage and debt ratios at the end of 2013 and 2014. Did the company improve, deteriorate, or remain about the same over the year?
3. Accounts payable at the end of 2012 was $190 million. Calculate accounts payable turnover as a ratio and days payable outstanding (DPO) for 2013 and 2014. Calculate current ratios for 2013 and 2014 as well. Evaluate whether the company improved or deteriorated from the standpoint of ability to cover accounts payable and current liabilities over the year.

LEARNING OBJECTIVE ❶❻❽

Analyze liabilities and debt-paying ability

E9-21 Mills Geothermal Ltd. installs environmental heating/cooling systems. The company's 2014 revenues totalled $360 million, and at December 31, 2014, the company had $65 million in current assets. The December 31, 2014, balance sheet reported the liabilities and shareholders' equity as follows:

At Year-End (in millions)	2014	2013
Liabilities and shareholders' equity		
Current liabilities		
Accounts payable..	$ 29	$ 26
Accrued expenses..	16	20
Employee compensation and benefits..........................	9	11
Current portion of long-term debt..............................	5	—
Total current liabilities..	59	57
Long-term debt	115	115
Post-retirement benefits payable..................................	31	27
Other liabilities...	21	17
Shareholders' equity..	73	70
Total liabilities and shareholders' equity	$299	$286

Requirements

1. Describe each of Mills Geothermal Ltd.'s liabilities, and state how the liability arose.
2. What were the company's total assets at December 31, 2014? Was the company's debt ratio at the end of 2014 high, low, or in a middle range?

E9-22 Companies that operate in different industries may have very different financial ratio values. These differences may grow even wider when we compare companies located in different countries.

LEARNING OBJECTIVE ❻
Evaluate debt-paying ability

Compare three leading companies on their current ratio, debt ratio, leverage ratio, and times-interest-earned ratio. Compute the ratios for Company B, Company N, and Company V.

(amounts in millions or billions)	Company B	Company N	Company V
Income data			
Total revenues	$9,732	¥7,320	€136,146
Operating income...	295	230	5,646
Interest expense..	41	27	655
Net income...	22	7	450
Balance sheet data			
(amounts in millions or billions)			
Total current assets..	429	5,321	144,720
Long-term assets...	81	592	65,828
Total current liabilities...	227	2,217	72,000
Long-term liabilities	77	2,277	111,177
Shareholders' equity...	206	1,419	27,371

Note: ¥ is the symbol for a Japanese yen; € for a euro.

Based on your computed ratio values, which company looks the least risky?

E9-23 Assume that Premium Golf Equipment completed these selected transactions during December 2014:

LEARNING OBJECTIVE ❶❽
Report current and long-term liabilities

a. Sales of $3,000,000 are subject to estimated warranty cost of 3%. The estimated warranty payable at the beginning of the year was $30,000, and warranty payments for the year totalled $60,000.
b. On December 1, 2014, Premium signed a $150,000 note that requires annual payments of $30,000 plus 5% interest on the unpaid balance each December 1.
c. Golf Town, a chain of golf stores, ordered $125,000 of golf equipment. With its order, Golf Town sent a cheque for $125,000, and Premium shipped $100,000 of the goods. Premium will ship the remainder of the goods on January 3, 2015.
d. The December payroll of $100,000 is subject to employee-withheld income tax, Canada Pension Plan and Employment Insurance, and the company's share of Canada Pension Plan and Employment Insurance totalling $25,000 and benefits of $9,000. On December 31, Premium pays employees their take-home pay and accrues all tax amounts.

Requirement

Classify each liability as current or long-term and report the liability and its amount that would appear on the Premium Golf Equipment balance sheet at December 31, 2014. Show a total for current liabilities.

E9-24 On January 31, 2014, Triumph Sports Cars issued 10-year, 6% bonds with a face value of $100,000. The bonds were issued at 97 and pay interest on January 31 and July 31. Triumph amortizes bonds by the straight-line method. Record (a) issuance of the bonds on January 31, (b) the semi-annual interest payment and discount amortization on July 31, and (c) the interest accrual and discount amortization on December 31.

LEARNING OBJECTIVE ❷❸❹
Record bond transactions and calculate interest using the straight-line method

E9-25 Moreau Manufacturing Inc. has $200,000 of 8% debenture bonds outstanding. The bonds were issued at 102 in 2014 and mature in 2034.

LEARNING OBJECTIVE ❷❸❹
Measure cash amounts for a bond; amortize the bonds by the straight-line method

Requirements

1. How much cash did Moreau receive when it issued these bonds?
2. How much cash *in total* will Moreau pay the bondholders through the maturity date of the bonds?

3. Take the difference between your answers to Requirements 1 and 2. This difference represents Moreau's total interest expense over the life of the bonds. (Challenge)
4. Compute Moreau's annual interest expense by the straight-line amortization method. Multiply this amount by 20. Your 20-year total should be the same as your answer to Requirement 3. (Challenge)

LEARNING OBJECTIVE ❷❸❹

Record bond transactions and calculate interest using the effective-interest method

E9-26 Family General Stores Inc. is authorized to issue $500,000 of 7%, 10-year bonds. On December 31, 2014, when the market interest rate is 8%, the company issues $400,000 of the bonds and receives cash of $372,660. Family General amortizes bonds by the effective-interest method. The semi-annual interest dates are January 31 and July 31.

Requirements

1. Prepare a bond amortization table for the first four semi-annual interest periods.
2. Record issuance of the bonds on December 31, 2014, and the semi-annual interest payments on January 31, 2015, and on July 31, 2015.

LEARNING OBJECTIVE ❷❸❹

Record bond transactions and calculate interest using the effective-interest method

E9-27 On June 30, 2014, the market interest rate is 7%. Dellaca Enterprises issues $500,000 of 8%, 20-year bonds at 110.625. The bonds pay interest on June 30 and December 31. Dellaca amortizes bonds by the effective-interest method.

Requirements

1. Prepare a bond amortization table for the first four semi-annual interest periods.
2. Record issuance of the bonds on June 30, 2014, the payment of interest at December 31, 2014, and the semi-annual interest payment on June 30, 2015.

LEARNING OBJECTIVE ❸❹

Create a debt payment and bond amortization schedule

E9-28 Carlson Candies issued $300,000 of 8⅜%, five-year bonds on January 1, 2014, when the market interest rate was 9½%. The company pays interest annually at year-end. The issue price of the bonds was $287,041.

Requirement

Create a spreadsheet model to prepare a schedule to amortize the bonds. Use the effective-interest method of amortization. Round to the nearest dollar, and format your answer as shown here.

	A	B	C	D	E	F
1						
2						Bond
3		Interest	Interest	Bond Discount	Bond Discount	Carrying
4	Date	Payment	Expense	Amortization	Balance	Amount
5	1-1-2014					287,041
6	12-31-2014	$ ⬜	$ ⬜	$ ⬜	$ ⬜	$ ⬜
7	12-31-2015					
8	12-31-2016					
9	12-31-2017					
10	12-31-2018					
		300,000 × 0.08375	+ F5 × 0.095	+ C6 − B6	300,000 − F5	+ F5 + D6

LEARNING OBJECTIVE ❶❻❽

Analyze current and long-term liabilities; evaluate debt-paying ability

E9-29 Green Earth Homes, Inc., builds environmentally sensitive structures. The company's 2014 revenues totalled $2,785 million. At December 31, 2014 and 2013, the company had $643 million and $610 million in current assets, respectively. The December 31, 2014 and 2013 balance sheets and income statements reported the following amounts:

At Year-End (in millions)	2014	2013
Liabilities and shareholders' equity		
Current liabilities		
Accounts payable	$ 137	$ 181
Accrued expenses	163	169
Employee compensation and benefits	51	16
Current portion of long-term debt	17	10
Total current liabilities	368	376
Long-term debt	1,497	1,326
Post-retirement benefits payable	138	112
Other liabilities	20	22
Shareholders' equity	2,027	1,492
Total liabilities and shareholders' equity	$4,050	3,328
Year-end (in millions)		
Cost of goods sold	$1,885	$2,196

Requirements

1. Describe each of Green Earth Homes, Inc.'s liabilities and state how the liability arose.
2. What were the company's total assets at December 31, 2014? Evaluate the company's leverage and debt ratios at the end of 2013 and 2014. Did the company improve, deteriorate, or remain about the same over the year?
3. Accounts payable at the end of 2012 was $195. Calculate accounts payable turnover as a ratio and days payable outstanding (DPO) for 2013 and 2014. Calculate current ratios for 2013 and 2014 as well. Evaluate whether the company improved or deteriorated from the standpoint of ability to cover accounts payable and current liabilities over the year.

E9-30 Companies that operate in different industries may have very different financial ratio values. These differences may grow even wider when we compare companies located in different countries.

LEARNING OBJECTIVE ❻
Use ratios to compare companies

Compare three leading companies on their current ratio, debt ratio, and times-interest-earned ratio. Compute three ratios for Sobeys (the Canadian grocery chain), Sony (the Japanese electronics manufacturer), and Daimler (the German auto company).

	(amounts in millions or billions)		
Income data	Sobeys	Sony	Daimler
Total revenues	$12,853	¥7,475	€151,589
Operating income	332	191	2,072
Interest expense	35	29	913
Net income	197	124	3,227
Asset and liability data			
Total current assets	$1,235	¥3,770	€93,131
Long-term assets	2,504	6,838	96,891
Total current liabilities	1,230	3,200	59,977
Long-term liabilities	674	4,204	95,890
Shareholders' equity	1,835	3,204	34,155

Based on your computed ratio values, which company looks the least risky? (Challenge)

E9-31 Companies that operate in different industries may have very different financial ratio values. These differences may grow even wider when we compare companies located in different countries.

LEARNING OBJECTIVE ❻
Evaluate debt-paying ability

Compare three leading companies on their current ratio, debt ratio, leverage ratio, and times-interest-earned ratio. Compute the ratios for Company F, Company K, and Company R.

	(amounts in millions or billions)		
Income data	Company F	Company K	Company R
Total revenues	$9,724	¥7,307	€136,492
Operating income	292	224	5,592
Interest expense	46	33	736
Net income	23	15	448
Assets and liability data			
Total current assets	434	5,383	148,526
Long-term assets	96	405	49,525
Total current liabilities	207	2,197	72,100
Long-term liabilities	107	2,318	110,107
Shareholders' equity	216	1,273	15,844

Based on your computed ratio values, which company looks the least risky?

CHALLENGE EXERCISES

LEARNING OBJECTIVE ❶❻❽

Report current and long-term liabilities; evaluate leverage

E9-32 The top management of Marquis Marketing Services examines the following company accounting records at August 29, immediately before the end of the year, August 31:

Total current assets	$ 324,500
Non-current assets	1,098,500
	$1,423,000
Total current liabilities	$ 173,800
Non-current liabilities	247,500
Shareholders' equity	1,001,700
	$1,423,000

1. Suppose Marquis's management wants to achieve a current ratio of 2. How much in current liabilities should Marquis pay off within the next two days in order to achieve its goal?

2. Calculate Marquis's leverage ratio and debt ratio. Evaluate the company's debt position. Is it low, high, or about average? What other information might help you to make a decision?

LEARNING OBJECTIVE ❺❻

Understand how structuring debt transactions can affect a company

E9-33 The Cola Company reported the following comparative information at December 31, 2014, and December 31, 2013 (amounts in millions and adapted):

	2014	2013
Current assets	$21,579	$17,551
Total assets	72,921	48,671
Current liabilities	18,508	13,721
Total stockholders' equity	31,317	25,346
Net sales	35,119	30,990
Net income	11,809	6,824

Requirements

1. Calculate the following ratios for 2014 and 2013:
   a. Current ratio
   b. Debt ratio

2. At the end of 2014, The Cola Company issued $1,590 million of long-term debt that was used to retire short-term debt. What would the current ratio and debt ratio have been if this transaction had not been made?

3. The Cola Company reports that its lease payments under operating leases will total $965 million in the future and $205 million will occur in the next year (2015). What would the current ratio and debt ratio have been if these leases had been capitalized?

E9-34 Mark IV Industries Inc. issued $100 million 13% debentures due March 15, 2019, with interest payable March 15 and September 15; the price was 96.5.

LEARNING OBJECTIVE ❷❸❹

Analyze bond transactions

Requirements

Answer these questions:

1. Journalize Mark IV Industries Inc.'s issuance of these bonds on March 15, 2014. No explanation is required, but describe the transaction in detail, indicating who received cash, who paid cash, and how much.

2. Why is the stated interest rate on these bonds so high?

3. Compute the semi-annual cash interest payment on the bonds.

4. Compute the semi-annual interest expense under the straight-line amortization method.

5. Compute both the first-year (from March 15, 2014, to March 15, 2015) and the second-year interest expense (March 15, 2015, to March 15, 2016) under the effective-interest amortization method. The market rate of interest at the date of issuance was 14%. Why is interest expense greater in the second year?

QUIZ

Test your understanding of accounting for liabilities by answering the following questions.

Q9-35 For the purpose of classifying liabilities as current or non-current, the term *operating cycle* refers to which of the following?

a. A period of one year

b. The time period between date of sale and the date the related revenue is collected

c. The time period between purchase of merchandise and the conversion of this merchandise back to cash

d. The average time period between business recessions

Q9-36 Failure to accrue interest expense results in which of the following?

a. An overstatement of net income and an overstatement of liabilities

b. An understatement of net income and an overstatement of liabilities

c. An understatement of net income and an understatement of liabilities

d. An overstatement of net income and an understatement of liabilities

Q9-37 Sportscar Warehouse operates in a province with a 6% sales tax. For convenience, Sportscar Warehouse credits Sales Revenue for the total amount (selling price plus sales tax) collected from each customer. If Sportscar Warehouse fails to make an adjustment for sales taxes, which of the following will be true?

a. Net income will be overstated, and liabilities will be overstated.

b. Net income will be overstated, and liabilities will be understated.

c. Net income will be understated, and liabilities will be overstated.

d. Net income will be understated, and liabilities will be understated.

Q9-38 What kind of account is *Unearned Revenue*?

a. Asset account

b. Liability account

c. Revenue account

d. Expense account

Q9-39 An end-of-period adjusting entry that debits Unearned Revenue will most likely credit which of the following?

a. A revenue

b. An asset

c. An expense

d. A liability

Q9-40 Adrian Inc. manufactures and sells computer monitors with a three-year warranty. Warranty costs are expected to average 8% of sales during the warranty period. The following table shows the sales and actual warranty payments during the first two years of operations:

Year	Sales	Warranty Payments
2013	$500,000	$ 4,000
2014	700,000	32,000

Based on these facts, what amount of warranty liability should Adrian Inc. report on its balance sheet at December 31, 2014?

a. $32,000

b. $36,000

c. $60,000

d. $96,000

Q9-41 Today's Fashions has a debt that has been properly reported as a long-term liability up to the present year (2014). Some of this debt comes due in 2014. If Today's Fashions continues to report the current position as a long-term liability, the effect will be to do which of the following?

a. Overstate the current ratio

b. Overstate net income

c. Understate total liabilities

d. Understate the debt ratio

Q9-42 A bond with a face amount of $10,000 has a current price quote of 102.875. What is the bond's price?

a. $1,028,750

b. $10,200.88

c. $10,028.75

d. $10,287.50

Q9-43 Bond carrying value equals Bonds Payable

a. minus Premium on Bonds Payable.

b. plus Discount on Bonds Payable.

c. plus Premium on Bonds Payable.

d. minus Discount on Bonds Payable.

e. Both a and b

f. Both c and d

Q9-44 What type of account is *Discount on Bonds Payable*, and what is its normal balance?

	Type of account	Normal balance
a.	Contra liability	Debit
b.	Reversing account	Debit
c.	Adjusting amount	Credit
d.	Contra liability	Credit

Questions Q9-45 through Q9-48 use the following data:

Q9-45 Sweetwater Company sells $100,000 of 10%, 15-year bonds for 97 on April 1, 2014. The market rate of interest on that day is 10½%. Interest is paid each year on April 1. The entry to record the sale of the bonds on April 1 would be which of the following?

a.	Cash	97,000	
	Bonds Payable		97,000
b.	Cash	100,000	
	Bonds Payable		100,000
c.	Cash	97,000	
	Discount on Bonds Payable	3,000	
	Bonds Payable		100,000
d.	Cash	100,000	
	Discount on Bonds Payable		3,000
	Bonds Payable		97,000

Q9-46 Sweetwater Company uses the straight-line amortization method. The sale price of the bonds was $97,000. The amount of interest expense on April 1 of each year will be which of the following?
a. $4,080
b. $4,000
c. $4,200
d. $10,200
e. None of these. The interest expense is _____.

Q9-47 Write the adjusting entry required at December 31, 2014. } nCF

Q9-48 Write the journal entry required at April 1, 2015.

Q9-49 McPherson Corporation issued $100,000 of 10%, five-year bonds on January 1, 2014, for $92,280. The market interest rate when the bonds were issued was 12%. Interest is paid semi-annually on January 1 and July 1. The first interest payment is July 1, 2014. Using the effective-interest amortization method, how much interest expense will McPherson record on July 1, 2014?
a. $6,000
b. $5,228
c. $6,772
d. $5,000
e. Some other amount ($5,537)

Q9-50 Using the facts in the preceding question, McPherson's journal entry to record the interest expense on July 1, 2014, will include a
a. debit to Bonds Payable.
b. credit to Interest Expense.
c. debit to Premium on Bonds Payable.
d. credit to Discount on Bonds Payable.

Q9-51 Amortizing the discount on bonds payable does which of the following?
a. Increases the recorded amount of interest expense
b. Is necessary only if the bonds were issued at more than face value
c. Reduces the semi-annual cash payment for interest
d. Reduces the carrying value of the bond liability

Q9-52 The journal entry on the maturity date to record the payment of $1,000,000 of bonds payable that were issued at a $70,000 discount includes
a. a debit to Discount on Bonds Payable for $70,000.
b. a credit to Cash for $1,070,000.
c. a debit to Bonds Payable for $1,000,000.
d. All of the above

Q9-53 The payment of the face amount of a bond on its maturity date is regarded as which of the following?
a. An operating activity
b. An investing activity
c. A financing activity

PROBLEMS

(Group A)

P9-54A Sea Spray Marina experienced these events during 2014.
a. December revenue totalled $110,000 and, in addition, Sea Spray collected sales tax of 7%. The sales tax amount will be remitted to the province of British Columbia early in January.
b. On October 31, Sea Spray signed a six-month, 7% note to purchase a boat costing $90,000. The note requires payment of principal and interest at maturity.
c. On August 31, Sea Spray received cash of $1,800 in advance for service revenue. This revenue will be earned evenly over six months.
d. Revenues of $900,000 were covered by Sea Spray's service warranty. At January 1, estimated warranty payable was $11,300. During the year, Sea Spray recorded warranty expense of $31,000 and paid warranty claims of $34,700.
e. Sea Spray owes $100,000 on a long-term note payable. At December 31, 6% interest for the year plus $20,000 of this principal are payable within one year.

LEARNING OBJECTIVE ❶❽
Measure current liabilities

Requirement

For each item, indicate the account and the related amount to be reported as a *current* liability on the Sea Spray Marina balance sheet at December 31, 2014.

LEARNING OBJECTIVE ❶

Record liability-related transactions

P9-55A The following transactions of Smooth Sounds Music Company occurred during 2014 and 2015:

2014	
Mar. 3	Purchased a Steinway piano (inventory) for $40,000, signing a six-month, 5% note.
Apr. 30	Borrowed $50,000 on a 9% note payable that calls for annual instalment payments of $25,000 principal plus interest. Record the short-term note payable in a separate account from the long-term note payable.
Sept. 3	Paid the six-month, 5% note at maturity.
Dec. 31	Accrued warranty expense, which is estimated at 2% of sales of $190,000.
31	Accrued interest on the outstanding note payable.
2015	
Apr. 30	Paid the first instalment plus interest for one year on the outstanding note payable.

Requirement

Record the transactions in Smooth Sounds' journal. Explanations are not required.

LEARNING OBJECTIVE ❷❸❹❽

Issue bonds at a discount, amortize by the straight-line method, and report bonds payable on the balance sheet

P9-56A On February 28, 2014, ETrade Inc. issues 8½%, 20-year bonds with a face value of $200,000. The bonds pay interest on February 28 and August 31. ETrade amortizes bonds by the straight-line method.

Requirements

1. If the market interest rate is 7⅝% when ETrade issues its bonds, will the bonds be priced at face value, a premium, or a discount? Explain.
2. If the market interest rate is 9% when ETrade issues its bonds, will the bonds be priced at face value, a premium, or a discount? Explain.
3. Assume that the issue price of the bonds is 97. Journalize the following bond transactions:
   a. Issuance of the bonds on February 28, 2014
   b. Payment of interest and amortization of the bonds on August 31, 2014
   c. Accrual of interest and amortization of the bonds on December 31, 2014
   d. Payment of interest and amortization of the bonds on February 28, 2015
4. Report interest payable and bonds payable as they would appear on the ETrade balance sheet at December 31, 2014.

LEARNING OBJECTIVE ❷❸❹

Account for bonds payable at a discount and amortize by the straight-line method

P9-57A

1. Journalize the following transactions of Trekker Boot Company:

2014	
Jan. 1	Issued $600,000 of 8%, 10-year bonds at 97.
July 1	Paid semi-annual interest and amortized bonds by the straight-line method on the 8% bonds payable.
Dec. 31	Accrued semi-annual interest expense and amortized bonds by the straight-line method on the 8% bonds payable.
2015	
Jan. 1	Paid semi-annual interest.
2024	
Jan. 1	Paid the 8% bonds at maturity.

2. At December 31, 2014, after all year-end adjustments, determine the carrying amount of Trekker's bonds payable, net.

3. For the six months ended July 1, 2014, determine the following for Trekker:
   a. Interest expense
   b. Cash interest paid

What causes interest expense on the bonds to exceed cash interest paid?

P9-58A Notes to the Maritime Industries Ltd. financial statements reported the following data on December 31, 2014 (the end of the fiscal year):

LEARNING OBJECTIVE ❷❸❹❽

Analyze a company's long-term debt and report long-term debt on the balance sheet (effective-interest method)

Note 6, Indebtedness		
Bonds payable, 5%, due in 2019	$600,000	
Less Discount	(25,274)	$574,726
Notes payable, 8.3%, payable in $50,000 annual instalments, starting in Year 2018		250,000

Maritime Industries amortizes bonds by the effective-interest method.

Requirements

1. Answer the following questions about Maritime's long-term liabilities:
   a. What is the maturity value of the 5% bonds?
   b. What are Maritime's annual cash interest payments on the 5% bonds?
   c. What is the carrying amount of the 5% bonds at December 31, 2014?
2. Prepare an amortization table through December 31, 2017, for the 5% bonds. The market interest rate for these bonds was 6%. Maritime pays interest annually on December 31. How much is Maritime's interest expense on the 5% bonds for the year ended December 31, 2017?
3. Show how Maritime Industries would report the bonds payable and notes payable at December 31, 2017.

P9-59A On December 31, 2014, Digital Connections issued 8%, 10-year bonds payable with a maturity value of $500,000. The semi-annual interest dates are June 30 and December 31. The market interest rate is 9%, and the issue price of the bonds is 94. Digital Connections amortizes bonds by the effective-interest method.

LEARNING OBJECTIVE ❷❸❹❽

Issuing bonds at a discount, amortizing by the effective-interest method, and reporting the bonds payable on the balance sheet

Requirements

1. Prepare an effective-interest-method amortization table for the first four semi-annual interest periods.
2. Journalize the following transactions:
   a. Issuance of the bonds on December 31, 2014. Credit Bonds Payable.
   b. Payment of interest and amortization of the bonds on June 30, 2015
   c. Payment of interest and amortization of the bonds on December 31, 2015
3. Show how Digital Connections would report the remaining bonds payable on its balance sheet at December 31, 2016.

P9-60A Outback Sporting Goods is embarking on a massive expansion. Assume plans call for opening 20 new stores during the next two years. Each store is scheduled to be 50% larger than the company's existing locations, offering more items of inventory, and with more elaborate displays. Management estimates that company operations will provide $1 million of the cash needed for expansion. Outback must raise the remaining $6 million from outsiders. The board of directors is considering obtaining the $6 million either through borrowing or by issuing common shares.

LEARNING OBJECTIVE ❺

Finance operations with debt or with shares

Requirement

Write a memo to Outback's management discussing the advantages and disadvantages of borrowing and of issuing common shares to raise the needed cash. Which method of raising the funds would you recommend?

LEARNING OBJECTIVE ❶❻❽

Report liabilities on the balance sheet; calculate the leverage ratio, debt ratio, and times-interest-earned ratio

P9-61A The accounting records of Brighton Foods, Inc., include the following items at December 31, 2014:

Mortgage note payable,			Total assets	$4,500,000
current portion	$ 92,000		Accumulated depreciation,	
Accumulated pension			equipment	166,000
benefit obligation	450,000		Discount on bonds payable	
Bonds payable, long-term	200,000		(all long-term)	25,000
Mortgage note payable,			Operating income	370,000
long-term	318,000		Equipment	744,000
Bonds payable, current portion	500,000		Pension plan assets	
Interest expense	229,000		(market value)	420,000
			Interest payable	75,000

Requirements

1. Show how each relevant item would be reported on the Brighton Foods, Inc., classified balance sheet, including headings and totals for current liabilities and long-term liabilities.
2. Answer the following questions about Brighton's financial position at December 31, 2014:
   a. What is the carrying amount of the bonds payable? (Combine the current and long-term amounts.)
   b. Why is the interest-payable amount so much less than the amount of interest expense?
3. How many times did Brighton cover its interest expense during 2014?
4. Assume that all of the existing liabilities are included in the information provided. Calculate the leverage ratio and debt ratio of the company. Evaluate the health of the company from a leverage point of view. What other information would be helpful in making your evaluation?
5. Independent of your answer to (4), assume that Footnote 8 of the financial statements includes commitments for operating leases over the next 15 years in the amount of $3,000,000. If the company had to capitalize these leases in 2014, how would it change the leverage ratio and the debt ratio? How would this change impact your assessment of the company's health from a leverage point of view?

LEARNING OBJECTIVE ❻❽

Report liabilities on the balance sheet; calculate times-interest-earned ratio

P9-62A The accounting records of Pacer Foods Inc. include the following items at December 31, 2014.

Mortgage note payable,			Accumulated depreciation,	
current	$ 50,000		equipment	$219,000
Bonds payable, long-term	490,000		Discount on bonds payable	
Mortgage note payable,			(all long-term)	7,000
long-term	150,000		Operating income	291,000
Bonds payable, current portion	70,000		Equipment	487,000
Interest expense	67,000		Interest payable	9,000

Requirements

1. Show how each relevant item would be reported on the Pacer Foods Inc. classified balance sheet, including headings and totals for current liabilities and long-term liabilities.
2. Answer the following questions about Pacer's financial position at December 31, 2014:
   a. What is the carrying amount of the bonds payable? (Combine the current and long-term amounts.)
   b. Why is the interest-payable amount so much less than the amount of interest expense?
3. How many times did Pacer cover its interest expense during 2014?

(Group B)

P9-63B Goldwater Corporation experienced these five events during 2014:

a. December sales totalled $50,000, and Goldwater collected harmonized sales tax (HST) of 13%. The HST will be remitted to CRA in January 2015. Reporting requirements are the segregation of the provincial portion (8%) and federal portion (5%).

b. On November 30, Goldwater received rent of $6,000 in advance for a lease on unused store space. This rent will be earned evenly over three months.

c. On September 30, Goldwater signed a six-month, 9% note to purchase store fixtures costing $12,000. The note requires payment of principal and interest at maturity.

d. Sales of $400,000 were covered by Goldwater's product warranty. At January 1, estimated warranty payable was $12,400. During the year, Goldwater recorded warranty expense of $22,300 and paid warranty claims of $24,600.

e. Goldwater owes $100,000 on a long-term note. At December 31, 5% interest since July 31 and $20,000 of this principal are payable within one year.

LEARNING OBJECTIVE ❶❽
Measure current liabilities

Requirement

For each item, indicate the account and the related amount to be reported as a *current* liability on the Goldwater Corporation balance sheet at December 31, 2014.

P9-64B Assume that the following transactions of Sleuth Book Store occurred during 2014 and 2015:

LEARNING OBJECTIVE ❶
Record liability-related transactions

2014		
Jan. 9	Purchased store fixtures at a cost of $50,000, signing an 8%, six-month note for that amount.
June 30	Borrowed $200,000 on a 9% note that calls for annual instalment payments of $50,000 principal plus interest. Record the short-term note payable in a separate account from the long-term note payable.
July 9	Paid the six-month, 8% note at maturity.
Dec. 31	Accrued warranty expense, which is estimated at 3% of sales of $600,000.
31	Accrued interest on the outstanding note payable.
2015		
June 30	Paid the first instalment and interest for one year on the outstanding note payable.

Requirement

Record the transactions in the company's journal. Explanations are not required.

P9-65B Assume the board of directors of The Saddledome Foundation authorizes the issue of $1 million of 8%, 20-year bonds. The semi-annual interest dates are March 31 and September 30. The bonds are issued on March 31, 2014, at face value.

LEARNING OBJECTIVE ❷❸❹❽
Record bond transactions (at face value) and report bonds payable on the balance sheet

Requirements

1. Journalize the following transactions:
   a. Issuance of the bonds on March 31, 2014
   b. Payment of interest on September 30, 2014
   c. Accrual of interest on December 31, 2014
   d. Payment of interest on March 31, 2015
2. Report interest payable and bonds payable as they would appear on the Saddledome Foundation balance sheet at December 31, 2014.

P9-66B On February 28, 2014, Panorama Ltd. issues 7%, 10-year notes with a face value of $300,000. The notes pay interest on February 28 and August 31, and Panorama amortizes notes by the straight-line method.

LEARNING OBJECTIVE ❷❸❹❽
Record bond transactions and calculate interest using the straight-line method; report notes payable on the balance sheet

Requirements

1. If the market interest rate is 6% when Panorama issues its notes, will the notes be priced at face value, a premium, or a discount? Explain.

2. If the market interest rate is 8% when Panorama issues its notes, will the notes be priced at face value, a premium, or a discount? Explain.

3. Assume that the issue price of the notes is 96. Journalize the following note payable transactions:

   a. Issuance of the notes on February 28, 2014

   b. Payment of interest and amortization of the bonds on August 31, 2014

   c. Accrual of interest and amortization of the bonds on December 31, 2014

   d. Payment of interest and amortization of the bonds on February 28, 2015

4. Report interest payable and notes payable as they would appear on Panorama's balance sheet at December 31, 2014.

LEARNING OBJECTIVE ❷❸❹

Account for bonds payable at a discount and amortize by the straight-line method

P9-67B

1. Journalize the following transactions of Farm Equipment Limited:

2014	
Jan. 1	Issued $100,000 of 8%, five-year bonds at 94.
July 1	Paid semi-annual interest and amortized the bonds by the straight-line method on our 8% bonds payable.
Dec. 31	Accrued semi-annual interest expense and amortized the bonds by the straight-line method on our 8% bonds payable.
2015	
Jan. 1	Paid semi-annual interest.
2019	
Jan. 1	Paid the 8% bonds at maturity.

2. At December 31, 2014, after all year-end adjustments, determine the carrying amount of Farm Equipment Limited's bonds payable, net.

3. For the six months ended July 1, 2014, determine the following for Farm Equipment Limited:

   a. Interest expense

   b. Cash interest paid

   What causes interest expense on the bonds to exceed cash interest paid?

LEARNING OBJECTIVE ❷❸❹❽

Analyze a company's long-term debt and report the long-term debt on the balance sheet (effective-interest method)

P9-68B The notes to the Community Charities financial statements reported the following data on December 31, 2014 (end of the fiscal year):

Note D—Long-Term Debt		
7% bonds payable, due in 2020	$ 500,000	
Less: Discount...	(26,032)	$473,968
6½% notes payable; principal due in annual amounts of		
$50,000 in 2018 through 2023		300,000

Community Charities amortizes bonds by the effective-interest method and pays all interest amounts at December 31.

Requirements

1. Answer the following questions about Community Charities' long-term liabilities:

   a. What is the maturity value of the 7% bonds?

   b. What is Community Charities' annual cash interest payment on the 7% bonds?

   c. What is the carrying amount of the 7% bonds at December 31, 2014?

2. Prepare an amortization table through December 31, 2017, for the 7% bonds. The market interest rate on the bonds was 8%. Round all amounts to the nearest dollar. How much is Community Charities' interest expense on the 7% bonds for the year ended December 31, 2017?

3. Show how Community Charities would report the 7% bonds payable and the 6½% notes payable at December 31, 2017.

P9-69B Two businesses in very different circumstances are pondering how to raise $2 million.

HighTech.com has fallen on hard times. Net income has been low for the last three years, even falling by 10% from last year's level of profits, and cash flow also took a nose dive. Top management has experienced some turnover and has stabilized only recently. To become competitive again, High Tech needs $2 million to invest in new technology.

Decorator Services is in the midst of its most successful period since it began operations in 2012. Net income has increased by 25%. The outlook for the future is bright with new markets opening up and competitors unable to compete with Decorator. As a result, Decorator is planning a large-scale expansion.

LEARNING OBJECTIVE ❺

Finance operations with debt or shares

Requirement

Propose a plan for each company to raise the needed cash. Which company should borrow? Which company should issue shares? Consider the advantages and disadvantages of raising money by borrowing and by issuing shares, and discuss them in your answer.

P9-70B The accounting records of Braintree Foods, Inc., include the following items at December 31, 2014:

LEARNING OBJECTIVE ❶❻❽

Report liabilities on the balance sheet; calculate the leverage ratio, debt ratio, and times-interest-earned ratio

Mortgage note payable, current portion	$ 97,000	Total assets	$4,200,000
Accumulated pension benefit obligation	470,000	Accumulated depreciation, equipment	162,000
Bonds payable, long-term	1,680,000	Discount on bonds payable (all long-term)	22,000
Mortgage note payable, long-term	314,000	Operating income	390,000
		Equipment	745,000
Bonds payable, current portion	420,000	Pension plan assets (market value)	425,000
Interest expense	227,000	Interest payable	74,000

Requirements

1. Show how each relevant item would be reported on the Braintree Foods, Inc., classified balance sheet, including headings and totals for current liabilities and long-term liabilities.
2. Answer the following questions about Braintree's financial position at December 31, 2014:
   a. What is the carrying amount of the bonds payable? (Combine the current and long-term amounts.)
   b. Why is the interest-payable amount so much less than the amount of interest expense?
3. How many times did Braintree cover its interest expense during 2014?
4. Assume that all of the existing liabilities are included in the information provided. Calculate the leverage ratio and debt ratio of the company. Evaluate the health of the company from a leverage point of view. What other information would be helpful in making your evaluation?
5. Independent of your answer to (4), assume that Footnote 8 of the financial statements includes commitments for operating leases over the next 15 years in the amount of $3,000,000. If the company had to capitalize these leases in 2014, how would it change the leverage ratio and the debt ratio? How would this change impact your assessment of the company's health from a leverage point of view?

P9-71B The accounting records of Toronto Financial Services include the following items at December 31, 2014:

Premium on bonds payable (all long-term)...	$ 13,000
Interest payable	3,900
Operating income...	104,000
Interest expense..	39,000
Bonds payable, current portion	50,000
Accumulated depreciation, building..	70,000
Mortgage note payable, long-term	215,000
Bonds payable, long-term...	250,000
Building	160,000

Requirements

1. Show how each relevant item would be reported on Toronto Financial Services' classified balance sheet. Include headings and totals for current liabilities and long-term liabilities.
2. Answer the following questions about the financial position of Toronto Financial Services at December 31, 2014:
   a. What is the carrying amount of the bonds payable? (Combine the current and long-term amounts.)
   b. Why is the interest payable amount so much less than the amount of interest expense? (Challenge)
3. How many times did Toronto cover its interest expense during 2014?

Apply Your Knowledge

Decision Cases

Case 1. In 2001, Enron Corporation filed for Chapter 11 bankruptcy protection, shocking the business community: How could a company this large and this successful go bankrupt? This case explores the causes and the effects of Enron's bankruptcy.

At December 31, 2000, and for the four years ended on that date, Enron reported the following (amounts in millions):

Balance Sheet (summarized)				
Total assets				$65,503
Total liabilities				54,033
Total shareholders' equity...				11,470

Income Statements (excerpts)				
	2000	**1999**	**1998**	**1997**
Net income	$ 979*	$893	$703	$105
Revenues	100,789			

*Operating Income = $1,953
Interest expense = $838

Unknown to investors and lenders, Enron also controlled hundreds of partnerships that owed vast amounts of money. These special-purpose entities (SPEs) did not appear on the Enron financial statements. Assume that the SPEs' assets totalled $7,000 million and their liabilities stood at $6,900 million; assume a 10% interest rate on these liabilities.

During the four-year period up to December 31, 2000, Enron's stock price shot up from $17.50 to $90.56. Enron used its escalating stock price to finance the purchase of the SPEs by guaranteeing lenders that Enron would give them Enron stock if the SPEs could not pay their loans.

In 2002, the SEC launched an investigation into Enron's accounting practices. It was alleged that Enron should have been including the SPEs in its financial statements all along. Enron then restated net income for years up to 2000, wiping out nearly $600 million of total net income (and total assets) for this four-year period. Assume that $300 million of this loss applied to 2000. Enron's stock price tumbled, and the guarantees to the SPEs' lenders added millions to Enron's liabilities (assume the full amount of the SPEs' debt). To make matters worse, the assets of the SPEs lost much of their value; assume that their market value is only $500 million.

Requirements

1. Compute the debt ratio that Enron reported at the end of 2000. By using the DuPont model, which we discussed in Chapter 7 (page 345), compute Enron's return on total assets (ROA) for 2000. For this purpose, use only total assets at the end of 2000, rather than the average of 1999 and 2000.
2. Compute Enron's leverage ratio. Now compute Enron's return on equity (ROE) by multiplying the ROA computed in part 1 by the leverage ratio. Can you see anything unusual in these ratios that might have caused you to question them? Why or why not?
3. Add the asset and liability information about the SPEs to the reported amounts provided in the table. Recompute all ratios after including the SPEs in Enron's financial statements. Also, compute Enron's times-interest-earned ratio both ways for 2000. Assume that the changes to Enron's financial position occurred during 2000.
4. Why does it appear that Enron failed to include the SPEs in its financial statements? How do you view Enron after including the SPEs in the company's financial statements? (Challenge)

Case 2. Business is going well for Park'N Fly, the company that operates remote parking lots near major airports. The board of directors of this family-owned company believes that Park'N Fly could earn an additional $2 million income before interest and taxes by expanding into new markets. However, the $5 million that the business needs for growth cannot be raised within the family. The directors, who strongly wish to retain family control of the company, must consider issuing securities to outsiders. The directors are considering three financing plans.

Plan A is to borrow at 6%. Plan B is to issue 100,000 common shares. Plan C is to issue 100,000 non-voting, $3.75 preferred shares ($3.75 is the annual dividend paid on each preferred share).[*] Park'N Fly currently has net income of $3.5 million and 1 million common shares outstanding. The company's income tax rate is 25%.

LEARNING OBJECTIVE ⑤

Analyze alternative ways of raising $5 million

Requirements

1. Prepare an analysis to determine which plan will result in the highest earnings per common share.
2. Recommend one plan to the board of directors. Give your reasons.

Ethical Issues

Issue 1. Microsoft Corporation is the defendant in numerous lawsuits claiming unfair trade practices. Microsoft has strong incentives not to disclose these contingent liabilities; however, IFRS and ASPE generally require that companies disclose their contingent liabilities in the notes to their financial statements.

---

[*]For a discussion of preferred shares, see Chapter 10.

Requirements

1. Why would a company prefer not to disclose its contingent liabilities?
2. Describe how a bank could be harmed if a company seeking a loan did not disclose its contingent liabilities.
3. What is the ethical tightrope that companies must walk when they report their contingent liabilities?

Issue 2. The top managers of Medtech.com borrowed heavily to develop a prescription-medicine distribution system. Medtech's outlook was bright, and investors poured millions into the company. Sadly, Medtech never lived up to its potential, and the company is in bankruptcy. It can't pay about half of its liabilities.

Requirement

Is it unethical for managers to saddle a company with a high level of debt? Or, is it just risky? Who could be hurt by a company's taking on too much debt? Discuss.

Focus on Financials

LEARNING OBJECTIVE ❶❽

Report current and long-term liabilities

TELUS Corporation

Refer to TELUS's financial statements in Appendix A at the end of this book.

1. TELUS's balance sheet reports a current portion of long-term debt under current liabilities. Why is this portion of long-term debt reported as a current liability?
2. TELUS's Notes to the Financial Statements include note 22, "Commitments and contingent liabilities." What information does this provide to the user of these financial statements?

Focus on Analysis

LEARNING OBJECTIVE ❶❻❽

Record and analyze liabilities

TELUS Corporation

1. The Financing Activities section of TELUS's 2011 statement of cash flows reports three items related to short-term and long-term debts. Assume that each of these items involved a single transaction and journalize each one. Did TELUS borrow more or pay off more debt in 2011? Journalize these transactions.
2. How would you rate TELUS's debt-paying ability at the end of 2011: excellent, neutral, or poor? Support your conclusion with relevant ratios.

Group Projects

Project 1. Use the Internet to locate financial statements for a company in each of the following industries:

1. A bank
2. A magazine publisher
3. A department store

For each business, list all its liabilities—both current and long-term. Then compare the three lists to identify the liabilities that the three businesses have in common. Also, identify the liabilities that are unique to each type of business.

Quick Check Answers

1. *a*
2. *e*
3. *c* ($200,000 × 0.025 = $5,000)
4. *c* [400 × 0.05 × $40 = *warranty expense of $800; repaired $40 × 6 = $240; year-end liability = $560 ($800 − $240)*]
5. *c*
6. *e*
7. *a*
8. *b*
9. *c*
10. *b*
11. *e*
12. *a* ($196,140 × 0.10 × 6/12 = $9,807)
13. *d* [*Int. exp.* = $9,807 *Int. payment* = $9,500 ($200,000 × 0.095 × 6/12) $9,807 − $9,500 = $307]
14. *b* ($200,000 × 0.095 = $19,000)
15. *c* (*See amortization schedule*)

Date	Interest Payment	Interest Expense	Discount Amortiz.	Bond Carry Amt.
1/1/14				$196,140
7/1/14	$9,500	$9,807	$307	196,447
1/1/15	9,500	9,822	322	196,769

16. *d* {$196,140 + [($200,000 − $196,140) × 1/5] = $196,912}

10 Shareholders' Equity

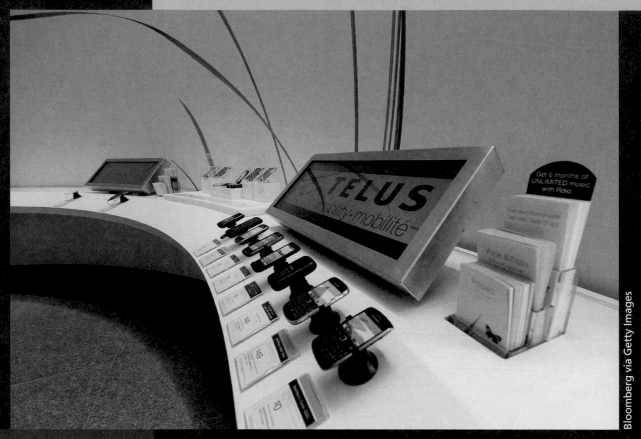

Bloomberg via Getty Images

SPOTLIGHT

Your parents have given you a $250 gift card from TELUS for your birthday. What will you buy: a tablet computer? A new smartphone with an extended service plan? We have featured TELUS in several places earlier in this text, so by now you're probably familiar with the company. During 2011, there were several changes in TELUS's shareholders' equity accounts. By the end of this chapter, you should be able to explain and account for many of these changes.

In this chapter, we'll show you how companies like TELUS account for the issuance of shares to investors. We'll also discuss other major components of shareholders' equity, such as Contributed Surplus and Retained Earnings, plus dividends and stock splits. In addition, you will learn how to interpret information about a company's share price and performance to decide if you'd want to buy shares in a company like TELUS. On the next page, you'll find details on the company's shareholders' equity as at December 31, 2011.

TELUS Corporation
Shareholders' Equity (Adapted)
As at December 31

	(in millions)	
	2011	**2010**
Non-voting share capital	3,337	3,327
Authorized: one billion non-voting shares without par value; issued and outstanding: 149,933,165 and 147,448,586 shares at December 31, 2011 and 2010, respectively		
Common share capital..	2,219	2,219
Authorized: one billion common shares without par value; issued and oustanding: 174,915,546 shares at December 31, 2011 and 2010		
Contributed surplus..	166	176
Accumulated other comprehensive income	11	1
Retained earnings...	1,780	2,126
	$7,513	$7,759

Chapters 4 to 9 discussed accounting for assets and liabilities. By this time, you should be familiar with most of the assets and liabilities listed on TELUS's balance sheet, so we will now focus on the major components of shareholders' equity. In this chapter, we discuss some of the issues a company faces when issuing shares and paying dividends.

Let's begin by looking at the key features of a corporation.

EXPLAIN THE MAIN FEATURES OF A CORPORATION

Anyone starting a business must decide how to organize the company. Corporations differ from proprietorships and partnerships in several ways.

SEPARATE LEGAL ENTITY. A corporation is a business entity formed under federal or provincial law. The federal or provincial government grants *articles of incorporation*, which consist of documents giving the governing body's permission to form a corporation. A corporation is a distinct entity, an artificial person that exists apart from its owners, the shareholders. The corporation has many of the same rights as a person. For example, a corporation may buy, own, and sell property. Assets and liabilities in the business belong to the corporation, not to its owners. The corporation may also enter into contracts, sue, and be sued.

Nearly all well-known companies, including TELUS, WestJet, and Shoppers Drug Mart, are corporations. Their legal names include *Limited*, *Corporation*, or *Incorporated* at the end (abbreviated *Ltd.*, *Corp.*, and *Inc.*) to indicate that they are corporations.

CONTINUOUS LIFE AND TRANSFERABILITY OF OWNERSHIP. Corporations have *continuous lives* regardless of changes in their ownership. The shareholders of a corporation may transfer shares as they wish. They may sell or trade the shares to another person, give them away, bequeath them in a will, or dispose of them in any other way. The transfer of the shares from one person to another does not affect the continuity of the corporation. In contrast, proprietorships and partnerships terminate when ownership changes.

LIMITED LIABILITY. Shareholders have **limited liability** for the corporation's debts, so they have no personal obligation to repay the company's liabilities. The most that a shareholder can lose on an investment in a corporation's shares is the cost of the investment. Limited liability is one of the most attractive features of the corporate form of organization. It enables corporations to raise more capital from a wider group of investors than proprietorships and partnerships. In contrast, proprietors and partners are personally liable for all the debts of their businesses (unless the business is organized as a limited liability partnership [LLP] or a limited liability company [LLC]).

SEPARATION OF OWNERSHIP AND MANAGEMENT. Shareholders own the corporation, but a *board of directors*—elected by the shareholders—appoints officers to manage the business. Thus, shareholders may invest $1,000 or $1 million in the corporation without having to manage it.

Company managers should run the business in the best interests of its shareholders, who rightfully own the company, but the separation between owners and managers may create problems. Corporate officers may run the business for their own benefit and not for the shareholders'. For example, the chief financial officer of Enron Corporation set up deals between Enron and several partnerships that he personally owned, enriching himself in the process, but harming the company and shareholders he worked for.

Some managers believe that their goal is to maximize the firm's value. Other managers believe that they should consider some or all of the other stakeholders of the corporation, such as employees, customers, the community where the company is located, and the environment.

CORPORATE TAXATION. Because corporations are separate legal entities, they must pay income taxes separate from those borne by their individual shareholders. Sole proprietors and partners pay individual income taxes based on their share of the business's income.

GOVERNMENT REGULATION. Because shareholders have only limited liability for corporation debts, outsiders doing business with the corporation can look no further than the corporation if it fails to pay. To protect a corporation's creditors and the shareholders, both federal and provincial governments monitor corporations. This regulation consists mainly of ensuring that corporations disclose the information in financial statements that investors and creditors need to make informed decisions.

Exhibit 10-1 summarizes the advantages and disadvantages of the corporate form of business organization.

EXHIBIT 10-1
Advantages and Disadvantages of a Corporation

Advantages	Disadvantages
1. Can raise more capital than a proprietorship or partnership	1. Separation of ownership and management
2. Continuous life	2. Corporate taxation
3. Ease of transferring ownership	3. Government regulation
4. Limited liability of shareholders	

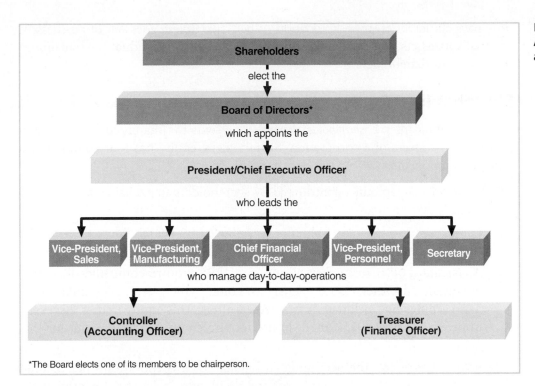

EXHIBIT 10-2
Authority Structure in a Large Corporation

*The Board elects one of its members to be chairperson.

Controlling and Managing a Corporation

The ultimate control of a corporation rests with the shareholders. The shareholders elect a *board of directors*, which sets the company policy and appoints officers. The board elects a **chairperson**, who usually is the most powerful person in the organization. The board also appoints the chief executive officer (CEO), who often also acts as the **president** in charge of day-to-day operations. Large corporations may also have vice-presidents in charge of sales, manufacturing, accounting and finance (the chief financial officer, or CFO), and other key areas. Exhibit 10-2 shows the authority structure in a large corporation.

Shareholders' Rights

Ownership of shares entitles shareholders to four basic rights, unless specific rights are withheld by agreement with the shareholders:

1. *The right to sell the shares.* Shareholders have the right to sell their shares to other parties when they no longer wish to own them.

2. *The right to vote.* Shareholders have the right to participate in management by voting on matters that come before them. This is the shareholder's sole voice in the management of the corporation. A shareholder is normally entitled to one vote for each common share owned. There are some classes of common shares that give the holder multiple votes or no vote.

3. *The right to receive dividends.* Shareholders have the right to receive a proportionate share of any distributions from the company's retained earnings. Each share in a particular class receives an equal dividend.

4. *The right to receive a residual interest upon liquidation.* Shareholders have the right to receive a proportionate share of any assets remaining after the corporation

pays all liabilities upon liquidation. When a company goes out of business, it sells its assets, pays its liabilities, and distributes any residual (or remaining) assets to shareholders.

Shareholders' Equity

As we saw in Chapter 1, *shareholders' equity* represents the shareholders' ownership interest in the assets of a corporation. Shareholders' equity has four common and separate components:

1. *Share capital*—amounts contributed by shareholders in exchange for shares in the corporation.

2. *Contributed surplus*—any amounts contributed by shareholders in excess of amounts allocated to share capital.

3. *Accumulated other comprehensive income*—IFRS require companies to report Accumulated Other Comprehensive Income, which is an accumulation of past earnings not included in retained earnings. This equity item is discussed in detail in Chapter 11. ASPE do not require companies to account for this item.

4. *Retained earning*—the accumulated balance of a corporation's net income since inception, less any net losses and dividends declared during this time. When the accumulation is a negative number, the term *deficit* is used to describe it.

A corporation issues *share certificates* to its owners in exchange for their investment in the business—usually cash. The basic unit of share capital is called a *share*. A corporation may issue a share certificate for any number of shares it wishes—one share, 100 shares, or any other number—but the total number of *authorized* shares is limited by charter. Shares are sometimes referred to as *stock*, particularly in the United States, but owning stock in a company means the same thing as owning shares in that company.

The terms *authorized*, *issued*, and *outstanding* are frequently used to describe a corporation's shares. *Authorized* refers to the maximum number of shares a corporation is allowed to distribute to shareholders. Companies incorporated under the *Canada Business Corporations Act* are permitted to issue an unlimited number of shares. *Issued* refers to the number of shares sold or transferred to shareholders. *Outstanding shares* are those actually in the hands of shareholders. Sometimes a company repurchases shares it has previously issued so that the number of shares outstanding will be less than the number of shares issued. For example, if a corporation issued 100,000 shares and later repurchased 20,000 shares, then the number of shares outstanding would be 80,000. The total number of shares outstanding at any time represents 100% ownership of the corporation.

Classes of Shares

Corporations issue different types of shares to appeal to a variety of investors. Every corporation issues *common shares*, which IFRS also refer to as *ordinary shares*, meaning they are subordinate to all other classes of shares a company is authorized to issue. Unless designated otherwise, the word *share* is understood to mean "common share." Common shareholders have the four basic rights of share ownership, unless a right is specifically withheld. For example, some companies, including TELUS, issue voting and non-voting common shares. In describing a corporation, we would say the common shareholders are the owners of the business. They stand to benefit the most if the corporation succeeds because they take the most risk by investing in common shares. The shares of a corporation may be either common shares or preferred shares.

Preferred shares give their owners certain advantages over common shareholders. Preferred shareholders receive dividends before the common shareholders and receive assets before the common shareholders if the corporation liquidates. Preferred shares are typically non-voting shares, but they have the other three basic shareholder rights. Companies may issue different classes of preferred shares (Class A and Class B or Series A and Series B, for example). Each class is recorded in a separate account.

Preferred shares are a hybrid of common shares and long-term debt. Like debt, preferred shares pay a fixed amount to the investor in the form of a dividend. Like common shares, the dividend does not have to be paid unless the board of directors has declared the dividend. Also, companies have no obligation to pay back true preferred shares. Preferred shares that must be redeemed (paid back) by the corporation are a liability masquerading as a stock and must be accounted for as such.

Preferred shares are much less frequently issued than common shares. A recent survey of over 600 companies found that fewer than 10% of them had issued preferred shares. TELUS, for example, is authorized to issue two billion preferred shares, but as at the end of 2011, none of them have actually been issued.

PAR VALUE AND STATED VALUE. **Par value shares** are shares of stock that have a value assigned to them by the articles of incorporation, which specify the legal details associated with a company's incorporation. *The Canada Business Corporations Act* and most provincial incorporating acts now require common and preferred shares to be issued without par value. Neither TELUS's common nor its non-voting shares have a par value. Instead, the shares are assigned a value when they are issued; this value is known as the **stated value**.

ACCOUNT FOR THE ISSUANCE OF SHARES

OBJECTIVE

❷ **Account** for the issuance of shares

Large corporations, such as Hudson's Bay Company and EnCana Corp., need huge amounts of money to operate. Such corporations usually sell their newly issued shares though an *underwriter*, such as the brokerage firms ScotiaMcLeod and BMO Nesbitt Burns.

ISSUING SHARES FOR CASH. Suppose that on January 8, 2014, George Weston Ltd. issued 100,000 common shares for cash for $50 each. The entry to record the issuance of these shares is:

```
2014
Jan. 8   Cash ...........................................................  5,000,000
             Common Share Capital ...............................              5,000,000
         To issue common shares at $50.00 per share
         (100,000 × $50.00).
```

ASSETS	=	LIABILITIES	+	SHAREHOLDERS' EQUITY
+5,000,000	=			+5,000,000 Share Capital

After this transaction, the number of common shares outstanding would increase by 100,000, and the company's common share capital would increase by $5,000,000.

It is important to note that when one shareholder of a company sells some of their shares to another shareholder, there is no impact on the accounts of the company due to the separate-entity concept, which was introduced in Chapter 1. Only when a company is party to a share transaction are its accounts affected.

<table>
<tr><td rowspan="6">STOP
+
THINK
(10-1)</td><td colspan="2">Examine the details of TELUS's Shareholders' Equity on page 475, then answer these questions:</td></tr>
<tr><td>1. How many more voting common shares is TELUS legally allowed to issue if it wants to raise more capital?</td><td>2. Assuming no shares were repurchased in 2011, how many shares did TELUS issue in 2011?

3. What is the average issue price of each of the two types of TELUS shares outstanding?</td></tr>
</table>

ISSUING SHARES FOR ASSETS OTHER THAN CASH. Companies sometimes issue shares in return for assets other than cash. When a transaction like this occurs, the company is required to measure the transaction based on the fair value of the assets received. If that fair value cannot be determined, the fair value of the shares given up will be the value assigned to the transaction.

For example, if on November 12, 2014, Kahn Corporation issued 15,000 common shares in return for equipment worth $4,000 and a building worth $120,000, it would record this entry:

```
2014
Nov. 12  Equipment.................................................    4,000
         Building...................................................  120,000
             Common Share Capital..............................               124,000
         To issue common shares in exchange for equipment
         and a building.
```

ASSETS	=	LIABILITIES	=	SHAREHOLDERS' EQUITY
+4,000 +120,000	=			+124,000 Share capital

Accounting for the issuance of preferred shares (or other kinds of non-voting shares) for cash or other assets is the same as that for common shares, except for the name of the share capital account used, which will match the type of shares being issued.

COOKING THE BOOKS
WITH SHARE CAPITAL

The issuance of shares for *cash* poses no ethical challenge. There is no difficulty in valuing shares issued for cash because the value of the cash—and therefore the shares—is obvious.

Issuing shares for *assets other than cash*, however, can pose an ethical challenge. The company issuing the shares often wishes to record a large amount for the non-cash asset received (such as land or a building) and for the shares that it is issuing. Why? Because large asset and shareholders' equity amounts on the balance sheet make the business look more prosperous and more creditworthy.

A company is supposed to record an asset received at its current fair value. But one person's perception of a particular asset's fair value can differ from another person's opinion. One person may appraise land at a fair value of $400,000. Another may honestly believe the land is worth only $300,000. A company receiving land in exchange for its shares must decide whether to record the land received and the shares issued at $300,000, at $400,000, or at some amount in between.

The ethical course of action is to record the asset at its current fair value, as determined by a good-faith estimate of fair value from independent appraisers. It is rare for a corporation to be found guilty of *understating* the asset values on its balance sheet, but companies have been embarrassed by *overstating* these values. Investors who rely on the financial statements may be able to prove in court that an overstatement of asset values caused them to pay too much for the company's shares. Creditors who rely on financial statements may also be able to prove in court that an overstatement of asset values caused them to loan the corporation more than if the asset values were correctly stated. In both cases, the court may render a judgment against the company. For this reason, companies often value assets conservatively.

MID-CHAPTER SUMMARY PROBLEM

1. Test your understanding of the first half of this chapter by deciding whether each of the following statements is true or false.

   a. The policy-making body in a corporation is called the board of directors.

   b. The owner of 100 preferred shares has greater voting rights than the owner of 100 common shares.

   c. Issuance of 1,000 common shares at $12 per share increases share capital by $12,000.

   d. A corporation issues its preferred shares in exchange for land and a building with a combined fair value of $200,000. This transaction increases the corporation's owners' equity by $200,000 regardless of the assets' prior book values.

   e. Preferred shares are a riskier investment than common shares.

2. Adolfo Inc., an auto parts manufacturer, has two classes of common shares. Class A shares are entitled to one vote, whereas Class B shares are entitled to 100 votes. The two classes rank equally for dividends. The following is extracted from a recent annual report:

Shareholders' Equity

Share capital	
Class A common shares, no stated value (authorized and issued 1,260 shares).....	$ 1,260
Class B common shares, no stated value (authorized and issued 46,200 shares).....	11,000
	12,260
Retained earnings...	872,403
	$884,663

Requirements

a. Record the issuance of the Class A common shares. Use the Adolfo Inc. account titles.

b. Record the issuance of the Class B common shares. Use the Adolfo Inc. account titles.

c. How much of Adolfo Inc.'s shareholders' equity was contributed by the shareholders? How much was provided by profitable operations? Does this division of equity suggest that the company has been successful? Why or why not?

d. Write a sentence to describe what Adolfo Inc.'s shareholders' equity balance means.

ANSWERS

1. a. True   b. False (preferred shares typically do not have voting rights)   c. True
   d. True   e. False (preferred shares typically have a fixed dividend right and first claim to residual assets upon dissolution or liquidation of the company)

2. a. Cash...   1,260
       Class A Common Shares   1,260
       To record issuance of Class A common shares.

   b. Cash...   11,000
       Class B Common Shares...   11,000
       To record issuance of Class B common shares.

   c. Contributed by the shareholders: $12,260 ($1,260 + $11,000).
   Provided by profitable operations: $872,403.
   This division suggests that the company has been successful because almost all of its shareholders' equity has come from profitable operations.

   d. The total of Adolfo's shareholders' equity indicates that the shareholders have a claim to $884,663 of the company's assets.

> a. and b. Share issuances increase assets (cash) and shareholders' equity.
>
> Compare the fraction of shareholders' equity contributed by shareholders to the fraction contributed by retained earnings. A greater retained earnings fraction is positive.
>
> Shareholders' equity is the net worth of the company (Assets − Liabilities).

OBJECTIVE

❸ **Explain** why a company repurchases shares

EXPLAIN WHY A COMPANY REPURCHASES SHARES

Corporations may repurchase their own shares for several reasons:

1. The company needs the **repurchased shares** to fulfill future share issuance commitments, such as those related to share option plans and conversions of bonds and preferred shares into common shares.

2. The purchase may help support the share's current **market price** by decreasing the supply of shares available to the public, which will usually result in an increase in the market price per share.

3. Management wants to avoid a takeover by an outside party, so it repurchases a significant proportion of its own shares to prevent the other party from acquiring them.

In basic terms, when a company repurchases shares, share capital and total shareholders' equity decrease, but the actual IFRS guidance on accounting for share repurchases is vague and sometimes difficult to interpret. In addition, ASPE offer two choices for how to account for repurchases, both of which differ from IFRS guidance. Given the complex and differing treatments of share repurchases, accounting for them will be left for those students who take intermediate financial accounting.

ACCOUNT FOR RETAINED EARNINGS, DIVIDENDS, AND STOCK SPLITS

The Retained Earnings account carries the accumulated balance of the corporation's net income less its net losses and any dividends declared over its lifetime. *The Retained Earnings account is not a reservoir of cash available for paying dividends or investing in other business activities.* In fact, the corporation may have a large balance in Retained Earnings, but not have any cash for dividends or investing. *Cash and Retained Earnings are two entirely separate accounts with no relationship to each other.* A $500,000 balance in Retained Earnings says nothing about the company's Cash balance.

A *credit* balance in Retained Earnings is normal, indicating that the corporation's lifetime earnings exceed its lifetime losses and dividends. A *debit* balance in Retained Earnings arises when a corporation's lifetime losses and dividends exceed its lifetime earnings. Called a **deficit**, this amount is subtracted from the sum of the other equity accounts to determine total shareholders' equity. Deficits are not uncommon.

Declaring and Paying Dividends

Corporations distribute past earnings to shareholders by declaring and then paying *dividends*. The majority of dividends are paid in cash, but companies sometimes pay stock dividends as well. In this section, we first present the accounting for cash dividends and then show you how to account for stock dividends.

Cash Dividends

Before a company can pay a cash dividend, it must have:

1. Retained Earnings in excess of the desired dividend and
2. Enough Cash to pay the dividend.

A corporation *declares* a dividend before paying it, and only the board of directors has the authority to declare a dividend. The corporation has no obligation to pay a dividend until the board declares one, but once declared, the dividend becomes a legal liability of the corporation. There are three relevant dates for dividends: the *date of declaration*, the *date of record,* and the *date of payment.* The following example illustrates the distinction between these dates.

1. The **date of declaration** is the date on which the board of directors officially declares the payment of a dividend, creating a liability for the amount declared. If the board declares a dividend of $50,000 on June 19, 2014, the entry to account for it is:

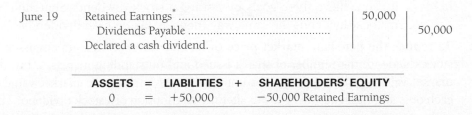

June 19	Retained Earnings*	50,000	
	Dividends Payable		50,000
	Declared a cash dividend.		

ASSETS	=	LIABILITIES	+	SHAREHOLDERS' EQUITY
0	=	+50,000		−50,000 Retained Earnings

---

*In Chapter 2, we debited a Dividends account to clearly identify the purpose of the payment. From here on, we follow the more common practice of debiting the Retained Earnings account for dividend declarations.

2. The **date of record** follows the declaration date. In order to receive the declared dividend, one must be officially registered as a shareholder of the company on this date. Let's assume the date of record in our illustration is July 1. This date has no accounting implications, so no entry is needed.

3. The **date of payment** is the date on which the dividend is actually paid to shareholders. If the $50,000 dividend declared on June 19 to shareholders of record on July 1 is paid on July 10, the entry would be:

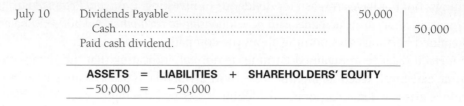

July 10	Dividends Payable	50,000	
	Cash		50,000
	Paid cash dividend.		

ASSETS	=	LIABILITIES	+	SHAREHOLDERS' EQUITY
−50,000	=	−50,000		

The preceding illustration applies to cash dividends declared and paid on any type of shares.

Stock Dividends

When a company declares a **stock dividend**, it eventually pays the dividend by issuing additional shares of the company instead of by distributing cash. The total dollar value of a stock dividend is determined by multiplying the number of shares to be issued by the market price of the shares on the date of declaration. For example, if a stock dividend totalling 100,000 shares is declared on a day when the shares are valued at $10 each, then the amount of the dividend would be $1,000,000.

The relevant dates for stock dividends are the same as those for cash dividends, but the journal entries differ. On the date of declaration, we debit Retained Earnings and credit Stock Dividends Distributable (a contra-equity account). On the date of payment, we debit Stock Dividends Distributable and credit the relevant Share Capital account. A stock dividend, therefore, has no impact on the total shareholders' equity balance because Share Capital increases and Retained Earnings decreases by the same amount.

The corporation distributes stock dividends to shareholders in proportion to the number of shares they already own. If you own 300 common shares of TELUS, for example, and TELUS distributes a 10% common shares dividend, you will receive 30 (300 × 0.10) additional shares. You would then own 330 common shares. All other TELUS shareholders would also receive additional shares equal to 10% of their prior holdings.

Why would a company issue a stock dividend instead of a cash dividend? A corporation may choose to distribute stock dividends for the following reasons:

1. **To continue dividends but conserve cash.** A company may wish to conserve cash to fund its business activities while still distributing dividends to its shareholders. It can achieve these goals by issuing a stock dividend. Shareholders pay tax on stock dividends the same way they pay tax on cash dividends.

2. **To reduce the per-share market price of its shares.** When a company issues a stock dividend, the number of shares issued and outstanding increases, but the market value of the company does not change. As a result, the market value of each outstanding share will be lower after the distribution of a stock dividend. This makes the company's shares less expensive, and therefore more affordable to some investors. Assume, for example, that a company with 100,000 common shares outstanding and a market value of $1,000,000 declares and pays a 10% stock dividend. Before the dividend, the market value per share is $10 ($1,000,000/100,000 shares), but after the dividend it is only $9.09 ($1,000,000/110,000 shares).

> **STOP + THINK (10-2)**
>
> Company A and Company B both have 200,000 common shares outstanding. On June 30, Company A declares a 10% stock dividend and Company B declares a 20% stock dividend. The common shares of both companies have a $10 market value per share on this date.
>
> 1. Which company's shareholders' equity will decrease the most after distributing these stock dividends?
> 2. Which company will have a lower market value per share after distributing these dividends?

Dividends on Preferred Shares

EXPRESSING THE DIVIDEND ON PREFERRED SHARES. Dividends on preferred shares are expressed as an annual dollar figure or as a percentage of the share's stated value. Scotiabank, for example, had some $1.20 preferred shares outstanding in July 2012, indicating that the holder of one of these shares could receive $1.20 in dividends per year.

DIVIDENDS ON PREFERRED AND COMMON SHARES. When a company has issued both preferred and common shares, the preferred shareholders receive their dividends first. The common shareholders receive dividends only if the total declared dividend is large enough to pay the preferred shareholders in full.

Pinecraft Industries Inc. has 100,000 shares of $1.50 cumulative preferred shares outstanding in addition to its common shares. Assume that in 2014, Pinecraft declares an annual dividend of $1,000,000. The allocation to preferred and common shareholders is as follows:

Preferred dividend (100,000 shares × $1.50 per share)	$ 150,000
Common dividend (remainder: $1,000,000 − $150,000)	850,000
Total dividend	$1,000,000

If Pinecraft declares only a $200,000 dividend, preferred shareholders receive $150,000, and the common shareholders receive the remaining, $50,000 ($200,000 − $150,000). A dividend of $150,000 or less would result in the common shareholders receiving no dividend.

DIVIDENDS ON CUMULATIVE AND NON-CUMULATIVE PREFERRED SHARES. The allocation of dividends may be complex if the preferred shares are *cumulative*. Corporations sometimes fail to pay a dividend to preferred shareholders. This is called *passing the dividend*, and any passed dividends on cumulative preferred shares are said to be *in arrears*. The owners of **cumulative preferred shares** must receive all dividends in arrears plus the current year's dividend before the corporation can pay dividends to the common shareholders. Preferred shares are assumed to be non-cumulative, unless otherwise stated.

The preferred shares of Pinecraft Industries Inc. are cumulative. Suppose the company passed the 2013 preferred dividend of $150,000. Before paying dividends to its common shareholders in 2014, the company must first pay preferred dividends of $150,000 for both 2013 and 2014, a total of $300,000. Assume that Pinecraft declared a dividend of $500,000 on September 6, 2014. The entry to record this declaration is:

2014			
Sept. 6	Retained Earnings	500,000	
	Dividends Payable, Preferred ($150,000 × 2)		300,000
	Dividends Payable, Common ($500,000 − $300,000)		200,000
	To declare a cash dividend.		

Note that even though dividends of $150,000 were in arrears at the end of 2013, no liability for these dividends is recorded until the board declares a dividend. If the preferred shares are *non-cumulative*, the corporation is not obligated to pay preferred dividends in arrears.

Stock Splits

When a company wishes to increase or decrease its market value per share without altering its assets, liabilities, or shareholders' equity, it can declare a **stock split**, which results in an increase or decrease in the number of issued and outstanding shares of the company, but does not affect any financial statement balances. On August 10, 2012, for example, The Coca-Cola Company (KO) executed a 2-for-1 stock split, which resulted in its shareholders receiving two company shares in exchange for each one they already owned. As a result of this split, the number of KO shares issued and outstanding doubled from 5.6 billion to 11.2 billion. Just prior to the split, KO shares were trading at around $78. With twice as many shares outstanding after the split, the price per share immediately declined to about $39 because neither the total market value nor the book value of Coca-Cola changed as a result of the stock split.

Companies typically split their stock when they think their share price has become too expensive or if the stock is trading too far above similar companies' stock. If a company wishes to alter its share price by something other than the 50% decrease seen in the Coca-Cola example, it merely has to change the split ratio. If, for example, a company wanted to decrease its share price from $400 to $100, it would execute a 4-for-1 stock split, which would result in there being four times as many shares issued and outstanding after the split.

Sometimes, companies want to *increase* their share price because a very low share price often deters investors from buying the stock. Assume, for instance, that a company wants to increase its share price from $0.50 to $1.50 so it is no longer considered a penny stock (an unflattering term for a stock trading below $1 per share). It could do this by executing a 1-for-3 stock split, which means the company would issue one share in exchange for every three shares owned by a shareholder. After this split, there would be one-third as many shares issued and outstanding, resulting in a tripling of the share price. Splits like this, where the number of shares issued and outstanding decreases, are often called *reverse stock splits*.

Regardless of whether a company executes a normal stock split or a reverse split, there is no impact *on the accounts of the company,* so no journal entries are needed in the event of a stock split. From a record-keeping perspective, the only change is the number of shares issued and outstanding, and this change, along with a description of the stock split, would be disclosed in the statement of owners' equity and the notes to the financial statements.

Summary of the Effects on Assets, Liabilities, and Shareholders' Equity

We've seen how to account for the basic shareholders' equity transactions and events:

- Issuance of shares (pp. 479–481)
- Cash dividends (pp. 483–484)
- Stock dividends (pp. 484–485)
- Stock splits (p. 486)

EXHIBIT 10-5
Formats for Reporting Shareholders' Equity

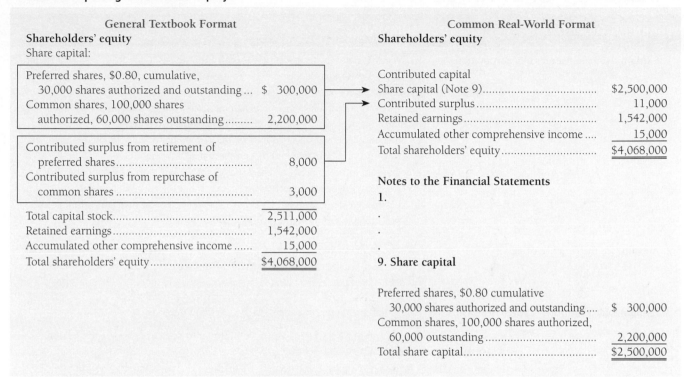

In general, the following are a few of the key pieces of equity information that must be disclosed in the balance sheet, statement of changes in owners' equity (see Chapter 11), or the notes:

- Number of authorized, issued, and outstanding shares, and changes in these amounts during the year, for each class of share capital; their par value, if any; dividend rights and preferences; and other restrictions and features.
- Contributed surplus.
- Accumulated other comprehensive income (IFRS only).
- Retained earnings.

Summary of IFRS-ASPE Differences

Concept	IFRS	ASPE
Accumulated other comprehensive income (p. 478)	Included as a component of shareholders' equity.	No accounting or reporting of this component is required.
Repurchase of shares (p. 492)	There are significant differences between IFRS and ASPE when accounting for share repurchases. These differences, and the inherent complexity of accounting for share repurchases in general, are beyond the scope of this textbook.	
Reporting of dividends on the statement of cash flows (p. 492)	May be reported as an operating activity or a financing activity at the company's discretion.	Must be reported as a financing activity.

SUMMARY OF CHAPTER 10

LEARNING OBJECTIVE	SUMMARY
1. **Explain** the main features of a corporation	1. A corporation is a separate legal entity that exists apart from its shareholders. 2. A corporation has a continuous life regardless of changes in ownership, and its shareholders may buy and sell their shares as they wish. 3. A corporation's shareholders have limited liability for the company's debts. The most they can lose is the amount of their initial investment. 4. Shareholders own the corporation, but company policy is set by the board of directors and implemented by company management. 5. Corporations pay income taxes separate from those borne by their shareholders. 6. Corporations are regulated by the government to ensure they report and disclose the information in their financial statements that investors and creditors need to make informed decisions.
2. **Account** for the issuance of shares	Shares are normally issued for cash, but they can also be issued in exchange for other assets, such as land or equipment. When shares are issued, the relevant Asset account is debited and the relevant Share Capital account is credited.
3. **Explain** why a company repurchases shares	Corporations repurchase their shares for several reasons: 1. To fulfill future share issuance commitments, such as those related to stock option plans. 2. To help support the corporation's market price per share by reducing the number of shares outstanding. 3. To avoid a takeover by an outside party.
4. **Account** for retained earnings, dividends, and stock splits	Retained earnings are the accumulation of a corporation's net income since inception less any net losses and dividends distributed. Dividends are commonly paid in cash, but they can also be distributed in the form of additional stock in the corporation, which is known as a stock dividend. On the date of declaration, Retained Earnings is debited and Dividends Payable is credited for the amount of the cash dividend declared. Parties officially registered as shareholders of the corporation on the date of record will receive the dividend when it is paid (no journal entry is needed in connection with the date of record). On the date of payment of a cash dividend, Dividends Payable is debited and Cash is credited. For a stock dividend, on the date of declaration, we debit Retained Earnings and credit Stock Dividends Distributable (a contra-equity account). On the date of payment, we debit Stock Dividends Distributable and credit the relevant Share Capital account. Stock splits are executed to increase or decrease the number of shares issued and outstanding, thereby decreasing or increasing the market price per share. An X-for-Y stock split, when X is greater than Y, increases the number of shares issued and outstanding and reduces the market price per share. If X is less than Y, the number of shares issued and outstanding decreases, and the market price per share increases. Stock splits have no effect on the corporation's shareholders' equity balances.
5. **Distinguish** between fair value and book value per share	The fair value (or market price) of a share of a company's stock is the price that a willing buyer would pay a willing seller to acquire the share. The book value of a share of a company's common stock indicates the dollar value of net assets a common shareholder would receive for each share *after* the preferred shareholders (if any) have received their share of the net assets.

| 6. **Evaluate** a company's return on equity using DuPont analysis | A company's return on equity (ROE) indicates how much profit it has generated for each dollar of common shareholder's equity it has. It can be calculated and analyzed using DuPont analysis, which incorporates three ratios introduced in prior chapters:

ROE = Net profit margin × Asset turnover × Leverage ratio

It can also be calculated directly, as follows:

$$ROE = \frac{\text{Net income} - \text{Preferred dividends}}{\text{Average common shareholders' equity}}$$

Generally, the higher a company's ROE, the better its profitability. A company's ROE is best evaluated by comparing it to prior years' returns and to the returns of major competitors. |
| 7. **Report** equity transactions and events in the financial statements | A corporation's equity transactions and events are reported in the Financing Activities section of its statement of cash flows. Common equity transactions and events include:

• Issuances of shares
• Repurchases of shares
• Payment of cash dividends (may instead be reported as operating activity under IFRS)

A corporation must also disclose the following equity information in its balance sheet, statement of changes in owners' equity (see Chapter 11), or the notes:

• Number of authorized, issued, and outstanding shares and changes in these amounts during the year for each class of share capital; their par value, if any; dividend rights and preferences; and other restrictions and features
• Contributed surplus
• Accumulated other comprehensive income (IFRS only)
• Retained earnings |

END-OF-CHAPTER SUMMARY PROBLEM

1. The balance sheet of Quetico Inc. reported the following at December 31, 2014:

Shareholders' Equity

Preferred shares, $0.40, 10,000 shares authorized and issued	$ 100,000
Common shares, 100,000 shares authorized*	400,000
Accumulated other comprehensive income	224,000
Retained earnings	476,500
Total shareholders' equity	$1,200,500

*The common shares were issued at a stated value of $8.00 per share.

Requirements

    a. Are the preferred shares cumulative or non-cumulative? How can you tell?

    b. What is the total amount of the annual preferred dividend?

    c. How many common shares are outstanding?

    d. Compute the book value per share of the common shares. No preferred dividends are in arrears, and Quetico Inc. has not yet declared the 2014 dividend.

2. Use the following accounts and related balances to prepare the classified balance sheet of Gandhi Ltd. at September 30, 2014. Use the account format of the balance sheet.

Common shares,		Property, plant, and	
50,000 shares authorized,		equipment, net	$266,000
20,000 shares issued	$100,000	Accounts receivable, net	23,000
Dividends payable	4,000	Preferred shares, $3.75,	
Cash	9,000	10,000 shares authorized,	
Accounts payable	28,000	2,000 shares issued	24,000
Long-term note payable	80,000	Accrued liabilities	3,000
Inventory	85,000	Retained earnings	104,000
Accumulated other			
comprehensive income	40,000		

All features must be specified in the financial statements.

Details should be given on the balance sheet.

ANSWERS

1. a. The preferred shares are not cumulative because they are not specifically labelled cumulative.

Each common share was sold for the $8 stated value.

b. Total annual preferred dividend: $4,000 (10,000 × $0.40).

c. Common shares outstanding: 50,000 shares ($400,000 ÷ $8 stated value).

d. Book value per common share:

Book value per common share must exclude any amounts pertaining to preferred shares.

Common:	
Total shareholders' equity	$1,200,500
Less shareholders' equity allocated to preferred	(100,000)
Shareholders' equity allocated to common	$1,100,500
Book value per share ($1,100,500 ÷ 50,000 shares)	$ 22.01

The classified balance sheet must specify current assets and current liabilities. Make sure that Total assets = Total liabilities + Shareholders' equity.

2.

Gandhi Ltd.
Balance Sheet
As at September 30, 2014

Assets		Liabilities		
Current		Current		
Cash	$ 9,000	Accounts payable	$ 28,000	
Accounts receivable, net	23,000	Dividends payable	4,000	
Inventory	85,000	Accrued liabilities	3,000	
Total current assets	117,000	Total current liabilities	35,000	
Property, plant, and equipment, net	266,000	Long-term note payable	80,000	
		Total liabilities		$115,000
		Shareholders' Equity		
		Preferred shares, $3.75,		
		10,000 shares authorized,		
		2,000 shares issued	$ 24,000	
		Common shares,		
		50,000 shares authorized,		
		20,000 shares issued	100,000	
		Retained earnings	104,000	
		Accumulated other		
		comprehensive income	40,000	
		Total shareholders' equity		268,000
		Total liabilities and		
Total assets	$383,000	shareholders' equity		$383,000

STOP + THINK (10-1)	ANSWERS

1. 825,084,454 shares (1 billion authorized − 174,915,546 issued and outstanding)
2. No common shares were issued in 2011, as indicated by there being the same number of common shares issued and outstanding at the end of 2010 and 2011. The number of non-voting shares issued and outstanding did increase in 2011, from 147,448,586 to 149,933,165, indicating 2,484,579 of these shares were issued during the year.

3. Average issue price per non-voting share = $22.26 ($3,337 million of non-voting share capital/149,933,165 shares outstanding).

   Average issue price per common share = $12.69 ($2,219 million of common share capital/174,915,546 shares outstanding).

STOP + THINK (10-2)	ANSWERS

1. There will be no decrease in shareholders' equity for either company because stock dividends have no net impact on this total. Share capital increases and retained earnings decrease by the same amount, regardless of the size of the stock dividend.
2. Company A's market value per share after stock dividend = $9.09 ($2,000,000 total market value/220,000 shares issued and outstanding).

Company B's market value per share after stock dividend = $8.33 ($2,000,000 total market value/240,000 shares issued and outstanding).

Company B will have a lower market value per share after the stock dividends are distributed.

STOP + THINK (10-3)	ANSWERS

1. $7,250,000 ($500,000 from preferred shareholders + $6,750,000 from common shareholders)
2. $4,900,000 (Retained Earnings of $3,250,000 + Dividends Paid of $1,650,000)
3. Unknown (Cash balance not provided; *Retained Earnings does not equal cash*)
4. $10,000,000 or $20/share (Total shareholders' equity of $10,500,000 − Preferred shareholders' equity

of $500,000 = Common shareholders' equity of $10,000,000 /500,000 shares = $20/share)
5. $260,000 ($310,000 total − $50,000 to preferred shareholders)
6. 750,000 (500,000 common shares outstanding divided by 2, then multiplied by 3). The split would have no effect on shareholders' equity, as only the number of shares issued and outstanding changes.

Review Shareholders' Equity

QUICK CHECK (ANSWERS ARE GIVEN ON PAGE 520.)

1. Copeland Company is authorized to issue 40,000 $10 common shares. On January 15, 2014, Copeland issued 10,000 shares at $15 per share. Copeland's journal entry to record these facts should include a
   a. credit to Common Shares for $100,000.
   b. credit to Common Shares for $150,000.
   c. debit to Common Shares for $150,000.
   d. Both a and b

Questions 2 through 5 use the following account balances of Casio Co. at March 31, 2014:

Number of common shares authorized	1,000,000	Number of common shares issued	180,000
		Cash	$ 74,000
Dividends Payable	$ 22,000	Common Shares	180,000
Preferred Shares	100,000	Retained Earnings	200,000

2. Casio has issued _____ common shares.
   a. 74,000
   (b.) 180,000
   c. 225,000
   d. some other amount
3. Casio's total share capital at March 31, 2014, is
   a. $495,000.
   b. $180,000.
   c. $1,175,000.
   (d.) some other amount. *280,000*
4. Casio's total shareholders' equity as of March 31, 2014, is
   a. $1,406,000.
   b. $1,249,000.
   (c.) $480,000. *180+200+100*
   d. $1,480,000.
5. What would Casio's total shareholders' equity be if it executed a 2-for-1 stock split on April 1, 2014? ___*480,000*___
6. Woodstock Corporation executed a 3-for-1 stock split on a day when its shares had a market price of $0.75 per share. After the split, what would you expect its share price to be? __*.75*__
7. The shareholders' equity section of a corporation's balance sheet reports

Common Shares	Discount on Bonds Payable
(a.) Yes	No
b. No	Yes
c. Yes	Yes
d. No	No

8. The repurchase of a company's own shares
   a. increases one asset and decreases another asset.
   (b.) decreases total assets and decreases total shareholders' equity.
   c. has no effect on total assets total liabilities, or total shareholders' equity.
   d. decreases total assets and increases total shareholders' equity.
9. When does a cash dividend become a legal liability?
   a. On date of payment
   b. On date of record
   (c.) On date of declaration
   d. It never becomes a liability because it is paid.
10. When do dividends increase shareholders' equity?
    (a.) Never
    b. On date of declaration
    c. On date of record
    d. On date of payment
11. Willow Run Mall Inc. has 5,000 $2 cumulative preferred shares and 100,000 common shares outstanding. At the beginning of the current year, preferred dividends were three years in arrears. Willow Run's board of directors wants to pay a $1.25 cash dividend on each share of outstanding common shares. To accomplish this, what total amount of dividends must Willow Run declare?
    a. $170,000
    b. $185,000
    (c.) $165,000
    d. Some other amount $_____
12. Which of the following is true of stock dividends?
    (a.) They have no effect on total shareholders' equity.
    b. They are distributions of cash to shareholders.
    c. They reduce the total assets of the company.
    d. They increase the corporation's total liabilities.

13. What is the effect of a stock split and a stock dividend on total assets?

Stock Split	Stock Dividend
a. Decrease	No effect
b. Decrease	Decrease
c. No effect	Decrease
d. No effect	No effect

14. A 2-for-1 stock split has the same effect on the number of shares being issued as a
   a. 20% stock dividend.
   b. 50% stock dividend.
   c. 100% stock dividend.
   d. 200% stock dividend.

15. The denominator for computing the return on equity is
   a. average common shareholders' equity.
   b. average total assets.
   c. net sales.
   d. net income.

Accounting Vocabulary

book value (of a share) Amount of owners' equity on the company's books for each share of its stock.   (p. 487)

chairperson Elected by a corporation's board of directors, usually the most powerful person in the corporation.   (p. 477)

cumulative preferred shares Preferred shares whose owners must receive all dividends in arrears plus the current year's dividend before the corporation can pay dividends to the common shareholders.   (p. 485)

date of declaration The date on which the Board of Directors declares a dividend to shareholders.   (p. 483)

date of payment The date on which a dividend is actually paid to shareholders.   (p. 484)

date of record The date on which a person must be recorded as a shareholder in order to receive a dividend.   (p. 484)

deficit Debit balance in the Retained Earnings account.   (p. 483)

DuPont analysis A detailed approach to analyzing rate of return on equity (ROE), calculated as follows: Net profit margin (net income/net sales) × Total asset turnover (net sales/average total assets) × Leverage ratio (average total assets/average common shareholders' equity). The first two components of the model comprise return on assets (ROA).   (p. 489)

fair value (of a share) The price that a willing buyer would pay a willing seller to acquire a share.   (p. 487)

limited liability No personal obligation of a shareholder for corporation debts. A shareholder can lose no more on an investment in a corporation's shares than the cost of the investment.   (p. 476)

market price (of a share) The price that a willing buyer would pay a willing seller to acquire a share.   (p. 482)

par value shares Shares of stock that do not have a value assigned to them by articles of the corporation.   (p. 479)

preferred shares Shares that give their owners certain advantages, such as the priority to receive dividends before the common shareholders and the priority to receive assets before the common shareholders if the corporation liquidates.   (p. 479)

president Chief executive officer in charge of managing the day-to-day operations of a corporation.   (p. 477)

repurchased shares A corporation's own shares that it has issued and later reacquired.   (p. 482)

return on assets (ROA) Measures how profitably management has used the assets that shareholders and creditors have provided the company.   (p. 489)

return on equity (ROE) Measures how well management has used equity to generate profits for shareholders.   (p. 489)

stated value An arbitrary amount assigned by a company to a share of its stock at the time of issue.   (p. 479)

stock dividend A proportional distribution by a corporation of its own shares to its shareholders.   (p. 484)

stock split An increase in the number of authorized, issued, and outstanding shares of stock coupled with a proportionate reduction in the share's book value.   (p. 486)

Assess Your Progress

MyAccountingLab

Make the grade with MyAccountingLab: The Exercises, Quizzes, and Problems (A set) marked in red can be found on MyAccountingLab. You can practise them as often as you want, and most feature step-by-step guided instructions to help you find the right answer.

SHORT EXERCISES

LEARNING OBJECTIVE ❶

Understand the advantages and disadvantages of a corporation

S10-1 What are two main advantages that a corporation has over a proprietorship and a partnership? What are two main disadvantages of a corporation?

LEARNING OBJECTIVE ❶

Summarize the characteristics of authority structure in a corporation

S10-2 Consider the authority structure in a corporation, as diagrammed in Exhibit 10-2, page 477.

1. What group holds the ultimate power in a corporation?
2. Who is the most powerful person in the corporation? What's the abbreviation of this person's title?
3. Who is in charge of day-to-day operations? What's the abbreviation of this person's title?
4. Who is in charge of accounting and finance? What's the abbreviation of this person's title?

LEARNING OBJECTIVE ❶

Identify the characteristics of preferred and common shares

S10-3 Answer the following questions about the characteristics of a corporation's shares:

1. Who are the real owners of a corporation?
2. What privileges do preferred shareholders have over common shareholders?
3. Which class of shareholders reaps greater benefits from a highly profitable corporation? Explain.

LEARNING OBJECTIVE ❷

Understand the effect of a share issuance on net income

S10-4 Study George Weston Ltd.'s January 8, 2014, share issuance entry given on page 479, and answer these questions about the nature of the transaction:

1. If George Weston had sold the shares for $80, would the $30 ($80 − $50) be profit for George Weston?
2. Suppose the shares had been issued at different times and different prices. Will shares issued at higher prices have more rights than those issued at lower prices? Give the reason for your answer.

LEARNING OBJECTIVE ❷❹

Issue shares and analyze retained earnings

S10-5 On December 31, 2014, shareholders' equity accounts of Green Products Inc. (GPI) had the balances shown below. GPI paid dividends of $4,096 on December 1, 2014.

	2014	2013
Common shares	$ 82,968	$ 64,968
Retained earnings	80,435	78,881
Total shareholders' equity	$163,403	$143,849

1. GPI sold 10,000 common shares on June 30, 2014. What was the average selling price of these shares if this was the only common-shares transaction during 2014?
2. Journalize GPI's sale of the common shares on June 30, 2014.
3. Based only on the above information, did GPI earn a profit or suffer a loss during 2014? Calculate the profit or loss.

LEARNING OBJECTIVE ❷

Issue shares to finance the purchase of assets

S10-6 This Short Exercise demonstrates the similarity and the difference between two ways to acquire capital assets.

Case A—Issue shares and buy the assets in separate transactions:	*Case B—Issue shares to acquire the assets in a single transaction:*
Longview Corporation issued 10,000 common shares for cash of $200,000. In a separate transaction, Longview used the cash to purchase a warehouse building for $160,000 and equipment for $40,000. Journalize the two transactions.	Tyler Corporation issued 10,000 common shares to acquire a warehouse valued at $160,000 and equipment worth $40,000. Journalize this transaction.

Compare the balances in all the accounts after making both sets of entries. Are the account balances the same or different?

S10-7 The financial statements of Eppley Employment Services Inc. reported the following accounts (adapted, with dollar amounts in thousands):

LEARNING OBJECTIVE ❷❹

Prepare the shareholders' equity section of a balance sheet

Common shares:			Total revenues	$1,390
600 shares issued	$600		Accounts payable	420
Long-term debt	25		Retained earnings	646
			Other current liabilities	2,566
			Total expenses	805

Prepare the shareholders' equity section of Eppley's balance sheet. Net income has already been closed to Retained Earnings.

S10-8 Use the Eppley Employment Services data in exercise S10-7 to compute Eppley's:
a. Net income
b. Total liabilities
c. Total assets (use the accounting equation)

LEARNING OBJECTIVE ❷❹

Use shareholders' equity data

S10-9 Karen Knox Exports, Inc., is located in Clancy, New Mexico. Knox is the only company with reliable sources for its imported gifts. The company does a brisk business with specialty stores such as Neiman Marcus. Knox's recent success has made the company a prime target for a takeover. An investment group in Alberton is attempting to buy 52% of Knox's outstanding shares against the wishes of Knox's board of directors. Board members are convinced that the Alberton investors would sell the most desirable pieces of the business and leave little of value.

LEARNING OBJECTIVE ❸

Explain the repurchase of shares to fight off a takeover of the corporation

At the most recent board meeting, several suggestions were advanced to fight off the hostile takeover bid. The suggestion with the most promise is to repurchase a significant quantity of outstanding shares. Knox has the cash to carry out this plan.

Requirement

Suppose you are a significant shareholder of Karen Knox Exports, Inc. Write a memorandum to explain to the board how the repurchase of shares would make it difficult for the Alberton group to take over Knox. Include in your memo a discussion of the effect that repurchasing shares would have on shares outstanding and on the size of the corporation.

S10-10 Gleneagles Corporation earned net income of $70,000 during the year ended December 31, 2014. On December 15, Gleneagles had declared the annual cash dividend on its $0.50 preferred shares (10,000 shares issued for $100,000) and a $0.60 per share cash dividend on its common shares (25,000 shares issued for $50,000). Gleneagles then paid the dividends on January 4, 2015.

LEARNING OBJECTIVE ❹

Account for cash dividends

Journalize the following for Gleneagles Corporation:
a. Declaring the cash dividends on December 15, 2014
b. Paying the cash dividends on January 4, 2015
Did Retained Earnings increase or decrease during 2014? If so, by how much?

S10-11 Refer to the allocation of dividends for Pinecraft Industries Inc. on page 485. Answer these questions about Pinecraft's cash dividends:

LEARNING OBJECTIVE ❹

Divide cash dividends between preferred and common shares

1. How much in dividends must Pinecraft declare each year before the common shareholders receive any cash dividends for the year?
2. Suppose Pinecraft declares cash dividends of $300,000 for 2014. How much of the dividends go to preferred? How much go to common?
3. Are Pinecraft's preferred shares cumulative or non-cumulative? How can you tell?
4. Pinecraft passed the preferred dividend in 2012 and 2013. Then in 2014, Pinecraft declares cash dividends of $800,000. How much of the dividends go to preferred? How much go to common?

LEARNING OBJECTIVE ❹

Record a small stock dividend

S10-12 Fidelity Software Ltd. has 80,000 common shares issued. Suppose Fidelity distributes a 10% stock dividend on May 11 when the market price (fair value) of its shares is $10.50 per share.

1. Journalize Fidelity's distribution of the shares dividend. An explanation is not required.
2. What was the overall effect of the stock dividend on Fidelity's total assets? What about on its total liabilities and its total shareholders' equity?

LEARNING OBJECTIVE ❺

Compute book value per share

S10-13 Refer to the real-world format of shareholders' equity in Exhibit 10-5, page 493. That company has passed its preferred dividends for three years including the current year. Compute the book value of one of the company's common shares.

LEARNING OBJECTIVE ❻

Compute and explain return on assets and return on equity

S10-14 Give the DuPont model formula for computing (a) rate of return on total assets (ROA) and (b) rate of return on common shareholders' equity (ROE). Then answer these questions about the rate-of-return computations:

1. Explain the meaning of the component driver ratios in the computation of ROA.
2. What impact does the leverage ratio have on ROA?
3. Under what circumstances will ROE be higher than ROA? Under what circumstances would ROE be lower than ROA?

LEARNING OBJECTIVE ❻

Compute return on assets and return on equity

S10-15 POLA Corporation's 2015 financial statements reported the following items, with 2014 figures given for comparison (adapted and in millions):

	2015	2014
Balance sheet		
Total assets	¥10,632	¥9,523
Total liabilities..	¥ 7,414	¥6,639
Total shareholders' equity (all common).....................	3,218	2,884
Total liabilities and shareholders' equity	¥10,632	¥9,523
Income statement		
Revenues and other income.....................................	¥ 7,632	
Operating expense...	7,289	
Interest expense..	31	
Other expense	194	
Net income...	¥ 118	

Use the DuPont model to compute POLA's return on assets and return on common equity for 2015. Evaluate the rates of return as being strong or weak. What additional information would be helpful in making this decision? ¥ is the symbol for the Japanese yen.

LEARNING OBJECTIVE ❼

Measure cash flows from financing activities

S10-16 During 2014, Robertson Inc. earned net income of $5.6 billion and paid off $2.7 billion of long-term notes payable. Robertson Inc. raised $1.2 billion by issuing common shares, paid $3.0 billion to repurchase shares, and paid cash dividends of $1.9 billion. Report Robertson's *cash flows from financing activities* on the statement of cash flows for 2014. Roberston reports under ASPE.

EXERCISES

LEARNING OBJECTIVE ❻

Evaluate return on equity

E10-17 Lofty Inns reported these figures for 2014 and 2013 (in millions):

	2014	2013
Balance sheet		
Total assets	$27,000	$18,400
Common share capital	43	389
Retained earnings	11,525	16,523
Other shareholders' equity	(3,008)	(9,300)
Income statement		
Net sales	$30,500	$28,200
Operating income	4,022	3,819
Net income	2,100	1,546

Requirements

1. Use DuPont analysis to compute Lofty's return on assets and return on equity for 2014.
2. Do these rates of return suggest strength or weakness? Give your reason.
3. What additional information do you need to make the decision in requirement 2?

E10-18 Burgers & Fries, Inc., is authorized to issue an unlimited number of common shares and 10,000 preferred shares. During its first year, the business completed the following share issuance transactions:

LEARNING OBJECTIVE ❷❹

Issue shares and report shareholders' equity

July	19	Issued 10,000 common shares for cash of $6.50 per share.
Oct.	3	Issued 500 $1.50 preferred shares for $50,000 cash.
	11	Received inventory valued at $11,000 and equipment with fair value of $8,500 for 3,300 common shares.

Requirements

1. Journalize the transactions. Explanations are not required.
2. Prepare the shareholders' equity section of Burgers & Fries' balance sheet. The ending balance of Retained Earnings is a deficit of $42,000.

E10-19 Citadel Sporting Goods is authorized to issue 5,000 preferred shares and 10,000 common shares. During a two-month period, Citadel completed these share-issuance transactions:

LEARNING OBJECTIVE ❷❹

Prepare the shareholders' equity section of a balance sheet

Sept.	23	Issued 1,000 common shares for cash of $16 per share.
Oct.	2	Issued 300 $4.50 preferred shares for $20,000 cash.
	12	Received inventory valued at $15,000 and equipment with fair value of $43,000 for 4,000 common shares.

Requirement

Prepare the shareholders' equity section of the Citadel Sporting Goods balance sheet for the transactions given in this exercise. Retained Earnings has a balance of $49,000. Journal entries are not required.

E10-20 Trans World Publishing Inc. was recently organized. The company issued common shares to a lawyer who provided legal services of $15,000 to help organize the corporation. Trans World also issued common shares to an inventor in exchange for his patent with a fair value of $80,000. In addition, Trans World received cash both for the issuance of 5,000 of its preferred shares at $110 per share and for the issuance of 20,000 common shares at $20 per share. During the first year of operations, Trans World earned net income of $55,000 and declared a cash dividend of $20,000. Without making journal entries, determine the total share capital created by these transactions.

LEARNING OBJECTIVE ❷❹

Measure the share capital of a corporation

LEARNING OBJECTIVE ❷❹

Prepare shareholders' equity section of a balance sheet

E10-21 Sagebrush Software Ltd. had the following selected account balances at December 31, 2014 (in thousands). Prepare the shareholders' equity section of Sagebrush Software's balance sheet (in thousands).

Inventory	$ 653	Class A common shares,	
Property, plant, and equipment, net...	857	unlimited number authorized,	
Contributed surplus	901	3,600 shares issued	$ 90
Class B common shares,		Deficit	2,400
unlimited number authorized,		Accounts receivable, net	600
5,000 shares issued	1,380	Notes payable	1,122

Explain what is meant by "deficit."

LEARNING OBJECTIVE ❷❹

Record share transactions and measure their effects on shareholders' equity

E10-22 Journalize the following transactions of Concilio Video Productions Inc.:

April	19	Issued 2,000 common shares at $10 per share.
July	22	Declared and paid a cash dividend of $0.50 per common share (21,000 common shares outstanding).
Nov.	11	Issued 800 common shares at $12 per share.

What was the overall effect of these transactions on Concilio's shareholders' equity?

LEARNING OBJECTIVE ❷❹

Record share issuance and dividend transactions

E10-23 At December 31, 2014, Blumenthall Corporation reported the shareholders' equity accounts shown here (as adapted, with dollar amounts in millions):

Common shares	
1,800 million shares issued	$2,700
Retained earnings	1,200
Total shareholders' equity	$3,900

Blumenthall's 2014 transactions included the following:
a. Net income, $350 million
b. Issuance of 6 million common shares for $12.50 per share
c. Declaration and payment of cash dividends of $25 million
   Journalize Blumenthall's transactions. Explanations are not required.

LEARNING OBJECTIVE ❷❹

Report shareholders' equity after a sequence of transactions

E10-24 Use the Blumenthall Corporation data in exercise E10-23 to prepare the shareholders' equity section of the company's balance sheet at December 31, 2014.

LEARNING OBJECTIVE ❷❸❹

Infer transactions from a company's shareholders' equity

E10-25 Optical Products Company reported the following shareholders' equity on its balance sheet:

	December 31,	
Shareholders' Equity (dollars and shares in millions)	**2014**	**2013**
Preferred shares; authorized 20 shares;		
Convertible Preferred shares; issued and outstanding:		
2014 and 2013—0 and 2 shares, respectively	$ 0	$ 12
Common shares; authorized unlimited shares; issued:		
2014 and 2013—564 and 364 shares, respectively	3,270	1,900
Retained earnings	6,280	5,006
Total shareholders' equity	$ 9,550	$ 6,918
Total liabilities and shareholders' equity	$48,918	$45,549

Requirements

1. What caused Optical Products' preferred shares to decrease during 2014? Cite all the possible causes.
2. What caused Optical Products' common shares to increase during 2014? Identify all the possible causes.
3. How many shares of Optical Products were outstanding at December 31, 2014?
4. Optical Products' net income during 2014 was $1,410 million. How much were Optical Products' dividends during the year?

E10-26 Great Lakes Manufacturing Inc. reported the following:

LEARNING OBJECTIVE ❹

Compute dividends on preferred and common shares

Shareholders' Equity	
Preferred shares, cumulative, $0.10, 80,000 shares issued....................	$ 80,000
Common shares, 8,130,000 shares issued	813,000

Great Lakes Manufacturing has paid all preferred dividends through <u>2010</u>.

Requirement

Compute the total amounts of dividends to both preferred and common shareholders for 2013 and 2014 if total dividends are $50,000 in 2013 and $100,000 in 2014.

E10-27 The shareholders' equity for Best in Show Cinemas Ltd. (BSC) (adapted) at December 31, 2013, appears as follows:

LEARNING OBJECTIVE ❹

Record a stock dividend and report shareholders' equity

Shareholders' Equity	
Common shares, 2,000,000 shares authorized,	
500,000 shares issued	$1,012,000
Retained earnings...	7,122,000
Total shareholders' equity	$8,134,000

On April 15, 2014, the market price of BSC common shares was $17 per share. Assume BSC distributed a 10% stock dividend on this date.

Requirements

1. Journalize the distribution of the stock dividend.
2. Prepare the shareholders' equity section of the balance sheet after the stock dividend.
3. Why is total shareholders' equity unchanged by the stock dividend?
4. Suppose BSC had a cash balance of $540,000 on April 16, 2014. What is the maximum amount of cash dividends BSC can declare?

E10-28 Identify the effects—both the direction and the dollar amount—of the following assumed transactions on the total shareholders' equity of a large corporation. Each transaction is independent.

LEARNING OBJECTIVE ❷❹

Measure the effects of share issuance, dividends, and share transactions

a. Declaration of cash dividends of $80 million
b. Payment of the cash dividend declared
c. 10% stock dividend. Before the dividend, 69 million common shares were outstanding; the market price was $7.625 at the time of the dividend.
d. A 50% stock dividend. Before the dividend, 69 million common shares were outstanding; the market price was $13.75 at the time of the dividend.
e. Sale of 600 common shares for $5.00 per share
f. A 3-for-l stock split. Prior to the split, 69 million common shares were outstanding.

LEARNING OBJECTIVE ❹

Report shareholders' equity after a
stock split

E10-29 Solartech Inc. had the following shareholders' equity at January 31 (dollars in millions):

Common shares, 500 million shares authorized,	
440 million shares issued	$ 318
Contributed surplus	44
Retained earnings...	2,393
Total shareholders' equity	$2,755

Assume that on March 7, Solartech split its common shares 2 for 1. Prepare the shareholders' equity section of the balance sheet immediately after the split.

LEARNING OBJECTIVE ❺

Measure the book value per share
of common shares

E10-30 The balance sheet of Oriental Rug Company reported the following:

Cumulative preferred shares, $0.06,	
outstanding 6,000 shares..	$ 10,000
Common shareholders' equity:	
8,000 shares issued and outstanding	87,200
Total shareholders' equity..	$ 97,200

Requirements

1. Compute the book value per share for the common shares, assuming all preferred dividends are fully paid up (none in arrears).
2. Compute the book value per share of the common shares, assuming that three years' preferred dividends, including the current year, are in arrears.
3. Oriental Rug's common shares recently traded at a market price of $7.75 per share. Does this mean that Oriental Rug's shares are a good buy at $7.75?

LEARNING OBJECTIVE ❻

Evaluate profitability

E10-31 Lexington Inns reported these figures for 2014 and 2013 (in millions):

	2014	2013
Balance sheet		
Total assets	$15,702	$13,728
Common share capital.......................................	80	680
Retained earnings	11,519	16,499
Other shareholders' equity.................................	(3,005)	(9,095)
Income statement		
Net sales..	$25,500	$27,500
Operating income..	4,025	3,813
Net income..	1,500	1,550

Requirements

1. Use DuPont analysis to compute Lexington's return on assets and return on equity for 2014.
2. Do these rates of return suggest strength or weakness? Give your reason.
3. What additional information do you need to make the decision in requirement 2?

E10-32 Easton Company included the following items in its financial statements for 2014, the current year (amounts in millions):

LEARNING OBJECTIVE ⑥

Evaluate profitability

Payment of long-term debt	$17,200	Dividends paid	$ 195
Proceeds from issuance		Net sales:	
of common shares	8,405	Current year	65,000
Total liabilities:		Preceding year	62,000
Current year-end	32,309	Net income:	
Preceding year-end	38,033	Current year	2,200
Total shareholders' equity:		Preceding year	1,995
Current year-end	23,471	Operating income:	
Preceding year-end	14,037	Current year	9,125
Borrowings	6,585	Preceding year	4,002

Requirements

1. Use DuPont analysis to compute Easton's return on assets and return on equity during 2014 (the current year). Easton has no preferred stock outstanding.
2. Do the company's rates of return look strong or weak? Give your reason.

E10-33 Use the Easton data in exercise E10-32 to show how the company reported cash flows from financing activities during 2014 (the current year). List items in descending order from largest to smallest dollar amount. Easton reports under ASPE.

LEARNING OBJECTIVE ⑦

Report cash flows from financing activities

CHALLENGE EXERCISES

E10-34 A-1 Networking Solutions Inc. began operations on January 1, 2014, and immediately issued its shares, receiving cash. A-1's balance sheet at December 31, 2014, reported the following shareholders' equity:

LEARNING OBJECTIVE ❷❹

Reconstruct transactions from the financial statements

Common shares	$253,500
Retained earnings	38,000
Total shareholders' equity	$291,500

During 2014, A-1:
a. Issued 50,000 common shares for $5 per share.
b. Issued common shares for $7 each.
c. Earned net income of $56,000 and declared and paid cash dividends. Revenues were $171,000 and expenses totalled $115,000.

Requirement

Journalize all A-1's shareholders' equity transactions during the year. A-1's entry in part (c) to close net income to Retained Earnings was:

Revenues	171,000	
Expenses		115,000
Retained Earnings		56,000

LEARNING OBJECTIVE 7

Report financing activities on the statement of cash flows

LEARNING OBJECTIVE 2 4

Explain the changes in shareholders' equity

E10-35 Use the data in exercise E10-34 to report all A-1 Networking Solutions' financing activities on the company's statement of cash flows for 2014 (journal entries and/or T-accounts may aid your approach to a solution). A-1 reports under ASPE.

E10-36 Startech Limited reported the following shareholders' equity data (all dollars in millions):

	December 31,	
	2014	2013
Preferred shares	$ 604	$ 740
Common shares	2,390	2,130
Retained earnings	20,661	19,108

Startech earned net income of $2,960 during 2014. Common shares were issued for $20.00 each. For each account except Retained Earnings, one transaction explains the change from the December 31, 2013, balance to the December 31, 2014, balance. Two transactions affected Retained Earnings. Give a full explanation, including the dollar amount, for the change in each account.

LEARNING OBJECTIVE 2 4

Account for changes in shareholders' equity

E10-37 Fun City Inc. ended 2013 with 8 million common shares issued and outstanding. The average issue price was $1.50. Beginning retained earnings totalled $40 million.
- In March 2014, Fun City issued 2 million common shares at a price of $2 per share.
- In May, the company distributed a 10% stock dividend at a time when Fun City's common shares had a fair value of $3 per share.
- Then in October, Fun City's stock price dropped to $1 per share and the company executed a 1-for-2 stock split.
- For the year, Fun City earned net income of $26 million and declared cash dividends of $17 million.

Determine what Fun City should report for shareholders' equity at December 31, 2014. Journal entries are not required.

QUIZ

Test your understanding of shareholders' equity by answering the following questions. Select the best choice from among the possible answers given.

Q10-38 Which of the following is a characteristic of a corporation?
a. Mutual agency
b. No income tax
c. Limited liability of shareholders
d. Both a and b

Q10-39 Team Spirit Inc. issues 240,000 common shares for $5 per share. The journal entry is:

a. Cash	240,000	
Common Shares		240,000
b. Cash	1,200,000	
Common Shares		240,000
Gain on the Sale of Shares		960,000
c. Cash	1,200,000	
Common Shares		1,200,000
d. Cash	1,200,000	
Common Shares		480,000
Contributed Surplus on Common Shares		720,000

Q10-40 Which of the following is true about stated value?
a. It represents what a share is worth.
b. It represents the original selling price for a share.
c. It is established for a share after it is issued.
d. It is an arbitrary amount assigned by a company to a share at the time of issue.
e. It may exist for common shares but not for preferred shares.

Q10-41 The contributed capital portion of shareholders' equity does not include
a. Preferred Shares.   c. Retained Earnings.
b. Contributed Surplus.   d. Common Shares.

Q10-42 Preferred shares are *least* likely to have which of the following characteristics?
a. Preference as to assets on liquidation of the corporation
b. Extra liability for the preferred shareholders
c. The right of the holder to convert to common shares
d. Preference as to dividends

Q10-43 Which of the following classifications represents the largest quantity of common shares?
a. Issued shares   c. Unissued shares
b. Outstanding shares   d. Authorized shares

Use the following information for questions Q10-44 through Q10-49:

These account balances at December 31 relate to Sportaid Inc.:

Accounts Payable............................	$ 51,700	Preferred shares, $0.10,	
Accounts Receivable.........................	81,350	890,000 shares issued.................	89,000
Common Shares..............................	593,000	Retained Earnings	71,800
Bonds Payable	3,400	Notes Receivable	12,500

Q10-44 What is total share capital for Sportaid Inc.?
a. $682,000   d. $753,800
b. $701,345   e. None of the above
c. $694,445

Q10-45 What is total shareholders' equity for Sportaid Inc.?
a. $766,300   d. $764,735
b. $758,800   e. None of the above
c. $753,800

Q10-46 Sportaid's net income for the period is $119,600 and beginning common shareholders' equity is $681,400. What is Sportaid's return on common shareholders' equity?
a. 15.7%   c. 17.5%
b. 16.4%   d. 18.6%

Q10-47 If the average issue price of Sportaid's outstanding common shares is $11.86, how many common shares are issued and outstanding?
a. 50,000   c. 593,000
b. 100,000   d. Unknown

Q10-48 If Sportaid's board of directors decided to declare a dividend on December 31, what is the largest dividend it could declare?
a. $753,800   c. $8,900
b. $71,800   d. $593,000

Q10-49 If the board of directors declare a dividend of $20,000 on December 31, how much of this total would the common shareholders receive? No other dividends have been declared during the year.

a. $8,900

b. $0

c. $20,000

d. $11,100

Q10-50 Shareholders are eligible for a dividend if they own the shares on the date of

a. declaration.

b. record.

c. payment.

d. issuance.

Q10-51 Mario's Foods has outstanding 500 $7.00 preferred shares and 1,200 common shares. Mario's declares dividends of $14,300. The correct entry is:

a. Retained Earnings...	14,300	
Dividends Payable, Preferred		3,500
Dividends Payable, Common.....................................		10,800
b. Dividends Expense...	14,300	
Cash		14,300
c. Retained Earnings...	14,300	
Dividends Payable, Preferred		7,150
Dividends Payable, Common....,.....................................		7,150
d. Dividends Payable, Preferred...	3,500	
Dividends Payable, Common	10,800	
Cash		14,300

Q10-52 A corporation has 20,000 $8.00 preferred shares outstanding with a stated value of $2,000,000. Also, there are 20,000 common shares outstanding. If a $350,000 dividend is paid, how much goes to the preferred shareholders?

a. $0

b. $350,000

c. $160,000

d. $120,000

e. $320,000

Q10-53 Assume the same facts as in question Q10-52. What is the amount of dividends per share on common shares?

a. $9.50

b. $8.00

c. $17.50

d. $1.50

e. None of the above

Q10-54 Which of the following is *not* true about a 10% stock dividend?

a. Shareholders do not receive additional shares.

b. No assets are affected.

c. Retained Earnings decreases.

d. The market price of the share is needed to record the stock dividend.

e. Total shareholders' equity remains the same.

Q10-55 A company declares a 5% stock dividend. The debit to Retained Earnings is an amount equal to the

a. stated value of original shares.

b. excess of the market price over the original issue price of the shares to be issued.

c. book value of the shares to be issued.

d. fair value of the shares to be issued.

Q10-56 Which of the following statements is *not* true about a 3-for-1 stock split?

a. Stated value is reduced to one-third of what it was before the split.

b. Total shareholders' equity increases.

c. The market price of each share will decrease.

d. A shareholder with 10 shares before the split owns 30 shares after the split.

e. Retained Earnings remains the same.

Q10-57 Franco Company's net income and preferred dividends are $44,000 and $4,000, respectively, and average total common shareholders' equity is $384,000. How much is Franco's return on equity?

a. 10.4%   c. 12.5%

b. 11.5%   d. 13.1%

PROBLEMS

(Group A)

P10-58A The board of directors of Freestroke Swim Centres Inc. is meeting to address the concerns of shareholders. Shareholders have submitted the following questions for discussion at the board meeting. Answer each question.

LEARNING OBJECTIVE ❶❹

Explain the features of a corporation's shares

1. Why did Freestroke organize as a corporation if a corporation must pay an additional layer of income tax?

2. How are preferred shares similar to common shares? How are preferred shares similar to debt?

3. Would Freestroke investors prefer to receive cash dividends or stock dividends? Explain your reasoning.

P10-59A The articles of incorporation from the province of Ontario authorize Challenger Canoes Inc. to issue 10,000 shares of $6 preferred shares and 100,000 common shares. In its first month, Challenger completed the following transactions:

LEARNING OBJECTIVE ❷❹

Record corporate transactions and prepare the shareholders' equity section of the balance sheet

2014

Oct. 6 Issued 300 common shares to the lawyer for assistance with chartering the corporation. The lawyer's fee was $1,500. Debit Organization Expense.

9 Issued 9,000 common shares to Jerry Spence and 12,000 shares to Sheila Markle in return for cash equal to the shares, market price of $5 per share. Spence and Markle are executives of the company.

10 Issued 400 preferred shares to acquire a patent with a fair value of $40,000.

26 Issued 2,000 common shares for cash of $12,000.

Requirements

1. Record the transactions in the journal.
2. Prepare the shareholders' equity section of the Challenger balance sheet at October 31, 2014. The ending balance of Retained Earnings is $49,000.

P10-60A Samuells' Sportswear's articles of incorporation authorize the company to issue 5,000 $5 preferred shares and 500,000 common shares. Samuells' issued 1,000 preferred shares at $100 per share. It issued 100,000 common shares for $427,000. The company's Retained Earnings balance at the beginning of 2014 was $61,000. Net income for 2014 was $80,000, and the company declared a $5 cash dividend on preferred shares for 2014.

LEARNING OBJECTIVE ❷❹

Prepare the shareholders' equity section of the balance sheet

Requirement

Prepare the shareholders' equity section of Samuells' Sportswear Inc.'s balance sheet at December 31, 2014. Show the computation of all amounts. Journal entries are not required.

P10-61A Calpak Winter Sports Ltd. is positioned ideally in the winter business. Located in Whistler, B.C., Calpak is the only company with a distribution network for its imported goods. The company did a brisk business around the 2010 Winter Olympics held in Whistler. Calpak's recent success has made the company a prime target for a takeover. Against the

LEARNING OBJECTIVE ❸

Fight off a takeover of the corporation

wishes of Calpak's board of directors, an investment group from Vancouver is attempting to buy 51% of Calpak's outstanding shares. Board members are convinced that the Vancouver investors would sell off the most desirable pieces of the business and leave little of value. At the most recent board meeting, several suggestions were advanced to fight off the hostile takeover bid.

Requirement

Suppose you are a significant shareholder of Calpak Winter Sports. Write a short memo to the board to propose an action that would make it difficult for the investor group to take over Calpak. Include in your memo a discussion of the effect your proposed action would have on the company's assets, liabilities, and total shareholders' equity.

LEARNING OBJECTIVE ❷❹

Measure the effects of share issuance and dividend transactions on shareholders' equity

P10-62A Wholegrain Health Foods Inc. is authorized to issue 5,000,000 common shares. In its initial public offering during 2010, Wholegrain issued 500,000 common shares for $7.00 per share. Over the next year, Wholegrain's share price increased and the company issued 400,000 more shares at an average price of $8.50.

During the five years from 2010 through 2014, Wholegrain earned net income of $920,000 and declared and paid cash dividends of $140,000. A 10% stock dividend was distributed to the shareholders in 2014 on the shares outstanding. The market price was $8.00 per share when the stock dividend was distributed. At December 31, 2014, the company has total assets of $14,500,000 and total liabilities of $6,820,000.

Requirement

Show the computation of Wholegrain's total shareholders' equity at December 31, 2014. Present a detailed computation of each element of shareholders' equity.

LEARNING OBJECTIVE ❷❹

Analyze the shareholders' equity and dividends of a corporation

P10-63A Steeltrap Security Inc. included the following shareholders' equity on its balance sheet at December 31, 2014:

Shareholders' Equity	($ millions)
Preferred Shares:	
Authorized 20,000 shares in each class:	
$5.00 Cumulative Preferred Shares, 2,500 shares issued	$ 125,000
$2.50 Cumulative Preferred Shares, 4,000 shares issued	100,000
Common Shares:	
Authorized 80,000 shares, issued 48,000 shares................................	384,000
Retained earnings..	529,000
	$1,138,000

Requirements

1. Identify the different issues of shares Steeltrap Security has outstanding.
2. What was the value at which the $2.50 Cumulative Preferred Shares were issued?
3. Suppose Steeltrap decided not to pay its preferred dividends for one year. Would the company have to pay these dividends in arrears before paying dividends to the common shareholders? Why?
4. What amount of preferred dividends must Steeltrap declare and pay each year to avoid having preferred dividends in arrears?
5. Assume preferred dividends are in arrears for 2013. Journalize the declaration of a $50,000 cash dividend for 2014. No explanation is needed.

LEARNING OBJECTIVE ❷❹

Account for share issuance and dividends

P10-64A Exquisite Jewellery Limited reported the following summarized balance sheet at December 31, 2013:

Assets

Current assets	$33,400
Property and equipment, net	51,800
Total assets	$85,200

Liabilities and Equity

Liabilities	$37,800
Shareholders' equity:	
$0.50 cumulative preferred shares, 400 shares issued	2,000
Common shares, 6,000 shares issued	23,400
Retained earnings	22,000
Total liabilities and equity	$85,200

During 2014, Exquisite completed these transactions that affected shareholders' equity:

Feb.	13	Issued 5,000 common shares for $4 per share.
June	7	Declared the regular cash dividend on the preferred shares.
July	24	Paid the cash dividend.
Aug.	9	Distributed a 10% stock dividend on the common shares. Market price of the common shares was $5 per share.
Nov.	20	Issued 200 common shares for $8 per share.

Requirements

1. Journalize Exquisite's transactions. Explanations are not required.
2. Report Exquisite Jewellery Limited's shareholders' equity at December 31, 2014. Net income for 2014 was $27,000.

P10-65A Niles Corporation completed the following selected transactions during the current year:

LEARNING OBJECTIVE ❷❹

Measure the effects of dividend and share transactions on a company

Mar.	3	Distributed a 10% stock dividend on the 90,000 common shares outstanding. The market price of the common shares was $25 per share.
May	16	Declared a cash dividend on the $5 preferred shares (5,000 shares outstanding).
	30	Paid the cash dividends.
Dec.	8	Issued 1,500 common shares for $27 per share.
	19	Issued 10,000 common shares for $28 per share.

Requirement

Analyze each transaction in terms of its effect (in dollars) on the accounting equation of Niles Corporation.

P10-66A The following accounts and related balances of Bluebird Designers, Inc., as of December 31, 2014, are arranged in no particular order.

LEARNING OBJECTIVE ❷❹❻

Prepare a corporation's balance sheet; measure profitability

Cash	$ 45,000	Interest expense		$ 16,300
Accounts receivable, net	25,000	Property, plant, and		
Contributed surplus	53,800	equipment, net		359,000
Accrued liabilities	22,000	Common shares		
Long-term note payable	97,000	500,000 shares authorized,		
Inventory	89,000	110,000 shares issued		197,000
Dividends payable	9,000	Prepaid expenses		14,000
Retained earnings	?	Common shareholders'		
Accounts payable	135,000	equity, December 31, 2013		220,000
Trademarks, net	9,000	Net income		90,000
Goodwill	18,000	Total assets,		
		December 31, 2013		500,000
		Net sales		750,000

Requirements

1. Prepare Bluebird's classified balance sheet in the account format at December 31, 2014.
2. Use DuPont analysis to compute Bluebird's rate of return on total assets and rate of return on equity for the year ended December 31, 2014.
3. Do these rates of return suggest strength or weakness? Give your reason.

LEARNING OBJECTIVE ❼

Analyze the statement of cash flows

P10-67A The statement of cash flows of Picture Perfect Photography reported the following for the year ended December 31, 2014:

Cash flows from financing activities	
Dividends [declared and] paid...	$(8,300)
Proceeds from issuance of common shares	14,100
Payments of short-term notes payable	(6,900)
Payments of long-term notes payable..	(1,300)
Proceeds from issuance of long-term notes payable	2,100

Requirement

Make the journal entry that Picture Perfect used to record each of these transactions.

(Group B)

LEARNING OBJECTIVE ❶❷❺

Explain the features of a corporation's shares

P10-68B Reinhart Industries Limited is conducting a special meeting of its board of directors to address some concerns raised by the shareholders. Shareholders have submitted the following questions. Answer each question.

1. Why are common shares and retained earnings shown separately in the shareholders' equity section of the balance sheet?
2. Lou Harris, a Reinhart shareholder, proposes to give some land she owns to the company in exchange for company shares. How should Reinhart Industries Limited determine the number of shares to issue for the land?
3. Preferred shares generally are preferred with respect to dividends and in the event of a liquidation. Why would investors buy *common* shares when *preferred* shares are available?
4. One of the Reinhart shareholders owns 100 shares of Reinhart, and someone has offered to buy her shares for their book value. What formula should be used to compute the book value of her shares?

LEARNING OBJECTIVE ❷❹

Record corporate transactions and prepare the shareholders' equity section of the balance sheet

P10-69B The partners who own Bassett Furniture Co. wished to avoid the unlimited personal liability of the partnership form of business, so they incorporated as BFC Inc. The articles of incorporation from the province of Manitoba authorize the corporation to issue 10,000 $6 preferred shares and 250,000 common shares. In its first month, BFC completed the following transactions:

2014		
Jan.	3	Issued 1,000 common shares to the promoter for assistance with issuance of the common shares. The promotional fee was $10,000. Debit Organization Expense.
	6	Issued 5,000 common shares to Jo Bassett, and 3,800 shares to Mel Bassett in return for cash equal to the market price of $11 per share. (The Bassetts were partners in Bassett Furniture Co.)
	12	Issued 1,000 preferred shares to acquire a patent with a fair value of $110,000.
	22	Issued 1,500 common shares for $12 cash per share.

Requirements

1. Record the transactions in the journal.
2. Prepare the shareholders' equity section of the BFC Inc. balance sheet at January 31. The ending balance of Retained Earnings is $89,000.

P10-70B Northwest Territories Inc. has the following shareholders' equity information:

LEARNING OBJECTIVE ❷❹

Prepare the shareholders' equity section of the balance sheet

Northwest's incorporation authorizes the company to issue 10,000 $5 cumulative preferred shares and 400,000 common shares. The company issued 1,000 preferred shares at $100 per share. It issued 100,000 common shares for a total of $370,000. The company's Retained Earnings balance at the beginning of 2014 was $40,000, and net income for the year was $90,000. During 2014, Northwest declared the specified dividend on preferred shares and a $0.50 per-share dividend on common shares. Preferred dividends for 2013 were in arrears.

Requirement

Prepare the shareholders' equity section of Northwest Territories Inc.'s balance sheet at December 31, 2014. Show the computation of all amounts. Journal entries are not required.

P10-71B Gary Swan Imports Inc. is located in Stratford, Ontario. Swan is the only company with reliable sources for its imported gifts. The company does a brisk business with specialty stores such as Bowring. Swan's recent success has made the company a prime target for a takeover. An investment group from Toronto is attempting to buy 51% of Swan's outstanding shares against the wishes of Swan's board of directors. Board members are convinced that the Toronto investors would sell the most desirable pieces of the business and leave little of value.

LEARNING OBJECTIVE ❸

Repurchase common shares to fight off a takeover of the corporation

At the most recent board meeting, several suggestions were made to fight off the hostile takeover bid. The suggestion with the most promise is to repurchase a huge quantity of common shares. Swan has the cash to carry out this plan.

Requirement

Suppose you are a significant shareholder of Gary Swan Imports Inc. Write a memorandum to explain to the board how the repurchase of common shares would make it difficult for the Toronto group to take over Swan. Include in your memo a discussion of the effect that repurchasing common shares would have on shares outstanding and on the size of the corporation.

P10-72B Western Agriculture Industries Ltd. is authorized by the province of Saskatchewan to issue 500,000 common shares.

LEARNING OBJECTIVE ❷❹

Measure the effects of share issuance, net income and dividend transactions on shareholders' equity

In its initial public offering during 2010, Western Agricultural issued 200,000 of its common shares for $12 per share. Over the next year, Western Agricultural's common share price increased, and the company issued 100,000 more shares at an average price of $14.50.

During the five years from 2010 to 2014, Western Agricultural earned net income of $395,000 and declared and paid cash dividends of $119,000. Stock dividends of $135,000 were distributed to the shareholders in 2013, when the share market price was $10. At December 31, 2014, total assets of the company are $7,030,000, and liabilities add up to $2,904,000.

Requirement

Show the computation of Western Agricultural Industries Ltd.'s total shareholders' equity at December 31, 2014. Present a detailed computation of each element of shareholders' equity.

P10-73B Teak Outdoor Furniture Limited included the following shareholders' equity on its year-end balance sheet at February 28, 2014:

LEARNING OBJECTIVE ❷❹

Analyze the shareholders' equity and dividends of a corporation

Shareholders' Equity	
Preferred shares, $1.10 cumulative; authorized 100,000 shares in each class	
Class A—issued 75,000 shares	$ 1,500,000
Class B—issued 92,000 shares..	1,840,000
Common shares; authorized 1,000,000 shares, issued 280,000 shares ...	6,940,000
Retained earnings...	8,330,000
	$18,610,000

Requirements

1. Identify the different issues of shares that Teak Outdoor Furniture Limited has outstanding.
2. Give the summary entries to record issuance of all the Teak shares. Assume that all the shares were issued for cash. Explanations are not required.
3. Suppose Teak did not pay its preferred dividends for three years. Would the company have to pay those dividends in arrears before paying dividends to the common shareholders? Give your reason.
4. What amount of preferred dividends must Teak declare and pay each year to avoid having preferred dividends in arrears?
5. Assume that preferred dividends are in arrears for 2013. Record the declaration of an $800,000 dividend on February 28, 2014. An explanation is not required.

LEARNING OBJECTIVE ❷❹
Account for share issuance and dividends

P10-74B Winnipeg Enterprises Inc. reported the following summarized balance sheet at December 31, 2013:

Assets	
Current assets	$18,200
Property and equipment, net	34,700
Total assets	$52,900
Liabilities and Equity	
Liabilities	$ 6,200
Shareholders' equity:	
$5 cumulative preferred shares, 180 shares issued	1,800
Common shares, 2,400 shares issued	25,900
Retained earnings	19,000
Total liabilities and equity	$52,900

During 2014, Winnipeg Enterprise completed these transactions that affected shareholders' equity:

Feb.	22	Issued 1,000 common shares for $16 per share.
May	4	Declared the regular cash dividend on the preferred shares.
	24	Paid the cash dividend.
July	9	Distributed a 10% stock dividend on the common shares. Market price of the common shares was $18 per share.
Dec.	8	Issued 600 common shares for $15 per share.

Requirements

1. Journalize Winnipeg Enterprise's transactions. Explanations are not required.
2. Report Winnipeg Enterprise's shareholders' equity at December 31, 2014. Net income for 2014 was $62,000.

LEARNING OBJECTIVE ❷❹
Measure the effects of dividend and share transactions on a company

P10-75B Cones Inc. of Baie-Comeau completed the following transactions during 2014, the company's 10th year of operations:

Feb.	2	Issued 10,000 common shares for cash of $250,000.
Apr.	22	Sold 700 common shares for $26 per share.
Aug.	6	Declared a cash dividend on the 10,000 $0.60 preferred shares.
Sept.	1	Paid the cash dividends.
Nov.	18	Distributed a 10% stock dividend on the 30,000 common shares outstanding. The market value of the common shares was $25 per share.

Requirement

Analyze each transaction in terms of its effect (in dollars) on the accounting equation of Cones Inc.

P10-76B The following accounts and related balances of Dove Designers, Inc., as of December 31, 2014, are arranged in no particular order.

LEARNING OBJECTIVE ❷❹❻

Prepare a corporation's balance sheet; measure profitability

Cash	$ 53,000	Interest expense	$ 16,200
Accounts receivable, net	27,000	Property, plant, and	
Contributed surplus	75,600	equipment, net	355,000
Accrued liabilities	25,000	Common shares,	
Long-term note payable	95,000	1,250,000 shares authorized,	
Inventory	98,000	118,000 shares issued	211,000
Dividends payable	6,000	Prepaid expenses	14,000
Retained earnings	?	Common shareholders'	
Accounts payable	130,000	equity, December 31, 2013	233,000
Trademark net	3,000	Net income	71,000
Goodwill	18,000	Total assets,	
		December 31, 2013	495,000
		Net sales	800,000

Requirements

1. Prepare Dove's classified balance sheet in the account format at December 31, 2014.
2. Use DuPont analysis to compute Dove's rate of return on total assets and rate of return on equity for the year ended December 31, 2014.
3. Do these rates of return suggest strength or weakness? Give your reason.

P10-77B The statement of cash flows of a large corporation reported the following (adapted) for the year ended December 31, 2014:

LEARNING OBJECTIVE ❼

Analyze the statement of cash flows

Cash flows from financing activities—*amounts in millions:*	
Cash dividends paid	$(1,854)
Issuance of common shares	1,194
Proceeds from issuance of long-term notes payable	51
Payments of long-term notes payable	(157)

Requirement

Make the journal entry that the corporation would use to record each of these transactions.

Apply Your Knowledge

Decision Cases

Case 1. Nate Smith and Darla Jones have written a smartphone app. They need additional capital to market the app, so they plan to incorporate their business. Smith and Jones are considering alternative capital structures for the corporation. Their primary goal is to raise as much capital as possible without giving up control of the business. Smith and Jones plan to receive 50,000 common shares of the corporation in return for the net assets of their old business. After the old company's books are closed and the assets adjusted to current fair value, Smith's and Jones's capital balances will each be $25,000.

The company's incorporation plans include an authorization to issue 10,000 preferred shares and 500,000 common shares. Smith and Jones are uncertain about the most desirable

LEARNING OBJECTIVE ❶❷❹

Evaluate alternative ways of raising capital

features for the preferred shares. Prior to incorporating, Smith and Jones are discussing their plans with two investment groups. The corporation can obtain capital from outside investors under either of the following plans:

- **Plan 1.** Group 1 will invest $80,000 to acquire 800 $6, non-voting preferred shares.
- **Plan 2.** Group 2 will invest $55,000 to acquire 500 $5 preferred shares and $35,000 to acquire 35,000 common shares. Each preferred share receives 50 votes on matters that come before the shareholders.

Requirements

Assume that the company is incorporated.

1. Journalize the issuance of common shares to Smith and Jones. Debit each person's capital account for its balance.
2. Journalize the issuance of shares to the outsiders under both plans.
3. Assume that net income for the first year is $120,000 and total dividends are $30,000. Prepare the shareholders' equity section of the corporation's balance sheet under both plans.
4. Recommend one of the plans to Smith and Jones. Give your reasons.

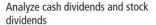

LEARNING OBJECTIVE ④

Analyze cash dividends and stock dividends

Case 2. Suppose the balance sheet of the financial statements you are analyzing had the following shareholders' equity amounts on December 31, 2013 (adapted, in millions):

Common Shares; 1,135 shares issued...	$ 278
Retained earnings	9,457
Total shareholders' equity	$ 9,735

During 2013, the corporation paid a cash dividend of $0.715 per share. Assume that, after paying the cash dividends, the corporation distributed a 10% stock dividend. Assume further that the following year, the corporation declared and paid a cash dividend of $0.65 per share. Suppose you own 10,000 of this corporation's common shares acquired three years ago, prior to the 10% stock dividend. The market price of the shares was $61.02 per share before the stock dividend.

Requirements

1. How does the stock dividend affect your proportionate ownership in the corporation? Explain.
2. What amount of cash dividends did you receive last year? What amount of cash dividends will you receive after the above dividend action?
3. Assume that immediately after the stock dividend was distributed, the market price of the corporation's shares decreased from $61.02 per share to $55.473 per share. Does this decrease represent a loss to you? Explain.
4. Suppose the corporation announces at the time of the stock dividend that the company will continue to pay the annual $0.715 *cash* dividend per share, even after distributing the *stock* dividend. Would you expect the market price of the common shares to decrease to $55.473 per share as in Requirement 3? Explain.

Ethical Issue

Ethical Issue 1. *Note:* This case is based on a real situation.
George Campbell paid $50,000 for a franchise that entitled him to market Success Associates software programs in the countries of the European Union. Campbell intended to sell individual franchises for the major language groups of Western Europe: German, French, English, Spanish, and Italian. Naturally, investors considering buying a franchise from Campbell asked to see the financial statements of his business.

Believing the value of the franchise to be greater than $50,000, Campbell sought to capitalize his own franchise at $500,000. The law firm of McDonald & LaDue helped Campbell form a corporation chartered to issue 500,000 common shares. Attorneys suggested the following chain of transactions:

a. A third party borrows $500,000 and purchases the franchise from Campbell.
b. Campbell pays the corporation $500,000 to acquire all its shares.
c. The corporation buys the franchise from the third party, who repays the loan.

In the final analysis, the third party is debt-free and out of the picture. Campbell owns all the corporation's shares, and the corporation owns the franchise. The corporation's balance sheet lists a franchise acquired at a cost of $500,000. This balance sheet is Campbell's most valuable marketing tool.

Requirements

1. What is unethical about this situation?
2. Who can be harmed in this situation? How can they be harmed? What role does accounting play here?

Ethical Issue 2. St. Genevieve Petroleum Corp. is a public, independent oil producer. St. Genevieve's year-end is June 30. In February 2014, company geologists discovered a pool of oil that tripled the company's proven reserves. The March 31, 2014, interim financial statements did not disclose the new pool of oil. During February and March 2014, St. Genevieve's managers quietly purchased most of its shares. The June 30, 2014, annual financial statements did disclose the new pool of oil, and the company's share price increased from $6 to $48.

Requirements

1. Did St. Genevieve's managers behave ethically? Explain your answer.
2. Identify the fundamental qualitative characteristic relevant to this situation.
3. Who was helped and who was harmed by management's actions?

Focus on Financials

TELUS Corporation

TELUS financial statements appear in Appendix A at the end of this book. Use information in the financial statements and the notes to the financial statements to answer the following:

1. Describe the classes of shares that TELUS has authorized? How many of each class are issued and outstanding at the end of 2011?
2. Did TELUS issue any new shares during 2011? If so, how many did it issue and what was the average issue price? (Challenge)
3. What was the total dollar value of dividends that TELUS declared in 2011? How much cash did it use to pay dividends in 2011? Why are these figures different? (Challenge)

LEARNING OBJECTIVE ❷❹❼

Analyze common shares and retained earnings

Focus on Analysis

TELUS Corporation

Using TELUS's financial statements that appear in Appendix A at the end of this book, answer the following: (Note: TELUS's total assets were $19,525 and its common shareholders' equity was $7,334 at the end of 2009.)

1. Use DuPont analysis to compute TELUS's return on equity and its components for 2011 and 2010. For simplicity, treat the non-voting share capital as a component of common shareholders' equity. Total assets at the end of 2009 were $19,525 million and total common shareholders' equity was $7,759 million at that date. Based on this information, what is your assessment of TELUS's performance in 2011 compared to 2010?

LEARNING OBJECTIVE ❻

Compute return on assets and return on equity

2. Based on the information from (1) and the 2011 data below for Bell Canada Enterprises (BCE), one of TELUS's major competitors, which company performed better in 2011? Explain your answer in detail.

	Net Profit Margin	×	Asset Turnover	×	Leverage Ratio	=	Return on Equity
BCE 2011	13.2%	×	0.52	×	4.17	=	28.6%

Group Project

LEARNING OBJECTIVE **6**

Evaluate companies' return on equity

Obtain the most recent financial statements of three Canadian companies operating in the same industry. Using the information in these statements, prepare a DuPont analysis for each company for each of the past two years. Based on this analysis, which company would you invest in and why?

Quick Check Answers

1. *b (10,000 shares × 15 = $150,000)*
2. *b*
3. *d ($180,000 + $100,000 = $280,000)*
4. *c ($180,000 + $200,000 + $100,000 = $480,000)*
5. *$480,000 [A stock split has no impact on total shareholders' equity.]*
6. *$0.25 [There are now three times as many shares outstanding, so the market price per share would decrease by approximately one-third.]*
7. *a*
8. *b*
9. *c*
10. *a*
11. *c [annual preferred dividend = $10,000 (5,000 × $2)] [($10,000 × 4) + (100,000 × $1.25) = $165,000]*
12. *a*
13. *d*
14. *c*
15. *a*

The Income Statement, the Statement of Comprehensive Income, and the Statement of Shareholders' Equity

REUTERS/Shaun Best

LEARNING OBJECTIVES

1. **Evaluate** the quality of earnings
2. **Account** for other items on the income statement
3. **Compute** earnings per share
4. **Analyze** the statement of comprehensive income and the statement of changes in shareholders' equity
5. **Differentiate** between management's and the auditor's responsibilities in financial reporting

SPOTLIGHT

TELUS Corporation is one of Canada's leading telecommunications companies. It has a 4G wireless network that provides wireless telephone and Internet access to 99% of Canadians. The company also sells leading smartphones, Wi-Fi devices, and tablets. Its landline networks in British Columbia, Alberta, and Quebec provide residential phone, Internet, television, and entertainment services. TELUS also provides IT, call centre, and outsourcing solutions for domestic and international businesses.

How much money did TELUS make selling these products and services in 2011? Its statements of income and other comprehensive income on page 523 show that its operating income was $1,968 million for the year. The company also reported net income of $1,215 million and comprehensive income of $374 million in 2011. What is the difference between all these income figures, and which one should you use to evaluate TELUS's 2011 operating performance? You are about to find out!

This chapter rounds out your coverage of the corporate income statement. After studying this material, you will have seen all the types of items that typically appear on an income statement. You will learn about income from operations (or operating income), which is often the basis for analysts' predictions about a company's future operations. You will also learn about earnings per share, the most often mentioned statistic in business. In addition, you will be introduced to the statement of comprehensive income and the statement of changes in shareholders' equity, which are financial statements required by IFRS. By the end of the chapter, you will also be able to distinguish between management's and the auditor's responsibilities in the financial reporting process. The knowledge you will get from this chapter will help you analyze financial statements and use the information in decision making.

We begin with a basic question: How do we evaluate the quality of a company's earnings? The term *quality of earnings* refers to the characteristics of an earnings number that make it most useful for decision making.

OBJECTIVE

❶ **Evaluate** the quality of earnings

EVALUATE THE QUALITY OF EARNINGS

A corporation's net income (including earnings per share) receives more attention than any other item in the financial statements. To shareholders, the larger the net income, the greater the likelihood of dividends. In addition, an upward trend in net income generally results in a higher share price over time. To creditors, a larger net income indicates a better ability to pay debts.

Suppose you are considering investing in the stock of either TELUS or Rogers. How do you make the decision? A knowledgeable investor will want to assess each company's **earnings quality**. A company's earnings quality provides insight into whether its earnings in the current period will persist into future periods. The higher the quality of a company's current earnings the more likely it is that the company is executing a successful business strategy that will generate healthy earnings in the future, which is a key determinant of its stock price.

There are many components of earnings quality. Among the most prominent are (1) proper revenue and expense recognition, (2) low operating expenses compared to sales, and (3) high and improving operating earnings as a percentage of sales. To explore the makeup and the quality of earnings, let's examine its various sources. Exhibit 11-1 shows the Consolidated Statements of Income and Other Comprehensive Income of TELUS Corporation for fiscal years 2011 and 2010. We'll use these statements as a basis for our discussion of earnings quality.

Revenue Recognition

The first component of earnings quality—revenue recognition—relates to the revenues that are reported in the first section of the income statement. You learned about the recognition and measurement of revenue in Chapters 3 through 6. In Chapter 3, you learned that the revenue recognition principle specifies three criteria that must be met before a business can recognize revenue from the sale of goods or services: (1) the control and benefits of the goods have been transferred to the customer, or the services have been provided to the customer; (2) the amount of revenue can be reliably measured; and (3) it is probable that the business will receive the economic benefits associated with the transaction, which usually come in the form of cash receipts. In Chapters 4 and 5, you learned how internal controls can prevent fraud related to improper revenue recognition and minimize the risk of not collecting cash

EXHIBIT 11-1
TELUS Corporation
Consolidated Statements
of Income and Other
Comprehensive Income

TELUS Corporation
Consolidated Statements of Income and Other Comprehensive Income (Adapted)
For the Years Ended December 31, 2011 and 2010

(in millions of dollars, except per share amounts)	2011	2010
Operating Revenues		
1. Service..	$9,606	$ 9,131
2. Equipment	719	611
3.	10,325	9,742
4. Other operating income (Note 6)	72	50
5.	10,397	9,792
Operating Expenses		
6. Goods and services purchased.................................	4,726	4,236
7. Employee benefits expense (Note 7)......................	1,893	1,906
8. Depreciation...	1,331	1,339
9. Amortization of intangible assets	479	402
10.	8,429	7,883
11. **Operating Income**	1,968	1,909
12. Financing costs (Note 8)..	377	522
13. **Income Before Income Taxes**	1,591	1,387
14. Income taxes (Note 9)	376	335
15. **Net Income**	1,215	1,052
Other Comprehensive Income (Note 10)		
16. Items that may subsequently be reclassified to income		
Change in unrealized fair value of derivatives		
designated as cash flow hedges	6	54
17. Foreign currency translation adjustment arising from		
translating financial statements of foreign operations.......	4	-
18.	10	54
19. Item never subsequently reclassified to income		
Employee defined benefit plans actuarial gains (losses)....	(851)	(214)
20.	(841)	(160)
21. **Comprehensive Income**..	$ 374	$ 892
Net Income (Loss) Attributable to:		
22. Common Shares and Non-Voting Shares	$1,219	$ 1,048
23. Non-controlling interests..	(4)	4
24.	$1,215	$ 1,052
Total Comprehensive Income (Loss) Attributable to:		
25. Common Shares and Non-Voting Shares	$ 378	$ 888
26. Non-controlling interests..	(4)	4
27.	$ 374	$ 892
Earnings Per Share		
28. Basic...	$ 3.76	$ 3.27
29. Diluted..	$ 3.74	$ 3.27
30. **Dividends Declared Per Share**	$2.205	$ 2.000
Total Weighted Average Shares Outstanding		
31. Basic...	324	320
32. Diluted..	326	321

from customers. In Chapter 5, you also learned that we must reduce reported revenues to account for any sales returns and sales discounts during the reporting period. Finally, in Chapter 6, you studied free on board (FOB) shipping terms, which dictate when the ownership of goods is transferred to the customer, a point that is critical to assessing whether the first revenue recognition criterion has been met. All of these concepts are crucial to the proper recognition and measurement of revenues on the income statement, and companies that rigorously adhere to them will enhance their quality of earnings.

In Exhibit 11-1, line 1 of TELUS's Statements of Income and Comprehensive Income reports its Service Revenues, which include revenues from local and long distance services, as well as data and wireless services. In Note 1 of TELUS's financial statements, we are told the company recognizes these revenues on the accrual basis, which includes an estimate of revenues earned but unbilled. In particular, these service revenues are recognized based on access to and usage of the company's telecommunications infrastructure, and on contract fees. Any advance billings are recorded as unearned revenue when billing occurs prior to rendering the associated service, and are then recognized as revenue in the period in which the services are provided. Similarly, when customers pay up-front activation and connection fees, these fees are deferred and recognized over the average expected term of the customer relationship. The Equipment Revenues reported on line 2, which include wireless handsets and other devices sold to resellers, and other customer premises equipment, are recognized when the products are delivered and accepted by the end-user customers. Any sales discounts and rebates are deducted from revenues. Based on this information, TELUS is properly recognizing and measuring its revenues, so the $10,325 million in revenues reported on line 3 will enhance the quality of TELUS's earnings reported on lines 15 (Net Income) and 21 (Comprehensive Income).

COOKING THE BOOKS WITH REVENUE

Research has shown that roughly half of all financial statement fraud over the past two decades has involved improper revenue recognition. Following are several of the more significant revenue recognition issues involving fraud:

- **Recognizing revenue prematurely (before it is earned).** One of the common fraud techniques is *channel stuffing*, where a company may ship inventory to regular customers in excess of amounts ordered. Bristol-Myers Squibb, a global pharmaceuticals company, was sued by the U.S. Securities and Exchange Commission in 2004 for channel stuffing during 2000 and 2001. The company allegedly stuffed its distribution channels with excess inventory near the end of every quarter in amounts sufficient to meet company sales targets (tied to executive bonuses), overstating revenue by about $1.5 billion. The company paid a civil fine of $100 million and established a $50 million fund to compensate shareholders for their losses.[*]

- **Providing incentives for customers to purchase more inventory than is needed, in exchange for future discounts and other benefits.**

- **Reporting revenue when significant services are still to be performed or goods delivered.**

- **Reporting sales to fictitious or nonexistent customers.** This may include falsified shipping and inventory records.

[*]Accounting and Auditing Enforcement Release No. 2075, August 4, 2004. *Securities and Exchange Commission v. Bristol-Myers Squibb Company*, 04-3680 DNJ (2004). See www.sec.gov.

Expense Recognition

Just as it is important to avoid premature or improper revenue recognition, it is equally important to make sure that *all expenses are accurately, completely, and transparently included* in the computation of net income. In Chapter 3, you learned that an expense must be recognized when two criteria have been met: (1) there has been a decrease in future economic benefits caused by a decrease in an asset *or* an increase in a liability, and (2) the expense can be reliably measured. We saw with the example of the WorldCom fraud in Chapter 7 what can happen when a company manipulates reported earnings by deliberately understating expenses. Without the information provided by full and complete disclosures of all existing expenses, the quality of earnings is reduced, making it difficult to properly assess a company's current and future operating performance.

Operating Expenses

Operating expenses consist of the ongoing costs incurred by a company to earn revenues and run its business on a day-to-day basis. These expenses include salaries and wages, depreciation, rent, marketing, and utilities. For a company that earns revenues from the sale of goods, they can also include the cost of goods sold if the company chooses not to report this item in a separate section preceding the operating expenses. TELUS does not report its cost of goods sold as a separate line item, but rather includes it in Goods and Services Purchased on line 6 of its income statement.

Again, the quality of earnings is enhanced when a company takes care to accurately measure and recognize operating expenses. In addition, the lower these expenses are as a percentage of operating revenues (or sales), the more efficiently and, therefore, the more profitably we can assume management is operating the business. As shown in line 10 of Exhibit 11-1, TELUS's operating expenses increased from $7,883 million in 2010 to $8,429 million in 2011, while total operating revenues grew from $9,792 million to $10,397 million (line 5). These changes resulted in a slight increase in operating expenses as a percentage of operating revenues, with the ratio going from 80.5% in 2010 to 81.1% in 2011. TELUS was therefore able to increase its revenues in 2011 without significantly increasing the cost of doing business.

Operating Income

We calculate a company's operating income (or income from continuing operations) by deducting its operating expenses from operating revenues. Because operating income is a function of a company's ongoing, day-to-day business activities, it is seen by many users as a more reliable predictor of future earnings than net income, which often includes one-time gains and losses, or other non-recurring items that will not persist into future years. When a company's operating revenues and expenses are accurately measured and properly recognized, the predictive value of operating income is even more reliable. On line 11 of Exhibit 11-1, we see that TELUS earned Operating Income of $1,968 million in 2011, which was up slightly from the $1,909 million it earned the previous year.

What Should You Analyze to Gain an Overall Picture of a Company?

While operating income is a key figure to use when analyzing a company's performance, it is also critical to examine its cash flow from operating activities, which gives us a different view of the company's operating performance. Because we record operating revenues and expenses on the accrual basis regardless of when we receive or pay cash, operating income may differ from cash flow from operating activities, which is based solely on cash receipts and payments. A company may report significant operating income, for example, but have poor operating cash flow because it cannot collect cash from its customers on a timely basis. The reverse may also be true: a company may generate significant operating cash flows but report little or no operating income. Generally, the higher the ratio of a company's cash flow from operations to its operating income, the better its quality of earnings.

The income statement and the statement of cash flows can therefore paint different pictures of the same company, so we must analyze both of them, along with the balance sheet and the statement of changes in shareholders' equity, to gain an overall picture of a company's operating performance and financial position.

OBJECTIVE

❷ **Account** for other items on the income statement

ACCOUNT FOR OTHER ITEMS ON THE INCOME STATEMENT

Interest Expense and Interest Income

Recall from Chapter 5 that interest income represents the return earned on invested money, and from Chapter 9 that interest expense represents the cost of borrowed money. Both items are reported outside of operating income because they are not part of the day-to-day operations of the business. These items can be netted against each other for presentation purposes, as long as the details are disclosed in the notes to the financial statements. On line 12 of TELUS's income statement in Exhibit 11-1, the company reports Finance Costs of $377 million in 2011 and $522 million in 2010. In Note 8 to the financial statements, we see that the 2011 finance costs consist of $380 million in interest expense and $3 million in interest income.

Corporate Income Taxes

Corporations, like individuals, must pay taxes on their incomes. Personal and corporate tax rates differ, and corporate tax rates also vary by type of company and by province.

The accounting for corporate income taxes is complicated by the fact that income for accounting purposes (or **pretax accounting income**) usually differs from income for tax purposes. We determine income for accounting purposes by applying IFRS or ASPE, whereas we determine income for tax purposes by applying the rules in federal and provincial Income Tax Acts. The differences between accounting standards and tax rules result in differences between accounting income, which is used to determine a corporation's *income tax expense*, and **taxable income**, which is the income figure used to determine a corporation's *income tax payable*.

In general, income tax expense and income tax payable can be computed as follows:[*]

$$
\begin{array}{ccc}
\text{Income} & & \text{Income before} \\
\text{tax} & = & \text{income tax} \\
\text{expense} & & \text{(from the \textit{income}} \\
& & \text{statement})
\end{array}
\times
\begin{array}{c}
\text{Income} \\
\text{tax} \\
\text{rate}
\end{array}
\qquad
\begin{array}{c}
\text{Income} \\
\text{tax} \\
\textit{payable}
\end{array}
=
\begin{array}{c}
\text{Taxable income} \\
\text{(from the} \\
\textit{income tax return} \\
\textit{filed with tax} \\
\textit{authorities)}
\end{array}
\times
\begin{array}{c}
\text{Income} \\
\text{tax} \\
\text{rate}
\end{array}
$$

---

[*]The authors thank Jean Marie Hudson for suggesting this presentation.

Income tax expense commonly differs from income tax payable because certain revenues and expenses are treated differently for accounting purposes than they are for tax purposes. The depreciation of capital assets is one area where such differences occur. Under IFRS and ASPE, companies have some leeway to choose the methods and rates they use to depreciate their assets, whereas tax rules specify the method and rate to be used for each asset type. We will use a simple example to illustrate the accounting impact of this kind of difference.

Suppose a company reports $10 million in pretax accounting income for the year ended December 31, 2014. Its operating expenses for 2014 include $2 million of depreciation, which was calculated using the straight-line method. The tax rules, however, require the use of an accelerated depreciation method, which results in depreciation for tax purposes of $2.8 million. If we assume there are no other accounting versus tax differences, then the company's taxable income for 2014 is $9.2 million, which is lower than its pretax accounting income due to the extra $800,000 ($2.8 million − $2 million) in depreciation for tax purposes. Assuming an income tax rate of 30%, the following journal entry is needed to account for the company's 2014 income taxes (dollar amounts in millions):

2014			
Dec. 31	Income Tax Expense ($10 × 0.30)	3.00	
	Income Tax Payable ($9.2 × 0.30)		2.76
	Deferred Income Tax Liability		0.24
	Recorded income tax for the year.		

ASSETS	=	LIABILITIES	+	SHAREHOLDERS' EQUITY	
0	=	$2.76 ⏐ $0.24		−$3.00	Income Tax Expense

The Income Tax Payable liability of $2.76 million (30% of taxable income of $9.2 million) represents the amount of income tax the company will actually have to remit to the government in 2015. The **Deferred Income Tax Liability** of $240,000, which is the difference between the company's income tax expense of $3 million and its income tax payable of $2.76 million, represents the amount of income taxes payable in future periods as a result of differences between accounting income and taxable income in the current and prior periods. When income tax payable exceeds income tax expense, the difference is debited to a Deferred Income Tax Asset account. Under ASPE, deferred income taxes are referred to as future income taxes. Deferred and future income taxes are covered in greater depth in intermediate accounting courses.

Discontinued Operations

Most large companies engage in several lines of business. TELUS, for example, has two major business lines: wireless and wireline. The wireless segment includes digital personal communications services, equipment sales, and wireless Internet services. The wireline segment includes local and long distance telephone services, TV and Internet access, and other telecommunications services that exclude wireless.

When a company sells or discontinues a component of its business, the income and expenses related to the component must be reported separately under the heading Discontinued Operations. Because the discontinuance of a business component is viewed as a one-time event, the income or loss from discontinued operations is reported outside of income from continuing operations on an after-tax basis. Users exclude income or losses from discontinued operations from their predictions of future income because the discontinued components will not continue to generate income or losses for the company.

Accounting Changes

Companies sometimes change the way they account for certain financial statement items. They may, for example, change from the diminishing-balance method of calculating depreciation to the straight-line method, or from the FIFO method of inventory costing to the weighted-average method. Without proper disclosure of such accounting changes, it would be difficult for users to compare the results of the current period with those of preceding periods. As a result, users may be misled into thinking that the current year is better or worse than preceding years, when in fact the year-over-year differences are being driven by accounting changes rather than by any meaningful change in business activities.

While the detailed treatment of accounting changes will be left for intermediate accounting courses, we will briefly introduce you to the treatment of the two types of changes mentioned above:

1. A *change in accounting estimate* is an adjustment of the carrying amount of an asset or a liability, or the amount of the periodic consumption of an asset, that results from new information or new developments in the current accounting period. Examples include changing the estimated useful life of a long-lived asset, changing depreciation methods, and changing the estimated collectibility of accounts receivable. The impacts of changes in accounting estimates are reported only for *current and future* accounting periods; we do not adjust balances from prior reporting periods after making a change in accounting estimate in the current period.

2. A *change in accounting principle* is an actual change in the application of a specific IFRS or ASPE accounting principle, such as a change from the FIFO to the weighted-average method of inventory costing, or a change in the way a specific type of revenue or expense is recognized. A change in accounting principle is applied *retrospectively*, meaning that the company reports figures for the current period and all reported comparative periods using the new accounting principle. This treatment results in all current and prior-period amounts being reported as though the new accounting principle had been in effect since the beginning of the earliest comparative period. This treatment enhances the comparability of the reported accounting information, making it more useful for decision makers.

Accounting Errors

Companies sometimes omit or misstate information in their financial statements. Such errors can be *inadvertently* caused by calculation mistakes, the inappropriate application of accounting principles, or the ignorance or misuse of facts. They may also be the *intentional* result of fraud, which you have seen many examples of in the Cooking the Books features of preceding chapters. Regardless of their cause, when companies subsequently discover that the financial statements of a prior period contain *material* errors, the errors must be corrected. We correct a *prior-period error* by restating the affected amounts in the comparative financial statements for the period

COOKING THE BOOKS
WITH ACCOUNTING CHANGES

Investment analysts follow companies to see if they meet their forecasted earnings targets, and managers sometimes take drastic actions to ensure they meet these targets. Assume, for example, that it's late in November and it looks like a company's earnings may fall *below* the forecasted target once the year ends on December 31. A reasonable thing for company management to do is to push for an increase in sales in December in an effort to improve revenues and net income by year-end. Management could also cut expenses in December to try to increase net income for the year. These actions are ethical and honest, so any additional net income generated from them is legitimate.

Management could also use an ethically questionable tactic to increase net income for the year. Suppose the company has been using the diminishing-balance method to depreciate its equipment, and that a change to the straight-line method would decrease depreciation expense and increase net income enough to meet the earnings forecast. By simply making this change in accounting estimate, the company could meet analysts' forecasts without management making any efforts to increase sales or legitimately reduce expenses. Accounting changes like this are a quick-and-dirty way to improve net income when the company can't earn enough from continuing operations. This is why IFRS and ASPE permit companies to make accounting changes only if the changes result in more relevant and reliable information. The standards also require companies to clearly disclose any changes in accounting estimates or policies, along with their effects on the financial statements. With full disclosure of such changes, users can more easily assess the effects of these changes on key financial statement items.

in which the error occurred. Suppose, for example, that when preparing its 2015 financial statements, a company discovers that it miscalculated depreciation expense in 2014, resulting in a $100,000 understatement of depreciation expense and a corresponding overstatement of the carrying amount of its capital assets. Before issuing its 2015 financial statements, the company would correct this error by increasing the 2014 depreciation expense by $100,000 and reducing the 2014 year-end carrying amount of its capital assets by the same amount. These revised comparative figures would be included in the 2014 comparative financial statements, along with a note describing the error. When an error relates to a period prior to the earliest reported comparative period, we correct it by restating the opening balances of assets, liabilities, and equity for the earliest comparative period.

COMPUTE EARNINGS PER SHARE

OBJECTIVE

❸ **Compute** earnings per share

The final segment of the Statements of Income and Comprehensive Income reports a company's **earnings per share (EPS)**, which represents the amount of net income earned per *outstanding common share*. IFRS require companies to report their EPS, whereas ASPE do not have this reporting requirement. The EPS is computed as follows:

$$\text{Earnings per share} = \frac{\text{Net income} - \text{Preferred dividends}}{\text{Weighted-average number of common shares outstanding}}$$

ADJUSTMENTS TO NET INCOME. Recall that the owners of a company's preferred shares have the first claim on any dividends paid out of the company's earnings. To account for this preference, we also deduct any preferred dividends from net income before computing the earnings per *common share*. TELUS does not have any preferred shares outstanding at the end of 2011, so the calculation of its 2011 EPS does not require any adjustment for preferred dividends.

The Net Income figure used to calculate EPS also excludes any income or loss from discontinued operations, as well as any income or loss pertaining to non-controlling interests (if the company reports discontinued operations, it must separately report EPS for these operations). TELUS had no income or loss from discontinued operations in 2011, but as reported on line 23, there was a $4 million loss attributable to non-controlling interests. TELUS's overall net income for 2011 was $1,215 million, so after adding back this loss, the 2011 net income attributable to common shareholders (including non-voting shareholders) is $1,219 million (line 22).

WEIGHTED-AVERAGE NUMBER OF COMMON SHARES OUTSTANDING. Notice that TELUS reports two EPS figures on its income statement: one for *basic* EPS (line 28) and one for *diluted* EPS (line 29). Each of these EPS figures is calculated using a different weighted-average number of common shares outstanding. Except in rare circumstances, the basic EPS is calculated based on the weighted average of the *actual* number of common shares outstanding during the period, whereas the diluted EPS also takes into account the *additional* number of common shares that would be outstanding if things like convertible preferred shares or common stock options were converted to issued and outstanding common shares, which would result in the *dilution* of the basic EPS. The computation of both weighted averages is beyond the scope of this textbook, so you will always be provided with these figures when asked to compute EPS in this book. Line 31 of TELUS's income statement reports that the basic weighted average number of common shares outstanding during 2011 was 324 million, while line 32 shows the diluted number was 326 million common shares.

Using the above information, we can now calculate TELUS's 2011 basic and diluted EPS:

Basic EPS ($1,219 million/324 million shares): $3.76 (line 28)

Diluted EPS ($1,219 million/326 million shares): $3.74 (line 29)

As an exercise, use the information in TELUS's 2010 income statement to recalculate the basic and diluted EPS figures it reports for the comparative period.

OBJECTIVE

❹ **Analyze** the statement of comprehensive income and the statement of changes in shareholders' equity

ANALYZE THE STATEMENT OF COMPREHENSIVE INCOME AND THE STATEMENT OF CHANGES IN SHAREHOLDERS' EQUITY

Reporting Comprehensive Income

In addition to reporting net income and its components, IFRS require companies to report **comprehensive income**, which includes additional items that cause a change in total shareholders' equity but that derive from sources other than the owners of the business. Specifically, comprehensive income includes net income plus:

- Gains and losses on certain types of investments (see line 16 of Exhibit 11-1 for an example)
- Foreign-currency translation adjustments (see line 17 of Exhibit 11-1)
- Actuarial gains and losses on defined benefit pension plans (see line 19 of Exhibit 11-1)
- Changes caused by the revaluation of capital assets

While some of the items from the first two categories were discussed briefly in Chapter 8, detailed coverage of the elements of comprehensive income will be left for more advanced accounting courses.

IFRS permit companies to report net income and comprehensive income in a single statement like the one used by TELUS in Exhibit 11-1. They also have the option of reporting the components of net income and comprehensive income in two separate statements: an income statement and a statement of comprehensive income. If this option is chosen, the income statement includes the components of net income as well as EPS data, while the statement of comprehensive income begins with net income from the income statement followed by the components of comprehensive income. Comprehensive income is excluded from the calculation of EPS, so no EPS data are reported on a separate statement of comprehensive income.

The concept of comprehensive income does not exist in ASPE, so there is no statement of comprehensive income required when reporting under these standards.

Reporting Changes in Shareholders' Equity

The **statement of changes in shareholders' equity** reports the details of all the changes in the shareholders' equity section of the balance sheet during the period. Exhibit 11-2 presents TELUS's statement for the year ended December 31, 2011. The statement contains a column for each major element of equity, starting with Share Capital on the left and ending with a column summarizing the total changes for the period. The top row (line 1) reports the beginning balance for each element as at December 31, 2010, while the next seven rows (lines 2–8) detail the causes of the changes in each element during the 2011 fiscal year.

Let's briefly examine some of the changes in TELUS's shareholders' equity during 2011. On line 2, we see the year's net income of $1,219 million (from line 22 of TELUS's income statement in Exhibit 11-1) being added to Retained Earnings, just as it would be in a stand-alone statement of retained earnings. Line 3 reports the components of comprehensive income that affect Retained Earnings and Accumulated Other Comprehensive Income. These items come from lines 19 and 18, respectively, of the

EXHIBIT 11-2
Statement of Changes in Shareholders' Equity

TELUS Corporation
Consolidated Statement of Changes in Owners' Equity (Adapted)
For the Year Ended December 31, 2011

(in millions)	Share capital	Contributed surplus	Retained earnings	Accumulated other comprehensive income	Total
1. **Balance as at January 1, 2011**	$5,456	$176	$2,126	$ 1	$7,759
2. Net income	-	-	1,219	-	1,219
3. Other comprehensive income	-	-	(851)	10	(841)
4. Dividends	-	-	(715)	-	(715)
5. Dividends reinvested in shares	54	-	-	-	54
6. Share option award expense	-	9	-	-	9
7. Acquisition of subsidiary	-	-	1	-	1
8. Shares issued pursuant to exercise of share options	46	(19)	-	-	27
9. **Balance as at December 31, 2011**	$5,556	$166	$1,780	$11	$7,513

EXHIBIT 11-3
TELUS Corporation—
Shareholders' Equity Section
of the Balance Sheet

TELUS Corporation
Consolidated Balance Sheet (Partial)
As at December 31, 2011

(in millions)

Shareholders' equity

Share capital	$5,556
Contributed surplus	166
Retained earnings	1,780
Accumulated other comprehensive income	11
Total shareholders' equity	**$7,513**

statement of comprehensive income in Exhibit 11-1. On line 4, we see dividends of $715 million being deducted from Retained Earnings—again, just like they would be in a separate statement of retained earnings. Line 5 reports that an additional $54 million in share capital was issued during 2011, pursuant to some shareholders using their dividend proceeds to purchase additional shares of the company. Lines 6 and 8 report the details of transactions related to TELUS stock options, while line 7 contains information on the impact of the acquisition of a subsidiary during the year.

The statement ends with the closing balances for each element as at December 31, 2011 (line 9). All of the closing balances are carried forward to the shareholders' equity section of the balance sheet, which is reported in Exhibit 11-3.

ASPE require only a statement of retained earnings, which you have seen in previous chapters. Such a statement for TELUS would contain only the information in the Retained Earnings column of Exhibit 11-2.

◀ DECISION GUIDELINES ▶

USING THE INCOME STATEMENT AND STATEMENT OF CHANGES IN SHAREHOLDERS' EQUITY

Suppose you've completed your studies, taken a job, and been fortunate to save $10,000, which you now wish to invest. These guidelines suggest some key information to examine on the income statement and the statement of changes in shareholders' equity before deciding where to invest your money.

Decision	Statement	Decision Factor
Has the company made any money recently?	Income statement	Net income
How much income can I expect the company to earn in the near future?	Income statement	Income from continuing operations
How much income can I expect to earn per share that I own?	Income statement	Earnings per share
Can I expect to earn dividend income from this company?	Statement of changes in shareholders' equity	Dividends paid
Has the company raised any additional capital recently?	Statement of changes in shareholders' equity	Increases in share capital pursuant to issuance of new shares

DIFFERENTIATE BETWEEN MANAGEMENT'S AND THE AUDITOR'S RESPONSIBILITIES IN FINANCIAL REPORTING

Management's Responsibility

A company's management is responsible for the internal controls over the financial reporting process and for the financial statements that result from this process. The managers of Canadian public companies must explicitly report these responsibilities to the users of their financial statements. Exhibit 11-4 presents an excerpt from TELUS's 2011 Report of Management on Internal Control Over Financial Reporting, which clearly describes management's financial reporting responsibilities.

The managers of private companies do not have to explicitly report their financial reporting responsibilities to users, but they bear the same set of responsibilities.

> **OBJECTIVE**
>
> ❺ **Differentiate** between management's and the auditor's responsibilities in financial reporting

Management of TELUS Corporation (TELUS) is responsible for establishing and maintaining adequate internal control over financial reporting and for its assessment of the effectiveness of internal control over financial reporting.

TELUS' Chief Executive Officer (CEO) and Chief Financial Officer (CFO) have assessed the effectiveness of the Company's internal control over financial reporting as of December 31, 2011, in accordance with the criteria established in *Internal Control—Integrated Framework* issued by the Committee of Sponsoring Organizations of the Treadway Commission (COSO).

Based on this assessment, management has determined that the Company's internal control over financial reporting is effective as of December 31, 2011. In connection with this assessment, no material weaknesses in the Company's internal control over financial reporting were identified by management as of December 31, 2011.

EXHIBIT 11-4
Excerpt from TELUS's Report of Management on Internal Control Over Financial Reporting

The Auditor's Responsibilities

All publicly accountable enterprises in Canada must have their financial statements audited by an independent public accountant, more commonly known as an **auditor**. In addition, many private companies are required by government incorporation acts, creditors, or other financial statement users to have their financial statements audited. The auditor's responsibility is to gather evidence regarding the financial information reported by management, and then decide whether the information reported in the financial statements complies with the applicable GAAP, which will usually be IFRS or ASPE. Upon completing its audit of a company's financial statements, the auditor provides a signed report to the board of directors and shareholders of the company.

The standard audit report has four sections, which contain the following information:

- The first section identifies the company being audited, the title and date or period of each audited financial statement, and an explicit statement that the financial statements have been audited.

- The second section clearly describes management's responsibilities for the internal controls over the financial reporting process and for the preparation and fair presentation of the financial statements in accordance with IFRS or ASPE.

- The third section clearly describes the auditor's responsibility to provide an opinion on the financial statements, and also briefly describes the process used to obtain the evidence on which the opinion is based.

- The final section contains the auditor's opinion on the fair presentation of the company's financial statements. When the evidence gathered suggests that the financial statements are in accordance with IFRS or ASPE, the auditor issues an **unmodified** (or **clean**) **opinion** on the fairness of the financial statements, which is the highest statement of assurance an auditor can express regarding the reliability of a company's financial statements.

Exhibit 11-5 contains an excerpt from TELUS's 2011 auditor's report. As you can see in the final section, Deloitte & Touche LLP, TELUS's auditor, issued an unmodified opinion on the company's 2011 financial statements, indicating they are in accordance with IFRS. Thus, users of these financial statements have a high degree of assurance that they are basing their decisions on reliable financial information.

EXHIBIT 11-5
Excerpt from Auditor's Report on TELUS's 2011 Financial Statements

To the Board of Directors and Shareholders of TELUS Corporation

We have audited the accompanying consolidated financial statements of TELUS Corporation and subsidiaries (the Company), which comprise the consolidated statements of financial position as at December 31, 2011, and the consolidated statements of income and other comprehensive income, changes in owners' equity and cash flows for the year ended December 31, 2011, and a summary of significant accounting policies and other explanatory information.

Management's Responsibility for the Consolidated Financial Statements

Management is responsible for the preparation and fair presentation of these consolidated financial statements in accordance with International Financial Reporting Standards as issued by the International Accounting Standards Board, and for such internal control as management determines is necessary to enable the preparation of consolidated financial statements that are free from material misstatement, whether due to fraud or error.

Auditors' Responsibility

Our responsibility is to express an opinion on these consolidated financial statements based on our audit. We conducted our audit in accordance with Canadian generally accepted auditing standards and the standards of the Public Company Accounting Oversight Board (United States). Those standards require that we comply with ethical requirements and plan and perform the audit to obtain reasonable assurance about whether the consolidated financial statements are free from material misstatement.

An audit involves performing procedures to obtain audit evidence about the amounts and disclosures in the consolidated financial statements. The procedures selected depend on the auditor's judgement, including the assessment of the risks of material misstatement of the consolidated financial statements, whether due to fraud or error. In making those risk assessments, the auditor considers internal control relevant to the entity's preparation and fair presentation of the consolidated financial statements in order to design audit procedures that are appropriate in the circumstances. An audit also includes evaluating the appropriateness of accounting policies used and the reasonableness of accounting estimates made by management, as well as evaluating the overall presentation of the consolidated financial statements.

We believe that the audit evidence we have obtained in our audit is sufficient and appropriate to provide a basis for our audit opinion.

Opinion

In our opinion, the consolidated financial statements present fairly, in all material respects, the financial position of TELUS Corporation and subsidiaries as at December 31, 2011, and their financial performance and their cash flows for the year ended December 31, 2011, in accordance with International Financial Reporting Standards as issued by the International Accounting Standards Board.

/s/Deloitte & Touche LLP
Vancouver, Canada
February 23, 2012

Summary of IFRS-ASPE Differences

Concept	IFRS	ASPE
Differences between income tax expense and income tax payable (p. 526)	Accounted for as deferred income taxes.	Accounted for as future income taxes.
Earnings per share (p. 529)	Companies must report this figure on their income statement.	Companies do not have to report this figure.
Statement of comprehensive income (p. 530)	Companies must report this statement, either on its own or in combination with the income statement.	The concept of comprehensive income does not exist in ASPE, so this statement is not reported.
Statement of changes in shareholders' (or owners') equity (p. 531)	Companies must report this statement.	Companies must report only a statement of retained earnings, which contains only a subset of the information reported in the statement of changes in shareholders' equity.

SUMMARY OF CHAPTER 11

LEARNING OBJECTIVE	SUMMARY
1. **Evaluate** the quality of earnings	Knowledgeable investors will analyze a company's earnings quality, which is a function of many factors, including: 1. Proper revenue and expense recognition. 2. Low operating expenses as a percentage of operating revenues. 3. High and increasing operating income (or income from continuing operations). The higher the quality of a company's current earnings, the more likely it is that the company is executing a successful business strategy that will generate healthy earnings in the future, which is a key determinant of its stock price.
2. **Account** for other items on the income statement	Interest income and interest expense are reported outside of operating income because they are not part of the day-to-day operations of a business. Corporations, like individuals, must pay taxes on their incomes. The accounting for corporate income taxes is complicated by the fact that differences between accounting standards and tax rules result in differences between accounting income, which is used to determine a corporation's income tax expense, and taxable income, which is the income figure used to determine a corporation's income tax payable. The differences between income tax expense and income tax payable are accounted for as deferred income tax under IFRS and future income tax under ASPE. When a company sells or discontinues a component of its business, the after-tax income or loss related to the component must be reported separately under the heading Discontinued Operations.

The impacts of changes in accounting estimates are reported only for current and future accounting periods; we do not adjust balances from prior reporting periods after making a change in accounting estimate in the current period.

A change in accounting principle is applied retrospectively, meaning that the company reports figures for the current period and all reported comparative periods using the new accounting principle. This treatment results in all current and prior-period amounts being reported as though the new accounting principle had been in effect since the beginning of the earliest comparative period.

We correct a prior-period error by restating the affected amounts in the comparative financial statements for the period in which the error occurred and also include a note describing the error.

3. **Compute** earnings per share

A company's earnings per share represents the amount of net income earned per outstanding common share, and can be used to help determine the fair value of its common shares. The EPS is computed as follows:

$$\text{Earnings per share} = \frac{\text{Net income} - \text{Preferred dividends}}{\text{Weighted-average number of common shares outstanding}}$$

The net income figure used to calculate EPS excludes any income or loss from discontinued operations, as well as any income or loss pertaining to non-controlling interests.

We calculate and report two EPS figures—a basic EPS and a diluted EPS. The basic EPS is calculated based on the weighted average of the actual number of common shares outstanding during the period, whereas the diluted EPS takes into account the additional number of common shares that would be outstanding if things like convertible preferred shares or stock options were converted to issued and outstanding common shares, which would result in the dilution of the basic EPS.

4. **Analyze** the statement of comprehensive income and the statement of changes in shareholders' equity

IFRS require companies to report comprehensive income, which includes items that cause a change in total shareholders' equity but that derive from sources other than the owners of the business. Specifically, comprehensive income includes net income plus:

- Gains and losses on certain types of investments
- Foreign-currency translation adjustments
- Actuarial gains and losses on defined benefit pension plans
- Changes caused by the revaluation of capital assets

IFRS permit companies to report net income and comprehensive income in a single statement, or separately in an income statement and a statement of comprehensive income.

The statement of changes in shareholders' equity reports the details of all the changes in the shareholders' equity section of the balance sheet during the period. It typically reports changes in the following equity items:

- Share capital
- Contributed surplus
- Retained earnings
- Accumulated other comprehensive income

5. **Differentiate** between management's and the auditor's responsibilities in financial reporting

A company's management is responsible for the internal controls over the financial reporting process and for the financial statements that result from this process.

The auditor's responsibility is to gather evidence regarding the financial information reported by management, and then decide whether the information reported in the financial statements complies with IFRS or ASPE. Upon completing its audit of a company's financial statements, the auditor provides a signed report to the board of directors and shareholders of the company. The report includes the auditor's opinion on the fairness of the company's financial statements.

END-OF-CHAPTER SUMMARY PROBLEM

The following information was taken from the ledger of Canmore Outdoor Products Ltd., a publicly accountable enterprise, as at December 31, 2014:

Gain on sale of property, plant, and equipment	21,000	Income tax expense, Unrealized gain on derivatives....	6,400
Cost of goods sold	380,000	Preferred shares, $8.00, 500 shares issued	50,000
Income tax expense, Continuing operations	25,600	Dividends	16,000
Selling expenses	78,000	Unrealized gain on derivatives	20,000
Common shares, 40,000 shares issued	165,000	Loss due to lawsuit	11,000
Sales revenue	620,000	General expenses	62,000
Interest expense	30,000		

Requirement

Prepare a multi-step statement of income and comprehensive income for the year ended December 31, 2014. Include the earnings-per-share presentation and show computations. Assume no changes in the share accounts during the year.

ANSWERS

Name: Canmore Outdoor Products Ltd.
Industry: Outdoor products corporation
Fiscal Period: Year ended December 31, 2014

Canmore Outdoor Products Ltd.
Statement of Income and Comprehensive Income
For the Year Ended December 31, 2014

Sales revenue	$620,000
Cost of goods sold	380,000
	240,000
Operating expenses	
Selling expenses	78,000
General expenses	62,000
	140,000
Operating income	100,000
Interest expense	(30,000)
Loss due to lawsuit	(11,000)
Gain on sale of property, plant, and equipment	21,000
Income before income taxes	80,000
Income tax expense	25,600
Net income	54,400
Other comprehensive income	
Unrealized gain on derivatives, net of tax	13,600
Comprehensive income	$ 68,000
Earnings per share: (40,000 shares outstanding)*	
Net income [($54,400 − $4,000)/40,000 shares]	$ 1.26

*Computations:

$$EPS = \frac{\text{Net income} - \text{Preferred dividends}}{\text{Common shares outstanding}}$$

Preferred dividends: 500 × $8.00 = $4,000
Common shares outstanding: 40,000 shares

Review the Income Statement, the Statement of Comprehensive Income, and the Statement of Shareholders' Equity

QUICK CHECK (ANSWERS ARE GIVEN ON PAGE 553.)

1. The quality of earnings suggests that
   a. net income is the best measure of the results of operations.
   b. income from continuing operations is better than income from one time transactions.
   c. continuing operations and one-time transactions are of equal importance.
   d. shareholders want the corporation to earn enough income to be able to pay its debts.

2. Which statement is true?
   a. Discontinued operations are a separate category on the income statement.
   b. Extraordinary items are part of discontinued operations.
   c. Cumulative effect of accounting changes is combined with continuing operations on the income statement.
   d. All of the above are true.

3. Marshall Transportation Ltd. reported a basic EPS of $5.94. The weighted-average number of common shares outstanding during the year was 111,000 and the company paid no preferred dividends. What was its net income for the year?
   a. $701,590   c. $659,340
   b. $695,430   d. Some other amount

4. Return to TELUS's income statement on page 523. TELUS has no preferred shares outstanding. How many common and non-voting shares did TELUS have outstanding during fiscal year 2011?
   a. 337 million   c. 324 million
   b. 326 million   d. 31 million

5. Why is it important for companies to report their accounting changes to the public?
   a. Accounting changes affect dividends, and investors want dividends.
   b. Some accounting changes are more extraordinary than others.
   c. Most accounting changes increase net income, and investors need to know why the increase in net income occurred.
   d. Without the reporting of accounting changes, investors could believe that all the company's income came from continuing operations.

6. Other comprehensive income
   a. affects earnings per share.
   b. includes extraordinary gains and losses.
   c. includes unrealized gains and losses on certain types of investments.
   d. has no effect on income tax.

7. OnStar, LLC, earned income before tax of $50,000. Taxable income was $40,000, and the income tax rate was 25%. OnStar recorded income tax with which journal entry?

a. Income Tax Expense	12,500	
Income Tax Payable		10,000
Deferred Income Tax Liability		2,500
b. Income Tax Expense	12,500	
Income Tax Payable		12,500
c. Income Tax Payable	10,000	
Income Tax Expense		10,000
d. Income Tax Payable	12,500	
Income Tax Expense		10,000
Deferred Income Tax Liability		2,500

8. Deferred Income Tax Liability is usually

       Type of Account   *Reported on the*
   - **a.** Short-term   Income statement
   - **b.** Short-term   Statement of shareholders' equity
   - **c.** Long-term   Income statement
   - **d.** Long-term   Balance statement

9. The main purpose of the statement of changes in shareholders' equity is to report
   - **a.** financial position.
   - **b.** reasons for changes in the equity accounts.
   - **c.** results of operations.
   - **d.** comprehensive income.

10. An unmodified auditor's opinion on a company's financial statements
    - **a.** ensures that the financial statements are error-free.
    - **b.** gives investors assurance that the company's shares are a safe investment.
    - **c.** gives investors assurance that the financial statements conform to GAAP.
    - **d.** is ultimately the responsibility of the management of the client company.

Accounting Vocabulary

auditor A person or firm that provides an objective opinion on whether an entity's financial statements have been prepared in accordance with generally accepted accounting principles. (p. 533)

clean audit opinion Another term for an *unmodified audit opinion*. (p. 534)

comprehensive income Includes net income and other items that cause a change in total shareholders' equity but that derive from sources other than from the owners of the business. (p. 530)

deferred income tax liability The amount of income taxes payable in future periods as a result of differences between accounting income and taxable income in current and prior periods. Under ASPE, this is known as a *future income tax liability*. (p. 527)

earnings per share (EPS) Amount of a company's net income per outstanding common share. (p. 529)

earnings quality Provides insight into whether a company's current-period earnings will persist into future periods. (p. 522)

pretax accounting income Income before tax on the income statement; the basis for computing income tax expense. (p. 526)

statement of changes in shareholders' equity Reports the changes in all categories of shareholders' equity during the period. (p. 531)

taxable income The basis for computing the amount of tax to pay the government. (p. 526)

unmodified audit opinion An audit opinion stating that the financial statements are in accordance with GAAP (IFRS or ASPE). (p. 534)

Assess Your Progress

MyAccountingLab   Make the grade with MyAccountingLab: The Exercises, Quizzes, and Problems (A set) marked in red can be found on MyAccountingLab. You can practise them as often as you want, and most feature step-by-step guided instructions to help you find the right answer.

SHORT EXERCISES

LEARNING OBJECTIVE ❶

Evaluate earnings quality

S11-1 Research has shown that over 50% of financial statement frauds include the improper recognition of revenue. What does this mean? Describe the most common ways companies improperly recognize revenue.

LEARNING OBJECTIVE ❷

Explain the items on a complex income statement

S11-2 Study the income statement of TELUS Corporation (page 523), and answer these questions about the company:

1. How much operating income did TELUS earn on operating revenue? How much was income before taxes? How much was net income?

2. What dollar amount of net income would most sophisticated investors use to predict TELUS's net income for the next year? Name this item, give its amount, and state your reason.

LEARNING OBJECTIVE **2**

Prepare a complex income statement

S11-3 Financial Resources Inc. reported the following items, listed in no particular order, at December 31, 2014 (in thousands):

Other gains (losses)	$ (2,000)	Cost of goods sold	$66,000
Net sales revenue	168,000	Operating expenses	56,000
Loss on discontinued operations	20,000	Accounts receivable	21,000

The company's income tax rate is 25%.

Prepare Financial Resources' income statement for the year ended December 31, 2014. Omit earnings per share.

LEARNING OBJECTIVE **3**

Report earnings per share

S11-4 Return to the Financial Resources data in exercise S11-3. Financial Resources had 10,000 common shares outstanding during 2014. Financial Resources declared and paid preferred dividends of $5,000 during 2014.

Report Financial Resources' earnings per share on the income statement.

LEARNING OBJECTIVE **4**

Report comprehensive income

S11-5 Use the Financial Resources data in exercise S11-3. In addition, Financial Resources had unrealized gains of $1,000 on derivatives and a $2,000 foreign-currency translation adjustment (a gain) during 2014. Start with Financial Resources' net income from S11-3 and show how the company would report additional comprehensive income on its 2014 comprehensive income statement.

Should Financial Resources report earnings per share for comprehensive income? State why or why not.

LEARNING OBJECTIVE **1**

Evaluate earnings quality

S11-6 Some companies fraudulently overstate their net income by intentionally understating their expenses. State three ways a company could understate its expenses.

LEARNING OBJECTIVE **3**

Interpret earnings-per-share data

S11-7 Marstaller Motor Limited has preferred shares outstanding and issued additional common shares during the year.

1. Give the basic equation to compute earnings per share.

2. What makes earnings per share so useful as a business statistic?

LEARNING OBJECTIVE **2**

Account for a corporation's income tax

S11-8 PEI Marine Inc. had income before income tax of $110,000 and taxable income of $90,000 for 2014, the company's first year of operations. The income tax rate is 25%. The company uses ASPE.

1. Make the entry to record PEI Marine's income taxes for 2014.

2. Show what PEI Marine will report on its 2014 income statement, starting with income before income tax. Also, show what PEI Marine will report for current and long-term liabilities on its December 31, 2014, balance sheet.

LEARNING OBJECTIVE **2**

Report a prior-period error

S11-9 Quick Pies Ltd. was set to report its financial statements for the year ended December 31, 2014, along with the comparative financial statements for 2013. Just prior to doing so, it discovered it had unintentionally overstated depreciation expense and understated the carrying amount of capital assets by $50,000 when it originally reported its 2013 financial statements last year. What must Quick Pies do to deal with this misstatement?

LEARNING OBJECTIVE **4**

Use the statement of changes in shareholders' equity

S11-10 Use the statement of changes in shareholders' equity in Exhibit 11-2 (p. 531) to answer the following questions:

1. How much additional share capital did the issuance of shares raise during 2011?

2. What effect did the payment of dividends have on shareholders' equity during 2011?

EXERCISES

E11-11 Mountain Cycles Inc. reported a number of special items on its income statement. The following data, listed in no particular order, came from Mountain's financial statements (amounts in thousands):

LEARNING OBJECTIVE ❹

Prepare a comprehensive income statement

Income tax expense (saving):			Net sales..	$18,300
Continuing operations....................	$	515	Foreign-currency translation	
Discontinued operations.................		56	adjustment (gain)..........................	320
Unrealized gain on derivatives............		15	Income from discontinued	
Short-term investments		25	operations......................................	311
			Dividends declared and paid	860
			Total operating expenses..................	16,250

Requirement

Prepare the Mountain Cycles Inc. comprehensive income statement for the year ended September 30, 2014. Omit earnings per share.

E11-12 The Golden Books Corporation accounting records include the following for 2014 (in thousands):

LEARNING OBJECTIVE ❷❸

Prepare an income statement; calculate EPS

Other revenues...	$ 1,400
Income tax expense—discontinued operations.....................................	600
Income tax expense—income from continuing operations	2,150
Income from discontinued operations	1,500
Sales revenue..	114,000
Total operating expenses...	106,800

Requirement

Prepare Golden Books' income statement for the year ended December 31, 2014, including earnings per share. Golden Books had 1,600 common shares and no preferred shares outstanding during the year.

E11-13 High Seas Cruise Lines Inc. reported the following income statement for the year ended December 31, 2014:

LEARNING OBJECTIVE ❶❷

Use an income statement

	millions
Operating revenues	$70,752
Operating expenses	60,258
Operating income...	10,494
Other revenue (expense), net	985
Income from continuing operations...	11,479
Discontinued operations, net of tax...	935
Net income...	$12,414

Requirements

1. Were High Seas' discontinued operations more like an income or an expense item? How can you tell?
2. Suppose you are working as a financial analyst and your job is to predict High Seas' income for 2015 and beyond. Which item from the income statement will you use for your prediction? Identify its amount. Why will you use this item?

E11-14 Refer to exercise E11-13. If High Seas had 150 million common shares outstanding throughout 2014, what were its earnings per share for the year?

LEARNING OBJECTIVE ❸

Compute earnings per share

LEARNING OBJECTIVE ❸

Compute earnings per share

E11-15 Tennyson Loan Corporation's balance sheet reports the following:

$6 Preferred shares, 10,000 shares issued..	$500,000
Common shares, 1,200,000 shares issued	600,000

During 2014, Tennyson earned net income of $5,800,000. Compute Tennyson's EPS for 2014. Assume there was no change in the number of common shares outstanding during the year.

LEARNING OBJECTIVE ❸

Compute earnings per share

E11-16 Midtown Holding Limited operates numerous businesses, including motel, auto rental, and real estate companies. The year 2014 was interesting for Midtown, which reported the following on its comprehensive income statement (in millions):

Net revenues	$3,930
Total expenses and other	3,354
Income from continuing operations......................................	576
Discontinued operations, net of tax	84
Net income..	660
Foreign-currency translation adjustment	8
Comprehensive income...	$ 668

Midtown had 900 common shares outstanding for the duration of 2014.

Requirement

Calculate Midtown's earnings per share for 2014.

LEARNING OBJECTIVE ❷

Account for income tax by a corporation

E11-17 For 2014, its first year of operations, Smartpages Advertising Ltd. earned pretax accounting income of $600,000. Taxable income is $550,000. The income tax rate is 25%. Record Smartpages' income tax for the year. Show what Smartpages will report on its 2014 income statement and balance sheet for this situation. Start the income statement with income before tax. The company uses ASPE.

LEARNING OBJECTIVE ❷

Account for income tax by a corporation

E11-18 During 2014, the Castle Heights Corp. income statement reported income of $300,000 before tax. The company's income tax return filed with the Canada Revenue Agency showed taxable income of $250,000. During 2014, Castle Heights was subject to an income tax rate of 25%. The company uses ASPE.

Requirements

1. Journalize Castle Heights' income taxes for 2014.
2. How much income tax did Castle Heights owe at the end of 2014?
3. At the beginning of 2014, Castle Heights' balance of Future Income Tax Liability was $40,000. How much Future Income Tax Liability did Castle Heights report on its balance sheet at December 31, 2014?

LEARNING OBJECTIVE ❷

Explain the impact of a prior-period error

E11-19 As Roy Beaty Products Inc. was finalizing its 2014 financial statements, it discovered that an accounting error caused the net income of 2013 to be understated by $10 million. Retained earnings at December 31, 2013, as previously reported, stood at $324 million. Net income for 2014 was $88 million, and 2014 dividends were $48 million.

Requirement

What impact will this prior-period error have on Roy Beaty's 2014 income statement and the 2013 comparative income statement?

E11-20 At December 31, 2013, Lake Air Mall Inc. reported shareholders' equity as follows:

LEARNING OBJECTIVE ❹

Prepare a statement of changes in shareholders' equity

Common shares, 500,000 shares authorized, 300,000 shares issued	$ 870,000
Retained earnings	680,000
	$1,550,000

During 2014, Lake Air Mall completed these transactions (listed in chronological order):

a. Declared and issued a 5% stock dividend on the outstanding shares. At the time, Lake Air Mall shares were quoted at a market price of $10 per share.

b. Issued 20,000 common shares at the price of $12 per share.

c. Net income for the year, $320,000.

d. Declared cash dividends of $100,000.

Requirement

Prepare Lake Air Mall's statement of changes in shareholders' equity for 2014, using the format of Exhibit 11-2 (p. 531) as a model.

E11-21 Spring Water Limited reported the following items on its statement of shareholders' equity for the year ended December 31, 2014 (in thousands):

LEARNING OBJECTIVE ❹

Use a company's statement of changes in shareholders' equity

	Common Shares	Retained Earnings	Accumulated Other Comprehensive Income	Total Shareholders' Equity
Balance, Dec. 31, 2013	$3,000	$5,000	$14	$8,014
Net earnings from operations		1,500		
Unrealized gain on investments			2	
Issuance of 15 shares	150			
Cash dividends		(220)		
Balance, Dec. 31, 2014				

Requirements

1. Determine the December 31, 2014, balances in Spring Water's shareholders' equity accounts and total shareholders' equity on this date.

2. Spring Water's total liabilities on December 31, 2014, are $7,500 thousand. What is Spring Water's debt ratio on this date?

3. Was there a profit or a loss for the year ended December 31, 2014? How can you tell?

4. At what price per share did Spring Water issue common shares during 2014?

E11-22 The 2014 financial statements of BigJet Airlines, Ltd. included the following:

LEARNING OBJECTIVE ❺

Identify responsibility for the financial statements

INDEPENDENT AUDITORS' REPORT to the Shareholders of BigJet Airlines Ltd.

We have audited the accompanying consolidated financial statements of BigJet Airlines Ltd., which comprise the consolidated statements of financial position as at December 31, 2014, December 31, 2013, and January 1, 2013, the consolidated statement of earnings, other comprehensive income, changes in equity and cash flows for the years ended December 31, 2014 and December 31, 2013, and notes, comprising a summary of significant accounting policies and other explanatory information.

Management's Responsibility for the Consolidated Financial Statements

Management is responsible for the preparation and fair presentation of these consolidated financial statements in accordance with International Financial Reporting Standards, and for such internal control as management determines is necessary to enable the preparation of consolidated financial statements that are free from material misstatement, whether due to fraud or error.

Auditors' Responsibility

Our responsibility is to express an opinion on these consolidated financial statements based on our audits. We conducted our audits in accordance with Canadian generally accepted auditing standards. Those standards require that we comply with ethical requirements and plan and perform the audit to obtain reasonable assurance about whether the consolidated financial statements are free from material misstatement.

An audit involves performing procedures to obtain audit evidence about the amounts and disclosures in the consolidated financial statements. The procedures selected depend on our judgment, including the assessment of the risks of material misstatement of the consolidated financial statements, whether due to fraud or error. In making those risk assessments, we consider internal controls relevant to the entity's preparation and fair presentation of the consolidated financial statements in order to design audit procedures that are appropriate in the circumstances, but not for the purpose of expressing an opinion on the effectiveness of the entity's internal controls. An audit also includes evaluating the appropriateness of accounting policies used and the reasonableness of accounting estimates made by management, as well as evaluating the overall presentation of the consolidated financial statements.

We believe that the audit evidence we have obtained in our audits is sufficient and appropriate to provide a basis for our audit opinion.

Opinion

In our opinion, the consolidated financial statements present fairly, in all material respects, the consolidated financial position of BigJet Airlines Ltd. as at December 31, 2014, December 31, 2013, and January 1, 2013, and its consolidated financial performance and its consolidated cash flows for the years then ended in accordance with International Financial Reporting Standards.

/s/ GPB LLP
Chartered Accountants

Calgary, Canada
February 7, 2015

1. Who is responsible for BigJet's financial statements?

2. By what accounting standard are the financial statements prepared?

3. Identify one concrete action that BigJet's management takes to fulfill its responsibility for the reliability of the company's financial information.

4. Which entity gave an outside, independent opinion on the BigJet financial statements? Where was this entity located, and when did it release its opinion to the public?

5. Exactly what did the audit cover? Give names and dates.

6. By what standard did the auditor conduct the audit?

7. What was the auditor's opinion on BigJet's financial statements?

QUIZ

Test your understanding of the corporate income statement and the statement of changes in shareholders' equity by answering the following questions. Select the best choice from among the possible answers given.

Q11-23 What is the best source of income for a corporation?
a. Prior-period error adjustments
b. Continuing operations
c. Foreign-currency translation adjustment
d. Discontinued operations

Q11-24 Jergens Lotion Limited reports several earnings numbers on its current-year income statement (parentheses indicate a loss):

Gross profit	$140,000	Income from continuing operations	$35,000
Comprehensive income	41,000	Foreign-currency translation adjustment	14,000
Income before income tax	60,000	Discontinued operations	(8,000)

How much income would most investment analysts predict for Jergens to earn next year?
a. $14,000
b. $35,000
c. $49,000
d. $41,000

Q11-25 Refer to question Q11-24. Based on the information provided, what was Jergens' net income for the year?
a. $35,000
b. $55,000
c. $41,000
d. $27,000

Q11-26 Hi-Valu Inc. reported the following items before income tax:

Loss from discontinued operations	$ 90,000
Gain on sale of discontinued assets	110,000

Operating income before income tax totals $260,000, and the income tax rate is 25%. Hi-Valu's net income is
a. $210,000.
b. $280,000.
c. $380,000.
d. $460,000.

Q11-27 Hi-Valu Inc. in question Q11-26 has 10,000 $5 preferred shares and 100,000 common shares outstanding. Assuming there were no changes in the number of outstanding shares during the year, Hi-Valu's EPS is
a. $1.02.
b. $1.60.
c. $1.68.
d. $2.02.

Q11-28 Earnings per share is based on
a. continuing operations.
b. discontinued operations.
c. number of common shares outstanding.
d. comprehensive income.

Q11-29 Copystar Corporation has income before income tax of $150,000 and taxable income of $100,000 during its first year of operations. The income tax rate is 25%. Copystar's income statement will report net income of
a. $40,000.
b. $60,000.
c. $112,500.
d. $120,000.

Q11-30 Based on the information in question Q11-29, Copystar Corporation must immediately pay income tax of
a. $60,000.
b. $8,000.
c. $32,000.
d. $25,000.

Q11-31 Use the Copystar Corporation data in question Q11-29. At the end of its first year of operations, Copystar's deferred income tax liability is
a. $12,500.
b. $28,000.
c. $32,000.
d. $40,000.

Q11-32 Which of the following items is most closely related to prior period adjustments?
a. Earnings per share
b. Retained earnings
c. Accounting errors
d. Preferred share dividends

Q11-33 Examine TELUS's statement of changes in owners' equity in Exhibit 11-2. If 1,243,679 shares were issued to shareholders who reinvested a portion of their dividends, what was the average value of the shares issued?

a. $80.41
b. $36.99

c. $54.40
d. $43.42

Q11-34 Which statement is true?
a. Management audits the financial statements.
b. Independent auditors prepare the financial statements.
c. An unmodified audit opinion indicates the financial statements are fairly presented.
d. Internal controls are not needed to ensure financial statements are free of material misstatements.

PROBLEMS

(Group A)

LEARNING OBJECTIVE ❷

Prepare a complex income statement

P11-35A The following information was taken from the records of Beauty Cosmetics Ltd. at December 31, 2014:

Income tax expense (saving):		Dividend revenue	$ 11,000
Continuing operations	$25,000	General expenses	71,000
Income from discontinued operations	2,000	Sales revenue	567,000
Loss on sale of discontinued assets	(8,900)	Retained earnings, beginning	63,000
Loss on sale of plant assets	10,000	Selling expenses	87,000
Income from discontinued operations	7,000	Common shares	
Preferred shares $1.50,		20,000 shares authorized	
4,000 shares issued	100,000	and issued	350,000
Dividends on common shares	37,000	Loss on sale of discontinued	
Interest expense	23,000	assets	27,000
Gain on lawsuit settlement	8,000	Cost of goods sold	319,000

Requirements

1. Prepare Beauty Cosmetics' multi-step income statement for the fiscal year ended December 31, 2014. Exclude earnings-per-share data.
2. Evaluate income for the year ended December 31, 2014. Beauty Cosmetics' top managers hoped to earn income from continuing operations equal to 10% of sales.

LEARNING OBJECTIVE ❹

Prepare a statement of changes in shareholder's equity

P11-36A Use the data in problem P11-35A and the format of Exhibit 11-2 to prepare the Beauty Cosmetics statement of changes in shareholders' equity for the year ended December 31.

LEARNING OBJECTIVE ❸

Compute earnings per share

P11-37A Based on the information in problem P11-35A, calculate Beauty Cosmetics' earnings per share. Assume there were no changes in the number of common shares outstanding during the year.

LEARNING OBJECTIVE ❸

Compute earnings per share

P11-38A Turnaround Specialists Ltd. (TSL) specializes in taking underperforming companies to a higher level of performance. TSL's capital structure at December 31, 2013, included 10,000 $2.50 preferred shares and 120,000 common shares. During 2014, TSL issued common shares and ended the year with 127,000 common shares outstanding. Average common shares outstanding during 2014 were 123,500. Income from continuing operations during 2014 was $219,000. The company discontinued a segment of the business at a loss of $69,000, and the sale of discontinued assets generated a gain of $49,500. All amounts are after income tax.

Requirement

Compute TSL's earnings per share.

P11-39A Richard Wright, accountant for Sweetie Pie Foods Inc., was injured in an auto accident. Another employee prepared the following income statement for the fiscal year ended
June 30, 2014:

LEARNING OBJECTIVE ❷❸❹

Prepare an income statement and
statement of comprehensive income

Sweetie Pie Foods Inc.	
Income Statement	
For the Year Ended June 30, 2014	

Revenue and gains:		
Sales		$733,000
Contributed surplus on common shares		100,000
Total revenues and gains		833,000
Expenses and losses:		
Cost of goods sold	$383,000	
Selling expenses	103,000	
General expenses	74,000	
Sales returns	22,000	
Unrealized loss on derivatives	4,000	
Dividends paid	15,000	
Sales discounts	10,000	
Income tax expense	46,500	
Total expenses and losses		657,500
Income from operations		175,500
Other gains and losses:		
Gain on sale of discontinued assets	30,000	
Loss on discontinued operations	(15,000)	
Total other gains (losses)		15,000
Net income		$190,500
Earnings per share		$ 4.76

The individual *amounts* listed on the income statement are correct. However, some
accounts are reported incorrectly, and some accounts do not belong on the income statement
at all. Also, income tax (33%) has not been applied to all appropriate figures. The weighted
average number of common shares outstanding during 2014 was 42,000.

Requirement
Prepare a corrected statement of income and comprehensive income for the 2014 fiscal year.
Include earnings per share.

P11-40A Haynes Publications Inc. reported pretax accounting income of $130,000 for its
2014 fiscal year. IFRS revenue recognition criteria prohibited the recognition of revenue
associated with $10,000 in cash received during 2014, but tax rules require Haynes to
pay tax on this amount in 2014. In addition, depreciation for tax purposes (capital cost
allowance) exceeds accounting depreciation by $20,000 for 2014. Haynes pays tax at a
rate of 33%.

LEARNING OBJECTIVE ❷

Account for a corporation's income
tax

Requirements
1. Compute Haynes' taxable income for 2014.
2. Journalize the corporation's income taxes for 2014.

P11-41A Asian Food Specialties Inc. reported the following statement of changes in shareholders' equity for the year ended June 30, 2014. The company was founded in 2011 and
issued 455 million common shares. There had been no further share transactions until
2014.

LEARNING OBJECTIVE ❹

Use a statement of changes in
shareholders' equity

Asian Food Specialties Inc.
Statement of Changes in Shareholders' Equity
For the Year Ended June 30, 2014

(in millions)	Common Shares	Retained Earnings	Total
Balance, June 30, 2013			
455 shares outstanding..................................	$2,275	$1,702	$3,977
Net income...		540	540
Cash dividends...		(117)	(117)
Issuance of shares (5 shares)............................	50		50
Stock dividend (36 shares)...............................	186	(186)	–
Issuance of shares (2 shares)............................	20		20
Balance, June 30, 2014....................................	$2,531	$1,939	$4,470

Requirements

Answer these questions about Asian Food Specialties' shareholders' equity transactions:

1. The income tax rate is 33%. How much income before income tax did Asian Food Specialties report on the income statement?
2. What is the stated value of a common share at June 30, 2013?
3. At what price per share did Asian Food Specialties issue its common shares during the year?
4. Asian Food Specialties' statement of changes in shareholders' equity lists the share transactions in the order in which they occurred. What was the percentage of the stock dividend? Round to the nearest percentage.

(Group B)

LEARNING OBJECTIVE ❷

Prepare a complex income statement

P11-42B The following information was taken from the records of Kendall Industries Ltd. at April 30, 2014. Kendall manufactures electronic controls for model airplanes.

Dividends..	$ 15,000	Common shares, 24,000 shares	
Interest revenue..................................	4,000	authorized and issued...................	$240,000
Foreign-currency translation		Sales revenue.....................................	833,000
adjustment	5,000	Interest expense................................	11,000
Income from discontinued operations...	30,000	Cost of goods sold	424,000
Loss on insurance settlement..............	12,000	Loss on sale of plant assets..............	8,000
General expenses................................	113,000	Income tax expense,	
Preferred shares—$2,		Continuing operations..................	33,250
10,000 shares authorized,		Discontinued operations..............	7,500
5,000 shares issued	200,000	Accumulated other	
Retained earnings, beginning..............	88,000	comprehensive income,	
Selling expenses	136,000	beginning	15,000

Requirements

1. Prepare Kendall's multi-step income statement for the fiscal year ended April 30, 2014. Exclude earnings-per-share data.
2. Evaluate income for the year ended April 30, 2014. Kendall's top managers hoped to earn income from continuing operations equal to 9% of sales.

LEARNING OBJECTIVE ❹

Prepare a statement of changes in shareholders' equity

P11-43B Use the data in problem P11-42B to prepare Kendall Industries Ltd.'s statement of changes in shareholders' equity for the year ended April 30, 2014.

P11-44B Based on the information from problem P11-42B, compute Kendall's earnings per share. Assume there were no changes in the number of common shares outstanding during the year.

LEARNING OBJECTIVE ❸
Compute earnings per share

P11-45B The capital structure of Morgan Products Inc. at December 31, 2013, included 20,000 $1.25 preferred shares and 44,000 common shares. During 2014, Morgan issued common shares and ended the year with 58,000 shares. The average number of common shares outstanding for the year was 51,000. Income from continuing operations during 2014 was $81,100. The company discontinued a segment of the business at a gain of $6,630, and unrealized losses on derivatives generated a loss of $16,000. All amounts are after income tax.

LEARNING OBJECTIVE ❸
Compute earnings per share

Requirement

Compute Morgan's earnings per share.

P11-46B Rhonda Sparks, accountant for Canon Pet Supplies Ltd., was injured in a skiing accident. Another employee prepared the accompanying income statement for the year ended December 31, 2014.

LEARNING OBJECTIVE ❷❹
Prepare a statement of income and comprehensive income

Canon Pet Supplies Ltd.
Income Statement
2014

Revenue and gains:		
Sales		$362,000
Unrealized gain on derivatives		10,000
Contributed surplus		80,000
Total revenues and gains		452,000
Expenses and losses:		
Cost of goods sold	$103,000	
Selling expenses	56,000	
General expenses	61,000	
Sales returns	11,000	
Dividends paid	7,000	
Sales discounts	6,000	
Income tax expense	37,500	
Total expenses and losses		281,500
Income from operations		170,500
Other gains and losses:		
Foreign-currency translation adjustment	(3,000)	
Loss on discontinued operations	(20,000)	
Total other losses		(23,000)
Net income		$147,500
Earnings per share		$ 2.95

The individual *amounts* listed on the income statement are correct. However, some *accounts* are reported incorrectly, and some accounts do not belong on the income statement at all. Also, income tax (30%) has not been applied to all appropriate figures. The weighted average number of common shares outstanding during 2014 was 51,000.

Requirement

Prepare a corrected statement of income and comprehensive income for 2014. Include earnings per share.

P11-47B Ottawa Rafting Inc. reported pretax accounting income of $200,000 for its 2014 fiscal year. IFRS revenue recognition criteria prohibited the recognition of revenue associated with

LEARNING OBJECTIVE ❷
Account for a corporation's income tax

$15,000 in cash received during 2014, but tax rules require the company to pay tax on this amount in 2014. In addition, depreciation for tax purposes (capital cost allowance) exceeds accounting depreciation by $30,000 for 2014. Ottawa Rafting pays tax at a rate of 25%.

Requirements
1. Compute Ottawa Rafting's taxable income for 2014.
2. Journalize the corporation's income taxes for 2014.

LEARNING OBJECTIVE ❹
Use a statement of shareholders' equity

P11-48B Datacom Services Inc. reported the following statement of changes in shareholders' equity for the year ended October 31, 2014.

Datacom Services Inc. Statement of Changes in Shareholders' Equity For the Year Ended October 31, 2014			
(in millions)	Common Shares	Retained Earnings	Total
Balance, Oct. 31, 2013,			
675 shares outstanding...............................	$2,025	$904	$2,929
Net income..		360	360
Cash dividends.......................................		(194)	(194)
Issuance of shares (13 shares)..........................	49		49
Stock dividend (55 shares)..............................	166	(166)	–
Balance, Oct. 31, 2014.................................	$2,240	$904	$3,144

Requirements
Answer these questions about Datacom Services' shareholders' equity transactions:
1. The income tax rate is 33%. How much income before income tax did Datacom report on the income statement?
2. What is the stated value of a common share at October 31, 2014?
3. At what price per share did Datacom Services issue its common shares during the year?
4. Datacom Services' statement lists the share transactions in the order they occurred. What was the percentage of the stock dividend?

Apply Your Knowledge

Decision Cases

LEARNING OBJECTIVE ❶❷
Evaluate the components of income

Case 1. Prudhoe Bay Oil Ltd. is having its initial public offering (IPO) of company shares. To create public interest in its shares, Prudhoe Bay's chief financial officer has blitzed the media with press releases. One in particular caught your eye. On September 19, Prudhoe Bay announced unaudited earnings per share (EPS) of $1.19, up 89% from last year's EPS of $0.63. An 89% increase in EPS is outstanding!

Before deciding whether to buy Prudhoe Bay stock, you investigated further and found that the company omitted several items from the determination of unaudited EPS:

- Unrealized loss on investments, $0.06 per share
- Gain on sale of building, $0.05 per share
- Cumulative effect of change in method of recognizing revenue, increase in retained earnings, $1.10 per share
- Restructuring expenses, $0.29 per share
- Loss on settlement of lawsuit begun five years ago, $0.12 per share
- Lost income due to employee labour strike, $0.24 per share
- Income from discontinued operations, $0.09 per share

Wondering how to treat these "special items," you called your stockbroker at Merrill Lynch. She thinks that these items are non-recurring and outside Prudhoe Bay's core operations. Furthermore, she suggests that you ignore the items and consider Prudhoe Bay's earnings of $1.19 per share to be a good estimate of long-term profitability.

Requirement

What EPS number will you use to predict Prudhoe Bay's future profits? Show your work, and explain your reasoning for each item.

Case 2. Mike Magid Toyota is an automobile dealership. Magid's annual report includes Note 1— Summary of Significant Accounting Policies, as follows:

LEARNING OBJECTIVE ❶

Evaluate earnings quality

Income Recognition

Sales are recognized when cash payment is received or, in the case of credit sales, which represent the majority of . . . sales, when a down payment is received and the customer enters into an instalment sales contract. These instalment sales contracts . . . are normally collectible over 36 to 60 months . . . .

Revenue from auto insurance policies sold to customers is recognized as income over the life of the contracts.

Bay Area Nissan, a competitor of Mike Magid Toyota, includes the following note in its Summary of Significant Accounting Policies:

Accounting Policies for Revenues

Sales are recognized when cash payment is received or, in the case of credit sales, which represent the majority of . . . sales, when the customer enters into an instalment sales contract. Customer down payments are rare. Most of these instalment sales contracts are normally collectible over 36 to 60 months . . . . Revenue from auto insurance policies sold to customers is recognized when the customer signs an insurance contract. Expenses are recognized over the life of the insurance contracts.

Suppose you have decided to invest in an auto dealership and you've narrowed your choices to Magid and Bay Area. Which company's earnings are of higher quality? Why? Will their accounting policies affect your investment decision? If so, how? Mention specific accounts in the financial statements that will differ between the two companies.

Ethical Issue

The income statement of Transparency Accounting Services Ltd. reported the following results of operations:

Earnings from operations	$178,064
Income from discontinued operations, net of tax	149,755
Income tax expense	58,761
Net earnings	269,058
Other comprehensive income:	
Unrealized loss on investments	(32,961)
Comprehensive net income	$236,097

Suppose Transparency's management had reported the company's results of operations in this manner:

Earnings before income taxes	$352,384
Income tax expense	116,287
Net earnings	$236,097

Requirements

1. Does it really matter how a company reports its operating results? Why? Who could be helped by management's action? Who could be hurt?
2. Suppose Transparency's management decides to report its operating results in the second manner. Evaluate the ethics of this decision.

Focus on Financials

LEARNING OBJECTIVE ❹❺

Analyze a corporate income statement and statement of changes in shareholders' equity, and understand managers'/auditors' responsibilities for financial statements

TELUS Corporation

Refer to the TELUS's financial statements in Appendix A at the end of this book.

Requirements

1. Review the Report of Management on Internal Control over Financial Reporting and answer the following questions:
   a. Who prepared the consolidated financial statements?
   b. What was management responsible for?
   c. Does management report any problems with internal controls during the year?
2. What was the difference between TELUS's net income and comprehensive income for 2011? What caused this difference?
3. What component of owners' equity changed the most during 2014? What caused this large change?

Focus on Analysis

LEARNING OBJECTIVE ❷❸

Evaluate income taxes and EPS

TELUS Corporation

Refer to the TELUS's financial statements in Appendix A at the end of this book.

Requirements

1. What was TELUS's Deferred Income Tax liability at the end of 2011? Did it increase or decrease during the year? Based on this information, what do you think was higher for 2011, TELUS's Income Tax Expense or its Income Tax Payable?
2. What was the percentage change in TELUS's Net Income Attributable to Common Shares and Non-voting Shares from 2010 to 2011? What was the percentage change in TELUS's basic EPS from 2010 to 2011? Why didn't the EPS increase at the same rate as the Net Income figure?

Group Project

Select a company and research its business. Search the business press for articles about this company. Obtain its annual report by requesting it directly from the company or from the company's website.

Requirements

1. Based on your group's analysis, come to class prepared to instruct the class on six interesting facts about the company that can be found in its financial statements and the related notes. Your group can mention only the obvious, such as net sales or total revenue, net income, total assets, total liabilities, total shareholders' equity, and dividends, in conjunction with other terms. Once you use an obvious item, you may not use that item again.
2. The group should write a paper discussing the facts that it has uncovered. Limit the paper to two double-spaced word-processed pages.

Quick Check Answers

1. *b*
2. *a*
3. *c* ($5.94 × 111,000)
4. *c*
5. *d*
6. *c*
7. *a*
8. *d*
9. *b*
10. *c*

12 The Statement of Cash Flows

© Oleksiy Maksymenko/Alamy

LEARNING OBJECTIVES

1. **Explain** the uses of the statement of cash flows

2. **Explain** and **classify** cash flows from operating, investing, and financing activities

3. **Prepare** a statement of cash flows using the indirect method of determining cash flows from operating activities

A-1. **Prepare** a statement of cash flows using the direct method of determining cash flows from operating activities

SPOTLIGHT

TELUS Corporation's statement of cash flows on the next page shows how much cash the company generated from and used in its operating, investing, and financing activities during 2011. The company generated over $2.5 billion in cash from its operating activities, which include the selling of smartphones, Internet access, and home phone services. During 2011, TELUS also used almost $2 billion in cash to perform investing activities, such as purchasing property, plant, and equipment. TELUS's financing activities, including the issuance of long-term debt and payment of dividends, resulted in net cash outflows of over $500 million. Combined, these cash flow activities netted the company $29 million in cash during 2011, leaving TELUS with $46 million in cash and temporary investments at the end of the year.

TELUS Corporation
Consolidated Statement of Cash Flows (Adapted)
For the Year Ended December 31, 2011

(in millions)	2011
Operating Activities	
Net income	$ 1,215
Adjustments to reconcile net income to cash provided by operating activities:	
Depreciation and amortization	1,810
Deferred income taxes	205
Share-based compensation	(12)
Net employee defined benefit plans expense	(32)
Employer contributions to employee defined benefit plans	(298)
Other	(83)
Changes in non-cash operating working capital accounts:	
Accounts receivable	(79)
Inventories	(69)
Prepaid expenses and deposits	(36)
Accounts payable and accrued liabilities	(47)
Income taxes receivable and payable, net	13
Advance billings and customer deposits	(3)
Provisions	(34)
Cash provided by operating activities	2,550
Investing Activities	
Capital expenditures	(1,847)
Acquisitions and other	(110)
Proceeds from the sale of property and other assets	4
Net change in non-cash investing working capital accounts	(15)
Cash used by investing activities	(1,968)
Financing Activities	
Non-voting shares issued	24
Dividends paid	(646)
Issuance and repayment of short-term borrowing	4
Long-term debt issued	4,068
Redemptions and repayment of long-term debt	(3,946)
Other	(57)
Cash used by financing activities	(553)
Cash Position	
Increase in cash and temporary investments, net	29
Cash and temporary investments, net, beginning of year	17
Cash and temporary investments, net, end of year	$ 46
Supplemental Disclosure of Cash Flows	
Interest (paid)	$ (378)
Interest received	$ 1
Income taxes paid, net	$ (150)

Source: TELUS Corporation 2011 Annual Report

In Chapter 1 we introduced you to the statement of cash flows, and in later chapters we briefly discussed cash flows from a variety of operating, investing, and financing activities, such as accounts receivable, long-lived assets, and long-term debt. In this chapter, we provide you with more detailed guidance on how to prepare and use the statement of cash flows. We begin by discussing how managers, investors, and creditors use the statement of cash flows to make business decisions. Following this introduction, we provide additional guidance on how to classify many of the common operating, investing, and financing activities performed by a company. We end the chapter by offering detailed instruction on how to prepare the statement of cash flows using *the indirect method* of determining cash flows from operating activities, which is the method used by the vast majority of companies to prepare their statements of cash flows. The chapter's Appendix provides details on how to prepare the statement of cash flows using *the direct method* of determining cash flows from operating activities, which is actually the method preferred (but not required) by IFRS and ASPE. This method is rarely used in practice, however, because the indirect method gained prominence in the past and now continues to be used for reasons of comparability and user familiarity. After working through this chapter, you will be able to prepare, analyze, and interpret a company's statement of cash flows.

OBJECTIVE

❶ **Explain** the uses of the statement of cash flows

EXPLAIN THE USES OF THE STATEMENT OF CASH FLOWS

A company's balance sheet reports its cash position at a specific date, and its balance sheets from consecutive financial periods show whether its cash balance increased or decreased over the interim period. But the balance sheet doesn't tell us *what caused the cash balance to change*. The income statement reports a company's revenues, expenses, and net income, but because it is prepared on an accrual basis, it provides limited information about *how cash flows were affected by the company's business activities* during the reporting period. To gain insight into how a company's cash flows affected its cash position during a reporting period, we need another financial statement: the statement of cash flows.

IFRS and ASPE, which provide similar guidance on the statement of cash flows, explain that the information disclosed by a company about its cash flows provides decision-relevant information to users of the company's financial statements. This statement includes details about a company's cash receipts and cash disbursements from operating, investing, and financing activities and permits a user to determine exactly what caused the company's cash balance to increase or decrease during the period. Because the statement describes cash flow activities *during a particular fiscal period* and not at a specific point in time, it is dated the same way as the income statement and the statement of changes in shareholders' equity. The TELUS statement of cash flows at the beginning of the chapter, for example, is dated "For the year ended December 31, 2011." Exhibit 12-1 illustrates the relative timing of the four basic financial statements.

The statement of cash flows helps managers, investors, and creditors perform the following functions:

1. **Predict future cash flows.** Past cash receipts and payments are reasonably good predictors of future cash flows.

2. **Evaluate management decisions.** Businesses that make wise investment decisions prosper, and those that make unwise decisions suffer losses. The statement of cash flows reports how managers got cash and how they used cash to run the business.

3. **Determine ability to pay dividends and interest.** Shareholders want dividends on their investments. Creditors collect interest and principal on their loans. The statement of cash flows reports on the ability to make these payments.

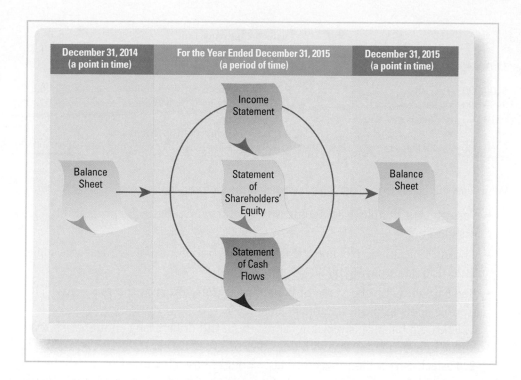

EXHIBIT 12-1
Timing of the Financial Statements

4. **Assess the relationship of net income to cash flows.** Usually, cash and net income move together. High levels of income tend to lead to increases in cash, and low levels of income tend to lead to decreases in cash. A company's cash flow can, however, suffer even when net income is high, or improve when it suffers a net loss.

5. **Compare the operating performance of different companies.** Because it eliminates the effects of using different accounting treatments for the same types of transactions and events, the statement of cash flows allows users to better compare the operating performance of multiple companies.

On a statement of cash flows, *cash* means more than just cash in the bank. It includes **cash equivalents**, which are short-term investments that are readily convertible to known amounts of cash, and which are very unlikely to change in value. Generally, only investments with maturities of three months or less meet these criteria. Examples include money-market investment accounts and three-month government Treasury bills. In the statement of cash flows at the beginning of the chapter, TELUS refers to its cash equivalents as *temporary investments*. *Bank overdraft* balances should also be included in the cash and cash equivalents total. Throughout this chapter, the term *cash* refers to cash and cash equivalents.

How Is a Company's Cash Flow? Telltale Signs of Financial Difficulty

Companies want to earn net income because profit measures success. Without net income, a business sinks. There will be no dividends, and the share price will likely suffer. High net income helps attract investors, but companies can't pay bills with net income—that requires cash.

A company needs both net income and strong cash flow. Income and cash flow usually move together because net income generates cash. Sometimes, however, net income and cash flow follow different patterns. To illustrate, consider Fastech Company Ltd.:

Fastech Company Ltd. Income Statement For the Year Ended December 31, 2014			Fastech Company Ltd. Balance Sheet As at December 31, 2014			
Sales revenue	$100,000		Cash	$ 3,000	Total current liabilities	$ 50,000
Cost of goods sold	30,000		Receivables	37,000	Long-term liabilities	20,000
Operating expenses	10,000		Inventory	40,000		
			PPE, net	60,000	Shareholders' equity	70,000
Net income	$ 60,000		Total assets	$140,000	Total liabilities and equity	$140,000

What can we glean from Fastech's income statement and balance sheet?

- Fastech is profitable. Net income is 60% of revenue. Fastech's profitability looks outstanding.
- The current ratio is 1.6, and the debt ratio is only 50%. These measures suggest little trouble in paying bills.
- But Fastech is on the verge of bankruptcy. Can you spot the problems? Three trouble spots leap out to a financial analyst:
  1. The cash balance is very low. Three thousand dollars isn't enough cash to pay the bills of a company with sales of $100,000.
  2. Fastech isn't selling inventory fast enough. Fastech turned over its inventory only 0.75 times during the year. As we saw in Chapter 6, many companies have inventory turnover rates of 3 to 8 times a year. A turnover ratio of 0.75 times means it takes a very long time to sell inventory, and that delays cash collections.
  3. Fastech's days' sales in receivables ratio is 135 days. Very few companies can wait that long to collect from customers. With standard credit terms of net 30 days, Fastech should collect cash within around 45 days. Fastech cannot survive with a collection period of 135 days.

  The take-away lesson from this discussion is this: A company needs both net income and strong cash flow to succeed in business.

Let's now examine the three types of cash flow activities.

EXPLAIN AND CLASSIFY CASH FLOWS FROM OPERATING, INVESTING, AND FINANCING ACTIVITIES

A business engages in three types of business activities:

- Operating activities
- Investing activities
- Financing activities

Operating activities comprise the main revenue-producing activities of a company and generally result from the transactions and other events that determine net income. Other activities that are not *investing* or *financing* activities are also classified as operating activities.[1] Common operating activities include cash receipts from a company's sales of its primary goods and services and cash payments to suppliers

---

[1] A simplifying assumption was made throughout chapter 12 that **all** current asset accounts and **all** current liability accounts and their related cash flows should be classified as operating activities on the statement of cash flows.

There are, in fact, a number of current asset and current liability accounts that reflect investing and financing activities, respectively. For example, current assets may include short-term investments and short-term notes receivable. The cash flows from these accounts should be classified as investing activities on the statement of cash flows. Current liabilities may include short-term loans payable, and their related cash flows should be classified as financing activities on the statement of cash flows.

and employees for the goods and services they provide to generate these sales. When TELUS pays Apple for the iPhones it sells to its customers, for example, the payment is an operating activity that results in a cash outflow. Similarly, when a customer pays TELUS for one of these iPhones, a cash inflow from operating activities results. If a company is in the business of buying and selling long-lived assets, such as buildings or equipment, or trading investments, such as bonds and stocks, the cash flows from these transactions are classified as investing activities.

In TELUS's statement of cash flows on page 555, we see that the company generated over $2.5 billion in cash flows from operating activities in 2011, despite earning only $1.2 billion in net income on an accrual basis. This is a sign of excellent financial health because it indicates TELUS has generated enough cash from its operating activities to fund capital expenditures, pay dividends, and finance its day-to-day operations without the aid of outside financing. A company that does not regularly generate sufficient cash flows from operating activities will eventually suffer liquidity and solvency problems.

Investing activities include the purchase and sale of long-term assets and other investments that do not qualify as cash equivalents. They generally consist of transactions that result in cash inflows or outflows related to resources used for generating future income and cash flows. IFRS and ASPE state that only expenditures related to assets that are recognized on the balance sheet qualify as investing activities. Cash payments to acquire tangible and intangible long-lived assets, and the cash received on the sale of these assets, are common investing activities. Investing activities also include cash flows from the purchase and sale of equity and debt instruments of other companies, and those related to both short-term and long-term advances and loans made to other entities. Any short-term investments that qualify as cash equivalents are excluded from investing activities.

In 2011, TELUS spent over $1.8 billion in cash on capital expenditures and another $110 million to acquire other entities. It also received $4 million in cash proceeds from the sale of property and other assets. Like its operating activities, TELUS's 2011 investing activities indicate excellent future prospects for the company because they show that the company invested almost $2 billion in new long-term assets that will help it earn additional revenues in coming years.

Financing activities result in changes in the size and composition of a company's contributed equity and borrowings. Common financing activities include the issuance and acquisition of the company's shares; the payment of cash dividends; the cash proceeds from loans, bonds, and notes; and the repayment of amounts borrowed. With the exception of bank overdrafts, which are included in cash and cash equivalents, both short-term and long-term borrowings are included in financing activities.

The Financing Activities section of TELUS's 2011 statement of cash flows contains more good news for the company's investors: it was able to pay them over $600 million in cash dividends while issuing only $24 million in non-voting shares and $122 million in long-term debt ($4,068 million in long-term debt issued less $3,946 million repaid or redeemed).

In sum, TELUS's 2011 statement of cash flows portrays a company with very high cash flows from operating activities, which it used to make significant investments in assets that will hopefully produce more income and cash in the future, while also having enough cash left over to pay a significant dividend to current shareholders without taking on much new debt or equity. In fact, even after net cash outflows from investing and financing activities of over $2.5 billion ($1,968 million in investing outflows and $553 million in financing outflows), TELUS ended 2011 with $46 million in cash and temporary investments, which was $29 million more than the $17 million it had at the end of 2010.

Classifying Interest and Dividends

IFRS and ASPE offer different guidance on classifying cash flows related to interest and dividends. IFRS note that there is no consensus on the classification of interest paid or interest and dividends received. Under IFRS, interest paid and interest and dividends received may be classified as operating cash flows because they enter into the determination of net income. Alternatively, interest paid may be classified as a financing cash flow because it is a cost of obtaining financial resources, while interest and dividends received may be classified as investing cash flows because they represent returns on investments. Under IFRS, a company is free to choose either classification scheme but must use it consistently from then onward. ASPE require that all interest paid and all interest and dividends received and included in the determination of net income be classified as operating activities.

IFRS also offer a choice when classifying dividends paid: they may either be classified as a financing cash flow because they are a cost of obtaining financial resources, or they may be classified as cash flows from operating activities so that users may determine the company's ability to pay dividends out of operating cash flows. ASPE, however, require that any dividends paid and charged against retained earnings be classified as a financing activity.

For the sake of simplicity and consistency, this text classifies all interest paid and interest and dividends received as operating activities, while classifying dividends paid as a financing activity. All questions and problems in this chapter should be answered using this convention.

STOP + THINK (12-1)

Classify each of the following as an operating activity, an investing activity, or a financing activity on the statement of cash flows prepared by the *indirect* method.

a. Issuance of shares

b. Borrowing

c. Sales revenue

d. Payment of dividends

e. Purchase of land

f. Repurchase of shares

g. Paying bonds payable

h. Interest expense

i. Sale of equipment

j. Cost of goods sold

k. Purchase of another company

l. Making a loan

Two Methods of Determining Cash Flows from Operating Activities

There are two methods of determining cash flows from operating activities on the statement of cash flows:

- **Indirect method**, in which net income is adjusted for non-cash transactions, for any deferrals or accruals of past or future operating cash receipts or payments, and for items of income or expense associated with investing or financing cash flows. (pp. 561 to 569)

- **Direct method**, which reports all cash receipts and cash payments from operating activities. (pp. 600 to 606)

The two methods use different computations, but they produce the same figure for cash from *operating activities*. IFRS and ASPE suggest that the direct method provides the most useful information to users, but this method is rarely used in practice because of the historical prominence of the indirect method. We present the indirect method below and detail the direct method in the Appendix to this chapter. The two methods do not affect *investing* or *financing* activities.

PREPARE A STATEMENT OF CASH FLOWS USING THE INDIRECT METHOD OF DETERMINING CASH FLOWS FROM OPERATING ACTIVITIES

OBJECTIVE

❸ **Prepare** a statement of cash flows using the indirect method of determining cash flows from operating activities

To illustrate the statement of cash flows we use Bradshaw Corporation, a dealer in playground equipment. Proceed as shown in the following steps to prepare the statement of cash flows by the indirect method.

> STEP 1 Lay out the template as shown in Exhibit 12-2. The exhibit is comprehensive. The diagram in Exhibit 12-3 (p. 562) gives a visual picture of the statement.

Bradshaw Corporation
Statement of Cash Flows
For the Year Ended December 31, 2014

Cash flows from operating activities:
  Net income
    Adjustments to reconcile net income to net cash provided by (used for) operating activities:
    + Depreciation and amortization expense
    + Loss on sale of investing assets
    − Gain on sale of investing assets
    − Increases in operating current assets other than cash
    + Decreases in operating current assets other than cash
    + Increases in operating current liabilities
    − Decreases in operating current liabilities
  Net cash provided by (used for) operating activities

Cash flows from investing activities:
    + Proceeds from sales of tangible and intangible assets
    − Purchases of tangible and intangible assets
    + Sales of investments that are not cash equivalents
    − Purchases of investments that are not cash equivalents
    + Collecting on loans and advances to others
    − New loans and advances to others
  Net cash provided by (used for) investing activities

Cash flows from financing activities:
    + Proceeds from issuance of shares
    − Repurchase of shares
    + Borrowing money (loans, bonds, notes)
    − Repaying debts (loans, bonds, notes)
    − Payment of dividends
  Net cash provided by (used for) financing activities

Net increase (decrease) in cash and cash equivalents during the year
    + Cash and cash equivalents at December 31, 2013
    = Cash and cash equivalents at December 31, 2014

EXHIBIT 12-2
Template of the Statement of Cash Flows: Indirect Method

EXHIBIT 12-3
Positive and Negative Items on the Statement of Cash Flows: Indirect Method

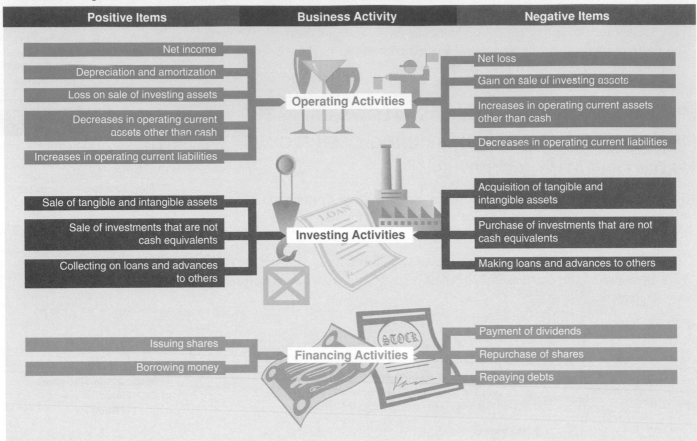

STEP 2 Use the comparative balance sheet to determine the increase or decrease in cash during the period. The change in cash is the "check figure" for the statement of cash flows. Exhibit 12-4 (p. 563) gives Bradshaw Corporation's comparative balance sheet with cash highlighted. Bradshaw's cash decreased by $20,000 during 2014. *Why* did cash decrease? The statement of cash flows provides the answer.

STEP 3 From the income statement, take net income, depreciation and amortization expense, and any gains or losses on the sale of long-term assets. Print these items on the statement of cash flows. Exhibit 12-5 (p. 563) gives Bradshaw Corporation's income statement, with relevant items highlighted.

STEP 4 Use the income statement and the balance sheet data to prepare the statement of cash flows. The statement of cash flows is complete only after you have explained the year-to-year changes in all the balance sheet accounts.

Cash Flows From Operating Activities

Operating activities comprise the main revenue-producing activities of a company, and generally result from the transactions and other events that determine net income.

The operating section of the statement of cash flows begins with net income, taken from the income statement (Exhibit 12-5), and is followed by "Adjustments to reconcile net income to net cash provided by (used for) operating activities" (Exhibit 12-6). Let's discuss these adjustments.

EXHIBIT 12-4
Comparative Balance Sheet for Bradshaw Corporation

Bradshaw Corporation
Comparative Balance Sheet
As at December 31, 2014 and 2013

(in thousands)	2014	2013	Increase (Decrease)	
Assets				
Current:				
Cash..	$ 22	$ 42	$ (20)	⎫
Accounts receivable...	93	80	13	⎪
Interest receivable...	3	1	2	⎬ Changes in current assets—Operating
Inventory..	135	138	(3)	⎪
Prepaid expenses...	8	7	1	⎭
Long-term note receivable from another company.........	11	—	11	⎫
Property, plant, and equipment				⎬ Changes in non-current assets—Investing
assets, net of depreciation...	353	219	134	⎪
Total..	$625	$487	$138	⎭
Liabilities				
Current:				
Accounts payable	$ 91	$ 57	$ 34	⎫
Salary and wages payable	4	6	(2)	⎬ Changes in current liabilities—Operating
Accrued liabilities...	1	3	(2)	⎭
Long-term debt..	160	77	83	⎫ Change in long-term liabilities and
Shareholders' Equity				⎬ contributed capital accounts—Financing
Share capital...	259	258	1	⎭
Retained earnings..	110	86	24	} Change due to net income—Operating
Total...	$625	$487	$138	Change due to dividends—Financing

Bradshaw Corporation
Income Statement
For the Year Ended December 31, 2014

EXHIBIT 12-5
Income Statement for Bradshaw Corporation

	(in thousands)	
Revenues and gains:		
Sales revenue..	$284	
Interest revenue...	12	
Dividend revenue	9	
Gain on sale of property, plant, and equipment	8	
Total revenues and gains...		$313
Expenses:		
Cost of goods sold..	150	
Salary and wages expense..	56	
Depreciation expense	18	
Other operating expense	17	
Interest expense...	16	
Income tax expense..	15	
Total expenses		272
Net income		$ 41

EXHIBIT 12-6
Statement of Cash Flows—
Operating Activities by the
Indirect Method

Bradshaw Corporation
Statement of Cash Flows
For the Year Ended December 31, 2014

	(in thousands)
Cash flows from operating activities:	
Net income..	$41
Adjustments to reconcile net income to net cash	
provided by operating activities:	
(A) Depreciation..	$ 18
(B) Gain on sale of property, plant, and equipment	(8)
Increase in accounts receivable	(13)
Increase in interest receivable	(2)
Decrease in inventory	3
(C) Increase in prepaid expenses	(1)
Increase in accounts payable...	34
Decrease in salary and wages payable	(2)
Decrease in accrued liabilities..	(2) 27
Net cash provided by operating activities.................................	$68

(A) **DEPRECIATION AND AMORTIZATION EXPENSES.** When we record these expenses, we debit depreciation/amortization expense and credit accumulated depreciation/amortization. As a result, net income decreases, but there is no corresponding outflow of cash. To reverse these non-cash expenses, we add them back to net income when determining operating cash flows.

Example: Suppose you had only two transactions during the period, a $1,000 cash sale and depreciation expense of $300. Net income is $700 ($1,000 − $300). Cash flow from operations is $1,000. To go from net income ($700) to cash flow ($1,000), we must add back the depreciation ($300).

(B) **GAINS AND LOSSES ON THE SALE OF INVESTING ASSETS.** Sales of tangible and intangible assets and investments other than cash equivalents are *investing* activities, and there is often a gain or loss on these sales. On the statement of cash flows, a gain or loss on the sale is an adjustment to net income. Exhibit 12-6 includes an adjustment for a gain. During 2014, Bradshaw sold equipment for $62,000. The carrying amount was $54,000 (see calculation of carrying amount on page 570), so there was a gain of $8,000.

The $62,000 of cash received from the sale, which includes the $8,000 gain, is an investing activity. Net income also includes the gain, so we must subtract the gain from net cash provided from operations, as shown in Bradshaw Corporation's statement of cash flows (Exhibit 12-6). (We explain investing activities in the next section.)

A loss on the sale of investing assets also creates an adjustment in the operating section. Losses are *added back* to net income to compute cash flow from operations, because the amount of the loss does not represent an actual outflow of cash. Assume, for example, that the asset with the $54,000 carrying amount was sold for $50,000 instead of $62,000, yielding a loss of $4,000. The only cash involved in this transaction is the receipt of the $50,000 proceeds, which is recorded as an inflow in the investing section, just like the $62,000 above. The $4,000 loss is added back to net income in the operating section, because there is no corresponding outflow of cash.

Ⓒ **CHANGES IN NON-CASH OPERATING WORKING CAPITAL ACCOUNTS.** A company's operating activities affect many of its non-cash current asset and liability accounts. When a company sells goods on credit, for example, accounts receivable increase and inventory decreases. Similarly, when a company incurs an expense but doesn't pay for it until later, accounts payable increase. As in TELUS's statement of cash flows at the beginning of the chapter, these accounts are commonly referred to as **non-cash operating working capital accounts**. In this case, *non-cash* does not necessarily mean the underlying activity did not involve cash, because it often does. Instead, it simply means that the *account* itself (e.g., accounts receivable, unearned revenue) is not one that is included in the *cash and cash equivalents* balance on the statement of cash flows. These accounts are described as *operating* accounts because they derive from *operating activities*, and they are all components of a company's *working capital* balance (current assets − current liabilities). Let's examine how transactions and events in some of the common non-cash operating working capital accounts affect the operating section of the statement of cash flows.

Accounts receivable When a company makes a sale on credit, net income increases via the increase in revenue, but there is no corresponding increase in cash. So, to reconcile net income to cash flows from operations (CFO), we must *deduct* any *increase* in accounts receivable during the year. When a customer pays down its account, however, cash increases but net income is not affected. In this case, any *decrease* in accounts receivable during the year must be *added* to net income to reconcile it with CFO. Changes in other types of *non-investing* receivables (e.g., income taxes receivable) are treated the same way.

Inventory When a company purchases inventory, cash decreases but there is no impact on net income. So, to reconcile net income to CFO, we must *deduct* an *increase* in inventory from net income. Adjustments to CFO for inventory purchased on account are made via the change in *accounts payable and accrued liabilities*, which is discussed below. When inventory is sold, net income decreases via an increase in cost of goods sold, but there is no corresponding decrease in cash. Any *decrease* in inventory is therefore *added* to net income to arrive at CFO.

Prepaid expenses If a company prepays an expense, there is a cash outflow with no consequent decrease in net income, so an *increase* in prepaid expenses must be *deducted* from net income to get CFO. When we adjust prepaid expenses at the end of a reporting period to recognize the expenses related to the period, expenses increase and net income decreases, but cash is not affected. We must therefore *add* a *decrease* in prepaids to net income to reconcile it with CFO.

Accounts payable and accrued liabilities When a company incurs an expense but does not pay for it until later, net income decreases via an increase in the affected expense account, but cash does not decrease. So we must *add* any *increases* in accounts payable and accrued liabilities to net income to get CFO. When the company eventually pays the debt, cash decreases but net income is not affected, so *decreases* in accounts payable and accrued liabilities are *deducted* from net income to reconcile it with CFO. Changes in similar types of *non-financing* liabilities (e.g., provisions) are treated the same way.

Unearned revenue If a customer pays a company before receiving the related goods or services, then cash increases, but there is no impact on net income. Any *increases* in unearned revenue must therefore be *added* to net income when reconciling it with CFO. When the company eventually provides the related goods or services, net income increases via the increase in revenue, but cash is not affected. So we must *deduct* any *decrease* in unearned revenue from net income to get CFO.

As a rule, increases (decreases) in non-cash operating current asset accounts result in decreases (increases) to net income when determining CFO— *the account impact is the opposite of the CFO impact*. In contrast, increases (decreases) in non-cash operating current liability accounts result in increases (decreases) to net income when reconciling to CFO— *the account impact is consistent with the CFO impact*. Exhibit 12-7 summarizes the impacts of these changes in non-cash operating working capital

EXHIBIT 12-7
Impacts of Changes in Non-cash Operating Working Capital Accounts on Cash Flows from Operations

Account	Transaction or Event	Account Impact	Cash Impact	Non-cash Net Income Impact	Cash Flows From Operations Impact
Current assets					
Accounts receivable	Sale on account	**Increase**	None	Increase	**Decrease**
Accounts receivable	Collection of account	**Decrease**	Increase	None	**Increase**
Inventory	Purchase	**Increase**	Decrease	None	**Decrease**
Inventory	Sale	**Decrease**	Increase	Decrease	**Increase**
Prepaid expenses	Prepayment of expense	**Increase**	Decrease	None	**Decrease**
Prepaid expenses	Recognition of expense	**Decrease**	None	Decrease	**Increase**
Current liabilities					
Payables and accruals	Purchase on account or accrual of expense	**Increase**	None	Decrease	**Increase**
Payables and accruals	Payment	**Decrease**	Decrease	None	**Decrease**
Unearned revenue	Cash received in advance of sale	**Increase**	Increase	None	**Increase**
Unearned revenue	Goods or services delivered	**Decrease**	None	Increase	**Decrease**

accounts on cash and net income, as well as the adjustments needed to reconcile net income to CFO. We can apply these rules to Bradshaw's balance sheet data in Exhibit 12-4, which results in the CFO impacts disclosed in the Operating Activities section of its statement of cash flows in Exhibit 12-6.

EVALUATING CASH FLOWS FROM OPERATING ACTIVITIES. Let's step back and evaluate Bradshaw's operating cash flows during 2014. Bradshaw generated $68,000 in cash flows from operating activities, which is $27,000 more than it reported in net income. This is a sign that Bradshaw has a high quality of earnings and is not using accruals and other estimates to inflate its net income. Now let's examine Bradshaw's investing and financing activities, as reported in Exhibit 12-8.

EXHIBIT 12-8
Statement of Cash Flows—Indirect Method

Bradshaw Corporation
Statement of Cash Flows
For the Year Ended December 31, 2014

	(in thousands)	
Cash flows from operating activities:		
Net income		$ 41
Adjustments to reconcile net income to net cash provided by operating activities:		
(A) Depreciation	$ 18	
(B) Gain on sale of property, plant, and equipment	(8)	
(C) Increase in accounts receivable	(13)	
Increase in interest receivable	(2)	
Decrease in inventory	3	
Increase in prepaid expenses	(1)	
Increase in accounts payable	34	
Decrease in salary and wages payable	(2)	
Decrease in accrued liabilities	(2)	27
Net cash provided by operating activities		68
Cash flows from investing activities:		
Acquisition of property, plant, and equipment	(206)	
Loan to another company	(11)	
Proceeds from sale of property, plant, and equipment	62	
Net cash used for investing activities		(155)
Cash flows from financing activities:		
Proceeds from issuance of common shares	1	
Proceeds from issuance of long-term debt	94	
Repayment of long-term debt	(11)	
Payment of dividends	(17)	
Net cash provided by financing activities		67
Net decrease in cash		(20)
Cash balance, December 31, 2013		42
Cash balance, December 31, 2014		$ 22

MID-CHAPTER SUMMARY PROBLEM

Lucas Corporation reported the following income statement and comparative balance sheets, along with transaction data for 2014:

Lucas Corporation
Income Statement
Year Ended December 31, 2014

Sales revenue		$662,000
Cost of goods sold		560,000
Gross profit		102,000
Operating expenses		
Salary expenses	$46,000	
Depreciation expense— equipment	7,000	
Amortization expense— patent	3,000	
Rent expense	2,000	
Total operating expenses		58,000
Income from operations		44,000
Other items:		
Loss on sale of equipment		(2,000)
Income before income tax		42,000
Income tax expense		16,000
Net income		$ 26,000

Lucas Corporation
Comparative Balance Sheets
December 31, 2014 and 2013

Assets	2014	2013	Liabilities and Shareholders' Equity	2014	2013
Current:			Current:		
Cash and equivalents	$ 19,000	$ 3,000	Accounts payable	$ 35,000	$ 26,000
Accounts receivable	22,000	23,000	Accrued liabilities	7,000	9,000
Inventories	34,000	31,000	Income tax payable	10,000	10,000
Prepaid expenses	1,000	3,000	Total current liabilities	52,000	45,000
Total current assets	76,000	60,000	Long-term note payable	44,000	—
Long-term investments	18,000	10,000	Bonds payable	40,000	53,000
Equipment, net	67,000	52,000	Shareholders' equity:		
Patent, net	44,000	10,000	Share capital	52,000	20,000
			Retained earnings	27,000	19,000
			Less: Treasury stock	(10,000)	(5,000)
Total assets	$205,000	$132,000	Total liabilities and equity	$205,000	$132,000

Requirement

Use the indirect method to prepare the Operating Activities section of Lucas Corporation's 2014 statement of cash flows.

ANSWER

Lucas Corporation
Statement of Cash Flows
Year Ended December 31, 2014

Cash flows from operating activities:		
Net income..		$26,000
Adjustments to reconcile net income to		
net cash provided by operating activities:		
Depreciation	$ 7,000	
Amortization...	3,000	
Loss on sale of equipment..	2,000	
Changes in non-cash operating working capital		
Decrease in accounts receivable	1,000	
Increase in inventories	(3,000)	
Decrease in prepaid expenses...	2,000	
Increase in accounts payable..	9,000	
Decrease in accrued liabilities	(2,000)	19,000
Net cash provided by operating activities.........................		45,000

Cash Flows From Investing Activities

Investing activities include the purchase and sale of long-term assets and other investments that do not qualify as cash equivalents. Purchases result in cash outflows from investing activities, whereas sales yield cash inflows. Cash inflows and outflows related to the same type of investing activity must be reported separately in the statement of cash flows.

ACQUISITIONS AND SALES OF TANGIBLE AND INTANGIBLE ASSETS. Companies with significant quantities of tangible assets typically keep track of them in a subledger, which details the cost, accumulated depreciation, and carrying amount of each item of property, plant, and equipment. When an asset is sold, its carrying amount can be deducted from the cash sale proceeds to determine the gain or loss on the sale of the asset. These details on individual asset sales can be accumulated to arrive at the total cash sale proceeds and net gain or loss on sales to be reported on the statement of cash flows for a given fiscal period. Without the detailed information from a company's asset subledger, we can use an alternative method to calculate this information.

To illustrate, we will use information from Bradshaw's balance sheet and income statement in Exhibits 12-4 and 12-5.

- At the beginning of 2014, Bradshaw's balance sheet shows that its carrying amount of property, plant, and equipment was $219,000. By the end of the year, it had increased to $353,000 (Exhibit 12-4).

- Bradshaw's income statement discloses depreciation expense of $18,000 and a gain on sale of property, plant, and equipment of $8,000 for 2014 (Exhibit 12-5).

Bradshaw's purchases of property, plant, and equipment total $206,000 (take this amount as given; see Exhibit 12-8). How much, then, are the proceeds from the sale of property, plant, and equipment? First, we must determine the carrying amount of property, plant, and equipment sold, as follows:

Property, plant, and equipment (net)						
Beginning balance	+ Acquisitions	− Depreciation	−	Carrying amount of assets sold	=	Ending balance
$219,000	+ $206,000	− $18,000		−X	=	$353,000
				−X	=	$353,000 − $219,000 − $206,000 + $18,000
				X	=	$54,000

The sale proceeds are $62,000, determined as follows:

$$
\begin{aligned}
\text{Sale proceeds} &= \text{Carrying amount of assets sold} + \text{Gain} - \text{Loss} \\
&= \$54,000 + \$8,000 - \$0 \\
&= \$62,000
\end{aligned}
$$

Trace the sale proceeds of $62,000 to the statement of cash flows in Exhibit 12-8. The Property, Plant, and Equipment T-account provides another look at the computation of the carrying amount of the assets sold.

Property, Plant, and Equipment, Net			
Beginning balance	219,000	Depreciation	18,000
Acquisitions	206,000	Carrying amount of assets sold	54,000
Ending balance	353,000		

If the sale had resulted in a loss of $3,000, the sale proceeds would have been $51,000 ($54,000 − $3,000), and the statement would report $51,000 as a cash receipt from this investing activity.

The same process can be used to determine cash proceeds from the sale of intangible assets, although there would be no amortization to deal with in the case of intangibles with indefinite useful lives.

ACQUISITIONS AND SALES OF INVESTMENTS OTHER THAN CASH EQUIVALENTS. The carrying amount of investments sold can be computed in the manner illustrated for property, plant, and equipment. Investment carrying amounts are easier to calculate because there is no depreciation to account for, as shown in the following equation (Bradshaw has no investments, so the information below is for illustration only):

Investments					
Beginning balance	+ Purchases	−	Carrying amount of investments sold	=	Ending balance
$100,000	+ $50,000		−X	=	$140,000
			−X	=	$140,000 − $100,000 − $50,000
			X	=	$10,000

The Investments T-account provides another look:

Investments			
Beginning balance	100		
Purchases	50	Carrying amount of investments sold	10
Ending balance	140		

If Bradshaw had realized a $15,000 gain on the sale of these investments, then the cash sale proceeds would have been $25,000 ($10,000 carrying amount + $15,000 gain), which we would report as a cash inflow in the Investing Activities section. The investment purchases of $50,000 in the illustration above would be reported as a cash outflow in the Investing section.

MAKING AND COLLECTING LOANS AND ADVANCES TO OTHERS. The beginning and ending balances of (short-term and long-term) Loans or Notes Receivable can be found on the balance sheet. If the amount of either the new loans/advances or the collections of loans/advances is known, the other amount can be computed. Bradshaw has a long-term note receivable of $11,000 at the end of 2014; this balance was zero at the end of 2013 (Exhibit 12-4; assume there were no collections during 2014). Using this information, we can determine the amount of loans/advances made during 2014 as follows:

Notes Receivable

Beginning balance	+	New loans made	−	Collections	=	Ending balance
$0	+	$X		−0	=	$11,000
		X			=	$11,000

Notes Receivable			
Beginning balance	0		
New loans made	11	Collections	0
Ending balance	11		

This $11,000 loan to another company can be seen as a cash outflow in the Investing Activities section of Bradshaw's statement of cash flows in Exhibit 12-8.

Cash Flows From Financing Activities

Financing activities result in changes in the size and composition of a company's contributed equity and borrowings. The issuance of equity or borrowings results in a cash inflow; the repurchase of equity and repayment of borrowings are cash outflows. Cash inflows and outflows related to the same type of financing activity must be reported separately in the statement of cash flows.

BORROWING MONEY AND REPAYING DEBTS. The beginning and ending balances of (short-term and long-term) borrowings, such as Loans, Bonds, and Notes Payable, can be found on the balance sheet. If the amount of either the new borrowings or the repayment of debts is known, the other amount can be computed. Bradshaw's long-term debt increased from $77,000 at the end of 2013 to $160,000 by the end of 2014 (Exhibit 12-4; assume new borrowings of long-term debt were $94,000 in 2014).

Using this information, we can determine the amount of long-term debt repayments made during 2014 as follows:

Long-Term Debt

Beginning balance	+	Borrowing of new debt	−	Repayments of debt	=	Ending balance
$77,000	+	$94,000		−X	=	$160,000
				−X	=	$160,000 − $77,000 − $94,000
				X	=	$11,000

This same information can be determined using a T-account as follows:

Long-Term Debt

		Beginning balance	77,000
Payments	11,000	Issuance of new debt	94,000
		Ending balance	160,000

The $94,000 cash inflow from new borrowing and the $11,000 cash outflow from the repayment of debts can be seen in the Financing Activities section in Exhibit 12-8.

Common Shares

Beginning balance	+	Issuance of new shares	−	Repurchase of shares	=	Ending balance
$258,000	+	$X	−	$0	=	$259,000
					=	$1,000

Here is the same information presented in a T-account:

Common Shares

		Beginning balance	258,000
		Issuance of new shares	1,000
		Ending	259,000

The $1,000 cash inflow from issuing new shares can also be seen in the Financing Activities section of Exhibit 12-8.

PAYMENT OF DIVIDENDS. Dividend payments can usually be found in the Statement of Retained Earnings (or Statement of Changes in Owners' Equity), but they can also be determined as follows, using information from Bradshaw's balance sheet (Exhibit 12-4) and income statement (Exhibit 12-5):

Retained Earnings

Beginning balance	+	Net income	−	Dividends declared	=	Ending balance
$86,000	+	$41,000		−X	=	$110,000
				−X	=	$110,000 − $86,000 − $41,000
				X	=	$17,000

The T-account provides another view of the dividend payment computation:

Retained Earnings

		Beginning balance	86,000
Dividend declarations	17,000	Net income	41,000
		Ending balance	110,000

The $17,000 dividend payment can be seen as a cash outflow in the Financing Activities section in Exhibit 12-8. Any increase or decrease in a Dividend Payable account is treated the same way as a change in a non-cash operating current liability account, except that the adjustment to cash flows is included in the Financing Activities section. If, for example, Bradshaw had a Dividends Payable account that had increased by $5,000 during 2014, then we would add this increase as a *Change in non-cash financing working capital* to the Financing Activities section of its statement of cash flows.

STOP + THINK (12-2)

Midwest Airlines
Statement of Cash Flows

(in millions)	2015	2014	2013
Cash Flows from Operating Activities			
Net income	548	313	442
Items not affecting cash:			
Depreciation and amortization	502	467	417
Loss (gain) on disposal of equipment	(25)	101	-
Changes in non-cash operating working capital items:			
(Increase) decrease in accounts receivable	(9)	(75)	43
(Increase) decrease in inventory	(13)	6	(19)
Increase (decrease) in accounts payable	855	231	129
Net Cash Inflow (Outflow) from Operating Activities	1,858	1,043	1,012
Cash Flows from Investing Activities			
Business acquisitions	-	(400)	-
Proceeds from sale of investments	6	-	23
Purchase of property, plant, and equipment	(1,316)	(1,505)	(1,261)
Proceeds from disposal of equipment	100	55	-
Net Cash Inflow (Outflow) from Investing Activities	(1,210)	(1,850)	(1,238)
Cash Flows from Financing Activities			
Payment of dividends	(14)	(14)	(14)
Proceeds from sale of capital stock	132	88	93
Repurchase of capital stock	(55)	(246)	-
Proceeds from long-term debt	300	520	-
Repayment of long-term debt	(150)	(215)	(127)
Net Cash Inflow (Outflow) from Financing Activities	213	133	(48)
Increase (Decrease) in Cash and Cash Equivalents	861	(674)	(274)
Cash and Cash Equivalents, Beginning of Year	3	677	951
Cash and Cash Equivalents, End of Year	864	3	677

Based on the information in Midwest Airlines' statements of cash flows for 2013–2015, answer the following questions:

1. Has Midwest been expanding or down-sizing its business?
2. What was the carrying amount of the equipment Midwest sold in 2014?
3. If you were a financial analyst following Midwest, would you be pleased with its operating cash flows?
4. Has Midwest been relying more on debt or equity financing in recent years? Cite information about both debt and equity to support your conclusion.
5. Overall, does Midwest have a strong or poor cash position? Cite two pieces of information to support your conclusion.

Non-cash Investing and Financing Activities

Companies sometimes engage in financing and investing activities that do not involve cash flows. An example of a non-cash transaction that involves both investing and financing is the acquisition of a subsidiary company in exchange for shares of the acquiring company. In this transaction, the acquiring company has *invested* in a new asset, the subsidiary company, and *financed* it with its own shares, but because the transaction does not involve cash, these activities are not included in the statement of cash flows. IFRS and ASPE do, however, require note disclosure of non-cash investing and financing activities. A sample disclosure of the above transaction and two other non-cash transactions is included in Exhibit 12-9.

EXHIBIT 12-9
Sample Disclosure on Non-cash Investing and Financing Activities

	(amounts in thousands)
Note 22: Non-Cash Investing and Financing Activities	
Acquisition of subsidiary by issuing common shares	$320
Acquisition of equipment by finance lease	70
Conversion of bonds payable to common shares	150
Total non-cash investing and financing activities	$540

Measuring Cash Adequacy: Free Cash Flow

Throughout this chapter, we have focused on cash flows from operating, investing, and financing activities. Some investors, creditors, and managers want to know how much cash a company can "free up" for new opportunities. The business world changes so quickly that new possibilities arise almost daily. A company with a significant free cash flow is better able to respond to new opportunities. **Free cash flow** is the amount of cash available from operations after paying for property, plant, and equipment. Free cash flow can be computed as follows:

$$\text{Free cash flow} = \frac{\text{Net cash flow provided by}}{\text{operating activities}} - \frac{\text{Capital expenditures on}}{\text{property, plant,}\atop\text{and equipment}}$$

Using information from TELUS's statement of cash flows on page 555, we can calculate its free cash flow for 2011. It generated cash from operating activities of $2,550 million and spent $1,847 million on capital expenditures, leaving $703 million in free cash flow for 2011. This information suggests that TELUS is well poised to take advantage of new business opportunities—even after spending over $1.8 billion on property, plant, and equipment in 2011, it still had over $700 million of free cash flow to spend on future investments.

It is important to note, however, that a negative free cash flow is not necessarily a bad sign for investors. It could mean that the company has made a significant investment in property, plant, and equipment that will pay off in the form of increased future revenues and profits.

◀ DECISION GUIDELINES ▶

INVESTORS' AND CREDITORS' USE OF CASH-FLOW AND RELATED INFORMATION

Jan Childres is a private investor. Through years of experience she has devised some guidelines for evaluating both stock investments and bond investments. Childres uses a combination of accrual-accounting data and cash-flow information. Here are her decision guidelines for both investors and creditors.

INVESTORS

Questions	Factors to Consider	Financial Statement Predictor*
1. How much in dividends can I expect to receive from an investment in stock?	Expected future net income	Income from continuing operations**
	Expected future cash balance	Net cash flows from (in order): • operating activities • investing activities • financing activities
	Future dividend policy	Current and past dividend policy
2. Is the stock price likely to increase or decrease?	Expected future income from continuing operations	Income from continuing operations**
	Expected future cash flows from operating activities	Income from continuing operations** Net cash flow from operating activities

CREDITORS

Question	Factors to Consider	Financial Statement Predictor*
Can the company pay the interest and principal at the maturity of a loan?	Expected future net cash flow from operating activities	Income from continuing operations** Net cash flow from operating activities

*There are many other factors to consider in making these decisions. These are some of the more common ones.
**See Chapter 11.

Summary of IFRS-ASPE Differences

Concepts	IFRS	ASPE
Classification of interest paid and interest and dividends received (p. 560)	Interest paid may be classified as either an operating activity or a financing activity.	Interest paid must be classified as an operating activity.
Classification of interest and dividends received (p. 560)	Interest and dividends received may be classified as either operating activities or investing activities.	Interest and dividends received must be classified as operating activities.
Classification of dividends paid (p. 560)	Dividends paid may be classified as either an operating activity or a financing activity. *Note: Once a classification scheme has been chosen for each of the above items, it must be used consistently thereafter.*	Dividends paid must be classified as a financing activity.

SUMMARY OF CHAPTER 12

LEARNING OBJECTIVE	SUMMARY
1. **Explain** the uses of the statement of cash flows	The information disclosed by a company in its statement of cash flows provides decision-relevant information to users of the company's financial statements. This statement includes details about a company's cash receipts and cash disbursements from operating, investing, and financing activities, and permits a user to determine exactly what caused the company's cash balance to increase or decrease during the period. Specifically, the statement of cash flows helps users do the following: 1. Predict future cash flows. 2. Evaluate management decisions. 3. Determine ability to pay interest and dividends. 4. Assess the relationship of net income to cash flows. 5. Compare the operating performance of different companies. Cash includes cash equivalents, which are short-term investments that are readily convertible to known amounts of cash, and which are very unlikely to change in value.
2. **Explain** and **classify** cash flows from operating, investing, and financing activities	Operating activities comprise the main revenue-producing activities of a company, and generally result from the transactions and other events that determine net income. Other activities that are not *investing* or *financing* activities are also classified as operating activities. There are two methods of determining cash flows from operating activities, both resulting in the same net cash flows from operating activities: • Indirect method, in which net income is adjusted for non-cash transactions, any deferrals or accruals of past or future operating cash receipts or payments, and items of income or expense associated with investing or financing cash flows • Direct method, which explicitly reports all cash receipts and cash payments from operating activities

Investing activities include the purchase and sale of long-term assets and other investments that do not qualify as cash equivalents. They generally consist of transactions that result in cash inflows or outflows related to resources used for generating future income and cash flows. Only expenditures related to assets that are recognized on the balance sheet qualify as investing activities.

Financing activities result in changes in the size and composition of a company's contributed equity and borrowings.

3. **Prepare** a statement of cash flows using the indirect method of determining cash flows from operating activities

To determine cash flows from operating activities using the indirect method, begin with net income and adjust it as follows:

- Add non-cash expenses, such as depreciation and amortization
- Add losses (deduct gains) on sales of tangible and intangible assets and investments
- Add decreases (deduct increases) in non-cash operating current asset accounts
- Add increases (deduct decreases) in non-cash operating current liability accounts

To determine cash flows from investing activities:

- Add sales (deduct purchases) of tangible and intangible assets and investments other than cash equivalents
- Add collection (deduct issuance) of loans and advances to others

To determine cash flows from financing activities:

- Add issuance (deduct repurchase) of shares
- Add borrowing (deduct repayment) of short-term and long-term debts
- (Deduct payment) of dividends

Non-cash investing and financing activities, such as the acquisition of a business using common shares, are excluded from the statement of cash flows, but must be disclosed in the notes to the financial statements.

END-OF-CHAPTER SUMMARY PROBLEM

Lucas Corporation, a private company, reported the following income statement and comparative balance sheet, along with transaction data for 2014:

Lucas Corporation
Income Statement
For the Year Ended December 31, 2014

Sales revenue		$662,000
Cost of goods sold		560,000
Gross margin		102,000
Operating expenses:		
Salary expense	$46,000	
Depreciation expense, equipment	7,000	
Amortization expense, patent	3,000	
Rent expense	2,000	
Total operating expenses		58,000
Income from operations		44,000
Other items:		
Loss on sale of equipment		(2,000)
Income before income tax		42,000
Income tax expense		16,000
Net income		$ 26,000

Lucas Corporation
Balance Sheet
As at December 31, 2014 and 2013

Assets	2014	2013	Liabilities and Shareholders' Equity	2014	2013
Current:			Current:		
Cash and equivalents......................	$ 19,000	$ 3,000	Accounts payable............................	$ 35,000	$ 26,000
Accounts receivable........................	22,000	23,000	Accrued liabilities...........................	7,000	9,000
Inventories	34,000	31,000	Income tax payable.........................	10,000	10,000
Prepaid expenses............................	1,000	3,000	Total current liabilities...............	52,000	45,000
Total current assets	76,000	60,000	Long-term note payable....................	44,000	—
Long-term investments......................	18,000	10,000	Bonds payable	40,000	53,000
Equipment, net	67,000	52,000	Shareholders' equity:		
Patent, net.......................................	44,000	10,000	Share capital...	42,000	15,000
			Retained earnings................................	27,000	19,000
			Total liabilities and		
Total assets...	$205,000	$132,000	shareholders' equity........................	$205,000	$132,000

Transaction Data for 2014:

Purchase of equipment...	$98,000
Payment of cash dividends	18,000
Issuance of common shares to repay bonds payable	13,000
Purchase of long-term investment	8,000
Issuance of long-term note payable to purchase patent...	37,000
Issuance of long-term note payable to borrow cash	7,000
Issuance of common shares for cash..	19,000
Proceeds on sale of equipment (carrying amount, $76,000)	74,000
Repurchase of common shares..	5,000

Requirements

Prepare Lucas Corporation's statement of cash flows for the year ended December 31, 2014. Determine operating cash flows by the indirect method. Follow the four steps outlined below. For Step 4, prepare a T-account to show the transaction activity in each long-term balance sheet account. For each capital asset, use a single account, net of accumulated depreciation or amortization (for example: Equipment, net).

Name: Lucas Corporation
Fiscal Period: Year ended December 31, 2014

STEP 1 Lay out the template of the statement of cash flows.
STEP 2 From the comparative balance sheet, determine the increase in cash during the year.
STEP 3 From the income statement, take net income, depreciation and amortization, and the loss on sale of equipment, to the statement of cash flows.
STEP 4 Complete the statement of cash flows. Account for the year-to-year change in each balance sheet account.

ANSWER

Lucas Corporation
Statement of Cash Flows
For the Year Ended December 31, 2014

Cash flows from operating activities:		
Net income...		$ 26,000
Adjustments to reconcile net income to net cash provided by operating activities:		
Depreciation	$ 7,000	
Amortization..	3,000	
Loss on sale of equipment......................................	2,000	
Changes in non-cash operating working capital accounts:		
Decrease in accounts receivable	1,000	
Increase in inventories..	(3,000)	
Decrease in prepaid expenses..	2,000	
Increase in accounts payable...	9,000	
Decrease in accrued liabilities	(2,000)	19,000
Net cash provided by operating activities............................		45,000
Cash flows from investing activities:		
Purchase of equipment	(98,000)	
Sale of equipment..	74,000	
Purchase of long-term investment.................................	(8,000)	
Net cash used for investing activities		(32,000)
Cash flows from financing activities:		
Issuance of common shares	19,000	
Payment of cash dividends	(18,000)	
Issuance of long-term note payable.................................	7,000	
Repurchase of common shares..	(5,000)	
Net cash provided by financing activities.............................		3,000
Net increase in cash		16,000
Cash balance, December 31, 2013...................................		3,000
Cash balance, December 31, 2014...................................		$ 19,000
Non-cash investing and financing activities:		
Issuance of long-term note payable to purchase patent........................		$ 37,000
Issuance of common shares to repay bonds payable		13,000
Total non-cash investing and financing activities		$ 50,000

Side notes:

The title must include the name of the company, "Statement of Cash Flows," and the specific period of time covered. There are three sections: Cash flows from operating, investing, and financing activities.

Add back non-cash items: depreciation, amortization; and deduct gains/add loss from sales of long-term assets.

$2,000 = $76,000 − $74,000

Any changes in current assets and current liabilities are included in the operating activities section. Calculate as 2014 balance − 2013 balance from the balance sheets.

Any cash changes in the long-term assets are included in the investing activities section. Check "Transaction Data for 2014."

Any cash changes in the long-term liabilities and contributed capital accounts are included in the financing activities section. Check "Transaction Data for 2014."

This result should equal the Dec. 31, 2014 balance sheet Cash amount.

Check "Transaction Data for 2014."

Long-Term Investments		
Bal.	10,000	
	8,000	
Bal.	18,000	

Equipment, Net		
Bal.	52,000	
	98,000	76,000
		7,000
Bal.	67,000	

Patent, Net		
Bal.	10,000	
	37,000	3,000
Bal.	44,000	

Long-Term Note Payable		
	Bal.	0
		37,000
		7,000
	Bal.	44,000

Bonds Payable		
	Bal.	53,000
13,000		
	Bal.	40,000

Share Capital		
	Bal.	15,000
		13,000
5,000		19,000
	Bal.	42,000

Retained Earnings		
	Bal.	19,000
18,000		26,000
	Bal.	27,000

Use the 2013 and 2014 balance sheet amounts and the transaction data for 2014 to complete these T-accounts.

STOP + THINK (12-1)

ANSWER

a. Financing
b. Financing
c. Operating

d. Financing
e. Investing
f. Financing

g. Financing
h. Operating
i. Investing

j. Operating
k. Investing
l. Investing

STOP + THINK (12-2)

ANSWER

1. Midwest has been expanding. It has acquired new business(es) for $400, with no significant disposals over three years. It also has total property, plant, and equipment purchases of $4,082 over the three years, with no significant disposals.

2. $156 (Proceeds of $55 − Carrying amount = loss of $101)

3. Yes, I would be pleased with Midwest's operating cash flows, as they are consistently higher than net income, which indicates a high quality of earnings. The company also has net cash inflows from operations of over $1,000 in each year, with a significant increase in 2015.

4. Midwest has been relying more on debt, as its net proceeds from equity issuances are only $10 over the three years, whereas its net proceeds from borrowing are $330 during this period.

5. Midwest has a strong cash position. It has over $850 in cash at the end of 2015, which is almost $200 more than it had at the end of 2013. Also, its cash flows from operations are its most significant source of cash in all three years.

Review the Statement of Cash Flows

QUICK CHECK (ANSWERS ARE GIVEN ON PAGE 599.)

1. All the following activities are explicitly reported on the statement of cash flows, except
   a. operating activities.
   b. investing activities.
   c. financing activities.
   d. marketing activities.

2. Activities that create long-term liabilities are usually
   a. operating activities.
   b. investing activities.
   c. financing activities.
   d. non-cash investing and financing activities.

3. Activities affecting long-term assets are
   a. operating activities.
   b. investing activities.
   c. financing activities.
   d. marketing activities.

4. Hilltop Company borrowed $50,000, paid dividends of $12,000, issued 2,000 shares for $30 per share, purchased land for $24,000, and received dividends of $6,000. Net income was $80,000 and depreciation for the year totalled $5,000. How much should be reported as net cash provided by financing activities?
   a. $85,000
   b. $98,000
   c. $110,000
   d. $104,000

5. Activities that obtain the cash needed to launch and sustain a company are
   a. income activities.
   b. investing activities.
   c. financing activities.
   d. marketing activities.

6. The exchange of shares for land would be reported as
   a. exchanges are not reported on the statement of cash flows.
   b. non-cash investing and financing activities.
   c. investing activities.
   d. financing activities.

Use the following Baycraft Ltd. information for questions 7 through 10.

Net Income	$47,000	Decrease in Inventories	$ 2,000
Depreciation Expense	8,000	Increase in Accounts Payable	7,000
Payment of Dividends	2,000	Acquisition of Equipment	24,000
Increase in Accounts Receivable	4,000	Sale of Shares	3,000
Collection of Notes Receivable	6,000	Payment of Long-Term Debt	9,000
Loss on Sale of Land	12,000	Proceeds from Sale of Land	36,000

7. Under the indirect method, net cash provided by operating activities would be
   a. $72,000.
   b. $76,000.
   c. $83,000.
   d. $84,000.

8. Net cash provided by (used for) investing activities would be
   a. $18,000.
   b. $(12,000).
   c. $(6,000).
   d. $24,000.

9. Net cash provided by (used for) financing activities would be
   a. $4,000.
   b. $2,000.
   c. $(8,000).
   d. $(11,000).

10. The cost of land must have been
   a. $30,000.
   b. $48,000.
   c. $54,000.
   d. Cannot be determined from the data given.

11. Merryhill Industries began the year with $45,000 in accounts receivable and ended the year with $31,000 in accounts receivable. If sales for the year were $650,000, the cash collected from customers during the year amounted to
    a. $664,000.
    b. $672,000.
    c. $733,000.
    d. $695,000.

12. Mouton Cheese Ltée made sales of $690,000 and had cost of goods sold of $390,000. Inventory increased by $15,000, and accounts payable increased by $9,000. Operating expenses were $175,000. How much was Mouton's net income for the year?
    a. $110,000
    b. $116,000
    c. $125,000
    d. $300,000

13. Use the Mouton Cheese Ltée data from question 12. How much cash did Mouton pay for inventory during the year?
    a. $374,000
    b. $390,000
    c. $396,000
    d. Some other amount ($_____)

Accounting Vocabulary

cash equivalents Short-term investments that are readily convertible to known amounts of cash, and which are very unlikely to change in value. Generally, only investments with maturities of three months or less meet these criteria. (p. 557)

direct method A method of determining cash flows from operating activities in which all cash receipts and cash payments from operating activities are directly reported on the statement of cash flows. (p. 560)

financing activities Activities that result in changes in the size and composition of a company's contributed equity and borrowings. (p. 559)

free cash flow A measure of how much cash a company has available to pursue new business opportunities. Calculated by deducting capital expenditures from cash flow from operating activities. (p. 574)

indirect method A method of determining cash flows from operating activities in which net income is adjusted for non-cash

transactions, any deferrals or accruals of past or future operating cash receipts or payments, and items of income or expense associated with investing or financing cash flows. (p. 560)

investing activities The purchase and sale of long-term assets and other investments that do not qualify as cash equivalents. They generally consist of transactions that result in cash inflows or outflows related to resources used for generating future income and cash flows. Only expenditures related to assets that are recognized on the balance sheet qualify as investing activities. (p. 559)

non-cash operating working capital account A current asset or current liability account that derives from an operating activity and is not included in cash and cash equivalents. (p. 565)

operating activities The main revenue-producing activities of a company, which generally result from the transactions and other events that determine net income. Other activities that are not *investing* or *financing* activities are also classified as operating activities. (p. 558)

Assess Your Progress

MyAccountingLab   Make the grade with MyAccountingLab: The Exercises, Quizzes, and Problems (A set) marked in red can be found on MyAccountingLab. You can practise them as often as you want, and most feature step-by-step guided instructions to help you find the right answer.

Recall that for the sake of simplicity and consistency, this text classifies all interest paid and interest and dividends received as operating activities, and classifies dividends paid as a financing activity. All questions and problems in this chapter should be answered using this convention.

SHORT EXERCISES

LEARNING OBJECTIVE ❶
Understand purposes of the statement of cash flows

S12-1 State how the statement of cash flows helps investors and creditors perform each of the following functions:
a. Predict future cash flows.
b. Evaluate management decisions.

LEARNING OBJECTIVE ❷
Evaluate operating cash flows—indirect method

S12-2 Examine the TELUS statement of cash flows on page 555. Suppose TELUS's operating activities *used*, rather than *provided*, cash. Identify three things under the indirect method that could cause operating cash flows to be negative.

S12-3 Canada Wide Transportation (CWT) began 2014 with accounts receivable, inventory, and prepaid expenses totalling $65,000. At the end of the year, CWT had a total of $78,000 for these current assets. At the beginning of 2014, CWT owed current liabilities of $42,000, and at year-end, current liabilities totalled $40,000.

Net income for the year was $80,000. Included in net income were a $4,000 gain on the sale of land and depreciation expense of $9,000.

Show how CWT should report cash flows from operating activities for 2014. CWT uses the *indirect* method. Use Exhibit 12-6 (p. 564) as a guide.

LEARNING OBJECTIVE ❸
Report cash flows from operating activities—indirect method

S12-4 Bewell Clinic Inc. is preparing its statement of cash flows (indirect method) for the year ended November 30, 2014. Consider the following items in preparing the company's statement of cash flows. Identify each item as an operating activity—addition to net income (O+), or subtraction from net income (O–); an investing activity (I); a financing activity (F); or an activity that is not used to prepare the statement of cash flows by the indirect method (N). Place the appropriate symbol in the blank space.

LEARNING OBJECTIVE ❷
Identify items for reporting cash flows from operations—indirect method

___ a. Loss on sale of land	___ h. Increase in accounts payable
___ b. Depreciation expense	___ i. Net income
___ c. Increase in inventory	___ j. Payment of dividends
___ d. Decrease in prepaid expense	___ k. Decrease in accrued liabilities
___ e. Decrease in accounts receivable	___ l. Issuance of common shares
___ f. Purchase of equipment	___ m. Gain on sale of building
___ g. Collection of cash from customers	___ n. Retained earnings

S12-5 (Exercise S12-6 is an alternative exercise.) Edwards Corporation Inc. accountants have assembled the following data for the year ended June 30, 2014:

LEARNING OBJECTIVE ❸
Compute operating cash flows—indirect method

Payment of dividends	$ 6,000	Other operating expenses	35,000
Proceeds from issuance of		Purchase of equipment	40,000
common shares	20,000	Decrease in operating current	
Sales revenue	224,000	liabilities	5,000
Increase in operating current assets		Payment of note payable	30,000
other than cash	30,000	Proceeds from sale of land	60,000
Repurchase of common shares	5,000	Depreciation expense	8,000
Cost of goods sold	$100,000		

Prepare the *operating activities section* of Edwards' statement of cash flows for the year ended June 30, 2014. Edwards uses the *indirect* method for operating cash flows.

S12-6 Use the data in exercise S12-5 to prepare Edwards Corporation's statement of cash flows for the year ended June 30, 2014. Edwards uses the *indirect* method for operating activities. Use Exhibit 12-8, page 567, as a guide, but you may stop after determining the net increase (or decrease) in cash.

LEARNING OBJECTIVE ❸
Prepare a statement of cash flows—indirect method

S12-7 Autos of Red Deer Inc. reported the following financial statements for 2014:

LEARNING OBJECTIVE ❸
Compute investing cash flows

Autos of Red Deer Inc.
Income Statement
For the Year Ended December 31, 2014

(in thousands)	
Sales revenue	$710
Cost of goods sold	340
Salary expense	70
Depreciation expense	20
Other expenses	130
Total expenses	560
Net income	$150

Autos of Red Deer Inc. Comparative Balance Sheet As at December 31, 2014 and 2013						
(in thousands)						
Assets	**2014**	**2013**	**Liabilities**	**2014**	**2013**	
Current:			Current:			
Cash	$ 19	$ 16	Accounts payable..................	$ 47	$ 42	
Accounts receivable	59	48	Salary payable.......................	23	21	
Inventory..................................	75	84	Accrued liabilities.................	8	11	
Prepaid expenses	3	2	Long-term notes payable	68	58	
Long-term investments................	55	75	**Shareholders' Equity**			
Property, plant, and			Common shares	40	32	
equipment...............................	225	185	Retained earnings....................	250	246	
Total..	$436	$410	Total..	$436	$410	

Compute the following investing cash flows:

a. Acquisitions of plant and equipment (all were for cash). Autos of Red Deer sold no plant and equipment.

b. Proceeds from the sale of investments. Autos of Red Deer purchased no investments.

LEARNING OBJECTIVE ❸

Compute financing cash flows

S12-8 Use the Autos of Red Deer data in exercise S12-7 to compute:

a. New borrowing or payment of long-term notes payable. Autos of Red Deer had only one long-term note payable transaction during the year.

b. Issuance of common shares or repurchase of common shares. Autos of Red Deer had only one common share transaction during the year.

c. Payment of cash dividends (same as dividends declared).

EXERCISES

LEARNING OBJECTIVE ❶

Identify the purposes of the statement of cash flows

E12-9 B.C. Plating Inc. has experienced an unbroken string of 10 years of growth in net income. Nevertheless, the company is facing bankruptcy. Creditors are calling all B.C. Plating's loans for immediate payment, and the cash is simply not available. It is clear that the company's top managers overemphasized profits and gave too little attention to cash flow.

Requirement

Write a brief memo, in your own words, to explain to the managers of B.C. Plating the purposes of the statement of cash flows.

LEARNING OBJECTIVE ❷

Identify activities for the statement of cash flows—indirect method

E12-10 Carter-Pierce Investments specializes in low-risk government bonds. Identify each of Carter-Pierce's transactions as operating (O), investing (I), financing (F), non-cash investing and financing (NIF), or a transaction that is not reported on the statement of cash flows (N). Indicate whether each item increases (+) or decreases (–) cash. The *indirect* method is used for operating activities.

___	a. Acquisition of building by cash payment		___	j. Acquisition of equipment by issuance of note payable
___	b. Decrease in merchandise inventory		___	k. Sale of long-term investment
___	c. Depreciation of equipment		___	l. Issuance of common share for cash
___	d. Decrease in accrued liabilities		___	m. Increase in accounts payable
___	e. Payment of cash dividend		___	n. Amortization of intangible assets
___	f. Purchase of long-term investment		___	o. Loss on sale of equipment
___	g. Issuance of long-term note payable to borrow cash		___	p. Payment of long-term debt
___	h. Increase in prepaid expenses		___	q. Cash sale of land
___	i. Accrual of salary expense		___	r. Repurchase of common shares
			___	s. Net income

E12-11 Indicate whether each of the following transactions affects an operating activity, an investing activity, a financing activity, or a non-cash investing and financing activity:

LEARNING OBJECTIVE ❷
Classify transactions for the statement of cash flows—indirect method

a.	Cash	61,000		g.	Equipment	11,000	
	Common Shares		61,000		Cash		11,000
b.	Furniture and Fixtures	18,000		h.	Dividends Payable	13,000	
	Cash		18,000		Cash		13,000
c.	Cash	52,000		i.	Salary Expense	14,000	
	Accounts Receivable	11,000			Cash		14,000
	Service Revenue		63,000	j.	Building	105,000	
d.	Cash	7,000			Note Payable—Long-Term		105,000
	Long-Term Investment		7,000	k.	Common Shares	12,000	
e.	Loss on Disposal of Equipment	1,000			Cash		12,000
	Equipment, Net		1,000	l.	Depreciation Expense	5,000	
f.	Land	15,000			Accumulated Depreciation		5,000
	Cash		15,000	m.	Bonds Payable	35,000	
					Cash		35,000

E12-12 The accounting records of South Central Distributors, Inc., reveal the following:

LEARNING OBJECTIVE ❸
Compute cash flows from operating activities—indirect method

Net income....................................	$ 42,000	Depreciation	$ 6,000
Collection of dividend revenue.......	7,100	Decrease in current liabilities.........	25,000
Payment of interest.........................	12,000	Increase in current assets other	
Sales revenue..................................	307,000	than cash	29,000
Gain on sale of land........................	26,000	Payment of dividends	7,700
Acquisition of land	35,000	Payment of income tax	14,000

Requirement

Compute cash flows from operating activities by the *indirect* method. Use the format of the operating activities section of Exhibit 12-6. Also evaluate the operating cash flow of South Central Distributors. Give the reason for your evaluation.

E12-13 The accounting records of Ashby Fur Traders include these accounts:

LEARNING OBJECTIVE ❸
Compute cash flows from operating activities—indirect method

Cash					Accounts Receivable			
Aug. 1	80,000				Aug. 1	8,000		
Receipts	418,000	Payments	450,000		Receipts	522,000	Collections	418,000
Aug. 31	48,000				Aug. 31	112,000		

Inventory					Equipment		
Aug. 1	6,000				Aug. 1	181,000	
Purchases	433,000	Cost of Sales	333,000		Acquisition	4,000	
Aug. 31	106,000				Aug. 31	185,000	

Accumulated Depreciation—Equipment					Accounts Payable		
		Aug. 1	45,000			Aug. 1	15,000
		Depreciation	5,000	Payments	334,000	Purchases	433,000
		Aug. 31	50,000			Aug. 31	114,000

Accrued Liabilities					Retained Earnings		
		Aug. 1	14,000	Quarterly		Aug. 1	63,000
Payments	35,000	Receipts	30,000	Dividend	20,000	Net Income	25,000
		Aug. 31	9,000			Aug. 31	68,000

Requirement

Compute Ashby's net cash provided by (used for) operating activities during August. Use the *indirect* method. Do you see any potential problems in Ashby's cash flows from operations? How can you tell?

LEARNING OBJECTIVE ❸

Prepare the statement of cash flows—indirect method

E12-14 The income statement and additional data of Breen Travel Products, Inc., follow:

Breen Travel Products, Inc.
Income Statement
Year Ended December 31, 2014

Revenues:		
Sales revenue	$283,000	
Dividend revenue	8,700	$291,700
Expenses:		
Cost of goods sold	96,000	
Salary expense	54,000	
Depreciation expense	27,000	
Advertising expense	4,300	
Interest expense	2,100	
Income tax expense	6,000	189,400
Net income		$102,300

Additional data:

a. Acquisition of plant assets was $200,000. Of this amount, $160,000 was paid in cash and $40,000 by signing a note payable.
b. Proceeds from sale of land totalled $23,000.
c. Proceeds from issuance of common share totalled $60,000.
d. Payment of long-term note payable was $13,000.
e. Payment of dividends was $10,000.
f. From the balance sheets:

	December 31,	
	2014	2013
Current assets:		
Cash	$150,000	$138,900
Accounts receivable	44,000	57,000
Inventory	104,000	72,000
Prepaid expenses	9,500	8,300
Current liabilities:		
Accounts payable	$ 38,000	$ 23,000
Accrued liabilities	11,000	24,000

Requirements

1. Prepare Breen's statement of cash flows for the year ended December 31, 2014, using the *indirect* method.
2. Evaluate Breen's cash flows for the year. In your evaluation, mention all three categories of cash flows and give the reason for your evaluation.

E12-15 Consider three independent cases for the cash flows of Texas Tires Corp. For each case, identify from the statement of cash flows how Texas Tires Corp. generated the cash to acquire new plant assets. Rank the three cases from the most healthy financially to the least healthy.

LEARNING OBJECTIVE ❸

Interpret a statement of cash flows—indirect method

	Case A	Case B	Case C
Cash flows from operating activities:			
Net income..	$ 14,000	$ 14,000	$ 14,000
Depreciation and amortization...........................	17,000	17,000	17,000
Increase in operating current assets	(1,000)	(7,000)	(3,000)
Decrease in operating current liabilities	(3,000)	(27,000)	(4,000)
	27,000	(3,000)	24,000
Cash flows from investing activities:			
Acquisition of plant assets	(141,000)	(141,000)	(141,000)
Sales of plant assets	148,000	28,000	47,000
	7,000	(113,000)	(94,000)
Cash flows from financing activities:			
Issuance of share	26,000	149,000	104,000
Payment of debt	(38,000)	(28,000)	(45,000)
	(12,000)	121,000	59,000
Net increase (decrease) in cash	$ 22,000	$ 5,000	$ (11,000)

E12-16 Compute the following items for the statement of cash flows:

a. Beginning and ending Plant Assets, Net, are $125,000 and $115,000, respectively. Depreciation for the period was $19,000, and purchases of new plant assets were $45,000. Plant assets were sold at a $10,000 gain. What were the cash proceeds of the sale?

b. Beginning and ending Retained Earnings are $44,000 and $69,000, respectively. Net income for the period was $61,000, and stock dividends were $10,000. How much were cash dividends?

LEARNING OBJECTIVE ❸

Compute investing and financing amounts for the statement of cash flows

CHALLENGE EXERCISES

E12-17 Crown Specialties Ltd. reported the following at December 31, 2014 (in thousands):

LEARNING OBJECTIVE ❸

Use the balance sheet and the statement of cash flows together

	2014	2013
From the comparative balance sheet:		
Property and equipment, net	$11,150	$9,590
Long-term notes payable	4,400	3,080
From the statement of cash flows:		
Depreciation...	$ 1,920	
Capital expenditures..	(4,130)	
Proceeds from sale of property and equipment	770	
Proceeds from issuance of long-term note payable................	1,190	
Payment of long-term note payable	(110)	
Issuance of common shares	383	

Determine the following items for Crown Specialties during 2014:

1. Gain or loss on the sale of property and equipment

2. Amount of long-term debt issued for something other than cash

QUIZ

Test your understanding of the statement of cash flows by answering the following questions.

Q12-18 Paying off bonds payable is reported on the statement of cash flows under
a. operating activities.
b. investing activities.
c. financing activities.
d. non-cash investing and financing activities.

Q12-19 The sale of inventory for cash is reported on the statement of cash flows under
a. operating activities.
b. investing activities.
c. financing activities.
d. non-cash investing and financing activities.

Q12-20 Selling equipment is reported on the statement of cash flows under
a. operating activities.
b. investing activities.
c. financing activities.
d. non-cash investing and financing activities.

Q12-21 Which of the following terms appears on a statement of cash flows—indirect method?
a. Payments to suppliers
b. Amortization expense
c. Collections from customers
d. Cash receipt of interest revenue

Q12-22 On an indirect-method statement of cash flows, an increase in prepaid insurance would be
a. included in payments to suppliers.
b. added to net income.
c. added to increases in current assets.
d. deducted from net income.

Q12-23 On an indirect-method statement of cash flows, an increase in accounts payable would be
a. reported in the investing activities section.
b. reported in the financing activities section.
c. added to net income in the operating activities section.
d. deducted from net income in the operating activities section.

Q12-24 On an indirect-method statement of cash flows, a gain on the sale of plant assets would be
a. ignored, because the gain did not generate any cash.
b. reported in the investing activities section.
c. deducted from net income in the operating activities section.
d. added to net income in the operating activities section.

Q12-25 Paying cash dividends is a/an _____ activity.
        Receiving cash dividends is a/an _____ activity.

Q12-26 Matlock Camera Co. sold equipment with a cost of $20,000 and accumulated depreciation of $8,000 for an amount that resulted in a gain of $3,000. What amount should Matlock report on the statement of cash flows as "proceeds from sale of plant and equipment"?
a. $9,000
b. $17,000
c. $15,000
d. Some other amount ($_____)

Questions 27 through 35 use the following data. Trudeau Corporation determines operating cash flows by the indirect method.

Trudeau Corporation
Income Statement for the Year Ended December 31, 2014

Sales revenue	$180,000	
Gain on sale of equipment	8,000	$188,000
Cost of goods sold	110,000	
Depreciation	6,000	
Other operating expenses	25,000	141,000
Net income		$ 47,000

Trudeau Corporation
Comparative Balance Sheet as at December 31, 2014 and 2013

Assets	2014	2013	Liabilities and Shareholders' Equity	2014	2013
Cash.................................	$ 4,000	$ 1,000	Accounts payable	$ 6,000	$ 7,000
Accounts receivable...........	7,000	11,000	Accrued liabilities............	7,000	3,000
Inventory	10,000	9,000	Common shares..............	20,000	10,000
Plant and equipment, net ..	93,000	69,000	Retained earnings...........	81,000	70,000
	$114,000	$90,000		$114,000	$90,000

Q12-27 How many items enter into the computation of Trudeau's net cash provided by operating activities?

a. 2

b. 3

c. 5

d. 7

Q12-28 How do Trudeau's accrued liabilities affect the company's statement of cash flows for 2014?

a. They don't because the accrued liabilities are not yet paid

b. Increase in cash provided by operating activities

c. Increase in cash used by investing activities

d. Increase in cash used by financing activities

Q12-29 How do accounts receivable affect Trudeau's cash flows from operating activities for 2014?

a. Increase in cash provided by operating activities

b. Decrease in cash provided by operating activities

c. They don't because accounts receivable result from investing activities

d. Decrease in cash used by investing activities

Q12-30 Trudeau's net cash provided by operating activities during 2014 was

a. $3,000.

b. $47,000.

c. $51,000.

d. $58,000.

Q12-31 How many items enter into the computation of Trudeau's net cash flow from investing activities for 2014?

a. 2

b. 3

c. 5

d. 7

Q12-32 The carrying amount of equipment sold during 2014 was $20,000. Trudeau's net cash flow from investing activities for 2014 was

a. net cash used of $22,000.

b. net cash used of $28,000.

c. net cash used of $50,000.

d. net cash provided of $28,000.

Q12-33 How many items enter into the computation of Trudeau's net cash flow from financing activities for 2014?

a. 2

b. 3

c. 5

d. 7

Q12-34 Trudeau's largest financing cash flow for 2014 resulted from the

a. sale of equipment.

b. purchase of equipment.

c. issuance of common shares.

d. payment of dividends.

Q12-35 Trudeau's net cash flow from financing activities for 2014 was

a. net cash used of $25,000.

b. net cash used of $20,000.

c. net cash provided of $10,000.

d. net cash used of $26,000.

Q12-36 Sales totalled $800,000, accounts receivable increased by $40,000, and accounts payable decreased by $35,000. How much cash did this company collect from customers?

a. $760,000
b. $795,000
c. $800,000
d. $840,000

Q12-37 Income Tax Payable was $5,000 at the end of the year and $2,800 at the beginning. Income tax expense for the year totalled $59,100. What amount of cash did this company pay for income tax during the year?

a. $56,900
b. $59,100
c. $61,300
d. $61,900

PROBLEMS

(Group A)

LEARNING OBJECTIVE ❶❷

Use cash-flow data to evaluate performance

P12-38A Top managers of Relax Inns are reviewing company performance for 2014. The income statement reports a 20% increase in net income over 2013. However, most of the increase resulted from a gain on insurance proceeds from fire damage to a building. The balance sheet shows a large increase in receivables. The statement of cash flows, in summarized form, reports the following:

Net cash used for operating activities	$(80,000)
Net cash provided by investing activities	40,000
Net cash provided by financing activities	50,000
Increase in cash during 2014	$ 10,000

Requirement

Write a memo giving Relax Inns' managers your assessment of 2014 operations and your outlook for the future. Focus on the information content of the cash-flow data.

LEARNING OBJECTIVE ❷❸

Prepare an income statement, balance sheet, and statement of cash flows—indirect method

P12-39A Vintage Automobiles of Orangeville Ltd. was formed on January 1, 2014, when Vintage issued common shares for $300,000. Early in January 2014, Vintage made the following cash payments:

a. $150,000 for equipment
b. $120,000 for inventory (four cars at $30,000 each)
c. $20,000 for 2014 rent on a store building

In February 2014, Vintage purchased six cars for inventory on account. Cost of this inventory was $260,000 ($43,333.33 each). Before year-end, Vintage paid $208,000 of this debt. Vintage uses the FIFO method to account for inventory.

During 2014, Vintage sold eight vintage autos for a total of $500,000. Before year-end, Vintage collected 80% of this amount.

The business employs three people. The combined annual payroll is $95,000, of which Vintage owes $4,000 at year-end. At the end of the year, Vintage paid income tax of $10,000.

Late in 2014, Vintage declared and paid cash dividends of $11,000.

For equipment, Vintage uses the straight-line depreciation method over five years with zero residual value.

Requirements

1. Prepare Vintage Automobiles of Orangeville Ltd.'s income statement for the year ended December 31, 2014. Use the single-step format, with all revenues listed together and all expenses listed together.
2. Prepare Vintage's balance sheet at December 31, 2014.
3. Prepare Vintage's statement of cash flows for the year ended December 31, 2014. Format cash flows from operating activities by using the *indirect* method.
4. Comment on the business performance based on the statement of cash flows.

P12-40A Primrose Software Inc. has assembled the following data for the year ended December 31, 2014.

LEARNING OBJECTIVE ❷❸

Prepare the statement of cash flows—indirect method

	December 31	
	2014	2013
Current Accounts:		
Current assets:		
Cash and cash equivalents	$38,700	$22,700
Accounts receivable	69,700	64,200
Inventories	88,600	83,000
Prepaid expenses	5,300	4,100
Current liabilities:		
Accounts payable	57,200	55,800
Income tax payable	18,600	16,700
Accrued liabilities	15,500	27,200

Transaction Data for 2014:

Acquisition of land by issuing		Repurchase of common shares	$14,300
long-term note payable	$ 95,000	Loss on sale of equipment	11,700
Stock dividends	31,800	Payment of cash dividends	18,300
Collection of loan	8,700	Issuance of long-term note payable	
Depreciation expense	27,100	to borrow cash	34,400
Purchase of building	125,300	Net income	45,100
Repayment of bonds payable by		Issuance of common shares	
issuing common shares	65,000	for cash	41,200
Purchase of long-term investment	31,600	Proceeds from sale of equipment	58,000

Requirement

Prepare Primrose Software Inc.'s statement of cash flows using the *indirect* method to report operating activities. Include an accompanying schedule of non-cash investing and financing activities. How much of the cash used for investing activities was provided by operations?

P12-41A The comparative balance sheet of Northern Movie Theatre Company at March 31, 2014, reported the following:

LEARNING OBJECTIVE ❷❸

Prepare the statement of cash flows—indirect method

	March 31,	
	2014	2013
Current assets:		
Cash and cash equivalents	$9,900	$14,000
Accounts receivable	14,900	21,700
Inventories	63,200	60,600
Prepaid expenses	1,900	1,700
Current liabilities:		
Accounts payable	30,300	27,600
Accrued liabilities	10,700	11,100
Income tax payable	8,000	4,700

Northern's transactions during the year ended March 31, 2014, included the following:

Acquisition of land by		Sale of long-term investment	$13,700
issuing note payable	$101,000	Depreciation expense	17,300
Payment of cash dividend	30,000	Cash purchase of building	47,000
Cash purchase of equipment	78,700	Net income	50,000
Issuance of long-term note		Issuance of common shares for cash	11,000
payable to borrow cash	50,000	Stock dividend	18,000

Requirements

1. Prepare Northern Movie Theatre Company's statement of cash flows for the year ended March 31, 2014, using the *indirect* method to report cash flows from operating activities. Report non-cash investing and financing activities in an accompanying schedule.
2. Evaluate Northern's cash flows for the year. Mention all three categories of cash flows and give the reason for your evaluation.

LEARNING OBJECTIVE ❷❸

Prepare the statement of cash flows—indirect method

P12-42A The 2014 comparative balance sheet and income statement of 4 Seasons Supply Corp. follow. 4 Seasons had no non-cash investing and financing transactions during 2014. During the year, there were no sales of land or equipment, no issuance of notes payable, and no repurchase of shares transactions

4 Seasons Supply Corp.
Comparative Balance Sheet
As at December 31, 2014 and 2013

	December 31,		Increase
	2014	2013	(Decrease)
Current assets:			
Cash and cash equivalents	$ 17,600	$ 5,300	$12,300
Accounts receivable	27,200	27,600	(400)
Inventories	83,600	87,200	(3,600)
Prepaid expenses	2,500	1,900	600
Property, plant, and equipment:			
Land	89,000	60,000	29,000
Equipment, net	53,500	49,400	4,100
Total assets	$273,400	$231,400	$42,000
Current liabilities:			
Accounts payable	$ 35,800	$ 33,700	$ 2,100
Salary payable	3,100	6,600	(3,500)
Other accrued liabilities	22,600	23,700	(1,100)
Long-term liabilities:			
Notes payable	75,000	100,000	(25,000)
Shareholders' equity:			
Common shares	88,300	64,700	23,600
Retained earnings	48,600	2,700	45,900
Total liabilities and shareholders' equity	$273,400	$231,400	$42,000

4 Seasons Supply Corp.
Income Statement
For the Year Ended December 31, 2014

Revenues:		
Sales revenue		$228,700
Expenses:		
Cost of goods sold	$70,600	
Salary expense	27,800	
Depreciation expense	4,000	
Other operating expense	10,500	
Interest expense	11,600	
Income tax expense	29,100	
Total expenses		153,600
Net income		$ 75,100

Requirements

1. Prepare the 2014 statement of cash flows, formatting operating activities by using the *indirect* method.
2. How will what you learned in this problem help you evaluate an investment?

(Group B)

P12-43B Top managers of Culinary Imports Limited are reviewing company performance for 2014. The income statement reports a 15% increase in net income, the fourth consecutive year showing an income increase above 10%. The income statement includes a non-recurring loss without which net income would have increased by 16%. The balance sheet shows modest increases in assets, liabilities, and shareholders' equity. The assets posting the largest increases are plant and equipment because the company is halfway through a five-year expansion program. No other asset and no liabilities are increasing dramatically. A summarized version of the statement of cash flows reports the following:

LEARNING OBJECTIVE ❶❷
Use cash-flow information to evaluate performance

Net cash provided by operating activities	$ 310,000
Net cash used for investing activities	(290,000)
Net cash provided by financing activities..	50,000
Increase in cash during 2014..	$ 70,000

Requirement

Write a memo giving top managers of Culinary Imports Limited your assessment of 2014 operations and your outlook for the future. Focus on the net income and the cash-flow data.

P12-44B Cruise Canada Motorhomes Inc. (CCM) was formed on January 1, 2014, when the company issued its common shares for $200,000. Early in January, CCM made the following cash payments:
a. For showroom fixtures, $50,000
b. For inventory, two motorhomes at $60,000 each, a total of $120,000
c. For rent on a store building, $12,000

LEARNING OBJECTIVE ❷❸
Prepare an income statement, balance sheet, and statement of cash flows—indirect method

In February, CCM purchased three motorhomes on account. Cost of this inventory was $160,000 ($53,333.33 each). Before year-end, CCM paid $140,000 of this debt. CCM uses the FIFO method to account for inventory.

During 2014, CCM sold four motorhomes for a total of $560,000. Before year-end, CCM collected 90% of this amount.

The store employs three people. The combined annual payroll is $90,000, of which CCM owes $3,000 at year-end. At the end of the year, CCM paid income tax of $64,000.

Late in 2014, CCM declared and paid cash dividends of $40,000.

For showroom fixtures, CCM uses the straight-line depreciation method over five years with zero residual value.

Requirements

1. Prepare CCM's income statement for the year ended December 31, 2014. Use the single-step format, with all revenues listed together and all expenses listed together.
2. Prepare CCM's balance sheet at December 31, 2014.
3. Prepare CCM's statement of cash flows for the year ended December 31, 2014. Format cash flows from operating activities by the indirect method.
4. Comment on the business performance based on the statement of cash flows.

LEARNING OBJECTIVE ❷❸

Prepare the statement of cash flows—indirect method

P12-45B Accountants for Crowne Plaza Products Inc. have assembled the following data for the year ended December 31, 2014:

	December 31	
	2014	2013
Current Accounts:		
Current assets:		
Cash and cash equivalents	$29,100	$34,800
Accounts receivable	70,100	73,700
Inventories	90,600	96,500
Prepaid expenses	3,200	2,100
Current liabilities:		
Accounts payable	71,600	67,500
Income tax payable	5,900	6,800
Accrued liabilities	28,300	23,200

Transaction Data for 2014:

Payment of cash dividends	$48,300	Stock dividends	$ 12,600
Issuance of long-term note		Collection of loan	10,300
payable to borrow cash	71,000	Purchase of equipment	69,000
Net income	31,000	Payment of note payable by	
Issuance of preferred shares for cash	36,200	issuing common shares	89,400
Sale of long-term investment	12,200	Purchase of long-term investment	44,800
Depreciation expense	30,300	Acquisition of building by issuing	
Payment of long-term note payable	47,800	long-term note payable	201,000
Gain on sale of investment	3,500		

Requirement

Prepare Crowne Plaza Products' statement of cash flows using the *indirect* method to report operating activities. Include an accompanying schedule of non-cash investing and financing activities. How much of the cash used for investing activities was provided by operations?

LEARNING OBJECTIVE ❷❸

Prepare the statement of cash flows—indirect method

P12-46B The comparative balance sheet of Crossbow Novelties Corp. at December 31, 2014, reported the following:

	December 31	
	2014	2013
Current Assets:		
Cash and cash equivalents	$28,800	$12,500
Accounts receivable	28,600	29,300
Inventories	51,600	53,000
Prepaid expenses	4,200	3,700
Current Liabilities:		
Accounts payable	31,100	28,000
Accrued liabilities	14,300	16,800
Income tax payable	11,000	14,300

Crossbow's transactions during 2014 included the following:

Cash purchase of building	$124,000	Depreciation expense	$17,800
Net income	52,000	Payment of cash dividends	17,000
Issuance of common shares		Cash purchase of equipment	55,000
for cash	105,600	Issuance of long-term note	
Stock dividend	13,000	payable to borrow cash	32,000
Sale of long-term investment	6,000	Repayment of note payable by	
		issuing common shares	30,000

Requirements

1. Prepare the statement of cash flows of Crossbow Novelties Corp. for the year ended December 31, 2014. Use the *indirect* method to report cash flows from operating activities. Report non-cash investing and financing activities in an accompanying schedule.
2. Evaluate Crossbow's cash flows for the year. Mention all three categories of cash flows, and give the reason for your evaluation.

P12-47B The 2014 comparative balance sheet and income statement of Riverbend Pools Inc. follow. Riverbend had no non-cash investing and financing transactions during 2014. During the year, there were no sales of land or equipment, no issuances of notes payable, and no share repurchase transactions.

LEARNING OBJECTIVE ❷❸

Prepare the statement of cash flows—indirect method

Riverbend Pools Inc.
Comparative Balance Sheet
As at December 31, 2014 and 2013

	2014	2013	Increase (Decrease)
Current assets:			
Cash and cash equivalents	$ 28,700	$ 15,600	$ 13,100
Accounts receivable	47,100	44,000	3,100
Inventories	94,300	89,900	4,400
Prepaid expenses	1,700	2,200	(500)
Property, plant, and equipment:			
Land	35,100	10,000	25,100
Equipment, net	100,900	93,700	7,200
Total assets	$307,800	$255,400	$ 52,400
Current liabilities:			
Accounts payable	$ 22,700	$ 24,600	$ (1,900)
Salary payable	2,100	1,400	700
Other accrued liabilities	24,400	22,500	1,900
Long-term liabilities:			
Notes payable	55,000	65,000	(10,000)
Shareholders' equity:			
Common shares	131,100	122,300	8,800
Retained earnings	72,500	19,600	52,900
Total liabilities and shareholders' equity	$307,800	$255,400	$ 52,400

Riverbend Pools Inc.
Income Statement
For the Year Ended December 31, 2014

Revenues:		
Sales revenue		$438,000
Interest revenue		11,700
Total revenues		449,700
Expenses:		
Cost of goods sold	$185,200	
Salary expense	76,400	
Depreciation expense	15,300	
Other operating expense	49,700	
Interest expense	24,600	
Income tax expense	16,900	
Total expense		368,100
Net income		$ 81,600

Requirements

1. Prepare the statement of cash flows of Riverbend Pools Inc. for the year ended December 31, 2014. Determine cash flows from operating activities by the indirect method.
2. How will what you learned in this problem help you evaluate an investment?

Apply Your Knowledge

Decision Cases

LEARNING OBJECTIVE ❸

Prepare and use the statement of cash flows to evaluate operations

Case 1. The 2014 income statement and the 2014 comparative balance sheet of T-Bar-M Camp Inc. have just been distributed at a meeting of the camp's board of directors. The directors raise a fundamental question: Why is the cash balance so low? This question is especially troublesome because 2014 showed record profits. As the controller of the company, you must answer the question.

T-Bar-M Camp Inc.
Income Statement
For the Year Ended December 31, 2014

	(in thousands)
Revenues:	
Sales revenue	$436
Expenses:	
Cost of goods sold	$221
Salary expense	48
Depreciation expense	57
Interest expense	13
Total expenses	339
Net income	$ 97

T-Bar-M Camp Inc.
Comparative Balance Sheet
As at December 31, 2014 and 2013

(in thousands)	2014	2013
Assets		
Cash	$ 17	$ 63
Accounts receivable, net	72	61
Inventories	194	181
Long-term investments	31	0
Property, plant, and equipment	369	259
Accumulated depreciation	(244)	(198)
Patents, net	177	188
Totals	$616	$554
Liabilities and Shareholders' Equity		
Accounts payable	$ 63	$ 56
Accrued liabilities	12	17
Notes payable, long-term	179	264
Common shares	149	61
Retained earnings	213	156
Totals	$616	$554

Requirements

1. Prepare a statement of cash flows for 2014 in the format that best shows the relationship between net income and operating cash flow. The company sold no plant and equipment or long-term investments and issued no notes payable during 2014. There were *no* non-cash investing and financing transactions during the year. Show all amounts in thousands.
2. Answer the board members' question: Why is the cash balance so low? Point out the two largest cash payments during 2014.
3. Considering net income and the company's cash flows during 2014, was it a good year or a bad year? Give your reasons. Explain the format you chose for the statement of cash flows.

Case 2. Applied Technology Inc. and Four-Star Catering Ltd. are asking you to recommend their shares to your clients. Because Applied and Four-Star earn about the same net income and have similar financial positions, your decision depends on their statements of cash flows, which are summarized as follows:

LEARNING OBJECTIVE ❶❷

Use cash-flow data to evaluate an investment

	Applied Technology Inc.		Four-Star Catering Ltd.	
Net cash provided by operating activities		$ 30,000		$ 70,000
Cash provided by (used for) investing activities:				
Purchase of property, plant, and equipment	$(20,000)		$(100,000)	
Sale of property, plant, and equipment	40,000	20,000	10,000	(90,000)
Cash provided by (used for) financing activities:				
Issuance of common shares		—		30,000
Paying off long-term debt		(40,000)		—
Net increase in cash		$ 10,000		$ 10,000

Based on their cash flows, which company looks better? Give your reasons.

Ethical Issue

Columbia Industries is having a bad year. Net income is only $37,000. Also, two important overseas customers are falling behind in their payments to Columbia, and Columbia's accounts receivable are ballooning. The company desperately needs a loan. The Columbia board of directors is considering ways to put the best face on the company's financial statements. Columbia's bank closely examines cash flow from operations. Daniel Peavey, Columbia's controller, suggests reclassifying the receivables from the slow-paying clients as long-term. He explains to the board that removing the $80,000 rise in accounts receivable from current assets will increase net cash provided by operations. This approach may help Columbia get the loan.

Requirements

1. Identify the ethical issue(s) in this situation.
2. Who are the stakeholders in this situation?
3. What is the potential impact of this reporting issue on each stakeholder?
4. What should the board do?
5. Under what conditions would the reclassification of the receivables be considered ethical?

Focus on Financials

LEARNING OBJECTIVE ❶❷❸

Use the statement of cash flows

TELUS Corporation

Use TELUS's statement of cash flows along with the company's other financial statements, all in Appendix A at the end of the book, to answer the following questions.

Requirements

1. By which method does TELUS report cash flows from operating activities? Explain your answer.
2. Evaluate TELUS's change in cash in fiscal year 2011 compared with 2010 and 2009.

Focus on Analysis

LEARNING OBJECTIVE ❶❷❸

Analyze cash flows

TELUS Corporation

Refer to the TELUS's financial statements in Appendix A at the end of this book. Focus on the fiscal year 2011.

Requirements

1. What was TELUS's main source of cash? Is this a positive result? What was TELUS's main use of cash? What sources of information contributed to your analysis?
2. Explain in detail the three main reasons why net cash from operations differs from net income.
3. There are two statements on which companies report declaration of dividends. Identify the two statements, review these statements, and determine what dividends TELUS paid shareholders in 2011.

Group Project

Project 1. Each member of the group should obtain the annual report of a different company. Select companies in different industries. Evaluate each company's trend of cash flows for the most recent two years. In your evaluation of the companies' cash flows, you may use any other information that is publicly available—for example, the other financial statements (income statement, balance sheet, statement of shareholders' equity, and the related notes) and news stories from magazines and newspapers. Rank the companies' cash flows from best to worst and write a two-page report on your findings.

Project 2. Select a company, and obtain its annual report, including all the financial statements. Focus on the statement of cash flows and, in particular, the cash flows from operating activities. Specify whether the company uses the direct method or the indirect method to report operating cash flows. As necessary, use the other financial statements (income statement, balance sheet, and statement of shareholders' equity) and the notes to prepare the company's cash flows from operating activities by using the *other* method.

Quick Check Answers

1. *d*
2. *c*
3. *b*
4. *b* ($50,000 − $12,000 + $60,000 = $98,000)
5. *c*
6. *b*
7. *a* ($47,000 + $8,000 − $4,000 + $12,000 + $7,000 + $2,000 = $72,000)
8. *a* ($6,000 − $24,000 + $36,000 = $18,000)
9. *c* (−$2,000 + $3,000 − $9,000 = −$8,000)
10. *b* ($12,000 + $36,000 = $48,000)
11. *a* [$650,000 + ($45,000 − $31,000) = $664,000]
12. *c* ($690,000 − $390,000 − $175,000 = $125,000)
13. *d* ($390,000 − $15,000 + $9,000 = $384,000)

Appendix 12A

Preparing the Statement of Cash Flows: Direct Method

PREPARE A STATEMENT OF CASH FLOWS USING THE DIRECT METHOD OF DETERMINING CASH FLOWS FROM OPERATING ACTIVITIES

IFRS and ASPE encourage companies to prepare the statement of cash flows using the direct method because it provides clearer information about the sources and uses of cash. Very few companies use this method, however, because the indirect method gained prominence in the past and now continues to be used for reasons of comparability and user familiarity. Investing and financing cash flows are unaffected by the chosen method of reporting operating cash flows.

To illustrate the statement of cash flows, we use Bradshaw Corporation, a dealer in playground equipment. To prepare the statement of cash flows by the direct method, proceed as follows:

STEP 1 Lay out the template of the *operating activities* section of the statement of cash flows by the direct method, as shown in Exhibit 12A-1.

STEP 2 Use the comparative balance sheet to determine the increase or decrease in cash during the period. The change in cash is the "check figure" for the statement of cash flows. Bradshaw Corporation's comparative balance sheet indicates that Bradshaw's cash decreased by $20,000 during 2014 (Exhibit 12-4, p. 563). *Why* did Bradshaw's cash fall during 2014? The statement of cash flows explains.

STEP 3 Use the available data to prepare the statement of cash flows. Bradshaw's transaction data appear in Exhibit 12A-2. These transactions affected both the income statement (Exhibit 12-5, p. 563) and the statement of cash flows. Some transactions affect one statement and some, the other. For example, sales (item 1) are reported on the income statement. Cash collections (item 2) go on the statement of cash flows. Other transactions, such as the cash receipt of dividend revenue (item 5), affect both statements. *The statement of cash flows reports only those transactions with cash effects* (those with an asterisk in Exhibit 12A-2). Exhibit 12A-3 gives Bradshaw Corporation's statement of cash flows for 2014.

EXHIBIT 12A-1
Template of the Operating Activities Section of the Statement of Cash Flows: Direct Method

Bradshaw Corporation
Statement of Cash Flows
For the Year Ended December 31, 2014

Cash flows from operating activities:
  Receipts:
    Collections from customers
    Interest received on notes receivable
    Dividends received on investments in shares
    Other operating receipts
      Total cash receipts
  Payments:
    To suppliers
    To employees
    For interest
    For income tax
    Other operating payments
      Total cash payments
  Net cash provided by (used for) operating activities

Operating Activities
1. Sales on credit, $284,000
*2. Collections from customers, $271,000
3. Interest revenue on notes receivable, $12,000
*4. Collection of interest receivable, $10,000
*5. Cash receipt of dividend revenue on investments in shares, $9,000
6. Cost of goods sold, $150,000
7. Purchases of inventory on credit, $147,000
*8. Payments to suppliers, $133,000
9. Salary and wages expense, $56,000
*10. Payments of salary and wages, $58,000
11. Depreciation expense, $18,000
12. Other operating expense, $17,000
*13. Interest expense and payments, $16,000
*14. Income tax expense and payments, $15,000

*Indicates a cash flow to be reported on the statement of cash flows.
Note: Income statement data are taken from Exhibit 12-A6, page 604.

Bradshaw Corporation
Statement of Cash Flows
For the Year Ended December 31, 2014

	(in thousands)	
Cash flows from operating activities:		
Receipts:		
Collections from customers	$ 271	
Interest received on notes receivable	10	
Dividends received on investments in shares	9	
Total cash receipts		$ 290
Payments:		
To suppliers	(133)	
To employees	(58)	
For interest	(16)	
For income tax	(15)	
Total cash payments		(222)
Net cash provided by operating activities		68

Cash Flows From Operating Activities

Operating cash flows are listed first because they are the most important. Exhibit 12A-3 shows that Bradshaw is sound; operating activities were the largest source of cash.

CASH COLLECTIONS FROM CUSTOMERS. Both cash sales and collections of accounts receivable are reported on the statement of cash flows as "Collections from customers . . . $271,000" in Exhibit 12A-3.

CASH RECEIPTS OF INTEREST. The income statement reports interest revenue. Only the cash receipts of interest appear on the statement of cash flows—$10,000 in Exhibit 12A-3.

CASH RECEIPTS OF DIVIDENDS. Dividends are earned on investments in shares. Dividend revenue is reported on the income statement, and only cash receipts are reported on the statement of cash flows—$9,000 in Exhibit 12A-3. (Dividends *received* are operating activities, but dividends *paid* are financing activities.)

PAYMENTS TO SUPPLIERS. Payments to suppliers include all payments for inventory and operating expenses except employee compensation, interest, and income taxes. *Suppliers* are those entities that provide the business with its inventory and essential services. For example, a clothing store's suppliers may include Arrow Shirts, Gildan Activewear, and Levi Strauss. Other suppliers provide advertising, utilities, and various services that are operating expenses. Exhibit 12A-3 shows that Bradshaw Corporation paid suppliers $133,000.

PAYMENTS TO EMPLOYEES. This category includes payments for salaries, wages, commissions, and other forms of employee compensation. Accrued amounts are excluded because they have not yet been paid. The statement of cash flows in Exhibit 12A-3 reports only the cash payments ($58,000).

PAYMENTS FOR INTEREST EXPENSE AND INCOME TAX EXPENSE. Interest and income tax payments are reported separately. Bradshaw Corporation paid all its interest and income tax expenses in cash. Therefore, the same amount appears on the income statement and the statement of cash flows. Interest payments are operating cash flows because the interest is an expense.

DEPRECIATION EXPENSE. This expense is *not* listed on the statement of cash flows in Exhibit 12A-3 because it does not affect cash.

GAIN ON SALE OF PROPERTY, PLANT, AND EQUIPMENT. This gain is not listed on the statement of cash flows in Exhibit 12A-3 because it does not affect cash. The proceeds from selling the property, plant, and equipment will be included as a cash inflow under investing activities.

STOP + THINK (12A-1)

Classify each of the following as an operating activity, an investing activity, or a financing activity. Also identify those items that are not reported on the statement of cash flows prepared by the *direct* method.

a. Net income

b. Payment of dividends

c. Borrowing

d. Payment of cash to suppliers

e. Making a loan

f. Receipt of cash dividends

g. Depreciation expense

h. Purchase of equipment

i. Issuance of shares

j. Purchase of another company

k. Payment of a note payable

l. Payment of income taxes

m. Collections from customers

n. Accrual of interest revenue

o. Expiration of prepaid expense

Now let's see how to compute the amounts of the operating cash flows by the direct method.

Computing Operating Cash Flows by the Direct Method

To compute operating cash flows by the direct method, we use the income statement and the *changes* in the related balance sheet accounts. Exhibit 12A-4 diagrams the process. Exhibit 12A-5 is Bradshaw Corporation's income statement and Exhibit 12A-6 (page 604) is the comparative balance sheet.

EXHIBIT 12A-4
Direct Method of Computing Cash Flows From Operating Activities

RECEIPTS/PAYMENTS	From Income Statement Account	Change in Related Balance Sheet Account	
RECEIPTS:			
From customers	Sales Revenue	+ Decrease in Accounts Receivable − Increase in Accounts Receivable	
Of interest	Interest Revenue	+ Decrease in Interest Receivable − Increase in Interest Receivable	
PAYMENTS:			
To suppliers	Cost of Goods Sold	+ Increase in Inventory − Decrease in Inventory	+ Decrease in Accounts Payable − Increase in Accounts Payable
	Operating Expense	+ Increase in Prepaids − Decrease in Prepaids	+ Decrease in Accrued Liabilities − Increase in Accrued Liabilities
To employees	Salary (Wages) Expense	+ Decrease in Salary (Wages) Payable − Increase in Salary (Wages) Payable	
For interest	Interest Expense	+ Decrease in Interest Payable − Increase in Interest Payable	
For income tax	Income Tax Expense	+ Decrease in Income Tax Payable − Increase in Income Tax Payable	

We thank Barbara Gerrity for suggesting this exhibit.

EXHIBIT 12A-5
Income Statement for the Bradshaw Corporation

Bradshaw Corporation
Income Statement
For the Year Ended December 31, 2014

	(in thousands)
Revenues and gains:	
Sales revenue	$284
Interest revenue	12
Dividend revenue	9
Gain on sale of property, plant, and equipment	8
Total revenues and gains	$313
Expenses:	
Cost of goods sold	150
Salary and wages expense	56
Depreciation expense	18
Other operating expense	17
Interest expense	16
Income tax expense	15
Total expenses	272
Net income	$ 41

COMPUTING CASH COLLECTIONS FROM CUSTOMERS. Collections start with sales revenue (an accrual-basis amount). Bradshaw Corporation's income statement (Exhibit 12A-5) reports sales of $284,000. Accounts Receivable increased from $80,000 at the beginning of the year to $93,000 at year-end, a $13,000 increase

EXHIBIT 12A-6
Comparative Balance Sheet for Bradshaw Corporation

Bradshaw Corporation
Comparative Balance Sheet
As at December 31, 2014 and 2013

(amuonts in thousands)	2014	2013	Increase (Decrease)	
Assets				
Current:				
Cash	$ 22	$ 42	$ (20)	⎫
Accounts receivable	93	80	13	⎬
Interest receivable	3	1	2	*Changes in current assets—Operating*
Inventory	135	138	(3)	⎬
Prepaid expenses	8	7	1	⎭
Long-term note receivable from another company	11	—	11	⎫
Property, plant, and equipment, net of depreciation	353	219	134	⎬ *Changes in non-current assets—Investing*
Totals	$625	$487	$138	
Liabilities				
Current:				
Accounts payable	$ 91	$ 57	$ 34	⎫
Salary and wages payable	4	6	(2)	⎬ *Changes in current liabilities—Operating*
Accrued liabilities	1	3	(2)	⎭
Long-term debt	160	77	83	⎫ *Change in long-term liabilities and*
Shareholders' Equity				⎬ *contributed capital accounts—Financing*
Share capital	259	258	1	⎭
Retained earnings	110	86	24	⎬ *Change due to net income—Operating*
Totals	$625	$487	$138	*Change due to dividends—Financing*

(Exhibit 12A-6). Based on those amounts, Cash Collections equal $271,000. We must solve for cash collections (X).

Accounts Receivable					
Beginning balance	+	Sales	−	Collections	= Ending balance
$80,000	+	$284,000		−X	= $93,000
				−X	= $93,000 − $80,000 − $284,000
				−X	= $271,000

The T-account for Accounts Receivable provides another view of the same computation:

Accounts Receivable			
Beginning balance	80,000		
Sales	284,000	Collections	271,000
Ending balance	93,000		

Accounts Receivable increased, so collections must be less than sales.

All collections of receivables are computed in this way. Let's turn now to other cash receipts. In our example, Bradshaw Corporation earned interest revenue. Interest Receivable's balance increased by $2,000 (Exhibit 12A-6). Cash receipts of interest were $10,000 (Interest Revenue of $12,000 minus the $2,000 increase in Interest Receivable). Exhibit 12A-4 shows how to make this computation.

COMPUTING PAYMENTS TO SUPPLIERS. This computation includes two parts:

- Payments for inventory
- Payments for operating expenses (other than interest and income tax)

Payments for inventory are computed by converting cost of goods sold to the cash basis. We use Cost of Goods Sold, Inventory, and Accounts Payable. First, we must solve for purchases. All amounts come from Exhibits 12A-5 and 12A-6.

Cost of Goods Sold					
Beginning inventory	+ Purchases	−	Ending inventory	=	Cost of goods sold
$138,000	+ X		$135,000	=	$150,000
	X			=	$150,000 − $138,000 + $135,000
	X			=	$147,000

Now we can compute cash payments for inventory (Y), as follows:

Accounts Payable					
Beginning balance	+ Purchases	−	Payments for inventory	=	Ending balance
$57,000	+ $147,000		−Y	=	$91,000
			−Y	=	$91,000 − $57,000 − $147,000
			−Y	=	$113,000

The T-accounts show where the data come from:

Inventory					Accounts Payable			
Beg. inventory	138,000	Cost of goods sold	150,000		Payments for		Beg. bal.	57,000
Purchases	147,000				inventory	113,000	Purchases	147,000
End. inventory	$135,000						End bal.	91,000

Accounts Payable increased, so payments are less than purchases.

COMPUTING PAYMENTS FOR OPERATING EXPENSES. Payments for operating expenses other than interest and income tax can be computed from three accounts: Prepaid Expenses, Accrued Liabilities, and Other Operating Expenses. All Bradshaw Corporation data come from Exhibits 12A-5 and 12A-6.[2]

Prepaid Expenses					
Beginning balance	+ Payments	−	Expiration of prepaid expense	=	Ending balance
$7,000	+ X		$7,000	=	$8,000
	X			=	$8,000 − $7,000 + $7,000
	X			=	$8,000

---

[2]A simplifying assumption has been made in this example that the entire opening prepaid expenses will expire during the year and that all opening accrued liabilities will be paid during the year.

Accrued Liabilities

Beginning balance	+	Accrual of expense at year-end	−	Payments	=	Ending balance
$3,000	+	$1,000		−X	=	$1,000
				−X	=	$1,000 − $3,000 − $1,000
				−X	=	$3,000

Other Operating Expenses

Accrual of expense at year-end	+	Expiration of prepaid expense	+	Payments	=	Ending balance
$1,000	+	$7,000	+	X	=	$17,000
				X	=	$17,000 − $1,000 − $7,000
				X	=	$9,000
		Total payments for operating expenses			=	$8,000 + $3,000 + $9,000
					=	$20,000

The T-accounts give another picture of the same data:

Prepaid Expenses			
Beg. bal.	7,000	Expiration of prepaid expense	7,000
Payments	8,000		
End. bal.	8,000		

Accrued Liabilities			
Payment	3,000	Beg. bal.	3,000
		Accrual of expense at year-end	1,000
		End. bal.	1,000

Operating Expenses		
Accrual of expense at year-end	1,000	
Expiration of prepaid expense	7,000	
Payments	9,000	
End. bal.	17,000	

COMPUTING PAYMENTS TO EMPLOYEES. It is convenient to combine all payments to employees into one account, Salary and Wages Expense. We then adjust the expense for the change in Salary and Wages Payable, as shown here:

Salary and Wages Payable

Beginning balance	+	Salary and wages expense	−	Payments	=	Ending balance
$6,000	+	$56,000		−X	=	$4,000
				−X	=	$4,000 − $6,000 − $56,000
				−X	=	$58,000

The T-account gives another picture of the same data:

Salary and Wages Payable			
Payments to employees	58,000	Beginning balance	6,000
		Salary and wages expense	56,000
		Ending balance	4,000

COMPUTING PAYMENTS OF INTEREST AND INCOME TAXES. Bradshaw Corporation's expense and payment amounts are the same for interest and income tax, so no analysis is required. If the expense and the payment differ, the payment can be computed as shown in Exhibit 12A-4.

Cash Flows From Investing and Financing Activities

Investing and financing cash flows are explained on pages 558–559. These computations are the same for both the direct and indirect methods.

**STOP
+
THINK
(12A-2)**

Fidelity Company reported the following for 2014 and 2013 (in millions):

As at December 31,	2014	2013
Receivables, net	$ 3,500	$3,900
Inventory	5,200	5,000
Accounts payable	900	1,200
Income taxes payable	600	700

Year Ended December 31,	2014
Revenues	$23,000
Cost of goods sold	14,100
Income tax expense	900

Based on these figures, how much cash did

- Fidelity collect from customers during 2014?
- Fidelity pay for inventory during 2014?
- Fidelity pay for income taxes during 2014?

SUMMARY OF APPENDIX 12A

LEARNING OBJECTIVE	SUMMARY
A-1. **Prepare** a statement of cash flows using the direct method of determining cash flows from operating activities	To determine cash flows from operating activities using the direct method, sum cash receipts from operating activities and deduct cash payments for operating activities.

Cash receipts from operating activities include:

- Collections from customers
- Interest received from loans and advances to others and from investments
- Dividends received

Cash payments for operating activities include:

- Payments to suppliers
- Payments to employees
- Payments of interest
- Payment of income taxes

The net cash flows from operating activities determined using the direct method will always equal the net cash flows from operating activities determined using the indirect method.

Cash flows from investing and financing activities are not affected by the method used to determine cash flows from operating activities.

Kapoor Products Inc. reported the following comparative balance sheet and income statement for 2014:

Kapoor Products Inc.
Balance Sheet
As at December 31, 2014 and 2013

	2014	2013
Cash	$ 19,000	$ 3,000
Accounts receivable	22,000	23,000
Inventories	34,000	31,000
Prepaid expenses	1,000	3,000
Equipment (net)	90,000	79,000
Intangible assets	9,000	9,000
	$175,000	$148,000
Accounts payable	$ 14,000	$ 9,000
Accrued liabilities	16,000	19,000
Income tax payable	14,000	12,000
Long-term debt	45,000	50,000
Share capital	22,000	18,000
Retained earnings	64,000	40,000
	$175,000	$148,000

Kapoor Products Inc.
Income Statement
For the Years Ended December 31, 2014 and 2013

	2014	2013
Sales revenue	$190,000	$165,000
Gain on sale of equipment	6,000	—
Total revenue and gains	196,000	165,000
Cost of goods sold	85,000	70,000
Depreciation expense	19,000	17,000
Other operating expenses	36,000	33,000
Total expenses	140,000	120,000
Income before income tax	56,000	45,000
Income tax expense	18,000	15,000
Net income	$ 38,000	$ 30,000

Assume that you are an investment analyst for Canmore Investments Ltd. and have been tasked with analyzing Kapoor Products Inc. as Canmore is considering purchasing it. You determine that you need the following Kapoor cash-flow data for 2014. There were no non-cash investing and financing activities.

a. Collections from customers
b. Cash payments for inventory
c. Cash payments for operating expenses
d. Cash payment for income tax

e. Cash received from the sale of equipment, with Kapoor Products Inc. paying $40,000 for new equipment during the year

f. Issuance of common shares

g. Issuance of long-term debt, with Kapoor Products Inc. paying off $20,000 of long-term debt during the year

h. Cash dividends, with no stock dividends

Provide your colleagues with the needed data. Show your work.

Name: Kapoor Products Inc.
Fiscal Period: Year ended December 31, 2014

ANSWER

a. Analyze Accounts Receivable (let X = Collections from customers):

Beginning	+	Sales	−	Collections	=	Ending
$23,000	+	$190,000	−	X	=	$22,000
				X	=	$191,000

The change in Accounts Receivable of $1,000 ($22,000 − $23,000) is a result of sales and collections from customers.

b. Analyze Inventory and Accounts Payable (let X = Purchases, and let Y = Payments for inventory):

Beginning Inventory	+	Purchases	−	Ending Inventory	=	Cost of Goods Sold
$31,000	+	X	−	$34,000	=	$85,000
		X			=	$88,000

Beginning Accounts Payable	+	Purchases	−	Payments	=	Ending Accounts Payable
$9,000	+	$88,000	−	Y	=	$14,000
				Y	=	$83,000

First calculate the amount of purchases. Then calculate the change in Accounts Payable that relates to cash payments.

c. Start with Other Operating Expenses, and adjust for the changes in Prepaid Expenses and Accrued Liabilities:

Other Operating Expenses		+ Increase, or − Decrease in Prepaid Expenses		− Increase, or + Decrease in Accrued Liabilities	=	Payments for Operating Expenses
$36,000	−	$2,000	+	3,000	=	$37,000

Cash payments for operating expenses must account for the changes that relate to prepaid expenses and accrued liabilities.

d. Analyze Income Tax Payable (let X = Payments of income tax):

Beginning	+	Income Tax Expense	−	Payments	=	Ending
$12,000	+	$18,000	−	X	=	$14,000
				X	=	$16,000

The change in Income Tax Payable of $2,000 ($14,000 − $12,000) is a result of income tax expense and income tax payments made.

e. Analyze Equipment (Net) (Let X = Carrying amount of equipment sold. Then combine with gain or loss on sale to compute cash received from sale.)

Beginning	+	Acquisitions	−	Depreciation	−	Carrying Amount Sold	=	Ending
$79,000	+	$40,000	−	$19,000	−	X	=	$90,000
						X	=	$10,000

Cash received from sale	=	Carrying Amount Sold	+	Gain, or − Loss on Sale
$16,000	=	$10,000	+	$6,000

Cash received from the sale of equipment is the carrying amount of the equipment plus the gain or minus the loss on the sale. First determine the carrying amount of the equipment sold.

The change in Common Shares of $4,000 ($22,000 − $18,000) is a result of issuing shares.

f. Analyze Common Shares (let X = issuance):

Beginning	+	Issuance	=	Ending
$18,000	+	X	=	$22,000
		X	=	$ 4,000

Long-Term Debt declined by $5,000 ($45,000 − $50,000). However, because a $20,000 payment was made during the year, $15,000 of long-term debt must have been issued.

g. Analyze Long-Term Debt (let X = issuance):

Beginning	+	Issuance	−	Payment	=	Ending
$50,000	+	X	−	$20,000	=	$45,000
		X			=	$15,000

The change in Retained Earnings of $24,000 ($64,000 − $40,000) is a result of net income ($38,000 from the 2014 income statement) and the payment of cash dividends. The same information is shown on the statement of retained earnings.

h. Analyze Retained Earnings (let X = dividends):

Beginning	+	Net Income	−	Dividends	=	Ending
$40,000	+	$38,000	−	X	=	$64,000
				X	=	$14,000

STOP + THINK (12A-1)

ANSWERS

a. Not reported	e. Investing	i. Financing	m. Operating
b. Financing	f. Operating	j. Investing	n. Not reported
c. Financing	g. Not reported	k. Financing	o. Not reported
d. Operating	h. Investing	l. Operating	

STOP + THINK (12A-2)

ANSWERS

		Beginning receivables	+	Revenues	−	Collections	=	Ending receivables
Collections from customers	= $23,400:	$3,900	+	$23,000	−	$23,400	=	$3,500

		Cost of goods sold	+	Increase in inventory	+	Decrease in accounts payable	=	Payments
Payments for inventory	= $14,600:	$14,100	+	($5,200 − $5,000)	+	($1,200 − $900)	=	$14,600

		Beginning income taxes payable	+	Income tax expense	−	Payment	=	Ending income taxes payable
Payment of income taxes	= $1,000:	$700	+	$900	−	$1,000	=	$600

Assess Your Progress

Recall that for the sake of simplicity and consistency, this text classifies all interest paid and interest and dividends received as operating activities, and classifies dividends paid as a financing activity. All questions and problems in this chapter should be answered using this convention.

SHORT EXERCISES

LEARNING OBJECTIVE A-1

Prepare a statement of cash flows—direct method

S12A-1 Tally-Ho Horse Farm Inc. began 2014 with cash of $44,000. During the year, Tally-Ho earned service revenue of $500,000 and collected $510,000 from customers. Expenses for the year totalled $420,000, with $400,000 paid in cash to suppliers and employees. Tally-Ho also paid $100,000 to purchase equipment and a cash dividend of $50,000 to shareholders. During 2014, Tally-Ho borrowed $20,000 by issuing a note payable.

Prepare the company's statement of cash flows for the year. Format operating activities by the direct method.

LEARNING OBJECTIVE A-1

Compute operating cash flows—direct method

S12A-2 (Exercise S12A-3 is an alternative exercise.) Maritime Fisheries Ltd. provides the following data for the year ended June 30, 2014:

Cost of goods sold	$100,000	Payment of dividends	$ 6,000
Payments to suppliers	87,000	Proceeds from issuance of	
Purchase of equipment	40,000	common shares	20,000
Payments to employees	70,000	Sales revenue	210,000
Payment of note payable	30,000	Collections from customers	180,000
Proceeds from sale of land	60,000	Payment of income tax	10,000
Depreciation expense	8,000	Repurchase of common shares	5,000

Prepare the *operating activities section* of Maritime Fisheries Ltd.'s statement of cash flows for the year ended June 30, 2014. Maritime Fisheries uses the *direct* method for operating cash flows.

LEARNING OBJECTIVE A-1

Prepare a statement of cash flows—direct method

S12A-3 Use the data in exercise S12-A2 to prepare Maritime Fisheries Ltd.'s statement of cash flows for the year ended June 30, 2014. Maritime Fisheries uses the *direct* method for operating activities. Use Exhibit 12A-3, page 601, as a guide, but you may stop after determining the net increase (or decrease) in cash.

LEARNING OBJECTIVE A-1

Compute operating cash flows—direct method

S12A-4 Autos of Red Deer Inc. reported the following financial statements for 2014:

Autos of Red Deer Inc.
Income Statement
For the Year Ended December 31, 2014

(in thousands)	
Sales revenue	$710
Cost of goods sold	340
Salary expense	70
Depreciation expense	20
Other expenses	130
Total expenses	560
Net income	$150

Autos of Red Deer Inc.
Comparative Balance Sheet
As at December 31, 2014 and 2013

(in thousands)

Assets	2014	2013	Liabilities	2014	2013
Current:			Current:		
Cash	$ 19	$ 16	Accounts payable	$ 47	$ 42
Accounts receivable	59	48	Salary payable	23	21
Inventory	75	84	Accrued liabilities	8	11
Prepaid expenses	3	2	Long-term notes payable	68	58
Long-term investments	55	75	**Shareholders' Equity**		
Property, plant, and			Share capital	40	32
equipment	225	185	Retained earnings	250	246
Totals	$436	$410	Totals	$436	$410

Compute the following:

a. Collections from customers

b. Payments for inventory

LEARNING OBJECTIVE

Compute operating cash flows—
direct method

S12A-5 Use the Autos of Red Deer data in exercise S12A-4 to compute the following:

a. Payments to employees

b. Payments of other expenses

EXERCISES

LEARNING OBJECTIVE ❷

Identify activities for the statement
of cash flows—direct method

E12A-6 Identify each of the following transactions as operating (O), investing (I), financing (F), non-cash investing and financing (NIF), or not reported on the statement of cash flows (N). Indicate whether each transaction increases (+) or decreases (−) cash. The *direct* method is used for operating activities.

___ a. Repurchase of common shares	___ k. Acquisition of equipment by issuance of note payable
___ b. Issuance of common shares for cash	
___ c. Payment of accounts payable	___ l. Payment of long-term debt
___ d. Issuance of preferred shares for cash	___ m. Acquisition of building by payment of cash
___ e. Payment of cash dividend	
___ f. Sale of long-term investment	___ n. Accrual of salary expense
___ g. Amortization of patent	___ o. Purchase of long-term investment
___ h. Collection of accounts receivable	___ p. Payment of wages to employees
___ i. Issuance of long-term note payable to borrow cash	___ q. Collection of cash interest
	___ r. Cash sale of land
___ j. Depreciation of equipment	___ s. Distribution of stock dividend

LEARNING OBJECTIVE ❷ A-1

Classify transactions for the
statement of cash flows—direct
method

E12A-7 Indicate where, if at all, each of the following transactions would be reported on a statement of cash flows prepared by the *direct* method and the accompanying schedule of non-cash investing and financing activities.

a.	Equipment.............................	18,000		h.	Retained Earnings	36,000
	Cash		18,000		Common Shares		36,000
b.	Cash......................................	7,200		i.	Cash...	2,000
	Long-Term Investment...........		7,200		Interest Revenue		2,000
c.	Bonds Payable...........................	45,000		j.	Land...	87,700
	Cash		45,000		Cash		87,700
d.	Building	164,000		k.	Accounts Payable	8,300
	Cash		164,000		Cash		8,300
e.	Cash...	1,400		l.	Salary Expense	4,300
	Accounts Receivable		1,400		Cash		4,300
f.	Dividends Payable......................	16,500		m.	Cash...	81,000
	Cash		16,500		Common Shares		81,000
g.	Furniture and Fixtures...............	22,100		n.	Common Shares........................	13,000
	Note Payable, Short-Term		22,100		Cash		13,000

E12A-8 The accounting records of Jasmine Pharmaceuticals Inc. reveal the following:

LEARNING OBJECTIVE

Compute cash flows from operating activities—direct method

Payment of salaries and wages............	$34,000	Net income...	$34,000
Depreciation.......................................	22,000	Payment of income tax	13,000
Decrease in current liabilities..............	20,000	Collection of dividend revenue..........	7,000
Increase in current assets		Payment of interest............................	16,000
other than cash.............................	27,000	Cash sales...	38,000
Payment of dividends.........................	12,000	Loss on sale of land	5,000
Collection of		Acquisition of land	37,000
accounts receivable.........................	93,000	Payment of accounts payable............	54,000

Requirement

Compute cash flows from operating activities by the *direct* method. Use the format of the operating activities section of Exhibit 12A-3. Also, evaluate Jasmine's operating cash flow. Give the reason for your evaluation.

E12A-9 Selected accounts of Fishbowl Antiques Inc. show the following:

LEARNING OBJECTIVE

Identify items for the statement of cash flows—direct method

Salary Payable

		Beginning balance	9,000
Payments	40,000	Salary expense	38,000
		Ending balance	7,000

Buildings

Beginning balance	90,000	Depreciation	18,000
Acquisitions	145,000	Carrying amount of	
		building sold	109,000*
Ending balance	108,000		

   *Sale price was 140,000

Notes Payable

		Beginning balance	273,000
Payments	69,000	Issuance of note payable	
		for cash	83,000
		Ending balance	287,000

Requirement

For each account, identify the item or items that should appear on a statement of cash flows prepared by the *direct* method. State where to report the item.

LEARNING OBJECTIVE

Prepare the statement of cash
flows—direct method

E12A-10 The income statement and additional data of Floral World Ltd. follow:

Floral World Ltd. Income Statement For the Year Ended June 30, 2014		
Revenues:		
Sales revenue	$229,000	
Dividend revenue	15,000	$244,000
Expenses:		
Cost of goods sold	103,000	
Salary expense	45,000	
Depreciation expense	29,000	
Advertising expense	11,000	
Interest expense	2,000	
Income tax expense	9,000	199,000
Net income		$ 45,000

Additional data:
a. Collections from customers are $30,000 more than sales.
b. Payments to suppliers are $1,000 more than the sum of cost of goods sold plus advertising expense.
c. Payments to employees are $1,000 more than salary expense.
d. Dividend revenue, interest expense, and income tax expense equal their cash amounts.
e. Acquisition of plant and equipment is $150,000. Of this amount, $101,000 is paid in cash and $49,000 by signing a note payable.
f. Proceeds from sale of land total $24,000.
g. Proceeds from issuance of common shares total $30,000.
h. Payment of long-term note payable is $15,000.
i. Payment of dividends is $11,000.
j. Cash balance, June 30, 2013, was $20,000.

Requirements
1. Prepare Floral World Ltd.'s statement of cash flows and accompanying schedule of non-cash investing and financing activities. Report operating activities by the *direct* method.
2. Evaluate Floral World's cash flows for the year. In your evaluation, mention all three categories of cash flows and give the reason for your evaluation.

LEARNING OBJECTIVE

Compute amounts for the statement
of cash flows—direct method

E12A-11 Compute the following items for the statement of cash flows:
a. Beginning and ending Accounts Receivable are $22,000 and $32,000, respectively. Credit sales for the period total $60,000. How much are cash collections from customers?
b. Cost of goods sold is $111,000. Beginning Inventory was $25,000, and ending Inventory is $21,000. Beginning and ending Accounts Payable are $14,000 and $8,000, respectively. How much are cash payments for inventory?

CHALLENGE EXERCISE

LEARNING OBJECTIVE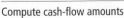

Compute cash-flow amounts

E12A-12 Morgan Industries Inc. reported the following in its financial statements for the year ended August 31, 2014 (in thousands):

	2014	2013
Income Statement		
Net sales	$24,623	$21,207
Cost of sales	18,048	15,466
Depreciation	269	230
Other operating expenses	3,883	4,248
Income tax expense	537	486
Net income	$ 1,886	$ 777
Balance Sheet		
Cash and cash equivalents	$ 17	$ 13
Accounts receivable	601	615
Inventory	3,100	2,831
Property and equipment, net	4,345	3,428
Accounts payable	1,547	1,364
Accrued liabilities	938	631
Income tax payable	201	194
Long-term liabilities	478	464
Common shares	519	446
Retained earnings	4,380	3,788

Determine the following cash receipts and payments for Morgan Industries Inc. during 2014:

a. Collections from customers
b. Payments for inventory
c. Payments for other operating expenses
d. Payment of income tax
e. Proceeds from issuance of common shares
f. Payment of cash dividends

PROBLEMS

(Group A)

P12A-13A World Mosaic Furniture Gallery Inc. provided the following data from the company's records for the year ended April 30, 2014:

a. Credit sales, $583,900
b. Loan to another company, $12,500
c. Cash payments to purchase property, plant, and equipment, $59,400
d. Cost of goods sold, $382,600
e. Proceeds from issuance of common shares, $8,000
f. Payment of cash dividends, $48,400
g. Collection of interest, $4,400
h. Acquisition of equipment by issuing short-term note payable, $16,400
i. Payments of salaries, $93,600
j. Proceeds from sale of property, plant, and equipment, $22,400, including $6,800 loss
k. Collections on accounts receivable, $428,600
l. Interest revenue, $3,800
m. Cash receipt of dividend revenue, $4,100

n. Payments to suppliers, $368,500
o. Cash sales, $171,900
p. Depreciation expense, $59,900
q. Proceeds from issuance of note payable, $19,600
r. Payments of long-term notes payable, $50,000
s. Interest expense and payments, $13,300
t. Salary expense, $95,300
u. Loan collections, $12,800
v. Proceeds from sale of investments, $9,100, including $2,000 gain
w. Payment of short-term note payable by issuing long-term note payable, $63,000
x. Depreciation expense, $2,900
y. Income tax expense and payments, $37,900
z. Cash balance: April 30, 2013, $39,300; April 30, 2014, $36,600

LEARNING OBJECTIVE

Prepare the statement of cash flows—direct method

Requirements

1. Prepare World Mosaic Furniture Gallery Inc.'s statement of cash flows for the year ended April 30, 2014. Use the *direct* method for cash flows from operating activities. Follow the format of Exhibit 12A-3 (p. 601), but do *not* show amounts in thousands. Include an accompanying schedule of non-cash investing and financing activities.

2. Evaluate 2014 from a cash-flow standpoint. Give your reasons.

LEARNING OBJECTIVE ❷ Ⓐ-1

Prepare an income statement, balance sheet, and statement of cash flows—direct method

P12A-14A Vintage Automobiles of Orangeville Ltd. was formed on January 1, 2014, when Vintage issued common shares for $300,000. Early in January 2014, Vintage made the following cash payments:

a. $150,000 for equipment
b. $120,000 for inventory (four cars at $30,000 each)
c. $20,000 for 2014 rent on a store building

In February 2014, Vintage purchased six cars for inventory on account. Cost of this inventory was $260,000 ($43,333.33 each). Before year-end, Vintage paid $208,000 of this debt. Vintage uses the FIFO method to account for inventory.

During 2014, Vintage sold eight vintage autos for a total of $500,000. Before year-end, Vintage collected 80% of this amount.

The business employs three people. The combined annual payroll is $95,000, of which Vintage owes $4,000 at year-end. At the end of the year, Vintage paid income tax of $10,000.

Late in 2014, Vintage declared and paid cash dividends of $11,000.

For equipment, Vintage uses the straight-line depreciation method over five years with zero residual value.

Requirements

1. Prepare Vintage's income statement for the year ended December 31, 2014. Use the single-step format, with all revenues listed together and all expenses listed together.
2. Prepare Vintage's balance sheet at December 31, 2014.
3. Prepare Vintage's statement of cash flows for the year ended December 31, 2014. Format cash flows from operating activities by using the *direct* method.

LEARNING OBJECTIVE ❷ Ⓐ-1

Prepare the statement of cash flows—direct method

P12A-15A The 2014 comparative balance sheet and income statement of 4 Seasons Supply Corp. follow. 4 Seasons had no non-cash investing and financing transactions during 2014. During the year, there were no sales of land or equipment, no issuance of notes payable, and no repurchase of shares transactions.

4 Seasons Supply Corp. Comparative Balance Sheet as at December 31, 2014 and 2013			
	December 31,		**Increase**
	2014	**2013**	**(Decrease)**
Current assets:			
Cash and cash equivalents	$ 17,600	$ 5,300	$12,300
Accounts receivable	27,200	27,600	(400)
Inventories	83,600	87,200	(3,600)
Prepaid expenses	2,500	1,900	600
Property, plant, and equipment:			
Land	89,000	60,000	29,000
Equipment, net	53,500	49,400	4,100
Total assets	$273,400	$231,400	$42,000
Current liabilities:			
Accounts payable	$ 35,800	$ 33,700	$ 2,100
Salary payable	3,100	6,600	(3,500)
Other accrued liabilities	22,600	23,700	(1,100)
Long-term liabilities:			
Notes payable	75,000	100,000	(25,000)
Shareholders' equity:			
Common shares	88,300	64,700	23,600
Retained earnings	48,600	2,700	45,900
Total liabilities and shareholders' equity	$273,400	$231,400	$42,000

4 Seasons Supply Corp.
Income Statement for the Year Ended December 31, 2014

Revenues:		
Sales revenue..		$228,700
Expenses:		
Cost of goods sold..	$70,600	
Salary expense..	27,800	
Depreciation expense..	4,000	
Other operating expense...	10,500	
Interest expense..	11,600	
Income tax expense	29,100	
Total expenses		153,600
Net income..		$ 75,100

Requirements

1. Prepare the 2014 statement of cash flows using the *direct* method.
2. How will what you learned in this problem help you evaluate an investment?

P12A-16A To prepare the statement of cash flows, accountants for Franklin Electric Limited have summarized 2014 activity in two accounts as follows:

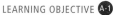

LEARNING OBJECTIVE A-1

Prepare the statement of cash flows—direct method

Cash

Beginning balance	53,600	Payments on accounts payable	399,100
Sale of long-term investment	21,200	Payments of dividends	27,200
Collections from customers	661,700	Payments of salaries and wages	143,800
Issuance of common shares	47,300	Payments of interest	26,900
Receipts of dividends	17,100	Purchase of equipment	31,400
		Payments of operating expenses	34,300
		Payment of long-term note payable	41,300
		Repurchase of common shares	26,400
		Payment of income tax	18,900
Ending balance	51,600		

Common Shares

Repurchase of common shares	26,400	Beginning balance	110,800
for cancellation		Issuance for cash	47,300
		Issuance to acquire land	80,100
		Issuance to retire note payable	19,000
		Ending balance	230,800

Requirement

Prepare the statement of cash flows of Franklin Electric Limited for the year ended December 31, 2014, using the *direct* method to report operating activities. Also prepare the accompanying schedule of non-cash investing and financing activities.

Franklin Electric Limited
Income Statement
For the Year Ended December 31, 2014

Revenues:		
Sales revenue..		$689,300
Dividend revenue		17,100
Total revenue		706,400
Expenses and losses:		
Cost of goods sold..	$402,600	
Salary and wage expense	150,800	
Depreciation expense..	19,300	
Other operating expense...	44,100	
Interest expense..	28,800	
Income tax expense	16,200	
Loss on sale of investments.......................................	1,100	
Total expenses and losses.....................................		662,900
Net income..		$ 43,500

Franklin Electric Limited
Selected Balance Sheet Data

	2014 Increase (Decrease)
Current assets:	
Cash and cash equivalents	$ (2,000)
Accounts receivable	27,600
Inventories	(11,800)
Prepaid expenses	600
Long-term investments	(22,300)
Equipment, net	12,100
Land	80,100
Current liabilities:	
Accounts payable	(8,300)
Interest payable	1,900
Salary payable	7,000
Other accrued liabilities	10,400
Income tax payable	(2,700)
Long-term note payable	(60,300)
Share capital	120,000
Retained earnings	16,300

LEARNING OBJECTIVE

Prepare the statement of cash flows—direct method

P12A-17A The comparative balance sheet of Graphic Design Studio Inc. at June 30, 2014, included these amounts:

Graphic Design Studio Inc.
Balance Sheet
As at June 30, 2014 and 2013

	2014	2013	Increase (Decrease)
Current assets:			
Cash	$ 28,600	$ 8,600	$ 20,000
Accounts receivable	48,800	51,900	(3,100)
Inventories	68,600	60,200	8,400
Prepaid expenses	3,700	2,800	900
Long-term investment	10,100	5,200	4,900
Equipment, net	74,500	73,600	900
Land	42,400	96,000	(53,600)
	$276,700	$298,300	$(21,600)
Current liabilities:			
Notes payable, short-term	$ 13,400	$ 18,100	$ (4,700)
Accounts payable	42,400	40,300	2,100
Income tax payable	13,800	14,500	(700)
Accrued liabilities	8,200	9,700	(1,500)
Interest payable	3,700	2,900	800
Salary payable	900	2,600	(1,700)
Long-term note payable	47,400	94,100	(46,700)
Share capital	59,800	51,200	8,600
Retained earnings	87,100	64,900	22,200
	$276,700	$298,300	$(21,600)

Transaction data for the year ended June 30, 2014 were:
a. Net income, $60,300
b. Depreciation expense on equipment, $13,400
c. Purchased long-term investment, $4,900
d. Sold land for $46,900, including $6,700 loss
e. Acquired equipment by issuing long-term note payable, $14,300
f. Paid long-term note payable, $61,000
g. Received cash for issuance of common shares, $3,900
h. Paid cash dividends, $38,100
i. Paid short-term note payable by issuing common shares, $4,700

Requirement

Prepare the statement of cash flows of Graphic Design Studio Inc. for the year ended June 30, 2014, using the *direct* method to report operating activities. Also, prepare the accompanying schedule of non-cash investing and financing activities. All current accounts except short-term notes payable result from operating transactions. The accounting records provide the following: collections from customers, $261,800; interest received, $1,300; payments to suppliers, $133,500; payments to employees, $40,500; payments for income tax, $10,600; payment of interest, $5,300.

(Group B)

P12A-18B Rocco's Gourmet Foods Inc. provides the following data from the company's records for the year ended July 31, 2014:

LEARNING OBJECTIVE A-1
Prepare the statement of cash flows—direct method

a. Salary expense, $105,300
b. Cash payments to purchase property, plant, and equipment, $181,000
c. Proceeds from issuance of note payable, $44,100
d. Payments of long-term note payable, $18,800
e. Proceeds from sale of property, plant, and equipment, $59,700, including $10,600 gain
f. Interest revenue, $12,100
g. Cash receipt of dividend revenue on investments, $2,700
h. Payments to suppliers, $673,300
i. Interest expense and payments, $37,800
j. Cost of goods sold, $481,100
k. Collection of interest revenue, $11,700
l. Acquisition of equipment by issuing short-term note payable, $35,500

m. Payments of salaries, $104,000
n. Credit sales, $768,100
o. Loan to another company, $35,000
p. Income tax expense and payments, $56,400
q. Advertising expense, $27,700
r. Collections on accounts receivable, $741,100
s. Loan collections, $74,400
t. Proceeds from sale of investments, $34,700, including $3,800 loss
u. Payment of long-term note payable by issuing preferred shares, $107,300
v. Depreciation expense, $23,900
w. Cash sales, $146,000
x. Proceeds from issuance of common shares, $50,000
y. Payment of cash dividends, $50,500
z. Cash balance: July 31, 2013—$23,800; July 31, 2014—$31,400

Requirements

1. Prepare Rocco's Gourmet Foods Inc.'s statement of cash flows for the year ended July 31, 2014. Use the *direct* method for cash flows from operating activities. Follow the format of Exhibit 12A-3, but do *not* show amounts in thousands. Include an accompanying schedule of non-cash investing and financing activities.
2. Evaluate 2014 in terms of cash flow. Give reasons for your evaluation.

P12A-19B Cruise Canada Motorhomes Inc. (CCM) was formed on January 1, 2014, when the company issued its common shares for $200,000. Early in January, CCM made the following cash payments:
a. For showroom fixtures, $50,000
b. For inventory, two motorhomes at $60,000 each, a total of $120,000
c. For rent on a store building, $12,000

LEARNING OBJECTIVE A-1
Prepare an income statement, balance sheet, and statement of cash flows—direct method

In February, CCM purchased three motorhomes on account. Cost of this inventory was $160,000 ($53,333.33 each). Before year-end, CCM paid $140,000 of this debt. CCM uses the FIFO method to account for inventory.

During 2014, CCM sold four motorhomes for a total of $560,000. Before year-end, CCM collected 90% of this amount.

The store employs three people. The combined annual payroll is $90,000, of which CCM owes $3,000 at year-end. At the end of the year, CCM paid income tax of $64,000.

Late in 2014, CCM declared and paid cash dividends of $40,000.

For showroom fixtures, CCM uses the straight-line depreciation method over five years with zero residual value.

Requirements

1. Prepare CCM's income statement for the year ended December 31, 2014. Use the single-step format, with all the revenues listed together and all expenses listed together.
2. Prepare CCM's balance sheet at December 31, 2014.
3. Prepare CCM's statement of cash flows for the year ended December 31, 2014. Format cash flows from operating activities by using the *direct* method.

LEARNING OBJECTIVE

Prepare the statement of cash flows—direct method

P12A-20B The 2014 comparative balance sheet and income statement of Riverbend Pools Inc. follow. Riverbend had no non-cash investing and financing transactions during 2014. During the year, there were no sales of land or equipment, no issuances of notes payable, and no share repurchase transactions.

Riverbend Pools Inc.
Comparative Balance Sheet
As at December 31, 2014 and 2013

	2014	2013	Increase (Decrease)
Current assets:			
Cash and cash equivalents..............................	$ 28,700	$ 15,600	$13,100
Accounts receivable.......................................	47,100	44,000	3,100
Inventories	94,300	89,900	4,400
Prepaid expenses...	1,700	2,200	(500)
Property, plant, and equipment:			
Land..	35,100	10,000	25,100
Equipment, net..	100,900	93,700	7,200
Total assets	$307,800	$255,400	$52,400
Current liabilities:			
Accounts payable...	$ 22,700	$ 24,600	$ (1,900)
Salary payable..	2,100	1,400	700
Other accrued liabilities................................	24,400	22,500	1,900
Long-term liabilities:			
Notes payable	55,000	65,000	(10,000)
Shareholders' equity:			
Common shares..	131,100	122,300	8,800
Retained earnings	72,500	19,600	52,900
Total liabilities and shareholders' equity	$307,800	$255,400	$52,400

Riverbend Pools Inc.
Income Statement
For the year ended December 31, 2014

Revenues:		
Sales revenue		$438,000
Interest revenue		11,700
Total revenues		449,700
Expenses:		
Cost of goods sold	$185,200	
Salary expense	76,400	
Depreciation expense	15,300	
Other operating expense	49,700	
Interest expense	24,600	
Income tax expense	16,900	
Total expense		368,100
Net income		$ 81,600

Requirements

1. Prepare the 2014 statement of cash flows by using the *direct* method.
2. How will what you learned in this problem help you evaluate an investment?

P12A-21B To prepare the statement of cash flows, accountants for Powers Art Gallery Inc. have summarized 2014 activity in two accounts as follows:

Cash

Beginning balance	87,100	Payments of operating expenses	46,100
Issuance of common shares	60,800	Payment of long-term note payable	78,900
Receipts of dividends	1,900	Repurchase of common shares	10,400
Collection of loan	18,500	Payment of income tax	8,000
Sale of long-term investments	9,900	Payments on accounts payable	101,600
Receipts of interest	12,200	Payments of dividends	1,800
Collections from customers	308,100	Payments of salaries and wages	67,500
		Payments of interest	21,800
		Purchase of equipment	79,900
Ending balance	82,500		

Common Shares

	Beginning balance	103,500
	Issuance for cash	60,800
	Issuance to acquire land	62,100
	Issuance to retire long-term note payable	21,100
	Ending balance	247,500

Requirement

Prepare Powers' statement of cash flows for the year ended December 31, 2014, using the *direct* method to report operating activities. Also, prepare the accompanying schedule of non-cash investing and financing activities. Powers' 2014 income statement and selected balance sheet data follow.

Powers Art Gallery Inc.
Income Statement
For the Year Ended December 31, 2014

Revenues and gains:		
Sales revenue		$291,800
Interest revenue		12,200
Dividend revenue		1,900
Gain on sale of investments		700
Total revenues and gains		306,600
Expenses:		
Cost of goods sold	$103,600	
Salary and wage expense	66,800	
Depreciation expense	20,900	
Other operating expense	44,700	
Interest expense	24,100	
Income tax expense	2,600	
Total expenses		262,700
Net income		$ 43,900

Powers Art Gallery Inc.
Selected Balance Sheet Data

	2014 Increase (Decrease)
Current assets:	
Cash and cash equivalents	$ (4,600)
Accounts receivable	(16,300)
Inventories	5,700
Prepaid expenses	(1,900)
Loan receivable	(18,500)
Long-term investments	(9,200)
Equipment, net	59,000
Land	62,100
Current liabilities:	
Accounts payable	$ 7,700
Interest payable	2,300
Salary payable	(700)
Other accrued liabilities	(3,300)
Income tax payable	(5,400)
Long-term note payable	(100,000)
Share capital	133,600
Retained earnings	42,100

P12A-22B Arts de France Ltée's comparative balance sheet at September 30, 2014, included the following balances:

LEARNING OBJECTIVE A-1

Prepare the statement of cash flows—direct method

Arts de France Ltée
Balance Sheet
As at September 30, 2014 and 2013

	2014	2013	Increase (Decrease)
Current assets:			
Cash	$ 21,700	$ 17,600	$ 4,100
Accounts receivable	46,000	46,800	(800)
Inventories	121,700	116,900	4,800
Prepaid expenses	8,600	9,300	(700)
Long-term investments	51,100	13,800	37,300
Equipment, net	131,900	92,100	39,800
Land	47,100	74,300	(27,200)
	$428,100	$370,800	$ 57,300
Current liabilities:			
Notes payable, short-term	$ 22,000	$ 0	$ 22,000
Accounts payable	88,100	98,100	(10,000)
Accrued liabilities	17,900	29,100	(11,200)
Salary payable	1,500	1,100	400
Long-term note payable	123,000	121,400	1,600
Common shares	113,900	62,000	51,900
Retained earnings	61,700	59,100	2,600
	$428,100	$370,800	$ 57,300

Transaction data for the year ended September 30, 2014 were:
a. Net income, $66,900
b. Depreciation expense on equipment, $8,500
c. Purchased long-term investments, $37,300
d. Sold land for $38,100, including $10,900 gain
e. Acquired equipment by issuing long-term note payable, $26,300
f. Paid long-term note payable, $24,700
g. Received cash of $51,900 for issuance of common shares
h. Paid cash dividends, $64,300
i. Acquired equipment by issuing short-term note payable, $22,000

Requirement

Prepare Arts de France's statement of cash flows for the year ended September 30, 2014, using the *direct* method to report operating activities. Also, prepare the accompanying schedule of non-cash investing and financing activities. All current accounts except short-term notes payable result from operating transactions. Prepare a supplementary schedule showing cash flows from operations by using the *direct* method. The accounting records provide the following: collections from customers, $343,100; interest received, $8,600; payments to suppliers, $216,400; payments to employees, $63,000; payment of income tax, $21,200; payment of interest, $10,700.

Financial Statement Analysis

The Canadian Press Images/J.P. Moczulski

LEARNING OBJECTIVES

1. **Perform** a horizontal analysis of financial statements
2. **Perform** a vertical analysis of financial statements
3. **Prepare** common-size financial statements
4. **Use** the statement of cash flows in decision making
5. **Use** ratios to make business decisions

SPOTLIGHT

This book began with the financial statements of TELUS, a company that provides a full range of communication products and services. Throughout this book we have shown you how to account for the operations, financial position, and cash flows of a variety of companies, such as Le Château, CGI, Canadian Tire, Leon's, and ONEX. Only one aspect of the course remains: the overall analysis of financial statements.

In this chapter, we analyze the financial statements of Empire Company Limited, which owns Sobeys, one of Canada's leading grocery chains. Empire's revenues and net earnings look good, but how good *are* they? The analytical tools you learn in this chapter will help you answer this question.

Empire Company Limited
Consolidated Statements of Earnings (Adapted)
For the Years Ended May 5, 2012 and May 7, 2011

(In millions of dollars)	2012	2011
Sales	$16,249.1	$15,956.8
Other revenue	83.1	84.6
Operating expenses		
Cost of sales	12,220.5	11,976.8
Selling & administrative expenses	3,577.4	3,538.9
Operating income	534.3	525.7
Finance costs, net	59.9	75.4
Gain on sale of Wajax	0.0	81.3
Earnings before income taxes	474.4	531.6
Income taxes	122.3	122.0
Net earnings	$ 352.1	$ 409.6

This chapter covers the basic tools of financial analysis. The first part of the chapter shows how to evaluate Empire Company Limited from year to year and also how to compare Empire to its competitor, Metro, another of Canada's leading grocery chains. The second part of the chapter discusses the most widely used financial ratios. You have seen many of these ratios in earlier chapters; however, we have yet to use all of them in a comprehensive analysis of a company. We will use the financial statements of Apple Inc. to perform this analysis.

By studying all these ratios together, you will do the following:

- Learn the basic tools of financial analysis.
- Enhance your business education.

Regardless of your chosen field—marketing, management, finance, entrepreneurship, or accounting—you will find these analytical tools useful as you move through your career.

How Is a Company Evaluated?

Investors and creditors for both public and private corporations cannot evaluate a company by examining only one year's data. This is why most financial statements cover at least two periods, like Empire's statement of earnings that begins this chapter. In fact, most financial analysis covers trends of three to five years. The goal of financial analysis is to predict the future by examining the past.

The graphs in Exhibit 13-1 show Empire's three-year trend of sales and operating income. Empire's sales and operating income increased steadily for the past three years. These are good signs. How would you predict Empire's sales and operating income for 2013 and beyond? Based on the recent past, you would probably extend the sales line and the operating income line upward.

Let's examine some of the tools of financial analysis. We begin with horizontal analysis.

EXHIBIT 13-1
Sales and Operating Income
of Empire Company Limited
(Adapted)

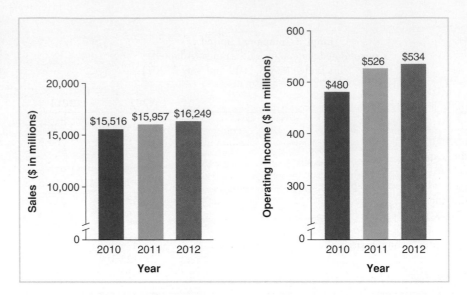

❶ **Perform** a horizontal analysis of financial statements

PERFORM A HORIZONTAL ANALYSIS OF FINANCIAL STATEMENTS

Many decisions hinge on the trends of a company's sales, expenses, net income, and other key financial statement figures. Has the sales figure risen from last year? If so, by how much? Suppose that sales have increased by $200,000. Considered alone, this fact is not very informative, but the *percentage change* in sales over time helps a lot. It is better to know that sales have increased by 20% than to know only that the increase is $200,000.

The study of percentage changes from year to year is called **horizontal analysis**. Computing a percentage change requires two steps:

1. Compute the dollar amount of the change from one period (the base period) to the next.

2. Divide the dollar amount of change by the base-period amount.

Illustration: Empire Company Limited

Horizontal analysis is illustrated for Empire as follows (dollars in millions):

	2012	2011	Increase (Decrease) Amount	Percentage
Sales	$16,249	$15,957	$292	1.8%

Empire's sales increased by 1.8% during 2012, computed as follows:

STEP 1 Compute the dollar amount of change in sales from 2011 to 2012:

$$2012 - 2011 = \text{Increase}$$
$$\$16,249 - \$15,957 = \$292$$

EXHIBIT 13-2
Comparative Income
Statement—Horizontal
Analysis

Empire Company Limited
Consolidated Statements of Earnings (Adapted)
For the Years Ended May 5, 2012 and May 7, 2011

(in millions of dollars)	2012	2011	Increase (Decrease) Amount	Percentage
Sales	$16,249.1	$15,956.8	$292.3	1.8
Other revenue	83.1	84.6	(1.5)	(1.8)
Operating expenses				
Cost of sales	12,220.5	11,976.8	243.7	2.0
Selling & administrative expenses	3,577.4	3,538.9	38.5	1.1
Operating income	534.3	525.7	8.6	1.6
Finance costs, net	59.9	75.4	(15.5)	(20.6)
Gain on sale of Wajax	0.0	81.3	(81.3)	(100.0)
Earnings before income taxes	474.4	531.6	(57.2)	(10.8)
Income taxes	122.3	122.0	0.3	0.2
Net earnings	$ 352.1	$ 409.6	$(57.5)	(14.0)

Note: Any increase from zero to a positive number is treated as an increase of 100%; any decrease to zero is treated as a decrease of 100%. Any decrease in a negative number is treated as an increase; any increase in a negative number is treated as a decrease.

STEP 2 Divide the dollar amount of change by the base-period amount. This computes the percentage change for the period:

$$\text{Percentage change} = \frac{\text{Dollar amount of change}}{\text{Base-year amount}} \times 100$$

$$= \frac{\$292}{\$15,957} \times 100 = 0.0182 \times 100 = 1.8\%$$

Exhibits 13-2 and 13-3 present horizontal analyses of Empire Company Ltd. The comparative statement of earnings shows that sales increased by 1.8% during 2012; however, cost of sales grew by 2%, faster than sales. While selling and administrative expenses increased by 1.1%, there was a 20.6% decrease in the finance cost, suggesting a decrease in the overall cost of debt. Operating income increased by 1.6% even though cost of sales and selling and administrative expenses increased by 2% and 1.1%, respectively. Net earnings decreased by 14%. Why was there such a large decrease in net earnings in 2012? In 2011, there was a $81.3 million gain from the sale of Wajax that caused net earnings in 2011 to be higher than 2012. Management may need to keep a closer eye on expenses in the future to help keep profits growing at a healthy pace.

STOP + THINK (13-1)	Assume you are a financial analyst for an investment bank and have been charged with gathering information about Empire Company Limited for a client. You have performed a horizontal analysis of Empire's statements of earnings for 2012 and 2011, similar to that in Exhibit 13-2. What do you think is the most important information for your analysis?

Studying changes in the balance sheet accounts can enhance our understanding of the current and long-term financial position of the entity. Let's look at a few of the balance sheet changes in Exhibit 13-3. First, cash decreased by 17.2%. While the state-

EXHIBIT 13-3
Comparative Balance Sheet—
Horizontal Analysis

Empire Company Limited
Consolidated Balance Sheets (Adapted)
As at May 5, 2012 and May 7, 2011

(in millions of dollars)	2012	2011	Increase (Decrease) Amount	Increase (Decrease) Percentage
ASSETS				
Current assets				
Cash and cash equivalents............................	$ 510.2	$ 615.9	$(105.7)	(17.2)
Receivables...	362.0	346.6	15.4	4.4
Inventories..	825.3	823.0	2.3	0.3
Prepaid expenses....................................	77.6	69.6	8.0	11.5
Loans and other receivables........................	41.0	52.4	(11.4)	(21.8)
Income taxes receivable............................	46.8	27.4	19.4	70.8
Assets held for sale	28.2	59.4	(31.2)	(52.5)
	$1,891.1	$1,994.3	(103.2)	(5.2)
Loans and other receivables........................	60.6	71.7	(11.1)	(15.5)
Investments..	326.4	226.4	(100)	(44.2)
Other assets..	68.5	55.3	13.2	23.9
Property and equipment.............................	2,679.2	2,398.1	281.1	11.7
Investment property..............................	86.9	73.8	13.1	17.8
Intangibles	461.8	449.2	12.6	2.8
Goodwill..	1,302.1	1,220.0	82.1	6.7
Deferred tax assets....................................	36.5	29.8	6.7	22.5
	$6,913.1	$6,518.6	394.5	6.1
LIABILITIES AND SHAREHOLDERS' EQUITY				
Current liabilities				
Bank indebtedness	$ 4.4	$ 0	4.4	100
Accounts payable and accrued liabilities.......	1,729.8	1,629.1	100.7	6.2
Income taxes payable	16.7	27.8	(11.1)	(39.9)
Current portion of long-term debt...............	237.3	49.4	187.9	380.4
Other liabilities	30.1	42.6	(12.5)	(29.3)
	2,018.3	1,748.9	269.4	15.4
Long-term debt..	889.1	1,090.3	(201.2)	(18.5)
Employee future benefits obligation	143.3	122.3	21.0	17.2
Deferred tax liabilities	190.0	177.0	13.0	7.3
Other long-term liabilities...........................	241.0	182.2	58.8	32.3
	3,481.7	3,320.7	161.0	4.8
Shareholders' equity				
Share capital..	319.3	323.4	(4.1)	(1.3)
Contributed surplus....................................	6.1	4.7	1.4	29.8
Retained earnings..	3,081.7	2,852.1	229.6	8.1
Accumulated other comprehensive loss........	(10.8)	(18.1)	7.3	(40.3)
	3,396.3	3,162.1	234.2	7.4
Minority interest...	35.1	35.8	(0.7)	(2.0)
	3,431.4	3,197.9	233.5	7.3
Total Liabilities & Shareholders' Equity...	$6,913.1	$6,518.6	$ 394.5	6.1

ment of cash flow would show why cash decreased, we are reserving that discussion for later. Reviewing the balance sheet, we can see that cash was used to prepay expenses (increase of 11.5%) and pay back long-term debt (decrease of 18.5%). Current Loans and other receivables decreased by 21.8%, while long-term Loans and other receivables declined by 15.5%. Income taxes receivable increased by 70.8%, meaning that the company is expecting to receive a refund from the Canada Revenue Agency.

Accounts receivable increased by 4.4%, faster than sales (1.8%). Accounts payable also increased by more than sales (6.2%), indicating that the company's payments of short-term debt are not quite keeping pace with its overall rate of growth in sales. On the whole, current assets decreased by 5.2%, while current liabilities increased by 15.4%, resulting in negative working capital for 2012.

Property, plant, and equipment grew by 11.7%, meaning the company invested in long-term assets. Other assets grew by 23.9%, but there is no indication what they are without reading the notes. Note 7 provides a schedule of the components of this category: the major items include investments and restricted cash, which the company is reserving for future use. While long-term debt decreased by 18.5% (the company has paid back some debt), other long-term liabilities increased by 32.3%, indicating the company borrowed more money. There was a decrease in share capital of 29.8% because the company bought back some stock; this may have resulted in an increase in contributed surplus. Net income of $352.1 contributed to the increase in retained earnings.

Trend Percentages

Trend percentages are a form of horizontal analysis. Trends indicate the direction a business is taking. How have sales changed over a five-year period? What trend does income from continuing operations show? These questions can be answered by trend percentages over a representative period, such as the most recent five years.

Trend percentages are computed by selecting a base year whose amounts are set equal to 100%. The amount for each following year is expressed as a percentage of the base amount. To compute a trend percentage, divide an item for a later year by the base-year amount:

$$\text{Trend } \% = \frac{\text{Any-year \$}}{\text{Base-year \$}}$$

Operating income represents a company's best predictor of the future net inflows from its core business units. Empire showed operating income from continuing operations for the past five years as follows:

(in millions)	2012	2011	2010	2009	2008
Operating income	$534	$526	$480	$466	$473

We would like to calculate trend percentages for the four-year period 2009 to 2012. The base year is 2008. Trend percentages are computed by dividing each year's amount by the 2008 amount. The trend percentages for the past five years are:

	2012	2011	2010	2009	2008
Operating income	113%	111%	101%	98%	100%

Looking at the trend percentages for Empire, we can see that operating income declined in 2009 but has risen since, most notably in 2011.

You can perform a trend analysis on any item you consider important. Trend analysis is widely used for predicting the future.

Horizontal analysis highlights changes in an item over time. However, no single technique gives a complete picture of a business.

OBJECTIVE

❷ **Perform** a vertical analysis of financial statements

PERFORM A VERTICAL ANALYSIS OF FINANCIAL STATEMENTS

Vertical analysis shows the relationship of a financial statement item to a base amount from the same statement. All items on the financial statement are reported as a percentage of that base. One use of vertical analysis is to reveal items that need to be investigated further. For example, if cost of goods sold as a percentage of sales is 50% in the previous year and 55% in the current year, management is now aware that expenses have increased in a particular area and can take measures to reduce these costs. You can also use a form of vertical analysis by preparing common-size financial statements and using them to compare one company with another. This will be discussed further in the next section.

To perform a vertical analysis using the income statement, total revenue is usually the base. Suppose, for example, a company's net income is 8% of revenue under normal conditions. A drop to 6% may cause the company's share price to fall.

Illustration: Empire Company Limited

Exhibit 13-4 shows the vertical analysis of Empire's statement of earnings as a percentage of sales. In this case,

$$\text{Vertical analysis } \% = \frac{\text{Each statement item}}{\text{Sales}}$$

For Empire, the vertical-analysis percentage for cost of sales is 74.8% ($12,220.5/16,332.2) in 2012, which is only a slight change from 74.7% in 2011. Even though it is only a slight increase, it may signal to management that this cost is beginning to rise and should be examined further. Operating income, as a percentage of sales, increased slightly from 3.2% to 3.3%, but net earnings as a percentage of sales decreased slightly from 2.5% in 2011 to 2.2% in 2012. This indicates to management that overall expenses have increased as a percentage of sales, and that action should be taken to reduce costs.

EXHIBIT 13-4
Comparative Statement of Earnings—Vertical Analysis

Empire Company Limited
Consolidated Statements of Earnings (Adapted)
For the Years Ended May 5, 2012 and May 7, 2011

(in millions of dollars)	2012 Amount	Percentage of Sales	2011 Amount	Percentage of Sales
Sales and other revenue	$16,332.2	100.0%	$16,041.4	100.0%
Operating expenses				
Cost of sales	12,220.5	74.8	11,976.8	74.7
Selling & administrative expenses	3,577.4	21.9	3,538.9	22.1
Operating income	534.3	3.3	525.7	3.2*
Finance costs, net	59.9	0.4	75.4	0.5
Gain on sale of Wajax	0.0	0.0	81.3	0.5
Earnings before income taxes	474.4	2.9	531.6	3.3
Income taxes	122.3	0.7	122.0	0.8
Net earnings	$ 352.1	2.2	$ 409.6	2.5*

*differences due to rounding

Exhibit 13-5 shows the vertical analysis of Empire's consolidated balance sheets. The base amount is total assets. The vertical analysis of Empire's balance sheet reveals several things about Empire's financial position at December 31, 2012, relative to 2011:

- While cash decreased by 17.2% from 2011, it also decreased as a percentage of total assets from 9.4% to 7.4%. At the same time, receivables decreased slightly from 5.3% to 5.2%.

- Inventories as a percentage of total assets decreased from 12.6% to 11.9%.

- The company's debt to total assets of 50.4% in 2012 decreased slightly from 50.9% in 2011. Of the total debt, current liabilities increased from 26.8% in 2011 to 29.2% in 2012, and long-term liabilities decreased from 24.1% to 21.2%. These debt ratios are still comfortably within reasonable limits for a retail concern.

EXHIBIT 13-5
Comparative Balance Sheet—Vertical Analysis

Empire Company Limited
Consolidated Balance Sheet (Adapted)
As at May 5, 2012 and May 7, 2011

	2012		2011	
(in millions of dollars)	Amount	Percentage of Total	Amount	Percentage of Total
ASSETS				
Current assets				
Cash and cash equivalents	$ 510.2	7.4	$ 615.9	9.4
Receivables	362.0	5.2	346.6	5.3
Inventories	825.3	11.9	823.0	12.6
Prepaid expenses	77.6	1.1	69.6	1.1
Loans and other receivables	41.0	0.6	52.4	0.8
Income taxes receivable	46.8	0.6	27.4	0.4
Assets held for sale	28.2	0.4	59.4	0.9
	$1,891.1	27.4	$1,994.3	30.6
Loans and other receivables	60.6	0.9	71.7	1.1
Investments	326.4	4.7	226.4	3.5
Other assets	68.5	0.9	55.3	0.8
Property and equipment	2,679.2	38.8	2,398.1	36.8
Investment property	86.9	1.3	73.8	1.1
Intangibles	461.8	6.7	449.2	6.9
Goodwill	1,302.1	18.8	1,220.0	18.7
Deferred tax assets	36.5	0.5	29.8	0.5
	$6,913.1	100.0	$6,518.6	100.0
LIABILITIES AND SHAREHOLDERS' EQUITY				
Current liabilities				
Bank indebtedness	$ 4.4	0.1	$ 0	0
Accounts payable and accrued liabilities	1,729.8	25.0	1,629.1	25.0
Income taxes payable	16.7	0.2	27.8	0.4
Current portion of long-term debt	237.3	3.4	49.4	0.8
Other liabilities	30.1	0.4	42.6	0.7
	2,018.3	29.2	1,748.9	26.8
Long-term debt	889.1	12.9	1,090.3	16.7
Employee future benefits obligation	143.3	2.1	122.3	1.9
Deferred tax liabilities	190.0	2.7	177.0	2.7
Other long-term liabilities	241.0	3.5	182.2	2.8
	3,481.7	50.4	3,320.7	50.9
Shareholders' equity				
Share capital	319.3	4.6	323.4	5.0
Contributed surplus	6.1	0.1	4.7	0.1
Retained earnings	3,081.7	44.6	2,852.1	43.8
Accumulated other comprehensive loss	(10.8)	(0.2)	(18.1)	(0.3)
	3,396.3	49.1	3,162.1	48.5
Minority interest	35.1	0.5	35.8	0.5
	3,431.4	49.6	3,197.9	49.1
Total Liabilities & Shareholders' Equity	$6,913.1	100.0	$6,518.6	100.0

PREPARE COMMON-SIZE FINANCIAL STATEMENTS

The percentages in Exhibits 13-4 and 13-5 can be presented as separate statements that report only percentages (no dollar amounts). These statements are called **common-size financial statements**.

On a common-size income statement, each item is expressed as a percentage of the net sales amount. Net sales is the *common size* to which we relate the other amounts. In the balance sheet, the common size is total assets. A common-size statement aids the comparison of different companies because their amounts are stated in percentages, thus expressing the financial results of each comparative company in terms of a common denominator.

Benchmarking

Benchmarking is the comparison of a company to a standard set by others. The goal of benchmarking is improvement. Suppose you are a financial analyst for ScotiaMcLeod. You are considering an investment in the shares of a grocery chain, and you are choosing between Empire Company Limited and Metro Inc. A direct comparison of their financial statements in dollar amounts is not meaningful because the companies differ greatly in size. We can, however, convert the income statements to common size and compare the percentages. The comparison is meaningful, as we shall see.

Benchmarking Against a Key Competitor

Exhibit 13-6 presents the common-size income statements of Empire Company Limited and Metro Inc. Metro serves as an excellent benchmark because it and Empire are both large, successful Canadian grocery chains. Empire's cost of goods sold, operating and other expenses as a percentage of sales are 1.7% higher than Metro's. Metro's net income as a percentage of sales is 1.1% is higher than Empire. When compared to Empire, it would appear that Metro is able to keep their costs down resulting in a higher percentage of net income to sales.

EXHIBIT 13-6
Common-Size Income Statement Compared With a Key Competitor

Empire Company Limited		
Common-Size Income Statement (Adapted) for Comparison With a Key Competitor		
For the Years Ended as Indicated		
	Empire Company Limited (Adapted) May 5, 2012	Metro Inc. (Adapted) September 24, 2011
Sales..	100.0%	100.0%
Cost of goods sold, operating and other expenses..	97.1	95.4
Income before income tax........................	2.9	4.6
Income tax expense..................................	0.7	1.3
Net earnings	2.2%	3.3%

Assume you are a financial analyst for an investment bank and have been charged with gathering information about K-M Inc. for a client. You have been provided with the following 2014 income statement by K-M and have decided to calculate the common-size percentages. What does this tell you about the company? Show your calculations.

Net sales	$150,000
Cost of goods sold	60,000
Gross profit	90,000
Operating expense	40,000
Operating income	50,000
Income tax expense	15,000
Net income	$ 35,000

USE THE STATEMENT OF CASH FLOWS IN DECISION MAKING

The chapter has focused on the income statement and balance sheet. To continue our analysis of financial statements, let's examine the comparative consolidated statements of cash flows for Empire, which are presented in Exhibit 13-7.

OBJECTIVE

4 **Use** the statement of cash flows in decision making

Empire Company Limited
Consolidated Statements of Cash Flows (Adapted)
For the Years Ended May 5, 2012 and May 7, 2011

(in millions of dollars)	2012	2011
Operating Activities		
Net earnings	352.1	409.6
Adjustments for:		
Depreciation	304.1	299.5
Income taxes	122.3	122.0
Finance costs, net	59.9	75.4
Amortization of intangibles	38.2	37.8
Gain on disposal of assets	(32.6)	(24.5)
Impairment of non-financial assets	5.2	34.3
Amortization of deferred items	1.1	1.2
Employee future benefits obligation	3.4	(19.4)
Other	4.5	38.6
Stock-based compensation	1.4	1.6
Gain on sale of Wajax	—	(81.3)
	859.6	894.8

EXHIBIT 13-7
Consolidated Statements of Cash Flows—Empire Company Limited

Net change in non-cash working capital	86.2	(7.2)
Income taxes, paid, net	(131.1)	(124.8)
Dividends paid, preferred shares	(0.1)	(0.1)
Cash flows from operating activities	814.6	762.7
Investing Activities		
Net increase in investments	(87.1)	(42.0)
Net proceeds from sale of Wajax		115.3
Property, equipment, and investment property	(589.5)	(552.4)
Proceeds on disposal of property, equipment, and investment property	196.0	168.3
Additions to intangibles	(29.1)	(34.2)
Loans and other receivables	22.5	35.4
Other assets and long-term liabilities	(23.8)	(8.3)
Business acquisitions	(247.7)	(17.0)
Interest received	3.8	2.8
Decrease in minority interest	(13.4)	(7.4)
Cash flows used in investing activities	(768.3)	(339.5)
Financing Activities		
Increase (decrease) in bank indebtedness	4.4	(4.1)
Issue of long-term debt	102.6	217.9
Repayment of long-term debt	(133.3)	(269.7)
Redemption of preferred shares	(4.1)	(0.1)
Repurchase of non-voting class A shares	—	(27.6)
Interest paid	(60.5)	(66.6)
Dividends paid, common shares	(61.1)	(54.4)
Cash flows used in financing activities	(152.0)	(204.6)
(Decrease) increase in cash & cash equivalents	(105.7)	218.6
Cash & cash equivalents, beginning of year	615.9	397.3
Cash & cash equivalents, end of year	$ 510.2	$ 615.9

For both 2012 and 2011, net cash provided by operating activities was the largest source of cash for the company. In addition, net cash provided by operating activities exceeded net income. Both of these relationships are signs of a healthy company.

The next thing to look at is how the company used this cash generated from operations. Focus on the investing activities section, which normally shows a net use of cash. Total investing activities were up by 126% [(768.3 − 339.5)/339.5] in 2012 (you'll notice that purchases of property and equipment increased year over year). This is a signal that the company is putting cash back into the business, and that excess cash generated from operations is being invested for future use. These uses of cash are also signs of financial strength from a cash-flow perspective.

Analysts find that the statement of cash flows is more helpful for spotting weakness than for gauging success. Why? Because a *shortage* of cash can throw a company into bankruptcy, but lots of cash doesn't ensure success. Let's now take a look at the cash flow statement for SK Corporation—see if you can find signals of cash flow weakness.

SK Corporation
Statement of Cash Flows
For the Year Ended June 30, 2014

		(in millions)
Operating activities:		
Net income...		$ 35,000
Adjustments for non-cash items:		
Depreciation	$ 14,000	
Net increase in current assets other than cash......................	(24,000)	
Net increase in current liabilities...	8,000	(2,000)
Net cash provided by operating activities.................................		33,000
Investing activities:		
Sale of property, plant, and equipment	91,000	
Net cash provided by investing activities		91,000
Financing activities:		
Borrowing	22,000	
Payment of long-term debt	(90,000)	
Repurchase of shares	(9,000)	
Payment of dividends...	(23,000)	
Net cash used for financing activities.....................................		(100,000)
Increase in cash...		$ 24,000

- SK Corporation's net cash provided by operations is less than net income. Ordinarily, cash provided by operations exceeds net income because of the add-back of depreciation and amortization. The increases in current assets and current liabilities should cancel out over time. For SK, current assets increased far more than current liabilities during the year. This may be harmless, or it may signal difficulty in collecting receivables or selling inventory. Either event may cause trouble.

- The sale of property, plant, and equipment is SK's major source of cash. This is okay if it is a one-time situation. SK may be shifting from one line of business to another, and it may be selling off old assets. But, if the sale of property, plant, and equipment is the major source of cash for several periods, SK will face a cash shortage. A company cannot continue to sell off its property, plant, and equipment forever. Soon, it will go out of business.

- The only strength shown by the statement of cash flows is that SK paid off more long-term debt than it took on in new borrowing. This will improve the debt ratio and SK's credit standing.

Here are some cash flow signs of a healthy company:

- Operations are a major *source* of cash (not a *use* of cash).

- Investing activities include more purchases than sales of long-term assets.

- Financing activities are not dominated by borrowing.

MID-CHAPTER SUMMARY PROBLEM

You, an employee at a bank lending office, are deciding whether to grant Jamate Corporation, which makes metal detectors, a large loan. You decide to perform a horizontal analysis and a vertical analysis of the comparative income statement of Jamate Corporation. State whether 2014 was a good year or a bad year and give your reasons.

Name: Jamate Corporation
Fiscal Period: Years ended December 31, 2014 and 2013

Jamate Corporation
Comparative Income Statement
For the Years Ended December 31, 2014 and 2013

	2014	2013
Total revenues	$275,000	$225,000
Expenses:		
Cost of products sold	194,000	165,000
Engineering, selling, and administrative expenses	54,000	48,000
Interest expense	5,000	5,000
Income tax expense	9,000	3,000
Other expense (income)	1,000	(1,000)
Total expenses	263,000	220,000
Net earnings	$ 12,000	$ 5,000

ANSWER

The horizontal analysis shows that total revenues increased 22.2%. This was greater than the 19.5% increase in total expenses, resulting in a 140% increase in net earnings.

Horizontal analysis compares 2014 with 2013 to determine the changes in each income statement item in dollar amounts and percent ($ and %). Large or unusual changes in $ or % should be investigated.

The net earnings increase of 140% occurred because the dollar amounts are quite small. Income tax expense increased 200%; this would be investigated.

Jamate Corporation
Horizontal Analysis of Comparative Income Statement
For the Years Ended December 31, 2014 and 2013

			Increase (Decrease)	
	2014	2013	Amount	Percent
Total revenues	$275,000	$225,000	$50,000	22.2%
Expenses:				
Cost of products sold	194,000	165,000	29,000	17.6
Engineering, selling, and administrative expenses	54,000	48,000	6,000	12.5
Interest expense	5,000	5,000	—	—
Income tax expense	9,000	3,000	6,000	200.0
Other expense (income)	1,000	(1,000)	2,000	—*
Total expenses	263,000	220,000	43,000	19.5
Net earnings	$ 12,000	$ 5,000	$ 7,000	140.0%

*Percentage changes are typically not computed for shifts from a negative to a positive amount, and vice versa.

The vertical analysis shows decreases in the percentages of net sales consumed by the cost of products sold (from 73.3% to 70.5%) and by the engineering, selling, and administrative expenses (from 21.3% to 19.6%). Because these two items are Jamate's largest dollar expenses, their percentage decreases are quite important. The relative reduction in expenses raised 2014's net earnings to 4.4% of sales, compared with 2.2% the preceding year. The overall analysis indicates that 2014 was significantly better than 2013.

Jamate Corporation
Vertical Analysis of Comparative Income Statement
For the Years Ended December 31, 2014 and 2013

	2014		2013	
	Amount	Percent	Amount	Percent
Total revenues	$275,000	100.0%	$225,000	100.0%
Expenses:				
Cost of products sold................................	194,000	70.5	165,000	73.3
Engineering, selling, and				
administrative expenses........................	54,000	19.6	48,000	21.3
Interest expense..	5,000	1.8	5,000	2.2
Income tax expense	9,000	3.3	3,000	1.4*
Other expense (income)	1,000	0.4	(1,000)	(0.4)
Total expenses	263,000	95.6	220,000	97.8
Net earnings..	$ 12,000	4.4%	$ 5,000	2.2%

*Number rounded up.

> Vertical analysis expresses net earnings and expenses as a percentage of total revenues. The percentages for 2014 are compared with those of 2013. Any large or unexpected differences would be reviewed.

USE RATIOS TO MAKE BUSINESS DECISIONS

OBJECTIVE

Ratios are a major tool of financial analysis. We have discussed the use of many ratios in financial analysis in various chapters throughout the book. A ratio expresses the relationship between various types of financial information. In this section, we review how ratios are computed and used to make business decisions, using Apple Inc.

⑤ Use ratios to make business decisions

Many companies include ratios in a special section of their annual reports. Exhibit 13-8 shows a summary of selected data from previous Apple Inc. annual reports.

The ratios we discuss in this chapter are classified as follows:

1. Measuring the ability to pay current liabilities
2. Measuring turnover and cash conversion
3. Measuring leverage: overall ability to pay debts
4. Measuring profitability
5. Analyzing stock as an investment

EXHIBIT 13-8
Financial Summary—Apple Inc.

Apple Inc.			
Results of operations (dollar amounts in millions):	FY 2011	FY 2010	FY 2009
Net sales			
Domestic	$ 41,812	$28,633	$22,325
International	66,437	36,592	20,580
Total net sales	108,249	65,225	42,905
Gross margin	43,818	25,684	17,222
Gross margin as percent of net sales	40%	39%	40%
Operating income	33,790	18,385	11,740
Operating income as percent of net sales	31%	28%	27%
Net income after provision for income taxes	25,922	14,013	8,235
Net income as percent of sales	24%	21%	19%
Earnings per weighted-average common share, basic	$ 28.05	$ 15.41	$ 9.22
Return on average stockholders' equity	41.7%	35.3%	23.8%
Financial position (dollar amounts in millions):			
Current assets	$ 44,988	$41,678	$31,555
Current liabilities	27,970	20,722	11,506
Working capital	17,018	20,956	20,049
Current ratio	1.61	2.01	2.74
Quick ratio	1.12	1.5	2.33
Total assets	116,371	75,183	47,501
Total liabilities	39,756	27,392	15,861
Debt ratio	0.34	0.36	0.33

There are a number of ratios that managers and analysts use to assess the health and strength of a company. In this section, you will learn that it's important to consider all ratios over a period of time to get a more accurate picture of a company. Let's analyze Apple Inc. with this in mind.

How do you determine whether a company's performance has been strong or weak, based on its current-period ratios? You can only make that decision if you have the following ratios to compare the current period against: (1) prior-year ratios; and (2) industry comparables, either in the form of an industry average or the ratios of a strong competitor. In the case of all the ratios in the following sections, we compare Apple's current-year ratios with (1) its prior years' ratios and (2) ratios for the industry (if available) or ratios of one of Apple Inc.'s competitors.

Measuring the Ability to Pay Current Liabilities

Working capital is defined as follows:

$$\text{Working capital} = \text{Current assets} - \text{Current liabilities}$$

Working capital measures the ability to pay current liabilities with current assets. In general, the larger the working capital, the better the ability to pay debts. Recall that capital is total assets minus total liabilities. Working capital is like a "current" version of total capital. Consider two companies with equal working capital:

	Company	
	Jones	Smith
Current assets............................	$100,000	$200,000
Current liabilities	50,000	150,000
Working capital.........................	$ 50,000	$ 50,000

Both companies have working capital of $50,000, but Jones's working capital is as large as its current liabilities. Smith's working capital is only one-third as large as current liabilities. Jones is in a better position because its working capital is a higher percentage of current liabilities. As shown in Exhibit 13-8, Apple's working capital as of September 24, 2011 (the end of its 2011 fiscal year), was $17,018 million. This compares with $20,956 million and $20,049 million at the end of its 2010 and 2009 fiscal years, respectively. In comparison, the working capital of Dell Inc., a strong competitor of Apple, as of the end of its 2011 fiscal year was $7,747 million. Apple appears to be in a very strong position from the standpoint of working capital, but the picture is incomplete. Let's look at two key ratios that help tell the rest of the story.

CURRENT RATIO. The most common ratio for evaluating current assets and current liabilities is the **current ratio**, which is current assets divided by current liabilities. As discussed in Chapter 3, the current ratio measures the ability to pay current liabilities with current assets. Exhibit 13-9 and Exhibit 13-10 show the consolidated statements of operations and the consolidated balance sheets of Apple Inc.

EXHIBIT 13-9
Comparative Consolidated Statements of Operations—Apple Inc.

Apple Inc.
Consolidated Statements of Operations (USD $)
For the Years Ended 2011, 2010, and 2009

(in millions, except share data in thousands, unless otherwise specified)	Sept. 24, 2011	Sept. 25, 2010	Sept. 26, 2009
Net sales	$108,249	$ 65,225	$ 42,905
Cost of sales	64,431	39,541	25,683
Gross margin	43,818	25,684	17,222
Operating expenses:			
Research and development	2,429	1,782	1,333
Selling, general, and administrative	7,599	5,517	4,149
Total operating expenses	10,028	7,299	5,482
Operating income	33,790	18,385	11,740
Other income and expense	415	155	326
Income before provision for income taxes	34,205	18,540	12,066
Provision for income taxes	8,283	4,527	3,831
Net income	25,922	$ 14,013	$ 8,235
Earnings per common share:			
Basic	$ 28.05	$ 15.41	$ 9.22
Diluted	$ 27.68	$ 15.15	$ 9.08
Shares used in computing earnings per share:			
Basic	924,258	909,461	893,016
Diluted	936,645	924,712	907,005

EXHIBIT 13-10
Comparative Consolidated Balance Sheets—Apple Inc.

Apple Inc.
Consolidated Balance Sheets (USD $)
As at September 24, 2011, and September 25, 2010

(in millions)	Sept. 24, 2011	Sept. 25, 2010
Current assets:		
Cash and cash equivalents	$ 9,815	$11,261
Short-term investments	16,137	14,359
Accounts receivable, less allowance of $55 and $52, respectively	5,369	5,510
Inventories	776	1,051
Deferred tax assets	2,014	1,636
Vendor non-trade receivables	6,348	4,414
Other current assets	4,529	3,447
Total current assets	44,988	41,678
Long-term marketable securities	55,618	25,391
Property, plant, and equipment, net	7,777	4,768
Goodwill	896	741
Acquired intangible assets, net	3,536	342
Other assets	3,556	2,263
Total assets	116,371	75,183
Current liabilities:		
Accounts payable	14,632	12,015
Accrued expenses	9,247	5,723
Deferred revenue	4,091	2,984
Total current liabilities	27,970	20,722
Deferred revenue—non-current	1,686	1,139
Other non-current liabilities	10,100	5,531
Total liabilities	39,756	27,392
Commitments and contingencies		
Shareholders' equity:		
Common stock, no par value, 1,800,000,000 shares authorized, 929,277,000 and 915,970,000 shares issued and outstanding, respectively	13,331	10,668
Retained earnings	62,841	37,169
Accumulated other comprehensive (loss)/income	443	(46)
Total shareholders' equity	76,615	47,791
Total liabilities and shareholders' equity	$116,371	$75,183

Using figures from Exhibit 13-10, the current ratios of Apple at September 24, 2011, and September 25, 2010, follow, along with the average for the computer manufacturing industry:

		Apple Inc.'s Current Ratio		Industry
	Formula	2011	2010	Average
Current ratio =	$\dfrac{\text{Current assets}}{\text{Current liabilities}}$	$\dfrac{\$44,988}{\$27,970} = 1.61$	$\dfrac{\$41,678}{\$20,722} = 2.01$	1.30

Although still strong, Apple's current ratio decreased during 2011, from 2.01 to 1.61. Further examination of current assets and current liabilities in Exhibit 13-10 shows that current liabilities increased by 34.9% during 2011, while current assets increased by only 7.9%. Accrued expenses increased by 61.6% during 2011. It will be necessary to dig into the footnotes further to discover why the company allowed this to happen. This is not necessarily a bad thing, especially since the current ratio is well within the bounds of what is considered healthy from the standpoint of the ability to pay current liabilities. In general, a higher current ratio indicates a stronger financial position. Apple certainly has more than sufficient current assets to maintain its operations. Apple's current ratio of 1.61 compares quite favourably with the current ratios of the industry as well as with two well-known competitors:

Company	Current Ratio
Dell Inc.	1.34
Hewlett-Packard Company	1.01

Note: These figures show that ratio values vary widely from one company to another in the same industry.

What is an acceptable current ratio? The answer depends on the industry. The norm for companies in most industries is around 1.50, as reported by the Risk Management Association. Apple Inc.'s current ratio of 1.61 is better than average.

QUICK (ACID-TEST) RATIO. As discussed in Chapter 5, the **quick (acid-test) ratio** tells us whether the entity could pass the acid test of paying all its current liabilities if they came due immediately (quickly). The quick ratio uses a narrower base to measure liquidity than the current ratio does.

To compute the quick ratio, we add cash, short-term investments, and accounts receivable (net of allowances), and divide by current liabilities. Inventory and prepaid expenses are excluded because they are less liquid. A business may be unable to convert inventory to cash immediately.

Using the information in Exhibit 13-10, Apple's quick ratios for 2011 and 2010 follow:

Formula	Apple Inc.'s Quick Ratio		Industry Average
	2011	2010	
Quick ratio = $\dfrac{\text{Cash + Short-term investments + Net current receivables}}{\text{Current liabilities}}$	$\dfrac{\$9,815 + \$16,137 + \$5,369}{\$27,970} = 1.12$	$\dfrac{\$11,261 + \$14,359 + \$5,510}{\$20,722} = 1.50$	0.80

Like the current ratio, the company's quick ratio deteriorated during 2011, but is still significantly better than the industry average. Compare Apple's quick ratio with the values of its competitors:

Company	Quick (Acid-Test) Ratio
Dell Inc.	1.12
Hewlett-Packard Company	0.58

A quick ratio of 0.90 to 1.00 is acceptable in most industries. How can many retail companies like Walmart function with low quick ratios? Because they price their inventories to turn over (sell) quickly and because they collect most of the revenues in cash. This points us to the next group of ratios, which measure turnover.

Measuring Turnover and the Cash Conversion Cycle

The ability to sell inventory and collect receivables, as well as pay accounts payable, is the lifeblood of any retail, wholesale, or manufacturing concern. In this section, we discuss three ratios that measure this ability—inventory turnover, accounts receivable turnover, and accounts payable turnover—as well as the relationship between them, called the *cash conversion cycle*.

INVENTORY TURNOVER. Companies generally strive to sell their inventory as quickly as possible. The faster inventory sells, the sooner cash comes in.

Inventory turnover, discussed in Chapter 6, measures the number of times a company sells its average level of inventory during a year. A fast turnover indicates ease in selling inventory; a low turnover indicates difficulty. A value of 6 means that the company's average level of inventory has been sold six times during the year, and that's usually better than a turnover of three times. But too high a value can mean that the business is not keeping enough inventory on hand, which can lead to lost sales if the company can't fill orders. Therefore, a business strives for the most *profitable* rate of turnover, not necessarily the *highest* rate.

To compute inventory turnover, divide cost of goods sold by the average inventory for the period. We use the cost of goods sold—*not sales*—in the computation because both cost of goods sold and inventory are stated *at cost*. Apple Inc.'s inventory turnover for 2011 is as follows:

Formula		Apple Inc.'s Inventory Turnover	Competitor (Dell Inc.)
Inventory turnover $=$	$\dfrac{\text{Cost of goods sold}}{\text{Average inventory}}$	$\dfrac{\$64,431}{\$914} = 70.5$	35.7
Days' inventory outstanding (DIO) $=$	$\dfrac{365}{\text{Turnover}}$	$\dfrac{365}{70.5} = 5$ days	10 days

Cost of goods sold comes from the consolidated statement of operations (Exhibit 13-9). Average inventory is the average of beginning ($1,051) and ending inventory ($776). (See the balance sheet, Exhibit 13-10.) If inventory levels vary greatly from month to month, you should compute the average by adding the 12 monthly balances and dividing the sum by 12.

Inventory turnover varies widely with the nature of the business. For example, Apple's inventory turned over 70.5 times in 2011! On a daily basis (days' inventory outstanding), that means once every 5 days (365/70.5)! In 2010, Apple's inventory turned over 52.5 times. Dell's inventory turnover for 2011 was 35.7 times (once every 10 days). Computer manufacturers purposely keep very low inventory levels because of their ability to manufacture inventory quickly and because technology is subject to rapid obsolescence.

To evaluate inventory turnover, compare the ratio over time as well as with industry averages or competitors. A sharp decline suggests the need for corrective action.

ACCOUNTS RECEIVABLE TURNOVER. Accounts receivable turnover measures the ability to collect cash from customers. In general, the higher the ratio, the better. However, a receivable turnover that is too high may indicate that credit is too tight, and that may cause a company to lose sales to good customers.

To compute accounts receivable turnover, divide net sales by average net accounts receivable. Ideally, net credit sales should be used but it cannot always be obtained. The ratio tells how many times during the year average receivables were turned into cash. Apple's accounts receivable turnover ratio for 2011 was as follows:

Formula		Apple Inc.'s Accounts Receivable Turnover	Competitor (Dell Inc.)
Accounts receivable turnover	$= \dfrac{\text{Net sales}}{\text{Average net accounts receivable}}$	$\dfrac{\$108{,}249}{\$5{,}440} = 19.8$	9.6
Days' sales outstanding (DSO) (or days'-sales-in-receivables)	$= \dfrac{365}{\text{Turnover}}$	$\dfrac{365}{19.8} = 18$ days	38 days

Net sales comes from Exhibit 13-9. Average net accounts receivable (Exhibit 13-10) is figured by adding beginning ($5,510) and ending receivables ($5,369), then dividing by 2. If accounts receivable vary widely during the year, compute the average by using the 12 monthly balances. Apple collected its average accounts receivable 19.8 times during 2011. The comparable ratio for Apple for 2010 was 14.7 times. Dell's accounts receivable turnover for 2011 was 9.6.

Apple's accounts receivable turnover of 19.8 times per year is much faster than the industry average. Apple owns and operates a large number of retail stores, and much of its sales are for cash, which makes the receivables balance very low relative to the sales balance.

DAYS' SALES IN RECEIVABLES. Businesses must convert accounts receivable to cash. All else being equal, the lower the receivable balance, the better the cash flow.

The *days' sales outstanding (DSO)* or **days' sales in receivables ratio**, discussed in Chapter 5, shows how many days' sales remain in accounts receivable. Days' sales in receivables can be calculated two different ways, each of which produces the identical result. First, if you have already calculated receivables turnover (see the previous section), simply divide the turnover into 365. For Apple, days' sales in receivables works out to 18.4 (rounded to 18) days (365/19.8). The second way to compute the ratio, described in Chapter 5, merely works from a different angle, by a two-step process:

1. Divide net sales by 365 days to figure average daily sales.
2. Divide average net receivables by average daily sales.

The data to compute this ratio for Apple are taken from the 2011 income statement (Exhibit 13-9) and balance sheet (Exhibit 13-10):

Formula		Apple Inc.'s Days' Sales in Accounts Receivable	Competitor (Dell Inc.)
Days' sales outstanding (DSO) or days' sales in receivables:			
1. Average daily sales	$= \dfrac{\text{Net sales}}{365 \text{ days}}$	$\dfrac{\$108{,}249}{365 \text{ days}} = \$296.6$	
2. Convert average daily sales to DSO	$= \dfrac{\text{Average net accounts receivable}}{\text{Average daily sales}}$	$\dfrac{\$5{,}440}{\$296.6} = 18$ days	38 days

In comparison, Dell's DSO in 2011 was 38 days (365/9.6 turnover).

ACCOUNTS PAYABLE TURNOVER. Discussed in Chapter 9, *accounts payable turnover* measures the number of times per year that the entity pays off its accounts payable. To compute accounts payable turnover, divide cost of goods sold by average accounts payable. For Apple, this ratio is as follows:

Formula			Apple Inc.'s Accounts Payable Turnover	Competitor (Dell Inc.)
Accounts payable turnover	=	$\dfrac{\text{Cost of goods sold}}{\text{Average accounts payable}}$	$\dfrac{\$64,431}{\$13,324}$ = 4.84	4.2
Days' payable outstanding (DPO)	=	$\dfrac{365}{\text{Turnover}}$	$\dfrac{365}{4.84}$ = 75 days	87 days

On average, Apple pays off its accounts payable 4.84 times per year, which is about every 75 days. To convert accounts payable turnover to days' payable outstanding (DPO), divide the turnover into 365 (365 ÷ 4.84 = 75 days). In comparison, Dell's accounts payable turnover is 4.2 times per year, or about every 87 days.

CASH CONVERSION CYCLE. By expressing the three turnover ratios in days, we can compute a company's **cash conversion cycle** as follows:

Formula			Apple Inc.'s Cash Conversion Cycle	Competitor (Dell Inc.)
Cash conversion cycle	=	DIO + DSO − DPO	5 + 18 − 75 = −52 days	−39 days
where DIO	=	Days' inventory outstanding		
DSO	=	Days' sales outstanding		
DPO	=	Days' payable outstanding		

At first glance, a negative amount for the cash conversion cycle looks odd. What does it mean? Apple is in the enviable position of being able to sell inventory and collect from its customers 52 days before it has to pay its suppliers who provided the parts and materials to produce those inventories. This means that Apple can stock less inventory and hold onto cash longer than other companies. It also helps explain why the company could afford to keep over $16 billion in short-term investments (Exhibit 13-10)—to "sop up" its excess cash—and using it to make still more money while waiting to pay off suppliers. Apple's competitor Dell has a similar situation, with a cash conversion cycle of −39 days. Retail companies that have a more "normal" inventory turnover (about four times per year, or about every 90 days) have cash conversion cycles in the range of 30 to 60 days, depending on how long it takes to collect from customers. The cash conversion cycle for service-oriented businesses consists only of (DSO − DPO) because service businesses typically do not carry inventory.

Measuring Leverage: Overall Ability to Pay Debts

The ratios discussed so far relate to current assets and current liabilities. They measure the ability to sell inventory, collect receivables, and pay current bills. Two indicators of the ability to pay total liabilities are the *debt ratio* and the *times-interest-earned ratio*.

DEBT RATIO. Suppose you are a bank loan officer and you have received loan applications for $500,000 from two similar companies. The first company already owes $600,000, and the second owes only $250,000. Which company gets the loan? Company 2 may look like the stronger candidate, because it owes less.

This relationship between total liabilities and total assets is called the **debt ratio**. Discussed in Chapters 3 and 9, the debt ratio tells us the proportion of assets financed with debt. A debt ratio of 1 reveals that debt has financed all the assets. A debt ratio of 0.50 means that debt finances half the assets. The higher the debt ratio, the greater the pressure to pay interest and principal. The lower the debt ratio, the lower the company's credit risk.

The debt ratios for Apple in 2011 and 2010 follow:

Formula	Apple Inc.'s Debt Ratio		Competitor
	2011	2010	(Dell Inc.)
Debt ratio = $\dfrac{\text{Total liabilities}}{\text{Total assets}}$	$\dfrac{\$39,756}{\$116,371} = 0.34$	$\dfrac{\$27,392}{\$75,183} = 0.36$	0.80

This is an extremely low debt ratio, because of Apple's unusually healthy cash position described in the previous section. Notice that Dell has a much higher debt ratio than Apple. The Risk Management Association reports that the average debt ratio for most companies ranges around 0.62, with relatively little variation from company to company. However, companies in certain industries such as airlines usually have higher debt ratios. The debt ratio is related to the leverage ratio discussed in the next section, which is used in DuPont analysis to compute return on assets and return on equity.

TIMES-INTEREST-EARNED RATIO. Analysts use a second ratio—the **times-interest-earned ratio** (introduced in Chapter 9)—to relate income to interest expense. To compute the times interest-earned ratio, divide income from operations (operating income) by interest expense. This ratio measures the number of times operating income can *cover* interest expense, and is also called the *interest-coverage ratio*. A high ratio indicates ease in paying interest; a low value suggests difficulty.

Formula	Apple Inc.'s Times-Interest-Earned Ratio		Competitor
	2011	2010	(Dell Inc.)
Times-interest-earned ratio = $\dfrac{\text{Income from operations}}{\text{Interest expense}}$	N/A	N/A	23.2

It is not possible to compute the times-interest-earned ratio for Apple for one simple reason: The company has no interest-bearing debt. Why should it borrow money and pay interest, when the company has so much cash on the balance sheet and the ability to generate cash from sales 52 days before having to pay creditors? From Exhibit 13-10, notice that $27 billion of the total $39 billion in liabilities is current, which is usually non-interest bearing. In addition, an examination of the financial statement footnotes reveals that, of the $10.1 billion of "other non-current liabilities," none are interest bearing. Although Apple's competitor Dell has a relatively high debt ratio (0.80), its times-interest-earned ratio is high (23.2), meaning that Dell is quite capable of servicing its interest payments. In summary, the judgment about the adequacy of interest coverage, like so many other factors of financial statement analysis, is very much dependent on the industry, as well as the company being studied.

Measuring Profitability

The fundamental goal of business is to earn a profit, and so the ratios that measure profitability are reported widely in the media.

GROSS (PROFIT) MARGIN. In Chapter 6, we defined gross profit as net sales – cost of goods sold. That is, gross profit is the amount of profit that the entity makes from merely selling a product before other operating costs are subtracted. In Chapter 11, we emphasized that a persistently improving gross profit is one important element of earnings quality. Let's look at Apple's gross margin percentages:

Formula	Apple Inc.'s Gross Margin		Competitor (Dell Inc.)
	2011	2010	
Gross profit % = $\dfrac{\text{Gross profit}}{\text{Net sales}}$	40%	39.4%	22.3%

Apple is known as *the* innovator in the technology field. The company is constantly inventing new technology that everyone literally stands in line to purchase! Do you remember the last time you visited an Apple store (perhaps when a new version of the iPhone was introduced)? How much were you willing to pay for your new iPhone, iPad, or iMac? Do you remember how crowded the store was? As we discussed in Chapter 7, because of the creative talents of their people, some companies have been able to adopt a "product differentiation" business strategy, which allows them to sell their products for more than their competitors. When everyone wants the product, they are usually willing to pay more for it. Although Apple's gross profit of 40% in 2011 is slightly more than the 39.4% it earned in 2010, this is quite an impressive number, and is higher than any competitor. In contrast, Dell, with a 22.3% gross profit, is known as a low-cost provider of computer equipment. Dell sells a lot of products, but it is usually not the first to introduce new products, so it has to sell products for lower prices, thus lowering its gross profit.

OPERATING INCOME (PROFIT) PERCENTAGE. Operating income (profit) percentage is net income from operations as a percentage of net sales. It is an important statistic because it measures the percentage of profit earned from each sales dollar in a company's core business operations. In Chapter 11, we pointed out that a persistently high operating income compared to net sales is an important determinant of earnings quality. The first component of high operating earnings is a high gross margin percentage. After that, maximizing operating income depends on keeping operating costs as low as possible, given the level of desired product quality and customer service. Apple's operating income percentages, compared with Dell follow:

		Apple Inc.'s Operating Income %		Competitor
Formula		2011	2010	(Dell Inc.)
Operating income % $= \dfrac{\text{Operating income}}{\text{Net sales}}$		31.2%	28.2%	7.1%

Apple is far ahead of the competition on earnings from its core operations, and the company is also improving steadily over prior years.

DUPONT ANALYSIS. In Chapter 7 we introduced **DuPont analysis**, which is a detailed analysis of rate of return on total assets (ROA) and return on common shareholders' equity (ROE). It might prove valuable to reread those pages before you proceed with the following material. In Exhibit 13-11, we review the basic driver ratios for DuPont analysis to provide a template that will be used for the analysis by component that follows.

Notice that the ultimate goal of DuPont analysis is to explain the rate of return on common shareholders' equity in a detailed fashion (far-right-hand column) by breaking it down into its component elements: return on sales, asset turnover, and leverage. The first two components of the model combine to give return on total assets (ROA). When the last component (leverage) is combined into the model, it produces (by cross cancellation) return on common shareholders' equity (ROE). We now explain each component of the model, using figures for Apple Inc. to illustrate.

EXHIBIT 13-11
DuPont Analysis Model

ROA			×	Leverage ratio (Equity multiplier)	=	ROE
Return on sales (Net profit margin)	×	Asset turnover	×	Leverage ratio (Equity multiplier)	=	Return on equity (ROE)
$\dfrac{\text{Net income}}{\text{Net sales}}$	×	$\dfrac{\text{Net sales}}{\text{Average total assets}}$	×	$\dfrac{\text{Average total assets}}{\text{Average common shareholders' equity}}$	=	$\dfrac{\text{Net income}}{\text{Average common shareholders' equity}}$

RETURN (NET PROFIT MARGIN) ON SALES. In business, *return* refers to profitability. Consider the **return on net sales**, or simply *return on sales* (ROS). (The word *net* is usually omitted for convenience.) In Chapter 7, we referred to this ratio as net profit margin. The initial element of DuPont analysis, this ratio shows the percentage of each sales dollar earned as net income. The return-on-sales ratios for Apple are as follows:

Formula		Apple Inc.'s Return on Sales		Competitor
		2011	2010	(Dell Inc.)
Return on sales (Net profit margin)	$= \dfrac{\text{Net income}}{\text{Net sales}}$	$\dfrac{\$25,922}{\$108,249} = 23.9\%$	$\dfrac{\$14,013}{\$65,225} = 21.5\%$	5.6%

Companies strive for a high return on sales. The higher the percentage, the more profit is being generated by sales dollars. Apple's return on sales is astoundingly high in 2011 (23.9%) and is over two percentage points higher than it was in 2010.

ASSET TURNOVER. As discussed in Chapter 7, **asset turnover** measures the amount of net sales generated for each dollar invested in assets. As such, it is a measure of how efficiently management is operating the company. Companies with high asset turnover tend to be more productive than companies with low asset turnover. Let's examine Apple's asset turnover for 2011 compared with 2010, and then compare it to competitor Dell's asset turnover:

Formula		Apple Inc.'s Asset Turnover		Competitor
		2011	2010	(Dell Inc.)
Asset turnover $=$	$\dfrac{\text{Net sales}}{\text{Average total assets}}$	$\dfrac{\$108,249}{\$95,777} = 1.13$	$\dfrac{\$65,225}{\$61,342} = 1.063$	1.49

Compared to Dell, Apple has invested more in assets per dollar of sales. This is often the case with innovative companies, as opposed to companies that focus on low cost. To make major product innovations requires a significant investment in both tangible and intangible assets. So, while Apple is significantly more profitable than Dell, it is less efficiently managed, at least by this measure.

RETURN ON TOTAL ASSETS (ROA). Having computed the "driver ratios"—rate of return on net sales and asset turnover—we are now prepared to combine them into the DuPont analysis to compute the **return on assets (ROA)** as follows:

Return on	Apple Inc.'s ROA		Competitor
assets (ROA)	2011	2010	(Dell Inc.)
Rate of return on sales*	23.9%	21.5%	5.6%
×	×	×	×
Asset turnover	1.13	1.063	1.49
=	=	=	=
ROA	27%	22.9%	8.3%

---

*Some analysts use net income before interest expense to compute ROA, because interest expense measures the return earned by creditors who provide the portion of total assets for which the company has used borrowed capital.

Again, the raw figures for our computations are based on income and asset figures from Exhibits 13.9 and 13-10, but the component ratios are based on the previous two illustrations. We see from these computations that for Apple, ROA is driven principally by its high profitability based on product differentiation, rather than efficiency. In contrast, Dell's ROA is based more on efficiency than profitability. Dell is a low-margin provider of basic computer technology, and as the low-cost provider, it is more efficient, generating more sales per dollar invested in total assets than Apple.

LEVERAGE (EQUITY MULTIPLIER) RATIO. The final element of DuPont analysis is **leverage**, which measures the impact of debt financing on profitability. You learned in Chapters 9 and 10 that it can be advantageous to use borrowed capital to finance a business. Earlier, we expressed the debt ratio as the ratio of total liabilities to total assets. The **leverage ratio**, or equity multiplier, measures the proportion of each dollar of assets financed with shareholders' equity. Because total assets – shareholders' equity = total liabilities, the leverage ratio is a way of inversely expressing the debt ratio—it merely looks at financing from the other side of the fundamental accounting equation. Let's examine Apple's leverage ratios for 2011 and 2010, compared with those of its competitor, Dell.

Formula	Apple Inc.'s Leverage Ratios		Competitor (Dell Inc.)
	2011	2010	
Leverage ratio $= \dfrac{\text{Average total assets}}{\text{Average common shareholders' equity}}$	$\dfrac{\$95,777}{\$62,203} = 1.539$	$\dfrac{\$61,342}{\$39,715} = 1.545$	4.98

As we pointed out in a previous section, Apple has a comparatively low debt ratio (34% and 36% for 2011 and 2010, respectively). This translates to very low leverage ratios for Apple (1.539 and 1.545 for 2011 and 2010, respectively). In comparison, Dell has a comparatively high debt ratio (80% for 2011). Therefore, Dell uses much more borrowed capital than equity capital to finance its operations, and its leverage ratio is much higher (4.98).

RETURN ON COMMON SHAREHOLDERS' EQUITY (ROE). A popular measure of profitability is **return on common shareholders' equity**, often shortened to *return on equity* (ROE). Also discussed in Chapter 10, this ratio shows the relationship between net income and common shareholders' investment in the company—how much income is earned for every $1 invested.

To compute this ratio, first subtract preferred dividends, if any, from net income to measure income available to the common shareholders. Then divide income available to common shareholders' by average common equity during the year. Common equity is total equity minus preferred equity. The 2011 return on common shareholders' equity for Apple is as follows:

Formula	Apple Inc.'s 2011 Return on Common Shareholders' Equity	Competitor (Dell Inc.)
Rate of return on common shareholders' equity $= \dfrac{\text{Net income} - \text{Preferred dividends}}{\text{Average common shareholders' equity}}$	$\dfrac{\$25,922 - \$0}{\$62,203} = 41.6\%$	$\$41.9\%$

Now observe something interesting: Apple has beaten its competitor (Dell) on virtually every measure so far, right? But here we see that Dell's ROE (41.9%) is slightly higher than Apple's ROE (41.6%). How can this be? If we hadn't considered the impact of leverage, we might have missed it. By using DuPont analysis to analyze the final components of ROE, we see it right away:

Rate of Return on Shareholders' Equity (ROE)	Apple Inc.'s ROE 2011	Apple Inc.'s ROE 2010	Competitor (Dell Inc.)
ROA	27%	22.9%	8.3%
×	×	×	×
Leverage ratio	1.539	1.545	4.98
=	=	=	=
ROE	(rounded) 41.6%	(rounded) 35.4%	41.3

Apple is by far the more profitable company. However, Dell is more highly leveraged than Apple, having an 80% debt ratio and a leverage ratio of $4.98 of assets per dollar of shareholders' equity. Thus, the detailed analysis provided by the DuPont model gives far more information on which to judge the quality of earnings than just the ROE ratio alone.

To be sure, the use of leverage by a company is often a good thing, as long as it is kept within reasonable limits. The practice of using leverage is called **trading on the equity**. Companies like Dell that finance operations with debt are said to *leverage* their positions.

As we pointed out in Chapter 10, leverage can hurt ROE as well as help. If revenues drop, debts still must be paid. Therefore, leverage is a double-edged sword. It increases profits during good times but also compounds losses during bad times.

EARNINGS PER SHARE OF COMMON STOCK. Discussed in Chapters 9 and 11, *earnings per share of common stock,* or simply **earnings per share (EPS)**, is the amount of net income earned for each share of outstanding *common* stock. EPS is the most widely quoted of all financial statistics. It's the only ratio that appears on the income statement of a publicly traded company. For private companies that follow ASPE, EPS is not required to be reported.

Earnings per share is computed by dividing net income available to common shareholders by the average number of common shares outstanding during the year. Preferred dividends are subtracted from net income because the preferred shareholders have a prior claim to their dividends. Apple Inc. has no preferred stock and thus has no preferred dividends. The firm's EPS for 2011 and 2010 follows (based on Exhibit 13-9):

	Formula	Apple Inc.'s Earnings Per Share (Basic) 2011	Apple Inc.'s Earnings Per Share (Basic) 2010
Earnings per share of common stock =	$\dfrac{\text{Net income} - \text{Preferred dividends (in thousands)}}{\text{Average number of common shares outstanding (in thousands)}}$	$\dfrac{\$25,922,000}{924,258} = \$28.05$	$\dfrac{\$14,013,000}{909,461} = \$15.41$

Apple's EPS increased 82% during 2011, and that's good news. That's more than double the percentage increase in EPS from 2009 to 2010 ($15.41 vs. $9.22). Such huge increases in earnings have certainly had an impact on the company's stock price. Apple Inc. shareholders have been enjoying huge appreciation in their investment for several years. In mid-2012, the stock was selling for over $500 per share! That's tremendous appreciation if you had purchased the stock five years prior, when the stock was selling for less than $100 per share. But is it still a good buy at this price? That's the relevant question a prospective shareholder wants to know. The next section gives you some information on how analysts make this decision.

Analyzing Stock Shares As an Investment

Investors buy stock shares to earn a return on their investment. This return consists of two parts: (1) gains (or losses) from selling the stock shares, and (2) dividends.

PRICE/EARNINGS RATIO (MULTIPLE). The **price/earnings ratio (multiple)** is the ratio of common stock price to earnings per share. This ratio, abbreviated P/E, appears in stock listings of many newspapers and online. It shows the market price of $1 of earnings.

Calculations for the P/E ratios of Apple follow. The market price of Apple's common stock was $404.30 at September 24, 2011 (the end of its 2011 fiscal year), and $292.32 at September 25, 2010 (the end of its 2010 fiscal year). Stock prices can be obtained from a company's website or various other financial websites.

	Formula	Apple Inc.'s Price/Earnings Ratio	
		2011	**2010**
P/E ratio	= $\dfrac{\text{Market price per share of common stock}}{\text{Earnings per share}}$	$\dfrac{\$404.30}{\$28.05} = 14.4$	$\dfrac{\$292.32}{\$15.41} = 19.0$

Given Apple's 2011 P/E ratio of 14 (rounded), we would say that the company's stock is selling at about 14 times earnings. Each $1 of Apple's earnings is worth $14 to the stock market. Stocks trade in ranges, and public companies report updated EPS quarterly. These earnings are annualized and projected for the upcoming year (quarterly earnings multiplied by 4). Because Apple's yearly earnings were reported in 2011, its stock has traded in the range of $363 to $705 per share. As of June 30, 2012, the latest quarterly (annualized) EPS for Apple was $9.32 and the stock closed at $584. As of June 30, 2012, therefore, the P/E ratio for Apple was 13.29. You can see by this that P/E ratios fluctuate daily. Certainly, reported earnings play a role in these fluctuations. However, market prices of stocks are based on consensus estimations of what may happen in the future—business cycles, government policies, new product announcements, foreign trade deals, currency fluctuations—even the health of key company executives may significantly impact the estimates. Markets run on sentiment and are very difficult to predict. Some analysts study past trends in P/E multiples and try to estimate future trading ranges. If the P/E multiple of a particular stock drifts towards the low end of a range, and if its projected earnings are increasing, it means that the price of the stock is becoming more attractive, which may be a signal to buy. As P/E multiples drift higher given projected earnings, the stock becomes too expensive, and the analyst would recommend a "hold" or "sell." Would you buy it?

DIVIDEND YIELD. **Dividend yield** is the ratio of dividends per share of stock to the stock's market price. This ratio measures the percentage of a stock's market value returned annually to the shareholders as dividends. Although dividends are never guaranteed, some well-established companies have continued to pay dividends even through turbulent economic times. *Preferred* shareholders pay special attention to this ratio because they invest primarily to receive dividends. However, certain companies, such as TELUS, Bank of Montreal, or Rogers Communications, also pay attractive dividends on their common stock. In periods of low interest rates on certificates of deposit or money-market funds, dividend-paying stocks become more attractive alternatives for conservative investors.

Apple Inc. has never paid dividends (in the technology industry, dividends are rare), but in 2012, Apple announced they would be paying a $2.65 dividend beginning in the fourth quarter of 2012. Annualized, the per-share dividend works out to be $10.60 ($2.65 × 4 quarters). So, Apple's dividend yield on its common stock was as follows:

	Formula	Dividend Yield on Apple Common Stock
		2012
Dividend yield on common stock*	$= \dfrac{\text{Dividend per share of common stock}}{\text{Market price per share of common stock}}$	$\dfrac{\$10.60}{\$584} = 0.018$

*Dividend yields may also be calculated for preferred stock.

An investor who buys Apple common stock for $584 can expect to receive around 1.8% of the investment annually in the form of cash dividends. You might think that's a very low rate, but compared to current yields on certificates of deposit or bonds, it's pretty attractive. Dividend yields vary widely among companies. They are generally higher for older, established firms and lower to nonexistent for young, growth-oriented companies.

BOOK VALUE PER SHARE OF COMMON STOCK. **Book value per share of common stock** is simply common shareholders' equity divided by the number of shares of common stock outstanding. Common equity equals total equity less preferred equity. Apple has no preferred stock outstanding. Calculations of its book value per common share follow. Numbers are based on Exhibits 13.9 and 13-10, using weighted-average number of shares outstanding.

		Book Value Per Share of Apple Inc.	
Formula (figures in thousands)		2011	2010
Book value per common share	$= \dfrac{\text{Total shareholders' equity} - \text{Preferred equity}}{\text{Weighted-average number of common shares outstanding (basic)}}$	$\dfrac{\$76,615,000}{924,258} = \$82.89$	$\dfrac{\$47,791,000}{909,461} = \$52.55$

Book value per share indicates the recorded accounting amount for each share of common stock outstanding. Many experts believe book value is not useful for investment analysis because it bears no relationship to market value and provides little information beyond what's reported on the balance sheet. But some investors base their investment decisions on book value. For example, some investors rank stocks by the ratio of market price per share to book value per share. The lower the ratio, the more attractive the stock. These investors are called "value" investors, as contrasted with "growth" investors, who focus more on trends in net income.

What does the outlook for the future look like for Apple? If the company can stay on the same path it has followed for the past several years, it looks bright. Its earnings per share are solid, and its ROS and ROA lead the industry. ROE for Apple is second to a competitor that is highly leveraged, so in comparison, Apple still looks preferable. From the standpoint of liquidity and leverage, the company is in stellar shape. It has a negative cash conversion cycle, meaning that it sells out inventory and collects cash weeks before accounts payable are due. It has no interest-bearing debt and virtually no long-term debt. The company's recent P/E ratio of 14.4 is relatively low. Beyond that, Apple is one of the most innovative companies in the world, continually putting out personal electronics products that everyone wants. All of these factors make Apple Inc. stock look like a good investment.

The Limitations of Ratio Analysis

Business decisions are made in a world of uncertainty. As useful as ratios are, they aren't a cure-all. Consider a physician's use of a thermometer. A reading of 38.9° Celsius tells a doctor that something is wrong with the patient but doesn't indicate what the problem is or how to cure it.

In financial analysis, a sudden drop in the current ratio signals that *something* is wrong, but it doesn't identify the problem. A manager must analyze the figures to learn what caused the ratio to fall. A drop in current assets may mean a cash shortage or that sales are slow. The manager must evaluate all the ratios in the light of factors such as increased competition or a slowdown in the economy.

Legislation, international affairs, scandals, and other factors can turn profits into losses. To be useful, ratios should be analyzed over a period of years to consider all relevant factors. Any one year, or even any two years, may not represent the company's performance over the long term. The investment decision, whether in stocks, bonds, real estate, cash, or more exotic instruments, depends on one's tolerance for risk, and risk is the one factor that is always a certainty!

Red Flags in Financial Statement Analysis

Recent accounting scandals have highlighted the importance of being alert when analyzing financial statements. Signs of trouble that may raise red flags include:

- **Earnings Problems.** Has income from continuing operations and net income decreased significantly for several years in a row? Has income turned into a loss? This may be okay for a company in a cyclical industry, such as an airline or a home builder, but most companies cannot survive consecutive loss years.

- **Decreased Cash Flow.** Cash flow validates earnings. Is cash flow from operations consistently lower than net income? Are the sales of capital assets a major source of cash? If so, the company may be facing a cash shortage.

- **Too Much Debt.** How does the company's debt ratio compare to that of major competitors and to the industry average? If the debt ratio is much higher than average, the company may be unable to pay debts during tough times.
- **Inability to Collect Receivables.** Are days' sales in receivables growing faster than for other companies in the industry? A cash shortage may be looming.
- **Buildup of Inventories.** Is inventory turnover slowing down? If so, the company may be unable to move products, or it may be overstating inventory. Recall from the cost-of-goods-sold model that one of the easiest ways to overstate net income is to overstate ending inventory.
- **Trends of Sales, Inventory, and Receivables.** Sales, receivables, and inventory generally move together. Increased sales lead to higher receivables and require more inventory to meet demand. Strange movements among these items may spell trouble.

The Decision Guidelines summarize the most widely used ratios.

◄ DECISION GUIDELINES ►

USING RATIOS IN FINANCIAL STATEMENT ANALYSIS

As we have seen in this chapter, ratio analysis is one tool that managers, investors, and creditors use when analyzing a company. How do they determine if a company is able to pay its bills, sell inventory, collect receivables, and so on? They use the standard ratios discussed in this book.

Ratio	Computation	Information Provided
Measuring ability to pay current liabilities:		
Managers must make sure there is enough cash on hand to pay the company's current liabilities.		
Investors know that a company that cannot pay its debts is not a good investment because it could go bankrupt.		
Creditors want to make sure they will be repaid if they loan the company money.		
1. Current ratio	$\dfrac{\text{Current assets}}{\text{Current liabilities}}$	Measures ability to pay current liabilities with current assets
2. Quick (acid-test) ratio	$\dfrac{\text{Cash} + \text{Short-term investments} + \text{Net current receivables}}{\text{Current liabilities}}$	Shows ability to pay all current liabilities if they come due immediately

Ratio	Computation	Information Provided
Measuring turnover and cash conversion:		
Managers need to know if there is too much or too little inventory on hand. This helps them decide how much inventory to buy. They also need to monitor their accounts receivable and accounts payable to ensure that cash is being received soon after sales and bills are being paid in a timely fashion.		
Investors like to see inventory being sold quickly because unsold inventory generates no profit. The time it takes to turn accounts receivable into cash and then use it to pay bills can be used to evaluate the company's liquidity.		
Creditors know that collecting cash soon after the sale enables the company to pay its bills and loans on time.		
3. Inventory turnover and days' inventory outstanding (DIO)	$$\text{Inventory turnover} = \frac{\text{Cost of goods sold}}{\text{Average inventory}}$$ $$\text{Days' inventory outstanding (DIO)} = \frac{365}{\text{Inventory turnover}}$$	Indicates saleability of inventory—the number of times a company sells its average level of inventory during a year
4. Accounts receivable turnover	$$\frac{\text{Net credit sales}}{\text{Average net accounts receivable}}$$	Measures ability to collect cash from credit customers
5. Days' sales in receivables or days' sales outstanding (DSO)	$$\frac{\text{Average net accounts receivable}}{\text{Average daily sales}}$$ or $$\frac{365}{\text{Accounts receivable turnover}}$$	Shows how many days' sales remain in Accounts Receivable—how many days it takes to collect the average level of receivables
6. Payables turnover and days' payable outstanding (DPO)	$$\text{Accounts payable turnover} = \frac{\text{Cost of goods sold}}{\text{Average accounts payable}}$$ $$\text{Days' payable outstanding (DPO)} = \frac{365}{\text{Accounts payable turnover}}$$	Shows how many times a year accounts payable turn over, and how many days it takes the company to pay off accounts payable

Ratio	Computation	Information Provided
7. Cash conversion cycle	Cash conversion cycle = DIO + DSO − DPO where DIO = Days' inventory outstanding DSO = Days' sales outstanding DPO = Days' payable outstanding	Shows overall liquidity by computing the total days it takes to convert inventory to receivables and back to cash, less the days to pay off creditors
Measuring ability to pay long-term debt: *Managers* must make sure they have enough assets on hand to pay the company's debts. *Investors* know that a business may be generating a profit but still be low on cash. They want to be sure they are investing in a company that can pay back its debts. *Creditors* loan the company money with the anticipation of being paid back. If a company is not able to pay its debts as they come due, they could face serious financial difficulty, and even be forced into bankruptcy.		
8. Debt ratio	$$\frac{\text{Total liabilities}}{\text{Total assets}}$$	Indicates percentage of assets financed with debt
9. Times-interest-earned ratio	$$\frac{\text{Income from operations}}{\text{Interest expense}}$$	Measures the number of times operating income can cover interest expense
Measuring profitability: *Managers* are evaluated based on how well a company has performed financially. *Investors* look to see if a company is able to generate a profit, which could mean an increase in the price of their shares. *Creditors* know that a profitable company is able to pay back their debt.		

Ratio	Computation	Information Provided
10. Gross profit %	$$\frac{\text{Gross profit}}{\text{Net sales}}$$	Shows the percentage of profit that a company makes from merely selling the product, before any other operating costs are subtracted
11. Operating income %	$$\frac{\text{Income from operations}}{\text{Net sales}}$$	Shows the percentage of profit earned from each dollar in the company's core business, after operating costs have been subtracted
12. DuPont model	Exhibit 13-11	A detailed analysis of return on assets (ROA) and return on common shareholders' equity (ROE)
13. Return on net sales	$$\frac{\text{Net income}}{\text{Net sales}}$$	Shows the percentage of each sales dollar earned as net income
14. Asset turnover	$$\frac{\text{Net sales}}{\text{Average total assets}}$$	Measures the amount of net sales generated for each dollar invested in assets
15. Return on total assets	Return on total assets (ROA) DuPont method: Return on net sales × Asset turnover or $$\frac{\text{Net income}}{\text{Average total assets}}$$	Measures how profitably a company uses its assets
16. Leverage ratio	$$\frac{\text{Average total assets}}{\text{Average common shareholders' equity}}$$	Otherwise known as the *equity multiplier*, measures the ratio of average total assets to average common shareholders' equity
17. Return on common shareholders' equity	Rate of return on common shareholders' equity (ROE) DuPont method: ROA × Leverage ratio or $$\frac{\text{Net income} - \text{preferred dividends}}{\text{Average common shareholders' equity}}$$	Measures how much income is earned for every dollar invested by the company's common shareholders
18. Earnings per share of common stock	$$\frac{\text{Net income} - \text{Preferred dividends}}{\text{Average number of common shares outstanding}}$$	Measures the amount of net income earned for each share of the company's common stock outstanding

Ratio	Computation	Information Provided
Analyzing shares as an investment:		
Investors purchase shares to earn a return on their investment. This return consists of two parts: (1) gains (or losses) from selling their shares, and (2) dividends (if any). They want to know if the shares are a worthwhile investment.		
19. Price/earnings ratio	$$\frac{\text{Market price per common share}}{\text{Earnings per share}}$$	Indicates the market price of $1 of earnings
20. Dividend yield	$$\frac{\text{Dividend per share of common (or preferred) stock}}{\text{Market price per share of common (or preferred) stock}}$$	Shows the percentage of a stock's market value returned as dividends to stockholders each period
21. Book value per share of common stock	$$\frac{\text{Total shareholders' equity} - \text{Preferred equity}}{\text{Number of shares of common stock outstanding}}$$	Indicates the recorded accounting amount for each share of common stock outstanding

SUMMARY OF CHAPTER 13

LEARNING OBJECTIVE	SUMMARY
1. **Perform** a horizontal analysis of financial statements	A horizontal analysis is used to study percentage changes in financial statement items, such as sales or net income, from year to year. The dollar amount of the change from one period to the next is divided by the base-year amount. A form of horizontal analysis is a trend percentage that shows how something (such as sales or net income, for example) has changed over a period of time.
2. **Perform** a vertical analysis of financial statements	Vertical analysis reveals the relationship of a financial statement item to a specified base. For example, using the income statement, total revenue is usually the base when analyzing income statement relationships.
3. **Prepare** common-size financial statements	A common-size statement reports only percentages (no dollar amounts). For example, on a common-size balance sheet, each item is expressed as a percentage of total assets. A common-size statement eases the comparison of different companies because their amounts are stated as percentages.
4. **Use** the statement of cash flows in decision making	Analyzing a cash flow statement helps to reveal whether or not the company is experiencing cash problems. Generally speaking, a company's main source of cash should come from its operations. If the major source of cash over several periods is from investing (for example, selling property, plant, and equipment), it may signal a cash shortage.
5. **Use** ratios to make business decisions **There are no differences between IFRS and ASPE in this chapter.**	Ratios discussed in this chapter to measure the "well being" of a business include: ability to pay current liabilities, ability to sell inventory and collect receivables, ability to pay long-term debt, profitability, and analysis of shares as an investment. Ratios are an important tool of financial analysis, but should be considered as only one source of information when analyzing a company.

The following financial data are adapted from the annual reports of Lampeer Corporation:

Lampeer Corporation
Four-Year Select Financial Data
Years Ended January 31, 2014, 2013, 2012, and 2011

Operating Results*	2014	2013	2012	2011
Net sales..	$13,848	$13,673	$11,635	$9,054
Cost of goods sold and occupancy expenses,				
excluding depreciation and amortization........	9,704	8,599	6,775	5,318
Interest expense..	109	75	45	46
Income from operations.......................................	338	1,445	1,817	1,333
Net earnings (net loss)...	(8)	877	1,127	824
Cash dividends..	76	75	76	77
Financial Position:				
Merchandise inventory	1,677	1,904	1,462	1,056
Total assets	7,591	7,012	5,189	3,963
Current ratio	1.48:1	0.95:1	1.25:1	1.20:1
Shareholders' equity	3,010	2,928	2,630	1,574
Average number of shares of common stock				
outstanding (in thousands).............................	860	879	895	576

*Dollar amounts are in thousands.

Requirement

1. Compute the following ratios for 2012 through 2014, and evaluate Lampeer's operating results. Are operating results strong or weak? Did they improve or deteriorate during the three-year period? Your analysis will reveal a clear trend.
   a. Inventory turnover (assume occupancy expenses are included in cost of goods sold)
   b. Gross margin (profit) percentage
   c. Operating income (profit) percentage
   d. Return on sales
   e. Asset turnover
   f. Rate of return on assets
   g. Leverage ratio
   h. Return on shareholders' equity
   i. Times-interest-earned ratio
   j. Earnings per share

ANSWER

	2014	2013	2012
a. Inventory turnover	$\dfrac{\$9,704}{(\$1,677 + \$1,904)/2} = 5.4$ times	$\dfrac{\$8,599}{(\$1,904 + \$1,462)/2} = 5.1$ times	$\dfrac{\$6,775}{(\$1,462 + \$1,056)/2} = 5.4$ times
b. Gross profit percentage	$\dfrac{\$13,848 - \$9,704}{\$13,848} = 29.9\%$	$\dfrac{\$13,673 - \$8,599}{\$13,673} = 37.1\%$	$\dfrac{\$11,635 - \$6,775}{\$11,635} = 41.8\%$
c. Operating income percentage	$\dfrac{\$338}{\$13,848} = 2.4\%$	$\dfrac{\$1,445}{\$13,673} = 10.6\%$	$\dfrac{\$1,817}{\$11,635} = 15.6\%$
d. Return on sales	$\dfrac{\$(8)}{\$13,848} = (0.06)\%$	$\dfrac{\$877}{\$13,673} = 6.4\%$	$\dfrac{\$1,127}{\$11,635} = 9.7\%$
e. Asset turnover	$\dfrac{\$13,848}{(\$7,591 + \$7,012)/2} = 1.897$	$\dfrac{\$13,673}{(\$7,012 + \$5,189)/2} = 2.241$	$\dfrac{\$11,635}{(\$5,189 + \$3,963)/2} = 2.543$
f. Rate of return on assets	$(0.06)\% \times 1.897 = (.114\%)$	$6.4\% \times 2.241 = 14.3\%$	$9.7\% \times 2.543 = 24.7\%$
g. Leverage ratio	$\dfrac{\$7,301.50}{(\$3,010 + \$2,928)/2} = 2.459$	$\dfrac{\$6,100.50}{(\$2,928 + \$2,630)/2} = 2.195$	$\dfrac{\$4,576}{(\$2,630 + \$1,574)/2} = 2.176$
h. Return on shareholders' equity	$(.114)\% \times 2.459 = (0.3\%)$	$14.3\% \times 2.195 = 31.4\%$	$24.7\% \times 2.176 = 53.7\%$
i. Times-interest-earned ratio	$\dfrac{\$338}{\$109} = 3.1$ times	$\dfrac{\$1,445}{\$75} = 19.3$ times	$\dfrac{\$1,817}{\$45} = 40.4$ times
j. Earnings per share	$\dfrac{\$(8)}{860} = \$(0.01)$	$\dfrac{\$877}{879} = \$1.00$	$\dfrac{\$1,127}{895} = \$1.26$

Evaluation:

During this period, Lampeer's operating results deteriorated on all these measures except inventory turnover. The gross profit percentage is down sharply, as are the times-interest-earned ratio and all the return measures. From these data it is clear that Lampeer could sell its merchandise, but not at the markups the company enjoyed in the past. The final result, in 2014, was a net loss for the year. This yielded a negative ROA, and because of leverage, an even more negative ROE.

STOP + THINK (13-1)	**ANSWER**
	The most important information in the analysis is the fact that net income decreased by 14%. A further examination of the statements will help	to determine what might have contributed to this decrease.

STOP + THINK (13-2)	**ANSWER**

Net sales	100%	(= $150,000 ÷ $150,000)
Cost of goods sold	40	(= $60,000 ÷ $150,000)
Gross profit	60	(= $90,000 ÷ $150,000)
Operating expense	27	(= $40,000 ÷ $150,000)
Operating income	33	(= $50,000 ÷ $150,000)
Income tax expense	10	(= $15,000 ÷ $150,000)
Net income	23%	(= $35,000 ÷ $150,000)

The company's expenses comprise 77% of net sales (40% + 27% + 10%), leaving 23% net income as a percentage of sales. The lower the expenses, the higher the net income. To determine if this percentage is reasonable, it should be compared with other companies in the same industry.

Review Financial Statement Analysis

QUICK CHECK **(ANSWERS ARE GIVEN ON PAGE 690.)**

Analyze the Donaldson Limited financial statements by answering the questions that follow. Donaldson owns a chain of restaurants.

Donaldson Limited
Consolidated Statement of Income (Adapted)
For the Years Ended December 31, 2014, 2013, and 2012

(in millions, except per share data)	2014	2013	2012
Revenues:			
Sales by company-operated restaurants	$12,795.4	$11,499.6	$11,040.7
Revenues from franchised and affiliated restaurants	4,345.1	3,906.1	3,829.3
Total revenues	17,140.5	15,405.7	14,870.0
Operating Expenses			
Company-operated restaurant expenses			
Food and paper (Cost of goods sold)	4,314.8	3,917.4	3,802.1
Payroll and employee benefits	3,411.4	3,078.2	2,901.2
Occupancy and other operating expenses	3,279.8	2,911.0	2,750.4
Franchised restaurants—occupancy expenses	937.7	840.1	800.2
Selling, general, and administrative expenses	1,833.0	1,712.8	1,661.7
Other operating expense, net	531.6	833.3	257.4
Total operating expenses	14,308.3	13,292.8	12,173.0

Operating income	2,832.2	2,112.9	2,697.0
Interest expense	388.0	374.1	452.4
Gain on sale of subsidiary	—	—	(137.1)
Non-operating expense, net	97.8	76.7	52.0
Income before income taxes and cumulative effect of accounting changes	2,346.4	1,662.1	2,329.7
Income tax expense	838.2	670.0	693.1
Income before cumulative effect of accounting changes	1,508.2	992.1	1,636.6
Cumulative effect of accounting changes, net of tax benefits of $9.4 and $17.6	(36.8)	(98.6)	—
Net income	$ 1,471.4	$ 893.5	$ 1,636.6
Per common share—basic:			
Income before cumulative effect of accounting changes	$ 1.19	$ 0.78	$ 1.27
Cumulative effect of accounting changes	(0.03)	(0.08)	
Net income	$ 1.16	$ 0.70	$ 1.27
Dividends per common share	$ 0.40	$ 0.24	$ 0.23

Donaldson Limited
Consolidated Balance Sheet
For the Years Ended December 31, 2014 and 2013

(in millions, except per share data)	2014	2013
Assets:		
Current assets		
Cash and equivalents	$ 492.8	$ 330.4
Accounts and notes receivable	734.5	855.3
Inventories, at cost	129.4	111.7
Prepaid expenses and other current assets	528.7	418.0
Total current assets	1,885.4	1,715.4
Other assets		
Investments in affiliates	1,089.6	1,037.7
Goodwill, net	1,665.1	1,558.5
Miscellaneous	960.3	1,075.5
Total other assets	3,715.0	3,671.7
Property and equipment		
Property and equipment, at cost	28,740.2	26,218.6
Accumulated depreciation	(8,815.5)	(7,635.2)
Net property and equipment	19,924.7	18,583.4
Total assets	$25,525.1	$23,970.5
Liabilities and Shareholders' Equity:		
Current liabilities		
Accounts payable	$ 577.4	$ 635.8
Income taxes	71.5	16.3
Other taxes	222.0	191.8
Accrued interest	193.1	199.4
Accrued restructuring and restaurant closing costs	115.7	328.5
Accrued payroll and other liabilities	918.1	774.7
Current maturities of long-term debt	388.0	275.8
Total current liabilities	2,485.8	2,422.3
Long-term debt	9,342.5	9,703.6
Other long-term liabilities and non-controlling interests	699.8	560.0
Deferred income taxes	1,015.1	1,003.7
Total liabilities	13,543.2	13,689.6

Shareholders' equity		
Preferred shares authorized—165.0 million shares; issued—none		
Common shares authorized—3.5 billion shares;		
issued—1,261.9 million shares......................................	1,854.1	1,763.9
Retained earnings...	10,763.3	10,118.3
Accumulated other comprehensive income (loss)..............	(635.5)	(1,601.3)
Total shareholders' equity...	11,981.9	10,280.9
Total liabilities and shareholders' equity	$25,525.1	$23,970.5

1. The trend precentage for selling, general, and administrative expenses using 2013 as the base year for Donaldson is
   a. 1.14.
   b. 1.10.
   c. 1.07.
   d. None of the above ($_____)

2. Vertical analysis of Donaldson's income statement for 2013 would show which of the following for selling, general, and administrative expenses?
   a. 1.144
   b. 0.143
   c. 0.107
   d. None of the above ($_____)

3. Which item on Donaldson's income statement has the most favourable trend during 2012–2014?
   a. Total revenues
   b. Net income
   c. Food and paper costs
   d. Payroll and employee benefits

4. On Donaldson's common-size balance sheet for 2014, goodwill would appear as
   a. 0.065.
   b. up by 6.8%.
   c. $1,665.1 million.
   d. 9.7% of total revenues.

5. A good benchmark for Donaldson Limited would be
   a. Whataburger.
   b. Boeing.
   c. Intel.
   d. All of the above

6. Donaldson's inventory turnover for 2014 was
   a. 91 times.
   b. 62 times.
   c. 21 times.
   d. 36 times.

7. Donaldson's acid-test ratio at the end of 2014 was
   a. 1.49.
   b. 0.49.
   c. 0.30.
   d. 0.20.

8. Donaldson's average collection period for accounts and notes receivables for 2014 is
   a. 1 day.
   b. 2 days.
   c. 30 days.
   d. 17 days.

9. Donaldson's total debt position looks
   a. safe.
   b. middle-ground.
   c. risky.
   d. None of the above.

10. Donaldson's return on sales for 2014 was
    a. 13.2%.
    b. $1.16.
    c. 5.9%.
    d. 8.6%.

11. Donaldson's return on shareholders' equity for 2014 was
    a. 13.2%.
    b. 8.6%.
    c. 5.9%.
    d. $1,471.4 million.

12. On June 30, 2014, Donaldson's common shares sold for $26 per share. At that price, how much did investors say $1 of the company's net income was worth?
    a. $1.00
    b. $22.41
    c. $21.85
    d. $26.00

13. Use Donaldson's financial statements and the data in question 12 to compute Donaldson's dividend yield during 2014.
    a. 3.1%
    b. 2.4%
    c. 2.2%
    d. 1.5%

Accounting Vocabulary

accounts receivable turnover Measures a company's ability to collect cash from credit customers. To compute accounts receivable turnover, divide net credit sales by average net accounts receivable. (p. 642)

acid-test ratio Ratio of the sum of cash plus short-term investments plus net current receivables to total current liabilities. Tells whether the entity can pay all its current liabilities if they come due immediately. Also called the *quick ratio*. (p. 641)

asset turnover The dollars of sales generated per dollar of assets invested. Net sales divided by Average total assets. (p. 648)

benchmarking The comparison of a company to a standard set by other companies, with a view towards improvement. (p. 632)

book value per share of common stock Common stockholders' equity divided by the number of shares of common stock outstanding. The recorded amount for each share of common stock outstanding. (p. 652)

cash conversion cycle The number of days it takes to convert cash into inventory, inventory to receivables, and receivables back into cash, after paying off payables. Days inventory outstanding + days sales outstanding – days payables outstanding. (p. 644)

common-size statement A financial statement that reports only percentages (no dollar amounts). (p. 632)

current ratio Current assets divided by current liabilities. Measures a company's ability to pay current liabilities with current assets. (p. 639)

days' sales in receivables Ratio of average net accounts receivable to one day's sales. Indicates how many days' sales remain in Accounts Receivable awaiting collection. Also called the *collection period* and *days sales outstanding*. (p. 643)

debt ratio Ratio of total liabilities to total assets. States the proportion of a company's assets that is financed with debt. (p. 645)

dividend yield Ratio of dividends per share of stock to the stock's market price per share. Tells the percentage of a stock's market value that the company returns to shareholders as dividends. (p. 652)

DuPont analysis Detailed method of analyzing return on common shareholders' equity. Return on sales × Asset turnover × Leverage = Return on average common shareholders' equity. (p. 647)

earnings per share (EPS) Amount of a company's net income earned for each share of its outstanding common stock. (p. 650)

horizontal analysis Study of percentage changes over time through comparative financial statements. (p. 626)

inventory turnover Ratio of cost of goods sold to average inventory. Indicates how rapidly inventory is sold. (p. 642)

leverage Earning more income on borrowed money than the related interest expense, thereby increasing the earnings for the owners of the business. Also called *trading on the equity*. (p. 649)

leverage ratio Ratio of average total assets to average common shareholders' equity. Measures the proportion of average total assets actually owned by the shareholders. (p. 649)

price/earnings ratio (multiple) Ratio of the market price of a common to the company's earnings per share. Measures the value that the stock market places on $1 of a company's earnings. (p. 651)

quick ratio Ratio of the sum of cash plus short-term investments plus net current receivables to total current liabilities. Tells whether the entity can pay all its current liabilities if they come due immediately. Another name for the *acid-test ratio*. (p. 641)

return on assets Net income divided by average total assets. This ratio measures a company's success in using its assets to earn income for the persons who finance the business, and tells whether a company can pay all its current liabilities if they come due immediately. Also called *return on total assets*. (p. 648)

return on common shareholders' equity Net income minus preferred dividends, divided by average common shareholders' equity. A measure of profitability. Also called *return on equity (ROE)*. (p. 649)

return on net sales Ratio of net income to net sales. A measure of profitability. Also called *return on sales*. (p. 648)

times-interest-earned ratio Ratio of income from operations to interest expense. Measures the number of times that operating income can cover interest expense. Also called the *interest-coverage ratio*. (p. 645)

trading on the equity Another name for *leverage*. (p. 650)

trend percentages A form of horizontal analysis that indicates the direction a business is taking. (p. 629)

vertical analysis Analysis of a financial statement that reveals the relationship of each statement item to a specified base, which is the 100% figure. (p. 630)

working capital Current assets minus current liabilities; measures a business's ability to meet its short-term obligations with its current assets. Also called *net working capital*. (p. 638)

Assess Your Progress

MyAccountingLab	Make the grade with MyAccountingLab: The Exercises, Quizzes, and Problems (A set) marked in red can be found on MyAccountingLab. You can practise them as often as you want, and most feature step-by-step guided instructions to help you find the right answer.

SHORT EXERCISES

LEARNING OBJECTIVE ❶

Perform a horizontal analysis of revenues and net income

S13-1 Cannes Corporation reported the following amounts on its 2014 comparative income statement:

(in thousands)	2014	2013	2012
Revenues	$10,889	$10,095	$9,777
Total expenses	5,985	5,604	5,194

Perform a horizontal analysis of revenues and net income—both in dollar amounts and in percentages—for 2014 and 2013.

S13-2 Zoobilee Inc. reported the following sales and net income amounts:

LEARNING OBJECTIVE ❶
Perform a trend analysis of sales and net income

(in thousands)	2014	2013	2012	2011
Sales	$9,180	$8,990	$8,770	$8,550
Net income	520	500	460	400

Show Zoobilee's trend percentages for sales and net income. Use 2011 as the base year.

S13-3 Vision Software Limited reported the following amounts on its balance sheets at December 31, 2014, 2013, and 2012:

LEARNING OBJECTIVE ❷
Perform a vertical analysis to understand a cash shortage

	2014	2013	2012
Cash	$ 6,000	$ 6,000	$ 5,000
Receivables, net	30,000	22,000	19,000
Inventory	148,000	106,000	74,000
Prepaid expenses	2,000	2,000	1,000
Property, plant, and equipment, net	96,000	88,000	87,000
Total assets	$282,000	$224,000	$186,000

Sales and profits are high. Nevertheless, Vision is experiencing a cash shortage. Perform a vertical analysis of Vision Software's assets at the end of years 2014, 2013, and 2012. Use the analysis to explain the reason for the cash shortage.

S13-4 Porterfield Inc. and Beasley Ltd. are competitors. Compare the two companies by converting their condensed income statements to common size.

LEARNING OBJECTIVE ❸
Compare common-size income statements of two companies

(in millions)	Porterfield	Beasley
Net sales	$9,489	$19,536
Cost of goods sold	5,785	14,101
Selling and administrative expenses	2,690	3,846
Interest expense	59	16
Other expense	34	38
Income tax expense	331	597
Net income	$ 590	$ 938

Which company earned more net income? Which company's net income was a higher percentage of its net sales? Which company is more profitable? Explain your answer.

Black Corporation			
	Years ended December 31		
(Dollar amounts in millions)	2014	2013	2012
Consolidated Financial Measures and Ratios			
Operating results			
Net earnings	$ 769	$ 675	$ 656
Per common share	$ 2.73	$ 2.43	$ 2.39
Operating income	1,312	$ 1,239	$ 1,205
Operating margin	4.4%	4.4%	3.9%
Gross profit percentage	22.2%	22.4%	23.4%
Return on net assets	12%	12%	12%
Return on shareholders' equity	13.2%	12.6%	10.9%
Interest coverage	4.2 times	4.2 times	4.2 times
Financial position			
Working capital	$ 1,744	$ 1,061	$ 972
Current assets	$ 6,462	$ 6,092	$ 5,995
Current liabilities	$ 4,718	$ 5,031	$ 5,023

LEARNING OBJECTIVE ❺

Evaluate the trend in a company's current ratio

LEARNING OBJECTIVE ❺

Evaluate a company's quick (acid-test) ratio

S13-5 Examine the financial data of Black Corporation above. Show how to compute Black's current ratio from 2013 to 2014. Is the company's ability to pay its current liabilities improving or deteriorating?

S13-6 Use the Allstott, Inc., balance sheet data below.

1. Compute Allstott, Inc.'s quick (acid-test) ratio at December 31, 2014 and 2013.
2. Use the comparative information from the table on page 667 for Baker, Inc., Colvin Company, and Dunn Companies Limited. Is Allstott's quick (acid-test) ratio for 2014 and 2013 strong, average, or weak in comparison?

Allstott, Inc. Balance Sheets (Adapted) As at December 31, 2014 and 2013				
			Increase (Decrease)	
(dollar amounts in millions)	2014	2013	Amount	Percentage
Assets				
Current assets:				
Cash and cash equivalents	$1,200	$ 900	$ 300	33.3 %
Short-term investments	6	70	(64)	(91.4)
Receivables, net	240	250	(10)	(4.0)
Inventories	96	81	15	18.5
Prepaid expenses and other assets	243	363	(120)	(33.1)
Total current assets	1,785	1,664	121	7.3
Property, plant, and equipment, net	3,611	3,376	235	7.0
Intangible assets	1,011	878	133	15.1
Other assets	828	722	106	14.7
Total assets	$7,235	$6,640	$ 595	9.0 %
Liabilities and Shareholders' Equity				
Current liabilities:				
Accounts payable	$1,000	$ 900	$ 100	11.1 %
Income tax payable	39	61	(22)	(36.1)
Short-term debt	118	111	7	6.3
Other	70	73	(3)	(4.1)
Total current liabilities	1,227	1,145	82	7.2

Long-term debt....................................	3,500	2,944	556	18.9
Other liabilities..................................	1,117	1,036	81	7.8
Total liabilities	5,844	5,125	719	14.0
Shareholders' equity:				
Common shares.................................	2	2	—	—
Retained earnings	1,543	1,689	(146)	(8.6)
Accumulated other comprehensive (loss)	(154)	(176)	22	12.5
Total shareholders' equity	1,391	1,515	(124)	(8.2)
Total liabilities and shareholders' equity..........	$7,235	$6,640	$ 595	9.0 %

Company	Quick (Acid-Test) Ratio
Baker, Inc. (Utility)..	0.71
Calvin Company (Department store)..........................	1.01
Dunn Companies Limited (Grocery store)..................	1.05

S13-7 Use the Allstott 2014 income statement that follows and the balance sheet from exercise S13-6 to compute the following:

LEARNING OBJECTIVE ⑤
Compute and evaluate turnover and the cash conversion cycle

Allstott, Inc.
Statements of Income (Adapted)
Year Ended December 31, 2014 and 2013

(dollar amounts in millions)	2014	2013
Revenues..	$9,500	$9,309
Expenses:		
Food and paper (Cost of goods sold)..	2,509	2,644
Payroll and employee benefits	2,138	2,211
Occupancy and other operating expenses...	2,413	2,375
General and administrative expenses...	1,217	1,148
Interest expense...	184	117
Other expense (income), net	19	(34)
Income before income taxes	1,020	848
Income tax expense...	285	267
Net income..	$ 735	$ 581

a. Allstott's rate of inventory turnover and days inventory outstanding for 2014

b. Days' sales in average receivables (days sales outstanding) during 2014 (round dollar amounts to one decimal place)

c. Accounts payable turnover and days' payables outstanding

d. Length of cash conversion cycle in days

Do these measures look strong or weak? Give the reason for your answer.

S13-8 Use the financial statements of Allstott, Inc., in exercises S13-6 and S13-7.

LEARNING OBJECTIVE ⑤
Measure ability to pay long-term debt

1. Compute the company's debt ratio at December 31, 2014.

2. Compute the company's times-interest-earned ratio for 2014. For operating income, use income before both interest expense and income taxes. You can simply add interest expense back to income before taxes.

3. Is Allstott's ability to pay liabilities and interest expense strong or weak? Comment on the value of each ratio computed for questions 1 and 2.

S13-9 Use the financial statements of Allstott, Inc., in exercises S13-6 and S13-7 to compute the following profitability measures for 2014. Show each computation.
a. Return on sales
b. Asset turnover
c. Return on assets
d. Leverage (equity multiplier) ratio
e. Return on common shareholders' equity
f. Is Allstott, Inc.'s profitability strong, medium, or weak?

S13-10 The annual report of Classic Cars Inc. for the year ended December 31, 2014, included the following items (in thousands):

Preferred shares outstanding, $4; 5,000 issued	$500
Net income	$990
Number of common shares outstanding	200

1. Compute earnings per share (EPS) and the price/earnings ratio for Classic Cars' common shares. Round to the nearest cent. The price of a common share of Classic Cars is $77.60.
2. How much does the stock market say $1 of Classic Cars' net income is worth?

S13-11 A skeleton of Hill Country Florist Limited's income statement appears as follows (amounts in thousands):

Income Statement	
Net sales	$7,278
Cost of goods sold	(a)
Selling expenses	1,510
Administrative expenses	351
Interest expense	(b)
Other expenses	126
Income before taxes	1,042
Income tax expense	(c)
Net income	$ (d)

Use the following ratio data to complete Hill Country Florist's income statement:
a. Inventory turnover was 5 (beginning inventory was $775, ending inventory was $767).
b. Return on sales is 0.12.

S13-12 A skeleton of Hill Country Florist Limited's balance sheet appears as follows (amounts in thousands):

Balance Sheet			
Cash	$ 253	Total current liabilities	$1,164
Receivables	(a)	Long-term debt	(e)
Inventories	555	Other long-term liabilities	826
Prepaid expenses	(b)		
Total current assets	(c)		
Property, plant, and		Common shares	185
equipment, net	(d)	Retained earnings	2,846
Other assets	1,150	Total liabilities and	
Total assets	$6,315	shareholders' equity	$ (f)

Use the following ratio data to complete Hill Country Florist's balance sheet:
a. Debt ratio is 0.52.
b. Current ratio is 1.20.
c. Acid-test ratio is 0.70.

EXERCISES

E13-13 Using the given balance sheet data, what were the dollar amount of change and the percentage of each change in Rocky Mountain Lodge Limited's working capital during 2014 and 2013? Is this trend favourable or unfavourable?

LEARNING OBJECTIVE ❶
Compute year-to-year changes in working capital

Rocky Mountain Lodge Limited	2014	2013	2012
Total current assets...	$326,000	$290,000	$280,000
Total current liabilities...	170,000	167,000	150,000

E13-14 Prepare a horizontal analysis of the comparative income statement of Stamps Music Ltd. Round percentage changes to the nearest one-tenth percent (three decimal places).

LEARNING OBJECTIVE ❶
Prepare a horizontal analysis of an income statement

Stamps Music Ltd. Comparative Income Statement For the Years Ended December 31, 2014 and 2013		
	2014	2013
Total revenue...	$403,000	$430,000
Expenses:		
Cost of goods sold..	$188,000	$202,000
Selling and general expenses.....................................	93,000	90,000
Interest expense..	4,000	10,000
Income tax expense	37,000	42,000
Total expenses	322,000	344,000
Net income..	$ 81,000	$ 86,000

E13-15 Compute trend percentages for Carmel Valley Sales & Service Ltd.'s total revenue and net income for the following five-year period, using year 0 as the base year. Round to the nearest full percent.

LEARNING OBJECTIVE ❶
Compute trend percentages

(in thousands)	Year 4	Year 3	Year 2	Year 1	Year 0
Total revenue..	$1,418	$1,287	$1,106	$1,009	$1,043
Net income..	125	104	93	81	85

Which grew faster during the period, total revenue or net income?

E13-16 Cobra Golf Limited has requested that you perform a vertical analysis of its balance sheet to determine the component percentages of its assets, liabilities, and shareholders' equity.

LEARNING OBJECTIVE ❷
Perform a vertical analysis of a balance sheet

Cobra Golf Limited Balance Sheet As at December 31, 2014	
Assets	
Total current assets..	$ 92,000
Property, plant, and equipment, net..	247,000
Other assets..	35,000
Total assets	$374,000

Liabilities

Total current liabilities	$ 48,000
Long-term debt	108,000
Total liabilities	156,000

Shareholders' Equity

Total shareholders' equity	218,000
Total liabilities and shareholders' equity	$374,000

LEARNING OBJECTIVE ❸

Prepare a common-size income statement

E13-17 Prepare a comparative common-size income statement for Stamps Music Ltd. using the 2014 and 2013 data of exercise E13-14 and rounding percentages to one-tenth percent (three decimal places).

LEARNING OBJECTIVE ❹

Analyze the statement of cash flows

E13-18 Identify any weaknesses revealed by the following statement of cash flows of Holland Marsh Farms Limited.

Holland Marsh Farms Limited
Statement of Cash Flows
For the Current Year

Operating activities:		
Income from operations		$ 42,000
Add (subtract) non-cash items:		
Depreciation	$ 23,000	
Net increase in current assets other than cash	(45,000)	
Net decrease in current liabilities exclusive of short-term debt	(7,000)	(29,000)
Net cash provided by operating activities		13,000
Investing activities:		
Sale of property, plant, and equipment		101,000
Financing activities:		
Issuance of bonds payable	$ 102,000	
Payment of short-term debt	(159,000)	
Payment of long-term debt	(79,000)	
Payment of dividends	(42,000)	
Net cash used for financing activities		(178,000)
Increase (decrease) in cash		$ (64,000)

LEARNING OBJECTIVE ❺

Compute five ratios

E13-19 The financial statements of National News Inc. include the following items:

	Current Year	Preceding Year
Balance Sheet:		
Cash	$ 17,000	$ 22,000
Short-term investments	11,000	26,000
Net receivables	64,000	73,000
Inventory	77,000	71,000
Prepaid expenses	16,000	8,000
Total current assets	$185,000	$200,000
Total current liabilities	$111,000	$ 91,000
Income Statement:		
Net credit sales	$654,000	
Cost of goods sold	327,000	

Requirement

Compute the following ratios for the current year:

a. Current ratio
b. Quick (acid-test) ratio
c. Inventory turnover

d. Accounts receivable turnover
e. Days' sales in receivables

E13-20 Patio Furniture Inc. has asked you to determine whether the company's ability to pay its current liabilities and long-term debts improved or deteriorated during 2014. To answer this question, compute the following ratios for 2014 and 2013.

a. Current ratio
b. Quick (acid-test) ratio

c. Debt ratio
d. Times-interest-earned ratio

LEARNING OBJECTIVE ❺

Analyze the ability to pay current liabilities

Summarize the results of your analysis of the following financial statement data in a written report.

	2014	2013
Cash	$ 61,000	$ 47,000
Short-term investments	28,000	—
Net receivables	142,000	116,000
Inventory	286,000	263,000
Prepaid expenses	11,000	9,000
Total assets	643,000	489,000
Total current liabilities	255,000	221,000
Long-term debt	46,000	52,000
Income from operations	165,000	158,000
Interest expense	40,000	39,000

E13-21 Compute four ratios that measure ability to earn profits for PGI Decor Inc., whose comparative income statement follows:

LEARNING OBJECTIVE ❺

Analyze profitability

PGI Decor Inc.
Comparative Income Statement
For the Years Ended December 31, 2014 and 2013

(in thousands)	2014	2013
Net sales	$174,000	$158,000
Cost of goods sold	93,000	86,000
Gross profit	81,000	72,000
Selling and general expenses	46,000	41,000
Income from operations	35,000	31,000
Interest expense	9,000	10,000
Income before income tax	26,000	21,000
Income tax expense	9,000	8,000
Net income	$ 17,000	$ 13,000

Additional data:

	2014	2013	2012
Total assets	$204,000	$191,000	$171,000
Common shareholders' equity	$ 96,000	$ 89,000	$ 79,000
Preferred dividends	$ 3,000	$ 3,000	$ 0
Average common shares outstanding during the year	21,000	20,000	18,000

Did the company's operating performance improve or deteriorate during 2014?

LEARNING OBJECTIVE ⑤

Evaluate shares as an investment

E13-22 Evaluate the common shares of Phillips Distributing Limited as an investment. Specifically, use the three share ratios to determine whether the common shares increased or decreased in attractiveness during the past year.

	2014	2013
Net income...	$112,000	$ 96,000
Common share dividends..	25,000	20,000
Total shareholders' equity at year-end		
(includes 80,000 common shares)..	580,000	500,000
Preferred shares, $8; 1,000 shares issued.................................	100,000	100,000
Market price per common share at year-end.............................	$ 22.50	$ 16.75

CHALLENGE EXERCISES

LEARNING OBJECTIVE ⑤

Use ratio data to reconstruct a
company's balance sheet

E13-23 The following data (dollar amounts in millions) are taken from the financial statements of Phase 1 Industries Inc.:

Total liabilities..	$11,800
Preferred shares...	$ 0
Total current assets..	$10,200
Accumulated depreciation...	$ 1,400
Debt ratio..	59%
Current ratio..	1.50

Requirement

Complete the following condensed balance sheet. Report amounts to the nearest million dollars.

Current assets..		$?
Property, plant, and equipment	$?	
Less accumulated depreciation	(?)	?
Total assets		$?
Current liabilities..		$?
Long-term liabilities		?
Shareholders' equity		?
Total liabilities and shareholders' equity		$?

LEARNING OBJECTIVE ⑤

Use ratio data to reconstruct a
company's income statement

E13-24 The following data (dollar amounts in millions) are from the financial statements of Provincial Industry Limited:

Average shareholders' equity..	$3,600
Interest expense...	$ 400
Preferred shares...	$ 0
Operating income as a percent of sales	25%
Return on equity	20%
Income tax rate...	40%

Requirement

Complete the following condensed income statement. Report amounts to the nearest million dollars.

Sales	$?
Operating expense	?
Operating income	?
Interest expense	?
Pretax income	?
Income tax expense	?
Net income	$?

QUIZ

Test your understanding of financial statement analysis by answering the following questions. Select the best choice from among the possible answers given. Use the Canada Technology Corporation (CTC) financial statements to answer the questions that follow.

Canada Technology Corporation
Consolidated Statements of Financial Position
(in millions)

	December 31,	
	2014	2013
Assets		
Current assets:		
Cash and cash equivalents	$ 4,317	$ 4,232
Short-term investments	835	406
Accounts receivable, net	3,635	2,586
Inventories	327	306
Other	1,519	1,394
Total current assets	10,633	8,924
Property, plant, and equipment, net	1,517	913
Investments	6,770	5,267
Other non-current assets	391	366
Total assets	$19,311	$15,470
Liabilities and Shareholders' Equity		
Current liabilities:		
Accounts payable	$ 7,316	$ 5,989
Accrued and other	3,580	2,944
Total current liabilities	10,896	8,933
Long-term debt	505	506
Other non-current liabilities	1,630	1,158
Commitments and contingent liabilities	—	—
Total liabilities	13,031	10,597
Shareholders' equity:		
Preferred shares; shares issued: 0	—	—
Common shares; shares authorized: 7,000; shares issued:		
2,556 and 2,579, respectively	284	1,479
Retained earnings	6,131	3,486
Other comprehensive loss	(83)	(33)
Other	(52)	(59)
Total shareholders' equity	6,280	4,873
Total liabilities and shareholders' equity	$19,311	$15,470

Canada Technology Corporation
Consolidated Statements of Income
(in millions, except per share amounts)

	Years Ended December 31,		
	2014	2013	2012
Net revenue...	$41,444	$35,404	$31,168
Cost of goods sold..	33,892	29,055	25,661
Gross profit	7,552	6,349	5,507
Operating expenses:			
Selling, general, and administrative	3,544	3,050	2,784
Research, development, and engineering....................	464	455	452
Special charges	—	—	482
Total operating expenses.....................................	4,008	3,505	3,718
Operating income...	3,544	2,844	1,789
Investment and other income (loss), net.........................	180	183	(58)
Income before income taxes	3,724	3,027	1,731
Income tax expense..	1,079	905	485
Net income...	$ 2,645	$ 2,122	$ 1,246
Earnings per common share:			
Basic...	$ 1.03	$ 0.82	$ 0.48

Q13-25 During 2014, CTC's total assets
a. increased by $8,341 million.   c. Both a and b.
b. increased by 24.8%.   d. increased by 19.9%.

Q13-26 CTC's current ratio at year-end 2014 is closest to
a. 1.2.   c. 1.0.
b. 1.1.   d. 0.8.

Q13-27 CTC's quick (acid-test) ratio at year-end 2014 is closest to
a. 0.80.   c. 0.47.
b. 0.65.   d. $8,787 million.

Q13-28 What is the largest single item included in CTC's debt ratio at December 31, 2014?
a. Cash and cash equivalents   c. Investments
b. Accounts payable   d. Common shares

Q13-29 Using the earliest year available as the base year, the trend percentage for CTC's net revenue during 2014 was
a. 117%.   c. up by 17.1%.
b. up by $10,276 million.   d. 133%.

Q13-30 CTC's common-size income statement for 2014 would report cost of goods sold as
a. $33,892 million.   c. 81.8%.
b. up by 16.6%.   d. 132.1%.

Q13-31 CTC's days' sales in receivables during 2014 was
a. 22 days.   c. 32 days.
b. 27 days.   d. 114 days.

Q13-32 CTC's inventory turnover during fiscal year 2014 was
a. very slow.
b. 54 times.
c. 107 times.
d. 129 times.

Q13-33 CTC's long-term debt bears interest at 6%. During the year ended December 31, 2014, CTC's times-interest-earned ratio was
a. 117 times.
b. 110 times.
c. 100 times.
d. 125 times.

Q13-34 CTC's trend of return on sales is
a. improving.
b. declining.
c. stuck at 6%.
d. worrisome.

Q13-35 How many common shares did CTC have outstanding, on average, during 2014? Hint: Use the earnings per share formula.
a. 2,721 million
b. 2,701 million
c. 2,645 million
d. 2,568 million

Q13-36 Book value per common share of CTC outstanding at December 31, 2014, was
a. $2.72.
b. $4.37.
c. $6,280.
d. $2.46.

PROBLEMS

(Group A)

P13-37A Net sales, net income, and total assets for Aaron Shipping, Inc., for a five-year period follow:

LEARNING OBJECTIVE ❶❺

Compute trend percentages, return on sales, asset turnover, and ROA, and compare with industry

(in thousands)	2014	2013	2012	2011	2010
Net sales	$900	$400	$352	$314	$296
Net income	50	39	46	37	24
Total assets	308	269	252	231	209

Requirements
1. Compute trend percentages for each item for 2011 through 2014. Use 2010 as the base year and round to the nearest percent.
2. Compute the return on net sales for 2012 through 2014, rounding to three decimal places. Explain what this means.
3. Compute asset turnover for 2012 through 2014. Explain what this means.
4. Use DuPont analysis to compute return on average total assets (ROA) for 2012 through 2014.
5. How does Aaron Shipping's return on net sales for 2014 compare with previous years? How does it compare with that of the industry? In the shipping industry, rates above 5% are considered good, and rates above 7% are outstanding.
6. Evaluate Aaron Shipping, Inc.'s ROA for 2014, compared with previous years, and against a 15% benchmark for the industry.

P13-38A Top managers of Medical Products Inc. have asked for your help in comparing the company's profit performance and financial position with the average for the industry. The accountant has given you the company's income statement and balance sheet and also the following data for the industry:

LEARNING OBJECTIVE ❶❺

Prepare common size financial statements and analyze ratios

Medical Products Inc.
Income Statement Compared With Industry Average
For the Year Ended December 31, 2014

	Medical Products	Industry Average
Net sales...	$957,000	100.0%
Cost of goods sold..	652,000	55.9
Gross profit	305,000	44.1
Operating expenses...	200,000	28.1
Operating income..	105,000	16.0
Other expenses..	3,000	2.4
Net income..	$102,000	13.6%

Medical Products Inc.
Balance Sheet Compared With Industry Average
As at December 31, 2014

	Medical Products	Industry Average
Current assets...	$486,000	74.4%
Fixed assets, net	117,000	20.0
Intangible assets, net	24,000	0.6
Other assets...	3,000	5.0
Total..	$630,000	100.0%
Current liabilities...	$245,000	45.6%
Long-term liabilities	114,000	19.0
Shareholders' equity...	271,000	35.4
Total..	$630,000	100.0%

Requirements

1. Prepare a common-size income statement and balance sheet for Medical Products. The first column of each statement should present Medical Products' common-size statement, and the second column should show the industry averages.
2. For the profitability analysis, compute Medical Products' (a) ratio of gross profit to net sales, (b) ratio of operating income to net sales, and (c) ratio of net income to net sales. Compare these figures with the industry average. Is Medical Products' profit performance better or worse than the average for the industry?
3. For the analysis of financial position, compute Medical Products' (a) ratios of current assets and current liabilities to total assets and (b) ratio of shareholders' equity to total assets. Compare these ratios with the industry averages. Is Medical Products' financial position better or worse than the average for the industry?

LEARNING OBJECTIVE ❹

Use the statement of cash flows for decision making

P13-39A You are evaluating two companies as possible investments. The two companies, similar in size, are commuter airlines that fly passengers up and down the West Coast. All other available information has been analyzed and your investment decision depends on the statement of cash flows.

Commonwealth Airlines (Comair) Limited
Statement of Cash Flows
For the Years Ended November 30, 2014 and 2013

	2014	2013
Operating activities:		
Net income (net loss)..	$(67,000)	$154,000
Adjustments for non-cash items:		
Total..	84,000	(23,000)
Net cash provided by operating activities.........	17,000	131,000
Investing activities:		
Purchase of property, plant, and equipment.....	$ (50,000)	$(91,000)
Sale of long-term investments..........................	52,000	4,000
Net cash provided by (used for)		
investing activities	2,000	(87,000)
Financing activities:		
Issuance of short-term notes payable	122,000	143,000
Payment of short-term notes payable...............	(179,000)	(134,000)
Payment of cash dividends	(45,000)	(64,000)
Net cash used for financing activities...............	(102,000)	(55,000)
Increase (decrease) in cash	(83,000)	(11,000)
Cash balance at beginning of year.......................	92,000	103,000
Cash balance at end of year	$ 9,000	$ 92,000

Jetway Inc.
Statement of Cash Flows
For the Years Ended November 30, 2014 and 2013

	2014	2013
Operating activities:		
Net income...	$184,000	$ 131,000
Adjustments for non-cash items:		
Total..	64,000	62,000
Net cash provided by operating activities.........	248,000	193,000
Investing activities:		
Purchase of property, plant, and equipment.....	$(303,000)	$(453,000)
Sale of property, plant, and equipment	46,000	72,000
Net cash used for investing activities	(257,000)	(381,000)
Financing activities:		
Issuance of long-term notes payable	174,000	118,000
Payment of short-term notes payable...............	(66,000)	(18,000)
Net cash provided by financing activities.........	108,000	100,000
Increase (decrease) in cash	99,000	(88,000)
Cash balance at beginning of year.......................	116,000	204,000
Cash balance at end of year	$215,000	$ 116,000

Requirement

Discuss the relative strengths and weaknesses of Comair and Jetway. Conclude your discussion by recommending one of the companies' shares as an investment.

LEARNING OBJECTIVE ❺

Understand the effects of business
transactions on selected ratios

P13-40A Financial statement data of Metro Engineering Limited include the following items:

Cash	$ 47,000	Accounts payable	$142,000
Short-term investments	21,000	Accrued liabilities	50,000
Accounts receivable, net	102,000	Long-term notes payable	146,000
Inventories	274,000	Other long-term liabilities	78,000
Prepaid expenses	15,000	Net income	104,000
Total assets	933,000	Number of common shares	
Short-term notes payable	72,000	outstanding	22,000

Requirements

1. Compute Metro's current ratio, debt ratio, and earnings per share. Use the following format for your answer (use dollar and share amounts in thousands except for EPS):

Requirement 1		
Current ratio	Debt ratio	Earnings per share

2. Compute the three ratios after evaluating the effect of each transaction that follows. Consider each transaction *separately*.
   a. Borrowed $27,000 on a long-term note payable
   b. Issued 10,000 common shares, receiving cash of $108,000
   c. Paid short-term notes payable, $51,000
   d. Purchased merchandise of $48,000 on account, debiting Inventory
   e. Received cash on account, $6,000

   Format your answer as follows:

Requirement 2			
Transaction (letter)	Current ratio	Debt ratio	Earnings per share

LEARNING OBJECTIVE ❺

Use ratios to evaluate a share
investment

P13-41A Comparative financial statement data of Hamden Optical Mart follow:

Hamden Optical Mart
Comparative Income Statement
Years Ended December 31, 2014 and 2013

	2014	2013
Net sales	$687,000	$595,000
Cost of goods sold	375,000	276,000
Gross profit	312,000	319,000
Operating expenses	129,000	142,000
Income from operations	183,000	177,000
Interest expense	37,000	45,000
Income before income tax	146,000	132,000
Income tax expense	36,000	51,000
Net income	$110,000	$ 81,000

Hamden Optical Mart
Comparative Balance Sheet
December 31, 2014 and 2013

	2014	2013	2012*
Current assets:			
Cash..	$ 45,000	$ 49,000	
Current receivables, net.................................	212,000	158,000	$200,000
Inventories..	297,000	281,000	181,000
Prepaid expenses...	4,000	29,000	
Total current assets..................................	558,000	517,000	
Property, plant, and equipment, net................	285,000	277,000	
Total assets..	$843,000	$794,000	700,000
Accounts payable...	150,000	105,000	112,000
Other current liabilities.................................	135,000	188,000	
Total current liabilities..................................	$285,000	$293,000	
Long-term liabilities......................................	243,000	231,000	
Total liabilities..	528,000	524,000	
Common shareholders' equity, no par............	315,000	270,000	199,000
Total liabilities and shareholders' equity..........	$843,000	$794,000	

*Selected 2012 amounts.

Other information:

1. Market price of Hamden common shares: $102.17 at December 31, 2014; and $77.01 at December 31, 2013
2. Average common shares outstanding: 18,000 during 2014 and 17,500 during 2013
3. All sales on credit

Requirements

1. Compute the following ratios for 2014 and 2013:
    a. Current ratio
    b. Quick (acid-test) ratio
    c. Receivables turnover and days' sales outstanding (DSO) (round to the nearest whole day)
    d. Inventory turnover and days' inventory outstanding (DIO) (round to the nearest whole day)
    e. Accounts payable turnover and days' payable outstanding (DPO) (round to the nearest whole day)
    f. Cash conversion cycle (in days)
    g. Times-interest-earned ratio
    h. Return on assets (use DuPont analysis)
    i. Return on common shareholders' equity (use DuPont analysis)
    j. Earnings per share of common shares
    k. Price/earnings ratio
2. Decide whether (a) Hamden's financial position improved or deteriorated during 2014 and (b) the investment attractiveness of Hamden's common shares appears to have increased or decreased.
3. How will what you learned in this problem help you evaluate an investment?

P13-42A Assume that you are considering purchasing shares as an investment. You have narrowed the choice to two Internet firms, Video.com Inc. and On-Line Express Ltd., and have assembled the following data.

LEARNING OBJECTIVE ⑤

Use ratios to decide between two share investments

Selected income statement data for current year:

	Video	Express
Net sales (all on credit)	$603,000	$519,000
Cost of goods sold	454,000	387,000
Income from operations	93,000	72,000
Interest expense	—	12,000
Net income	56,000	38,000

Selected balance sheet and market price data at *end* of current year:

	Video	Express
Current assets:		
Cash	$ 25,000	$ 39,000
Short-term investments	6,000	13,000
Current receivables, net	189,000	164,000
Inventories	211,000	183,000
Prepaid expenses	19,000	15,000
Total current assets	$450,000	$414,000
Total assets	$974,000	$938,000
Total current liabilities	366,000	338,000
Total liabilities	667,000*	691,000*
Preferred shares $4.00 (250 shares)		25,000
Common shares (150,000 shares)	150,000	
(20,000 shares)		100,000
Total shareholders' equity	307,000	247,000
Market price per common share	$ 9.00	$ 47.50

*Includes long-term debt; Video, $-0-; and Express, $350,000

Selected balance sheet data at *beginning* of current year:

	Video	Express
Current receivables, net	$142,000	$193,000
Inventories	209,000	197,000
Total assets	842,000	909,000
Long-term debt	—	303,000
Preferred shares, $4.00 (250 shares)		25,000
Common shares (150,000 shares)	150,000	
(20,000 shares)		100,000
Total shareholders' equity	263,000	215,000

Your strategy is to invest in companies that have low price/earnings ratios but appear to be in good shape financially. Assume that you have analyzed all other factors and that your decision depends on the results of ratio analysis.

Requirement

Compute the following ratios for both companies for the current year and decide which company's shares better fit your investment strategy:

a. Quick (acid-test) ratio

b. Inventory turnover

c. Days' sales in receivables

d. Debt ratio

e. Times-interest-earned ratio

f. Return on equity

g. Earnings per share

h. Price/earnings ratio

P13-43A Take the role of an investment analyst at Merrill Lynch. It is your job to recommend investments for your client. The only information you have is the following ratio values for two companies in the direct mail industry:

LEARNING OBJECTIVE ❺

Analyze a company based on its ratios

Ratio	Fast Mail Ltd.	Message Direct Inc.
Days' sales in receivables	51	43
Inventory turnover	9	7
Gross profit percentage	62%	71%
Net income as a percent of sales	16%	14%
Times interest earned	12	18
Return on equity	29%	36%
Return on assets	19%	14%

Write a report to the Merrill Lynch investment committee. Recommend one company's shares over the other. State the reasons for your recommendation.

(Group B)

P13-44B Net sales, net income, and total assets for Azbell Shipping, Inc., for a five-year period follow:

LEARNING OBJECTIVE ❶❺

Compute trend percentages, return on sales, asset turnover, and ROA, and compare with industry

(in thousands)	2014	2013	2012	2011	2010
Net sales	$700	$618	$325	$309	$299
Net income	41	39	41	34	27
Total assets	300	262	253	223	201

Requirements

1. Compute trend percentages for each item for 2011 through 2014. Use 2010 as the base year and round to the nearest percent.
2. Compute the return on net sales for 2012 through 2014, rounding to three decimal places. Explain what this means.
3. Compute asset turnover for 2012 through 2014. Explain what this means.
4. Use DuPont analysis to compute return on average total assets (ROA) for 2012 through 2014.
5. How does Azbell Shipping's return on net sales compare with previous years? How does it compare with that of the industry? In the shipping industry, rates above 5% are considered good, and rates above 7% are outstanding.
6. Evaluate Azbell Shipping, Inc.'s ROA for 2014, compared with previous years, and against a 15% benchmark for the industry.

P13-45B Pathfinder Inc. has asked you to compare the company's profit performance and financial position with the industry average. The proprietor has given you the company's income statement and balance sheet as well as the industry average data for retailers.

LEARNING OBJECTIVE ❷❸❺

Prepare and evaluate common-size financial statements

Pathfinder Inc.
Income Statement Compared with Industry Average
For the Year Ended December 31, 2014

	Pathfinder	Industry Average
Net sales	$700,000	100.0%
Cost of goods sold	497,000	65.8
Gross profit	203,000	34.2
Operating expenses	163,000	19.7
Operating income	40,000	14.5
Other expenses	3,000	0.4
Net income	$ 37,000	14.1%

Pathfinder Inc.
Balance Sheet Compared with Industry Average
As at December 31, 2014

	Pathfinder	Industry Average
Current assets	$300,000	70.9%
Fixed assets, net	74,000	23.6
Intangible assets, net	4,000	0.8
Other assets	22,000	4.7
Total	$400,000	100.0%
Current liabilities	$206,000	48.1%
Long-term liabilities	64,000	16.6
Shareholders' equity	130,000	35.3
Total	$400,000	100.0%

Requirements

1. Prepare a common-size income statement and a balance sheet for Pathfinder. The first column of each statement should present Pathfinder's common-size statement, and the second column, the industry averages.
2. For the profitability analysis, compute Pathfinder's (a) ratio of gross profit to net sales, (b) ratio of operating income to net sales, and (c) ratio of net income to net sales. Compare these figures with the industry averages. Is Pathfinder's profit performance better or worse than the industry average?
3. For the analysis of financial position, compute Pathfinder's (a) ratio of current assets to total assets, and (b) ratio of shareholders' equity to total assets. Compare these ratios with the industry averages. Is Pathfinder's financial position better or worse than the industry averages?

LEARNING OBJECTIVE ④

Use the statement of cash flows for decision making

P13-46B You have been asked to evaluate two companies as possible investments. The two companies, Norfolk Industries Inc. and Strafford Crystal Limited, are similar in size. Assume that all other available information has been analyzed, and the decision concerning which company's shares to purchase depends on their cash flow data.

Norfolk Industries Inc.
Statement of Cash Flows
For the Years Ended September 30, 2014 and 2013

	2014	2013
Operating activities:		
Net income..	$ 17,000	$ 44,000
Adjustments for non-cash items:		
Total	(14,000)	(4,000)
Net cash provided by operating activities..............	3,000	40,000
Investing activities:		
Purchase of property, plant, and equipment.......... $ (13,000)		$ (3,000)
Sale of property, plant, and equipment 86,000		79,000
Net cash provided by investing activities	73,000	76,000
Financing activities:		
Issuance of short-term notes payable 43,000		19,000
Payment of short-term notes payable................... (101,000)		(108,000)
Net cash used for financing activities...................	(58,000)	(89,000)
Increase in cash..	18,000	27,000
Cash balance at beginning of year...........................	31,000	4,000
Cash balance at end of year	$ 49,000	$ 31,000

Strafford Crystal Limited
Statement of Cash Flows
For the Years Ended September 30, 2014 and 2013

	2014	2013
Operating activities:		
Net income..	$ 89,000	$ 71,000
Adjustments for non-cash items:		
Total	19,000	—
Net cash provided by operating activities..............	108,000	71,000
Investing activities:		
Purchase of property, plant, and equipment.......... $(121,000)		$(91,000)
Net cash used for investing activities	(121,000)	(91,000)
Financing activities:		
Issuance of long-term notes payable 46,000		43,000
Payment of short-term notes payable................... (15,000)		(40,000)
Payment of cash dividends .... (12,000)		(9,000)
Net cash provided by (used for) financing activities...	19,000	(6,000)
Increase (decrease) in cash	6,000	(26,000)
Cash balance at beginning of year...........................	54,000	80,000
Cash balance at end of year	$ 60,000	$ 54,000

Requirement

Discuss the relative strengths and weaknesses of each company. Conclude your discussion by recommending one company's shares as an investment.

P13-47B Financial statement data of HiFlite Electronics Limited include the following items (dollars in thousands):

LEARNING OBJECTIVE

Understand the effects of business transactions on selected ratios

Cash..	$ 22,000
Short-term investments	39,000
Accounts receivable, net	83,000
Inventories	141,000
Prepaid expenses	8,000
Total assets	677,000
Short-term notes payable..	49,000
Accounts payable	103,000
Accrued liabilities...	38,000
Long-term notes payable	160,000
Other long-term liabilities	31,000
Net income..	91,000
Number of common shares outstanding.....................................	40,000

Requirements

1. Compute HiFlite's current ratio, debt ratio, and earnings per share. Use the following format for your answer:

Requirement 1		
Current ratio	**Debt ratio**	**Earnings per share**

2. Compute the three ratios after evaluating the effect of each transaction that follows. Consider each transaction *separately*.
   a. Purchased store supplies of $46,000 on account
   b. Borrowed $125,000 on a long-term note payable
   c. Issued 5,000 common shares, receiving cash of $120,000
   d. Paid short-term notes payable, $32,000
   e. Received cash on account, $19,000

   Format your answer as follows:

Requirement 2			
Transaction (letter)	**Current ratio**	**Debt ratio**	**Earnings per share**

LEARNING OBJECTIVE ❺

Use ratios to evaluate a share investment

P13-48B Comparative financial statement data of Panfield Optical Mart follow:

Panfield Optical Mart
Comparative Income Statement
Years Ended December 31, 2014 and 2013

	2014	2013
Net sales...	$686,000	$592,000
Cost of goods sold..	380,000	281,000
Gross profit	306,000	311,000
Operating expenses	127,000	148,000
Income from operations	179,000	163,000
Interest expense..	30,000	50,000
Income before income tax	149,000	113,000
Income tax expense...	38,000	45,000
Net income..	$111,000	$ 68,000

Panfield Optical Mart
Comparative Balance Sheet
As at December 31, 2014 and 2013

	2014	2013	2012*
Current assets:			
Cash	$ 32,000	$ 82,000	
Current receivables, net	217,000	157,000	$200,000
Inventories	297,000	284,000	188,000
Prepaid expenses	7,000	29,000	
Total current assets	553,000	552,000	
Property, plant, and equipment, net	283,000	271,000	
Total assets	$836,000	$823,000	701,000
Accounts Payable	150,000	105,000	112,000
Other current liabilities	135,000	187,000	
Total current liabilities	$285,000	$292,000	
Long-term liabilities	240,000	233,000	
Total liabilities	525,000	525,000	
Common shareholders' equity, no par	311,000	298,000	199,000
Total liabilities and shareholders' equity	$836,000	$823,000	

*Selected 2012 amounts.

Other information:

1. Market price of Panfield common stock: $94.38 at December 31, 2014; and $85.67 at December 31, 2013

2. Common shares outstanding: 15,000 during 2014 and 10,000 during 2013

3. All sales on credit

Requirements

1. Compute the following ratios for 2014 and 2013:
   a. Current ratio
   b. Quick (acid-test) ratio
   c. Receivables turnover and days' sales outstanding (DSO) (round to nearest whole day)
   d. Inventory turnover and days' inventory outstanding (DIO) (round to nearest whole day)
   e. Accounts payable turnover and days' payable outstanding (DPO) (round to nearest whole day).
   f. Cash conversion cycle (in days)
   g. Times-interest-earned ratio
   h. Return on assets (use DuPont analysis)
   i. Return on common shareholders' equity (use DuPont analysis)
   j. Earnings per share of common stock
   k. Price/earnings ratio

2. Decide whether (a) Panfield's financial position improved or deteriorated during 2014, and (b) the investment attractiveness of Panfield's common stock appears to have increased or decreased.

3. How will what you learned in this problem help you evaluate an investment?

P13-49B Assume that you are purchasing an investment and have decided to invest in a company in the publishing business. You have narrowed the choice to Thrifty Nickel Corp. and The Village Cryer Limited and have assembled the following data.

LEARNING OBJECTIVE ❺

Use ratios to decide between two share investments

Selected income statement data for the current year:

	Thrifty Nickel	Village Cryer
Net sales (all on credit)	$371,000	$497,000
Cost of goods sold	209,000	258,000
Income from operations	79,000	138,000
Interest expense	—	19,000
Net income	48,000	72,000

Selected balance sheet data at *beginning* of the current year:

	Thrifty Nickel	Village Cryer
Current receivables, net	$ 40,000	$ 48,000
Inventories	93,000	88,000
Total assets	259,000	270,000
Long-term debt	—	86,000
Preferred shares: $5.00 (200 shares) issued	—	20,000
Common shares: (10,000 shares)	10,000	
(5,000 shares)		12,500
Total shareholders' equity	118,000	126,000

Selected balance sheet and market price data at *end* of the current year:

	Thrifty Nickel	Village Cryer
Current assets:		
Cash	$ 22,000	$ 19,000
Short-term investments	20,000	18,000
Current receivables, net	42,000	46,000
Inventories	87,000	100,000
Prepaid expenses	2,000	3,000
Total current assets	$173,000	$186,000
Total assets	265,000	328,000
Total current liabilities	108,000	98,000
Total liabilities	108,000*	131,000*
Preferred shares: $5.00 (200 shares)		20,000
Common shares: (10,000 shares)	10,000	
(5,000 shares)		12,500
Total shareholders' equity	157,000	197,000
Market price per share of common share	$ 51	$ 112

*Includes long-term debt: Thrifty Nickel, $-0-; and Village Cryer, $86,000

Your strategy is to invest in companies that have low price/earnings ratios but appear to be in good shape financially. Assume that you have analyzed all other factors and your decision depends on the results of ratio analysis.

Requirement
Compute the following ratios for both companies for the current year, and decide which company's shares better fit your investment strategy:
    a. Quick (acid-test) ratio
    b. Inventory turnover

c. Days' sales in average receivables

d. Debt ratio

e. Times-interest-earned ratio

f. Return on equity

g. Earnings per share

h. Price/earnings ratio

P13-50B Take the role of an investment analyst at RBC Dominion Securities. It is your job to recommend investments for your clients. The only information you have is the following ratio values for two companies in the pharmaceuticals industry:

LEARNING OBJECTIVE ⑤

Analyze a company based on its ratios

Ratio	Pain Free Ltd.	Remedy Inc.
Days' sales in receivables	36	42
Inventory turnover	6	8
Gross profit percentage	49%	51%
Net income as a percent of sales	7.2%	8.3%
Times interest earned	16	9
Return on equity	32.3%	21.5%
Return on assets	12.1%	16.4%

Write a report to your investment committee. Recommend one company's shares over the other's. State the reasons for your recommendation.

Apply Your Knowledge

Decision Cases

Case 1. Assume a major Canadian company had a bad year in 2014, when it suffered a $4.9 billion net loss. The loss pushed most of the return measures into the negative column and the current ratio dropped below 1.0. The company's debt ratio is still only 0.27. Assume top management is pondering ways to improve the company's ratios. In particular, management is considering the following transactions:

LEARNING OBJECTIVE ⑤

Assess the effects of transactions on a company

1. Sell off a segment of the business for $30 million (receiving half in cash and half in the form of a long-term note receivable). Book value of the segment business is $27 million.

2. Borrow $100 million on long-term debt.

3. Repurchase common shares for $500 million cash.

4. Write off one-fourth of goodwill carried on the books at $128 million.

5. Sell advertising at the normal gross profit of 60%. The advertisements run immediately.

6. Purchase trademarks from a competitor, paying $20 million cash and signing a one-year note payable for $80 million.

Requirements

1. Top management wants to know the effects of these transactions (increase, decrease, or no effect) on the following ratios of the company:
   a. Current ratio
   b. Debt ratio
   c. Times-interest-earned ratio
   d. Return on equity
   e. Book value per common share

2. Some of these transactions have an immediately positive effect on the company's financial condition. Some are definitely negative. Others have an effect that cannot be judged as clearly positive or negative. Evaluate each transaction's effect as positive, negative, or unclear.

LEARNING OBJECTIVE ⑤

Analyze the effects of an accounting difference on the ratios

Case 2. Company A uses the first-in, first-out (FIFO) method to account for its inventory, and Company B uses weighted-average cost. Analyze the effect of this difference in accounting methods on the two companies' ratio values. For each ratio discussed in this chapter, indicate which company will have the higher (and the lower) ratio value. Also, identify those ratios that are unaffected by the inventory valuation difference. Ignore the effects of income taxes, and assume inventory costs are increasing. Then, based on your analysis of the ratios, summarize your conclusions as to which company looks better overall.

LEARNING OBJECTIVE ②⑤

Identify action to cut losses and establish profitability

Case 3. Suppose you manage The Runner's Store Inc., a sporting goods store that lost money during the past year. To turn the business around, you must analyze the company and industry data for the current year to learn what is wrong. The company's and industry average data follow:

The Runner's Store Inc.
Common-Size Balance Sheet Data

	Runner's Store	Industry Average
Cash and short-term investments	3.0%	6.8%
Trade receivables, net	15.2	11.0
Inventory	64.2	60.5
Prepaid expenses	1.0	0.0
Total current assets	83.4	78.3
Fixed assets, net	12.6	15.2
Other assets	4.0	6.5
Total assets	100.0%	100.0%
Notes payable, short-term 12%	17.1%	14.0%
Accounts payable	21.1	25.1
Accrued liabilities	7.8	7.9
Total current liabilities	46.0	47.0
Long-term debt, 11%	19.7	16.4
Total liabilities	65.7	63.4
Common shareholders' equity	34.3	36.6
Total liabilities and shareholders' equity	100.0%	100.0%

The Runner's Store Inc.
Common-Size Income Statement Data

	Runner's Store	Industry Average
Net sales	100.0%	100.0%
Cost of sales	(68.2)	(64.8)
Gross profit	3 1.8	35.2
Operating expense	(37.1)	(32.3)
Operating income (loss)	(5.3)	2.9
Interest expense	(5.8)	(1.3)
Other revenue	1.1	0.3
Income (loss) before income tax	(10.0)	1.9
Income tax (expense) saving	4.4	(0.8)
Net income (loss)	(5.6)%	1.1%

Requirement

On the basis of your analysis of these figures, suggest four courses of action The Runner's Store might take to reduce its losses and establish profitable operations. Give your reason for each suggestion.

Ethical Issue

Turnberry Golf Corporation's long-term debt agreements make certain demands on the business. For example, Turnberry may not repurchase common shares in excess of the balance of retained earnings. Also, long-term debt may not exceed shareholders' equity, and the current ratio may not fall below 1.50. If Turnberry fails to meet any of these requirements, the company's lenders have the authority to take over management of the company.

Changes in consumer demand have made it hard for Turnberry to attract customers. Current liabilities have mounted faster than current assets, causing the current ratio to fall to 1.47. Before releasing financial statements, Turnberry management is scrambling to improve the current ratio. The controller points out that an investment can be classified as either long-term or short-term, depending on management's intention. By deciding to convert an investment to cash within one year, Turnberry can classify the investment as short-term: a current asset. On the controller's recommendation, Turnberry's board of directors votes to reclassify long-term investments as short-term.

Requirements

1. What effect will reclassifying the investments have on the current ratio? Is Turnberry's financial position stronger as a result of reclassifying the investments?
2. Shortly after the financial statements are released, sales improve; so, too, does the current ratio. As a result, Turnberry management decides not to sell the investments it had reclassified as short-term. Accordingly, the company reclassifies the investments as long-term. Has management behaved unethically? Give the reasoning underlying your answer.

Focus on Financials

TELUS Corporation

Use the five-year summary of selected financial data for TELUS to answer the following questions.

LEARNING OBJECTIVE ⑤
Measure profitability and analyze shares as an investment

	2011	2010	2009	2008	2007
Net sales.	$10,397	$9,792	$9,606	$9,653	$9,074
Net earnings.	1,215	1,052	1,002	1,128	1,258
Cash from operations.	2,550	2,670	2,904	2,819	3,712
Total assets.	19,931	19,624	19,219	19,160	16,988
Total long-term debt.	8,573	7,745	8,680	8,898	7,350

Requirements

1. Using 2007 as the base year, perform trend analysis of TELUS's selected Financial Highlights for net sales, net earnings, and cash from operations for each year 2007 through 2011.
2. Evaluate TELUS's operating performance during 2007 through 2011. Comment on each item computed.

Focus on Analysis

TELUS Corporation

Use the TELUS financial statements in Appendix A to address the following questions.

LEARNING OBJECTIVE ③
Prepare common-size statements

Requirements

1. During fiscal 2011, TELUS's net earnings increased over 2011. Prepare a common-size income statement for 2011 and 2010.

2. Discuss the results of TELUS based on the common-size income statement.

3. Consider this information from the CFO's letter to investors in the 2011 Annual Report:

> TELUS' long-term strategy of investing in our core network assets to drive data growth in both wireline and wireless has generated significant momentum and positions the Company for continued success. In 2011, we surpassed $10 billion of revenue with higher than expected revenue growth of six per cent and generated earnings per share (EPS) growth of 15 percent due to significant lower financing costs and higher operating income.

Given the common-size income statement prepared in Requirement 2 and the comments made by the CFO's letter to investors, what is the company's outlook for the future?

Group Project

Project 1. Select an industry in which you are interested, and use the leading company in that industry as the benchmark. Then select two other companies in the same industry. For each category of ratios in Exhibit 13-10 on page 640, compute at least two ratios for all three companies. Write a two-page report that compares the two companies with the benchmark company.

Project 2. Select a company and obtain its financial statements. Convert the income statement and the balance sheet to common size, and compare the company you selected to the industry average. Risk Management Association's *Annual Statement Studies*, Dun & Bradstreet's *Industry Norms & Key Business Ratios*, and Prentice Hall's *Almanac of Business and Industrial Financial Ratios* by Leo Troy publish common-size statements for most industries.

Quick Check Answers

1. *c* ($1,833/$1,712.8 = 1.070)
2. *c* ($1,833/$17,140.5 = 0.107)
3. *b* (Net income: $1,471.4 − $893.5 = $577.9; $577.9/$893.5 = Increase of 64.7%)
4. *a* ($1,665.1/$25,525.1 = 0.065)
5. *a*
6. *d* $\left[\dfrac{\$4,314.8}{(\$129.4 + \$111.7)/2}\right] = 35.8 \approx 36$ times
7. *b* [($492.8 + $734.5)/$2,485.8 = 0.49]
8. *d* $\left[\dfrac{(\$734.5 + \$855.3)/2}{\$17,140.5/365}\right] = 16.9 \approx 17$ days
9. *a* (Debt ratio is ($25,525.1 − $11,981.9)/$25,525.1 = 0.53. This debt ratio is lower than the average for most companies, given in the chapter as 0.62.)
10. *d* ($1,471.4/$17,140.5 = 0.086)
11. *a* $\left[\dfrac{\$1,471.4}{(\$11,981 + \$10,280.9)/2}\right] = 0.132$
12. *b* ($26/$1.16 = $22.41)
13. *d* ($0.40/$26.00 = 0.015)

REPORT OF MANAGEMENT ON INTERNAL CONTROL
OVER FINANCIAL REPORTING

Management of TELUS Corporation (TELUS) is responsible for establishing and maintaining adequate internal control over financial reporting and for its assessment of the effectiveness of internal control over financial reporting.

TELUS' Chief Executive Officer (CEO) and Chief Financial Officer (CFO) have assessed the effectiveness of the Company's internal control over financial reporting as of December 31, 2011, in accordance with the criteria established in *Internal Control – Integrated Framework* issued by the Committee of Sponsoring Organizations of the Treadway Commission (COSO). Internal control over financial reporting is a process designed by, or under the supervision of, the Chief Executive Officer and the Executive Vice-President and Chief Financial Officer and effected by the Board of Directors, management and other personnel to provide reasonable assurance regarding the reliability of financial reporting and the preparation of financial statements for external purposes in accordance with generally accepted accounting principles.

Due to its inherent limitations, internal control over financial reporting may not prevent or detect misstatements on a timely basis. Also, projections of any evaluation of the effectiveness of internal control over financial reporting to future periods are subject to the risk that the controls may become inadequate because of changes in conditions, or that the degree of compliance with the policies or procedures may deteriorate.

Based on this assessment, management has determined that the Company's internal control over financial reporting is effective as of December 31, 2011. In connection with this assessment, no material weaknesses in the Company's internal control over financial reporting were identified by management as of December 31, 2011.

Deloitte & Touche LLP, the Company's Independent Registered Chartered Accountants, audited the Company's Consolidated financial statements for the year ended December 31, 2011, and as stated in the Report of Independent Registered Chartered Accountants, they have expressed an unqualified opinion on the effectiveness of the Company's internal control over financial reporting as of December 31, 2011.

Robert G. McFarlane
Executive Vice-President
and Chief Financial Officer
February 23, 2012

Darren Entwistle
President
and Chief Executive Officer
February 23, 2012

CONSOLIDATED STATEMENTS OF INCOME AND OTHER COMPREHENSIVE INCOME

Years ended December 31 (millions except per share amounts)	Note	2011	2010
			(adjusted – Note 25(c))
Operating Revenues			
Service		$ 9,606	$ 9,131
Equipment		719	611
		10,325	9,742
Other operating income	6	72	50
		10,397	9,792
Operating Expenses			
Goods and services purchased		4,726	4,236
Employee benefits expense	7	1,893	1,906
Depreciation		1,331	1,339
Amortization of intangible assets		479	402
		8,429	7,883
Operating Income		1,968	1,909
Financing costs	8	377	522
Income Before Income Taxes		1,591	1,387
Income taxes	9	376	335
Net Income		1,215	1,052
Other Comprehensive Income	10		
Items that may subsequently be reclassified to income			
Change in unrealized fair value of derivatives designated as cash flow hedges		6	54
Foreign currency translation adjustment arising from translating financial statements of foreign operations		4	–
		10	54
Item never subsequently reclassified to income			
Employee defined benefit plans actuarial gains (losses)		(851)	(214)
		(841)	(160)
Comprehensive Income		$ 374	$ 892
Net Income (Loss) Attributable to:			
Common Shares and Non-Voting Shares		$ 1,219	$ 1,048
Non-controlling interests		(4)	4
		$ 1,215	$ 1,052
Total Comprehensive Income (Loss) Attributable to:			
Common Shares and Non-Voting Shares		$ 378	$ 888
Non-controlling interests		(4)	4
		$ 374	$ 892
Net Income Per Common Share and Non-Voting Share	11		
Basic		$ 3.76	$ 3.27
Diluted		$ 3.74	$ 3.27
Dividends Declared Per Common Share and Non-Voting Share	12	$ 2.205	$ 2.000
Total Weighted Average Common Shares and Non-Voting Shares Outstanding			
Basic		324	320
Diluted		326	321

The accompanying notes are an integral part of these consolidated financial statements.

CONSOLIDATED STATEMENTS OF FINANCIAL POSITION

(en millions)	Note	December 31, 2011	December 31, 2010	January 1, 2010
			(adjusted – Note 25(d))	(Note 25(d))
Assets				
Current assets				
Cash and temporary investments, net		$ 46	$ 17	$ 41
Accounts receivable	24(a)	1,428	1,318	1,195
Income and other taxes receivable		66	62	16
Inventories	24(a)	353	283	270
Prepaid expenses		144	113	105
Derivative assets	4(h)	14	4	1
		2,051	1,797	1,628
Non-current assets				
Property, plant and equipment, net	15	7,964	7,831	7,832
Intangible assets, net	16	6,153	6,152	6,166
Goodwill, net	16	3,661	3,572	3,572
Other long-term assets	24(a)	81	235	286
Investments		21	37	41
		17,880	17,827	17,897
		$ 19,931	$ 19,624	$ 19,525
Liabilities and Owners' Equity				
Current liabilities				
Short-term borrowings	18	$ 404	$ 400	$ 500
Accounts payable and accrued liabilities	24(a)	1,419	1,477	1,336
Income and other taxes payable		25	6	174
Dividends payable	12	188	169	150
Advance billings and customer deposits	24(a)	655	658	530
Provisions	19	88	122	299
Current maturities of long-term debt	20	1,066	847	549
Current portion of derivative liabilities	4(h)	–	419	62
		3,845	4,098	3,600
Non-current liabilities				
Provisions	19	122	204	91
Long-term debt	20	5,508	5,209	5,623
Other long-term liabilities	24(a)	1,343	649	1,334
Deferred income taxes		1,600	1,683	1,522
		8,573	7,745	8,570
Liabilities		12,418	11,843	12,170
Owners' equity				
Common Share and Non-Voting Share equity	21	7,513	7,759	7,334
Non-controlling interests		–	22	21
		7,513	7,781	7,355
		$ 19,931	$ 19,624	$ 19,525
Commitments and Contingent Liabilities	22			

The accompanying notes are an integral part of these consolidated financial statements.

Approved by the Directors:

William A. MacKinnon
Director

Brian A. Canfield
Director

CONSOLIDATED STATEMENTS OF CHANGES IN OWNERS' EQUITY

(millions except number of shares)	Note	Common Shares		Non-Voting Shares	
		Number of shares	Share capital	Number of shares	Share capital
Balance as at January 1, 2010		174,819,020	$ 2,216	142,875,516	$ 3,070
Net income		–	–	–	–
Other comprehensive income		–	–	–	–
Dividends	12(a)	–	–	–	–
Dividend Reinvestment and Share Purchase Plan	12(b)				
– Dividends reinvested in shares		–	–	4,091,865	150
– Optional cash payments		–	–	31,565	1
Share option award expense	13	–	–	–	–
Shares issued pursuant to cash exercise of share options	21(b)	96,526	3	372,579	15
Shares issued pursuant to use of share option award net-equity settlement feature	21(b)	–	–	77,061	1
Balance as at December 31, 2010		174,915,546	$ 2,219	147,448,586	$ 3,237
Balance as at January 1, 2011		**174,915,546**	**$ 2,219**	**147,448,586**	**$ 3,237**
Net income		–	–	–	–
Other comprehensive income		–	–	–	–
Dividends	12(a)	–	–	–	–
Dividend Reinvestment and Share Purchase Plan	12(b)				
– Dividends reinvested in shares		–	–	**1,243,679**	**54**
– Optional cash payments		–	–	**5,990**	–
Share option award expense	13	–	–	–	–
Reclassification of subsidiary as held for sale	16(a)	–	–	–	–
Acquisition of subsidiary	16(e)	–	–	–	–
Shares issued pursuant to cash exercise of share options	21(b)	–	–	**812,834**	**44**
Shares issued pursuant to use of share option award net-equity settlement feature	21(b)	–	–	**422,076**	**2**
Balance as at December 31, 2011		**174,915,546**	**$ 2,219**	**149,933,165**	**$ 3,337**

The accompanying notes are an integral part of these consolidated financial statements.

		Common Share and Non-Voting Share equity					
Equity contributed							
Share capital				Accumulated other comprehensive income			
Total	Contributed surplus	Retained earnings			Total	Non-controlling interests	Total
		(adjusted – Note 25)					
$ 5,286	$ 167	$ 1,934	$ (53)		$ 7,334	$ 21	$ 7,355
–	–	1,048	–		1,048	4	1,052
–	–	(214)	54		(160)	–	(160)
–	–	(642)	–		(642)	(3)	(645)
150	–	–	–		150	–	150
1	–	–	–		1	–	1
–	11	–	–		11	–	11
18	(1)	–	–		17	–	17
1	(1)	–	–		–	–	–
$ 5,456	$ 176	$ 2,126	$ 1		$ 7,759	$ 22	$ 7,781
$ 5,456	$ 176	$ 2,126	$ 1		$ 7,759	$ 22	$ 7,781
–	–	1,219	–		1,219	(4)	1,215
–	–	(851)	10		(841)	–	(841)
–	–	(715)	–		(715)	(4)	(719)
54	–	–	–		54	–	54
–	–	–	–		–	–	–
–	9	–	–		9	–	9
–	–	–	–		–	(12)	(12)
–	–	1	–		1	(2)	(1)
44	(17)	–	–		27	–	27
2	(2)	–	–		–	–	–
$ 5,556	$ 166	$ 1,780	$ 11		$ 7,513	$ –	$ 7,513

CONSOLIDATED STATEMENTS OF CASH FLOWS

Years ended December 31 (millions)	Note	2011	2010
			(adjusted – Note 25)
Operating Activities			
Net income		$ 1,215	$ 1,052
Adjustments to reconcile net income to cash provided by operating activities:			
Depreciation and amortization		1,810	1,741
Deferred income taxes		205	217
Share-based compensation	13	(12)	(30)
Net employee defined benefit plans expense	14(b)–(c)	(32)	(9)
Employer contributions to employee defined benefit plans		(298)	(140)
Gain on 51% Transactel (Barbados) Inc. interest re-measured at acquisition-date fair value and subsequent adjustment to contingent consideration	6, 16(e)	(17)	–
Other		(66)	(42)
Net change in non-cash operating working capital	24(b)	(255)	(119)
Cash provided by operating activities		2,550	2,670
Investing Activities			
Capital expenditures	5, 15, 16	(1,847)	(1,721)
Acquisitions and other	16(e)	(110)	–
Proceeds from the sale of property and other assets		4	10
Other		–	4
Net change in non-cash investing working capital		(15)	(24)
Cash used by investing activities		(1,968)	(1,731)
Financing Activities			
Non-Voting Shares issued		24	15
Dividends paid to holders of Common Shares and Non-Voting Shares	12(a)	(642)	(473)
Issuance and repayment of short-term borrowing	18	4	(100)
Long-term debt issued	20, 24(b)	4,068	3,725
Redemptions and repayment of long-term debt	20, 24(b)	(3,946)	(4,119)
Acquisition of additional equity interest in subsidiary from non-controlling interest	16(e)	(51)	–
Dividends paid by a subsidiary to non-controlling interest		(4)	(3)
Other		(6)	(8)
Cash used by financing activities		(553)	(963)
Cash Position			
Increase (decrease) in cash and temporary investments, net		29	(24)
Cash and temporary investments, net, beginning of period		17	41
Cash and temporary investments, net, end of period		$ 46	$ 17
Supplemental Disclosure of Cash Flows			
Interest (paid)	24(b)	$ (378)	$ (479)
Interest received		$ 1	$ 3
Income taxes (inclusive of Investment Tax Credits) (paid), net	9	$ (150)	$ (311)

The accompanying notes are an integral part of these consolidated financial statements.

NOTES TO CONSOLIDATED FINANCIAL STATEMENTS

December 31, 2011

TELUS Corporation was incorporated under the *Company Act* (British Columbia) on October 26, 1998, under the name BCT.TELUS Communications Inc. (BCT). On January 31, 1999, pursuant to a court-approved plan of arrangement under the *Canada Business Corporations Act* among BCT, BC TELECOM Inc. and the former Alberta-based TELUS Corporation (TC), BCT acquired all of the shares of BC TELECOM Inc. and TC in exchange for Common Shares and Non-Voting Shares of BCT, and BC TELECOM Inc. was dissolved. On May 3, 2000, BCT changed its name to TELUS Corporation and in February 2005, TELUS Corporation transitioned under the *Business Corporations Act* (British Columbia), successor to the *Company Act* (British Columbia). TELUS Corporation maintains its registered office at 3777 Kingsway, Burnaby, British Columbia, V5H 3Z7.

TELUS Corporation is one of Canada's largest telecommunications companies providing a wide range of telecommunications services and products incuding wireless, data, Internet protocol, voice and television.

The terms "TELUS" or "Company" are used to mean TELUS Corporation and, where the context of the narrative permits, or requires, its subsidiaries.

1

SUMMARY OF SIGNIFICANT ACCOUNTING PRINCIPLES
Summary review of accounting policies and principles and the methods used
in their application by the Company

The accompanying consolidated financial statements are expressed in Canadian dollars. The generally accepted accounting principles (GAAP) used by TELUS are International Financial Reporting Standards as issued by the International Accounting Standards Board and these consolidated financial statements comply with International Financial Reporting Standards as issued by the International Accounting Standards Board (IFRS-IASB) and Canadian generally accepted accounting principles.

The consolidated financial statements of TELUS for the years ended December 31, 2011 and 2010, were authorized by TELUS's Board of Directors for issue on February 23, 2012.

(a) Consolidation
The consolidated financial statements include the accounts of the Company and all of the Company's subsidiaries, of which the principal one is TELUS Communications Inc. Currently, through the TELUS Communications Company partnership and the TELE-MOBILE COMPANY partnership, TELUS Communications Inc. includes substantially all of the Company's Wireline segment's operations and substantially all of the Wireless segment's operations. With the exception of non-controlling interests in an immaterial subsidiary held for sale, all of the Company's subsidiaries are wholly owned.

The financing arrangements of the Company and all of its subsidiaries do not impose restrictions on inter-corporate dividends.

On a continuing basis, TELUS reviews its corporate organization and effects changes as appropriate so as to enhance its value. This process can, and does, affect which of the Company's subsidiaries are considered principal subsidiaries at any particular point in time.

(b) Use of estimates and judgements
The preparation of financial statements in conformity with generally accepted accounting principles requires management to make estimates, assumptions and judgements that affect: the reported amounts of assets and liabilities at the date of the financial statements;

the disclosure of contingent assets and liabilities at the date of the financial statements; and the reported amounts of revenues and expenses during the reporting period. Actual results could differ from those estimates.

Estimates
Examples of significant estimates and assumptions include:
- the allowance for doubtful accounts;
- the allowance for inventory obsolescence;
- the estimated useful lives of assets;
- the recoverability of tangible assets;
- the recoverability of intangible assets with indefinite lives;
- the recoverability of goodwill;
- the recoverability of long-term investments;
- the amount and composition of income tax assets and income tax liabilities, including the amount of unrecognized tax benefits; and
- certain actuarial and economic assumptions used in determining defined benefit pension costs, accrued pension benefit obligations and pension plan assets.

Judgements
Examples of significant judgements, apart from those involving estimation, include:
- The Company's choice to depreciate and amortize its property, plant, equipment and intangible assets subject to amortization on a straight-line basis as it believes that this method reflects the consumption of resources related to the economic lifespan of those assets better than an accelerated method and is more representative of the economic substance of the underlying use of those assets.
- The Company's view that its spectrum licences granted by Industry Canada will likely be renewed by Industry Canada; that the Company intends to renew them; and that the Company believes it has the financial and operational ability to renew them and, thus, they are deemed to have an indefinite life, as discussed further in Note 16(c).

FINANCIAL STATEMENTS & NOTES: 1

(c) Financial instruments – recognition and measurement*

In respect of the recognition and measurement of financial instruments, the Company has adopted the following policies:

Financial instrument	Fair value through net income[1][2]	Loans and receivables	Available-for-sale[3]	Amortized cost	Part of a cash flow hedging relationship[3]
Measured at amortized cost					
Accounts receivable		X			
Short-term obligations				X	
Accounts payable				X	
Provisions				X	
Long-term debt				X	
Measured at fair value					
Cash and temporary investments	X				
Short-term investments	X				
Long-term investments (not subject to significant influence)[4]			X		
Foreign exchange derivatives	X				X
Share-based compensation derivatives	X				X
Cross currency interest rate swap derivatives					X

(1) Classification includes financial instruments held for trading. Certain qualifying financial instruments that are not required to be classified as held for trading may be classified as held for trading if the Company so chooses.

(2) *Unrealized* changes in the fair values of financial instruments are included in net income.

(3) *Unrealized* changes in the fair values of financial instruments classified as available-for-sale, or the effective portion of *unrealized* changes in the fair values of financial instruments held for hedging, are included in other comprehensive income.

(4) Long-term investments that are not subject to significant influence of the Company are classified as available-for-sale. In respect of investments in securities for which the fair values can be reliably measured, the Company determines the classification on an instrument-by-instrument basis at time of initial recognition.

- Accounts receivable that may be sold to an arm's-length securitization trust are accounted for as loans and receivables. The Company has selected this classification as the benefits that would have been expected to arise from selecting the available-for-sale method were not expected to exceed the costs of selecting and implementing that method.

- Short-term marketable securities investments are accounted for as held for trading and thus are measured at fair value through net income. Long-term investments not subject to significant influence of the Company are accounted for as available-for-sale. The Company has selected these classifications as they better reflect management's investment intentions.

- Derivatives that are part of an established and documented cash flow hedging relationship are accounted for as held for hedging. The Company believes that classification as held for hedging results in a better matching of the change in the fair value of the derivative financial instrument with the risk exposure being hedged.

  Derivatives that are not part of a documented cash flow hedging relationship are accounted for as held for trading and thus are measured at fair value through net income.

- Regular-way purchases or sales (those which require actual delivery of financial assets or financial liabilities) are recognized on the settlement date. The Company has selected this method as the benefits that would have been expected to arise from using the trade date method were not expected to exceed the costs of selecting and implementing that method.

- Transaction costs, other than in respect of held for trading items, are added to the initial fair value of the acquired financial asset or financial liability. The Company has selected this method as it believes that this results in a better matching of the transaction costs with the periods benefiting from the transaction costs.

- In respect of hedges of anticipated transactions, which in the Company's specific instance currently relate to inventory purchase commitments, hedge gains/losses will be included in the cost of the inventory and will be expensed when the inventory is sold. The Company has selected this method as it believes that a better matching with the risk exposure being hedged is achieved.

(d) Hedge accounting

General

The Company applies hedge accounting to the financial instruments used to:

- establish designated currency hedging relationships for its U.S. dollar denominated long-term debt, which matured in fiscal 2011, as set out in Note 4 and further discussed in Note 20(b);

- establish designated currency hedging relationships for certain U.S. dollar denominated future purchase commitments, as set out in Note 4; and

- fix the compensation cost arising from specific grants of restricted stock units, as set out in Note 4 and further discussed in Note 13(c).

Hedge accounting

The purpose of hedge accounting, in respect of the Company's designated hedging relationships, is to ensure that counterbalancing gains and losses are recognized in the same periods. The Company chose to apply hedge accounting, as it believes this is more representative of the economic substance of the underlying transactions.

In order to apply hedge accounting, a high correlation (which indicates effectiveness) is required in the offsetting changes in the values of the financial instruments (the hedging items) used to establish the designated hedging relationships and all, or a part, of the asset, liability or transaction having an identified risk exposure that the Company has taken steps to modify (the hedged items). The Company assesses

*Denotes accounting policy affected in the years ended December 31, 2011 and 2010, by the convergence of Canadian GAAP for publicly accountable enterprises with IFRS-IASB, as discussed further in Note 2 and Note 25.

the anticipated effectiveness of designated hedging relationships at inception and actual effectiveness for each reporting period thereafter. A designated hedging relationship is considered effective by the Company if the following critical terms match between the hedging item and the hedged item: the notional amount of the hedging item and the principal of the hedged item; maturity dates; payment dates; and interest rate index (if, and as, applicable). As set out in Note 4(i), any ineffectiveness, such as would result from a difference between the notional amount of the hedging item and the principal of the hedged item, or from a previously effective designated hedging relationship becoming ineffective, is reflected in the Consolidated Statements of Income and Other Comprehensive Income as Financing costs if in respect of long-term debt, as Goods and services purchased if in respect of U.S. dollar denominated future purchase commitments or as Employee benefits expense if in respect of share-based compensation.

Hedging assets and liabilities

In the application of hedge accounting, an amount (the hedge value) is recorded on the Consolidated Statements of Financial Position in respect of the fair value of the hedging items. The net difference, if any, between the amounts recognized in the determination of net income and the amount necessary to reflect the fair value of the designated cash flow hedging items on the Consolidated Statements of Financial Position is effectively recognized as a component of other comprehensive income, as set out in Note 10.

In the application of hedge accounting to U.S. dollar denominated long-term debt that matured in fiscal 2011, the amount recognized in the determination of net income was the amount that counterbalanced the difference between the Canadian dollar equivalent of the value of the hedged items at the rate of exchange at the statement of financial position date and the Canadian dollar equivalent of the value of the hedged items at the rate of exchange in the hedging items.

In the application of hedge accounting to the compensation cost arising from share-based compensation, the amount recognized in the determination of net income is the amount that counterbalances the difference between the quoted market price of the Company's Non-Voting Shares at the statement of financial position date and the price of the Company's Non-Voting Shares in the hedging items.

(e) Revenue recognition

General

The Company earns the majority of its revenue (wireless network, data (including television, Internet, data and information technology managed services), voice local and voice long distance) from access to, and usage of, the Company's telecommunications infrastructure. The majority of the balance of the Company's revenue (other and wireless equipment) arises from providing services and products facilitating access to, and usage of, the Company's telecommunications infrastructure.

The Company offers complete and integrated solutions to meet its customers' needs. These solutions may involve the delivery of multiple services and products occurring at different points in time and/or over different periods of time. As appropriate, these multiple element arrangements are separated into their component accounting units, consideration is measured and allocated amongst the accounting units based upon their relative fair values (derived using Company-specific objective evidence) and then the Company's relevant revenue recognition policies are applied to the accounting units. A limitation cap restricts the consideration allocated to services or products currently transferred in multiple element arrangements to an amount that is not contingent upon the delivery of additional items or meeting other specified performance conditions. The Company's view is that the limitation cap results in a faithful depiction of the transfer of services and products as it reflects the telecommunications industry's generally accepted understanding of the transfer of services and products as well as reflecting the related cash flows.

Multiple contracts with a single customer are normally accounted for as separate arrangements. In instances where multiple contracts are entered into with a customer in a short period of time, they are reviewed as a group to ensure that, as with multiple element arrangements, relative fair values are appropriate.

Lease accounting is applied to an accounting unit if it conveys the right to use a specific asset to a customer but does not convey the risks and/or benefits of ownership.

The Company's revenues are recorded net of any value-added, sales and/or use taxes billed to the customer concurrent with a revenue-producing transaction.

When the Company receives no identifiable, separable benefit for consideration given to a customer (e.g. discounts and rebates), the consideration is recorded as a reduction of revenue rather than as an expense.

Voice local, voice long distance, data and wireless network

The Company recognizes revenues on the accrual basis and includes an estimate of revenues earned but unbilled. Wireline and wireless service revenues are recognized based upon access to, and usage of, the Company's telecommunications infrastructure and upon contract fees.

Advance billings are recorded when billing occurs prior to rendering the associated service; such advance billings are recognized as revenue in the period in which the services are provided. Similarly, and as appropriate, upfront customer activation and connection fees are deferred and recognized over the average expected term of the customer relationship.

The Company follows the liability method of accounting for its quality of service rate rebate amounts that arise from the jurisdiction of the Canadian Radio-television and Telecommunications Commission (CRTC).

The CRTC has established a portable subsidy mechanism to subsidize local exchange carriers, such as the Company, that provide residential basic telephone service to high cost serving areas. The CRTC has determined the per network access line/per band portable subsidy rate for all local exchange carriers. The Company recognizes the portable subsidy on an accrual basis by applying the subsidy rate to the number of residential network access lines it has in high cost serving areas, as further discussed in Note 6. Differences, if any, between interim and final subsidy rates set by the CRTC are accounted for as a change in estimate in the period in which the CRTC finalizes the subsidy rate.

Other and wireless equipment

The Company recognizes product revenues, including wireless handsets sold to re-sellers and customer premises equipment, when the products are delivered and accepted by the end-user customers. Revenues from operating leases of equipment are recognized on a systematic and rational basis (normally a straight-line basis) over the term of the lease.

Non-high cost serving area deferral account

On May 30, 2002, and on July 31, 2002, the CRTC issued Decision 2002-34 and Decision 2002-43, respectively, pronouncements that affected regulated services in the Company's Wireline segment. In an effort to foster competition for residential basic service in non-high cost serving areas, the concept of a deferral account mechanism was introduced by the CRTC, as an alternative to mandating price reductions.

The deferral account arises from the CRTC requiring the Company to defer the statement of income recognition of a portion of the monies received in respect of residential basic services provided to non-high cost serving areas. The Company has adopted the liability method of accounting for the deferral account. This resulted in the Company recording incremental liability amounts, subject to reductions for the mitigating activities, during the Decisions' initial four-year periods. The deferral account balance also reflects an interest expense component based on the Company's applicable short-term cost of borrowing, such expense being included in the Consolidated Statements of Income and Other Comprehensive Income as Financing costs.

The Company discharges the deferral account liability by undertaking qualifying actions including providing broadband services to rural and remote communities, enhancing the accessibility to telecommunications services for individuals with disabilities and providing customer rebates for the balance. The Company recognizes the drawdown and amortization (over a period no longer than three years) of a proportionate share of the deferral account as qualifying actions are completed; such amortization is included in Other operating income.

(f) Government assistance*

The Company recognizes government assistance on an accrual basis as the subsidized services are provided or as the subsidized costs are incurred. As set out in Note 6, government assistance is included in the Consolidated Statements of Income and Other Comprehensive Income as Other operating income.

(g) Cost of acquisition and advertising costs

Costs of acquiring customers, that are expensed as incurred, include the total cost of hardware sold to customers, commissions, advertising and promotion related to the initial customer acquisition. Costs of acquiring customers, that are capitalized as incurred, include Company-owned hardware situated at customers' premises and associated installation costs. Costs of acquisition that are expensed are included in the Consolidated Statements of Income and Other Comprehensive Income as a component of Goods and services purchased except for commissions paid to Company employees, which are included as Employee benefits expense. Costs of advertising production, advertising airtime and advertising space are expensed as incurred.

(h) Research and development

Research and development costs are expensed except in cases where development costs meet certain identifiable criteria for capitalization. Capitalized development costs are amortized over the life of the commercial production, or in the case of serviceable property, plant and equipment, are included in the appropriate property group and are depreciated over its estimated useful life.

(i) Leases

Leases are classified as finance or operating depending upon the terms and conditions of the contracts.

Where the Company is the lessee, asset values recorded under finance leases are amortized on a straight-line basis over the period of expected use. Obligations recorded under finance leases are reduced by lease payments net of imputed interest.

For the year ended December 31, 2011, real estate and vehicle operating lease expenses, which are net of the amortization of the deferred gain on the sale-leaseback of buildings, were $250 million (2010 – $266 million (adjusted – Note 25(c))); of these amounts, less than $1 million (2010 – less than $1 million) was in respect of real estate leased from the Company's pension plans, as discussed further in Note 14(b). The unamortized balances of the deferred gains on the sale-leaseback of buildings are set out in Note 24(a).

(j) Depreciation, amortization and impairment*

Depreciation and amortization

Assets are depreciated on a straight-line basis over their estimated useful lives as determined by a continuing program of asset life studies. Depreciation includes amortization of assets under finance leases and amortization of leasehold improvements. Leasehold improvements are normally amortized over the lesser of their expected average service life or the term of the lease. Intangible assets with finite lives (intangible assets subject to amortization) are amortized on a straight-line basis over their estimated lives; estimated lives are reviewed at least annually and are adjusted as appropriate.

Estimated useful lives for the majority of the Company's property, plant and equipment subject to depreciation are as follows:

	Estimated useful lives[1]
Network assets	
Outside plant	17 to 40 years
Inside plant	4 to 16 years
Wireless site equipment	6.5 to 8 years
Balance of depreciable property, plant and equipment	3 to 40 years

(1) The composite depreciation rate for the year ended December 31, 2011, was 5.0% (2010 – 5.1%). The rate is calculated by dividing depreciation expense by an average gross book value of depreciable assets for the reporting period. One result of this methodology is that the composite depreciation rate will be lower in a period that has a higher proportion of fully depreciated assets remaining in use (Note 15).

Estimated useful lives for the majority of the Company's intangible assets subject to amortization are as follows:

	Estimated useful lives
Wireline subscriber base	40 years
Customer contracts, related customer relationships and leasehold interests	6 to 10 years
Software	3 to 5 years
Access to rights-of-way and other	8 to 30 years

Impairment – general

Impairment testing compares the carrying values of the assets or cash-generating units being tested with their recoverable amounts (recoverable amounts being the greater of the assets' or cash-generating units' values in use or their fair values less costs to sell). Impairment losses are immediately recognized to the extent that the asset or cash-generating unit carrying values exceed their recoverable amounts. Should the recoverable amounts for previously impaired assets or cash-generating units subsequently increase, the impairment losses previously recognized (other than in respect of goodwill) may be reversed to the extent that the reversal is not a result of "unwinding of the discount" and that the resulting carrying value does not exceed the carrying value that would have been the result if no impairment losses had been previously recognized.

*Denotes accounting policy affected in the years ended December 31, 2011 and 2010, by the convergence of Canadian GAAP for publicly accountable enterprises with IFRS-IASB, as discussed further in Note 2 and Note 25.

Impairment – property, plant and equipment; intangible assets subject to amortization

The continuing program of asset life studies considers such items as timing of technological obsolescence, competitive pressures and future infrastructure utilization plans; such considerations could also indicate that carrying values of assets may not be recoverable. If the carrying values of assets were not considered recoverable, an impairment loss would be recorded.

Impairment – intangible assets with indefinite lives; goodwill

The carrying values of intangible assets with indefinite lives and goodwill are periodically tested for impairment. The frequency of the impairment tests generally is the reciprocal of the stability of the relevant events and circumstances, but intangible assets with indefinite lives and goodwill must, at a minimum, be tested annually; the Company has selected December as its annual test time.

The Company assesses its intangible assets with indefinite lives by comparing the recoverable amounts of the cash-generating units to the carrying amounts of its cash-generating units (including the intangible assets with indefinite lives allocated to the cash-generating unit, but excluding any goodwill allocated to the cash-generating unit). To the extent that the carrying values of the cash-generating units (including the intangible assets with indefinite lives allocated to the cash-generating unit, but excluding any goodwill allocated to the cash-generating unit) exceed their recoverable amounts, the excess would reduce the carrying value of intangible assets with indefinite lives.

Subsequent to assessing its intangible assets with indefinite lives, the Company then assesses its goodwill by comparing the recoverable amounts of the cash-generating units to the carrying amounts of its cash-generating units (including the intangible assets with indefinite lives and the goodwill allocated to the cash-generating unit). To the extent that the carrying values of the cash-generating units (including the intangible assets with indefinite lives and the goodwill allocated to the cash-generating unit) exceed their recoverable amounts, the excess would first reduce the carrying value of goodwill and any remainder would reduce the carrying value of the assets of the cash-generating unit on a pro-rated basis.

The Company has determined that its current cash-generating units are its reportable segments, Wireless and Wireline, as the reportable segments are the smallest identifiable groups of assets that generate net cash inflows that are largely independent of each other.

(k) Translation of foreign currencies

Trade transactions completed in foreign currencies are translated into Canadian dollars at the rates prevailing at the time of the transactions. Monetary assets and liabilities denominated in foreign currencies are translated into Canadian dollars at the rate of exchange in effect at the statement of financial position date with any resulting gain or loss being included in the Consolidated Statements of Income and Other Comprehensive Income as a component of Financing costs, as set out in Note 8. Hedge accounting is applied in specific instances as further discussed in Note 1(d).

The Company has minor foreign subsidiaries that do not have the Canadian dollar as their functional currency. Accordingly, foreign exchange gains and losses arising from the translation of the minor foreign subsidiaries' accounts into Canadian dollars are reported as a component of other comprehensive income, as set out in Note 10.

(l) Income taxes*

The Company follows the liability method of accounting for income taxes. Under this method, current income taxes are recognized for the estimated income taxes payable for the current year. Deferred income tax assets and liabilities are recognized for temporary differences between the tax and accounting bases of assets and liabilities, as well as for the benefit of losses and Investment Tax Credits available to be carried forward to future years for tax purposes that are more likely than not to be realized. The amounts recognized in respect of deferred income tax assets and liabilities are based upon the expected timing of the reversal of temporary differences or usage of tax losses and application of the substantively enacted tax rates at the time of reversal or usage.

The Company accounts for changes in substantively enacted tax rates affecting deferred income tax assets and liabilities in full in the period in which the changes were substantively enacted; the Company has selected this method as its emphasis on the statement of financial position is more consistent with the liability method of accounting for income taxes. The Company accounts for changes in the estimates of prior year(s) tax balances as estimate revisions in the period in which the changes in estimate arose; the Company has selected this method as its emphasis on the statement of financial position is more consistent with the liability method of accounting for income taxes.

The operations of the Company are complex and the related tax interpretations, regulations and legislation are continually changing. As a result, there are usually some tax matters in question that result in uncertain tax positions. The Company only recognizes the income tax benefit of an uncertain tax position when it is more likely than not that the ultimate determination of the tax treatment of the position will result in that benefit being realized. The Company accrues for interest charges on current tax liabilities that have not been funded, which would include interest and penalties arising from uncertain tax positions. The Company includes such charges in the Consolidated Statements of Income and Other Comprehensive Income as a component of Financing costs.

The Company's research and development activities may be eligible to earn Investment Tax Credits; the determination of eligibility is a complex matter. The Company only recognizes Investment Tax Credits when there is reasonable assurance that the ultimate determination of the eligibility of the Company's research and development activities will result in the Investment Tax Credits being received. When there is reasonable assurance that the Investment Tax Credits will be received, they are accounted for using the cost reduction method whereby such credits are deducted from the expenditures or assets to which they relate, as set out in Note 9.

(m) Share-based compensation

For share option awards granted after 2001, a fair value is determined for share option awards at the date of grant and that fair value is recognized in the financial statements. Proceeds arising from the exercise of share option awards are credited to share capital, as are the recognized grant-date fair values of the exercised share option awards.

Share option awards which have a net-equity settlement feature, as set out in Note 13(b), and which do *not* also have a net-cash settlement feature, are accounted for as equity instruments. The Company has selected the equity instrument fair value method of accounting for the net-equity settlement feature as it is consistent with the accounting treatment afforded to the associated share option awards.

*Denotes accounting policy affected in the years ended December 31, 2011 and 2010, by the convergence of Canadian GAAP for publicly accountable enterprises with IFRS-IASB, as discussed further in Note 2 and Note 25.

Share option awards which have a net-cash settlement feature, as set out in Note 13(b), are accounted for as liability instruments. If share option awards which have the net-cash settlement feature and which were granted subsequent to 2001 were to be settled using other than the net-cash settlement feature, they would be accounted for as equity instruments.

In respect of restricted stock units, as set out in Note 13(c), the Company accrues a liability equal to the product of the vesting restricted stock units multiplied by the fair market value of the corresponding shares at the end of the reporting period (unless hedge accounting is applied, as set out in Note 1(d)). The expense for restricted stock units that do not ultimately vest is reversed against the expense that had been previously recorded in their respect.

When share-based compensation vests in its entirety at one future point in time (cliff vesting), the expense is recognized by the Company on a straight-line basis over the vesting period. When share-based compensation vests in tranches (graded vesting), the expense is recognized by the Company using the accelerated expense attribution method. An estimate of forfeitures during the vesting period is made at the date of grant; such estimate is adjusted for actual experience.

(n) Employee future benefit plans*

Defined benefit plans

The Company accrues for its obligations under employee defined benefit plans, and the related costs, net of plan assets. The cost of pensions and other retirement benefits earned by employees is actuarially determined using the projected benefit method pro-rated on service and management's best estimate of expected plan investment performance, salary escalation and retirement ages of employees. For the purpose of calculating the expected return on plan assets, those assets are valued at fair value. Actuarial gains (losses) arising subsequent to, or on, January 1, 2010, the date of the Company's transition to IFRS-IASB, are recognized in other comprehensive income in the period in which they arise as the Company believes that this better reflects the long-term nature of employee future benefits. See Note 2(b) for significant amendments to the employee benefits accounting standard which are not yet effective and have not yet been applied.

As discussed further in Note 25, unamortized actuarial gains (losses), past service costs and transitional assets (obligations) at January 1, 2010, were recognized directly in retained earnings at the transition date to, and as permitted by, IFRS-IASB.

On an annual basis, at a minimum, the defined benefit plan key assumptions are assessed and revised as appropriate. When the defined benefit plan key assumptions fluctuate significantly relative to their immediately preceding year-end values, actuarial gains (losses) arising from such significant fluctuations are recognized on an interim basis.

Defined contribution plans

The Company uses defined contribution accounting for the Telecommunication Workers Pension Plan and the British Columbia Public Service Pension Plan that cover certain of the Company's employees, both of which provide defined benefits to their members. In the absence of any regulations governing the calculation of the share of the underlying financial position and plan performance attributable to each employer-participant, and in the absence of contractual agreements between the plans and the employer-participants related to the financing of any shortfall (or distribution of any surplus), these plans are treated by the Company as defined contribution plans in accordance with International Accounting Standard 19, *Employee Benefits*.

(o) Cash and temporary investments, net

Cash and temporary investments, which may include investments in money market instruments that are purchased three months or less from maturity, are presented net of outstanding items including cheques written but not cleared by the bank as at the statement of financial position date. Cash and temporary investments, net, are classified as a liability on the statement of financial position when the amount of the cheques written but not cleared by the bank exceeds the amount of cash and temporary investments. When cash and temporary investments, net, are classified as a liability, they may also include overdraft amounts drawn on the Company's bilateral bank facilities, which revolve daily and are discussed further in Note 17.

(p) Sales of trade receivables*

Sales of trade receivables in securitization transactions are recognized as collateralized short-term borrowings and thus do not result in the Company's derecognition of the trade receivables sold.

(q) Inventories

The Company's inventory consists primarily of wireless handsets, parts and accessories and telecommunications equipment held for resale. Inventories are valued at the lower of cost and net realizable value, with cost being determined on an average cost basis. Previous write-downs to net realizable value are reversed if there is a subsequent increase in the value of the related inventories.

(r) Property, plant and equipment; intangible assets*

General

Property, plant and equipment and intangible assets are recorded at historical cost and, with respect to self-constructed property, plant and equipment, include materials, direct labour and applicable overhead costs. With respect to internally developed, internal-use software, recorded historical costs include materials, direct labour and direct labour-related costs. Where property, plant and equipment construction projects are of a sufficient size and duration, an amount is capitalized for the cost of funds used to finance construction. The rate for calculating the capitalized financing costs is based on the Company's weighted-average cost of borrowing experienced during the reporting period.

When property, plant and/or equipment are sold by the Company, the net book value is netted against the sale proceeds and the difference, as set out in Note 6, is included in the Consolidated Statements of Income and Other Comprehensive Income as Other operating income.

Asset retirement obligations

Provisions for liabilities, as set out in Note 19, are recognized for statutory, contractual or legal obligations, normally when incurred, associated with the retirement of property, plant and equipment (primarily certain items of outside plant and wireless site equipment) when those obligations result from the acquisition, construction, development and/or normal operation of the assets. The obligations are measured initially at fair value, determined using present value methodology, and the resulting costs are capitalized into the carrying amount of the related asset. In subsequent periods, the liability is adjusted for the accretion of discount, for any changes in the market-based discount rate and

*Denotes accounting policy affected in the years ended December 31, 2011 and 2010, by the convergence of Canadian GAAP for publicly accountable enterprises with IFRS-IASB, as discussed further in Note 2 and Note 25.

for any changes in the amount or timing of the underlying future cash flows. The capitalized asset retirement cost is depreciated on the same basis as the related asset and the discount accretion, as set out in Note 8, is included in the Consolidated Statements of Income and Other Comprehensive Income as a component of Financing costs.

(s) Investments

The Company accounts for its investments in companies over which it has significant influence using the equity basis of accounting whereby the investments are initially recorded at cost and subsequently adjusted to recognize the Company's share of earnings or losses of the investee companies and dividends received. The excess of the cost of equity investments over the underlying book value at the date of acquisition, except for goodwill, is amortized over the estimated useful lives of the underlying assets to which it is attributed.

The Company accounts for its other investments as available-for-sale at their fair values unless the investment securities do not have quoted market prices in an active market, in which case the Company uses the cost basis of accounting whereby the investments are initially recorded at cost and earnings from such investments are recognized only to the extent received or receivable. The cost of investments sold or amounts reclassified out of other comprehensive income into earnings are determined on a specific identification basis.

Unless there is an other than temporary decline in the value of an available-for-sale investment, the carrying values of available-for-sale investments are adjusted to estimated fair values with such adjustment being included in the Consolidated Statements of Income and Other Comprehensive Income as a component of other comprehensive income. When there is an other than temporary decline in the value of an investment, the carrying values of investments accounted for using the equity, available-for-sale and cost methods are reduced to estimated fair values with any such reduction being included in the Consolidated Statements of Income and Other Comprehensive Income as Other operating income.

6 OTHER OPERATING INCOME
Summary schedule and review of items comprising other operating income

Years ended December 31 (millions)	2011	2010
Government assistance, including deferral account amortization (Note 1(e))	$ 54	$ 48
Investment income (loss)	(2)	(2)
Gain on disposal of assets	3	4
Gain on 51% Transactel (Barbados) Inc. interest re-measured at acquisition-date fair value and subsequent adjustment to contingent consideration (Notes 16(e), 19(a))	17	–
	$ 72	$ 50

The Company receives government assistance, as defined by IFRS-IASB, from a number of sources and includes such receipts in Other operating income.

CRTC portable subsidy

Local exchange carriers' costs of providing the level of residential basic telephone services that the CRTC requires to be provided in high cost serving areas are more than the CRTC allows the local exchange carriers to charge for the level of service. To ameliorate the situation, the CRTC directs the collection of contribution payments, in a central fund, from all registered Canadian telecommunications service providers (including voice, data and wireless service providers) that are then disbursed to incumbent local exchange carriers as portable subsidy payments to subsidize the costs of providing residential basic telephone services in non-forborne high cost serving areas. The portable subsidy payments are paid based upon a total subsidy requirement calculated on a per network access line/per band subsidy rate. For the year ended December 31, 2011, the Company's portable subsidy receipts were $32 million (2010 – $37 million).

The CRTC currently determines, at a national level, the total annual contribution requirement necessary to pay the portable subsidies and then collects contribution payments from the Canadian telecommunications service providers, calculated as a percentage of their CRTC-defined telecommunications service revenue. The final contribution expense rate for 2011 was 0.66% and the interim rate for 2012 has been similarly set at 0.66%. For the year ended December 31, 2011, the Company's contributions to the central fund, which are accounted for as goods and services purchased, were $40 million (2010 – $46 million).

Government of Québec

Salaries for qualifying employment positions in the province of Quebec, mainly in the information technology sector, are eligible for tax credits. In respect of such tax credits, for the year ended December 31, 2011, the Company recorded $14 million (2010 – $11 million).

8

FINANCING COSTS
Summary schedule of items comprising financing costs

Years ended December 31 (millions)	2011	2010
		(adjusted – Note 25(c))
Interest expense		
Interest on long-term debt	$ 374	$ 442
Interest on short-term borrowings and other	11	29
Interest accretion on asset retirement obligation (Note 19(a))	4	4
Loss on redemption of debt[1]	–	52
	389	527
Foreign exchange	(9)	(1)
	380	526
Interest income	(3)	(4)
	$ 377	$ 522

(1) This amount includes a loss of $16 which arose from the associated settlement of financial instruments that were used to manage the foreign exchange rate risk associated with U.S. dollar denominated debt that was redeemed during the third quarter of 2010.

10

OTHER COMPREHENSIVE INCOME
Details of other comprehensive income and accumulated amounts

Years ended December 31				2011						2010 (adjusted – Note 25)	
	Other comprehensive income (loss)			Accumulated income (loss)		Other comprehensive income (loss)			Accumulated income (loss)		
(millions)	Amount arising	Income taxes	Net	Beginning of period	End of period	Amount arising	Income taxes	Net	Beginning of period	End of period
Items that may subsequently be reclassified to income										
Change in unrealized fair value of derivatives designated as cash flow hedges (Note 4(i))										
Gains (losses) arising in current period	$ 15	$ 5	$ 10			$ 15	$ 11	$ 4		
(Gains) losses arising in prior periods and transferred to net income in the current period	(7)	(3)	(4)			59	9	50		
	8	2	6	$ 1	$ 7	74	20	54	$ (53)	$ 1
Cumulative foreign currency translation adjustment	4	–	4	–	4	–	–	–	–	–
	12	2	10	1	11	74	20	54	(53)	1
Item never subsequently reclassified to income										
Cumulative employee defined benefit plan actuarial gains (losses)[1]	(1,139)	(288)	(851)	(214)	(1,065)	(287)	(73)	(214)	–	(214)
	$ (1,127)	$ (286)	$ (841)	$ (213)	$ (1,054)	$ (213)	$ (53)	$ (160)	$ (53)	$ (213)

(1) Cumulative employee defined benefit plan actuarial gains (losses) are only those amounts arising on or after January 1, 2010 (see Note 25); excluding the tax effects thereon, the cumulative net gain (loss) charged to other comprehensive income at December 31, 2011, was $(1,426) (2010 – $(287)).

As at December 31, 2011, the Company's estimate of the net amount of existing gains (losses) arising from the unrealized fair value of derivatives designated as cash flow hedges which are reported in accumulated other comprehensive income and are expected to be reclassified to net income in the next twelve months, excluding tax effects, is $3 million.

12

DIVIDENDS PER SHARE
Summary schedule of dividends declared and review of dividend reinvestment plan

(a) Dividends declared

Years ended December 31
(millions except per share amounts)

Common Share and Non-Voting Share dividends	Declared		Paid to		Declared		Paid to	
				2011				**2010**
	Effective	Per share	shareholders	Total	Effective	Per share	shareholders	Total
	Mar. 11, 2011	$ 0.525	Apr. 1, 2011	$ 170	Mar. 11, 2010	$ 0.475	Apr. 1, 2010	$ 152
	June 10, 2011	0.550	July 4, 2011	178	June 10, 2010	0.500	July 2, 2010	161
	Sep. 9, 2011	0.550	Oct. 3, 2011	179	Sep. 10, 2010	0.500	Oct. 1, 2010	160
	Dec. 9, 2011	0.580	Jan. 3, 2012	188	Dec. 10, 2010	0.525	Jan. 4, 2011	169
		$ 2.205		$ 715		$ 2.000		$ 642

Years ended December 31 (millions)

	Dividends declared in			Dividends declared in		
			2011			**2010**
	Prior fiscal year	Current fiscal year	Total	Prior fiscal year	Current fiscal year	Total
Common Share and Non-Voting Share dividends						
Payable, beginning of period	$ 169	$ –	$ 169	$ 150	$ –	$ 150
Declared	n.a.	715	715	n.a.	642	642
Paid in cash	(115)	(527)	(642)	(129)	(344)	(473)
Reinvested in Non-Voting Shares issued from Treasury	(54)	–	(54)	(21)	(129)	(150)
Payable, end of period	$ –	$ 188	$ 188	$ –	$ 169	$ 169

On February 8, 2012, the Board of Directors declared a quarterly dividend of $0.58 per share on the issued and outstanding Common Shares and Non-Voting Shares of the Company payable on April 2, 2012, to holders of record at the close of business on March 9, 2012. The final amount of the dividend payment depends upon the number of Common Shares and Non-Voting Shares issued and outstanding at the close of business on March 9, 2012.

On February 21, 2012, the Board of Directors declared a quarterly dividend of $0.61 per share on the issued and outstanding Common Shares and Non-Voting Shares of the Company, payable on July 3, 2012, to holders of record at the close of business on June 8, 2012. In the event that the proposed share conversion of Non-Voting Shares to Common Shares on a one-for-one basis receives all requisite approvals (see Note 21(a)) and is effective prior to the dividend record date of June 8, 2012, holders of record on such date who previously held Non-Voting Shares would hold Common Shares and would therefore receive the same dividend as all other holders of Common Shares.

(b) Dividend Reinvestment and Share Purchase Plan

General
The Company has a Dividend Reinvestment and Share Purchase Plan under which eligible holders of Common Shares and Non-Voting Shares may acquire Non-Voting Shares through the reinvestment of dividends and by making additional optional cash payments to the trustee. Under this Plan, the Company has the option of offering shares from Treasury or having the trustee acquire shares in the stock market.

Reinvestment of dividends
The Company, at its discretion, may offer the Non-Voting Shares at up to a 5% discount from the market price. In respect of dividends reinvested during the three-month period ended March 31, 2011, the Company issued Non-Voting Shares from Treasury at a discount of 3%. The Company opted to have the trustee acquire the Non-Voting Shares in the stock market commencing March 1, 2011, with no discount. In respect of Common Share and Non-Voting Share dividends declared during the year ended December 31, 2011, $34 million (2010 – $183 million) was to be reinvested in Non-Voting Shares.

Optional cash payments
Shares purchased through optional cash payments are subject to a minimum investment of $100 per transaction and a maximum investment of $20,000 per calendar year.

15 PROPERTY, PLANT AND EQUIPMENT
Summary schedule of items comprising property, plant and equipment

(millions)	Network assets	Buildings and leasehold improvements	Assets under finance lease	Other	Land	Assets under construction	Total
	(adjusted – Note 25(d))						
At cost							
As at January 1, 2010	$ 22,141	$ 2,244	$ 13	$ 1,644	$ 49	$ 431	$ 26,522
Additions(1)	443	15	10	35	–	840	1,343
Dispositions, retirements and other	(568)	(13)	(2)	(182)	–	–	(765)
Reclassifications	675	105	–	53	–	(833)	–
As at December 31, 2010	22,691	2,351	21	1,550	49	438	27,100
Additions(1)	502	19	1	41	7	887	1,457
Additions arising from business acquisitions (Note 16(e))	–	11	–	7	–	–	18
Dispositions, retirements and other	(206)	(7)	1	(51)	(1)	–	(264)
Reclassifications	779	99	–	75	–	(953)	–
As at December 31, 2011	**$ 23,766**	**$ 2,473**	**$ 23**	**$ 1,622**	**$ 55**	**$ 372**	**$ 28,311**
Accumulated depreciation							
As at January 1, 2010	$ 16,040	$ 1,333	$ 9	$ 1,308	$ –	$ –	$ 18,690
Depreciation	1,088	118	2	131	–	–	1,339
Dispositions, retirements and other	(573)	(8)	(1)	(178)	–	–	(760)
As at December 31, 2010	16,555	1,443	10	1,261	–	–	19,269
Depreciation	1,091	121	2	117	–	–	1,331
Dispositions, retirements and other	(218)	(4)	8	(39)	–	–	(253)
As at December 31, 2011	**$ 17,428**	**$ 1,560**	**$ 20**	**$ 1,339**	**$ –**	**$ –**	**$ 20,347**
Net book value							
As at January 1, 2010	$ 6,101	$ 911	$ 4	$ 336	$ 49	$ 431	$ 7,832
As at December 31, 2010	$ 6,136	$ 908	$ 11	$ 289	$ 49	$ 438	$ 7,831
As at December 31, 2011	**$ 6,338**	**$ 913**	**$ 3**	**$ 283**	**$ 55**	**$ 372**	**$ 7,964**

(1) For the year ended December 31, 2011, additions include $15 (2010 – $12) in respect of asset retirement obligations.

The gross carrying amount of fully depreciated property, plant and equipment that was still in use as at December 31, 2011, was $3.0 billion (December 31, 2010 – $3.0 billion; January 1, 2010 – $2.6 billion).

As at December 31, 2011, the Company's contractual commitments for the acquisition of property, plant and equipment were $188 million over a period through to 2013 (December 31, 2010 – $170 million over a period through to 2013).

16 INTANGIBLE ASSETS AND GOODWILL
Summary schedule of items comprising intangible assets, including goodwill and review of reported fiscal year acquisitions from which goodwill arose

(a) Intangible assets and goodwill, net

(millions)	Subscriber base	Customer contracts, related customer relationships and lease-hold interests	Software	Access to rights-of-way and other	Assets under construction	Total	Spectrum licences	Acquired brand	Total	Total intangible assets	Goodwill[1]	Total intangible assets and goodwill
						(adjusted – Note 25(d))						
At cost												
As at January 1, 2010	$ 245	$ 137	$ 2,408	$ 104	$ 158	$ 3,052	$ 4,867	$ 7	$ 4,874	$ 7,926	$ 3,936	$ 11,862
Additions	–	–	38	8	344	390	–	–	–	390	–	390
Dispositions, retirements and other	–	–	(213)	–	–	(213)	–	–	–	(213)	–	(213)
Reclassifications	–	–	262	–	(262)	–	–	–	–	–	–	–
As at December 31, 2010	245	137	2,495	112	240	3,229	4,867	7	4,874	8,103	3,936	12,039
Additions	–	–	39	4	347	390	–	–	–	390	–	390
Additions arising from business acquisitions (e)	–	60	1	–	–	61	–	–	–	61	110	171
Dispositions, retirements and other	–	–	(256)	(23)	–	(279)	–	–	–	(279)	(21)	(300)
Reclassifications	–	–	422	–	(422)	–	–	–	–	–	–	–
As at December 31, 2011	**$ 245**	**$ 197**	**$ 2,701**	**$ 93**	**$ 165**	**$ 3,401**	**$ 4,867**	**$ 7**	**$ 4,874**	**$ 8,275**	**$ 4,025**	**$ 12,300**
Accumulated amortization												
As at January 1, 2010	$ 52	$ 27	$ 1,605	$ 76	$ –	$ 1,760	$ –	$ –	$ –	$ 1,760	$ 364	$ 2,124
Amortization	6	14	378	4	–	402	–	–	–	402	–	402
Dispositions, retirements and other	–	–	(211)	–	–	(211)	–	–	–	(211)	–	(211)
As at December 31, 2010	58	41	1,772	80	–	1,951	–	–	–	1,951	364	2,315
Amortization[2]	6	19	431	4	–	460	–	–	–	460	19	479
Dispositions, retirements and other	–	–	(267)	(22)	–	(289)	–	–	–	(289)	(19)	(308)
As at December 31, 2011	**$ 64**	**$ 60**	**$ 1,936**	**$ 62**	**$ –**	**$ 2,122**	**$ –**	**$ –**	**$ –**	**$ 2,122**	**$ 364**	**$ 2,486**
Net book value												
As at January 1, 2010	$ 193	$ 110	$ 803	$ 28	$ 158	$ 1,292	$ 4,867	$ 7	$ 4,874	$ 6,166	$ 3,572	$ 9,738
As at December 31, 2010	$ 187	$ 96	$ 723	$ 32	$ 240	$ 1,278	$ 4,867	$ 7	$ 4,874	$ 6,152	$ 3,572	$ 9,724
As at December 31, 2011	**$ 181**	**$ 137**	**$ 765**	**$ 31**	**$ 165**	**$ 1,279**	**$ 4,867**	**$ 7**	**$ 4,874**	**$ 6,153**	**$ 3,661**	**$ 9,814**

Intangible assets subject to amortization comprise the columns Subscriber base through Total. *Intangible assets with indefinite lives* comprise Spectrum licences, Acquired brand and Total.

(1) Accumulated amortization of goodwill is amortization recorded prior to 2002.
(2) Includes a goodwill impairment relating to an immaterial Wireline segment subsidiary classified as held for sale at, and disposed of subsequent to, December 31, 2011.

The gross carrying amount of fully amortized intangible assets subject to amortization that were still in use as at December 31, 2011, was $662 million (December 31, 2010 – $772 million; January 1, 2010 – $752 million).

As at December 31, 2011, the Company's contractual commitments for the acquisition of intangible assets were $142 million over a period through to 2018 (December 31, 2010 – $134 million over a period through to 2018).

(b) Intangible assets subject to amortization

Estimated aggregate amortization expense for intangible assets subject to amortization, calculated for such assets held as at December 31, 2011, for each of the next five fiscal years is as follows:

Years ending December 31 (millions)

2012	$ 406
2013	248
2014	104
2015	44
2016	32

(c) Intangible assets with indefinite lives – spectrum licences

The Company's intangible assets with indefinite lives include spectrum licences granted by Industry Canada. Industry Canada's spectrum licence policy terms indicate that the spectrum licences will likely be renewed. The Company's spectrum licences are expected to be renewed every 20 years (December 31, 2010 – every 5 years or every 10 years; January 1, 2010 – every 5 years or every 10 years) following a review by Industry Canada of the Company's compliance with licence terms. In addition to current usage, the Company's licensed spectrum can be used for planned and new technologies. As a result of the combination of these significant factors, the Company's spectrum licences are currently considered to have indefinite lives.

(d) Impairment testing of intangible assets with indefinite lives and goodwill

As referred to in Note 1(j), the carrying values of intangible assets with indefinite lives and goodwill are periodically tested for impairment and this test represents a significant estimate for the Company.

The carrying amounts of intangible assets with indefinite lives and goodwill allocated to each cash-generating unit are as set out in the following table.

As at (millions)	Intangible assets with indefinite lives			Goodwill			Total		
	Dec. 31, 2011	Dec. 31, 2010	Jan. 1, 2010	Dec. 31, 2011	Dec. 31, 2010	Jan. 1, 2010	Dec. 31, 2011	Dec. 31, 2010	Jan. 1, 2010
		(adjusted – Note 25(d))	(Note 25(d))						
Wireless	$ 4,874	$ 4,874	$ 4,874	$ 2,644	$ 2,606	$ 2,606	$ 7,518	$ 7,480	$ 7,480
Wireline	–	–	–	1,017	966	966	1,017	966	966
	$ 4,874	$ 4,874	$ 4,874	$ 3,661	$ 3,572	$ 3,572	$ 8,535	$ 8,446	$ 8,446

The recoverable amounts of the cash-generating units' assets have been determined based on a value in use calculation. There is a material degree of uncertainty with respect to the estimates of the recoverable amounts of the cash-generating units' assets given the necessity of making key economic assumptions about the future. The value in use calculation uses discounted cash flow projections which employ the following key assumptions: future cash flows and growth projections, including economic risk assumptions and estimates of achieving key operating metrics and drivers; the future weighted average cost of capital; and earnings multiples. The Company considers a range of reasonably possible amounts to use for key assumptions and decides upon amounts that represent management's best estimates. In the normal course, changes are made to key assumptions to reflect current (at time of test) economic conditions, updating of historical information used to develop the key assumptions and changes in the Company's debt ratings.

The cash flow projection key assumptions are based upon the Company's approved financial forecasts which span a period of three years and are discounted, for December 2011 annual test purposes, at a consolidated pre-tax notional rate of 9.39% (December 2010 – 9.49%; January 1, 2010 – 8.89%). For impairment testing valuation purposes, the cash flows subsequent to the three-year projection period are extrapolated, for December 2011 annual test purposes, using perpetual growth rates of 1.75% (December 2010 – 1.75%; January 1, 2010 – 1.75%) for the wireless cash-generating unit and zero (December 2010 – zero; January 1, 2010 – zero) for the wireline cash-generating unit; these growth rates do not exceed the observed long-term average growth rates for the markets in which the Company operates.

The Company validates its value in use results through the use of the market-comparable approach and analytical review of industry and Company-specific facts. The market-comparable approach uses current (at the time of test) market consensus estimates and equity trading prices for U.S. and Canadian firms in the same industry. In addition, the Company ensures that the combination of the valuations of the cash-generating units is reasonable based on current market values of the Company.

The Company believes that any *reasonably possible* change in the key assumptions on which its cash-generating units recoverable amounts are based would not cause the cash-generating units' carrying amounts (including the intangible assets with indefinite lives and the goodwill allocated to the cash-generating unit) to exceed their recoverable amounts. If the future were to *adversely* differ from management's best estimate of key assumptions and associated cash flows were to be materially adversely affected, the Company could potentially experience future material impairment charges in respect of its intangible assets with indefinite lives and goodwill.

Sensitivity testing was conducted as a part of the December 2011 annual test. A component of the sensitivity testing was a break-even analysis. Stress testing included moderate declines in annual cash flows with all other assumptions being held constant; this too resulted in the Company continuing to be able to recover the carrying value of its intangible assets with indefinite lives and goodwill for the foreseeable future.

(e) Business acquisitions

Transactel (Barbados) Inc.

During the three-month period ended March 31, 2011, the Company acquired control of Transactel (Barbados) Inc., a business process outsourcing and call centre company with facilities in two Central American countries. The investment was made with a view to enhancing the Company's business process outsourcing capacity, particularly regarding

Spanish-language capabilities, and acquiring multi-site redundancy in support of other facilities. The primary factor that contributed to the recognition of goodwill was the earnings capacity of the acquiree in excess of the net tangible assets and net intangible assets acquired (such excess arising from: the assembled workforce; the established operation with certain capabilities in the industry; and the geographic location of the acquiree). The amount assigned to goodwill is not expected to be deductible for tax purposes.

The Company's investment in Transactel (Barbados) Inc. is summarized as follows:

	Interest in Transactel (Barbados) Inc. attributable to:					
	Common Shares and Non-Voting Shares		Non-controlling interest[2]		Total	
($ in millions)		Economic interest		Economic interest		Economic interest
December 2008 tranche						
Cash	$ 19					
Contingent consideration	10					
	29	29.99%				
January 2011 tranche	20	21.01%				
Equity accounting adjustments through						
February 1, 2011	(2)					
	47	51.00%				
Gain on 51% interest re-measured						
at acquisition-date fair value	16					
Relative acquisition-date (February 1, 2011)						
fair values	63	51.00%	$ 60	49.00%	$ 123	100.00%
May 2011 equity transaction[1]	56	44.00%	(56)	(44.00%)	–	–
	$ 119	95.00%	$ 4	5.00%	$ 123	100.00%

(1) The difference between the amount paid by the Company for the incremental 44% economic interest and the associated proportionate share of the non-controlling interest in the net assets of Transactel (Barbados) Inc. was recorded as a credit to retained earnings in the Consolidated Statements of Changes in Owners' Equity.

(2) The non-controlling interest at December 31, 2011, is included in the Consolidated Statements of Financial Position as a non-current provision due to the provision of a written put option for the 5% economic interest not owned by the Company.

The acquisition was effected as follows:

■ On December 22, 2008, the Company acquired an initial 29.99% economic interest in Transactel (Barbados) Inc. for $19 million cash. Additional contingent consideration could become payable depending upon Transactel (Barbados) Inc. earnings for the year ended December 31, 2011.

Concurrent with acquiring the initial interest in Transactel (Barbados) Inc., the Company provided two written put options to the vendor. The first written put option became exercisable on December 31, 2009, expiring June 30, 2011, and allowed the vendor to put up to a further 21.01% economic interest to the Company (the Company's effective economic interest in Transactel (Barbados) Inc. would become 51% assuming the written put option was exercised in full). The second written put option became exercisable on December 31, 2010, it had no expiry, and it allowed the vendor to put whatever interest was not put under the first written put option plus up to an incremental 44% economic interest to the Company. The written put options set out the share pricing methodology, which was dependent upon Transactel (Barbados) Inc. future earnings.

The vendor provided the Company with two purchased call options which substantially mirrored the written put options except that they were only exercisable upon Transactel (Barbados) Inc. achieving certain business growth targets.

The Company initially accounted for its investment in Transactel (Barbados) Inc. using the equity method.

■ On January 7, 2011, the Company exercised its first purchased call option to acquire an additional 21.01% economic interest in Transactel (Barbados) Inc. from the vendor for $20 million cash.

Upon such exercise, the Company continued to account for its resulting direct 51% economic interest in Transactel (Barbados) Inc. using the equity method. Transactel (Barbados) Inc.'s board of directors "super-majority" provisions affected the Company's assessment of control as the continuing power to determine the strategic operating, investing and financing policies of Transactel (Barbados) Inc. resided with the board of directors "super-majority". Although the Company had the right to elect a simple majority of the board of directors at the direct 51% economic interest level, the vendor's remaining direct 49% economic interest effectively had a veto right over the strategic operating, investing and financing policies of Transactel (Barbados) Inc. and thus the Company did not have the control necessary to apply consolidation accounting.

- Subsequently in the first quarter of 2011, Transactel (Barbados) Inc. achieved the business growth target necessary for the Company to exercise its second purchased call option. The Company exercised its second purchased call option and asserted its control effective February 1, 2011 (the acquisition date). The effects of the second purchased call option exercise included that the Company:
  - accounted for its 51% economic interest in Transactel (Barbados) Inc. on a consolidated basis (as the vendor no longer had an effective veto over the strategic operating, investing and financing policies of Transactel (Barbados) Inc.) and thus included Transactel (Barbados) Inc.'s results in the Company's Wireline segment effective February 1, 2011;
  - was required to re-measure its pre-acquisition 51% economic interest at acquisition-date fair value, resulting in the recognition of a gain of $16 million (see Note 6) (such gain being net of a contingent consideration liability estimate of $10 million; concurrent with preparing the Company's 2011 financial statements, the contingent consideration liability was confirmed at $9 million, as discussed further in Note 19(a), and the gain was thus revised to $17 million);
  - was required to initially measure the non-controlling interest's 49% economic interest at acquisition-date fair value, resulting in an increase of $60 million in the non-controlling interest; and
  - recorded, in the second quarter of 2011, a post-acquisition equity transaction with the vendor for the incremental 44% economic interest for $51 million cash.

Concurrent with acquiring the incremental 44% economic interest, the Company provided a written put option to the vendor. This third written put option becomes exercisable on December 22, 2015, and allows the vendor to put the remaining 5% economic interest to the Company (the Company's effective interest in Transactel (Barbados) Inc. would become 100%). The written put option sets out that the pricing methodology is to use an independent party using common practice valuation techniques. Also concurrently, the vendor has provided the Company with a purchased call option which substantially mirrors the third written put option.

TELUS-branded wireless dealership businesses

During the year ended December 31, 2011, the Company acquired 100% ownership of certain TELUS-branded wireless dealership businesses for $81 million cash ($81 million net of cash acquired). There was no contingent consideration in the transactions. The investments were made with a view to enhancing the Company's distribution of wireless products and customer services across Western Canada.

The primary factor that contributed to the recognition of goodwill was the earnings capacity of the acquired businesses in excess of the net tangible assets and net intangible assets acquired (such excess arising from the acquired workforce and the benefits of acquiring established businesses in multiple locations). Approximately $16 million assigned to goodwill during the year ended December 31, 2011, may be deductible for tax purposes.

Acquisition-date fair values

The acquisition-date fair values assigned to assets acquired and liabilities assumed are as set out in the following table.

As at (millions)	Transactel (Barbados) Inc. February 1, 2011	TELUS-branded wireless dealership businesses Various 2011
Assets		
Current assets		
Accounts receivable[1]	$ 25	$ 2
Other	5	1
	30	3
Non-current assets		
Property, plant and equipment	12	6
Intangible assets		
Intangible assets subject to amortization[2]		
Customer contracts, related customer relationships and leasehold interests	21	39
Software	1	–
	22	39
Deferred income taxes	–	2
Total non-current assets	34	47
Total identifiable assets acquired	64	50
Liabilities		
Current liabilities	13	5
Non-current liabilities		
Other long-term liabilities	–	1
Deferred income taxes	–	1
Total non-current liabilities	–	2
Total liabilities assumed	13	7
Net identifiable assets acquired	51	43
Goodwill	72	38
Net assets acquired	$ 123	$ 81
Acquisition effected by way of:		
Cash consideration	$ –	$ 81
Re-measured pre-acquisition 51% interest at acquisition-date fair value[3]	63	n.a.
	63	81
Non-controlling interest measured at fair value[4]	60	n.a.
	$ 123	$ 81

(1) The fair value of the accounts receivable is equal to the gross contractual amounts receivable and reflects the best estimates at the acquisition dates of the contractual cash flows expected to be collected.

(2) The customer contracts and the related customer relationships and the software acquired in conjunction with Transactel (Barbados) Inc. are being amortized over periods of six years and three years, respectively. The customer contracts, related customer relationships and leasehold interests acquired in conjunction with the TELUS-branded wireless dealership businesses are being amortized over a period of six years.

(3) Re-measurement of the Company's previously held 51% economic interest resulted in the recognition of an acquisition-date gain of $16 which is included in the Consolidated Statements of Income and Other Comprehensive Income as a component of Other operating income (see Note 6). The previously held 51% economic interest was comprised of an initial 29.99% acquired December 22, 2008, and a 21.01% economic interest obtained January 7, 2011.

The acquisition-date fair value of the Company's 51% interest included the recognition of $10 for contingent consideration, which was contractually based upon a multiple of an estimate of Transactel (Barbados) Inc. fiscal 2011 earnings in excess of a threshold amount.

Concurrent with preparing the Company's 2011 financial statements, the contingent consideration liability was confirmed at $9, as discussed further in Note 19(a), and the gain was thus revised to $17.

(4) The remaining non-controlling interest, representing a 49% economic interest, had a fair value of $60 as of February 1, 2011 (acquisition-date fair value). The non-controlling interest fair value (the recorded amount of which is based upon net assets acquired) was determined by discounted cash flows. The fair value estimate is based upon: a going-concern basis; market participant synergies; a perpetuity terminal value based on sustaining cash flows; and costs (taxes) associated with future repatriation of funds.

Pro forma disclosures

The following pro forma supplemental information represents certain results of operations as if the business acquisitions noted above had been completed at the beginning of the fiscal years presented.

Years ended December 31		2011		2010
(millions except per share amounts)	As reported[1]	Pro forma[2]	As reported	Pro forma[2]
			(adjusted – Note 25(c))	
Operating revenues	$ 10,397	$ 10,419	$ 9,792	$ 9,891
Net income	$ 1,215	$ 1,208	$ 1,052	$ 1,045
Net income per Common Share and Non-Voting Share				
– Basic	$ 3.76	$ 3.73	$ 3.27	$ 3.26
– Diluted	$ 3.74	$ 3.71	$ 3.27	$ 3.25

(1) Operating revenues and net income for the year ended December 31, 2011, include $39 and $NIL, respectively, in respect of the acquisition of Transactel (Barbados) Inc. Operating revenues and net income (loss) for the year ended December 31, 2011, include $11 and $(2), respectively, in respect of the acquisition of the TELUS-branded wireless dealership businesses.

(2) Pro forma amounts for the years ended December 31, 2011 and 2010, reflect Transactel (Barbados) Inc. and the TELUS-branded wireless dealership businesses. The pro forma amounts for the year ended December 31, 2010, do not reflect a re-measurement gain on the 29.99% interest in Transactel (Barbados) Inc. that the Company held during that period. Transactel (Barbados) Inc. was acquired on February 1, 2011, and the TELUS-branded wireless dealership businesses were acquired on various dates in 2011; their results have been included in the Company's Consolidated Statements of Income and Other Comprehensive Income effective the dates of acquisition.

The pro forma supplemental information is based on estimates and assumptions which are believed to be reasonable. The pro forma supplemental information is not necessarily indicative of the Company's consolidated financial results in future periods or the results that actually would have been realized had the business acquisitions been completed at the beginning of the periods presented. The pro forma supplemental information includes incremental intangible asset amortization, financing and other charges as a result of the acquisitions, net of the related tax effects.

18 SHORT-TERM BORROWINGS
Review of short-term borrowings and related disclosures

On July 26, 2002, TELUS subsidiary TELUS Communications Inc. (see Note 23(a)) entered into an agreement with an arm's-length securitization trust associated with a major Schedule I bank under which TELUS Communications Inc. is able to sell an interest in certain of its trade receivables up to a maximum of $500 million (December 31, 2010 – $500 million; January 1, 2010 – $500 million). This revolving-period securitization agreement's current term ends August 1, 2014. TELUS Communications Inc. is required to maintain at least a BBB (low) credit rating by Dominion Bond Rating Service or the securitization trust may require the sale program to be wound down prior to the end of the term.

When the Company sells its trade receivables, it retains reserve accounts, which are retained interests in the securitized trade receivables, and servicing rights. As at December 31, 2011, the Company had transferred, but continued to recognize, trade receivables of $456 million (December 31, 2010 – $465 million; January 1, 2010 – $598 million). Short-term borrowings of $400 million (December 31, 2010 – $400 million; January 1, 2010 – $500 million) are comprised of amounts loaned to the Company from the arm's-length securitization trust pursuant to the sale of trade receivables.

The balance of short-term borrowings (if any) comprised amounts drawn on the Company's bilateral bank facilities.

20 | LONG-TERM DEBT
Summary schedule of long-term debt and related disclosures

(a) Details of long-term debt

As at ($ in millions) Series	Rate of interest	Maturity	December 31, 2011	December 31, 2010	January 1, 2010
TELUS Corporation Notes					
U.S.[2]	8.00%[1]	June 2011	$ –	$ 736	$ 1,411
CB	5.00%[1]	June 2013	300	299	299
CC	4.50%[1]	March 2012	300	300	299
CD	4.95%[1]	March 2017	692	691	690
CE	5.95%[1]	April 2015	498	498	498
CF	4.95%[1]	May 2014	698	698	697
CG	5.05%[1]	December 2019	991	990	989
CH	5.05%[1]	July 2020	993	992	–
CI	3.65%[1]	May 2016	595	–	–
			5,067	5,204	4,883
TELUS Corporation Commercial Paper	1.16%	Through April 2012	**766**	104	467
TELUS Communications Inc. Debentures					
1	12.00%[1]	May 2010	**–**	–	50
2	11.90%[1]	November 2015	**124**	124	124
3	10.65%[1]	June 2021	**174**	174	173
5	9.65%[1]	April 2022	**245**	245	245
B	8.80%[1]	September 2025	**198**	198	198
			741	741	790
TELUS Communications Inc. First Mortgage Bonds					
U	11.50%[1]	July 2010	**–**	–	30
Finance leases			**–**	7	2
Long-Term Debt			**$ 6,574**	$ 6,056	$ 6,172
Current			**$ 1,066**	$ 847	$ 549
Non-current			**5,508**	5,209	5,623
Long-Term Debt			**$ 6,574**	$ 6,056	$ 6,172

(1) Interest is payable semi-annually.
(2) Principal face value of notes is U.S.$NIL (December 31, 2010 – U.S.$741; January 1, 2010 – U.S.$1,348).

(b) TELUS Corporation notes

General

The notes are senior, unsecured and unsubordinated obligations of the Company and rank equally in right of payment with all existing and future unsecured, unsubordinated obligations of the Company, are senior in right of payment to all existing and future subordinated indebtedness of the Company, and are effectively subordinated to all existing and future obligations of, or guaranteed by, the Company's subsidiaries.

The indentures governing the notes contain certain covenants which, among other things, place limitations on the ability of TELUS and certain of its subsidiaries to: grant security in respect of indebtedness, enter into sale and lease-back transactions and incur new indebtedness.

Series	Issued	Maturity	Issue price	Principal face amount		Redemption present value spread (basis points)[1]
				Originally issued	Outstanding at financial statement date	
5.00% Notes, Series CB	May 2006	June 2013	$998.80	$300 million	$300 million	16
4.50% Notes, Series CC	March 2007	March 2012	$999.91	$300 million	$300 million	15
4.95% Notes, Series CD	March 2007	March 2017	$999.53	$700 million	$700 million	24
5.95% Notes, Series CE[2]	April 2008	April 2015	$998.97	$500 million	$500 million	66
4.95% Notes, Series CF[2]	May 2009	May 2014	$999.96	$700 million	$700 million	71
5.05% Notes, Series CG[2]	December 2009	December 2019	$994.19	$1.0 billion	$1.0 billion	45.5
5.05% Notes, Series CH[2]	July 2010	July 2020	$997.44	$1.0 billion	$1.0 billion	47
3.65% Notes, Series CI[2]	May 2011	May 2016	$996.29	$600 million	$600 million	29.5

(1) The notes are redeemable at the option of the Company, in whole at any time, or in part from time to time, on not fewer than 30 and not more than 60 days' prior notice. The redemption price is equal to the greater of (i) the present value of the notes discounted at the Government of Canada yield plus the redemption present value spread, or (ii) 100% of the principal amount thereof. In addition, accrued and unpaid interest, if any, will be paid to the date fixed for redemption.

(2) This series of notes requires the Company to make an offer to repurchase the series of notes at a price equal to 101% of their principal plus accrued and unpaid interest to the date of repurchase upon the occurrence of a change in control triggering event, as defined in the supplemental trust indenture.

On July 27, 2010, the Company exercised its right to early and partially redeem, on September 2, 2010, U.S.$607 million of its publicly held 2011 (U.S. Dollar) Notes. The loss on redemption, which included the loss arising on early settlement of the associated cross currency interest rate swap agreements, was $52 million.

On December 1, 2009, the Company exercised its right to early and partially redeem, on December 31, 2009, U.S.$577 million of its publicly held 2011 (U.S. Dollar) Notes. The loss on redemption, which included the loss arising on early settlement of the associated cross currency interest rate swap agreements, was $99 million.

2011 Cross Currency Interest Rate Swap Agreements

With respect to the 2011 (U.S. Dollar) Notes, U.S.$NIL (December 31, 2010 – U.S.$0.7 billion; January 1, 2010 – U.S.$1.3 billion) in aggregate, the Company entered into cross currency interest rate swap agreements which effectively converted the principal repayments and interest obligations to Canadian dollar obligations with an effective fixed interest rate of 8.493% and an effective fixed economic exchange rate of $1.5327.

The counterparties of the swap agreements were highly rated financial institutions and the Company did not anticipate any non-performance. TELUS did not require collateral or other security from the counterparties due to its assessment of their creditworthiness.

The Company translates items such as the U.S. Dollar Notes into equivalent Canadian dollars at the rate of exchange in effect at the statement of financial position date. The swap agreements at December 31, 2011, comprised a net derivative liability of $NIL (December 31, 2010 – $404 million; January 1, 2010 – $721 million), as set out in Note 4(h). The asset value of the swap agreements increased (decreased) when the statement of financial position date exchange rate increased (decreased) the Canadian dollar equivalent of the U.S. Dollar Notes.

(c) TELUS Corporation commercial paper

On May 15, 2007, TELUS Corporation entered into an unsecured commercial paper program, which is backstopped by a portion of its $2.0 billion syndicated credit facility, enabling it to issue commercial paper up to a maximum aggregate of $800 million (or U.S. dollar equivalent), to be used for general corporate purposes, including capital expenditures and investments; in August 2008, the program was expanded to $1.2 billion. Commercial paper debt is due within one year and is classified as a current portion of long-term debt as the amounts are fully supported, and the Company expects that they will continue to be supported, by the revolving credit facility, which has no repayment requirements within the next year.

(d) TELUS Corporation credit facility

On November 3, 2011, TELUS Corporation entered into a $2.0 billion bank credit facility with a syndicate of financial institutions. The credit facility consists of a $2.0 billion (or U.S. dollar equivalent) revolving credit facility expiring on November 3, 2016, to be used for general corporate purposes including the backstop of commercial paper. This new facility replaced the Company's pre-existing committed credit facility prior to its expiry in May 2012.

TELUS Corporation's credit facility expiring on November 3, 2016, is unsecured and bears interest at prime rate, U.S. Dollar Base Rate, a bankers' acceptance rate or London interbank offered rate (LIBOR) (all such terms as used or defined in the credit facility), plus applicable margins. The credit facility contains customary representations, warranties and covenants, including two financial quarter-end financial ratio tests. The financial ratio tests are that the Company may not permit its net debt to operating cash flow ratio to exceed 4.0:1 and may not permit its operating cash flow to interest expense ratio to be less than 2.0:1, each as defined under the credit facility.

On June 19, 2009, TELUS Corporation entered into an amended $300 million revolving credit facility with a syndicate of financial institutions, expiring December 31, 2010; during the quarter ended September 30, 2010, the Company exercised its right to cancel the facility in its entirety. The credit facility was unsecured and bore interest at prime rate or bankers' acceptance rate (all such terms as used or defined in the credit facility), plus applicable margins.

Continued access to TELUS Corporation's credit facility is not contingent on the maintenance by TELUS Corporation of a specific credit rating.

As at (millions)	Dec. 31, 2011	Dec. 31, 2010			January 1, 2010
Revolving credit facility expiring	Nov. 3, 2016	May 1, 2012	May 1, 2012	Dec. 31, 2010	Total
Net available	$ 1,234	$ 1,779	$ 1,410	$ 300	$ 1,710
Outstanding, undrawn letters of credit	–	117	123	–	123
Backstop of commercial paper	766	104	467	–	467
Gross available	$ 2,000	$ 2,000	$ 2,000	$ 300	$ 2,300

In addition to the ability to provide letters of credit pursuant to its $2.0 billion bank credit facility, the Company has $115 million of letter of credit facilities expiring mid-2013, all of which were utilized at December 31, 2011.

(e) TELUS Communications Inc. debentures

The outstanding Series 1 through 5 debentures were issued by a predecessor corporation of TELUS Communications Inc., BC TEL, under a Trust Indenture dated May 31, 1990, and are non-redeemable.

The outstanding Series B Debentures were issued by a predecessor corporation of TELUS Communications Inc., AGT Limited, under a Trust Indenture dated August 24, 1994, and a supplemental trust indenture dated September 22, 1995. They are redeemable at the option of the Company, in whole at any time or in part from time to time, on not less than 30 days' notice at the higher of par and the price calculated to provide the Government of Canada Yield plus 15 basis points.

Pursuant to an amalgamation on January 1, 2001, the Debentures became obligations of TELUS Communications Inc. The debentures are not secured by any mortgage, pledge or other charge and are governed by certain covenants, including a negative pledge and a limitation on issues of additional debt, subject to a debt to capitalization ratio and interest coverage test. Effective June 12, 2009, TELUS Corporation guaranteed the payment of the debentures' principal and interest.

(f) TELUS Communications Inc. first mortgage bonds

The first mortgage bonds were issued by TELUS Communications (Québec) Inc. and were secured by an immovable hypothec and by a movable hypothec charging specifically certain immovable and movable property of the subsidiary TELUS Communications Inc., such as land,

buildings, equipment, apparatus, telephone lines, rights-of-way and similar rights limited to certain assets located in the province of Quebec. The first mortgage bonds were non-redeemable. Pursuant to a corporate reorganization effected July 1, 2004, the outstanding first mortgage bonds became obligations of TELUS Communications Inc. Effective June 12, 2009, TELUS Corporation guaranteed the payment of the first mortgage bonds' principal and interest.

(g) Long-term debt maturities

Anticipated requirements to meet long-term debt repayments, calculated upon such long-term debts owing as at December 31, 2011, for each of the next five fiscal years are as follows:

Years ending December 31 (millions)

2012	$ 1,066
2013	300
2014	700
2015	625
2016	600
Thereafter	3,324
Future cash outflows in respect of long-term debt principal repayments	6,615
Future cash outflows in respect of associated interest and like carrying costs[1]	2,107
Undiscounted contractual maturities (Note 4(c))	$ 8,722

(1) Future cash outflows in respect of associated interest and like carrying costs for commercial paper and amounts drawn under the Company's credit facilities (if any) have been calculated based upon the rates in effect as at December 31, 2011.

---

21 | COMMON SHARE AND NON-VOTING SHARE EQUITY
Review of Common Share and Non-Voting Share equity items, including share option price stratification

(a) Authorized share capital

As at December 31, 2011, December 31, 2010, and January 1, 2010, the Company's authorized share capital consisted of one billion no par value shares of each of the following classes: First Preferred Shares; Second Preferred Shares; Common Shares; and Non-Voting Shares. Only holders of Common Shares may vote at general meetings of the Company with each holder of Common Shares being entitled to one vote per Common Share held at all such meetings. Non-Voting Shares have conversion rights in certain instances, such as if there are changes in Canadian telecommunications, radiocommunication and broadcasting regulations so that there is no restriction on non-Canadians owning or controlling Common Shares of the Company. In that instance, shareholders have the right to convert their Non-Voting Shares into Common Shares on a one-for-one basis, and the Company has the right to require conversion on the same basis.

With respect to priority in payment of dividends and in the distribution of assets in the event of liquidation, dissolution or winding-up of the Company, whether voluntary or involuntary, or any other distribution of the assets of the Company among its shareholders for the purpose of winding-up its affairs, preferences are as follows: First Preferred Shares; Second Preferred Shares; and finally Common Shares and Non-Voting Shares participating equally, without preference or distinction.

Subsequent to December 31, 2011, the Company announced that holders of its Common Shares and Non-Voting Shares will have the opportunity to decide whether to eliminate the Company's Non-Voting Share class at the Company's annual and special meeting to be held May 9, 2012. Under the terms of the proposal, each Non-Voting Share would be converted into a Common Share on a one-for-one basis, effected by way of a court-approved plan of arrangement and will be subject to the approval of two-thirds of the votes cast by the holders of Common Shares and two-thirds of the votes cast by the holders of Non-Voting Shares, each voting separately as a class.

22 COMMITMENTS AND CONTINGENT LIABILITIES
Summary review of lease obligations, contingent liabilities, claims and lawsuits

(a) Leases

The Company occupies leased premises in various centres and has land, buildings and equipment under operating leases. As set out in Note 19(b), the Company has consolidated administrative real estate and, in some instances, this has resulted in sub-letting land and buildings. The future minimum lease payments under finance leases and operating leases are as follows:

| | Operating lease payments | | | | | |
| | Land and buildings[1] | | | Vehicles and other equipment | | Operating lease receipts from sub-let land and buildings |
Years ending December 31 (millions)	Rent	Occupancy costs	Gross		Total	
2012	$ 179	$ 92	$ 271	$ 16	$ 287	$ 11
2013	165	88	253	8	261	14
2014	151	80	231	4	235	21
2015	136	76	212	3	215	20
2016	123	73	196	1	197	18
Thereafter	665	466	1,131	–	1,131	82
Total future minimum lease payments as at December 31, 2011	$ 1,419	$ 875	$ 2,294	$ 32	$ 2,326	$ 166

(1) Subsequent to December 31, 2011, the Company entered into a lease for its new national headquarter premises from a real estate joint venture as set out in Note 17(b); the associated operating lease payments, totalling $163 (including occupancy costs of $63), have not been included in this table.

| | | Operating lease payments | | | | | |
| | Finance lease payments | Land and buildings | | | Vehicles and other equipment | | Operating lease receipts from sub-let land and buildings |
Years ending December 31 (millions)		Rent	Occupancy costs	Gross		Total	
2011	$ 8	$ 169	$ 96	$ 265	$ 20	$ 285	$ 7
2012	–	153	88	241	12	253	12
2013	–	142	87	229	6	235	12
2014	–	129	83	212	2	214	12
2015	–	118	81	199	1	200	12
Thereafter	–	661	484	1,145	1	1,146	15
Total future minimum lease payments as at December 31, 2010	8	$ 1,372	$ 919	$ 2,291	$ 42	$ 2,333	$ 70
Less imputed interest	1						
Finance lease liability	$ 7						

Of the amount in respect of land and buildings, as at December 31, 2011, approximately 56% (December 31, 2010 – 57%; January 1, 2010 – 55%) of this amount was in respect of the Company's five largest leases, all of which were for office premises over various terms, with expiry dates that range from 2016 to 2026.

(b) Concentration of labour

In 2010, TELUS commenced collective bargaining with the Telecommunications Workers Union to renew the collective agreement which expired November 19, 2010; the expired contract covered approximately 31% of the Company's workforce as at December 31, 2010.

On April 11, 2011, the Telecommunications Workers Union and the Company reached a tentative agreement for a collective agreement subject to ratification by members of the Telecommunications Workers Union. On June 7, 2011, the Telecommunications Workers Union announced that its members voted to accept the April 11, 2011, tentative agreement. The terms and conditions of the new collective agreement are effective from June 9, 2011, to December 31, 2015; the contract covered approximately 27% of the Company's workforce as at December 31, 2011.

(c) Indemnification obligations

In the normal course of operations, the Company may provide indemnification in conjunction with certain transactions. The terms of these indemnification obligations range in duration and often are not explicitly defined. Where appropriate, an indemnification obligation is recorded as a liability. In many cases, there is no maximum limit on these indemnification obligations and the overall maximum amount of such indemnification obligations cannot be reasonably estimated. Other than obligations recorded as liabilities at the time of the transaction, historically the Company has not made significant payments under these indemnifications.

In connection with its 2001 disposition of TELUS' directory business, the Company agreed to bear a proportionate share of the new owner's increased directory publication costs if the increased costs were to arise from a change in the applicable CRTC regulatory requirements. The Company's proportionate share is 15% through, and ending, May 2016. As well, should the CRTC take any action which would result in the owner being prevented from carrying on the directory business as specified in the agreement, TELUS would indemnify the owner in respect of any losses that the owner incurred.

As at December 31, 2011, the Company has no liability recorded in respect of indemnification obligations.

(d) Claims and lawsuits

General

A number of claims and lawsuits (including class actions) seeking damages and other relief are pending against the Company. As well, the Company has received or is aware of certain possible claims (including intellectual property infringement claims) against the Company and, in some cases, numerous other wireless carriers and telecommunications service providers. In some instances, the matters are at a preliminary stage and the potential for liability and magnitude of potential loss currently cannot be readily determined. It is impossible at this time for the Company to predict with any certainty the outcome of any such claims, possible claims and lawsuits. However, subject to the foregoing limitations, management is of the opinion, based upon legal assessment and information presently available, that it is unlikely that any liability, to the extent not provided for through insurance or otherwise, would be material in relation to the Company's consolidated financial position, excepting the following items.

Certified class actions

Certified class actions against the Company include a class action brought in August 2004, in Saskatchewan, against a number of past and present wireless service providers including the Company. The claim alleges that each of the carriers is in breach of contract and has violated competition, trade practices and consumer protection legislation across Canada in connection with the collection of system access fees, and seeks to recover direct and punitive damages in an unspecified amount; similar proceedings were commenced in other provinces. In September 2007, a national class was certified by the Saskatchewan Court of Queen's Bench. The Company's appeal of the certification order was dismissed on November 15, 2011. An application for leave to appeal this decision to the Supreme Court of Canada was filed on January 13, 2012. Since the enactment of opt-out class action legislation in Saskatchewan, Plaintiffs' counsel applied to certify a new national class in Saskatchewan making substantially the same allegations. That application was stayed by the court in December 2009 upon an application by the defendants to dismiss it for abuse of process, conditional on possible future changes in circumstance. In March 2010, the plaintiffs applied for leave to appeal the stay decision and that application was adjourned pending the outcome of the 2004 class action. In late 2011, a further class action relating to system access fees was filed in British Columbia; this action is not yet certified. The Company believes that it has good defences to these actions.

Should the ultimate resolution of these actions differ from management's assessments and assumptions, a material adjustment to the Company's financial position and the results of its operations could result; management's assessments and assumptions include that a reliable estimate of the exposure cannot be made at this preliminary stage of the lawsuit.

Uncertified class actions

Uncertified class actions against the Company include a 2008 class action brought in Saskatchewan (with similar proceedings having also been filed by plaintiffs' counsel in Alberta) alleging that, among other things, Canadian telecommunications carriers including the Company have failed to provide proper notice of 9-1-1 charges to the public and have been deceitfully passing them off as government charges, as well as a 2008 class action brought in Ontario alleging that the Company has misrepresented its practice of "rounding up" wireless airtime to the nearest minute and charging for the full minute. The plaintiffs in these actions seek direct and punitive damages and other relief. The Company is assessing the merits of these claims but the potential for liability and magnitude of potential loss cannot be readily determined at this time.

Intellectual property infringement claims

Claims and possible claims received by the Company include notice of one claim that certain wireless products used on the Company's network infringe two third-party patents. The Company is assessing the merits of this claim but the potential for liability and magnitude of potential loss cannot be readily determined at this time.

24 ADDITIONAL FINANCIAL INFORMATION
Summary schedules of items comprising certain primary financial statement line items

(a) Statement of financial position

As at (millions)	December 31, 2011	December 31, 2010	January 1, 2010
Accounts receivable (adjusted – Note 25(d))			
Customer accounts receivable	$ 1,178	$ 1,142	$ 1,057
Accrued receivables – customer	111	102	103
Allowance for doubtful accounts	(36)	(41)	(59)
	1,253	1,203	1,101
Accrued receivables – other	172	113	93
Other	3	2	1
	$ 1,428	$ 1,318	$ 1,195
Inventories[1]			
Wireless handsets, parts and accessories	$ 307	$ 236	$ 226
Other	46	47	44
	$ 353	$ 283	$ 270
Other long-term assets (adjusted – Note 25(d))			
Pension and other post-retirement assets	$ –	$ 179	$ 251
Other	81	56	35
	$ 81	$ 235	$ 286
Accounts payable and accrued liabilities (adjusted – Note 25(d))			
Accrued liabilities	$ 579	$ 555	$ 520
Payroll and other employee related liabilities	287	284	252
Restricted stock units liability	29	20	20
Accrual for net-cash settlement feature for share option awards (Note 13(b))	3	18	14
	898	877	806
Trade accounts payable	406	448	382
Interest payable	68	73	60
Other	47	79	88
	$ 1,419	$ 1,477	$ 1,336
Advance billings and customer deposits (adjusted – Note 25(d))			
Advance billings	$ 575	$ 536	$ 470
Regulatory deferral accounts	24	62	–
Deferred customer activation and connection fees	32	35	40
Customer deposits	24	25	20
	$ 655	$ 658	$ 530

As at (millions)	December 31, 2011	December 31, 2010	January 1, 2010
Other long-term liabilities (adjusted – Note 25(d))			
Derivative liabilities (Note 4(h))	$ –	$ –	$ 721
Pension and other post-retirement liabilities	1,053	423	357
Other	116	123	131
Restricted stock units and deferred share units liabilities	35	29	38
	1,204	575	1,247
Regulatory deferral accounts	77	–	–
Deferred customer activation and connection fees	59	67	80
Deferred gain on sale-leaseback of buildings	3	7	7
	$ 1,343	$ 649	$ 1,334

(1) Cost of goods sold for the year ended December 31, 2011 was $1,522 (2010 – $1,189).

(b) Supplementary cash flow information

Years ended December 31 (millions)	2011	2010
Net change in non-cash working capital		
Accounts receivable	$ (79)	$ (123)
Inventories	(69)	(13)
Prepaid expenses	(36)	(8)
Accounts payable and accrued liabilities	(47)	160
Income and other taxes receivable and payable, net	13	(214)
Advance billings and customer deposits	(3)	128
Provisions	(34)	(49)
	$ (255)	$ (119)
Long-term debt issued		
TELUS Corporation Commercial Paper	$ 3,468	$ 2,725
Other	600	1,000
	$ 4,068	$ 3,725
Redemptions and repayment of long-term debt		
TELUS Corporation Commercial Paper	$ (2,806)	$ (3,088)
Other	(1,140)	(1,031)
	$ (3,946)	$ (4,119)
Interest (paid)		
Amount (paid) in respect of interest expense	$ (378)	$ (427)
Amount (paid) in respect of loss on redemption of long-term debt	–	(52)
	$ (378)	$ (479)

Summary of Differences Between International Financial Reporting Standards and Accounting Standards for Private Enterprises

Appendix B

Canada has two main sets of generally accepted accounting principles: the International Financial Reporting Standards (IFRS) that must be applied by publicly accountable enterprises, and the Accounting Standards for Private Enterprises (ASPE) that are applied by most other Canadian companies. The following table provides a chapter-by-chapter summary of the IFRS-ASPE differences that appear in this textbook. There are many more differences between the two sets of standards, but they are left to be discussed in senior accounting courses.

CHAPTER 1

Summary of IFRS-ASPE Differences

Concepts	IFRS	ASPE
Application of IFRS and ASPE (p. 7)	Publicly accountable enterprises or those enterprises planning to become one must apply IFRS.	Private enterprises have the option of applying IFRS, but almost all apply ASPE, which is simpler and less costly for these smaller enterprises.
Historical-cost assumption (p. 10)	Certain assets and liabilities are permitted to be recorded at their fair values rather than being kept on the books at their historical costs.	With rare exceptions, assets and liabilities are carried at their historical costs for as long as the company owns or owes them.
Changes in retained earnings during an accounting period (p. 14)	These changes are reported in the statement of changes in owners' equity.	These changes are reported in the statement of retained earnings.
The balance sheet (p. 15)	This financial statement is called the statement of financial position.	This financial statement is called the balance sheet.
The income statement (p. 11)	This financial statement is called the statement of profit or loss.	This financial statement is called the income statement.
The cash flow statement (p. 20)	This financial statement is called the statement of cash flows.	This financial statement is called the cash flow statement.
The statement of other comprehensive income (p. 14)	This statement is required.	This statement is not required.

CHAPTER 5

Summary of IFRS-ASPE Differences

Concept	IFRS	ASPE
Short-term investments (p. 223)	These investments are reported at fair value, with unrealized and realized gains and losses reported in net income, unless the company elects to report them in other comprehensive income.	These investments are reported at fair value, with unrealized and realized gains and losses reported in net income.

CHAPTER 7

Summary of IFRS-ASPE Differences

Concepts	IFRS	ASPE
Depreciation (p. 322)	This concept is called depreciation.	This concept is called amortization.
Significant components of an item of property, plant, or equipment (p. 340)	Significant components shall be depreciated separately.	Significant components are amortized separately only when it is practical to do so.
Impairment (p. 340)	A company shall assess at the end of each reporting period whether there are any signs that an asset may be impaired. Irrespective of any signs of impairment, a company must annually review goodwill and intangible assets with indefinite useful lives for impairment. If an impaired asset subsequently increases in value, a company may reverse all or part of any previous write-down but not on goodwill.	A company shall test an asset for impairment whenever events or circumstances indicate its carrying amount may not be recoverable. A company may not reverse any write-downs, even if an impaired asset subsequently increases in value.
Revaluation (p. 340)	A company may choose to use the revaluation model to measure its property, plant, and equipment.	A company must use the cost method; no revaluation is permitted.

CHAPTER 8

Summary of IFRS-ASPE Differences

Concepts	IFRS	ASPE
Non-strategic investments (p. 377)	These investments are reported at fair value, with unrealized and realized gains and losses reported in net income, unless the company elects to report them in other comprehensive income.	These investments are reported at fair value, with unrealized and realized gains and losses reported in net income.
Investments subject to significant influence (p. 377)	A company shall apply the equity method to account for these investments.	A company may choose to apply either the equity method or the cost method. If the share investments are quoted in an active market, then the fair value method replaces the cost method as an option, with any changes in fair value reported through net income.
Investments in controlled subsidiaries (p. 383)	A company shall consolidate its financial statements with those of its subsidiaries.	A company may choose to account for its subsidiaries using the cost method, the equity method, or the consolidation method. If share investments are quoted in an active market, then the fair value method replaces the cost method, with any changes in fair value reported through net income.
Amortization of the discount or premium relating to long-term investments in bonds (p. 385)	The effective-interest method must be used to amortize discounts and premiums.	The straight-line method or the effective-interest method may be used to amortize discounts and premiums.
Foreign-currency translation resulting from consolidation (p. 389)	Translation adjustments are included in other comprehensive income.	Translation adjustments are included in a separate category in shareholders' equity, unless they relate to a self-sustaining subsidiary in a highly inflationary environment, in which case they are included in the determination of net income.

CHAPTER 9

Summary of IFRS-ASPE Differences

Concepts	IFRS	ASPE
Provisions and contingent liabilities (p. 424)	A contingent liability is recorded as a provision when it is probable that an outflow of economic benefits will be required to settle the liability. *Probable* is generally considered to mean that an outflow is *more likely than not* to occur.	A contingent liability is recorded as a liability when it is likely that an outflow of economic benefits will be required to settle the liability. *Likely* is generally considered to be a higher threshold to meet than *probable*, so fewer contingent liabilities will be recorded under ASPE than under IFRS.
Government remittances (p. 425)	No separate disclosure of these liabilities is required.	Government remittances (other than income taxes) such as sales taxes, Employment Insurance, and Canada Pension Plan payable must be disclosed separately, either on the balance sheet or in the notes.
Amortization of discounts and premiums (p. 431)	The effective-interest method must be used to amortize discounts and premiums.	The straight-line method is available as an amortization option.
Finance leases (p. 442)	Leases that transfer substantially all the risks and rewards incidental to the ownership of assets to the lessee are called finance leases.	The equivalent term is capital leases. There are no differences in accounting for these leases.

CHAPTER 10

Summary of IFRS-ASPE Differences

Concept	IFRS	ASPE
Accumulated other comprehensive income (p. 478)	Included as a component of shareholders' equity.	No accounting or reporting of this component is required.
Repurchase of shares (p. 492)	There are significant differences between IFRS and ASPE when accounting for share repurchases. These differences, and the inherent complexity of accounting for share repurchases in general, are beyond the scope of this textbook.	
Reporting of dividends on the statement of cash flows (p. 492)	May be reported as an operating activity or a financing activity at the company's discretion.	Must be reported as a financing activity.

CHAPTER 11

Summary of IFRS-ASPE Differences

Concepts	IFRS	ASPE
Differences between income tax expense and income tax payable (p. 526)	Accounted for as deferred income taxes.	Accounted for as future income taxes.
Earnings per share (p. 529)	Companies must report this figure on their income statement.	Companies do not have to report this figure.
Statement of comprehensive income (p. 530)	Companies must report this statement, either on its own or in combination with the income statement.	The concept of comprehensive income does not exist in ASPE, so this statement is not reported.
Statement of changes in shareholders' (or owners') equity (p. 531)	Companies must report this statement.	Companies must report only a statement of retained earnings, which contains only a subset of the information reported in the statement of changes in shareholders' equity.

CHAPTER 12

Summary of IFRS-ASPE Differences

Concepts	IFRS	ASPE
Classification of interest paid and interest and dividends received (p. 560)	Interest paid may be classified as either an operating activity or a financing activity.	Interest paid must be classified as an operating activity.
Classification of interest and dividends received (p. 560)	Interest and dividends received may be classified as either operating activities or investing activities.	Interest and dividends received must be classified as operating activities.
Classification of dividends paid (p. 560)	Dividends paid may be classified as either an operating activity or a financing activity. *Note: Once a classification scheme has been chosen for each of the above items, it must be used consistently thereafter.*	Dividends paid must be classified as a financing activity.

Check Figures

CHAPTER 1

S1-1	NCF
S1-2	a. $300,000 b. 200,000 c. 100,000
S1-3	NCF
S1-4	NCF
S1-5	NCF
S1-6	Net income $70
S1-7	R/E, end $260
S1-8	Total assets $140,000
S1-9	CB, Dec. 31, 2011, $19,000
S1-10	NCF
S1-11	NCF
S1-12	NCF
E1-13	NCF
E1-14	NCF
E1-15	NCF
E1-16	Telus Total assets $16,987 mil.
E1-17	2. $2,997.8 mil. 3. $1,836.4 mil.
E1-18	1. No net loss 2. No net loss 3. Net loss of $1 mil.
E1-19	1. Total assets $840,000 2. SE $400,000
E1-20	NCF
E1-21	R/E $25 mil.
E1-22	1. Net inc. before tax $9 mil. 2. Dividends $3 mil.
E1-23	Net cash provided by operations $360 thou. End Cash $125,000
E1-24	R/E, July 31, 2011, $5,900
E1-25	Total assets $44,100
E1-26	Net cash provided by operations $11,100. End Cash $8,100

E1-27	NCF
E1-28	NCF
Q1-29	a
Q1-30	a
Q1-31	c
Q1-32	a ($20,000 − $4,000 = $16,000)
Q1-33	b
Q1-34	d
Q1-35	b
Q1-36	b
Q1-37	d
Q1-38	b ($140,000 − $59,000 − $8,000 − $3,000 = $70,000)
Q1-39	a ($145,000 + $90,000 − $30,000 = $205,000)
Q1-40	c
Q1-41	c
Q1-42	a (Total assets $25,000 + $11,000 =$36,000)
Q1-43	c ($450,000 + $50,000 − $320,000 = $180,000)
P1-44A	1. Net inc. $28,000
P1-45A	Chain Inc.
P1-46A	1. Total assets $99,000
P1-47A	1. Total assets $160,000
P1-48A	1. Net inc. $86,000
	2. R/E, end. $116,000
	3. Total assets $180,000
P1-49A	1. Net decrease in cash $41 mil.
P1-50A	1. b. $2.4 thou. g. $5,700 thou. m. $2,600 thou. s. $17,400 thou.

P1-51B 1. Net inc. $0.8 mil.

P1-52B Groceries Inc. ending assets $3,389 mil.

Bottlers Corp. repurchase of shares $20 mil

Gas Limited expenses $10,036 mil.

P1-53B 1. Total assets $114,000

P1-54B 1. Total assets $199,000

P1-55B 1. Net inc. $100,000

2. R/E, end. $90,000

3. Total assets $293,000

P1-56B 1. Net increase in cash $34,000

P1-57B 1. b. $5,850 thou. g. $15,400 thou. n. $3,670 thou. v. $43,490 thou.

DC1 NCF

DC2 1. Net inc. $0;

Total assets $70,000

FOF 3. Total resources: $19,931 mil.

Amt. owed $12,418 mil.

Equity $7,513 mil.

FOA 2. Net earnings of $1,215 mil. Is 15% increase

CHAPTER 2

S2-1 NCF

S2-2 a. $12,000 b. $2,000

S2-3 Cash bal. $23,000

S2-4 NCF

S2-5 NCF

S2-6 2. A/P bal. $2,000

S2-7 2. Cash bal. $100

A/R bal. $400, Service Rev. bal. $500

3. Total assets $500

S2-8 T/B total $398 mil. Net income, $31 mil.

S2-9 1. $95,000 2. $39,000

3. $56,000 4. $38,500

S2-10 T/B total $70,900

S2-11 NCF

S2-12 Total debits $160,000

E2-13 Cash $10,000

B/S Total assets $270,000

E2-14 NCF

E2-15 NCF

E2-16 2. a. $68,300 b. $5,000

c. $11,000 d. $57,050 ($50,000 + $7,050)
e. $7,050

E2-17 NCF

E2-18 NCF

E2-19 2. T/B total $32,200

3. Total assets $30,700

E2-20 Cash bal. $10,700; Owing $30,600

E2-21 1. T/B total $71,200

2. Net inc. $14,300

E2-22 T/B total $94,200

E2-23 Cash bal. $4,200

E2-24 1. T/B total $27,500

2. Net income $8,500

E2-25 4. T/B total $14,400

E2-26 a. Cash paid $85,000

b. Cash collections $52,000

c. Cash paid on a note payable $17,000

E2-27 1. T/B out of balance by $2,200

2. T/B total $118,200

3. Total assets $111,500, Total liabilities $71,800, Net inc. $12,400

E2-28 NCF

Q2-29 c

Q2-30 d

Q2-31 c

Q2-32 a

Q2-33 d

Q2-34 b

Q2-35 c

Q2-36 a

Q2-37 b

Q2-38 d

Q2-39 d

Q2-40 c

Q2-41 a

Q2-42 b

Q2-43 a

Q2-44 d

Q2-45 c

Q2-46 b

Q2-47 a

Q2-48 b

P2-49A Total assets $300,000, Total liabilities $150,000, Net inc. $30,000

P2-50A 2. Net inc. $8,900

4. Total assets 23,700

P2-51A 3. Cash bal. $7,700; A/P bal. $5,500

P2-52A 2. Total assets $56,500

P2-53A 3. Cash bal. $10,800; Amt. owed $35,600

P2-54A 3. T/B total $35,000

4. Net inc. $2,205

P2-55A 3. T/B total $116,800

4. Net inc. $1,400

P2-56B Total assets $292,000

Net inc. $33,000

P2-57B 2. Net inc. $16,400 4. Total assets $73,900

P2-58B 3. Cash bal. $32,500; A/P bal. $5,200

P2-59B 3. b. Total assets $56,400

P2-60B 3. Cash bal. $26,300; Amt. owed $30,000

P2-61B 3. T/B total $29,300

4. Net inc. $7,290

P2-62B 3. T/B total $174,600

DC1 3. T/B total $27,900

4. Net inc. $6,400

DC2 Net inc. $3,000; Total assets $21,000

FOF 4. Cash $46 mil; A/R $1,428 mil. Inventories $353 mil. A/P $1,419 mil

FOA 3. Net income increase $163 mil. (15.5%)

Operating revenues increase $583 (6.0%)

CHAPTER 3

S3-1 a. Net inc. $50 mil.

b. Ending cash $90 mil.

S3-2 NCF

S3-3 NCF

S3-4 1. Prepaid Rent bal. $2,000

2. Prepaid Supplies $500

S3-5 3. $20,000 Carrying amount

S3-6 Income statement, $42,000,000; Balance sheet $2,000,000

S3-7 3. Interest Payable Dec. 31 bal. $1,500

S3-8 3. Interest Receivable Dec. 31 bal. $1,500

S3-9 NCF

S3-10 Prepaid Rent: a. $6,000 b. $0; RentExpense: a. $0 b. $6,000.

S3-11 NCF

S3-12 Net inc. $3,500 thou.; R/E $4,800 thou. Total assets $97,900 thou.

S3-13 Retained earnings $4,800 thou.

S3-14 a. 1.24 b. 0.69

S3-15 NCF

E3-16 NCF

E3-17 a. Net Inc. $10,000

b. Net Inc. $80,000

E3-18 NCF

E3-19 NCF

E3-20 NCF

E3-21 2. Net inc. overstated by $17,200

E3-22 NCF

E3-23 Carrying amount $48,000

E3-24 Service Revenue $15,700

E3-25 Net inc. $4,000 thou.; Total assets $22,200 thou.; R/E $6,800 thou.

E3-26 Sales rev. $20,900 mil.; Insurance expense $330 mil; other operating expense $4,200 mil.

E3-27 Mountain B/S: Unearned service rev. $3,000; Squamish I/S: Consulting expense $9,000

E3-28 1. B/S: Unearned service rev. $90 mil. I/S service rev. $310 mil.

2. B/S: Unearned service rev. $90 mil. I/S service rev. $390 mil.

E3-29 Net Inc. $1,200 thou.

Dec. 31, 2009, bal. of R/E $2,700 thou.

E3-30 NCF

E3-31 1. Total assets $39,100

2. Current ratio Current Yr. 1.26

Debt ratio Current Yr. 0.48

E3-32 1. 2014 Current ratio 2.0; Debt ratio 0.40;

2013 Current ratio 1.88; Debt ratio 0.35;

2012 Current ratio 1.33; Debt ratio 0.29

E3-33 7. Net inc. $1,200, Total assets $12,800; R/E $200

E3-34 2013: 1.868; 2014: 2.174

E3-35 a. Net inc. $108,000

b. Total assets $158,000

c. Total liabilities $13,000

d. Total shareholders' equity
$145,000

Q3-36 b

Q3-37 b

Q3-38 a

Q3-39 b

Q3-40 d

Q3-41 d

Q3-42 c

Q3-43 c

Q3-44 c

Q3-45 d

Q3-46 b

Q3-47 c

Q3-48 a

Q3-49 d

Q3-50 c

P3-51A 1. $27 mil. 3. End. rec. $6 mil. 4. End.
Payable $8 mil.

P3-52A 2. Cash basis—loss $700, Accrual basis—inc. $3,240

P3-53A NCF

P3-54A a. Insurance Exp. $3,100

d. Supplies Exp. $6,600

P3-55A 2. Net inc. $6,000, Total assets $54,000;
R/E $15,000

P3-56A 2. Total assets $68,600,
Net inc. $4,100, Total Liabilities $7,400

P3-57A 1. Net inc. $39,200, Total assets $47,000,
Debt ratio 0.549

P3-58A 2. March 31, 2014 bal. of R/E $47,300

P3-59A 1. Total assets $83,300

2. Current ratio 2014,
1.60, Debt ratio 2014, 0.32

P3-60A 1. Current ratio 2014,
1.692. Debt ratio 2014, 0.571

P3-61B 1. $15; 3. End. rec. $5 End Acc. Payable $6

P3-62B 2. Cash basis—loss $2,700, Accrual basis—inc.
$1,100

P3-63B NCF

P3-64B c. Supplies Exp. $11,400

f. Insurance Exp. $2,700

P3-65B 2. Net inc. $19,800, Total assets $61,600,
R/E $36,200

P3-66B 2. Total assets $30,400, Net inc. $25,500, Total
liabilities $14,700

P3-67B 1. Net inc. $78,600, Total assets $109,000

2. Debt ratio 0.42

P3-68B 2. Dec. 31, 2014 bal. of R/E $16,800

P3-69B 1. Total assets $55,000

2. Current ratio 2014, 1.71 Debt ratio 2014, 0.42

P3-70B 1. 2014, Current ratio 1.36, 2. Debt ratio 0.681

DC1 1. $2,000 3. Current ratio 1.748

DC2 Net inc. $7,000, Total assets $32,000

DC3 1. $260,000 2. Shareholder Equity $148,000

FOF 5. 2011: Current ratio 0.53; Debt ratio 0.62

FOA 2. Deprec. Expense, $1,331 mil.

CHAPTER 4

S4-1 NCF

S4-2 NCF

S4-3 NCF

S4-4 NCF

S4-5 Adj. bal. $3,005

S4-6 NCF

S4-7 $1,000 stolen

S4-8 NCF

S4-9	NCF		P4-49B	NCF
S4-10	NCF		P4-50B	1. Adj. bal. $5,960
S4-11	Cash available $29 mil.		P4-51B	1. Adj. bal. $8,239.00
S4-12	NCF		P4-52B	NCF
E4-13	NCF		P4-53B	1. (New financing needed) $(5,490)
E4-14	NCF		P4-54B	NCF
E4-15	NCF		DC1	Bookkeeper stole $1,000
E4-16	NCF		DC2	NCF
E4-17	NCF		FOF	1.Adj. bal. $46,000 mil.
E4-18	NCF		FOA	Purchase of property, plant, and equipment $1,847
E4-19	Adj. bal. $1,150			
E4-20	Adj. bal. $1,780			Payment of long term debt $3,946
E4-21	NCF			Issued long term debt, $4,068
E4-22	NCF			Payment of dividends, $642
E4-23	NCF			

CHAPTER 5

E4-24	New financing needed $(64) mil.		S5-1	NCF
E4-25	NCF		S5-2	I/S Unrealized gain $4,000
E4-26	NCF			B/S Short term investment at fair value of $84,000
E4-27	1. Cash available $45 thou. 2. Current ratio 1.60; Debt ratio 0.50		S5-3	Dr. Unrealized Loss $6,000
Q4-29	c		S5-4	NCF
Q4-30	b		S5-5	2. A/R, net $62,500
Q4-31	a		S5-6	Dr. Bad debt Exp. $15,000
Q4-32	d			Bal. for Allowance for Uncollectible Accounts $16,500
Q4-33	d			
Q4-34	a		S5-7	1. A/R balance, $184,000
Q4-35	b			2. Allowance for Uncollectible Accounts $16,500
Q4-36	c			
Q4-37	d			3. A/R, net $167,500
Q4-38	a		S5-8	d. Bad debt expense $12,000
Q4-39	d		S5-9	3. A/R, net $123,000
Q4-40	c		S5-10	b. Dr. Cash $93,600
P4-41A	NCF		S5-11	3. $102,667
P4-42A	NCF		S5-12	c. Dr. Cash $6,480
P4-43A	1. Adj. bal. $6,090		S5-13	a. Notes receivable $6,000; Interest receivable $280
P4-44A	1. Adj. bal. $2,242.16			
P4-45A	NCF			b. Interest rev. $280
P4-46A	1. (New financing needed) $(3,700) thou.			c. Nothing to report d. Interest rev. $200
P4-47A	NCF		S5-14	1. 0.95 2. 24 days
P4-48B	NCF		S5-15	2. Net inc. $4,424 thou. 3. 1.60

E5-16	3. B/S: Short-term invest. $195,000	**P5-50A**	4. Allowance for Uncollectible Accounts $318, A/R $4,517
	I/S: Unrealized gain $10,000		5. I/S: Bad debt. exp. $380
E5-17	I/S: Div. rev. $500; Unrealized(loss) $(500); B/S Short-term invest. $49,500	**P5-51A**	3. A/R, net: 2014, $221,000; 2013, $207,800
E5-18	Unrealized Gain on Invest. $5,000	**P5-52A**	2. Corrected ratios: Current 1.48; Acid-test 0.75;
	Gain on Sale of Invest. $1,000		3. Net inc., corrected $82,000
E5-19	NCF	**P5-53A**	2. 12/31/14 Note rec. $25,000; Interest rec. $82
E5-20	A/R, net $91,000	**P5-54A**	1. 2014 ratios: a. 1.98 b. 1.14 c. 31 days
E5-21	3. A/R, net $49,500	**P5-55B**	3. 40,000 4. Div rev. $1,250; Unrealized gain on invest. $2,500
E5-22	2. A/R, net $52,800	**P5-56B**	NCF
E5-23	3. A/R, net $224,850	**P5-57B**	5. I/S: Bad debt. exp. $335 thou.
E5-24	Bad debt Exp. $150; Write offs $148	**P5-58B**	3. A/R, net: 2014, $109,200; 2013 $107,300
E5-25	Dec. 31 Dr. Interest Rec. $1,326	**P5-59B**	2. Corrected ratios: Current 1.39; Acid-test 0.85
E5-26	I/S: Interest rev. $750 for 2013 and $250 for 2014		3. Net inc., corrected $84,000
E5-27	NCF	**P5-60B**	2. 12/31/14 Note rec. $20,000; Interest rec. $247
E5-28	a. 1.89 b. 53 days	**P5-61B**	1. 2014 ratios: a. 1.87 b. 0.87 c. 35 days
E5-29	1. 10 days	**DC1**	Net inc. $223,000
E5-30	Expected net inc. w/bank cards $129,800	**DC2**	2014: Days' sales in rec. 26 days; Cash collections $1,456 thou.
E5-31	a. $28 mil. b. $11,148 mil.	**FOF**	1. $50 mil. 2. Customers owed Telus $1,428 (2011) and $1,318 mil. (2010) 3. Collected $10,183 FOA One day sales = $28.48 mil.
Q5-32	c		
Q5-33	c		Days in receivables = 48 days
Q5-34	d		Acid-test ratio = 0.40
Q5-35	b		
Q5-36	$201,000		

CHAPTER 6

Q5-37	d		
Q5-38	b	**S6-1**	NCF
Q5-39	$1,000	**S6-2**	GP $160,000
Q5-40	c	**S6-3**	COGS: Weighted-Avg. $3,760; FIFO $3,740
Q5-41	b	**S6-4**	Net inc.: Weighted-Avg. $3,060; FIFO $3,100
Q5-42	a	**S6-5**	Inc. tax exp: Weighted-Avg. $551; FIFO $558
Q5-43	a	**S6-6**	NCF
Q5-44	Dr. Cash $10,450	**S6-7**	COGS $421,000
Q5-45	a	**S6-8**	GP% 0.321; Inv TO 3.0 times
Q5-46	c	**S6-9**	Estimated ending inv. $100,000
Q5-47	c	**S6-10**	c. COGS $1,190 mil. d. GP $510 mil.
P5-48A	3. $7,500 4. Div. rev. $260; Unrealized (loss) on invest. $(1,500)	**S6-11**	1. Correct GP $5.7 mil.
P5-49A	NCF		2. Correct GP $5.1 mil.

S6-12	NCF
S6-13	NCF
S6-14	2. $90,000 3. GP $50,000
E6-15	2. GP $1,100 thou.
E6-16	3. GP $3,790
E6-17	1. COGS: a. $1,730 b. $1,760 c. $1,710
E6-18	$12.50
E6-19	2. Net inc. $132
E6-20	1. GP: FIFO $0.2 mil.; Weighted-avg. cost $0.6 mil.
E6-21	NCF
E6-22	NCF
E6-23	GP $45,000
E6-24	a. $475 c. $56 f. $2 g. $3; Myers (net loss) $(136) mil.
E6-25	Myers GP% 0.125; Inv. TO 17.9 times
E6-26	GP $16.3 bil.; GP% 29.7; Invy. TO 5.3 times
E6-27	$1,272 mil.
E6-28	$33,000
E6-29	Net inc.: 2014 $65,000; 2013 $69,000
E6-30	1. Ending inv. $1,320 COGS $2,890; 2. Ending inv. $1,347 COGS $2,863; 3. Ending Inv. $1,410 COGS $2,800
E6-31	4. COGS $2,863
E6-32	1. COGS $2,843 2. GP $2,843
E6-33	COGS $3,010
E6-34	NCF
E6-35	1. COGS $150,410; 2. COGS $152,750
E6-36	GP 2014, $8.3 thou.; GP% 0.202, Inv TO 3.7 times
Q6-37	b
Q6-38	b
Q6-39	d
Q6-40	d
Q6-41	c
Q6-42	a
Q6-43	c
Q6-44	b
Q6-45	a
Q6-46	d $200,000
Q6-47	a
Q6-48	d
Q6-49	d
Q6-50	c
Q6-51	a
Q6-52	c
Q6-53	c
P6-54A	2. Inv. ending balance $700,000 3. Net inc. $603,000
P6-55A	i) GP $2,409 Ending Inv. $2,437 ii) GP $2,400 Ending Inv. $2,428
P6-56A	1. COGS: Weighted-Avg. $7,290; FIFO $7,200 3. Net inc. $2,457
P6-57A	1. GP: Weighted-Avg. $60,286; FIFO $60,785
P6-58A	NCF
P6-59A	1. Chocolate Treats: GP% 12.5%; Inv. TO 17.9 times
P6-60A	1. $476,500 2. GP $332,000
P6-61A	1. $771,000 2. Net inc. $160,000
P6-62A	1. Net inc. each yr. $2 mil.
P6-63B	2. Inv ending balance $1,750,000 3. Net inc. $1,448,400
P6-64B	i) GP $1,173 Ending inv. $340 ii) GP $1,169 Ending Inv. $336
P6-65B	1. COGS: Weighted-Avg. $40,678; FIFO $40,530 3. Net inc. $11,028
P6-66B	1. GP: Weighted-Avg. $291,571; FIFO $299,500
P6-67B	NCF
P6-68B	1. 2012: TC Motors: GP% 24.7%; Inv. TO 8.0 times; X-Country Trucks: GP% 33.8%; Inv. TO 45.4 times
P6-69B	1. Ending Inv. $2,442,000 2. GP $3,432,000
P6-70B	1. $802,000 2. $160,000
P6-71B	1. Net inc. (thou): 2014, $150; 2013, $320; 2012, $50

DC1 1. Net inc.: FIFO $370,300,
Weighted-avg. $364,161

DC2 NCF

FOF 3. Purchases $4,796

4. GP% 2011 54.2%, Inv. TO 2011 14.86 times

CHAPTER 7

S7-1 2. Carrying amount $29,893 mil.

S7-2 NCF

S7-3 Building cost $56,000

S7-4 Net inc. overstated

S7-5 2. Carrying amount: SL $21 mil.; UOP $22 mil.; DDB $15 mil.

S7-6 Dep.: UOP yr. 5, $2 mil.; SL $4 mil. DDB yr. 5, none.

S7-7 a. Dep. SL 1.25 mil. b. Dep. UOP 3.5 mil. c. Dep. DDB 2,857,143 mil.

S7-8 Dep'n. Exp. $12,000

S7-9 1. $13,000

S7-10 NCF

S7-11 1. Goodwill $19.7 mil.

S7-12 1. Net inc. $2,100,000

S7-13 1. Net cash provided by investing $6 mil.

S7-14 ROA 15%

S7-15 ROA 2012 17.7%, ROA 2013 18%

E7-16 Land $283,000 Building $3,820,000

E7-17 Machine cost 1 $25,000; 2 $41,700; 3 $33,300

E7-18 NCF

E7-19 2. Building, net $737,160

E7-20 Yr 1: SL $9,000, UOP $7,200 DDB $19,980

E7-21 I/S: Dep. Exp.–building $6,000; B/S: Building net $194,000

E7-22 Profit margin 4.12%; Asset TO 1.45; ROA 5.96%

E7-23 Dep. yr. 12, $55,833

E7-24 Loss on sale $2,200

E7-25 Carrying amount $140,800

E7-26 NCF

E7-27 Amort. yr. 3, $200,000

E7-28 NCF

E7-29 1. Cost of goodwill $17,000,000

E7-30 NCF

E7-31 NCF

E7-32 Profit margin 1.36%; Asset TO 3.5; ROA 4.75%

E7-33 Hours 5,600

E7-34 Sale price $20.2 mil.

E7-35 Expected net inc. for 2014, $21,426

E7-36 2013 Effects on: 2. Equip. $50,000 under; 3. Net inc. $50,000 over; 4. Equity $50,000 under

Q7-37 c

Q7-38 a

Q7-39 c

Q7-40 b

Q7-41 c

Q7-42 c

Q7-43 d

Q7-44 b

Q7-45 d

Q7-46 b

Q7-47 b

Q7-48 c

Q7-49 c

Q7-50 a

Q7-51 d

P7-52A 1. Land $296,600; Land Improve. $103,800; Warehouse $1,241,000

P7-53A 2. A/Dep.–Building. $105,000; A/Dep.-Equip. $338,000

P7-54A Dec. 31 Dep. Exp.–Motor CarrierEquip. $58,667; Dep.Exp.–Building. $1,050

P7-55A NCF

P7-56A Dep. SL $44,000; UOP 2017, $33,000, DDB, 2017, $11,104

P7-57A 1. Carrying amount $41,497 thou., 3. PPE bal. $68,406; A/Dep. bal. $26,909; Long term investment bal. $108,302

P7-58A Part 1. 2. Goodwill $1.2 mil.

Part 2. 2. Net inc. $3,720,000

P7-59A 1. Loss on sale $0.1 mil.

2. P.P, & E, net $0.7 mil.

P7-60A 2014 Profit margin 4.33%; Asset TO 1.53; ROA 6.62%

P7-61B 1. Land $143,450; Land Improve. $86,000; Garage $654,000

P7-62B 2. A/Dep.–Building. $52,000; A/Dep.–Equip. $437,500

P7-63B Dec. 31 Dep. Exp.–Comm.; Equip. $4,000; Dep. Exp.–Televideo Equip. $1,333

P7-64B NCF

P7-65B Dep. SL $9,000; UOP 2014, $9,720, DDB, 2017, $4,741

P7-66B 1. Carrying amount $2,131 mil.; 2. Premises and Equip. bal. $5,941; A/Dep. bal. $3,810

P7-67B Part 1. 2. Goodwill $5,500;

Part 2. 3. Amort. $300,000

P7-68B 1. Gain on sale $0.02 bil.

2. PPE net $7.26 bil.

P7-69B 2014 Profit margin 6.06%; Asset TO 1.38; ROA 8.34%

DC1 1. Net inc.: LPF $142,125;

BA $128,250

DC2 NCF

FOF 4. Proportion of property, plant, & equipment used up in 2011, 78.1%

FOA 2. Amortization expense $479 mil.

CHAPTER 8

S8-1 1. Unrealized loss on invest. $5,000

2. LT investment at fair value $7,000

S8-2 Gain on sale $300

S8-3 LT investment bal. $42.6 mil.

S8-4 Loss on sale $7.3 mil.

S8-5 NCF

S8-6 NCF

S8-7 2. Cash Interest $70,000 4. Interest revenue $68,175

S8-8 c. Dr. Interest Revenue $1,825

S8-9 1. PV $6,810

2. PV $39,930

S8-10 PV $6,145,000

S8-11 NCF

E8-12 d. Loss on sale $4,000

E8-13 2. Unrealized loss $63,560

3. LT investments $242,644

E8-14 Invest. End. Bal. $1,055,000

E8-15 Gain on sale $1,645,000

E8-16 2. Long term investment at equity $525,000

E8-17 3. Interest rec. $350; LT investment in bonds $18,214

E8-18 PV of bond investment $10,521

E8-19 FC translation adj. $23,000

E8-20 Net cash used inv. $(11.8) mil.

E8-21 NCF

E8-22 PV of investment at 5%, $103,890

PV of investment at 10%, $90,855

E8-23 Accum. Other comprehensive loss Dec 31. 2014, $(40) mil.

Q8-24 a

Q8-25 d

Q8-26 Gain on sale $8,000

Q8-27 b

Q8-28 c

Q8-29 a

Q8-30 d

Q8-31 b

Q8-32 a

Q8-33 b

Q8-34 d

Q8-35 c

P8-36A 2. B/S LT invest. at equity $523,300

I/S Equity method invest. rev. $178,500, Div. Rev. $240 Unrealized loss $2,600

P8-37A 2. LT invest. in MSC bal. $659,000

P8-38A 3. Consolidated debt ratio 0.898

P8-39A B/S LT investment in bonds $622,031; I/S Interest rev. $25,031

P8-40A　Choose Investment A, PV $19,578

P8-41A　FC translation adj. $46,000

P8-42A　NCF

P8-43B　B/S Invest. at equity $526,300; I/S Equity method inv. Rev. $87,500 Div rev. $750, Unrealized (loss) $(3,300)

P8-44B　LT invest. in Affil. Bal. $535,000

P8-45B　2. LT invest. in bonds $445,304; Int. rev. $35,304

P8-46B　Choose Investment X, PV $25,650

P8-47B　1. FC translation adj. $230,000

P8-48B　NCF

DC1　NCF

DC2　2. Gain on sale $4,200 3. Gain on sale $80,000

FOF　NCF

FOA　NCF

CHAPTER 9

S9-1　3/31/2015 Debits include interest expense $250

S9-22.　Interest exp. $250

S9-3　2. Est. Warranty Payable bal. $50,000

S9-4　NCF

S9-5　2014, A/P TO=9; Days payable outstanding 41 days

S9-6　a. $897,500; b. $551,875

S9-7　NCF

S9-8　10/31/2014, Interest expense $313

S9-9　2. 07/31/2014 Interest expense $3,915

S9-10　3. 07/31/2014, Interest expense $3,915; 01/31/2015 Interest expense $3,934

S9-11　1. $9,400; 2. $10,000 on July 2021; 3. $325; 4. $355

S9-12　b. 12/31/2014 Interest expense $375

S9-13　Leverage ratio Best Buy 2.45, Wal-Mart 2.53; Debt ratio Best Buy .59 Wal-Mart .60

S9-14　Lev. Ratio 2.5; Debt ratio .60; Time interest Earned 3.73 times

S9-15　Total liabilities $501,000

E9-16　2. Warranty expense $9,000; Est. Warranty Pay. $7,600

E9-17　Unearned subscription rev. $1,000

E9-18　Payroll tax expense $9,000; Payroll payable $6,400

E9-19　3. Interest expense for 2014, $1,250 and for 2015, $1,750

E9-20　2. 2014 Debt ratio 0.47; Leverage ratio 1.90

E9-21　2. Debt ratio 0.76

E9-22　Company B: Current ratio 1.89; debt ratio 0.60; Leverage ratio 2.48; interest coverage ratio 7.2 times

E9-23　d. Total current liabilities $149,625

E9-24　c. 12/31/2014 Interest expense $2,625

E9-25　4. Annual interest expense by the straight-line $15,800

E 9-26　01/31/2015 Bond carrying amount $372,811

E9-27　06/30/2014 Bond carrying amount $553,125

E9-28　01/01/2014 Bond Carrying amount $287,041

E9-29　2. 2014 Debt ratio 0.50; Leverage ratio 2

E9-30　Sobeys ratios: Current 1; Debt 0.51; Times int. earned 9.49 times

E9-31　Company F ratios: current 2.1; Debt 0.59; Leverage 2.45; Times Int. earned 6.4 times

E9-32　2. Leverage ratio 4.52; debt ratio .30

E9-33　1. 2014 Current ratio 1.17; Debt ratio .571

E9-34　5. 3/15/2016 Bond Carrying amount $97,632

Q9-35　a

Q9-36　d

Q9-37　b

Q9-38　b

Q9-39　a

Q9-40　c

Q9-41　a

Q9-42　d

Q9-43　f

Q9-44　a

Q9-45　c

Q9-46　d

Q9-47　NCF

Q9-48　NCF

Q9-49　e: $5,537

Q9-50　d

Q9-51　a

Q9-52	c
Q9-53	c
P9-54A	e. Note pay. due in 1 year $20,000; Interest pay. $6,000
P9-55A	12/31/2014 Warranty Expense $3,800; 4/30/2015 Interest Expense $1,500
P9-56A	Interest pay. $5,667; Bonds pay. net $194,250
P9-57A	2. $583,800; 3. a. $24,900; b. $24,000
P9-58A	12/31/2017 Bond carrying amt. $589,001
P9-59A	12/31/2016 Bond Carrying amt. $474,920; 3. Bond pay. net $472,352
P9-60A	NCF
P9-61A	2. a. Carrying amt. $675,000; 3. Time interest earned ratio 1.62 times; 4. Leverage ratio 1.36; Debt ratio 0.26
P9-62A	2. a. Carrying amt. $553,000; 3. Time interest earned ratio 4.3 times
P9-63B	e. Long term notes pay. due in 1 year $20,000; Interest pay. $2,083
P9-64B	12/31/2014 Warranty expense $18,000; 6/30/2015 Interest expense $9,000
P9-65B	a. Bonds pay. $1,000,000; c. Interest pay. $20,000
P9-66B	4. Interest pay. $7,000; Notes pay. net $289,000
P9-67B	2. $95,200; 3. a. $4,600; b. $4,000
P9-68B	2.12/31/2017 Bond carrying amt. $483,439
P9-69B	NCF
P9-70B	1. Pension liability $45,000; 2. Bonds pay. carrying amt. $2,078,000; 3. Times interest earned ratio 1.72 times; 4. Leverage ratio 2.63; debt ratio 0.62
P9-71B	2. Bonds pay. carrying amt. $313,000; 3. Times interest earned ratio 2.7 times
DC1	1.Debt ratio 0.82; ROA 1.5%; 2. Leverage ratio 5.71; ROE 8.5%; 3. Debt ratio 0.92; ROA 0.1%
DC2	EPS plan A $4.78; plan B $4.54; plan C $4.63
FOF	NCF
FOA	2. Current ratio 0.5333; Debt ratio 0.623

CHAPTER 10

S10-1	NCF
S10-2	NCF
S10-3	NCF
S10-4	NCF

S10-5	1. $1.80 3. $5,650 profit
S10-6	NCF
S10-7	Total SE $1,246 thou.
S10-8	a. $585 thou. b. $3,011 thou. c. $4,257 thou.
S10-9	NCF
S10-10	R/E increased $50,000
S10-11	1. $150,000 4. Pfd. $450,000
S10-12	No effect
S10-13	BV per share $61.60
S10-14	NCF
S10-15	ROA 1.2%; ROE 3.96%
S10-16	Cash used by financing $(6.4) bil.
E10-17	ROA 9.2%; ROE 25.9%
E10-18	2. Total SE $92,500
E10-19	Total SE $143,000
E10-20	Total PIC $1,045,000
E10-21	SE $(29) deficit
E10-22	Overall increase in SE $19,700
E10-23	NCF
E10-24	Total SE $4,300 mil.
E10-25	3.564 mil. shares 4. $136 mil.
E10-26	2013: Pfd. $24,000; Com. $26,000
E10-27	2. Total SE $8,134,000
E10-28	a. Decrease SE $80 mil. e. Increase SE $3,000
E10-29	Total SE $2,755 mil.
E10-30	1. $10.40 2. $10.27
E10-31	ROA 10.2%; ROE 18%
E10-32	ROA 4.1%; ROE 11.8%
E10-33	Cash used by financing $(2,405)
E10-34	b. Issued 500 shares
E10-35	Cash generated by financing activities $232,300
E10-36	Div. $1,407 mil.
E10-37	12/31/14 Total equity $65 mil.
Q10-38	c
Q10-39	c
Q10-40	d
Q10-41	c

Q10-42 b

Q10-43 d

Q10-44 a

Q10-45 c

Q10-46 b

Q10-47 a

Q10-48 b

Q10-49 d

Q10-50 b

Q10-51 a

Q10-52 c

Q10-53 a

Q10-54 a

Q10-55 d

Q10-56 b

Q10-57 a

P10-58A NCF

P10-59A 2. Total SE $207,500

P10-60A Total SE $663,000

P10-61A NCF

P10-62A Total SE $7,680,000

P10-63A 4. $22,500

P10-64A 2. Total SE $95,800

P10-65A NCF

P10-66A 1. Total assets $559,000, Total SE $296,000
              2. ROA 17%; ROE 34.9%

P10-67A NCF

P10-68B NCF

P10-69B 2. Total SE $323,800

P10-70B Total SE $540,000

P10-71B NCF

P10-72B Total SE $4,126,000

P10-73B 4. $183,700

P10-74B 2. Total SE $132,800

P10-75B NCF

P10-76B 1. Total assets $568,000,
              Total SE $312,000 2. ROA 13.4%; ROE 26.1%

P10-77B NCF

DC1   3. Total SE: Plan 1, $220,000 Plan 2, $230,000

DC2   NCF

FOF   1. 174,915,546 common shares
         3. Avg. share price $40.25

FOA   1. 2011: ROA 6.1%; ROE 15.8%

CHAPTER 11

S11-1   NCF

S11-2   1. Operating inc. $1,968; Net inc. $1,215

S11-3   Net inc. $18,000

S11-4   EPS $2.80

S11-5   Comp. inc. $21,000

S11-6   NCF

S11-7   NCF

S11-8   2. Net inc. $82,500, Future income tax liab.
         $5,000

S11-9   NCF

S11-10   1. $100 mil.; 2. Decrease in SE by $715 mil.

E11-11   Comp. inc. $2,125 thou.

E11-12   1. Net inc. $7,350 EPS $4.03

E11-13   NCF

E11-14   EPS $76.53

E11-15   EPS $4.78

E11-16   EPS $0.64

E11-17   Net inc. $450,000, Future income tax liab.
         $12,500

E11-18   2. $62,500 3. $52,500

E11-19   NCF

E11-20   Total SE 12/31/14, $2,010,000

E11-21   1. Total SE 12/31/14, $9,446 thou.
         2. Debt ratio 44.3% 4. $10.00 per share

E11-22   NCF

Q11-23   b

Q11-24   b

Q11-25   d

Q11-26   a

Q11-27   b

Q11-28 c

Q11-29 c

Q11-30 d

Q11-31 a

Q11-32 b

Q11-33 d

Q11-34 c

P11-35A 1. Net. inc. $37,900

P11-36A R/E, 12/31/14 $57,900

P11-37A EPS $2.25

P11-38A 1. EPS $1.57

P11-39A Comp. inc. $100,550, EPS $2.25

P11-40A 1. $120,000 2. Cr. future inc. tax liab. $3,300

P11-41A 1. $806 mil. 2. $5 per share 3. $10.00 per share 4. 7.8%

P11-42B 1. Comp. inc. $72,250

P11-43B R/E, 4/30/14 $187,750

P11-44B EPS $3.74

P11-45B 1. EPS $1.1

P11-46B Comp. inc. $80,500, EPS $1.72

P11-47B 1. $185,000 2. Cr. future inc. tax liab. $3,750

P11-48B 1. $537 mil. 2. $3.01 per share 3. $3.77 per share 4. 8%

DC1 Use $0.59

DC2 NCF

FOF NCF

FOA 1. Deferred income tax liab. $1,600 mil.

CHAPTER 12

S12-1 NCF

S12-2 NCF

S12-3 Net cash oper. $70,000

S12-4 NCF

S12-5 Net cash oper. $54,000

S12-6 Net cash oper. $54,000

Net increase in cash $53,000

S12-7 a. $60,000; b. $20,000

S121-8 a. New borrowing $10,000

b. Issuance $8,000

c. Dividends $146,000

E12-9 NCF

E12-10 NCF

E12-11 NCF

E12-12 Net cash oper. $32,000

E12-13 Net cash oper. $80,000

E12-14 Net cash oper. $111,100

Net increase in cash $11,100

E12-15 NCF

E12-16 a. Cash proceeds of sale $46,000;

b. Cash dividends $26,000

E12-17 Gain on sale of property and equipment $120; LT debt issued $240

Q12-18 c

Q12-19 a

Q12-20 b

Q12-21 b

Q12-22 d

Q12-23 c

Q12-24 c

Q12-25 NCF

Q12-26 c

Q12-27 d

Q12-28 b

Q12-29 a

Q12-30 c

Q12-31 a

Q12-32 a

Q12-33 a

Q12-34 d

Q12-35 d

Q12-36 a

Q12-37 a

P12-38A NCF

P12-39A 1. Net inc. $56,667

2. Total assets $396,667

3. Net cash oper. $(49,000) Net increase in cash $90,000

P12-40A Net cash oper. $63,200

Net increase in cash $16,000

Non-cash inv. and fin. $160,000

P12-41A Net cash oper. $76,900

Net (decrease) in cash $(4,100)

Non-cash inv. and fin. $101,000

P12-42A Net cash oper. $80,000

Net increase in cash $12,300

P12-43B NCF

P12-44B 1. Net inc. $157,333

2. Total assets $340,333

3. Net cash oper. $81,000 Net increase in cash $191,000

P12-45B Net cash oper. $75,400

Net (decrease) in cash $(5,700)

Non-cash inv. and fin. $290,400

P12-46B Net cash oper. $68,700

Net increase in cash $16,300

Non-cash inv. and fin. $30,000

P12-47B Net cash oper. $90,600

Net increase in cash $13,100

DC1 (in thousands)1. Net cash oper. $132, Net (decrease) in cash $(46)

DC2 NCF

FOF NCF

FOA NCF

APPENDIX 12A

S12A-1 Net cash oper. $110,000

Net (decrease) in cash $(20,000)

S12A-2 Net cash oper. $13,000

S12A-3 Net cash oper. $13,000

Net increase in cash $12,000

S12A-4 a. $699,000; b. $326,000

S12A-5 a. $68,000; b. $134,000

E12A-6 NCF

E12A-7 NCF

E12A-8 Net cash oper. $21,000

E12A-9 NCF

E12A-10 Net cash oper. $102,000 Net increase in cash $29,000

E12A-11 a. $50,000; b. $113,000

E12A-12 (in thousands) a. $24,637; b. $18,134; c. $3,576; d. $530; e. $73; f. $1,294

P12A-13A Net cash oper. $95,700

Net (decrease) in cash $(2,700)

Non-cash inv. and fin. $79,400

P12A-14A 1. Net inc. $51,667

2. Total assets $396,667

3. Net cash oper. $49,000 Net increase in cash $90,000

P12A-15A Net cash oper. $80,000; Net increase in cash $12,300

P12A-16A Net cash oper. $55,800; Net (decrease) in cash $(2,000); Non-cash inv. and fin. $99,100

P12A-17A Net cash oper. $73,200; Net increase in cash $20,000; Non-cash inv. and fin. $19,000

P12A-18B Net cash oper. $30,000; Net increase in cash $7,600; Non-cash inv. and fin. $142,800

P12A-19B 1. Net inc. $157,333

2. Total assets $340,333

3. Net cash oper. $81,000 Net increase in cash $191,000

P12A-20B Net cash oper. $90,600; Net increase in cash $13,100

P12A-21B Net cash oper. $77,200; Net (decrease) in cash $(4,600); Non-cash inv. and fin. $83,200

P12A-22B Net cash oper. $40,400; Net increase in cash $4,100; Non-cash inv. and fin. $48,300

CHAPTER 13

S13-1 2014 Net inc.(increase) 9.2%

S13-2 2014 Sales trend 107%

S13-3 2014 Cash 2.3%

S13-4 Net inc. Porterfield 6.22%

S13-5 2011 Current ratio 1.36

S13-6 2014 Allstott Inc. Quick ratio 1.17

S13-7 a. 28.3 times; 12.8 days; b. 9 days; c. 2.64 times; 138.2 days

S13-8 1. 1.23; 2. 4.57

S13-9   a. 7.73% b. 0.9 times

c. 6.95% d. 4.77 e. 33.1%

S13-10   1. EPS $4.85 P/E 16

S13-11   a. $3,855 thou. d. $873 thou.

S13-12   a. $562 thou. d. $3,768 thou. e. $1,294 thou.

E13-13   2014 WC increase 26.8%

E13-14   Net inc. decreased 5.8%

E13-15   Yr.4 Net inc. trend 147%

E13-16   Current assets 24.6% Total liabilities 41.7%

E13-17   Net. Inc 20% both years

E13-18   NCF

E13-19   a. 1.67; b.0.83; c. 4.4 times; d. 9.5 times;
e. 38 days

E13-20   2014 ratios a. 2.07; b. 0.91; c. 0.47; d. 4.13

E13-21   2014 ratios a. 0.098; b. 0.132; c. 0.151; d. 0.67

E13-22   2014 ratios a. 17.3; b. 0.014; c. $6

E13-23   No solution provided

E13-24   No solution provided

Q13-25   b

Q13-26   c

Q13-27   a

Q13-28   b

Q13-29   d

Q13-30   c

Q13-31   b

Q13-32   c

Q13-33   a

Q13-34   a

Q13-35   d

Q13-36   d

P13-37A No solution provided

P13-38A 1. Net inc. 10.7%, Current assets 77.1%

P13-39A NCF

P13-40A Current ratio before 1.74; a. current ratio after 1.84

P13-41   No solution provided

P13-42A 1. Video a. 0.60; b. 2.16; c. 100; d. 0.68; f. 0.196

P13-43A NCF

P13-44B No solution provided

P13-45B 1. Net inc. 5.3%, Current assets 75%

P13-46B NCF

P13-47B Current ratio before 1.54; a. Current ratio after 1.44

P13-48B No solution provided

P13-49B 2014 ratios a. 0.78; b. 2.32; c. 40; d. 0.41; f. 0.349

P13-50B NCF

DC1   NCF

DC2   NCF

DC3   NCF

Glossary

accelerated depreciation method A depreciation method that writes off a relatively larger amount of the asset's cost nearer the start of its useful life than the straight-line method does. (p. 330)

account format A balance sheet format that lists assets on the left side and liabilities above shareholders' equity on the right side. (p. 122)

account payable A liability for goods or services purchased on credit and backed by the general reputation and credit standing of the debtor. (p. 417)

account The record of the changes that have occurred in a particular asset, liability, or element of shareholders' equity during a period. (p. 55)

accounting An information system that measures and records business activities, processes data into reports, and reports results to decision makers. (p. 3)

accounting equation Assets = Liabilities + Owners' Equity. Provides the foundation for the double-entry method of accounting. (p. 15)

Accounting Standards for Private Enterprises (ASPE) Canadian accounting standards that specify the *generally accepted accounting principles* applicable to *private enterprises* that are required to follow *GAAP* and choose not to apply *IFRS*. (p. 7)

accounts payable turnover (T/O) A liquidity ratio that measures the number of times per year a company was able to repay its accounts payable in full. Calculated by dividing the cost of goods sold by the average accounts payable balance for the year. (p. 439)

accounts receivable turnover Net sales divided by average net accounts receivable. (p. 246)

accrual accounting A basis of accounting that records transactions based on whether a business has acquired an asset, earned revenue, taken on a liability, or incurred an expense, regardless of whether cash is involved. (p. 106)

accrual An adjustment related to revenues earned or expenses incurred prior to any cash or invoice changing hands. (p. 115)

accrued expense An expense that has been incurred but not yet paid or invoiced. (p. 115)

accrued revenue A revenue that has been earned but not yet collected or invoiced. (p. 116)

accumulated depreciation The account showing the sum of all depreciation expense from the date of acquiring a capital asset. (p. 114)

acid-test ratio Ratio of the sum of cash plus short-term investments plus net current receivables to total current liabilities. Tells whether the entity can pay all its current liabilities if they come due immediately. Also called the *quick ratio*. (p. 244)

adjusted trial balance A list of all the ledger accounts with their adjusted balances. (p. 118)

aging-of-receivables method A way to estimate bad debts by analyzing accounts receivable according to the length of time they have been receivable from the customer. Also called the *balance-sheet approach* because it focuses on accounts receivable. (p. 233)

allowance for bad debts Another name for *allowance for uncollectible accounts*. (p. 232)

allowance for doubtful accounts Another name for *allowance for uncollectible accounts*. (p. 232)

allowance for uncollectible accounts A contra account, related to accounts receivable, that holds the estimated amount of collection losses. (p. 232)

allowance method A method of recording collection losses based on estimates of how much money the business will not collect from its customers. (p. 231)

amortization Allocation of the cost of an intangible asset with a finite life over its useful life. (p. 342)

asset A resource owned or controlled by a company as a result of past events and from which the company expects to receive future economic benefits. (p. 15)

asset turnover The dollars of sales generated per dollar of assets invested. Net sales divided by Average total assets. (p. 648)

audit A periodic examination of a company's financial statements and the accounting systems, controls, and records that produce them. (p. 181)

auditor A person or firm that provides an objective opinion on whether an entity's financial statements have been prepared in accordance with generally accepted accounting principles. (p. 533)

bad debt expense A cost to the seller of extending credit to customers. Arises from a failure to collect an account receivable in full. (p. 231)

balance sheet Reports a company's financial position as at a specific date. In particular, it reports a company's assets, liabilities, and owners' equity. Also called the *statement of financial position*. (p. 15)

bank collections Collections of money by the bank on behalf of a depositor. (p. 188)

bank reconciliation A document explaining the reasons for the difference between a depositor's records and the bank's records about the depositor's cash. (p. 188)

bank statement Document showing the beginning and ending balances of a particular bank account and listing the month's transactions that affected the account. (p. 186)

benchmarking The comparison of a company to a standard set by other companies, with a view towards improvement. (p. 632)

board of directors Group elected by the shareholders to set policy for a corporation and to appoint its officers. (p. 6)

bond discount Excess of a bond's face (par) value over its issue price.   (p. 427)

bond investments Bonds and notes are debt instruments that an investor intends to hold until maturity.   (p. 387)

bond market price The price investors are willing to pay for the bond. It is equal to the present value of the principal payment plus the present value of the interest payments. (p. 427)

bond premium Excess of a bond's issue price over its face value.   (p. 427)

bonds payable Groups of notes payable issued to multiple lenders called *bondholders*.   (p. 420)

book value (of a share) Amount of owners' equity on the company's books for each share of its stock.   (p. 487)

book value per share of common stock Common stockholders' equity divided by the number of shares of common stock outstanding. The recorded amount for each share of common stock outstanding.   (p. 652)

brand name A distinctive identification of a product or service. Also called a *trademark* or *trade name*.   (p. 343)

budget A quantitative expression of a plan that helps managers coordinate the entity's activities.   (p. 180)

capital expenditure Expenditure that increases an asset's capacity or efficiency, or extends its useful life. Capital expenditures are debited to an asset account. Also called *betterments*.   (p. 325)

carrying amount (of a capital asset) The asset's cost minus accumulated depreciation.   (p. 114)

carrying amount The historical cost of an asset net of its accumulated depreciation.   (p. 17)

cash budget A budget that helps a company or an individual manage cash by planning receipts and payments during a future period.   (p. 198)

cash conversion cycle The number of days it takes to convert cash into inventory, inventory to receivables, and receivables back into cash, after paying off payables. Days inventory outstanding + days sales outstanding – days payables outstanding.   (p. 652)

cash equivalents Short-term investments that are readily convertible to known amounts of cash, and which are very unlikely to change in value. Generally, only investments with maturities of three months or less meet these criteria.   (p. 557)

cash-basis accounting Accounting that records only transactions in which cash is received or paid.   (p. 106)

chairperson Elected by a corporation's board of directors, usually the most powerful person in the corporation.   (p. 477)

chart of accounts List of a company's accounts and their account numbers.   (p. 66)

cheque Document instructing a bank to pay the designated person or business the specified amount of money.   (p. 186)

classified balance sheet A balance sheet that shows current assets separate from long-term assets, and current liabilities separate from long-term liabilities.   (p. 122)

clean audit opinion Another term for an *unmodified audit opinion*.   (p. 534)

closing entries Entries that transfer the revenue, expense, and dividend balances from these respective accounts to the Retained Earnings account.   (p. 129)

common-size statement A financial statement that reports only percentages (no dollar amounts).   (p. 632)

comparability Investors like to compare a company's financial statements from one year to the next. Therefore, a company must consistently use the same accounting method each year.   (p. 8)

comprehensive income Includes net income and other items that cause a change in total shareholders' equity but that derive from sources other than from the owners of the business.   (p. 530)

computer virus A malicious program that enters a company's computer system by e-mail or other means and destroys program and data files.   (p. 184)

consistency principle A business must use the same accounting methods and procedures from period to period.   (p. 286)

consolidated statements Financial statements of the parent company plus those of majority-owned subsidiaries as if the combination were a single legal entity.   (p. 383)

contingent liability A possible obligation that arises from past events and whose existence will be confirmed only by the occurrence or non-occurrence of one or more uncertain future events not wholly within the control of the company.   (p. 424)

contra account An account that always has a companion account and whose normal balance is opposite that of the companion account.   (p. 114)

controller The chief accounting officer of a business who accounts for cash.   (p. 180)

controlling (majority) interest Ownership of more than 50% of an investee company's voting shares and can exercise control over the investee.   (p. 383)

copyright Exclusive right to reproduce and sell a book, musical composition, film, other work of art, or computer program. Issued by the federal government, copyrights extend 50 years beyond the author's life.   (p. 342)

corporation An incorporated business owned by one or more *shareholders*, which according to the law is a legal "person" separate from its owners.   (p. 6)

cost of goods sold Cost of the inventory the business has sold to customers. Also called *cost of sales*.   (p. 271)

cost-of-goods-sold model Formula that brings together all the inventory data for the entire accounting period: Beginning inventory + Purchases = Goods available for sale. Then, Goods available for sale − Ending inventory = Cost of goods sold. (p. 290)

credit The right side of an account.   (p. 67)

creditor The party to whom money is owed.   (p. 237)

cumulative preferred shares Preferred shares whose owners must receive all dividends in arrears plus the current year's dividend before the corporation can pay dividends to the common shareholders.   (p. 485)

current asset An asset that is expected to be converted to cash, sold, or consumed during the next 12 months, or within the business's normal operating cycle if longer than a year.   (p. 16)

current liability A debt due to be paid within one year or within the entity's operating cycle if the cycle is longer than a year. (p. 18)

current portion of long-term debt The amount of the principal that is payable within one year. Also called *current instalment of long-term debt*.   (p. 422)

current ratio Current assets divided by current liabilities. Measures a company's ability to pay current liabilities with current assets.   (p. 131)

date of declaration The date on which the Board of Directors declares a dividend to shareholders. (p. 483)

date of payment The date on which a dividend is actually paid to shareholders. (p. 484)

date of record The date on which a person must be recorded as a shareholder in order to receive a dividend. (p. 484)

days payable outstanding (DPO) Another way of expressing the accounts payable turnover ratio, this measure indicates how many days it will take to pay off the accounts payable balance in full. Calculated by dividing the *accounts payable turnover* into 365. (p. 439)

days' sales in receivables Ratio of average net accounts receivable to one day's sales. Indicates how many days' sales remain in Accounts Receivable awaiting collection. Also called the *collection period* and *days sales outstanding*. (p. 430)

debentures Unsecured bonds—bonds backed only by the good faith of the borrower. (p. 427)

debit The left side of an account. (p. 67)

debt ratio Ratio of total liabilities to total assets. States the proportion of a company's assets that is financed with debt. (p. 132)

debtor The party who owes money. (p. 237)

deferral An adjustment related to a transaction for which a business has received or paid cash in advance of delivering or receiving goods or services. (p. 111)

deferred income tax liability The amount of income taxes payable in future periods as a result of differences between accounting income and taxable income in current and prior periods. Under ASPE, this is known as a *future income tax liability*. (p. 527)

deficit The term used when *retained earnings* is a negative balance. (p. 14)

deposits in transit A deposit recorded by the company but not yet recorded by its bank. (p. 188)

depreciable cost The cost of a tangible asset minus its estimated residual value. (p. 328)

depreciation Allocation of the cost of property, plant, and equipment for its useful life. (p. 326)

depreciation An expense to recognize the portion of a capital asset's economic benefits that has been used up during an accounting period. (p. 113)

direct method A method of determining cash flows from operating activities in which all cash receipts and cash payments from operating activities are directly reported on the statement of cash flows. (p. 560)

direct write-off method A method of accounting for bad debts in which the company waits until a customer's account receivable proves uncollectible and then debits Uncollectible-Account Expense and credits the customer's Account Receivable. (p. 235)

disclosure principle A business's financial statements must report enough information for outsiders to make knowledgeable decisions about the business. The company should report relevant, reliable, and comparable information about its economic affairs. (p. 286)

dividend yield Ratio of dividends per share of stock to the stock's market price per share. Tells the percentage of a stock's market value that the company returns to shareholders as dividends. (p. 652)

double-diminishing-balance (DDB) method An accelerated depreciation method that computes annual depreciation by multiplying the asset's decreasing carrying amount by a constant percentage, which is two times the straight-line rate. (p. 331)

double-entry system An accounting system that uses debits and credits to record the dual effects of each business transaction. (p. 66)

doubtful account expense Another name for bad debt expense. (p. 231)

DuPont analysis A detailed approach to analyzing rate of return on equity (ROE), calculated as follows: Net profit margin (net income/net sales) × Total asset turnover (net sales/average total assets) × Leverage ratio (average total assets/average common shareholders' equity). The first two components of the model comprise return on assets (ROA). (p. 489)

earnings per share (EPS) Amount of a company's net income earned for each share of its outstanding common stock. (p. 437)

earnings quality Provides insight into whether a company's current-period earnings will persist into future periods. (p. 522)

electronic funds transfer (EFT) System that transfers cash by electronic communication rather than by paper documents. (p. 186)

encryption Mathematical rearranging of data within an electronic file to prevent unauthorized access to information. (p. 184)

equity method The method used to account for investments in which the investor has 20–50% of the investee's voting shares and can significantly influence the decisions of the investee. (p. 381)

estimated residual value Expected cash value of an asset at the end of its useful life. Also called *scrap value* or *salvage value*. (p. 328)

estimated useful life Length of service that a business expects to get from an asset. May be expressed in years, units of output, kilometres, or other measures. (p. 328)

ethical standards Standards that govern the way we treat others and the way we restrain our selfish desires. They are shaped by our cultural, socioeconomic, and religious backgrounds. (p. 25)

exception reporting Identifying data that is not within "normal limits" so that managers can follow up and take corrective action. Exception reporting is used in operating and cash budgets to keep company profits and cash flow in line with management's plans. (p. 181)

expense A cost incurred to purchase the goods and services a company needs to run its business on a day-to-day basis. The opposite of revenue. (p. 12)

face value of bond The principal amount payable by the issuer. Also called *maturity value*. (p. 427)

fair value (of a share) The price that a willing buyer would pay a willing seller to acquire a share. (p. 487)

fair value The amount that a business could sell an asset for, or the amount that a business could pay to settle a liability. (p. 10)

faithful representation A fundamental qualitative characteristic of accounting information. Information is a faithful representation if it is complete, neutral, accurate, and reflects the economic substance of the underlying transaction or event. (p. 7)

finance lease Under IFRS, a lease that transfers substantially all the risks and rewards incidental to ownership of assets to the lessee.   (p. 422)

financial accounting The branch of accounting that provides information for managers inside a business and for decision makers outside the business.   (p. 5)

financial statements The reports that companies use to convey the financial results of their business activities to various user groups, which can include managers, investors, creditors, and regulatory agencies.   (p. 2)

financing activities Activities that result in changes in the size and composition of a company's contributed equity and borrowings.   (p. 559)

firewall An electronic barrier, usually protected by passwords, around computerized data files to protect local area networks of computers from unauthorized access.   (p. 184)

first-in, first-out (FIFO) cost method Inventory costing method by which the first costs into inventory are the first costs out to cost of goods sold. Ending inventory is based on the costs of the most recent purchases.   (p. 281)

foreign-currency exchange rate The measure of one country's currency against another country's currency.   (p. 385)

franchises and licences Privileges granted by a private business or a government to sell a product or service in accordance with specified conditions.   (p. 343)

fraud An intentional misrepresentation of facts, made for the purpose of persuading another party to act in a way that causes injury or damage to that party.   (p. 173)

fraud triangle The three elements that are present in almost all cases of fraud. These elements are motive, opportunity, and rationalization on the part of the perpetrator.   (p. 174)

fraudulent financial reporting Fraud perpetrated by management by preparing misleading financial statements.   (p. 173)

free cash flow A measure of how much cash a company has available to pursue new business opportunities. Calculated by deducting capital expenditures from cash flow from operating activities.   (p. 574)

future value Measures the future sum of money that a given current investment is "worth" at a specified time in the future, assuming a certain interest rate.   (p. 391)

gain A type of income other than revenue that results in an increase in economic benefits to a company, and usually occurs outside the course of the company's ordinary business activities.   (p. 12)

generally accepted accounting principles (GAAP) The guidelines of financial accounting, which specify the standards for how accountants must record, measure, and report financial information.   (p. 6)

going-concern assumption The assumption that an entity will continue operating normally for the foreseeable future.   (p. 9)

goodwill Excess of the cost of an acquired company over the sum of the market values of its net assets (assets minus liabilities).   (p. 343)

gross margin Another name for *gross profit*.   (p. 273)

gross profit method A way to estimate inventory based on a rearrangement of the cost-of-goods-sold model: Beginning inventory + Net purchases = Goods available for sale − Cost of goods sold = Ending inventory. Also called the *gross margin method*.   (p. 291)

gross profit Sales revenue minus cost of goods sold. Also called *gross margin*.   (p. 273)

gross profit percentage Gross profit divided by net sales revenue. Also called the *gross margin percentage*.   (p. 288)

held-for-trading investment A share or bond investment that is to be sold in the near future with the intent of generating profits on the sale.   (p. 224)

historical-cost assumption Holds that assets should be recorded at their actual cost, measured on the date of purchase as the amount of cash paid plus the dollar value of all non-cash consideration (other assets, privileges, or rights) also given in exchange.   (p. 10)

horizontal analysis Study of percentage changes over time through comparative financial statements.   (p. 626)

imprest system A way to account for petty cash by maintaining a constant balance in the petty cash account, supported by the fund (cash plus payment slips) totalling the same amount.   (p. 198)

income Consists of a company's *revenues* and *gains*.   (p. 12)

income statement The financial statement that measures a company's operating performance for a specified period of time. In particular, it reports income, expenses, and net income. Also called the *statement of profit or loss*.   (p. 11)

indirect method A method of determining cash flows from operating activities in which net income is adjusted for non-cash transactions, any deferrals or accruals of past or future operating cash receipts or payments, and items of income or expense associated with investing or financing cash flows.   (p. 560)

intangible assets Long-lived assets with no physical form that convey a special right to current and expected future benefits.   (p. 322)

interest The borrower's cost of renting money from a lender. Interest is revenue for the lender and expense for the borrower.   (p. 237)

interest-coverage ratio Another name for the *times-interest-earned ratio*.   (p. 441)

internal control Organizational plan and related measures adopted by an entity to safeguard assets, encourage adherence to company policies, promote operational efficiency, ensure accurate and reliable accounting records, and comply with legal requirements.   (p. 177)

International Financial Reporting Standards (IFRS) International accounting standards that specify the *generally accepted accounting principles* which must be applied by *publicly accountable enterprises* in Canada and over 100 other countries.   (p. 7)

inventory turnover Ratio of cost of goods sold to average inventory. Indicates how rapidly inventory is sold.   (p. 289)

investing activities The purchase and sale of long-term assets and other investments that do not qualify as cash equivalents. They generally consist of transactions that result in cash inflows or outflows related to resources used for generating future income and cash flows. Only expenditures related to assets that are recognized on the balance sheet qualify as investing activities.   (p. 559)

journal The chronological accounting record of an entity's transactions.   (p. 70)

lapping A fraudulent scheme to steal cash through misappropriating certain customer payments and posting payments from other customers to the affected accounts to cover it up. Lapping is caused by weak internal controls (i.e., not segregating the duties of cash handling and accounts receivable bookkeeping, allowing the bookkeeper improper access to cash, and not appropriately monitoring the activities of those who handle cash).   (p. 171)

lease Rental agreement in which the tenant (lessee) agrees to make rent payments to the property owner (lessor) in exchange for the use of the asset.   (p. 442)

ledger The book of accounts and their balances.   (p. 71)

lessee Tenant in a lease agreement.   (p. 442)

lessor Property owner in a lease agreement.   (p. 442)

leverage Earning more income on borrowed money than the related interest expense, thereby increasing the earnings for the owners of the business. Also called *trading on the equity*.   (p. 649)

leverage ratio Shows the ratio of a company's total assets to total shareholders' equity. It is an alternative way of expressing how much debt a company has used to fund its assets, or in other words, how much leverage it has used.   (p. 440)

liability An obligation (or debt) owed by a company, which it expects to pay off in the future using some of its assets.   (p. 18)

limited liability No personal obligation of a shareholder for corporation debts. A shareholder can lose no more on an investment in a corporation's shares than the cost of the investment.   (p. 476)

line of credit A method of short-term borrowing that provides a company with as-needed access to credit up to a maximum amount specified by its lender.   (p. 417)

liquidity A measure of how quickly an asset can be converted to cash. The higher an asset's liquidity, the more quickly it can be converted to cash.   (p. 16)

lockbox system A system of handling cash receipts by mail whereby customers remit payment directly to the bank, rather than through the entity's mail system.   (p. 172)

long-term asset Another term for *non-current asset*.   (p. 17)

long-term investments Any investment that does not meet the criteria of a short-term investment; any investment that the investor expects to hold for longer than a year.   (p. 376)

long-term liability Another term for *non-current liability*.   (p. 19)

loss A type of expense that results in a decrease in economic benefits to a company, and usually occurs outside the course of the company's ordinary business activities. The opposite of a gain.   (p. 13)

lower-of-cost-and-net-realizable-value (LCNRV) rule Requires that an asset be reported in the financial statements at whichever is lower—its historical cost or its net realizable value.   (p. 286)

majority interest Ownership of more than 50% of an investee company's voting shares.   (p. 383)

management accounting The branch of accounting that generates information for the internal decision makers of a business, such as top executives.   (p. 5)

market interest rate Interest rate that investors demand for loaning their money. Also called *effective interest rate*.   (p. 428)

market price (of a share) The price that a willing buyer would pay a willing seller to acquire a share.   (p. 482)

marketable securities Another name for *short-term investments*.   (p. 223)

material Accounting information is material if it is significant enough in nature or magnitude that omitting or misstating it could affect the decisions of an informed user.   (p. 7)

maturity date The date on which a debt instrument must be paid.   (p. 237)

misappropriation of assets Fraud committed by employees by stealing assets from the company.   (p. 173)

mortgage A *term loan* secured by real property, such as land and buildings.   (p. 442)

multi-step income statement An income statement that contains subtotals to highlight important relationships between revenues and expenses.   (p. 123)

net assets Another name for *owners' equity*.   (p. 19)

net earnings Another name for *net income*.   (p. 14)

net income The excess of a company's total income over its total expenses.   (p. 14)

net loss Occurs when a company's total expenses exceed its total income.   (p. 14)

net profit Another term for *net income*.   (p. 13)

net profit margin Computed by the formula Net income/Net sales. This ratio measures the portion of each sales dollar generated in net profit.   (p. 345)

net realizable value The amount a business could get if it sold the inventory less the costs of selling it.   (p. 286)

net working capital Current assets – current liabilities. Measures the ease with which a company will be able to use its current assets to pay off its current liabilities.   (p. 131)

non-cash operating working capital account A current asset or current liability account that derives from an operating activity and is not included in cash and cash equivalents.   (p. 565)

non-controlling interest A subsidiary company's equity that is held by shareholders other than the parent company.   (p. 384)

non-current asset Any asset that is not classified as a current asset.   (p. 16)

non-current liability A liability a company expects to pay off beyond one year from the balance sheet date.   (p. 18)

non-strategic investments Investments in which the investor owns less than 20% of the voting shares of the investee and is presumed to exercise no influence.   (p. 376)

nonsufficient funds (NSF) cheque A cheque for which the payer's bank account has insufficient money to pay the cheque. NSF cheques are cash receipts that turn out to be worthless.   (p. 189)

obsolescence Occurs when an asset becomes outdated or no longer produces revenue for the company.   (p. 327)

operating activities Activities that comprise the main revenue-producing activities of a company, and generally result from the transactions and other events that determine net income.   (p. 20)

operating budget A budget of future net income. The operating budget projects a company's future revenue and expenses. It is usually prepared by line item of the company's income statement.   (p. 180)

operating lease A lease in which the risks and rewards of asset ownership are not transferred to the lessee.   (p. 442)

outstanding cheques Cheques issued by the company and recorded on its books but not yet paid by its bank.   (p. 188)

owners' equity The company owners' remaining interest in the assets of the company after deducting all its liabilities. (p. 19)

par value shares Shares of stock that do not have a value assigned to them by articles of the corporation. (p. 479)

parent company An investor company that owns more than 50% of the voting shares of a subsidiary company. (p. 383)

partnership An unincorporated business with two or more parties as co-owners, with each owner being a partner in the business. (p. 5)

password A special set of characters that must be provided by the user of computerized program or data files to prevent unauthorized access to those files. (p. 182)

patent A federal government grant giving the holder the exclusive right for 20 years to produce and sell an invention. (p. 342)

payroll Employee compensation, a major expense of many businesses. (p. 421)

percentage-of-sales method Computes bad debt expense as a percentage of net sales. Also called the *income-statement approach* because it focuses on the amount of expense to be reported on the income statement. (p. 232)

periodic inventory system An inventory system in which the business does not keep a continuous record of the inventory on hand. Instead, at the end of the period, the business makes a physical count of the inventory on hand and applies the appropriate unit costs to determine the cost of the ending inventory. (p. 274)

permanent accounts Assets, liabilities, and shareholders' equity accounts, which all have balances that carry forward to the next fiscal year. (p. 129)

perpetual inventory system An inventory system in which the business keeps a continuous record for each inventory item to show the inventory on hand at all times. (p. 275)

petty cash Fund containing a small amount of cash that is used to pay minor amounts. (p. 197)

phishing Creating bogus Web sites or sending phony e-mails for the purpose of stealing unauthorized data, such as names, addresses, social security numbers, bank account, and credit card numbers. (p. 183)

physical wear and tear Occurs when the usefulness of the asset deteriorates. (p. 326)

post-employment benefits A special type of employee benefits that do not become payable until after a person has completed employment with the company. They include such things as pension benefits, medical and dental insurance, and prescription drug benefits. (p. 443)

posting Transferring amounts from the journal to the ledger. (p. 71)

preferred shares Shares that give their owners certain advantages, such as the priority to receive dividends before the common shareholders and the priority to receive assets before the common shareholders if the corporation liquidates. (p. 479)

present value The value on a given date of a future payment or series of future payments, discounted to reflect the time value of money. (p. 392)

president Chief executive officer in charge of managing the day-to-day operations of a corporation. (p. 477)

pretax accounting income Income before tax on the income statement; the basis for computing income tax expense. (p. 526)

price/earnings ratio (multiple) Ratio of the market price of a common to the company's earnings per share. Measures the value that the stock market places on $1 of a company's earnings. (p. 651)

principal The amount borrowed by a debtor and lent by a creditor. (p. 237)

private enterprise An entity that has not issued and does not plan to issue shares or debt on public markets. (p. 7)

proprietorship An unincorporated business with a single owner, called the proprietor. (p. 5)

provision Under IFRS, a present obligation of uncertain timing or amount that is recorded as a liability because it is probable that economic resources will be required to settle it. (p. 423)

publicly accountable enterprises (PAEs) Corporations that have issued or plan to issue shares or debt in a public market. (p. 7)

purchase allowance A decrease in the cost of purchases because the seller has granted the buyer a discount (an allowance) from the amount owed. (p. 277)

purchase discount A decrease in the cost of purchases earned by making an early payment to the vendor. (p. 277)

purchase return A decrease in the cost of purchases because the buyer returned the goods to the seller. (p. 277)

quick ratio Ratio of the sum of cash plus short-term investments plus net current receivables to total current liabilities. Tells whether the entity can pay all its current liabilities if they come due immediately. Another name for the *acid-test ratio*. (p. 641)

receivables Monetary claims against a business or an individual, acquired mainly by selling goods or services and by lending money. (p. 228)

relevance A fundamental qualitative characteristic of accounting information. Information is relevant if it has predictive value, confirmatory value, or both, and is *material*. (p. 7)

remittance advice An optional attachment to a cheque (sometimes a perforated tear-off document and sometimes capable of being electronically scanned) that indicates the payer, date, and purpose of the cash payment. The remittance advice is often used as the source document for posting cash receipts or payments. (p. 186)

report format A balance sheet format that lists assets at the top, followed by liabilities and then shareholders' equity. (p. 122)

repurchased shares A corporation's own shares that it has issued and later reacquired. (p. 482)

retained earnings Represent the accumulated net income of a company since the day it started business, less any net losses and dividends declared during this time. (p. 14)

return on assets Net income divided by average total assets. This ratio measures a company's success in using its assets to earn income for the persons who finance the business, and tells whether a company can pay all its current liabilities if they come due immediately. Also called *return on total assets*. (p. 648)

return on common shareholders' equity Net income minus preferred dividends, divided by average common shareholders' equity. A measure of profitability. Also called *return on equity (ROE)*. (p. 649)

return on equity (ROE) Measures how well management has used equity to generate profits for shareholders. (p. 489)

return on net sales Ratio of net income to net sales. A measure of profitability. Also called *return on sales*.   (p. 648)

revenue Consists of amounts earned by a company in the course of its ordinary, day-to-day business activities. The vast majority of a company's revenue is earned through the sale of its primary goods and services.   (p. 12)

sales discount Percentage reduction of sale price by the seller as an incentive for early payment before the due date. A typical way to express a sales discount is "2/10, n/30." This means the seller will grant a 2% discount if the invoice is paid within 10 days, or the full amount is due within 30 days.   (p. 242)

sales returns and allowances Merchandise returned for credit or refunds for services provided.   (p. 242)

sales tax payable The amount of HST, GST, and provincial sales tax owing to government bodies.   (p. 419)

separate-entity assumption Holds that the business activities of the reporting entity are separate from the activities of its owners.   (p. 9)

serial bonds Bonds that mature in instalments over a period of time.   (p. 427)

shareholder A party who owns shares of a corporation.   (p. 6)

shareholders' equity Another term for *owners' equity*.   (p. 19)

shares Legal units of ownership in a corporation.   (p. 6)

short-term investments Investments that a company plans to hold for one year or less. Also called *marketable securities*.   (p. 223)

short-term notes payable Notes payable due within one year.   (p. 418)

single-step income statement Lists all revenues together and all expenses together; there is only one step in arriving at net income.   (p. 122)

specific identification cost method Inventory costing method based on the specific cost of particular units of inventory.   (p. 279)

stable-monetary-unit assumption Holds that regardless of the reporting currency used, financial information is always reported under the assumption that the value of the currency is stable, despite the fact that its value does change due to economic factors such as inflation.   (p. 10)

stated interest rate Interest rate printed on the bond certificate that determines the amount of cash interest the borrower pays and the investor receives each year. Also called the *coupon rate* or *contract interest rate*.   (p. 428)

stated value An arbitrary amount assigned by a company to a share of its stock at the time of issue.   (p. 479)

statement of cash flows Reports cash receipts and cash payments classified according to the entity's major activities: operating, investing, and financing.   (p. 20)

statement of changes in shareholders' equity Reports the changes in all categories of shareholders' equity during the period.   (p. 531)

statement of financial position Another name for the *balance sheet*.   (p. 15)

statement of profit or loss Another name for the *income statement*.   (p. 11)

statement of retained earnings Summary of the changes in the retained earnings of a corporation during a specific period.   (p. 14)

stock dividend A proportional distribution by a corporation of its own shares to its shareholders.   (p. 484)

stock split An increase in the number of authorized, issued, and outstanding shares of stock coupled with a proportionate reduction in the share's book value.   (p. 486)

straight-line (SL) method Depreciation method in which an equal amount of depreciation expense is assigned to each year of asset use.   (p. 329)

subsidiary company An investee company in which a parent company owns more than 50% of the voting shares and can exercise control over the subsidiary.   (p. 383)

tangible long-lived assets Also called property, plant, and equipment.   (p. 322)

taxable income The basis for computing the amount of tax to pay the government.   (p. 526)

temporary accounts Revenue, expense, and dividend accounts, which do not have balances that carry forward to the next fiscal year.   (p. 129)

term The length of time from inception to maturity.   (p. 442)

term bonds Bonds that all mature at the same time for a particular issue.   (p. 427)

term loan A long-term loan at a stated interest rate, typically from a single lender such as a bank, which must be repaid over a specified number of years. Usually secured by specific assets of the borrower, often the ones acquired using the loan proceeds.   (p. 237)

times-interest-earned ratio Ratio of income from operations to interest expense. Measures the number of times that operating income can cover interest expense. Also called the *interest-coverage ratio*.   (p. 441)

total asset turnover It measures a a company's success in using assets to earn a profit. The formula is Net sales/Average total assets. Also known as asset turnover.   (p. 345)

trademark, trade name A distinctive identification of a product or service. Also called a *brand name*.   (p. 343)

trading on the equity Another name for *leverage*.   (p. 650)

transaction An event that has a financial impact on a business and that can be reliably measured.   (p. 55)

trend percentages A form of horizontal analysis that indicates the direction a business is taking.   (p. 629)

trial balance A list of all the ledger accounts with their balances.   (p. 76)

Trojan horse A malicious program that hides within legitimate programs and acts like a computer virus.   (p. 183)

underwriter Organization that purchases the bonds from an issuing company and resells them to its clients or sells the bonds for a commission, agreeing to buy all unsold bonds.   (p. 427)

unearned revenue A liability that arises when a business receives cash from a customer prior to providing the related goods or services.   (p. 112)

units-of-production (UOP) method Depreciation method by which a fixed amount of depreciation is assigned to each unit of output produced by the plant asset.   (p. 330)

unmodified audit opinion An audit opinion stating that the financial statements are in accordance with GAAP (IFRS or ASPE).   (p. 534)

verifiability The ability to check financial information for accuracy, completeness, and reliability.   (p. 8)

vertical analysis Analysis of a financial statement that reveals the relationship of each statement item to a specified base, which is the 100% figure.   (p. 630)

weighted-average-cost method Inventory costing method based on the average cost of inventory for the period. Weighted-average cost is determined by dividing the cost of goods available by the number of units available. Also called the *average cost method*.   (p. 279)

working capital Current assets minus current liabilities; measures a business's ability to meet its short-term obligations with its current assets. Also called *net working capital*.   (p. 638)

Index

Note: Page numbers with *f* indicate figures.

A

accelerated depreciation method, 330–331, 331*f*, 332, 332*f*
account format, 122
accounting
  conceptual framework of, 7, 8*f* (*see also* assumptions)
  data, flow of, 71–74, 71*f*
  defined, 3
  as language of business, 3–6
accounting changes
  cooking the books and, 529
  cooking the books with, 524
  income statement and, 528
accounting errors
  income statement and, 528 , 529
accounting equation
  expanded, 68–69, 69*f*
  illustration of, 17*f*
  impact of transactions on, 57–63
  liabilities and, 18
  overview of, 15
  owners' equity and, 19, 20
  rules of debit and credit and, 67–69, 67*f*, 70*f*
accounting information
  cost constraint and, 9
  enhancing qualitative characteristics of, 8–9
  fundamental qualitative characteristics of, 7, 8
  GAAP and, 6–7
  using, 2–3
accounting records
  access to, limiting, 181
  adequate, 181
  internal control and, 177, 181
  safeguarding, 177
Accounting Standards for Private Enterprises (ASPE), 7
  accumulated other comprehensive income, 478
  amortization of discounts and premiums, 431
  amortization of the discount or premium relating to long-term investments in bonds, 385
  application of, 7
  balance sheet, 15
  changes in retained earnings during accounting period, 14
  classification of dividends paid, 560
  classification of interest and dividends received, 560
  classification of interest paid and interest and dividends received, 560
  depreciation, 322
  differences between income tax expense and income tax payable, 526
  earnings per share, 526, 529
  finance leases, 442

  foreign-currency translation resulting from consolidation, 389
  government remittances, 425
  historical-cost assumption, 10
  impairment, 349
  income statement, 11
  income tax expense *vs.* income tax payable and, 529
  investments in controlled subsidiaries, 383
  investments subject to significant influence, 377
  non-strategic investments, 377
  provisions and contingent liabilities, 424
  repurchase of shares, 492
  revaluation, 349
  short-term investments, 226
  significant components of an item of property, plant, or equipment, 340
  statement of changes in shareholders' equity, 531
  statement of changes in shareholders' (or owners') equity, 531
  statement of comprehensive income, 526, 535
accounts
  Accumulated Depreciation account, 114
  analyzing, 74, 75–76
  asset account, 55–56
  chart of, 66, 67*f*
  decreases in, 67–68
  defined, 55
  increases in, 67–68
  liability account, 56
  rules of debit and credit and, 67–69, 67*f*
  shareholders' equity account, 56–57
  T-accounts, 67–70, 67*f*, 68*f*, 70*f*
accounts payable
  cash flows and, 565–566, 566*f*
  current liabilities and, 417–418
Accounts Payable account, 56
accounts payable turnover, 439–440, 644
Accounts Receivable account, 55
accounts receivables. *See* receivables
accounts receivable turnover, 246*n*, 642–643
accrual accounting, 105–106
  vs. cash-basis accounting, 106–108
  closing entries, 129–130
  cooking the books and, 118
  debt-paying ability and, 131–134
  defined, 106
  entries, adjusting (*See* adjusting entries)
  financial statements and, 120–124
  issues in, 118
  revenue recognition principle and, 108–110
accruals, 115–117
  accrued expenses, 115–116
  accrued revenues, 116–117
  defined, 110